Jesus and Archaeology

Jesus and Archaeology

edited by

James H. Charlesworth

WILLIAM B. EERDMANS PUBLISHING COMPANY
GRAND RAPIDS, MICHIGAN / CAMBRIDGE, U.K.

Wm. B. Eerdmans Publishing Co.
2140 Oak Industrial Drive N.E., Grand Rapids, Michigan 49505 /
P.O. Box 163, Cambridge CB3 9PU U.K.

Printed in the United States of America

11 10 09 08 07 06   7 6 5 4 3 2 1

Library of Congress Cataloging-in-Publication Data

Jesus and archaeology / edited by James H. Charlesworth.
        p.   cm.
    Includes bibliographical references and indexes.
    ISBN-10: 0-8028-4880-X / ISBN-13: 978-0-8028-4880-2 (pbk.: alk. paper)
    1. Bible. N.T. — Antiquities.   2. Jesus Christ.
    I. Charlesworth, James H.

    BS621.J47 2006
    225.9′3 — dc22

                                                    2006006712

www.eerdmans.com

Dedicated to and in Honor of
Thomas and Ann Cousins

Contents

Archaeology and Theology

Abbreviations

Modern Publications

AA	*Archäologischer Anzeiger*
AASOR	Annual of the American Schools of Oriental Research
AB	Anchor Bible
ABD	*Anchor Bible Dictionary*, ed. D. N. Freedman, 6 vols. (New York, 1992)
ABRL	Anchor Bible Reference Library
ABW	*Archaeology in the Biblical World*
ACNT	Augsburg Commentaries on the New Testament
ADAJ	*Annual of the Department of Antiquities, Jordan*
ADPV	Abhandlungen des Deutschen Palästina-Vereins
AE	*L'Année épigraphique* (Paris: Presses Universitaires de France, 1988-)
AEHL	*Archaeological Encyclopedia of the Holy Land*, ed. A. Negev and S. Gibson, rev. ed. (New York and London: Continuum, 2001)
AGJU	Arbeiten zur Geschichte des antiken Judentums und des Urchristentums
AJA	*American Journal of Archaeology*
AJBA	*Australian Journal of Biblical Archaeology*
AJPA	*American Journal of Physical Anthropology*
AJT	*American Journal of Theology*
AnBib	Analecta biblica
ANF	*The Ante-Nicene Fathers*
ANRW	*Aufstieg und Niedergang der römischen Welt,* ed. W. Haase and H. Temporini (Berlin and New York, 1979-)
ANTC	Abingdon New Testament Commentaries
ArF	Archäologische Forschungen
ASOR	American School of Oriental Research
ASORER	American Schools of Oriental Research Excavation Report
ASTI	*Annual of the Swedish Theological Institute*
AV	Authorized Version of the Bible (KJV)
BA	*Biblical Archaeologist*

BAGD	Bauer, Arndt, Gingrich, and Danker, *Greek-English Lexicon of the New Testament*
BAIAS	*Bulletin of the Anglo-Israel Archeological Society*
BAMA	British Academy Monographs in Archaeology
BAR	*Biblical Archaeology Review*
BASOR	*Bulletin of the American Schools of Oriental Research*
BAZ	Biblische Archäologie und Zeitgeschichte
BCH	*Bulletin de correspondance hellénique*
BEATAJ	Beiträge zur Erforschung des Alten Testaments und des antiken Judentum
BIES	*Bulletin of the Israel Exploration Society*
BJ	*Bonner Jahrbücher*
BJRL	*Bulletin of the John Rylands University Library of Manchester*
BJS	Brown Judaic Studies
BK	*Bibel und Kirche*
BSac	*Bibliothecha Sacra*
BSJS	Brill's Series in Jewish Studies
BTAVO	Beihefte zum Tübinger Atlas des Vorderen Orients
BZ	*Biblische Zeitschrift*
CahRB	Cahiers de la Revue biblique
CB	*Cultura bíblica*
CBQ	*Catholic Biblical Quarterly*
CBQMS	Catholic Biblical Quarterly Monograph Series
CCL	Corpus Christianorum, Series Latina
CIJ	*Corpus inscriptionum judaicarum*
CIL	*Corpus inscriptionum latinarum*
CJA	Christianity and Judaism in Antiquity
CJZC	*Corpus jüdischer Zeugnisse aus der Cyrenaika,* by G. Lüderitz and J. M. Reynolds (Wiesbaden: Ludwig Reichert, 1983)
CL	Collection Latomus
CPJ	*Corpus papyrorum Judaicarum,* ed. V. Tcherikover, A. Fuks, and D. M. Lewis, 3 vols. (Cambridge: Harvard University Press, 1957-64)
CRAIBL	*Comptes rendus de l'Académie des inscriptions et belles-lettres*
CRINT	Compendia rerum iudaicarum ad Novum Testamentum
CSCO	Corpus scriptorum christianorum orientalium, ed. I. B. Chabot et al. (Paris, 1903-)
CSCOSA	Corpus scriptorum christianorum orientalium. Scriptores aethiopici
CSEL	Corpus scriptorum ecclesiasticorum latinorum
CurBS	*Currents in Research: Biblical Studies*
DACL	*Dictionnaire d'archéologie chrétienne et de liturgie,* ed. F. Cabrol, 15 vols. (Paris, 1907-53)
DBSup	*Dictionnaire de la Bible: Supplément,* ed. L. Pirot and A. Robert (Paris, 1928-)
DFSJ	*Donateurs et fondateurs dans les synagogues juives,* by B. Lifshitz (Paris: J. Gabalda et Cie, 1967)
DHGE	*Dictionnaire d'histoire et de géographie ecclésiastiques*

DJD	Discoveries in the Judaean Desert
DJSS	Duke Judaic Studies Series
DNTB	*Dictionary of New Testament Background,* ed. C. E. Evans and S. E. Porter (2000)
DOP	*Dumbarton Oaks Papers*
DSD	*Dead Sea Discoveries*
DTMT	Dictionary of Talmud, Midrash and Targum
EAEHL	*Encyclopedia of Archaeological Excavations in the Holy Land,* ed. M. Avi-Yonah, 4 vols. (Jerusalem, 1975)
EBib	Etudes bibliques
EH	Europäische Hochschulschriften
ErFor	Erträge der Forschung
ErIsr	*Eretz-Israel*
ESI	*Excavations and Surveys in Israel*
ESt	Eichstätter Studien
EstBib	*Estudios bíblicos*
ET	*Expository Times*
ETL	*Ephemerides theologicae lovanienses*
EWNT	*Exegetisches Wörterbuch zum Neuen Testament,* ed. H. Balz and G. Schneider
FD	*Fouilles de Delphos,* ed. T. Homolle et al., 6 vols. (Paris: E. de Boccard, 1902-87)
FMSt	*Frühmittelalterliche Studien*
FRLANT	Forschungen zur Religion und Literatur des Alten und Neuen Testaments
FSC	Faith and Scholarship Colloquies
GCS	Griechischen christlichen Schriftsteller
GerasaCBW	C. B. Welles, "Inscriptions," in *Gerasa: City of the Decapolis,* ed. C. H. Kraeling, pp. 355-69 (New Haven: Yale University Press, 1938)
GerasaPLG	P.-L. Gatier, "Gouverneurs et Procurateurs à Gérasa," *Syria* 73 (1996): 47-56
GNS	Good News Studies
GRBS	*Greek, Roman, and Byzantine Studies*
HA	Handbuch der Archäologie
HAlt	Handbuch der Altertumswissenschaft
HBT	*Horizons in Biblical Theology*
HdO	Handbuch der Orientalistik
HNT	Handbuch zum Neuen Testament
HSCP	*Harvard Studies in Classical Philology*
HTR	*Harvard Theological Review*
HTS	Harvard Theological Studies
HUCA	*Hebrew Union College Annual*
IA	Internationale Archäologie
IAlexandriaK	*Recueil des inscriptions grecques et latines (non funéraires) d'Alexandrie impériale (Ier-IIIer s. apr. J.-C.),* by F. Kayser (Cairo: Institut français d'archéologie orientale du Caire, 1994)

IBeth She'arim	*Beth She'arim II: The Greek Inscriptions,* by M. Schwabe and B. Lifshitz (New Brunswick, N.J.: Rutgers University Press, 1967)
IBS	*Irish Biblical Studies*
ICC	International Critical Commentary
IDB	*Interpreter's Dictionary of the Bible,* ed. G. A. Buttrick, 5 vols. (Nashville, 1962)
IDBSup	*Interpreter's Dictionary of the Bible, Supplement*
IDelta	*Le delta égyptien d'après les textes grecs,* by A. Bernand, 3 vols. (Cairo: Institut français d'archéologie orientale, 1970-)
IEJ	*Israel Exploration Journal*
IFayum	*Recueil des inscriptions grecques du Fayoum,* by E. Bernand, 3 vols. (Leiden: Brill, 1975-81)
IG	*Inscriptiones graecae.* Editio minor (Berlin 1924-)
IG ii²	*Inscriptiones Atticae Euclidis anno posteriores,* ed. J. Kirchner, 4 vols., Inscriptiones Graecae ii-iii (Berlin: Walter de Gruyter, 1913-40)
IGLSyria xiii/1	*Inscriptions grecques et latines de la Syrie. Tome XIII/1: Bostra,* by M. Sartre (Paris: Paul Geuthner, 1982)
IGLSyria xxi/2	*Inscriptions grecques et latines de la Syrie. Tome XXI: Inscriptions de la Jordanie. 2: Région centrale,* by P.-L. Gatier (Paris: Paul Geuthner, 1986)
IGRR	*Inscriptiones Graecae ad Res Romanas Pertinentes,* ed. R. L. Cagnat et al., 4 vols. (Paris: E. Leroux, 1906-27)
IJNAUE	*International Journal of Nautical Archaeology and Underwater Exploration*
IJudEg	*Jewish Inscriptions of Graeco-Roman Egypt,* ed. W. Horbury and D. Noy (Cambridge: Cambridge University Press, 1992)
IJudEu	*Jewish Inscriptions of Western Europe,* ed. D. Noy, 2 vols. (Cambridge: Cambridge University Press, 1993-95)
ILS	*Inscriptiones Latinae Selectae,* ed. H. Dessau, 3 vols. in 5 (Berlin, 1892-1916)
IMagMai	*Die Inschriften von Magnesia am Maeander,* by O. Kern (Berlin: W. Spemann, 1900)
Int	*Interpretation*
IoRJ	Iconography of Religions, Judaism
ISmyrna	*Die Inschriften von Smyrna,* ed. G. Petzl, Inschriften griechischer Städte aus Kleinasien 23-24/1-2 (Bonn: Rudolf Habelt, 1982-90)
JAC	*Jahrbuch für Antike und Christentum*
JANES	*Journal of the Ancient Near Eastern Society of Columbia University*
JBL	*Journal of Biblical Literature*
JdI	*Jahrbuch des deutschen archäologischen Instituts*
JDSK	*Jahrbuch der Deutschen Sporthochschule Köln*
JebelBlât	"Les inscriptions de l'église de Blât: Essai de relecture," by F. Alpi and L. Nordiguian, *Syria* 73 (1996): 5-14
JES	*Journal of Ecumenical Studies*
JJS	*Journal of Jewish Studies*
JNES	*Journal of Near Eastern Studies*

JPOS	*Journal of the Palestine Oriental Society*
JQR	*Jewish Quarterly Review*
JRA	*Journal of Roman Archaeology*
JRASS	*Journal of Roman Archaeology Supplementary Series*
JRS	*Journal of Roman Studies*
JSJ	*Journal for the Study of Judaism in the Persian, Hellenistic, and Roman Periods*
JSNT	*Journal for the Study of the New Testament*
JSNTSS	Journal for the Study of the New Testament: Supplement Series
JSOTSS	Journal for the Study of the Old Testament: Supplement Series
JSPSup	Journal for the Study of the Pseudepigrapha: Supplement Series
JTC	*Journal for Theology and the Church*
JTS	*Journal of Theological Studies*
JTSA	*Journal of Theology for Southern Africa*
LASBF	*Liber annuus Studii biblici franciscani*
LCL	Loeb Classical Library
LXX	Septuagint
MAMA	*Monumenta Asiae Minoris antiqua*, ed. W. M. Calder et al., 10 vols. (London: Published for the Society by the Manchester University Press, 1928-93)
MB	Middle Bronze
MDAI	*Mitteilungen des Deutschen archäologischen Instituts*
MdB	*Le Monde de la Bible*
NEAEHL	*New Encyclopedia of Archaeological Excavations in the Holy Land*, ed. E. Stern, 4 vols. (New York, 1993)
NewDocs	*New Documents Illustrating Early Christianity*, ed. G. H. R. Horsley, 7 vols. (North Ryde, New South Wales: Macquarrie University, 1981-96)
NovT	*Novum Testamentum*
NovTSup	Novum Testamentum Supplements
NRSV	New Revised Standard Version
NTAM	New Testament Archaeology Monograph
NTOA	Novum Testamentum et Orbis Antiquus
NTS	*New Testament Studies*
NTSMS	New Testament Studies Monograph Series
NTT	*Norsk Teologisk Tidsskrift*
NTTS	New Testament Tools and Studies
OBO	Orbis biblicus et orientalis
OEANE	*The Oxford Encyclopedia of Archaeology in the Near East*, ed. E. Meyers, 5 vols. (Oxford, 1997)
OTP	Old Testament Pseudepigrapha
OTP	*Old Testament Pseudepigrapha*, ed. J. H. Charlesworth, 2 vols. (New York, 1983-85)
PEQ	*Palestine Exploration Quarterly*
PG	Patrologia Graeca, ed. J.-P. Migne, 162 vols. (Paris, 1857-66)
PGL	*Patristic Greek Lexicon*, ed. G. W. H. Lampe

PGM	*Papyri graecae magicae,* ed. K. Preisendanz
PIR[1]	*Prosopographia Imperii Romani Saec. I.II.III,* by E. Klebs, P. de Rohden, and H. Dessau, 3 vols. (Berlin: Georg Reimer, 1897-98)
PL	Patrologia Latina, ed. J.-P. Migne, 221 vols. (Paris, 1844-64)
PLRE	*The Prosopography of the Later Roman Empire,* by A. H. M. Jones, J. R. Martindale, and J. Morris, 3 vols. (Cambridge: Cambridge University Press, 1971-92)
POxy	*The Oxyrhynchus Papyri,* ed. A. S. Grenfell, B. P. Hunt, et al. (London: Egypt Exploration Society, 1898-)
PRyl	*Catalogue of the Greek Papyri in the John Rylands Library,* ed. A. S. Hunt et al., 4 vols. (Manchester: Manchester University Press, 1911-52)
PSB	*Princeton Seminary Bulletin*
PTS	Patristische Texte und Studien
PTSDSSP	Princeton Theological Seminary Dead Sea Scrolls Project
PW	A. F. Pauly, *Paulys Realencyclopädie der classischen Altertumswissenschaft,* ed. G. Wissowa, new ed., 49 vols. (Munich, 1980)
Qad	*Qadmoniot*
QDAP	*Quarterly of the Department of Antiquities in Palestine*
QRT	*Quaker Religious Thought*
RA	*Revue d'assyriologie et d'archéologie orientale*
RAC	*Reallexikon für Antike und Christentum,* ed. T. Kluser et al. (Stuttgart, 1950-)
RB	*Revue biblique*
REA	*Revue des études anciennes*
REG	*Revue des études grecques*
REJ	*Revue des études juives*
RevQ	*Revue de Qumran*
RRP	Religion der Römischen Provinzen
RSR	*Recherches de science religieuse*
RSV	Revised Standard Version
RVV	Religionsgeschichtliche Versuche und Vorarbeiten
SB	*Sammelbuch griechischer Urkunden aus Ägypten,* ed. F. Preisigke and F. Bilabel (Strassburg: K. J. Trubner, 1915-)
SBEC	Studies in the Bible and Early Christianity
SBF.CMa	Studium biblicum Franciscanum — Collection Major
SBF.CMi	Studium biblicum Franciscanum — Collection Minor
SBLDS	Society of Biblical Literature Dissertation Series
SBLSP	*Society of Biblical Literature Seminar Papers*
SBLTT	Society of Biblical Literature Texts and Translations
SBS	Stuttgarter Bibelstudien
SBT	Studies in Biblical Theology
SC	Sources Chrétiennes
SCI	*Scripta Classica Israelica*
SCJ	Studies in Christianity and Judaism

ScrHier	*Scripta hierosolymitana*
SE	*Studia evangelica I, II, III* (= TU 73 [1959], 87 [1964], 88 [1964], etc.)
SEG	*Supplementum Epigraphicum Graecum* (Leiden: A. W. Sijthoff, 1923-)
SFSHJ	South Florida Studies in the History of Judaism
SHANE	Studies in the History of the Ancient Near East
SHR	Studies in the History of Religions
SJLA	Studies in Judaism in Late Antiquity
SNTSMS	Society for New Testament Studies Monograph Series
SNTSU	Studien zum Neuen Testament und seiner Umwelt
SPB	Studia postbiblica
SSKA	Schriften des Seminars für Klassische Archäologie der Freien Universität Berlin
STDJ	Studies on the Texts of the Desert of Judah
Str-B	H. L. Strack and P. Billerbeck, *Kommentar zum Neuen Testament aus Talmud und Midrasch,* 6 vols. (Munich, 1922-61)
SUNT	Studien zur Umwelt des Neuen Testaments
SwJT	*Southwestern Journal of Theology*
Syll³	*Sylloge Inscriptionum Graecarum,* by W. Dittenberger, 3rd ed., 4 vols. (Leipzig: S. Hirzel, 1915-24)
TA	*Tel Aviv*
TANZ	Texte und Arbeiten zum neutestamentlichen Zeitalter
TBei	*Theologische Beiträge*
TDNT	*Theological Dictionary of the New Testament,* ed. G. Kittel and G. Friedrich, trans. G. W. Bromiley, 10 vols. (Grand Rapids, 1974-)
TDOT	*Theological Dictionary of the Old Testament,* ed. G. J. Botterweck and H. Ringgren, trans. D. E. Green, 6 vols. (Grand Rapids, 1974-)
TEV	Today's English Version
TIR	*Tabula Imperii Romani: Iudaea-Palestina: Eretz Israel in the Hellenistic, Roman, and Byzantine Periods: Maps and Gazetteer,* Y. Tsafrir, L. di Segni, and J. Green (Jerusalem: Israel Academy of Sciences and Humanities, 1994)
TRu	*Theologische Rundschau*
TSAJ	Texte und Studien zum antiken Judentum
TTS	Theologische Texte und Studien
TU	Texte und Untersuchungen
TWNT	*Theologisches Wörterbuch zum Neuen Testament,* ed. G. Kittel and G. Friedrich, 10 vols. (Stuttgart, 1932-79)
TynBul	*Tyndale Bulletin*
UCPH	University of California Publications in History
UTY	Übersetzung des Talmud Yerushalmi
VC	*Vigiliae christianae*
VS	*Verbum Salutis*
VT	*Vetus Testamentum*
WBC	Word Biblical Commentary
WdF	Wege der Forschung
WuD	*Wort und Dienst*

WUNT	Wissenschaftliche Untersuchungen zum Neuen Testament
ZABR	*Zeitschrfit für altorientalische und biblische Rechtgeschichte*
ZDPV	*Zeitschrift des deutschen Palästina-Vereins*
ZKG	*Zeitschrift für Kirchengeschichte*
ZNW	*Zeitschrift für die neutestamentliche Wissenschaft*
ZPE	*Zeitschrift für Papyrologie und Epigraphik*

Ancient Documents

BIBLE

Gen	Genesis	Nah	Nahum
Ex	Exodus	Hab	Habakkuk
Lev	Leviticus	Zeph	Zephaniah
Num	Numbers	Hag	Haggai
Deut	Deuteronomy	Zech	Zechariah
Josh	Joshua	Mal	Malachi
Judg	Judges	Mt	Matthew
Ruth	Ruth	Mk	Mark
1 Sam	1 Samuel	Lk	Luke
2 Sam	2 Samuel	Jn	John
1 Kgs	1 Kings	Acts	Acts of the Apostles
2 Kgs	2 Kings	Rom	Romans
1 Chr	1 Chronicles	1 Cor	1 Corinthians
2 Chr	2 Chronicles	2 Cor	2 Corinthians
Ezra	Ezra	Gal	Galatians
Neh	Nehemiah	Eph	Ephesians
Esth	Esther	Phil	Philippians
Job	Job	Col	Colossians
Ps(s)	Psalm(s)	1 Thess	1 Thessalonians
Prov	Proverbs	2 Thess	2 Thessalonians
Eccl	Ecclesiastes	1 Tim	1 Timothy
Song	Song of Solomon	2 Tim	2 Timothy
Isa	Isaiah	Titus	Titus
Jer	Jeremiah	Philem	Philemon
Lam	Lamentations	Heb	Hebrews
Ezek	Ezekiel	Jas	James
Dan	Daniel	1 Pet	1 Peter
Hos	Hosea	2 Pet	2 Peter
Joel	Joel	1 Jn	1 John
Am	Amos	2 Jn	2 John
Ob	Obadiah	3 Jn	3 John
Jon	Jonah	Jude	Jude
Mic	Micah	Rev	Revelation

Old Testament Apocrypha and Pseudepigrapha

(Also, see abbreviations in Charlesworth, ed., *Old Testament Pseudepigrapha*, 2 vols.)

1 En	*1 Enoch*
1 Macc	1 Maccabees
2 Macc	2 Maccabees
4 Macc	4 Maccabees
Jdt	Judith
Jub	*Jubilees*
Pss Sol	*Psalms of Solomon*
Sib Or	*Sibylline Oracles*
T Benj	*Testament of Benjamin*
Wis	Wisdom of Solomon

New Testament Apocrypha and Pseudepigrapha

(Also, see abbreviations in Charlesworth, *The New Testament Apocrypha and Pseudepigrapha*)

ActsPet	*Acts of Peter*
ActsThom	*Acts of Thomas*
(Arab) GosInf	*Arabic Gospel of the Infancy*

Ancient Writers

Agr	Philo, *De agricultura*
Ann	Tacitus, *Annals*
Ant	Josephus, *Jewish Antiquities*
Apion	Josephus, *Against Apion*
Ep Const	Eusebius, *Epistula ad Constantium*
HE	Eusebius, *Ecclesiastical History*
Geogr	Strabo, *Geography*
Hist	Herodotus, *History*
OmnProbLib	Philo, *Quod omnis probus liber sit*
Post	Philo, *De posteritate Caini*
Quir	Cyprian, *Ad Quirinum*
QuisRerDivHer	Philo, *Quis rerum divinarum heres sit*
Scorp	Tertullian, *Scorpiace*
Tranq	Seneca, *De tranquillitate animi*
War	Josephus, *Jewish War*

Contributors

Paul N. Anderson is Professor of Biblical and Quaker Studies at George Fox University in Newberg, Oregon.

Rami Arav is Director of the Bethsaida Excavations Project at the University of Nebraska at Omaha, where he also teaches in the Department of Philosophy and Religion.

Dan Bahat is Senior Lecturer in the Department of Land of Israel Studies, Bar-Ilan University, Ramat-Gan, Israel.

Richard A. Batey is Professor of Religious Studies at Rhodes College.

Avraham Biran is Director of the Nelson Glueck School of Biblical Archaeology at Hebrew Union College–Jewish Institute of Religion in Jerusalem.

Brian J. Capper is Reader in Christian Origins at Canterbury Christ Church University College.

James H. Charlesworth is George L. Collord Professor of New Testament Language and Literature and Editor of the Dead Sea Scrolls Project at Princeton Theological Seminary.

Bruce Chilton is Bernard Iddings Bell Professor of Philosophy and Religion and Executive Director of the Institute of Advanced Theology at Bard College.

James D. G. Dunn is Lightfoot Professor of Divinity Emeritus at the University of Durham, England.

J. K. Elliott is Professor of New Testament Textual Criticism at the University of Leeds, England.

Esther Eshel is Senior Lecturer in the Department of Bible, Bar-Ilan University, Ramat-Gan, Israel.

Craig A. Evans is Payzant Distinguished Professor of New Testament Studies at Acadia Divinity College.

Sean Freyne is Director of Mediterranean and Near Eastern Studies and Professor of Theology Emeritus at Trinity College, Dublin.

Yizhar Hirschfeld is Associate Professor in the Institute of Archaeology at the Hebrew University of Jerusalem, where he is Director of the Tiberias Excavation.

William Klassen is Professor of Religious Studies Emeritus at the University of Waterloo.

John S. Kloppenborg is Professor in the Department and Centre for the Study of Religion at the University of Toronto.

Achim Lichtenberger is Scientific Assistant in the Archäologisches Seminar und Museum at Westfälischen Wilhelms-Universität Münster.

Frédéric Manns, O.F.M., is Director of the Studium Biblicum Franciscanum, Jerusalem.

John Painter is Professor of Theology and Research Biblical Scholar at St. Mark's National Theological Centre, Charles Sturt University, Australia.

Michele Piccirillo, O.F.M., is Ordinary Professor of Biblical Geography and History at the Studium Biblicum Franciscanum, where he is also director of the museum.

Bargil Pixner, O.S.B., was Professor of New Testament and Biblical Studies at the Jerusalem Center for Biblical Studies and a member of the Hagia Maria Sion Abbey in Jerusalem before his death in April 2002.

Emile Puech is Professor at the École Biblique et Archéologique Française de Jérusalem.

John Reumann is Professor of New Testament Studies Emeritus at the Lutheran Seminary at Philadelphia.

Peter Richardson is Professor of Religion Emeritus at the University of Toronto.

Henry W. M. Rietz is Associate Professor of Religious Studies at Grinnell College.

Daniel R. Schwartz is Professor in the Department of Jewish History at the Hebrew University of Jerusalem.

Benedict T. Viviano, O.P., is Professor of Biblical Studies at the University of Fribourg, Switzerland.

Urban C. von Wahlde is Professor of Theology at Loyola University of Chicago.

John W. Welch is Robert K. Thomas Professor of Law at Brigham Young University's J. Reuben Clark Law School.

Jürgen Zangenberg is *Privatdozent* jointly in the theological faculties of the Universities of Frankfurt, Germany, and Tilburg, the Netherlands.

Joseph E. Zias works in the Science and Archaeology Group at the Hebrew University of Jerusalem.

The Historical Jesus and
Biblical Archaeology: Questions

The beginnings of historical Jesus research may be dated to the late eighteenth century with the publication of portions of the *magnum opus* of Hermann Samuel Reimarus (1694-1768) in 1778.[1] Interest in the historical Jesus waned between the wars (ca. 1913-45) and sputtered again to new life in the New Quest of the Historical Jesus sometime after 1953. Only recently, however, has the new interest in the study of the historical Jesus — "Jesus Research" — been challenged and even enriched by archaeological research.

New Testament experts rightly agree that they are theologians. The study of Jesus begins with theological texts, the intra-canonical Gospels. These texts are clearly shaped by the desire to proclaim that Jesus from (of) Nazareth is the Christ (the Messiah) and that one should believe in him as the Savior. The impression is often given that history is not important; what is significant is theology.

Archaeologists like to claim that they are scientists. They excavate a circumscribed area and seek to learn what might be known about life in the past in that particular place and during the periods revealed by each stratum (level of occupation). They habitually claim that *realia* (what is recovered by excavations, like pots, arrowheads, bronze or iron utensils, and coins) take precedence over any text that refers to the site, or area being excavated.

Actually, New Testament scholars are more than theologians. They admit that history is imperative for understanding the theologies presented in the New Testament. They recognize that the Gospels habitually refer to sites and

---

1. A. Schweitzer correctly reported, "BEFORE REIMARUS, NO ONE HAD ATTEMPTED TO FORM A HISTORICAL CONCEPTION OF THE LIFE OF JESUS" (capitalization in the original). Schweitzer, *The Quest of the Historical Jesus: A Critical Study of Its Progress from Reimarus to Wrede,* trans. W. Montgomery (New York: Macmillan, 1906, 1964 [reprinted often]), p. 13. Schweitzer reported that Reimarus's full manuscript is in the Hamburg municipal library and "runs to 4000 pages" (p. 14).

realia (references to physical things in a text). Thus, Jesus is reputed to have visited and done certain things in specific sites, like Nazareth, Cana, and Bethsaida, as well as places such as a synagogue. Jesus refers to specific things *(realia)* like pots, utensils, and coins. No reputable scholar today questions that a Jew named Jesus son of Joseph lived; most readily admit that we now know a considerable amount about his actions and his basic teachings (the proclamation that the rule of God [the kingdom of God] was dawning on earth).

Archaeologists seldom misrepresent themselves by suggesting that they are disinterested in what is discovered. They are usually interested in more than some object from the past; they often get excited (and rightly so) about the possibility of being in touch with and bringing life again to the past. One reason for this energy is that our culture celebrates in many ways what is reputed to have happened in ancient Palestine, which is Israel today, and "the Holy Land." Most archaeologists are Jews and Christians, and while many are more secular than religious, they are not uninfluenced by the ways our culture and values enable meaning to shine into dark balks.

Neither archaeologists nor biblical scholars are "objective" observers. Each person shapes what is being seen and examined according to subjective norms, as Merleau-Ponty and Michael Polanyi demonstrated.[2] One should not imagine that biblical scholars are subjective theologians and archaeologists objective scientists. Faith in methodology, which is constantly being revised, and a set of presuppositions (often unperceived) guide each human search for truth and understanding. On the one hand, an archaeological discovery does limit discussion; but on the other hand, it does not come self-interpreted and usually challenges the interpreters. In my late twenties and during the time I was studying in the Ecole biblique, I was surprised by a fiery debate between K. Kenyon and R. de Vaux, and later by a fervent exchange between Glueck and Mazar in a balk south of the Temple Mount. Archaeological discoveries brought up volcanic tempers. Hence, archaeological discoveries usually demand discussion before any synthesis and historical reconstruction are acceptable.

The following chapters disclose how New Testament scholars learn from archaeologists, who are expert stratigraphers of archaeological sites, and how archaeologists garner knowledge from New Testament scholars, who are experts in the stratification of texts. I have noted and experienced a close and respectful relationship among biblical scholars and archaeologists. After all, it is often clear that some scholars are both, including Petrie, Albright, Wright,

---

2. For my personal reflections, see Charlesworth, "Polanyi, Merleau-Ponty, Arendt, and the Foundation of Biblical Hermeneutics," in *Interpretation of the Bible,* ed. J. Krašovec (Ljubljana: Slovenska akademija znanosti in umetnosti; Sheffield: Sheffield Academic Press, 1998), pp. 1531-56.

Cross, Kenyon, de Vaux, Benoit, Murphy-O'Connor, Corbo, Strange, and virtually all who participated in the millennium symposium and prepared chapters for the present volume.

Thus, it is relevant to ask numerous questions about how and in what ways, if at all, archaeological discoveries can help us reconstruct and understand the life and teachings of Jesus, son of Joseph (Jn 1:45 and 6:42).[3] Among the stellar questions are the following selected few:

- What can be known about Nazareth during the time Jesus lived there as a youth, and where he read scripture in a synagogue, grew up, and perhaps worked in a builder's shop?
- What archaeological evidence has been recovered that helps us re-create and locate the activity of John the Baptizer?
- Where is Cana, is there any evidence of Jewish life there during the time of Jesus, and have stone vessels for the Jewish rites of purification been discovered?
- Where is Bethsaida, what evidence indicates fishermen were living there, and do we get a glimpse of what Jesus and his earliest disciples might have seen before 30 C.E.?
- What can be known about life in Sepphoris when Jesus was a youth, and how might he have been influenced by its culture?
- What can be known about synagogues during the time of Jesus?
- What was Samaria like during Jesus' time, and what has been discovered that helps us re-create that territory?
- What was Jerusalem like when Jesus visited there?
- How majestic was the Temple and the area near it, and what remains to help us comprehend what a Jew, at Passover, in 30 C.E., walking up to the Temple, might have seen?
- Does archaeology provide any supporting data regarding Caiaphas, Pilate, and Simon of Cyrene?
- Where was Jesus crucified and what can be known about crucifixion in ancient Palestine at that time?

Obviously, we will always have more questions than answers. The process of being educated, in many ways, entails replacing a few small questions with many large ones. Archaeological research impacts Jesus Research — as the following chapters disclose — and helps us ask honest questions. Eventually, we will ob-

---

3. Jesus as "the son of Joseph" is a designation found only in the Gospel of John. It is claimed by the genealogies in Matthew and Luke.

tain more mature reflections on life in ancient Palestine from the time of Herod to the time of the destruction of 70 C.E.

I am grateful to those who made sacrifices so they could attend the millennium conference in Jerusalem. Many came early in the morning from their excavations and returned to their archaeological teams immediately after presenting their papers. I am also grateful for the support of Mayor Teddy Kollek, who was able to attend the opening luncheon. I was honored by the presence of Bill Eerdmans and Tom Cousins; I appreciate their presence and interest in Jesus and archaeology. Walter Weaver helped me improve my drafts. The papers were edited by me with the assistance of numerous students; three were especially helpful in working with me daily for a year to complete the task of editing. James J. Foster helped me correct the page proofs. Joe Eason helped me edit and complete the notes. Jacob Cherian helped me polish each chapter and compiled the glossary. Jonathan Soyars worked with me at the final stage, polishing the volume for publication, providing significant computer assistance, and completing the selected bibliography. To each and all I express my deep appreciation.

Princeton   JHC
January 2005

INTRODUCTION:
What Is Biblical Archaeology?

Avraham Biran

The subject of this lecture is a challenging one since it encompasses two fields of research — the Bible and archaeology. It is usually clear what is meant by "the Bible." As for archaeology, in view of the extensive and intensive archaeological activities in Israel, especially in recent years, and in view of certain misconceptions among a number of scholars, let me start by saying what biblical archaeology is not. In doing so, I go back to my great teacher, William Foxwell Albright.

Albright devoted himself to archaeological research and developed to perfection the principle of sequentially dating different accumulated layers of earth in ancient sites. He did so by a careful and detached study of the ceramic remains found in each layer and thus established the archaeological discipline on scientific foundations. Albright, a biblical scholar, is generally considered the father of biblical archaeology and, as I recall, included in biblical archaeology the whole Mediterranean area from North Africa to beyond Persia. He insisted that archaeology does not prove or disprove the Bible; the Bible, as a book of divine inspiration, needs no proof. Hence, biblical archaeology is not a discipline proving or disproving the Bible.

Nelson Glueck, a disciple of Albright, stated emphatically that the moral and spiritual values of the teachings or traditions in the Bible transcend the changes of time or the vagaries of human affairs. These values are inseparably connected with belief in the one God eternal. The finds of archaeological research, exploration, and excavation in Bible lands have a relevance to historical elements in the Bible, but in no wise affect its religious propositions or ethical decrees that are applicable to all peoples in all lands at all times. Glueck added that many source materials are to be found in the Bible, and it furnishes us with our main body of knowledge about the ancient history of Israel, the Holy Land, and the forces that affected them both.

Biblical archaeology in essence is only one among many legitimate specializations within the broader field of Near Eastern studies. It should be clearly stated that the discipline governing the study of the Bible and the discipline governing archaeological research are two separate and different disciplines based on independent principles, methodology, and training. Neither can be used to prove or disprove the other. At the same time, we are not at liberty to ignore either one. Indeed, they complement each other. Enigmatic biblical statements can often be illustrated by archaeological finds, and the more archaeological research is undertaken, the more our understanding of the biblical record is increased. Thus, biblical archaeology is a synthesis between the meager historical information drawn from the Bible and the extensive results of archaeology research. *Biblical archaeology may then be defined as archaeology of Bible lands in general and of the Holy Land in particular.* By establishing a dialogue between biblical studies and archaeological research, we are able to obtain a better picture of the historical and cultural setting of the Bible.

I would like to stress that biblical archaeology, with its two indispensable disciplines — archaeological research and biblical studies — is the base on which we set out our own excavations with a most positive effect on our work. Let me illustrate how the disciplines are intertwined. No doubt there are many pertinent examples of this from Old Testament sites, as well as from the New Testament period. I have chosen a few from our own excavations at Tel Dan, the longest ongoing archaeological project in Israel. The excavations of Tel Dan have uncovered significant remains that provide considerable evidence to illustrate the points I am making.

The first question to ask is if this site, Tel Dan (in Arabic Tell el Qadi, the mound of the judge), is correctly identified with the ancient city of Dan, mentioned in the Bible many times and well-known from the phrase "from Dan to Beersheba."

Over a hundred years ago Edward Robinson suggested the identification, basing it on the correspondence between two words that mean Judge, the Arabic word *Qadi* and the Hebrew Dan, and on Eusebius, who stated that Dan is located four miles from Banias. We had no doubt that the site was ancient Dan. Nevertheless, it was gratifying to have the identification confirmed when, during the excavations, a bilingual dedicatory inscription was discovered inscribed with the name Dan (fig. 1).

In the Bible the first reference to Dan is in Gen 14:14, but we know from Judg 18:29 that before its conquest by the tribe of Dan it was called "Laish." Laish also appears in the eighteenth century B.C.E. Egyptian execration texts with the name of its king — Horon Ab. Gen 14 relates events in the days of Abraham. Archaeological research is not concerned with proving or disproving what the patriarch Abraham did or whether he existed. However, what our ar-

Figure 1. Bilingual Greek and Aramaic inscription: "To the God who is in Dan."
Courtesy of Tel Dan Excavations, Hebrew Union College, Jerusalem

chaeological excavations did reveal are the remains of a large city of the Middle Bronze Age, defended in the eighteenth century B.C.E. by formidable sloping-earth ramparts. This discovery led to many seasons of excavations devoted to the investigation of these ramparts. We now know that the principle of construction — a central core with layers of earth abutting it — was the same in the southern, eastern, and northern flanks of the site. However, in the northern and eastern flanks, earlier Early Bronze Age structures served as a core, while in the southern flank a 10-meter-high, 5-to-6-meter-wide stone structure had to be built. It extended beyond the southern tower of the city gate. The gate, built of mud brick with three arches, is still standing as originally built.

The identification of these remains with Laish, the precursor of Dan, seems most reasonable. The purpose for such a complex defense system is a fascinating archaeological puzzle. For the student of the Bible, it is interesting that a few centuries later the people of Laish, according to Judg 18:7, were a people "quiet and secure." They must have trusted their formidable sloping-earth embankments to provide the necessary security.

The discovery of the gate and the steps leading up to it from the east, as well as the steps going down into the city in the west, allows our imagination flights of fancy. Would not the king of Laish, perhaps the same Horon Ab mentioned in the Egyptian execration text, greet Abraham, who had just defeated the kings who took his nephew Lot prisoner, and invite him to enter the city?

3

As the excavations progressed, the story of Tel Dan continued to unfold. The excavations also uncovered remains of a large city from the third as well as the second millennium B.C.E. The rich Canaanite culture is best illustrated by Mycenaean imports (fig. 2). We are thus able to obtain a picture of the city so briefly mentioned in the Bible — a city in existence long before the arrival there of the tribe of Dan.

Sometime toward the first half of the twelfth century B.C.E. a change occurs in the character of the settlement. The excavation uncovered a layer of pits, some stone lined, which are associated with nomadic people living in huts and storing their food in these pits. The pottery found in these pits included collared rim jars, and is dated to the beginning of the Iron Age. This is all that archaeology reveals, without telling much about the people who made these pits. However, in Judg 18:12 we read that the Danites pitched camp in Kiryat Yearim and called that place "*Mahaneh* Dan," tent camp of Dan, a statement that indicates seminomadic character. We had no doubt in assigning this level of occupation to the tribe of Dan.

The discovery during the excavations of crucibles, tuyeres, furnaces, and metal slag (fig. 3) indicates that this seminomadic people also engaged in metalwork. To a student of the Bible this should not be surprising. We learn from Ex 35:34 that the man assisting Bezalel in the construction of the tabernacle in the wilderness of Sinai was Aholiab, son of Ahisamach of the tribe of Dan. In other words, the members of the tribe of Dan were more than just shepherds. The archaeological discovery of metalwork at Tel Dan also enables us to appreciate an enigmatic reference in 2 Chr 2:13-14. Hiram, king of Tyre, tells Solomon that the expert he is sending is "the son of a woman of the daughters of Dan." By mentioning this fact the king of Tyre tells Solomon that this man comes from a place with a long tradition of metalwork.

The urbanization of the inhabitants of Tel Dan takes place, according to the archaeological evidence, in the eleventh to tenth century B.C.E. The Bible tells us that in the tenth century B.C.E. Jeroboam sets a golden calf at Dan (1 Kgs 12:29). We suggest that Jeroboam chose Dan not only because it is his northernmost city, but because Dan had a tradition of worship going back to the period of the settlement of the tribe, which had in Dan a statue and priests, as is related in Judg 18:30. Our excavations have now uncovered a layer of flat blocks of stone with pottery dated to the end of the tenth century B.C.E. and a large number of cult objects. Assigned to the reign of King Jeroboam, it represents the first stage of construction of the sanctuary and may well be the "house of High Places" mentioned in 1 Kgs 12:31. The centrality and importance of the sanctuary at Dan, revealed by the excavations, help us appreciate the somewhat obscure reference in 1 Kgs 12:30: "For the people went to worship before the one, even unto Dan."

The archaeological evidence leads to the conclusion that the sanctuary of

Figure 2. Imported Mycenaean Late Bronze Age vessels.

Courtesy of Tel Dan Excavations, Hebrew Union College, Jerusalem

Figure 3. The evidence for metalwork.

Courtesy of Tel Dan Excavations, Hebrew Union College, Jerusalem

Dan lasted for over a thousand years, from the days of Jeroboam to the Roman period. The second stage of construction is dated to the ninth century B.C.E. This is the period of the reign of King Ahab. The sanctuary, built of headers and stretchers, was enlarged. The discovery of a row of leaning stones was puzzling. But then we recalled a detail of how Solomon built the Temple. In 1 Kgs 6:36 we are told: "and he built the inner course with three rows of hewed stones and a row of cedar beams." We learn from Ezra 6:4 that this was common. Some five hundred years after Solomon, Cyrus, king of Persia, tells the exiles returning to Jerusalem to build the Temple in Jerusalem "with three rows of great stones and a row of new timber." At Dan we can actually see the principle of this construction. Can the construction of this sanctuary be assigned to a known historical figure?

The student of biblical archaeology knows of the accomplishments of King Ahab, who fought the Arameans and the Assyrians, and was also a great builder (1 Kgs 22:39). Thus we have no hesitancy in assigning to Ahab Stage B of the sanctuary and the construction of the fortifications of Dan.

The excavations uncovered at the foot of the rampart a massive stone wall and complex gate structure dated to the ninth century. They include a main gate, an outer gate, large paved areas, and a processional road that led from the gate to the city (fig. 4). These fortifications may have been built to ward off further attacks by the Arameans, whose king Ben-hadad of Damascus "smote Dan" at the beginning of the ninth century, according to 1 Kgs 15:20 and 2 Chr 16:4. The discovery of the outer and main gates provides the student of the Bible with a visual example of a king "who sits between the gates" (2 Sam 18:24).

The excavations also revealed evidence for considerable cultic activity at the gate. This included a canopied structure and three sets of five *masseboth* (sacred pillars), which may well be considered part of the "high place at the gate" mentioned only once in the Bible (2 Kgs 23:8). That they must have been a common feature at the entrance of the city can be adduced from the discovery of the structure built at Dan in the seventh century B.C.E. (fig. 5), on top of the accumulated debris from Tiglath-pileser III's conquest in 735/732. We suggest that this composite and well-preserved structure is a good example of what the "high place at the gate" may have looked like. The discoveries at Tel Dan indicate that the cultic activity at the gates was indeed much more common than the one reference in the Bible implies. Dan thus sets another example of the affinity of archaeological excavations to biblical studies.

The excavations at Tel Dan help us visualize also the *ḥuṣṣoth* mentioned in the Bible. Ben-hadad, king of Damascus, tells the victorious Ahab, "I will restore the towns that my father took from your father; and you may establish *ḥuṣṣoth* for yourself in Damascus, as my father did in Samaria" (1 Kgs 20:34). *Ḥuṣṣoth* is usually translated "streets" (or "bazaars"; RSV), but *ḥuṣṣoth* comes from the He-

Figure 4. Reconstruction of the ninth century B.C.E. city gate complex.

Courtesy of Tel Dan Excavations, Hebrew Union College, Jerusalem

Figure 5. Structure with *masseboth* built in the seventh B.C.E. century on top of the accumulated debris of the Assyrian conquest.

Courtesy of Tel Dan Excavations, Hebrew Union College, Jerusalem

brew *ḥûṣ*, meaning outside. Until now, no one could suggest what the *ḥuṣṣoth* looked like. At Dan we have an example of the *ḥuṣṣoth* (fig. 6), built outside the city wall and gate complex. They may well be found at other sites in the future.

It is necessary to conclude this presentation with references to two more discoveries at Tel Dan. First, the most elaborate stage of the Dan sanctuary is in the eighth century B.C.E. Steps were built leading to the top of the central platform, and additional structures were erected with an altar and jars for the ashes. Here iron shovels were found. Similar shovels may well have been used in the Temple in Jerusalem. The centrality of this sanctuary at Dan may well have aroused the wrath of the prophet Amos, who castigated the people for swearing by the "god of Dan" (Am 8:14). Also in the eighth century, an upper gate was built to strengthen the defenses of the city. To the student of biblical archaeology, Jeroboam II is the candidate who could have undertaken such projects. He conquered Damascus and "restored the coasts of Israel" as far north as "from the entering of Hamath" (2 Kgs 14:25), and had the means and ability to do so.

Second, an Aramaic victory stele dated to the second half of the ninth century mentions the "king of Israel" and the "king of the House of David" (i.e., Judah; see fig. 34 on p. 159). This inscription illustrates most strikingly how archaeological research and biblical studies complement each other. The examples from Tel Dan illustrate the essence and significance of biblical archaeology.

Figure 6. Paved courtyard and the *ḥuṣṣoth* outside the gate and city wall.
Courtesy of Tel Dan Excavations, Hebrew Union College, Jerusalem

STUDIES IN ARCHAEOLOGY

Jesus Research and Archaeology:
A New Perspective

James H. Charlesworth

How and in what significant ways may archaeology be important in Jesus Research?[1] The present attempt to answer this question is organized under three sequential sections: a brief scan of the preeminent publications in this field, an assessment of the archaeological discoveries in "the Holy Land"[2] that may be most helpful in Jesus Research, and a glimpse at three crucial debates among experts. Intermittently as well as in the conclusion, I shall indicate how we might grasp the fundamental importance of archaeology in re-creating the social and spiritual world of Jesus from Nazareth.[3] While Jesus lived in an apocalyptic world charged with cosmic spirits, he used earthly images that shaped his creative thoughts. Many of these images can be more accurately imagined two thousand years later, since we can hold or see first-century *realia*, like stone vessels,[4] lamps and "flasks" (actually oil fillers),[5] walled vineyards with towers,[6] coins (even the widow's mite),[7] and swords,[8] that shaped his pictorially rich teachings and parables.[9]

1. I capitalize "Jesus Research" since it has become a *terminus technicus*. And I use it to represent the study of the historical Jesus that began around 1980 (following the no-quest, and the two quests).

2. The concept of the Holy Land is not a Christian creation. It appeared before the first century c.e. in early Jewish literature. See Charlesworth, "The Jesus of History and the Topography of the Holy Land," in *The Handbook of the Study of the Historical Jesus*, ed. T. Holmén and S. E. Porter (Leiden: Brill, 2005).

3. See Mt 21:11; cf. Mt 4:13; Mk 1:9.

4. See Jn 2:6. Only the Fourth Evangelist refers to stone jars that are necessary for the Jewish rites of ritual purity. See esp. 11QTemple 50.

5. See Mt 25:1-12.

6. See Mk 12:1-9.

7. The widow's mite (or *Perutah*), two copper coins, is mentioned only in Mk 12:42-43 and Lk 21:2-3.

8. See esp. Mt 26:52, which is the only verse in which Jesus warns that those who take up the sword will perish by the sword. In fact, this warning appears twice in this one verse.

9. A form of this publication appeared in the Peder Borgen Festschrift (NovTSup 106). I

I. A Review of Publications

In 1988 I attempted to assess, inter alia, how archaeology was beginning to enrich Jesus Research. Some experts missed this point, since archaeology appeared only as a subtitle of *Jesus within Judaism: New Light from Exciting Archaeological Discoveries.*[10] Now, at the beginning of the twenty-first century, I shall focus primarily on the archaeological insights into Jesus' time obtained by trained archaeologists digging in Galilee, Judea, and the environs of ancient Palestine. How can scholars learn from archaeology as they engage in Jesus Research?

What is meant by "Jesus Research"? This term can be categorized as beginning in 1980, which followed the decline of the so-called new quest for the historical Jesus. The latter was shaped by theological, even existential, concerns. Jesus Research attracts not only Christian scholars but also Jewish experts — like Flusser, Vermes, Gruenwald, Mendels,[11] and Segal — who have no yearning to discover a Jesus deemed worthy to follow. Jesus Research proceeds with open questions; it is not shaped by theological agendas as were all the preceding studies of the historical Jesus.

Jesus Research contrasts to both the old quest of the historical Jesus and the new quest of the historical Jesus. The old quest was not defined by interrogatives; it was categorized by scholars (and others) who attempted to write a biography of Jesus. The new quest was more defined by questions, and the leading one was, "What does the historical Jesus mean to me as a Christian?"[12] The issues in Jesus Research contrast to these christological agendas.[13] It is almost always defined by interrogative investigations. Some of the most important questions in Jesus Research are the following:

---

am grateful to E. J. Brill and Professor Borgen for permission to publish a revised version of that work. An even earlier version of the present publication was delivered to the Jesus Seminar in the SNTSMS; it was dedicated to two archaeologists who teach in the Hebrew University, Jerusalem, namely, Lee I. Levine and Ehud Netzer. They were my colleagues during the two years I was Lady Davis Professor in the History Department at the Hebrew University.

10. Charlesworth, *Jesus within Judaism: New Light from Exciting Archaeological Discoveries,* ABRL 1 (Garden City, N.Y.: Doubleday, 1988).

11. See esp. D. Mendels, "Jesus and the Politics of His Day," in *Images of Jesus Today,* ed. Charlesworth and W. P. Weaver, FSC 3 (Valley Forge, Pa.: Trinity, 1994), pp. 98-112.

12. For further reflections see Charlesworth, "Archaeology, Jesus, and Christian Faith," in *What Has Archaeology to Do with Faith?* ed. Charlesworth and Weaver, FSC (Philadelphia: Trinity, 1992), pp. 1-22.

13. Of course, some of those engaged in Jesus Research are continuing a quest for Jesus for christological reasons. I shall not cite their works in this review, since they have shown no interest in archaeology.

Figure 7. Qumran; Loc. 48; large *mikveh*. Perhaps in this *mikveh* the young men were permitted for the first time to enter the waters that would purify them and allow them to pass over into the Community. Courtesy of J. H. Charlesworth

- Who was this Jew that is called "Jesus from (of) Nazareth"?
- How does archaeological research help re-create Jesus' time and place?
- How do these new insights help us understand Jesus' life and actions?
- How does archaeological research help us perceive Jesus' agenda?
- How do archaeological discoveries help us re-create his social environment?
- How do they assist us better to understand Jesus' teachings?
- How do *realia* from Jesus' time and place help us comprehend his teaching?
- How do they help us write Jesus' psychobiography?[14]

It becomes clearer that Jesus Research is primarily inquisitive. It is not primarily (or usually) shaped by theological agendas. It appeared after exceptional archaeological discoveries — like the Qumran scrolls and the Nag Hammadi

14. See Charlesworth, "Jesus Research and the Appearance of Psychobiography," in *Revelation, Reason, and Faith: Essays in Honor of Truman G. Madsen,* ed. D. W. Parry et al. (Provo, Utah: FARMS, 2002), pp. 55-84. Also, see the next note.

codices — and the often phenomenal disclosures from excavations especially in Galilee, Judea, and the Jordan Valley, and on the Mediterranean coast of ancient Palestine (modern Israel). The central question in Jesus Research is, "Who was Jesus of Nazareth, what can be learned about his time and place, and how do these new discoveries help us re-create his life and teachings?"

Thus, while the brilliant insights of Martin Heidegger (1889-1976) on "time and being" tended to shape the new quest, historiography, sociology, psychology, and especially archaeology are intermittently helping to define and shape Jesus Research.

What are some of the major sociological insights? It seems we have learned, from sociology and archaeology, that the major elements in traditional village life in Lower Galilee included kinship, nationality, various types of Judaism, gender, inheritance, property, occupation, economic level, and health. In terms of psychology, some specialists are learning that we can focus on Jesus' personality. On the one hand, we should distance such research from modern clinical methods. On the other hand, we might enrich Jesus Research by being informed of psychobiographical methodologies.[15]

The new quest assumed — and proclaimed — that a biography of Jesus was now simply impossible, since the Gospels were judged (incorrectly) to be a unique genre in antiquity. Moreover, Jesus scholars, during that period (ca. 1953-80), argued that any interest in Jesus' life by the Evangelists was only because of the kerygma. This proclamation that Jesus was the Messiah, God's Son, whom God raised from the dead, was judged to be significant because it brings life and meaning to our present existence. Now, especially under the influence of R. A. Burridge, many scholars would concur with G. Stanton's statement: "I do not think it is now possible to deny that the Gospels are a sub-set of the broad ancient literary genre of 'lives,' that is, biographies. Even if the evangelists were largely ignorant of the tradition of Greek and Roman 'lives,' that is how the Gospels were received and listened to in the first decades after their composition."[16] I would urge us to include in such discussions another comparison. Since Jesus was a Jew, and since his Judaism was obviously shaped by Greek (and other) cultures, we need to compare the Gospels with the biographical interest in ancient biblical ideal figures that characterize the OT Apocrypha and Pseudepigrapha; for example, Joseph is hailed "the son of God" by the author of

15. See Charlesworth, "Psychobiography: A New and Challenging Methodology in Jesus Research," in *Psychology and the Bible: A New Way to Read the Scriptures,* ed. J. H. Ellens and W. G. Rollins (Westport, Conn., and London: Praeger, 2004), 4:21-57.

16. See Stanton's statement on p. ix in R. A. Burridge, *What Are the Gospels? A Comparison with Graeco-Roman Biography* (Grand Rapids: Eerdmans, 2004).

the biographical romance called *Joseph and Aseneth,* which was written about the same time as the final edition of the Gospel of John.

While a consensus in historical research may always remain elusive, we New Testament scholars seem to agree that a paradigm shift has occurred in the study of the historical Jesus.[17] Few of us now wish to ignore what is being learned archaeologically about life in Galilee and Judea during the time of Jesus. But it is not yet clear what has been learned from archaeological excavations of sites known from the New Testament records and how such information helps us re-create the world of Jesus' time and his own life and message. That endeavor is both the subject of the present book, *Jesus and Archaeology,* and the primary focus of the present chapter.

Surveys

One confronts vast problems in attempting to survey the field of Jesus and archaeology. Foremost among them seems to be an awareness that there may not yet exist such a "field" of study. On the one hand, we are confronted with the vast number of publications on pre-70 Palestinian archaeology with virtually no concern for the New Testament, let alone Jesus of Nazareth. On the other hand, we are faced with the veritable flood of books and articles on Jesus, with shockingly little concern for or knowledge of archaeology. This focused survey of Jesus and archaeology is therefore organized so that the best surveys, the most reliable encyclopedias, and the most helpful one-volume works will be placed on center stage in Jesus Research.

The most helpful survey for our purposes seems to be Jonathan L. Reed's *Archaeology and the Galilean Jesus* (2000).[18] Reed has been involved in archaeological excavations in Galilee and served as codirector of the Sepphoris Acropolis Excavations. His major purpose is to share with a wide audience the developments in field archaeology in Galilee and to indicate how and why these are important in Jesus Research.

17. Long after this study had been completed, I heard about J. L. Reed and J. D. Crossan's collaborative effort on Jesus and archaeology; see their book entitled *Excavating Jesus* (San Francisco: HarperSanFrancisco, 2001).

18. J. L. Reed, *Archaeology and the Galilean Jesus: A Re-examination of the Evidence* (Harrisburg, Pa.: Trinity, 2000). For a less critical and informed treatment of archaeology and Jesus Research, but one that includes Judea and even the Diaspora, see J. McRay, *Archaeology and the New Testament* (Grand Rapids: Baker, 1991). Too out-of-date is J. Finegan's *Archaeology of the New Testament: The Life of Jesus and the Beginning of the Early Church* (Princeton: Princeton University Press, 1970 [1992, rev. ed.]).

Reed features Sepphoris and Capernaum in studying the historical Jesus. That is because he has spent over a decade helping to excavate and analyze these two sites.[19] He correctly warns that studies on Jesus and Sepphoris have been distorted by false dichotomies, such as Hellenism versus Judaism and urban versus rural. He points out that Antipas is the one who forced a tendency toward Hellenization in Galilee and that this fact is evident in later *realia* and architectural remains.

Reed organizes his book under three parts. First, he examines the diverse scholarly opinions regarding the identity of the Galileans. Were they primarily Jews or transplanted Judeans, as S. Klein and S. Freyne contend? Were they essentially Gentiles or Itureans forced to become "Jewish" by the Hasmoneans, as E. Schürer and W. Bauer claimed? Or were they descendants of the northern Israelites, as A. Alt and R. Horsley argue?[20] Reed points out that archaeological work discloses that there was no continuity from the Iron Age to the first century B.C.E. (*pace* Alt and Horsley). He shows that there is no evidence of the seminomadic Itureans in Lower Galilee (*pace* Schürer and Bauer). He demonstrates that Galilee and Judea were united culturally (Hasmonean coins are abundant only in Judea, Galilee, and the Golan), and that Galileans and Judeans shared a common heritage.

The shift in meaning of *Ioudaios* (which can mean "Judean" or "Jew") from the ethno-geographical term "Judean" to the religious designation "Jew" occurred during the Hasmonean period in the second century B.C.E.[21] Most likely, the earliest reference to *Ioudaios* as meaning "Jew" occurs in 2 Macc 6:6 and 9:17. This text was written shortly after 134 B.C.E., since it refers to the conferring of the high priesthood on John Hyrcanus, which occurred in that year.

Reed correctly states that there are four main religious indicators of a cultural homogeneity between Galilean Jews and Judean Jews. These are the discoveries in both provinces, and virtually nowhere else, of stone vessels, *mikvaot*

19. If he had been involved in the excavations at Bethsaida, Reed would probably have said more about that site than two sentences, as they are about its relevance for assessing why Jesus may not have visited Sepphoris (see Reed, *Archaeology*, p. 133). Periodic page references in the following paragraphs are to Reed's *Archaeology and the Galilean Jesus*.

20. See R. A. Horsley, *Archaeology, History, and Society in Galilee: The Social Context of Jesus and the Rabbis* (Valley Forge, Pa.: Trinity, 1996); Horsley, *Galilee: History, Politics, People* (Valley Forge, Pa.: Trinity, 1995); Horsley, *Jesus and the Spiral of Violence: Popular Jewish Resistance in Roman Palestine* (Minneapolis: Fortress, 1993); Horsley, *Bandits, Prophets, and Messiahs: Popular Movements in the Time of Jesus* (Minneapolis: Winston, 1985).

21. I am indebted to S. J. D. Cohen for this insight; see his *The Beginnings of Jewishness: Boundaries, Varieties, and Uncertainties* (Berkeley: University of California Press, 1999), pp. 70-71 and 82-106.

(Jewish baths for ritual purification), common burial techniques, and the lack of pig bones among discarded animal remains. It is now relatively certain that *mikvaot*, the most important architectural feature among these four indicators, were introduced to the Galileans by the Hasmoneans.

Many Galilean Jews adhered to the Torah's celebration of the Temple. Some most likely considered it the *axis mundi* (cf. *Jubilees*). Archaeological discoveries in Lower Galilee, where Jesus centered his ministry (according to the Synoptics), reveal how the religious roots of the Galilean Jews stretched southward into Judea and Jerusalem.

Second, Reed is interested in discerning the demographics of cities and villages in Galilee. He shows that scholars have inflated the population of Capernaum from 1,000 (Loffreda and Bagatti; Strange in *IDBSup*) to 15,000 (Meyers and Strange) and even to 25,000 inhabitants (H. C. Kee).[22] By measuring the circumscribed area of the ruins and the density of population, evident from extant private dwellings, and by comparing these with what can be known about *Ostia Antica* and Pompeii, Reed estimates that the population of Capernaum during the time of Jesus might have been as high as 1,700. Because of tombs 300 meters north of the shore, Reed estimates its size at only 6 to 10 hectares. Hence, most likely between 600 and 1,500 people dwelt in Capernaum during Jesus' time. If Nazareth contained fewer than 400 residents, then Capernaum was "one of the larger villages" (p. 152). It nevertheless contrasts with the largest cities in Lower Galilee: Sepphoris and Tiberias. They had slightly fewer than 12,000 inhabitants. This section on the demographics of Lower Galilee is one of the attractive dimensions of Reed's book.

Reed rightly states that the crucial question is "not where Jesus was in Capernaum, but what Capernaum of Jesus was like" (p. 143). I am convinced that much more data needs to be collected before we can be confident that Capernaum was not an urban center (Downing) but a small fishing village (Bagatti, Loffreda, Strange), as now seems probable.

In my judgment, the discoveries made by the Franciscans in the western section of Capernaum need to be compared with what has been unearthed in the eastern section of Capernaum. Pilgrims, visitors, and even scholars seldom visit the early Roman ruins in the Greek Orthodox section of ancient Capernaum. These are important, for one area contains an ancient Roman bathhouse with ceramic pipes still *in situ*. The bathhouse is clearly early Roman; but how early is it? Does it date before or after 70 C.E., and what criteria

---

22. H. C. Kee, "Early Christianity in the Galilee: Reassessing the Evidence from the Gospels," in *The Galilee in Late Antiquity*, ed. L. Levine (New York: Jewish Theological Seminary of America, 1992), pp. 3-22.

prove that claim? Thus, there is still much to do in the study of Jesus and the Capernaum he knew.

Capernaum is now about 4 kilometers west of the Jordan, the ancient border separating the territories of Antipas and of Philip.[23] While it did have a tollhouse, Capernaum was not on a major international route. It had no major public or civic buildings and grew randomly. It had no walls.

Reed cautions that the foundation under the fifth-century synagogue may be only the remains of a gathering place. He opines that the Roman *balneum* (bathhouse) should be dated to the second century c.e. The bathhouse thus does not provide evidence of Roman legionnaires during the time of Jesus; they were there only later, during the time of Hadrian. With these judgments Reed ventures close to the minimalists. A "gathering place" for Jews is exactly what a "synagogue" means etymologically. It should now be clear that before 70 c.e. a "synagogue" can mean not only a "gathering place" but also a structure, since inscriptions refer to repairing "the synagogue" (as I shall illustrate later). While most of the inscriptions come from the Diaspora, we are now wise enough to know that one must not think about vast distinctions between Diasporic customs[24] and Palestinian traditions.

Not one *mikveh* has been found in Capernaum. How do we explain this startling discovery? Reed contends it is because of the nearness of the lake, the toughness of the basalt, and the lack of affluence. Surely, these are insightful suggestions.

The dwellings at Capernaum are built of local basalt. Usually, the houses comprise a single room that opened out to a small courtyard that served more than one family unit.[25] Often the family lived in one room and perhaps in one large bed. Thus, intimate relations were often too public, and one could wake up and find that a loved one had become cold beside you (as noted in several OTP).

Reed is certainly correct to point out the lack of affluence at Capernaum. Houses were poorly constructed. The stones were not shaped by craftsmen as in Sepphoris, and the roofs would have been simply thatched with reeds. While Capernaum was probably a simple fishing and agricultural village, it was Jewish, as evidenced by Herodian stone vessels, which intimate the need for ritual purity. In contrast to Sepphoris, none of the latter was made on a large lathe.

23. For a photograph of Capernaum, see Charlesworth, *Jesus within Judaism,* illus. 6.

24. Diasporic Judaism now replaces the older and misleading "Hellenistic Judaism." Diasporic Judaism includes the Jews living in Persia, Syria, Egypt, Greece, Rome, and northwest Africa.

25. Y. Hirschfeld, *The Palestinian Dwelling in the Roman-Byzantine Period* (Jerusalem: Franciscan Printing Press and Israel Exploration Society, 1995).

According to Luke, a centurion was present in Capernaum (Lk 7:1-10). The historicity of this tradition — as is well known — has been hotly debated by New Testament scholars. Reed contends that a centurion was probably there, but he was not the head of 100 Roman legionnaires. Reed thinks he "was likely an official in Antipas's administrative and military apparatus" (p. 162).

This judgment is well founded. Unlike Nazareth, Capernaum was close to Gentile territory and a border crossing into ancient Palestine; it might have needed a Roman soldier, especially an experienced officer. A centurion could have been financially able and religiously motivated to help cover the costs of constructing a synagogue.

I thus concur with Safrai that the modest basalt foundations beneath the white limestone synagogue in Capernaum may be "vestiges of the synagogue that the centurion built."[26] Thus, I tend to follow Safrai against Reed, in imagining a synagogue under a later synagogue. Why? The more recent synagogue is not simply above an earlier building; it is aligned more accurately toward Jerusalem, perhaps due to better scientific alignment or to clarified laws in post-70 rabbinics that stressed that Jews, when praying in synagogues, must face Jerusalem.

Third, Reed completes his work with reflections on the provenience of the Q document. This lost document is a putative Jesus sayings source used only by Matthew and Luke. Since that study exceeds the focus of the present chapter, it will not be included.[27] Suffice it to state, Reed places Q in Galilee, most likely in "the region around Capernaum on the northern shore of the Sea of Galilee" (p. 182). The conclusion is based on the sites dominant and central in Q: Capernaum, Chorazin, and Bethsaida. Reed's conclusion regarding the archaeological importance of Q will not be so important if Q is only a modern imagined source, as numerous scholars are now contending.

Criticisms

Thanks to Reed's honesty, it is easy to contend that he has depended too much on anecdotal evidence, employed sociological models in far too eclectic a manner, and developed his thoughts from intuitions shaped while engaged in archaeological work in Sepphoris (p. xi).

The present book reports many archaeological discoveries and insights

26. S. Safrai, "The Synagogue the Centurion Built," *Jerusalem Perspective* 55 (1998): 12-14.

27. See, however, J. S. Kloppenborg, *Excavating Q: The History and Setting of the Sayings Gospel* (Minneapolis: Fortress, 2000).

that are not mentioned in Reed's book. Sometimes they postdate his book and he could not have known them. Reed's synthesis is thus not only premature but in need of refinement. In addition to the critiques supplied already, some improvement in assessing the importance of archaeology for Jesus Research will be necessary and in order. Some will be provided now, in this introduction, and some will be presented, or intimated, in the following chapters.

Reed intends to focus on examining "the patterns of evidence in the material culture that impinge on the study of Christian origins" (p. 3). It seems clear that one cannot focus only on Jesus Research, only on the Synoptics, and only on "one geographical area, Galilee" (p. 3), without distorting the study of Christian origins.[28] Surely, all portions of the New Testament should be included in Jesus Research; and obviously excavators in Judea, and Jerusalem especially, have unearthed data fundamental for assessing how archaeology enriches Jesus Research.

As the title of his book indicates, Reed has concentrated only on Galilee. That is fine, but forgetting his focus, he makes many statements that are misleading or false. He claims that "the major cities in Palestine" were Caesarea Maritima and Scythopolis (p. 94), that "the major urban centers in the Levant" were Caesarea Maritima, Scythopolis, and Tyre (p. 96). His view seldom moves below Galilee into Samaria and Judea.

Excavations in the Old City of Jerusalem prove that before 70 C.E. Jerusalem was a major metropolis with elegant houses; wide, impressively paved streets; palaces; monumental tombs; and perhaps the most magnificent temple in the world (see Bahat's chapter).[29] Jerusalem was the leading city in ancient Palestine and one of the major urban centers in the Levant. If Caesarea Maritima and Scythopolis respectively had 20,000 and 40,000 inhabitants (p. 94), Jerusalem may have held well over 40,000 people (Jews, Romans, and others [see Acts 2:9-11]). This metropolis would have included more inhabitants, if the ruins north of the Damascus Gate indicate pre-70 habitations within a greater Jerusalem (see sec. II below).

Other cities must also be included in any assessment of urban centers in ancient Palestine. In addition to those Reed mentions, we should include Gamla in the Golan (though Jesus never apparently went there), Tiberias (now

---

28. Reed's own preoccupation with Galilean archaeology leads him to miss the vast amount of archaeological work since 1968 that has exposed life and society in Jerusalem before 70 and during the time of Jesus. Thus, his comments are often off track; note, especially, his misleading claim that in Jesus Research the focus is "increasingly on the particularities of the region at hand, and in the case of Jesus, Galilee" (p. 7).

29. See Lane Ritmeyer's rendering of the Herodian Temple, in Charlesworth, *Jesus within Judaism*, illus. 14.

being excavated by Hirschfeld), Sebaste in Samaria (see Zangenberg's chapter), and perhaps Bethsaida (see Arav's chapter).

Scythopolis, thus, was certainly not "Palestine's largest and perhaps wealthiest city" (p. 95). While the grandeurs of Caesarea Maritima and Scythopolis are obvious, the architecture in these locations frequently postdates 70 C.E. These two cities only on exception equaled the opulence and grandeur of some of the pre-70 palaces and palatial dwellings in the Upper City of Jerusalem. Moreover, nothing in them compares to the Temple area and its surroundings. Some of Reed's judgments must be reshaped in light of the discoveries of a sumptuous palace and estate, with running water and a bathhouse, at Ramat Hanadiv (see Hirschfeld's chapter). In ancient Palestine, wealth was not represented only by Scythopolis, a city that grew markedly after Jesus' time.

Furthermore, Reed's numerical figures are presented without the requisite use of subjunctives. It is debatable that Italian cities, like Pompeii, provide a reliable grid for Galilean cities. There is no epigraphic evidence for ascertaining the demography of any city or village in pre-70 Galilee. Likewise, any estimate of Tiberias's size is now impossible; the excavations so far have neither clarified its perimeters nor intimated the density of population.[30] Moreover, it is often impossible to distinguish between Antipas's initial constructions and the expansions required later by the flow of Jews into Galilee, especially after the destruction of Jerusalem in 70 C.E. and then later after the defeat of Bar-Kokhba in 135/36 C.E. While various dates are given for the founding of Tiberias by Herod Antipas (4 B.C.E.–39 C.E.), neither Josephus nor Eusebius provides reliable information regarding that year. Numismatics, however, notably the Roman imperial city coins issued in Tiberias, proves that the city was founded between 17 and 22 C.E.[31]

The assessments of the population in each village and city is a herculean task. Perhaps we might in the twenty-first century be able to approximate more accurately the population of ancient Palestine before the destructions of 70 C.E. Most likely its population was near 3 million.[32]

Reed's archaeological excavations only in Galilee seem to have led him to claim that "Jesus' ministry is to be located in Galilee and that he was a Galilean" (p. 10). He has followed only the Synoptics' account of Jesus' career.

30. Hirschfeld is directing a new team of archaeologists at Tiberias. As of January 2005, they had not unearthed first-century, pre-70 layers of occupation in his area of excavations. Also, see U. C. von Wahlde's chapter in the present collection.

31. See M. Avi-Yonah, "The Founding of Tiberias," *IEJ* 1 (1950): 160-69, esp. p. 168; and Y. Meshorer, *Ancient Jewish Coinage* (New York: Amphora Books, 1982), 2:35.

32. M. Avi-Yonah estimated the population of Palestine was about two and a half million. See Avi-Yonah in *The Jewish People in the First Century* (Philadelphia: Fortress, 1974), 1:108-10. Also, see S. Applebaum in *ANRW* 2.8, p. 376.

The Fourth Gospel situates a significant part of Jesus' ministry in the south, in Samaria,[33] and in Judea. Is the Fourth Gospel devoid of historical data and importance? Many specialists in Jesus Research rightly now depend not only on the Synoptics but also on the Gospel of John. Among these scholars of the historical Jesus who conclude that John is reliable historically are P. Fredriksen in her *Jesus of Nazareth: King of the Jews*, B. Chilton in his *Rabbi Jesus*, and B. D. Ehrman in his *Jesus: Apocalyptic Prophet of the New Millennium*. Many of the experts who gathered in Jerusalem for the millennium celebration on Jesus and archaeology and have contributed to the present volume intermittently present a surprising number of links behind what is recorded in John and what is being unearthed in Galilee and Judea, especially in Herodian Jerusalem. Two of the best and most balanced assessments of reliable historical and topographical elements in the Gospel of John and the importance of archaeology for comprehending this text are presented by P. N. Anderson and U. C. von Wahlde in the present volume.[34]

These comments do not disparage Reed's book. It is superb and certainly deserves to be taken seriously. He intermittently shows how the different settings of the Evangelists altered traditions and how "their narrative worlds shape the picture of Galilee" (p. 160; cf. p. 212). Inter alia, he astutely shows why it is implausible that Cynic philosophical schools should be imagined at Sepphoris (p. 135); after all, it was a city populated by religious Jews.

Reed's work should be supplemented by an archaeological study of Jesus in Judea, especially Jerusalem, and enriched by the new discoveries presented and discussed in the present volume. He wisely points out that the main contribution of archaeology to Jesus Research is "in its ability to reconstruct his social world" (p. 18). That is, archaeology should be studied, along with anthropology, psychology, and sociology, in imagining and describing the social world of Jesus and the Palestinian Jesus Movement.

Reed rightly utters a "plea for giving archaeology a more prominent voice" in Jesus Research (p. 213). This timely task was anticipated by the present volume and facilitated by the publication of two major, multivolume encyclopedias. Each encyclopedia is important, but the contributors do not reflect on how archaeology may be important for Jesus Research.

In 1993 Ephraim Stern edited *The New Encyclopedia of Archaeological Excavations in the Holy Land (NEAEHL)*.[35] It is authoritative, arranged alphabeti-

---

33. Zangenberg clarifies the importance and complexity of Samaria before and during the time of Jesus. See his chapter in the present volume.

34. Anderson focuses on history and archaeology; von Wahlde examines the topography of the Gospel of John and archaeological research and the topography of ancient Palestine.

35. E. Stern, ed., *The New Encyclopedia of Archaeological Excavations in the Holy Land*, 4 vols. (New York and London: Simon and Schuster, 1993).

cally, and richly illustrated. In this four-volume encyclopedia, scholars will find some of the most erudite discussions of major archaeological sites associated with the life and teachings of Jesus, namely, Jerusalem, Caesarea Maritima, Capernaum, Nazareth, Bethlehem, Scythopolis, Jericho, and Sepphoris. These volumes are the most important and authoritative source for studying the archaeology of "the Holy Land." The contributions are composed usually by experts who have excavated at the site included for discussion; the focus of the encyclopedia is on biblical sites. Yet, as is so obvious in the world of archaeology, almost all entries are rapidly becoming dated. Sadly, however, in *NEAEHL* there is virtually no interest either in Jesus' life and teachings or in the Palestinian Jesus Movement.

The second major encyclopedia on archaeology was edited in 1997 by Eric Meyers. It consists of five volumes and is entitled *The Oxford Encyclopedia of Archaeology in the Near East.*[36] This work is not limited to biblical archaeology, and it has valuable entries on some sites essential for a study of Jesus and archaeology. Singularly important are the entries on Bethsaida, the biblical Temple, burial practices, Capernaum, ceramics of the Hellenistic and Roman periods (vol. 1); cities of the Hellenistic and Roman periods, coins, the First Jewish Revolt, Galilee, the Galilee boat (vol. 2); Herodian Jericho, inscriptions of the Hellenistic and Roman periods, Jericho, Jerusalem, lamps, Magdala, medicine (vol. 3); Nabateans, Nag Hammadi, ossuary, Palestine in the Persian through Roman periods, Parthians, ritual baths, roads, Roman Empire, Sepphoris (vol. 4); synagogue inscriptions and synagogues, and finally Tiberias (vol. 5).

Perhaps the most reliable, insightful, and user-friendly one-volume encyclopedia for biblical archaeology has been Avraham Negev's *The Archaeological Encyclopedia of the Holy Land.*[37] Now, with the help of about one hundred experts, Simon Gibson has revised and expanded this valuable resource.[38] New or revised entries and sections include the following: Jesus (pp. 268-69), John the Baptist (pp. 271-72),[39] Josephus (pp. 272-73), Philo, Dead Sea Scrolls (pp. 134-36), Old Testament Apocrypha (p. 39), Old Testament Pseudepigrapha (p. 413), astrology, and serpents (pp. 457-58). The volume will be especially helpful to New Testament specialists, since it avoids jargon, opaque *termini technici,* and is

36. E. M. Meyers, ed., *The Oxford Encyclopedia of Archaeology in the Near East,* 5 vols. (New York and Oxford: Oxford University Press, 1997).

37. See A. Negev, *The Archaeological Encyclopedia of the Holy Land,* 3rd ed. (New York and London: Prentice-Hall, 1990).

38. See A. Negev and S. Gibson, eds., *Archaeological Encyclopedia of the Holy Land,* rev. ed. (New York and London: Continuum, 2001). Page numbers in the remainder of this paragraph come from this updated edition.

39. Also, see the chapter by M. Piccirillo in the present work.

designed for a wide audience. It is also more current than the multivolumed encyclopedias just reviewed; yet, it needs to be updated in light of the information
contained in the following chapters.

As I come to the end of a brief survey of publications relevant for a study of
the importance of archaeology for Jesus Research, I am impressed with two observations.

The first observation — which was intimated earlier — is that archaeologists are not usually interested in Jesus. Such a concern seems to be either too
faith-oriented for most of them or they assume that the Gospels and the New
Testament documents, like Acts, are devoid of historical information. For example, I witnessed a paradigm shift during my thirty-plus years in Jerusalem in
what is now the Albright Institute. In the late sixties, when I was Thayer Fellow,
biblical studies and archaeology were discussed daily in an engaging manner. In
the late nineties, when I was Annual Professor, biblical issues surfaced rarely
and when I mentioned them a polite silence often appeared, until what might
be deemed more scientific issues should be discussed. This diffidence to biblical
studies may be due to two factors. First, biblical study is frequently equated
with confessional theology. Second, and more importantly, far too many people
have enlisted archaeology to prove the historicity of the biblical stories or even
to create faith.

Now, however, something new is appearing, and scholars are beginning
again, after forty years perhaps, to include Jesus in historical research. In the
twenty-first century, more and more scholars are taking the historical Jesus seriously, as they did, perhaps as an exception, during the Jerusalem congress on
Jesus and Hillel in 1992.[40]

The second observation is that New Testament scholars are not usually devoted to archaeology and are sometimes wary and even hostile to the field (if
not the discipline). Why? There are probably two main reasons. The foremost
reason is the absurd claims made about the significance and alleged superiority
of archaeology over biblical studies. Second, the distrust seems to be because
archaeological methodologies are too foreign to New Testament specialists and
too far removed from theology; that is, New Testament scholars are trained in
languages (especially Greek, but also Coptic, Syriac, Aramaic, and Hebrew),
textual studies, exegesis of the biblical texts, biblical and church history, and
theology. Only later, almost always after formal training, do some New Testament specialists learn about the methods and purposes of archaeology. Archaeology is not a curricular course in most departments of religion in universities;

---

40. The proceedings appeared in Charlesworth and L. L. Johns, eds., *Hillel and Jesus: Comparative Studies of Two Major Religious Leaders* (Minneapolis: Fortress, 1997).

the discipline is almost nonexistent in seminaries.[41] Generally speaking, in most standard courses on the historical Jesus archaeology continues to be considered irrelevant.

New Testament scholars are not usually conversant with such terms as "ashlar," "balk," eastern *terra sigillata, mikvaot, opus reticulatum,* and "tournette." Few New Testament experts have trimmed the balk, analyzed stratigraphical layers, found *realia in situ,* cleaned pottery, discerned their chronological information, or served as area supervisors. Most have never been involved in neutron activation analysis, thermoluminescence dating, AMS C-14 analysis, computer-enhanced resolution of images, or the distinguishing of faience from glass.

How many New Testament scholars know how to read archaeological reports or understand why archaeologists can differ so markedly? Along with many specialists, they confront nomenclature that is foreboding and acronyms that are unfamiliar; some, like "BAR," can represent *Biblical Archaeology Review* or British Archaeological Reports.

Many New Testament scholars would agree with me that our work entails not only Jesus Research but also an attempt to re-create and understand early Judaism and Christian origins. I think we would tend to agree that our perspective has often been too myopic; that is, it is characteristically focused only on texts. Seeking the context too often means examining only the literary context. Most scholars would surely agree with me that too often New Testament texts have been interpreted without controls obtained from discerning a phenomenological context by means of archaeological and sociological insights. We might even agree that a text must not be allowed to mean anything or nothing at all.

These comments do suggest that New Testament scholars — and not just New Testament historians — cannot work oblivious of the insights obtained by archaeologists. In one real sense, all New Testament scholars will henceforth be fundamentally indebted to (but not dependent upon) archaeologists. For example, we derive our texts from textual critics who create canonical and extracanonical texts that receive their present shapes because of archaeological discoveries, such as the Bodmer Papyri, the Nag Hammadi codices, and the Dead Sea Scrolls (broadly defined). In such a statement lies an irony. Many of the most important archaeological discoveries are not made by archaeologists; hence, archaeological methodology has not been employed, and to a great ex-

41. An attempt to correct this situation led to the papers that are published in M. C. Moreland, ed., *Between Text and Artifact: Integrating Archaeology in Biblical Studies Teaching* (Atlanta: Society of Biblical Literature, 2003).

tent an archaeologist cannot help solve critical issues, like the source and stratum in which so many of our fundamental texts or *realia* were found.

Over the past fifty years, the fields of archaeology and biblical research have frequently separated like oil and water. Thus, the task of assessing the importance of archaeology for the study of the historical Jesus is frustrated by a dual recognition, which adds to the previous reflections. First, Jesus Research may be nontheological by intent, but it is grounded in documents that are shaped by theological concerns. The character of the Gospel accounts has, until recently, seemed too mythological to many archaeologists. Second, Jesus Research is becoming increasingly influenced by archaeological research and discoveries, as the present volume proves. This demands a marriage of two disciplines that have, over the past four decades, tended to move away from each other.

One of my present tasks is to seek ways to catch the new spirit that I find appearing in the method and work of experts in Jesus Research and in archaeology. To help evaluate this spirit I contacted Professor John Meier of Notre Dame. He has devoted the past two decades to Jesus Research; he has just completed his third volume of *A Marginal Jew* for the Anchor Bible Reference Library. I thus asked him to comment on the "impact of archaeology on that volume." In late June 2001 he sent me the following statement:

> In general, my use of archaeological data varies greatly depending on the subject under review. Since the initial Jesus movement was a small band of largely itinerant Jews moving between Galilee and Judea for some two years and some months, direct knowledge of the movement from archaeology is basically nil. What archaeology does is help fill in the background and larger context in Jewish Palestine at the time. This may at times be individual tidbits, e.g., the Pontius Pilate inscription from Caesarea Maritima or the supposed Caiaphas inscription on an ossuary. This may at times touch on the socio-religious situation of the Galilee in which Jesus worked, e.g., the present-day debate over how hellenized was Sepphoris (apparently much less around the time of Jesus than some have claimed). This may relate to a major find that has transformed our whole view of Palestinian Judaism, the prime example being the Dead Sea Scrolls. They naturally impact on a good part of my Chapter 30, most of which deals with the question of the relation of Jesus with the Essenes and/or Qumranites (with an attempt to balance similarities and yet great differences). Here vast questions may intersect with small bits of data, e.g., the Aramaic qorban inscription or an ossuary, which relates directly to Jesus' statement about qorban in Mark 7 and indirectly to various statements on oaths and vows found in the *Damascus Document* and also in the Mishna.

It is clear that Meier does now use archaeological data. Exceedingly important in Meier's personal letter to me are three points. First, archaeology is intermittently important in studying the historical Jesus, but it should not be supposed that archaeology can directly throw clarifying light on the Jesus of history or his initial movement. Second, archaeology helps us reconstruct the sociological and religious situation of Jesus' Galilee. Third, it is incorrect to conclude that archaeology only serves to clarify the landscape of Jesus' itinerancy; indeed, archaeological discoveries and research have demanded a new perception of Jesus' Judaism. While Meier's judgments certainly do not represent a minimalist viewpoint, I would (and shall) speak more positively about the essential nature of archaeology in Jesus Research today.

I agree with L. I. Levine that archaeology can sometimes confirm literary data, sometimes supplement it, and at other times raise new questions and perspectives.[42] I would add that sometimes archaeology reveals that a section of a text cannot be historical. With an open mind, let us continue to ask how and in what ways, if at all, archaeological discoveries can help and are helping us reconstruct the setting of Jesus, as well as his life and some of his sayings.

II. Archaeological Discoveries and Jesus Research

A convenient way to begin a survey of the most recent archaeological developments important for Jesus Research is to *focus on sites, villages, and cities.* My book *Jesus within Judaism: New Light from Exciting Archaeological Discoveries* signaled seven primary discoveries for Jesus Research. These will be assessed in light of developments since the book was published in 1988. The presentation will be from the least important to the most important discoveries for Jesus Research.

The *seventh*-most-significant discovery is the first identification of synagogues in the land that antedate 70 C.E. On the one hand, it is surprising that no pre-70 synagogues have been identified at Caesarea Maritima, Jerusalem, Machaerus, or Tiberias. On the other hand, pre-70 synagogues are now clearly exposed at Gamla,[43] Masada (but a renovation by Zealots),[44] and the

---

42. L. I. Levine, "Archaeological Discoveries from the Greco-Roman Era," in *Recent Archaeology in the Land of Israel,* ed. B. Mazar and H. Shanks (Washington, D.C.: Biblical Archaeology Society; Jerusalem: Israel Exploration Society, 1984), pp. 75-87.

43. See S. Gutman, *Gamla: A City in Rebellion* (in Hebrew) (Israel: Ministry of Defence, 1994), pp. 18-19, 88-89, 143; see esp. pp. 99-108; and Gutman, in *NEAEHL* 2:459-63.

44. E. Netzer, "The Synagogue of Masada (Loci 1042-1043)," in *Masada III: The Yigael Yadin Excavations, 1963-1965; Final Reports* (Jerusalem: Israel Exploration Society, 1991), pp. 402-38. For

Herodium (again, only in a renovation by Zealots).[45] Of course, there are scholars who contend that there is no evidence that the structures identified as synagogues in these places were designed for religious purposes;[46] some experts claim that no building can be identified as a synagogue until the third century C.E.[47] Such voices represent the minority; the majority of scholars have now concluded that archaeologists have uncovered first-century synagogues in ancient Palestine. I am also persuaded that in some areas of Galilee and Judea worship and reading the Torah were aspects of synagogue life long before 70, and that the New Testament witness to Jesus' reading from the Torah on Shabbat in a synagogue (and not just a meeting house) is trustworthy (cf. Lk 4:16-22).[48]

To the list of pre-70 synagogues at least one more might be added. It is at Jericho, and according to E. Netzer, it may be the oldest, since it was destroyed by the earthquake of 31 B.C.E. and was not restored. He argues that the synagogue building "developed in two or three stages, starting either in the reign of Jannaeus (103-76 B.C.E.), in that of his widow Queen Salome (76-67 B.C.E.), or in that of one of her rival sons (67 B.C.E. onward)."[49] In the western part of the building, there is a large hall (16.2 × 11.1 m.). In the eastern part are seven rooms and a small courtyard (8.4 × 5.1 m.). To the south of the "syna-

---

a photograph see Charlesworth, *The Millennium Guide for Pilgrims to the Holy Land* (North Richland Hills, Tex.: BIBAL, 2000), p. 181.

45. See esp. G. Foerster, "The Synagogues at Masada and Herodium," in *Ancient Synagogues Revealed*, ed. L. I. Levine (Jerusalem: Israel Exploration Society, 1981), pp. 24-29. For recent research on pre-70 synagogues, see the following: D. Urman and P. V. M. Flesher, eds., *Ancient Synagogues: Historical Analyses and Archaeological Discovery*, 2 vols., SPB 47.1-2 (Leiden and New York: Brill, 1995); L. I. Levine, *The Ancient Synagogue* (New Haven and London: Yale University Press, 2000); Levine, ed., *The Synagogue in Late Antiquity* (Philadelphia: American Schools of Oriental Research, 1987); S. Fine and E. M. Meyers, "Synagogues," in *OEANE* 4:118-23; H. Bloedhorn and G. Hüttenmeister, "The Synagogue," in *The Early Roman Period*, ed. W. Horbury, W. D. Davies, and J. Sturdy, Cambridge History of Judaism, vol. 3 (Cambridge and New York: Cambridge University Press, 1999), pp. 267-97; C. Claußen, *Versammlung, Gemeinde, Synagoge*, SUNT 27 (Göttingen: Vandenhoeck & Ruprecht, 2002). Especially, see the most recent discussions in R. Olsson and M. Zetterholm, eds., *The Ancient Synagogue from Its Origins until 200 C.E.*, CB NT Series 39 (Stockholm: Almqvist & Wiksell International, 2003).

46. See esp. H. C. Kee, "The Transformation of the Synagogue after 70 C.E.: Its Import for Early Christianity," *NTS* 36 (1990): 8.

47. J. Gutmann, "Ancient Synagogues: Archaeological Fact and Scholarly Assumption," *Bulletin of the Asia Institute* 9 (1997): 226-27.

48. See, now, the proceedings of the conference in Lund University in 2001, published in Olsson and Zetterholm, *The Ancient Synagogue from Its Origins until 200 C.E.*

49. E. Netzer, "A Synagogue from the Hasmonean Period Recently Exposed in the Western Plain of Jericho," *IEJ* 49 (1999): 203-21; the quotation is from p. 205.

gogue" is a *mikveh.* The latter helps identify the building as a synagogue; recall that in Gamla a *mikveh* is situated just east of the synagogue and contiguous with it.

Perhaps, however, the building unearthed in Herodian Jericho was not a place of worship but a building to serve public needs; if so, it may not have been a synagogue. A minor water channel bisected the so-called synagogue; this would be unexpected, indeed exceptional, in a synagogue from any date. The alleged "niche" may be merely a cupboard for storing documents. Finally, the additions of a triclinium and a "kitchen" to the "synagogue hall" during its "last phase" would desecrate a synagogue.[50] Since it would probably be Jews who renovated an earlier Jewish structure, the architectural features mentioned give me pause in recognizing the Jericho building as a synagogue.

There are no other ruins in ancient Palestine that suggest a pre-70 synagogue. The gathering place recently uncovered at Khirbet Qana, as indicated by P. Richardson's chapter in this book, is most likely a synagogue. What is open now for discussion seems to be the date of this synagogue. It dates to the Roman period, but does it antedate 70 C.E. so that we can imagine its importance for Jesus' life?

Two final words on the ancient synagogue are appropriate.[51] It was certainly developed by Jews before 70 C.E., attested by archaeological excavations at Gamla especially and citations in Josephus and the New Testament. That is, the synagogue (called a *proseuchē* by Philo, and in places like Tiberias) was "the gathering place" for Jews to read the Torah, study, pray, and perhaps fast. Second, New Testament scholars should jettison the assumption that women were separated from men in ancient synagogues; this phenomenon appears in the Middle Ages.[52]

In summation, the structures unearthed in Gamla, Masada, and the Herodium are *pre-70 synagogues.* Thus, there is archaeological evidence to support the Gospel record that there were buildings identifiable as synagogues elsewhere in Palestine in which Jesus could have taught. In particular, note

---

50. Levine is also skeptical about the building in Jericho being a synagogue: "some of the interior elements found in this building — a triclinium in the main hall and the niche with its cupboard (which Netzer suggests might have held Torah scrolls) — would clearly constitute finds of revolutionary proportions." Levine, *The Ancient Synagogue,* p. 69.

51. For studies on the ancient synagogue, besides those noted, see the following: I. Levy, *The Synagogue: Its History and Function* (London: Vallentine, Mitchell, 1963); K. Hruby, *Die Synagoge: Geschichtliche Entwicklung einer Institution* (Zürich: Theologischer Verlag, 1971); W. Schrage, "συναγωγή (etc.)," in *TDNT* 7 (1971), pp. 798-852. Also, see the major publications listed in the bibliography of Levine, *The Ancient Synagogue,* pp. 615-84.

52. See esp. Levine, "Synagogues," in *NEAEHL* 4:1423.

Mark's summary: and Jesus "went throughout Galilee preaching in the synagogues" (κηρύσσων εἰς τὰς συναγωγὰς [Mk 1:39]). The extant archaeological evidence discloses that pre-70 synagogues were rectangular rooms in larger buildings, as in the Herodium, or more public areas, such as at Masada and Gamla. Thus, it seems proper to assume that Jesus did teach in synagogues,[53] provided that we do not imagine an architectural edifice as is evident in post-third-century Palestine.

The last point elicits two emphases. First, the pre-70 synagogues are not similar to a basilica, a broadhouse, or an apsidal structure. They are diverse and often unimpressive. Second, typology cannot be aligned with chronology, as so many experts once claimed (viz., Kohl, Watzinger, Sukenik, Avi-Yonah, and Goodenough). In the same area and at the same time we see both typologies: a Galilean-type structure at Meiron and a broadhouse-type at Khirbet Shemaʿ.[54] During the time of Jesus, most likely, many synagogues ("gathering places" to study and read Torah) were rooms in large houses.

The *sixth*-most-significant archaeological discovery concerns the walls and gates of Jerusalem. The northern wall and gate that Jesus knew is most likely under or near the present Turkish wall near the Damascus Gate (but not farther west, near the "New Gate" — that is part of the "third wall").[55] This northern wall, which may not have been completed before 70 C.E.,[56] may well be exposed now about 450 meters from the Turkish wall and northward up Nablus Road. This wall ("the third wall") was probably begun by Herod Agrippa I (37-44 C.E.) sometime between 41 and 44 (*War* 5.152). The dating of this "wall" is important for Jesus Research, because of the extent and population of Jerusalem in Jesus' time. Even if Jerusalem's walls were, at the northern extent, identical to those of Old Jerusalem today, there probably were numerous people living beyond the northern walls. The population of Jerusalem during Jesus' time has been variously estimated: 25,000-35,000 (Jeremias and Wilkinson),[57] 40,000 (Broshi),[58] 90,000 (Avi-Yonah).[59] With any of these numbers, Jerusalem was a large city

53. See J. D. G. Dunn's chapter in this book.

54. See the superb discussion by Levine in *The Ancient Synagogue*, pp. 296-98.

55. See D. Bahat, "Does the Holy Sepulchre Church Mark the Burial of Jesus?" in *Archaeology in the World of Herod, Jesus, and Paul*, ed. H. Shanks and D. P. Cole (Washington, D.C.: Biblical Archaeology Society, 1990, 1992), pp. 248-70; see esp. the map on p. 257.

56. So also, H. Geva, in *NEAEHL* 2:719.

57. J. Jeremias, *Jerusalem in the Time of Jesus* (Philadelphia: Fortress, 1969), pp. 27, 83-84; J. Wilkinson, "Jerusalem: Its Water System and Population," *PEQ* 106 (1974): 33-51.

58. M. Broshi, "Estimating the Population of Ancient Jerusalem," *BAR* 4 (1978): 10-15.

59. M. Avi-Yonah, "Survey of the Density and Numbers of the Population in Ancient Eretz Israel" (in Hebrew), in *Essays and Studies in the Lore of the Holy Land* (Jerusalem: Neumann, 1964), pp. 114-24.

when Jesus visited it; but it certainly was not as populous as Josephus claimed, having 120,000 residents (*Apion* 1.22).

Southwest of the Zion Gate and the Domitian Abbey are the remains of a gate. It is visible beneath a later Byzantine threshold. Is this gate to be identified as the "Essene Gate" mentioned by Josephus (*War* 5.145; cf. the *Temple Scroll* 46.14), as B. Pixner argued?[60] Or is the Essene Gate to be identified with a monumental staircase that leads into the western section of Jerusalem's walls, farther to the north, as S. Gibson has claimed? Gibson also suggests that the Essenes would be outside the gate, since gates are usually defined by what is outside them, as with the Damascus Gate, the Jaffa Gate, and the Sheep Gate.

If the more southern gate is the Essene Gate,[61] does that suggest Essenes lived in the southwest section of Jerusalem? Some scholars have speculated that Essenes lived in the southwestern section of Herodian Jerusalem.[62] If so, that would be significant for Jesus Research, since this is the part of the city occupied by Jesus' followers after 30 C.E. Were the members of the Palestinian Jesus Movement living contiguous with Jerusalem Essenes?[63] To what extent is this suggestion romantic or fanciful? There is certainly a need for further research, excavation, and discussion.[64]

Archaeologists have also found the remains of a city wall to the east of the Church of the Holy Sepulchre. It was built sometime before Herod the Great. What is surprising is the discovery that the present city wall to the west of the Church of the Holy Sepulchre is the "third wall" built by Agrippa between 41 and 44.[65] This wall reveals that Golgotha was outside Jerusalem's walls before the early forties, and Jesus was crucified on Golgotha in 30 (or perhaps 33). The importance of this discovery will be reserved until our final, "most significant" archaeological discovery for Jesus Research.

The *fifth* major archaeological discovery concerns the Temple Mount. The seam in the eastern section of the Temple Mount reveals the extent to which

60. Also, see Pixner's chapter in this volume.

61. For a photograph see Charlesworth, *The Millennium Guide*, p. 149.

62. See esp. R. Riesner, "Jesus, the Primitive Community, and the Essene Quarter of Jerusalem," in J. H. Charlesworth, *Jesus and the Dead Sea Scrolls*, ABRL (New York: Doubleday, 1992), pp. 198-234.

63. For the Judean Essene communities and Jesus Research, see the chapter in the present collection by B. J. Capper.

64. The most reliable discussion of an Essene community on Mount Zion, from the time of King Herod until the destruction in 70 C.E., is by B. Pixner, who mastered what could be known about this area of Jerusalem from written sources and excavations. See his contribution in the present volume.

65. See the map in Bahat's article in *Archaeology in the World of Herod, Jesus, and Paul*, p. 257.

Figure 8. The Essene Gate? The wall in the background is sixteenth century C.E., but the entrance outside of it contained Herodian plaster and may be the Gate of the Essenes.   Courtesy of J. H. Charlesworth

Herod extended the Temple area.[66] A stone found *in situ* in the western retaining wall of the Temple, north of the "Wailing Wall," may be even heavier than reported. It could weigh as much as 600 tons; that would make it close to the size of the gigantic stone sticking out of the quarry at Baalbek.[67] Perhaps there is some history behind Mk 13:1: "And as he (Jesus) was coming out of the Temple, one of his disciples said to him, 'Look, Teacher, what great (or wonderful) stones (ἴδε ποταποὶ λίθοι) and what great (or wonderful) buildings.'"

Monumental and pre-70 structures are now visible south of the southern retaining wall of the Temple. Jesus surely saw the double and triple Hulda Gates, the large esplanade, and the large *mikvaot* just to the south of the Temple Mount.[68] To the west, foundations were found that proved that Robinson's Arch, unlike Wilson's Arch, was not a corridor from the Upper City to the Temple, but a support for a massive staircase that turns toward the Temple Mount

66. For a photograph see Charlesworth, *The Millennium Guide*, p. 136.

67. For a photograph see W. Bell, *Rome in the East* (London and New York: Routledge, 2000), p. 46.

68. See the photograph in Charlesworth, *Jesus within Judaism*, illus. 15.

as it ascends. Near the Dung Gate, large Herodian sewers and an elegantly paved street have been recently exposed.[69]

Was the *Ḥanuth* (Heb. lit. "meat market"), the circumscribed area for holding large animals designated for sacrifice (*Ant* 15.393, 411-17), moved from the Mount of Olives to inside the Temple area only a few months before 30 C.E.?[70] If so, it becomes clearer why Jesus, on his final pilgrimage to Jerusalem,[71] exploded with rage inside the Temple.[72] Did he see large animals, such as a full-grown ox (see *m. Pesahim* 7.11), tethered inside the Temple area when they had been located outside it earlier?[73] Any Jew, like Jesus, might have been offended by the desecration and pollution accompanying large animals. For example, their bodily releases could not simply be contained in a cage, as with the doves.

Perhaps the corridor discovered that allegedly leads from "Solomon's Stables" to the large staircase inside the Hulda Gates was used for moving large animals up and into the Temple. I have not yet been able to examine this corridor. The political tension in this section of Jerusalem is now severe and too inhospitable for me to seek permissions and possible confirmations. Thus, the striking evidence that might give credence to John's unique account remains presently unavailable. If the *Ḥanuth* did move within the area beneath the Temple Mount shortly before Jesus' last visit to Jerusalem, then archaeology may help prove the historicity of Jn 2:15: "And making a (kind of) whip from cords, he [Jesus] drove them all, with the sheep and oxen, out of the Temple." That is, if oxen were moved into the area underneath the Temple and near the staircase just before Jesus visited the Temple for the last time, and if straw for such large animals were available for fashioning a whip, then the account in the Fourth Gospel seems less likely a product of theological imaginations.

The *fourth*-most-significant archaeological discovery for Jesus Research is the Pool of Bethesda (or Bethzatha) described in Jn 5:2-9. New developments strengthen the earlier report. Gibson is working on the artifacts found in this area north of the Temple Mount. He and I examined a large clay vessel with many

69. See the photograph by E. M. Charlesworth in Charlesworth, *The Millennium Guide,* p. 142.

70. I am indebted to David Flusser for this suggestion.

71. Clearly Jesus was in Jerusalem at this time to observe Passover, as prescribed by Torah. On pilgrimage, see S. Safrai, *Pilgrimage at the Time of the Second Temple* (Tel Aviv, 1965).

72. See C. A. Evans, "Opposition to the Temple: Jesus and the Dead Sea Scrolls," in *Jesus and the Dead Sea Scrolls,* pp. 235-53.

73. For rules regarding slaughtering large animals inside and outside the Temple courtyard, see *Hullin* 5.1 and 5.2.

snakes on it.[74] It was found in a cistern near Bethesda in the late nineteenth century by Clermont-Ganneau. The ophidian object, known as "the Bethesda Vase," is preserved in the Palestinian Exploration Fund Archives in London. This vessel increases the possibility that a shrine to Asclepius, who is characteristically depicted with serpents, existed at Bethesda. While this vessel was not found *in situ* and thus cannot be dated stratigraphically, there is abundant evidence in the cisterns within Bethesda and from the images of snakes found on objects found *in situ* in Bethesda that this site was a place set aside for healing before and during the Herodian period (the time of Jesus). More historical credence seems to be given to Jesus' statement in Jn 3:14 and also to the "story" in Jn 5:1-18.

The *third*-most-important archaeological insight for Jesus Research concerns the Praetorium, the official residence of the Roman *praetor* (governor). Many experts now agree that the dwelling for the *prefectus,* Pilate, was in the Upper City and not in the Antonia Fortress (the location of the Sisters of Zion today).[75] The *lithostrōton* (Jn 19:13) denotes the public square in front of the Praetorium; it was paved with large stones. The Aramaic *Gabbatha* (Jn 19:13)[76] denotes the "high" place or the setting of the Praetorium. This term probably denotes Herod's palace (cf. κατὰ τὴν ἄνω δειμάμενος πόλιν [*War* 1.402]) that is situated in the western elevated part of the city. Due to the Romans' desire to raze Jerusalem in 135/36 C.E., all that remains of Herod's Palace is a portion of the massive tower inside, and to the right of, Jaffa Gate. It is the remains of the Phasael tower built under Herod the Great.

The *second* significant archaeological data for understanding the historical Jesus is the remains of a crucified man named Jehoḥanan. The recent discussions, led by J. Zias, have revealed that the marks on this man's wrists may not have been caused by nails. One now ponders how someone was crucified. If the arms were tied to the horizontal bar, then we also have an answer why the bones of only one crucified person have been found. Ropes do not leave discernible marks on bones.[77] The bones of Jehoḥanan stimulate reflection on the various means of crucifying someone and how horrible the punishment was for the person crucified and for those related to him. In contrast to capital punishment

74. See the photograph and discussion in Charlesworth, *The Serpent: A Symbol of Life or Death?* ABRL (forthcoming).

75. See esp. M. Broshi, "The Topography and Archaeology of the Passion: A Reconstruction of the Via Dolorosa," in D. Flusser, in collaboration with R. S. Notley, *Jesus* (Jerusalem: Magnes Press, 1998), pp. 251-57.

76. See J. F. Wilson, "Archaeology and the Origins of the Fourth Gospel: Gabbatha," in *Johannine Studies: Essays in Honor of Frank Pack* (Malibu, Calif.: Pepperdine University Press, 1989), pp. 221-30.

77. I am grateful to Joe Zias for years of discussing how Romans crucified their victims.

Figure 9. The Bezetha Vase. Probably from the Asclepieion at Bezetha, Jerusalem, early Roman period. Palestine Exploration Fund AP 4149.

Courtesy of Dr. R. L. Chapman III

in the United States, Roman crucifixion was public and brutal (as indicated, but in an excessive manner, in *The Passion of the Christ*).

Finally, we come to the *most* significant archaeological discovery for Jesus Research. It is the archaeological evidence that Jesus was crucified on the rock now seen inside the Church of the Holy Sepulchre.[78] As mentioned earlier, a wall that was most likely built by Herod Agrippa I has been found east of this church; thus, in 30 c.e. — but not after 44 — the rock inside the church was outside the city walls.

There is now archaeological proof that Jesus was crucified outside the city's walls and probably on top of the white stone shown to visitors and pilgrims inside the Church of the Holy Sepulchre. There also seems to be a consensus among archaeologists that Jesus was possibly, and perhaps probably, crucified on this white stone to the right of the entrance to this church.[79]

Jesus may well have been buried near this site, identified as Golgotha. As a distinguished archaeologist of Jerusalem, and a Jew, Dan Bahat states, "We may not be absolutely certain that the site of the Holy Sepulchre Church is the site of

78. The published research on excavations is voluminous. For the most recent, and authoritative, see V. Corbo, *Il Santo Sepolcro di Gerusalemme: Aspetti archeologici dalle origini al periodo crociato,* 3 vols., Studium Biblicum Franciscanum 29 (Jerusalem: Franciscan Printing Press, 1981-82) — there is a sixteen-page summary in English by S. Loffreda. See Benoit's review in *RB* (1984): 281-87; C. Coüasnon, *The Church of the Holy Sepulchre in Jerusalem,* trans. C. Ross, Schweich Lectures (London: British Academy, 1974).

79. For photographs of the Church of the Holy Sepulchre, see Charlesworth, *Jesus within Judaism,* illus. 18 and 19.

Jesus' burial, but we certainly have no other site that can lay a claim nearly as weighty, and we really have no reason to reject the authenticity of the site."[80]

My own study of the site, from the late sixties to the present, leads me to agree fully with Bahat's assessment. Over the past fifty years archaeologists have excavated in, under, and near the Church of the Holy Sepulchre, and others have examined the architectural stratigraphy of the church.

One of the most assured results of this research is the proof that pilgrims were shown, beyond the crusader doors to the right, up the stairs, and then straight ahead to a white outcropping of stone, the site where Jesus probably had been crucified by Roman soldiers. And nearby, to the west and inside the church, are pre-70 tombs cut in the rock for burials. One can see still visible, before the well-carved openings in the stone, the cut horizontal groove for a rolling stone.

Excavations in the 1970s beneath the Armenian Chapel of St. Vartan revealed the drawing of a boat with an inscription that has been interpreted in various contradictory ways.[81] The image and the inscription should be interpreted together. Someone depicted a large Roman merchant ship (perhaps a *navis oneraria*).[82] The main mast of the boat is either lowered, suggesting the vessel is in harbor, or broken or fallen, indicating that the vessel had been "wrecked in a storm."[83] Thus, it seems best to take the verb to be in the first-person plural perfect form. The inscription seems to be *domine ivimus*. If the inscription was made by Christian pilgrims, perhaps from Rome (or from any Latin-speaking community), then it probably means "O Lord, we came (or have arrived)."[84]

The Latin also may mirror the first verse of Ps 122, the classical psalm of Christian pilgrims to Jerusalem. P. Benoit pointed out that the inscription seems to reflect the Latin of this psalm: *In domum domini ibimus.*[85] The meaning would then be "O Lord, we went," citing Ps 122's "Let us go (or, we are going [נלך]) to the house of the Lord." It is conceivable that Christians from the West, probably Rome, made the sign of a boat, an early Christian symbol, and saluted their arrival at (or near) the place at which they most likely thought Jesus had been crucified, buried, and resurrected.

80. Bahat in *Archaeology in the World of Herod, Jesus, and Paul,* p. 260.

81. I wish to express appreciation to Bishop Kapikian for taking me below the Armenian Chapel, showing me the drawing and inscription, and discussing its meaning with me.

82. I am indebted to Gibson for this information.

83. This is Broshi's interpretation. See his "Evidence of Earliest Christian Pilgrimage to the Holy Land Comes to Light in Holy Sepulchre Church," in *Archaeology in the World of Herod, Jesus, and Paul,* pp. 267-70.

84. See Geva, in *NEAEHL* 2:780.

85. I am grateful to Benoit for conversations on these issues. See also Broshi, in *Archaeology in the World of Herod, Jesus, and Paul,* p. 268.

Gibson and J. E. Taylor, however, rightly point out conceivable flaws in this interpretation. They note that the language of Aelia Capitolina, the name of Jerusalem when this inscription was added, was Latin and that the drawing and inscription probably date from the second century C.E. They suggest that perhaps some sailors from Caesarea Maritima, engaged in construction work in Jerusalem, proclaimed to their master that they went as instructed. They propose "master, we went." Rather than push one interpretation, they conclude by reporting that the "precise meaning of the inscription and the identity of the artist remains a mystery."[86]

It is clear that archaeological data need to be sifted and discussed by scholars representing different trainings, traditions, and skills. The focused search for *realia* that help situate Jesus in his time should be informed of diverse possibilities. It is clear that archaeologists have discovered pre-Constantinian structures, even remains of a Roman temple, beneath the present Church of the Holy Sepulchre. Archaeological work alone cannot solve puzzles left by the ancients.

While further discussion is required to ascertain if the boat and inscription reveal the presence of Christian pilgrims at Golgotha, in my judgment the most likely interpretation is the easiest one. Gibson and Taylor are informed and gifted scholars, but they present us with a difficult scenario. The easiest solution is also supported by the setting, or context, in which the boat and inscription are located. It is a site clearly referred to by early Christians as the place where Jesus was crucified, buried, and resurrected. Thus, most likely *domine ivimus* means "O Lord, we came" and was inscribed by a Christian pilgrim. The setting, the use of *domine* for "Lord," and the symbolic meaning of a ship to denote Christianity indicate that Christian pilgrims from Rome may have left this inscription.[87] In my judgment, the inscription means "O Lord, we have (finally) arrived [at the place where you died for us and were raised from the dead]."

Additional Archaeological Discoveries

The preceding pages review and update the seven most significant archaeological discoveries for Jesus Research, according to *Jesus within Judaism*, which was published in 1988. Do these seven remain as significant as I once thought? Should their order be altered? Perhaps, but any response would be rather subjective. The following discussion contains candidates for inclusion in such a list.

---

86. Gibson, "The Jerusalem Ship Drawing," in Gibson and J. E. Taylor, *Beneath the Church of the Holy Sepulchre, Jerusalem* (London: Palestine Exploration Fund, 1994), pp. 25-48. See especially the numerous photographs of the boat and inscription.

87. The date of the inscription cannot be discerned precisely.

Surveying briefly the additional most-significant archaeological discoveries for Jesus Research, I will strive when possible to move geographically in ancient Palestine, from north to south and west to east.

Nazareth   This city in which Jesus clearly spent his youth boasts evidence of veneration by Christians, but solid evidence of Jesus' time has been lacking. Tour buses often stopped on a hill above the modern city, so that visitors could view the bustling city and its churches from a distance.

Since the nineties, excavations less than half a mile from the center of first-century Nazareth reveal some challenging structures. A winepress has been exposed, and beautifully constructed stone-walled terraces are now visible. Most importantly, three circular stone towers only about fifty feet apart now rise majestically above the rocky terrain. These cannot be fortifications; they seem related to a vineyard. Working with Ross Voss, I cleared the eastern tower (which is now across a new road and thus separated from the winepress). The shards I collected from its base were all Roman; most of them were Herodian.[88]

These archaeological discoveries raise many questions that presently remain unanswerable. Were Joseph and Jesus "builders" (cf. Mk 6:3)? Did they know how to build terrace walls? Could they have built the terrace walls and towers now exposed in Nazareth? Could they be some of the builders of the winepress? Regardless of speculative responses to such possibilities, we now have evidence from Nazareth of vineyards with towers, which had seemed odd or misconceived by the compiler of Jesus' parable of the vineyard and the tenants.[89] Recall that parable: "A man planted a vineyard (ἀμπελών) and he encircled it with a stone-hedge (φραγμός), and he dug a winepress (ὑπολήνιον). Then he constructed a tower (πύργος). Finally, he leased it to farmers (γεωργός), and went away" (Mk 12:1). The absentee landlord and overtaxed tenant workers of a vineyard are easy to imagine in light of the sumptuous palace or manor house uncovered not too far to the southwest of Nazareth at Ramat Hanadiv (see the following discussion). Perhaps the new discoveries of a vineyard with walls, a winepress, and a tower just to the west of first-century Nazareth should be considered among the most important archaeological discoveries for Jesus Research.

Cana   Numerous sites are shown to tourists as the Cana in which Jesus performed the miracle described in Jn 2:1-11. In Galilee there are two major com-

---

88. For a photograph and further discussion, see Charlesworth, *The Millennium Guide*, pp. 188-91.

89. See J. S. Kloppenborg, *Reading Viticulture: The Social Context of the Parable of the Tenants in Mark and Thomas* (Claremont, Calif.: Institute for Antiquity and Christianity, 2002).

Figure 10. Nazareth,
tower of a vineyard,
Roman period.

Courtesy of J. H. Charlesworth

peting sites. In southern Lebanon, just southeast of Tyre, there is a "Cana" that some claim to be the authentic site for Jesus' miracle.[90] Both Eusebius and Jerome support that site, and the Lebanese point to vestiges of Christian saints carved on the "Khashna" rocks not far from Kâna el Jalil.[91] While early pilgrims celebrated this site as Jesus' Cana, and while Eusebius and Jerome present valuable witnesses for other sites, the archaeological evidence for this Cana to be Jesus' Cana is lacking.

Where is Jesus' Cana — the Cana mentioned in Jn 2? After three seasons of excavating, Peter Richardson and Douglas Edwards have most likely located the Cana of Josephus (*Life* 86) and of the New Testament (Jn 2:1-11; 4:46; 21:2).[92] It is Khirbet Qana. Since the sixth century c.e. it also has been venerated as the Cana of the Gospel of John. It sits on a hill on the north side of the Beth Netofa Valley at the Wadi Yodefat, and in sight of Nazareth. The village peaked during the early Roman and Byzantine periods. During Jesus' time it was without walls. The archaeologists discovered two pre-70 c.e. *columbaria*, glass wasters

90. It is clear, thanks to archaeological research, that Galileans, especially in Upper Galilee, traded with Tyre and Sepphoris.

91. El Hourani's publication is too popular and geared to lure tourists to warrant scholarly evaluation. See Y. El Hourani, *Cana of Galilee in South Lebanon* ([Beirut]: Ministry of Tourism, 1995). See rather, R. Dussaud, *Topographie historique de la Syrie antique et mediévale* (Paris: Paul Geuthner, 1927), p. 10.

92. See Richardson's contribution to the present volume.

from a glass-blowing factory, and large olive oil presses. The first century C.E. houses at Khirbet Qana are reminiscent of those at Capernaum and Yodefat.

Evidence of pre-70 Jewish habitation at Khirbet Qana is stoneware that is both turned on a lathe and handmade, a *mikveh*, and nearly 100 loculi of twelve or thirteen first-century tombs. The monumental features of rooms in the southwest parts of a trapezoidal wall from the seventh century C.E. are from the early Roman period. Rooms that are adjacent and with benches suggest to the archaeologists that they have found either a public building or more likely a synagogue. A capital with grape clusters such as those found at Gamla enhances this latter suggestion. It is unlikely, however, that the so-called synagogue dates to the time of Jesus, and probably was constructed in the late second or third century C.E. (see Richardson's chapter in the present volume).

Bethsaida   Bethsaida looms large in the Galilee of Jesus.[93] It is perhaps the home of James and John, the sons of Zebedee, and most likely the early home of Philip, Peter, and Andrew (cf. Jn 1:44; 12:21). The present site identified as Bethsaida has been challenged, because an insufficient amount of first-century pottery and coins has been recovered, and because Bethsaida, which means "house of the fishermen," is now about one and a half miles north of the Sea of Galilee and over 200 yards from the Jordan River.[94] Rami Arav and those convinced they are excavating et-Tel, the site proposed in 1838 by E. Robinson as Bethsaida, respond that a sufficient amount of first-century ware has been found, and that the Jordan River shifted course after Jesus' time, cutting Bethsaida off from the present shoreline (see Arav's chapter in the present volume).[95]

The houses in Bethsaida were more solidly built than the dwellings in Capernaum.[96] The walls are often two feet thick. Within one house (the "Fisherman's House") there is a large courtyard paved with basalt stones.[97] It seems that those who lived in Bethsaida were more affluent than those in Capernaum.

---

93. Charlesworth, "Tzer, Bethsaida, and Julias," in *Bethsaida*, ed. R. Arav and R. A. Freund, Bethsaida Excavations Project 3 (Kirksville, Mo.: Truman State University Press, 2004), pp. xi-xiii.

94. See esp. M. Nun, "Has Bethsaida Finally Been Found?" *Jerusalem Perspective* (July/August 1999). Also, see the reply to him by the Bethsaida Excavations Project in "The Case for el-Araj," *BAR* 26 (2000): 52.

95. See esp. R. Arav, R. A. Freund, and J. F. Shroder, "Bethsaida Rediscovered: Long-Lost City Found North of Galilee Shore," *BAR* 26 (2000): 45-56; see the two drawings clarifying the relation of Bethsaida to the Sea of Galilee today and two thousand years ago (on p. 46).

96. I have examined the houses on numerous visits to Bethsaida.

97. See the photograph in *The Millennium Guide*, p. 54.

In one house the excavators found weights for fishing nets, anchors, needles, and fishhooks. The house is thus called "the Fisherman's House." One fishhook had not yet been bent, indicating that fishhooks were probably manufactured in or near this place. An underground room with basalt slabs for a roof, and within which four large wine jars were unearthed, has been labeled "the Wine Maker House." Herodian coins, coins of the Prefect Gratus, a coin of Pontius Pilate from 29 C.E., and coins of Philip dating to 30 C.E. prove occupation near or during the time of Jesus.[98] Stone vessels suggest that some of the houses belonged to Jews. Arav contends that he may have discovered a temple built in honor of Julia-Livia, wife of the emperor Augustus and mother of the emperor Tiberius (see his chapter in this volume). Near what is judged to be the *adyton,* archaeologists found buried *instrumenta sacra,* including two bronze incense shovels.[99]

In 30 C.E. Bethsaida was elevated to a *polis* (city) and renamed Julia to honor the wife of Augustus and the mother of Tiberias. Josephus, after 70, calls the place both Bethsaida and Julia. The Evangelists use traditions that always cite the village as Bethsaida and never as Julia. Mark calls it a "village" (κώμη; 8:23), and much later Luke refers to the site as a "city" (πόλις; 9:10). What do these facts reveal to us about the reliability and editorial tendencies of these Gospel traditions?

The Galilean Boat   M. Nun has drawn attention to the Sea of Galilee (the Kinnereth) and archaeological research on ancient fishermen.[100] Some comment should be added now about a boat found in the mud of the northwestern shore of the Sea of Galilee. It was found by two brothers near Kibbutz Ginosar.[101] Unfortunately, it has sometimes been called "the Jesus Boat." That is misleading. The boat has no clear connection either with Jesus or with one of his early followers.

Yet, the boat may assist us in Jesus Research. It helps us imagine boating and fishing on the Sea of Galilee during Jesus' time.[102] The boat was built in the

---

98. See the drawings in F. Strickert, *Bethsaida: Home of the Apostles* (Collegeville, Minn.: Liturgical Press, 1998), pp. 80, 81, 85, 96, 97, 98, 100, 101, and 146.

99. See Arav's contribution in the present volume. For a photograph of the incense shovel, see Strickert, *Bethsaida,* p. 105.

100. M. Nun, *Der See Genezareth und die Evangelien: Archäologische Forschungen eines jüdischen Fischers,* Biblische Archäologie und Zeitgeschichte 10 (Basel: Brunnen, 2001).

101. I wish to express appreciation to the Israel Department of Antiquities and Museums for the permission to examine and study the boat shortly after it had been discovered. For a discussion and photograph, see Charlesworth, *The Millennium Guide,* p. 165.

102. See S. Wachsmann, "The Galilee Boat," in *Archaeology in the World of Herod, Jesus, and Paul,* pp. 209-23.

Figure 11. Bethsaida; the wine celler with the monoliths still in position to keep the wine cool.   Courtesy of J. H. Charlesworth

first century B.C.E. and was used until sometime around 70 C.E. It is poorly crafted and represents the possession of ordinary people. Perhaps about thirteen men could be crowded into it; but if so many were in the boat, they could not move about as would be necessary for casting nets. Perhaps the most important feature of the wooden boat is its shallow draft. It sat low to the water. Thus fishermen could easily pull nets full of fish into it; but it also would quickly fill with water when waves rose due to a storm. The latter is so well known from the Gospels that it needs no elaboration.

Ramat Hanadiv   At Ḥorvat ʿAqav or Ramat Hanadiv, excavators have unearthed ruins of a once-impressive Herodian palace or fortified manor house, with well-dressed thresholds. The complex dates to the end of the first century B.C.E. The excavations are reported in Y. Hirschfeld's magnificent *Ramat Hanadiv Excavations.*[103] The ruins contain stables, two winepresses, an oil

---

103. Y. Hirschfeld, *Ramat Hanadiv Excavations: Final Report of the 1984-1988 Seasons* (Jerusalem: Israel Exploration Society, 2000). The 768-page report contains the work of many archaeologists, and concludes with sixteen color plates.

press, a tower (perhaps a *columbarium*), and what looks like a rock-cut, single-person, Herodian *mikveh* (locus 343).

The site of the palace or manor was well chosen. It is nestled on the southern slopes of the Carmel hills. This elevated spot commands a pleasing view of the valley to the south and the coastal plain to the west. While the palace does not remind one of the sumptuousness of Hadrian's villa in ways that the palaces at Herodian Jericho might,[104] it nevertheless reveals the elegance of Herodian estates not far from Galilee, barely to the north. What seems strange is the absence of a large hall for greeting distinguished guests.[105] The palace or manor Horvat has a bathhouse with a *caldarium* and swimming pool; the complex is called 'Ein Tzur. The weather at this site and the views are superb.

The Herodian palace or manor (called Horvat 'Eleq) clearly dates from Herodian times, since the construction is Herodian with ashlars in the fortified palatial building and swimming pool. The *realia* found *in situ* in the area are Herodian, including beautiful and often decorated oil lamps (one with a female figure and another with a griffin), various pottery vessels, and three Herodian keys. The coins of Horvat 'Aqav include five from the Roman period, including one of Festus. The 223 coins from Horvat 'Eleq include coins of Herod the Great, Herod Archelaus, Agrippa I, numerous prefects or procurators (including Pilate and Festus), and Vespasian.

In light of the growing importance of ophidian iconography in the ancient world, it is worthwhile reporting that a caduceus appears on the coins of Herod the Great, Archelaus, and Vespasian.[106] It is clear that Horvat 'Eleq was a thriving palace or manor built during the time of Herod the Great, who may have helped finance it so that it would enhance Caesarea Maritima, not far away. This site was occupied until the First Jewish Revolt (66-70 C.E.), when it was abandoned.

The Herodian aqueduct is still covered in places, in ways reminiscent of some aqueducts within Khirbet Qumran. The ruins betray a palatial villa. The wealth came from the surrounding fertile valleys.

Reflections on life here among the elite and the vistas of vineyards below in the southern valley help contextualize the parable of the wicked tenant farmers. It was during the time of the Herods that absentee landlords, who lived in palatial dwellings like this one, overtaxed many Jews and forced some to become

---

104. The Herodian complex was immense; it covered 200 *dunams*. Contrast that figure with Herodian Jericho and its palaces; they covered 25 *dunams*. See E. Netzer et al., *Greater Herodium*, Qedem 13 (Jerusalem: Institute of Archaeology, Hebrew University of Jerusalem, 1981), p. 109.

105. I am most grateful to Hirschfeld for showing me the ruins and discussing the archaeology of the site with me.

106. The caduceus is two serpents facing each other.

tenant farmers. The presence of an unusual number of cattle bones seems to indicate the wealth of this palace or manor. The owner may well have had a herd of cattle. The affluence of the palace is now confirmed by the recent recovery of an elegantly crafted lion or panther, once part of a marble table that originally stood in the palace's garden.[107]

Caesarea Maritima   The Evangelists do not report that Jesus visited Caesarea Maritima, but the massive and major port built by Herod the Great should not go unmentioned in Jesus Research.[108] Jesus certainly would have known about the city, and not only because the Roman legions were usually quartered there. Caesarea, of course, played a major role in the life of Peter and Paul. It helps us contemplate how much ancient Palestine, in Jesus' time, was open to the flow of goods from all over the civilized world.

Jews most likely enjoyed chariot races. Two of the most impressive hippodromes are now exposed in Caesarea. A 100-ton red granite obelisk, discovered in the east hippodrome, has been reerected in the center of the racetrack on its original base and on a wall that divides the hippodrome. The obelisk originally stood 15 meters high but is now only 12 meters high.

Jerusalem   Much is being exposed now that should be considered among the most important archaeological discoveries for Jesus Research. The comments, of course, must continue to be very selective. Excavators working to the south and west of the Temple Mount have exposed first-century streets, well-crafted sewers, shops, and entrances into the Temple that clearly date from Jesus' time in Jerusalem.[109]

Seats that conceivably are from the Jerusalem theater mentioned by

---

107. Hirschfeld kindly showed me this marble lion or panther before it was published.

108. See an artist's rendering of Caesarea Maritima during the time of Jesus (p. 99) and the popular but scholarly discussions by leading experts who have excavated at Caesarea in K. G. Holum and R. L. Hohlfelder, eds., *King Herod's Dream* (New York and London: Norton, 1988). For more scholarly work, see Levine and Netzer, eds., *Excavations at Caesarea Maritima: 1975, 1976, 1979 — Final Report,* Qedem 21 (Jerusalem: Hebrew University of Jerusalem, 1986). For the western hippodrome, see p. 9. For photographs of the eastern hippodrome and a discussion, see Levine, "Sports Arenas," in *Roman Caesarea: An Archaeological-Topographical Study,* Qedem 2 (Jerusalem: Hebrew University of Jerusalem, 1975), pp. 27-29; pl. 5 (the obelisk can be seen *in situ* on photograph 3). The western hippodrome was not found until later in the excavations; for a color photograph see Charlesworth, *The Millennium Guide,* color section following p. 40.

109. For the most recent report, see R. Reich and Y. Billig, "Excavations Near the Temple Mount and Robinson's Arch, 1994-1996," in *Ancient Jerusalem Revealed,* expanded ed. (Jerusalem: Israel Exploration Society, 2000), pp. 340-52.

Figure 12. The tomb of Queen Helena of Adiabene, ca. 40 C.E. The tomb is just north of Herod's Gate, Jerusalem.

Courtesy of J. H. Charlesworth

Josephus (*Ant* 15.268-70) may have been discovered.[110] In the present collection, A. Lichtenberger discusses the theater built by Herod that was lavishly decorated with gold and silver trophies that were, of course, an offense to Jewish religious laws. Lichtenberger concludes that the shape of the seats recovered in Jerusalem, especially their bent profile, is typical of seats belonging to theaters built in the second century C.E., at the earliest.

A large cave, dug out of limestone, east of Jerusalem and north of Bethphage has been discovered. It was the site of a factory that produced both lathe-turned and hand-chiseled stone vessels. The factory antedates 70 C.E.[111]

An extensive quantity of exquisitely made Herodian glass, with stunning detail and color, some with a menorah,[112] has appeared in Jerusalem. Most of the glass comes from Hizma, slightly to the north of Jerusalem.

S. Gibson is presently excavating an area to the east of Zion Gate and just outside the present Turkish Walls. He has reached the Herodian layer, and what he is discovering may help us better estimate the location of Caiaphas's house. From earlier excavations in this part of Jerusalem, but more to the west, he has

110. Reich and Billig, "Appendix: A Group of Theater Seats from Jerusalem," in *Ancient Jerusalem Revealed*, pp. 350-52.

111. See D. Amit, J. Seligman, and I. Zilberbod, "Stone Vessel Workshops of the Second Temple Period East of Jerusalem," in *Ancient Jerusalem Revealed*, pp. 353-58. Also, see Gibson, "The Stone Vessel Industry at Hizma," *IEJ* 33 (1983): 176-88.

112. See Charlesworth, *The Millennium Guide*, the color section following p. 40.

much to publish. One item is especially well preserved: a Roman sword still in its scabbard.[113] Gibson and D. M. Jacobson's sourcebook on the subterranean chambers of the Temple Mount, especially the area inside the triple gates of the Herodian Temple, is replete with valuable information.[114]

While I was finalizing the present introduction, I saw a report that the first-century Siloam Pool has been discovered (Associated Press; December 24, 2004). According to the Fourth Evangelist, Jesus healed a man born blind in the vicinity of the Temple.[115] After Jesus spat on the ground, made clay, and anointed the man's eyes with it, he said, "'Go, wash yourself in the pool of Siloam' (which means Sent [in Hebrew]). So he went and washed and came back seeing" (Jn 9:7; cf. 9:11). In the Silwan suburb of present-day Jerusalem, archaeologists have discovered this first-century stone-lined pool (which is 50 yards long), an esplanade, a water channel that brought clean water from the Silwan spring, steps that lead down into the pool, and a paved street that leads up to the Temple. It is now much clearer that this pool — the Pool of Siloam — was used to perform the Jewish rites of ritual purification during the time of Jesus and until the destruction of 70 C.E.

Luke (and he alone) refers to a tower in Siloam. This Evangelist records a saying of Jesus in which he refers to eighteen people who died when "the tower in Siloam fell" (ὁ πύργος ἐν τῷ Σιλωὰμ; Lk 13:4). It will be interesting to observe if any evidence of this tower appears in the excavations south of the present walls of Jerusalem.

The water, which still flows there from out of the ground, is pure. It can not only cleanse the body but purify the soul, according to Jewish customs (Mishnah, Tosephta, and the Qumran scrolls). It is likely that the blind man was trying to purify himself so that he could ascend unto the Mount of the Lord. According to *Some Works of the Torah* (4QMMT [esp. 4Q396 frgs. 1-2, col. 2]), a blind man cannot enter the Temple because he is imperfect, and does not know what to do when he enters "into the purity of the sanctuary." According to the Fourth Evangelist, the man's impurity was removed by Jesus and the purifying waters of the Pool of Siloam. The site for this tradition has now been found.

The Herodium   The burial site of King Herod has not yet been located. No one has found a trace of Herod's tomb. Josephus describes in detail where

113. I am most grateful to S. Gibson for sharing with me his insights and discoveries.

114. Gibson and D. M. Jacobson, *Below the Temple Mount in Jerusalem*, British Archaeological Reports International Series 637 (Oxford: Tempus Reparatum, 1996).

115. On the location of the miracle, see D. M. Smith, *John*, ANTC (Nashville: Abingdon, 1999), p. 191.

Herod was buried (*War* 1.667-73). It is the Herodium.[116] E. Netzer, who excavated the Herodium,[117] is convinced that Herod was not buried in the elevated hill (the Upper Herodium) but below it (the Lower Herodium).[118] Netzer presents two main arguments. First, no Jew would live within a circumscribed area in which a body was buried. Second, he has recovered elegant Herodian ashlars that were part of a Doric frieze, in one corner of the Monumental Building that once dominated the Lower Herodium.[119] A. Lichtenberger presented the same arguments, concluding that the Upper Herodium, most likely, cannot at the same time be a palace and a tomb.[120]

More recently J. Magness, however, has stressed that an examination of S. Loffreda's *La ceramica di Macheronte e dell'Herodion (90 a.C.–135 d.C.)*[121] reveals that from the time of Herod's death until the First Jewish Revolt, fine ware types are found in the Lower Herodium but not in the Upper Herodium. That discovery seems to suggest that the Upper Herodium ceased to be a palace after Herod's death.[122] Does that indicate that Herod was buried in the Upper Herodium, and that after his burial no one lived there?

How solid is Magness's conclusion? She herself admits that there is some evidence that might disprove her assumption. Loffreda did report the discovery in the Upper Herodium of the base of a carinated shallow cup or small plate, and it seems to postdate Herod's death (Loffreda, fig. 57.156). The dating of the pottery is imprecise, and the remains are not isolated into clear stratigraphical layers. Finally, since the Upper Herodium was used during the First and Second Revolts and later by Byzantine monks, one should ask if these people may have removed evidence of occupation from 4 B.C.E. to 66 C.E. Despite these reservations, I am impressed and influenced by Magness's insight.

Thus, we are left with challenging questions regarding the location of Herod's tomb. Where was Herod buried, and why have archaeologists failed to

116. For a photograph of the Herodium, see Charlesworth, *Jesus within Judaism*, illus. 7.

117. See esp. E. Netzer, "Herodium," in *NEAEHL* 2:618-26.

118. E. Netzer, *Greater Herodium*, Qedem 13 (Jerusalem: Institute of Archaeology, Hebrew University of Jerusalem, 1981), p. 43; and Netzer, *Die Paläst der Hasmonäer und Herodes' des Grossen* (Mainz am Rhein: Von Zabern, 1999), pp. 106-7.

119. Netzer, "Searching for Herod's Tomb," in *Archaeology in the World of Herod, Jesus, and Paul*, pp. 137-58; see esp. p. 157.

120. A. Lichtenberger, *Die Baupolitik Herodes des Grossen*, Abhandlungen des Deutschen Palästinavereins 26 (Wiesbaden: Harrassowitz, 1999), p. 111. Also, see Lichtenberger's chapter in the present volume.

121. S. Loffreda, *La ceramica di Macheronte e dell'Herodion (90 a.C.–135 d.C.)*, SBF.CMa 39 (Jerusalem: Franciscanum, 1996).

122. J. Magness, "Where Is Herod's Tomb at Herodium?" *BASOR* 322 (2001): 43-46.

Figure 13. The Herodium.

Courtesy of J. H. Charlesworth

find his burial site at the Herodium? Indeed, why have none of the tombs of the kings of Israel or Judea been located?[123]

Numerous other archaeological sites or discoveries should also be included. Among these would be Caesarea Philippi, where tradition reports that Peter confessed that Jesus was the Messiah. A cave with flowing water, shrines to Pan, and palaces of Antipas have been discovered and exposed in this area of Upper Galilee.

An inscription with the name of Pilate and his office, prefect, has been discovered in Caesarea Maritima.[124] A stone box (ossuary) bearing the name of Joseph Caiaphas was found south of the Old City of Jerusalem. Another stone box bears the inscription "James, the son of Joseph, the brother of Jesus." But I do not include it in this list, because I was convinced the moment it was announced that "the brother of Jesus" is not authentic to the ossuary.[125]

123. A stone slab with the name of Uzziah, who is identified as "Uzziah King of Judah," has been recovered. Most likely the slab dates from the time of Jesus, when the king's bones were reburied. See the photograph in J. A. Thompson, *Handbook of Life in Bible Times* (1986; reprint, Leicester: InterVarsity, 1999), p. 245.

124. For a photograph of the Pilate inscription, see Charlesworth, *Jesus within Judaism,* illus. 10.

125. The addition "the brother of [someone]" is almost undocumented, and a man is identified by his father. To me the handwriting is slightly different, but one cannot be certain, since no scribe makes consonants exactly the same each time. The dubious provenience of the ossuary, which is authentic, also raises major questions, and the addition "the brother of Jesus" would elevate the value of the object astronomically. Among the publications on the James ossuary, one of the best, most informed, and balanced is C. A. Evans's *Jesus and the Ossuaries* (Waco, Tex.: Baylor University Press, 2003).

III. Three Problematic Points in Scholarly Discussions

Three debates crucial for those engaged in Jesus Research are frequently found in archaeological reports and summaries. They will be introduced in order of importance.

Peter's House

Has Peter's house been found in Capernaum? This was the claim of V. Corbo and S. Loffreda, two Franciscan fathers, who excavated Capernaum from 1968 to 1985.[126] Some of their reading of the graffiti seems tendentious to some experts.[127] Reed gives some credence to these criticisms and opines that "the validity of Peter's house under the basilica" is "of marginal concern to the nature and character of Capernaum at the time of Jesus."[128] If the discovery of Peter's house at Capernaum is marginal to the character of Capernaum during Jesus' time, it is not necessarily insignificant for Jesus Research.

In favor of the site being the house of Peter are the following observations: (1) Peter clearly lived in Capernaum. (2) This is the only house in this area of Galilee that has been identified by archaeologists, pilgrims, and other early traditions as Peter's house. (3) An octagonal basilica was placed over sacred sites in the Holy Land; such a basilica was placed over this house, and in the sixth century, at least, the house below was celebrated as Peter's house. (4) Public rooms used for special purposes were plastered; the central room in this house was so plastered. Most likely, the walls already received such plaster in the first century c.e. (5) Graffiti left by Christians in the second century c.e., and perhaps earlier, was discovered on the plaster. One of them might have the name Peter.[129] (6) The narrow basalt walls of this house would have probably supported only a thatched roof; that architectural ele-

126. V. Corbo, *Cafarnao I,* and S. Loffreda, *Cafarnao II,* Studium Biblicum Franciscanum 19 (Jerusalem: Franciscan Printing Press, 1974); A. Spijkerman, *Cafarnao III,* Studium Biblicum Franciscanum 19 (Jerusalem: Franciscan Printing Press, 1975); E. Tesa, *Cafarnao IV,* Studium Biblicum Franciscanum 19 (Jerusalem: Franciscan Printing Press, 1972).

127. See J. Taylor, *Christians and the Holy Places: The Myth of Jewish-Christian Origins* (Oxford: Clarendon, 1993), pp. 284-88.

128. Reed, *Archaeology,* p. 143.

129. See the excellent reproduction and discussion in J. F. Strange and H. Shanks, "Has the House Where Jesus Stayed in Capernaum Been Found?" in *Archaeology in the World of Herod, Jesus, and Paul,* pp. 188-99, esp. p. 199. As Strange and Shanks contend, "a considerable amount of circumstantial evidence does point to its identification as St. Peter's house" (p. 199).

ment precisely fits Peter's house as described by the earliest Evangelist (Mk 2:1-12).[130]

Archaeological evidence is almost always hotly debated. What, then, is clear? The "house church" in Capernaum that is celebrated as Peter's house may well be the house in which Jesus taught. It is certainly not a "synagogue," but it seems to be Peter's house. Thus, I fully agree with J. Murphy-O'Connor, who is unusually well informed of data related to Jesus and archaeology and astutely critical; notice his judgment: "The most reasonable assumption is the one attested by the Byzantine pilgrims, namely, that it was the house of Peter in which Jesus may have lodged (Mt 5:20). Certainly, nothing in the excavations contradicts this identification."[131]

Theodotus Inscription

Does the Theodotus inscription, on display in the Rockefeller Museum in Jerusalem, postdate 70 C.E.? This inscription (Inv. S842 and *CIJ* II 1404) now seems, in the judgment of most experts, to be evidence of a pre-70 synagogue in Jerusalem. Three points seem fundamental.[132]

First, the claim by many scholars — including Reed — that *sunagōgē* (συναγωγή) before 70 C.E. denotes only a "gathering," never a building, is inaccurate. An inscription from Benghazi (Bernike, Cyrenaica) refers to "the renovation of the synagogue" (εἰς ἐπισκευὴν τῆς συναγωγῆς). Obviously, a building is denoted by a "renovation." The script dates from the time of Nero (55/56 C.E.), and the "synagogue" is thus pre-70.

Second, the paleography of the Theodotus inscription antedates 70 C.E. It is a lapidary script similar to the Herodian script found on manuscripts from the Qumran caves.

Third, the stratigraphy of the site in which the Theodotus inscription was recovered is Herodian. There is no reason to suggest a post-Herodian date for the object and its inscription.

Cumulatively, it becomes clear that a synagogue in Jerusalem, funded by a man named Theodotus, was constructed in the late first century B.C.E. or early

---

130. Other evidence may also point to Peter; for example, it may not be insignificant that fishing hooks were found in the house and that Peter was a fisherman and not a farmer (ample evidence for preparation of olive oil and wine is also seen at Capernaum).

131. J. Murphy-O'Connor, *The Holy Land,* 4th ed. (Oxford and New York: Oxford University Press, 1998), p. 220.

132. I wish to express indebtedness and appreciation to J. S. Kloppenborg for information and discussion. Also, see his chapter in the present volume.

first century C.E. Moreover, Theodotus's grandfather is also identified as leader of a synagogue (ἀρχισυνάγωγος). Hence, it seems wise to assume that the Theodotus inscription denotes a "synagogue" in Jerusalem that antedates 70 by decades (see also J. S. Kloppenborg's chapter in this book).

Date of the Sepphoris Theater

A storm center of debate in archaeology and Jesus Research concerns the date of the impressive theater in Sepphoris. What is the date of this theater? Does it date from Jesus' time? Did he and his father walk the four miles from Nazareth to Sepphoris to work there as builders? Did Jesus learn about "hypocrites" because of "actors" performing in the theater? Some scholars have answered these questions affirmatively; others have been critical of such assertions.

If the Sepphoris theater dates to Jesus' youth, then it should be considered one of the major archaeological discoveries for Jesus Research. Reed dates the theater to the late first century C.E. He rejects an earlier dating because the requisite stratification and dating of pottery shards are only announced and not defended.[133] If Reed is correct, then the theater cannot have been where Joseph or Jesus may have worked as a "builder" *(tektōn)*, and activity in it could not have influenced Jesus.

Does the theater date from the time of Jesus, and does it help us understand some of his sayings? Three main names seem to dominate in this debate. W. Bauer, in 1927, claimed that Sepphoris, like other cities in Galilee, namely, Chorazin, Bethsaida, and Tiberias, represented Gentile culture. He surmised that Jesus probably avoided this Hellenistic city because his message was discordant from the religion of those in Sepphoris.[134] Bauer contended that Jesus "most likely never preached in or visited Sepphoris."[135] S.-J. Case, probably the pioneer in the sociological study of Jesus and the scholar who stimulated Waterman's excavations at Sepphoris in 1926,[136] raised the question whether Jesus could have been involved as a builder in Antipas's grand rebuilding of Sepphoris, which (according to him) continued to 25 C.E. R. Batey, in 1991, answered this question positively in his popular *Jesus and the Forgotten City.*[137]

133. Reed, *Archaeology,* pp. 96, 108.

134. W. Bauer, "Jesus der Galiläer," in *Aufsätze und kleine Schriften,* ed. G. Stecker (Tübingen: Mohr-Siebeck, 1967), pp. 91-108. Of course, this work is a reprint of his 1927 article.

135. Bauer, "Jesus der Galiläer," p. 106.

136. S.-J. Case, "Jesus and Sepphoris," *JBL* 45 (1926): 14-22. For astute reflections on Bauer, Case, and Batey, see Reed, *Archaeology,* pp. 104-14.

137. R. Batey, *Jesus and the Forgotten City* (Grand Rapids: Baker, 1991). Also, see Batey's chapter in the present volume.

The criterion for discerning the correct answer to Jesus' possible involvement in the building of the theater at Sepphoris is appreciably distinct from dating a manuscript. The latest orthographic form reveals the date of a manuscript. The earliest clear evidence of a theater's construction dates its beginning, and should not be confused with possible later expansions or renovations.

For researching the historical Jesus, a date before 30 C.E. for the Sepphoris theater is imperative. A later date for this theater will not be helpful in Jesus Research, and will be significant primarily for an understanding of the theology of the Evangelist Matthew. That is, if "hypocrites" is a post-Jesus editorial addition by Matthew, then it will derive from Matthew's sociological setting and theology. If the mention of "hypocrites" — so evident in Matthew — is shaped by a post-70 theater, then this attribution to Jesus will be anachronistic, and derive from theaters far removed from and later than the Sepphoris Jesus would have known.

With these methodological clarifications, we can examine the evaluation of the archaeological evidence. The major protagonists in the debate are the leading excavators of Sepphoris. E. Meyers and C. Meyers opt for a second century C.E. date for the Roman theater. They report that the "theater, parts of which have been excavated by four expeditions, seems to date to a period later than Antipas." They suggest that it was constructed "as late as the early to mid-second century, when the city underwent extensive rebuilding after the First Jewish Revolt."[138]

This judgment is contradicted by another entry in the *OEANE*, of which E. M. Meyers is editor in chief. In the entry entitled "Theaters," A. Segal states: "Three theaters were erected in Herod the Great's kingdom (37-4 BCE); at Caesarea, in Jerusalem, and in Jericho. A fourth was presumably initiated by his son Antipas at Sepphoris" (5:201). This same opinion is offered by Z. Weiss, who with E. Netzer directed the Hebrew University excavations at Sepphoris until 1995 when he became sole director. In *NEAEHL*, Weiss reports that the Sepphoris "theater apparently was built in the early first century C.E., possibly in the reign of Antipas (4 B.C.E. to 39 C.E.), as part of his building activity at Sepphoris at the beginning of his rule in Galilee" (4:1325). Another director of excavations at Sepphoris, J. Strange, also dates the theater to the time of Antipas.[139] He claims to have found archaeological evidence that the theater was first constructed during the time of Antipas; that is, the theater was there during the time Jesus was nearby, either in Nazareth or in Capernaum.[140]

Which archaeologists should we follow? The argument cannot be settled

---

138. C. L. Meyers and E. M. Meyers, in *OEANE* 4:530 and 4:533.

139. Strange, "Sepphoris," in *ABD* 5:1091.

140. I am grateful to Strange for conversations on the dating of the theater at Sepphoris.

by studying Josephus or the New Testament. What is demanded is proof that the Sepphoris theater is datable archaeologically: that its dating is based on the discovery of some datable stratigraphic factor, something like a coin or a shard found *in situ* and beneath an extant portion of the theater. We need to see something at Sepphoris similar to what Benoit found in Jerusalem's alleged prison of Jesus. Benoit pointed out that the traditional site of Jesus' imprisonment is Hadrianic, since a pillar *in situ* dates the floor, with its game, to the time of Aelia Capitolina around 130 C.E.[141]

I have discussed this issue with both James Strange and Eric Meyers. Strange has no doubt that this proof has been found and that the theater originally dates from the time of Antipas.[142] He is digging on the northern or lower area of Sepphoris. He reports that the date of the theater in his area is the first half of the first century C.E.; the date is suggested by the dating of pottery shards found under the stage, the rear wall, and the perimeter outer wall. The theater was renovated sometime later, perhaps between 70 and 80 C.E.[143] Batey opines that the theater was constructed in the early years of Antipas's reign, and that the construction began in 3 B.C.E.[144]

Meyers, who has been excavating and studying the southern elevated part of Sepphoris, is adamant: the final date of the Sepphoris theater is post-70 C.E. and probably dates to sometime around 100 C.E.[145] This conclusion is also defended by M. Chancey, who points out that it is not clear that the Sepphoris theater "ever existed at the time of Jesus."[146] The date for the upper level does seem to be the early second century C.E., because of datable pottery at that point.[147] Weiss and Netzer have changed their minds; they now con-

141. During the millennium celebration in Jerusalem, two scholars presented such proofs for dating the Sepphoris theater. These studies appear in the present volume.

142. I am indebted to Strange for conversations on this point, many during visits to Sepphoris, and in November 2001.

143. See also Strange, "Six Campaigns at Sepphoris," in *The Galilee in Late Antiquity,* pp. 342-43.

144. Batey, "Sepphoris and the Jesus Movement," *NTS* 47 (2001): 402-9. Also, see Batey's chapter in this volume.

145. I am indebted to Eric Meyers for insights and information supplied on November 10, 2001. Also, see Meyers and M. Chancey, "How Jewish Was Sepphoris in Jesus' Time?" *BAR* 26 (2000): 18-33.

146. M. Chancey, "The Cultural Milieu of Ancient Sepphoris," *NTS* 47 (2001): 127-45; the quotation is on p. 136. Also, see Chancey, *The Myth of a Gentile Galilee: The Population of Galilee and New Testament Studies* (Cambridge: Cambridge University Press, 2002). Chancey is a student of Eric Meyers.

147. It is clear that the theater was not used in the Byzantine period; it was destroyed by the earthquake of 363 C.E.

clude that the date of the Sepphoris theater is the late first century c.e., at the earliest.[148]

How can these two conflicting discoveries and informed judgments be reconciled? Perhaps the theater was constructed in two different stages and periods. If the reading of the pottery finally solves this debate,[149] it is conceivable that the upper and southern level was an expansion of an earlier theater from the time of Herod Antipas (4 b.c.e. to 39 c.e.). Hence, if that conclusion is warranted, then Jesus and his contemporaries might have known a smaller theater at Sepphoris.

If this proof can be supplied and accepted as scientific evidence that an early theater dates from Jesus' youth, then we may turn again to Josephus and the New Testament records. According to Josephus, Antipas's building projects made Sepphoris "the ornament of all Galilee" (*Ant* 18.27). What does "ornament of all Galilee" (πρόσχημα τοῦ Γαλιλαίου) mean? According to E. Meyers and C. Meyers, πρόσχημα denotes an impregnable fortification.[150] The context in Josephus might suggest this interpretation; it refers to Antipas fortifying (τειχίσας) Sepphoris.

Antipas, however, also made Sepphoris an imperial city, and not just a fortress. He honored Augustus by calling Sepphoris "Autocratoris" (Αὐτοκρατορίδα). The Greek verb τειχίζω denotes building a wall (τεῖχος) and may be irrelevant for contemplating the construction of a theater. The noun "Autocratoris," however, denotes a royal city, and not just a walled city. The key term is πρόσχημα, which means generically anything "that is held before." Its primary meaning is "appearance"; its derived meaning is "ornament." The noun πρόσχημα is chosen by Polybius to describe the new city of Carthage; it was "the chief ornament and capital (πρόσχημα καὶ βασίλειον) of the Carthaginian empire" (*Histories* 3.15.3).[151] Thus "capital" and "ornament" seem also to describe Antipas's "Sepphoris."[152] If archaeological proof can be forth-

148. Weiss and Netzer, "Hellenistic and Roman Sepphoris," in *Sepphoris in Galilee*, ed. M. Nagy et al. (Winona Lake, Ind.: Eisenbrauns, 1996), pp. 32, 122.

149. As of November 2001, the pottery had not yet been scrutinized and dated. I am grateful to Eric Meyers for showing me the Sepphoris pottery in the basement of the Albright Institute.

150. Meyers and Meyers, in *OEANE* 4:530.

151. The text and translation is by W. R. Paton, *Polybius*, LCL (Cambridge, Mass., 1979), 2:36-37.

152. Antipas was married to Herodias, whose daughter was Salome. The latter married Philip, and when he died she married Aristobulus, the son of Herod king of Chalcis, who along with Agrippa I was the grandson of Herod the Great. We New Testament scholars too often forget about the extent of the Herodian dynasty that plagued Jesus and his followers. D. Flusser wisely warned against assuming Salome "was a morally depraved person" (p. 21). See Flusser, "A New Portrait of Salome," *Jerusalem Perspective* 55 (1998): 18-21.

coming for Antipas constructing a theater at Sepphoris during Jesus' youth, that would fit nicely with it being the "ornament of all Galilee."

The date of the theater does not settle the possible influence of Sepphoris on Jesus, especially during his youth. The presence of sophisticated *mikvaot* at Sepphoris indicates there were priests, who intermittently served in the Temple, probably living there, as evidenced by the ancient literature (*m. Yoma* 6.3; *y. Ber.* 3.6b; *t. Ta'an.* 1 end; *y. Yoma* 6.43c; *y. Ma'as. S.* 5.56a). Is it possible that Jesus' love for the Temple and Jerusalem may have been enhanced by conversations with priests in Sepphoris? These issues cannot be settled by archaeologists. In fact, virtually no conceivable discovery can supply answers to most of the questions that stimulate, and often plague, New Testament scholars. We historians too often wander in the opaqueness of recorded history.

Conclusion: The Fundamental Importance of Archaeology in Jesus Research

The archaeological evidence now available for reconstructing Jesus' time is not only abundant; it is impressive. Now, we know that Galilee was not defined by rural villages; at least Sepphoris and Tiberias were cities. Gamla was more like a city than a village. We are seeing, in some publications in Jesus Research, the importance not only of archaeology, but also of sociology, psychology, and iconography.

In the past decade, or more, serious scholars have argued that New Testament research has become too text-centered. Yet, some studies have become even more myopic, devolving into self-centered rhetorical studies. Rhetorical studies of New Testament texts are exceedingly important, if they are informed about ancient rhetoric;[153] but this is not always the case. It is disturbing to observe that while historical, sociological, and archaeological methodologies and insights are judged to be fundamental for New Testament studies, especially Jesus Research, some experts are still oblivious of such scientific foundations for research.

Jesus Research is paradigmatically different from the new quest of Ernst Käsemann, Günther Bornkamm, and James Robinson and even the old quest of Heinrich Holzmann, Adolf Harnack, and Albert Schweitzer. Whereas earlier scholars relied on source criticism and sought to ground the study of Jesus in the putative earliest sources, Mark and Q, more recent scholars see the danger

---

153. See the masterful studies by C. C. Black in *The Rhetoric of the Gospel* (St. Louis: Chalice, 2001).

of a text-centered approach, include the Gospel of John, and utilize sociology, psychology, and especially archaeology.

As I contemplate the many publications that pour forth on Jesus Research, I am surprised how cavalierly some experts treat sociology, as if it is a methodology designed to work with ancient texts. I am also concerned how suspicious so many scholars are about the historical reliability of the intra-canonical Gospels,[154] and their tendency to shun the demands placed on them by philology, sociology, psychology, and archaeology.

The study of psychology has recently enriched the study of the Bible, as evidenced by the four-volume *Psychology and the Bible: A New Way to Read the Scriptures* (2004). It is edited by J. H. Ellens and W. G. Rollins, and is introduced by D. Capps. Jesus Research is already being informed and enriched by the study of psychobiography.

As Jesus Research moves forward with the attempt to reconstruct Jesus' time, as well as a better comprehension of Jesus' acts and sayings, archaeological discoveries and insights are proving to be quintessential, as the present volume demonstrates. The New Testament documents from which we reconstruct what Jesus said and did, and why, obtain clearer meaning when examined within the settings in which he lived. I fully agree with the judgment of J. Strange: "Archaeology can aid in establishing the social context in which the New Testament reports that the ministry of Jesus took place. This context includes details of economics, village/city relationships, the organization of Roman taxation, the extent of gentile and Jewish settlement in Galilee, resources for gentile worship, resources for Jewish worship, educational programs, and many other social systems."[155] Clearly the New Testament texts need contexts — otherwise they can mean virtually anything a modern reader might suggest; or worse, they might mean nothing at all.

During his adult ministry, Jesus may have avoided Sepphoris because of his own Jewishness, as J. P. Meier and E. P. Sanders suggest. He may also have shunned the city for political reasons, that is, to avoid Antipas (Lk 13:31-33). Most likely Jesus knew this Herodian had killed John the Baptizer (probably Jesus' teacher and possible relative, as we know from previous exegesis of John and Luke). He may not have wished to avoid the Jews who characterized Sepphoris, but he may have judged that city not a suitable social setting for his revolutionary insights.

---

154. See esp. M. Sawicki, *Crossing Galilee: Architecture of Contact in the Occupied Land of Jesus* (Harrisburg, Pa.: Trinity, 2000), who rightly claims that those involved in Jesus Research apply sociology "too reverently" and approach the "texts too suspiciously"; see esp. pp. 64-67. Also see Freyne's chapter in the present collection.

155. J. Strange, "Some Implications of Archaeology for New Testament Studies," in *What Has Archaeology to Do with Faith?* pp. 23-59; the quotation is from p. 30.

Did Jesus choose Capernaum, a modest fishing village without evidence of conservative Judaism, and avoid Gamla, a conservative religious Jewish city, because his Jewishness was challengingly "liberal"? Such new questions are aroused by a study of Galilean archaeology, since first-century Jews in Capernaum apparently had no *mikvaot*, while Jews in Gamla frequented an impressive synagogue with a contiguous *mikveh*.

In light of archaeological research and especially the recovery of the Qumran scrolls as well as the appreciation of the Old Testament Pseudepigrapha, there should be no doubt that Jesus was an apocalyptic and eschatological prophet.[156] I would wish to add with D. Flusser a caveat: Jesus "is the only Jew of ancient times known to us, who preached not only that people were on the threshold of the end of time, but that the new age of salvation had already begun."[157] Jesus sought to reform Judaism, inter alia, by employing intermittently some anti-Judean sentiments and developing select pro-Israelite traditions.[158] As evidenced by the research and insights provided by Meyers, Strange, and Bowersock, it is clear that Hellenism was not necessarily antithetical or antagonistic to Judaism. Hellenism and Judaism mixed in various ways at different times and places, depending on economic, social, and religious factors. It is imperative to observe that the concept of a Jewish Galilee does not exclude older and more indigenous traditions,[159] such as those associated with ancient Israel (traditions before and after the northern kingdom) and the influence from Assyria (especially at Bethsaida). It is certainly clear now, thanks to archaeological research, that in Jesus' time many Galileans were Jews; they were descendants of the Judeans who settled in Galilee during the second and first centuries B.C.E.[160]

156. G. Theissen and A. Merz, in their superb and comprehensive guide to Jesus Research (*The Historical Jesus: A Comprehensive Guide,* trans. J. Bowden [Minneapolis: Fortress, 1998]), incorrectly assume that J. D. Crossan and M. J. Borg represent a consensus of Jesus specialists in the United States; they report that in "most recent North American exegesis, future eschatology is denied" (p. 245). E. P. Sanders, P. Fredriksen, B. Chilton, J. P. Meier, D. Allison, I, and others have no doubt that Jesus' teaching was shaped by Jewish eschatology. Perhaps most of those involved in Jesus Research in America, and not members of the Jesus Seminar, would agree with Theissen and Merz that in "his preaching of the kingly rule of God, Jesus revitalizes the traditional Israelite metaphor of the king in the framework of a modified eschatological expectation" (p. 246). For more reflections see Charlesworth, "The Historical Jesus and Exegetical Theology," *PSB* (2001): 45-63. Also, note B. D. Ehrman, *Jesus: Apocalyptic Prophet of the New Millennium* (Oxford and New York: Oxford University Press, 1999). Also, see the insights by H. W. M. Rietz in the present volume.

157. Flusser, *Jesus,* p. 110. The quotation appears in his earlier version, but with "men" instead of "people." See D. Flusser, *Jesus,* trans. R. Walls (New York: Herder and Herder, 1969), p. 90.

158. See the insightful comments by Reed, *Archaeology,* pp. 58-61.

159. See Freyne's chapter in the present volume.

160. See Dunn's chapter in the present volume.

Little consensus can be reported on some of the major issues in the burgeoning field of Jesus and archaeology. Do we agree with Strange and Batey, imagining that Jesus' life and message were shaped by urbanized Galilee? Or do we side with Horsley and attempt to reconstruct the historical Jesus in light of rural Galilee? Or, further, are we being forced to choose between false alternatives, since the data is too complex to close out either option?

What was the relation between the new urban centers, like Sepphoris and Tiberias, and the older villages? Do we side with Edwards and see a network of interaction and deny any parasitic function to the cities, or do we side with Freyne and see social and economic tensions caused by the heterogeneous cities, especially Sepphoris and Tiberias, and contemplate exploitation?[161] Perhaps both factors can be perceived, intermittently, in the life and teaching of Jesus.

The land of Jesus is no longer a *terra incognita*.[162] Archaeological excavations in places obviously frequented by this itinerant Galilean prophet have changed the map of Jesus Research. The present is the time for analysis and fruitful dialogue. We are learning to raise questions and correct an earlier text-based myopic reconstruction of Jesus' life and social environment. Scholars who ignore archaeology (as well as sociological and psychological studies) in pursuing Jesus Research will henceforth be charged with being misinformed. The data collected and the discussions presented now by the experts who contribute to the present volume have constructed a solid foundation for reflection and provided discussions to ponder, as we explore a relatively new field: Jesus and archaeology.

The research reviewed in this chapter demonstrates that a new perspective is beginning to enrich Jesus Research; it evolves from scientific research focused on archaeological discoveries, from the Dead Sea Scrolls to *realia*, like coins once held by Jesus' contemporaries, and the remains of a Jew who was crucified about the time of Jesus' death. The new perspective sometimes helps us better re-create the social and symbolic setting of Jesus' life and teachings, the rural and urban conditions he knew, and sometimes the new discoveries help us obtain a better understanding of Jesus' parables (e.g., a lamp and "flask" [actually an oil filler] that explain the "eschatology" of Jesus' parable, according to Mt 25:1-12).

---

161. Tiberias has not been the focus of a section of this review. Jesus perhaps never went there, and the early Roman ruins that remain almost always postdate him, belonging especially to the second and third centuries C.E. See the convenient booklet by Y. Hirschfeld entitled *A Guide to Antiquity Sites in Tiberias* (Jerusalem: Israel Antiquities Authority [1991]). Hirschfeld is presently excavating in Tiberias.

162. This is the Latin term used by E. Robinson. See his *Later Biblical Researches in Palestine and the Adjacent Region*, ed. J. Murray (London, 1856), p. 66.

Figure 14. Roman clay lamps with oil fillers (cf. Mt 25).

Courtesy of J. H. Charlesworth

Postscriptum

Obviously, Jesus Research must begin scientifically, without pondering its possible relevance for faith. Ultimately, any interest in the historical Jesus will entail, for the Christian, reflections on Christology.

Certainly, in this whole enterprise we should not forget that the study of the historical Jesus is also related, in some ways, to our own perspective on the importance of Jesus in the world of theology and our common world culture. What seems quintessentially important is that archaeological research dedicated to first-century Palestine and Jesus Research must be based on scientific methodologies. Only later should hermeneutical interests be allowed to enter the discussion. We should never be so naive as to think that such issues do not matter and were never present. After all, biblical or Near Eastern archaeology was and continues to be important primarily because of a psychic attachment to the origins of our culture and the religious or spiritual journey of many, not only Jews and Christians.

How and in which ways is archaeology important for a *homo religiosus?* This question is often ignored, since too many archaeologists now wish to distance themselves (wisely) from the sensationalists and (unwisely) from the first scholars in the field, like Albright, de Vaux, Wright, and Glueck.[163] As I stated in a similar fashion in *What Has Archaeology to Do with Faith?* archaeology is not irrelevant for faith.[164] It is also not essential for it. Yet, while archaeology cannot form faith, it can help inform faith.

---

163. See, however, the important section "Hermeneutics and Theology" (and the chapter by R. W. Younker) in J. K. Hoffmeier and A. Millard, eds., *The Future of Biblical Archaeology: Reassessing Methodologies and Assumptions* (Grand Rapids and Cambridge: Eerdmans, 2004).

164. Charlesworth and Weaver, *What Has Archaeology?* p. 19.

Appendix: Jesus, the *Mamzer*, and the Dead Sea Scrolls

In "Recovering Jesus' *Mamzerut*," B. Chilton insightfully argues that Jesus may well have been treated as a *mamzer* in Nazareth (see his chapter in this volume). His sources are the Mishnah, the Tosephta, the Talmudim, and the Hebrew Bible. In support of Chilton's research, I have decided to add an appendix to my chapter, drawing attention to the perception of the *mamzer* in the Qumran scrolls. These Jewish texts are clearly closer to Jesus' time than the texts Chilton cites, and they reflect a widespread Jewish perception of the *mamzer* (though it would be foolish to claim that all these scrolls were composed at Qumran and reflect the traditions known only there).

At the outset, let me report that it is now clear that the masculine noun *mamzer* (ממזר) does not simply mean "a bastard."[165] A *mamzer* is anyone who could not prove, to the satisfaction of the authorities, that one's mother and father were full-blooded Jews.[166] Thus, many issues are involved, and most of them impinge on the social setting of Jews in ancient Palestine.[167] The person being grilled about being a possible *mamzer* might have to prove to any questioning authority that his (or her) legitimate father was a full-blooded Jewish male, that the mother was a full-blooded Jewish female, and — to some Jewish authorities — that these two conceived him (or her) after a legally acceptable wedding.

It seems evident that both the virgin birth accounts and the claim of fornication intersect at one point: Jesus' birth seems exceptional and Joseph is not his biological father.[168] Both of these accounts appeared in the first century, and within decades of Jesus' life. The virgin birth of Jesus is proclaimed in Mt 1 and Lk 1–2. The charge of fornication appears in the Gospel of John.[169] The

---

165. The definition "bastard" given in many translations can be misleading. It appears also in M. G. Abegg, Jr., et al., but should not be considered representative of the full range of meanings. See Abegg, *The Dead Sea Scrolls Concordance* (Leiden: Brill, 2003), 1:454.

166. The Hebrew *mmzr* derives from the verb *mzr*, which denotes "to decay." Koehler and Baumgartner rightly report that *mamzer* denotes a "child of a prohibited mixed marriage" or a "half-breed" (*The Hebrew and Aramaic Lexicon of the Old Testament* [Leiden: Brill, 2001], 1:595). The full meaning of *mmzr* is not clear, and that would allow a high priest to define it to serve his purpose.

167. A. J. Avery-Peck rightly defines *mamzer(et)* as the "offspring of a man and a woman who could not legally marry one another." Thus, the judgment may depend on the priest's ruling. See Avery-Peck's glossary in J. Neusner, *The Mishnah: A New Translation* (New Haven and London: Yale University Press, 1988), p. 1141.

168. One of the most scholarly studies of the birth narratives in Matthew and Luke is R. E. Brown's *The Birth of the Messiah*, rev. ed. (New York and London: Doubleday, 1999).

169. In 178 C.E., in a polemic against Christianity, Celsus reports that he heard from a Jew that Jesus was illegitimate (Jesus' father was Ben Pendera [Ben Pantere]). Earlier, however,

Fourth Evangelist portrays Jesus in dialogue with the Jews who had believed in him. They say to Jesus, "We were not born of fornication" (*ek porneias;* Jn 8:41).[170] The clear implication is that Jesus was born of fornication; that is, his birth was illegitimate, according to some Jewish authorities, and that he was a *mamzer* (since in the Septuagint *pornēs* renders *mamzer*). In addition, if Joseph had died or abandoned the family, he could not appear in a synagogue and prove that Jesus could not be a *mamzer.*

The charge against Jesus would clearly have been especially harsh from many of the Judean priestly aristocrats, like the Sadducean high priests named Caiaphas and Annas (Jn 18:12-14, 24), who were not only his major adversaries, but were also raising the standards of purity and the requirements of the Torah.

One of the most important fresh sources for knowledge about the increased rigorousness of Jewish laws, based on the Torah, is the recently published *Temple Scroll.* According to col. 50, a woman with a dead fetus makes impure everything in a house that is in an earthen vessel, and the house is also impure.[171] The Torah legislation that defined the cemetery was now extended to include a woman who had a dead fetus within her. (I am told that this possibility could exist as long as the woman remained alive, so it should not be reduced to nine months.)[172]

Most importantly, for us now, is the reference to the *mamzer* in the Dead Sea Scrolls. In the *Hodayot* (1QH[a] 24.15 and 1QH[a] 2 ii 6), the term does not receive a context that helps us comprehend the intended meaning. In 4QIncantation (4Q444) frg. 2, col. 1, which has lacunae, the "b]astards" (if that is the appropriate translation) are linked with "the spirit of uncleanness." Likewise, in 4QSongs of the Sage[a] (4Q510) frg. 1, we learn about the categorizing of the *mamzer:* "And I, a Maskil (or Sage), proclaim the splendor of his radiance in order to frighten and terr[ify] all the spirits of the ravaging angels and the spirits of the *mmzrym* (bastards?), demons, Lilith, owls, and [. . .]."

More significant are the references to the *mamzer* in 4QSongs of the Sage[b] (4Q511), which is very fragmentary. In frg. 2 the author refers to "the congregation of the *mmzrym.*" The context is pejorative, since it includes "the shame of one's face." Later in the same scroll, in frg. 35, the author celebrates "the holy

---

Trypho never challenges Justin Martyr with Jesus' illegitimacy. For a good discussion and notes to recent publications, see Meier, "The Question of Illegitimacy," in *A Marginal Jew: Rethinking the Historical Jesus* (New York: Doubleday, 1991), 1:222-29.

170. This is the usual Greek equivalent in the LXX for *mamzer.*

171. N.B. *m. Ḥullin* 4.3 F.-G: "The woman whose foetus died in her womb, and [which foetus] the midwife put in her hand and touched — the midwife is unclean with a seven-day uncleanness, and the woman is clean until the foetus will emerge" (Neusner's translation).

172. On cemeteries in ancient Palestine, see the chapter by J. Zias in the present collection.

ones" whom God has chosen for "himself" as "an everlasting sanctuary," which most likely refers to the Qumranites since the text seems to echo *termini technici* found in the *Rule of the Community* and the *Hodayot*. If so, then the author's attempt to terrify "al[l] the spirits of the *mmzrym*" would most likely refer to his contempt of the illegitimate priests now controlling the Temple (i.e., the Hasmoneans). The same interpretation seems to apply to frgs. 48, 49, and 51 ("And through my mouth he shakes (with fear) [all the spirits of] the *mmzrym*" [cf. also 4Q511 frg. 182]).

Two scrolls are singularly important for our perception of what might be meant by *mamzer*. In 4QFlorilegium frg. 1, col. 1, we learn that the *mamzer* (*wmmzr*) shall not enter the Temple because God's "holy ones are there (*qdwshw shm*)." According to the author of *More Works of the Torah* (4Q397 frg. 5), which is unfortunately very fragmentary, the *mamzer*, along with others, especially those who have "cr[ushed testicles]," are most likely forbidden to enter into the Temple.

Cumulatively, from these Jewish texts roughly contemporaneous with Jesus we obtain three insights:

1. The legislation regarding the *mamzer* is more severe than that supplied by the Torah. According to Deut 23:2, no *mamzer* can enter the "congregation of the Lord." Some early Jews used this rule to prohibit a *mamzer* to enter into the Temple.
2. While the *mamzer* is not defined in any of these texts, it is clear that the authors assume the readers and audience knew who might be a *mamzer*, and that decision probably ultimately depended on priests, especially the high priest.
3. The *mamzer* cannot enter the Temple.[173]

In conclusion, it is helpful to use archaeology in Jesus Research and to reflect on how Jesus' life and teachings were impacted by his social contexts. What is important is to perceive Jesus within his Jewish environment. The question thus becomes, Did some of Jesus' fellow Jews consider that he could not prove that Joseph and Mary were each full-blooded Jews and were his legitimate biological parents? If not, some priestly authorities could claim he was a *mamzer*, and according to the traditions just examined, he could be banned from entering the Temple Mount.[174]

173. Contrast *m. Ḥullin* 1.2, which does not mention the *mamzer* and judges that a "blind person's" act of slaughtering is valid.
174. One should not confuse such traditions with the *mishnayot* and halakic traditions

The data now collected clarifies that some authoritative Jews most likely considered Jesus a *mamzer*. If the charge of *mamzer* appeared during Jesus' life, it most likely developed later during his public ministry, since he originally taught in Galilean synagogues. The Fourth Evangelist should be taken seriously; that is, the charge appeared later in his life and in Jerusalem, "as he taught in the Temple," as Jn 8:20 indicates. If so, then two scrolls may be exceptionally significant, since 4QFlorilegium and *Some Works of the Torah* record a ruling that the *mamzer* — like the deaf and blind — cannot enter the Temple. While the deaf might break Torah laws, since they could not hear the words of scripture, and while the blind might also break the sacred laws because they could not read scripture or see their way, the *mamzer* is excluded because he would pollute the Temple, because his birth was impure. Did some Temple authorities eventually obtain what they sought, a negative ruling on Jesus? Did they learn that a charge of *mamzerut* could be brought against Jesus?

If Jesus could not prove to the ruling priests that he was a legitimate Jew, that he had a pure lineage, they would have grounds for barring him from entering the Temple. Does this new insight shine a clearer light that dispels some of the shadows obscuring the reasons for his explosive rage in the Temple at the end of his ministry, an episode that has been hotly debated in recent Jesus Research (Mk 11:15-19 and par.)? Does a charge of being a *mamzer* and thus prohibited from entering the Temple, restore the original intent of Jesus' statement that the Temple is "my Father's house" (Jn 2:16)?

that provide no explicit information that an Israelite (would Jesus qualify?) was forbidden entry into the Temple or "the Court" (*'azara),* which was divided into the Court of Israelites and the Court of Priests. See a discussion of these rabbinic traditions in S. Safrai, "The Temple and the Divine Service," in *The Herodian Period,* ed. M. Avi-Yonah and Z. Baras, World History of the Jewish People 1.7 (Jerusalem and New Brunswick, N.J.: Rutgers University Press, 1975), pp. 282-337, plus notes.

Archaeology and the Historical Jesus

Sean Freyne

On first reflection, my title seems less than promising. We are currently en-gaged in the third wave of questing for the historical Jesus, an enterprise that has been largely conducted on the basis of the literary sources, but without a consensus any nearer, it would seem. How could archaeology, itself a discipline that is constantly developing, bring anything new and enlightening to the dis-cussion? For some New Testament scholars there is something slightly irrever-ent about the suggestion that it should be invoked at all. For those not used to looking beyond the boundary wall of their own narrowly defined discipline, "Archaeology and Jesus" smacks of a search for his relics — an idea that would be anathema to Christian faith and piety. Yet, the term "bedrock" has been uti-lized in historical approaches to the Gospels for some time now, without any great attention to the source of the metaphor, namely, the archaeological dig. It has a comforting ring about it for those who have found themselves foundering in the quicksands of Bultmannian and post-Bultmannian Gospel studies. It is reassuring to know that there are some "hard facts" that can be rescued from the debris once the form and redaction critics have had their say.

At the outset it is worthwhile recalling the major landmarks of historical Jesus studies in order to appreciate better the significance of current moves to introduce archaeology into the discussion. Archaeological exploration of Pales-tine was only in its infancy during the halcyon days of the liberal quest for Jesus

---

This article was completed in 2002 and dealt with the issues that were current in the litera-ture at that time with regard to debates about the historical Jesus. It has not been possible to revise the discussion to include some of the more recent publications dealing with the archaeology of Galilee. In my book *Jesus, a Jewish Galilean: A New Reading of the Jesus-Story* (London and New York: T. & T. Clark [Continuum], 2004), my discussion is in-formed by the most recent publications.

from the mid–nineteenth century onward. It is noteworthy that in Albert Schweitzer's rightly acclaimed account of the previous century's debate, *The Quest of the Historical Jesus* (1906), there is not a single mention of archaeology in his narrative. Ernest Renan's *Life of Jesus* (1863) receives a full discussion, but the romantic description of the landscape as a "fifth gospel" does not prompt Schweitzer's interest to discuss the context of Jesus' ministry more fully. The fact that "the liberal lives" sought to present Jesus as a universal figure whose lofty ethical teaching was universally applicable meant that the intellectual climate of the day was opposed to the narrow particularism that a local perspective might be seen to espouse.

Bultmann's designation of the Gospels as for the most part mythical and legendary was a reaction to the whole liberal agenda in the wake of the human catastrophe that was the First World War. In his view the very idea of the historical Jesus had to be abandoned, not just because of the status of the sources, but also because of its theological illegitimacy from his Lutheran perspective. Both he and the other pioneers of the form-critical study of the Gospels (K. L. Schmidt and M. Dibelius) saw the need for literary comparisons between the pre-Gospel traditions and analogous units from Greco-Roman pagan literature, but the demythologization program, with its emphasis on the meaning of the gospel for moderns, had little interest in the material and social culture of Jesus and the first Christians. There were alternative voices within German biblical scholarship of the period, particularly Albrecht Alt in Old Testament and Joachim Jeremias in the New Testament. Both scholars had actually lived in Palestine and had developed a genuine interest in the physical as well as the human geography, in the tradition of Gustav Dalman's monumental seven-volume *Arbeit und Sitte in Palästina*. Both Dalman and Alt turned their attention to Jesus in his environment, but their publications seem to have made little impact on the prevailing dominance of the kerygmatic approach to the New Testament.[1] Jeremias also confined himself entirely to the literary sources in his comprehensive *Jerusalem at the Time of Jesus* (original German ed. 1951), but not even this highly significant study, as well as his other impressive attempts to understand the parables and sayings of Jesus in their Palestinian milieu, were able to change the trend toward the historical and the contextual in Gospel studies.

The beginning of the "new quest" for the historical Jesus is generally attributed to Ernst Käsemann's programmatic lecture of 1954 in which he affirmed the

---

1. G. Dalman, *Orte und Wege Jesu* (Gütersloh: C. Bertelsmann, 1924); A. Alt, "Die Stätten des Wirkens Jesu in Galiläa Territorialgeschichtlich betrachtet," in *Kleine Schriften zur Geschichte des Volkes Israel,* 3 vols. (Munich: C. H. Beck, 1953), 2:436-55.

necessity of maintaining the historical nature of the kerygma.[2] Unlike the old, liberal quest, this new one was not concerned with writing a life of Jesus, but with showing how, as far as God's call and human response were concerned, the proclamation *about* Jesus was in essential agreement with the proclamation *of* Jesus. While this initial formulation of the new quest appears somewhat abstract and theological, it gave rise to a lively discussion of the criteria for identifying genuine Jesus material in the pool of tradition about him. Käsemann's formulation of the criterion of dissimilarity was to prove influential, namely, that Jesus' sayings are authentic "when there are no grounds for deriving a tradition from Judaism or of ascribing it to early Christianity." He acknowledges that the information thus obtained about Jesus merely gives us insight into what separated Jesus from his environment. Clearly, theological rather than genuinely historical concerns are paramount in this approach, and hence a critical dialogue with the emerging archaeology of ancient Palestine was still not possible.

Even the current "third wave" of historical Jesus studies was quite slow in picking up on the possibilities that archaeology had to offer to the discussion. Thus, while the Meiron Excavation Project, pioneered by Eric and Carol Meyers and James Strange, published their preliminary report of a survey of Upper Galilee and the Golan in 1978, and followed with a popular study that engaged with historians of early Judaism and early Christianity (1981), scholars interested in the historical Jesus did not see its immediate relevance. E. P. Sanders's important study, *Jesus and Judaism* (1985), broke definite new ground on the basis of his wide-ranging familiarity with the Jewish sources, as did Geza Vermes' earlier *Jesus the Jew* (1975), based on a particular Galilean type of *hasid* known from the rabbinic sources. It was, however, the establishment of the Jesus Seminar by Robert Funk and others in the early 1980s that again catapulted the historical Jesus issue to the top of the scholarly agenda in a new and provocative manner. Yet, despite the stated aim of liberating Jesus from the encrustations of canon, creed, and church, and therefore, presumably, setting him loose in his own original context, the discussions of the group as reported in *Forum*, the official organ of the Seminar between 1985 and 1994, were focused almost entirely on literary consideration of the sayings tradition, in an ongoing search to apply various criteria of authenticity. In an article entitled "Materials and Methods in Historical Jesus Research" by one of the main spokesmen for the Seminar, John Dominic Crossan, the materials in question are all literary.[3] In-

---

2. Reprinted in an English translation in E. Käsemann, *Essays on New Testament Themes* (London: SCM, 1964), pp. 15-47.

3. J. D. Crossan, "Materials and Methods in Historical Jesus Research," *Forum* 4, no. 4 (1988): 3-24.

deed, this was one of the criticisms that have been leveled at his own highly influential study on Jesus, something he has attempted to rectify in his more recent work, namely, its failure to engage other than minimally with the archaeological profile of early Roman Galilee.

Such reluctance, for whatever reason, was not due solely to the particular concerns and direction of the Jesus Seminar, however. In the first volume of his three-volume study of Jesus (1991), John Meier discusses thoroughly the sources for Jesus and engages at length with the debates about the historicity of the Gospel traditions. Again, however, there is a noteworthy absence of any recognition of the contribution that archaeology could make to the discussion, despite the impassioned plea in important contributions in 1985 and 1988 by James H. Charlesworth that historians of Jesus in a Jewish context should take account of the archaeological as well as the literary evidence.[4] Indeed, my own "conversion" to archaeology as an important tool in the armory of all ancient historians, has been gradual. When I first essayed a study of Galilean society at the suggestion of Martin Hengel in the 1970s, I quickly became aware that the literary sources alone could not contribute adequate information on many of the issues I wanted to explore. Thus, the standard archaeological journals (such as *Israel Exploration Journal, Palestine Exploration Quarterly, Zeitschrift des deutschen Palästina-Vereins, Bulletin of the American Schools of Oriental Research,* and *Biblical Archaeologist*) as well as the *Encyclopedia of Archaeological Excavations in the Holy Land* were constant resources to be explored. The systematic approach to the archaeology of Galilee during the Hellenistic and Roman periods was still only in its infancy, but in retrospect it is fair to say that my perspective was strongly influenced by the literary sources and archaeological data.

Due to the influence of various field archaeologists working in Galilee — namely, Eric Meyers, James Strange, Dan Urman, Gideon Foerster, Zvi Ma'oz, David Adan-Bayewitz, Mordechai Aviam, Ehud Netzer, Douglas Edwards, Jonathan Reed, and others — I gradually saw the need to broaden and deepen my knowledge of the field by visiting the important sites, having first read the relevant reports, and with direction from the field archaeologists mentioned above. Two international conferences on Galilean studies in 1989 and 1996 that

---

4. J. H. Charlesworth, "Research on the Historical Jesus Today: Jesus and the Pseudepigrapha, the Dead Sea Scrolls, the Nag Hammadi Codices, Josephus, and Archaeology," *PSB*, n.s., 6 (1985): 98-115; Charlesworth, "The Jesus of History and the Archaeology of Palestine," in *Jesus within Judaism: New Light from Exciting Archaeological Discoveries*, ABRL 1 (New York and London: Doubleday, 1988), pp. 103-30. See also Charlesworth, "Archaeology, Jesus, and Christian Faith," in *What Has Archaeology to Do with Faith?* ed. Charlesworth and W. P. Weaver, FSC (Philadelphia: Trinity, 1992), pp. 1-22.

brought together archaeologists, ancient historians, and literary scholars were for me important learning occasions also.[5] I still regard myself very much an amateur, but I would not otherwise have become so aware that archaeology should not be treated as the Cinderella discipline in the dialogue with the literary sources. It needs to be engaged with as an equal partner in the discussion. Of course, when archaeologists wander outside their field to discuss literary sources, they must be politely but firmly reminded that literary texts demand literary skills that their fieldwork may have inhibited them from honing, just as literary scholars must acknowledge that they have spent more time with the text than with the spade. When archaeologists and literary scholars alike embark in the larger task of profiling a region in terms of its economic, social, and cultural systems, then we all need to be both self-critical and aware that it is not just a matter of "mixing and matching." We should regard the systems theories we adopt as labeled "dangerous for the nonexpert."

Models or Muddles? Understanding Galilean Social Life

A joint meeting of the seminars for the archaeology of the New Testament and the historical Jesus that took place at the annual meeting of the Society for Biblical Literature (SBL) in Chicago in 1994 was to prove a watershed for the relationship between the two areas.[6] It became very clear that a North American secular rather than a German ecclesiastical context was now driving Jesus Research. Politics, economics, and class struggle were deemed more important than religion in evaluating Jesus and his message. Indeed, those who spoke of religion were judged to be importing an alien, enlightenment conception, since we should know, we were repeatedly told, that in the ancient world religion was embedded in other social realities. It was also very obvious that those engaged in Jesus Research and the archaeologists of Galilee were operating with very different methodologies and assumptions. Both Richard Horsley and John Dominic Crossan in particular were critical of the ways archaeologists such as Eric Meyers and James Strange interpreted their data within the larger picture of social relations in Lower Galilee. It gradually emerged that both sides were using the concept of model quite differently. Whereas an archaeologist thinks of model in isomorphic terms, that is, as an exact representation of a building

5. The proceedings of these two conferences are now published: L. Levine, ed., *The Galilee in Late Antiquity* (New York: Jewish Theological Seminary of America, 1992), and E. Meyers, ed., *Galilee through the Centuries: Confluence of Cultures* (Winona Lake, Ind.: Eisenbrauns, 1999).

6. The papers for this joint seminar were published in *SBL Seminar Papers, 1994* (Atlanta: Scholars, 1994).

or object, sociologists adopt a homomorphic understanding, thinking of it as an expression of a general likeness. The one demands exactitude and calls for constant revision as the pieces begin to emerge, whereas the other usage is analogous and allows for multiple variations in its application.

In her most recent book Marianne Sawicki, who was present at that SBL joint meeting, takes up this very issue of the models that Jesus scholars use and their implications. One comment is highly pertinent: "Jesus historians have been reading sociology too reverently and texts too suspiciously." She goes on to discuss the values and limits of models as well as pointing out their inbuilt biases. A philosopher of science by training, Sawicki has developed a deep interest in Galilean studies in relation to the historical Jesus, and her own most recent study has some important and original insights that I will presently discuss. She is well placed, therefore, to cast a cold eye on the various methodological moves of scholars in their efforts to come to a better understanding of Jesus in his context, and I personally have profited from her critical engagement with my own efforts. Helpfully, she reminds us that "the generalized model adds no evidence," but rather involves three steps: analyzing, analogizing, and hypothesizing. *Analysis* deals with states and processes leading to functions, which in turn give rise to feedback loops that maintain the balance of the whole social system. *Analogies* involve appropriate labeling of the various elements based on similar better-known societies, whereas *hypotheses* have to do with suggesting a framework and a set of questions for the gathering of further information. Thus, "the model provides a context and a range of expectable responses against which to assess the data that comes in from a particular society under investigation."[7]

In developing her own model for understanding Galilean life in terms of what she describes as "an archaeology of the Galilean mind," Sawicki comments critically on three different models currently employed in Jesus studies, the most significant one for the present discussion being the so-called Lenski-Kautsky model, which is the driving force behind both Crossan's and Horsley's debates with the archaeologists.[8] Horsley has not so far produced a full-blown account of the historical Jesus, though his studies of Galilean society are obviously highly pertinent, and the role he postulates for Jesus in that context, namely, the renewal of village life in accordance with the Israelite tradition, is very different

---

7. M. Sawicki, *Crossing Galilee: Architecture of Contact in the Occupied Land of Jesus* (Harrisburg, Pa.: Trinity, 2000); see esp. pp. 64-67.

8. The Lenski-Kautsky model is a composite of the insights of G. Lenski, *Power and Privilege: A Theory of Social Stratification* (New York: McGraw-Hill, 1966), dealing with social stratification in agrarian empires, and J. Kautsky, *The Politics of Aristocratic Empires* (Chapel Hill: University of North Carolina Press, 1982), which deals with the issue of class struggle from the perspective of historical sociology.

from that suggested in Crossan's best-selling book on Jesus (*The Historical Jesus: The Life of a Mediterranean Jewish Peasant,* 1991). This latter study was almost entirely based on the literary sources, though he does invoke the suggestions of Andrew Overman regarding the urbanization of Lower Galilee, a conclusion that neatly supports his Cynic-like Jesus operating in the villages of the region.[9]

Crossan's espousal of the Lenski-Kautsky model is explained in detail in his 1998 book, *The Birth of Christianity,* in which he devotes a chapter to Galilean archaeology. His aim is to provide as sharp a focus as possible for an under-standing of the tradition of Jesus' sayings and their transmission within early Christianity, which makes the chapter on Galilee an important step in the argu-ment of the work as a whole. His claim is that early Christianity developed along two quite separate trajectories, one based on the sayings traditions that moved from rural/small-town Galilee to Syria, and the other — the death and life traditions — originating in urban Jerusalem and developing further in the Pauline churches. A distinctive culture for Galilee is as important for this sce-nario as was the "urbanized" Galilee for the earlier book. Allowing for this larger agenda, Crossan develops a three-phased investigation of Galilean soci-ety, involving anthropology, history, and archaeology. The Lenski-Kautsky model is foundational in that it provides the framework within which the re-sults of the other two disciplines are judged. It is essential to his enterprise, in that without a model "I can interpret data almost at will." The question then becomes: "How does the early Roman culture look to Galilean archaeology, *es-pecially when that data is superimposed on the cross-cultural anthropology of agrarian empire and peasant society?*"[10]

In passing, it should be noted that this formulation would seem to intro-duce two foreign bodies into Galilee, one ancient and the other modern. Crossan does not seem to consider it important to see what archaeology might have to say about traditional or even Hasmonean Galilean culture, but only early Roman culture in the region. Surely this is too narrow a perspective for any conclusions to be drawn about the changing ethos of Galilee in the first century, something that is central to Crossan's argument subsequently, in line with what one might expect according to the Lenski-Kautsky model of com-mercializing empires. One must ask further, in view of Sawicki's comments about the limitations of modeling, whether the model or the data is now deter-mining the conclusions. The model in question is the second foreign body that

9. A. Overman, "Who Were the First Urban Christians? Urbanization in Galilee in the First Century," in *SBL Seminar Papers, 1988* (Atlanta: Scholars, 1988), pp. 160-68.

10. J. D. Crossan, *The Birth of Christianity: Discovering What Happened in the Years Imme-diately after the Execution of Jesus* (New York: HarperSanFrancisco, 1998); see esp. pp. 209-35. The quotation is from p. 210.

is being imposed, since as Sawicki explains, it is based on modern, Eurocentric assumptions and ignores "the practices of kinship, gender and inheritance that were key elements of traditional village life in Galilee."[11]

As Crossan's argument unfolds in the chapter dealing with Galilean archaeology, he does not really engage independently with the archaeological evidence but is content to criticize the way archaeologists such as Meyers, Strange, Longstaff, and Adan-Bayewitz, interpret their data in the light of the Lenski-Kautsky model that dictates the way things ought to be, in his view. The reality is that the data coming from the village contexts, as distinct from urban Sepphoris, give rather mixed messages in relation to what the model dictates. Earlier Crossan explains his preference for this very model because it is deemed to include a much greater concern for the conditions of the peasantry than do alternative ones. But that very notion of the peasantry is itself a modern construct, replacing "the primitive" as the representative of "the ideal other" in the constructions of twentieth-century postcolonial anthropologists.[12] Thus, Sawicki's proposal of attempting to discover "the indigenous principles of organization that were enacted in the everyday tasks of people, although never explicitly formulated by them,"[13] appears to be the better option, if we are interested in engaging archaeology in the task of understanding the village culture of Galilee that the historical Jesus encountered. At the very least, such an emic, or "native," approach should be used to counterbalance the etic, or "outside observer," perspective of the Lenski-Kautsky model.

Richard Horsley also employs this model in his study of Galilee. He explains the method he proposes to follow: "Simply to adapt a model of an agrarian society such as Lenski's and then test how it fits ancient Judea would not serve to illuminate ancient history so much as to provide yet another test of the model. More helpful in the long run, I believe, will be to work back and forth dialectically between our sources for ancient Judea and Galilee (critically considered) on the one hand, and comprehensive comparative studies such as Lenski's and Kautsky's on the other."[14] This formulation certainly takes full account of the heuristic value of models, while also acknowledging the importance of evidence. In particular, the mention of a dialectical process is important since it suggests a self-critical approach that operates with a hermeneutic of suspicion with regard to one's own conclusions. As Bernard Lonergan explains, "Every investigation is conducted from within horizons. . . . Whether

11. Sawicki, *Crossing Galilee*, p. 68.

12. Crossan, *The Birth of Christianity*, pp. 151-57; cf. M. Kearney, *Reconceptualizing the Peasantry: Anthropology in Global Perspective* (Boulder, Colo.: Westview Press, 1996).

13. Sawicki, *Crossing Galilee*, p. 37.

14. R. Horsley, *Galilee: History, Politics, People* (Valley Forge, Pa.: Trinity, 1995), p. 9.

they are acknowledged or not, dialectically opposed horizons lead to opposite value judgments, opposed accounts of historical movements, opposed interpretations of authors and different selections of relevant data in special research." To escape from this impasse, the aware (in Lonergan's terminology, "the converted") interpreter will develop positions and counterpositions, and test each against the evidence in an attempt to come to an informed and "objective" judgment of the meaning of acts, objects, or persons.[15] It comes as some surprise, therefore, that Horsley begins with a historical account of Galilean social-economic-cultural-religious life dictated directly by the model, since this would seem to prejudge the results of his subsequent investigation of that society. Rarely, if ever, does he explicitly engage in the dialectic exercise that the above citation implies, by allowing counterevidence from either the texts or archaeology to challenge the model. In judging the adequacy of various archaeologists' views about Galilean life (Meyers and Strange in particular), Horsley is dismissive of their reconstructions on the basis that, in his opinion, they are adopting anachronistic views of exchange mechanisms in antiquity, when all economies were, he believes, politically controlled.[16] The idea that some Galilean peasants may have been in a position to market their wares, thereby explaining the preponderance of Tyrian coins at Galilean sites excavated by the Meiron team, is ruled out *tout court* as impossible, just as Adan-Bayewitz's idea about the Kefar Hananya wares being marketed at Sepphoris is ruled out by Crossan for similar reasons.[17] Both Horsley and Crossan may be correct in their overall assessment of Galilean society. The point is that neither pays sufficient attention to the counterevidence to their own positions, which, one suspects, were virtually predetermined by the choice of model and the manner of its application. As a result, the changes within Galilean Jewish society in terms of two competing value systems are blurred or not picked up at all.

Douglas Oakman is another Jesus scholar who posed methodological questions from a social-systems perspective to the archaeologists at the Chicago

15. For a discussion of the role of dialectics in a hermeneutic of suspicion, see the still-important discussion of B. Lonergan, *Method in Theology* (London: Darton, Longman and Todd, 1971), pp. 235-66.

16. Cf. in particular the discussion in R. Horsley, *Archaeology, History, and Society in Galilee: The Social Context of Jesus and the Rabbis* (Valley Forge, Pa.: Trinity, 1996); see esp. pp. 66-85 on "Trade or Tribute: The Political Economy of Galilee," based on his earlier "Archaeology and the Villages of Upper Galilee: A Dialogue with the Archaeologists," *BASOR* 297 (1995): 5-16, with E. Meyers's response, pp. 17-26.

17. Crossan, *The Birth of Christianity*, pp. 22-30, discussing some of the conclusions of D. Adan-Bayewitz's important study of Galilean pottery: *Common Pottery in Roman Galilee: A Study of Local Trade* (Ramat-Gan: Bar-Ilan University Press, 1993).

meeting. He has been concerned with Jesus' attitude to the economic issues in first-century Galilee. Oakman is active in the Context Group that is led by Bruce Malina, John Elliott, and Philip Esler, among others. This implies a certain preference for the honor-shame model, based on the contemporary understanding of what are deemed to have been pivotal Mediterranean values. Unlike Crossan and Horsley, neither of whom have had any direct archaeological experience to the best of my knowledge, Oakman has taken part in various digs in Galilee, especially that at Jotapata, and more recently at Khirbet Qana. He may thus be more aware of the nature of the archaeological process and the constant need for revising one's opinions as new data are discovered and new methodologies are employed in their analysis. In his Chicago paper he is more understanding of the starting point and perspective of archaeologists and poses new kinds of questions that fall within their particular competence to answer.[18] Oakman proposes the need for a distinction between cultural and social indices as these manifest themselves in the material remains. The former have been the main focus of practitioners of the so-called Israeli method of archaeology that has focused particularly on the issue of the Jewish or Hellenistic ethos of Galilee. The latter are of greater significance to those attempting a complete account of the economic and social system, influenced by general anthropology of the North American variety. This approach makes it possible to detect the fault lines between various strata in terms of wealth, power, and prestige.

In line with this proposal, Oakman suggests what kinds of evidence archaeologists interested in the social description of Galilee should look for. In the consideration of buildings, for example, attention should be given to the variations between different settlements and within settlements, as a way of determining the social differentiation either between cities, towns, and villages or between different quarters of such settlements. In discussions of monumental structures, on the other hand, consideration should be given to the demands they made on both human and natural resources in a region, and the likely knock-on effects of these. More precise questions can be posed to discoveries of coins also, in terms of the distinction between various types of coinage (bronze and silver) and their social as well as economic significance. The various caches of coins that have been discovered pose a particularly interesting question for the monetary situation and the purposes for storing them. The location and distribution of the cultural indices of observant Jewishness such as *mikvaot*,

18. D. Oakman, "The Archaeology of First-Century Galilee and the Social Interpretation of the Historical Jesus," *SBL Seminar Papers, 1994,* pp. 220-51. Cf. also more recently K. C. Hanson and D. Oakman, *Palestine in the Time of Jesus: Social Structures and Social Conflicts* (Minneapolis: Fortress, 1998).

stone jars, animal bones, and burial practices also need to be attended to in order to determine their extent and class specificity within the Galilean Jewish population as a whole. These and other similar questions are well framed and likely to yield more information of a precise kind, even if in the end we are reduced to hypotheses in the absence of reliable data to answer all our queries. In these circumstances it will be important for all participants in the dialogue to remember that certain proposals are just that, hypotheses, not facts.

Space does not permit further discussion of Galilean archaeology, even though in addition to those already mentioned — Eric and Carol Meyers, James Strange and Thomas Longstaff (Meiron Project and Sepphoris), and David Adan-Bayewitz (Kefar Hananya and Yodefat) — there are many significant contributions bearing either directly or indirectly on the question of the historical Jesus by scholars such as Douglas Edwards (Sepphoris, Yodefat, and Khirbet Qana); Jonathan Reed (Sepphoris and Capernaum); Mordechai Aviam (Upper Galilee and Yodefat); Rami Arav and others (Bethsaida); Zvi Ma'oz (Banias); Danni Syon (Gamala); Vasillios Tzaferis (Capernaum and Caesarea Philippi); Ross Voss, Stephen Pfann, and James Charlesworth (Nazareth); and Virgilio Corbo (Capernaum). In the discussion so far, I have concentrated on those, coming from historical Jesus studies, who have attempted to engage critically with the archaeologists. Clearly, we are only at the very early stages of a dialogue that hopefully will develop fruitful collaboration while retaining a critical, if sympathetic, eye on the ways different disciplines engage with their particular evidence and the interpretative strategies that each adopts, especially in their use of the social sciences. We now turn to the results so far gained by examining the different profiles of Jesus that have emerged.

The Different Faces of Jesus the Galilean

One wonders what Albert Schweitzer would say if, after just one hundred years, he were asked to comment again on the current "quest for Jesus" and what advances, if any, have been made. I think he would have little difficulty reaffirming his oft-cited remark that the various lives of Jesus tell us more about the questers than they tell us about Jesus. However, I do not interpret this, nor did Schweitzer intend it to be interpreted, as an accusation of bad faith by the interpreters, but rather as an expression of the difficulty of the enterprise, given the nature of the sources. The rather naive hope of some more conservative scholars that somehow archaeology could deliver "hard facts" that are missing in the literary sources, has, of course, proved illusory. At best it can only provide indirect evidence of the way things were with the Galileans whom Jesus encoun-

Figure 15. The Arbel. This is where Herod the Great finally killed the last of those who opposed him in 37 B.C.E. N.B. the Kinnereth.

Courtesy of J. H. Charlesworth

tered, thus adding one more hermeneutical step to be taken by students of the historical Jesus. The more archaeology engages in the larger enterprise of ethno- and socio-archaeology, the more significant it becomes for the issue of the historical Jesus, however. Such interpretative activity by archaeologists suggests various systems that Jesus and the Palestinian Jesus Movement had to engage within a Galilean setting, and the judgments one makes in relation to these broader issues will directly influence one's views of Jesus and the particular emphasis and impact of his ministry.

This does not mean that we should all stop trying to understand better Jesus in his context, or that no progress can be achieved. The different approaches within archaeology as practiced today can give us a view from below of the way ordinary people lived their lives, in contrast to the more ideologically driven dimensions of the textual evidence. In attempting to assess this specific contribution of archaeology from below, it may be useful to look at three aspects of the contemporary debates, namely, culture, class, and gender, and see how these can lead to different perceptions of Jesus and his concerns.

Culture

In an article with a title similar to this one, I argued for the importance of a "Jewish" Galilee for understanding Jesus. In that contribution I was reacting strongly to the view of a Hellenized Galilee and the resultant picture of Jesus that emerged.[19] Nothing I have since read from either the archaeologists or the

---

19. S. Freyne, "Archaeology and the Historical Jesus," reprinted in *Galilee and Gospel: Collected Essays* (Tübingen: Mohr Siebeck, 2000), pp. 160-82.

Jesus scholars has changed my views on the issue. Indeed, the most up-to-date account of the evidence, that by Jonathan Reed, strengthens the case, in my opinion.[20] As I pointed out in my previous paper, a "Jewish" Galilee does not eliminate all aspects of other cultural influences there, given the proximity of the Greek cities in "the circle," and the remnants of an older, indigenous population (Assyrian or Israelite) as well as newer arrivals such as the Itureans. The difficulty with such a scenario, however, is that it is extremely difficult to find traces of these influences in the material culture; the literary evidence is also at best problematic. Andrea Berlin's important study tracing the distribution pattern of Phoenician semifine ware should make us cautious about assuming the range of influence from the Greek cities, at least in matters of cultural affiliation.[21] Nor does a "Jewish" Galilee imply no Greek influence in language, architectural styles, and other aspects of everyday life as this was lived in the whole region. Eric Meyers has repeatedly pointed out that Jews had adapted to Greek culture in many Diaspora situations, and there is no reason to doubt that the same was true of the Galilean Jews also. Indeed, the very notion of Judaism and Hellenism as opposed and competing cultural forces is now seen as an outmoded nineteenth-century construct that needs to be abandoned, or at least seriously revised.

However, there are further questions to be asked even about a Jewish Galilee. I still prefer the case for a Judean rather than a Babylonian source for the "Jewishness" of Galilean culture, despite the arrival of the Babylonian Jews in the Golan during the reign of Herod the Great.[22] Perhaps future archaeological research will be able to distinguish between the two provenances and suggest the markers for each in the material culture. That would certainly be a considerable contribution, and it would strengthen the case for a cultural diversity between Galilean and Judean Jews in the first century. Nor do I accept the idea of Richard Horsley that a Judean presence in Galilee must be seen as invasive and oppressive of an older Israelite culture. It would, however, imply a Judean/Jerusalem ideology of restoration shaping the ethos and aspirations of the dominant segment of the population there.[23] But where are these Jews to be found, and did they all share the same ideas of what that restoration implied and how it was to be achieved? It is impor-

20. J. Reed, *Archaeology and the Galilean Jesus: A Re-examination of the Evidence* (Harrisburg, Pa.: Trinity, 2000); see esp. pp. 23-62.

21. A. Berlin, "From Monarchy to Markets: The Phoenicians in Hellenistic Palestine," *BASOR* 306 (1997): 75-86.

22. This is the position of E. Nodet in E. Nodet and J. Taylor, *The Origins of Christianity: An Exploration* (Collegeville, Minn.: Liturgical Press, 1998), pp. 127-64.

23. S. Freyne, "The Geography of Restoration: Galilee-Jerusalem Relations in Early Jewish and Christian Experience," *NTS* 47 (2001): 289-311.

tant to reflect that the most significant ethnic markers — *mikvaot,* stone jars, burial customs, and the absence of pig bones — are to be found at Sepphoris, Jotapata, and Gamala, places that were not at the center of Jesus' ministry, it would seem. If Jesus appears in Galilee espousing the Judean restoration ideals, one might expect that his support base and following would have been among the more observant Jews of the region and not among the fishermen of the lakefront or the villagers of Upper Galilee, not to mention those living within the borders of "greater Israel" that territorially belonged to the surrounding cities.

It is this aspect of his ministry that has led to portrayals of Jesus more in a non-Jewish, or marginally Jewish, coloring, and the (partial) evidence from the material culture is summoned in support of this point of view. However, it must be remembered that "the Judean Jews" who in all probability had colonized Galilee were a complex mixture of those who espoused the exilic ideology of separateness and those who had seen the benefits of Hellenistic culture and were therefore less concerned with the strategies of strong boundary maintenance. This meant that there were in the Judean community itself divergent views of ethnic restoration and its implications, but that did not make them less "Jewish" or "Judean," in a Galilean context. Because he was a follower and former disciple of John the Baptizer, one might think Jesus espoused the former rather than the latter point of view, once he came to Galilee. Yet, for whatever reason, purity and its maintenance as an ethnic marker appears to have been less important to him than a more expansive view of Jewish ethnicity that brought him to the margins of both Galilean and Judean life, and on occasion even dared to transgress the outer boundary walls that separated Jew from non-Jew.[24] In stressing the fact that Jesus was a Galilean, some recent Jesus scholars seem to want to forget that he was a Galilean *with Judean roots,* if not actually born in Judea, and that it was in that guise that he "crossed Galilee," to borrow Sawicki's title.

Class

As already mentioned, Douglas Oakman has pointed to the need for archaeologists to attend to class as well as to cultural indices. While several surveys have been conducted, we still need a better profile of Galilean village life and the ways in which the limited goods in terms of land or other resources might have been distributed. Indeed, the project that Oakman and others are involved in at

---

24. See the discussion of the relationship between John and Jesus from a consideration of the geography of their ministries in J. Murphy-O'Connor, "John the Baptist and Jesus: History and Hypotheses," *NTS* 36 (1990): 359-74.

Khirbet Qana is intended to address this specific set of questions. The fact that the houses excavated in the acropolis of Sepphoris appear to have both storage silos and *mikvaot* suggests that these are elite houses, and one has to go to Capernaum to encounter the difference of nonelite housing. Here, there are no such private installations, and the houses, built of local basalt field stones, seem to consist of a single room opening onto a courtyard that was shared by several different family units.[25] This would mean that life for many in a village such as Capernaum was at subsistence level, despite the fertility of the plain of Gennesar (as described by Josephus [*War* 3.506-21]), the resource of the lake, and the fishing industry. Does this suggest that the resources of land and lake were unevenly distributed, and would it explain, at least in part, the apparent concentration of Jesus and his prophets in this and other towns in the region such as Chorazin and Bethsaida (Mt 11:21)? At the same time, there seems to be some indication that the present Byzantine period synagogue at Capernaum had a forerunner of comparable size if not grandeur. Presumably, this means that there were in the area some wealthy people who may have controlled the resources, and were therefore unreceptive to a radical egalitarian movement like that espoused by Jesus.[26]

The refurbishment of Sepphoris and the founding of Tiberias have played a major role in recent discussions of Jesus within the Galilean social context. Archaeology has been able to tell us much about Sepphoris, even if there has been a danger of exaggeration by projecting back to the first century conditions from the later period, and quite different estimations of its cultural and social ethos emerge from archaeologists reporting from different sections of the city and dealing with different historical periods. When used uncritically, these results can lead to a highly distorted view of the situation in the early first century c.e. It ignores the major changes in the population and the role of the city in the reorganization of Palestine after the two revolts, when Sepphoris became Diocaesarea with control of a greatly increased territory. My own approach has been to interpret the emergence of these two Herodian centers in Lower Galilee as symptomatic of rapid changes occurring in the social and economic system as a whole. Initially, at least, these changes can be characterized in terms of two competing systems, the one based on kinship and located in the village culture, and the other reflective of a politically controlled, distributive economy that seeks to exploit the resources for the benefit of the ruling elite. This scenario would explain the urban-rural tensions in Galilee as reflected in both the Gospels and Josephus's writings, espe-

---

25. See Y. Hirschfeld, *The Palestinian Dwelling in the Roman-Byzantine Period* (Jerusalem: Franciscan Printing Press/Israel Exploration Society, 1995); S. Guijarro Oporto, "La familia en la Galilea del siglo primero," *EstBib* 53 (1995): 461-88.

26. Reed, *Archaeology*, pp. 139-69.

cially his *Life,* since a serious displacement and disruption of the traditional rural way of life would have naturally ensued from Antipas's policy of Romanization.[27]

So far I am in agreement with Horsley, even though I do not subscribe to his views either that social banditry was endemic to Galilee or that popular kingship was a focal point for peasant resistance there.[28] Here Crossan's most recent ideas of differentiation within the peasant society itself can prove useful, in that they allow for various levels of exploitation by the elites but also indicate various alliances of convenience between rulers and ruled.[29] In this regard the policy established by Herod the Great had been one of honoring Roman patrons while maintaining stability of rule in Palestine by placating insofar as was feasible the demands of the Jewish subjects. Antipas seems to have been more successful in Galilee and Perea than was Archelaus in Judea in adhering to their father's style of rule. Thus, Mark's list of those attending Herod's birthday banquet, comprising military officers, great ones, and the *prōtoi tēs Galilaias* (6:21), is altogether realistic.[30] These are the same *prōtoi* Josephus claims he could rely on for support when he was appointed governor of Galilee in 66 C.E., suggesting a local Jewish retainer class that was not located at either of the Herodian centers and had ancestral attachments to the Jerusalem priestly elite. Obviously, archaeology cannot substantiate this account, but it can confirm the view of the prevailing social situation that is presupposed in the narrative. On the basis of the literary evidence and the style of Herodian rule generally, it seems highly plausible, and it would have direct implications for the way the politically controlled economy actually functioned. In that event, some element of "free market" practices may well have been operative, thereby explaining the archaeological data to which Meyers (coins) and Adan-Bayewitz (pottery) point. Thus, the idea of Galilean peasants trading with Tyre and Sepphoris, so summarily dismissed by both Crossan and Horsley on the basis of generalized notions of the peasantry and politically controlled economies, at least, needs to be assessed in terms of other possible scenarios.

This still left plenty of displaced and impoverished Galileans, as the needs and demands of a new ruling elite at both Sepphoris and Tiberias had to be met. What, according to the various accounts we have been examining, was Jesus' stance when faced with these victims of empire? According to Crossan, he confronted the brokered kingdom of Rome and the embattled brokerage of the Judean priestly

---

27. Cf. Freyne, *Galilee and Gospel,* pp. 45-58, 59-73, and 86-113.

28. For a recent discussion, see J. Kloppenborg Verbin, *Excavating Q: The History and Setting of the Sayings Gospel* (Edinburgh: T. & T. Clark, 2000), pp. 245-55.

29. Crossan, *The Birth of Christianity,* pp. 345-50.

30. S. Freyne, "The Geography, Politics and Economics of Galilee and the Quest for the Historical Jesus," in *Studying the Historical Jesus: Evaluations of the State of Current Research,* ed. B. Chilton and C. Evans (Leiden: Brill, 1994), pp. 75-121; see esp. pp. 96-99.

elite with the brokerless kingdom of God's universal care and immediacy to all human beings, symbolized by his policy of "open commensality." Put simply, Jesus espoused a world in which all mediation of power and privilege, religious and secular alike, was abolished, and in his own lifestyle enacted an alternative practice based on God's universal care, symbolized through shared meals and unlimited hospitality. Horsley opts for a much more local and less idealized proposal, namely, a program of renewal and revitalization based on Israelite covenantal traditions of local communities whose ethos had been eroded by the intervention in Galilee of Roman imperial power and its Judean retainers. This view seems curiously at odds with his conflictual model of active peasant resistance to imperial domination, but it is certainly more realistic and plausible than Crossan's idealized scenario. As Sawicki notes, this latter suggestion presumes that Jesus had been socialized into Greco-Roman dining practices, whereas most recently Crossan locates him on the lowest stratum of the peasant class as a *tektōn*, "builder."

Because the model both scholars operate with (despite Horsley's apparent drawing back from its full implications) is dominated by class conflict, neither pays particular attention to the way cultural affiliations might have mitigated the sense of oppression that otherwise would indeed have given rise to open conflict. Insofar as Jesus espoused a view of Jewish restoration that was inclusive rather than separatist, and was concerned as well with justice for all, he was in fact addressing two aspects of alienation at the same time as far as Galilean peasants were concerned. On the one hand a shared participation in the fruits of the land was intended for all according to the Pentateuchal ideal, and yet the peasants were being deprived by "Jewish" landowners and retainers. Equally, however, non-Jewish peasants in the region were also experiencing exploitation, giving rise to local hostilities, especially in urban situations. In other words, to profile accurately a social situation one needs to attend to the mitigating as well as the alienating factors in a given society. This means that in a Jewish context a shared symbolic worldview could be both oppressive and liberating, in that no matter how much the Jewish temple state was in thrall to an agrarian or commercializing empire, its prophetic voice could offer different horizons for those who felt marginalized or excluded. The Palestinian Jesus Movement not only addressed the issues of class deprivation in Roman Galilee, but also offered an inclusive alternative for all in terms of a new understanding of God's rule in the present.

Gender

The archaeology of gender has not featured prominently in reports from Roman Galilee, though in his most recent book Crossan does include the anthropology of gender in his consideration of the early Christian community, and Horsley also has noted the significance of Jesus' apparent lack of concern for purity as far as women were concerned.[31] Sawicki, however, has sought to integrate the archaeology of gender with the results of Galilean archaeology in novel ways. She eschews what she regards as the ideologically driven approaches of modern feminist theory in favor of an indigenous, caste model based on kinship that seeks to take account of the intergenerational roles of women in maintaining the purity system devised by the Judeans. Brides who conformed to the demands of purity associated with the priests were essential if the rules involving the matrilineal line as described in the (admittedly later) Mishnah were to be observed. The status of would-be brides needed to be publicly verifiable if the privileges of the purity system were to flow into the household to which they were attached; these privileges had an economic importance for priestly families due to the tithing of the agricultural crop that should accrue to them. The *mikvaot* and other observable institutions for purity maintenance introduced into Galilee by the Hasmoneans served this public function. However, Roman colonization of Palestine posed a serious threat by destroying the kinship patterns on which the system was based. Insofar as archaeology has identified these immersion pools both in private houses and at the points of crop harvesting, it has assisted in identifying the homes where suitable brides might be found for those who sought them, as well as confirming the overall concern with tithing and other regulations of the system.

While Sawicki focuses on indigenous gender roles — and the contribution of archaeology in bringing these to light as they operated on the ground is fascinating — her study does not bring us immediately closer to the historical Jesus. He seems to have avoided centers such as Sepphoris, not just because of the view of the *basileia* that was inscribed in its imperial architecture, but also because that was where one found traces of the caste system that sought to maintain the purity of Israel while collaborating with the alien imposition against the people of the land. The Gospels present Jesus as being just as much at odds with the propagators of this system as he was with "those who dwell in royal houses" (Mt 11:8). His life was lived in "the contact zone" between imperial power and the Jewish caste system, "the social frontier between the indigenous logic of 'circulating and grounding' and the imperial deployment of Roman colonial structures in Galilee."[32] Thus, according to Sawicki, Jesus' view of the kingdom was contrary to both of the prevailing systems in Galilee, Roman and Jewish alike, and yet he

---

31. Crossan, *The Birth of Christianity*, pp. 159-65; Horsley, *Galilee*, pp. 197ff.

32. Sawicki, "Magdalenes and Tiberiennes: City Women in the Entourage of Jesus," in *Transformative Encounters: Jesus and Women Re-viewed*, ed. I. Kitzberger (Leiden: Brill, 2000), p. 179.

draws elements from each. On the one hand, he supports the idea of universal governance of the universe, but it belongs to God not to Rome, and it involves justice for all, not for the elites only. On the other hand, he supports the indigenous system of "circulation and grounding" of the older Israelite system, but it should be a free and open one based on nature rather than on the built environment of humans (i.e., Judeans) that controls and separates pure from impure.[33]

By situating Jesus and his understanding of the *basileia* at this interface, Sawicki believes that Jesus was supporting the strategies of coping that were being fashioned in Galilean society at that time. He was therefore supporting *resistance to* rather than *liberation from* imperial oppression. At the coalface of this resistance were Galilean women, whom Sawicki identifies as Magdalenes and Tiberiennes, that is, city women in the entourage of Jesus as described by Luke. However, though possible, this scenario, in my view, lacks plausibility on several grounds: The mention of Joanna, the wife of Chuza, is attested only in Luke (8:3), and this at least must raise the suspicion of it being a Lukan retrojection from his own situation, especially in view of his interest in Herodians generally. In addition, one has to wonder whether the kind of friendly exchange that Sawicki suggests between the Magdalenes and the Herodian court women, namely, that of providers of supplies to organizers of court banquets, was likely to have taken place, at least in the terms Sawicki suggests. Judgment of that possibility will depend on how one views the urban-rural relations in terms of economic exchange as well as the likelihood of nonelite women (in the case of the Magdalenes) being engaged in independent commercial activity in Roman Galilee. Sawicki does present some archaeological evidence from Masada that points to such a possibility, yet this rather special situation cannot allay the suspicion that, for once, Sawicki's interest in providing a role for women at the origins of the Palestinian Jesus Movement has ruled her head.[34] At least I, for one, would like to see much more evidence to support the scenario that she presents. Nevertheless, she is to be commended for drawing the attention of both archaeologists and historians of Jesus to gender issues and the dangers of our misreading the indigenous script by introducing our ideas into a different social and cultural setting.

However, this raises a further issue. Sawicki's hypothesis locates Jesus at a higher rung on the social ladder than do other accounts based on social-scientific discussion of the peasantry. Indeed, Crossan locates him, a *tektōn*, lower than the

---

33. Sawicki, *Crossing Galilee*, pp. 176-84.

34. Sawicki, *Crossing Galilee*, pp. 143-47, 184-87; Sawicki, "Magdalenes and Tiberiennes," pp. 181-202. For an alternative viewpoint see S. Freyne, "Jesus the Wine-Drinker, Friend of Women," in *Transformative Encounters*, pp. 162-80.

small landowner on the social scale. In Sawicki's account, on the other hand, he has been socialized into Hellenistic-style banquets and the appropriate etiquette, and thus gains entrée to Herodian circles.[35] His mother's name (Miriam) suggests a Judean nationalistic family background that opposed the Herodian presence in Galilee, but since he himself was not married nor the head of a household, he was a defective male in terms of the caste system and the gender role he was expected to fulfill. In the end Sawicki's Jesus seems to have abandoned his Judean heritage in favor of an older Israelite one that is not encumbered with the strategies of maintaining Israelite purity devised by the Hasmoneans. Missing from this account is any trace of apocalyptic and messianic awareness of Jesus' ministry that would have suggested his concern with a radically alternative kingdom in accordance with Jewish-Israelite tradition, rather than resistance to the existing one. Has Sawicki's methodology ended in so prioritizing archaeology over texts that it skews the picture somewhat? This Jesus too, it would seem, is in danger of becoming a prisoner of his social environment, even if his prison is different from that constructed by the social sciences.

Conclusion

In this paper I have sought to discuss some of the recent attempts to correlate the findings of Galilean archaeology with the search for the historical Jesus. It is a dialogue that in reality is only in its infancy, but already it is apparent that there are real possibilities for advancement. Jesus Research can pose new and more precise questions to archaeology, whereas archaeology can provide a different kind of evidence to that of the literary accounts, which historians must also take seriously. The overarching role of the social sciences is likely to provide the framework within which such discussions will take place. Provided they are introduced for their heuristic possibilities, rather than as guarantor of a fixed and immutable framework that determines the data to be selected and the meaning to be ascribed to them, such systems will certainly be of genuine assistance in the ongoing quest for Jesus. What should not be forgotten, however, is that Jesus was a religious reformer, no matter how embedded religion was in the social structures. One must therefore hope that, irrespective of the model chosen, consideration of the symbolic universe as well as the social world of Jesus will not be excluded from the discussion.

---

35. Crossan, *The Birth of Christianity*, pp. 345-52; Sawicki, *Crossing Galilee*, pp. 182, 194.

Recovering Jesus' *Mamzerut*

Bruce Chilton

The New Testament offers not one but three theories of Jesus' conception. One presents it as the consequence of an intervention of the Holy Spirit (by an unspecified mechanism), when Mary had not had sexual relations with a man. That is the explanation of Luke's Gospel, most emphatically (Lk 1:34-35), and strongly seconded by the Gospel according to Matthew (Mt 1:18-25).

A second explanation, expressed by Philip in John's Gospel after he had become Jesus' disciple, maintains that Jesus was in fact the son of Joseph (Jn 1:45), and it is — rather oddly — repeated both by John's "Jews" in the synagogue at Capernaum (Jn 6:42) and by Luke's congregation in Nazareth (Lk 4:22). Although the latter references are dismissive, Philip's is not, and it is difficult to see how the genealogies of Jesus, variously presented by Matthew (1:1-17) and Luke (3:23-38), can have been developed except on the supposition of the second theory. (Mt 1:16 and Lk 3:23 try to finesse the issue, but these adjustments seem to be post hoc.) Further, Jesus' identity as David's son — recognized by the Gospels (Mt 1:1; 9:27; 12:23; 15:22; 20:30, 31; 21:9, 15; Mk 10:47-48; Lk 18:38-39) as well as by Paul and later sources (Rom 1:3; cf. 2 Tim 2:8; Rev 5:5; 22:16) — implicitly invokes this theory, since only Joseph (himself called David's son in Mt 1:20; cf. Lk 1:27, 32; 2:4) can have mediated that pedigree to Jesus.

Finally, in John's Gospel opponents appear to taunt Jesus with being born of "fornication" (*porneia;* Jn 8:41), and such an accusation is often seen as standing behind the pointed omission of Joseph, but a reference to mother and siblings, in the identification of Jesus in Mk 6:3. At that juncture Matthew's reference to Jesus as the son of the workman (Mt 13:55) has been construed to imply Joseph's paternity (but also as saying in a Semitic idiom that Jesus belonged to the class of such workers). But Lk 4:22, the apparent analogue of Mk 6:3 and Mt 13:55, has the people in Nazareth affirm that Jesus is *Joseph's* son (cf. Jn 6:42).

The New Testament can in no sense be said to support the charge in Jn 8:41 and Mk 6:3, although those texts attest to the existence of such an accusation. Indeed, it seems that Matthew, Luke, and John would prefer to imply that Joseph was Jesus' actual father, rather than approach Mark's admission that people referred to Jesus in a way that gave comfort to those who denigrated his descent. But the second theory of Jesus' conception — the assertion of Joseph's paternity, rather than a grudging acceptance — may legitimately be claimed to be more broadly supported in the New Testament than the theory of the virginal conception, and to be assumed in sources earlier than the infancy narratives of Matthew and Luke.

The purpose of this essay is not to make out a case for the superiority of the second theory, though it is arguably superior on exegetical grounds. Rather, our purpose is to explain how all three theories emerged. What were the conditions under which some of Jesus' followers would acclaim him as David's son and Joseph's, while others would make his birth even more miraculous than the prophet Samuel's (cf. 1 Sam 1:1–2:11), and opponents would scorn him as the offspring of fornication?

When rabbinic literature has been used at all to illuminate this issue, it has typically been cited in connection with the allegation, cited as early as the time of Celsus (see below), that Jesus' mother had had relations with a Roman soldier. As we will see, however, that tradition seems to be a late arrival within a skein of passages that deal with the overall question of *mamzerut*, or mixed genealogy. That is the first part of the discussion here. The second part deals with how the suspicion of mixed genealogy might arise; the third part considers how the charge of *mamzerut* might have come to be leveled at Jesus in particular. That will bring us by way of conclusion to a fourth part, where we will consider methodological issues in the study of Jesus, and the likely date of his escape from the consequences of being treated as a *mamzer* in Nazareth.

Defining *Mamzerut*

At base, a *mamzer* was the product of a union that was forbidden, because the couple was not permitted to marry and procreate according to the Torah. Whatever became of the man and the woman as the result of their sexual contact, their offspring was what we may call a changeling or mixling (terms that perhaps better convey the sense of *mamzer* than "bastard" or "mongrel," the traditional translations). The sense of abhorrence involved, at the mixture of lines that should never be mixed, was such that the stricture of *mamzerut* could also be applied to the offspring of a woman whose sexual partner was unidentified, and therefore was not known to have been permitted to her.

The practice of attributing the status of mixed genealogy to particular individuals varied over time. That is not surprising, since Deut 23:2, although specifying that a *mamzer* is to be excluded from the congregation until the tenth generation (see also *Yebamot* 8.3 in the Mishnah), does not actually define what such a mixed offspring might be. But however much the definition of *mamzerut* did change, it is striking that the precise description of Mary's pregnancy in Mt 1:18 (as occurring between the time a contract of marriage was exchanged and the actual cohabitation of the couple) would have put Jesus into the position of being considered a *mamzer* within a principle articulated in the Mishnah.

In what follows, we will cite and explain the major passages at issue, following the line of chronology critically assigned to rabbinics, first Mishnah (from the second century c.e.), then Tosephta (from the third century), and then Talmud (from the fifth century).[1]

Yebamot 4.13 in the Mishnah[2] attests to an established consensus by the second century that incest — under the terms of reference of Leviticus (which of course were more rigorous than in the Hellenistic world) — would produce a *mamzer*. At the same time, a rabbi named Joshua supported by Simeon ben Azzai (allegedly citing written evidence) broadens the definition, by including adultery as grounds for finding *mamzerut*:

> How is one a *mamzer* (Deuteronomy 23:2)? Any case of near of kin which is forbidden, the words of Rabbi Aqiba. Simeon of Teman says, Any case where they [that is, the parents] were liable to extirpation by heaven (Leviticus 18:29). And the *halakhah* is according to his words. Rabbi Joshua says, Any case where they were liable to death by a court. Said Rabbi Simeon ben Azzai, I found a scroll of descents in Jerusalem, and there was written in it: A certain man is a *mamzer*, from a man's wife (Leviticus 18:20) — confirming the words of Rabbi Joshua.

It is interesting that, in Matthew's Gospel, Joseph is portrayed as having decided to divorce Mary quietly (Mt 1:19). In the Mishnah, the possibility of such a dissolution of the contract between betrothal and common domicile is mentioned

---

1. See the now classic treatment of Jacob Neusner, *Introduction to Rabbinic Literature*, ABRL (New York: Doubleday, 1994).

2. See the translations of P. Blackman, *Mishnayoth* (Gateshead: Judaica, 1983), and Neusner, *The Mishnah: A New Translation* (New Haven: Yale University Press, 1988), which I have here revised.

(see *Soṭah* 4.1). In the present case, such an act would imply voiding the contract of marriage without a formal charge of her adultery and of the *mamzerut* of the child. This Mishnaic tractate cites Deut 23:2 explicitly, moving into a case of adulterous relations by way of application of the statute. The connection of ideas is easy to follow, because the themes of virginity, adultery, rape, and incest are developed in Deuteronomy (22:13-30) just before the mention of the *mamzer*, and the punishment for such crimes (sometimes expressly demanded in this chapter of Deuteronomy) is stoning.

Ketubot 1.9 in the Mishnah, however, is even more to the point, since it corresponds to Mary's predicament as specified in Mt 1:18: "She was pregnant, and they said to her, What kind of fetus is this? From a certain man, and he is a priest! Rabbi Gamaliel and Rabbi Eliezer say, 'She is believed.' And Rabbi Joshua says, 'We do not rely on her statement. But she remains in the assumption of having become pregnant by a *Netin* or a *mamzer*, until she brings evidence for her words.'" Here we have two opposed policies. In one (Gamaliel's and Eliezer's), the testimony of a mother suffices to establish fatherhood; in the other (Joshua's), evidence is required — for example, in the shape of knowledge of the couple's common domicile (as we shall see).

Joshua's opinion is consistent with his view in *Yebamot* 4.13, since a finding of adultery involves a witness (human or supernatural, see Num 5:11-31), and witnesses are just what he calls for in *Ketubot* 1.9. Logical consistency would approve this position. The opposition of Gamaliel and Eliezer, however, draws attention to a severe social problem inherent in Joshua's definition of *mamzerut* and his application of that definition. If the matter turns on being unable to establish a licit father, that extends the number of children who might be considered *mamzers* and opens a large number of women to the charge or the suspicion of adultery.

But the point of view attributed to Gamaliel and Eliezer does not represent all that much progress, from the point of view of well-ordered social relations. Since it permits a woman to name a licit father, by the terms of the Torah itself that man would be required to marry her without recourse to divorce (Deut 22:28-29). What the Mishnah is showing us, in the names of rabbis from the first century, is that *mamzerut* posed social as well as logical problems (see also *Qiddushin* 4.8). The attributions themselves need not be taken at face value here (although I am struck by the consistency of the views ascribed to Joshua at various junctures in the Mishnah); whether they are accepted or not, the Mishnah memory that *mamzerut* was a thorny issue remains. Indeed, the most direct proof of that is that the Mishnah not only recollects the problem, but also goes on to resolve it.

This resolution is beautifully represented in Mishnah *Qiddushin* 4.1-2 in a passage that will take some explaining, once we have cited it:

> Ten descents came up from Babylonia: (1) priest, (2) Levite, (3) Israelite, (4) impaired priest, (5) convert, and (6) freed slave, (7) *mamzer*, (8) *Netin*, (9) silenced [*shetuqi*], and (10) foundling. Priest, Levite, and Israelite intermarry among one another. Levite, Israelite, impaired priest, convert, and freed slave intermarry one another. Convert, freed slave, *mamzer*, *Netin*, silenced, and foundling all intermarry among one another. These are silenced — everyone who knows his mother but does not know his father; and foundling — everyone who was retrieved from the market and knows neither his father nor his mother. Abba Saul called a "silenced" [*shetuqi*] "to be *examined*" [*beduqi*].

This passage is a triumph of categorical thinking. In this list the status of a *mamzer* is neatly distinguished from that of one put to silence, although the two are also closely associated.

The category of *mamzerut* is evidently reserved for offspring of known instances of adultery, incest, or other illicit intercourse (see *Qiddushin* 3.12 in the Mishnah). In contrast, the "silenced" *(shetuqi)* caste permits mother and child not to be associated with adultery, incest, or illicit intercourse and the punishments they occasioned, a compassionate conclusion in the face of the uncertainty of fatherhood. From the point of view of mother and child, the *shetuqi* represents a signal advance over Joshua's perspective on the *mamzer* (in *Ketubot* 1.9); from the point of view of the alleged father, it also makes life easier than Gamaliel and Eliezer would have it. Even the foundling, whose licit birth could not be attested by a mother or by witnesses (again, under the provisions of *Ketubot* 1.9), is protected from the status of *mamzerut* here.

The manifest tolerance of this distinction between *mamzer* and *shetuqi* (or foundling, mutatis mutandis), and the elegant social adaptation it facilitated, comports well with the adjustment toward marriage that the passage as a whole conveys. The alignment of the differing castes is articulated in two senses. The first sense is the association of one caste with several others. Levites and Israelites can intermarry with one another and with priests. Proselytes and freed slaves can intermarry with impaired priests one notch further down the list, but also with the Levites and Israelites higher in the list. In much the same way, the *mamzer, Netin*, silenced, and foundling classes can intermarry with one another and with proselytes and freed slaves.

If this strong association is surprising in view of the treatment of *mamzerut* elsewhere in the Mishnah (and the Hebrew Bible, come to that), it is far from unambiguous. That brings us to the second sense of the articulation of caste alignment of the list. It is hierarchical — and literally so — because priests are assigned a unique position, without a higher association in the list, and emphatically without links to the other categories lower in the list that are not expressly Israelite. Taken together with the associative articulation, the hierarchical articulation conveys an ideal structure of marital preferences. A given arrangement is less desirable the more one moves down the list, so that any sense of preference all but disappears within the varying degrees of *mamzerut* cited (except in implicit contrast to a Gentile without any affiliation with Israel).

This relative disapprobation of the *mamzer* was such that, well after the Mishnah, it provoked the rule that when a Gentile or a slave had sexual relations with an Israelite woman, the result was a *mamzer* (*Qiddushin* 70a). This was the root of the growing sense that maternity rather than paternity governed one's identity as an Israelite, and also provided for a place for proselytes in procreation, even as it maintained their status as outsiders.[3]

The means by which *mamzerut* is attributed to those of non-Israelite paternity in the Talmudic passage is instructive. In two ways, the attempt is made to link the Mishnaic category referred to in *Qiddushin* 4.1 firmly to scripture (Talmud *Qiddushin* 70a):[4]

> Mamzers: from where do we know? From where it is written, And Sanballat the Horonite and Tobiah the slave, the Ammonite heard it (Nehemiah 2:10); and it is written, for there were many in Judah sworn unto him, because he was the son-in-law of Shechaniah the son of Arah, and his son Jehohanan had taken the daughter of Meshullam the son of Berechiah to wife (Nehemiah 6:17-18). This holds that when a gentile or a slave has sexual relations with an Israelite woman — the offspring is a *mamzer*. That is convenient for him who maintains that the offspring is a *mamzer,* but from the viewpoint of him who holds that the offspring is licit, what can be said? Furthermore, how do you know that they had children? Maybe they didn't have children? And furthermore, how do you know that they were originally here but then went up? Perhaps they were located there. Rather, from this: And these are the ones who went up from Tel-melah, Tel-harsha, Cherub, Addon, and Immer, but they could not show their fathers' houses nor their seed, whether they were of Israel (Nehemiah 7:61). Tel-melah: This refers to people whose deeds are like those of Sodom, which was turned into a salt heap. Tel-harsha: This refers to those who call "father," whom their mothers silence. But they could not show their fathers' houses nor their seed, whether they

3. See S. J. D. Cohen, *The Beginnings of Jewishness: Boundaries, Varieties, Uncertainties* (Berkeley: University of California Press, 1999), pp. 273-307.

4. See H. Freedman, *Kiddushin: The Babylonian Talmud* (London: Soncino, 1936); Neusner, *Bavli Tractate Qiddushin: The Talmud of Babylonia* (Atlanta: Scholars, 1996); *Qiddushin min Talmud Bavli* (Jerusalem: Vagshal, 1980).

were of Israel: This refers to a foundling, retrieved from the market. Cherub, Addon, and Immer: Said Rabbi Abbahu, Said the Lord, I said that the Israelites would be valued before me as a cherub, but they have made themselves into a leopard. There are those who say, said Rabbi Abbahu, Said the Lord, Even though they have made themselves into a leopard, nonetheless, the Israelites are valued before me as a cherub.

In the first case, Tobiah's status as an Ammonite and a slave is used to attribute *mamzerut* to his children. But then the objection is raised that not enough is known about the status of these children to know whether the prescription of Deut 23:2 had been applied. Instead, Neh 7:61 is invoked, on the assumption that the inability to specify one's father's house involved *mamzerut*. Not only does the Talmudic passage maintain this basic point as the straightforward reading of the Mishnah (*Ketubot* 1.9), it also associates slaves, silenced ones, and foundlings within the general category of the *mamzer*, as the list in the Mishnah does (*Qiddushin* 4.1).

Once this definition was accepted, it was a short step to the tradition that Jesus' father had been a Gentile, and a Roman soldier at that (*Shabbat* 104b and *Sanhedrin* 67a, according to manuscripts in Munich and Oxford). It had once been possible to accuse him of *mamzerut* in a Mishnaic sense, because the identity of his father was not established; according to the Talmudic tradition, his father was known, and known as non-Israelite, and for that reason he was a *mamzer*. Whatever the current definition, it could be and was applied to Jesus.[5]

Proximity and Sexual Contact

That then brings us to the question of how the status of a *mamzer* can have been applied to Jesus.

Well before the Talmud, a commonly cited tradition affirmed that Jesus' father was called "Panther," a Roman soldier with whom Mary had an adulterous affair (Origen, *Contra Celsum* 1.2).[6] This is a cunning haggadah, because it dou-

---

5. I owe this formulation to William Horbury, during discussions in the seminar on the Gospels and rabbinic literature that I chaired for the Studiorum Novi Testamenti Societas (August 2000 in Tel Aviv). I am grateful for the encouraging, engaged discussion that took place.

6. Dismissed by J. Maier in *Jesus von Nazareth in der talmudischen Überlieferung*, ErFor 82 (Darmstadt: Wissenschaftliche Buchgesellschaft, 1978), this legend that Celsus circulated circa 178 C.E. has recently been championed by J. J. Rousseau and R. Arav, *Jesus and His World: An Archaeological and Cultural Dictionary* (Minneapolis: Fortress, 1995), pp. 223-25. They maintain

bles Jesus' *mamzerut:* he is the product of adultery (and therefore a *mamzer* according to the definition of the Mishnah) and the offspring of a non-Israelite father (and therefore a *mamzer* according to the definition that later emerged in the Talmud).

This story is as hybrid as Jesus' birth is made out to be, but the idea has been taken up in recent discussions of Jesus' "illegitimacy": his irregular birth is explained by the rape of his mother in Sepphoris during the civil strife of 4 B.C.E.[7] Although this hypothesis has helped to move us along the right track, into a consideration of birth status in Judaism, in my opinion it demands more supposition about tight contact between Sepphoris and the hamlets that surrounded it than recent discussion warrants (see below). Further, the "Panther" tale suits the Mishnaic and Talmudic definition of *mamzerut* so well as to suggest it is a fiction.[8]

So why did some people accuse Jesus of being born of fornication (*porneia;* Jn 8:41)? Was it for the same reason he was called "son of Mary" in his own town (Mk 6:3) rather than "son of Joseph"? What emerges from both rabbinic literature (supplemented by Origen) and the New Testament is that Jesus' mother was clearly known, and that the identity of his father was contested. Whoever his natural father was — Joseph, another man to whom Mary was not married while Joseph was her husband (a soldier or not, a Gentile or not), or the power of the Most High (if some procreative event really is implied in Lk 1:35) — Jesus was a *mamzer* within the terms of reference established by the Mishnah in its discussion of traditional definitions (*Ketubot* 1.9 above all). This category provoked the disparate views of Jesus' birth attested in the New Testament (and to a lesser extent, in rabbinic discussion).

Although the relevance of *mamzerut* to the evaluation of Jesus might be as much as rabbinic literature can teach us, there is another step to take. The simple fact of proximity between a man and a woman is well attested with halakic

---

that an epitaph in Bingerbrück, probably from the time of Germanicus and bearing the name of a soldier whose sobriquet was "Panther," attests the identity of Jesus' real father. But if "Panther" was a common cognomen, that better explains the phraseology of the Talmudic legend than anything about Jesus' paternity.

7. See M. Sawicki, *Crossing Galilee: Architectures of Contact in the Occupied Land of Jesus* (Harrisburg, Pa.: Trinity, 2000); J. Schaberg, *The Illegitimacy of Jesus: A Feminist Theological Interpretation of the Infancy Narratives* (San Francisco: Harper and Row, 1987).

8. See Sawicki, *Crossing Galilee*, pp. 171-73; Schaberg, *The Illegitimacy of Jesus*. See Cohen, *The Beginnings of Jewishness*, pp. 276-80. But he goes too far when he says on p. 276, "M. Yevamot 7:5 states that the offspring of a Jewish mother and a gentile or slave father is a *mamzer.*" This text in fact relates to a woman of priestly descent (and was no doubt a precedent for the later, broader rule). The pertinent text, which Cohen cites and explains on pp. 277-80, is Talmudic, *b. Yebamot* 45b.

discussion as a cause for concluding that sexual contact has occurred. The most famous instance of that is the Mishnaic tractate *Soṭah,* where having been with a man other than her husband in a private place obliges a married woman to drink the bitter water of Num 5:11-31 (*Soṭah* 1.1-7).[9] In this case, Eliezer and Joshua are said to disagree, as in the question of believing a pregnant woman about the paternity of her child. Joshua demands two witnesses before she is required to drink, while Eliezer is content with the testimony of one witness, even the husband himself (*Soṭah* 1.1).

Just as proximity invokes the suspicion of forbidden sexual contact, so it may be used to suggest that permitted contact has occurred. This brings us to a discussion of the halakah most frequently discussed in connection with Mt 1:18.

Raymond Brown supports the argument of many commentators that there was a difference in marital custom between Galilee and Judea: he claims that in Galilee no sexual relation was tolerated between a woman and her husband before they lived together in their marital home, while in Judea intimate relations were not excluded in the interim between the agreement of contract and the couple's public cohabitation.[10] John P. Meier demurs, observing that "later rabbinic distinctions about differences of customs in Judea and Galilee are of questionable relevance."[11]

Yet Meier persists in the supposition that Mt 1:18 reflects a controversy over Mary's virginity, and for him rabbinic literature shows that virginity was such an important issue that the dispute over Jesus' birth should be seen as one over his mother's sexual experience at the time of her marriage. In this, Meier is far from alone, because the discussion about virginity was prompted by the widely cited compendium of Paul Billerbeck.[12] But the texts cited from that source

9. *Soṭah* 2.6 establishes by consensus that this applied only between the time of betrothal and divorce, not before or after.

10. R. E. Brown, *The Birth of the Messiah* (London: Chapman, 1993), p. 124: "According to later Jewish commentary [*sic*] (Mishnah *Ketuboth* 1:5; TalBab *Ketuboth* 9b, 12a), *in parts of Judea* it was not unusual for the husband to be alone with his wife on at least one occasion in the interval between exchange of consent and the move to the home (and so interim marital relations were not absolutely condemned). But *in Galilee* no such leniency was tolerated and the wife had to be taken to her husband's home as a virgin."

11. J. P. Meier, *A Marginal Jew: Rethinking the Historical Jesus* (New York: Doubleday, 1991), 1:245-46.

12. Hermann L. Strack and Paul Billerbeck, *Das Evangelium nach Mattäus erläutert aus Talmud und Midrasch,* Str-B 1 (Munich: Beck, 1922). W. D. Davies and D. C. Allison, *A Critical and Exegetical Commentary on the Gospel according to Saint Matthew,* ICC (Edinburgh: T. & T. Clark, 1988), pp. 199-200, cite comparable texts (*m. Yeb.* 4.10; *m. Ketub.* 1.5; 4.12; *b. Ketub.* 12a), and draw the same distinction between Galilean and Judean custom. See also C. S. Keener in *A Commentary on the Gospel of Matthew* (Grand Rapids: Eerdmans, 1999), p. 92; he makes reference to

have often been taken out of context in my view, and in any case their relevance for an understanding of Mt 1:18 seems only indirect.

First, the alleged difference in custom cited by Brown and other commentators is not supported by all the texts they cite. It is not the Mishnah (*Ketubot* 1.5) but the Talmud (*Ketubot* 9b, 12a) that claims a distinction between Galilee and Judea. The Mishnah speaks only of Judea, insisting that a man does not have the right, if he had lived with his father-in-law (and therefore with his fiancée) prior to marriage, to bring a complaint against his wife after the marriage because she was no longer a virgin. If there is a contrast with Galilee in this case, it is merely by implication. The source of an explicit contrast is the Tosephta (*Ketubot* 1.4), which the Talmud seems to adapt in this instance.

The significance of the contrast as drawn by Brown[13] — that in Galilee a bride's virginity was demanded, whatever the circumstances of the couple's domicile before their public cohabitation — may also be contested. If the economic development of Jewish Galilee was less rapid and less urban than in Judea, as contemporary archaeology would suggest,[14] the domicile of a groom with his father-in-law would have been so current that no complaint of the type envisaged in the Mishnah would have been feasible.

Perhaps it was especially in urban Judea, where more families had the means to offer their children their own marital domiciles, that there was the possibility — real or imagined — of a confusion of the customs of the rich and

---

S. Safrai, "Home and Family," in *The Jewish People in the First Century,* ed. S. Safrai and M. Stern, CRINT (Assen: Van Gorcum, 1976), 2:728-92, 756-57, and to L. Finkelstein, *The Pharisees: The Sociological Background of Their Faith* (Philadelphia: Jewish Publication Society of America, 1962), 1:45. These citations support Billerbeck's observation, but Tosephta remains crucial to any discussion of regional difference. Davies and Allison are less speculative when they observe: "To judge from the rabbinic sources (which may be late), betrothal or engagement (*'erusin* or *qiddushim*) in ancient Judaism took place at a very early age, usually at twelve to twelve and a half years (*b. Yeb.* 62b; SB 2, p. 274). Following courtship and the completion of the marriage contract (Tob 7:14), the marriage was considered established: the woman had passed from her father's authority to that of her husband. But about a year typically passed before the woman moved from her parents' house to her husband's house (*m. Ket.* 5.2; *m. Ned.* 10.5; *b. Ket.* 57b). During that time, although marriage was not yet consummated, the woman was 'wife' (Deut 20:7; 28:30; Judg 14:15; 15:1; 2 Sam 3:14) and she could become a widow (*m. Yeb.* 4.10; 6.4; *Ket.* 1.2) or be punished for adultery (Deut 22:23-4; 11QTemple 61). Thus betrothal was the legal equivalent of marriage, and its cancellation divorce (*m. Ket.* 1.2; 4.2; *m. Yeb.* 2.6; *m. Git.* 6.2)."

13. But the formulation is actually that of Finkelstein, *The Pharisees,* p. 45.

14. See S. Freyne, *Galilee, Jesus, and the Gospels* (Philadelphia: Fortress, 1988); R. A. Horsley, *Archaeology, History, and Society in Galilee: The Social Context of Jesus and the Rabbis* (Valley Forge, Pa.: Trinity, 1996); J. F. Strange, "First Century Galilee from Archaeology and from the Texts," in *Archaeology and the Galilee: Texts and Contexts in the Graeco-Roman and Byzantine Periods,* SFSHJ 143 (Atlanta: Scholars, 1997), pp. 39-48; Sawicki, *Crossing Galilee.*

the poor. Under these circumstances, the Mishnah lays down a rule in *Ketubot* 1.5 that brooks no double dealing: "He who eats with his father-in-law in Judea without a witness cannot bring a complaint for the cause of non-virginity, because he was alone with her."

Clearly, then, the rule that proximity allows of the finding of sexual contact (whether permitted or not) seems to have been well established. Just as women were protected against one custom being substituted for another, so there was an explicit caution against moving a woman away from her home (*Ketubot* 13.10). "There are three provinces in what concerns marriage: Judah, Beyond Jordan, and Galilee. They do not remove from town to town or from city to city. But in the same province, they do remove from town to town or from city to city, but not from a town to a city, and not from a city to a town. They remove from a bad dwelling to a pleasant dwelling but not from a pleasant dwelling to a bad dwelling. Rabban Simeon ben Gamaliel says, Also not from a bad dwelling to a pleasant one, since the pleasant dwelling tempts." Following this rule in a relatively undeveloped area (such as rural Galilee) would imply that a groom would "eat with his father-in-law" after his marriage as well as before. Although the husband brought a patriarchal construction of genealogy to the marriage, the location of household, which was the bride's domain, was determined by where she lived, and in most cases must actually have been under the control of her family.

Although Mishnah *Ketubot* 1.5 indirectly indicates how and why one might conclude that sexual contact had occurred, the fact remains that the problem specified in Mt 1:18 is not Mary's virginity, but her pregnancy.

This simple observation, by Marie-Joseph Lagrange,[15] invites another take on Mt 1:18. If Joseph and Mary were known not to be living together, even though they were betrothed, that would account for Jesus' repute as a *mamzer* in Nazareth. This brings us to the issue of locating Bethlehem.

Bethlehem

"Where was Jesus born?" Steve Mason and Jerome Murphy-O'Connor both answered that question for *Bible Review*,[16] and their remarks landed the editors a blizzard of mail. Not surprising, when you consider that *where* Jesus was born necessarily involves *how* he was born. The way these two scholars approached their assigned question takes us into that whole issue.

15. Lagrange, *Évangile selon Saint Matthieu*, EBib (Paris: Gabalda, 1941), p. 10.
16. Mason and Murphy-O'Connor, "Where Was Jesus Born?" *Bible Review* 16, no. 1 (2000): 31-51.

Mason represents the position that Nazareth was Jesus' birthplace. After all, he called it his *patris* (or fatherland; Mk 6:1; Mt 13:57; Lk 4:24), although this term might refer to Jesus' region generally more than to Nazareth in particular (see Jn 4:43-44). More to the point, John's Gospel has Philip identify Jesus as "Joseph's son from Nazareth" (Jn 1:45-46). Murphy-O'Connor, on the other hand, criticizes Mason for supposing that the messianic prophecy of a son of David (derived from Mic 5:2) caused Christians to make up the name "Bethlehem" as Jesus' natal village. He insists that Matthew and Luke used different sources that mentioned the place, so that it is more likely the name was remembered, rather than a Christian invention.

Both these contributors, for all their differences, follow the principle that a historical "fact" is an event that we surmise actually happened. History involves both the chain of events that historians study and the theories they use to understand them. In this case, our challenge is to see a coherent picture, without just discounting about one-half of the evidence (be it about Nazareth or Bethlehem).

But are we even arguing about the right Bethlehem? The Hebrew Bible itself mentions a Bethlehem far to the north of Jerusalem, assigned to Zebulun (Josh 19:15), and in Jn 7:41-42 some apparently well informed skeptics resist the idea that Jesus is Messiah on the grounds that he comes from Galilee and not from Davidic Bethlehem. In Hebrew the name means "house of bread," perhaps designating a settlement with mills capable of producing fine flour, rather than the coarse grade most people used for their daily needs. In 1975 I learned of a *Galilean* Bethlehem near Nazareth from a study of Talmudic geography published during the nineteenth century. I was disconcerted at the dearth of discussion about this place as the possible site of Jesus' birth.

I was intrigued but wary (conscious of how easily a new idea can be rejected out of hand, just because it *is* new. More than once in my career, I have been asked how an exegesis can possibly be correct if no one has thought of it before!). The Talmud was composed centuries after Jesus lived, so one cannot assume it accurately reflects ancient Galilee's geography. I appended my findings to my Ph.D. thesis and let the matter rest. Now, however, archaeological excavations show that Bethlehem in Galilee is a first-century site just seven miles from Nazareth, so my former reserve can be put aside.[17] There is good reason to surmise that the Bethlehem that Matthew and Luke remember, dimly and distantly (and through the lenses of scripture and legend), was actually in Galilee.

17. See A. Neubauer, *La Géographie du Talmud* (Paris, 1868), pp. 189-91, discussed in Chilton, *God in Strength: Jesus' Announcement of the Kingdom*, SNTSU 1 (Freistadt: F. Plöchl, 1979), reprinted in "The Biblical Seminar" (Sheffield: JSOT, 1987), pp. 311-13. For a recent, critical treatment of Bethlehem of Galilee in relation to other Jewish settlements, see Strange, "First Century Galilee," pp. 39-48.

With the evidence of excavation reports, an idea from the nineteenth century crosses the threshold of probability. Mt 1:18, as interpreted here, provides us with a clue to why Jesus' parents were in Galilean Bethlehem in the first place. Had Joseph been domiciled there, that would explain both why Mary's pregnancy in Nazareth was a scandal and why Joseph took her away from Nazareth to Bethlehem for Jesus' birth. (Such a change of site is, of course, much more plausible than having Joseph and Mary traveling to Judea for the birth, a journey that in any case would have violated the custom mentioned in *Ketubot* 13.10 in the Mishnah.) The conditions of Jesus' conception *as Matthew refers to them* made him a *mamzer* in the eyes of Mary's neighbors in Nazareth. Cultural preoccupation with sex before marriage in the West has caused scholarship to convert the issue of Jesus' status in Israel into the anachronistic question of his legitimacy, and to ignore one of the most powerful influences on his development. Cast aside as a *mamzer* or "silenced one" *(shetuqi)*, Jesus from the beginning of his life negotiated the treacherous terrain between belonging to Israel and the experience of ostracism within his own community. The aspirations of a restored Israel can only have been particularly poignant to those branded with the reputation of *mamzerut*.

The Jesus of Literary History

The nature of the Gospels is such that Jesus can be known only by means of literary inference, owing to the tenuous relationship between the sources and what we call historical information. There is a reasonable degree of consensus that Mark was the first of the Gospels to be written, around 73 C.E. in the environs of Rome. As convention has it, Matthew was subsequently composed, near 80, perhaps in Damascus (or elsewhere in Syria), while Luke came later, perhaps in 90, probably in Antioch. John is generally assigned to Ephesus, circa 100, and the *Gospel according to Thomas* may have been compiled in Edessa sometime during the middle of the second century.

The close relationship among the first three Gospels, in their wording, order, and content, has led to their designation as "Synoptic," and to the hypothesis of their literary relationship. The hypothesis that once enjoyed a commanding position in the discipline assigns Mark as the written source of Matthew and Luke, and holds that Matthew and Luke also used a source of Jesus' sayings, known as "Q[uelle, 'source']," as well as other written or oral sources.

The popularity of the hypothesis of a genetic, literary relationship among the Synoptic Gospels is predicated upon untested assumptions, and has produced several unfortunate results. Chief among the common fallacies of study is the notion that the verbal similarity among the Gospels demonstrates their literary connection: the fact is that the rate of correspondence is as great in rabbinic literature, where the influence of oral transmission is known to have been substantial.[18] The notion of "the Evangelists" as authors is another distortion. The Gospels simply were not produced within the sort of literary circles that gave us the Josephan corpus, and any critical reading reveals that there are layers of interpretative reflection within each of the Gospels, no single one of which can claim the authority of "the Evangelist."

Once "the Evangelist" is assumed to be an authorial scribe, his work is easily misconstrued as a mechanical compilation of documents. Moreover, the social function of the Gospels within the development of early Christianity tends to be ignored, because a model of professional, literary production is simply taken for granted. But the "hypothesis" (which among some scholars approaches the status of axiom) of Markan priority and the genetic relationship of the Synoptic Gospels has also left us with the most misleading apprehension of all: the supposition that there is a "real" Jesus "behind" the Gospels, who is to be identified by excavating and paring away "late" material and getting down to what is "primitive."

The persistence of the fallacious analogy between a critical reading of the Gospels and textual archaeology,[19] or stratigraphy (the more fashionable designation today),[20] requires that its inadequacy be identified. The point is obvious, but apparently it has not been taken to heart, that the analogy of texts to tells presupposes that inert matter overlays the "original" object beneath, which only requires to be uncovered to be discovered in its pristine primitivity. But a text is not a tell, and meaning is not conveyed from generation to generation of tradents by permitting the erection of whatever seems convenient upon what has gone before.

A text by definition conveys some set of meanings, and — for the Gospels — the complexity is that earlier meanings may be conveyed within later meanings, and that we have access to the former only through the latter. In the case to hand, we have access to Jesus only insofar as the texts that claim to convey him in fact do so. There is no "primitive," "historical," "authentic," or otherwise real Jesus apart from what texts promulgate. In the first instance, therefore, Jesus is knowable only as a literarily historical phenomenon: what the Gospels point to as their source.

In the instance of Jesus' occupation of the Temple, one of the best-attested

18. See Chilton, *Profiles of a Rabbi: Synoptic Opportunities in Reading about Jesus,* BJS 177 (Atlanta: Scholars, 1989).

19. So J. Jeremias, *New Testament Theology: The Proclamation of Jesus,* trans. J. Bowden (New York: Scribner, 1971).

20. So J. S. Kloppenborg, *The Formation of Q* (Philadelphia: Fortress, 1987).

events, the Gospels in fact present us with distinct portraits of Jesus. In Mark we are informed that Jesus "did not permit anyone to carry a vessel through the Temple" while he occupied it (11:16). The uniquely Markan assertion is that Jesus effectively brought sacrificial activity to a halt. In much the same way, a uniquely Markan explanation earlier in the Gospel (chap. 7) has it that "the Pharisees and all the Jews" (v. 3) keep many practices "of washings of cups and pots and bronze things and beds" (7:4): Mark's Jesus represents the end of all that.

By contrast, the Matthean Jesus, precisely in his occupation of the Temple, represents the fulfillment of Davidic hopes. He heals the blind and the lame, and is hailed as David's son (21:14, 15). Within Matthew particularly, the designation "son of David" alludes to Solomon's power to heal,[21] which Jesus also is understood to exert. The high priests and scribes become angry precisely because Jesus is so recognized in the Temple, and his response is to affirm that the praise itself fulfills God's intent (21:15, 16).

Luke presents the most condensed version of the occupation within the canonical Gospels, and yet here too there is unique matter. The notice is appended that Jesus taught every day in the Temple, and that the high priest and scribes were unable to act against him, owing to the support of "the people" (19:47, 48). The Temple is therefore established as a place where, as in the book of Acts, Christian teaching is a proper activity.

The simple, literary fact that the Synoptic Gospels are each substantially unique in their presentation of Jesus' action in the Temple, one of the most stable elements in the Synoptic tradition, ought long ago to have warned the discipline against a reductionistic, purely documentary solution of the "Synoptic problem." A more adequate approach would recognize that the similarity of the first three Gospels is a function of their shared origin in the catechesis of the early church, and that their uniqueness is a measure of the differences among the catechetical programs current in Antioch, Damascus, and Rome. Indeed, the "problem" is an artifact of the assumption that their relationship is a documentary cipher that can be solved as a puzzle; more plausibly, it is a matter of the consensus and distinctiveness of apostolic Christianity. Similarly, the dichotomy between oral and written transmission within the process of Synoptic formation, which is frequently assumed in recent discussion, is false: catechesis is essentially a matter of preparing baptisands, and whether one does so from written notes or from memory, the point of the exercise is to inculcate what is held to be vital.[22]

---

21. See D. Duling, "Solomon, Exorcism, and the Son of David: An Element in Matthew's Christological Apologetic," *NTS* 24 (1977-78): 392-410.

22. See P. J. Achtemeier, "*Omne verbum sonat:* The New Testament and the Oral Environment of Late Western Antiquity," *JBL* 109 (1990): 3-27.

The principal point of consensus among the Synoptic Gospels in their portrayal of the occupation of the Temple, which in turn makes them unique in comparison with John and *Thomas,* is the attribution to Jesus of some form of the biblical citation, a hybrid of passages in Isaiah and Jeremiah, "My house will be a house of prayer, but you have made it a den of thieves" (Lk 19:46; cf. Mt 21:13; Mk 11:17). The Synoptic placement of the occupation within the presentation of the passion of Jesus, preceding an extensive prediction of the destruction of the Temple, associates his action with the divine judgment against the cult, a judgment that is assumed to have been executed in 70 C.E. With a variety of narrative devices, the Synoptics bring out and vivify the connection between Jesus' occupation and subsequent death and the end of the Temple, but their stability in making that connection tends to suggest it was a prominent part of early catechesis.

The connection between Jesus' death and the destruction of the Temple is attenuated in John, and is transformed into the theme of the general irreconcilability of Jesus and "the Jews." Jesus' statement, "Destroy this Temple, and in three days I will raise it," is misunderstood by "the Jews" to refer to the building; Jesus is alleged thereby to have referred to his own resurrection (Jn 2:18-22). The scriptural citation of the Synoptics, and its apparent denunciation of commercialism, does not appear; instead, Jesus' disciples think of Ps 69:10(9), "Zeal for your house will consume me" (Jn 2:17). The plane of the Johannine presentation, in other words, is the thematic axiom, "he came into his own, and his own received him not" (1:11), and the placement of the occupation near the beginning of the Gospel demonstrates that a dominant concern of the Gospel is discursive. Discursive reflection upon central themes of belief is here more important than catechesis, and the impact is even less historical than in the Synoptics.

If John's logic is discursive, that of *Thomas* is aphoristic: sayings of Jesus are presented as if they provided their own contextual meaning, although in fact the questions that generally lead into a given section provide an interlocutory, and obviously artificial, context. *Thomas* is no mere hodgepodge of traditional materials, although association by catchword and topic is a feature of organization. Evidently, the sayings were handed on orally within the community of *Thomas,* but the peculiar shape of the Thomaean tradition as we know it, in a documentary form, was achieved when an interlocutory structure was developed for the whole. The structure of interlocutions has disciples ask questions or make statements, to which Jesus is alleged to respond in the sayings that follow. A governing context is thereby generated for each saying, shorn of any narrative context (such as in the canonical Gospels, to which the Thomaean logia are usually comparable).

The interlocutions of disciples target our attention on the particular issues

Figure 16. Titus Arch, Rome. N.B. the trumpets and menorah from the Temple, destroyed by Titus's troops in 70 C.E.   Courtesy of J. H. Charlesworth

raised by contextual definition throughout *Thomas*. Didymos Judas Thomas, that is, Judas "the Twin," is introduced as the guardian of Jesus' words, and the first saying immediately makes the correct interpretation of those words the guiding concern of the entire work (cf. 1, with the superscription). In that strings of sayings are made to reply to the disciples' remarks, those remarks are the primary determinants of the context — and therefore the meaning — of Jesus' aphorisms. Prayer, fasting, and almsgiving (6, 104), radically challenged by Jesus here, are made key issues, as are right leadership within the community (12); the purpose of discipleship (18); entering the kingdom and finding Jesus (20, 21, 22, 24, 113, 114); the identity of Jesus (43, 61.2); the world to come (51, 52, 53); human, especially physical relationships (79, 99); and human government (100). The interlocutory structure of the document makes it apparent that a community centered upon Jesus as an enduring, interpretative reality is the fundamental presupposition and aim of the whole. Full separation from Judaism is intimated not only by that exclusive perspective, but by the absence of reference to the Hebrew scriptures, the dismissal of prophetic testimony as the speech of "the dead" (52), and the rejection of literal circumcision (53). It is no accident that when the disciples ask who Jesus is, he responds sarcastically that, in even posing the question, they have come to be like "the Jews" who cannot understand the whole of revelation (43).

In 64.12 the laconic statement is made, "Tradesmen and merchants shall never enter the places of my father"; it follows the statement of Salome in 61.2, "Who are you, man, and whose (son)? You climbed on my couch and have eaten from my table." The interlocutory context establishes that the thematic interest is in the identity of Jesus, and the key to that identity is that he is a single "one," integrated with his heavenly counterpart, knowledge of which Salome's very question betrays an awareness. But 64 itself is immediately followed by the parable of the vineyard in 65, which is closely associated with the Temple within the Synoptic tradition; 66 is the key text concerning "the stone that the builders rejected," the climax of the parable in the Synoptics. The association of 64.12 with the Temple in the tradition before *Thomas* is therefore evident, and that association makes sense of the term "places" within the saying. The architectural complexity of the Temple appears to be reflected in the plural; the form of the saying is an instance of an independent tradition in *Thomas* closely associated with the catechesis that produced the Synoptics.

A brief review of the contents of the earliest Gospels (including *Thomas*) as they concern Jesus' occupation of the Temple, makes it evident that none of them (as it stands) is what could be called historical. A given Gospel might be catechetical, as in the Synoptics (but even then, the tenor of the catechesis involved varies greatly), theologically discursive (as in John), or aphoristically interpretative (as in *Thomas*). There is no stemma of the relationship among the five, so that the "most primitive" is identifiable from the outset, and even if there were, our experience of the texts to hand would make us suspicious of any claim that what was most primitive happened also to be the most historical. All the texts are programmatic, and in that sense tendentious; none of them is historical in its governing intention, even to the extent that, say, Josephus is.

Yet the Gospels are historical in effect, albeit not by intention. In the process of the Synoptic catechesis, the Johannine reflection, and the Thomaean revision of traditions, those traditions, some deriving from Jesus and his first followers, are permitted to come to speech. Moreover, the Gospels refer back to Jesus as their source: the literarily historical Jesus is a fact of which any reading of the Gospels must take account, even if the question of the historical Jesus remains problematic. That is to say, we cannot understand the documents at all unless we can identify what they believe they are referring to (whether or not we accept that they in fact do so). That reference constitutes the literarily historical Jesus for a particular document, and the community of tradents that produced it.

With or without wishing to, those tradents were in the best possible position to know things about Jesus, and their documents are sometimes historically informative in spite of their programs. *Thomas* 64.12 does not wish to tell us that the principal issue in the occupation was tradesmen and merchants; its concern is the lifestyle of disciples generally. But the logion nonetheless tells us something historical. Similarly, Jn 2:15 has Jesus make a whip of cords to drive animals away, and thereby confirms what an approach from the concern for purity in the Temple would suggest, that it was trade in the outer court that upset Jesus. And the Synoptic citation of Isaiah and Jeremiah (Mt 21:13; Mk 11:17; Lk 19:46) quite clearly indicates an enduring interest in the Temple, not an explanation for its imminent destruction. Because the ancient sources often speak historically despite themselves, no method can be commended that attempts to remove any Gospel from consideration because it is more secondary than another on literary grounds.

Critical method must rather reject the misleading analogy of archaeological strata, and attend to the historical unfolding of meaning by exegetical means. Our first and principal concern in the study of Jesus is for what we must presuppose of him to explain the shape of a given text. Sometimes, of course, nothing must be presupposed: on occasion the Gospels may simply speak the language of folk piety (as is, for the most part, the case in the narratives of Jesus' birth). But it is difficult to understand how the Gospels came to speak of the kingdom of God as they do, for example, had Jesus not been concerned with the topic. Jesus' position cannot be known directly, but by means of the sources to hand, we can "pentagulate" his theology; that is, in a process akin to triangulation in mapping, we may infer from our reading of texts what his position must have been to produce what we read in the five rich sources that are commonly used. That course is unquestionably tortuous, but it is the only course available for the historical apprehension of Jesus.

If we press the model of pentagulation further, another consideration presents itself. No cartographer can map a territory simply on the basis of the data of a survey. It is true that the measurement of angles from various perspectives will permit him to place objects, but only on the assumption of a certain geometry. Triangulation is as dependent upon Euclid for the conception of space that it assumes as it is for the method of measurement that is its more obvious feature. So in the Gospels we must appreciate from the outset that if we wish to speak of Jesus in historical terms, he must be located in the space of early Judaism. It should go without saying that reference here to Judaism in no sense excludes an appreciation of Hellenistic culture, since the two were not mutually exclusive at the stage of Jesus' activity, nor were they thereafter. Any language that alleges Jesus' rejection or transcendence of Judaism should be rejected at the outset as an instance of apologetic.

There are, then, precisely two indices of Jesus as he may be known historically: (1) what may be said of him in aggregate as the presupposition of the canonical Gospels and *Thomas;* and (2) within a critical understanding of Judaism prior to the destruction of the Temple. Other alleged measures, such as his distinction or dissimilarity from Judaism, or the alleged primitivity of a given source, are examples of ideology masquerading as science, attempts to define the Jesus to be discovered in advance of investigation. As the Gospels are read, it is crucial that they be assumed at no point (and at no hypothetical level) to convey a historical perspective directly. Rather, we may infer the literarily historical Jesus to which a given source refers on exegetical grounds, and then further conceive by inference of the historical Jesus who presumably gave rise within early Judaism to that source and the others. Throughout, an attempt is being made to identify, insofar as that is possible, the historical performance of meaning, the consciousness that is called Jesus and gave rise to the transformation of that meaning into a catechetical program (the earliest version of the tradition that became Synoptic), and a collection of sayings (the source known as Q), which by a further set of permutations, combinations, and fresh developments became — in chronological order — the Synoptic Gospels, John, and *Thomas.*

In the case of Jesus' *mamzerut,* then, the sources of Judaism, literary and anthropological (insofar as archaeological study has evinced Judaic anthropology), have provided a plausible social reality behind the genesis of the birth narratives, as well as the other theories of Jesus' birth. In a recent book I worked the implications of that status into an account of his life.[23] What is involved in that case is not only inference, but an inferential narrative. The narrative form was selected because it is the sole means by which development may be traced; without tracing development there can be no biography, and no justice can be done to dynamic factors such as *mamzerut* itself. The result has been an uncertainty as to the genre at issue. Is my *Rabbi Jesus,* to choose a few examples from reviews and my correspondence, a historical novel, true fiction, creative nonfiction, traditional biography, human myth, psychoanalysis, or something else?

I can understand how this perplexity arises, because I share it myself. From inference, the only critical purchase available on Jesus in literary historical terms, I moved to narrative, the only instrument available for recounting a life. Inferential narrative is, as inference itself, a thinking behind the evidence to hand in order to explain it. Unlike an inference in regard to an atomistic passage of the Gospels, however, an inference regarding Jesus' life must at one and the same time account for the textual evidence to hand, the movement that produced those texts, and the "Christianity" that emerged out of that mix. Naturally, when the object is to achieve an inference with explanatory power, the

23. Chilton, *Jesus: An Intimate Biography* (New York: Doubleday, 2000).

standards of assessment are not "certainty," "objectivity," "bearing the burden of proof," and all the other clichés of positivistic historiography that still plague our discipline, even as we celebrate our alleged postmodernism. Rather, the operative criteria involve how plausible a finding is within the environment of early Judaism (in all its various conditions) as well as how suitable it is as an explanation for why Jesus was remembered in the way he was.

One of the determinative issues of Jesus' development turns on the amount of time he is given to develop. The chronology has varied considerably over the years, although it is surprising how many scholars simply accept Lk 3:1-2 as timing the death of John the Baptist. When he is placed in his own context, and within Josephus's treatment, an earlier date becomes more likely, and that has radical implications for understanding how Jesus developed.

The purpose of John's baptism should be sought not in the apologetic presentation of the Synoptics, but in the nature of his activity as compared to ordinary practices of purification.[24] It is just here that contemporary students of John have been most misled by the supposition (derived from reading the Synoptics as history) that he was a prophet with a recoverable message that explains his activity. Historically, his activity is itself as much of his program as we are ever likely to grasp.

John practiced his baptism in natural sources of water. It is sometimes taken that his purpose was to use literally moving water, but that is not specified in any source, and the waters of the Jordan or a pool in Perea or an oasis in the valley of the Jordan would not necessarily be flowing. Indeed, Sanders has reminded us that water from a spring was equated with naturally collected water by the first century.[25] Moreover, even if John did use living water by preference, the especial corruption of what was thereby purified was not thereby marked, as is sometimes supposed:[26] corpse contamination, after all, was dealt with by means of the still water of the ashes of the red heifer, not living water (cf. Num 19 and *Para* 5.1–8.11). John's baptism made no statement as to the nature of what was to be purified: his activity took that as being self-evident. John's baptism was however an implicit claim that there was no advantage in the pools of Qumran, the double-vatted *mikvaot* of the Pharisees, or the private baths of aristocratic groups such as the Sadducees.[27] He enacted what amounted to generic purification, in contrast to the deliberate artifice involved

---

24. See J. E. Taylor, *The Immerser: John the Baptist within Second Temple Judaism,* Studying the Historical Jesus 2 (Grand Rapids: Eerdmans, 1997).

25. Sanders, *Jewish Law from Jesus to the Mishnah* (Philadelphia: Trinity, 1990), p. 215.

26. See R. Webb, *John the Baptizer and Prophet: A Socio-Historical Study,* JSNTSS 65 (Sheffield: Sheffield Academic Press, 1991), p. 193.

27. See Sanders, *Jewish Law,* pp. 214-27.

in several other movements, sectarian and nonsectarian. In that sense, his purpose was deliberately antisectarian.

Inferentially, it might be maintained that John's baptism was driven by an eschatological expectation, not necessarily of a messiah, but of divine judgment.[28] Of all the statements attributed to John, the claim that after him a baptism of spirit was to come stands out as possibly authentic, and a connection with Ezek 36:25-26 seems likely. Whether or not it is, the anticipation of imminent judgment would both supply a suitable motivation for John's activity and help to account for his appropriation within early Christianity. But whatever his own motivation, and those of subsequent interpreters, that he acted as a purifier on the basis of ritual bathing is the most certain — as well as the most obvious — feature of his public activity.

Josephus's famous report about John in *Ant* 18 (§116-119) is a flashback, related to explain the opinion among "some Jews" that the defeat of Antipas's army at the hands of Aretas, the king of Nabatea, was divine retribution for his treatment of John. How Josephus flashes back to the incident, and why it is important to him, are issues that need to be taken into account as much as the purposes of the Gospels and their sources. In his own way he is as tendentious as they are.[29] What Josephus does not say, but the Gospels do attest (Mk 6:17-29; Mt 14:3-12; Lk 3:19-20), is that John had criticized Antipas for marrying Herodias, who had been married to his brother Philip. Josephus's account dovetails with the Gospels,[30] in that he gives the details of Antipas's abortive divorce from Aretas's daughter in order to marry Herodias (§109-112).[31] But Josephus also explains that this was merely the initial source of the enmity, which was later exacerbated by a border dispute that preceded the outbreak of hostilities (§113).

In fact, he says Aretas "made this the start of a quarrel," as if it were something of a self-justification in retrospect. No delay of time is indicated in the compressed narrative between the divorce and John's death and the start

28. So Flusser, "The Magnificat, the Benedictus, and the War Scroll," in *Judaism and the Origins of Christianity* (Jerusalem: Magnes Press, 1988), pp. 126-49, 148.

29. But then, why should this surprise us? Long ago E. C. Colwell pointed out that every historian ought to know that the "only road to historical fact, even to the most narrowly objective fact, is through some human consciousness"; *Jesus and the Gospels* (New York: Oxford University Press, 1963), p. 11.

30. So R. L. Webb, "John the Baptist and His Relationship to Jesus," in *Studying the Historical Jesus: Evaluations of the State of Current Research*, ed. B. Chilton and C. A. Evans, NTTS 19 (Leiden: Brill, 1994), pp. 179-229, 209.

31. It is — as we will see — an important hint that Antipas planned to divorce his wife after his return from a visit to Rome (§110).

of the war, but mounting tension is indicated. It is also noteworthy that Josephus blames the defeat on the betrayal by some of Philip's troops, who had joined his army (§114). So, the delay is long enough for tension to have mounted with Aretas, and for Antipas, however unwisely, to believe that his brother's troops would loyally fight for him.[32] Philip died in 34 C.E. (see §106), and this defeat is usually dated to circa 36. The death of Philip would have provided ample motivation for the soldiers to join Antipas, and a delay of some fifteen years from the divorce would perhaps account for Antipas's acceptance of their services.

It has been suggested that John died as late as 32,[33] but that seems not to fit the case, or any accepted chronology of Jesus' life. Indeed, the late dating of John's death has caused Joan Taylor to imagine a radically revised chronology of Jesus' death: "John may have been killed as late as 33 or early in 34. For all we know, Jesus' death may have followed quite soon after, or as late as 36."[34] That view comes, however, of accepting Josephus's association of the death of John with the tenure of Vitellius, when Josephus himself introduces the material about John as a flashback. That analeptic technique is as natural to Josephus as compressed narration is in the Gospels. Account of both needs to be taken in establishing the time of John's death, which therefore need not be placed immediately before Antipas's defeat, nor near the time of Jesus' execution.

Long ago F. F. Bruce warned about pressing Josephus's presentation literally:

> It may well be, as Josephus says, that some of Antipas's subjects saw in this defeat the divine nemesis for Antipas's execution of John the Baptist; but it is unimaginative to conclude that John's execution must therefore have been much more recent than the Evangelists indicate. The Pharisees and many other Jews believed that the mills of God ground slowly; if divine nemesis could wait fifteen years before punishing Pompey for violating the sanctity of the holy of holies in Jerusalem [here Bruce notes Pss Sol 2.30f.], it was not extraordinary that it should have waited a mere seven years before taking vengeance for the death of John.[35]

32. Commentators routinely argued that the Philip involved was not the tetrarch, but another brother; see, for example, A. Durand, *Evangile selon Saint Matthew*, VS (Paris: Beauchesne, 1948), pp. 274-75. The behavior of the troops (and of Antipas) as described by Josephus supports the Gospels' identification.

33. See B. Witherington, "John the Baptist," in *Dictionary of Jesus and the Gospels*, ed. J. B. Green and S. McKnight (Downers Grove, Ill.: InverVarsity, 1992), pp. 383-91; see esp. p. 388.

34. Taylor, *The Immerser*, pp. 255-58.

35. F. F. Bruce, *New Testament History* (Garden City, N.Y.: Doubleday, 1972), pp. 30-31.

What I find interesting about this disagreement is that in their opposition over whether to take the notice of time in Lk 3:1-3 as accurate, the lines of discussion represented by Taylor and Bruce nonetheless accept it as the *terminus post quem*. That seems to me odd, because that same reference to the fifteen years of Tiberius is also taken as the standard point of departure for Jesus' public activity. Luke is evidently compressing, and the compression extends to conflating John and Jesus. What if we were to entertain the possibility of a Josephan chronology for John, and dispense with the Synoptic chronology?

Bruce actually opens this line of investigation early in his discussion, with his remark that Antipas would have sought to divorce Aretas's daughter "after living with her twenty years or more."[36] "Or more" is an understatement, because the marriage with her was presumably undertaken shortly after the Nabatean involvement in violence following the death of Herod the Great, as part of Antipas's attempt to solidify his position. On Bruce's chronology, the marriage would have been nearly thirty years old by the time Antipas decided to divorce the daughter of Aretas.

Whenever Antipas made his decision, it was a bold move. It involved him in breaking with Aretas, and it inflamed Jewish opinion, bringing not only John's censure but even that of Josephus (*Ant* 18 §110). Nor was there any mystery about the likely Jewish reaction against the marriage; after all, Archelaus had run afoul of popular opinion when he married the wife of a *dead* brother (*Ant* 17 §340-341). Antipas is usually credited with more sensitivity than that to the demands of the Torah, and it is doubtful he acted out of simple passion. Still, it was a rash and immature act, and to this extent the suggestion by Christiane Saulnier that the divorce and the new marriage were over and done with by the early twenties is plausible.[37]

Saulnier proceeds on the basis that Josephus is better informed chronologically about Agrippa I than about other Herodians. Note her thoughts: "Ce récit laisse entendre que Hérode Antipas et Hérodiade étaient déjà officiellement mariés au moment du retour d'Hérode Agrippa, c'est-à-dire au printemps 24, et implique que le séjour du tétrarque à Rome était antérieur d'un ou deux ans au moins. Cette date présente l'avantage de ne pas être en desaccord avec la tradition évangélique, néanmoins le visite d'Hérode Antipas à la cour impériale entre 21 et 23 est-elle vraisemblable?"[38] She finds that it is not difficult to imagine Antipas visiting Rome between 21 and 23 C.E., and associates that visit with a

36. Bruce, *New Testament History*, p. 28.

37. See L. C. Saulnier, "Hérode Antipas et Jean le Baptiste: Quelques remarques sur les confusions chronologiques de Flavius Josèphe," *RB* 91 (1984): 362-76.

38. Saulnier, "Hérode Antipas et Jean le Baptiste," pp. 365-66.

supposed intervention on behalf of Roman Jews who had been exiled to Sardinia (*Ant* 18 §81-84).[39]

I personally do not see Antipas having the influence or the inclination to help Jews in Rome, so I identify other reasons for the visit below. That change causes me to place the marriage with Herodias slightly earlier than Saulnier suggests, although my proposal is in line with her proposal as a whole. I also depart from other aspects of Saulnier's chronology, which still tries too hard in my view to vindicate the presentation in the Synoptics, but it is still well worth considering as a whole.[40]

A reading of Josephus with due account of his narrative technique largely supports Saulnier, and permits a somewhat more specific dating. Prior to dealing with Vitellius (from *Ant* 18 §88), and therefore flashing back to Antipas's various trials, Josephus last spoke of Antipas in connection with the establishment of Tiberias in 19 c.e. (*Ant* 18 §36-38). Here, too, Josephus criticizes Antipas, because the city was partially established on the site of tombs, and he complains elsewhere that the palace there incorporated idolatrous representations of animals, which Josephus himself undertook to destroy (*Life* 64-69). Why, then, do we see Antipas in such an uncharacteristically trenchant philo-Roman mode, flouting commandments of the Torah in a way that could only have alienated his subjects?

At the opening of his section on Tiberias, Josephus provides an answer: Antipas had advanced considerably within the circle of Tiberius's friendship (*Ant* 18 §36). Having been educated in Rome, his contacts with the city were no doubt good, but it is unlikely that this advance was accomplished without an actual visit. Was this the visit Josephus refers to in connection with Herodias in *Ant* 18 §110-111?

There is good reason to think so. After all, his tenure came to an abrupt end when, prodded by Herodias, Antipas made another trip to Rome in 39 c.e. to plead for the title of king (*Ant* 18 §240-256). Indeed, Gaius is said to have

---

39. Saulnier, "Hérode Antipas et Jean le Baptiste," pp. 367-68.

40. Saulnier, "Hérode Antipas et Jean le Baptiste," pp. 375-76. She summarizes her own analysis as follows: "Hérode Antipas et Hérodiade se sont mariés au plus tard en 23; Jean le Baptiste a été exécuté en 27 ou 28 et il est plausible qu'il ait publiquement critiqué cette union. A la suite de l'affront fait à sa fille, Arétas a vaincu l'armée du tétrarque vers 29. Hérode Antipas s'est trouvé à Jérusalem avec Vitellius au printemps 37, après le renvoi de Ponce Pilate; la même année il a participé aux négociations menées avec les Parthes mais, par sa maladresse, s'est attiré l'inimitié du légat. En outre il s'était brouillé avec Hérode Agrippa, alors qu'il séjournait à Rome en 21 ou 22 pour intercéder en faveur des Juifs déportés en Sardaigne. En 39, son neveu l'avait accusé d'avoir comploté avec Séjan avant 23 et d'être entré en collusion avec les Parthes en 36 our 37; le crédit, dont jouissait Hérode Agrippa auprès de Caligula, avait fait accepter ces charges, justifiant la déchéance et l'exil du tétrarque."

personally exiled Herodias along with her husband for her ambition. Josephus opines that exile served Antipas right for his attention to the nattering of his wife. But her ploy was consistent with her marriage in the first place, and with the foundation of Tiberias, as part of a policy of establishing Antipas as a Herodian king on a good footing in Rome. She underestimated the cunning of Herod Agrippa, her own brother, but her influence was part of a strategic desire. That same desire had worked earlier, when her husband had returned from Rome to marry her, and the no doubt happy couple were ensconced in Tiberias. At that time, it only remained to see to the death of John (around 21 c.e., contrary to the Synoptic chronology and Saulnier)[41] to make her happiness complete.

John's status as a prophet derives from the tradition of Christian apologetics (indeed, from Jesus himself, to judge from Mt 11:9; Lk 7:26), but his activity and program within the terms of reference of Judaism made him a purifier. He was certainly not a routine figure, because his take on purity was both distinctive and controversial, but Josephus shows us that John cut a recognizable profile as a practitioner and teacher.

A reading of Josephus also suggests that John need no longer be dated within the Synoptic chronology, whose usage as a catechetical instrument makes it an unreliable historical tool. Rather, John was put to death well before Jesus came to adulthood (perhaps in 21 c.e.), during a period when Herod Antipas was emboldened by his recent foundation of Tiberias as well as his marriage to the ever ambitious Herodias, once his brother's wife. That suggests that John affected Jesus more deeply than a passing visit from Galilee to Judea for baptism (Mt 3:13-17; Mk 1:9-11) would indicate. Jesus would have known John during his adolescence, and the purifier's perspective on cleanness and related matters proved to be a formative influence.[42] Far from Nazareth, Jesus' *mamzerut* was in all likelihood not an issue (and Philip's identification in Jn 1:45 reflects the acceptance of Joseph's paternity). But if it were in his own mind, what might he have thought at this point? A hint may be provided in Tosephta *Qiddushin* 5.4: "*Netins* and *Mamzers* will be clean in the world to come, the words of Rabbi Yosé. Rabbi Meir says, They will not be clean. Said to him R. Yosé. But has it not truly been said, I will sprinkle clean water upon you, and you shall be clean (Ezekiel 36:25)? Said to him Rabbi Meir, And you shall be clean from all your uncleannesses, and from all your idols I will cleanse you

41. My other departures from her dating all derive from my decision to infer the chronology from Josephus alone.

42. See Chilton, "The *Talmid* of John," in *Rabbi Jesus: An Intimate Biography* (New York: Doubleday, 2000), pp. 41-63.

(Ezekiel 36:25). Said to him R. Yosé, Why then does Scripture say, I shall clean you? It means, Even from the *Netins* and the *mamzers.*" In my *Rabbi Jesus* I did not cite this passage, because its attestation is late and because my inferential narrative, although devoted to development, does not aim to develop Jesus' actual psychology. His emotions are on the surface of all our texts (in stark contrast to the presentation of great religious figures of other traditions, and even in contrast to Christian hagiography as a whole), and therefore are among the data to be explained. A step from inferential narrative and development into inferential psychology might indeed be desirable,[43] but I would not pretend personally to have attempted that.[44]

43. For the beginnings of such an approach, see A. van Aarde, *Fatherless in Galilee: Jesus as Child of God* (Harrisburg, Pa.: Trinity, 2001).

44. See also Charlesworth's "Jesus, the *Mamzer,* and the Dead Sea Scrolls," which is appended to his earlier chapter.

Did Antipas Build the Sepphoris Theater?

Richard A. Batey

Introduction: Waterman Discovers the Sepphoris Theater

In his personal notebook Leroy Waterman, professor at the University of Michigan, made this handwritten entry for July 16, 1931: "worked till 11 am on letters went to dig and found that the escarped rock was from a huge theater. Mr. Huckelsby called and staid to lunch."[1] This matter-of-fact notation gave little indication of the far-reaching importance of this discovery. Waterman excavated for two months during the summer of 1931 at Sepphoris (Hebrew *Zippori*), once the capital of Galilee and Perea. Following the death of Herod the Great in 4 B.C.E., riots centered at Sepphoris caused Roman soldiers to destroy the city. Immediately rebuilt by Antipas, a son and heir of Herod the Great, Sepphoris became the largest and most important city in Galilee, described by the first-century Jewish historian Josephus, who had lived there on more than one occasion, as "the ornament of all Galilee." Well fortified, the seat of government, and the royal residence of Antipas the ruling Roman tetrarch, Sepphoris was less than four miles north of Nazareth, in full view across the valley.

Renewed archaeological excavations at Sepphoris beginning in 1983 have uncovered a major Greco-Roman metropolis and are bringing to light more information each year. This new evidence is radically changing the understanding of Galilee during the life and ministry of Jesus and the beginnings of Christianity. One of the most important and controversial issues arising at Sepphoris concerns the date for the construction of the theater. Waterman discovered Hasmonean coins from Alexander Jannaeus and other artifacts in the orchestra of the theater and concluded that Herod the Great may have erected the theater and Antipas (4

---

1. Waterman's notebook is preserved in the Kelsey Museum at the University of Michigan in Ann Arbor.

B.C.E.–39 C.E.) enlarged it later. Waterman wrote: "That the theater was in existence in the reign of Herod Antipas there can scarcely be a doubt. However, there are several considerations that favor his father as the original builder of the theater. Two things emerge as very certain. First, it is scarcely possible under the circumstances to place the theater later than Herod Antipas. Second, it is equally impossible to think of locating it earlier than Herod the Great, since no Hasmonean Jew could be conceived of as builder of a theater."[2] To Waterman's conclusion may be added the judgment of S. Yeivin, architect and field manager of the Waterman excavation, who wrote the historical and archaeological notes for the Waterman report. "There is no other period in the history of the town when the erection of a similar building was likely, whereas Herod Antipas tried, no doubt, to ape, on his own small-scale, the large program of public buildings initiated by his father."[3]

Controversial Date of the Theater

Waterman's "very certain" date for the construction of the theater has been challenged and modified by subsequent excavations. In 1983 the University of South Florida began excavations of the theater directed by James F. Strange; Richard Batey was administrative director. Two years later the Joint Sepphoris Project (JSP), directed by E. Netzer with E. M. Meyers, also began to excavate at different locations in the theater. The results of these two separate digs produced conflicting conclusions. A brief summary of the various dates assigned to the construction of the theater is revealing and valuable. The historical significance of the date for the founding of the theater is determined in part by the intriguing question of whether the theater was standing and in use during the life and ministry of Jesus. Were dramatic theatrical performances staged by Antipas at Sepphoris, an hour's walk from Jesus' home in Nazareth?

When the Waterman report was published in 1937, Yeivin wrote: "The second building, which was probably erected by Herod Antipas at the time when he rebuilt Sepphoris as the capital for his residence, was the theater, fully described in the archaeological report."[4] However, the following year W. F. Albright, after inspecting the cut stones of the exterior wall of the theater, expressed the judgment that a second-century date was more probable.[5]

---

2. L. Waterman et al., *Preliminary Report of the University of Michigan Excavations at Sepphoris, Palestine, in 1931* (Ann Arbor: University of Michigan Press, 1937), p. 29.

3. Waterman et al., *Preliminary Report*, p. 29.

4. Waterman et al., *Preliminary Report*, p. 29.

5. W. F. Albright, review of *Preliminary Report of the University of Michigan Excavations at Sepphoris, Palestine, in 1931*, by L. Waterman et al., *Classical Weekly* 31 (1938): 148.

Figure 17. Sepphoris, early Roman theater.

Courtesy of R. A. Batey

Strange and Batey worked on the theater in 1983; the following year Strange reported: "A second square, just east of the trench dug in 1931 [by Waterman], cut into the rubble fill beneath the robbed-out seats of the theater. The latest pottery found in the rubble seemed to date from the second century, suggesting that the theater was founded or extensively rebuilt during that period."[6] In that same year, a similar judgment was expressed by Strange in a letter to Batey: "The material from the undisturbed fill beneath the seats in probe II. 2 yielded a small corpus of sherds. In field readings a small but consistent number (8 percent) appear to be of the Middle Roman period. It is possible that further studying will alter the inferred date for the theater. However, it seems simplest to report in a preliminary fashion that the date of the theater is more likely second than first century C.E. Further excavations and study are needed to settle the matter."[7]

In 1985 the excavations of the JSP led to the conclusion: "However, in one section dug into the foundational sub-structure of the theater, pottery of only the late Hellenistic and early Roman periods was identified. Herod Antipas, therefore, is the likely builder of this theater. However, dating the theater requires further studying and additional soundings will be made in future seasons."[8] Soundings made the following year tended to support this date for Antipas as the theater's builder. The JSP reported: "A tentative first century date achieved by the JSP probes into the foundations probably means that the theater was one of

6. J. F. Strange and T. R. W. Longstaff, "Notes and News," *IEJ* 34 (1984): 52; R. A. Batey, "Jesus and the Theatre," *NTS* 30 (1984): 566.

7. Batey, "Jesus and the Theatre," p. 573 n. 11.

8. E. M. Meyers, C. L. Meyers, and E. Netzer, "Notes and News," *IEJ* 35 (1985): 297.

Figure 18. James F. Strange lectures to volunteers at Sepphoris Theater, 1985.
Courtesy of R. A. Batey

Herod Antipas' building projects."[9] Then in 1987 the Antipas date for the construction of the theater appeared to be confirmed. "Excavation was begun of the
side entrance corridor adjoining the stage to the east. . . . Excavated finds from
this area confirmed the date of the theater in the early Roman period."[10]

After further excavations, the JSP in 1992 expressed growing uncertainty
concerning the date for the founding of the theater and took an evasive stance.
"A date for the construction of this theater cannot be definitely established. . . .
On the basis of this pottery and of various soundings and probes in the building's foundations and substructures, it appears that the construction of the theater could have taken place during one of three periods: the early first century
C.E., possibly during the years in which Herod Antipas made Sepphoris his capital; the late first century C.E., when Sepphoris again became a regional capital
under Felix (52 C.E.); or possibly as late as the second century, when there
would have been a much larger pagan population. In our opinion one of the
second two alternatives is the more probable."[11]

9. E. M. Meyers, C. L. Meyers, and E. Netzer, "Sepphoris: 'Ornament of All Galilee,'" *BA* 49
(1986): 13-15.

10. E. M. Meyers, C. L. Meyers, and E. Netzer, "Notes and News," *IEJ* 37 (1987): 278.

11. E. M. Meyers, E. Netzer, and C. Meyers, *Sepphoris* (Winona Lake, Ind.: Eisenbrauns,
1992), p. 33; see also M. T. Boatwright, "Theaters in the Roman Empire," *BA* 53 (1990): 190-91.

Figure 19. Sepphoris Theater from top of the fortress/museum. Courtesy of R. A. Batey

E. M. Meyers, also in 1992, questioned the date for the construction of the theater offered by Batey eight years previously, when he stated that Antipas would have built the theater as a centerpiece for his new capital at Sepphoris: "Batey of course, assumes that the theater at Sepphoris had been completed in Jesus' day (p. 570, n. 35) and enlarged by the second century C.E. At the time Batey wrote the article, J. F. Strange provisionally maintained that the theater was originally built in the second century (p. 573, n. 11), a view espoused by Albright long ago."[12]

As Strange continued excavating the theater, the date of construction became increasingly clear to him. In reports published in 1992, Strange stated the results of nearly a decade of his work on the theater: "We were able to determine with certainty that the founding of the main internal wall [of the theater] took place in the first half of the Early Roman period, however, there is nothing in our evidence that would require a date later than Herod Antipas."[13] To this judgment must be added his later conclusion: "The finds at the northwest side of the the-

12. J. F. Strange, "Roman Sepphoris in Light of New Archaeological Evidence and Recent Research," in *The Galilee in Late Antiquity,* ed. L. I. Levine (New York: Jewish Theological Seminary of America, 1992), p. 325 n. 25.

13. J. F. Strange, "Six Campaigns at Sepphoris: The University of South Florida Excavations, 1983-1989," in *The Galilee in Late Antiquity,* p. 342.

ater, then, tend to support our finds of 1983: (1) the construction of the theater was certainly in the Early Roman period; (2) it continued in use and was probably renovated extensively in the Middle Roman period, or between 70 and 180 C.E. There is some evidence for a major overhaul in the Late Roman, perhaps in the late third or early fourth century; (3) the theater was abandoned and filled in about the middle of the fourth century C.E."[14] In the same year (1992) Strange stated: "The works of Herod Antipas at Sepphoris included a theater that seated 3,000, a palace, and an upper and lower city with an upper and lower market."[15]

Z. Weiss, who also excavated in the theater, concluded in 1993: "The theater apparently was built in the early first century C.E., possibly in the reign of Antipas (4 B.C.E.–39 C.E.), as part of his building activity at Sepphoris in the beginning of his rule in Galilee."[16] However, the following year (1994), Weiss coauthored a book with E. Netzer in which they proposed a very different date of construction: "It was generally assumed that the theater at Zippori had been constructed by Herod Antipas at the beginning of his reign; it is now becoming clear that it was built at a later date. Archaeological soundings conducted at the core of the theater and its foundations fix the date of its construction at no earlier than the second half of the first century C.E."[17]

In 1997 C. L. Meyers and E. M. Meyers again expressed uncertainty about the time of the building of the theater: "The theater, parts of which have been excavated by four expeditions, seems to date to a period later than Antipas, though there is no unanimity of opinion about the date, and no public buildings of any great size that have been recovered from the period of his rule."[18]

Is there a reasonable explanation for these different judgments arrived at by competent archaeologists who have excavated separate areas of the Sepphoris theater? It may be helpful to note some limitations of the methodology employed by the science of archaeology.

Archaeology as Science

Archaeology of the New Testament world is a science, but it is not an exact science. During the past two thousand years most of the artifacts have perished, and not all that remain are recovered in excavations. The care and precision with

---

14. Strange, "Six Campaigns at Sepphoris," p. 343. See also R. A. Batey, "Sepphoris — an Urban Portrait of Jesus," *BAR* 18 (1992): 60-61.

15. "Sepphoris," in *NEAEHL* 4:1325.

16. "Sepphoris," in *NEAEHL* 4:1325.

17. Z. Weiss and E. Netzer, *Zippori* (Jerusalem: Israel Exploration Society, 1994), pp. 18-19.

18. "Sepphoris," in *OEANE* 4:530.

which the archaeologists and the team work (often using volunteers) are crucial for a successful excavation. The recovered artifacts provide the archaeologists with only fragmentary evidence with which to attempt to understand and re-construct the site. Once a site has been excavated and the evidence disturbed, its value is greatly diminished. Some archaeologists are primarily interested in the recovery of structures and foundations. Once exposed, these ancient structures may be restored and prepared for viewing by tourists, which in turn provides funds for additional excavations. Other archaeologists are primarily focused on the recovery of the chronology and social import of an ancient site. They nor-mally excavate more methodically and with greater precision. Consequently the dates they assign to various strata are as a rule more reliable.

Of the various artifacts discovered in an excavation, e.g., pottery, coins, jewelry, bones, and stone inscriptions, pottery has proven to be especially valu-able. Pottery is one of the most durable substances that people have ever made and has become an important key to unlocking the secrets of ancient societies. Pottery forms and methods of manufacture evolved over wide geographical ar-eas within specific time frames. It is thus possible to determine the approximate time in which a vessel or artifact was created. However, once a potter intro-duced a new form or type of pottery, its acceptance by other potters and the marketplace was not immediate and universal. The new form gradually came into vogue and became widely accepted until it reached its height of popularity, and then it began to decline as other types replaced it. Therefore, even when a pottery form has been correctly identified, there remains some uncertainty as to the precise date of its manufacture. Additionally, there is the question of the exact length of time a particular vessel was in use.

As with most research, there is a subjective bias that the archaeologist brings to the task of interpreting the evidence. This personal perspective may have initially motivated the archaeologist to pursue this field of study as well as the choice of the particular site to be excavated. In addition to obvious personal considerations, there may well be professional, political, and religious interests that influence the way the evidence is handled, understood, interpreted, and published in archaeological reports. Scholars and historians study these reports to prepare scholarly or popular interpretations of the site.

Construction of the Theater

Once the archaeological evidence for the date of the theater is assembled, a rea-sonable history of its construction may be discerned. The evidence indicates that the theater originally built by Herod Antipas seated approximately 3,000.

For a city anticipated to have a population of between 20,000 and 30,000, this size would be appropriate. As a general rule, a theater would seat approximately one-tenth of the city's population. The original part of the theater constructed by Antipas would include the stage, the orchestra, and the first two sections of seats, i.e., rows 1 through 12, the crosswalk, and rows 13 through 24. The stepped foundations for these seats were cut into bedrock on the north face of the acropolis. The archaeologists who have worked in the area of the stage, orchestra, and the east entrance to the stage agreed in dating the theater to the early Roman period, i.e., to the reign of Antipas.

Excavations in the upper seats or third section of the *cavea* and around the foundations of the outer semicircular wall fix the date to the late first or early second century. The evidence demonstrates that an expansion of the original 3,000-seat theater occurred around the end of the first century. As the population grew, the necessary expansion took place in this way. The foundations of the exterior wall of the theater that remain today belong to the outer wall of this expansion. This is a massive wall approximately 5 meters thick, constructed of large well-dressed ashlars and built with engaged columns, which provided both additional strength and ornamentation. It was necessary to construct this wall across an older cistern by building an arch founded on bedrock over the cistern. Without this arch, the large expansion wall would have seriously cracked. However, this arch still stands today. This outer wall is the wall that Albright dated to the second century C.E.

Inside this huge exterior expansion wall is a corridor approximately 5 meters wide. The interior wall of this corridor was the exterior wall of the original theater built by Antipas. Spanning these two walls, an extended semicircular vault provided the support for the third tier of seats in the upper *cavea*, i.e., rows 25 through 35. These additional rows increased the seating capacity by about two thousand. To maintain the angle of inclination of the first two sections of seats, it was necessary to haul in, fill, and cover this large vault connecting the original wall with the expansion wall. This is the reason that excavations in and around the corridor and its foundations as well as in the upper seats and *vomitoria* uncovered remains dating from the late first century. When the angle of inclination from the first two sections of seats in the *cavea* is projected over the third section of seats, the height of the expansion wall can be determined and how much fill was necessary to maintain the required slope in the *cavea*. The height of this expansion wall, the weight of the massive arch connecting it to the original exterior wall of the Antipas theater, as well as the additional fill pressing against the concaved surface of the expansion wall required that the expansion wall be strongly constructed. The remaining massive foundations demonstrate that this was the case.

Antipas Builds a Theater

An important question for this chapter is: Would Antipas have built a theater as a centerpiece for his new capital at Sepphoris? The answer is an affirmative one. Following the victory of Augustus over Mark Antony and Cleopatra at the Battle of Actium on September 2, 31 B.C.E., Herod the Great celebrated the Actium Games in Jerusalem. In preparation for this celebration, Herod built a beautiful theater at Jerusalem along with several other necessary venues. These games were celebrated every four years with elaborate preparations and large expenditures. Antipas was born about 20 B.C.E. and may well have been familiar with these extravagant celebrations. Herod the Great built other theaters at Caesarea Maritima, Samaria (Sebaste), Jericho, and even presented the Phoenician city of Sidon with the gift of a theater.[19]

As a young teenager, Antipas studied in Rome at a time when Augustus was concerned to promote the theater as a part of his policy of cultural enrichment. To the beautiful theater of Pompey constructed in 55 B.C.E. were added the theater of Balbus built in 13 B.C.E. and the theater of Marcellus, dedicated in 11 B.C.E. by Augustus to his nephew. Not only did Augustus support the theater, he attended and enjoyed the performances. Augustus even wrote a drama, *Ajax,* which he later destroyed. On his deathbed he called together some of his closest friends and advisers and asked if he had played well his role in life's brief comedy. "Yes," they answered. Then Augustus said, "Since well I have played my part, all clap your hands and from the stage dismiss me with applause." Augustus received a standing ovation as he made his final exit.

This is the cultural environment in which Antipas matured and received his education in preparation for becoming a ruler in his father's kingdom. When Herod the Great died, Augustus and the Roman Senate ratified Herod's last will and testament that made Antipas tetrarch of the districts of Galilee and Perea. After Antipas returned to Galilee from Rome and found Sepphoris destroyed by the Roman army, he selected this strategic central location with its important history as the site for his new capital. A beautiful theater as a central feature of this new city would have been a virtual necessity for this young ruler.

---

19. A. Segal, "Theaters," in *OEANE* 5:201. R. A. Batey, *Jesus and the Forgotten City* (Grand Rapids: Baker, 1991), pp. 93-100.

Khirbet Qana (and Other Villages) as a Context for Jesus

Peter Richardson

The Cana of Josephus[1] is no doubt the same site as New Testament Cana (Jn 2:1-11; 4:46; 21:2 with 1:43-45), but there has been some disagreement over which site is the correct site. Recent excavations have tipped the scales decisively in favor of Khirbet Qana as the location of Cana.[2] The site is on a 100-meter hill on the north side of the Beth Netofa (Battauf) Valley, across from Sepphoris (8 km. south-southwest) and within sight of Nazareth Illit (13 km. due south), at the mouth of the Wadi Yodefat. It was occupied from the Neolithic to the Ottoman periods, with peaks of settlement in the early Roman and Byzantine periods. Sometime in the Byzantine period a cave halfway up the hill was adapted to meet the needs of pilgrims, presenting a tableau of Jesus' water-to-wine incident.

The extensive literature describing pilgrimages to the Holy Land contains numerous references to Cana, some of which (both in the Byzantine period and in the period of the Crusades) presuppose that Khirbet Qana was the pilgrim site. Sometime during the Middle Ages, it seems, attention began to shift to Kefr Kanna, today's tourist stop northeast of Nazareth. By the early modern period both sites were known; in the early seventeenth century Francisco Quaresmius decided between the two sites on the grounds that Kefr Kanna had a church and Khirbet Qana did not.[3] It is likely that an important factor in this shift was the main road from Sepphoris to Tiberias, which passed by Kefr Kanna. Khirbet Qana, however, was not on any major road,[4] and even what-

---

1. Josephus, *Vita* 86.

2. Excavations have been under the direction of Douglas Edwards (University of Puget Sound) and Jack Olive (Pacific Lutheran University) in association with the Israel Antiquities Authority.

3. J. Herrojo, *Cana de Galilea y su localización*, CahRB 45 (Paris: Gabalda, 1999), pp. 115-20.

4. It has been argued that a major "Jewish road" went from Tiberias through Arbela, and thence along the north side of the Beth Netofa Valley to Cana, at which point the road split, one

ever minor roads may have served it earlier must have gone out of use by the early modern period. Beginning with the nineteenth-century investigations of the Holy Land,[5] scholarly opinion has shifted to Khirbet Qana as New Testament Cana, a deduction now being borne out by the excavations (begun in 1998).

Jesus' context within first-century Palestine can be illuminated by an appreciation of small towns and villages, both those associated with him, such as Cana, and others that might be useful for comparative purposes, such as Yodefat and Gamla. The present study presumes that a more sophisticated and nuanced understanding of the architectural and urban features of towns (using those adjectives generally) will provide a sounder basis for literary scholars who interpret the texts,[6] especially the social, economic, domestic, religious, architectural, and urban features of small-town life, as evidenced by places such as Cana, Yodefat, and Gamla. There are, of course, other relevant towns (Capernaum and Chorazin), small villages (Nazareth), and capital cities (Bethsaida, Panias, Tiberias, and Sepphoris). Cana is an especially intriguing case study because the Gospel of John presents it almost as Jesus' early center, much as the Synoptic Gospels portray Capernaum.

Towns and villages in all regions associated with Jesus might be drawn into this discussion,[7] especially where archaeological work has taken a broad approach, as in the Meiron project in Upper Galilee, including Gush Halav and Khirbet Shema.[8] In Lower Galilee comparisons of small towns with capital cities *(poleis)*, especially Sepphoris, are of fundamental importance, and comparisons among the four capital cities (Sepphoris and Tiberias in Galilee, Bethsaida and Panias in Gaulanitis) could help in interpreting some of Jesus'

---

branch going northwest up the Wadi Yodefat and the other south to Sepphoris. The claim is not borne out by any presently visible evidence today.

5. E. Robinson, *Biblical Researches in Palestine: Mount Sinai and Arabia Petraea* (Boston: Crocker and Brewster, 1841), 3:204-5.

6. H. Moxnes, "Placing Jesus of Nazareth: Toward a Theory of Place in the Study of the Historical Jesus," in *Text and Artifact in the Religions of Mediterranean Antiquity: Essays in Honour of Peter Richardson,* ed. S. G. Wilson and M. Desjardins (Waterloo, Ont.: Wilfrid Laurier University Press, 2000), pp. 158-75; P. Richardson, with C. Hixon and A. Spurling, "3-D Visualizations of a First-Century Galilean Town," in *Virtual Reality in Archaeology,* ed. J. Barceló, M. Forte, and D. H. Sanders, BAR International Series 843 (Oxford: Archaeopress, 2000), pp. 195-204.

7. M. Aviam and P. Richardson, "Josephus's Galilee in *Life* and *War* in Archaeological Perspective," in *Josephus, Translation and Commentary,* ed. S. N. Mason (Leiden: Brill, 2000), 8:177-217.

8. E. M. Meyers et al., *The Excavations at Ancient Meiron, Upper Galilee, Israel, 1971-72, 1974-75, 1977* (Cambridge, Mass.: American Schools of Oriental Research, 1981).

back-and-forth movements between the regions of Antipas and Philip. Comparisons with Samaritan and Judean towns should isolate distinctive characteristics, if any, of the Galilee. This chapter, however, has the limited goal of describing the character of small towns in the light of the new excavations at Khirbet Qana.

Overall Character

Cana persisted through several occupational periods with few major changes. It was a hilltop village, approached from a saddle to the north, whose plan was set by general considerations of access and topography (fig. 20). The plan was informal. Natural contours and slopes established its general layout, though some aspects of its plan are now partly obscured by a later trapezoidal wall that hides some hilltop features of the late Hellenistic and Roman period. Cana spread naturally partway down both eastern and western slopes, and somewhat farther down on the shallower north side. The steeper south slope — facing Sepphoris and the Beth Netofa — had no buildings until one reaches a plateau halfway down, where a separate small village was built later, laid out on approximately rectangular coordinates with informal *insulae*.

Nearby Yodefat provides an instructive comparison.[9] Its occupation period was much shorter, late Hellenistic to early Roman, but it had a somewhat similar layout. It was a hilltop town (but walled from the Hellenistic period to the Revolt of 66-74 C.E.), approached from a saddle to the north, with a late first century B.C.E. or early first century C.E. extension onto a lower plateau, which had an approximately rectangular layout. Gamla, in the Golan, was also a hilltop town, though its site was a steeply inclined plane that had an informally rectilinear plan. Thus, all three towns shared a kind of "quasi-Hippodamian" plan in some parts, not unlike the layouts of Capernaum and Chorazin, with their roughly rectangular coordinates that give an informal, late Hellenistic feel to some parts of the towns. Whether it is correct to refer to this as Hippodamian (or even quasi-Hippodamian) planning needs careful consideration.

The interpretation of Cana's hilltop, after three seasons of excavations, has become clearer but more complex. The Roman-Byzantine structures below the later trapezoidal wall (see further below) were (where investigated) arranged almost exactly due north to south, though on the slopes below the hilltop a natural contour-hugging layout and street arrangement was used. It is too soon to

---

9. D. Adan-Bayewitz and M. Aviam, "Jotapata, Josephus, and the Siege of 67: Preliminary Report on the 1992-94 Seasons," *JRA* 10 (1997): 131-65.

Figure 20. Cana from the southwest, across the Beth Netofa Valley.
Courtesy of P. Richardson

say whether the hilltop buildings formed a coherent plan in the first century, organized in *insulae,* or whether its generally orthogonal layout was simply a function of the hill's shape. In the two hilltop areas within the trapezoidal walls investigated in detail (the northeast and southwest corners), the layout seems more than accidental, though the site's contours might well have prompted such an arrangement.

A number of small towns, it appears, including towns whose character was set by the second/first century B.C.E., had informal or quasi-Hippodamian elements, though in no case the formal Hippodamian plans of Hippos, Dor, or Caesarea Maritima at the same period, or of Sepphoris and Tiberias at a later period. This seems to indicate one element in late Hellenistic cultural influences in the Galilee and Golan. While it would go too far to argue that there was a uniform late Hellenistic urban design throughout the Galilee and Golan, in rural towns and villages as well as in major cities, there may be some general planning influence in a number of towns, at a relatively early period, certainly well before the second century C.E. The highly formal rectilinear plans at major Roman sites more clearly draw on late Hellenistic and Roman urbanism, while the towns have a vaguely similar but much less clear influence.

Road Patterns and Connections to Main Systems

A main approach road, identifiable by a retaining wall on the lower edge of the roadbed, came into Khirbet Qana on the east from a small wadi; it doubled back and approached the town from the northeast (fig. 21). A second road may have come into Cana from the west (Wadi Yodefat), though the evidence is less strong. Both approaches utilized the northern saddle, where there was a public reservoir. At the northeast edge of town there appears to have been both an outer informal "gate" (between bedrock and a large standing stone) and a more formal inner gate (with ramp and right-angled turn); the area is unexcavated, so it is not possible to say from what period this arrangement derived.

Road connections with other towns are uncertain. There would have been a minor road west and north to Yodefat along the wadi, but the main roads of the Galilee (even before 70 C.E.) lay 6 kilometers away across the Beth Netofa Valley. Major roads connected Sepphoris with Tiberias and Ptolemais, and beyond those with Lebanon, Samaria, Gaulanitis, and the Decapolis. In the early first century, such roads were still unpaved and perhaps relatively informal.[10] Like Cana, neither Yodefat nor Gamla was on a major road, a feature common and perhaps important to all three towns. They were rural communities, though in all three cases within easy distance of one of the capitals. They were not exactly remote, but neither were they urban *poleis*.

Walls

Cana was unwalled for most of its life, including the early Roman period. Cana is absent from Josephus's list of walled towns,[11] and Vespasian ignored it in the Revolt of 66-74 C.E., though he probably marched right by it going to Yodefat. No ballista stones or arrowheads or catapult bolts have been found, though there are sling stones for ordinary hunting. Josephus's silence on military engagements at Cana during the Revolt seems accurate.

There are, however, meter-wide walls forming a trapezoidal structure on the hilltop (fig. 22). Initially we thought these were the walls of a monastery referred to in the pilgrim literature. Where the walls' foundations have been exposed on the east and north sides, they were poorly built, founded on dirt or

10. J. F. Strange, "First Century Galilee from Archaeology and from the Texts," in *Archaeology and the Galilee: Texts and Contexts in the Greco-Roman and Byzantine Periods,* ed. D. R. Edwards and C. T. McCollough, SFSHJ 143 (Atlanta: Scholars, 1997), pp. 39-48.

11. Josephus, *War* 2.573-776; *Life* 185-188; See Aviam and Richardson, "Josephus's Galilee in *Life* and *War* in Archaeological Perspective."

Figure 21. Access road on the northeast side of the site, looking south. The diagonal wall retains the lower edge of the roadway. Courtesy of P. Richardson

Figure 22. The northwest corner of the "Trapezoidal Walls," looking south across the hilltop. Courtesy of P. Richardson

rock tumble; cross walls were not bonded to the trapezoidal wall, and some were earlier than the trapezoidal wall, which was merely fill between them (cf. the first-century walls of Gamla and Yodefat, below). The large trapezoidal structure was in fact a shoddy late defensive wall enclosing the hilltop — and presumably the extent of the town during the unsettled seventh century c.e. In contrast to the north and east, the walls at the southwest corner were earlier and much better built (perhaps middle Roman period), and it is likely (see below) that there was an earlier public building on the southwest hilltop. The later portions of the wall were an extension of — and took their orientation from — the walls of the earlier southwest building.

One obvious fact should be underlined: the density of buildings in an unwalled town results from traditional social organization and principles of layout, not from containment. The tight clustering of buildings in towns and villages in early Roman Galilee was simply the way towns developed, and reconstructions that show dispersed buildings in a built-up area are likely to be wrong.

The walls at both Gamla and Yodefat, despite the impressions found in Josephus and the Mishnah, were built mainly at the time of the Revolt, under pressure of Roman attack, primarily by joining existing walls with short pieces of new walls to present a continuous front to the enemy.[12] Gamla's walls did not predate the Revolt. Yodefat's walls had a more complicated history: the hilltop, but only the hilltop, was fortified both in the Hellenistic and the Hasmonean periods, so that Yodefat was always a partly walled town — no doubt a main reason why it was chosen as one of the villages to be further fortified and defended at all costs during the Revolt of 66-74.

The northwest walls at Yodefat, where the Roman siege ramp was built, are of special interest. Walls from four or five periods have been identified (from Hellenistic to Early Roman II). The latest walls were additional fortifications built under the threat of Vespasian's attack, presumably Josephus's walls.[13] In places, use of existing houses resulted in a casemate wall. Deposits of stone chips formed a makeshift glacis outside the walls on the northwest.[14] Excavations on the east, southeast, and southwest sides disclosed simpler walls, 2 meters or less wide, in relatively straight segments, though on the east there was a redoubt and on the southeast there were towers, about 50 meters apart, projecting 2-3 meters from the line of the wall. Construction was of rough fieldstones,

12. See Aviam and Richardson, "Josephus's Galilee in *Life* and *War* in Archaeological Perspective."

13. Adan-Bayewitz and Aviam, "Jotapata, Josephus, and the Siege of 67."

14. In one square there were glacis in two different strata, suggesting that the defenses had been reinforced earlier as well, undoubtedly in the Hasmonean period.

with hewn stones limited mainly to the projecting towers. Though the towers suggest more carefully planned fortifications, in the very same area the wall cuts across pottery kilns, suggesting a very hastily built wall. At places on the west, the walls intersect or parallel domestic walls. In general, the walls of the southern plateau were built in one period, before or during the Revolt.

Towns and villages of the first century had no walls (cf. Capernaum and Chorazin). Yodefat and Gamla were exceptions that highlight the norm. Major cities or *poleis,* however, were walled as a matter of course. Thus Sepphoris, Tiberias, Bethsaida, and Panias/Caesarea Philippi were walled, if not from their foundation as capitals, then soon after.[15] Three typical conditions can be established: capital cities and *poleis* were walled; towns and villages were typically not walled; untypically, a very few towns or villages were walled, some from earlier periods (Yodefat) and some from the time of the Revolt (Gamla).

Agoras and Commercial Structures

Sepphoris and Tiberias had one or more marketplaces at least by the second century. By contrast, there seems to have been no marketplace *(forum* or *agora)* at Cana, or at Gamla, Yodefat, Capernaum, Chorazin, and most other small towns and villages. In the first centuries B.C.E. and C.E., market forces had not, by and large, led to the creation of a forum in the center of rural towns where goods were bought and sold, along the lines of a Hellenistic or Roman town,[16] though the economy could have been changing in that direction. Commercial activity was conducted, no doubt, from houses or from near the town's entrance — the "gate" as it was described in earlier periods, especially the Iron Age.[17] The popular view that there should be a formal prescribed space for commerce does not apply to small towns and villages; it is conditioned by Hellenistic and Roman patterns, as the terms *agora* and *forum* suggest. Several possible locations, where commerce might be carried on in Cana, can be identified on the town's north side, informal spaces at the edge of town, where access roads entered the built-up area. The likeliest location is in the northeast, where

15. Tiberias was unusual. Though the city had a major gate on the south between it and Hammat, no walls were connected to the gate until later; in the first century C.E. it was unwalled.

16. See D. Perring, "Spatial Organization and Social Change in Roman Towns," in *City and Country in the Ancient World,* ed. J. Rich and A. Wallace-Hadrill (London: Routledge, 1991), pp. 273-93.

17. Z. Herzog, "Fortifications (Levant)," in *ABD* 2:844-52; Herzog, "Cities in the Levant," in *ABD* 1:1032-42.

an irregular area could have served the village's needs well. Huge rough boulders, intended to define spaces, not serving as the base of walls, surrounded the area. This was probably a commercial area for itinerant travelers and townspeople alike. Presumably "shops" were in dwellings where pottery, glass, or other goods were manufactured, though no such shop-dwelling has yet been identified at Cana.

A shift to monetization is frequently mentioned as an aspect of the first century C.E. economy. Excavations such as Cana, however, have provided almost uniform negative results. At Cana, like other sites, many more Hasmonean than Herodian coins are found; relatively few Roman coins are found in first-century contexts. The claims to a highly monetized economy (which seems intuitively attractive) are not being borne out by the archaeological results from towns and villages of Galilee and the Golan; serious revisions may be called for on this question.

Street Patterns

The town core at Cana in the late Hellenistic and·early Roman period was a fairly densely packed hilltop in the parts excavated, organized relatively regularly. Streets and lanes are being defined in the excavations that provide a sense of how the town's circulation patterns worked (fig. 23). Around the hilltop, the housing on slopes on three sides followed the contours, with streets along the contours *(vici)* wider than the streets climbing the slopes *(clivi)*. Stairs are still visible in a few of the *clivi*.

At Yodefat it is impossible to trace a street plan on the hilltop because of erosion, though the plan was probably adapted to the hill's contours. On the hillsides to the east and the south, the street pattern was like that at Cana. When the town expanded onto a relatively level plateau to the south (late first century B.C.E./early first century C.E.), the "suburb" was laid out roughly on a gridiron, either because that naturally suited the shape of the site (east and west sides of the plateau were nearly parallel) or because of cultural preferences. Certainty is impossible.

At Gamla the *vici* followed the contours in a more or less parallel layout and were the main streets of the town, though there were irregularities in the layout due to the topography. The *clivi* were narrower and stepped, like Cana, because of the steep hillside. Capernaum and Chorazin had flatter sites, and as a result the street layout was more rectangular, with somewhat irregular *insulae*. The same was true at Sepphoris, even in the older (western) parts of the *polis*. It is safe to make two contrasting statements: (1) topography was a determining factor, shaping the layout of the town in traditional ways; (2) ir-

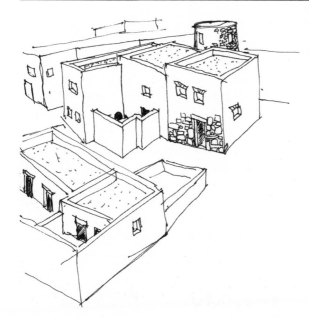

Figure 23. Perspective sketch of courtyard housing on the north, viewed to the northeast. Behind the jogged wall in the center are the *mikveh* and the doorway to the room with bench and storage cave.

Courtesy of P. Richardson

regular orthogonal layouts ("quasi-Hippodamian" plans) appear more frequently than expected, so that imported cultural factors may also have shaped urban plans.

Cisterns and Reservoirs

Villages and towns were differentiated from *poleis* by water supply. *Poleis* such as Hippos, Beth Shean, Ptolemais, Dor, Caesarea Maritima, Tiberias, and Sepphoris had aqueducts with a permanent water source and extensive communal water storage facilities to ensure regular supply. In most towns and villages, however, households subsisted on water stored in domestic cisterns filled during the winter rains. Towns may have provided public cisterns and reservoirs for the population at large, whether for regular needs or emergencies. Cana had a public reservoir (undated) in the saddle north of the town, at a level where it was of relatively little use except to water animals.[18] Some of the cisterns on the hilltop are much larger than domestic scale, probably providing a publicly available water supply on the top. Most of the cisterns at Cana were older bell-shaped designs; some of the exceptions were obviously later, such as a

18. Samples of plaster have been taken for carbon dating, so many of the features mentioned in this article as undated should soon be given dates.

large rectangular cistern near the lower village; the dominant bell-shape may derive from earlier phases of the town.

Yodefat had two public reservoirs, one on the southern plateau (first century) and another, like Cana, on the northern saddle (undated). The one on the southern plateau was a large rectangular pool, open, stepped, plastered, partly rock-cut and partly built, with remains of a rock-cut balustrade at one corner. This communal water supply may have been for watering animals, doing laundry, and emergencies, as Vespasian observed.[19] It was filled by runoff water from streets, lanes, and roofs. Yodefat's assemblage of cisterns included a mix of household cisterns and large public cisterns. Like Cana, the public cisterns were in the older parts of town at the top of the hill. Yodefat's cistern typology was richer than Cana's, with several styles and shapes. The reason for the differences in cistern typology is not immediately apparent, but may have to do in part with Yodefat's Tyrian background and Cana's lengthier occupation.

Industrial Areas

Cana had several industrial areas. On the eastern slope a bell-shaped plastered dovecote *(columbarium)* was hewn from bedrock (fig. 24). A second tower-style *columbarium* may have been located on the northern slope. Both *columbaria* were in domestic areas and typical first century b.c.e./c.e. forms.[20] East of the trapezoidal wall several natural caves have collapsed; some were probably industrial installations (perhaps an olive press, for example). Glass wasters have been found on the hilltop, suggesting a small glass-blowing activity. On the southeastern shoulder between two large cisterns was a two-room industrial installation of uncertain date — perhaps for dyeing wool or leather — with four or five vats or pools in each room.

The most important industry at Yodefat was pottery manufacturing on the southern plateau, where several kilns produced a pottery similar to Kefar Hananiah ware. One kiln was destroyed when Josephus's wall was built hastily right through it. Just outside the wall, also on the southeast, a natural cave held a large olive oil factory with two intact presses. The main industry at Gamla was also olive oil; a large two-press factory was located at the western end of town in a well-built, roofed structure near a wealthy residential area. There was also a substantial number of flour mills in the same general area.

19. Josephus, *War* 3.181-185.
20. B. Zissu, "Two Herodian Dovecotes: Horvat Abu Haf and Horvat 'Aleq," *JRASS* 14 (1995): 56-69.

Figure 24. Bell-shaped dovecote or *columbarium* on the east side of the site, with rock-cut recesses for doves.   Courtesy of P. Richardson

Economic Differentiation

Such a brief summary raises general economic issues. Cana controlled visually one of the most fertile areas in the Galilee, second only to the Jezreel Valley. The site was occupied through a very long period, with peaks of settlement in early Roman and Byzantine periods and smaller peaks in the Iron Age and the Arab period; the long occupation suggests a town whose location was prompted by natural agricultural advantages, probably crop farming similar to Bedouin practices today.[21] To date, however, there is no evidence of large flour mills, threshing floors, or traditional storage bins, as one might expect, but there is a large repertoire of basalt grinders of various sizes and shapes.

Comparisons of economic activities in adjacent towns or villages should reveal whether and how neighboring towns differentiated their roles by developing complementary activities. Cana and Yodefat, 2.5 kilometers apart, offer an excellent opportunity to add to our limited knowledge of such differentiations, so a trial comparison of the two sites might be helpful.

21. Soil cores taken in the 2000 season should provide information both about grain crops in the Beth Netofa Valley and environmental fluctuations.

	Yodefat (6 seasons)	**Cana** (3 seasons)
Olives	Double press	Household size only (to date)
Grapes	—	—
Pottery	Three kilns	None
Grain crops	Some terraces	Probably in valley
Sheep and wool	Numerous loom weights and spindle whorls	Relatively few loom weights
Dyeing	—	Major installation
Glass	—	Some wasters
Lime	?	?
Quarrying	Some	Some
Goats	?	?
Doves (dovecotes)	—	One certain, another probable
Other domestic animals	?	?

This table (which needs to be amplified by full information from the excavations to date) suggests that there was relatively little overlap in industrial and agricultural activity in the two villages. Part of the reason may be that, despite their proximity, they are situated in geographically different regions, so they developed appropriately different economies. This may be only a partial explanation, however; the implied picture suggests a more general complementarity of adjacent towns. It would be helpful to know — and could only be known from fuller comparisons that included other nearby towns and villages — the region's ability to function as a coherent economic unit. Such an analysis would assist scholars of the social setting to understand better economic exploitation (frequently claimed for this period in the Galilee), city-rural relationships, peasant social protests, and the like.[22]

22. Richardson and Edwards, "Jesus and Palestinian Social Protest," in *A Handbook of Early Christianity and the Social Sciences,* ed. A. J. Blasi, P.-A. Turcotte, and J. Duhaime (Lanham, Md.: Altamira Press, 2000), chap. 11.

Differentiated Neighborhoods

In both Cana and Yodefat, and less clearly at Gamla, major industries were located on the edges of the town, with a preference for the eastern side of built-up areas because of the prevailing westerly winds. Pottery kilns, olive presses, *columbaria*, and dyeing facilities were situated on the eastern sides in Cana or Yodefat or both; the same would be expected of lime kilns, glass blowing, forges, and other industries that produced smoke or waste products. Industrial activity shaped neighborhood patterns.

Housing neighborhoods were differentiated; at Cana a housing typology is gradually emerging. The structures on the hilltop under the Byzantine reconstruction of the town were mainly early Roman, with occasional small finds suggesting longer occupancy (Persian and Iron Age; mostly in first-century fills). The east and west slopes were occupied at least from late Hellenistic through early Roman and Byzantine periods (fig. 25). The walls of houses were reused continuously, with evidence of alterations but little evidence of destruction. These hillside houses were terraced, as at Yodefat and Gamla. For example, on the east slope a basement-level party wall between two houses had joist supports for the floor of the house lower down the slope. In these cases families in the houses higher up the slope used the roof of a house below as an extension of their living and working areas. Terrace houses in the three towns ordinarily did not have courtyards, so the roof served that function, more or less.[23]

Neighborhood and housing differentiation is only beginning to get the attention it deserves. Recent excavations and concentrated work will eventually illuminate the social character of the towns and identify social strata. The strong scholarly opinions sometimes expressed on the basis of a study of texts have rarely had adequate roots in archaeological evidence.[24] At Cana, houses on the less steep northern slope were larger and better equipped (e.g., with a *mikveh* and storage cave attached to one from the Byzantine period; fig. 26), and in most cases had a side courtyard. While we have no evidence of columns for a peristyle, we anticipate that as the North Slope flattens more, we will find still larger houses organized around a central courtyard. So we are gradually developing a three-item typology: terrace housing without courtyards, side courtyard houses,

---

23. Josephus, *War* 4.23-26.

24. For contrasting essays, see W. E. Arnal, "The Parable of the Tenants and the Class Consciousness of the Peasantry," and J. S. Kloppenborg Verbin, "Isaiah 5:1-7, the Parable of the Tenants and Vineyard Leases on Papyrus," both in *Text and Artifact in the Religions of Mediterranean Antiquity*, pp. 135-57 and 111-34, respectively.

Figure 25. Perspective
sketch of terrace
housing on the east,
viewed to the northwest.
The houses in squares
5 and 9 are at the top
of the slope.

Courtesy of P. Richardson

and central courtyard houses.[25] All the houses excavated to date were built of simple materials and according to typical Galilean construction.

Houses at Yodefat were equally simple, one or two stories, possibly three in the terrace housing. About the same range of houses can be distinguished as at Cana: terrace housing, houses with informal courtyards, and central courtyard houses. A remarkable frescoed house was discovered on the eastern slope, with a Pompeian-style decoration and a painted plaster floor. The top end of the social scale thus appears higher than anticipated at a rural site. The lower end of the social scale was a pottery-making neighborhood on the southern plateau. At Gamla the steep slope makes all the houses terrace housing. But there are still differences among neighborhoods, identifiable by size, finishes, artifacts, and location. A wealthy neighborhood to the west was better built:

25. For different typologies, see Y. Hirschfeld, *The Palestinian Dwelling in the Roman-Byzantine Period* (Jerusalem: Franciscan Printing Press/IES, 1995); S. Guijarro, "The Family in First-Century Galilee," in *Constructing Early Christian Families,* ed. Halvor Moxnes (London and New York: Routledge, 1997), pp. 42-65; S. Guijarro Oporto, *Fidelidades en Conflicto: La Ruptura con la Familia por Causa del Discipulado y de la Mission en la Tradición Sinóptica,* Plenitudo Temporis 4 (Salamanca: Pulicaciones Universidad Pontificia, 1998).

Figure 26. Squares 22 and 24, to the northeast. The opening on the left is a *mikveh;* inside the room on the right is a low bench, and on the extreme right the opening to a storage cave.   Courtesy of P. Richardson

flagstone courtyards, stone stairs, better finishes, and larger floor areas. Near the synagogue houses were smaller, without courtyards, and with fewer significant artifacts.

Comparisons with Capernaum and Chorazin are helpful. The first century C.E. housing at Capernaum was relatively modest, analogous to but different from the houses at Yodefat and Cana. Several of the houses had small central courtyards. In the southerly parts of Chorazin near the synagogue, there were two (later) *insulae,* where housing units were grouped around a large common central courtyard. (No information is available on first-second centuries C.E. northerly areas.) The clearest results to date are from Yodefat, where a spectrum of wealth and status has emerged. Further examination of these housing types needs to be undertaken before definitive results can shed light on Jesus' context in rural towns and villages in the Galilee and the Golan. Comparisons should include material artifacts and house styles in different areas within the same site, and comparisons more broadly from one site to another. Careful consideration also needs to be given to change over time in the towns and villages of rural Galilee. Were they contracting or still expanding? Were houses being abandoned in the first century or still being occupied?

Religion/Tombs

Religiously significant finds at Cana include a well-preserved *mikveh,* an unusual mock-Ionic capital from a monumental structure, stoneware (both turned and chiseled), pottery, and coins from the late Hellenistic and early Roman periods. The most important evidence is a set of twelve or thirteen undecorated tombs with between fifty and one hundred loculi, none excavated but all similar in style to first-century tombs (fig. 27). These tombs may represent the largest village or town family necropolis in the Galilee. The tombs were distributed in four areas around the main hilltop: southwest (5), southeast (3 or 4), northwest (3), and east (1). All were between 200 and 400 meters from built-up areas. All appear to be typical loculus-type Jewish tombs from the early Roman period. All but one (the one on the east) shared an unusual entrance design, with shallow vertical shafts (about 1.5 m. deep) without steps down or other means of access from ground level. This arrangement may have been borrowed from elsewhere and adapted to Jewish use; if so, it would represent an important variation derived from a nearby culture.

Though no decorations or inscriptions have been found in the tombs, several were architecturally embellished on the exterior, with evidences of walls and water installations, possibly including a monument or two, in rock cuttings on the bedrock. Forty-two loculi were counted, though the total number must be nearer seventy-five or eighty, since only about half the chambers could be entered. This assemblage of tombs represents a very substantial body of information about rural burial practices in the Galilee — much more than most other small towns and villages — and will become an important feature of Cana's contribution to knowledge of religion at the time of Jesus. The relative status of the families who built the tombs cannot be ascertained from a superficial examination, nor can we say whether the tombs were intended for all Cana's inhabitants or only for the higher echelons.[26]

Synagogues/Public Buildings

The trapezoidal wall, which enclosed an area of approximately 45 × 75 m on the crown of the hill with an orientation about 18 or 20 degrees east of true

---

26. This evidence may bear on the question of population (which on grounds of area might be calculated as about 2 hectares times 250 persons per hectare = 500 persons maximum). If there were, say, seventy-five loculi, if a body remained in a loculus for a year, if life expectancy was about thirty-five years, and if the death rate was more or less uniform, on a very crude estimate the tombs would be sufficient for burial of as many as 1,500 persons.

Figure 27. Unexcavated tomb with loculi on the lower east slope of the site. None of the tombs had any decoration.   Courtesy of P. Richardson

north (in fact, oriented directly to Sepphoris and approximately toward Jerusalem), was mentioned above, where it was suggested that it dated from the seventh century C.E., either because of the Persian invasion of 614 or the Muslim conquest of 636. It was not the perimeter wall of a monumental public building complex.

The southwest parts of the trapezoidal wall, however, were carefully built with genuinely monumental features. Its regular courses were founded on bedrock, and the wall intersections that can be examined were well bonded. This portion of the wall was relatively early, and probably formed part of the walls of a public building complex of three or more rooms. The main room (10 × 15 m) was in the middle; it had regular 5 × 5 m bays in the nave, with 2.5 × 5.0 m bays in the aisles, and its columns sat on three dressed foundation stones apiece (fig. 28). The floors in the aisles were plastered, but flattened bedrock in the nave. This larger room had a single bench of varying widths on parts of three sides. The smallest room (3 × 4 m), east of and higher than the larger room, had a single low bench on three sides, and probably on all four, with a floor of bedrock. An entrance area (3.5 × 5.0 m) with a monumental threshold was west of and lower than the large room, with several successive plaster floors. The juxtaposition of two adjacent benched rooms suggests a synagogue and *beth midrash*. A soft,

Figure 28. The small benched room (Beth ha-Midrash?), to the southwest. The doorway was later blocked up, from the seam to the rear corner; the floor is bedrock.   Courtesy of P. Richardson

chalky limestone mock-Ionic capital — decorated with what look like grape clusters in low relief — found in secondary usage as part of a later rebuilt wall, supports this identification, for the capital has formal analogies with capitals at Beth Shearim and Gamla (fig. 29). The date of the complex has not yet been determined; it was in use for some time, judging from the successive plaster floors, but there is little likelihood that it will be as early as the first century C.E. (fig. 48 on p. 248). If this Roman-period structure is a public complex, the much later trapezoidal walls adopted its orientation, suggesting that there was still occupation in this sector in the seventh century C.E.

In the northeast section where the trapezoidal walls were so flimsy, there was a pilaster made from well-dressed plastered stones with a finely carved rectangular capital in hard limestone, whose top surface was only about 1.5 meters off the floor. This hints at either another public building (originally we hypothesized a monastery room) or more likely a well-appointed house. No *voussoirs* and no matching capital have been found, so an arch that springs from the pilaster and supports a second floor cannot be confirmed yet. In the adjacent square a finely bossed lintel, perhaps a door lintel, was discovered. There were a well-laid flagstone floor and an entry room off the street, with a large bell-

Figure 29. The chalky limestone capital (analogies at Gamla and Beth Shearim synagogues), found in secondary use in square 1, was rolled out of place by robbers (the photo has been rotated).   Courtesy of P. Richardson

shaped cistern and another rectangular pit, the latter filled with first-century debris (fig. 30).

In the lower village, halfway down the hill, a cave complex with two *in situ* stone water pots (and room for four more) was venerated in the Byzantine period. One of the signs of veneration was Greek graffiti on the ceiling on several of the multiple layers of plaster. There may have been a church, perhaps with associated monastic structures, contiguous to the cave. The explanation of the character of these buildings awaits further excavations, and is in any case not relevant to questions about Jesus, except that this Byzantine evidence confirms that in the sixth century Khirbet Qana was identified as the Cana of the Gospels and Josephus.[27]

At Gamla there are one certain public communal building and a second

27. The veneration site was an altarlike construction, into which stone pots were plastered. Most of the front face of the altar was constructed from a sarcophagus lid on edge, with the flat inside surface facing out; this had "Maltese" crosses inscribed into it. Part of the bottom of the sarcophagus was found 40 or 50 meters away. The complex has four caves that communicate with each other; stairs and a tunnel suggest a deliberate processional way through three of the four caves.

Figure 30. Flagstone floor in square 29, looking west, with line of an earlier wall clearly visible.   Courtesy of P. Richardson

likely one. The well-known synagogue (17 × 25 m) was a multipurpose space with attached *beth midrash,* not unlike the proposed combination at Cana. In fact, Gamla's small benched room is the closest analogy to Cana's. There were columns on four sides of the synagogue, heart-shaped columns at the corners, variously designed capitals (one similar to the Cana capital), columns founded on stylobates on a beaten earth floor (also somewhat analogous to Cana). The main room had three benches on three sides, and five benches at the front; a small cupboard may have held Torah scrolls. There were also a nearby *mikveh* and *otzer.* A second large building has been excavated on the west side of town, with three square rooms side by side, connected with each other by doors, and with wide openings to other spaces in front. Several competing suggestions have been made as to its purpose: a wealthy house or a basilica? Its architectural form, however, is not villa-like (nor is it basilica-like in form). It was likely a second public building of some sort. What purpose it served is not at all clear (it had no columns, benches, or associated ancillary structures). It did, however, have refined moldings and larger spaces than is typical of domestic architecture.

No *in situ* evidence of a synagogue at Yodefat has survived, but there is scattered evidence of a public building, whether Jewish or pagan is hard to say: a monumental doorjamb in secondary usage, several column drums found in destruction layers, column drums and capitals reused in a Byzantine synagogue at the bottom of the hill to the north, a piece of architrave lying loose on the site (now lost). These could be the remains of a Tyrian late Hellenistic structure, though it would be surprising for its fragments to be found in early Roman destruction layers. It seems more likely that these are remains of a public building from the immediate predestruction period, perhaps a synagogue, at the top of the hill.

The question of predestruction synagogues continues to be debated. On the one hand, inscriptional evidence confirms the presence of "synagogues" or Jewish public buildings.[28] On the other hand, the paucity of archaeological data suggests a relatively limited presence of synagogues in first century C.E. towns. One thing seems clear: in assessing structures as possible first-century Jewish public buildings, we must avoid establishing a Procrustean bed that demands some combination of essential elements before the name "synagogue" can be used. There was a range of types and styles of buildings that defies simple categorization or typologies.

Architecture and Construction

The major architectural remains in these villages are housing, with the limited exceptions of some fine architectural fragments from public buildings; the most significant results of their scientific excavation and analysis will be to increase substantially understanding of first-century housing in the Galilee and the Golan. Houses were one or two stories; walls were constructed in rough masonry rubble with relatively few dressed stones even around the openings, and very few genuine ashlars. Only one very finely dressed lintel (with central boss) has been found at Cana, along with a substantial number of well-dressed thresholds and doorjambs, including several that are monumental in scale. Except in the lower village, the walls do not survive high enough to show windows; even in the lower village, the wall openings seem to be for cupboards.

There has been little indication of mortar, plaster, or stucco; the walls must have been bonded and finished with a mud mortar, all of which has washed away. There is substantial evidence, however, of plastered (and replastered) floors,[29] and flagstone floors (in most cases rather rough flags), though most floors were beaten earth, cobbles, or bedrock. No construction evidence has

---

28. See J. S. Kloppenborg Verbin, "Dating Theodotus (CIJ II 1404)," *JJS* 51, no. 2 (2000): 243-80; P. Richardson, "Early Synagogues as Collegia in the Diaspora and Palestine," in *Voluntary Associations in the Ancient World,* ed. S. G. Wilson and J. Kloppenborg (London: Routledge, 1996), pp. 90-109.

29. This suggests some lime-burning activity, though no evidence has yet been found.

survived of upper floors and roofs; they would have been made from small, locally cut wooden beams with sticks, branches, or reeds forming the basis for mud floors and roofs. No domestic stone beams or arches have been found, though the pilaster capital suggests an arch. A large number of roof tiles have been found on the hilltop within the trapezoidal walls (in contrast to Yodefat and Gamla), using several late Roman and Byzantine forms, suggesting one or more institutional buildings.

Conclusion

Few conclusions but several questions emerge from this survey, bearing on issues related to the study of Jesus. I offer provisional comments on those questions, though the answers have still to be determined.

To what extent were the towns of rural Lower Galilee and the Golan planned towns of a kind characteristic of centralized economies and centralized control? There is evidence for modified or quasi-Hippodamian plans, especially in the early Roman period, and this is just a little surprising in areas of Lower Galilee and Gaulanitis, where one might expect more traditional, informally laid out towns. This may suggest influence from Hellenistic cultures.

Have we exaggerated those differences (other than size and facilities) between the major urban centers such as Sepphoris, Tiberias, Panias, and Bethsaida, on the one hand, and rural villages such as Cana, Yodefat, and Capernaum on the other? The differences, which seem real and pervasive, are most persuasively seen in the small finds from Tiberias or Sepphoris or Panias (Bethsaida is less clear), which reflect a quality of sophistication and urbanity that we do not find regularly in small towns. The frescoed wall in a Yodefat house is a genuine surprise, for it fits more easily into the artistic and decorative vocabulary of a *polis* than a rural village. There are a few bits of fresco work at Cana from a public building; perhaps it is a Jewish public building.

Was there a substantial difference in the degree of "Hellenization" evident in the urban centers and the rural villages? In a word, yes. Hellenistic influence was by no means absent in rural villages; indeed, Yodefat's origins lay in a late Hellenistic settlement. But once "Judaized" (mostly in the Hasmonean period), small towns and villages were both more conservative religiously and more constrained in expressions of wealth and culture. That is to say, even though a city such as Sepphoris might have had *mikvaot*, as Cana and Yodefat and Gamla also did, Sepphoris had more objects that suggest diversity of religious affiliations and more wealth for acquiring objects that reflected those mixed elements in the population.

Did rural towns and villages have a planned economy? There were elements of "planning" perhaps in such features of town life as the expansion of Yodefat onto the lower plateau, where the layout seems rather more regular than might be expected of an unplanned gradual expansion. Cana seems to have no similar elements. In general, there is not much to suggest a planned economy.

What evidence is there for exploitation and for economic development? Two factors point to economic development: a substantial number of new towns in the post-Hasmonean period, and new areas of development within existing towns. Both factors may have been due to an influx of Judean settlers. There is little evidence of evacuation of houses because of economic exploitation. Those interested in questions of social protest and peasant exploitation will need to accumulate the data in helpful ways to address this question of the balance between development and deprivation.

What does the material evidence in villages and small towns suggest about the overall economy, and about dependence upon agriculture on the one hand and a manufacturing or industrial economy on the other? Most small towns were self-sufficient agriculturally, or had interlocking agriculturally based economies. Most Galilean towns probably depended on either olives or grapes, perhaps occasionally both. Most would have grown some root crops, and those that could likely grew grain crops. Adjacent towns may have developed differentiated economies, perhaps both in the agricultural and industrial-manufacturing fields. Since much manufacturing and industry was household based and since labor was episodic, most towns had some balance between the two forms of employment and occupation. The balance at Cana was probably typical of the balance at most other small towns: grain crop farming, herding of sheep and goats, wool and leather production, raising of doves, glass manufacture; these are different from but similar to what was found at Yodefat and at Gamla. More attention needs to be given to the complementary and interlocking features of adjacent small towns.

Is there material evidence of social differentiation and social stratification in the organization and layout of these towns, and how would this bear on a study of Jesus? Cana has hints of social differentiation, especially in the variety of the village's housing types, as at Yodefat and Gamla. Gamla's evidence is somewhat clearer, and Yodefat's fresco is important evidence for an upper class. Abstractly one might have suspected this and questioned a uniform "peasant" model. More careful attention needs to be given to this issue, for an accurate answer to this question would substantially influence the way in which Jesus' context is understood and the way his words were interpreted.

Is there evidence of socioreligious differences in first-century towns, or should we think of an undifferentiated "common Judaism"? If we can homogenize the data from the three main sites we have discussed, the answer is yes to both questions. There was a dominant "common Judaism," along the lines Sanders has suggested, though his picture needs modification: this common religious understanding included use in many places of a communal meeting hall or public building and access to a communal *mikveh;* wealthier citizens who wished to highlight their concern for ritual purity built private *mikvaot.* Some used stoneware if they could afford it. Not all Jews had a private *mikveh,* not all used stoneware; some had objects drawn from the pagan Roman world that broke the laws in the Torah. In burial practices, Cana followed Jewish customs more extensively than can be verified for other similarly sized towns.

In summation, Cana has begun to provide another touchstone site for study of the historical Jesus, one that, like Capernaum, is identified in the literary traditions as a place frequented by Jesus. While its evidence is not as stratigraphically limited as Yodefat or Gamla, like those towns it gives strong evidence of first-century life in a village whose occupation extended from the Iron Age to the Crusades and beyond. In the long run its evidence will take on special importance when seen alongside the evidence of other nearby towns and villages such as Yodefat, Shikhim, Ruma, Nazareth, and by contrast with cities such as Sepphoris and Tiberias. Through such comparative analyses, we may eventually be able to make more precise statements about some of the cities, towns, and villages linked with Jesus and the Palestinian Jesus Movement.

Postscript. A revised but abbreviated form of this chapter appeared in Peter Richardson, *Building Jewish in the Roman East* (Waco: Baylor University Press, 2004), chap. 4. The question of a synagogue at Khirbet Qana, discussed above, has been clarified since 2000: the public building in the southwest corner of the hilltop is certainly a synagogue, from the second century c.e. at the latest.

Bethsaida

Rami Arav

History, Location, and Identification

Bethsaida is located on a basalt extension, which descends from the Golan plateau to the Sea of Galilee. One of the largest mounds in Israel, Bethsaida is now about a mile and a half away from the seashore and a few hundred yards away from the river Jordan. Its ruins occupy an area of 8 hectares and are situated 30 meters above the Bethsaida Plain, also known as the Bateiha Plain. On a clear day, a magnificent view of the entire lake is seen from the summit of the mound. When the city was founded, sometime during the tenth century B.C.E., it was presumably called "Zer" (rocks), or "Zed" (fishing), if the enigmatic verse of Josh 19:35 can be interpreted in this way: "And these are the fortified towns of the fishermen: Zer, Hammath, Rakkath and Chinnereth." The verse describes the fishing towns around the Sea of Galilee in a clockwise direction and opens with Zer, presumably the largest of all fishing towns.[1]

During the First Temple period the northeast section of the Sea of Galilee was part of the Aramean kingdom of Geshur. The excavation finds indicate that Bethsaida was the capital of this kingdom. Geshur is first mentioned in the letters written to the Egyptian king Akhenaton, known also as the El Amarna Letters (fourteenth century B.C.E.). Apparently, during this period the Geshurites were but one of many ethnic groups organized as city-states, on the eastern side of the Sea of Galilee as part of the Egyptian province of Canaan. Seven different cities were mentioned in these letters. Claire Epstein suggested that all of them

---

1. See R. Arav, "Bethsaida, Tzer, and the Fortified Cities of Naphtali," in *Bethsaida*, vol. 1, ed. R. Arav and R. Freund (Kirksville, Mo.: Thomas Jefferson University Press, 1995), pp. 193-201. It was never suggested in literature before mainly because the magnitude of the settlement of Bethsaida was not known before the excavations.

Figure 31. Map of Bethsaida.

Courtesy of R. Arav

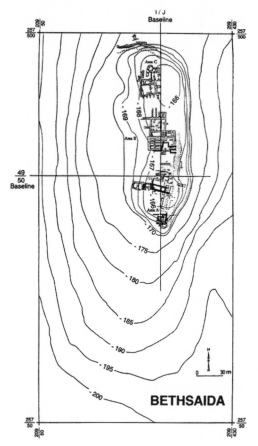

were located in the southeast region of the Sea of Galilee.[2] It seems that during the tenth century B.C.E., these city-states were consolidated into an independent kingdom under the name of Geshur by a Hurrian dynasty.

Names of two Geshurite kings survived in the Bible: Amihud (or Ami-Hur) and his son Talmai. The latter is the latest Hurrian name known to us in the Bible.[3] The Geshurites had a special and interesting relationship with the Davidic dynasty, and their involvement lasted at least five generations. David married Maacah, the daughter of Talmai, presumably as part of a peace treaty between the two countries (2 Sam 3:3). Already in the time of David this treaty

2. C. Epstein, "The Cities in the Land of Garu-Gesher Mentioned in EA 256 Reconsidered," in *Studies in the Archaeology and History of Ancient Israel in Honor of Moshe Dothan*, ed. M. Heltzer (Haifa: Haifa University Press, 1993), pp. 83-90.

3. See R. Hess, "'Geshurite' Onomastica of the Bronze and Iron Ages," in *Bethsaida*, vol. 3, ed. R. Arav and R. Freund (Kirksville, Mo.: Truman State University Press, 2004), pp. 49-62.

benefited him. The Geshurites refused to join the Aramean coalition, which attempted to rescue Hanun, the king of the Ammonites, from the hands of David (2 Sam 10). Scholars who investigate political marriages of biblical times indicate that the stronger party in such a treaty marries his daughter to the weaker one, to establish a loyal branch in the weaker dynasty, which will look after the interests of the stronger party in future generations. If this is the case, then the marriage of David and Maacah indicates that the Geshurites had a remarkably strong position in the region.[4]

In addition, in a royal marriage such as this the new bride would bring with her an entourage, which would include her court men, architects, and masons who would build her a new palace and court. If Maacah was not different from what we know, then she brought with her to Hebron and later to Jerusalem the Aramean architectural tradition. This is an important observation, which will be discussed subsequently.

The son of David and Maacah was the famous Absalom. After Absalom murdered his half brother Amnon, who was also the crown prince, he fled to Geshur and stayed there three years and perhaps married a wife there. After his return to Jerusalem, David (his father) still did not want to see him for four years. Finally he turned to Joab to complain: "Why have I come from Geshur? It would be better for me to be there still" (2 Sam 14:32b). In light of what we have found at the Bethsaida excavations, we understand this statement to have greater significance.

Bethsaida was near a lake; Jerusalem was not. Bethsaida was much larger and more magnificently adorned with lavish and great public buildings than Jerusalem in the time of David. Absalom died attempting to seize power and left a daughter also named Maacah, just like his mother. A generation later, King Rehoboam, the son of King Solomon, married Maacah the daughter of Absalom, and he loved her "more than all his other wives and concubines" (2 Chr 11:21). The reasons for this "love" were related, perhaps, to the political connection Maacah could provide — the connections to the Aramean kingdoms of Damascus and Maacah. Rehoboam needed these links to press his rival king, Jeroboam of Israel, because there was a lifelong war between them (1 Kgs 15:6). Maacah daughter of Absalom was the queen mother of the next king, King Abijam, the son of Rehoboam, and later the grandmother of King Asa. According to the Bible, she introduced "foreign worship" to Jerusalem. King Asa removed the "abomination" she made for Asherah by burning it in the Kidron Valley and deposing her from her position (1 Kgs 15:13). At the same time, he

---

4. See K. Spanier, "The Two Maachas," in *Bethsaida*, vol. 2, ed. R. Arav and R. Freund (Kirksville, Mo.: Truman State University Press, 1999), pp. 295-305.

used his old connection to the Aramean kingdoms in order to enlist them against his rival, King Baasha of Israel, who threatened the kingdom of Judah by building a town near Jerusalem (1 Kgs 15:17-21). The Aramean king picked up the challenge and charged the northern kingdom of Israel, taking all the towns down to the Sea of Galilee. The Israelite king discerned the message and removed the siege from Jerusalem. The Davidic dynasty was thus saved with the aid of the ancient Geshurite connections.

In the following period, we witness a typical archaeological phenomenon. While during the Hellenistic and Roman periods the historical documents of Bethsaida become more prolific, the archaeological finds turn poor and fragmentary. During the Iron Age the situation was reversed: the archaeological finds were abundant compared with scanty and fragmentary historical documents.

According to the NT, at least three apostles were from Bethsaida — Peter (the founder of the papacy at Rome), Andrew (the patron of the Greek Orthodox Church), and Philip. Early in the first century c.e., Jesus came to Bethsaida and performed some of his "mighty works," including the miracle of healing a blind man (Mk 8:22-25)[5] and the feeding of the multitude (Lk 9:10-17).[6] Additionally, Jesus' woes on Chorazin and Bethsaida are well known and attributed to the hypothetical Q source (Mt 11:21; Lk 10:13).

Josephus relates that Philip, the son of Herod the Great, inherited the Golan territory from his father upon his death in 4 b.c.e., and in the thirty-fourth year of his reign (30 c.e.) he elevated the fishing village of Bethsaida to the status of a city (the Greek *polis*) and renamed it Julias, in honor of Livia-Julia, the wife of the emperor Augustus and the mother of the reigning emperor Tiberius. Livia-Julia had died a few months earlier, and similar to many eastern Roman provinces where the emperor and his wife were venerated as a divine couple, the renaming of Bethsaida to Julias was an attempt to take part in the Roman imperial cult and to promote the attempts of Livia-Julia to be deified. Bethsaida-Julias never flourished as a town, never minted coins, and never played a major part in the historical affairs of the country.

Four years after its foundation, Philip, the founder of the city, died at Bethsaida and was buried in a costly burial; unfortunately, Josephus, our source of information, does not indicate where Philip was buried. Thirty-five years after this event, the city witnessed clashes between Jewish rebels led by Josephus and the Roman mercenaries of Agrippa II. As a result of this episode the city

---

5. J. J. Rousseau, "The Healing of a Blind Man in Bethsaida," in *Bethsaida*, 1:257-66. See J. M. Robinson, "A Down-to-Earth Jesus," in *Jesus and His World*, ed. J. J. Rousseau and R. Arav (Minneapolis: Fortress, 1995), pp. xiii-xviii.

6. H. W. Kuhn, "Bethsaida in the Gospels: The Feeding Story in Luke 9 and the Q Sayings in Luke 10," in *Bethsaida*, 1:243-56.

was partly deserted and ruined (Josephus, *Vita* 71, 72). It is important to mention in this context that Mk 8:23 preserves the tradition of Bethsaida as being a village *(kōmē)* and not a town *(polis)*. Luke refers to Bethsaida as a *polis* (Lk 9:10), and it seems that he was not careful in his definition of the place.[7] Bethsaida as a town named Julias did not exist for more than a few years.

Bethsaida was called Saidan and was mentioned in Jewish rabbinical sources. It was known as a town located near the highway to Mesopotamia (*Sifre Debarim* 80) that had a bounty of fish. Rabbi Shimon Ben Gamaliel counted 300 fish in one single vessel (*Sheqalim* 50.1). The emperor Hadrian (129-130 C.E.) was served pheasants caught for him at Saidan upon his visit to Palestine (*Kohelet Rabbah* 2.11). In the light of the archaeological finds, it is extremely interesting to read in the Mishnah that under the heaps of stones at Bethsaida there were pagan idols (*Abodah Zarah* 3.7). They did not, or perhaps did, know how correct they were.[8]

The direct literary sources on Bethsaida cease in the third century C.E., as do the archaeological finds, but because the place was mentioned frequently in the NT the site was never forgotten. From the fourth century C.E. onward, pilgrims and travelers believed they had been at the place where the apostles were born and Jesus performed his miracles. From this period until the modern age, Bethsaida is mentioned in pilgrims' accounts in every century. A thorough examination, however, discovered that none of the visitors actually had been at the authentic site of Bethsaida. An eighth-century pilgrim named Willibaldus described a church built on the house of Peter at Bethsaida. He spent the night there and continued on his way to Chorazin. This description fits the finds at Capernaum better than Bethsaida, but he has a totally different report on Capernaum.[9]

Starting in the nineteenth century, scholars and visitors searched more critically for the location of Bethsaida.[10] In 1838 Edward Robinson, the famous American scholar, climbed a nameless mound, known as et-Tell (the mound), located on the northern corner of "the Beteiha Plain" (today called the Bethsaida Plain), a mile and a half away from the seashore, and identified this mound with Bethsaida, following the German visitor Sitzen. In the 1870s

7. See Kuhn, "Bethsaida in the Gospels," p. 248.

8. R. Freund, "The Search for Bethsaida in Rabbinic Literature," in *Bethsaida*, 1:267-311.

9. E. McNamer, "Medieval Pilgrim Accounts of Bethsaida and the Bethsaida Controversy," in *Bethsaida*, 2:397-411.

10. For a summary of the research until the current excavations, see H. W. Kuhn and R. Arav, "The Bethsaida Excavations: Historical and Archaeological Approaches," in *The Future of Early Christianity: Essays in Honor of Helmut Koester*, ed. B. A. Pearson (Minneapolis: Fortress, 1991), pp. 77-106.

Gotlieb Schumacher, the German scholar and engineer, visited the area and questioned this identification. He claimed that "Bethsaida," which translates as "house of the fishermen," should be located closer to the seashore and suggested a ruin by the name of el-Araj, located nearer the seashore, as a possible identification for Bethsaida. From the days of Schumacher until 1987, there was no significant change in the research on Bethsaida. Some scholars tended to support Robinson, and others aligned with Schumacher. There were, however, some who suggested a compromise: Bethsaida at et-Tell, and Julias near the seashore. There were also those who suggested two places by the name of Bethsaida: one on the Galilean shores of the lake and the other on the Golan shores. These proposals originated from the Gospel of John, which indicated that Peter, Andrew, and Philip were born in Bethsaida that is located in Galilee (Jn 12:21). B. Pixner investigated this issue prior to the excavations and asserted a different compromise.[11] Accordingly, the Jordan River diverted its course so that Bethsaida once appeared on the Golan shores of the lake and at another time in Galilee. In 1987 the Bethsaida Excavations Project, led by me, began its work to locate Bethsaida. The excavations initially began on behalf of the Golan Research Institute, under the auspices of Haifa University. In 1991 the Consortium of the Bethsaida Excavations Project (CBEP) was formed, housed at the University of Nebraska at Omaha. Today the CBEP consists of eighteen universities and colleges throughout the USA, Europe, and Israel.[12] Our investigations and research of both contenders (Wilson and Schumacher) indicate conclusively that a level of occupation dating from the time of Jesus exists only at et-Tell. El-Araj is a ruin dating from the Byzantine period only, which is a few hundred years later. We also conducted a ground penetration radar (GPR) survey, in which we realized that at el-Araj there is only beach sedimentation below the single Byzantine level of occupation. Ultimately, we have found that Robinson was correct; et-Tell is the elusive Bethsaida.

The Geological Investigations

Now, after it was discovered where Bethsaida was actually located, a puzzle remained: Why is a fishing village located so far away from the seashore? This is basically a geological and geomorphological question, and to answer it the De-

---

11. B. Pixner, "Searching for the New Testament Site of Bethsaida," *BA* 48 (1986): 207-16.

12. Popular reports were published in R. Arav, R. Freund, and J. Shroder, "Bethsaida Rediscovered," *BAR* 26 (2000): 44-56. See also R. Arav, "Bethsaida" (in Hebrew), *Qadmoniot* 32 (1999): 78-91.

partment of Geology and Geography at the University of Nebraska at Omaha was called upon. In three years of investigation, carried out under the direction of John F. Shroder, Jr., from UN-Omaha and Moshe Inbar from Haifa University, the geologists clarified the picture.[13] Evidently, 5,000 years ago the Sea of Galilee was much larger than it is today and covered the entire Bethsaida Plain. Earthquakes along the Syro-African rift, where Bethsaida is located, caused landslides and avalanches in the area north of Bethsaida. These landslides dammed the Jordan River and later filled up the area with silt, created the plain, and shifted the shoreline farther south. The duration of these processes was short, lasting a few weeks, after which the shoreline was established farther south. Four major landslides occurred in the past 15,000 years; the largest at the end of the Iron Age dammed the river to an elevation of 70 meters. As a result, large lagoons were created in the plain. Remnants of these lagoons are still seen in a few places in the plain. A very significant landslide occurred in the mid–third century c.e., and consequently the lagoons dried out. The fishermen were left with no seashore and migrated farther south.

The Results of the Excavations

The Iron Age

Bethsaida was first founded in the tenth century b.c.e. on top of a rocky basalt extension, which descended to the lake and created a small peninsula. A very short and steep ravine marks the extension on the east, the lake surrounds the hill from the south and the west sides, and the easiest access to the hill was from the north. The city was built in two stages, the upper city and the lower city. The upper city was situated on the northeast side of the mound and consisted mainly of public structures: city walls and fortifications, monumental city gates, a palace in the style known as *Bit Hilani,* and perhaps a temple as well.

The massive fortification system was aimed at resisting the major offensive power of that time: the Assyrian battering rams. It consisted of a rampart built with crushed limestone and dirt and ended in a short, steep glacis. On top of the rampart, a few meters from the glacis, there was the impregnable city wall, 6-8 meters thick, filled with fieldstones of all sizes and coated with large and heavy boulders. A very similar fortification system was found at other Iron Age

---

13. J. F. Shroder and M. Inbar, "Geological and Geographical Background to the Excavations," in *Bethsaida,* 1:65-98; J. F. Shroder, M. P. Bishop, K. J. Cornwell, and M. Inbar, "Catastrophic Geomorphic Process and Bethsaida Archaeology, Israel," in *Bethsaida,* 2:115-73.

Figure 32. Bethsaida; tenth century B.C.E. city walls.
Courtesy of R. Arav

cities in the region: especially at Dan, Hazor, and Megiddo. The width and state of preservation of the Bethsaida walls, however, have no parallel in the military architecture of the period. At the northeastern corner of the city wall there was a large tower that measures 7 meters long and 8 meters wide. Every few meters there were buttresses and bastions, which protruded from the wall and added to its fortification. This system was used in other towns as well, but unlike other towns, the buttresses and bastions had parallel offsets in the inner side of the wall. This system created an uneven line of the wall and made the width of the wall vary between 6 and 8 meters.

Farther south of the city gate, a small segment of a retaining tower was discovered running in an east-west direction, which distinguished the upper city from the lower one. Tenth century B.C.E. Cypro-Phoenician vessels were discovered on the floor of this wall, which help date the founding of the city to this period. The tenth-century city gate has not yet been found, although there are many indications that it is buried under the monumental ninth-century city gate. GPR tests, a few seasons of excavations that have revealed the city gate complex retaining walls, and paved floor deep under the paved courtyard of the later gate, together with a stela in a secondary use in the ninth-century gate, support this assumption. A thick layer of destruction separates the two levels of occupation and is due, most probably, to the consolidation and annexation act of the Aramean king of Damascus, Hazael, in the first half of the ninth century.[14]

14. Finkelstein tentatively suggested that the city was founded by Hazael. I. Finkelstein, "Hazor and the North in the Iron Age: A Low Chronology Perspective," *BASOR* 314 (1999): 55-

A small gate fortified by a tower leads from the northeast corner of the city gate to a well-built, spacious plaza. Behind the plaza there is the palace, which is perhaps the most monumental structure of this period. The palace was built in the type known by the Assyrians as *Bit Hilani,* which is a palace with very distinctive features.[15] It consists of a closed rectangular structure without an inner courtyard or a patio. The entrance is always at the long wall, making the building appear as a broadhouse. Frequently, the *Bit Hilani* palaces were situated near the city walls, adjacent to the city gate. Because they were closed structures, there was no way to enlarge them by adding a new wing without damaging their form, function, and perhaps also light and ventilation. Therefore the builders of these palaces preferred, in many cases, to erect a new palace next to the existing one rather than enlarge the older one.

In all palaces there is a rectangular vestibule leading to the main room situated parallel to the rectangular form of the palace. A few scholars suggested that *Bit Hilani* palaces were adorned with columns; however, this was not a common feature to all. Some palaces were equipped with columns and others were not. The *Bit Hilani* palace of Bethsaida fulfills all the features of a palace of this kind. It is a large rectangular structure that measures 15 × 28 meters. Its walls, built of very large boulders and located near the city gate, measure 1.4 meters. Behind the vestibule, which is parallel to the facade, there is the main room, perhaps the throne hall. Eight rooms, some of which are well preserved, surrounded this hall.

Unlike the ninth century B.C.E. city gate, the palace did not suffer heavy destruction, and so it survived in new, renovated forms for the entire millennium. Among the spectacular discoveries there was a small Egyptian figurine made of faience, which probably represents the dwarf Egyptian god Pataekos. One of the chambers contained dozens of intact vessels. Behind the northern wall of the palace there was a Phoenician-style bulla, which arrived at Bethsaida with a certain official letter from one of the Phoenician coastal cities or perhaps from Samaria, the capital of the kingdom of Israel.

The Gate Complex

Thus far the ninth-eighth century B.C.E. city gate is the most spectacular and monumental structure unearthed at the site. It is located on the east side of the

70; see esp. p. 61. However, the dates obtained by carbon 14 testing suggest that the city was founded in the tenth century, a century before Hazael.

15. See R. Arav and M. Bernett, "An Egyptian Figurine of Pataikos at Bethsaida," *IEJ* 47 (1997): 198-213. See R. Arav and M. Bernett, "The *Bit Hilani* at Bethsaida: Its place in Aramaean/Neo-Hittite and Israelite Palace Architecture in the Iron Age II," *IEJ* 50 (2000): 47-81.

city, on top of an artificial rampart facing a steep ravine. Its position there was rather challenging for the excavators, not only because the easiest access to the city was from the north, and a gate in the east was highly unexpected, but also because prior to the excavations a high heap of dirt covered the gate and made the place the highest spot of the entire mound. It seemed rather inconceivable that a gate would be located at this spot. During the excavations, it became apparent that the heap was created by the destruction caused by the Assyrian soldiers. This heap was used during the Roman period as a podium to erect a temple (as we shall see).

The gate consists of two elements, an external gate and an internal gate. We investigated the external gate only very briefly. It consists of a tower that measures 10 × 8 meters, which is probably one of two towers flanking the entryway. A plaza of 30 meters separates the two gates. The well-preserved plaza was paved in large basalt flagstones — which show signs of erosion created by many years of walking — with small stones filling the gaps.

The inner gate was of the type known as "the Four Chamber Gate." It is the largest and best preserved of its kind ever found in Israel. It measures 17.5 × 35 meters and is preserved to an elevation of 3 meters. It is built of partly dressed basalt stones, plastered in red and covered with whitewash. The upper stories (two or three) were built out of large, clay, sun-dried bricks, which were also plastered and whitewashed. When the gate stood in its glorious days during the ninth and eighth centuries, the dominating color was plain white; nothing of the black basalt core was seen to the outside. This gate consists of two strong towers (10 × 6 m.) flanking a flagstone entryway, with four large chambers behind it. There were no traces of any rooms in the first floor of the tower. In front of the towers was a low bench used as the seat of the court, perhaps, by the elders of the city.

The High Places

Two deep niches were built in the two towers of the gate. The southern niche contained a high place in the shape of a high shelf. It demonstrates very vividly the biblical rule about the high place preferred by God for his worship (Lev 21:23).

The northern niche contained a surprise, one which archaeologists rarely come across. It contained the best-preserved high place ever discovered. The high place was built with basalt stones and was plastered and whitewashed like the rest of the gate. It is 2.1 meters long and 1.58 meters wide. Two steps lead to the top of the high place where a dressed basalt basin, sunken in the high place, was discovered. Behind the basin there was a decorated stela.

The stela was not in its original place. It was found destroyed and scattered in five large pieces along the altar. The top of the stela was found upside down near the foot of the high place. Evidently this destruction was caused by a deliberate, violent action of the Assyrian soldiers. There is perhaps nothing better to illustrate Lam 4:1 ("How the gold has grown dim, how the pure gold is changed! The sacred stones lie scattered at the head of every street") than what lay before the eyes of the excavators. Because the stela covered the basin, the finds inside the basin were sealed since the time of the destruction and may perfectly help to date the destruction. Two perforated, tripod cups known as incense burners were found there. They date to the second half of the eighth century B.C.E. and confirm our assumption that the gate was destroyed in 734 by the Assyrian king Tiglath-pileser III.

Four other stelae were discovered at the gate. They were all made of basalt stones and bear no icons. They all measure about 1.2 × 0.5 × 25.0 meters. One stela was discovered at the courtyard, which leads to the entrance opposite the northern tower; two were found on both sides of the entrance, and one was found behind the gate inside the city. The stelae at the entrance were all "beheaded" (possibly due to the violent Assyrian military actions).

Another high place was discovered at the southern end of the south tower. This portion was built in haste in the latter days of the city, close to the time of the Assyrian conquest. The high place contained three steps leading to a shallow podium, and nothing was found in and around this high place. The construction of it was in connection with the construction of an external wall built on the pavement to reinforce the gate against the assault of the Assyrians.

The Threshold

The threshold is built of large and dressed stones; it is located 1.5 meters inside the niches. In the center of the threshold is a dressed, semicircular stop-stone. In its center there are traces of the wooden door. The door's pivots were 30 centimeters below the threshold to prevent it from being uprooted. Nothing of the pivots was preserved; this part of the door was completely burnt. Traces of the oak wooden doors were found carbonated near the threshold.

The Hall of the Gate

The threshold was built 30 centimeters above the floor of the corridor that connects the entrance to the exit. This is presumably the "Hall of the Gate" mentioned in Ezek 40:8-9. The hall was meticulously paved and bears traces of erosion created by long usage. It is noteworthy that unlike pavements dated much later, there are no traces of wheels on the pavement, which would indicate that chariots and wagons were not frequently used in the city. A 25-centimeter niche alongside the walls of the hall bear witness to wooden beams that were installed into the walls and provided flexibility in case of earthquakes. We did not observe any damage resulting from earthquakes, as we have seen elsewhere where this technique was not in use.

Chamber 1 measures 10.70 × 3.65 meters and was partly destroyed by a modern Syrian military trench dug in the 1950s and 1960s. Very few finds were discovered in this chamber. The walls separating the chambers are extremely thick (2.5 m.).

Chamber 2 — identical in size to chamber 1 — was used for different purposes. A brick wall was built next to its threshold and its floor was plastered. Traces of grain prints on the plaster testify that the room was used as a granary. Similar to the rest of the gate, the chamber burnt to ashes during the Assyrian conquest. Carbonated oak beams, which came from the ceiling, were found on the floor.

Chamber 3 measures 10 × 3.65 meters and served as a granary as well. One ton of carbonated pure barley, without any other mixed grain, was found in the room. Our attempts to find burnt insects in the grain, which would help us determine the season of the destruction, were not successful. No remains of insects were found, nor were remains of other grain. The harvest of this barley was clean and pure.

Chamber 4 was identical in size to chamber 3. It contained a thick level of ash and a large amount of broken pottery, a small portion of grain, and about fifteen iron arrowheads that witnessed the last battle the Geshurites fought for independence. In addition to these finds, remains of ritual vessels, such as incense burners and a jug bearing an inscription "in the name of" followed by an ankh symbol design (perhaps the moon god), indicate that the purpose of chamber 4 was to contain the offering vessels from the high place at the gate.

Behind the gate a stela was found next to a long bench or a high place and a paved rampart, which descended to the floor of the area behind the gate. This was perhaps a large high place used for large offerings. Traces of fire were all over the rampart and may derive from the Assyrian assault.

The Decorated Stela and the Worship of the Moon God

Similar to the other stelae, also made of basalt stone, the decorated stela is 115 centimeters high and 59 centimeters wide and 31 centimeters thick, and describes in a high relief a very schematic figure with concave limbs wearing a bull's head and equipped with a dagger. A line across the width of the body connects the figure to the frame. The bull is depicted coarsely, but very explicitly, and bears very long horns, which recall the crescent of the moon. Four projections are seen near the "chest" of the figure.

Only three stelae with similar depiction exist. Two were found in south Hauran and one was found in south Turkey. In the Hauranian stelae the sun disk is seen between the horns of the bull. Other similar works on other materials show the bull-headed figure on a high place or on a standard. A very interesting parallel is seen on a bronze incense burner from a private, unknown origin. It shows, in addition to the bull-headed figure, the moon, the sun, a snake, and a round object divided into four. The Swiss archaeologist Othmar Keel suggested that the bull-headed figure is the image of the moon god. Keel maintains that Mesopotamian texts refer to the moon god sometimes as a bull. Therefore the moon god was worshiped on the northern niche of the gate of Bethsaida.[16] What his name was in the Geshurite Aramean dialect is still unknown. "Sin" was the Akkadian name of this god. The main Aramean god was Hadad. Whether he identified with Hadad or had another name is a subject for further research and discussion.

The significance of this discovery of the moon god at Bethsaida cannot be exaggerated. Moon god worship was one of the most popular cults in Mesopotamia. Two centers were particularly famous for it: one in the city of Ur in lower Mesopotamia, and the other in Haran in upper Mesopotamia. The moon god was the main character in the creation stories of Mesopotamia. His worshipers were puzzled over the question of creation and the problem of what came first and how the universe was created. They concluded that darkness was the primeval situation, and the moon god, as the god of darkness, was the first and therefore the great creator of the universe. He (the moon god was male) also created the sun, which is why it appears between its crescents in the Hauranian stelae. This theology had a significant influence on the religion of ancient Israel, and we observe its impact in theology and liturgy. It was commonly believed that the center in Haran radiated its influence on Jerusalem. Today, with the discovery of a moon god worship center at Bethsaida, it seems reasonable to

---

16. M. Bernett and O. Keel, *Mond, Stier und Kult am Stadttor. Die Stele von Betsaida (et Tell)*, OBO 161 (Freiburg: Universitätsverlag; Göttingen: Vandenhoeck & Ruprecht, 1998).

Figure 33. Moon god.
Courtesy of R. Arav

suggest that Bethsaida was among a few other mediators of this cult and religion. The Geshurite involvement in the Davidic dynasty may have contributed a great deal to this influence. We have seen above how this involvement may have had an influence on the palace of Solomon; now we observe it working in religion.

The *Bit Hilani* palace was altered during this period and the period following the Assyrian conquest. The main hall was divided into two separate halls, and a thick wall was built in the facade of the palace, so its function was presumably altered. Only a few written documents were found in the excavations. An ostracon bearing the name AKIBA (the Aramaic form of Jacob) was found that dates to the eighth century B.C.E. Another fragment shows two letters only, and an incision on a handle carries the name MAKY, which is the shortening of the name Michiahu. In another area, a handle with a stamp carrying the name ZECHARIO was found. The same stamp was found in Tel Dan a few years ago. A. Biran has suggested that this name can be identified with Zacharia, the son of Jeroboam II, who reigned over Israel only six months. Royal stamps, however, always bear a title, which is absent in this seal.

Figure 34. The ancient entrance to Dan. The *byt dwd* inscription was found to the right of the three visitors.   Courtesy of A. Biran

Bethsaida in the Time of Jesus

In 734 B.C.E., Tiglath-pileser III stormed the Near East and conquered the kingdom of Aram, Damascus, the Golan, Galilee, and Gilead. His conquest brought destruction to all the strong, fortified cities in this area. The destruction in Bethsaida did not bring an end to the settlement but certainly reduced it drastically. The city never rose again to the same position it had. The Assyrians moved the capital of the region farther east, creating a new administrative center — Pahva — and its capital, Ashtarot Karnaim, which is located on the main highway, also called the King's Highway, between Damascus and Rabbat Ammon, which is about 40 kilometers east of Bethsaida.

The city gate of Bethsaida was burnt by the Assyrians. Its second and third floors collapsed into the first story and helped to preserve it very well. The gate was never rebuilt. The palace was altered, and its rooms were blocked. Simple structures were built on the big plaza in front of the palace. Assyrian cylinder seals and some vessels testify that there was still some administrative use for the structure.

The Persian period saw some revival when compared to the previous one.

Figure 35. Reconstruction of Hellenistic house, Area B; Bethsaida. Courtesy of R. Arav

Some new houses were built on the foundation of the old ones, which penetrated from the ground. Cylinder seals and other glass seals are witness to the role the rural settlement played in the Persian administration.

A meaningful change occurred only with the Hellenistic era. The new markets in Greece and Asia Minor opened new opportunities for the merchants in the Phoenician coastal cities. Their prosperity brought about development and expansion of the Phoenician hinterland.[17] The new settlers of Bethsaida were either Phoenicians or affiliated with the Phoenician commerce and trade, as the abundance of Phoenician coins and pottery testifies. The change between the Egyptian-based Ptolemaic regime and the Syrian Seleucid regime in 200 B.C.E. further contributed to the prosperity of Bethsaida. The number of Seleucid coins, which date from the first half of the second century B.C.E., is the highest found at the site.

The excavations reveal a residential quarter with some private homes. The houses were built in a very simple style and in a single ground plan. In the center of the house there was a spacious courtyard surrounded by some rooms. The kitchen was built on the east side of the courtyard. At the north was the dining room, and the bedrooms were probably on the second floor. The courtyard was paved, but the difference between the domestic character of the Hellenistic-Roman period and the royal Iron Age was obvious. In most cases

17. G. E. Markoe, *Phoenicians* (Los Angeles: University of California Press, 2000), pp. 63-67.

the older and better-constructed pavement survived longer than the pavement made hundreds of years later. The private homes had, almost as a rule, walls of 70 centimeters, which, in places where it was possible, were placed over older foundations. We called one of these homes "the Fisherman's House" because of the plethora of fishing implements discovered there. Among the finds there were lead, fishing-net weights, anchors, needles, and fishhooks. A most interesting discovery was a fishhook that had not been bent, which testifies to a small fishing gear industry.

North of this house we discovered another house, which we called the "Wine Maker's House." In addition to the fishing gear, there was also a wine cellar, as well as pruning hooks, which indicate the profession of the landlord. A small, paved segment of a street was found just east of this house and the remains of another house. South of the Fisherman's House, situated on the Iron Age palace, there were remains of another house. This house, unfortunately, was partly destroyed by the modern Syrian military earthworks. It is noteworthy that the back wall of this house was the ancient city wall, which stood there since the tenth century B.C.E. The city wall was in use in this area for longer than a millennium. There were attempts during the Roman period to renovate it. In the south, a 2-meter-wide segment was built over the ancient city wall, and next to it there were remains of a small tower.

The conquest of Galilee, Gaulanitis, and Hauranitis by Alexander Jannaeus in 84-83 B.C.E. followed a major change in the life of these districts. The local population was either converted to Judaism or was altogether "switched" to Jewish; from that time and for several centuries the population remained Jewish. This switch meant a change in local and distant trade and orientation. Phoenician coins were replaced with Hasmonean coins, and pottery disappeared from Bethsaida. It is presumed that trade with the coastal cities was reduced. Instead, we observe trade with pottery manufacturers, which later would be identified as thoroughly Jewish centers of manufacture, such as Kefar Hanania and Kefar Shikhin. A short-term change ensued with the conquest of the Romans, headed by Pompey in 63 B.C.E., but twenty years later the area was given to Herod the Great and the Jewish presence at the site resumed. A slight increase in the number of Herodian coins versus Hasmonean coins indicates that the place was revitalized under Herodian rule. Limestone vessels from the site are the best marker of Jewish presence and testify to the Jewish populations that continued through the Herodian period. However, lifestyle at Bethsaida did not change greatly from one population to the other. The same courtyard houses were built in the Hellenistic–Early Roman period, and the standard of living remained the same.

Figure 36. The spout
of a Herodian oil
lamp; Bethsaida.
Courtesy of R. Arav

The Temple of Livia-Julia

Josephus relates that Philip, the son of Herod the Great, elevated the fishing village to the status of a city and renamed it Julias. We asked ourselves what the actual meaning of this act was when we set to excavate the site, and indeed, on top of the mound, we believe we have found a substantial answer. In this area we discovered very sparse remains of a structure that could be interpreted as a temple built in honor of Livia-Julia. She was the wife of the emperor Augustus and the mother of the emperor Tiberius, who reigned in 30 C.E., when this renaming occurred.[18] The temple was very modest in size, and without all the circumstantial evidence no one would imagine that the renovated and converted house is indeed a temple.[19] It is only 20 × 6 meters and faces east. The width of its walls is 1.1 meters, which is larger than most of the residential walls we know. Only one foundation was discovered from a column in the porch of the temple. Behind the porch was a small "pro-*naos*," heavily destroyed by modern Syrian military, and behind that a long rectangular room — most probably the *naos*,

18. See M. Bernett, "Der Kaiserkult als Teil der politischen Geschichte Iudeas unter den Herodianern und Römern (30 v.Chr.–66 n.Chr.)" (Habilitationsschrift, University of Munich, 2001).

19. H. W. Kuhn discusses the temple in length and arrives at the conclusion that it could have been earlier than the Roman period. The temple obviously uses old walls in a secondary use. See H. W. Kuhn, "Jesu Hinwendung zu den Heiden im Markusevangelium im Verhältnis zu Jesu historischem Wiren in Betsaida, mit einem Zwischenbericht zur Ausgrabung eines vermuteten heidnischen Tempels auf et-Tell (Betsaida)," in *Die Weite des Mysteriums, Christliche Identität im Dialog für Horst Buerkle*, ed. K. Kraemer and A. Paus (Freiburg, 2000), pp. 222-29.

Figure 37. Bethsaida; wine cellar with jars *in situ*. Courtesy of R. Arav

Figure 38. Incense shovel; Bethsaida. Courtesy of R. Arav

Figure 39. Reconstruction of the Roman imperial cult temple; Bethsaida. Courtesy of R. Arav

the holy of holies of the temple. A small opening at the rear wall leads to a small room at the back porch. This room is called *adyton* in Roman temples. Behind the *adyton* and surrounding the temple there were plenty of the temple's utensils and vessels buried in pits. Among them were some extremely rare objects, such as a rare oil lamp filler and vessels similar to the ritual vessels found both in temples at Caesarea Philippi (Banias) and at the Cave of Letters. Other important finds were two bronze incense shovels, one of which was almost identical to the shovels discovered at the Cave of Letters. The impression one gets from the vessels at Bethsaida and the Cave of Letters is that they formed a collection of *instrumenta sacra* of Roman temples.[20]

In addition to this, five rare coins of Philip, which commemorate this renaming and the elevation of the status of the city, were found, and figurines, one of a woman with red hair wearing a veil. The veil indicates a woman fulfilling a religious position. And indeed, Livia-Julia was the first priestess in the cult of Augustus at Rome and was frequently identified with the goddess Roma and the mother of god. Another figurine depicts a woman wearing a veil over a tiara, which is adorned by a diadem. There is no doubt that this is a royal female who holds a religious position. It again recalls the description of Livia-Julia. Other interesting finds were a group of small anchor-shaped basalt stones, known as votive anchors. These anchors were presumably given by the temple to fishermen as talismans or given to the temple by worshipers. A small anchor-shaped seal with illegible depiction shows perhaps a boat with one or two figures on deck with round and semiround objects above them and a reed in front of the ship.

The temple structure was embellished with dressed and decorated stones, some of which were found in the secondary use in the Bedouin tombs scattered around the building. It is noteworthy that no single dressed stone was found incorporated in the private homes dating from the Roman and Hellenistic period. In the vicinity of the building there were also dressed limestones and column fragments. A large decorated lintel that contains a frieze with meander and floral motives was also found nearby. Other stone decorations contained two fragments of scrolls of leaves and floral decoration and a stone containing an acanthus floral decoration. All these stones perhaps originated in the temple. The secondary use of these stones is undoubtedly connected to the Roman *spolia* — stones dismantled from old buildings to be used in new ones. Because basalt stones are hard and strong and last indefinitely, *spolia* of basalt stones

20. A. V. Siebert, *Instrumenta Sacra: Untersuchungen zu römischen Opfer-, Kult- und Priestergeräten* (Berlin and New York: W. de Gruyter, 1999). Siebert deals with sacred vessels in the Roman period. However, she does not present incense shovels. An incense shovel rarely appears in Roman art. I would like to thank M. Bernett for bringing to my attention a rare example from North Africa of a stela describing an incense shovel on a tombstone of a priest.

were very popular. The Talmud deals with rules of *spolia* of ancient synagogues, again demonstrating how popular this was. It is noteworthy that very similar stones to the decorated stones of Bethsaida were discovered at the synagogue of Chorazin. The absence of a Byzantine level of occupation at Bethsaida eliminates the possibility that the stones came from Chorazin; they most probably traveled from Bethsaida to Chorazin. An amazing find is the pediment of the synagogue at Chorazin, which fits perfectly well the width of the temple of Bethsaida, and in three dimensions it describes in its gable a tree and eagle — the most obvious Roman imperial symbol. The temple ceased to function at the end of the Julio-Claudian dynasty. A floor with second century C.E. finds seals the walls of the temple.

Summary

Bethsaida excavations, carried on since 1987, help to shed new light on some of the most important topics of research in the Hebrew Bible and the New Testament. This town offers a rare opportunity to gaze at a royal city, which was situated near the kingdom of Israel. We have an unusual opportunity to look closely at the cult of the high places of the gate. We can inspect its meaning and reconstruct accordingly the fragmentary high places that were discovered elsewhere in the country. We are able, with the decorated stela, to properly date the other stelae and to suggest the archaeological context of this discovery.

The *Bit Hilani* palace is perhaps the best-preserved structure of its kind in Israel. Its state of preservation enables us to investigate other structures that may also be *Bit Hilani*–styled palaces.

The palace at Bethsaida is connected with another important issue related to the monumental buildings of the tenth century in Jerusalem. The tenth century B.C.E. yielded no Davidic or Solomonic remains. The Temple in Jerusalem can only be conjectured from the biblical description, and the palace of Solomon is described only briefly. It was larger than the Temple at 50 × 100 cubits, which means it was a broad structure, and its construction lasted many years. Many scholars suggested that it was built in a *Bit Hilani* style. The *Bit Hilani* in Bethsaida offers not only the closest parallel we know for the palace of Solomon, but also the historical background to this activity; it thereby reinforces the assumption that Solomon's palace at Jerusalem was a *Bit Hilani* structure.

The destruction of the Assyrian king Tiglath-pileser III was something archaeologists have encountered in the past. However, not all the destroyed cities appear in his list. Bethsaida is now added to cities such as Dan, Hazor, Megiddo, and the recently discovered Rehob, which was not mentioned in his list.

The conclusions relating to New Testament research are interesting as well, because they help elucidate a few difficult passages and help to clear some presumptions scholars have had for a long time. First and foremost, the excavations enable us to observe a village from the Hellenistic and Roman periods, which was a base for the activities of Jesus in the northern Sea of Galilee region, and to study some of its components. The excavations enable one to check how Hellenized this village was, and to deduce from this concerning the level of Hellenization that surrounded Jesus and his disciples in their ministry in Galilee. The degree of Hellenization around Jesus is a topic that has stood at the midst of scholarship for quite a long time.

For this purpose one has to remember that Bethsaida is the only place that is directly connected to the ministry of Jesus and is accessible to archaeological investigations. Other sites, such as Nazareth, Capernaum, or Chorazin, yielded very few remains from the first centuries B.C.E. and C.E. that have implications for Jesus research. Bethsaida provides an example of a rural settlement with very little Hellenization. If there was any degree of Hellenization, it was imposed on the inhabitants from above in the shape of a small and modest Roman imperial cult temple and not an initiation from the populace. It is therefore correct to assume that Jesus' address to the Gentiles was made in the front of the temple of the Roman emperor and perhaps oriented toward it.

Mount Tabor

Frédéric Manns

Modern scholars generally express skepticism about the localization of the transfiguration on Mount Tabor in Galilee. J. Murphy-O'Connor, in his guide to the Holy Land, speaks of a late tradition: "Eusebius (d. 340) hesitates between Tabor and Mount Hermon, while the Pilgrim of Bordeaux (333) places it on the Mount of Olives. In 348 Cyril of Jerusalem decided on Tabor and the support of Epiphanius and Jerome established the tradition firmly."[1] Since we do not have early traditions, one may hesitate and define this localization as a Byzantine one.

J. Taylor, in her dissertation on the holy places (in which she criticizes the Bagatti-Testa hypothesis on the Judeo-Christian traditions), does not take Tabor into consideration. Only in one small footnote does she present the problem linked with this place: "The transfiguration appears to have been fixed to Mount Tabor in Galilee by the time of Cyril (Cat. XII, 16)."[2] The implicit conclusion seems to be that the place does not present any historical importance.

P. Maraval repeats that only from the fourth century onward is Mount Tabor presented as the place of the transfiguration of the Lord.[3] While during the fourth century no churches are mentioned,[4] in the sixth century three churches

---

1. J. Murphy-O'Connor, *The Holy Land: An Archaeological Guide from Earliest Times to 1700* (Oxford: Oxford University Press, 1992), p. 370. The Pilgrim of Bordeaux was confused or influenced by the *Apocalypse of Peter*, in which an event like the transfiguration precedes the final ascension of Jesus. See also F. Santini, *È il Carmelo il monte della trasfigurazione non il Tabor?* (Rome: Bardi, 1979).

2. Taylor, "The Myth of the Judeo-Christian Origins" (Ph.D. diss., University of Edinburgh, 1993), p. 151 n. 30.

3. Maraval, *Lieux saints et pèlerinages d'Orient* (Paris: Éditions du Cerf, 1985), p. 292.

4. Jerome, *Epistulae* 46.13 and 108.13; Peter the Deacon, *De locis* 5.1.

(representing the three tents Peter wanted to build) were shown to pilgrims.[5] The place was chosen because it was a natural holy place.[6]

1. Methodology

Behind the skepticism regarding the localization of Mount Tabor there is a more general problem. Many modern authors are convinced that we do not know anything about Christianity in the Holy Land before the fourth century.[7] As far as topography is concerned, we have to wait for the *Onomasticon* of Eusebius to become a serious source of knowledge.[8] Many historians forget that pilgrims came to the holy places starting in the second century:[9] Melito, the bishop of Sardis,[10] Origen,[11] and Alexander from Cappadocia[12] are only a few of the famous pilgrims who visited the holy places after the second century. In fact, if we know very little about the first centuries of Christianity, it is because many Christian sources were destroyed during the persecutions;[13] it does not mean that no Christian communities existed in the Holy Land, or that the traditions about the holy places are late. Even if three wars destroyed many places during the first two centuries, Christian traditions did survive.

A second assumption of many modern historians is that the apocryphal literature does not contain much serious geographical information, and since the New Testament Apocrypha was rejected from the canon, it should not be consid-

---

5. Anonym of Piacenza, *Itinerarium* 6.2. E. Vardapet, "Traité sur la Transfiguration," *JTS* 18 (1967): 31-32. This Armenian pilgrim places the apparition of the risen Christ to his disciples on Mount Tabor.

6. Maraval, *Lieux saints*, p. 51.

7. The Israel Museum organized for the new millennium an archaeological exhibition called "Cradle of Christianity." The catalogue has been published by Yael Israeli and David Mevorah. According to this exhibition, the archaeologic history of Christianity in the Holy Land starts only with the Byzantine period. It seems that the Christians were imported by Constantine during the fourth century in the Holy Land.

8. M. Noth, "Die topographischen Angaben im Onomastikon des Eusebios," *ZDPV* 66 (1943): 32-63; J. Wilkinson, "L'apport de S. Jérôme à la topographie," *RB* 81 (1974): 245-57.

9. H. Windisch, "Die ältesten christlichen Palästinapilger," *ZDPV* 48 (1925): 145-58; E. Burger, "Die Anfänge des Pilgerwesen in Palästina," *Palestina Jahrbuch* 27 (1931): 84-111; J. Vilar, "Peregrini antiquissimi," *Verbum Domini* 6 (1926): 123-26.

10. Eusebius, *HE* 4.26, 13-14: SC 41:211.

11. Origen, *In Joh com* 6.204: SC 157:286.

12. Eusebius, *HE* 6.11, 12: SC 41:100.

13. Justin, *1 Apology* 44.12-13; Eusebius, *HE* 8.2; Arnobius, *Adversus gentes* 4.36: PL 5:1076. See 1 Macc 1:56-57; 4 Ezra 14:20-21.

ered in a scientific investigation.[14] Nevertheless, even if the books of the Apocrypha were not accepted into the canon, they must be studied as haggadic material.

Another difficulty arises from the literary genre of the Gospel accounts of the transfiguration.[15] For many authors these texts are not historical.[16] They are symbolic, representing an apparition account of the resurrected Christ with apocalyptic scenery. Thus there is no need to investigate any geographical correlations. The text of the Gospels speaks about a high mountain without specification. It could be a theological theme that must be interpreted, as some artists did, as corresponding to the mountain of the Old Testament, Mount Sinai. In fact, Byzantine artists adorned the Church of St. Catherina at the foot of Sinai with a beautiful mosaic of the transfiguration.[17]

Those who admit that the text could contain some historical elements usually locate it on Mount Hermon. According to Mk 8:27, Jesus was in the vicinity of Caesarea Philippi, which he leaves only in 9:30. The transfiguration is recorded in 9:1-13. The event must therefore be located on Mount Hermon.[18] Besides, on top of Mount Tabor there was a Roman fortress during the time of Jesus, a place not very convenient for the transfiguration. This hypothesis assumes that the Gospels are biographies and that all the geographical notations are authentic.

A last difficulty comes from the fact that the church at Jerusalem seems to have celebrated the memory of the transfiguration on the Mount of Olives. The Pilgrim of Bordeaux is a witness to this tradition.[19]

14. Recently this kind of attitude toward the Apocrypha has changed.

15. J. Blinzler, *Die Neutestamentliche Berichte über die Verklärung Jesu* (Münster: Aschendorff, 1937); B. D. Chilton, "The Transfiguration: Dominical Assurance and Apostolic Vision," *NTS* 27 (1981): 115-24; A. Del Agua, "Transfiguration as a Derashic Scenification of the Faith Confession (Mk 9:2-8)," *NTS* 39 (1993): 340-54; H. C. Kee, "The Transfiguration in Mark: Epiphany or Apocalyptic Vision?" in *Understanding the Sacred Text*, ed. J. Reumann (Valley Forge, Pa.: Judson, 1972), pp. 135-52; J. H. Neyrey, "The Apocalyptic Use of the Transfiguration in 2 Pet 1:16-21," *CBQ* 42 (1980): 504-19.

16. Even for Origen (*Com in Mt* 12.35–13.2; *Com in Luc* 20.121; *Hom in Jer* 17.21; *Com in Gen* 1.7, 10), the transfiguration is more the paradigm of Christian spirituality than a historic reality. The soul has to transcend the physical realm in its contemplation of the Logos.

17. For the artistic representations of the transfiguration, see F. Bisconti, *Temi di iconografia paleocristiana* (Vatican City, 2000), p. 293. The earliest artistic representation of the transfiguration is found in Ravenna in the apse of S. Appolinare in classe (549).

18. H. B. Swete, *The Gospel according to St. Mark* (London: Macmillan, 1927), p. 187.

19. *Itinéraire du Pèlerin de Bordeaux*, Publications de l'Orient latin (Geneva, 1979), 1:14. The Georgian lectionary of Jerusalem of the tenth century could confirm this belief since it does not specify the place of the transfiguration. G. Garitte, *Le calendrier palestino-géorgien du Sinaïticus 34 (Xe siècle)* (Brussels: Société des Bollandistes, 1958). But in the lectionary of Latal, p. 494, one reads for August 6: *synaxis in loco Ascensionis: in Thabor transfiguratio Salvatoris*. The lectionary

Monuments and documents are the two sources every historian must consider seriously. But each of these two disciplines uses a different methodology. Archaeology has its own techniques and its own problems, while literary sources must be studied in a critical way according to historico-critical methods. It is only after these two disciplines have solved their inner problems that their results can be compared. A dialogue can then be started between monuments and documents. Archaeological research on Mount Tabor has not been very active, even if a few excavations have been done recently.[20]

2. The Biblical Concept of the Mountain

The account of the transfiguration mentions a high mountain that Jesus climbed with three disciples. Semitic cosmology implies that eternal mountains sustain the vault of heaven, and on the peak of these mountains is the hidden dwelling of God. For most religions, mountains are considered to be the dwelling place of the divinities. On the sacred mountains, the Canaanites offered sacrifices (Hos 4:13) and participated in sacred meals (Deut 12:2; Jer 3:23). Mountains usually evoke the experience of the divine. The mount of the Temple is called "the mountain of the Lord" (Mic 4:2; Zech 8:3; Ps 24:3). At the end of time all people would flow there to take part in the banquet of the Lord (Isa 25:6). In the eschatological times Mount Zion will be higher than all the mountains. Ps 67:17 (LXX) affirms that the Lord will dwell there.[21] Mountains are also places of revelation in the New Testament. The apocalyptic discourse of Jesus takes place on the Mount of Olives (Mk 13:3), the new explanation of the Law is given upon a mountain (Mt 5:1), and Jesus reveals himself on the mountains of

---

of Paris, fol. 266r, has this note for August 6: *Transfiguratio Salvatoris quam fecit super montem in Thabor.* The *Book of the Resurrection of Our Lord by Bartholomew the Apostle* 8.1 mentions the descent of Jesus from the Mount of Olives when he healed Simon. It is possible that this passage comments on Mk 9:14-29 where Jesus, descending the mountain after the transfiguration, healed a child.

20. A. Battista and B. Bagatti, *La fortezza saracena del Monte Tabor (AH. 609-15; AD. 1212-18)*, SBF.CMi 18 (Jerusalem: Franciscan Printing Press, 1976); S. Loffreda, "Una tomba romana al Monte Tabor," *Liber Annuus* 28 (1978): 241-46; N. Tsori, "Remains of Iron Age Sites in the Beth Shean and Jezreel Valleys, Mt. Gilboa, Mt. Tabor, Giv'at Hamore and the Plain of Issachar," in Collectif, *Sixth Archaeological Conference in Israel (Tel-Aviv, 14-15 March 1979)* (Jerusalem: Israel Exploration Society, 1979), p. 12; B. Bagatti, "Una grotta bizantina sul Monte Tabor," *Liber Annuus* 27 (1977): 119-22; J. Lewy, "Tabor, Tibar, Atabyros," *HUCA* 23 (1951): 357-86; E. Alliata, "Elementi del culto pagano sul Monte della Trasfigurazione," in *Memoriam Sanctorum venerantes. Miscellanea in onore di Mons. Victor Saxer* (Vatican City, 1992), pp. 1-10.

21. *kataskēnōsei eis telos.*

Figure 40. Mount Tabor, from the southeast. Courtesy of J. H. Charlesworth

Galilee (Mt 28:16). For Luke, a mountain is a place of prayer (Lk 6:12; 9:28), and the ascension is from the Mount of Olives (Acts 1:2).

In the text of the transfiguration the mountain as a place of theophany is connected with the Sinai theophany.[22] In the transfiguration scene, Jesus goes up to the mountain with three disciples just as Moses went up with Aaron, Nadab, and Abihu (Ex 24:1, 9). Moses entered the cloud (Ex 24:16-18). In Ex 34:29-30 the face of Moses became radiant. The descent of both Moses and Jesus from a mountain is well known.

3. Mount Tabor, a Jewish Holy Place

Mount Tabor is mentioned for the first time in the Bible in connection with the defeat of the army of the king of Hazor at the hands of Deborah and Barak. There the Israelites captured 900 Canaanite chariots that were traveling across the valley of Jezreel (Judg 4:12-16). The name Tabor seems to be derived from Phoenician and recalls the name of the Semitic God, known in Greek as Zeus

22. Eusebius draws a contrast with Moses on Sinai: *Demonstratio evangelica* 3.2, 19-20; cf. Origen, *Com in Ex* 3.2, 165; *Com in Num* 7.2-4, 40-44.

Atabyros. The heterodox worship on Tabor is condemned in Hos 5:1. It is interesting to note that the Targumim, the Aramaic version of the Bible, translate Tabor by "a high mountain."[23] For Jeremiah (46:18) Tabor symbolizes the mighty of Nebuchadnezzar. In 218 B.C.E. Antiochus III feigned a retreat, enticing the Egyptian garrison from its position at the summit. His strategy succeeded and he won the battle. A similar strategy was used by Placidus, the Roman general who defeated the Jews under Josephus. According to him (*War* 4.54-61), there was a village on the summit in the first century, which was probably inhabited by the descendants of a garrison left behind by Alexander Jannaeus.

Mount Tabor may be the holy mountain mentioned in the blessing of Moses (Deut 33:19).[24] The tribes of Zebulun and Issachar used to meet there to offer sacrifices. It is interesting to note that the Targum, in the Song of Deborah (Judg 5:5), preserves a story about a discussion between Mount Tabor, Mount Hermon, and Mount Carmel. Each of these mountains wanted the privilege of receiving the Shekinah: "The mountains shook from before the Lord. Sinai was shaken up, its smoke went up like the smoke of the furnace because the Lord, the God of Israel, was revealed upon it." Codex Reuchlianus (f 16) has a long addition about the contest among these three mountains regarding the proper place for the Shekinah, and the ultimate choice of Sinai.[25] Midrash *Mekilta de R. Ismael* on Ex 20:2 and *Genesis Rabbah* 99:1 repeat this tradition on the basis of their exegesis of Ps 68:17. This liturgical tradition shows that Mount Tabor and Mount Hermon symbolized in a certain way a place of revelation. The victory of Deborah near Mount Tabor was most likely commemorated in the Jewish world.

This Jewish tradition of the revelation of the Shekinah was probably taken over by Christians. There are many examples of Christianization of Jewish traditions. Sometimes Jewish worship places have been taken over by Christians.[26] The mountain is singled out for its beauty in Ps 89:13(12), where it is mentioned together with Mount Hermon.

The Midrash *Yalqut Shimoni* on Deut 33:18 knows a curious tradition according to which the Temple would have been built on the top of Mount Tabor.

---

23. *tor ram.*

24. According to *Targum Neofiti* and *Jerushalmi I*, the mountain is the mountain of the Temple.

25. D. J. Harrington, "The Prophecy of Deborah: Interpretative Homiletics in Targum Jonathan of Judges 5," *CBQ* 48 (1986): 432-42. According to Harrington, this Targum contains a possible reference to conditions of the land of Israel either in early stages of the Jewish Revolt (67 C.E.) or in the Bar-Kokhba revolt (132-135 C.E.).

26. See Maraval, *Lieux saints et pèlerinages d'Orient.*

There was, however, another revelation that required the Temple to be built on Mount Moriah. Mount Hermon, proposed by others as the mount of transfiguration, is also linked with deities and pagan cults. Hermon is the mount of "curse" that provided hospitality to the rebellious angels who rebelled against God. Descending on Hermon, the angels sinned with women and became the cause of the spread of evil in the world.[27]

4. The Literary Sources

Let us begin an examination of the Christian literary sources in favor of Mount Tabor as the place of the transfiguration.[28]

2 Pet 1:18 states that the Christian faith is not based upon myths, but on historical facts. Christ's glory was seen and a prophetic word accompanied it: "We heard it on the holy mountain."[29] The presence of the article in this text indicates that the mountain was known as *the* holy mountain. Pss 2:6; 3:4; 15:1; 42(43):3; 98:9; Wis 9:8; Joel 2:1; 3:17; Zeph 3:11; Zech 8:3; Isa 11:9; 27:13; 56:7; 63:18; 65:9, 11; Jer 38:23; Ezek 20:40; 28:14; Dan 9:16, 17, 20 give this title to Mount Zion. But the Synoptic Gospels mention only that Jesus climbed up a high mountain. This unspecified mention could point to Mount Tabor, since Tabor was called a high mountain in the Targum of Hos 5:1.

Those who choose Mount Tabor remember that Origen knew the tradition of Tabor. They cite the passage of *In Joh* 2.12[30] and *Hom Jer* 15.10[31] where Origen quotes the *Gospel according to the Hebrews*: "Jesus said: 'The Holy Spirit, my mother, took me by the hair and brought me to Mount Tabor.'"[32] The text does not speak about the transfiguration, but it does not exclude it either. It belongs to the account of the temptation of Jesus. It is possible that the author of the *Gospel according to the Hebrews* wanted to place in parallel the theophany following the baptism of Jesus and the theophany of the transfiguration. Mount

---

27. *1 En* 6.6–7.4.

28. From the archaeological point of view, it must be remembered that a wall found on Mount Tabor has been dated to the Hellenistic period; it is probably the wall Josephus claims to have built in only forty days, using the remains of ancient walls (*War* 2.572-576; *Life* 187-188). The Byzantine remains on the summit of Mount Tabor belong to a church and a monastery attached to it. The caves around the summit may have been used by hermits. See M. Aviam, "Galilee: The Hellenistic and Byzantine Periods," in *NEAEHL* 2:453-57.

29. *en tō hagiō orei.*

30. PG 14:132.

31. PG 13:433.

32. Origen, *In Joh,* t.2, 12. The text of the *Gospel according to the Hebrews* is found in Resh, *Agrapha: aussercanonische Schriftfragmente* (Leipzig: J. C. Hinrichs, 1906), p. 383.

Tabor seems to be the place of the temptation of Jesus,[33] as in Mt 4:8, where the last temptation is located upon a high mountain. The Spirit, like Wisdom, is a feminine entity. Jesus, like Ezekiel (Ezek 8:3), is taken to Tabor.

How do we date the *Gospel according to the Hebrews*? It could be from the second century C.E., according to most scholars,[34] since Hegesippus quotes it. The mention of Mount Tabor in this work shows that it was a Judeo-Christian holy place.

In *Selecta in Psalmos* Ps 88:13(89:12) Origen writes: "Tabor and Hermon shall exult in thy name. Tabor *eklekton,* the chosen one. Tabor is the Mount of Galilee where Jesus was transfigured."[35] R. Devresse doubts the authenticity of the attribution to Origen of the *Selecta in Psalmos.*[36] In his many references to the transfiguration Origen does not suggest a location for this event, but he may have used Ps 88 as a text that summarized the two most likely possibilities.

In the apocryphon called *Transitus B. V. Mariae,*[37] the author, while describing the death of Mary, says: "The light and the perfume were so great that all those who were present fell upon their faces like the apostles when Christ transfigured himself in their presence upon Mount Tabor." The last detail is not known by the oldest version of the *Dormition,* the Greek version of Vaticanus 1982.

In the *Apocalypse of John, the Theologian,* the author knows of a revelation made to John on Mount Tabor: "I, John, went upon Mount Tabor, where he showed us his pure divinity."[38] Mount Tabor seems to be the mount of the apparition of the risen Christ.[39] Again, the problem of dating the Apocrypha remains controversial. Probably the redaction of the two apocrypha quoted is late, but the tradition they contain seems to be ancient.

Eusebius saw the transfiguration more in its historical terms as a revelation of Christ. He refers to Mount Tabor thirteen times in his *Onomasticon,*[40] and frequently discusses the transfiguration as an event (*Com in Luc* [9.28] 549cd; *Demonstratio evangelica* 3.2, 19-20; *Com in Is* [17.6] 116.10-14; *Ep Const* 1545bc).

---

33. J. B. Fuliga, "The Temptation on the Mount of Transfiguration," *AJT* 9 (1995): 331-40.

34. A. F. J. Klijn, "Das Hebräer- und Nazoräerevangelium," *ANRW* 2.25.5 (Berlin: W. de Gruyter, 1988), pp. 3997-4033.

35. *Metemorphōthē.*

36. Devresse, "Chaînes exégétiques grecques," in L. Pirot, *Supplément du Dictionnaire de la Bible* (Paris), 1:1121.

37. M. Craveri, ed., *I Vangeli apocrifi* (Turin: G. Einaudi, 1969), p. 468.

38. M. Erbetta, ed., *Gli Apocrifi del Nuovo Testamento* (Turin: Marietti, 1969), 3:410.

39. B. Meistermann, *La montagne de Galilée où le Seigneur apparut aux apôtres (Math 28,16) est le mont Thabor* (Jerusalem, 1901).

40. But there is no mention of the transfiguration in these quotations of the *Onomasticon.*

Quoting Ps 88:13, he puts Tabor and Hermon together.[41] He does not conclude where the transfiguration took place. After discussing all the academic arguments, he suggests Mount Tabor as his personal opinion. He is very close to the Jewish tradition of Targum Judg 5:5, where the mountains discuss among themselves the privilege of receiving the glory of God.

Epiphanius in his *De Gemmis* writes: "Mount Tabor which the Lord climbed, where Moses and Elijah and some disciples stayed with him, there the great divine visions took place."[42] Again Epiphanius seems to locate the visions of the resurrection upon Mount Tabor.

Ephrem in two hymns on the transfiguration mentions Mount Tabor as the place where it happened. The church of Edessa celebrated the feast of transfiguration in the fourth century C.E. Ephrem in his Hymn 21.5 of *De virginitate* remembers that Simon climbed Mount Tabor and said, "It is good for us to stay here."[43]

Cyril the bishop of Jerusalem puts the transfiguration on the top of Mount Tabor.[44] He presents this opinion as a common tradition. As a pastor of the church of Jerusalem, he did not have the luxury of discussing all the arguments. Liturgy demands places. Pilgrims desire a precise identification. Cyril chose the place because Jewish Christians gave importance to Mount Tabor. Till today the Eastern churches call the festival *To Taburion*.

Jerome, in his *Letter* 46.12, invites Marcella to come to the Holy Land: "We shall climb upon Mount Itabyrion, to see the tents of the Lord and we shall contemplate him not with Moses and Elijah as did Peter, but with the Father and the Spirit."[45] In his *Letter* 108.13 he remembers that Paola went up Mount Tabor where Jesus was transfigured.[46] In his *Letter* 58.8 he mentions Mount Tabor with Mount Zion and Mount Sinai, showing that all three mountains were sacred for him.[47]

Theodosius in 530 mentions Tabor as the place where Jesus appeared to his disciples after the resurrection.[48] The Anonym of Piacenza in 570 recognizes Tabor as the mount of the transfiguration. In the Georgian lectionary of

---

41. PG 23:1092D.

42. R. P. Blake and H. de Vis, eds., Epiphanius, "De Gemmis," *Studies and Documents* (London, 1943), 2:152.

43. CSCO 95:66.

44. Cyril, *Catecheses* 12.16: PG 33:744B.

45. PL 22:491.

46. PL 22:889.

47. PL 22:585.

48. Geyer, *De situ Terrae Sanctae*, ed. P. Geyer, *Itineroi Hierosdymitana saeculi IV-VIII*, CSEL 39 (Vindobonae: F. Tempsky, 1898), p. 139.

the church of Jerusalem from the fifth century, there is a short mention of the feast: "6 of August, the Transfiguration of the Lord which happened on Mount Tabor."[49]

5. Modern Research

This tradition had been accepted till the sixteenth century. In 1596 Maldonatus doubted this localization.[50] R. H. Fuller and J. Lightfoot proposed Mount Hermon as the mount of the transfiguration, because the place mentioned in the Gospels before the transfiguration is Caesarea Philippi.[51] J. Wilson and Conder-Kitchener repeated the tradition of the transfiguration on Mount Hermon.[52]

But many other places were presented as possible candidates for the mountain. G. Dalman chose tell el Akhmar on the Golan Heights as the place of transfiguration.[53] R. W. Stewart preferred the Horn of Hattin.[54] W. Ewing thought Gebel Germaq was the place where Jesus showed his glory to the apostles.[55]

A. Loisy concluded that those who look for a geographical place for the transfiguration are like Peter who asked to build three tents. They do not understand anything of the real message of the text.[56] Nevertheless, C. W. van de Velde ended his research with this sentence: "If anyone on the base of Mk 8:27 and 9:2-30 can show me that the Lord was glorified not upon Mount Tabor but upon a Mountain close to Caesarea Philippi, I am ready to reconsider it."[57] But till now nobody has proved it. M. Halbwachs was convinced that the topography of the Gospels in the Holy Land contains a lot of legendary characteristics.[58]

49. "Grand lectionnaire de l'Eglise de Jérusalem (5-8 siècle)," CSCO 205:25.

50. Maldonatus, *Commentarii in quatuor Evangelistas* (Moguntiae, 1863).

51. Fuller, *A Pisgah-Sight of Palestine* (London, 1869), p. 145; Lightfoot, *Horae hebraicae et talmudicae i quatuor Evangelistas* (Leipzig, 1675), p. 624.

52. Wilson, *The Lands of the Bible* (Edinburgh: William Whyte & Co., 1847), vol. 2; Conder-Kitchener, *The Survey of Western Palestine* (London: Committee of the Palestine Exploration Fund, 1881), vol. 1.

53. Dalman, *Orte und Wege Jesu* (Gütersloh: Bertelsmann, 1924).

54. Stewart, *The Tent and the Khan: A Journey to Sinai and Palestine* (Edinburgh: W. Oliphant and Sons, 1857), pp. 434-35.

55. Ewing, "The Mount of Transfiguration," *ET* 18 (1906-7): 220.

56. Loisy, *Les Evangiles synoptiques* (Ceffonds, 1908), 2:34.

57. Velde, *Narrative of a Journey Through Syria and Palestine in 1851 and 1852* (Edinburgh: W. Blackwood and Sons, 1854), vol. 2.

58. Halbwachs, *La topographie légendaire des Evangiles en Terre sainte* (Paris: Presses universitaires de France, 1941). See the criticism of H. Vincent, "La topographie des Evangiles," *Vivre et penser*, 1943-44, p. 50 n. 1.

Conclusion

It is interesting to note the variety of traditions linked to Mount Tabor: the temptation, the apparitions of the risen Christ, and the transfiguration. Maybe the two latest traditions present some common elements. That could be a reason that the transfiguration was placed on Mount Tabor.

Why was Mount Tabor chosen as the place of the transfiguration in the Byzantine period? It seems clear that they took over a Judeo-Christian place of cult. The *Gospel according to the Hebrews* and other apocrypha show that the place was sacred to the Jewish Christians who themselves took over a Jewish tradition.

Jesus the Exorcist in Light of Epigraphic Sources

Esther Eshel

The belief in demons was a widespread and accepted part of the Jewish milieu in the Second Temple period, and for certain circles even a central feature of their worldview. In this paper I will discuss stories of possession and exorcism in the Synoptic Gospels in the light of epigraphic sources, dating from the Hellenistic and early Roman periods.

One of the aspects of demonology is descriptions of demonic possession and exorcism. These descriptions are known from Jewish sources as well as from Christian and pagan ones.[1]

The Synoptic Gospels include six possession and exorcism stories, some in two or three versions. The main source is Mark, whereas the Fourth Gospel mentions none. Another detailed story is included in the Acts of the Apostles. Some of the stories of possession and exorcism found in the New Testament include both simple and compound stories of exorcism. These stories reflect a developed form of exorcism with fixed elements.

The earliest description of possession and exorcism in biblical sources is found in 1 Sam 16:14-23, where an evil spirit sent by God attacks King Saul and is exorcised through David's employment of his musical gifts:

> Now the spirit of the Lord had departed from Saul, and an evil spirit from the Lord began to terrify him. Saul's courtiers said to him: "An evil spirit of God is terrifying you. Let our lord give the order [and] the courtiers in attendance on you will look for someone who is skilled at playing the lyre; whenever the evil spirit of God comes over you, he will play it and you will

---

1. See J. F. M. Middleton, "Magic," in *The New Encyclopaedia Britannica*, 11:298-302; Middleton, "Magic: Theories of Magic," and D. R. Hill, "Magic: Magic in Primitive Societies," both in *The Encyclopedia of Religion*, ed. M. Eliade (New York and London: Collier Macmillan, 1989), pp. 81-89 and 89-92 respectively.

feel better." So Saul said to his courtiers, "Find me someone who can play well and bring him to me." One of the attendants spoke up, "I have observed a son of Jesse the Bethlehemite who is skilled in music; he is a stalwart fellow and a warrior, sensible in speech, and handsome in appearance, and the Lord is with him." . . . So David came to Saul and entered his service. . . . Whenever the [evil] spirit of God came upon Saul, David would take the lyre and play it; Saul would find relief and feel better, and the evil spirit would leave him.

This story underwent expansion in some Second Temple period documents, including Pseudo-Philo's *Biblical Antiquities:* "And in that time the spirit of the Lord was taken away from Saul, and an evil spirit was choking him. And Saul sent and brought David, and he played a song on his lyre by night" (60.1; *OTP* 2:373).

This description is followed by the words of the song David played, which served as an exorcism. The same event is also referred to in Josephus's *Jewish Antiquities:* "But as for Saul, he was beset by strange disorders and evil spirits which caused him such suffocation and strangling that the physicians could devise no other remedy save to order search to be made for one with power to charm away spirits and play upon the harp, and, whensoever the evil spirits should assail and torment Saul, to have him stand over the king and strike the strings and chant his songs" (3.166).

In these works the evil spirit is portrayed as an independent entity, and the harm it inflicts has parallels in contemporary descriptions of demonic possession.

Some scrolls from Qumran portray other biblical figures possessed by demons, among them Pharaoh. In the biblical story of Abram and Sarai's descent to Egypt, Sarai was taken into Pharaoh's palace, "But the Lord afflicted Pharaoh and his household with mighty plagues on account of Sarai, the wife of Abram" (Gen 12:17).

In the *Genesis Apocryphon* this affliction is attributed to an evil spirit: "(But) that night God Most High sent him a pestilential spirit to afflict him and all the men of his household, an evil spirit, that kept afflicting him and all his household" (1QapGen 20.16-17).[2] The evil spirit was exorcised by Abram himself, as described later in the scroll (line 29, see discussion below).

These descriptions essentially perpetuate the biblical worldview that evil spirits are sent by God to strike people with various afflictions, such as boils.

---

2. J. A. Fitzmyer, ed., *The Genesis Apocryphon of Qumran Cave 1*, 2nd rev. ed. (Rome: Biblical Institute Press, 1971), pp. 64-65.

The earliest Jewish sources that attest to the existence of evil spirits as independent entities are the exorcism of the demon Asmodeus in the book of Tobit. This demon caused the death of Sarah's six husbands on their wedding night.

A more detailed exorcism of a demon, performed by a Jew named Eleazar, is documented in Josephus:

> I have seen a certain Eleazar, a countryman of mine, in the presence of Vespasian, his sons, tribunes and a number of other soldiers, free men possessed by demons, and this is the manner of the cure: he put to the nose of the possessed man a ring which had under its seal one of the roots prescribed by Solomon, and then, as the man smelled it, drew out the demon through his nostrils, and, when the man at once fell down, adjured the demon never to come back into him, speaking Solomon's name and reciting the incantations which he had composed. Then, wishing to convince the bystanders and prove to them that he had this power, Eleazar placed a cup or foot basin full of water a little way off and commanded the demon, as it went out of the man, to overturn it and make known to the spectators that he had left the man. (*Ant* 8.46-48)

Both these sources describe the ceremonial act of exorcism in detail. Nevertheless, our main sources of possession and exorcism as practiced in Palestine during that period are the Synoptic Gospels and the Acts of the Apostles.[3]

Comparison of the descriptions in the Synoptic Gospels with Jewish sources reveals similarities as well as differences, the latter existing mainly in the function ascribed to Jesus and his audience.[4] The points of comparison between the Jewish and Christian sources are: the epithets for the evil forces; the terminology used describing exorcism; the typology of exorcism stories; various practices and acts added to the exorcism. We will briefly discuss these four elements.

---

3. For a general description, see M. Smith, *Jesus the Magician* (New York: Harper and Row, 1978); J. P. Meier, "Jesus' Exorcisms," in *A Marginal Jew*, ABRL (New York: Doubleday, 1991), 2:646-77. For the history of research see G. H. Twelftree, *Jesus the Exorcist* (Tübingen: J. C. B. Mohr [Paul Siebeck], 1993), pp. 4-10, and bibliography there.

4. For a study of the shared elements of exorcism stories found in both Jewish and Christian sources, and the various story types, see G. Theissen, *The Miracle Stories in the Early Christian Tradition*, trans. F. McDonagh (Philadelphia: Fortress, 1983); R. W. Funk, "The Form of the New Testament Healing Miracle Story," *Semeia* 12 (1978): 57-96.

Epithets of the Evil Forces

In the Synoptic Gospels one finds "demon" (δαιμόνιον), sometimes with the adjective "impure" or "evil," alongside "spirit" (πνεῦμα πονηρόν), which is sometimes also accompanied by the adjective "evil."[5]

The evil forces were named in the early Jewish sources by the general name "evil spirit."[6] Such is the case in the story of Saul, as we saw, in 1 Sam 16. The parallel epithet can also be found in various Aramaic sources from Qumran, where "the evil spirit" (רוחא באישתא), "a striking spirit" (רוח מכדש), and "the spirit of purulence" (רוח שחלניא) are mentioned in the *Genesis Apocryphon* (Cave 1, col. 20.16-17, 26). The Septuagint translation of the book of Samuel remains faithful to the Hebrew sources, using "evil spirit" (πνεῦμα πονηρόν), and the same term is used by Josephus's description of the same event (*Ant* 6.214).

Demons (δαιμόνιον) were first mentioned in other references to David exorcising the evil spirit from King Saul, in Josephus (*Ant* 6.166, 211). An early mention of "a demon" (שד) is attested in a Qumran scroll numbered 11Q11, which is a collection of incantations;[7] in a collection of apotropaic prayers (4Q510-511);[8] as well as in the fragments of book of Tobit found at Qumran.[9] Thus we have seen that both terms "evil spirit" and "demon" appear side by side in numerous early Jewish sources.

This leads to the conclusion that "evil spirits" and "demons" were understood in antiquity as parallel terms. Exception to the usage of these general terms can be found in the mentioning of the proper name Asmodeus in the book of Tobit and Legion in the story of the Gerasean demoniac in Mark and Luke.

---

5. A. Plummer, *A Critical and Exegetical Commentary on the Gospel according to Luke,* ICC (Edinburgh: T. & T. Clark, 1898), p. 133.

6. J. A. Fitzmyer, *The Gospel according to Luke (I–IX),* AB (Garden City, N.Y.: Doubleday, 1981), pp. 544-45.

7. Cols. 1.10; 2.3. See A. S. van der Woude, "11Qapocryphal Psalms," in *Qumran Cave 11: II (11Q2-18, 11Q20-31),* ed. F. García Martínez, E. C. J. Tigchelaar, and A. van der Woude, DJD 33 (Oxford: Clarendon, 1998), pp. 188-91.

8. 4Q510 frg. 1.5 (שד אים for שרים = demons); M. Baillet, *Qumran Grotte 4, III,* DJD 7 (Oxford: Clarendon, 1982), p. 216.

9. 4QpapTob[a] ar frg. 14 i.5, 12; 4QpapTob[b] ar frg. 4 i 13, ii.9; see J. A. Fitzmyer, "Tobit," in M. Broshe et al., *Qumran Cave 4: XIV, Parabiblical Texts, Part 2,* DJD 19 (Oxford: Clarendon, 1995), pp. 20, 44, 48.

Figure 41. Qumran
Caves 4A and 4B, as
seen from the
Wadi Qumran.
Courtesy of J. H. Charlesworth

Terminology Used for Describing Possession

In the early sources one cannot find a detailed description of the act of the demon entering the body, but only a general description of the person stricken by it, while the later ones add more details to the possession. Such is the case, for example, in the stories of the Gerasean demonic and the epileptic boy. The most expanded version is found in Mark: "And when he had stepped out of the boat, immediately a man out of the tombs with an unclean spirit met him. He lived among the tombs; and no one could restrain him any more, even with a chain; for he had often been restrained with shackles and chains, but the chains he wrenched apart, and the shackles he broke in pieces; and no one had the strength to subdue him. Night and day among the tombs and on the mountains he was always howling and bruising himself with stones" (Mk 5:2-5; cf. Mt 8:28; Lk 8:27).

In the Jewish sources the effect of the demon is usually described by one verb, for example, "torment" or "afflict" (כתש in Aramaic).[10] A special terminology for descriptions of exorcism began to be developed later, and was used for description of nonbiblical figures. The most important verb used is "to possess" (λαμβάνω in Greek), used in the story of Eleazar the exorcist (*Ant* 8.46). This term is shared by some of the Synoptic exorcism stories, such as the description of the epileptic boy in Luke: "Suddenly a spirit seizes him" (Lk 9:39).

---

10. See 1QApGen 20.16-18: "(But) that night God Most High sent him a pestilential spirit *to afflict him* (למכתשה) . . . an evil spirit that kept *afflicting* him (והואת כתשא לה). . . . At the end of two years the plagues and *afflictions* (מכתשיא) became more severe"; Fitzmyer, *The Genesis Apocryphon*, pp. 64-65, 131-32.

Typology of Exorcism Stories

The two basic literary elements of the genre of possession-exorcism stories are an introduction, which serves as a frame and includes a short description of the possession, and a nucleus story that contains the description of the exorcism itself. The exorcism process was initiated by invoking the demon and calling its name, and concluded with the demon's departure, often not before it performed a violent act that left an impact on the possessed person or the onlookers, or both. These descriptions were sometimes supplemented by physical acts, such as using magical rings, burning fish innards, the laying on of hands, and the like. These practical acts also have shared elements with the depictions found in Jewish, Christian, and pagan sources.

These stories were studied by Robert Funk, who divided them into different categories. Two of these categories consist of "R Type," which includes a dialogue between the exorcist and a relative of the possessed person, and "D Type," in which the dialogue is carried on between the exorcist and the demon himself.[11] These developed types cannot be found in the Jewish stories of exorcism, but one example of the exorcist approaching the demon can be found in 11Q11. In one of the incantations the exorcist says to the demon: "Who are you, oh offspring of man and of the seed of the holy ones ([תנולד מ[אדם ומזרע] [הקד]ו[שים]): your face is a face of delusion ([ש]ו פניך פני) and your horns are horns of illusion (וקרניך קרני חלוף), you are darkness and not light, [injust]ice and not justice."[12]

Various Practices and Acts Added to the Exorcism

Exorcism of evil spirits was usually accomplished by a prayer, in both Jewish and Christian sources, sometimes supplemented by practical actions. Such acts, including use of a magical ring, usually go back to King Solomon. Such is the case in the story of Eleazar the exorcist, according to Josephus (*Ant* 8.46-48), and later found in the *Testament of Solomon* (1.6-7; 10-13). The magical ring of Solomon is well attested in various amulets and Greek magical papyri.[13] Some-

---

11. Funk, "The Form of the New Testament Healing Miracle Story."

12. 11Q11, col. 5, 6-8, van der Woude, "11Qapocryphal Psalms," pp. 198-200.

13. *The Great Paris Magical Papyrus,* line 3039, see R. Merkelbach, *Abrasax: Ausgewählte Papyri religiösen und magischen Inhalts; Band 4: Exorzismen und jüdisch/christlich beeinflusste Texte,* Papyrologica Coloniensia 17 (Opladen: Westdeutscher Verlag, 1996). It can also be found in incantations of the Byzantine period, e.g., Incantation no. 27, line 2: ". . . and the signet-ring of Solomon"; see J. Naveh and S. Shaked, *Magic Spells and Formulae* (Jerusalem: Magnes Press,

times the exorcist uses roots with magical power, for example, in the story of Baaras in Josephus (*War* 7.178-189).

Another applied technique found in Acts is the use of handkerchiefs or pieces of linen, carried away from Paul to the possessed person: "God worked extraordinary miracles through Paul: when handkerchiefs and scarves which had been in contact with his skin were carried to the sick, they were cured of their diseases and the evil spirits came out of them" (Acts 19:11-12).

This technique is also mentioned in the Greek magical papyri (*PGM* 7:826),[14] which testify that sometimes incantations were written on them.[15]

From the story of the demon Asmodeus, told in the book of Tobit, we learn of yet another act of exorcism, that is, smoking the heart and liver of a fish: "and [the angel] s[aid to him: 'Sl]it it (namely: the fish) open and take out [its gall, its [heart,] and its liver. Keep them w]ith you, but [throw away] it[s] inwards. [A medicine is its gall], its [heart], and its liver.' . . . If you smoke it (namely, the heart of the fish, its liver) in the presence of a man or a woman afflicted by a demon or an [evil] spirit, [and] thei[r] encounters will [nev]er occur again" (4QTobitb ar frg. 4 i.8-13).[16]

Reference to this act can be found in Justin's *Dialogue of Trypho,* chapter 85: "Now assuredly your exorcists, I have said, make use of crafts when they exorcise, even as the Gentiles do, and employ *fumigations* and incantations" (*ANF* 1:241).

The last act to be discussed is the laying on of hands. Such is the case, for example, in the expanded story in the *Genesis Apocryphon,* according to which Abram descended to Egypt because of the famine in the land of Canaan. When Sarai was taken to Pharaoh, a plague struck Pharaoh and his household in answer to Abram's prayer. This plague is described as a "deadly spirit" or "an evil spirit," which prevented Pharaoh from touching Sarai. After all the magicians failed to cure Pharaoh, he was cured by the prayer and exorcism of Abram. The last act was performed by laying hands upon Pharaoh, as described by Abram: "I laid my hand upon his (namely, Pharaoh's) [he]ad. The plague was removed

---

1993), pp. 91-94; R. Kotansky, J. Naveh, and S. Shaked, "A Greek-Aramaic Silver Amulet from Egypt in the Ashmolean Museum," *Le Muséon* 105 (1992): 5-24.

14. A handkerchief is also mentioned in *PGM* 36:269, which is an untitled spell; see H. D. Betz, ed., *The Greek Magical Papyri in Translation, Including the Demotic Spells* (Chicago: University of Chicago Press, 1986), p. 275.

15. See R. Kotansky, "Incantations and Prayers for Salvation on Inscribed Greek Amulets," in *Magika Hiera: Ancient Greek Magic and Religion,* ed. C. A. Faraone and D. Obbink (New York and Oxford: Oxford University Press, 1991), pp. 107-37; see esp. pp. 108-10. It might be connected to the stripes of the phylactery.

16. See Fitzmyer, "Tobit," pp. 44-46.

from him and the evil [spirit] was commanded (to depart) [from him], and he was cured" (20.29).

As noted by David Flusser,[17] the same technique is mentioned in Luke, in the description of Jesus healing sick and possessed people: "As the sun was setting, all those who had any who were sick with various kinds of diseases brought them to him; and he laid his hands on each of them and cured them. Demons also came out of many, shouting, 'You are the Son of God!' But he rebuked them and would not allow them to speak, because they knew that he was the Messiah" (Lk 4:40-41).

Another act of exorcism practiced by Jesus is described later in the book: "And just then there appeared a woman with a spirit that had crippled her for eighteen years. She was bent over and was quite unable to stand up straight. When Jesus saw her, he called her over and said: 'Woman, you are set free from your ailment.' When he laid his hands on her, immediately she stood up straight and began praising God" (Lk 13:11-13).

In conclusion, early Jewish sources of the Second Temple period shed light on the stories of Jesus' exorcisms, and enrich them with some details concerning technique used at that period.

---

17. D. Flusser, "Healing through the Laying On of Hands in a Dead Sea Scroll," in *Judaism and the Origins of Christianity* (Jerusalem: Magnes Press, 1988), pp. 21-22.

Reflections on Jesus' Eschatology in Light of Qumran

Henry W. M. Rietz

Strange as it may seem, I will suggest that one of the first steps in investigating Jesus' eschatology in light of Qumran is to move away from the language and conceptions of "eschatology" and even "apocalypticism." In my opinion, the real value of the sectarian Dead Sea Scrolls for the study of Jesus is that they give us insights into practices and thoughts of other Jews of the first century. As it will become apparent in this paper, I will argue that those insights are clearer if one avoids, at least initially, importing connotations often associated with eschatology and apocalypticism. In particular, such a move allows us to discern emphases and perspectives that more accurately reflect the context of early Judaism, namely, those of halakoth, ritual, cosmology, and divine presence.

The discovery of the Dead Sea Scrolls beginning in 1947 is one of the most important archaeological finds for understanding the context of the historical Jesus. Many scholars have discussed the many significant similarities as well as contrasts between the Qumran Community and Jesus. In particular, both the Qumran Community[1] and the historical Jesus[2] have been characterized as "es-

---

1. See the standard synthetic treatments of the Qumran Community: J. C. VanderKam, *The Dead Sea Scrolls Today* (Grand Rapids: Eerdmans, 1994); L. H. Schiffman, *Reclaiming the Dead Sea Scrolls: The History of Judaism, the Background of Christianity, the Lost Library of Qumran* (Philadelphia and Jerusalem: Jewish Publication Society, 1994); F. García Martínez and J. Trebolle Barrera, *The People of the Dead Sea Scrolls*, trans. W. G. E. Watson (Leiden: Brill, 1995), originally published as *Los Hombres de Qumrán* (1993); H. Stegemann, *The Library of Qumran: On the Essenes, Qumran, John the Baptist, and Jesus* (Grand Rapids: Eerdmans; Leiden: Brill, 1998), originally published as *Die Essener, Qumran, Johannes der Täufer und Jesus* (1993); M. A. Knibb, *The Qumran Community*, Cambridge Commentaries on Writings of the Jewish and Christian World, 200 BC to AD 200, vol. 2 (Cambridge: Cambridge University Press, 1987); D. Dimant, "Qumran Sectarian Literature," in *Jewish Writings of the Second Temple Period: Apocrypha, Pseudepigrapha, Qumran Sectarian Writings, Philo, Josephus*, ed. M. E. Stone, CRINT 2.2 (Assen: Van Gorcum; Philadelphia: Fortress, 1984), pp. 483-550; G. Vermes, *The Dead Sea*

chatological" and "apocalyptic."³ However, for reasons discussed below, the application of eschatology and apocalyptic to the Qumran Community and the his-

Scrolls: Qumran in Perspective, rev. ed. (Philadelphia: Fortress, 1977); F. M. Cross, *The Ancient Library of Qumran*, 3rd ed. (Minneapolis: Fortress, 1995 [rev. ed. 1961; 1st ed. 1958; the 3rd ed. is a revised reprint of the 1st ed.]); J. T. Milik, *Ten Years of Discovery in the Wilderness of Judaea*, trans. J. Strugnell (Naperville, Ill.: A. R. Allenson, 1959).

2. The identification of the historical Jesus as an apocalyptic or eschatological prophet has been a point of consensus among critical scholars for much of the twentieth century. See esp. A. Schweitzer, *The Quest of the Historical Jesus: A Critical Study of Its Progress from Reimarus to Wrede* (New York: Macmillan, 1968), originally published as *Von Reimarus zu Wrede* (1906); E. P. Sanders, *Jesus and Judaism* (Philadelphia: Fortress, 1985); J. H. Charlesworth, *Jesus within Judaism: New Light from Exciting Archaeological Discoveries*, ABRL (New York: Doubleday, 1988); B. D. Ehrman, *Jesus: Apocalyptic Prophet of the New Millennium* (Oxford: Oxford University Press, 1999). This consensus is challenged by many members of the Jesus Seminar group; for a survey of recent positions, see M. J. Borg, *Jesus in Contemporary Scholarship* (Valley Forge, Pa.: Trinity, 1994).

3. Among the focal points of discussion of the Qumranites' "eschatology" have been their expectation of two messiahs, the "eschatological" war, and the resurrection of the dead. For a general overview, see J. J. Collins, *Apocalypticism in the Dead Sea Scrolls*, Literature of the Dead Sea Scrolls (London and New York: Routledge, 1997), and "Patterns of Eschatology at Qumran," in *Traditions in Transformation: Turning Points in Biblical Faith*, ed. B. Halpern and J. D. Levenson, F. M. Cross Festschrift (Winona Lake, Ind.: Eisenbrauns, 1981), pp. 351-75. For discussion of the expectation of two messiahs, a priestly "messiah of Aaron" and a royal "messiah of Israel" (1QS 9.11; 1QSa 2; but compare CD MS B 19.10-11), see J. J. Collins, *The Scepter and the Star: The Messiahs of the Dead Sea Scrolls and Other Ancient Literature*, ABRL (New York: Doubleday, 1995); J. J. Collins, "The Works of the Messiah," *DSD* 1 (1994): 98-112; J. H. Charlesworth, ed., *Jesus and the Dead Sea Scrolls*, ABRL (New York: Doubleday, 1992); J. H. Charlesworth and L. L. Johns, eds., *The Messiah: Developments in Earliest Judaism and Christianity*, First Princeton Symposium on Judaism and Christian Origins (Minneapolis: Fortress, 1992); Sh. Talmon, "Waiting for the Messiah: The Spiritual Universe of the Qumran Covenanters," in *Judaisms and Their Messiahs*, ed. J. Neusner, W. S. Green, and E. Frerichs (New York: Cambridge University Press, 1988), pp. 111-37, reprinted in *The World of Qumran from Within: Collected Studies* (Jerusalem: Magnes Press; Leiden: Brill, 1989), pp. 273-300; J. Starcky, "Les quatre étapes du messianisme à Qumran," *RB* 70 (1963): 481-505; K. G. Kuhn, "The Two Messiahs of Aaron and Israel," in *The Scrolls and the New Testament*, ed. K. Stendahl, with J. H. Charlesworth, Christian Origins Library (New York: Crossroad, 1992), pp. 54-64, compilation originally published in 1957; essay originally published as "Die beiden Messias Aarons und Israels," *NTS* 1 (1954-55): 168-79. For discussion of the "eschatological" war, see esp. J. J. Collins, "The Eschatological War," in *Apocalypticism in the Dead Sea Scrolls*, pp. 91-109; Y. Yadin, *The Scroll of the War of the Sons of Light against the Sons of Darkness*, trans. B. Rabin and Ch. Rabin (Oxford: Oxford University Press, 1962), originally published in Hebrew in 1955; see also J. J. Collins, "The Mythology of Holy War in Daniel and the Qumran War Scroll: A Point of Transition in Jewish Apocalyptic," *VT* 25 (1975): 596-612; P. R. Davies, "Dualism and Eschatology in the Qumran War Scroll," *VT* 28 (1978): 28-36; J. J. Collins, "Dualism and Eschatology in 1QM: A Reply to P. R. Davies," *VT* 29 (1979): 212-16; P. R. Davies, "Dualism and Eschatology: A Rejoinder," *VT* 30 (1980): 93-97. With respect to the resurrection of the dead, J. J. Collins articulates the po-

torical Jesus is problematic. Rather, I would suggest that an investigation into the Qumran Community's conception of time may be a more profitable venture.[4]

Criteria of Dissimilarity

Why would an examination of the Qumran Community provide insights for the study of the historical Jesus? In fact, two of the criteria commonly used to reconstruct images of the historical Jesus are discontinuity from first-century Judaism and discontinuity from the early followers of Jesus.[5] While these criteria are useful, many scholars have rightly pointed out that using these criteria alone produces reconstructions of the historical Jesus in which Jesus inherits nothing from his traditions, nor does he have a positive effect on the subsequent movement that deified him.[6] These criteria proceed from the often implicit assumption that the goal of historical Jesus research is to discover the uniqueness of Jesus. Ironically, these criteria alone produce a historical Jesus

---

sition that there is no positive evidence in the sectarian Dead Sea Scrolls for the belief in the resurrection of the dead; contrast É. Puech, who argues for a belief in a bodily resurrection at Qumran (*La Croyance des Esséniens en la vie future: immortalité, résurrection, vie éternelle? Historie d'une croyance dans le Judaïsme ancien,* EBib, n.s., 21-22 [Paris: Gabalda, 1993]); see the significant review by J. J. Collins (*DSD* 1 [1994]: 246-52); see also G. W. E. Nickelsburg, Jr., *Resurrection, Immortality, and Eternal Life in Intertestamental Judaism,* HTS 26 (Cambridge: Harvard University Press; London: Oxford University Press, 1972), pp. 144-69.

4. For a fuller discussion, see Rietz, *Time in the Sectarian Dead Sea Scrolls,* WUNT II (Tübingen: Mohr Siebeck, forthcoming). The value of the heuristic category of time is determined by how well the concept enables one to discern relationships that are latent in the religious tradition. Such heuristic categories are legitimate tools used by modern scholars of religion and are as basic as the terms "religion," "culture," and "identity." That is not to say that all such categories are equally useful or valid; see, for instance, the discussion by D. S. Lopez, Jr., who convincingly challenges the notion that "belief" is the basic category for investigating all religions ("Belief," in *Critical Terms for Religious Studies,* ed. M. C. Taylor [Chicago: University of Chicago Press, 1998], pp. 21-35). The use of the heuristic category of time does not indicate that this project is a development of "the so-called etymologizing school" of biblical theology. For this approach see, e.g., T. Boman, *Hebrew Thought Compared with Greek* (Philadelphia: Westminster, 1960), and O. Cullmann, *Christ and Time: The Primitive Christian Conception of Time and History,* trans. F. V. Filson, 3rd ed. (London: SCM, 1962). For a substantive critique see J. Barr, *The Semantics of Biblical Language* (Oxford: Oxford University Press, 1961); for the description of this approach in biblical theology as the so-called etymologizing school, see S. J. DeVries, *Yesterday, Today, and Tomorrow: Time and History in the Old Testament* (Grand Rapids: Eerdmans, 1975), p. 31.

5. For a concise summary of common criteria, see J. P. Meier, *A Marginal Jew: Rethinking the Historical Jesus,* ABRL (New York: Doubleday, 1991), 1:167-95; for discussion of the criteria of dissimilarity, see esp. pp. 171-74.

6. See Meier, *A Marginal Jew,* 1:172-73.

Figure 42. Qumran, Caves 4A and 4B.   Courtesy of J. H. Charlesworth

who is removed from history, a certainly untenable prospect. In contrast, I would suggest that the goal of historical Jesus research, and indeed all historical research, is not to discover the uniqueness of a person, movement, or period. Instead of *uniqueness,* the goal is to discern *particularity.* The quest for uniqueness leaves undone the first half of the basic investigative approach of comparison and contrast. Describing the particularity of Jesus involves discerning both continuities and discontinuities. A reconstruction of particularities grounds a subject in the historical contingencies within time and space rather than abstracts a uniqueness that seems to transcend reality.

The historical Jesus was a first-century Jew living in Palestine, and the immediate context for understanding him is the early Judaism of the late Second Temple period. While Jesus' opponents were often other Jews, so were most — if not all — of his followers. In fact, the movement into which his followers developed remained within Judaism for at least a generation or two. Thus, one should expect significant continuities between Jesus and other Jews of the same period. The Dead Sea Scrolls, found near the ruins of Qumran, are one of the richest sources for understanding Jews in Judea in the time of Jesus.[7] That is not

7. Scholars have long recognized that the collection of documents found in eleven caves

to say that the Qumran Community or the documents found in its library are representative of all Jews of the period;[8] in fact, the Qumran Community was a sectarian movement that had separated itself to some degree from the rest of society.[9] Rather, through a process of comparison and contrast with the historical Jesus, elements will arise that may be indicative of a "common Judaism."

Were the Teachings of Jesus and the Qumran Community Eschatological and Apocalyptic?

Many scholars characterize the Qumran Community and the historical Jesus as "eschatological" and "apocalyptic." One of the problems with these adjectives, however, is that they have complex, even contradictory, uses in the history of scholarship. M. Borg aptly illustrates the confusion:

> Both ["eschatology" and "apocalyptic"] were initially used in Jesus studies to refer to the end of the world of ordinary history. But subsequent scholarship

near Khirbet Qumran constitutes a sort of "library" of the community whose ruins are adjacent to the caves. It is recognized as a library because the documents are from a variety of sources; not all the documents are compositions of the Qumran Community.

8. There are indications that the contents of the library have been shaped by the tendencies of the community. It is significant that certain categories of documents have not been found at Qumran. These include pre-70 Jewish Greek compositions such as the Wisdom of Solomon, the *Letter of Aristeas,* and the *Psalms of Solomon.* Scholars also have not found pro-Hasmonean documents such as 1 Maccabees and Judith. The only probable exception is the so-called *Prayer for King Jonathan* (4Q448). While it is hazardous to argue from silence, the sheer number of manuscripts found at Qumran reduces the statistical possibility that these omissions are the result of chance. Rather, it is probable that the omissions reflect the tendencies of the community. In particular, excluded are the partisan documents of the so-called Hellenizers of the early second century B.C.E., as well as those of their Hasmonean opponents. Cf. the comments of D. Dimant: "One cannot, then, escape the conclusion that the collection was intentional and not a haphazard assemblage of disparate works" ("The Qumran Manuscripts: Contents and Significance," in *Time to Prepare the Way in the Wilderness: Papers on the Qumran Scrolls by Fellows of the Institute for Advanced Studies of the Hebrew University, Jerusalem, 1989-1990,* ed. D. Dimant and L. H. Schiffman, STDJ 16 [Leiden: Brill, 1995], pp. 23-58, quotation from pp. 32-33).

9. According to 4QMMT, the community has "separated" themselves "from the multitude of the people": [אתם יודעים" ש]פרשנו מרוב העם ו]מהתערב בדברים האלה ומלבוא ע]מהם [לגב אלח" = "[And you know that] we have separated ourselves from the multitude of the peo[ple . . . and] from sharing in these things and from going wi[th them] in these" (C 7-8; text adapted from DJD 10, p. 58). The expression "we have separated ourselves from the multitude of the peo[ple]" seems parallel to the ones who "turned aside from the way of the people" (סרו מדרך העם) in the *Damascus Document* (CD MS A 8.16 and CD MS B 19.29). In the *Damascus Document,* the expression "the ones departing from the way of the people" is parallel to "the repenting ones of Israel" (שבי ישראל), a reference to the members of the community.

190

in this century has given the terms many different senses. "Eschatological" can be used metaphorically in a non–end of the world sense: as a nuanced synonym for "decisive," or as "earth-shattering," or to point to the *telos* of history. Even "apocalyptic," we are discovering, need not refer to the end of the world; some apocalyptic literature describes experiences of another world (visions or other-worldly journeys) and does not refer to the imminent end of the world of ordinary history.[10]

In addition to lacking precision, these terms tend to import completely otherworldly or transhistorical conceptions that do not accurately reflect the subjects.

Use of the adjective "apocalyptic" is best informed by the distinctions drawn by J. Collins[11] and J. Carmignac. They identify "apocalypse" as a specific literary genre. Collins defines the genre of apocalypse as follows: "Apocalypse is a genre of revelatory literature with a narrative framework, in which a revelation is mediated by an otherworldly being to an human recipient, disclosing a transcendent reality which is both temporal, insofar as it envisages eschatological salvation, and spatial, insofar as it involves another supernatural world."[12]

---

10. M. Borg, "A Renaissance in Jesus Studies," in *Jesus in Contemporary Scholarship* (Valley Forge, Pa.: Trinity, 1994), pp. 3-17, quotation from pp. 8-9; see also his "Jesus and Eschatology: A Reassessment," in *Images of Jesus Today*, ed. J. H. Charlesworth and W. P. Weaver, FSC 3 (Valley Forge, Pa.: Trinity, 1994), pp. 42-67.

11. Collins, in turn, is dependent on the distinctions drawn by M. E. Stone ("List of Revealed Things in the Apocalyptic Literature," in *Magnalia Dei: The Mighty Acts of God*, ed. F. M. Cross, W. E. Lemke, and P. D. Miller, Jr. [Garden City, N.Y.: Doubleday, 1976], p. 439) and P. D. Hanson ("Apocalypticism," in *IDBSup*, pp. 29-30).

12. J. J. Collins, "Apocalypse: The Morphology of a Genre," *Semeia* 14 (1979): 9. Collins's definition is comparable to that proposed by Carmignac; "Ainsi l'on pourrait proposer comme définition de l'Apocalyptique: genre littéraire qui présente, à travers des symboles typiques, des revelations soit sur Dieu, soit sur anges ou les demons, soit sur leurs partisans, soit sur les instruments de leur action" (J. Carmignac, "Qu'est-ce que l'Apocalyptique? Son emploi à Qumran," *RevQ* 10 [1979]: 20). Carmignac acknowledges his basic agreement with Collins's definition of apocalypse "qui est un genre littéraire et non pas une théologie particulière" (p. 33). Carmignac's only point of contention with Collins concerns the eschatological element that Collins includes; "Personnellement, je préférerais terminer cette définition après '. . . transcendent reality,' car l'eschatological salvation est un contenu théologique qui est possible, mais qui n'est pas du tout essentiel à l'Apocalyptique" (p. 33). Collins's definition focused on form and content, purposefully leaving aside function, which was subsequently picked up by D. Hellholm ("The Problem of Apocalyptic Genre and the Apocalypse of John," *Semeia* 36 [1986]: 13-64) and D. Aune ("The Apocalypse of John and the Problem of Genre," *Semeia* 36 [1986]: 65-96). Their work has led A. Yarbro Collins to propose an amendment to J. J. Collins's definition: "intended to interpret present, earthly circumstances in light of the supernatural world, and of the future, and to influence both the understanding and the behavior of the audience by means of divine

Subsequently, they distinguish apocalypticism as a sociological movement[13] and apocalyptic eschatology as "the kind of eschatology found in the apocalypses."[14] The pivotal point for Collins's and Carmignac's definitions is genre. While Collins does not restrict the adjective "apocalyptic" to the genre, the genre still remains the controlling point: "The use of the term should be controlled by analogy with the apocalyptic texts, and not allowed to float freely as an intuitive 'theological concept.'"[15]

The association of the adjective "apocalyptic" with the genre is critical for discussing the historical Jesus and the Qumran Community. Jesus did not produce any literary works, much less apocalypses. As for the Qumran Community, while a number of apocalypses were found in their library, probably none of them were composed by them.[16] Nevertheless, at least two apocalypses were

---

authority" (A. Yarbro Collins, "Introduction: Early Christian Apocalypticism," *Semeia* 36 [1986]: 7), which J. J. Collins accepts ("Genre, Ideology and Social Movements in Jewish Apocalypticism," in *Mysteries and Revelations: Apocalyptic Studies since the Uppsala Colloquium*, ed. J. J. Collins and J. H. Charlesworth, JSPSup 9 [Sheffield: JSOT, 1991], p. 19).

13. "A movement might reasonably be called apocalyptic if it shared the conceptual framework of the genre, endorsing a world view in which supernatural revelation, the heavenly world, and eschatological judgment played essential parts." J. J. Collins, *The Apocalyptic Imagination: An Introduction to the Jewish Matrix of Christianity* (New York: Crossroad, 1992), p. 10.

14. J. J. Collins, *The Apocalyptic Imagination*, p. 9. However, many scholars doubt whether a "common intellectual or ideational system" can be discerned in the apocalypses (P. R. Davies, "Qumran and Apocalyptic or *Obscurum per Obscurius*," *JNES* 49 [1990]: 127-34; see esp. 128-31), much less a distinctive eschatology (C. Rowland, *The Open Heaven: A Study of Apocalyptic in Judaism and Early Christianity* [New York: Crossroad, 1982], see esp. pp. 23-29, 47-48, 71).

15. J. J. Collins, "Genre, Ideology," p. 24; cf. *The Apocalyptic Imagination*, p. 10. Compare F. García Martínez, who emphasizes apocalyptic thought over the genre: "La apocalíptica es una corriente de pensamiento que nace en el contexto religioso y cultural concreto del judaísmo posexílico, que se desarrolla durante un largo período de tiempo reaccionando interactivamente con otras corrientes de pensamiento del medio ambiente judío, como la tradición profética o la tradición sapiencial, y que se plasma en las distintas obras que designamos como 'apocalipsis'" (*Qumran and Apocalyptic: Studies on the Aramaic Texts from Qumran* [Leiden: Brill, 1992], p. x n. 9). While García Martínez may be correctly describing the historical train of causality (i.e., apocalyptic thought produced the genre apocalypse), from a methodological standpoint the historian must work back from the genre to the thought.

16. See also D. Dimant, "Apocalyptic Texts at Qumran," in *The Community of the Renewed Covenant: The Notre Dame Symposium on the Dead Sea Scrolls*, ed. E. Ulrich and J. VanderKam (Notre Dame: University of Notre Dame Press, 1994), pp. 175-91. In contrast, García Martínez considers the *New Jerusalem, Visions of Amram* and 4QpsDan ar to be examples of apocalypses produced by the Qumran Community (*Qumran and Apocalyptic*, see esp. pp. 212-13). H. Stegemann suggests that there may be two possible exceptions, the *Book of Giants* and the *New Jerusalem*, which may be apocalypses and which may be products of the community. Nevertheless, even if these are Qumran-produced apocalypses, they account for such a small percentage of

authoritative traditions used by the community, namely, the books of Enoch[17] and Daniel.[18] Therefore, because of the centrality of the genre, use of the cognates of "apocalypse" ("apocalyptic" and "apocalypticism") is problematic with respect to the sectarian Dead Sea Scrolls and the historical Jesus. Collins, however, is willing to apply the adjective to communities that did not produce apocalypses, including the Qumran Community: "A movement or community might also be apocalyptic if it were shaped to a significant degree by a specific apocalyptic tradition, or if its world-view could be shown to be similar to that of the apocalypses in a distinctive way. The Essene movement and Qumran community would seem to qualify on both counts."[19] While ultimately I might agree, in my opinion more research on both the sectarian Dead Sea Scrolls and the historical Jesus as well as on the various apocalypses is necessary before we can broaden our use of the adjective "apocalyptic." In other words, if the adjective is to be applied at all, I suggest that it be applied at the end of inductive analysis rather than at the beginning. Thus, I find myself in agreement with R. L. Webb's conclusions, which are appropriate for discussions of the historical Jesus as well:

> Because Qumran was not an apocalypse-producing Community, however, the question of apocalypticism and Qumran becomes somewhat more complicated. We are examining literature written in other genres to determine the presence of an ideology defined by a separate genre. But since some of the motifs and ideas are not *unique* to apocalypses, then to what extent can we identify the presence of a particular motif or idea to constitute the presence of apocalypticism in a particular text? Perhaps a more cautious approach

the community's writings that "the Qumran community can in no way be regarded as an 'apocalyptic movement'" (H. Stegemann, "Some Aspects of Eschatology in Texts from the Qumran Community and in the Teachings of Jesus," in *Biblical Archaeology Today: Proceedings of the International Congress on Biblical Archaeology, Jerusalem, April 1984* [Jerusalem: Israel Exploration Society, 1985], p. 410). For an opposing position, see F. García Martínez and J. Trebolle Barrera, who emphatically describe the Qumran Community as "apocalyptic" (García Martínez and Barrera, *The People of the Dead Sea Scrolls,* and García Martínez, *Qumran and Apocalyptic*).

17. The traditional character of the Enoch material is indicated by a variety of evidence, including the number of manuscripts found at Qumran (4Q201-202, 4Q204-212). Influence of the story of the Watchers, which the Enochic material develops from Gen 6:1-4, is found in the *Damascus Document* (e.g., CD MS A 2.17-21) and the *Interpretation concerning the Periods* (4Q180 and possibly 4Q181).

18. The traditional character of Daniel also is indicated by the number of manuscripts found at Qumran (1Q71-72 [1QDan[a-b]], 4Q112-116 [4QDan[a-e]], 6Q7 [6QDan]). Note also the presence of the "pseudo-Daniel" compositions attested in 4Q243-245. For a brief discussion of Daniel and the "pseudo-Daniel" traditions, see J. J. Collins, *Apocalypticism,* pp. 12-18.

19. J. J. Collins, "Genre, Ideology," p. 23.

would look for a combination of motifs and ideas functioning together and would examine their interplay with one another and their function within the text before identifying the presence of apocalypticism in that text.[20]

This is not to say that comparisons between apocalypses on the one hand and the sectarian Dead Sea Scrolls and the historical Jesus are illegitimate. Rather, such comparisons should take place only after the sectarian Dead Sea Scrolls and the historical Jesus have been analyzed without importing connotations of apocalypticism.

The imposition of the term "eschatology" in discussions of the historical Jesus and the Qumran Community is even more problematic. The category of eschatology was developed in the context of Christian dogmatic theology.[21] It is historically illegitimate to apply a Christian dogmatic category to early Jewish texts and sources in order to investigate their worldview, which in turn may be used to understand the documents of the New Testament. Such a circular methodology skews the results produced by such analysis.[22] This circularity is illustrated when eschatology (the study of the "last things," from the Greek ἔσχατα) is used to classify a Hebrew concept such as אחרית הימים (literally the "latter days"). Eschatology often refers to a posthistorical reality, whereas אחרית הימים does not necessarily have such connotations. The situation is further complicated by the atemporal understanding of the term by dialectical theologians such as Bultmann.[23] Even within Semitic circles, a dualistic conception of his-

---

20. R. L. Webb, "'Apocalyptic': Observations on a Slippery Term," *JNES* 49 (1990): 115-26; quotation is from p. 126.

21. Carmignac denies the legitimacy of using the term "eschatology" with regard to the New Testament documents: "Quiconque parle d'Eschatologie (même dans le sens admissible) doit reconnaître que sa pensée ne part pas de Nouveau Testament mais qu'elle impose à ce Nouveau Testament un concept non-biblique." J. Carmignac, *Le Mirage de l'Eschatologie: Royauté, Règne et Royaume de Dieu . . . sans Eschatologie* (Paris: Letouzey et Ané, 1979), p. 200.

22. See, for example, H. Stegemann, who first defines eschatology, which he then exemplifies with a citation from Barnabas: "What is the meaning of eschatology? Eschatology belongs to a specific idea of history, which runs in a 'linear' way from a 'beginning' to an 'end.' . . . Basic for each conception of 'eschatology' is a pattern, in which specific elements of the 'beginning' and of the 'end' of a given history correspond to one another. Ἰδού, ποιῶ τὰ ἔσχατα ὡς τὰ πρῶτα, 'See, I make the last things according to the first things,' is an extremely apt description of this mode of thinking in the Early Christian letter of Barnabas 6:13" (Stegemann, "Some Aspects," p. 411).

23. E.g., "Thus eschatological existence has become possible. God has *acted,* and the world — 'this world' — has come to an end. *Man himself has been made new*" (R. Bultmann, "New Testament and Mythology," in *Kerygma and Myth: A Theological Debate,* ed. H. W. Bartsch, rev. ed. [New York: Harper and Row, 1961], p. 32); cf. *Jesus Christ and Mythology* (London: SCM, 1958), pp. 80-82.

tory may be problematic. Many descriptions of the Qumran Community and early Jewish apocalypses posit, either implicitly or explicitly, a contrast between "This World" (העולם הזה) and "The World to Come" (העולם הבא).[24] While such a conception may be implied by the documents, J. Licht argues that the situation is more complex as he illustrates with the Apocalypse of the Ten Weeks in *1 Enoch*.[25] In my opinion, Talmon captures the perspective of the Qumranites' (whom he calls "Covenanters") conception of the "New Age": "It needs to be stressed that the Covenanters invested their conceptions of the messianic age with the same real-historical character which biblical thinkers give to their visions of the future. The new eon was seen by the founding members to be only one step away from their own days. They were standing on the threshold of a new epoch in history, infinitely sublime, but basically not different from the preceding stages in actual experienced history."[26]

The Qumran Community's Conception of Time

The concept of time provides insight into the religious matrix of the Qumran Community. The community members' preoccupation with time is expressed by, and brings together, their distinctive calendrical system and perception of history. These two elements, in turn, are related to other aspects of the community's thought and praxis, namely, its halakah (or interpretations of Jewish Law), ritual practices, cosmology (especially the relationship between the heavens and the earth), and the affirmation of the divine presence in its midst. Moreover, the Qumranites' disputes over these issues with other Jews, especially those controlling the Jerusalem Temple, led them to believe they were living in the last days of an evil era, and to await the dawning of a new era *in history* when evil would be eradicated.

The community inherited traditions asserting that God commanded the use of a specific 364-day calendar.[27] The use of this calendar enabled the community

---

24. Rather, there is a tendency among scholars "to view the whole of apocalyptic literature in light of its later stages and, of course, that of its successors; for both the Rabbis and the New Testament use the terms *this World* and the [*sic*] *The World to Come*" (J. Licht, "Time and Eschatology in Apocalyptic Literature and in Qumran," *JJS* 16 [1965]: 178).

25. Licht, "Time and Eschatology," pp. 177-82.

26. Talmon, "Waiting for the Messiah," p. 126.

27. See, for example:

> (Thus) now, my son, I have revealed to you everything; (so) the rules concerning all the stars of heaven are concluded (here). (Indeed) he showed me all their respective rules for every day, for every season, and for every year; the procession of each according to

members to keep the Torah commandments to observe the various festivals while at the same time honoring the commandments concerning the Sabbath. In particular, the Qumranites restricted sacrifice on the Sabbath to only the Sabbath burnt offering, a prescription they were able to observe because of the 364-day calendar.

אל יעל איש למזבח בשבת כי אם עולת השבת כי כן בתוב מלבד שבתותיכם

Let no man offer at the altar[28] on the sabbath except the burnt offering of the sabbath, for thus it is written, "Apart from your sabbaths." (CD MS A 11.17b-18a)[29]

The passage grounds the halakah by citing Lev 23:38.[30] As Schiffman observes, the interpretation understands Lev 23:37-38 as one sentence[31] and the preposition מלבד in Lev 23:38 as excluding, "apart," rather than including, "besides,"

---

the commandment, every month and every week. (1 En 79.1-2, translated by E. Isaac in OTP 1:58)

And you, command the children of Israel so that they shall guard the years in this number, three hundred and sixty-four days, and it will be a complete year. (Jub 6.32, translated by O. S. Wintermute in OTP 2:68)

For identification of the 364-day calendar, see Sh. Talmon, "Yom Hakippurim in the Habakkuk Scroll," Biblica 32 (1951): 549-63, reprinted in a slightly revised form in The World of Qumran from Within, pp. 186-99; D. Barthélemy, "Notes en marge de publications récentes sur les manuscrits de Qumran," RB 59 (1952): 187-218; see esp. 199-203; A. Jaubert, "Le calendrier des Jubilés et de la secte de Qumrân. Ses origines bibliques," VT 3 (1953): 250-64; "Le calendrier de Jubilés et les jours liturgiques de la semaine," VT 7 (1957): 35-61; The Date of the Last Supper (Staten Island, N.Y.: Alba House, 1965), English translation of La Date de la Cène: Calendrier biblique et liturgie chrétienne (1957), by I. Rafferty. See also, J. C. VanderKam, "The Origin, Character, and Early History of the 364-Day Calendar: A Reassessment of Jaubert's Hypotheses," CBQ 41 (1979): 390-411. For detailed reviews of the scholarship, see J. C. VanderKam, Calendars in the Dead Sea Scrolls: Measuring Time, Literature of the Dead Sea Scrolls (London and New York: Routledge, 1998), pp. 52-70; and earlier VanderKam, "Calendrical Texts and the Origins of the Dead Sea Community," in Methods of Investigation of the Dead Sea Scrolls and the Khirbet Qumran Site: Present Realities and Future Prospects, ed. M. O. Wise, N. Golb, J. J. Collins, and D. G. Pardee, Annals of the New York Academy of Sciences 722 (New York: New York Academy of Sciences, 1994), pp. 371-88; D. Barthélemy, "Notes en marge de publications récentes sur les manuscrits de Qumran," RB 59 (1952): 187-218; see esp. 199-203.

28. Or "on the altar"; for the root עלה followed מזבח with a prefixed ל-, see 2 Chr 29:27 (Schiffman, The Halakah at Qumran [Leiden: Brill, 1975], p. 128).

29. Text and translation adapted from Baumgarten and Schwartz, PTSDSSP 2:48-49. A fragmentary parallel is preserved in 4Q266 frg. 9 1.2-3 (DJD 18, pp. 67-68).

30. The MT reads שבתת יהוה. Unfortunately, Lev 23:38 has not been identified among the biblical Dead Sea Scrolls.

31. Schiffman, The Halakah at Qumran, p. 128 n. 298.

other sacrifices.[32] This halakah corresponds to the community's use of the 364-day calendar, which prevented festivals, and thus offerings, other than the burnt offering of the Sabbath, from occurring on the Sabbath.[33] Thus, the adherence to the 364-day solar-based calendar is rooted in their halakic interpretations, and is focused on praxis.

In addition to the halakic significance, observance of the 364-day calendar also has cosmic dimensions. The Qumran Community shared the cosmology common in early Judaism, namely, that the cosmos consists of the heavens above and the earth below.[34] Despite the bifurcation of the two realms, the structures and inhabitants of each realm are conceived as paralleling the other. Humans on earth are paralleled by divine angelic beings in the heavens.[35] The

32. Baumgarten and Schwartz, PTSDSSP 2:49 n. 176. See also מלבד שבתית in 4Q513 frg. 4 line 3, where there seems to be a polemic against the reaping and offering of barley for the Omer celebration (J. M. Baumgarten, "Halakhic Polemics in New Fragments from Qumran Cave 4," in *Biblical Archaeology Today*, Proceedings of the International Congress on Biblical Archaeology, Jerusalem, April 1984 [Jerusalem: Israel Exploration Society, 1985], pp. 390-99; see esp. pp. 395-97; see also L. H. Schiffman, PTSDSSP 1:145-49, 158-75; M. Baillet, DJD 7, 1982, pp. 287-295 and pls. LXXII-LXXIII).

33. See Schiffman's discussion of how this halakah relates to Num 28:10, which is usually interpreted by non-Qumran Jews as enjoining the daily sacrifice to be performed on the Sabbath: this decision flies in the face of Num 28:10, which indicates that this offering (i.e., the Sabbath burnt offering [עולה השבת]) was to be brought in addition to the regular daily offerings *(tamid)*. One can only assume that the sect interpreted the word *'al* ("in addition to") in Num 28:10 to mean "instead of." Hence, there was no contradiction according to their interpretation. If the sect actually perceived this problem and worked it out as set forth above, this is a clear example of *midrash halakhah*. It may be, however, that the two explanations were developed independently, that of Num 28:10 coming first, so that no one asked about the apparent contradiction (Schiffman, *The Halakah at Qumran*, p. 128). Baumgarten, however, disputes that the *tamid* offering would be affected ("Halakic Polemics," pp. 395 and 398 n. 23). Similarly, Ch. Rabin cites Num 28:10 and comments that the prohibition does not refer to the *tamid* (*The Zadokite Documents* [Oxford: Clarendon, 1958], p. 58).

34. Cf. J. G. Gammie, who refers to this as a "spatial dualism" ("Spatial and Ethical Dualism in Jewish Wisdom and Apocalyptic Literature," *JBL* 93 [1974]: 356-85; see esp. pp. 360-72).

35. See esp. the *Rule of the Community* (1QS 3.13–4.26). The anthropological, or "ethical," dualism is expressed by the two categories of humans, the "Sons of Light" and the "Sons of Darkness." This anthropological dualism corresponds to an angelic dualism such that human actions are determined by their heavenly counterparts, called the "Spirit of Truth," who is synonymous with the "Prince of Light," and the "Spirit of Perversity," who is synonymous with the "Angel of Darkness." Each of these two corresponding dualisms comprises a polarity of warring factions and has been called a "cosmic dualism." For discussion of the Qumranites' various dualisms, see esp. J. H. Charlesworth, "A Critical Comparison of the Dualism in 1QS 3:13–4:26 and the 'Dualism' Contained in the Gospel of John," in *John and the Dead Sea Scrolls*, ed. J. H. Charlesworth, Christian Origins Library (New York: Crossroad, 1990 [1972]), pp. 76-106, originally published in *NTS* 15 (1968-69): 389-418; P. von der Osten-Sacken, *Gott und*

Jerusalem Temple corresponds to a celestial sanctuary. Members of the Qumran Community believed that the commandments regarding the Sabbath and the festivals had been given not only to Israel, but also to the celestial beings and the angels;[36] the Sabbath and the festivals are to be celebrated in the heavens as well as on earth.[37] Thus, the liturgy of the two sanctuaries is to be coordinated not only in actions, but also in timing. That is, worship in the Jerusalem Temple is to be synchronized with the heavenly worship.[38] In this way a connection, even an experience of community, is established between the celestial and the terrestrial beings. Thus, the 364-day calendar was understood not only as an expression of God's will, but also as God's ordering of the cosmos.

Belial: Traditionsgeschichtliche Untersuchungen zum Dualismus in den Texten aus Qumran, SUNT 6 (Göttingen: Vandenhoeck & Ruprecht, 1969), see esp. pp. 116-89; M. Treves, "The Two Spirits of the Rule of the Community," *RevQ* 3 (1962): 449-52; P. Wernberg-Møller, "A Reconsideration of the Two Spirits in the Rule of the Community (1QSerek III,13–IV,26)," *RevQ* 3 (1961): 413-41; H. W. Huppenbauer, *Der Mensch zwischen zwei Welten: Der Dualismus der Texte von Qumran (Höhle I) und der Damaskusfragmente; Ein Beitrag zur Vorgeschichte des Evangeliums,* Abhandlungen zur Theologie des Alten und Neuen Testaments 34 (Zürich: Zwingli, 1959); J. Licht, "An Analysis of the Treatise of the Two Spirits in DSD," in *Aspects of the Dead Sea Scrolls,* ed. Ch. Rabin and Y. Yadin, 2nd ed., ScrHier 4 (Jerusalem: Magnes Press, 1965), pp. 88-99.

36. Distinct from the biblical tradition, the command to observe the Sabbath in *Jubilees* was first given to the angels and the Sabbath is observed in the heavens:

> And he gave us a great sign, the sabbath day, so that we might work six days and observe a sabbath from all work on the seventh day. And he told us — all of the angels of the presence and all of the angels of sanctification, these two great kinds — that we might keep the sabbath with him in heaven and on earth. (*Jub* 2.17-18; translation by Wintermute in *OTP* 2:57)

> On this day we kept the sabbath in heaven before it was made known to any human to keep the sabbath thereon upon the earth. (*Jub* 2.30b; translation by Wintermute in *OTP* 2:58)

> Among humans, the Sabbath was only made known to the chosen people of Israel, and they were instructed to observe the Sabbath with the angels. (*Jub* 2.19-20, 30b; 50.9-10)

> And thus he created therein a sign by which they (i.e., the Israelites) might keep the sabbath *with us* (i.e., the angels) on the seventh day, to eat and drink and bless the one who created all things just as he blessed and sanctified for himself a people who appeared from all the nations so that they might keep the sabbath *together with us*. (*Jub* 2.21; translation by Wintermute in *OTP* 2:57, emphasis added)

37. See the *Songs of the Sabbath Sacrifice* (4Q400-4Q407, 11Q17, Masık).

38. See the arguments developed in Rietz, "Collapsing of the Heavens and the Earth: Conceptions of Time in the Sectarian Dead Sea Scrolls" (Ph.D. diss., Princeton Theological Seminary, 2000).

The members of the Qumran Community, however, were living during a time when a lunar-based 354-day, not a solar-based 364-day, calendar was being observed in the Jerusalem Temple.[39] The Qumranites interpreted this situation in light of the traditions they inherited. Since they believed that the heavens and the earth were supposed to be brought together and synchronized, when the commandments were not performed at the appropriate time the sacred continuity between the heavens and the earth would be severed. They interpreted the use of the 354-day calendar in the Temple as breaking the continuity between the heavens and the earth. Since the heavens and the earth represent not only spatial but also ontological categories, that is, the categories of human and divine, breaking the synchronicity results in the alienation of the human from the divine. For members of the community, human praxis had cosmic implications; failure to observe the community's halakoth in the Temple created a cosmic disturbance. To be "out of sync" with God's ordering of the cosmos by not observing the Sabbath and the festivals at the correct time was sin and made one liable to God's wrath.

The Qumranites interpreted their halakic conflict with the priests controlling the Temple in light of their understanding of history. From their perspective, God has not only ordered the cosmos according to the annual cycles of the 364-day calendar, but God has also ordered the course of history. "From the God of knowledge (comes) all that is and (all) that shall be."[40] Specifically, members of the community believed that God has arranged history into "periods" (קצים) and has predetermined the character, duration, and events of each of these periods. Within this understanding of history, the regnant priests' fail-

---

39. Sh. Talmon concluded from his reading of 1QpHab 11.4-8 that the Qumran community followed a different calendrical system than the one being observed in the Jerusalem Temple. The passage, interpreting Hab 2:15, describes a conflict between the leader of the Qumran Community — the "Righteous Teacher" — and the high priest who is referred to in the passage as the "Wicked Priest"; its interpretation concerns the Wicked Priest who pursued after the Righteous Teacher to devour him with his poisonous vexation to the house of his exile. And at the end of the festival, the rest-(day) of the Day of Atonement, he appeared to them to devour them and to cause them to stumble on the day of fasting, their restful Sabbath (שבת מנוחתם; 1QpHab 11.4-8). As Talmon argued, the high priest (the "Wicked Priest") could not have launched an attack on a day he considered a festival. Thus, the high priest could not have recognized that particular day as a holy day. That the community was observing the Day of Atonement on a different day than the high priest indicated to Talmon that the community was following a different calendrical system. He supported his interpretation further by noting the significance of the third-person pronominal suffix ("their") restricting observation of the "restful Sabbath" (שבת מנוחתם) to the community. See Sh. Talmon, "Yom Hakippurim in the Habakkuk Scroll," *Biblica* 32 (1951): 549-63, reprinted in a slightly revised form in *The World of Qumran from Within*, pp. 186-99.

40. 1QS (1Q28) 3.15; cf. *Sabbath Song 5* and 4Q180 frg. 1 lines 1-2a.

Figure 43. Qumran toilet in Northeast Quarter. Were the Roman soldiers, after 68 C.E., the ones who moved the latrine within the buildings?
Courtesy of J. H. Charlesworth

ure to observe the community's halakoth — especially the calendar — in the Jerusalem Temple indicated to the Qumranites that they were living in "the latter days" (אחרית הימים) of an "evil period" (קץ הרשיע) in history.[41]

This concept of predeterminism is cast within the framework of the spatial dualism of the heavens and the earth and the ontological dualism of human and divine. Superimposed over this framework is an ethical dualism of good and evil, with good angelic beings in the heavens allied with the community and evil angelic beings corresponding to the community's opponents.[42] Thus, within this matrix, the community's terrestrial conflict reflects a celestial conflict among the angelic beings. Ultimately, Qumranites predicted that the pe-

41. See, e.g., 4QMMT C12-14; CD MS A 12.23; 1QS 3.13–4.26; 1QSa 1.1; 1QpHab 5.7-8; 4Q181 frg. 1 2.1-6.

42. See 1QS 3.13–4.26; 1QM 1.13b-16a. In the *War Scroll*, the angelic figures include the "Prince of Light" (שר מאור; 1QM 13.10; cf. שר אורים in 1QS 3.20), Michael, Gabriel, Sariel, Raphael (1QM 9.15-16), and others who are waging war "against the army of Belial" (בחיל בליעל; 1QM 1.1), which includes "the spirits of his lot, the angels of emptiness" (רוחי גורלו מלאכי חבל; 1QM 13.11-12//4QM5 frg. 2 line 4).

riod of evil would culminate in a full-blown war between the forces of good and evil in the heavens and on the earth.[43]

Because of the strong spatial dualism, references to the war often portray two parallel battles occurring, one on earth and the other in the heavens. Nevertheless, within the context of the war, there are also claims that divine beings — angels and even God — are present in the community. Significantly, the wording of some of these claims echoes affirmations of communion with the divine associated with worshiping God at the correct time: "for the holy angels (are) together with their hosts."[44] These echoes suggest that as members of the community believed that terrestrial worshipers should be synchronized with the heavenly counterparts, they also conceived of their combatants on earth as needing to be synchronized with their heavenly allies.

The association of the community's worship on the Sabbath, for instance, and battle is supported by the common ritual contexts. War in many cultures, including the ancient Near East and especially in early Judaism, is a religious phenomenon requiring cultic rituals and purity. This aspect of war is well attested at Qumran by compositions such as the *War Scroll* and the *Rule of War,* which are primarily liturgies for battle. Formally, liturgy consists of music (i.e., songs, chants, as well as the playing of instruments) and ritual actions (i.e., choreographed movements and even dance). Group performance of music and ritual actions often involves a synchronization of participants. The phenomenology of music suggests that perhaps the Qumranites' perception of community and even unity with the divine is a product of the synchronicity facilitated by their rituals and liturgies. Within a worldview in which members of the community believed they were "in time" with the heavens, the experience of unity among members of the community in liturgy would have been understood as including the divine.

Summary of the Qumran Community's Concept of Time

This study has attempted to present a brief description of the religion of the Qumran Community through its "concept of time." As with other forms of Ju-

43. See, e.g., 1QM 1.13b-16a: "During the war, the Sons of Light shall strengthen (for) three lots and smite wickedness, and (for) three (lots) the army of Belial shall gird itself for the return of the lot of [. . .]. . . . And during the seventh lot, the great hand of God shall subdue [. . .] the angels of his dominion and for all the men of [. . .] (vacat) [. . .] the holy ones, he shall appear in help [. . .] truth for the destruction of the Sons of Darkness" (translation adapted from Duhaime, PTSDSSP 2:96-99).

44. 1QM (1Q33) 7.3-6; cf. 1QSa 2.3-9 and a composite of 4QDᵃ (4Q266) frg. 8 1.7-9, CD MS A 15.15-18, and 4QDᵉ (4Q270) frg. 6 2.8-9.

Figure 44. Qumran, Locus 30. Most Qumranologists judge this to be the scriptorium.   Courtesy of J. H. Charlesworth

daism, the primary expression of the Qumran Community was the observance of the Torah, praxis. So the community's adherence to the 364-day calendar was driven by a desire to fulfill the commandments according to their interpretation of the Torah, their halakoth. Thus, their practice reflected their theological study and speculation. The Qumranites' use of the 364-day calendar was set in the context of a complex theological framework whereby they understood themselves to be participating with the cosmic beings in fulfilling God's will. Thus, their praxis and theology were situated within a perception of their place in history, at a time when they believed the connection between the heavens and the earth had been ruptured. In this context their liturgies, performed "in sync" with the heavens, facilitated and anticipated God's reconciliation of the heavens and the earth. For the Qumranites, the cyclical observance of "sacred time" was situated within a linear conception of history, and it was through the cyclical observance that the progression of linear time was anticipated. The reconciliation of the heavens and the earth included the experience of the divine in the midst of the human community. The experience of the divine in worship represented an in-breaking or even a collapsing of the heavens and the earth.

A Comparison and Contrast of the Qumran Community with the Historical Jesus

Exploration of the Qumran Community's conceptions of time provides a perspective from which to comprehend better the historical Jesus. Of foremost importance is the centrality of halakoth, the interpretation and practice of the Torah, in the Qumran Community's thought. Rather than opposed to their theology, cosmology, and ritual mysticism, halakoth should be seen in dynamic relationship with their understanding of cosmology and their place in history. In particular, the community's halakic disputes with other Jews and especially with the priests controlling the Jerusalem Temple led its members to believe they were living in the last days of an evil generation and world. The perception of the historical Jesus changes dramatically when the understanding of his conflict with other Jews moves away from anachronistic concerns about his identity to differing interpretations of halakoth. There is no evidence that Jesus purposely broke the Torah; rather, his words and actions represent interpretations of how to fulfill it. Clearly, Jesus and members of the Qumran Community differ sharply on their specific interpretations,[45] not least in their interpretation of the Sabbath halakoth, but the fact that they sought to do God's will by honoring what they considered to be the true meaning of the Sabbath reflects their commonality as Jews. Moreover, I would suggest that the shift from understanding Jesus' teachings as intra-Jewish halakic disputes to belief versus works reflects the tendencies of a period after Jesus when the inclusion of Gentiles becomes a major concern for the followers of Jesus.

Second, the investigation of the Qumran Community lifts up ritual practice as an important, if not integral, aspect of fulfilling the will of God and experiencing the divine. This provides another potentially fruitful perspective for imaging the historical Jesus. While at first blush the Gospel accounts do not seem to emphasize Jesus' ritual activity, there are indications that his life was indeed ordered by ritual practice. There is ample evidence that prayer was an important component of his daily life, and one should not anachronistically presuppose that his prayers were primarily extemporaneous, devoid of liturgical structure. Moreover, Jesus submitted to the ritual lustration of John, a practice clearly adopted by his followers and possibly performed by Jesus himself.[46] As with his halakic disputes, Jesus' polemics against the development of elaborate rituals not prescribed in the Torah[47] need not be read as a *rejection* of ritual, but rather as a different interpreta-

---

45. Cf., e.g., D. Flusser, "The Parable of the Unjust Steward: Jesus' Criticism of the Essenes," in *Jesus and the Dead Sea Scrolls*, pp. 176-97.

46. See, e.g., the contradictory testimonies of Jn 3:22; 4:1-3.

47. E.g., Mt 6:1-18 and parallels. Notice that in Mt 6:7 the attack on "heaping up empty phrases" while praying is directed against the Gentiles.

tion of how to *perform* rituals, thus affirming their importance. Indeed, the Gospel accounts consistently portray Jesus as observing Jewish festivals and holidays, including his final journey to Jerusalem to observe the Passover.

Third, members of the Qumran Community believed it was God's will that events in the heavens and on the earth be synchronized. For members of the community, following what they considered to be improper halakoth, particularly by the priests in the Jerusalem Temple, severed the synchronistic relationship between the heavens and the earth and led them to believe they were living in the last days of an evil generation. This cosmic dualism was complicated by ethical and ontological dualisms of good and evil, or, in the language of the community, of the forces of "light" (אור) and "darkness" (חשך).[48] Moreover, this ethical dualism was related to the community's monotheistic belief in an all-encompassing divine predestination of people and events.[49] Ultimately this complex cosmology served not to devalue events and practices on earth; instead, it tended to heighten their importance. For example, ritual practices in the Jerusalem Temple on the Sabbath were not viewed as mere reflections of angelic worship in the heavens; rather, they were viewed as reflections of celestial worship. Thus, terrestrial worship had cosmic implications.

While Jesus' thought was not characterized by such a complex cosmology as the Qumran Community with its strict notions of ontological dualism and predestination, his thought presupposed a similar cosmic dualism between the heavens and the earth. Neither the Qumran Community's nor Jesus' cosmic dualism promoted an otherworldly escapism. Rather, the cosmology provided the context in which this-worldly events and actions came under divine scrutiny. For example, in his teachings and disputes Jesus insisted that human actions on earth are of ultimate importance. For Jesus, unjust acts and relationships that transgressed his interpretations of the Torah estranged institutions, such as the Temple, and people, such as the political and religious elite, from God. Moreover, the just order observed in the heavens provided the model for realizing the kingdom of God on earth. So Jesus prayed, "Your kingdom come, your will be done on earth as it is in the heavens."

Fourth, another commonality between Jesus' and the Qumranites' cosmic dualism is their affirmation that the divine was present in the midst of their respective communities. For the Qumran Community the experience of the divine presence — often represented by angelic beings — was associated with the proper observance of rituals such as the Sabbath worship, ritual meals, and the performance of battle liturgies. Jesus also affirmed the in-breaking of the divine pres-

---

48. See especially the *Rule of the Community*, 1QS 3.13–4.26.

49. See, e.g., 1QS (1Q28) 3.15, quoted earlier; cf. *Sabbath Song* 5 and 4Q180 frg. 1 lines 1-2a.

ence he called the "kingdom of God," where God's will for just social relations was realized. Thus, while both Jesus and the Qumranites claimed to experience the presence of God on earth, their emphasis on how or where that experience would be manifested differed. For the Qumranites, the divine was experienced usually in ritual. For Jesus, it was realized primarily in just relationships.

The different emphases are demonstrated by their respective conflicts with other Jews, especially with the Temple authorities. As a priestly movement, the Qumran Community objected to specific ritual practices as well as the lineage of the ruling priests. Jesus, in contrast, seems to have opposed the economic and social effects that the building and maintenance of the massive Temple complex and infrastructure had on the people at large.[50] According to the *Pesher Habakkuk,* the Righteous Teacher was physically attacked by the Wicked Priest, presumably the high priest of the Jerusalem Temple.[51] Jesus, in turn, actively protested in the Temple, creating a disturbance that probably set the stage for his arrest and execution by the Roman authorities. Thus, it is their respective rejection of the practices of the Temple leadership that was a major factor in their belief that they were living in the last days of an evil generation. Their conflicts with the Temple, however, bring to the fore the particularities that distinguish them. While both sought reforms to bring the Temple in line with the will of God expressed in the Torah, they differed on specifics of their interpretations of the Torah. In particular, the Qumranites argued with the Temple authorities about sacerdotal issues while Jesus opposed the socioeconomic effects of the Temple administration on the people.

Conclusion

In this discussion I have tried to provide a balanced comparison and contrast between Jesus and the members of the Qumran Community. Commonalities shared by the sectarian Qumran Community and Jesus demonstrate how much both Jesus and the Qumranites had in common with other Jews of the period. While I have attempted to preserve the particularities of both Jesus and the Qumran Community, the contrasts should not be overdrawn. The priestly emphases of the separatist Qumran Community were not necessarily antithetical to the emphasis on social justice by the populist Jesus. Rather, I would suggest that they are two varying interpretations of the same Torah. Indeed, this study suggests that examining the interrelations of the two emphases would provide fruitful results.

50. See C. A. Evans, "Opposition to the Temple: Jesus and the Dead Sea Scrolls," in *Jesus and the Dead Sea Scrolls,* pp. 235-53.

51. See 1QpHab 11.4-8, quoted in an earlier note.

Did Jesus Attend the Synagogue?

James D. G. Dunn

Did Jesus attend the synagogue? The question appears simple, and the answer seems straightforward in the light of the testimony of the Gospels. The Gospels refer a number of times to *synagōgai*,[1] and particularly speak of Jesus quite regularly teaching and preaching in Galilean *synagōgai*.[2] What, then, is the problem?

The problem is twofold. First, there is the interrelated issue of terminology and archaeology. Does the Greek term *synagōgē* mean "synagogue"? That is, does it refer to a building set apart for religious purposes? And is there archaeological evidence for such buildings in the Galilee of Jesus? Second, behind that lies the far-reaching question, whether we should expect to find synagogues in Galilee at that time. The question could be posed thus: Was Galilee sufficiently Jewish to support any assumption that Galileans would have attended the synagogue Sabbath by Sabbath?

In both cases recent archaeological findings have a direct relation to the problem. They help to clarify the issues, shed light on what it must have meant to grow up in Lower Galilee in the first decades of the common era, and effectively undermine some of the wilder hypotheses that have grown out of the earlier confused state of the evidence. It will be most convenient to take the two issues in reverse order: (1) Can we speak of "Galilean Judaism"? (2) Were there synagogues in first-century Galilee?

---

1. Note particularly reference to "the best seats in the synagogues" (Mk 12:39 pars.; Lk 11:43) and being beaten/flogged in synagogues (Mk 13:9/Mt 10:17). [Also, see the chapter in this collection by J. S. Kloppenborg. — JHC.]

2. Mt 4:23; 9:35; 13:54; Mk 1:39; 6:2; Lk 4:15-16; 4:44; 6:6; 13:10; Jn 6:59.

Can We Speak of "Galilean Judaism"?

The initial problem concerns the terms "Jew" and "Judaism." For the term usually translated "Jew" *(Ioudaios)* is first to be translated "Judean" — someone who comes from the territory known as "Judea" *(Ioudaia)*. And "Judaism" *(Ioudaismos)* first appears as the national religion of those who lived in Judea.[3] The "Jews" were first "Judeans." But Jesus is remembered as a Galilean,[4] and no one disputes that most of his mission was centered in the Galilee.[5] And Galilee is not Judea. Does that mean that the Galileans were also not part of Judaism, that it is actually improper to call Jesus a Jew? The issue has potentially far-reaching implications and cannot be avoided. There are two aspects to the issue: Was Galilee "Jewish"? and to what extent was Galilee "Hellenized"?

Was Galilee Jewish?

The first issue can be posed quite sharply in terms of early Judaism's own historical records. As part of the northern kingdom (Israel), Galilee had been separated from Judea since the division of the Davidic kingdom following Solomon's death (about 922 B.C.E.). When finally overrun by the Assyrians (722 or 721), "the Israelites" were transported to Assyria (2 Kgs 17:6), "exiled from their own land to Assyria until this day" (17:23), and replaced "in the cities of Samaria" by settlers from Mesopotamia (17:24). According to 1 Maccabees, it was only in the course of the internecine warfare that marked the decline of the Syrian empire that Samaria and Galilee were added (offered?) to Judea (1 Macc 10:30) in about 152 B.C.E.[6] But it was nearly another fifty years before the Hasmoneans, under Aristobulus I (104-103), regained full control of the area.

---

3. The Greek term *Ioudaismos* first appears in literature in 2 Maccabees, in three passages — 2:21, 8:1, and 14:38. 2:21 describes the Maccabean rebels as "those who fought bravely for Judaism"; 8:1 refers to their supporters as "those who had continued in Judaism"; and 14:38 calls the martyr Razis one who had formerly been accused of Judaism and had eagerly risked body and life "for Judaism." Reflecting the same traditions, 4 Macc 4:26 describes the attempt of the Syrian overlord Antiochus Epiphanes "to compel each member of the nation to eat defiling foods and to renounce Judaism."

4. Mk 1:9; Mt 2:22; 21:11; 26:69; 27:55; Lk 2:39; 23:6; Jn 7:41, 52.

5. E.g., Mk 1:14, 16, 28, 39; 3:7; Lk 4:14, 31; 23:5, 49, 55; Acts 10:37.

6. Emil Schürer, *A History of the Jewish People in the Time of Jesus Christ* (Jerusalem: Raritas [1970?]), 1:141 and n. 9. In an earlier campaign, Simon, brother of Judas Maccabeus, had rescued "the Jews (Judeans) of Galilee" and brought them back to Judea (1 Macc 5:23); "the early Maccabees by no means set out to Judaize those regions, but on the contrary, withdrew their Jewish population" (Schürer, 1:142).

Josephus's description of the forcible accession is noteworthy: Aristobulus "compelled the inhabitants, if they wished to remain in the territory, to be circumcised and to live in accordance with the laws of the Jews (= Judeans)" (*Ant* 13.318).[7] Then, after less than one hundred years of rule from Jerusalem, at the death of Herod the Great, Herod's kingdom was divided up and Galilee with Perea was given to Herod Antipas (4 B.C.E.–39 C.E.), while Judea was soon taken under direct imperial rule (6-41 C.E.). So the obvious question arises: Was Jesus brought up in an only superficially "Judaized" Galilee?

In the first thorough English-language study of Galilee, Sean Freyne strongly argued that, despite the above data, Galileans retained a firmly Jewish identity.[8] Under the Ptolemies (Egypt) and Seleucids (Syria), the administrative region (eparchy) of Samaria included both Galilee and Judea.[9] Josephus reports a decree of the Seleucid king Antiochus III that "all the members of the nation shall be governed in accordance with their ancestral laws" (*Ant* 12.142), which Freyne thinks would have included Galilee.[10] Consequently, there was no need for a "Judaization" of Galilee under the Hasmoneans.[11] Rather, "Galilean Judaism was now politically reunited with what had always been its cultural and religious center"; "the Jerusalem temple continued to exercise a powerful attraction for them."[12] Richard Horsley, however, has protested that Galilee was not integrated into a culturally unified "Common Judaism."[13] Rather we should recognize a cultural divide between Galilean peasants and imported aristocrats, initially Hasmonean "Judeans" and subsequently the Hellenized appointees of the Herods.[14] The

---

7. Schürer, *History,* 1:217-18.

8. S. Freyne, *Galilee from Alexander the Great to Hadrian, 323 BCE to 135 CE: A Study of Second Temple Judaism* (Wilmington, Del.: Michael Glazier, 1980). Freyne has consistently updated his views in the light particularly of fuller archaeological evidence. See his collected essays: *Galilee and Gospel,* WUNT 125 (Tübingen: Mohr-Siebeck, 2000), especially "Archaeology and the Historical Jesus" (pp. 160-82) and "Jesus and the Urban Culture of Galilee" (pp. 183-207); see also "The Geography, Politics, and Economics of Galilee and the Quest for the Historical Jesus," in *Studying the Historical Jesus: Evaluations of the State of Current Research,* ed. B. Chilton and C. A. Evans (Leiden: Brill, 1994), pp. 75-121.

9. Freyne, *Galilee,* pp. 33-35.

10. Freyne, *Galilee,* pp. 35-36.

11. The area taken over by Aristobulus is described as Iturea, and Freyne questions Schürer's conclusion that Iturea included any of Lower Galilee (*Galilee,* pp. 43-44).

12. Freyne, *Galilee,* pp. 392-93 (quoting from his conclusions).

13. R. A. Horsley, *Galilee: History, Politics, People* (Valley Forge, Pa.: Trinity, 1995). Like Freyne, Horsley has updated his views in light of increasing archaeological data; see esp. *Archaeology, History, and Society in Galilee: The Social Context of Jesus and the Rabbis* (Valley Forge, Pa.: Trinity, 1996). Horsley's basic thesis has remained largely unchanged throughout.

14. Horsley argues that the requirement to live "according to the laws of the Judeans"

continuity was more at the level of ancient Israelite traditions stemming from the period of the northern kingdom.[15]

Recent archaeological findings, however, have transformed the debate, and when correlated with the literary data seem to settle the issue fairly conclusively.[16] Study of the settlement patterns of Galilean sites reveals two striking features. First, the data indicate an almost complete abandonment of the region, painting "a picture of a totally devastated and depopulated Galilee in the wake of the Assyrian campaigns of 733/732 B.C.E."[17] Second, the sudden burgeoning of data around the end of the second century B.C.E. (architecture, pottery, and Hasmonean coins) indicates that there was a rapid rise in new settlements in the wake of the Hasmonean conquest, attesting also economic and political ties between Galilee and Jerusalem.[18] These data refute Horsley's idea of a Hasmonean aristocracy imposing themselves over a continuing Israelite population, and point clearly to a wave of Judean settlements spreading over a depopulated territory.

To this has to be added what Reed calls four indicators of Jewish religious identity: stone vessels (chalk or soft limestone), attesting a concern for ritual purity;[19] plastered stepped pools, that is, Jewish ritual baths *(mikvaot)*; burial practices, reflecting Jewish views of the afterlife;[20] and bone profiles that include no pig bones, indicating conformity to Jewish dietary laws. Such finds

---

"meant political-economic-religious subordination to the Hasmonean high priesthood in Jerusalem"; similarly, recircumcision was "a sign of being joined to the 'body-politic'"; but Galileans were not thereby "integrated into the Judean *ethnos*" (*Galilee*, pp. 46-52). The disagreement between Freyne and Horsley is highlighted by the unresolved question of whether *Ioudaioi* in Josephus should be translated "Jews" (Freyne) or "Judeans" (Horsley).

15. Horsley has further developed his case in finding "Israelite traditions in Q" as reflecting popular tradition in Galilee (R. A. Horsley and J. A. Draper, *Whoever Hears You Hears Me: Prophets, Performance, and Tradition in Q* [Harrisburg, Pa.: Trinity, 1999], chap. 5).

16. I draw particularly on J. L. Reed, *Archaeology and the Galilean Jesus* (Harrisburg, Pa.: Trinity, 2000), pp. 23-61, "The Identity of the Galileans: Ethnic and Religious Consideration."

17. Reed, *Archaeology,* pp. 28-35 (here p. 29); "in the Galilean heartland . . . every single excavated site . . . was destroyed or abandoned at the end of the eighth century" (p. 31); "there is no archaeological evidence for an indigenous population in the centuries after 733/2 B.C.E." (p. 33).

18. Reed, *Archaeology,* pp. 39-43. Reed also notes the (Hasmonean) destruction of Gentile sites between Judea and Galilee and on Galilee's periphery (pp. 42-43). The evidence also confirms Freyne's rejection of Schürer's hypothesis ("Archaeology," pp. 177-79) that the Galileans were converted Itureans (Reed, pp. 34-39, referring to n. 11 above).

19. According to the Mishnah, stone vessels are impervious to ritual impurity (*m. Kelim* 10.1; *'Ohal.* 5.5; *Para* 6.5).

20. "Placing ossuaries inside so-called *kokhim* or loculi, horizontally shafted underground family tombs, was a distinctly Jewish phenomenon at the end of the Second Temple period" (Reed, *Archaeology,* p. 47).

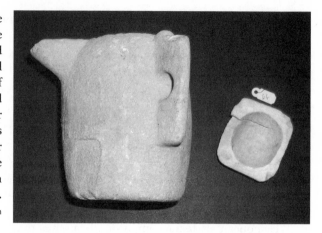

Figure 45. Stone pitcher from the Herodian period designed to fulfill the Jewish rites of purification, and a small alabaster vessel, perhaps for cosmetics or medicine. Both are from Jerusalem or its environs.

Courtesy of J. H. Charlesworth

have been made across Galilee, whereas they are lacking at sites outside the Galilee and the Golan.[21] In the light of such finds we can hardly do other than speak of the characteristically *Jewish* population of Galilee in the late Second Temple period.

This archaeological picture is confirmed by the literary data. Galilean regard for the Jerusalem Temple is fairly well attested. During the reign of Herod Antipas (which covers the adult life of Jesus), there are indications that Galileans were expected to pay tithes and other dues to the priests and Temple, even if in the event they were notably slack in doing so.[22] According to Mk 1:44 (pars.), there were priests in Galilee, who could expect to benefit from the tithes due to priests. Galilean participation is also attested in the great pilgrim festivals (in Jerusalem):[23] following the death of Herod the Great, Josephus speaks of "a countless multitude" from Galilee and elsewhere that flocked into Jerusalem at Pentecost (*War* 2.43; *Ant* 17.254); later on he notes "the custom of the Galileans at the time of a festival to pass through the Samaritan territory on their way to the holy city" (*Ant* 20.118; *War* 2.232); and the tradition of some Galilean participation in the pilgrim festivals echoed in Lk 2:41-43 and Jn 7:10 is no doubt soundly based. In addition, the reference to Pilate mingling the blood of Galileans with their sacrifices (Lk 13:1) suggests that at least some Galileans did participate in the Temple cult; and according to Mk 7:11 and Mt 5:23-24, Jesus assumed similar participation for his hearers.

21. Reed, *Archaeology*, pp. 43-52.

22. Freyne, *Galilee*, pp. 281-87, 294; Horsley, *Galilee*, pp. 142-44.

23. Freyne, *Galilee*, pp. 287-93; Horsley, *Galilee*, pp. 144-47.

As for Galilean loyalty to the Torah, we need simply note here that Jesus' own knowledge and use of the Torah presumably implies that schooling in Torah was practiced in Galilee. Some of the issues confronting Jesus were matters of Torah and Torah interpretation (including fasting and Sabbath, purity laws, and Temple offerings)[24] and imply a similar breadth of concern regarding the Law. As attested by Mk 1:44 (pars.), the local priests would be responsible for administering the Law. Beyond the Gospel accounts, and over against later rabbinic disdain for "the people of the land," we should note Josephus's account of Eleazar, "who came from Galilee and who had a reputation for being extremely strict *(akribēs)* with regard to the ancestral laws" (*Ant* 20.43-44). And we should certainly recall the striking episode occasioned by Emperor Caligula's order for a statue of himself to be erected in the Jerusalem Temple (39-40 c.e.). It evidently triggered just as vehement a response among the Galilean peasantry in Tiberias as it would have in Judea, the mass protest before the Roman legate (Petronius) declaring, "We will die sooner than violate our laws" (*Ant* 18.271-272).[25] The pillars of Second Temple Judaism[26] — Temple, monotheism, and Torah (the second of the Ten Commandments) — were evidently as deeply embedded in Galilean as in Judean soil.

Does all this mean that the Galileans can be described straightforwardly as "Jews"? The implication that first century c.e. Galileans were descendants of the Judean settlers a century earlier suggests a clear affirmative answer. At the same time, we need to recall the degree of ambivalence in the term "Judean" or "Jew." Shaye Cohen has suggested that the shift in meaning of *Ioudaios* from (ethnic-geographical) "Judean" to (religious) "Jew" took place in the Hasmonean period,[27] which correlates well with the archaeological evidence regarding Galilee's Jewish character. But he also notes Josephus's readiness to regard "Judea" as the name for the entire land of Israel, including Galilee,[28] and

---

24. E.g., Mk 2:18–3:5; 7:1-23.

25. Josephus explicitly notes that the protesters "neglected their fields, and that, too, though it was time to sow the seed." Horsley accepts that this probably indicates a "peasant strike" in Galilee (*Galilee*, p. 71).

26. I refer to my *The Partings of the Ways between Christianity and Judaism* (London: SCM, 1991), chap. 2, "The Four Pillars of Second Temple Judaism," pp. 18-36.

27. S. J. D. Cohen, *The Beginnings of Jewishness: Boundaries, Varieties, Uncertainties* (Berkeley: University of California Press, 1999), concludes that prior to the Hasmonean period *Ioudaios* should always be translated "Judean," and never as "Jew," pp. 70-71, 82-106; the shift from a purely ethno-geographical term to one of religious significance is first evident in 2 Macc 6:6 and 9:17, where for the first time *Ioudaios* can properly be translated "Jew"; and in Greco-Roman writers the first use of *Ioudaios* as a religious term appears at the end of the first century c.e. (pp. 90-96, 127, 133-36).

28. Similarly Luke uses "Judea" when he was probably thinking of Galilee (Lk 4:44); and he

various occasions on which Josephus calls Galileans *Ioudaioi*,[29] while in other passages *Galilaioi* seem to be distinct from the *Ioudaioi*.[30] Probably, then, the designation of Galilee as part of Judea was a matter of perspective, the dominant element in the state standing for the whole.[31] Ironically, "Israel," though applicable primarily to the northern kingdom in the period of the divided kingdoms, was too precious an expression of Jewish self-identity not to be used by all who claimed to stand in the line of inheritance from the patriarchs.[32]

The upshot is that we should have no qualms about calling Galileans in general "Jews," including Jesus of Nazareth. And even if the propriety and overtones of the epithet are less clear-cut, the implication of the term itself, that the Galileans in general were practitioners of the so-called Common Judaism, should be allowed to stand, whatever qualifications might be called for in particular instances.

How Hellenized Was Galilee?

This is obviously the other side of the same coin. The question arises from the same data noted in posing the first question, summed up now in the ancient description of Galilee as "Galilee of the nations/Gentiles."[33] In the light of this description and the corollary of Galilean syncretism, Walter Grundmann could infamously argue: "Galilee was gentile," "Jesus was no Jew."[34] "The issue with regard to Jesus is reinforced by the presence of two cities in lower Galilee, Sepphoris and Tiberias, (re)established by Herod Antipas within Jesus' lifetime

---

certainly seems to think of Judea as including Galilee (Lk 23:5; Acts 10:37). In Luke's Gospel Jesus does not leave Galilee till 17:11 and does not enter Judea proper till 18:35–19:10.

29. Particularly *War* 2.232; 3.229; *Ant* 13.154; 20.43; *Life* 113. Cohen also observes that Diaspora *Ioudaioi* continued to be regarded as citizens of Judea (*The Beginnings of Jewishness*, pp. 72-76).

30. See esp. *Life* 346, 349.

31. We may compare the use of "Holland" for the Netherlands, of "Russia" for a wider territory, including, e.g., the Ukraine, and of "England" for the whole of the United Kingdom. Cohen speaks of *Ioudaioi* as either "broadly defined" (including Galileans) or "narrowly defined" (living only in Judea) (*The Beginnings of Jewishness*, p. 73).

32. "Israel implies the religious claim to be God's chosen people even when it is used in secular contexts, within religious emphasis, as the accepted designation" (K. G. Kuhn, "Israel," in *TDNT* 3:362, with examples). S. Zeitlin, *The Jews: Race, Nation, or Religion?* (Philadelphia: Dropsie College, 1936), p. 10, notes that the prophets of Judah (the southern kingdom) always delivered their messages in the name of the God of Israel, over the God of Judah.

33. Isa 9:1; 1 Macc 5:15; Mt 4:15.

34. W. Grundmann, *Jesus der Galiläer und das Judentum* (Leipzig: George Wigand, 1941), pp. 166-75.

as administrative centers. From the model of the hellenistic cities of the Decapolis and the Mediterranean coast it becomes possible to argue that the Galilean cities were themselves 'hellenistic' in character and culture."[35] A further inference readily drawn is that Sepphoris would have attracted villagers from the locality for trade and social outings;[36] also that the young Jesus would have (regularly?) visited Sepphoris, only two hours (5 km.) from Nazareth, perhaps even as a young builder assisting in the construction of its theater.[37] Sepphoris was also a natural stop on the trade route from Tiberias to Ptolemais on the coast; so the potential for still wider influence on a young Galilean can readily be imagined.[38] A final layer of presupposition frequently added in the last decade or so is that the attitudes and principles of Cynic philosophy must have been familiar in such an urbanized culture,[39] no doubt including Sepphoris,[40] and must have substantially shaped Jesus' own ideas, as evident particularly from the Q tradition of his teaching.[41]

---

35. "Galilee was . . . an epitome of Hellenistic culture on the eve of the Roman era"; "the Hellenistic ethos known to have prevailed in Galilee" (B. L. Mack, *A Myth of Innocence: Mark and Christian Origins* [Philadelphia: Fortress, 1988], pp. 66, 73-74).

36. "People from the surrounding area probably also flocked to Sepphoris on such occasions, either to attend the theater or to hawk their wares" (E. M. Meyers, "Roman Sepphoris in Light of New Archaeological Evidence and Recent Research," in *The Galilee in Late Antiquity*, ed. L. I. Levine [New York: Jewish Theological Seminary of America, 1992], pp. 321-38 [here p. 333]).

37. R. A. Batey, *Jesus and the Forgotten City: New Light on Sepphoris and the Urban World of Jesus* (Grand Rapids: Baker, 1991): "it requires no very daring flight of the imagination to picture the youthful Jesus seeking and finding employment in the neighboring city of Sepphoris" (p. 70); "The stage on which he acted out his ministry was cosmopolitan and sophisticated and his understanding of urban life more relevant than previously imagined" (p. 103).

38. E. M. Meyers and J. F. Strange, *Archaeology, the Rabbis, and Early Christianity* (Nashville: Abingdon, 1981), p. 43; J. D. Crossan, *The Historical Jesus: The Life of a Mediterranean Jewish Peasant* (San Francisco: HarperSanFrancisco, 1991), pp. 17-19.

39. Three Cynic teachers are associated with Transjordan Gadara: Menippus (third century B.C.E.), but he learned and taught his Cynicism elsewhere; Meleager (first century B.C.E.), who flourished in Tyre; and Oenomaus (early second century C.E.).

40. In his *Cynics and Christian Origins* (Edinburgh: T. & T. Clark, 1992), F. G. Downing's speculation becomes steadily more confident and far-reaching by dint of repetition: Cynic influence was possible (pp. 146, 148); "the most likely explanation is that Jesus was formed in response to native Cynic . . . influences" (pp. 150, 153); "a Cynic-influenced Galilean Jewish culture" (p. 157); "an existing Cynic influence among ordinary people in the Galilee of his own day" (p. 161); "Cynic tradition in some form had permeated ordinary Jewish society in southern Galilee" (p. 164). According to Mack, Jesus "may have read some scriptures, just as he may have read Meleager" (*A Myth of Innocence*, p. 64).

41. So especially Downing, *Cynics and Christian Origins*, chap. 5; B. L. Mack, *The Lost Gospel: The Book Q and Christian Origins* (San Francisco: HarperSanFrancisco, 1993), pp. 45-46, 114-23; L. E. Vaage, *Galilean Upstarts: Jesus' First Followers according to Q* (Valley Forge, Pa.: Trinity, 1994).

Unfortunately, such hypotheses have failed to consider the historical evidence regarding Lower Galilee, as Horsley has again been quick to point out. Sepphoris and Tiberias were not in fact like the Hellenistic cities of the Decapolis: they were built as administrative capitals, not as independent Hellenistic *poleis;* and unlike the latter, they had no territorial jurisdiction over the surrounding districts.[42] More to the point, they were not major Hellenistic cities (like Scythopolis or Caesarea Maritima) but minor provincial centers, quite lacking in the typical marks or wealth of a Hellenistic city.[43] The road running from Tiberias to Ptolemais through Sepphoris was not a major international trade route but carried only interregional traffic.[44] And the archaeological evidence for Sepphoris is as clear as for the rest of Galilee: no indications of large numbers of non-Jews; and plenty of evidence of the same four indicators of Jewish religious identity (stone vessels, *mikvaot,* absence of pig remains, burial in shafted tombs with ossuaries).[45] The conclusion that Sepphoris contained a predominantly Jewish and devout Jewish population is hard to avoid.[46]

All this tells against the Cynic hypothesis regarding Galilee and Sepphoris in particular. Sepphoris's "thin veneer of cosmopolitan culture" was hardly conducive to Cynic philosophers;[47] and for their presence in Galilee there is no evidence whatsoever.[48] Of course, the hypothesis that Jesus was influenced by Cynicism has been built primarily on the Q material. But the attempt to restrict a Greek document like Q to Galilee ignores the evidence that Jesus' sayings were

42. Horsley, *Galilee,* pp. 214-15 and n. 36, citing A. H. M. Jones, *The Greek City* (Oxford: Clarendon, 1966), p. 80; Freyne, "Urban Culture of Galilee," p. 195.

43. Freyne notes that unlike the major Hellenistic cities, Sepphoris and Tiberias had no power to mint their own coins ("Urban Culture of Galilee," pp. 193-94). Reed estimates the population of Scythopolis and Caesarea Maritima as between 20,000 and 40,000, in contrast to Sepphoris and Tiberias (8,000-12,000) (*Archaeology,* pp. 79-81, 89, 93-96, 117-24); "no temple, no gymnasium, no hippodrome, no *odeon,* no *nymphaeum,* no euergistic inscriptions" (p. 95); Sepphoris "could not afford marble or imported columns" (p. 124); its theater, dating to the latter half of the first century C.E., was one of the more modest theaters in the eastern Mediterranean, with seating capacity of around 4,000 (pp. 108, 119-20); the inhabitants' private possessions do not appear to have been expensive (p. 126). We should remember, however, that the excavation of Sepphoris is incomplete and that it has been possible to excavate only a small part of Tiberias.

44. Reed, *Archaeology,* pp. 146-48.

45. Reed, *Archaeology,* pp. 84, 127-28, 134; similarly Freyne, "Urban Culture of Galilee," p. 191.

46. Similarly Meyers, "Roman Sepphoris": archaeological excavations "point to a Torah-true population, judging by the number of ritual baths '*miqva'ot*' in houses and by the strict practice of burial outside the city precincts" (p. 325).

47. Horsley, *Archaeology,* pp. 59, 179-80; similarly Reed, *Archaeology,* p. 218.

48. As Downing readily acknowledges (*Cynics and Christian Origins,* pp. 146-47).

much more widely known.[49] Moreover, the argument that the Q teachings presuppose what Gerald Downing repeatedly insists is "distinctively Cynic" influence is flawed.[50] It invites the obvious response that such Q material reflects rather a prophetic lifestyle that echoes that of Elijah, and a prophetic critique of rich oppressors that echoes many oracles of the classical prophets.[51] In this case, as in others, *we must not confuse analogy with genealogy:* protests against the lifestyles and inconsiderateness of the wealthy establishment will always tend to sound similar, whatever the context. Suffice it here to say that the historical context envisaged to explain Jesus' alleged indebtedness to Cynicism is poorly supported by what we know of that context.

The relationships predicated between Sepphoris and its surrounding villages (including Nazareth) are more difficult to assess. Horsley disputes with those who assume the traditional European pattern of market towns serving as focal points for buying and selling rural produce.[52] On the contrary, he argues, the Galilean villages were basically self-sufficient; any surplus produce would go in taxes and tithes, which were paid and collected in kind from the threshing floors; the local economy was not heavily monetized.[53] And the picture of villagers flocking into Sepphoris ignores the hostility with which Sepphoris was viewed in the Galilean villages, as illustrated most dramatically by the devastation of Sepphoris in the revolt of 66 C.E., "the Galileans . . . venting their hatred on one of the cities which they detested" (Josephus, *Life* 375).[54] Perhaps the silence of the Jesus tradition as to any contact of Jesus with Sepphoris is eloquent after all!

On the other hand, Jonathan Reed points out that Nazareth was bound to be oriented more to Sepphoris than to the south: Nazareth was one of the

49. H. Koester, "The Sayings of Q and Their Image of Jesus," in *Sayings of Jesus: Canonical and Non-canonical,* ed. W. L. Petersen et al., T. Baarda Festschrift, NovTSup 89 (Leiden: Brill, 1997), pp. 137-54 (here pp. 138-40).

50. Downing, *Cynics and Christian Origins,* pp. 143, 150, 152, 153, 160, 161.

51. See Freyne, "Urban Culture of Galilee," pp. 197-98. Mack sees the Cynics "as the Greek analogue to the Hebrew prophets" (*The Lost Gospel,* p. 114).

52. "Villagers go to town to sell produce, both to buy goods and to acquire cash to pay taxes and tolls. Market gossip filters back" (Downing, *Cynics and Christian Origins,* p. 149); Horsley, *Galilee,* p. 203 and n. 6, quotes similar assumptions of a European "market" economy made by M. Goodman, *State and Society in Roman Galilee,* AD 132-212 (Totowa, N.J.: Rowman and Allanheld, 1983), pp. 54-60; and Z. Safrai, *The Economy of Roman Palestine* (London: Routledge, 1994).

53. Horsley, *Galilee,* pp. 176-81, 202-7; also *Archaeology,* pp. 70-76, 83-85.

54. Horsley, *Archaeology,* pp. 118-30; in critique particularly of D. Edwards, "The Socio-Economic and Cultural Ethos of the Lower Galilee in the First Century: Implications for the Nascent Jesus Movement," in *The Galilee in Late Antiquity,* pp. 53-73.

southernmost villages in Galilee; travel south would encounter the steep incline of the south side of the Nazareth ridge, and so would probably have been via Sepphoris and Tiberias, to skirt Samaria as far as possible; and the lines of trade did not run southward from the Nazareth ridge.[55] Moreover, the rebuilding of Sepphoris and maintenance of it as an administrative center would presumably have required tax revenue and a shift in agricultural patterns in Lower Galilee (to feed its population).[56] The wine installations, olive presses, threshing floors, and millstones found around and even inside Sepphoris indicate that it must have served as some kind of local center.[57] And if the population as a whole was less Hellenized and more Jewish than has often been claimed, there would be less reason for devout Jewish villagers to bypass or avoid it.

In any case, the existence of some tension between city and village needs not be doubted. One can readily surmise that there will always be a tendency toward friction between local bureaucrats and administrators, on the one hand, and the producers of agricultural and other material goods on the other. This is all the more apposite if much of the good land close by a city like Sepphoris (particularly the Beth Netofah Valley) was being steadily acquired by Herod's elite. That such tensions did indeed exist between Sepphoris and inter alia Nazareth is strongly suggested by the social situations reflected in many of Jesus' parables — wealthy estate owners, resentment against absentee landlords, exploitative stewards of estates, family feuds over inheritance, debt, day laborers (forced to sell off family patrimony because of debt?), and so on.[58]

How all this bears on Jesus and his own relationship with Sepphoris and Tiberias remains unclear. The silence of the Jesus tradition in regard to both is still surprising and somewhat ominous. But at least it is clear that the answer does not lie in the blanket description of Sepphoris as "Hellenistic."

Were There Synagogues in First-Century Galilee?

As already noted, the term *synagōgē* occurs regularly in the Gospels, and in every case the term is translated, not surprisingly, as "synagogue." But this translation rests on a number of unexamined assumptions: particularly that there were buildings ("synagogues") at the time of Jesus that were dedicated places of wor-

55. Reed, *Archaeology*, pp. 115-17; Freyne, "Archaeology," pp. 169-70, 171-73.

56. See also Freyne, "Urban Culture of Galilee," pp. 191-93. Both Freyne (pp. 191-92) and Reed (*Archaeology*, p. 126) observe that Sepphoris's pottery and stone storage jars came from Galilean villages.

57. Reed, *Archaeology*, pp. 83-89.

58. Freyne, "Urban Culture of Galilee," pp. 195-96, 205-6.

ship, for Torah reading and prayer. The translation itself, "synagogue," can thus constitute evidence of Jesus' attachment to the synagogue as attesting his own Jewishness and initial willingness to work with the local religious authorities.

In the past twenty years, however, such assumptions have come under serious challenge.[59] The basic problem is that archaeology has failed to turn up clear evidence that would confirm the basis for such a historical reconstruction. In view of the relevance of this data to our central question, it is worth indicating the evidence with some care.

According to Eric Meyers, "Only three synagogue buildings within Israel Palestine have been securely dated to the Second Temple period: Gamla, Masada, and Herodium."[60] In addition, a structure at Magdala (or Migdal on the west shore of Galilee) is sometimes included, though it would at best be described as a "mini-synagogue."[61] Migdal is the only example in Galilee, although Gamla, like Bethsaida technically in Herod Philip's territory, was evidently in close communication with Galilee proper.[62]

The well-known synagogue in Capernaum most probably dates from the fourth or fifth century c.e.; though underneath there is evidence of walls of houses and stone pavements.[63] When these earlier structures are to be dated remains unclear. It is conceivable that a large house served for communal gatherings.[64] But it is also conceivable that there was an earlier synagogue, on the

59. See H. C. Kee and L. H. Cohick, eds., *Evolution of the Synagogue: Problems and Progress* (Harrisburg, Pa.: Trinity, 1999), particularly the essays by Kee, "Defining the First-Century c.e. Synagogue" (pp. 7-26), in debate with J. F. Strange, "Ancient Texts, Archaeology as Text, and the Problem of the First-Century Synagogue" (pp. 27-45), and R. H. Horsley, "Synagogues in Galilee and the Gospels" (pp. 46-69, a reworking of chap. 10 of his *Galilee* and chap. 6 of his *Archaeology, History, and Society in Galilee*); S. Fine, ed., *Jews, Christians, and Polytheists in the Ancient Synagogue: Cultural Interaction during the Greco-Roman Period* (London: Routledge, 1999), particularly the essays by E. P. Sanders, "Common Judaism and the Synagogue in the First Century" (pp. 1-17), and P. W. van der Horst, "Was the Synagogue a Place of Sabbath Worship before 70 c.e.?" (pp. 18-43). Earlier discussion is reviewed by H. A. McKay, "Ancient Synagogues: The Continuing Dialectic between Two Major Views," *CurBS* 6 (1998): 103-42.

60. E. M. Meyers, "Synagogue," in *ABD* 6:251-60 (here p. 255).

61. M. J. Chiat, "First-Century Synagogue Architecture: Methodological Problems," in *Ancient Synagogues: The State of Research*, ed. J. Gutmann, BJS 22 (Chico, Calif.: Scholars, 1981), pp. 49-60 (floor plans, p. 112); R. Hachlili, "Early Jewish Art and Architecture," in *ABD* 1:447-54 (here pp. 449-50; floor plans, p. 449); Strange, "Ancient Texts," pp. 35-45.

62. But see also Horsley, *Archaeology,* chap. 6, and those cited by him on p. 221 nn. 2-3.

63. S. Loffreda, "The Late Chronology of the Synagogue of Capernaum," in *Ancient Synagogues Revealed,* ed. L. I. Levine (Jerusalem: Israel Exploration Society, 1981), pp. 52-56.

64. Kee, "Defining," p. 22. Kee has also argued strenuously against a pre-70 date for the famous "Theodotus inscription" from Jerusalem ("The Transformation of the Synagogue after 70 c.e.," *NTS* 36 [1990]: 1-24); but see R. Riesner, "Synagogues in Jerusalem," in *The Book of Acts in*

Figure 46. Mosaic
showing an early boat,
from Magdala.
Courtesy of J. H. Charlesworth

same site or elsewhere, and Luke's report that the centurion had "built" (that is, presumably, paid for the building of) what must anyway have been a fairly unpretentious structure (Lk 7:5) cannot be dismissed out of hand. One could well imagine local personages trying to ape the benefactions of more prestigious cities, like Tiberias round the lake. But still it has to be said that deductions drawn from the archaeological evidence are hardly secure.

In consequence, a substantial body of opinion has emerged that *synagōgē* in the Gospels should be translated not as "synagogue," precisely because of the (now traditional) implications of that term, but as "assembly" or "congregation" (the word's more literal meaning).[65] There is certainly something in this.

Its Palestinian Setting, ed. R. Bauckham (Grand Rapids: Eerdmans, 1995), pp. 179-210 (here pp. 192-200); and Sanders remains unpersuaded ("Common Judaism," p. 16 n. 70).

65. Kee illustrates the (for him) false assumption that has hitherto been made regarding the meaning of *synagōgē* by reference to Josephus, *Ant* 19.305, where the Greek actually speaks of the Jews prevented from "being" *(einai)* a *synagōgē* and of "the place of the *synagōgē,*" where the obvious sense of "assembly" is obscured by the Loeb translation ("Defining," p. 13). It is worth

Synagōgē is a term that denotes in the first place the village gathering or town assembly, with the *archisynagōgos* more accurately described as "leader of the assembly," the "head man," rather than "ruler of the synagogue."[66] Presumably assemblies would be called to discuss the community's affairs, including the hammering out of disputes and local administration of justice.[67]

But equally we can deduce that one of the purposes of a communal gathering would no doubt have been the hearing of Torah read and expounded (usually by a priest or elder, but others could contribute). This is certainly the clear testimony of Philo, the Jewish philosopher and leading citizen in Alexandria, contemporary with Jesus. At one point he asks, "Will you sit in your assemblies [*synagōgais*] . . . and read in security our sacred books, expounding any obscure point and in leisurely comfort discussing at length your ancestral philosophy?"[68] And elsewhere he reports that the Jews "assemble in the same place on these seventh days . . . (and) some priest or one of the elders reads the holy laws to them and expounds them point by point."[69] The Jewish historian Josephus, who knew Galilee well, writing two generations later, likewise reports that Moses "appointed the Law to be the most excellent and necessary form of instruction, ordaining . . . that every week men should desert their other occupations and assemble to listen to the Law and to obtain a thorough and accurate knowledge of it."[70] And from the fact that the places of assembly were described as "prayer houses" in the Diaspora we can certainly deduce that communal gatherings on Sabbaths and feast days also included the saying of prayers.[71]

---

noting that the equivalent word in Christian circles, *ekklēsia,* had similar force, as is evident in 1 Cor 11:18, "when you come together in assembly" (not "in the church"). In the LXX *synagōgē* and *ekklēsia* are both used to translate the Hebrew *qahal,* denoting the "assembly or congregation" of Israel (W. Schrage, *"synagōgē,"* in *TDNT* 7:798-852 [here p. 802]). See further Schürer, *History,* 2:429-31 (nn. 12-14).

66. *Archisynagōgos* was a common name for the officer in charge of a Hellenistic association *(synagōgē)*; see, e.g., R. E. Oster, "Supposed Anachronism in Luke-Acts' Use of *synagōgē*: A Rejoinder to H. C. Kee," *NTS* 39 (1993): 178-208 (here pp. 202-4); see also Horsley, *Galilee,* pp. 223-33; *Archaeology,* pp. 145-51; and "Synagogues," pp. 48-61.

67. See also L. I. Levine, "The Second Temple Synagogue: The Formative Years," in *The Synagogue in Late Antiquity,* ed. L. I. Levine (Philadelphia: Fortress, 1987), pp. 7-31.

68. Philo, *De somniis* 2.127; similarly *De vita Mosis* 2.216; *De legatione ad Gaium* 156-157 (Kee, "Defining," pp. 13-14). See also *CIJ* 2:1404 (the Theodotus inscription — above, n. 64).

69. Eusebius, quoting Philo's otherwise lost *Hypothetica* 7.12-13 (*Praeparatio evangelica* 8.7, 11-13). See also E. P. Sanders, *Jewish Law from Jesus to the Mishnah: Five Studies* (London: SCM, 1990), pp. 78-81; and *Judaism: Practice and Belief, 63 BCE–66 CE* (London: SCM, 1992), pp. 199-202.

70. Josephus, *Apion* 2.175.

71. Thus Philo speaks of "many" *proseuchas* ("prayers" in the extended sense of "prayer houses") "in each section of the city" of Alexandria (*De legatione ad Gaium* 132, 134, 137–138) and

But where would such assemblies have met in Galilee? Certainly we must accept the likelihood that in some places the gatherings would have taken place in a large house,[72] as did the earliest Christian gatherings.[73] At the same time, there is no good reason to discount the literary evidence that there were buildings evidently set aside for communal gatherings, and called either "synagogues" or "prayer houses" — in Palestine as well as abroad. The reference in Lk 7:5 to the centurion who "built the synagogue for us" in Capernaum is arguably a less well-founded deduction made by Luke. But Josephus also recalls a general assembly *(sunagōntai pantes)* in Tiberias in the 60s in the prayer house *(proseuchē)*, a very large house or building *(megiston oikēma)*.[74] And the floor plans of the buildings in the lands of Israel most securely identified as "synagogues," with rows of benches along one or more of the walls, are hardly what we would expect for private dwellings.[75] These were no doubt buildings used for town assemblies, but probably also as a schoolroom[76] and for social and fes-

regarded such places as "all holy" *(panieros)* (911); see further *Contra Flaccum* 41-49. In Josephus, see *Ant* 14.258 and further below. For epigraphical references to "prayer houses" see Schürer, *History*, 2:425-26 n. 5, 439-40 n. 61; *NewDocs* 3:121-22.

72. The "apparent contradiction" between the dearth of early Second Temple synagogue remains and the large number of references to synagogues in ancient literary sources "disappears if we assume that, in the first centuries, large private houses were used as places of worship alongside other buildings that came to be utilized for worship and other matters requiring public assembly" (Meyers, "Synagogue," 6:255). Similarly Hachlili, "Early Jewish Art," pp. 449-50; Riesner, "Synagogues in Jerusalem," p. 186.

73. Acts 2:46; 12:12; 18:7; Rom 16:5; 1 Cor 16:19; Col 4:15.

74. Josephus, *Life* 277; also 280, 293. See also Philo, *OmnProbLib* 81 ("sacred places which they call synagogues"); *Contra Flaccum* 48 ("sacred buildings"); Acts 18:7; Josephus, *War* 2.285, 289; 7.44. A first century c.e. inscription from Berenike (Libya) uses the term *synagōgē* twice, once in the sense "congregation," the other in the sense of "building" (conveniently in Oster, "Supposed Anachronism," pp. 187-88; on p. 186 he lists the range of terms used in inscriptions and papyri as well as Philo and Josephus). See also Schürer, *History*, 2:439-40. Kee is much too resolute in his unwillingness to recognize that a building may be referred to in some of the NT texts other than Lk 7:5 ("Defining," pp. 14-20); see particularly Oster's rejoinder to Kee (Oster, pp. 194-97). M. Hengel's argument is plausible that the term "synagogue" came to be used for the place of assembly, not just the assembly itself, during the first century c.e. — "Proseuche und Synagoge, Jüdische Gemeinde, Gotteshaus und Gottesdienst in der Diaspora und in Palästina," in *Tradition und Glaube: Das frühe Christentum in seiner Umwelt*, ed. G. Jeremias et al., K. G. Kuhn Festschrift (Göttingen: Vandenhoeck & Ruprecht, 1971), pp. 157-84.

75. See n. 61 above. Sanders is particularly critical of Kee's arguments (*Jewish Law*, pp. 77-78, 341-43 n. 29; *Judaism*, pp. 198-202; "Common Judaism and the Synagogue in the First Century"); also K. Atkinson, "On Further Defining the First Century c.e. Synagogue: Fact or Fiction? A Rejoinder to H. C. Kee," *NTS* 43 (1997): 491-502 (here, particularly pp. 499-501).

76. Philo calls the meeting house *didaskaleion*, that is, "place of teaching" (*De vita Mosis* 2.216; *De specialibus legibus* 2.62; also *De legatione ad Gaium* 312). See also Schürer, *History*, 2:417-22.

tive events — in modern parlance, not so much the village church as the village hall. The difference, like the difference between "church" = people and "church" = building, may seem insubstantial. But it may also involve a significant shift in orientation for some, and is another reminder of the need for Jesus historians to jerk themselves consciously out of their contemporary perspective in order to gain a more sound historical perspective.

Conclusion

Archaeology strengthens an impression already strong from the literary evidence. The son of an artisan brought up in Nazareth in Lower Galilee in the early years of the first century C.E. is properly described as a "Jew." That description would have included education in Torah at the local village (Nazareth) assembly/synagogue.[77] Second Temple Judaism put a great emphasis on the study of Torah, and according to Josephus (*Apion* 2.204), it was expected that children should be taught to read (learn their letters, *grammata paideuein*). There is no difficulty, then, in recognizing Jesus' knowledge of and familiarity with scripture, as indicated in the Synoptic tradition.[78] And it is quite plausible to conceive that even a Galilean villager (of some ability) might well have learned to read.[79] Jesus' quite widely attested challenge, "Have you not read?"[80] probably presupposes his own reading ability.[81] And the presence of scripture scrolls is attested in Palestinian villages as early as 1 Macc 1:56-57, and confirmed by Josephus for both Judea (*War* 2.229) and Galilee (*Life* 134). So the picture painted in Lk 4:16-17 is in essence quite credible.

Similarly we can deduce without strain that Jesus was brought up to recite the Shema (Deut 6:4), probably as a daily obligation (cf. Mk 12:29-30 pars.), and that he prayed, probably two or three times a day (cf. Josephus, *Ant* 4.2, 12).[82] We can also assume that the adult Jesus observed the Sabbath, attended the synagogue, and "gave every seventh day over to the study of our customs and law" (Josephus, *Ant* 16.43), even though only Lk 4:16 indicates that synagogue atten-

77. There is no archaeological evidence of a first-century synagogue at Nazareth, but very little archaeological investigation has been possible since, unlike Capernaum, later and modern buildings largely obscure the site.

78. E.g., Mk 2:25-26; 7:6-8; 10:5-8; 12:26.

79. For the broad picture see, e.g., Schürer, *History,* 2:417-22.

80. Mk 2:25 pars.; 12:10 pars.; 12:26 par.; Mt 12:5; 19:4; 21:16; Lk 10:26.

81. The great number and range of scrolls at Qumran presumably implies a substantial reading ability among its members.

82. Sanders, *Judaism,* pp. 196-97, 202-8.

dance was his normal custom. The references to the "tassels" of his garment suggest that he himself[83] was a pious Jew who took his religious obligations seriously.

Our simple question, then, has proved more complicated than at first seemed likely. But one of the great benefits of recent archaeological discoveries is that we can now give the question a much more confidently positive answer than had seemed possible even a few years ago. Yes, in all probability Jesus did attend the synagogue.

83. Mt 9:20/Lk 8:44; Mk 6:56/Mt 14:36; with reference to the instructions of Num 15:38-39 and Deut 22:12 (note also Zech 8:23).

Synagogues and Spirituality:
The Case of Beth Alfa

Benedict Thomas Viviano, O.P.

Why should anyone be interested in ancient synagogues? For Jews the answer is obvious: synagogues are an ancient expression of their religion. For Christians, it suffices to mention that neither Jesus nor Paul ever worshiped in a church building. Both began their ministries in synagogues. For Jesus it begins in the synagogue of his hometown, Nazareth, according to Lk 4:16-30, a programmatic moment in Jesus' life. In Mark, the ministry of healing begins in the synagogue of Capernaum (Mk 1:21-28; cf. Lk 4:31-37). In the longest chapter in John, the major "bread of life" discourse takes place in the synagogue at Capernaum (Jn 6:59). Little wonder then that the rediscovery of this synagogue by the Franciscans at the turn of the century (1905) was sensational. (To be sure, the synagogue they discovered was built several centuries later than the time of Jesus. But one reckons in such cases with the continuity of sacred places, and perhaps the earlier synagogue is beneath the later one.)

As for Paul, the author of Acts depicts him regularly beginning his ministry in a town by speaking in the synagogue. The great set piece for this is his address in Pisidian Antioch (Acts 13; see especially vv. 14-15): "On the Sabbath they entered the synagogue and took their seats. After the reading of the law and the prophets, the synagogue officials sent word to them, 'My brothers, if one of you has a word of exhortation for the people, please speak.'" (See also Acts 9:20; 14:1; 15:21; 17:1, 10, 17; 18:4, 7, 19, 26; 22:19; 24:12; 26:11.) Over 100 ancient synagogues have been unearthed and identified in Israel/Palestine, and 20 elsewhere, though nowadays some of these identifications have been contested.

The origins of the synagogue are a subject of lively controversy and great uncertainty. In fact, Deut 31:9-13 can be considered the earliest description of what became the synagogue service, if not the building. This description is then developed in the liturgically crucial Neh 8. There Ezra seems to be the founder. Ezekiel and the exile have also been listed as agents. See the *miqdash m$^{e\varsigma}$at* of

Figure 47. The third-century synagogue at Bar'am with its elaborate facade that faces Jerusalem (cf. *Megillah* 2:18). Courtesy of J. H. Charlesworth

Ezek 11:16, variously translated as a "little sanctuary," a "diminished sanctuary," or "a sanctuary for a time." Given the later dating of the Pentateuch to the Persian period, which is currently popular, these various options may not be so chronologically diverse as might at first appear. Hard-nosed scholars refuse to admit any physical evidence of a synagogue before 100 B.C.E. But the New Testament takes the existence of synagogues so totally for granted that there can be no reasonable doubt that they existed prior to the birth of Christianity. What went on in them is another hotly contested issue. A consensus seems to be forming that the reading and exposition of Scripture preceded the formulation of fixed prayers to be recited repeatedly. Qumran may have contributed something to this formulation.[1]

---

1. For the earlier literature, see B. T. Viviano, "Hillel and Jesus on Prayer," in *Hillel and Jesus,* ed. J. H. Charlesworth and L. L. Johns (Minneapolis: Fortress, 1997), pp. 427-57; W. Schrage, in *TDNT* 7:798-852, s.v. *synagōgē;* K. Hruby, "La synagogue dans la littérature rabbinique," *L'orient Syrien* 9 (1964): 473-514; J. Gutmann, ed., *Ancient Synagogues: The State of Research,* BJS 22 (Chico, Calif.: Scholars, 1981); J. G. Griffiths, "Egypt and the Rise of the Synagogue," *JTS* 38 (1987): 1-15; E. M. Meyers and R. Hachlili, "Synagogue," in *ABD* 6:252-63; H. C.

I

The mosaic floor of the Beth Alfa synagogue was excavated by E. L. Sukenik in 1929; it was one of the first successes of Jewish archaeology in the Holy Land. It lies in the Beth Shean Valley in Lower Galilee and is located in what is today a collective farm called Kvuzat Hefzibah.[2] The building is on the basilican, not the broadhouse, model. The outer court contained a font, perhaps for the washing of hands. There are a series of raised floors: from court to atrium, from atrium to nave, from nave to niche. There is one row of benches, not steps (i.e., multiple seats) as elsewhere. There is a possible base for a bema (reading stand) near the niche. There is no specimen of carved stone. The aisles and court were covered with mosaics in geometric patterns, indicating that the figures in the central section of the floor were a deliberate choice. The main mosaic consists of three panels and a border; the result gives the impression of a carpet.

At the entrance to the main mosaic there are two inscriptions. The first, in Aramaic, half of which is damaged beyond recovery, reads: "This mosaic was laid down in the [. . .] year of the emperor Justin . . . ," and goes on to record gifts for the building. The second inscription is in Greek. Its letters are well formed and preserved intact: "May the craftsmen who carried out this work, Marianos and his son Hanina, be held in remembrance." A third language, Hebrew, is used in the first and second of the three main panels; in the first, the Hebrew Bible is briefly quoted; in the second panel, the Hebrew names of the signs of the zodiac and of the four seasons are given. This means that the mo-

---

Kee, "The Transformation of the Synagogue after 70 C.E.," *NTS* 36 (1990): 1-24; R. E. Oster, "Supposed Anachronism in Luke-Acts: Use of *synagōgē;* A Rejoinder to H. C. Kee," *NTS* 39 (1993): 178-208; H. C. Kee, "The Changing Meaning of Synagogue: A Response to Richard Oster," *NTS* 40 (1994): 281-82; H. C. Kee and L. H. Cohick, eds., *The Evolution of the Synagogue: Problems and Progress* (Harrisburg, Pa.: Trinity, 1999); the four essays in sec. 5, "Die Synagoge und die rabbinische Literatur," in Beate Ego et al., eds., *Gemeinde ohne Tempel*, WUNT 118 (Tübingen: Mohr Siebeck, 1999): E. Eshel, "Prayer in Qumran and the Synagogues," pp. 323-34; Folker Siegert, "Die Synagoge und das Postulat eines unblutigen Opfers," pp. 335-56; F. G. Hüttenmeister, "Die Synagoge. Ihre Entwicklung von einer multifunktionalen Einrichtung zum reinen Kultbau," pp. 357-70; and S. Schreiner, "Wo man Tora lernt, braucht man keinen Tempel: Einige Anmerkungen zum Problem der Tempelsubstitution in rabbinischen Judentum," pp. 371-92.

2. E. L. Sukenik, *Ancient Synagogues in Palestine and Greece* (London: British Academy, 1934). For more general and recent introductions to the archaeology of ancient synagogues, see E. M. Meyers and J. F. Strange, *Archaeology: The Rabbis and Early Christianity* (Nashville: Abingdon, 1981), pp. 140-54; L. J. Hoppe, *What Are They Saying about Biblical Archaeology?* (New York: Paulist, 1984), pp. 58-89; A. T. Kraabel, "The Diaspora Synagogues: Archeological and Epigraphic Evidence Since Sukenik," in *ANRW* II.19.1 (1979), pp. 477-510; P. R. Trebilco, *Jewish Communities in Asia Minor* (Cambridge: Cambridge University Press, 1991).

saic is trilingual. This fact further substantiates J. A. Fitzmyer's thesis that the most commonly used language of Palestine in the first century C.E. was Aramaic, but that many Palestinian Jews used Greek, and not only in the big cities. Hebrew was also known and used, at least as a written language.[3]

Thanks to the Aramaic inscription, we are able to date the Beth Alfa synagogue to the sixth century C.E., since the text mentions the Byzantine emperor Justin. (Justin I reigned from 518 to 527, and Justin II from 565 to 578.) The synagogue was probably built during the reign of Justin I. The lion-and-the-bull designs flanking the inscriptions look upside down to a person entering the synagogue. This odd arrangement suggests that they are meant to guard the inner design, not the door. The border mosaics consist mostly of geometric patterns, but two squares show grape clusters and a breadbasket; others show a pomegranate, a hen with four chicks (quails?), a tree with three pomegranates, three goblets or drinking horns (containing the water of life?). The hen and chicks may suggest the security provided by religious faith and community (cf. Ruth 2:12; Pss 17:8; 36:7; 55:6; 57:1; 61:4; 63:7; 91:4; Mt 23:37, par. Lk 13:34).

The first of the three main panels represents the binding of Isaac, known in Hebrew as the *Aqedah* (binding), as recounted in Gen 22:1-19:[4] Abraham in a chiton (and himation?) and the boy Isaac held near the altar, with a fierce flame on it. Both of them are identified by their names in Hebrew. In the upper middle of the panel is a small black cloud (the cloud of unknowing of apophatic theology? cf. 1 Kgs 8:12, "The Lord has said that he would dwell in thick darkness"). From the black cloud extends a hand, and rays. All these elements represent God. Underneath the hand, two Hebrew words are visible: 'al-tishlah; they are the first words of the divine command to Abraham, knife poised in obedience, to spare Isaac's life: "*Do not lay* your hand on the boy or do anything to him; for now I know that you fear God, since you have not withheld your son, your only son, from me" (Gen 22:12). In the center is a tree or thicket from which is suspended a ram. Gen 22:13 is quoted in Hebrew: "and behold a ram" *(wᵉ-hinnēh — 'ayil)*. Because the ram is hanging from the tree, some interpreters have suspected Christian influence (so Michael Krupp, viva voce). This cannot be excluded (see below), but it could also simply be due to lack of space. To the left are two servants holding the ass (Gen 22:3-5). The upper border con-

3. J. A. Fitzmyer, "The Languages of Palestine in the First Century A.D.," *CBQ* 32 (1970): 501-31, reprinted in his *A Wandering Aramean: Collected Aramaic Essays* (Missoula, Mont.: Scholars, 1979), pp. 29-56.

4. The literature on the *Aqedah* is abundant. The works that have most influenced me are: R. Le Déaut, *La Nuit Pascale*, AnBib 22 (Rome: Biblical Institute, 1963); S. Spiegel, *The Last Trial* (New York: Behrman House, 1967); J. D. Levenson, *The Death and Resurrection of the Beloved Son* (New Haven and London: Yale University Press, 1993).

tains eight stylized palm trees, perhaps representing paradise (Elysian fields). It is unclear whether Abraham's head is surrounded by a halo, or not.

A word on the dark cloud. In Acts 1:9 a cloud takes Jesus out of sight of the apostles. In the transfiguration narrative, a cloud comes and casts a shadow over the apostles and a voice speaks from it (Mk 9:7; Mt 17:5; the cloud is *phōteinos*, light filled, luminous; Lk 9:34-35). The cloud functions then as an aniconic icon; that is, in biblical religion icons of God are forbidden, yet somehow God's presence and activity must be indicated. This is done by the cloud, the hand, and the words. In Neoplatonic philosophy and in theology influenced by it (Augustine, Dionysius the Pseudo-Areopagite, ca. 500 C.E.), and already in Philo, there is a view that we know more what God is not than what he is, so we attribute negative attributes to him such as infinite, that is, not finite, not limited. This is called the *via negativa*, or negative way of knowing God. This is also called apophatic, as opposed to kataphatic, theology. These terms were developed by Dionysius the Pseudo-Areopagite, an anonymous, semi-Monophysite Christian theologian, hiding out in the region of Gaza and Beth Guvrin (Eleutheropolis) in the late fifth century. His spirituality will be relevant when we turn to the meaning of the Beth Alfa mosaic as a whole. Here, in relation to the dark cloud found in the mosaic, I want only to clarify the two terms he introduced. Apophatic refers to the modest way of knowing God by negative attributes, a way of confessing that we do not know him so as to be able to control or possess him, even mentally. Kataphatic discourse about God boldly dares to attribute positive predicates to him; e.g., God is good, God is just, God is holy. Both ways of speaking about God are found in the Bible. But the two terms, "apophatic" and "kataphatic," though having a background in Philo, Plotinus, Proclus, and Cappadocian thought, are first found, so far as I can determine, in Dionysius's *Mystical Theology*, chapters 1–3.

The point of the first panel is to present the offering of Isaac (and the ram) as a symbol of atonement or winning forgiveness for sin and further divine blessing (Gen 22:16-18). For further considerations it will not be irrelevant to note here that the moving story of the binding of Isaac was found meaningful by Jews as well as Christians (see Rom 8:32; Heb 6:13-14). Christians, very early on, saw Isaac as a type of Christ.[5]

---

5. H.-P. Stahli, "'. . . was die Welt im Innersten zusammenhält': Die Mosaike von Beth-Alpha — Bildliche Darstellungen zentraler Aussagen jüdischen Glaubens," *Judaica* 41 (1985): 79-98, with plates; on the Isaac typology see J. Swetnam, *Jesus and Isaac: A Study of the Epistle to the Hebrews in the Light of the Aqedah*, AnBib 94 (Rome: Biblical Institute Press, 1981). See also M. Bachmann, *Antijudaismus im Galaterbrief? Exegetische Studien zu einem polemischen Schreiben und zur Theologie des Apostels Paulus*, NTOA 40 (Freiburg: Universitätsverlag; Göttingen: Vandenhoeck & Ruprecht, 1999), chap. 3: "Jüdischer Bundesnomismus und

At the center of the second panel is the sun god Helios or Apollo riding across the sky in a chariot. Apollo wears a complicated halo, consisting of seven red rays and six trapezoids. The chariot has two wheels and is pulled by four horses with different color combinations. (Think of the four horses of the Apocalypse, Rev 6:1-8, each a different color.) The moon and twenty-four or twenty-three stars are also represented. Placed around this central scene are the twelve signs of the zodiac, each in its own segment, with its symbol and its name in Hebrew: (1) Aries, the ram, to the right of Apollo; *talah,* a different word for ram than that found in the first panel, *'ayil.* (2) Taurus, bull, upward, to the left; *shôr,* with hump. (3) Gemini, the twins, *tô^amim.* (4) Cancer, the crab, *sartan.* (5) Leo, the lion, *'ariyah.* (6) Virgo, the virgin, *bethulah,* seated on a (royal?) throne, with red shoes. (7) Libra, the balance, *moznayim.* (8) Scorpio, the scorpion, *'aqrab.* (9) Sagittarius, the archer, *gashet.* (10) Capricorn, the goat. Its name is damaged, lost beyond recovery. Perhaps the Hebrew was *tayish.* (11) Aquarius, the water bearer; *we-dali:* "and water-drawer or bucket-boy." Someone is drawing from a well; there is a bucket at the end of a rope. (12) Pisces, the fish (two are shown), *we-dagim.*

In the four corners of the second panel are figures representing the four seasons, four winged females (cherubs?). (1) Spring, in white, is in the upper left-hand corner. The accompanying Hebrew lettering is damaged. One can make out *tequphat,* which means season, but not the word for spring. Perhaps *Nisan* once stood there. (2) Summer, with fruit; *tequphat Tammuz* (not *qayitz,* the normal biblical word for summer). (3) Autumn, more fruit, plus a bird on the wing, and amphorae for winemaking; *tequphat Tishri.* (4) Winter, *tequphat Tebet.* The four seasons are not synchronized with the twelve months, whether due to error or by intention is hard to say. Helios or Sol Invictus (unconquered Sun) was the most important god of the late empire. Constantine identified himself with Sol Invictus. Helios is explicitly worshiped in a Hebrew magical handbook of the early Talmudic period, the *Sepher ha-Razim* or *Book of the Mysteries.*[6]

Two quotes are relevant here. "If you wish to view the sun during the day, seated in his chariot and ascending; guard yourself, take care, and keep pure for seven days from all [impure] food, from all [impure] drink, and from every unclean thing. Then on the seventh day stand facing [the sun] when he rises and

---

paulinisches Gesetzesverständnis, das Fussbodenmosaik von Bet Alfa und das Textsegment Gal 3,15-29."

6. The Hebrew has been published in an eclectic edition by M. Margalioth, *Sepher ha-Razim* (Jerusalem: Yediot Achronot, 1966). An English translation has been done by M. A. Morgan, *Sepher ha-Razim, the Book of the Mysteries,* SBLTT 25, Pseudepigrapha Series 11 (Chico, Calif.: Scholars, 1983).

burn incense of spices weighing three shekels before him, and invoke seven times the names of the angels that lead him during the day."[7] The sun is then addressed in prayer: "Holy Helios who rises in the east, good mariner, trustworthy leader of the sun's rays, reliable [witness], who of old didst establish the mighty wheel [of the heavens], holy orderer, ruler of the axis [of heaven], Lord, Brilliant Leader, King, Soldier."[8]

There is no necessary connection between the Beth Alfa mosaic and this magical text. These passages are quoted simply to illustrate how some Jews at the time (marginal to pure Judaism?) regarded Helios. The mosaic further poses the problem of how Jews who caused the synagogue floor of Beth Alfa (and of Tiberias Hammat) to be built related to the biblical commandments to avoid idolatry as the supreme evil. We will return to this problem in our final remarks. It is possible that these common astral motifs were dead symbols, without pagan associations by the time of Beth Alfa.[9] Some of the astronomical values current at the time were cyclic determinism, hope of immortality (death from life, and life from death), and the great ladder to the world beyond, that is, the great pilgrimage or journey through life to the beyond. For Greek thought, notably Aristotle's *Nicomachean Ethics,* we need the virtues to accompany us on this journey.

The third panel at Beth Alfa, although it contains no human figures, represents the high point of religious significance from a Jewish aniconic point of view. On the right side we see the curtain drawn. (The curtain veiled the synagogue ark that contained the Torah scroll, the word of God for believers. We think of the curtain[s] in the Jerusalem Temple and in Mk 15:38 and its parallels.) In the center stands the Torah ark. Its doors are shut. Three cups stand on top of three pillars from which hang the ark doors or curtains. Above the ark is a roof from which hangs the *ner tamid,* or eternal lamp. To either side of the ark are a series of Jewish religious symbols: two menorahs (seven-branched candelabras, the oldest symbol of Judaism), the lion (of Judah?), the shofar or ram's horn, the lulab with ethrog (linked with the great feast of Sukkah or Tabernacles), the incense shovel, and the tree. Only the tree is not a cult instrument in Judaism. The tree represents life, the bird in the tree represents hope of life in heaven.

---

7. Morgan, *Sepher ha-Razim,* p. 69.

8. Morgan, *Sepher ha-Razim,* p. 71.

9. See E. E. Urbach, "The Rabbinic Laws of Idolatry in the Second and Third Centuries in the Light of Archaeological and Historial Facts," *IEJ* 9 (1959): 149-65, 229-45; S. Lieberman, *Hellenism in Jewish Palestine* (New York: Jewish Theological Seminary, 1950; reprint, 1962), pp. 115-27; for the biblical period the indispensable work is O. Keel and C. Uehlinger, *Gods, Goddesses, and Images of God in Ancient Israel* (Minneapolis: Fortress, 1998).

In summation, the third panel is trying to represent God, in an indirect way, out of reverence — or better: the third panel is trying to represent Jewish ways of attempting to contact God through word and festal liturgy. The three panels may be understood to form a unity in which three phases or aspects of religious experience are depicted in crude but effective images: the need for purification or forgiveness of sins before one can come into the divine presence; the long process of growth and maturation through the practice of the virtues *(imitatio Dei);* union or communion with the divine through faith, love (Deut 6:5), and standing in the divine favor or grace, where one shares in the divine liturgy.

According to E. R. Goodenough, the design of the three panels is influenced by the then popular (just coming into circulation) spirituality of an anonymous Byzantine author, Dionysius, already mentioned. For him the mystic way or spiritual life consists of three "ages": the *purgative* way when the believer tries to be rid of deliberate sin; the *illuminative* way in which the believer makes progress in the virtues while journeying along the spheres of light (zodiac) to the source of light (the sun = God); finally the *unitive* way in which the believer arrives at unification or communion with the divine.[10]

Before we leave the description of this mosaic, we should add as a coda that there is a second such mosaic floor at Tiberias Hammat, just south of the main city of Tiberias. Unfortunately, only the last two of the panels are preserved, those containing the astral symbolism of the sun's chariot and the Torah shrine. The level of artistic execution is of a much higher order than the rather naive workmanship at Beth Alfa. This one would expect closer to an urban center. The fact of the duplication suggests that Beth Alfa is not a totally isolated phenomenon. The spiritual interest lying behind the Beth Alfa floor was shared by other Jews in Byzantine Palestine.[11]

II

My thesis is twofold. (1) The interpretation of the Beth Alfa mosaic by E. R. Goodenough is substantially correct. The mosaic depicts the mystic path as worked out by Dionysius a few years before the mosaic was built. But the mosaic does this by means of Jewish religious symbols, not Christian ones. This is

10. E. R. Goodenough, *Jewish Symbols in the Greco-Roman Period,* vol. 1 of *The Archeological Evidence from Palestine,* Bollingen 37 (New York: Pantheon Books, 1953), pp. 241-53.

11. See the study by B. Lifshitz, "L'ancienne synagogue de Tibériade, sa mosaïque et ses inscriptions," *JSJ* 4 (1973): 43-55.

so even though Dionysius is a Christian author, full of references to the Scriptures of both Testaments, the main Christian sacraments, church order, and monasticism. (To be sure, he is also deeply influenced by the Neoplatonic philosophy of the pagan Proclus.) (2) This set of facts can be taken as an illustration of the second part of the thesis: dogmas are truths that partly serve the social purpose of defining one religious community over against others. They create barriers, hedges, fences, not necessarily uncrossable, but requiring negotiation at least. Their social function is to help decide the vexing question: Who is in, who is out? In contrast to all this, spiritualities, more personal approaches to religious experience, easily leap over doctrinal hedges and are readily adapted by people of other religious traditions. There are many examples of this in all ages. In the seventeenth and eighteenth centuries there was much (not always acknowledged) borrowing of spiritual methods and images between French Catholic devotees, German Protestant Pietists, and British Evangelicals (notably John Wesley). There were Protestant editions of Thomas à Kempis's *Imitation of Christ,* and Greek and Russian Orthodox editions of Lorenzo Scupoli's *Spiritual Combat.* The hymns of Angelus Silesius, a Catholic layman, were sung by Protestants. John Bunyan's allegory *Pilgrim's Progress* was read for edification by Christians of all denominations. Closer to our own day, the spiritual writings of Thomas Merton and Henri Nouwen have been enjoyed by Catholic, Protestant, and Jewish readers alike. The same could be said for the works of Buber and Scholem, Bonhoeffer and Kenneth Leech. Beth Alfa is a striking visual example of this phenomenon of spirituality borrowing and cross-fertilization.

That is the thesis. Can it be proven? No, not beyond a shadow of doubt. That would be possible only if the mosaic explicitly cited terminology from Dionysius to explain the panels. That is not the case. All that can be done is to argue that this is the hypothesis that best fits the facts, an argument that can attain a high degree of probability, so that one sees that the hypothesis is reasonable. Further, one can eliminate rival hypotheses, should there be any, so that the Dionysian explanation would stand for want of a better alternative. As it happens, no rival global explanation has been proposed, so far as the present writer is aware.

A first step is to develop the hypothesis so that one sees what is at stake. The donors were probably lay Jews with sufficient means to pay for the construction, but also with sufficient interest in the then current trends in spirituality to involve themselves in the working out of the design of the mosaic floor. These "laypeople" were not necessarily totally submissive to the directives of the priests or rabbis. That would explain the boldness of the imagery borrowed from paganism as well as the underlying Christian ground plan. One could even think of a powerful, independent woman behind the project, a Lydia (see Acts 16:13-15 and 40).[12] The donors would also need to be bilingual, since the Dionysian corpus circulated at that time in its own, rather cryptic Greek. (There were translations into Syriac, Arabic, and Latin after Beth Alfa was built.) Such bilingualism was not uncommon in Byzantine Palestine.

The next step is to note the psychological insight underlying the Dionysian scheme. The Neoplatonists were psychologists. They were interested in the journey inward. The reason the Dionysian pattern of the three ages or degrees of the spiritual life caught on and spread even beyond Christian confines is that it corresponded to what today would be called developmental psychology. We are not exactly the same people at seventy that we were at twenty or at forty-five, not even religiously. We grow and change. It is as simple as that. And it is a universal human truth that does not stop at denominational frontiers. The Dionysian scheme is often judged too simple. And it is. But there had been earlier schemes that were too complicated. Origen, in his great commentary on Numbers, develops a scheme with forty-two stages. This is based on the forty-two starting points or way stations (LXX *stathmoi*) that Moses recorded in Num 33 that occurred during the Israelite marches in the desert (Origen, *Hom. Num.* 27). But this was too long and complicated. People preferred the simple, tripartite scheme of Dionysius. The contemporary psychological value of this scheme has been well explained by Karl Rahner.[13]

The biblical basis of this schema can be rapidly sketched as follows. Christians divided up Ps 34:15(14) to correspond to the three ages: shun evil (= purgative); and do good (= illuminative); seek amity (integrity, peace, well-being, *shalom*) and pursue it (unitive). They saw a three-step progression in the OT priesthood: Levites, priests *(kohanim)*, high priest, and soon applied this to church leaders: deacons, presbyters, bishops (1 *Clement* 32 and 44; Ignatius, *Letter to the Magnesians* 2 and 6; *Letter to the Philadelphians* 4 and 7). These schemes influenced Dionysius, because in his view the clergy were to help the people to attain to perfection. In Lk 9:23 the disciple must (1) deny himself, (2) take up his cross daily, and (3) follow Jesus. In Matthew the story of the rich young man (19:16-30) divides Christian life into two stages or levels: (1) keeping the commandments (Decalogue and Lev 19:18) and (2) perfection: "Go, sell what you have and give to the poor . . . follow me" (Mt 19:21). This scheme had an enormous influence due to its role in Athanasius's *Life of Anthony of the*

12. On women synagogue leaders, see the study by B. J. Brooten, *Women Leaders in the Ancient Synagogue*, BJS 36 (Chico, Calif.: Scholars, 1982).

13. K. Rahner, "Reflections on the Problem of the Gradual Ascent to Christian Perfection," in his *Theological Investigations*, vol. 3, *The Theology of the Spiritual Life* (Baltimore: Helicon; London: DLT, 1967), pp. 3-23.

Desert, and was used to justify the monastic order. It is so influential that I am tempted to call it the basic schema of Christian spiritual life. But it needed a middle step to become tripartite. This was found in Paul's famous metaphor of the runner who has not reached the goal but presses forward to the prize (Phil 3:13-17). This metaphor suggests the possibility of progress, forward movement, in the spiritual life, an intermediate phase of the proficient, of people making progress. Paul also can distinguish between fleshly *(sarkikoi),* infant Christians and spiritual *(pneumatikoi)* people (1 Cor 3:1-2). He can also speak of the perfect (*teleioi;* 1 Cor 2:6; cf. Mt 5:48; Eph 4:13; Col 1:28; 4:12). The letter to the Hebrews, first in 6:1, exhorts us to "leave behind the basic teaching about Christ and advance to maturity" (AV: "go on unto perfection"). Then, in Heb 12:1-2, the letter proposes what may be read as a three-part program: (1) "let us rid ourselves of every burden and sin"; (2) "and persevere in running the race that lies before us"; (3) "while keeping our eyes fixed on Jesus, the leader and *perfecter* of faith." Heb 6:1 had a great influence on John Wesley's views of Christian spiritual life. Jn 14:23 may also be read as implying some growth or development: "Whoever loves me will keep my word, and my Father will love him, and we will come to him and make our dwelling with him."

The reader will have sensed that while Heb 12:1-2 and Lk 9:23 may be read in a way that leads to a three-step developmental sequence in time, such a reading is not imposed by the texts themselves. They could just as easily be read as recommending three actions that could be pursued more or less simultaneously. The three-stage reading was therefore probably due to the influence of Dionysius and his schema and occurred only after his works were in circulation. (By contrast, Mt 19:21 and 1 Cor 3:1-2 really do have two built-in, explicit degrees, even though it has become fashionable to deny this, or to play it down.)

Before leaving the New Testament period, it might be beneficial to look briefly at the Hellenistic Jewish author Philo of Alexandria (d. ca. 40 C.E.). In his *De somniis* (1.129), he describes the athlete first as a trainee or pupil, then as a wrestler, finally as a victor. In *De sacrificiis Abelis et Caini* 7, he distinguishes the common people from the pupil and the perfect. In several works Philo describes the journey of the soul along the *basilik' hodos,* the *via regis,* the royal road or king's highway, in three stages: through (1) the visible world, to (2) the spiritual world, to (3) God. It is a journey of the spirit to God.[14] This way of thinking may have influenced the Letter to the Hebrews.[15]

14. Philo, *De opicifio mundi* 69; *De mutatione nominis* 179-182; *De immutabilitate Dei* 143. On this aspect of Philo, see J. Pascher, *Η ΒΑΣΙΛΙΚΗ ΟΔΟΣ: Königsweg zur Wiedergeburt und Vergöttung bei Philon von Alexandria* (Paderborn: Schöningh, 1931), pp. 23-28.

15. On Philo's influence on Hebrews, see E. Käsemann, *Das wandernde Gottesvolk,* FRLANT 55 (Göttingen: Vandenhoeck & Ruprecht, 1938); translated by R. Harrisville as *The*

Among the early church fathers, Clement of Alexandria distinguished between children, men, and true gnostics. Evagrius of Pontus divided the Christian life into the practical, the theoretical, and the theological. John Cassian divided it into three stages: servile fear, mercenary hope, filial love (*Collationes* 11.6-12). Dionysius the Pseudo-Areopagite, deeply influenced by the Neoplatonic philosopher Proclus, and choosing pseudonymity because of his moderately Monophysite leanings, was obsessed with order *(taxis)*. He wanted to see the entire cosmos as a *taxis,* in the sense of a hierarchy. "Hierarchy" is a word Dionysius invented for the administration of holy things, and it expresses his concern with order. Orders, like a Greek play, must have a beginning, a middle, and an end.

For Dionysius, hierarchies existed both among the angels and among the members of the church. He drew up a list of nine choirs of angels, one above the other, derived from data scattered in the Bible. These shared in the thearchy or divine government of the universe. In the church on earth he saw gradations toward perfection among the clergy in the familiar series of deacons, priests, bishops. Among the laity he saw the steps of catechumens/penitents, the baptized laypeople, and monks. To all these groups applies the *imitatio Dei* in the three stages we have already seen: purgation *(katharsis)* and illumination *(ellampsis).* Both of these are related to the illumination *(phōtismos)* of baptism. The perfection of union is all-encompassing; it embraces all three stages. Each order or rank is purified, illumined, and perfected by the higher preceding rank, and in turn purifies, illumines, and perfects the rank below. The scheme is Neoplatonic but not Pelagian. Saint Paul says we are "co-workers with God" (1 Cor 3:9), and for Dionysius we are helped by divine grace. We receive the three operations by grace. Thus he says: "I call hierarchy a holy order, a knowing and an acting as close as possible to the divine form, raised up to the imitation of God according to the divine illuminations" (*Celestial Hierarchy,* chap. 3, par. 1; PG 1:164D).[16] The triadic scheme will continue to be developed, not only

---

Wandering People of God (Minneapolis: Augsburg, 1984), p. 76; J. W. Thompson, *The Beginnings of Christian Philosophy: The Epistle to the Hebrews,* CBQMS 13 (Washington, D.C.: Catholic Biblical Association of America, 1982), p. 153 and passim.

16. G. W. H. Lampe, *A Patristic Greek Lexicon* (Oxford: Clarendon, 1961), p. 669. The standard older edition of Dionysius is in Migne, PG 1 or 3 and 4. The current critical edition is B. R. Suchla, G. Heil, and A. M. Ritter, eds., *Corpus Dionysiacum,* 2 vols., PTS 36 (Berlin and New York: de Gruyter, 1991). The most recent English translation is by C. Luibheid and P. Rorem, *Classics of Western Spirituality Series* (New York: Paulist, 1987). Studies include R. Rogues, *L'univers dionysien,* Théologie 29 (Paris: Aubier-Montagne, 1954). The same author in *RAC* 3 (1957), cols. 1075-1121, s.v. "Dionysius Areopagita"; with others in *Dict. Sp.* 3 (1957), cols. 244-429, s.v. "Denys (2), l'Aréopagite (Le Pseudo-)"; R. Rogues, W. M. Cappuyns, and R. Aubert, in

by Greek theologians like Maximus the Confessor, but also by major medieval thinkers in the West. Saint Bonaventure wrote a treatise called *De triplici via* (1259 or 1260), which had a wide distribution.

Saint Thomas Aquinas was not satisfied with the unbiblical labels that Dionysius gave to these stages of Christian life. Thomas therefore avoids the vocabulary of purgative, illuminative, unitive steps. He prefers the more biblical terms "beginners, proficient, perfect" *(incipientes, proficientes, perfecti),* which are set in relation to the supreme value, charity, or love of God and neighbor. To avoid illusions, Thomas distinguishes between the relative perfection of this life, where venial sins are unavoidable, and the absolute perfection possible only in heaven. His whole analysis is geared to growth in charity.[17]

By way of conclusion, it will suffice to recall our basic thesis that dogmas tend to divide, to define communities, while spiritualities can sometimes leap over dogmatic barriers to unite nonprofessional believers. The mosaic synagogue floor of Beth Alfa, which expresses a Christian analysis of the spiritual life in Jewish religious symbols, is a good illustration of this kind of cross-fertilization. And then, we should add, the whole phenomenon of Jewish figurative art came to an abrupt end in the region with the arrival of Islam and its associated return to aniconism.

DHGE 14 (1960), cols. 265-310, s.v. "Denys (14) le Pseudo-Aréopagite"; A. Louth, *Denys the Areopagite* (London: G. Chapman, 1989); H. U. von Balthasar, *The Glory of the Lord* 2 (San Francisco: Ignatius, 1984), pp. 144-210; I. P. Sheldon-Williams, in *The Cambridge History of Later Greek and Early Medieval Philosophy,* ed. A. H. Armstrong (Cambridge: Cambridge University Press, 1967), pp. 457-72.

17. *Summa theologiae* 1-2, q. 61, art. 5; 2-2, q. 24, arts. 8 and 9; q. 183, art. 4; q. 184, art. 2; 3; *Sentences* D. 29, q. 1, a. 8. A. Solignac, "Voies," in *Dictionnaire de Spiritualité* (Paris: Beauchesne, 1994), pp. 16, 1200-1215; J. de Guibert, *The Theology of the Spiritual Life* (New York: Sheed and Ward, 1953), part 6, chap. 1; R. Garrigou-Lagrange, *The Three Ages of the Spiritual Life,* trans. M. T. Doyle, 2 vols. (St. Louis: Herder, 1956).

The Theodotos Synagogue Inscription and the Problem of First-Century Synagogue Buildings

John S. Kloppenborg

The Gospels make frequent reference to Jesus' activities in *synagōgai* (synagogues). Since these activities include teaching, preaching, and healing in places where Jews gathered, often on the Sabbath, it is a natural inference that *synagōgē* refers to a building of some kind. This impression is made even stronger by Luke's mention of a centurion who had a *synagōgē* constructed (ᾠκοδόμησεν) in Capernaum (Lk 7:5). Nevertheless, the ordinary sense of the term *synagōgē* is "meeting" or "assembly" and need not refer to a building at all. This has led some scholars to conclude that *synagōgē* in the intra-canonical Gospels should be translated as "assembly" or "congregation" and that for most of the first century at least, no identifiable architectural structure called a "synagogue" existed. Texts that imply the existence of purpose-built buildings in first-century Judea and Galilee are anachronistic projections from a later time or from the Diaspora.

The most prominent advocate of this view is Howard Clark Kee, who has defended the hypothesis that in the first century C.E. *synagōgē* referred to assem-

A longer version of this paper was published in *JJS* 51 (2000): 243-80, and is reprinted and revised here with the kind permission of the editors, Geza Vermes and Tessa Rajak. Much of the paper was written while I was a visiting fellow at Clare Hall, Cambridge; a shorter version was presented at the annual meeting of the Studiorum Novi Testamenti Societas in Tel Aviv (August 2000). I am indebted to Fellows of Clare Hall for electing me a fellow, to the Faculty of Classics and Tyndale House for extending me library privileges, to the Social Sciences and Humanities Research Council of Canada for a travel grant, and to various respondents to the paper at Tel Aviv. J. M. Reynolds and E. M. Meyers graciously read earlier drafts of the paper, providing many helpful comments and sparing me from various errors and overstatements. D. Bahat clarified some points on the excavations of the Ophel; Y. Barschak of the Israel Antiquities Authority kindly supplied a photograph of the Rockefeller inv. S 842; and B. Isaac assisted me in locating a photograph of a squeeze of *SEG* xxxiii 1277.

blies or congregations rather than to buildings, both in the land of Israel and in the Diaspora.[1] In Eretz Israel, he argued, it is impossible to identify any structure before 200 C.E. as a *synagōgē* with architecturally distinguishable features.[2] In the Diaspora, he says, the earliest literary references to *synagōgē* as a building date from the late third century C.E.: "[F]rom the first century C.E. on to the time of Diocletian, inscriptions from the Bosphorus and the Black Sea area use *synagōgē* for the community and *proseuchē* [prayer house] for the place where they gather. Analogously, in Greek literature of the period, *synagōgai* are designations for group gatherings, rather than for the places where they assemble."[3]

Only at the end of the first century or beginning of the second did a linguistic shift begin to occur, with *synagōgē* being applied to buildings as well as to assemblies. This implies, according to Kee, that in referring to two pre-70 C.E. buildings as *synagōgai* (Lk 7:5; Acts 18:7), Luke inadvertently read back later usage into an earlier period.

Kee's thesis on the meaning of *synagōgē* in the first century C.E. has attracted both severe criticism[4] and favorable notice.[5] The issue he raises has lit-

---

1. H. C. Kee, "The Transformation of the Synagogue after 70 C.E.: Its Import for Early Christianity," *NTS* 36 (1990): 1-24; Kee, "Early Christianity in the Galilee: Reassessing the Evidence from the Gospels," in *The Galilee in Late Antiquity*, ed. L. I. Levine (New York: Jewish Theological Seminary of America, 1992), pp. 3-22; Kee, "The Changing Meaning of Synagogue: A Response to Richard Oster," *NTS* 40 (1994): 281-83; Kee, "Defining the First Century C.E. Synagogue: Problems and Progress," *NTS* 41 (1995): 481-500, reprinted essentially unchanged in H. C. Kee and L. H. Cohick, eds., *The Evolution of the Synagogue: Problems and Progress* (Harrisburg, Pa.: Trinity, 1999), pp. 7-26.

2. This view, as E. M. Meyers has pointed out to me (*per litt.* 20.12.99), ignores the first phase of Nabratein (building one), dated no later than the mid–second century C.E. on the basis of stratigraphic and ceramic evidence. This building, a broadhouse (11.2 × 9.35 m.), has two rows of benches on three sides (but not on the Jerusalem-facing south wall), a bema (against the southern wall), and an impression at the center of the plastered floor, probably made by a lectern. See E. M. Meyers, J. F. Strange, and C. L. Meyers, "Preliminary Report on the 1980 Excavations at en-Nabratein, Israel," *BASOR* 244 (1981): 1-26; Meyers, Strange, and Meyers, "Second Preliminary Report on the 1981 Excavations at en-Nabratein, Israel," *BASOR* 246 (1982): 35-54; E. M. Meyers, "Nabratein (Kefar Neburaya)," in *NEAEHL* 3:1077-79; M. J. Chiat, *Handbook of Synagogue Architecture*, BJS 29 (Chico, Calif.: Scholars, 1982), pp. 41-45.

3. Kee, "Transformation," p. 6. See also p. 9: "Thus there is simply no evidence to speak of synagogues in Palestine as architecturally distinguishable edifices prior to 200 C.E. Evidence of meeting places: 'Yes,' both in private homes and in public buildings. Evidence of distinctive architectural features of a place of worship or the study of Torah: 'No'"; p. 13: "In every other case [in the Diaspora except Sardis], what became a synagogue building by the end of the second or in the third century C.E., with identifiable features as such, was originally a residence."

4. E. P. Sanders, *Jewish Law from Jesus to the Mishnah: Five Studies* (Philadelphia: Trinity, 1990), pp. 341-43 nn. 28-29 (who describes Kee's 1990 article as "remarkably ill-informed and often incoherent"); R. Oster, "Supposed Anachronism in Luke-Acts' Use of *sunagōgē*: A Rejoinder

erary, lexicographic, archaeological, and epigraphical dimensions. First, although the Gospels frequently use the term *synagōgē* and sometimes seem to have in mind a building, the evidence requires careful evaluation, since some of the occurrences of the term are probably editorial and hence probably do not reflect practices at the time of Jesus. Second, since the primary meaning of *synagōgē* has to do with assemblies and not with the buildings in which they occur, one must take care both to construe the term as a building *only* when the context makes this clear and to be attentive to the point in the historical development of the Greek language when the latter meaning was introduced. Third, archaeologists have unearthed several structures in Israel that date from prior to the First Revolt that are often called "synagogues." None of these, however, bears an inscription that designates it as a *synagōgē* or as a *bet keneset*.[6] Apart from benches on two or more sides, none contains the architectural features typical of later purpose-built synagogues such as a bema (platform), Torah niche or chest, lectern, cathedra of Moses or mosaic or other inscriptions with *menorot*, or other obviously Jewish symbols. That these buildings were designed for public rather than private (domestic) use is obvious from their floor

to H. C. Kee," *NTS* 39 (1993): 178-208; R. Riesner, "Synagogues in Jerusalem," in *The Book of Acts in Its Palestinian Setting,* ed. R. J. Bauckham, Book of Acts in Its First Century Setting 4 (Grand Rapids: Eerdmans; Carlisle: Paternoster, 1995), pp. 179-211; K. Atkinson, "On Further Defining the First-Century C.E. Synagogue: Fact or Fiction? A Rejoinder to H. C. Kee," *NTS* 43 (1997): 491-502; S. J. D. Cohen, "Were Pharisees and Rabbis the Leaders of Communal Prayer and Torah Study in Antiquity?" in *The Echoes of Many Texts: Reflections on Jewish and Christian Traditions; Essays in Honor of Lou H. Silberman,* ed. W. G. Dever and J. E. Wright, BJS 313 (Atlanta: Scholars, 1997), pp. 99-114; and P. W. van der Horst, "Was the Ancient Synagogue a Place of Sabbath Worship?" in *Jews, Christians, and Polytheists in the Ancient Synagogue,* ed. S. Fine (London and New York: Routledge, 1999), pp. 18-43.

5. Kee is cited favorably by H. A. McKay, "Ancient Synagogues: The Continuing Dialectic between Two Major Views," *CurBS* 6 (1998): 103-42. R. A. Horsley (*Galilee: History, Politics, People* [Valley Forge, Pa.: Trinity, 1995], pp. 223-25) agrees that there is "no archaeological or literary evidence for synagogue buildings in Judean or Galilean towns and villages until the third century or later" (p. 225). Similarly, Horsley, "Synagogues in Galilee and the Gospels," in *The Evolution of the Synagogue,* p. 47. McKay (p. 106) schematizes views on the ancient synagogue as "maximalist" and "minimalist": the former view affirms substantial continuity between "synagogues" of the first century C.E. and the established institutions of the third and following centuries, while the latter holds "that the synagogue did not reach a form more or less in recognizable continuity with that of the present day until the third and fourth centuries C.E." Apropos of the Theodotos inscription, McKay characterizes the "maximalist" view as maintaining a pre-70 C.E. date for the *synagōgē,* and the "minimalists" (among whom she groups herself) as dissatisfied with this date (pp. 109, 126-27). See also H. A. McKay, *Sabbath and Synagogue: The Question of Sabbath Worship in Ancient Judaism,* Religions in the Graeco-Roman World 122 (Leiden: Brill, 1994), pp. 242-45.

6. בת כנסת.

plan; but it is far from clear what sorts of public functions were intended. Finally, there is a single piece of epigraphical evidence, the Theodotos synagogue inscription (Rockefeller inv. S842 = *CIJ* ii 1404), that uses the term *synagōgē* with reference to a building. There is, however, a question of its date. While it was originally dated to the first century c.e., it was not found *in situ* where other kinds of ceramic, numismatic, and stratigraphical evidence could be called upon to corroborate this early date. Kee places the inscription much later, sometime between the late second and fourth centuries. If such a date could be sustained, our one bit of "hard" evidence would vanish.[7]

Literary Evidence

Evidence from the Gospels

The Synoptic Gospels and John locate synagogues at Capernaum,[8] Nazareth,[9] and two unnamed locations,[10] and their summary statements and general comments suggest that synagogues were a general feature of towns and villages in Galilee and Judea.[11] But close investigation of these literary references renders them more problematic than one might first imagine.

Lk 7:5, the most obvious reference to a *synagōgē* as a building, belongs to a text from the Sayings Gospel Q,[12] used independently by Matthew and Luke in the

---

7. J. F. Strange ("Ancient Texts, Archaeology as Text, and the Problem of the First-Century Synagogue," in *The Evolution of the Synagogue*, p. 28) cites Kee's "reevaluation" of the date of the Theodotos inscription, but in the note (p. 28 n. 10) appears to accept Riesner's criticism of Kee. R. Hachlili ("The Origin of the Synagogue: A Re-assessment," *JSJ* 28 [1997]: 38 n. 27) reports Kee's redating of the Theodotos inscription, apparently considering it to be viable. P. V. M. Flesher ("Palestinian Synagogues before 70 c.e.: A Review of the Evidence," in *Ancient Synagogues: Historical Analyses and Archaeological Discovery*, ed. D. Urman and P. V. M. Flesher, SPB 47/1-2, 2 vols. [Leiden: Brill, 1995], 1:27-39) comments that the Theodotos inscription "could even be from the late third or early fourth century" (p. 33 n. 21). His criticisms of the methods of the "archaeologists who found the inscription" appear to be influenced by Kee's statements, although he does not cite Kee. Flesher erroneously states that the stone was found "at the bottom of a well" (p. 33).

8. Capernaum: Mk 1:21; 1:23 (= Lk 4:33); 1:29 (= Lk 4:38); 3:1 (= Mt 12:9; Lk 6:6); Lk 7:5; Jn 6:59.

9. Nazareth: Mk 6:2 (Mt 13:54); Lk 4:15, 16, 20, 28.

10. Unnamed locations: Lk 8:41 (somewhere in Galilee); 13:10 (either in Galilee or Judah).

11. Summary and general comments: Mk 1:39 (= Mt 4:23/9:35; Lk 4:44, which refers to the synagogues of Judah); 12:39 (Mt 23:6; Lk 20:46); 13:9 (Mt 10:17; Lk 21:12); Q 11:43 (Mt 23:6; Lk 11:43); Mt 6:2, 5; 23:34; Lk 12:11; Jn 18:20.

12. Texts from the Sayings Gospel Q are cited by their *Lukan* versification. E.g., Q 11:43 is the Q text used by Mt 23:6 and Lk 11:43. The convention does not necessarily imply that Luke's

construction of their Gospels.[13] Luke's version of the story is complicated: the centurion *built (oikodomein)* a synagogue for the Jews of Capernaum, and it is this deed that a delegation of town elders cite in recommending to Jesus that he comply with the centurion's request to heal his slave *(doulos)*. He then sent a second delegation of friends to convey a (first-person!) speech about his unworthiness. The difficulty with this text is that Matthew's version of the story (Mt 8:5-10, 13) lacks any mention of the building of a synagogue and both delegations, instead having the centurion confront Jesus directly with his request for healing his serving boy *(pais)* and his declarations of unworthiness. This raises serious doubts as to whether the building of the synagogue was part of Q's story or an addition by Luke. Suspicions are heightened when it is observed that Luke tells the story of another centurion, Cornelius, whom he describes as pious and a God-fearer, used to giving alms to Jews (Acts 10:2). Cornelius also sent two delegates to Peter, who describe him in much the same terms used by the Jewish delegates of Lk 7:5:

Lk 7:4-5	Acts 10:22
He is worthy to have you do this thing for him, for he loves our nation and he himself built the synagogue for us.	Cornelius, a centurion, a pious man and a God-fearer, publicly acknowledged by the entire nation of Jews. . . .

Although there is some division among Lukan critics and in the various reconstructions of Q, the Lukan vocabulary and interests displayed in verses 3b-6a and the difficulty in accounting for Matthew's omission of the delegation of elders, had he seen it in Q, make it likely that Luke added these verses to underscore the centurion's piety and humility and to enhance the parallels with the Cornelius story.[14] But this means that Lk 7:5 ceases to be compelling early evidence of *synagōgē* meaning "building."[15]

---

wording or sequence is to be preferred, although in general Q reconstructions have preferred Lukan sequence.

13. See J. M. Robinson, P. Hoffmann, and J. S. Kloppenborg, eds., *The Critical Edition of Q: A Synopsis, Including the Gospels of Matthew and Luke, Mark and Thomas*, Hermeneia Supplements (Leuven: Uitgeverij Peeters; Minneapolis: Fortress, 2000).

14. For a tabulation of opinion, see J. S. Kloppenborg, *Q Parallels*, Foundations and Facets, Reference Series (Sonoma, Calif.: Polebridge, 1988), p. 50. The International Q Project (based on a database prepared by S. R. Johnson and evaluations by J. M. Robinson, J. S. Kloppenborg, and P. Hoffmann) treats Lk 7:3b-6a as Lukan editorial. See also I. Dunderberg, *Johannes und die Synoptiker: Studien zu Joh 1–9*, Annales Academiae Scientiarum Fennicae, Dissertationes Humanarum Litterarum 69 (Helsinki: Suomalainen Tiedeakatemia, 1994), pp. 85-89; F. Neirynck, review of *Johannes und die Synoptiker*, by Dunderberg, *ETL* 72 (1996): 454-56.

15. Kee, "Transformation," p. 17: "The very fact that 'synagogue' here alone in the gospel

Other occurrences of *synagōgē* in the Gospels are much less clear: Mk 1:21, 23, 29, 39; 3:1; 6:2; 13:9 (and their respective parallels); Mt 6:2, 5; Lk 8:41; 13:10; and Jn 6:59 use *synagōgē* in a manner that could be rendered "assembly." Such assemblies must have been held in a definite place, but the context does not require us to assume that they took place in a special building; an open-air assembly or a meeting in a large house might do just as well. Mk 12:39 and Q 11:43 speak of the "front seats" *(prōtokathedriai)* in the *synagōgē*, which is certainly consistent with a building with specially designated seating. Indeed, in a third century C.E. inscription from Phocaea (Ionia, Asia Minor), a woman who constructed part of a synagogue was voted a golden crown and the honor of sitting in the front seat *(proedria)*.[16] It might still be objected, nevertheless, that *prōtokathedriai* refer only to the honored places in an assembly, wherever it might take place, rather than to designated seats in a purpose-built building.[17]

Lk 4:15-30 presupposes a fairly elaborate synagogue structure, where scrolls of the Tanak are kept and made available for reading and where an attendant *(hypēretēs)* gives the scroll to the reader (4:17) and takes it back once the reading is completed (4:20). The role of the attendant seems to correspond to the *ḥazzan* mentioned in later rabbinic and inscriptional sources and the administrator *(phrontistēs)* or assistant *(diakonos)* mentioned in others.[18] But again it could be objected that some or all of these details might be the work of Luke, probably writing in the Diaspora and representing late first-century Diaspora rather than early first-century Galilean practices.

Despite the density of references to *synagōgai* in the Gospels, none of them provides compelling evidence of the existence of an architectural institution

---

tradition pointed unequivocally to a building, rather than to a gathering, serves to confirm the impression that Luke-Acts is a document from a Hellenistic center, where (as the archaeological evidence we have examined suggests) Jews in the Diaspora had begun to modify house or public structures in order to serve more effectively the needs of the local Jewish community."

16. *DFSJ* 13 (pp. 21-22) = *CIJ* ii 738: "Tation daughter of Straton son of Empedon, having constructed (furnished?) the assembly hall and the wall enclosing the atrium from her own resources, gave them as a gift to the Jews. The congregation *(synagōgē)* of Judaeans honoured Tation, daughter of Straton son of Empedon with a golden crown and (the privilege of sitting in) the front seat *(proedria)*."

17. Kee, "Transformation," p. 14: "Mark 12:38-39 hints at nothing more than a gathered community, in which some seek front seats and favoured positions at the common meals." Similarly, Kee, "Defining," p. 489: "But [front seats] can mean only the most visible location in the gathering taking place in a home or public meeting hall."

18. See L. I. Levine, *The Ancient Synagogue: The First Thousand Years* (New Haven: Yale University Press, 1999), pp. 410-17, and *DFSJ* 40 (Apamea, Syria; 391 C.E.): "During the administration of Nemias, hazzan *(azzana)* and assistant *(diakonos)* . . ."; *DFSJ* 36 (Side, Pamphylia; IV C.E.): "Isakis, administrator *(phrontistēs)* of the most holy first synagogue. . . ."

called a "synagogue" in the early first century. Lk 7:5 indeed refers precisely to such a building, and Lk 4:15-30 presupposes the existence of a structure with storage for scrolls and an attendant, but these might well be Luke's *assumptions* about Galilean synagogues rather than a reflection of Galilean practice at the time of Jesus. All that these tell us is that by the late first century when Luke wrote, such institutions existed in Luke's part of the world. Mk 12:39 and Q 11:43 are compatible with the assumption of the existence of buildings called "synagogues" with designated seating arrangements, but other readings of these texts are possible too.

Josephus

The other source of references to Palestinian *synagōgai* in the first century is Josephus. In *Life* (277, 280, 293) Josephus mentions a very large building (μέγιστον οἴκημα) in Tiberias. This building was used for meetings — Josephus mentions one held on the Sabbath and the two following days to discuss political matters. The term he uses for this building, however, is not *synagōgē* but rather *proseuchē* (prayer hall), the term customarily used for Jewish meeting halls in the Diaspora, especially in Egypt and on Delos.[19]

Josephus's references to buildings called *synagōgai* occur in his discussion of Gentile-Jewish conflict in the coastal cities of Dora and Caesarea Maritima. In 41 C.E. some Gentile youths from Dora set up a statue of Caligula in the synagogue (εἰς τὴν τῶν Ἰουδαίων συναγωγήν) (*Ant* 19.300). Agrippa I objected to Petronius the legate of Syria, who treated the matter as a violation of the law of sacrilege (ἔκρινεν ἀσέβειαν τὴν τῶν ἐννόμων παράβασιν) and wrote to the leaders of Dora: "You have prevented the Jews from having a synagogue (συναγωγὴν Ἰουδαίων κωλύοντας εἶναι) by transferring to it an image of Caesar." He continued: the youths offended against the emperor, "whose image was better placed in its own sanctuary than in that of another, especially in the place of assembly" (οὗ ὁ ἀνδριὰς βέλτιον ἐν τῷ ἰδίῳ ναῷ ἢ ἐν ἀλλοτρίῳ ἐτίθετο καὶ ταῦτα ἐν τῷ τῆς συναγωγῆς τόπῳ) (19.305). Thus it is clear that the meeting place for the Jews of Dora was not a private house, and that it was regarded, both by the Jews and Petronius, as holy, on par with a pagan temple, and therefore susceptible to defilement.

19. See M. Hengel, "Proseuchē und Synagōgē: Jüdische Gemeinde, Gotteshaus und Gottesdienst in der Diaspora und in Palästina," in *Tradition und Glaube: Das frühe Christentum in seiner Umwelt. Festgabe für Karl Georg Kuhn*, ed. G. Jeremias, H.-W. Kuhn, and H. Stegemann (Göttingen: Vandenhoeck & Ruprecht, 1971), pp. 157-84, reprinted in J. Gutmann, ed., *The Synagogue: Studies in Origins, Archaeology, and Architecture* (New York: Ktav, 1975), pp. 27-54 (all citations are from the 1971 version).

Josephus's use of the term *synagōgē* varies. In *Ant* 19.300 its most obvious meaning is a building (in which an image could be set up). In *Ant* 19.305, he uses instead the phrase "the place of gathering [*synagōgēs*]." Nevertheless, the account makes clear that the building in question was identifiable by Jews and others and was used for specifically cultic purposes (as were Greek and Roman sanctuaries).

Josephus uses *synagōgē* yet again in his description of the hostilities between Greeks and Jews in Caesarea Maritima in 66 c.e., including conflict over access to a *synagōgē*. He states that Caesarean Jews had a *synagōgē* adjoining land owned by a Greek.[20] They had tried in vain to purchase the land and the owner instead built workshops, thereby impeding access to the *synagōgē*. Following a violent conflict, some Caesarean youths placed a bird sacrifice beside the entrance to the *synagōgē* (παρὰ τὴν εἴσοδον αὐτῶν), which the Jews discovered when they assembled at the synagogue on Sabbath (τῶν Ἰουδαίων εἰς τὴν συναγωγὴν συναθροισθέντων; *War* 2.289). The conclusion of Richard Oster seems entirely reasonable: "It appears much easier to conceptualize the details of this narrative if *synagōgē* refers to a meeting-place rather than to the people themselves."[21]

To this Kee had two answers. In a 1994 rejoinder, Kee merely noted that Josephus was writing at the same time as Luke, or later, and hence it was hardly surprising to find the same terminological shift.[22] In the following year Kee offered a different interpretation of *War* 2.285-289: "Here the phrase *eis tēn synagōgēn* [in *War* 2.289] almost certainly means 'into the meeting,' but it cannot be completely excluded that, following the destruction of the temple in 70 c.e., the term *synagōgē*, which earlier had been used with reference to the Jewish group meetings, began to be used to refer as well to the structure where they met."[23]

The first part of this conclusion is based on a mistaken reading of the context, for Kee assumes that the intent of the Caesarean Jews was "to buy a plot where they could erect a building."[24] If this were so, and they did not yet possess a building, *synagōgē* can only mean "meeting." But the text of *War* 2.285-289 indicates nothing of the sort. All that is said is that the Greek owner began to erect

20. *War* 2.285: *hoi en Kaisareia Ioudaioi, synagōgēn exontes para chōrion hou despotēs ēn tis Hellēn Kaisareus.*

21. Oster, "Supposed Anachronism," p. 189. Oster also adduced *War* 7.43-44, where Josephus describes the offerings Antiochus IV Epiphanes confiscated and which his successors returned to the Jews of Antioch to set them up in their *synagōgē*. *Synagōgē* here *could* mean "assembly," but clearly it is in a location where offerings can be set up.

22. Kee, "Changing Meaning," p. 282 (in reference to *Ant* 19.300-305; *War* 2.289; 7.44): "But writing as he is around and after the turn of the second century, Josephus occasionally uses *synagōgē* to refer to the gathering places of pious Jews. By the late first century therefore, the word was well on its way to becoming the common term referring to the gathering place of Jews."

23. Kee, "Defining," p. 488.

24. Kee, "Defining," p. 488.

buildings and thereby restricted access to the *synagōgē*. The Caesarean Jews may have wanted to purchase the land because they intended to expand the current building or merely to secure access by creating a plaza — the text of Josephus gives us no hint. Elsewhere Josephus indicates that Caesarean Jews of the mid–first century had considerable wealth and were thus in a position to do either. Josephus's description of the Caesarean *synagōgē* leaves little real doubt that it was a building, not a congregation: it was located in a definite place (παρὰ χωρίον); it had an entrance (εἴσοδος); and it was a place where Jews could assemble on the Sabbath. Whether the existing building was a purpose-built assembly hall or a converted house makes little difference.

The dating of Josephus's works to the latter part of the first century means, nonetheless, that Kee might yet be right, and that Josephus, no less than Luke, was being anachronistic in referring to the Caesarean assembly hall as a *synagōgē*. The fact that Philo, writing in the early first century c.e. and describing Essene gatherings in Palestine (*Quod omnis probus liber sit* 81), had to explain the term *synagōgē* to his readers is explicable if this designation for a building was unusual in Philo's Alexandria, where *proseuchē* still dominated.[25]

Lexicographic Data

A second aspect of Kee's argument has to do with historical lexicography — the point at which one can document *synagōgē* used of a building rather than a congregation or meeting. Kee claimed that "the oldest direct reference in the papyri to the synagogue as a structure is dated from 291 c.e."[26] The claim is mistaken: the oldest papyrus reference is much later, from the mid–sixth century c.e.[27] As

25. See below, n. 35.

26. Kee, "Transformation," p. 6. Although Kee does not document his claim, his reference is presumably to a manumission document, *POxy* ix 1205.6-8 (Oxyrhynchus; 291 c.e.) = *CPJ* iii 473.6-8: *arithmē[thentōn hēmin hyper tēs eleutherōseōs kai apolus]eōs para tēs syna[g]ōgēs tōn Ioudaiōn dia Aurēliōn [Dioskorou kai Ious]tou*, "(The money) having been paid to us by the congregation *(synagōgē)* of Judaeans by Aurelius Dioskoros [*vacat*] and Aurelius Justus, for the manumission and release (of a slave)." As the context makes clear, *synagōgē* refers not to a building but to the congregation paying for manumission.

27. Kee's appeal to papyrus evidence is problematic, since occurrences of *synagōgē* to designate either a building or a congregation are very rare, and hence any generalization from papyri alone is bound to be precarious. Setting aside the occurrences of *synagōgē* that have to do with collections of money, wheat, and other agricultural products, the term most commonly occurs in respect to the *meeting* of an association (rather than the designation of the association itself): *PRyl* iv 590.1 (provenance unknown; reign of Cleopatra VII?): "at the meeting *(synagōgē)* that was held in the *proseuchē*." The group (perhaps a Jewish group) apparently referred to itself as a

Oster pointed out,[28] however, the impression Kee left by citing only papyri is misleading, for we have much earlier epigraphical evidence from Benghazi (= Bernike, Cyrenaica) that uses *synagōgē* to mean *both* a congregation and a building.[29] *CJZC* 72, dated to the second year of Nero's principate (55/56 C.E.), has the phrase *eis episkeuēn tēs synagōgēs* in lines 4/5, which can only refer to the repair of a building:[30]

col. 1

 (ἔτει) β Νέρωνος Κλαυδίου Καίσαρος Δρούσου
 Γερμανικοῦ αὐτοκράτος Χόσιαχ ις
 ἐφάνη τῇ συναγωγῇ τῶν ἐν Βερνεικίδι
 Ἰουδαίων τοὺς ἐπιδιδόντες εἰς ἐπισκευ-
5 ὴν τῆς συναγωγῆς ἀναγράψαι αὐτοὺς εἰστή-
 λην λίθου Παρίου.

(Year) 2 of Nero Claudius Caesar Drusus Germanicus, Imperator, sixth of Chosiak. It seemed good to the congregation *(synagōgē)* of Judaeans (living)

---

synodos (lines 4, 8, 16), a common designation of a club or association. For variations of the formulae "at the meeting of" *(epi tēs synagōgēs)* + club name in Greco-Egyptian inscriptions, see *SB* v 8929.1-3 (Memphis; 112-111 B.C.E.); *SEG* viii 641.16-18 (104 B.C.E.); *IDelta* i 446.2-4 (Psenamosis; II B.C.E.); *IDelta* i 899.2-4 (Psenemphaia; 5 B.C.E.) and *IAlexandriaK* 91.2-4 (Alexandria; 4/5 C.E.).

 The earliest papyrus reference to a *synagōgē* as a *building* is in fact a ledger of rents, *POxy* lv 3805.v.56-57 (Oxyrhynchus; after 566 C.E.): "(Paid) through Lazar(os) the Judaean, for the rent of the *synagōgē*: by public standard, 1 solidus + ¼ carat; and for the *rhope* and *incrementum*, nil, by custom; and for conversion of the public standard to Alexandrian (standard), at ⅙ carat per solidus: 1 solidus, ¼ carat. Total by Alexandrian standard: 1 solidus, ½ carat."

 28. Oster, "Supposed Anachronism," pp. 187-88.

 29. *CJZC* 72 (pp. 155-58) = Joyce M. Reynolds, "Inscriptions," in *Excavations at Sidi Khrebish, Benghazi (Bernice)*, vol. 1, *Buildings, Coins, Inscriptions, Architectural Decoration*, ed. J. A. Lloyd, Supplements to Libya Antiqua 5 (Tripoli: Department of Antiquities, 1977), 1:242-44 n. 12. The inscription, now lost, was originally published by G. Caputo, "La sinagoga di Berenice in Cirenaica in una iscrizione greca inedita," *Parola del Passato* 12 (1957): 132-34 (with a photograph), and S. Applebaum, "A New Jewish Inscription from Bernike in Cyrenaica" (in Hebrew), *BIES* 25 (1961): 167-74 (with a photograph), and by Lifshitz, *DFSJ* 81-83 (no. 100).

 30. Compare a similar decree of a club of Rhamnousian demesmen regarding the repairs needed to their temple: *IG* ii² 1322.10-13 (Rhamnous, Attica; III/II B.C.E.): *agathei tychei dedochthai tois Amphieraïstais epidounai men hekaston eis tēn episkeuēn tou hierou hoson an boulētai, tōn d' epidontōn anagrapsai ta onomata en stēlei lithinei kai stēsai para ton theon*, "For good fortune, the Amphieranistai have resolved that each member who is so willing shall make contributions for the repair of the sanctuary, and that the names of those who contribute shall be inscribed on a stone stele to be set up beside the god." A list of donors follows. For other instances of ἐπισκευή, "repairs," see *IG* ii² 1361.10-11 (Piraeus; IV B.C.E.); *Syll*³ 1106 B.69 (Cos; 300 B.C.E.); *ISmyrna* ii 721.1-4 (Smyrna; n.d.); *IG* xii/7 937.9-10 (Malona, Rhodes; n.d.).

in Bernike to inscribe this stele of Parian marble with (the names of) those who contributed to the renovation of the synagogue.

(The names of eighteen donors follow, with the amounts of their donations, which range from five to twenty-eight drachmae.)

The Benghazi inscription indicates that already in the mid–first century, *synagōgē* could be used of both social gatherings (congregations) and buildings. Thus, in its crudest form, Kee's thesis requires modification.[31] At the very least, *CJZC* 72 is an exception to the rule that Kee proposes, and at worst it is fatal to his thesis.[32]

Second, Oster observed that contrary to Kee's claims, Philo uses the term *synagōgē* in a way that can only refer to buildings. In 1990 Kee noted with Hengel that in Egypt where Jewish assembly buildings are regularly called prayer houses (προσευχαί), Philo also preferred the term *proseuchē*.[33] Kee,

31. Oddly, both in his rejoinder to Oster ("Changing Meaning," pp. 281-83) and in the article of the next year ("Defining the First Century C.E. Synagogue") Kee completely ignored *CJZC* 72 and simply reiterated his original thesis. The double significance of *synagōgē*, however, had already been noted by Hengel ("Proseuchē," p. 182): "The third mention [of the Jewish community in the inscriptions from Cyrenaica], about 31 years later (56 C.E.), does not speak any longer of a *politeuma* [ethnic community], but of the *synagōgē tōn en Berneikidi Ioudaiōn* [Judean community in Bernike], who set up a marble stele. Now *synagōgē* suddenly means both the community and the synagogue building" (my translation).

32. McKay ("Ancient Synagogues," p. 125) suggests a possible mitigation of the significance of *CJZC* 72: "[A]ny discussion of the Bernice inscription would have to take more notice than is usually taken of its uniqueness, rather than assume that many similar inscriptions could well await discovery. Such a discussion would have to posit either the restriction of the double use of the term 'synagogue' as community and building to that one site only; or, contrarily, it would have to argue for its representativeness of many other buildings of which we now have no evidence. Many scholars imply that they assume representativeness, but they neither say so explicitly, nor do they argue the case." J. M. Reynolds points out to me *(per litt.)* that the possibility that συναγωγή of buildings was a local (Cyrenaic) usage must be balanced against the fact that the term eventually became a standard designation for a building and it would be curious, at least, if its origin was solely Cyrenaic. Moreover, there is good evidence of close contacts between Cyrenaica and Jerusalem in the first century C.E.: not only the New Testament references to Simon of Cyrenaica (Mk 15:21) and to Jews from Cyrene (Acts 2:10; 6:9), but epigraphical records of Cyrenians buried in Jerusalem (N. Avigad, "A Depository of Inscribed Ossuaries in the Kidron Valley," *IEJ* 12 [1962]: 1-12) and Josephus's (*War* 7.437-453; *Life* 424) mention of Jonathan, a weaver, who fled from Judea and was involved in an uprising in Cyrenaica. Such contacts raise the clear possibility that regular movement to and fro accounted for the common use of *synagōgē*. On these contacts, see S. Applebaum, *Jews and Greeks in Ancient Cyrene*, SJLA 28 (Leiden: Brill, 1979), pp. 215-16; J. M. G. Barclay, *Jews in the Mediterranean Diaspora from Alexander to Trajan (323 B.C.E.–117 C.E.)* (Edinburgh: T. & T. Clark, 1996), pp. 239-41.

33. See Hengel, "Proseuchē," pp. 158-59 + nn. 1-6 for a list of inscriptions and papyri. Philo

however, also asserted that *synagōgē* "appears only twice in the surviving Philonic corpus, and refers to the gathered community rather than to the place of meeting."[34] Oster pointed out that Philo used *synagōgē* five times[35] and that in Philo's description of Essene *synagōgai* in *OmnProbLib* 81,[36] the term can refer only to buildings. In his 1994 response to Oster, Kee seemed to concede the point that "Philo does use the term for places where Jews gather to study the scriptures" and that *OmnProbLib* 81 refers to Essene buildings.[37] Yet in his later (1995) summary, Kee merely reiterated his earlier conclusion that, "with the single exception of Lk 7:5, the synagogue is depicted in the New Testament and in pre-70 Jewish writings as a gathering rather than as a distinctive type of religious structure."[38] This conclusion appears to be contradicted by the evidence

---

uses *proseuchē*, always designating assembly halls: *Contra Flaccum* 41, 45, 47-49, 53, 122; *De legatione ad Gaium* 132, 134, 137, 138, 148, 152, 156-57, 165, 191, 346, 371.

34. Kee, "Transformation," p. 5. Kee's reference is puzzling, since συναγωγή occurs four times in Philo's citations of Num 27:16-17 (*Post* 27 [*bis*]; *Agr* 44 [*bis*]) and once in *OmnProbLib* 81. Kee appears to be dependent on Hengel, "Proseuchē," p. 169, who, however, was commenting on *synagōgion* rather than *synagōgē*, and whose point was more nuanced: "In the two cases where [Philo] uses the concept of *synagōgion* it is disputed whether he is referring to a synagogue building or to a synagogue gathering" (my translation). Hengel cites (p. 169 n. 50) *De somniis* 2.127 ("and will you sit in your assemblies (?) [*synagōgia*] and convene your regular association [*thiasos*] and read your holy books in security?") and *De legatione ad Gaium* 311 ("[Augustus] ordered that the Jews alone should be permitted by [the provincial governors] to assemble in *synagōgia*. These gatherings [*synodoi*], he said, were not based on drunkenness or carousing to promote conspiracy . . . but were schools of temperance and justice"). But Hengel continues: "Only in a single instance does he use *synagōgē* and, significantly, in a description of the Essenes in Palestine: *eis hierous aphikoumenoi topous, hous kalountai synagōgai* [*OmnProbLib* 81]. Besides the Theodotos inscription, this may be the oldest occurrence of *synagōgē* as a synagogue building" (my translation).

35. Oster, "Supposed Anachronism," pp. 190-91. In fact, Philo uses it seven times. In addition to *Post* 67 (2x); *Agr* 44 (2x, both quoting Num 27:16-17) and *OmnProbLib* 81, note *Quaestiones in Genesim* 2.66 (*hydōr eis synagōgēn mian*) and *Quaestiones in Exodum* 1.19 (*synagōgōn hēdonōn*). In his response to Oster, Kee ("Changing Meaning," p. 282) noted *Quaestiones in Genesin* 2.66 (as well as *Post* 67; *Agr* 44; and *OmnProbLib* 81), but failed to note *Quaestiones in Exodum* 1.19.

36. *OmnProbLib* 81: "they gather at holy places which they call synagogues" (*eis hierous aphikoumenoi topous, hous kalountai synagōgai*). That Philo has buildings in mind is not completely clear; *hieroi topoi* could refer to open spaces used for meeting. But Oster's main point stands: *synagōgē* here refers to space rather than to social groupings.

37. Kee, "Changing Meaning," p. 282. "The process of change of terminology for places of Jewish study and worship has begun."

38. Kee, "Defining," p. 493. Noteworthy is the absence of Acts 18:7 from the list of alleged Lukan anachronisms (contrast Kee, "Transformation," p. 18). In the more recent (1995) discussion of Acts 18:1-8, Kee argued that the fact that the house of Titus Justus was next door to the synagogue suggests that "the synagogue itself was a meeting in a house rather than a special building" ("Defining," p. 492). This assertion muddies the waters by confusing the issue of

Figure 48. Excavation at Cana, looking east from square 11 across square 16 to square 1, with balks removed. If this is a synagogue complex, the entrance is in the foreground, and the Beth ha-Midrash is where the people are standing in the background. Courtesy of Peter Richardson

of Josephus, cited above, by the Benghazi inscription, and by Philo's reference in *OmnProbLib* 81.

Archaeology

One of the more controverted parts of Kee's argument concerns archaeological data. Public assembly halls dating from prior to 70 c.e. have been unearthed at

whether there were purpose-built structures called *synagōgai* in the first century with that of whether *any buildings* — regardless of their original use — were called *synagōgai*. The prayer house *(proseuchē)* in Delos — originally a house modified for assembly use — is located in a residential area, but its design, with walls lined with benches, excludes the possibility that it continued to function as a house. See L. M. White, "The Delos Synagogue Revisited: Recent Fieldwork in the Graeco-Roman Diaspora," *HTR* 80 (1987): 133-60; B. H. McLean, "The Place of Cult in Voluntary Associations and Christian Churches on Delos," in *Voluntary Associations in the Graeco-Roman World,* ed. J. S. Kloppenborg and S. G. Wilson (London and New York: Routledge, 1996), pp. 186-225; see esp. pp. 192-95.

Gamla,[39] the Herodium, Masada,[40] Magdala,[41] Jericho,[42] Kiryat Sepher,[43] and probably at Capernaum.[44] Many archaeologists have taken these to be "synagogues," thereby implying a continuity between these unnamed first century C.E. structures and the buildings expressly called *synagōgai* from the third and fourth centuries C.E.[45] Reconsideration of the archaeological evidence has however underscored the fact that these pre-70 structures lack the architectural adaptations most characteristic of later synagogues: a Torah shrine[46] or chest, a

39. See in general, R. Hachlili, *Ancient Jewish Art and Archaeology in the Land of Israel*, Handbuch der Orientalistik, 7. Abt.: Kunst und Archäologie, 1. Bd.: Der alte Vordere Orient, 2. Abschnitt: Die Denkmäler, B: Vorderasien, Lieferung 4 (Leiden: Brill, 1988), pp. 84-86. On Gamla, see S. Gutman, "The Synagogue at Gamla," in *Ancient Synagogues Revealed*, ed. L. I. Levine (Jerusalem: Israel Exploration Society; Detroit: Wayne State University Press, 1981), pp. 30-34; Gutman, "Gamala," in *NEAEHL* 2:459-63, and S. Gutman and Y. Rapel, *Gamla* (in Hebrew) (Tel Aviv: Misrad Ha-bitahon, 1994), pp. 99-126.

40. On the Herodium and Masada, see G. Foerster, "The Synagogues at Masada and Herodium," in *Ancient Synagogues Revealed*, pp. 24-29.

41. The structure at Migdal (Magdala), thought to be a synagogue by the excavator, V. Corbo ("Scavi archeologici a Magdala [1971-1973]," *Liber Annuus* 24 [1974]: 5-37), has now been interpreted as a nymphaeum or fountain house by E. Netzer, "Did the Fountain House at Magdala Serve as a Synagogue?" (in Hebrew); and A. Oppenheimer, A. Kasher, and U. Rappaport, eds., *Synagogues in Antiquity* (in Hebrew) (Jerusalem: Yad Yitzak Ben-Zvi, 1987), pp. 165-72.

42. See E. Netzer, Y. Kalman, and R. Laureys, "A Synagogue from the Hasmonean Period Recently Discovered in the Western Plain of Jericho," *IEJ* 49 (1999): 203-21.

43. An excavation report has not yet been published. For a general description and photograph, see Levine, *The Ancient Synagogue*, pp. 65-66.

44. Excavations beneath the central nave of the III/IV C.E. building at Capernaum (trench 1) revealed a large pavement continuing southward under the facade. Another pavement to the north supports the northern stylobate (trench 2) and continues to the east (trench 11) and north (trench 6) (V. Corbo, *Cafarnao 1: Gli Edifici della Città*, Pubblicazioni dello Studium Biblicum Franciscanum 19 [Jerusalem: Franciscan Printing Press, 1975], pp. 118-24, 127-28, and Tav. XI). S. Loffreda ("The Late Chronology of the Synagogue at Capernaum," in *Ancient Synagogues Revealed*, pp. 52-56) suggested that the synagogue was built over private houses, but this conclusion, as Loffreda makes clear, applies only to the structures lying beneath the northeast corner of the later synagogue (trenches 2, 6, and 11). M. Avi-Yonah ("Some Comments on the Capernaum Excavations," in *Ancient Synagogues Revealed*, p. 60) argued that this pavement was too large for a private house and suggested that it was part of an earlier public building, presumably a synagogue. Loffreda ("Capernaum," in *NEAEHL* 1:294) now accepts this view. Kee ("Defining," p. 495) thinks the structure was a house, apparently unaware of Avi-Yonah's dissent or Loffreda's more recent views.

45. *DFSJ* 1 = *IG* iv 190.3-4 (Aegina; IV C.E.): "I built this synagogue from its foundations"; *CIJ* ii 861.3 (Tafas, Syria; IV C.E.): "they built the synagogue."

46. Netzer, Kalman, and Laureys ("A Synagogue from the Hasmonean Period Recently Discovered in the Western Plain of Jericho") describe a small cupboard in the northeastern corner of the hall, which they think might have been a Torah niche.

bema (platform), obviously Jewish iconography, and orientation toward Jerusalem.[47] Kee interprets this to mean that the buildings at Gamla, Masada, and the Herodium were assembly halls without any special "religious" function.[48]

This conclusion overreaches the evidence. First, it presumes a division in ancient Jewish society between "religious" and "nonreligious" activities that is hardly defensible. Josephus's description of the prayer house *(proseuchē)* in Tiberias indicates that it was used not only for political discussions, but for prayer and *ta nomima*, a standard term for religious rites (*Life* 295). Second, since we do not know the specific functions of *any* of these buildings beyond the obvious fact that they were used for public assemblies, it is hardly justified a priori to exclude liturgical or other cultic functions. Nor, conversely, is it justified to conclude that the buildings were used *exclusively* for such functions. Again, Josephus's description of the prayer house in Tiberias is apropos. Since *mikvaot* (stepped pools) are located adjacent to the buildings at Gamla and Jericho, and near the structures at the Herodium and Masada, it is hardly unreasonable to imagine some cultic functions occurring there.[49] Nonetheless, insofar as the structures at Gamla, Masada, and the Herodium bear no inscriptions, we have no idea whether they were called *synagōgai, proseuchai,* or some other term. To the extent that Kee's point is a lexicographic one, it is correct that archaeological findings — apart from the Theodotos and Benghazi inscriptions — neither confirm nor disconfirm the existence of buildings called *synagōgai.*

A second part of Kee's argument is architectural. He asserts that in the first century both Jews and Christians most likely used private homes for "worship" rather than purpose-built or specially converted buildings.[50] This conviction

---

47. See Hachlili, *Ancient Jewish Art,* p. 141, who distinguishes three types of synagogues: (1) the earliest structures in the Galilee and the Golan, with an ornamental facade and (presumably) a movable Torah shrine; (2) a transitional form (IV-V C.E.) of broadhouse design with a fixed Torah shrine on the Jerusalem-oriented wall, and a shift from reliefs to mosaic pavements; and (3) the V-VII C.E. longhouse or apsidal basilica structures, with mosaic pavements. See also L. I. Levine, "The Nature and Origin of the Palestinian Synagogue Reconsidered," *JBL* 115 (1996): 425-48, esp. pp. 445-46; S. Fine and E. M. Meyers, "Synagogues," in *OEANE* 5:118-23, esp. pp. 120-21.

48. Kee, "Defining," p. 494, citing J. Gutmann, "Prolegomenon," in Gutmann, ed., *The Synagogue,* p. xi. What Kee quotes as Gutmann's view is that of S. B. Hoenig, "Review of Yigael Yadin, *Bar Kochba," Jewish Bookland,* April 1973, p. 8: "There is no proof of piety or of a definite place of worship other than [Yadin's] wishful thinking." Gutmann ("The Origins of the Synagogue: The Current State of Research," in *The Synagogue,* p. 76) only observes that "no building dating from the first century has so far been positively identified as a synagogue."

49. This point is made by Atkinson, "On Further Defining," pp. 496-97. Atkinson (p. 498) curiously denies that the three buildings were "assembly halls," insisting that they were "synagogues." The distinction is rather odd, since "synagogue" in this sense means precisely "assembly hall."

50. Kee cites as his authority E. M. Meyers, "Synagogue," in *ABD* 6 (1992), pp. 251-60, esp.

leads him either to treat the structures at Gamla and Magdala as private houses,[51] or to dismiss them as merely meeting halls with no particular "religious" function. That Gamla and Magdala were *not* private houses is obvious, however, from their floor plans.[52] Neither are the structures at the Herodium, Masada, Jericho, and Kiryat Sepher. And the latter opinion, that they were meeting halls with no religious function, is, as I have already noted, problematic because of the nature of the archaeological evidence, which scarcely allows for secure conclusions regarding the activities that did or did not occur in these public structures.

Epigraphy: The Theodotos Inscription

The single piece of epigraphical evidence that bears on this problem is the Theodotos synagogue inscription (pl. 1: Rockefeller inv. S842 = *CIJ* ii 1404). This inscription, discovered by Raimund Weill in his 1913-14 excavations at the southern end of the eastern ridge of the Ophel (City of David),[53] is of considerable potential importance, not only regarding the date at which a building might be called a "synagogue," but to the discussion of the nomenclature, leadership, and function of ancient synagogues. For unlike many *proseuchē* and *synagōgē* in-

---

p. 255: "[I]n the first centuries [c.e.] large private houses were used as places of worship alongside other buildings that could be utilized for worship and other matters requiring public assembly. In Palestine, it would seem, it was about a hundred years after the destruction of the Temple that the synagogue *as a building* began to emerge as a central feature of Jewish communal life." Kee, however, misconstrues Meyers's comment, whose intent was to point out only that in Temple times, private houses were used *along with* purpose-built structures and other public buildings, not that purpose-built structures did not exist. (I am indebted to Meyers for correspondence [September 21, 1999] on this matter.)

51. Kee, "Transformation," p. 8: "Other sites that were first identified as synagogues — at Magdala and Gamala — turn out to be nothing more than private houses in which the pious gathered for prayer." In "Defining," p. 494, Kee seems to have corrected his erroneous view of the structure at Gamla, though he says nothing of Magdala.

52. See Gutman, "The Synagogue at Gamla," p. 34: "The interior layout of this building clearly indicates that it was intended for public assembly. The benches and the surrounding floors obviously served some public function," and Gutman, "Gamala," 2:459-63. On the structure at Magdala (a colonnaded building with benches on three sides), see above, n. 41.

53. R. Weill, "La Cité de David: Compte rendu des fouilles exécutées à Jérusalem sur le site de la ville primitive. Campagne de 1913-14 [I-IV]," *REJ* 69 (1919): 3-85 [I]; 70 (1920): 1-36 [II]; 149-179 [III]; 71 (1920): 1-45 [IV] + plates (published as an "annexe" to part II). The four *REJ* articles were revised completely and published as *La Cité de David: Compte rendu des fouilles exécutées à Jérusalem sur le site de la ville primitive. Campagne de 1913-14*, 2 vols. with plates (Paris: Paul Geuthner, 1920).

scriptions, which provide little data beyond the name or title of a dedicator or the name of a building or congregation,[54] *CIJ* ii 1404 not only records the terms *synagōgē* (used of a building) and *archisynagōgos* (ἀρχισυνάγωγος, 3x), but lists the intended functions of this *synagōgē* as a place for "the reading of the Law and teaching of the commandments" and as a hostel for visitors to Jerusalem.[55] The inscription reads:[56]

Θ[ε]όδοτος Οὐττήνου, ἱερὺς καὶ
ἀ[ρ]χισυνάγωγος, υἱὸς ἀρχισυν[αγώ]-
γ[ο]υ, υἱωνὶος ἀρκισυν[α]γώγου, ᾠκο-
δήμησε τὴν συναγωγὴν εἰς ἀν[άγν]ωⅡ-
5   σ[ιν] νόμου καὶ εἰς [διδαχ[ὴ]ν ἐντολῶν, καὶ
τ[ὸ]ν ξενῶνα, κα[ὶ τὰ] δώματα καὶ τὰ χρη-
σ[τ]ήρια τῶν ὑδάτων εἰς κατάλυμα τοῖ-
ς [χ]ρήζουσιν ἀπὸ τῆς ξέ[ν]ης, ἣν ἐθεμε-
λ[ίω]σαν οἱ πατέρες [α]ὐτοῦ καὶ οἱ πρεⅡ-
10   σ[β]ύτεροι καὶ Σιμων[ί]δης.

Theodotos son of Vettenus, priest and *archisynagōgos,* son of an *archisynagōgos* and grandson of an *archisynagōgos,* built the assembly hall

54. Many of the relevant epigraphical materials were assembled by J.-B. Frey in *CIJ* i-ii. B. Lifshitz provided a new prolegomenon to the first volume in his 1975 reissue of *CIJ* i, suggesting numerous improvements (unfortunately the same was not done for vol. ii). Lifshitz's *DFSJ* collects most of the donative inscriptions bearing on synagogues, but was published without photographs and should be used only in conjunction with other editions with photographs and facsimiles. The inscriptions from Egypt and western Europe have now been reedited, along with more recent discoveries, in *IJudEg* and *IJudEu* i-ii. Inscriptions from Cyrenaica are available in *CJZC* and synagogue inscriptions from Israel have now been reedited by Leah Roth-Gerson, *The Greek Inscriptions from Synagogues in Eretz Israel* (in Hebrew) (Jerusalem: Yad Yitzak Ben-Zvi, 1987).

55. *Editio princeps:* Weill, "La Cité de David [IV]," *REJ* 71 (1920): 1-45; see esp. pp. 30-34 + pl. XXVA = *La Cité de David,* 1:186-90 + 2:plate XXVA. The photograph appeared first in mid-1920, published as an "annexe" of plates with Weill's "La cité de David [II]" (*REJ* 70 [1920]). In the next volume of *REJ* (71 [1920]), Weill's own discussion appeared (pp. 30-34), along with T. Reinach, "L'inscription de Théodotus," *REJ* 71 (1920): 46-56. In the meantime, however, C. Clermont-Ganneau had presented an analysis at the Académie des Inscriptions et Belles-Lettres (*CRAIBL,* June 1920, pp. 187-88), summarized in "Une synagogue de l'époque hérodienne à Jérusalem," *RB* 58 (1920): 509-10 and subsequently published as "Découverte à Jérusalem d'une synagogue de l'époque hérodienne," *Syria* 1 (1920): 190-97 + photo (pl. XVIIIA).

56. I print the text of Lifshitz (*DFSJ* 79, following Frey, *CIJ* ii 1404), checking it against Weill's photograph (1920:plate XXVa) and the photograph supplied by the Israel Antiquities Authority.

(synagōgē) for the reading of the Law and for the teaching of the command-ments, and the guest room, the chambers, and the water fittings, as an inn for those in need from foreign parts, (the synagogue) which his fathers founded with the elders and Simonides.[57]

When the stone was first discovered, it was dated to prior to the First Revolt (70 C.E.), although, as we shall see, on perhaps less than adequate grounds. The dating of the inscription is crucial to Kee's case, however. If it turns out, as Kee claims, to be from a much later period, we would be left with much more con-trovertible attestations of *synagōgē* in reference to buildings: in addition to Gos-pels, only attestations from the Jewish Diaspora (the Benghazi inscription and Philo's discussion of the Essenes of Palestine in *OmnProbLib* 81) and Josephus's references in works composed between the mid-70s *(War)* and the mid-90s *(Antiquities).* To date, there has been no thorough review of the epigraphy of the Theodotos inscription, and since it is crucial to Kee's thesis, this seems a good point at which to conduct a review.

A Revised Date for CIJ ii 1404?

Kee's case for redating the inscription has five bases: (1) epigraphic remarks; (2) the nature of the discovery locus; (3) linguistic observations; (4) observa-tions about synagogue architecture in general; and (5) the likelihood of Jewish (re)settlement of Jerusalem at least by the late second century C.E.

1. First, Kee claimed that "[s]everal responsible archaeologists and epigraphers who saw [the inscription] prior to publication dated it to the time of Trajan or of Hadrian in the second quarter of the second century C.E.,"[58] and further, "When the Theodotus inscription was first found, the initial assess-ment of it by archaeologists knowledgeable about Palestinian finds was that it was from the later Roman period, as Deissmann himself notes."[59] Kee con-cluded: "There is, therefore, no reason to question that the Theodotus inscrip-tion was indeed associated with a building of the era to which the archaeolo-gists initially assigned it: the second half [*sic*] of the second century C.E. The epigraphic assessment may even have erred on the early side, so that the in-

---

57. The rendering of *dōma* is uncertain, since it can refer to a house in general, the main hall of a house, a roof terrace, or a chamber. Although the first portion of the inscription de-scribes various portions of the building, the final relative clause *(hēn ethemel[iō]san . . .)* treats all these features collectively, as part of the *synagōgē.*

58. Kee, "Transformation," p. 7.

59. Kee, "Defining," p. 482.

scription could be from as late as the third century. This latter date would fit well with the evidence that we shall now assess: the archaeological remains of synagogues in Palestine."[60]

Kee seems to have taken the supposed dispute between "responsible archaeologists and epigraphers" as license to date the inscription far later than any of these had proposed: in 1994 he declared that his examination of the inscription led him to the conclusion that it dated "from no earlier than the fourth century,"[61] though he adduced no epigraphical or paleographical evidence. A year later he returned to a somewhat earlier date, claiming that epigraphical analysis of the stone now confirmed a mid-second to late third century C.E. dating.[62] Again, he adduced no evidence.

Kee's claims about the dispute among "epigraphers" are misleading. Deissmann mentioned several discussions of the dating of the inscription, but only one scholar, Gustaf Dalman, suggested a date in the "late Roman period." Dalman's suggestion appeared in his 1915 notice of the discovery, i.e., *prior* to the publication of the photograph and the *editio princeps.* In his 1922 essay on Weill's excavations Dalman accepted the pre-70 date on the basis of the paleographical observations of Clermont-Ganneau, Reinach, and Vincent.[63] Vincent's initial examination of the stone led him to suggest a date early in the second century (*not* the late Roman period), but he eventually acceded to the judgments of Clermont-Ganneau and Reinach in favor of a date before 70 C.E.[64] In his brief

60. Kee, "Transformation," p. 8. It is not clear from Kee's reference in the first sentence of this quotation who the "archaeologists" are. Weill dated the building to the first century, and Vincent, who observed Weill's excavations at close hand, initially dated it to the early second century C.E. No one, to my knowledge, suggested the late second century.

61. Kee, "Changing Meaning," p. 283.

62. Kee, "Defining," p. 482: "Estimates of the date of the inscription by a number of distinguished epigraphers whom I consulted informally converge on the period from the mid-second to the late third century C.E."

63. A. Deissmann, *Light from the Ancient East*, rev. ed. (London: Hodder and Stoughton, 1927), p. 439 n. 2. Dalman's note appeared in "Zion, die Burg Jerusalems," *Palästinajahrbuch* 11 (1915): 75-76: "Also wurde wohl in der spätrömischen Zeit hier auf dem Boden der alten Davidstadt weitab von der Aelia Capitolina jüdischer Gottesdienst geübt, entweder weil man Synagogen in der Stadt nicht zuließ, oder weil das Bethaus sich an seinem Orte in der Nähe von Wasser befinden sollte, wie auch das galiläische Gishala die eine seiner beiden Synagogen entfernt von der Stadt in nächsten Tale hatte" (p. 76). Compare the 1922 assessment by G. Dalman, "Die Ausgrabungen von Raymond Weill in der Davidstadt," *ZDPV* 45 (1922): 22-30; see esp. p. 30: "Der Charakter der Schrift weist in die Zeit vor 70 n.Chr."

64. L.-H. Vincent recounts his earlier reasoning in favor of a date during the principate of Trajan in "Découverte de la 'synagogue des affranchis' à Jérusalem," *RB* 30 (1921): 247-77. McKay ("Ancient Synagogues," pp. 126-27) rightly observes that Vincent's initial proposal of a date in the early second century was rejected and ridiculed by Reinach on less than adequate grounds.

notice about the discovery, Bees agreed with Vincent's initial assessment; his opinion, however, was not based on an analysis of the stone itself but rather on Vincent's report and photograph.[65] Hence, only Vincent and Bees registered serious dissents from the earlier dating, and neither suggested a date in the late Roman period. Other critics uniformly favored a date prior to 70 C.E.[66]

The dating of inscriptions — especially imperial period inscriptions — by paleographical means is a far more complicated and subtle matter than Kee imagines. As I shall indicate below, the style of lettering does not allow so dogmatic a conclusion as that drawn by Clermont-Ganneau and Vincent. In this

Vincent's epigraphical comments were far more rigorous and careful than those of Clermont-Ganneau or Reinach, and one suspects that his retraction and endorsement of the early date were less than wholehearted.

65. N. A. Bees, "Epigraphik," *Byzantinisch-neugriechische Jahrbücher* 2 (1921): 259: "ME ist die Inschrift nicht älters als die Trajanzeit."

66. Weill, "Cité de David [IV]," p. 34 = *Cité de David*, 1:190: "antérieurs à la date de 70"; Clermont-Ganneau, "Découverte," p. 193: "soit du règne d'Hérode le Grand . . . soit, tout au moins, de la période de 66 ans, comprise entre la mort de ce roi et la destruction de Jérusalem"; Reinach, "L'inscription de Théodotus," p. 53: "vers 45 après J.-C."; Samuel Klein, *Jüdisch-Palästinischen Corpus Inscriptionum (Ossuar-, Grab- und Synagōgēninschriften)* (Vienna and Berlin: Lowit, 1920), 102: "Aller Wahrscheinlichkeit nach, lebte [Theodotos] jedoch zur Tempelzeit"; Cagnat and Besnier, in *AE*, 1922, 117 (p. 37): "vers l'année 45 ap. J.-C.; il est antérieur, en tout cas, à la prise de Jérusalem par Titus en 70"; Gerald M. FitzGerald, "Notes on Recent Discoveries," *Palestine Exploration Fund Quarterly Statement*, 1921, 179: "well into the first century without going beyond . . . the critical year 70"; Hans Lietzmann, "Notizen," *ZNW* 20 (1921): 172-73: "frühe Kaiserzeit"; Peter Thomsen, "Die lateinischen und griechischen Inschriften der Stadt Jerusalem und ihrer nächsten Umgebung," *ZPDV* 44 (1921): 143: "Vor 70 n.Chr."; Deissmann, *Light*, p. 441: "before 70 C.E." This dating is followed by virtually all recent editions: E. L. Sukenik, *Ancient Synagogues in Palestine and Greece* (London: Oxford University Press, 1934), p. 69; *SEG* viii (1937), p. 170; Frey, *CIJ* ii 1404 (2:333): "sans doute"; Schwabe, *IBeth She'arim*, p. 362: "the time of Herod the Great or the time immediately after him"; Emilio Gabba, *Iscrizioni greche e latine per lo studio della Bibbia*, Sintesi dell'oriente e della Bibbia 3 (Rome: Marietti, 1958), p. 79; Lifshitz, *DFSJ* 71; F. Hüttenmeister and G. Reeg, *Die antiken Synagōgēn in Israel*, 2 vols., BTAVO, Reihe B, Geisteswissenschaften, no. 12 (Wiesbaden: Reichert, 1977), 1:195: "zwar aus der Zeit vor der Zerstörung des Tempels"; Leah Roth-Gerson, *The Greek Inscriptions from Synagogues in Eretz Israel* (in Hebrew) (Jerusalem: Yad Yitzak Ben-Zvi, 1987), p. 76: "end of the first century B.C.E. or beginning of the first century C.E."; Laura Boffo, *Iscrizioni greche e latine per lo studio della Bibbia*, Biblioteca di storia e storiografia dei tempi biblici 9 (Brescia: Paideia, 1994), p. 275: "*terminus ante quem* il 70 d.C." For a full bibliography, see the appendix to this chapter: "Major Publications of the Theodotos Inscription."

Until the issue of dating was reopened by Kee, the only scholar to suggest a later date was I. Press, *A Topographical-Historical Encyclopaedia of Palestine* (in Hebrew), 4 vols. (Jerusalem: Rubin Mass, 1948-55), 2:414, who conjectured (without analysis or argument) that the hostel mentioned in the inscription was designed for Jews returning to Jerusalem following the First Revolt, hence, sometime between 70 C.E. and 135 C.E.

limited sense Kee is right (though perhaps inadvertently so), that paleo-graphical observations might permit a later dating. Epigraphical dating, how-ever, is not based solely (or even principally) on observations on the cutter's hand, and it is these other evidences, neglected by Kee, that must also be taken into account when assigning a date to an inscription.

2. Kee's second point concerns the site of discovery. The inscription was not found *in situ*, but in a cistern, in a pile of other building materials. Thus, there is no indication of the original function of the stone in the building, nor, as Kee rightly notes, do we have an enclosed locus where ceramic and numismatic finds can assist in dating. He asserts, moreover, that the complex in which Weill discovered the inscription was a *Roman* bath,[67] the inference being that the building materials and inscription found piled in the cistern (presumably a part of the Roman bath complex) must be dated after the construction of the baths. "On purely inferential grounds, the finding of the inscription among rubbish in the bottom of the cistern increases the probability that it is from a later date than the second or third century Roman bath complex in which it was found. One possibility is that the inscription was dumped there in the fourth century at the time that the city was being rebuilt in the post-Constantinian period, when anti-Jewish sentiment and activities soared."[68]

The difficulty with this supposition is that the excavator made no reference to the structure as a *Roman* bath; he described only a series of cisterns and pools, all part of an "installation balnéaire." There is no report of a hypocaust or the standard parts of a Roman bath *(caldarium, tepidarium, frigidarium)*. Moreover, Weill noted that the pools and water installations were built on the site of older and disused tombs; and they were later disturbed by open quarry-ing.[69] A few meters to the east of the cistern, Weill unearthed two or three courses of "well worked" blocks and the remains of paving stones sitting di-rectly on bedrock.[70] Although Weill considered the possibility that this building

67. Kee, "Defining," p. 481; similarly, p. 483.

68. Kee, "Defining," p. 483.

69. Weill, "Cité de David [IV]," p. 18 = *Cité de David*, 1:174: "nous avons parlé d'une vaste organization dont subsistent des éléments profondément excavés, piscenes et citernes, installés dans le champ des tombeaux antiques et curieusement imbriqués avec eux, en plan, mais qui, non moins remarquablement, prennent le soin de respecter les souterrains funéraires; et par-tout, aussi, nous avons mentionné les carrières ouvertes, ultérieurement, sur toute la surface du site et dont les coupes ont dévasté, indifféremment, les monuments primitifs et les installations hydrauliques de deuxième stade."

70. Weill, "Cité de David [II]," p. 9 = *Cité de David*, 1:99: "Il devait donc y avoir, à cette place, une assez vaste installation balnéaire, qui fut détruite, à l'époque romaine, par l'ouverture de carrière le long de certains lits de roche de bonne qualité. Nous avons signalé certaines des piscines et des citernes qui faisaient partie de l'ensemble; par la suite, la fouille en découvrira

— presumably the *synagōgē* of *CIJ* ii 1404 — had been constructed after the quarrying, he also noted that parts of the building had been disturbed by quarrying and thus it should be dated *before* the quarry.[71] The quarrying, evidence of which Weill found throughout his site on the southeastern ridge,[72] was so extensive that scarcely was a stone left in place. Kenyon's later excavations in areas K and V, adjoining Weill's 1913-14 site, as well as in areas R and S (at the northern end of the southeastern ridge), produced evidence that the quarrying took place in the early second century, probably the result of Hadrian's rebuilding activities.[73] Although Weill himself did not date the quarrying beyond saying that it was "Roman," he was able to propose a relative stratigraphy that placed the bath installation prior to the quarrying: "Thus we have a kind of precision or confirmation of the history of these bathing chambers and of the building of which they are a part: prior to the Roman quarrying which destroyed them, and subsequent to the great tombs."[74]

As to the nature of the pools themselves, Ronny Reich has now noted the presence of a low divider on the steps of the largest pool (P1 [Pool 1]: 6.2 × 5.5–8.2 m.),[75] which suggests that the stepped pool was a *mikveh*.[76] Reich is duly cautious about identifying the water installations mentioned in the inscription with the stepped baths discovered to the north of the cistern. In any event, there

---

d'autres encore. Aux constations déjà faites est venue se joindre, en dernier lieu, la mise à jour de ruines proprement dites, de portions d'édifices en maçonnerie quie reposaient sur le roc et dont il subsiste (S2 du plan) deux ou trois assises de grands blocs de calcaire bien appareillés, et en un autre point (S1), une sorte de dallage ou de radier en grand blocs, reposant sur un épais lit de béton établi sur la surface rocheuse."

71. Weill, "Cité de David [II]," p. 9 = *Cité de David,* 1:99: "Certains indices porteraient à croire que l'édifice dont nous avons ces restes a été construit postérieurement aux carrières; mais il est également possible que certaines parties de constructions aient été perturbées par les carrières en même temps que les chambres balnéaires, et il faudrait alors reconnaître en elles, sans doute, les constructions dont il fait mention dans un important document historique, sorti de la fouille dans les conditions que nous allons rapporter."

72. Weill, "Cité de David [II]," pp. 1-9 = *Cité de David,* 1:91-99.

73. K. Kenyon, *Digging Up Jerusalem* (London and Tonbridge: Ernest Benn, 1974), pp. 263-64: "The most dramatic quarrying evidence is in the area excavated by Weill towards the southern end of the eastern ridge. In our adjoining area V, we were able to date this quarrying to the second century C.E. Hadrian thus very literally abolished Jewish Jerusalem with his construction of Aelia Capitolina. Within his city he buried it to level up the site for his regular layout. Outside it he threw it away in order to use the very rock on which it was built for his own city."

74. Weill, "Cité de David [IV]," p. 21 = *Cité de David,* 1:177 (my translation).

75. See Weill, "Cité de David [IV]," pp. 20-21 = *Cité de David,* 1:176-77 and plate XX:B.

76. R. Reich, "The Synagogue and the *miqveh* in Eretz-Israel in the Second-Temple, Mishnaic and Talmudic Periods," in *Ancient Synagogues,* 1:289-97; see esp. pp. 291-92.

is no indication that the baths belonged to a Roman bathhouse or were posterior to the second century C.E. quarrying.

3. Third, Kee offers an extensive review of the use of *synagōgē* in literature before 70 C.E., concluding that the sole reference to *synagōgē* as a building is Luke's anachronism in Lk 7:5. The logic of the argument is sound: an inscription that employs a term with a meaning that has a definable terminus a quo should not be dated prior to that terminus. The difficulty, however, is not with the logic of the argument but with its neglect of important data in establishing that terminus a quo, notably *CJZC* 72 (55/56 C.E.) and literary evidence from Philo, Josephus, and the Gospels discussed above.[77]

4. As I have already indicated, Kee is essentially right that the pre-70 structures found in Israel and often identified as "synagogues" do not provide very clear indications of their intended or actual uses or their nomenclature. He overstates matters, however, when he excludes a religious or liturgical function for these structures.

5. The final part of Kee's argument is a refutation of the notion that an absolute ban existed on Jewish presence in Aelia Capitolina. This false supposition, Kee thinks, is at the root of the misdating of *CIJ* ii 1404, and Kee lays the blame at the feet of Deissmann, who "arbitrarily" assigned a pre-70 C.E. date on the assumption that Jews would not have been permitted to live in Jerusalem after 70.[78] "Astonishingly, most scholars have simply accepted that wholly unwarranted date."[79]

A careful review of the early literature on the inscription shows that Deissmann's comments were far from the decisive factor in swaying opinion on

77. See also Oster, "Supposed Anachronism in Luke-Acts' Use of *sunagōgē*"; Riesner, "Synagogues in Jerusalem," pp. 181-84; Horst, "Was the Ancient Synagogue?" pp. 19-23.

78. Kee ("Transformation," p. 7; "Defining," p. 482) seems unaware of the genealogy of Deissmann's error. Deissmann (*Light*, p. 441) claimed that from 70 C.E. on, "no Jew could settle within the city area — to say nothing of building, and even erecting a synagogue there." His authority (p. 441 n. 1) was E. Schürer, *Geschichte des judischen Volkes im Zeitalter Jesu Christi*, 3-4. Aufl., 4 vols. (Leipzig: J. C. Hinrichs, 1901-11), 1:649, 703. Apropos of the situation after 70 C.E., however, Schürer had only observed, "Jerusalem had been so completely razed to the ground that there was left nothing to make those that came thither believe that it had ever been inhabited [citing Josephus, *Vita* 7.3-4]. It was first of all only a Roman camp, in which, if not the whole of the tenth legion, yet at least the chief portions of it, had its headquarters, together with its baggage and followers" (1:649, ET: *The History of the Jewish People in the Age of Jesus Christ*, 2nd ed., 6 vols. [Edinburgh: T. & T. Clark, 1898-1910], 1/2:265). It is only apropos of the situation *after the Second Revolt* that Schürer stated that Jews were driven from Jerusalem: "No Jew was allowed thereafter to enter the territory of the city; if any one should be discovered there he was put to death" (1:699, ET 1/2:315), quoting Jerome, *In Jeremiam* 4.971 (PL 24:798): "By law no Jew is permitted to enter the land or the holy city" (nullus Judaeorum terram quondam et urbem sanctam ingredi lege permittitur).

79. Kee, "Transformation," p. 7.

dating;[80] Clermont-Ganneau's paleographical observations and his comments on the name Vettenus were far more influential. But a critical part of Kee's case for dating *CIJ* ii 1404 to the second or third century is the possibility of Jewish presence in Aelia Capitolina after 135.[81]

Little directly is known of the Jewish population of Jerusalem between the two revolts. It is likely that in Judea Jews who had not participated in the revolt maintained their landholdings or were able to purchase land that Vespasian confiscated and subsequently auctioned.[82] Jerusalem, however, became a camp for the tenth legion, Legio X Fretensis. This would not have automatically implied the exclusion of the Jewish population from the city; the camp would normally rely upon locals for produce and labor. Moreover, Hadrian's ban on Jews entering Jerusalem after Bar-Kokhba presupposes that there had been a Jewish population in and around Jerusalem prior to the Second Revolt.[83]

Hadrian's ban on Jewish presence in Aelia Capitolina (except perhaps for the ninth of Av) may have been relaxed during the Antonine period,[84] since the

---

80. Already in 1927 K. Galling ("Archäologischer Jahresbericht," *ZDPV* 50 [1927]: 298-319) remarked, "Für die Theodot-Inschrift hat man Entstehung vor 70 n.Chr angenommen, doch ist dafür kein Beweis zu führen" (p. 315). "Bei A. Deissmann, Licht vom Osten⁴, 1923, S. 380 vermißt man ihn jedenfalls. Die dort gegebene Ansetzung ist durch eine petitio principii bestimmt" (p. 315 n. 5).

81. Kee ("Transformation," pp. 7-8) countered Deissmann's supposition about the situation for Jews after 70 C.E. by adducing Safrai's discussion of Jewish self-government after 70: "[Safrai] asserts that in *Jerusalem* as early as the time of Nerva and Trajan, the Jewish system of self-government was operative, not only in relation to religious issues (such as the setting of the date of the new moon), but also on such legal matters as property, fines, modes of punishment in accord with Jewish law" (emphasis added). Safrai's comments, however, have nothing to do with Jewish presence in *Jerusalem;* they concern Jewish self-government at *Yavneh,* first under Yohanan ben Zakkai and then under Gamaliel II. See S. Safrai, "Jewish Self-Government," in *The Jewish People in the First Century,* ed. S. Safrai and M. Stern, CRINT 1/1 (Philadelphia: Fortress, 1974), pp. 377-419; see esp. pp. 406-9.

82. On this, and on the reading of Josephus, *Vita* 7.216, see B. Isaac, "Judaea after 70 C.E.," in *The Near East under Roman Rule: Selected Papers,* Mnemosyne Supplements 177 (Leiden: Brill, 1998), pp. 112-21 = *JJS* 35 (1984): 44-50.

83. Eusebius's statement in *HE* 4.6.3-4 (citing Ariston of Pella) that Hadrian's ban extended even to the area about Jerusalem "so that the ancestral home could not even be seen [by Jews] even from afar" implies that Jews had been in and around Jerusalem up to that time. Likewise, Eusebius's statement that from the time of Hadrian the church in Jerusalem was composed of Gentiles and that the earlier Jewish bishops were succeeded by Marcus (4.6.4) assumes that before Bar-Kokhba, there had been Jews in Jerusalem. Other reports of Hadrian's ban are found in Eusebius, *HE* 5.12.1 and Tertullian, *Adversus Iudaeos* 13. On these texts see J. R. Harris, "Hadrian's Decree of Expulsion of the Jews from Jerusalem," *HTR* 19 (1926): 199-206.

84. The ban, however, seems not to have been rescinded, for Jerome describes it as in force in his day (*In Sophoniam* 1.15-16 [CCL 76a:673]).

Talmuds contain stories of occasional visits to Jerusalem.[85] From the Severan period onward, there are more reports of Jews visiting Jerusalem unimpeded by Roman officials.[86] There is even a report of a group of disciples of R. Meir settling in Jerusalem, but, as Avi-Yonah points out, the community seems to have lasted only one generation and left no traces thereafter.[87] Based on a comment of R. Meir that the stones of the walls were sacred and that no profit was to be had from them, Avi-Yonah surmises that there may have been some building activities.[88]

This evidence leaves some room for Kee's late dating of *CIJ* ii 1404, and even allows for the possibility of the building of a synagogue during the Severan period.[89] What is decisive, however, is not whether Jews during the Antonine and Severan periods might have visited the city (or even taken up temporary residence) but, as we shall see below, the specific areas of the city that were occupied from the second to the fourth centuries C.E. The Ophel was in fact unoccupied before the Byzantine period, and hence it seems unlikely that the remains of the synagogue discovered in the cistern come from those centuries.

Dating Theodotos

The dating of inscriptions is a matter of diverse factors, ideally converging on the same general date. (a) First is the provenance of the inscription. Inscriptions are not normally dated earlier than the foundation or later than the destruction of the city in which they are found (although it is certainly imaginable that a village may have preceded a city's foundation or followed its

85. M. Avi-Yonah, *The Jews of Palestine: A Political History from the Bar Kokhba War to the Arab Conquest* (Oxford: Basil Blackwell; New York: Schocken Books, 1976), p. 80; E. M. Smallwood, *The Jews under Roman Rule from Pompey to Diocletian,* SJLA 20 (Leiden: Brill, 1976), pp. 478-81.

86. For documentation, see Avi-Yonah, *The Jews of Palestine,* p. 80; and Smallwood, *Jews under Roman Rule,* pp. 499-500.

87. Avi-Yonah, *The Jews of Palestine,* pp. 80-81; on the community, see S. Safrai, "The Holy Congregation in Jerusalem," *Scripta Hierosolymitana* 23 (1973): 62-78.

88. *b. Qidd.* 54a: "R. Ishmael b. R. Isaac said: 'If the stones of Jerusalem fall out [of the place in the wall] trespass is incurred with them [if they are used for another purpose].' This is R. Meir's view." This occurs in a section dealing with the misuse of money or things devoted to the Temple.

89. Kee ("Defining," pp. 498-99) describes Hadrian's efforts to exclude Jews from Aelia as having "utterly failed within decades of the promulgation of his decrees"; this is rather an overstatement, given the scanty evidence we have of permanent Jewish *occupation* in Jerusalem.

destruction). (b) The character of the document must be considered. Some types of monuments are datable — elaborate Athenian funerary reliefs, for example, which were banned under sumptuary legislation about 312 B.C.E. (c) Inscriptions may refer to datable events or persons or contain other prosopographic data. (d) Certain formulae or names may be datable. For example, a high frequency of names with the nomen Aurelius could be an indication of a date after the edict of Caracalla in 212 C.E.[90] (e) Finally and least decisively, the style and shape of the letters must be considered.[91]

Not all these factors are relevant to *CIJ* ii 1404. Dedicatory inscriptions are found in the Levant from well before the earliest dating of the inscription to very much later. Obviously, it begs the question to date the inscription, as Kee wishes to do, to the late second or early third century C.E. on the grounds that *synagōgē* in line 4 refers to a building. This is especially the case since *synagōgē* clearly has that meaning in *CJZC* 72 (55/56 C.E.). Nor is the designation of Theodotos as a priest *(hiereus)* decisive for dating; Jewish inscriptions from 27 B.C.E. to the fourth century C.E. identify persons as "priests" even though they presumably no longer functioned as such after 70 C.E..[92]

The more relevant criteria are considerations of the provenance of the inscription, references to datable persons, and paleography.

The Provenance of the Inscription   The site of discovery makes a Herodian date highly likely. In 1978 a major excavation of various sites on the Ophel (City of David) was begun, issuing in a reasonably clear and consistent stratigraphy of the area, including sites directly adjacent to Weill's 1913-14 excavations.[93]

---

90. This is not an entirely reliable index, since both Marcus Aurelius and Commodus franchised a number of persons, who would have become Aurelii. (I owe this observation to J. Reynolds.)

91. See A. G. Woodhead, *The Study of Greek Inscriptions,* 2nd ed. (Cambridge and New York: Cambridge University Press, 1981), pp. 52-66.

92. *IJudEg* 84 (= *CIJ* ii 1514) (Leontopolis; 27 B.C.E.); *CJZC* 72 (Bernike, Cyrenaica; 55/56); *IJudEg* 149 (= *CIJ* ii 930) (Jaffa; II-IV C.E.); *IJudEu* ii 11 (= *CIJ* i 315) (Monteverde, Rome; III-IV C.E.); *IJudEu* ii 80 (= *CIJ* i 346) (Monteverde, Rome; III-IV C.E.); *IJudEu* ii 109 (= *CIJ* i 375) (Monteverde, Rome; III-IV C.E.); *IJudEu* ii 124 (= *CIJ* i 347) (Monteverde, Rome; III-IV C.E.); *IJudEu* ii 125 (= *CIJ* i 355) (Monteverde, Rome; III-IV C.E.); *IJudEu* ii 558 (= *CIJ* i 504) (Italy; III-IV C.E.?); *IBeth She'arim* ii 180 (Beth She'arim; III-IV C.E.); *IBeth She'arim* ii 181 (Beth She'arim; III-IV C.E.).

93. Y. Shiloh, *Excavations at the City of David: Volume I; 1978-1982; Interim Report of the First Five Seasons,* Qedem 19 (Jerusalem: Institute of Archaeology, Hebrew University of Jerusalem, 1984); D. T. Ariel, ed., *Excavations at the City of David, 1978-1985, Directed by Yigal Shiloh: Volume II; Imported Stamped Amphora Handles, Coins, Worked Bone and Ivory, and Glass,* City of David Excavations, Final Report ii = Qedem 30 (Jerusalem: Institute of Archaeology, Hebrew University

As a generalization, the late Roman period (Stratum 4) is badly represented throughout the entire City of David. Areas B, D1, and D2 — respectively east, northeast, and north of Weill's area, the first two of these containing the dumps of Weill's excavations — bore clear signs of the destruction of Stratum 6 (27 B.C.E.–70 C.E.). Nothing was discovered, however, that dated from later than 70 C.E. Shiloh's preliminary report noted that the destruction layer (Stratum 5), a constant feature of most areas of the eastern slope, often reached a depth of 5 meters.[94] He concluded:

> With the destruction of Jerusalem at the end of Stratum 6, the hill of the City of David was neglected. The structures of the "Lower City" on its ridge, and the supporting walls on its slope, collapsed and tumbled down. The eastern slope for its entire length became covered with a layer of debris several meters thick. This debris included many finds from Stratum 6, carried down from the buildings at the top of the slope. They have been defined by us as a separate stratum, Stratum 5, which also contains almost nothing later than 70 C.E.[95]

The next occupational level (Stratum 3; Byzantine period) was evidenced only in the central valley, in areas G, at the north end, and A1 and A2, above the Siloam Pool. The Byzantine stratum was absent in areas B, D1, and D2.[96]

The final report provides a more comprehensive picture of the history of the area. There is evidence of fortifications from the early Hellenistic (Stratum 8), Hellenistic (Strata 7B, 7A), and early Roman periods (Stratum 6), but only debris in Stratum 5 (early Roman, after 70 C.E.). No architectural remains survived from Stratum 6, thus apparently confirming the thorough destruction wreaked on the site by Titus.[97] Coins and pottery, none dated later than 70 C.E., formed part of the rubble accumulated from the destruction of Stratum 6. A

---

of Jerusalem, 1990); A. De Groot and D. T. Ariel, eds., *Excavations at the City of David, 1978-1985, Directed by Yigal Shiloh: Volume III; Stratigraphical, Environmental, and Other Reports*, City of David Excavations, Final Report iii = Qedem 33 (Jerusalem: Institute of Archaeology, Hebrew University of Jerusalem, 1992); D. T. Ariel and A. De Groot, eds., *Excavations at the City of David, 1978-1985, Directed by Yigal Shiloh: Volume IV; Various Reports*, City of David Excavations, Final Report iv = Qedem 35 (Jerusalem: Institute of Archaeology, Hebrew University of Jerusalem, 1996).

94. Shiloh, *Excavations*, 1:8.

95. Shiloh, *Excavations*, 1:30.

96. Shiloh, *Excavations*, 1:30-31. See also D. T. Ariel and J. Magness ("Area K," in De Groot and Ariel, *Excavations*, 3:63-97; see esp. p. 91), who report "intensive occupation" in the Byzantine period (Stratum 3) in the vicinity of the Siloam Pool; but "remains of pre-Byzantine strata are scanty."

97. Josephus (*Vita* 6.363-364) describes the destruction of the lower town "as far as Siloam" by Titus's troops.

small amount of pottery belonging to the later Roman period (Stratum 4) appeared in areas H and K (in the valley to the west of Weill's excavations), but no architectural remains were discovered. Signs of later (Byzantine) occupation were discovered only near the Siloam Pool and at the northern extremity of the southeast hill (area G).[98]

In areas B, D, and E (near Weill's site) the picture is similar: Stratum 5 comprises the rubble of the walls and terraces of Stratum 6 that had collapsed due to deliberate destruction and neglect during the winter rains. There were no finds that could be dated later than 70 c.e.

The nature of the archaeological evidence makes it extremely difficult to imagine the presence of a building on the south end of the eastern ridge of the Ophel at any time after 70 c.e., since by all accounts the site was unoccupied. Kenyon's evidence from areas K and V (due east of Weill's area) indicates that it was used as a quarry after 135 c.e. It seems a reasonable conclusion that the quarrying that Weill had seen in his area and that had destroyed the pools and cisterns belonged to the period: Hadrian's quarrying of the Ophel to provide building materials for Aelia. The City of David was itself seemingly unoccupied after 135, becoming part of Jerusalem only after circa 460.[99]

References to Datable Persons   Of the three names mentioned in the inscription, only Simonides and Vettenus[100] have attracted significant attention. The name Theodotos is of little assistance in dating the inscription, since it was a common name, especially in Jewish inscriptions of the Hellenistic and Roman periods.[101]

Simonides would not otherwise be of interest were it not for a coincidence noted by Vincent: one of the consuls for the year 107/8 c.e. was C. Vettennius Severus,[102] and about the same time, Josephus's son, Flavius Agrippa (also

98. Shiloh, "Stratigraphical Introduction to Parts I and II," in Ariel, *Excavations*, 2:1-12; see esp. pp. 2-3, 6-7.

99. Dan Bahat, *per litt.* 3.08.99.

100. The transliteration of the Latin name may be an indication of an early date for the inscription. Prior to the second century c.e., *v* was commonly rendered *ou* (e.g., Vespasianus → Ouespasianos), but by the III/IV c.e., both the initial and medial *v* were transliterated as a *B* (e.g., Valerius → Balerius). See B. H. McLean, *An Introduction to Greek Epigraphy of the Hellenistic and Roman Periods from Alexander the Great Down to the Reign of Constantine (323 b.c.e.–337 c.e.)* (Ann Arbor: University of Michigan Press, 2001), §5.11.

101. See the indices in *CPJ* iii; *IJudEg* and *IJudEu* I-ii. The name is also borne by a freedman of Queen Agrippina in an inscription from Jericho *(Theodotou apeleutherou basilissēs Agrippeinēs)*: R. Hachlili, "The Goliath Family in Jericho: Funerary Inscriptions from a First Century c.e. Jewish Monumental Tomb," *BASOR* 235 (1979): 31-66; see esp. pp. 33, 46-47 (no. 3).

102. See *PIR*[1] iii 410 (V313), consul with C. Minicus Fundanus. The nomen Vettennius is,

known as Simonides), was a Roman priest at Caesarea Maritima.[103] "Would this Agrippa-Simonides," Vincent asks, "who had a Roman pontifical function at Caesarea in Palestine, not have been in the position to offer easy assistance to the Jewish religious enterprise [of building a synagogue] in Jerusalem?"[104] He assumed that an ancestor of Theodotos had been among Titus's prisoners and that C. Vettennius Severus or someone of his *gens* had manumitted him. Hence, *Ouettēnou* was not a patronym but instead the name of Theodotos's patron.[105]

There are some difficulties with this conjecture. First, had Theodotos been a freedman of Vettennius, the more likely form of the name would have been, e.g., C(aius) Vettennius C(aii) l(ibertus) Theodotos, or simply C. Vettennius Theodotos, with both the nomen and the cognomen in the nominative.[106] Indeed, the names of five freedmen and freedwomen of C. Vettenus in an inscription from Samnium take just this form.[107] Second, since the manumitted slave of a Roman citizen became a citizen, it seems rather unlikely that a provincial who had attained citizenship would have used a name-form that disguised that fact. C. Vettennius [C.l.] Theodotos would have displayed the enviable social status that attended citizenship — just the sort of display that is frequent in dedicatory inscriptions.[108] The form of the name in *CIJ* ii 1404 (nominative +

---

however, also attested in the third century C.E. as the name of a vestal virgin, Vettenia Sabinilla (*ILS* 1446 = *CIL* vi 1587: *PIR*[1] iii 410 [V314]; *PLRE* i 790).

103. Josephus, *Vita* 76 (*Simōnidēs ho kai Agrippas epiklēseis*); *CIL* iii Supplement ii 12082 (Caesarea Maritima): m Fl(avium) Agrippam pontif(icem), II viral(em) col(oniae primae) Fl(aviae) Aug(ustae) Caesareae oratorem ex dec(urionum) dec(reto) pec(unia) publ(ica).

104. Vincent, "Dé,couverte" p. 260.

105. Vincent, "Découverte," p. 261: "Que l'on suppose notre Théodote, descendant de captifs de 70, affranchi au début du second siècle par un Vettenius tel que le personnage consulaire de l'an 107; sa dépendance aurait pu n'être exprimée — par un euphémisme intentionnel ou quelque prétentieux retour au plus ancien usage romain — tout comme pour un ingénu, que par le nom individuel de son patron, mis au génitif de propriété."

106. A manumitted slave normally adopted the praenomen and nomen of his patron, followed by the praenomen of the patron in the genitive, *l(ibertus)* and the slave name, now, used as a cognomen. Thus Cicero's slave Tiro became m Tullius M(arci) l(ibertus) Tiro. Since a woman normally had no praenomen, she used a feminized form of the patron's gentilicial name along with her own slave name: Aurelia C(aii) l(iberta) Nais (*ILS* 7500) = (Nais, who was manumitted by Gaius Aurelius).

107. *CIL* ix 4157: C. Vettenus C.l. Aphrodisius | C. Vettenus C.l. Tertius | C. Vettenus C.l. Sextus | C. Vettena C.l. Hilara | C. Vettena C.l. Maxima.

108. E.g., the honorific inscription from Benghazi (*CJZC* 70), honoring Dekmos Oulerios Gaiou Dionysios (lines 6, 21), i.e., Decimus Valerius Gaii (f./l.?) Dionysios, a Jewish benefactor. J. Roux and G. Roux ("Un décret du politeuma des Juifs de Béréniké en Cyrénaïque," *REG* 62 [1949]: 281-96, 290) argued that the Dionysios was a freedman, since there is no mention of his

genitive) suggests rather that Theodotos was freeborn, since normally only freeborn persons were entitled to use a patronym.

Other conjectured identifications are not any more compelling. Clermont-Ganneau and Reinach suggested that *Ouettēnos* more likely represented Vettienus.[109] Clermont-Ganneau speculated that Theodotos's father or grandfather had been enslaved at the time of Pompey's conquest of Judea and that subsequently he was manumitted or adopted by a member of the Vettia *gens*.[110] This made natural the supposition that the synagogue of *CIJ* ii 1404 was the synagogue of freedmen of Acts 6:9.[111] With more hesitation he connected the synagogue builder's ancestor with a Vettienus mentioned in Cicero's letters to Atticus.[112]

This suggestion also runs afoul of the point raised against Vincent: if Theodotos's father was manumitted by someone from the Vettiena *gens*, one ought to expect a name like C. Vettienus (C.f.) Theodotos, again with the cognomen in the nominative.[113] Moreover, it is difficult to connect the *Ouettēnos* of *CIJ* ii 1404 with any specific figure of the first century B.C.E. or C.E.: we know the nomina Vettenus from one first-century inscription and several undated texts,[114]

Roman tribe; Reynolds ("Inscriptions," pp. 246-47), however, points out that "Greek practice in naming tribes was so unsystematic that this is not compelling. He [Decius] appears to be given filiation, though in the Greek, not the Roman manner (i.e., without the word *huios* for filius), and it seems improbable that this would appear if he were not freeborn."

109. Reinach ("L'inscription de Théodotus," p. 5) observed that Gallienus appears in Greek as Gallenos. Since the eta seems to have been vocalized as an ī, the *ei/ie* combination would easily reduce to an eta.

110. Vettenus, Vettienus, and Vettius are in fact three distinct nomina. Vettius, which is by far the most common of the three (*PIR*¹ iii V318-346; *PLRE* 955), would not, however, yield Vett(i)enus, as Clermont-Ganneau believed.

111. Clermont-Ganneau's suggestion is followed widely. See, e.g., Hüttenmeister and Reeg, *Die antiken Synagogen in Israel*, 1:195.

112. Clermont-Ganneau ("Découverte," pp. 193, 196) does not provide references, but presumably was thinking of the Vettienus who helped Cicero purchase a lodge (*Atticus* 196.3 [49 B.C.E.]) and to whom Cicero owed money (202.5 [49 B.C.E.]; cf. 205.2 [49 B.C.E]; 207.4 [49 B.C.E.]; 239.2 [45 B.C.E.]; 397.1 [44 B.C.E.]; 416.3 [44 B.C.E.]; 417.1 [44 B.C.E.]). Vettienus is said to be *ut monetalis*, "like a mint-master" (417.1 [44 B.C.E.]). Clermont-Ganneau (p. 197) took this as an indication that Vettienus was Jewish: "Ce Vettienus exerçait un métier qui répond assez bien aux aptitudes caractéristiques de la race juive." Reinach ("L'inscription de Théodotus," pp. 53-54) commented: "Si ce n'est là une simple boutade, c'est un grave anachronisme, qu'on s'étonne de recontrer dans la bouche d'un érudit éminent."

113. I.e., C(aius) Vettienus C(aii) f(ilius) Theodotos. In this form, both the servile origins of Theodotos's biological father and his cognomen are hidden. The latter would have been mentioned only if his father was particularly distinguished.

114. Lucius Vettenus M[—]: *AE*, 1966, 61 (Rome; beginning of first century C.E.); L. Vettenus L. l. Anteros: *CIL* vi 9137 = *ILS* 7684 (Rome); C. Vettenus C. l. Aphrodisius, with four

and Vettieni are known not only in the time of Cicero, but during the principates of Trajan[115] and Hadrian[116] and in several undated inscriptions.[117] Hence, there is little purchase for an identification of *Ouettēnos* with a specific member of the Vett(i)eni, still less with the Vett(i)eni of a particular century.

If, as I have argued, neither Theodotos nor his father was a freedman, we might ask how his father came to have a Latin name. There is evidence from Egypt, Cyrenaica, and Rome of fathers who bore Hebrew or Greek names giving their children Latin names (as Vettenus's father presumably did), and fathers with Latin names giving their children Greek names (as Theodotos's father did).[118] The giving of a Latin name that in Italy would have been a *nomen gentilicium* is imaginable if Vettenus's father had some reason to be grateful to one of the Vetteni (presumably active in Palestine). An analogous suggestion might be made apropos of Cornelius, the father of one of the donors (Karnedas) to the synagogue at Benghazi (*CJZC* 72). Hence, there is no compelling reason to suppose that either Theodotos or Vettenus had servile origins and therefore no special reason to connect the synagogue of *CIJ* ii 1404 with the "synagogue of the freedmen and or the Cyrenaicans and Alexandrians" of Acts 6:9. And although we might suspect that Vettenus's father had some connection with a Vett(i)enus, the name is attested from the first century B.C.E. to the second century C.E., and hence is no real help in dating the inscription.

Paleography   The dating of undated inscriptions by script type is far from an exact science. Ideally, good paleographical dating requires a dossier of comparative materials that (a) are securely dated by internal means — normally, by ref-

other Vetteni: *CIL* ix 4157 (Samnium [Italy]); C. Vettenus Dionysius, and Vettena Zmyrna (presumably freedmen/women): *CIL* x 3094; C. Vettenus Timotheus: *CIL* x 3095; P. Vettenus Atilianus: *CIL* ix 6083.166.

115. C. Vettienus Modestus: *AE*, 1984, 15 (Rome; I C.E.); *ILS* 9054 (= *CIL* xvi 46) (Pannonia Superior; 100 C.E.); *AE*, 1980, 992 (Mauretania [Lixus]; 100-107 C.E.); *ILS* 2001 (Deva [Britain]; 103 C.E.): *AE*, 1990, 798 (Pannonia Superior [Carnuntum]; 103-7 C.E.); *ILS* 2002 (Germania; 107 C.E.); *CIL* V 4091.

116. C. Vettienus Hermes: *CIL* x 7855; *AE*, 1967, 395 (Tibiscum [Dacia]; 126 C.E.); *AE*, 1974, 569 [= *AE*, 1965, 131] (Aquae Calidae [Moesia Inferior]; 121 C.E.); *AE*, 1994, 1519 (Moesia Inferior; 133 C.E.); *AE*, 1968, 407 (Abisina [Raetia]; 135 C.E.).

117. C. Vettienus C. l. Metro[—]: *CIL* xii 5226 (Narbonensis; n.d.) (along with a son and another freedman of C. Vettienus); C. Vettienus C. f. Pupin[—]: *ILS* 2351 (Colonia Agrippinensis [Germania Inferior], n.d.); C. Vettienus Placidus: *CIL* vi 28656; C. Vettienus C.l. Nedymus: *AE*, 1990, 341 (Etruria [Italy]; n.d.), with his wife, Vettiena Libas.

118. Hebrew/Greek (father) → Latin (son/daughter): *IJudEg* 148 [= *CIJ* ii 928]; 151; *CIJ* ii 929; 1011; *CJZC* 7a; 11; 13a; 45c; 51c; 57b; 58f; 59c; 68; *IJudEu* i 35; 48; 68; 69; 76; 85; 90; 103; 107; 118; 183; Latin (father) → Greek (son/daughter): *CJZC* 33d; 53c; 57g; 57h; 67e, f; 70; 72; *IJudEu* 28; 62; 120; 134.

erence to regnal years of kings or emperors or city dates — (b) come from the same site and (c) include several examples of the same category of text, and (d) show a continuous development of script types. Such a dossier exists for Attica, and Steven Tracy has even been able to identify the hands of individual Attic cutters and thus (re)date some undated stones to the period of activity of these cutters.[119]

For other locations, more limited dossiers are available. C. Bradford Welles analyzed the inscriptions from Gerasa, identifying four early alphabets (and three Byzantine alphabets) and observing some development of the scripts.[120] At other sites, however, it has proved more difficult to show a continuous development of scripts and thus to produce a template against which to compare undated inscriptions. At Aphrodisias, for example, while the scripts of contemporaneous public inscriptions are mainly homogeneous, private inscriptions are much more variable, sometimes anticipating features that entered the "public" scripts only later.[121] Moreover, for the late Roman period, Rouché notes that private inscriptions honoring the same individual often exhibit differing epigraphic styles, thus making it difficult to speak of a "development" of script types.[122] Sartre made

119. S. V. Tracy, "Identifying Epigraphical Hands," *GRBS* 11 (1970): 321-33; Tracy, "Identifying Epigraphical Hands, II," *GRBS* 14 (1973): 189-95; Tracy, "The Date of the Grain Decree from Samos," *Chiron* 20 (1990): 97-100; Tracy, *Attic Letter-Cutters of 229 to 86 b.c.*, Hellenistic Culture and Society 6 (Berkeley: University of California Press, 1990); Tracy, *Athenian Democracy in Transition: Attic Letter-Cutters of 340 to 290 b.c.*, Hellenistic Culture and Society 20 (Berkeley: University of California Press, 1995). Tracy's method applied only to letters ranging from circa .005 meters to circa .01 meters in height.

120. C. B. Welles, "Inscriptions," in *Gerasa: City of the Decapolis,* ed. C. H. Kraeling (New Haven: American Schools of Oriental Research, 1938), pp. 355-69. Welles identified four early alphabets: (1) square (appearing in Syria in the first century b.c.e. and in Gerasa from 22/23 c.e., and continuing until ca. 150 c.e.); (2) monumental (from the first century to Caracalla); (3) the rounded alphabet, with three subforms: (3a) round (third quarter of the first century c.e. to the late third century); (3b) tall-narrow (second quarter of the second century c.e. to the second quarter of the third century); (3c) oval (second quarter of the second century c.e. to the second quarter of the third century); and (4) the revised square (late second century c.e. to the third century). Welles argued that the large number of dated inscriptions from Gerasa made it possible to date Gerasene Greek hands within "a period of a half-century or closer" (p. 358).

121. See C. Rouché, *Aphrodisias in Late Antiquity,* Journal of Roman Studies Monographs 5 (London: Society for the Promotion of Roman Studies, 1989), pp. xxi-xxii; J. M. Reynolds and R. Tannenbaum, *Jews and God-fearers at Aphrodisias: Greek Inscriptions with Commentary,* Proceedings of the Cambridge Philological Society, Supplementary Series 12 (Cambridge: Cambridge Philological Society, 1987), pp. 3-5. For the public script of Aphrodisias, see J. M. Reynolds, *Aphrodisias and Rome: Documents from the Excavation of the Theatre at Aphrodisias,* Journal of Roman Studies Monographs 1 (London: Society for the Promotion of Roman Studies, 1982), p. 33.

122. Rouché, *Aphrodisias in Late Antiquity,* pp. 331-32.

similar observations apropos of the inscriptions of Bostra (Syria) from the time of Roman occupation (117-120 C.E.) to Justinian. Developments in the form of certain letters could be observed, but several scripts coexisted at any given time, their use dependent upon the tastes of individual cutters.[123]

It is important to observe several cautions when dating undated inscriptions. First, it is a precarious procedure to extrapolate from the local scripts of, say, Athens to other parts of the classical world, since regional differences abound. Second, it is not possible to rule out either traditionalism, deliberate archaizing, or innovation on the part of the cutter. The entire imperial period is characterized by both variety and inconsistency of scripts.[124] Third, the studies of Rouché and Sartre have drawn attention to the coexistence of several scripts.[125] Finally, the scripts of public documents are likely to display a more consistent and homogeneous style than those of private documents, where a greater range of scripts is possible.

The initial epigraphical analysis of the Theodotos inscription (hereafter Θ) was very limited, though widely assumed to be decisive. Clermont-Ganneau dated the inscription to the Herodian period on the basis of similarities with the balustrade inscription of the Herodian Temple (pl. 2 = CIJ ii 1400, hereafter H[1]).[126] He noted only two features: (a) in both inscriptions the outer strokes of the mu and sigma diverge slightly; and (b) the bar on the epsilon does not touch the vertical. These observations sufficed for Clermont-Ganneau to establish a date in the Herodian period or shortly thereafter.[127] Reinach concurred with this dating, adding only that both inscriptions exhibited a broken-bar alpha.[128]

Vincent's analysis was by contrast careful and extensive, noting many differences between H[1] and Θ. Most obvious was the fact that while the letters of H[1]

---

123. Sartre, *IGLSyria* xiii/1, pp. 31-32.

124. W. Larfeld, *Handbuch der griechischen Epigraphik* (Leipzig: Reisland, 1902-7), 2:484.

125. In first century C.E. Palestine it is possible to see the use of the lunate epsilon and sigma and other cursive forms (alpha, delta, lambda, omega) in the texts scratched on ossuaries, even though incised texts of an official or semiofficial nature still employ classical letter forms. Lunate forms are attested in public scripts only much later.

126. The inscription, mentioned by Josephus (*Ant* 15.417), was found and published by C. Clermont-Ganneau, "Une stèle du temple de Jérusalem," *RA* 23 (1872): 214-34, 290-96 + pl. X (= *CIJ* ii 1400 + photo). For a second copy of this inscription, see below, n. 138.

127. Clermont-Ganneau, "Découverte," pp. 192-93. Commenting on a second-century Bithynian inscription (= *SEG* ii [1924] 663), Holleaux pointed out that there the medial bar was always attached to the vertical (Maurice Holleaux, "Inscription trouvée à Brousse," *BCH* 48 [1924]: 1-57; see esp. p. 6). He added that the form of the epsilon in *CIJ* ii 1404 "suffices to show that it is impossible to bring this inscription down, as someone [i.e., Vincent] rashly tried, to the second century C.E., and that it is hardly later than the beginning of the first century" (p. 6 n. 2).

128. Reinach, "L'inscription de Théodotus," p. 52.

are regular and well spaced, the letter height and width of Θ vary: the first three lines are regular and evenly spaced; the letters of lines 4-8 are visibly smaller; line 9 has slightly larger letters, and the final line begins small but the final letters (ΚΑΙΣΙΜΩΝΙΔΗΣ) gradually increase in size. It would appear that the cutter of Θ feared he would run out of space after the third line, and so compressed the letters of lines 4-8. Only in lines 9-10 did he realize that he had sufficient room for the whole inscription and expanded the final line significantly.

Vincent's comparison of H[1] with Θ was designed to underscore the significant differences in lettering, thereby allowing for a different (and later) dating of Θ. The most important observations are:[129]

Alpha: in H[1] the form (a broken-bar alpha) is constant, with the bar always higher than the midpoint of the *hastae* (diagonal strokes). In Θ the letter is sometimes wide, sometimes smaller than the neighboring letters (ll. 6, 8), and the bar deeply broken and always low.

Epsilon: in H[1] the bar is joined to the vertical; in Θ the bar is detached (except in l. 8, *bis*).

Eta: in H[1] the letter is usually narrow with parallel and equal *hastae*; in Θ the letter is almost always wide, with unequal *hastae*.[130]

Kappa: the only instance in H[1] (l. 3) has very open diagonal strokes touching the vertical and aligned exactly with the base line and top line. The κ in Θ has irregular diagonals that do not always reach the lines (l. 5); they are attached high to the vertical (l. 3) or low (9, 10). In line 6 the branches are disjointed.

Mu: Vincent points out (against Clermont-Ganneau) that the sole μ in H[1] has completely vertical *hastae*; Θ has the (archaizing) splayed outer strokes in lines 5, 6, 7, 8, and 10, but the strokes are almost vertical in line 4.

Xi: the sole instance in H[1] (l. 6) has two equal bars, top and bottom, while in the two occurrences in Θ (ll. 6, 8) the lower bar is shorter.

Omicron: the letter in H[1] is perfectly circular; in Θ there are some deformations (ll. 1, 6).

Rho: in H[1] the upper stroke of the loop is attached to the vertical at an angle and the loop is rounded; in Θ the loop is small and attached high on the vertical.

Sigma: Clermont-Ganneau made much of the archaizing sigma in both inscriptions; but in H[1] the letter is generally rectangular, with the lower horizontal declining only slightly (ll. 1, 4, 5; straight in l. 2 [*bis*]). The decline is much more obvious in lines 1 and 2 of Θ, but as Vincent rightly states, "I do not see

129. Vincent, "Découverte," pp. 263-65. I have added line numbers to Vincent's comments and made some observations more precise.

130. Vincent, "Découverte," p. 264, also states that the eta in H[1] is barred in the middle (ll. 1, 4, 5) while the bar is high in 1. But while the bar is high in line 1, it is in the middle in lines 4, 6, 7, 8 (*bis*) (p. 10).

that [Clermont-Ganneau's observation] is justified in any of the other cases where the letter appears."[131]

Omega: in H[1] the letter is very open (l. 5), with its branches ending in a slight curve; a distant resemblance is found in Θ (l. 6), but elsewhere the terminal strokes are either horizontal (ll. 2, 3, 6, 7, 10) or slightly diagonal (upward) (l. 4), and in one case the horizontal completely closes the letter at the bottom (l. 7).

Vincent was rightly critical of Clermont-Ganneau's limited comparison and suggested three other comparisons. *IG* xii/5 739 (Andros; time of Augustus)[132] compared favorably to H[1] but not to Θ. Better analogies to Θ, Vincent suggested, were offered by *FD* iii/ii 106 (Delphi; 129 c.e.)[133] and *IMagMai* 171 (Magnesia ad Maeander; 104 c.e.),[134] both dating from several decades after 70 c.e. An examination of both *FD* iii/ii 106[135] and *IMagMai* 171,[136] however, shows as many divergences from the hand of Θ as it does similarities.

Rather than drawing on Delphic and Carian inscriptions, a more appropriate set of comparative materials for Θ is provided by *dated* Greek inscriptions from Roman Palestine. This is unfortunately a rather small corpus; there are only a handful of Greek inscriptions from Herodian and early Roman Jerusalem — probably the result of Titus's assault on the city. Fewer still bear dates. In the period following 70 c.e. there are many Latin inscriptions (many coming from the legionary camp established there). Greek inscriptions reappear only much later. There are, however, a few Greek inscriptions from Herodian Jerusalem and more from other parts of Roman Palestine and southern Syria that may be used for comparative purposes.[137]

131. Vincent, "Découverte," p. 265.

132. Incorrectly cited as *CIG* xii v[1] 739.

133. *FD* iii/ii 106 (pp. 114-15 + pl. IX:2). Vincent cited this incorrectly as *FD* iii iii 106.

134. *IMagMai* 171 (p. 126 + pl. 171).

135. *FD* iii/ii 106 has a broken-bar alpha with the bar sometimes high (l. 2), sometimes medial (ll. 2, 3, 4), and occasionally low on the *hastae* (l. 3). Unlike Θ, the medial stroke of the epsilon is attached to the vertical (ll. 1, 3, 5). Like Θ, the loop of the rho is small and attached high. Quite unlike Θ, the right *hastae* of the delta and lambda are elongated, extending past the left *hastae* (a shift toward cursive letters). And the sigma of *FD* iii/ii 106 is neither the archaizing splayed form nor the rectangular form of H[1] but square, like an epsilon without the medial stroke.

136. *IMagMai* 171 shares with Θ an alpha with a deeply broken bar, but other letters exhibit differences: the medial stroke of the epsilon always joins the vertical; while the delta of Θ is triangular, in *IMagMai* 171 the two *hastae* cross at the top and then curve slightly downward; the middle bar on the theta has apices (serifs) and does not touch the circle; both the mu and the sigma are rectangular, with no hints of splayed outer strokes; and the rho, while rounded, has a much larger loop than Θ and the vertical descends below the base line. Moreover, in *IMagMai* 171 ligatures — rarely attested before the second century c.e. — make their appearance (H-M, H-K) and the terminal strokes of many letters have apices.

137. According to P. Thomsen's tabulation of inscriptions from Jerusalem ("Die

Herodian Cutters and CIJ ii 1404

The second fragmentary copy of the Herodian balustrade inscription (hereafter H^2)[138] provides a remarkable opportunity to see the variability in cutters' styles in the same period (pl. 3). Unlike the cutter of H^1, whose letters are even and regular, the cutter of H^2 crowded the first two lines both vertically and horizontally, apparently fearing he would run out of space for the entire inscription. The first editor, Iliffe, took this to be a sign of the cutter's inexperience. A similar conclusion might follow from the inconsistency of letters: the bar of the alpha in line 1 is straight, but those in lines 3, 4, 5, 6 are broken; and the upsilon in line 2 is almost V-shaped, while that in line 4 has a tall vertical base.

The similarities with and divergences from H^1 are particularly noteworthy: as in H^1, the upper and lower strokes on the sigma are parallel.[139] Unlike H^1, however, H^2's bar on the epsilon (l. 1) does not touch the vertical and has apices. The horizontal bar on the tau is very long (ll. 2, 3, 5, 6), and the terminal strokes

---

lateinischen und griechischen Inschriften der Stadt Jerusalem und ihrer nächsten Umgebung," *ZDPV* 43 [1920]: 138-58; 44 [1921]: 1-61, 90-168), the following Greek inscriptions are extant: *II B.C.E.*: no. 241-45, 263 (all stamped amphorae handles); *100 B.C.E.–150 C.E.*: no. 190-206 (graffiti on ossuaries); *I C.E.* (1-50 C.E.): no. 11 (= *CIJ* ii 1400 [=H^1]); no. 261 (= *CIJ* ii 1404); *II C.E.*: no. 209 (inscribed gem); no. 220 (dedication [to Jupiter Sarapis?]); no. 250 (pottery stamp); *III C.E.*: no. 181 (graffito); no. 207 (metal band); no. 208 (gold leaf); no. 238-240 (amphora stamps); no. 254 (cast); no. 256 (brick stamps). None bears a date and all but numbers 11 and 261 are either too short to be useful for comparison or are not inscribed stones.

Thomsen's list of Greek inscriptions from Jerusalem can now be supplemented by dated or datable inscriptions from *SEG*: *I C.E.*: viii 169 [=H^2] (second copy of *CIJ* ii 1400); *SEG* xxxiii 1277 (Herodian period); *III C.E.*: viii 204 (= *CIJ* ii 1414); viii 206 (= *CIJ* ii 1405). I have excluded from this list fragmentary undated inscriptions, pottery stamps, mosaic inscriptions, and most ossuary inscriptions, which are scratched on the stone rather than inscribed. An exception is *CIJ* ii 1385, an ossuary inscription cut in a hand comparable to that of *SEG* viii 169 [H^2].

Other inscriptions of a reasonable length from Hellenistic and Roman Palestine include: *III B.C.E.*: *SEG* xx 467 (Jaffa; 217 B.C.E.); *II B.C.E.*: xix 904 (Ptolemais; 130/129 B.C.E.); xxix 1613 (Hefzibah; 199-195 B.C.E.); xli 1556 (Jamnia; 163 B.C.E.); *I C.E.*: viii 13 (Nazareth; time of Augustus); viii 84 (Kh. Bene Malek; 73/74 C.E.); xxi 1266 (Dora; after 70 C.E.); xviii 1048 (Caesarea Maritima; after 71 C.E.); *II C.E.*: viii 2 (Kedesh; 117/18 C.E.); viii 3 (Kedesh; 114/15 C.E.); viii 91 (Bêt Raš; 180-92 C.E.); xx 456 (Scythopolis; 139/40 C.E.); xx 494 (Madaba; 108/9 C.E.); xxxix 1624 (Gadara; 139-51 C.E.); xli 1547 (Dora; 119/20–130/31 C.E.); xlii 1409 (Caesarea Panias [Senaim]; 165/66 C.E.); xlii 1410 (Caesarea Panias [Senaim]; 148/49 C.E.); xlv 1947 (Dora; time of Trajan); *III C.E.*: viii 11 (Tiberias); xix 923 (Kibbutz Erez; 210/11 C.E.).

138. The inscription was discovered in 1935 in secondary usage and published by J. H. Iliffe, "The ΘΑΝΑΤΟΣ from Herod's Temple: Fragment of a Second Copy," *Quarterly of the Department of Antiquities in Palestine* 6, no. 1 (1936): 1-3 + 2 plates (cf. *SEG* viii [1937] 169).

139. Iliffe's facsimile ("THANATOS," p. 2) indicates a square sigma (l. 2), but the photograph shows a medial stroke and damaged left side.

of most letters of H^2 have apices. In both the formation of the epsilon and in the use of apices, H^2 is closer in style to Θ (though the apices in Θ are more restrained). These observations confirm Iliffe's suggestion that the cutter of H^2 was not the same as that of H^1. At the same time, they suggest that many of the differences between H^1 and Θ, which Vincent took to be indications that the two inscriptions are from different periods, need not be interpreted in this way. Instead, they indicate that the two could be from *different cutters*.

A third Herodian-period inscription (pl. 4 = *SEG* xxxiii 1277), discovered in Benjamin Mazar's excavations south of the Temple Mount, confirms this point.[140] The inscription is securely dated to 18/17 B.C.E. and records the donation by a Rhodian Jew, Paris son of Akeson, for paving the Temple complex. The cutter's hand resembles in some respects that of H^1: the letters are evenly spaced; there are few apices; the bar on the epsilon (ll. 1, 2) touches the vertical; and the outer strokes of the mu are completely vertical (l. 5). On the other hand, the bar on the alpha is broken and begins at or below the midpoint of the *hastae* (ll. 1, 2, 5); the kappa has irregular diagonals that do not reach the base or top lines (ll. 1, 2); the loop on the rho is small and attached high on the vertical (ll. 1, 2, 3, 4, 5); and the omega has terminal strokes resembling Θ but is smaller than surrounding letters (ll. 1, 2, 3, 4).

Because it is securely dated to the same period as H^1 and H^2, *SEG* xxxiii 1277 illustrates the variability in lettering styles in contemporary public documents. The variations among H^1 and H^2 and *SEG* xxxiii 1277 are due to the tastes of individual cutters, all presumably employed at public expense in the building of the Temple. Such variations are not indicative of the lettering styles of diverse eras. Θ, a private dedication and therefore probably not the product of the shops that produced the three public inscriptions,[141] nonetheless shows affinities with H^1, H^2, and *SEG* xxxiii 1277. Thus, most of the differences between H^1 and Θ that Vincent adduced are not probative for establishing that Θ was cut a half-century after H^1.[142] Although it is impossible to identify the cutter of the Theodotos in-

140. B. Isaac, "A Donation for Herod's Temple in Jerusalem," *IEJ* 33 (1983): 86-92 + photograph (*SEG* xxxiii 1277); reprinted in *The Near East under Roman Rule*, pp. 21-28 (+ photograph).

141. Tracy (*Attic Letter-Cutters*, pp. 223-36) provides a helpful glimpse of cutters' activities in Athens between 230 and 90 B.C.E. He has identified thirty-eight individual cutters, each responsible for between two and eighty-three inscriptions. There are, in addition, a large number of inscriptions (sixty-four) that represent the work of individual cutters who cannot be identified with any other. He estimates that at any given time, between fifteen and twenty cutters were able to produce long decrees between 200 and 160 B.C.E., and twice that many between 140 and 100 B.C.E. Some cutters traveled to the Piraeus, Eleusis, and even Sounion, but there were probably also local cutters at the Piraeus and Rhamnous.

142. Reynolds (*per litt.* 31.12.99) noted that while the cutter of H^1 probably laid the inscription out with a ruler or a compass, the cutter of Θ seems to have designed letters freehand, and

scription with any of the Herodian Temple cutters, the style of lettering falls within the range illustrated by these three public documents.

Inscriptions from Early to Late Roman Palestine and Syria

Other documents from Hellenistic and Roman Palestine and southern Syria help to set some general parameters for dating the Theodotos inscription. Examination of these dated and datable inscriptions suggests *both* that the lettering of *CIJ* ii 1404 is thoroughly consistent with that of first century c.e. inscriptions from the Levant and that it *lacks* the transformations that are characteristic of inscriptions of the second century and later.

Alpha: the broken-bar alpha with apices is found in Levantine inscriptions from the late Hellenistic period, through the first century and well beyond.[143] In the second and following centuries, however, two developments are common: the elongation of the right *hasta*[144] and the (re)appearance of the straight medial stroke,[145] or even a diagonal, descending right to left.[146]

---

if he ruled the lines, he did so as he got to each one. She suggests that "[the cutter of Θ] was a good deal less competent than the cutter of the Balustrade text — and it is his weaknesses that have misled some into thinking him rather late."

143. *SEG* xx 467 (Jaffa; 217 b.c.e.); *SEG* xli 1556 (Jamnia; 163 b.c.e.); *SEG* xix 904 (Ptolemais; 130/129 b.c.e.); *SEG* viii 13 (Nazareth; time of Augustus); *GerasaCBW* 49 (67/68 c.e.); *GerasaPLG* 1 (75/76 c.e.); *GerasaCBW* 51 (81-83 c.e.); *GerasaCBW* 52 (81-96 c.e.); *GerasaCBW* 29 (98 c.e.); *GerasaCBW* 141 (102-14 c.e.); *GerasaCBW* 56/57 (115 c.e.); *SEG* xxxix 1624 (Gadara; 139-51 c.e.); *JebelBlât* A, B, C (all 148/49 c.e.); *IGLSyria* 21/2 17 (150 c.e.); *GerasaCBW* 11 (163 c.e.); *GerasaPLG* 4 (177-80 c.e.). The broken-bar alpha first appears in Attic inscriptions late III b.c.e. and supplants the earlier A form in the mid-II b.c.e. (Larfeld, *Handbuch,* 2:472, 478). Apices are attested already in the I b.c.e. (*IG* ii² 1339 [57/56 b.c.e.]; *IG* ii² 1046 [52/51 b.c.e.]; *IG* ii² 1343 [37/36 b.c.e.]).

144. *SEG* xx 494 (Madaba; 108/9 c.e.); *SEG* xlv (1995), 1947 (Dora; 102-17 c.e.); *GerasaCBW* 144 (130 c.e.); *GerasaCBW* 21 (150 c.e.); *SEG* viii 91 (Bêt Raš [Capitolias]; 180-92 c.e.); *GerasaCBW* 170 (210-12 c.e.); *IEJ* 38 (1988): 177-80 (161-305 c.e.). In Attic inscriptions, this is attested first about 20 b.c.e. and becomes more common in the period after 50-120 c.e.: *IG* ii² 1099 (121 c.e.); *IG* ii² 3733 (126/27 c.e.); *IG* ii² 3764 (217/18 c.e.); *IG* ii² 2245 (262/63 c.e.).

145. Already in *SEG* xxix 1613 (Hefzibah; 199-195 b.c.e.). See also *SEG* viii 84 (Kh. Bene Malek; 73/74 c.e.); *SEG* xviii 1048 (Caesarea Maritima; after 71 c.e.); *GerasaCBW* 58 (130 c.e.); *SEG* xx 456 (Scythopolis; 139/40 c.e.); *GerasaCBW* 11 (163 c.e.); *CIJ* ii 891 (Apollonias; 176 c.e.); *GerasaCBW* 155 (212-17 c.e.). According to Larfeld's now-somewhat-dated treatment (*Handbuch,* 2:483-90), in Attic inscriptions the straight bar form, largely eclipsed by the broken bar in the mid-II b.c.e., reappears in the period after 50 c.e. and begins to dominate after Hadrian: e.g., *IG* ii² 1099 (121 c.e.); *IG* ii² 3764 (217/18 c.e.).

146. Already seen in *SEG* xxxi 1266 (Dora; after 70 c.e.), in a square script resembling the square script of Gadara. See also Yoram Tsafrir, *ErIsr* 19 (1987): 282-83 (+ photo); Tsafrir, "Further Evidence of the Cult of Zeus Akraios at Beth Shean (Scythopolis)," *IEJ* 39 (1989): 76-78 + pl.

Delta (and lambda): the classical forms of the delta (Δ) and the lambda (Λ) are dominant in the first and second centuries C.E. but also occur later.[147] In the mid–second century, a development parallel to that seen in the alpha occurs: under the influence of cursive forms in nonmonumental lettering, the right *hasta* is elongated.[148]

Epsilon: the epsilon of the Hellenistic and early Roman periods takes two basic forms: a rectangular letter with detached medial stroke, attested in H[2] and Θ and common in Gerasene inscriptions to the time of Trajan;[149] and a rectangular form with attached medial stroke, attested in the Hellenistic period,[150] the Herodian period,[151] and supplanting the detached forms in the second century.[152] The more significant development is the introduction of the lunate epsilon, seen at Dora and Gerasa in the fourth quarter of the first

---

10. The photograph published in *IEJ* is too small to read, but that in *ErIsr* is legible. The inscription appears to come from the mid-II C.E., related to other dedications to Zeus Akraios dated 139/40 (= year 203 of the city, founded in 64 B.C.E.); see B. Lifshitz, "Der Kult des Zeus Akraios und des Zeus Bakchos in Beisan (Scythopolis)," *ZDPV* 77 (1961): 186-90 + pl. 8 (= *SEG* xx 456) (who mistakenly dated the inscription to 159 C.E.).

147. *SEG* xix 904 (Ptolemais; 130/129 B.C.E.); *SEG* viii 13 (Nazareth; time of Augustus); *SEG* viii 84 (Kh. Bene Malek; 73/74 C.E.); *GerasaCBW* 49 (67/68 C.E.); *GerasaPLG* 1 (75/76 C.E.); *GerasaCBW* 181 (117 C.E.); *SEG* xxxix 1624 (Gadara; 139-51 C.E.); *JebelBlât* A, B (148/49 C.E.); *SEG* xlii (1992), 1410 (Senaim [near Panias] 148/49 C.E.). Sartre (*IGLSyria* xiii/1, p. 32) notes that the classical Δ is found at Bostra in the II C.E. (9005), III C.E. (9006, 9007), IV C.E. (9445), and V C.E. (9046; 9119).

148. *GerasaCBW* 13 (mid-II C.E.); *GerasaCBW* 150 (153/54 C.E.); *SEG* viii 91 (Bêt Raš [Capitolias]; 180-92 C.E.); *GerasaCBW* 150 (193-211 C.E.); *IEJ* 38 (1988): 177-80 (161-305 C.E.). Sartre (*IGLSyria* xiii/1, p. 32) notes that this is the only trait in the delta that is typical of Bostran inscriptions, found in the mid-III C.E. (9088) to the VI C.E. (9132). The elongation of the right *hasta* of the delta and lambda is already seen, however, in first-century ossuary texts: Hachlili, "Goliath Family," figs. 27, 35, 41. In Attic inscriptions, the crossing of the two *hastae* is seen in the early imperial period (e.g., *IG* ii[2] 1973; 40/41–53/54 C.E.) and the elongation of the right *hasta* appears at the same time (*IG* ii[2] 1970; 45/46 C.E.), becoming common in the second century (e.g., *IG* ii[2] 1996 [84/85–92/93 C.E.]; 1099 [121 C.E.]; 3733 [126/27 C.E.]; 3316 [132 C.E.]; 1368 [177 C.E.]).

149. *SEG* xix 904 (Ptolemais; 130/129 B.C.E.); *GerasaPLG* 1 (75/76 C.E.); *GerasaCBW* 49 (67/68 C.E.); *GerasaCBW* 51 (81-83 C.E.); *GerasaCBW* 52 (83-96 C.E.); *GerasaCBW* 29 (98 C.E.); *GerasaCBW* 141 (102-14 C.E.); *GerasaCBW* 119 (115/16 C.E.); *GerasaCBW* 10 (time of Trajan). The latest attestation is *GerasaCBW* 132 (212-17 C.E.).

150. *SEG* xx 467 (Jaffa; 217 B.C.E.); *SEG* xxix 1613 (Hefzibah; 199-195 B.C.E.); *SEG* xli 1556 (Jamnia; 163 B.C.E.).

151. H[1]; *SEG* xxxiii 1277; *SEG* viii 13 (Nazareth; time of Augustus).

152. *SEG* xviii 1048 (Caesarea Maritima; after 71 C.E.); *IGLSyria* xxi/2 17 (150 C.E.); *GerasaCBW* 120 (115/16 C.E.); *GerasaCBW* 58 (130 C.E.); *SEG* xxxix 1624 (Gadara; 139-51 C.E.); *GerasaCBW* 11 (163 C.E., alongside a lunate form); *GerasaPLG* 4 (177-80 C.E.). A rectangular form without a medial stroke occurs at *JebelBlât* A, B (148/49 C.E.), perhaps the cutter's mistake.

century C.E., becoming common in the second, and dominant in Syria after the third century C.E.[153]

Mu: the older form, with splayed outer strokes,[154] continues in Palestine and Syria until the second century C.E.,[155] but it existed alongside and was supplanted by a form with parallel verticals.[156] A shift toward rounded, cursive forms is also seen in the mu: a rounded medial stroke is seen in the second century C.E.,[157] a development seen in Syrian inscriptions in the third century C.E., eventually resulting in a cursive mu.[158]

Sigma: in the late Hellenistic and early imperial periods, the sigma is often encountered with the splayed outer strokes,[159] although in both Θ and H[1] it is

153. *SEG* xxxi 1266 (Dora; after 70 C.E.); *SEG* viii 84 (Kh. Bene Malek; 73/74 C.E.); *GerasaCBW* 117 (73/74 C.E.); *SEG* xx 494 (Madaba; 108/9 C.E.); *GerasaPLG* 2 (ca. 130/31 C.E.); *SEG* xx 456 (Scythopolis; 139/40 C.E.); *JebelBlât* C (148/49 C.E.); *SEG* xlii (1992), 1410 (Senaim [near Panias]; 148/49 C.E.); *ErIsr* 19 (1987): 282-83 (mid-II C.E.); *GerasaCBW* 63 (150 C.E.); *GerasaCBW* 65 (162-66 C.E.); *GerasaCBW* 11 (163 C.E., alongside rectangular forms); *SEG* xlii (1992), 1409 (Senaim [near Panias]; 163/64 C.E.); *CIJ* ii 891 (Apollonias; 176 C.E.); *SEG* viii 91 (Bêt Raš [Capitolias]; 180-92 C.E.); *IEJ* 38 (1988): 177-80 (161-305 C.E.); *GerasaCBW* 148 (193 C.E.). The epsilon is always lunate in the inscriptions of Bostra (*IGLSyria* xiii/1; III C.E.–VI C.E.). The lunate forms are attested in Attic inscriptions as early as the fourth century B.C.E. and increase in frequency in the early imperial period (Larfeld, *Handbuch,* 2:484). They become common in the second and third centuries C.E., e.g., *IG* ii² 1368 (177 C.E.; the Iobacchoi inscription). However, first-century ossuary inscriptions attest lunate forms: Hachlili, "Goliath Family," figs. 7-8, 27, 30, 31, 34-35, 39, 41-42.

154. The splayed form appears alongside quadratic forms in Attic inscriptions starting in the period 225-150 B.C.E. (Larfeld, *Handbuch,* 2:472) and continuing into the early imperial period; see, e.g., *IG* ii² 1029 (95/94 or 94/93 B.C.E.); *IG* ii² 1339 (57/56 B.C.E.); *IG* ii² 1715 (14/13 B.C.E.); *IG* ii² 2292 (36/37 C.E.); *IG* ii² (45/46 C.E.).

155. *SEG* xx 467 (Jaffa; 217 B.C.E.); *SEG* xxix 1613 (Hefzibah; 199-195 B.C.E.); *SEG* viii 13 (Nazareth; time of Augustus) (some mus); *GerasaCBW* 141 (102-14 C.E.); *JebelBlât* A, B (148/49 C.E.); *GerasaPLG* 4 (177-80 C.E.).

156. *SEG* xli 1556 (Jamnia; 163 B.C.E.); *SEG* viii 13 (Nazareth; time of Augustus) (some mus); *GerasaCBW* 49 (67/68 C.E.); *SEG* xxxi 1266 (Dora; after 70 C.E.); *SEG* xviii 1048 (Caesarea Maritima; after 71 C.E.); *GerasaPLG* 1 (75/76 C.E.); *GerasaCBW* 51 (81-83 C.E.); *GerasaCBW* 52 (83-96 C.E.); *GerasaCBW* 29 (98 C.E.); *GerasaCBW* 120 (115/16 C.E.); *GerasaCBW* 58 (130 C.E.); *SEG* xxxix 1624 (Gadara; 139-51 C.E.); *GerasaPLG* 3 (early III C.E.). Sartre (*IGLSyria* xiii/1, p. 33) notes that the mu with splayed outer strokes is attested in the II C.E. (*IGLSyria* xiii/1 9049), but beginning with the III C.E., the outer strokes are more usually vertical (*IGLSyria* xiii/1 9054, 9055).

157. *SEG* xx 494 (Madaba; 108/9 C.E.); *SEG* xlii (1992), 1410 (Senaim [near Panias]; 148/49 C.E.): with splayed outer strokes and rounded medial; *SEG* viii 91 (Bêt Raš [Capitolias]; 180-92 C.E.): a fully cursive form.

158. Sartre, *IGLSyria* xiii/1, p. 33: the medial bar begins to appear round circa 210-20 C.E. (*IGLSyria* xiii/1 9007 [217/18]); then curved vertical and inner strokes (*IGLSyria* xiii/1 9108 [278/79 C.E.]); then cursive mu in the IV C.E. (*IGLSyria* xiii/1 9111 [320 C.E.]).

159. According to Larfeld (*Handbuch,* 2:481), this form of the sigma makes its appearance in Attic inscriptions circa 90 B.C.E.

only the lower stroke that descends slightly.[160] Other inscriptions from the third century B.C.E. to the second century C.E. attest a quadrilateral form with parallel final strokes.[161] From the first century C.E., however, one finds a square sigma (like an epsilon without a medial stroke),[162] and in the second and following centuries the lunate form comes to dominate.[163] Sartre notes that the sigma at Bostra is always lunate.[164]

Omega: the omega is generally in its classical form (Ω) in the inscriptions of Palestine and Syria up to the mid–second century C.E., at which point the square and rounded cursive forms appear.[165] This corresponds generally to the trend in Attic inscriptions, where the cursive forms, attested in the first century (*IG* ii² 3264 [37 C.E.]), become more common in monumental inscriptions in the second (e.g., *IG* ii² 1368).[166] This transition is, again, probably the result of the influence of popular letter-forms on the cutters. Sartre comments that in Bostra, the classical omega is found only in the second century C.E. (the earliest

160. A similar form is seen in *SEG* xx 467.3 (Jaffa; 217 B.C.E.) and *SEG* xli 1556 (Jamnia; 163 B.C.E.) and in Attic inscriptions, e.g., *IG* ii² 1029 (95/94 or 94/93 B.C.E.); *IG* ii² 1339 (57/56 B.C.E.).

161. *SEG* xx 467.2, 5 (Jaffa; 217 B.C.E.); *SEG* xxix 1613 (Hefzibah; 199-195 B.C.E.); *SEG* xix 904 (Ptolemais; 130/129 B.C.E.); *SEG* viii 13 (Nazareth; time of Augustus); *GerasaCBW* 49 (67/68 C.E.); *SEG* xviii 1048 (Caesarea Maritima; after 71 C.E.); *GerasaCBW* 51 (81-83 C.E.); *GerasaCBW* 52 (83-96 C.E.); *GerasaCBW* 29 (98 C.E.); *GerasaCBW* 141 (102-14 C.E.); *GerasaCBW* 119 (115/16 C.E.); *GerasaCBW* 181 (117 C.E.); *GerasaCBW* 10 (Trajan); *SEG* xxxix 1624 (Gadara; 139-51 C.E.); *JebelBlât* A, B (148/49 C.E.); *IGLSyria* xxi/2 17 (150 C.E.); *GerasaPLG* 4 (177-80 C.E.); *GerasaPLG* 3 (early III C.E.).

162. *GerasaPLG* 1 (75/76 C.E.); *SEG* xlv (1995), 1947 (Dora; 102-17 C.E.).

163. Already in the first century in *SEG* xxxi 1266 (Dora; after 70 C.E.) and *SEG* viii 84 (Kh. Bene Malek; 73/74 C.E.). Again, lunate forms are attested on ossuary texts in the first century, e.g., Hachlili, "Goliath Family," figs. 8-10, 12, 27, 31, 34-35, 39, 41. In the second: *SEG* xx 494 (Madaba; 108/9 C.E.); *SEG* xx 456 (Scythopolis; 139/40 C.E.); *JebelBlât* C (148/49 C.E.); *ErIsr* 19 (1987): 282-83 (mid-II C.E.); *SEG* xlii (1992), 1409 (Senaim [near Panias]; 163/64 C.E.); *CIJ* ii 891 (Apollonias; 176 C.E.); *SEG* viii 91 (Bêt Raš [Capitolias]; 180-92 C.E.); *IEJ* 38 (1988): 177-80 (161-305 C.E.).

164. Sartre, *IGLSyria* xiii/1, p. 33.

165. Classical: *SEG* xx 467 (Jaffa; 217 B.C.E.); *SEG* xxix 1613 (Hefzibah; 199-195 B.C.E.); *SEG* xli 1556 (Jamnia; 163 B.C.E.); *SEG* xix 904 (Ptolemais; 130/129 B.C.E.); *SEG* viii 13 (Nazareth; time of Augustus); *GerasaCBW* 49 (67/68 C.E.); *SEG* xviii 1048 (Caesarea Maritima; after 71 C.E.) (closed at the bottom); *GerasaCBW* 81 (81-83 C.E.); *GerasaCBW* 52 (83-96 C.E.); *GerasaCBW* 29 (98 C.E.); *GerasaCBW* 119 (115/16 C.E.); *GerasaCBW* 120 (115/16 C.E.); *GerasaCBW* 10 (Trajan); *SEG* xxxix 1624 (Gadara; 139-51 C.E.); *GerasaCBW* 12 (ca. 163 C.E.). Square cursive: *SEG* xxxi 1266 (Dora; after 70 C.E.); *GerasaPLG* 1 (75/76 C.E.); *JebelBlât* B (148/49 C.E.). Cursive: *SEG* xx 494 (Madaba; 108/9 C.E.); *GerasaCBW* 58 (130 C.E.); *ErIsr* 19 (1987): 282-83 (mid-II C.E.); *GerasaCBW* 11 (163 C.E., alongside the classical form); *SEG* xlii (1992), 1409 (Senaim [near Panias]; 163/64 C.E.); *GerasaCBW* 155 (212-17 C.E.); *IEJ* 38 (1988): 177-80 (161-305 C.E.).

166. See Larfeld, *Handbuch*, 2:487.

of his inscriptions), where it appears alongside the lunate forms, which dominate thereafter.[167]

In addition to the shifts in letter form, the second and third centuries also attest the appearance of ligatures and monograms at Gadara, Gerasa, and Bostra.[168]

In situating the Theodotos inscription within this range of letter styles, it is important to note again that shifts in lettering styles are not sufficiently sharply defined to enable one to exclude a second-century date or one even later. The broken-bar alpha and nonlunate epsilon and sigma, for example, are attested beyond the first century. Nevertheless, the above description of lettering forms should make clear that the lettering style of *CIJ* ii 1404 is completely consistent with an early imperial period date. Moreover, *none* of the transformations regularly attested in the second and following centuries is in evidence: the bar on the alpha is always broken, never straight; the right *hastae* on the alpha, delta, and lambda show no lengthening; the epsilon and sigma are quadrilateral rather than lunate; the mu and sigma have splayed outer strokes rather than parallel strokes; still less do these letters display any tendency toward cursive forms; the omega is classical; and no ligatures or monograms are to be seen. Hence, while it is still possible that the lettering is from later than the first century C.E. — the result of traditionalism or deliberate archaizing — nothing requires such a dating, and all the indications are consistent with the Herodian period.

Conclusion and Epilogue

Kee's argument against the early dating of *CIJ* ii 1404 and in favor of a second-century to late third-century dating is based on several faulty premises and a misleading presentation of the history of scholarship on the inscription. An examination of the features of the inscription germane to its dating favors an early date. Although the names Theodotos, Vettenus, and Simonides provide no secure basis for dating, both the provenance of *CIJ* ii 1404 and its paleography point to a date in the Herodian or early Roman periods (prior to 70 C.E.). Consideration of the stratigraphy of the site of discovery virtually rules out a date later than 70 C.E., and the paleography of the inscription is both consistent

---

167. Sartre, *IGLSyria* xiii/1, p. 33.

168. *SEG* xxix 1624 (Gadara; 139-51 C.E.) (an o-υ monogram written as an *O* with a *V* inside) and an ō-*n* monogram (with the nun inside the omega); Welles, "Inscriptions," p. 360; Sartre, *IGLSyria* xiii/1, 34. The *o-y* monogram (*o* with a *y* on top) appears for the first time at Bostra in 501/2 (*IGLSyria* xiii/1 9124).

with the Herodian to early Roman periods and shows none of the paleographical transformations characteristic of later inscriptions from Roman Palestine and Syria.

CIJ ii 1404 thus attests a synagogue building in Jerusalem, probably constructed in the early first century C.E. or perhaps the latter part of the first century B.C.E. Theodotos's family, besides being priestly, was wealthy enough to undertake the building project and apparently enjoyed a long-standing connection with the aristocracy in Jerusalem (οἱ πρεσβύτεροι: ll. 9/10), a Roman family, and an otherwise unknown Simonides.

The securing of the date of the inscription is important for a number of reasons: first, it confirms that *synagōgē* was used of buildings not only in Egypt and Cyrenaica but also in early Roman Palestine. Second, Theodotos's grandfather is also identified as an *archisynagōgos,* which implies that he held this position sometime in the first century B.C.E. Hence *CIJ* ii 1404 provides the earliest datable attestation for the term *archisynagōgos* used in Jewish associations,[169] perhaps half a century prior to other epigraphical and literary attestations of the term and contemporary with our earliest pagan attestations of that term.

Finally, the Theodotos inscription provides a unique insight into the function of early synagogues, or at least those in Jerusalem. It lists the study of the Torah and teaching as primary functions, and hence is in general agreement with the description of Galilean synagogues mentioned in the Gospels, where Jesus also teaches.[170] Interestingly, the inscription lacks any mention of prayer. This is perhaps because the synagogue was located a few hundred meters from the Temple, the more natural place of prayer. But we should not conclude from the Theodotos inscription that synagogues did not feature prayer. Prayer was a function of the *proseuchē* in Tiberias (Josephus, *Life* 295) and is mentioned by

---

169. Aside from *CIJ* ii 1404 and the mention of *archisynagōgos* in the New Testament (Mk 5:22, 35, 36, 38; Lk 8:49; 13:14; Acts 13:15; 18:8, 17), the earliest attestations of the term apropos of Jewish groups are *MAMA* vi 264.3, 4 (Ammonia; late I C.E.), *IJudEu* i 14.2 (Ostia; I-II C.E.), and *MAMA* iv 90.1-2 (Synnada, Phrygia; I/II C.E.). Pagan *archisynagōgoi* are attested from the first century B.C.E.: *IFayum* i 9.7 (Crocodilopolis-Arsinoe, Fayûm; 80/79–69/67 B.C.E.); *IAlexandriaK* 91.4 (Alexandria; 4/5 C.E.); E. Voutiras, "Berufs- und Kultverein: Ein ΔΟΥΜΟΣ Thessalonike," *ZPE* 90 (1992): 87-96 (Thessalonica; 90/91 C.E.); and *IGRR* i 782.3-4 (Perinthus, Thrace; I C.E.?). For recent discussions of the title, see T. Rajak and D. Noy, "*Archisynagōgoi:* Office, Title and Social Status in Greco-Jewish Synagogue," *JRS* 83 (1993): 75-93 (who fail to note both *MAMA* iv 90.1-2 and the Thessalonican inscription in their list of inscriptions); G. H. R. Horsley, "An *archisynagogos* of Corinth?" in *NewDocs* 4:213-20; and L. I. Levine, "Synagogue Leadership: The Case of the Archisynagogue," in *Jews in a Graeco-Roman World,* ed. M. Goodman (Oxford and New York: Clarendon, 1998), pp. 195-213.

170. Mk 1:21; 6:2; Mt 9:35 (a redactional addition to Mk 1:39); Lk 4:15-30; 6:6 (a redactional addition to Mk 3:1); 13:10; and Jn 6:59.

Mt 6:5 as a part of synagogue activities (even though Matthew is written after the First Revolt). One might surmise that in synagogues in Galilee and other locations outside Jerusalem prayer was part of synagogue activities, and that after 70 C.E. other functions of the Herodian Temple devolved on synagogues.

This does not mean that all aspects of the Gospels' description of Galilean synagogues are to be taken at face value. The Theodotos inscription does not link the role of the synagogue leader *(archisynagōgos)* with the Pharisees, and there is no other early evidence to suggest that the Pharisees had control of the leadership of synagogues. Even later rabbinic sources contain various criticisms of synagogue practices — an indication that in the second century C.E. the synagogue was not a center of rabbinic activities or control.[171] This means that the single Markan instance of Pharisees in a synagogue (Mk 3:1) should not be generalized for the time of Jesus, and that impressions conveyed by Matthew (Mt 6:2, 5; 23:6, expanding Mk 12:39) and Jn 9:22 that Pharisees were ubiquitous in synagogues are functions either of the polemical interests of these authors in creating occasions for controversy, or of the specific locales of Matthew and John, or of a late first-century date when some Pharisees may have developed connections with synagogues known to Matthew and John.

The Theodotos inscription thus not only helps to solve a lexicographic issue — the point at which the term *synagōgē* came to be used in Palestine of buildings — but also provides important controls on the descriptions of synagogues encountered in the Gospels.

Appendix: Major Publications of the Theodotos Inscription (in Chronological Order)

Editio princeps: Raimund Weill, "La Cité de David: Compte rendu des fouilles exécutées à Jérusalem sur le site de la ville primitive. Campaigne de 1913-14 [IV]," *REJ* 71 (1920): 1-45, esp. 30-34 + pl. XXVA = *La Cité de David: Compte rendu des fouilles exécutées à Jérusalem sur le site de la ville primitive. Campaigne de 1913-14,* 2 vols. with plates (Paris: Paul Geuthner, 1920), 1:186-90 + 2:pl. XXVA.

Following Weill: Samuel Klein, *Jüdisch-Palästinischen Corpus Inscriptionum (Ossuar-, Grab- und Synagōgēninschriften)* (Vienna and Berlin: Lowit, 1920), pp. 101-4 (no. 17); L.-H. Vincent, "Découverte de la 'synagogue des affranchis' à

---

171. See Levine, *The Ancient Synagogue,* pp. 37-38, 440-70; Cohen, "Were Pharisees and Rabbis the Leaders of Communal Prayer and Torah Study in Antiquity?" in *Echoes of Many Texts,* pp. 99-114.

Jérusalem," *RB* 30 (1921): 247-77 + photo (pl. III); S. A. Cook, "The Synagogue of Theodotus at Jerusalem," *Palestine Exploration Fund Quarterly Statement,* 1921, pp. 22-23; N. A. Bees, "Epigraphik," *Byzantinisch-neugriechische Jahrbücher* 2 (1921): 259 (reviewing Vincent); Gerald M. FitzGerald, "Notes on Recent Discoveries," *Palestine Exploration Fund Quarterly Statement,* 1921, pp. 175-81; Hans Lietzmann, "Notizen," *ZNW* 20 (1921): 171-73 (reviewing Vincent); Peter Thomsen, "Die lateinischen und griechischen Inschriften der Stadt Jerusalem und ihrer nächsten Umgebung," *ZPDV* 44 (1921): 143-44 (no. 261); R. Cagnat and M. Besnier, *AE* (1922), 117 (pp. 36-37) = "Revue des publications épigraphiques," *Revue archéologique* 16 (1922): 365-421, no. 117 (pp. 400-401); Adolf Deissmann, *Light from the Ancient East,* rev. ed. (London: Hodder and Stoughton, 1927), app. V, pp. 439-41 + photo (fig. 80); Eleazar L. Sukenik, *Ancient Synagogues in Palestine and Greece* (London: Oxford University Press, 1934), pp. 69-70 + photo (pl. XVIa); *SEG* viii (1937), 170; *CIJ* ii 1404 (2:332-35 + ph.); I. Press, *A Topographical-Historical Encyclopaedia of Palestine* (in Hebrew), 4 vols. (Jerusalem: Rubin Mass, 1948-55), 2:414-15; Moshe Schwabe, *Greek Inscriptions of Jerusalem* (in Hebrew), in Michael Avi-Yonah, ed., *The Book of Jerusalem* (in Hebrew) (Jerusalem and Tel Aviv: Bialik; Dvir, 1956), pp. 358-69, esp. 362-65 (photo); Emilio Gabba, *Iscrizioni greche e latine per lo studio della Bibbia,* Sintesi dell'oriente e della Bibbia 3 (Rome: Marietti, 1958), pp. 79-82 (no. 23); Lifshitz, *DFSJ* 79 (pp. 70-71); Frohwald Hüttenmeister and Gottfried Reeg, *Die antiken Synagōgēn in Israel,* 2 vols., Beihefte zum Tübinger Atlas des Vorderen Orients. Reihe B, Geisteswissenschaften 12 (Wiesbaden: Reichert, 1977), 1:192-95; Leah Roth-Gerson, *The Greek Inscriptions from Synagogues in Eretz Israel* (in Hebrew) (Jerusalem: Yad Yitzak Ben-Zvi, 1987), pp. 76-86 (no. 19) + photo; Laura Boffo, *Iscrizioni greche e latine per lo studio della Bibbia,* Biblioteca di storia e storiografia dei tempi biblici 9 (Brescia: Paideia, 1994), pp. 274-82 (no. XXIII).

Selected Bibliography

Binder, D. D. *Into the Temple Courts: The Place of the Synagogues in the Second Temple Period.* SBLDS 162. Atlanta: Society of Biblical Literature, 1999.

Bloedhorn, H., and G. Hüttenmeister. "The Synagogue." In *The Cambridge History of Judaism.* Vol. 3, *The Early Roman Period,* edited by W. Horbury, W. D. Davies, and J. Sturdy, pp. 267-97. Cambridge and New York: Cambridge University Press, 1999.

Chiat, M. J. *Handbook of Synagogue Architecture.* BJS 29. Chico, Calif.: Scholars, 1982.

Cohen, S. J. D. "Were Pharisees and Rabbis the Leaders of Communal Prayer and Torah Study in Antiquity?" In *The Echoes of Many Texts: Reflections on Jewish and Christian Traditions; Essays in Honor of Lou H. Silberman,* edited by William G. Dever and J. E. Wright, pp. 99-114. BJS 313. Atlanta: Scholars, 1997.

Fine, S. *This Holy Place: On the Sanctity of the Synagogue during the Greco-Roman Period.* Christianity and Judaism in Antiquity 11. Notre Dame: University of Notre Dame Press, 1998.

———. *Sacred Realm: The Emergence of the Synagogue in the Ancient World.* London and New York: Oxford University Press, 1996.

———, ed. *Jews, Christians, and Polytheists in the Ancient Synagogue.* London and New York: Routledge, 1999.

Fine, S., and E. M. Meyers. "Synagogues." In *OEANE* 5:118-23.

Frey, J.-B., ed. *Corpus inscriptionum iudaicarum: Recueil des inscriptions juives qui vont du IIIe siècle avant J.-C.* 2 vols. Rome: Pontificio Istituto di archeologia cristiana, 1936-52.

Grabbe, L. L. "Synagogues in Pre-70 Palestine: A Reassessment." *JTS* 38 (1988): 401-10.

Griffiths, J. G. "Egypt and the Rise of the Synagogue." *JTS* 38 (1987): 1-15.

Gutmann, J., ed. *Ancient Synagogues: The State of Research.* BJS 22. Chico, Calif.: Scholars, 1981.

———, ed. *The Synagogue: Studies in Origins, Archaeology, and Architecture.* Library of Biblical Studies. New York: Ktav Publishing House, 1975.

Hachlili, R. *Ancient Jewish Art and Archaeology in the Land of Israel.* Handbuch der Orientalistik. 7. Abteilung: Kunst und Archäologie, 1. Band: Der alte Vordere Orient, 2. Abschnitt: Die Denkmäler, B: Vorderasien, Lieferung 4. Leiden, New York, Copenhagen, and Cologne: Brill, 1988.

———. "The Origin of the Synagogue: A Re-assessment." *JSJ* 28 (1997): 34-47.

———, ed. *Ancient Synagogues in Israel: Third–Seventh Century C.E.* Proceedings of Symposium, University of Haifa, May 1987. BAR International Series 499. Oxford: BAR, 1989.

Hengel, M. "Proseuchē und Synagōgē: Jüdische Gemeinde, Gotteshaus und Gottesdienst in der Diaspora und in Palästina." In *Tradition und Glaube: Das frühe Christentum in seiner Umwelt. Festgabe für Karl Georg Kuhn,* edited by G. Jeremias, H.-W. Kuhn, and H. Stegemann, pp. 157-84. Göttingen: Vandenhoeck & Ruprecht, 1971.

Hüttenmeister, F., and G. Reeg. *Die antiken Synagōgēn in Israel.* 2 vols. Beihefte zum Tübinger Atlas des Vorderen Orients. Reihe B, Geisteswissenschaften, no. 12. Wiesbaden: Reichert, 1977.

Kee, H. C. "Defining the First Century C.E. Synagogue: Problems and Progress." *NTS* 41 (1995): 481-500.

———. "The Transformation of the Synagogue after 70 C.E.: Its Import for Early Christianity." *NTS* 36 (1990): 1-24.

Kee, H. C., and L. H. Cohick, eds. *Evolution of the Synagogue: Problems and Progress.* Harrisburg, Pa.: Trinity, 1999.

Levine, L. I. *The Ancient Synagogue: The First Thousand Years.* New Haven: Yale University Press, 2000.

———, ed. *Ancient Synagogues Revealed.* Jerusalem: Israel Exploration Society; Detroit: Wayne State University Press, 1981.

———, ed. *The Synagogue in Late Antiquity.* Philadelphia: American Schools of Oriental Research, 1987.

McKay, H. A. "Ancient Synagogues: The Continuing Dialectic between Two Major Views." *CurBS* 6 (1998): 103-42.

Meyers, E. M. "Synagogue." In *ABD* 6:251-60.

Oster, R. "Supposed Anachronism in Luke-Acts' Use of συναγωγή: A Rejoinder to H. C. Kee." *NTS* 39 (1993): 178-208.

Rajak, T., and D. Noy. "*Archisynagōgoi:* Office, Title and Social Status in Greco-Jewish Synagogue." *JRS* 83 (1993): 75-93.

Riesner, R. "Synagogues in Jerusalem." In *The Book of Acts in Its Palestinian Setting*, edited by R. J. Bauckham, pp. 179-211. Book of Acts in Its First Century Setting 4. Grand Rapids: Eerdmans; Carlisle: Paternoster, 1995.

Sukenik, E. L. *Ancient Synagogues in Palestine and Greece.* London: Oxford University Press, 1934.

Urman, D., and P. V. M. Flesher, eds. *Ancient Synagogues: Historical Analyses and Archaeological Discovery.* 2 vols. SPB 47/1-2. Leiden, New York, and Cologne: Brill, 1995.

Jesus and the Theater in Jerusalem

Achim Lichtenberger

Archaeology is the study of *that which is no longer here.*[1] This statement documents in a drastic way the difficulty connected with the recovery and reconstruction of archaeological monuments. This difficulty is especially acute when no material remains of the archaeological monuments exist, and their existence is derived entirely from literary sources. Such is the case with the theater and the amphitheater in Jerusalem, built by Herod the Great, according to the Jewish historian Josephus.[2] As Greco-Roman institutions, both buildings are of major interest for the cultural climate of Jerusalem in the Second Temple period, and in the time of Jesus.

Most of the events during the time of Herod the Great are handed down to us in parallel records in the *Jewish War* and in the *Antiquities.* However, the theater and the amphitheater in Jerusalem are mentioned only in *Ant* 15.7.1 §268, §272; 15.7.4 §284, and not in *War.* For the chapters on Herod (in both of Josephus's historical works), Herod's court historian and adviser Nicolaus of Damascus is the most important source.[3] But also Jewish sources inimical to

1. See A. von Salis, "Klassische Komposition," in *Concinnitas: Beiträge zum Problem des Klassischen,* Heinrich Wölfflin zum achzigsten Geburtstag am 21. Juni 1944 zugeeignet (Basel: Benno Schwabe Verlag, 1944), p. 177.

2. The hippodrome is also occasionally mentioned in this context by some scholars. Josephus locates it southwest of the Temple and lists it in the context of the unrest after Herod's death. It cannot be proven that this building goes back to Herod's time; it should rather be presumed to be identical with the xystos, a part of the Hasmonean palace. P. Richardson, *Herod: King of the Jews and Friend of the Romans* (Minneapolis: Fortress, 1996), p. 186, and Z. Weiss, "Buildings for Entertainment," in *The City in Roman Palestine,* ed. D. Sperber (New York: Oxford University Press, 1998), p. 85, refer to the hippodrome as one of Herod's buildings. They are of the opinion that it is identical with the amphitheater.

3. Concerning Nicolaus and the sources of Josephus, cf. B. Z. Wacholder, *Nikolaus of Damascus,* UCPH 75 (Berkeley: University of California Press, 1962); M. Toher, "Nicolaus and

Herod are used, especially in the *Antiquities,* and the report mentioning both buildings in Jerusalem appears to go back to such. It is quoted in detail as follows:

> Herod went still farther in departing from the native customs, and through foreign practices he gradually corrupted the ancient way of life, which had hitherto been inviolable. As a result of this we suffered considerable harm at a later time as well, because those things were neglected which had formerly induced piety in the masses. For in the first place he established athletic contests every fifth year in honor of Caesar, and he built a theater in Jerusalem, and after that a very large amphitheater in the plain, both being spectacularly lavish but foreign to Jewish custom, for the use of such buildings and the exhibition of such spectacles have not been traditional (with the Jews). Herod, however, celebrated the quinquennial festival in the most splendid way, sending notices of it to the neighboring peoples and inviting participants from the whole nation. Athletes and other classes of contestants were invited from every land, being attracted by the hope of winning the prizes offered and by the glory of victory. And the leading men in various fields were assembled, for Herod offered very great prizes not only to the winners in gymnastic games but also to those who engaged in music and those who are called *thymelikoi.* And an effort was made to have all the most famous persons come to the contest. He also offered considerable gifts to drivers of four-horse and two-horse chariots and to those mounted on racehorses. And whatever costly or magnificent efforts had been made by others, all these did Herod imitate in his ambition to see his spectacle become famous. All round the theater were inscriptions concerning Caesar and trophies of the nations that he had won in war, all of them made for Herod of pure gold and silver. As for serviceable objects, there was no valuable garment or vessel of precious stones that was not also on exhibition along with the contests. There was also a supply of wild beasts, a great many lions and other animals having been brought together for him, such as were of extraordinary strength or of very rare kinds. When the practice began of involving them in combat with one another or setting condemned men to fight against them, foreigners were astonished at the expense and at the same time entertained by the dangerous spectacle, but to the natives it meant an open break with the customs held in honor by them. For it seemed glaring impiety to throw men to wild beasts for the pleasure of other men as spectators, and it seemed a further impiety to change their established ways for foreign practices. But more than

---

Herod in the *Antiquitates Judaicae,*" *HSCP* 101 (2003): 427-47. See also A. Lichtenberger, *Die Baupolitik Herodes des Großen,* ADPV 26 (Wiesbaden: Harrassowitz, 1999), pp. 11-13.

all else it was the trophies that irked them, for in the belief that these were images surrounded by weapons, which it was against their national custom to worship, they were exceedingly angry.[4]

As a result, there were protests against the presumed images, which Herod managed to calm by having the trophies *(tropaia)* dismantled, and by showing the outraged Jews that these were weapons on wooden poles and not human images.[5] Although the problem was resolved in laughter for the greater part of the protesters, a small minority of Zealots remained so upset over the matter that they plotted the assassination of Herod in the theater.[6] The rest of the story follows a typical pattern: It is told how the conspirators were given away by a traitor and brought before Herod, where they heroically confessed their plan and died as martyrs. The betrayer was then murdered by other Jews. This popular end of the story, relating the betrayer's swift punishment, probably shows that the story is an independent tradition in itself. That it is relating a Jewish tradition is hinted at by the subtly differentiated description of the problem, which, according to the Jewish view, arose in holding Greco-Roman spectacles. This would have hardly aroused the interest of Nicolaus of Damascus or his readers. Still, the detailed description of the Hellenistic-Roman splendor of the festival games shows that Josephus also would have used a further source that laid emphasis on the Greek character of the sporting event.[7]

Josephus's criticism is noteworthy in his account, in which he, as a matter of introduction, explains: "Herod went still farther in departing from the native customs, and through foreign practices he gradually corrupted the ancient way of life, which had hitherto been inviolable. As a result of this we suffered considerable harm at a later time as well, because those things were neglected which had formerly induced piety in the masses."[8]

This alludes to the Jewish War and puts the blame of guilt on Herod for the revolt and the resultant destruction of the Temple by the Romans. The games are seen as the prelude to the disaster of the Jewish War.

4. *Ant* 15.8.1 §267-276.

5. This misunderstanding is amazing because *tropaia* could not have been totally unknown to the Jews in the land of Israel, as they had already been used to adorn the family grave of the Maccabeans in Modein (1 Macc 13:29). Concerning the *tropaia*, see Lichtenberger, *Baupolitik*, p. 76.

6. On this see M. Hengel, *Die Zeloten: Untersuchungen zur jüdischen Freiheitsbewegung in der Zeit von Herodes I. bis 70 n. Chr.*, 2nd ed., AGJU 1 (Leiden: Brill, 1976), pp. 263-64.

7. This could have been Nicolaus with an account of the festival in which the conflict with the Jews was not described at all or in such detail. On the problems concerning non-Jewish sources in the *Antiquities*, see Toher, "Nicolaus," pp. 428-31.

8. *Ant* 15.8.1 §267.

Figure 49. Roman
arrowheads, from
Jerusalem and the
siege of 70 C.E.
Courtesy of J. H. Charlesworth

What then can we learn about both buildings, the Herodian theater and the amphitheater in Jerusalem? According to Josephus's account, they were built for the occasion of the festival games, which took place, as the context shows, in 28/27 B.C.E. and which could have been games honoring Caesar Octavian, the later Augustus. At least, the point in time and the direct reference to the Roman emperor in the inscriptions, naming the peoples he conquered, placed next to the theater, point to such games, which in memory of the victory over Mark Antony at Actium in 31 B.C.E., were also held in other places in the Roman Empire.[9] Everywhere we find lots of *tropaia* that hint at the Augustan victory at Actium.[10] The games in Jerusalem were, like Actia in other places, to take place every four years, yet we hear nothing more of them, neither in Josephus's subsequent historical work nor in other sources, and the theater and amphitheater also disappear from the records without a trace.

This disappearance can presumably be explained by the fact that, because of the popular protests directed not only at the supposed human images set up

9. Compare the following studies on the Actia: E. Reisch, "Aktia," in PW (1894), vol. I.1, pp. 1213-14; R. Rieks, "Sebasta und Aktia," *Hermes* 98 (1970): 96-116; M. Lämmer, "Die Aktischen Spiele von Nikopolis," *Stadion* 12/13 (1986/87): 27-38. On Herod's Actia see W. Otto, "Herodes," in PW (1913), vol. S.2, pp. 64-65; A. Schalit, *König Herodes: Der Mann und sein Werk*, 2. Auflage mit einem Vorwort von Daniel R. Schwartz (Berlin: de Gruyter, 2001), p. 371; M. Lämmer, "Griechische Wettkämpfe in Jerusalem und ihre politischen Hintergründe," *JDSK* (1973): 182-227; Lämmer, "Die Aktischen Spiele," p. 35; R. A. Gurval, *Actium and Augustus: The Politics and Emotions of Civil War* (Ann Arbor: University of Michigan Press, 1995), pp. 74-85; Richardson, *Herod*, pp. 223-24. See also S. Japp, *Die Baupolitik Herodes' des Großen. Die Bedeutung der Architektur für die Herrschaftslegitimation eines römischen Klientelkönigs*, IA 64 (Rahden: Verlag Maria Leidorf GmbH, 2000), pp. 23-26.

10. See, e.g., T. Hölscher, "Denkmäler der Schlacht von Actium. Propaganda und Resonanz," *Klio* 67 (1985): 83-97. See now also K. L. Zachos, "The *tropaeum* of the Sea-Battle of Actium at Nicopolis: Interim Report," *JRA* 16 (2003): 84-85.

but also at the gladiator contests, the games were no longer held in Jerusalem. M. Lämmer assumes that they took place thereafter in Sebaste, which had a greater pagan influence.[11] However, there is no reference to this.

Josephus writes surprisingly little about both buildings. According to him, the theater was located in Jerusalem, the large amphitheater "in the plain." He writes nothing about how the architecture looked. In describing other buildings constructed by Herod, Josephus's detail is noticeable; for example, in describing the expensive materials used, especially marble, which in Herodian building projects can be proven only in exceptional cases.[12] In describing the games in Jerusalem, on the other hand, significantly more emphasis is placed on the magnificence of the event, which is related in detail and which makes the silence about the architecture of the theater and the amphitheater even more necessary to explain. It can be presumed that the gymnastic and equestrian contests took place in the amphitheater while the music events were held in the theater. Where the animals were riled up is unclear, but it is likely this also occurred in the theater.[13]

In describing the festive games, the traces of two models for the event can be shown: one with a Roman influence and the other following Hellenistic form. Not only do the inscriptions in honor of Octavian point to Rome, but also the agitation of animals, which is of Roman character and, as such, could be seen as a diminished form of gladiator games, which Herod felt confident enough to hold only in pagan Caesarea.[14] But also the Hellenistic character of the event is clearly evident. It had as its goal the display of wealth and opulence *(polyteleia* or *tryphē),* and sought models in the Hellenistic representation of royalty.[15] The display of expensive materials, dishes, as well as the rare and dan-

---

11. M. Lämmer, "Die Kaiserspiele von Caesarea im Dienste der Politik des Königs Herodes," *JDSK,* 1974, p. 99; Lämmer, "Griechische Wettkämpfe," pp. 206-7; E. Paltiel, *Vassals and Rebels in the Roman Empire: Julio-Claudian Policies in Judaea and the Kingdoms of the East,* CL 212 (Brussels: Latomus, 1991), p. 70.

12. See M. L. Fischer and A. Stein, "Josephus on the Use of Marble in Building Projects of Herod the Great," *JJS* 44 (1994): 79-85.

13. See on that topic M. Junkelmann, "Familia Gladiatoria: Die Helden des Amphitheaters," in *Caesaren und Gladiatoren: Die Macht der Unterhaltung im antiken Rom,* ed. E. Köhne and C. Ewigleben (Mainz: Philipp von Zabern, 2000), pp. 77-79.

14. See Lichtenberger, *Baupolitik,* pp. 126-27.

15. For the demonstration of wealth and splendor in the Hellenistic presentation of royalty, cf. J. Tondriau, "La Tryphé, philosophie royale ptolémaique," *REA* 50 (1948): 49-54; C. Préaux, *Le monde hellénistique: La Grèce et l'Orient de la mort d'Alexandre à la conquête romaine de la Grèce (323-146 av. J.-C.),* Nouvelle Clio 6 (Paris: Presses Universitaires de France, 1978), 1:208-12; H. Heinen, "Die Tryphē des Ptolemaios VIII. Euergetes II. Beobachtungen zum ptolemäischen Herrscherideal und zu einer römischen Gesandtschaft in Ägypten (140/39 v. Chr.)," in

gerous exotic animals was designed to impress the audience. This is reminiscent of the display tables of Hellenistic kings at symposia and the procession of Ptolemy Philadelphos II in Alexandria in which he presented these kinds of objects and animals.[16] With this *conspicuous consumption,* Herod placed himself within the tradition of Hellenistic kings, a tradition he also took up with the maintenance of his court and his construction projects.[17] He invited an international audience of spectators and participants and thereby won kingly prestige that was intended to have an effect on his subjects as well as the inhabitants of the Roman Empire, and certainly not least of all, on Rome itself. While he accomplished this with the international guests, the event was resisted by the Jewish population of Jerusalem.

Though the participants and visitors, the kinds of games and prizes, the objects of splendor presented at the event, and the conflict with Jewish spectators are depicted in a detailed fashion, every kind of reference to the architecture of the theater and the amphitheater is lacking in Josephus's account. In the following, I will present arguments for the assertion that both buildings were only temporary, i.e., wooden constructions erected for the occasion of the games and torn down afterward.

To begin, it is necessary to review briefly the status of research on the matter. As far back as I can retrace, the permanent existence of the theater and the amphitheater is not doubted, except in a noteworthy study by A. L. Hirt (1819) that, in this respect, has received no response.[18] "Permanent" here means stone

---

Althistorische Studien: Hermann Bengtson zum 70. Geburtstag dargebracht von Kollegen und Schülern, ed. H. Heinen, Historia. Einzelschriften 40 (Wiesbaden: Steiner, 1983), pp. 116-28. Concerning Herod, cf. D. M. Jacobson, "King Herod's 'Heroic' Public Image," *RB* 95 (1988): 386-403; Lichtenberger, *Baupolitik,* passim.

16. For more information on the display tables of Hellenistic rulers, see F. Studniczka, *Das Symposion Ptolemaios II: Nach der Beschreibung des Kallixeinos wiederhergestellt* (Leipzig: Teubner, 1914), pp. 162-69; G. Zimmer, "Prunkgeschirr hellenistischer Herrscher," in *Basileia: Die Paläste der hellenistischen Könige. Internationales Symposion in Berlin vom 16.12.1992 bis 20.12.1992,* ed. W. Hoepfner and G. Brands, SSKA (Mainz: Philipp von Zabern, 1996), pp. 130-35. Concerning the procession of Ptolemy II Philadelphos, see Studniczka, *Das Symposion Ptolemaios II;* E. E. Rice, *The Grand Procession of Ptolemy Philadelphus* (Oxford: Oxford University Press, 1983); J. Köhler, *Pompai. Untersuchungen zur hellenistischen Festkultur,* EH XXXVIII/ 61 (Frankfurt: Peter Lang, 1996), pp. 35-45. For more on the animals, see Athenaeus 5.200; Diodorus 3.36-37; Rice, pp. 82-99; Köhler, pp. 106-7.

17. Regarding conspicuous consumption, see T. Veblen, *The Theory of the Leisure Class: An Economic Study of Institutions* (New York: Random House, 1899). For more on Herod, see Lichtenberger, *Baupolitik,* passim; Japp, *Baupolitik,* passim.

18. A. L. Hirt, "Ueber die Baue Herodes des Großen überhaupt, und über seinen Tempelbau in Jerusalem ins besondere," in *Abhandlungen der historisch-philologischen Klasse der Königlich-Preußischen Akademie der Wissenschaften aus dem Jahre 1816-1817* (Berlin: Realschul-

buildings that lasted longer than the games described, and that were possibly used further. Hirt came to the conclusion that both buildings were constructed of wood.

The majority of scholars do not doubt that there were a theater and amphitheater from Herod over a long period of time in Jerusalem. The authors do not always write explicitly that these were stone constructions because they often seem not to be aware of the possibility of a temporary construction. Yet, in topographical descriptions of the city, for example, from the Herodian period or that of the Second Temple, the theater and the amphitheater are treated in such a way that the authors seem to presume that the buildings were designed as permanent constructions. The following authors believe in such an existence of both buildings: F. de Saulcy, C. Schick, Schürer, G. A. Smith, G. Dalman, C. Watzinger, L.-H. Vincent and M.-A. Steve, M. Avi-Yonah, A. Schalit, K. M. Kenyon, B. Mazar, N. Avigad, T. A. Busink, E. Netzer, W. H. Mare, L. L. Grabbe, K. Bieberstein and H. Bloedhorn, A. Segal, D. W. Roller, P. Richardson, M. Hengel, as well as L. I. Levine.[19] Some authors think the theater fell into de-

Buchhandlung, 1819), p. 6. After the completion of this paper in 2000, an article was published by J. Patrich in which he also argued that there did not exist a Herodian theater of stone in Jerusalem: J. Patrich, "Herod's Theater in Jerusalem: A New Proposal," *IEJ* 52 (2002): 231-39. But see already Lichtenberger, *Baupolitik*, pp. 78-79.

19. F. de Saulcy, *Jerusalem* (Paris: Vve A. Morel et Cie, éditeurs, 1882), pp. 167-71; C. Schick, "Herod's Amphitheater," *PEQ* 19 (1887): 161-66; E. Schürer, *Die Geschichte des jüdischen Volkes im Zeitalter Jesu Christi* (Leipzig: J. C. Hinrichs'sche Buchhandlung, 1901), 1:387-88; Schürer, *The History of the Jewish People in the Age of Jesus Christ (175 B.C.–A.D. 135)*, rev. and ed. G. Vermes and F. Millar (Edinburgh: T. & T. Clark, 1973), 1:304; G. A. Smith, *Jerusalem: The Topography, Economics, and History from the Earliest Times to A.D. 70* (London: Hodder and Stoughton, 1908), 2:492-94; G. Dalman, *Jerusalem und sein Gelände* (Gütersloh: Mohn, 1930), pp. 149-50; C. Watzinger, *Denkmäler Palästinas: Eine Einführung in die Archäologie des heiligen Landes* (Leipzig: J. C. Hinrichs'sche Buchhandlung, 1935), 2:31; L.-H. Vincent and M.-A. Steve, *Jérusalem de l'ancien testament. Recherches d'Archéologie et d'histoire* (Paris: Lecoffre, 1956), pp. 708-9; Y. Aharoni and M. Avi-Yonah, *The Macmillan Bible Atlas* (New York: Macmillan, 1968), p. 139; Schalit, *König Herodes*, pp. 370-71; K. M. Kenyon, *Digging Up Jerusalem* (London: Ernest Benn, 1974), p. 207; B. Mazar, *The Mountain of the Lord* (New York: Doubleday, 1975), pp. 215-56; N. Avigad, *Discovering Jerusalem* (Nashville: Nelson, 1980), p. 81; T. A. Busink, *Der Tempel von Jerusalem. Von Salomo bis Herodes: Eine archäologisch-historische Studie unter Berücksichtigung des westsemitischen Tempelbaus* (Leiden: Brill, 1980), 2:1021-22; E. Netzer, "Herod's Building Projects: State Necessity or Personal Need?" *Jerusalem Cathedra* 1 (1981): 49, 59; W. H. Mare, *The Archaeology of the Jerusalem Area* (Grand Rapids: Baker, 1987), p. 140; L. L. Grabbe, *Judaism from Cyrus to Hadrian* (Minneapolis: Fortress, 1992), p. 356; K. Bieberstein and H. Bloedhorn, *Jerusalem: Grundzüge der Baugeschichte vom Chalkolithikum bis zur Frühzeit der osmanischen Herrschaft*, BTAVO B100/3 (Wiesbaden: Dr. Ludwig Reichert, 1994), 3:400-401; A. Segal, *Theaters in Roman Palestine and Provincia Arabia*, Mnemosyne 140 (Leiden: Brill, 1995), p. 4; D. W. Roller, *The Building Program of Herod the Great* (Berkeley: University of California Press, 1998), p. 178;

cay after Herod's death and would like to explain the silence of the later sources based on that.[20] In their view, both buildings fit in well with Herod's Hellenizing endeavors. This is true: Herod must be seen as one of the pioneers of theater construction in the ancient Near East.[21] A stone theater in Caesarea and one in the context of the royal palace in Jericho can also be shown as being from him.[22] These two theaters are the oldest archaeologically documented theater buildings in the Near East.[23]

There is much disagreement in the literature on the location of the buildings in Jerusalem. Because of the lack of archaeological evidence and Josephus's scanty description, it is wide open to speculation where the theater was located in Jerusalem, and what was meant by "in the plain" for the location of the amphitheater. De Saulcy tried to identify an *opus reticulatum* building north of the Damascus Gate as the theater.[24] But this building is most likely a Herodian funeral monument.[25] The location of the theater that has found the most adherents is that of Schick, who places it in a descending slope in Wadi Yasul, southwest of the Kidron Valley.[26] This view was agreed to, for example, by Schürer, Smith, Schalit, Busink, and Richardson,[27] although Dalman had already explained the evidence as a natural descending valley,[28] and archaeological investigations there of more recent years have resulted in nothing pointing to a the-

Richardson, *Herod*, pp. 186-87, 223-24; M. Hengel, "Jerusalem als jüdische und hellenistische Stadt," in *Judaica, Hellenistica et Christiana: Kleine Schriften II*, WUNT 109 (Tübingen: Mohr-Siebeck, 1999), p. 145; L. I. Levine, "Second Temple Jerusalem: A Jewish City in the Greco-Roman Orbit," in *Jerusalem: Its Sanctity and Centrality to Judaism, Christianity, and Islam* (New York: Continuum, 1999), p. 63.

20. Segal, *Theaters*, p. 4.

21. See also Japp, *Baupolitik*, p. 25.

22. For more information on Caesarea see A. Frova et al., *Scavi di Caesarea Maritima* (Rome: L'Erma di Bretschneider, 1966), pp. 157-234, and Segal, *Theaters*, pp. 64-69. For more on Jericho see E. Netzer, *Die Paläste der Hasmonäer und Herodes' des Großen* (Mainz: Philipp von Zabern, 1999), pp. 56-59. See, though, H.-P. Kuhnen's critical remarks in *Palästina in griechisch-römischer Zeit*, HA II/2 (Munich: Beck, 1990), p. 202. Patrich, "Herod's Theater in Jerusalem," pp. 236-37, thinks even the theater in Jericho was partly constructed of wood.

23. On the theaters in Palestine, see Kuhnen, *Palästina*, pp. 193-202; Segal, *Theaters in Roman Palestine and Provincia Arabia*; Weiss, "Buildings for Entertainment," pp. 79-85.

24. De Saulcy, *Jerusalem*, pp. 167-71.

25. E. Netzer and S. Ben-Arieh, "Remains of an Opus Reticulatum Building in Jerusalem," *IEJ* 33 (1983): 163-75; S. Bonato-Baccari, "Le mausolée en *opus reticulatum* de Jérusalem: tombeau d'Hérode ou simple témoin d'un modèle romain?" *Latomus* 61 (2002): 67-87.

26. Schick, "Herod's Amphitheater," pp. 161-66.

27. E. Schürer, *Geschichte*, p. 388 n. 58; Schürer, *History*, pp. 304-5 n. 56; Smith, *Jerusalem*, p. 493; Schalit, *König Herodes*, pp. 370-71; Busink, *Tempel*, p. 1021; Richardson, *Herod*, pp. 186-87.

28. Dalman, *Jerusalem*, pp. 149-50.

ater.[29] Dalman thought the theater was at the southeastern slope of the Upper City in the area of the Hasmonean royal palaces in the Kidron Valley[30] — a thesis followed by Avi-Yonah, and thus the theater appears there in the model of Jerusalem in the Holyland Hotel and on the map of the Macmillan Bible atlas.[31] Again, for this location there is no supporting archaeological evidence.[32]

Regarding the amphitheater, there are only a few suggestions as to its location, and Josephus's reference to the plain appears to be accurate in placing it outside of Jerusalem — for example, in front of the city (Richardson), in Jericho (Dalman), or in Caesarea (Bieberstein/Bloedhorn).[33] Nevertheless, other suggestions have placed the amphitheater within Jerusalem, as is illustrated in the first edition of the Macmillan Bible atlas and in the model of Jerusalem in the Holyland Hotel. There the amphitheater is located south of the Temple in the Tyropoion Valley.[34] Still, all these considerations do not find any confirmation in the archaeological record. Therefore, it must be emphasized that until now there is no proof of a Herodian theater and a Herodian amphitheater in the archaeological record. Two pieces of archaeological evidence have however been brought out in support of a Herodian theater in Jerusalem. These deal with possible theater seats and with presumed theater tickets.

Recently excavated, a group of clear-cut elevated stone blocks, built into an Umayyad building on the southwest side of the Temple as spoils, have been interpreted by R. Reich and Y. Billig as theater seats.[35] These are supposed to

29. *Hadashot Arkheologiyot* 5 (1974): 15. See also R. Reich and Y. Billig, "Excavations near the Temple Mount and Robinson's Arch, 1994-1996: Appendix; A Group of Theater Seats from Jerusalem," in *Ancient Jerusalem Revealed*, ed. H. Geva (Jerusalem: Israel Exploration Society, 2000), p. 352; "A Group of Theater Seats Discovered Near the South-Western Corner of the Temple Mount," *IEJ* 50 (2000): 182.

30. Dalman, *Jerusalem*, p. 150.

31. Aharoni and Avi-Yonah, *The Macmillan Bible Atlas*, p. 139; M. Avi-Yonah, *Das Modell des alten Jerusalem zur Zeit des Zweiten Tempels auf dem Gelände des Holyland Hotels in Jerusalem* (Herzlia: Palphot, n.d.), pp. 5, 16-17, 20. See also D. Bahat, *Carta's Historical Atlas of Jerusalem: A Brief Illustrated Survey* (Jerusalem: Carta, 1973), p. 13.

32. Bieberstein and Bloedhorn, *Jerusalem*, pp. 400-401; Reich and Billig, "A Group," pp. 182-83.

33. Richardson, *Herod*, p. 187; Dalman, *Jerusalem*, p. 149; Bieberstein and Bloedhorn, *Jerusalem*, p. 401; see also J. Patrich, "On the Lost Circus of *Aelia Capitolina*," *SCI* 21 (2002): 185-86.

34. Aharoni and Avi-Yonah, *The Macmillan Bible Atlas*, p. 139; Avi-Yonah, *Das Modell*, pp. 5, 21-22. See also Bahat, *Carta's*, p. 13. Locating the amphitheater in the Tyropoion Valley goes back, presumably, to the excavations performed by K. Kenyon, who assumed the amphitheater was there. However, this has not been confirmed. The revised edition of the Bible atlas again deleted the hippodrome. See Y. Aharoni and M. Avi-Yonah, *The Macmillan Bible Atlas*, rev. ed. (New York: Macmillan, 1977), p. 149.

35. Reich and Billig, "Excavations," pp. 350-52; "A Group," pp. 175-84.

have been part of a stone theater located in this region, although the excavators do not want to decide if the seats stem from the Herodian theater or from Hadrian's theater in Jerusalem mentioned in the Chronicon Paschale.[36] On top of one of the seats were carved the Greek letters ΔI, and on another ΔIO. Reich and Billig interpret ΔI as number fourteen in the Greek numerals alphabet, and in their view it designates a specific row or group of rows in the theater.[37] Although the stone seats have so far been published only in a brief preliminary report, their identification as the seats of a theater-like building appears to be correct. As such, they could have been used in any round building, e.g., in theaters, *odeia*, amphitheaters, circuses, stadia, or *bouleutēria*.[38] In case they stem from a theater, we have to check if the theater could have been that of Herod.

The only possible reference for dating the seats is their defined shape. They have a simple profile and hang out over the front. At the point where the seats once met the stairs of the "theater," the upper part of the profile breaks off at the bottom and is led down the steps sideways.[39] If one tries to look for examples to compare with this detail, one cannot observe it at the Herodian theater in Caesarea Maritima. There (as is typical for Hellenistic theaters) the horizontal profile runs straight to the steps of the stairs, and this is also found in the south theater in Gerasa, begun in the later part of the first century C.E. The same is true for the large theater of the early imperial period in Petra, which because it was hewn directly out of the rock, can only be compared with caution.[40] We find the bent profile (which is characteristic for the Jerusalem seats) in the theater in Philadelphia-Amman, which is probably from the time of

36. Chronicon Paschale P254. See on the theater and circus of Aelia Capitolina: Patrich, "Lost Circus," pp. 173-88. On Aelia Capitolina see now N. Belayche, *Iudaea-Palaestina: The Pagan Cults in Roman Palestine (Second to Fourth Century)*, RRP 1 (Tübingen: Mohr-Siebeck, 2001), pp. 108-70 (for the theater see p. 135).

37. Reich and Billig, "A Group," p. 181.

38. For the different types of buildings in which such seats could have been used, see P. Gros, *L'architecture romaine du début du IIIᵉ siècle av. J.-C. à la fin du Haut-Empire*. Vol. 1, *Les monuments publics* (Paris: Picard, 1996), pp. 272-361. For the *bouleutēria* see also D. Gneisz, *Das antike Rathaus. Das griechische Bouleuterion und die frührömische Curia* (Vienna: Verlag der wissenschaftlichen Gesellschaften Österreichs, 1990).

39. This detail does seem to be incorrect in the reconstruction by Reich and Billig, "Excavations," p. 352; "A Group," p. 181, fig. 6.

40. On Caesarea see Frova et al., *Scavi*, p. 80, illus. 52; p. 191, illus. 232. On Gerasa see I. Browning, *Jerash and the Decapolis* (London: Chatto and Windus, 1982), p. 127, illus. 62. The large theater in Petra from the early imperial period has no profile at all. See P. C. Hammond, *The Excavation of the Main Theater at Petra, 1961-1962: Final Report* (London: Bernhard Quaritch, 1965).

Antoninus Pius,[41] as well as in the Amman-Odeion (second century C.E.),[42] in the *odeion* of Canatha (second century C.E.?),[43] in the theater of Bosra (second century C.E.),[44] in the Severan theater in Nysa-Scythopolis,[45] and in the Severan theater in Samaria-Sebaste.[46] Thus this detail seems to indicate that in Jerusalem we are hardly dealing with a Herodian edifice, but instead, the seats point to a building, at the earliest, from the second century C.E. The theater of Aelia Capitolina named in the Chronicon Paschale, for example, must be considered here, though an *odeion,* a *bouleutērion,* or another building with round seating structures is also possible.[47] As we know very little about theater buildings in the Hellenized East during the early imperial period, the shape of the seats alone is inadequate to date them.[48] This also means the seats found by Reich and Billig in Jerusalem cannot be used as an argument for a Herodian stone theater in Jerusalem. Instead, it is much more likely that they stem from a second- or third-century building.

We mention only in passing the discovery of two so-called theater tickets from the Second Temple period in the Avigad Excavations in the Upper City of Jerusalem. In the excavations, two ornamented bone disks were found.[49] Their identification as theater tickets, and thus as an indirect reference to a permanent theater in

41. H. C. Butler, *Syria: Publications of the Princeton University Archaeological Expedition to Syria in 1904-5 and 1909; IIA* (Leiden: Brill, 1919), pl. IV; F. el-Fakharani, "Das Theater von Amman in Jordanien," *AA* (1975): 381, illus. 4 (for a different dating of the theater, cf. pp. 400-402); Segal, *Theaters,* pp. 82-85.

42. Butler, *Syria,* p. 51, illus. 34; Alastair Northedge, "Archaeological Topography," in *Studies on Roman and Islamic Amman, I: History, Site, and Architecture,* ed. A. Northedge, BAMA 3 (Oxford: Oxford University Press, 1992), p. 58.

43. Butler, *Syria,* p. 351, illus. 316; Segal, *Theaters,* pp. 43-44.

44. R. E. Brünnow and A. v. Domaszewski, *Die Provincia Arabia* (Strassburg: Verlag von Karl J. Trabner, 1909), 3:74-75, illus. 971, 973; Segal, *Theaters,* pp. 53-55.

45. S. Applebaum, "The Roman Theater of Scythopolis," *SCI* 4 (1978): 99.

46. J. W. Crowfoot, K. M. Kenyon, and E. L. Sukenik, *The Buildings at Samaria* (London: Palestine Exploration Society, 1942), p. 59, illus. 25.

47. The Chronicon Paschale P254 not only attributes a theater to Aelia Capitolina, but also gives the account of the construction of two public buildings *(dēmosia).* The rows of seats could also be from one of these buildings.

48. See El-Fakharani, "Theater," pp. 400-402, for an example of what it would look like to date the theater in Philadelphia in the last quarter of the first century B.C.E. This is criticized by F. Zayadine, "Amman," *MdB* 22 (1982): 27, who argues for a dating in the time of Antoninus Pius. See as well the dating of the capitals in the mid–second century C.E. by E. Frézouls, "Recherches sur les théatres de l'orient syrien I," *Syria* 36 (1959): 225.

49. Avigad, *Discovering Jerusalem,* pp. 193-94; p. 200, illus. 239; *The Herodian Quarter in Jerusalem: Wohl Archaeological Museum* (Jerusalem: Keter, 1991), p. 65. See the designation as "theater tickets" by Reich and Billig, "Excavations," p. 352; "A Group," p. 181.

Second Temple Jerusalem, can certainly be ruled out because both pieces (as E. Alföldi-Rosenbaum showed for the entire group) were clearly used as playing stone pieces for a board game and have nothing at all to do with the theater.[50]

In summary, we can say that we have neither a direct nor an indirect reference to a stone theater building or a permanent amphitheater during the Herodian period in Jerusalem.

What then about nonstone theater buildings in the Roman Empire during the early imperial period? Though there were numerous stone theaters in Greece, Asia Minor, and southern Italy, even in the Hellenistic age, a stone theater was built in Rome for the first time by Pompey the Great in 55 B.C.E.[51] Before that, all theater buildings in Rome were temporary structures made of wood, erected on the occasion of the festival games. Details on the building of the temporary theater of Scaurus in Rome in 58 B.C.E., shortly before the building of the theater of Pompey, are related: the theater is said to have had seats for 80,000 and fantastic decor and costumes for display.[52] Even after the building of the theater of Pompey, there were wooden theater buildings. One is attested in Rome in 17 B.C.E.,[53] and outside Rome, another is attested later.[54] In the context of the *ludi saeculares,* a *theatrum ligneum* is still mentioned in 204 C.E. in Rome.[55] Also,

---

50. E. Alföldi-Rosenbaum, "The Finger Calculus in Antiquity and in the Middle Ages: Studies on Roman Game Counters I," *FMSt* 5 (1971): 1-9. See here also the history of research on the subject. See also Avigad, *Discovering Jerusalem,* pp. 193-94. Reich and Billig, "A Group," p. 181, interpret the Greek letters ΔI on the theater seats as the Greek number fourteen. Because the bone disks have the Latin number fourteen (XIIII) and the Greek number fourteen (ΔI) as well, Reich and Billig think the correspondence proves that the bone disks must be theater tickets. Apart from the fact that game counters cannot be interpreted as theater tickets, it is not very probable that by chance exactly one out of two preserved seats that might show the number fourteen coincides with the bone disks. Besides, the letters ΔIO on another seat, which are only one more letter, can hardly be understood as a Greek number, so that even the interpretation of the ΔI as fourteen remains doubtful. On the Greek numerals alphabet cf. W. Larfeld, *Griechische Epigraphik,* HAlt I.5 (Munich: Beck, 1914), p. 293.

51. See A. Rumpf's thorough study, "Die Entstehung des römischen Theaters," *MDAI* 3 (1950): 40-50. See also M. Fuchs, *Untersuchungen zur Ausstattung römischer Theater in Italien und den Westprovinzen des Imperium Romanum* (Mainz: Philipp von Zabern, 1987), pp. 2-11; R. C. Beacham, *The Roman Theater and Its Audience* (London: Routledge, 1991), pp. 56-84; Gros, *L'architecture,* pp. 274-75; Patrich, "Herod's Theater in Jerusalem," pp. 233-35.

52. Pliny, *Natural History* 36.114. On the theater see also Rumpf, "Entstehung," pp. 47-48; Fuchs, *Untersuchungen,* p. 4; Köhler, *Pompai,* p. 102.

53. *ILS* 5050 (108), (154), (156). See Rumpf, "Entstehung," pp. 45-46; Fuchs, *Untersuchungen,* pp. 4-5.

54. *CIL* XIII 1642. See Rumpf, "Entstehung," p. 45; Fuchs, *Untersuchungen,* p. 5.

55. See H. Erkell, "Ludi saeculares und ludi Latini saeculares. Ein Beitrag zur römischen Theaterkunde und Religionsgeschichte," *Eranos* 67 (1969): 166-74.

Nero had a wooden amphitheater erected.[56] These buildings were by no means primitive wooden sheds, but complex and magnificent works of architecture.

The reason for the construction of temporary architecture in Rome was neither to save money[57] nor to reject Hellenistic culture, but, as A. Rumpf showed, because a permanent stone theater could serve as a place of public assembly outside the time of the games, and this was something Rome's Republican aristocrats were quite suspicious of.[58]

Also, in the classical and Hellenistic Greek world, temporary architecture, specially constructed for a festival, was not unusual. Particularly Hellenistic rulers erected splendid tents and magnificent ships of a temporary nature often as grand, costly displays.[59]

For Herod the Great, the late Hellenistic client king of Rome, both poles of his politics, his orientation to Rome and the presentation of himself as a Hellenistic monarch, would be links for the building of temporary architecture. For him as a Hellenistic king, temporary architecture would have been appropriate for a demonstrative presentation of his wealth, and the wish to construct no building that people could use as a place for political assembly. The respect for Jewish interests and particularities must be seen as a third parameter for Herod's politics. The clearly evident reservations of Jewish groups over a theater in Josephus's description of the games may have been even greater over a permanent stone theater. Besides these general considerations, further evidence can be brought forward for postulating a temporary theater and a temporary amphitheater built by Herod in Jerusalem.

Though it is methodologically questionable to use arguments *e silentio,* Josephus's silence concerning a theater and amphitheater in Jerusalem in the time after the games must once again be pointed out. It is amazing that the buildings are not only missing in his otherwise detailed descriptions of Herod's building activity,[60] but also in the context of the Jewish War (66-70 c.e.) and the siege of Jerusalem. This is very conspicuous because we are informed about most of the buildings constructed in Jerusalem during the Second Temple pe-

---

56. Tacitus, *Ann* 13.13; Pliny, *Natural History* 19.24; Suetonius, *Nero* 12.

57. Quite the contrary, as Tacitus, in *Ann* 14.21, shows that temporary architecture was definitely more expensive in the long run.

58. Rumpf, "Entstehung," pp. 44-45; Beacham, *Roman Theater,* p. 159. For information on the theater as a place of public assembly, see F. Kolb, *Agora und Theater, Volks- und Festversammlung,* ArF 9 (Berlin: Gebr. Mann, 1981).

59. See here extensively Köhler, *Pompai,* pp. 99-104. On the ships see the Ptolemaic Thalamegos (Fritz Caspari, "Das Nilschiff Ptolemaios IV," *JdI* 31 [1916]: 1-74) and the ship of Hieron II of Syracuse (Athenaios 206e, 208f).

60. See, for example, *War* 1.21.1-13 §401-430; *Ant* 15.9.5 §326-330; 16.5.4 §150-159.

riod, especially by the historical works of Josephus. It is important to note that buildings and places mentioned by him in direct connection with the Jewish War and the occupation of the city considerably increase our knowledge of Jerusalem's topography. By this we learn about an archive, a *bouleutērion*, the graves of Alexander Jannaeus, that of the high priest Ananias, that of the royal house of Adiabene, that of Hyrcanus, as well as the so-called monument of Herod. Furthermore, descriptions of numerous markets and pools of water, the palace of the royal house of Adiabene, the xystos, and several other aspects of the topography of Jerusalem are then (and often only then) recorded.[61]

Of the buildings named by Josephus in the time of Herod the Great, only David's tomb, the royal tombs, the hippodrome, and the theater and amphitheater are missing in a later context of the Jewish War. Because the hippodrome was presumably identical to the xystos[62] and, moreover, was also part of the Hasmonean palace mentioned in the context of the Jewish War, there exists an even later reference to it. Josephus also does not mention David's tomb and the royal tombs anymore. But for them we can find further references. David's tomb and the royal tombs were presumably very closely connected to one another or identical buildings. Both are referred to in later sources: Acts 2:29 still mentions David's tomb and Cassius Dio records Solomon's tomb shortly before the Bar-Kokhba rebellion.[63] This means that *only* the theater and the amphitheater in Jerusalem disappear completely from the later records. This is amazing because these were certainly no small monuments and must have had strategic significance in the battle for the city if they existed in stone during the Jewish War.[64] Yet, not a word is mentioned about them. The silence of the sources indicates that the buildings did not exist in Jerusalem during the time of the Jewish War. This can only be explained by a complete demolition of stone buildings from which we know nothing and which we probably can exclude, or there never were such stone buildings at all.

If they were not of stone, they must have been of wood. In the Mishnah, *Abodah Zarah*, we find a reference to wood architecture in connection with the-

---

61. The individual passages in Josephus here have not been listed. See the indices in Flavius Josephus, *De Bello Judaico. Der Jüdische Krieg. Griechisch und Deutsch. Bd. III: Ergänzungen und Register*, ed. O. Michel and O. Bauernfeind (Munich: Kösel, 1969), pp. 102-9; Josephus, with an English translation by L. H. Feldman, *Jewish Antiquities*, vol. IX, *Books XVIII-XX, General Index to Volumes I-IX* (London: William Heinemann; Cambridge: Harvard University Press, 1965), pp. 708-09.

62. See Lichtenberger, *Baupolitik*, p. 75.

63. Cassius Dio 69.14.2. See Lichtenberger, *Baupolitik*, p. 155 n. 789.

64. On the military campaign of the conquest of Jerusalem, see J. J. Price, *Jerusalem under Siege: The Collapse of the Jewish State, 66-70 C.E.*, BSJS 3 (Leiden: Brill, 1992), pp. 115-74.

ater plays.[65] There, after a list of dangerous animals kept for agitation and hounding, the loanword *gradus* (for forbidden buildings) is used. *Gradus* can refer to temporary architecture for games,[66] and is used in this way by Tacitus (*Ann* 14.20) even as an opposite to the permanent (stone) theater buildings.[67] The mention of this kind of structure in the Mishnah, of course, cannot be connected to Herod the Great, but the loanword does show that it must also be expected in Israel. Sometimes only parts of theater buildings were made of wood, as can be seen with the theater of Sepphoris.[68] In general, wood as a material for building is very well attested in ancient Palestine during the Second Temple period.[69]

That Josephus, in contrast to many modern historians, was aware of the possibility that theaters did not have to be built of stone is seen in *War* 15.9.6 §341, where he speaks of Herod's buildings in Caesarea Maritima. He writes, "Herod . . . built a theater of stone"; and a Herodian stone theater in Caesarea has been confirmed by archaeology.[70] Emphasizing that Herod built a theater of stone *(ek petras)* only makes sense if there were theaters not made of stone. Otherwise, specifying it seems superfluous. Josephus's distinction is possibly directly related to the theater in Jerusalem because in the parallel account for the theater in Caesarea Maritima (in *War* 1.21.8 §415), the qualification, that it was built of stone, is missing. This can be explained by the fact that *War* does not at all mention the theater and the amphitheater in Jerusalem, and thus a more precise description of the different material of the theater of Caesarea was not yet necessary in *War*.

If one doesn't presume a stone theater behind every theater, then it is also understandable how Josephus could ascribe the building of a theater in Berytos to Agrippa I as well as to Agrippa II.[71] Although in the Near East we sometimes

65. *m. Abod. Zar.* 1.7.

66. See H. Blaufuss, *Aboda zara. Mischna und Tosefta. Übersetzt und mit vornehmlicher Berücksichtigung der Altertümer erklärt* (Nürnberg: Buchdruckerei von J. L. Stich, 1916), pp. 10, 54. G. A. Wewers translates *gradus* incorrectly as "Richtplatz": *Avoda Zara: Götzendienst übersetzt von Gerd A. Wewers*, UTY IV/7 (Tübingen: Mohr, 1980), p. 27. See as well D. Sperber, *A Dictionary of Greek and Latin Legal Terms in Rabbinic Literature*, DTMT 1 (Jerusalem: Bar-Ilan University Press, 1984), p. 77, who translates *gradus* incorrectly as "basilica for holding court procedures." See also Sperber, *The City*, p. 75.

67. See for that Gros, *L'architecture*, p. 274.

68. See Segal, *Theaters*, p. 42.

69. See for this G. Dalman, *Arbeit und Sitte in Palästina*, VII (Gütersloh: Bertelsmann, 1942), pp. 28-45, and for further literature A. Lichtenberger, "Architektur und Bauwesen," in *Neues Testament und Antike Kultur* 2, ed. K. Erlemann et al. (Neukirchen-Vluyn: Neukirchener, 2004), pp. 199-205.

70. Frova et al., *Scavi*, pp. 57-234; Segal, *Theaters*, pp. 64-69.

71. *Ant* 19.7.5 §335; 20.9.4 §211. For that see also L. J. Hall, *Roman Berytus: Beirut in Late Antiquity* (London: Routledge, 2004), pp. 62-63.

find more than one theater in a city,[72] the building of Agrippa I may have been a wooden construction for onetime festival games (which are mentioned by Josephus in this context), and the theater founded by Agrippa II was possibly a stone theater in which games could be held annually. To me it seems quite unlikely that both kings gave money for such an expensive stone building in the same city.[73]

If one therefore presumes that Herod had a theater and an amphitheater built in Jerusalem only as temporary wooden constructions, then a number of problems are solved:

a. the lack of archaeological evidence for the buildings;
b. the silence of literary sources after the first mention of the buildings;
c. the emphasis of the stone construction of the Herodian theater of Caesarea;
d. the two-time theater construction under Agrippa I and Agrippa II in Berytos.

If one is furthermore reminded that theater buildings of wood in the Hellenistic and Roman world (as the Mishnah points out, even in the land of Israel) were common buildings, then we must conclude that Herod did not erect stone buildings in Jerusalem, but rather, built temporary contest facilities for the limited time of the festival games in honor of the emperor.

In the past few years, R. A. Batey has particularly taken up the old discussion whether or not Jesus could have visited the theater of Sepphoris.[74] Far-reaching

72. See, e.g., K. Butcher, *Roman Syria and the Near East* (London: British Museum Press, 2003), pp. 255-58.

73. For the donation of theaters by kings, see B. Schmidt-Dounas, *Geschenke erhalten die Freundschaft. Politik und Selbstdarstellung im Spiegel der Monumente* (Berlin: Akademie Verlag, 2000), pp. 61-68.

74. See R. A. Batey, "Jesus and the Theater," *NTS* 30 (1984): 563-74; Batey, *Jesus and the Forgotten City: New Light on Sepphoris and the Urban World of Jesus* (Grand Rapids: Baker, 1991), pp. 100-103. These ideas have primarily been met by rejection; see S. S. Miller, "Sepphoris the Well Remembered City," *BA* 55, no. 2 (1992): 76-78; L. H. Schiffman, review of *Jesus and the Forgotten City*, by R. A. Batey, *BA* 55, no. 2 (1992): 105-6; E. M. Meyers, "The Drawings of J. Robert Teringo in *Jesus and the Forgotten City*," *BA* 55, no. 2 (1992): 106-7; Meyers, "Roman Sepphoris in Light of New Archeological Evidence and Recent Research," in *The Galilee in Late Antiquity*, ed. L. I. Levine (Cambridge: Harvard University Press, 1992), p. 325; E. P. Sanders, "Jesus' Relation to Sepphoris," in *Sepphoris in Galilee: Crosscurrents of Culture*, ed. R. M. Nagy et al. (Raleigh: North Carolina Museum of Arts, 1996), pp. 75-79; J. L. Reed, *Archaeology and the Galilean Jesus: A Reexamination of the Evidence* (Harrisburg, Pa.: Trinity, 2000), pp. 120-21, with a good discussion of the history of research on the topic on pp. 104-8. [Also, see Batey's chapter in the present collection. — JHC.]

consequences for the cultural influence on Jesus and his use of the term *hypokritēs,* for which (in the opinion of Batey) Jesus had (as in the classical Greek usage) actors directly in view, have been postulated. Batey even imagines Jesus having visited the theater in Jerusalem as a twelve-year-old.[75] Apart from the fact that it is uncertain which word in which language Jesus could have used to attack his opponents, it seems that in literature contemporary to the Gospels the term *hypokritēs* was not limited to its technical meaning, and was used, for example, by Philo and Josephus and, especially, in the Septuagint already in a figurative sense.[76] The use of *hypokritēs* in the Gospels is thus tied to the Jewish use of language; deriving it directly from Greek theater terminology is unfounded. The discussion concerning the theater of Sepphoris seems also to have ended, in that it is likely it was built, at the earliest, in the late first century c.e., and therefore did not yet exist at the time of Jesus.[77] A history of Jesus and the theater thus cannot be written from this; while the stone theater in Sepphoris did not yet exist in Jesus' day, the wooden Herodian theater in Jerusalem was no more.

It is always more dangerous to dispute the hidden existence of something nonexistent than to postulate the existence of something nonexistent as invisible yet existent. While the latter position in theory can never be disproven with certainty, the former can not only never be proven with certainty, it is also in danger of one day being disproven by an archaeological discovery. The theoretical possibility that one day, in fact, a Herodian stone theater and a stone amphitheater will be found in Jerusalem must be pointed to. Still, this may not lead to an uncritical treatment of the sources. According to the present status of the sources available to us, there is no sufficient indication that Herod the Great built a permanent theater and a permanent amphitheater in Jerusalem. Everything we can derive from the sources speaks for the fact that Herod erected temporary wooden facilities for the contests dedicated to the emperor, which did not last longer than the games. In the Jerusalem of Jesus' day, there were no longer a theater and an amphitheater.

75. Batey, *Jesus,* p. 92.

76. U. Wilckens, ὑποκρίνομαι, in *TWNT* 8 (1969), pp. 558-68; H. Giesen, ὑπόκρισις, in *EWNT* 3 (1983), pp. 963-66.

77. See Meyers, "Roman Sepphoris," p. 325; Z. Weiss and E. Netzer, "Architectural Development of Sepphoris during the Roman and Byzantine Periods," in *Archaeology and the Galilee: Texts and Contexts in the Graeco-Roman and Byzantine Periods,* ed. D. R. Edwards and C. T. McCollough, SFSHJ 143 (Atlanta: Scholars, 1997), pp. 121-22; Reed, *Archaeology,* p. 120. The chronology of J. F. Strange is not convincing: J. F. Strange, "Six Campaigns at Sepphoris: The University of South Florida Excavations, 1983-1989," in *The Galilee in Late Antiquity,* p. 342. But see also M. A. Chancey, *The Myth of a Gentile Galilee,* SNTSMS 118 (Cambridge: Cambridge University Press, 2002), pp. 74-75, who leaves open the possibility that the theater of Sepphoris was already built in early Roman times. [Also, see the discussion by Charlesworth in the present collection. — JHC.]

Jesus and the Herodian Temple Mount

Dan Bahat

The Temple Mount played as important a role in Jesus' life in Jerusalem as it played in Jewish life altogether. The Gospels have valuable references to the Temple Mount, which may cast light on some queries pertaining to the topography and history of the Mount. There is no differentiation in the Gospels and Acts between the Temple Mount and the Temple proper. No doubt, the reference to the Temple in Jn 2:19-20 is to the Temple Mount and not to the Temple.

The excavations carried out along the Western Wall of the Temple's precinct show that Herod the Great did not bring the construction of its retaining walls to an end.[1] According to Josephus, Herod started to build the Temple in his fifteenth[2] or eighteenth regnal year,[3] namely, somewhere between 22 and 20 B.C.E. According to Jn 2:20, it took forty-six years to build the Temple. His reference, then, should be to about 26 C.E., when works had not yet terminated. There is no way to prove that the Temple itself was never finished, but the works on the Temple Mount definitely were not accomplished, as may be seen on the northern end of the Western Wall (in the Tunnels).[4] Hence it is clear that at least in the case of John, the Gospel speaks about the Mount and not the Temple, although John uses the word "Temple."

Several activities of Jesus took place in the Temple precincts (Mt 21:12, 23; 24:1; 26:55; Mk 11:15, 27; 12:35; 13:1-4; 14:49; etc.), and we need to clarify the precise location of these events. To cast light on the quest for the various sites mentioned in the Gospels, we have to understand the division of the Temple Mount area into sections where the events could have taken place.

---

1. See D. Bahat, "The Western Wall Tunnels," in *Ancient Jerusalem Revealed* (Jerusalem: Israel Exploration Society, 1994), pp. 177-90.

2. Josephus, *War* 1.401.

3. Josephus, *Ant* 15.380.

4. For a different opinion about the completion of the construction works of the Temple, see J. Jeremias, *Jerusalem in the Time of Jesus* (Philadelphia: Fortress, 1977), pp. 21-22.

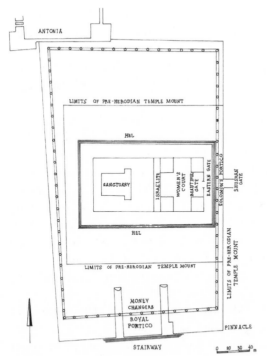

Figure 50. The Temple Mount.

Courtesy of D. Bahat

Solomon's Portico (Jn 10:22-23) and the Beautiful Gate (Acts 3:2)

Scholars who deal with the development of the Herodian Temple Mount agree that the eastern wall is the oldest one.[5] Josephus, who maintained that the eastern wall was built first, also reports this.[6] Since it was older than the other walls, it also looked different at that time: it was lower, presumably to enable the priest who burnt the red heifer on top of the Mount of Olives to see the entrance to the Temple when the blood was sprinkled.[7] We may thus understand that the eastern wall could not achieve the greatness of the other Herodian porticos. Since it was very old when the works of Josephus and the Gospels were written, the contemporary name given to the portico was Solomon's Portico, which most presumed was built by Solomon.[8] Surprisingly the name Solo-

5. For an extreme opinion, see most recently E.-M. Laperrousaz, *Les temples de Jérusalem* (Paris: Paris-Médit, 1999). By "extreme," I mean his opinion that the eastern wall was indeed built by King Solomon, an opinion that is difficult to accept. See there pp. 35-41, and elsewhere in that book.

6. Josephus, *War* 5.184.

7. *Middoth* 2.4 and Josephus, *Ant* 20.219-220.

8. See F. J. Hollis, *The Archeology of Herod's Temple* (London: Dent, 1934), p. 107 and n. 1.

mon's Portico is not mentioned in the Mishnah but only in the Gospels and Josephus.[9] This may prove that unlike the other two sources, the Mishnah speaks about the pre-Herodian Temple Mount, when all four porticos were of the same character. The description in the Gospel, then, will tell us that the Jews surrounded Jesus when he was walking in the eastern portico of the Temple Mount,[10] namely, Solomon's Portico.

In the eastern wall of the Mount there was one gate only "on which was portrayed the palace of Shushan."[11] This gate is not the gate named in Acts as *Beautiful*.[12] The identification of the Beautiful Gate underwent many vicissitudes, and the Golden Gate as well as the Gate of the Chain (both being gates of the Temple Mount) are usually identified with it.[13] The view that the gate referred to in Acts 3:2 is not the Shushan Gate follows from the fact that it only served the priests going to the Mount of Olives for the sacrifice of the red heifer, and therefore a beggar would not sit there, as almost no one went through there. The event in Acts took place in the eastern gate of the Women's Court, which was the main thoroughfare for every visitor to the Temple, and not in the eastern wall of the Mount.

This gate is referred to in the Mishnah as the Eastern Gate;[14] it speaks of the old Rabban Gamaliel standing "at the Eastern Gate."[15] It seems that there was a gathering place at the gate named Beautiful (in Acts). The importance of this gate may be deduced by the following reference: "A man should not behave himself unseemly while opposite the Eastern Gate."[16] I cannot say where the name Beautiful in the Gospels comes from, but as said, its prominence over the other gates of the Temple is clear.[17]

9. J. Simons, *Jerusalem in the Old Testament* (Leiden: Brill, 1952), pp. 402, 421.

10. Here again, John speaks about the portico while referring to the Temple, and it is clear that it is a reference to the Temple Mount.

11. *Middoth* 1.3. Shushan is the ancient Persian capital (= Susa in Greek).

12. In the Vulgate, *speciosa*; in the Greek, *hōraia*.

13. It is beyond the scope of the present paper to discuss the premedieval and medieval identifications of the gate (and see n. 17 below).

14. In *m. Soṭa* 1.5 the Eastern Gate is the gate between the Women's Court and the Court of the Israelites. In *Tamid* 5.6 it seems to refer to the eastern gate of the Women's Court, as there were impure standing.

15. *'Orla* 2.12.

16. *Berakot* 9.5.

17. The earliest known Christian pilgrim visiting Jerusalem — the anonymous Pilgrim of Bordeaux — is the first to mention the Beautiful Gate in the eastern wall of the Mount. See D. Baldi, *Enchiridion Locorum Sanctorum* (Jerusalem: Franciscan Printing Press, 1935), p. 539. Since the Golden Gate was not built yet, it may refer to the remains of the Herodian (or rather the pre-Herodian) gate. The description of the older remains is repeated frequently by the pilgrims — but the most detailed one is that of the Pilgrim of Piacenza, who says of the remains,

The Gentiles Court

From Josephus we know that there were four degrees of purity with regard to the Temple and the people (besides women in the time of their impurity) who may approach it.[18] The outer court was open also to the Gentiles. The second court was allotted to the pure, men and women alike; the third was allowed to Israelite men only; the fourth to the priests; and the innermost only to the high priest. The Mishnah describes the degrees of holiness as follows:[19] The first court restriction refers to impure women and to people inflicted by various contagious diseases. The second court is bordered by the *Hel*, beyond which the Gentiles and the impure (by the impurity of a corpse) are not allowed. The third court is where Israelite men are allowed, and then comes the priests' court. When we juxtapose the description of Josephus to that of the Mishnah, it is clear that the Gentiles were allowed as far as the *Hel* only.

Since it is clear today that Josephus's description of the Herodian Temple is the most precise, one should note that he divides the Temple's courts into inner and outer courts, which does not comply with his previous description.[20] The passage from one court to the other was through a screen on which inscriptions, in Greek and Latin respectively, were installed. The inscriptions warned Gentiles against passing into the inner court.[21] From his other description we may assume that Gentiles could go only into the outer court. According to the Mishnah, they could go into the second court bordered by the *Hel*. From this we may conclude that the outer court of Josephus is the same as the first and second courts of the Mishnah, and the inner court of Josephus stands for the women's and Israelites' courts of the Mishnah. The priests' court is the innermost. According to Josephus, the final phase of construction of the Temple's platform was the addition of more area to the existing platform from three sides.[22] His statement may be understood if he is claiming that the three sides form an addition to the eastern side. But this is not necessarily so, as his description is very specific about the northern side, which Herod annexed to the older platform. Josephus's description is perplexing, as it says the area enclosed in the screen is

---

"the threshold and the posts of the gate are still visible." For this see T. Tobler and A. Molinier, *Itinera Hierosolymitana* (Geneva: J. G. Fick, 1879; reprint, Osnabrueck, 1966), p. 101, chap. 17. The Golden Gate was constructed by Emperor Heraclius in 629-630 c.e. See also Simons, *Jerusalem*, p. 371 n. 3.

18. Josephus, *Apion* 2.103-105.

19. *m. Kelim* 1.8.

20. Josephus, *Ant* 15.380-425 and *War* 1.401-402; 5.184-227.

21. Josephus, *Ant* 15.417; *War* 5.193-194. Could this wall be the one mentioned in Eph 2:14?

22. Josephus, *War* 5.187.

named "holiness" and is reached by fourteen steps — which does not equal the Mishnaic *Hel,* which has, as is mentioned, twelve steps[23] — but it probably speaks of the same steps. Elsewhere,[24] the *Hel* is marked as the place where Gentiles and those contaminated by the impurity of the dead could not enter, and it marks the limits of the pre-Herodian Mount. Such an assumption may be deduced because the screen bearing the inscriptions was installed at the bottom of the steps composing a part of the *Hel.* This could create an impression that the *Hel* separates the outer and inner courts of Flavius; but intriguingly there is no mention of the inscriptions in the Mishnaic sources.[25] Josephus mentions the inner area of the Temple as *hieron,*[26] whereas when Titus pleaded with the Jews not to give him a reason to destroy the Temple, he said the inscriptions surrounded the area "of the holiness."[27] We may thus conclude that the *hieron* defines the Herodian extension.[28] According to Josephus, the screen bearing the inscription was made in a beautiful manner[29] and could add to the glory of the Temple as described in the Mishnah. There was no need for the inscriptions in the pre-Herodian Temple (or rather, the Temple Mount), as the entire Temple precinct was not allowed to the impure. Now, with the extension of the Temple Mount by Herod, the entire Mount was not forbidden to the impure — as may be understood from the absence of the inscriptions before Herod's time. This was already suggested in the nineteenth century.[30] All of the above is said so as to consider the possibility that the screen bearing the inscriptions was the innermost limit of the court allotted to the Gentiles, or the impure, and it marks the limits of the pre-Herodian Temple Mount and not the *Hel.*[31]

23. *m. Middoth* 2.3.

24. *m. Toharot, Kelim* 1.8.

25. Since two inscriptions were found, both of them in Greek, there is no need to dispute Josephus about it. For one inscription see J. H. Iliffe, "The Tanathos Inscription from Herod's Temple," *QDAP* 6 (1938): 1-3, and for the second, see C. Clermont-Ganneau, *CRAIBL,* 3e ser., 1 (1872): 170-96; and in many other publications. Hollis has an interesting opinion about the inscriptions in *Archeology of Herod's Temple,* p. 157.

26. Josephus, *War* 6.149. The Greek definitions to the various parts of the Temple and the Temple Mount are dealt with by Simons, *Jerusalem,* p. 392 n. 1. I believe the whole case should be restudied now in light of the differentiation between the pre-Herodian and the Herodian Temple Mounts as is agreed today by most of the scholars who deal with the problems of the Mount.

27. τῶν ἁγίων. Josephus, *War* 6.124.

28. The sanctuary proper Josephus names *naos* (see Hollis, *Archeology of Herod's Temple,* p. 172). See also in Hollis his plate X, on p. 160, for his suggestion on the confines of the outer and inner courts as well as the inscription wall, which is not acceptable anymore. In spite of it, his book is still of great value.

29. Josephus, *War* 5.193.

30. M. de Vogue, *Le Temple de Jerusalem* (Paris: Noblet and Baudrey, 1864), p. 54.

31. For a similar discussion see also Hollis, *Archeology of Herod's Temple,* pp. 153-61.

All scholars who deal with the Temple Mount agree that its eastern retaining wall also forms the eastern wall of the older, pre-Herodian Mount. This will serve as a starting point to understand the location of one or some of the places mentioned in the Gospels or in Acts. In the latter, Solomon's Portico is mentioned, which is the eastern portico, as mentioned by Josephus. The name of this portico stems no doubt from its ancient origin,[32] but it also required repairs in the time of Agrippa II. Four gates were installed in the western wall of the Temple Mount, all of which are known to the present. A recent study shows that Barclay's gate had a straight passage, and did not have a 90-degree bend as is usually depicted;[33] so also with Warren's gate. Since the two gates are known to their entire length, one must assume that the screen bearing the inscriptions was aligned in such a way as to enable a Gentile to pass through the gates to reach the Temple Mount platform, and still have enough space to be able to read the inscription. The western alignment was thus located about 30 meters east of the present Western Wall. As we assume that, we may estimate that the cubit by which the pre-Herodian Mount was measured (500 × 500 cubits) must be about 44.6 centimeters. In our excavations along the Western Wall, we could find some data pertaining to the alignment of the northern wall of the pre-Herodian Mount. Here there is some important data: the moat discovered by Warren;[34] the remains of foundation trenches of the Baris,[35] which was outside of the pre-Herodian Temple Mount; the northern rocky scarp bordering today's upper terrace of the Mount. The southern limit of the pre-Herodian Temple Mount should be located 500 cubits to the south of this alignment. This southern alignment should be located north of today's Aqsa mosque, and this is the largest open area within the pre-Herodian Temple Mount.

After delineating the pre-Herodian, older, Mount, we may say that it occupied the entire Mount Moriah, the reason for the sanctity of the Temple Mount;[36] and so the Herodian addition to the Temple Mount was out of Mount Moriah, and thus considered less holy.

32. Josephus, *War* 5.184; *Ant* 20.219-222; Jn 10:22-23.

33. D. M. Jacobson and S. Gibson, "The Original Form of Barclay's Gate," *PEQ* 129 (1997): 138-49.

34. See Warren's atlas, map 2, where it is marked *"Excavated Ditch,"* and map 4 where it is marked *"Ditch Cut in the Rock,"* etc.

35. See Bahat, "The Western Wall Tunnels," pp. 183-85.

36. The dimensions and the shape of Mount Moriah were studied by Charles Warren in the nineteenth century. By digging shafts around the Mount, he managed to trace the valleys surrounding it and thus to create the contours of the various hills in the area. Mount Moriah is the source of sanctity of the Temple Mount. Herod's extension of the Mount reached beyond Mount Moriah — and therefore was not considered holy; this may be the reason for the allowance for the impure to visit the parts added by him to the sacred Mount.

The Location of the Stalls of the Money Changers
(Mt 21:12-14; Mk 11:15-17)

As may be understood from the above, the laws of purity did not apply to the large area that was added by Herod the Great, and the secular activities of the Temple could be performed there. Even the money changers might have had their stalls there. This may well fit the description in *Sheqalim* 1.3: "on the 15th the tables of the money changers were set up in the provinces, and on the 25th they were set up in the Temple." Moreover, in the Talmud, *Berakot* (p. 62/2),[37] it says: "a man should not enter the Temple Mount with a stick in his hand . . . or with coins packed in his bag." So it is clear that the tables of the money changers were located outside the Temple Mount, an area in which one could not bring ordinary money;[38] only the annual tax could be brought into the holy place.[39] The reference here is to the 500 × 500 cubit area; so we have to look for the site of the changers outside of that. The most suitable area for the tables, in my opinion, and after considering the location of the 500 × 500 area, must have been the space which is more or less in the area occupied today by the Aqsa mosque. Herod's extension works created a vast area in the southern part of the Temple, where there must have been intensive activities pertaining to the Temple Mount, and yet, outside the holy place. Before the Herodian extension, it must have been in the immediate outskirts of the Temple Mount, but this does not refer to Jesus' time.

The money changers were indispensable for enabling the Temple to maintain the income level needed for its various functions such as initiator of public works.[40] Money changing was the only source of the Temple's income, and the system of the money changers ensured the validity of the contribution to it, even in periods of inflation. It is also believed that the coins used as tokens were minted in Jerusalem.[41] Tyrian money was so invested in life in Judah that "Whenever the Torah says *money,* then it is *Tyrian money, and what is Tyrian money? Tyrian money is Jerusalemite* [money]."[42] In the Talmudic sources, a place named *Hanuyoth* is mentioned as a site on the Mount.[43] The meaning of the word is

---

37. Also in *t. Berakot* 7.19.

38. For the reference in the Gospels, see Mt 21:12 — ἱερόν; Mk 11:15; Lk 19:45; Jn 2:13ff.

39. See Mk 12:41-44.

40. For which, see Josephus, *Ant* 18.60-62. Pontius Pilate penetrated the treasury to obtain money for the repair of the aqueduct bringing water to Jerusalem.

41. For a discussion about the whole matter, see Y. Meshorer, *A Treasury of Jewish Coins* (in Hebrew) (Jerusalem: Yad Yitshak Ben-Tsevi, 1997). See esp. pp. 68-73.

42. I wish to thank Y. Meshorer for discussing this matter with me.

43. E.g., *Sanhedrin* 41.1; *Aboda Zara* 8.2.

"shop/s." It must have been a place outside the limits of the holy place, as the supreme tribunal moved there forty years before the destruction of the Temple, probably because secular matters were discussed there. Because of the structure's name, one may ask whether this was not the place of the money changers.

The Boy Jesus and Rabbis (Lk 2:41-50)

The discovery of a grand stairway south of the southern wall of the Temple Mount[44] makes it clear that it was here that the young Jesus amazed the rabbis by his knowledge.[45] A fragment of an inscription found on the stairway, along with another fragment of it housed today in the Louvre in Paris, mentions the elders *(zeqenim)*.[46] Probably a place on the stairway was allotted to them. The Talmud refers to three tribunals in Jerusalem. One of these "used to sit at the gate of the Temple Mount."[47] The tribunal at the gate of the Temple Mount — "Har HaBait" — engaged in deliberations and expounding *(drisha)*. But the most decisive indication to the events that took place on the stairway is the tractate that says: "The story of Rabban Gamaliel[48] and the elders *(zeqenim)* who were sitting on the stairway *(al gav ma'aloth)* in the Temple Mount and this Johanan the scribe in front of them, and they said to him: *'write, we the people of the Upper Galilee and to the people of the Lower Galilee.'*" The place where the young Jesus heard the expoundings of the rabbis and disputed them, was on this stairway.

Other Events on the Temple Mount

A. An angel heralds the birth of John (Lk 1:5-25). The site of this event was in the Temple, and probably in the Women's Court or the Court of the Israelites.

44. B. Mazar, "The Archeological Excavations Near the Temple Mount," in *Jerusalem Revealed*, ed. Y. Yadin (Jerusalem: Israel Exploration Society, 1975), pp. 25-40. The stairway is mentioned on pp. 27-30.

45. Lk 2:41ff. has the most detailed description of the event. According to him, it took place in the ἱερόν.

46. For the term "elder" see Jeremias, *Jerusalem*, p. 222. See also p. 210.

47. *m. Sanhedrin* 11.2; *m. Yerushalmi* 11.3. In *Sanhedrin* it is mentioned: "In this way I have expounded [*darashti*] and in that way have my fellows expounded this way, in this way I have taught."

48. *t. Sanhedrin* 2.6. One may recall that Rabban Gamaliel was one of the foremost contemporary authorities in Judaism. He was also the traditional teacher of Saint Paul, and his teaching was thus reflected in the Christian thought.

B. Simeon presents Jesus in the Temple (Lk 2:25-35). Like the above, the Women's Court or the Court of the Israelites must have been the stage for the event. It is also possible that Luke did not differentiate between the Temple and the Temple Mount, and thus the entire Temple Mount could be the site of the event.

C. Jesus' teaching in the Temple during the Feast of Tabernacles (Jn 7:14-53).

D. The temptation of Jesus is another event that took place in the Temple Mount, although the mention in the text is "on the pinnacle of the Temple" (Mt 4:5-7; Lk 4:9-12).[49] It is clear that the reference is not to the Temple's roof, as only priests could go there, but to the Temple Mount. Usually the reference is assigned to the southeastern corner of the Mount, and is probably to the roof of the Royal Portico. The corner of the portico was, and still is, the most impressive point on the Mount — the Kidron Valley is so deep below — and Josephus goes out of his way to describe this corner.[50]

Indeed, the excavations carried out around the Temple Mount since 1967 afford fresh insight into the course of events on the Mount in the first century C.E., and give us a platform to discuss what would have been visible on the Mount in the time of Jesus.

49. The Hebrew translation of this description is: "The corner of the roof of the Temple," which may refer to the Royal Portico. In the Vulgata, Matthew: *Supra pinnaculum templi,* and Luke: *supra pinnam templi.* In Greek the text says: ἐπὶ τὸ πτερύγιον τοῦ ἱεροῦ. According to Matthew and Luke, ἐπὶ τὸ πτερύγιον τοῦ ἱεροῦ. As the Greek and the Latin agree, I don't know where the Hebrew stems from.

50. Josephus, *Ant* 15.411-416.

Mount Zion, Jesus, and Archaeology

Bargil Pixner, O.S.B.

The thesis proposed in this chapter is that toward the end of the Second Temple period there were two religious communities on Mount Zion: (1) an Essene community and (2) the primitive Christian community. We also seek to extract whatever possible information from archaeology about the existence and composition of these two communities.

An Essene Community on Mount Zion

What is the archaeological evidence of the existence of an Essene community on the southwestern hill of Jerusalem, today called Mount Zion?

In the city walls of Second Temple Jerusalem there was a gate referred to by Josephus as the "Gate of the Essenes" (*War* 5.145).[1] Since I was teaching archaeology and biblical topography at our Theological Faculty on Mount Zion, our abbot asked me to make a special study of the Mount Zion area.[2] Since the early seventies, when many were talking about the discoveries at Qumran and its

---

1. In describing the extent of the First Wall (the oldest of three), Josephus started with the Hippicus Tower, which was near today's Jaffa Gate: "This wall began in the north at the so-called Hippicus Tower and went on to the Xystos, it joined the Council House and ended at the western Wall of the Sanctuary. On the other side, facing west, it began at the same starting point [Hippicus Tower], extended to a place called Bethso to the Gate of the Essenes and turned hereafter facing south towards the Pool of Siloam. From there it bent again, facing east, towards Solomon's Pool, and reached as far as a certain place called Ophlas, where it was joined to the Eastern Wall of the Temple." Josephus, *War* 5.144-146.

2. B. Pixner, "An Essene Quarter on Mount Zion?" in *Studia Hierosolymitana in onore di P. Bellarmino Bagatti I: Studi archeologici,* SBF.CMa 22 (Jerusalem: Franciscan Printing Press, 1976), pp. 245-85.

possible connection with the Essene community, the citation of Josephus has fascinated me. I figured that the part of the wall with the Gate of the Essenes may well be in the neighborhood of our abbey, in the area of the Anglican-Lutheran cemetery. After obtaining permission from the owners of the cemetery to reexamine a dig of Frederick J. Bliss and Archibald C. Dickie at the end of the nineteenth century,[3] I also received the authorization of the Israeli Department of Antiquities. Based on some calculations, I guessed the approximate location of the "Gate-G" (the name given by Bliss) first found by the English excavators a hundred years ago. With the help of our theology students and much good fortune, I struck at the exact location of the gate. This was in the spring of 1977. Later I was joined by two Israeli archaeologists, Dr. Doron Chen and field archaeologist Shlomo Margalit. Professor Rainer Riesner did research on the historical implications of our finds.[4] Several articles were published about this excavation.[5] Let me give you a short résumé of the results of our examination.

We found a complex of three superimposed gate sills belonging to three different periods. Since the stratigraphy of the excavated area had been destroyed by Bliss's excavation, we had to use other methods to ascertain the chronology of the three gate sills. The top sill was easily ascribable to the Byzantine period. Its basic measurements were the Byzantine foot. It also showed rills in the threshold caused by wheels of heavily laden carts. While the two lower and older door sills could only be reached by a steep path ascending from the Gehinnom Valley, the top Byzantine sill was approachable by a road built around Mount Zion, leading toward Bethlehem. It has been suggested that this entrance into the city was used to bring heavy boulders from the Bethlehem quarries when the Nea church was built in the sixth century. The middle gate sill consisting of two stone slabs, superimposed and joined by mortar, was dated to the period of the Aelia Capitolina (the debris underneath the lower slab seems to suggest that). Coins found — one outside and one inside the gate

---

3. *Excavations at Jerusalem* (London: Palestine Exploration Fund, 1898), pp. 16-20, 322-24.

4. R. Riesner, "Jesus, the Primitive Community, and the Essene Quarter of Jerusalem," in *Jesus and the Dead Sea Scrolls*, ed. J. H. Charlesworth (New York: Doubleday, 1993), pp. 198-234; See also Riesner, *Essener und Urgemeinde in Jerusalem: Neue Funde und Quellen*, BAZ 6 (Giessen: Brunnen, 1998).

5. B. Pixner, D. Chen, and S. Margalit, "Mount Zion: The 'Gate of the Essenes' Reexcavated," *ZDPV* 105 (1989): 85-95 and pls. 6-16; B. Pixner, "The History of the 'Essene Gate' Area," *ZDPV* 105 (1989): 96-104; R. Riesner, "Josephus' 'Gate of the Essenes' in Modern Discussion," *ZDPV* 105 (1989): 105-9; B. Pixner, D. Chen, and S. Margalit, "Mount Zion: Discovery of Iron Age Fortifications Below the Gate of the Essenes," in *Ancient Jerusalem Revealed*, ed. H. Geva (Jerusalem: Israel Exploration Society, 1994), pp. 76-81.

— are of Emperor Heliogabalus (218-222 c.e.). Judging from the socket and the material used, it must have been a rather primitive gate, and can best be ascribed to the Judeo-Christian ghetto wall visited by the Pilgrim of Bordeaux (333 c.e.), who called it "murus Sion." There he entered and saw a synagogue (*Itinerarium* 16 [CSEL 39:22]).

The lowest sill is the one that most interests us. Again it was only possible to date its chronology by examining the pottery underneath the gate, since it had remained undisturbed by Bliss's excavation of 1894. The material examined by several experts was conclusively dated to the Roman period before 70 c.e., the time of the destruction of the gate by Titus's soldiers. Its basic unit of measurement is the Roman foot. In my opinion there can be no reasonable doubt that it is the gate referred to by Josephus as the "Gate of the Essenes." Judging from the elements still in existence (the gate socket, parts of the pillars, etc.), it must have been a handsome gate, though not very large, with an underground sewage channel emptying into the Gehinnom Valley. One of the six sections forming the two pillars of the gate is still preserved and has "H IIII" incised as a mason's mark. Could this Latin mark point to the originator of this gate, namely, Herod the Great, who used Roman engineers for his many works in Jerusalem and who is said to have had a special regard for the Essenes (*Ant* 15.371-379)?

What implication can be drawn from the fact that an ancient city gate was named after the Essenes?

Often city gates take their names after the towns toward which they are leading; examples for Jerusalem are the Damascus Gate or Sichem Gate and the Jaffa Gate or Bab el-Khalil (Hebron Gate). The same is true for most other cities. Could the "Gate of the Essenes" point in the direction of Qumran by the Dead Sea, as some have thought? I think this argument is false. This might be true when gates are called after cities of destination, but not when they are named after a group of people, or an object in the gate's neighborhood. A typical Jerusalem example is the so-called Gate of Mugrabins, which is the Arab name of both the Dung Gate and the present southern gate leading to the Temple. Before the Six-Day War, Arabs that originated from the Maghreb were living there between both gates. The Arabs call the Damascus Gate, Bab el-Amud, because in ancient times a pillar was standing there inside the wall. Other gates of ancient Jerusalem, to mention a few, were the Gate of the Women Tower, or in Nehemiah the Gate of the Furnace (3:11), so called because these two objects were close by. So it can safely be maintained that the Gate of the Essenes had its name from an Essene community living in that area.

This being so, is there other topographical evidence that Essenes were actually living there?
There are several tunnels still left from the excavations of Bliss. Creeping through the one leading from the gate to the city, along the road I noticed that several secondary channels were coming from the northwest ending in the larger sewage channel. Could this be an indication that the quarter of the Essenes lay in that direction? Indeed, in that area, which today is used as a football field for the Greek Orthodox seminarians, there are two very large *mikvaot*, both similar in outlay to those in Qumran. Especially the size (11 × 4 m.) of one of them (now roofed over by a concrete ceiling) would indicate that it was used by a community rather than by a family, as are most other *mikvaot* found in the city.

Josephus refers to a "place called Bethso" close to the Gate of the Essenes (*War* 5.145). With the help of a text in the *Temple Scroll* (11QTemple[a] 46.13-15), Bethso can be identified with the Essene latrines.

Furthermore, some hundred meters to the west of the Gate of the Essenes, outside the wall, there is an elevation cut out of the rock with two *mikvaot* apparently used for ritual washing before entering the compound (cf. Deut 23:11-12; 11QTemple[a] 50.15; 51.3). From there a narrow, maybe secret, small portico, possibly referred to in the *Copper Scroll* (3Q15 1.13-15: *manos*), leads to the interior, where there are the remains of a very large construction, which might have been the headquarters of the Essene establishment.

Allow me a word about the Qumran *Copper Scroll*. More scholars besides Professor Émile Puech of the École Biblique[6] are now convinced that it is a genuine product of the Essene community and that the hidden treasures were real. Now the first fourteen hiding places, those with Greek initials (3Q15 1.1-4.5), seem to have been located in and around Mount Zion.[7] Some of the described locations seem to exactly fit local conditions. From the statements of Philo (*Apologia pro Iudaeis* 1) and Josephus (*War* 2.124), it is quite clear that the Essene movement extended to many villages in Israel and certainly also to Jerusalem. The texts of Qumran also envisage a community in Jerusalem. A text from the *Damascus Document* seems to imply that the members of the Jerusalem community were, to a large extent, celibates (CD 12.1).

Recently to the southwest of the old city a large group of tombs was discovered. As described by Israeli archaeologist Boaz Zissu, these had been dug in the

---

6. E. Puech, "Quelques résultats d'un nouvel examen du *Rouleau de Cuivre (3Q15)*," *RevQ* 18 (1997): 163-90.

7. See B. Pixner, "Unravelling the Copper Scroll Code: A Study on the Topography of 3 Q 15," *RevQ* 11 (1983): 323-66.

same way as the graves in Qumran.[8] They could very well have been related to the Mount Zion Essene Quarter. On the basis of these different archaeological finds, it can safely be stated that there existed a quarter on Mount Zion where Essenes formed a close-knit community that lasted at least from the time of Herod the Great (37 to 4 B.C.E.) to 70 C.E.

Mount Zion as the Location of the Primitive Christian Community

First it should be stated that like all the great world religions, Judaism, Hinduism, Buddhism, Islam, so also the origins of Christianity are not so clear. Since the primitive "Christian church" was very small, it can hardly be expected to have left much archaeological evidence from the early years of its existence. All we have is a strong literary tradition that the cradle of Christianity was on Mount Zion. It is common to view the church's birthday as Pentecost of 30 C.E.

To reach firm archaeological ground for such a Christian Mount Zion tradition, we have to start rather late in the Byzantine period and try to trace back the tradition to the first century.
We start with the evidence we can derive from the Madaba Map (ca. 560 C.E.). The Jerusalem vignette of this mosaic map shows two sanctuaries in the area of Mount Zion. It is generally accepted that the larger one stands for the Hagia Sion Church (probable construction date, 415 C.E.);[9] the smaller one, adjacent to it, is the old Judeo-Christian sanctuary of the *Hyperōon* (Acts 1:13). At the time of the design of the map, that ancient synagogue was used as a Christian shrine, which, by order of Bishop John II of Jerusalem, was used to hold the relics of Saint Stephen. Inspired by a visionary dream, a certain presbyter Lucian found Stephen's tomb in Bet Jemal near Bet Shemesh and was asked to hand the relics of the famous saint to Jerusalem's bishop (*Epistula Luciani* 6-8 [PL 41:813-15]). It seems that an ancient niche, which today can be seen behind the cenotaph of David, served as depository for the urn. That niche gives also the prayer direction of that synagogue, which was no more as in Jewish synagogues the Temple, but the place of the resurrection (Golgotha and the Holy Sepulchre Church), as can be ascertained with the help of a compass.

8. B. Zissu, "'Qumran Type' Graves in Jerusalem: Archaeological Evidence of an Essene Community?" *DSD* 5 (1998): 158-71.

9. See M. de Esbroeck, *Les plus anciens homiliaires Géorgiens* (Louvain: Peeters, 1975), pp. 314-15.

When in the early twelfth century the Crusaders incorporated the ruins of that sanctuary into their church of Sancta Maria in Monte Sion, they built the present Upper Room *(coenaculum)*. The Crusaders seem to have had the luck to find approximately the right place for the Cenacle. Pope John Paul II at his pilgrimage in 2000 was the first after five centuries to have the legal permission to offer Mass at the place, where it was originally instituted. But the Crusaders made a rather foolish mistake by placing in front of the niche a cenotaph of King David. With the passing of time this pseudotomb was accepted as genuine by Jews, Christians, and Muslims, although it is well known that David's real tomb was in David's city on the Ophel. Like many other Jewish sites, it was destroyed by Hadrian after the Bar-Kokhba war (132–135/36 C.E.). The Romans quarried the excellent stone of the tomb area (Dio Cassius, *Roman History* 69.14). After that the Byzantines venerated David's tomb in Bethlehem. Still the Crusaders might have done a service to Christianity by putting that tomb on such a spot, for that led to the preservation of the ancient walls around it. These apparently are the remains of the ancient Judeo-Christian synagogue, which carries the honor of being the "mother of all the churches" *(mētēr pantōn ekklēsiōn)*.

The one and only archaeological excavation ever done in this neuralgic area was by the archaeologist Joseph Pinkerfeld, chief inspector of the Israel Department of Archaeology, in 1951. He was supposed to repair damages caused by a shell that had entered through the eastern window during the war of independence; but he also used his chance to do some archaeological exploration. Unfortunately, Pinkerfeld was killed in 1956 during a Jordanian attack, so that all we have is a preliminary report translated from Hebrew by Michael Avi-Yonah in the December 1960 issue of *Hebrew University Louis Rabinowitz Fund for the Exploration of Ancient Synagogues.*[10] Pinkerfeld found that of the three layers of floors (Crusader, Byzantine, Roman) below the present pavement of the "Tomb of David," the earliest one was late Roman. He concluded, and I believe rightly so, that the wall to the south, the east, and the north surrounding the tomb of David was from the Roman period after 70 C.E. Assuming that the large niche behind the cenotaph was facing the Temple, he believed that this could have been a Jewish synagogue. I am convinced he was mistaken about the direction of the niche. It also is most unlikely that the Jews were able to build a synagogue in Jerusalem after they had been expelled after the Bar-Kokhba war, and were kept away also during the early Byzantine period. If it was a synagogue, it must have been a Judeo-Christian one, for on closer examination the

10. J. Pinkerfeld, "'David's Tomb': Notes on the History of the Building," *Bulletin* 3 (1960): 41-43.

said niche is directed toward the place of the resurrection. We even have a literary source from about 440 C.E. expressly stating so (Eucherius of Lyons, *De situ Hierusolimae* 4 [CSEL 39:125]).

Let us try now to ascertain the origin of those beautiful ashlars around David's cenotaph.

Some expressed the opinion that they could only belong to the Byzantine Hagia Sion Basilica or to the later Crusader Sancta Maria in Monte Sion. There are several arguments that go against such an opinion. The Madaba Map shows two separate sanctuaries; the axis of the existing ruins of the Hagia Sion and the Cenacle building are not in alignment with what Léon-Hugues Vincent proved.[11] The most striking evidence, though, is in a photo showing the foundation of the northeast corner of those ancient walls. Those ashlars have no connection with an adjoining building, but belong to a building by itself, which was necessarily much older than the Hagia Sion.[12]

Before Bishop John II of Jerusalem built his Hagia Sion Basilica next to the ancient church-synagogue in 415, a portico leading into the *Hyperōon* synagogue must have stood on that spot. A pillar, said to have been the column of flagellation, was brought from the ruins of the house of the high priest Caiaphas and incorporated into it. That portico and the column are mentioned during visits to Sion by the pilgrim Egeria (*Peregrinatio* 39.5 [CSEL 39:88]) and Saint Paula in company with Saint Jerome (*Letter* 108.9 [PL 22:884]) at the end of the fourth century. Such a portico is also shown on the Jerusalem mosaic of the Pudentiana church in Rome (ca. 400). About that time the Judeo-Christians were apparently reconciled with the Byzantine church of the empire and consequently absorbed into it. Most of the preceding fourth century was marked by tension between the Gentile Christians and the Jewish Christians. Judging from the writings of the church fathers of that period (Eusebius, Epiphanius, Jerome), "the Hebrews" were suspected of leaning toward the Arian heresy and other superstitions. Epiphanius remarks that Mount Zion, which earlier had been in high esteem, was "cut off" from the rest of the church (*Panarion* 46.5 [GCS 31:208-10]).

In a very interesting text Eusebius (260-340), who had visited Mount Zion several times, apparently refers to those magnificent stones of the Judeo-Christian sanctuary. He ridicules the exaggerated pride with which the Jewish owners regarded those stones:

11. L. Vincent, *Jérusalem Nouvelle II* (Paris: Gabalda, 1922), pp. 451-55.
12. See Pinkerfeld, "David's Tomb," pl. IX/2.

How simple-minded and almost ridiculous is the opinion of those, who in a material sense expect that a stone of those, which are held to be very perfect and most praise-worthy *(lythōn tina toutōn de tōn polytelōn kai polytimōn einai nomizomenōn)*, will be inserted into the foundation of the real Sion by the action of the Lord himself and whoever shall put his trust in that stone will not be confounded as prophesied. Hence, while objecting to such foolish Jewish stories, which the Apostle calls myths [Col 2:18], we accept the prophecies as worthy of God and divinely inspired. For He says: Behold, I place a stone into the foundation of Sion etc. [Isa 28:16]. (*Eklogae propheticae* 4.13 [PG 22:1217])

Hereupon Eusebius gives his own spiritualized interpretation of the prophecy.

Now we have to ask the question: When was this church-synagogue (shown on the Madaba Map), whose impressive ashlar stones still can be observed forming the foundation of the Cenacle building on Mount Zion, first erected, and who built it? Another question begs for an answer: In the Prophets and Psalms, Zion is always the site of the Temple. How is it that for almost two thousand years this southwestern hill of Jerusalem is called "Zion"?
I believe in the accuracy of the persistent Christian tradition that the primitive Judeo-Christian community was behind both the building and the name giving.[13] Thinking back to the days of Jesus, we encounter the statements of two church fathers, Eusebius (*Church History* 3.5.3) and Epiphanius (*Panarion* 29.7.7 [GCS 25:330]). They relate that the Judeo-Christian community left Jerusalem (in 66-70 C.E.) on a flight to Pella, urged to do so by an oracle (probably the one recorded in Mk 13:1-32). Some scholars have questioned the historicity of this flight for purely circumstantial reasons. I believe that in our excavation on Mount Zion in 1981 we might have found an indication to the time of such a flight.[14] The director of the excavation below the annex of our Hagia Maria Sion Abbey was the Israeli archaeologist Emmanuel Eisenberg.[15] We discovered elements of the facade and the pillar bases of the northwestern Crusader church of Sancta Maria Sion. But the most interesting discovery was a street running in a northerly direction on the Zion rock itself. It had some poorly built houses

---

13. See B. Pixner, "The Apostolic Synagogue on Mount Zion," *BAR* 17, no. 3 (1990): 16-35, and several articles in B. Pixner, *Wege des Messias und Stätten der Urkirche*, ed. R. Riesner, 3rd ed., BAZ 2 (Giessen: Brunnen, 1996).

14. See B. Pixner, "Archäologische Beobachtungen zum Jerusalemer Essener-Viertel und zur Urgemeinde," in *Christen und Christliches in Qumran?* ed. B. Mayer, ESt, n.s., 32 (Regensburg: Pustet, 1992), pp. 89-113.

15. E. Eisenberg, "Church of Dormition," *ESI* 3 (1984): 47.

flanking both its sides. One had a small *mikveh*. All these buildings (dated to the first century C.E.) were destroyed in the great conflagration of 70 C.E. We found several coins along that street. The remarkable thing was that they all ended with the second year of the revolt (67/68 C.E.). I found one on a step of the *mikveh*. The *mikveh* itself had a section of a column, enabling older people to hold on to it while taking the ritual bath. We asked ourselves: Could this absence of coins of the third and fourth year of the revolt indicate that the rather poor inhabitants of that area had left Mount Zion just before Titus's soldiers reached Jerusalem? Could this be an indication of the flight of the primitive community to Pella?

The apocryphon *Ascension of Isaiah* mentions that this flight brought these Judeo-Christians not only to Pella, but from one place to the other in the region of Gilead and Bashan in the hope that the "Beloved One" (Jesus) might come back (3.21–4.13). This expectation was especially strong, when they heard that the Holy City and its Temple had been destroyed. They waited two or three years and finally, it is said in an ancient tradition (Euthychios of Alexandria, *Annales* [PL 111:985]), returned to Jerusalem under the leadership of Simon Bar-Kleopha, the cousin of Jesus (Eusebius, *Church History* 3.11), "during the fourth year of Vespasian" (73/74 C.E.). With the fall of Masada in 73/74 (*War* 7.252ff.), the hope of an early parousia had waned. On returning to Jerusalem they found the ruins of their former center on Mount Zion (the cenacle) destroyed with the rest of Jerusalem (as confirmed by our excavations).

Eusebius refers to this group of returnees as "a very large church of Jews in Jerusalem" (*Demonstratio evangelica* 3.5 [GCS 23:131]). They took courage and, overcoming the stifling hope of a proximate parousia, rebuilt their center as a synagogue. Judaism was then a *religio licita,* so they were allowed to build a prayer center. In doing so, they used those very large and beautiful ashlars, which can be seen to this day. They even seem to have figured out that this hill could have been the site of the ancient fortress of Zion conquered by King David, as is attested in an old apocryphon with Christian interpolations (*Lives of the Prophets* 13). Although archaeology proved them wrong, for that fortress stood on the highest point of the Ophel (City of David), they proudly named their site the Nea Sion, a designation that still remains. To make their point they possibly used stones from the Temple that lay in ruins. Among the ashlars of the Temple north of Robinson's Arch I have noticed the same measurements. The Judeo-Christian structure, no longer facing the Temple but rather the place of the resurrection, deserved the title "mother of all the churches." But how is Jesus himself connected with this cenacle sanctuary?

Jesus and the Essene Quarter on Mount Zion

How good is the tradition that Jesus celebrated there the Last Supper as a Passover meal with his disciples?

I believe that with the discovery of the "Gate of the Essenes" and the Essene Quarter on Mount Zion, we have a new opening to the last days of Jesus in Jerusalem. The first challenge is to solve the long-standing puzzle of the discrepancy between the Synoptics and the Gospel of John. According to John, the Passover meal was on Saturday of Passion Week; according to the Synoptic Gospels, Jesus celebrated the meal earlier in the week. Since the discovery of the Dead Sea Scrolls, we know that at the end of the Second Temple period two calendars were in use in Jerusalem. The Temple priesthood followed a lunar calendar of 350 days in the year. The ancient group of *kohanim* (priests) among them, the Essenes, followed a solar calendar of 364 days. Those following the solar calendar always had the meal on a Wednesday, while for the observers of the lunar calendar it varied from year to year.

I will now briefly note the events of Jesus' last days as explained, in greater detail, in other works of mine.[16] Jesus, like John the Baptist, came from a family influenced by Essenism. Like John, he broke with that ideology once he perceived that he had a mission for all of Israel and not only for the group that the Essenes considered the "Sons of Light." Jesus left his clan and family in Nazareth and established his own group in Capernaum, using the Pharisaic model, where he was the rabbi surrounded by the *ḥabura* of the Twelve. During the three years of his public life in Capernaum he followed the lifestyle of a normal Jew and regularly visited the feasts in the Temple. His Nazarene brothers, though, as one can conclude from the Gospel of John, continued to visit the Jewish festivals according to their solar calendar (7:2-6), as they were celebrated on Mount Zion. But Jesus made one exception. For the last Passover he returned to the practice of his natural family. Why?

Foreseeing his near end, he wanted to use the symbol-laden traditional meal as his farewell meal with his disciples: "I have greatly desired to eat this passover with you before I suffer" (Lk 22:15). But when the story of the raising up of Lazarus hit the city, people were agog with the news and so was the group of high priests, namely, the house of Annas, which had produced five high priests. This

16. B. Pixner, *With Jesus in Jerusalem: His First and Last Days in Judea* (Rosh Pina: Corazin, 1997); Pixner, "Jesus and His Community: Between Pharisees and Essenes," in *Hillel and Jesus: Comparisons of Two Major Religious Leaders*, ed. J. H. Charlesworth (Minneapolis: Fortress, 1997), pp. 193-224; Pixner, "Nazoreans on Mount Zion (Jerusalem)," in *Le judéo-christianisme ancien dans tous ses états: Actes du Colloque de Jérusalem 6-10 juillet 1998*, ed. S. C. Mimouni and F. S. Jones (Paris: Cerf, 2001), pp. 289-316.

central body of the Sanhedrin was worried that this messianic movement around Jesus might get out of hand and they as leaders would be blamed, the Romans might come, depose them, and take the Temple away (Jn 11:45-51). In unison with their acting high priest, Caiaphas, they decided to get rid of Jesus, and that before Passover: "It is expedient for you that one man should die for the people, instead of the whole nation perishing" (Jn 11:50). Jesus heard of this decision and went at first into hiding in Ephraim, a village close to the desert (Jn 11:54). With the Passover approaching, he returned with his disciples to Bethany near Jerusalem, where there was a meal in the house of Simon the leper. According to John's calculation, this meal took place "six days before Passover" (Jn 12:1). Jesus, knowing of the decision that before that Passover he was destined to die, announced right there to his disciples: "You shall know, in two days is Passover" (Mt 26:2; Mk 14:1). Because of such circumstances he decided in a way of exception to celebrate his last Passover according to the calendar used by his family — which was always on a Wednesday. I suspect that he had asked his brother James, who had always kept his connection with the Essenes on Mount Zion, to make the preparations. Such a decision was made easier by the fact that Bethany was one of the three villages chosen by the Essenes for the dwelling of Jews who were not pure enough to visit the Temple, like lepers and others. The grèat Israeli Qumran scholar Yigael Yadin thought so, basing his view on a passage from the *Temple Scroll* (11QTempleᵃ 46.16–47.5).[17]

As Jesus had announced, after two days it was Tuesday, the first day of the Feast of Unleavened Bread. Since this was the eve of Passover as celebrated by the Essenes on Mount Zion, Jesus had arranged to use one of the guesthouses of the Essenes for his Passover meal. Peter and John (Lk 22:8), not being Essenes, were told by Jesus to look for that guesthouse *(katalyma)* and were helped to locate it by the man (probably an Essene monk) carrying a water jar (Mk 14:12-16). The head of the community *(oikodespotēs)* led them to the designated guesthouse, adjoining their quarter, where the two apostles (probably with the help of the women) prepared the festive meal. They had to do without a lamb, it seems, since the paschal lambs were slaughtered in the Temple on Friday. It was Tuesday evening, the eve of the Essene Passover, when Jesus arrived with his apostles through the Gate of the Essenes. Out of respect to the Essene hosts, Jesus made sure everyone was ritually clean by washing the feet of his disciples (Jn 13:1-15).

Jesus and the disciples probably followed the traditional ritual of the seder. During the meal, using the unleavened bread *(matzot)*, Jesus took one loaf, blessed it, and gave it to his disciples, saying, "This is my body which will be

17. Y. Yadin, *The Temple Scroll I: Introduction* (Jerusalem: Hebrew University Press, 1983), p. 305.

Figure 51. The *Temple Scroll* (11Q19). Courtesy of J. H. Charlesworth

given up for you" (Mk 14:22). After the meal he used the fourth cup of wine to symbolize the new covenant in his blood. By his order: "Do this in memory of me" (Lk 22:19), he perpetuated his presence with those believing in him for all times. Descending through the Gate of the Essenes into the Gehinnom Valley, he crossed the Kedron brook (Jn 18:1) and reached the Garden of Gethsemane. During Wednesday night he was taken prisoner and brought to the house of the high priest Caiaphas. After some delaying tactics (by sending Jesus to his father-in-law, Hannas [Jn 18:12-14]), Caiaphas succeeded in gathering the members of the Sanhedrin. They found Jesus guilty of blasphemy (Mk 14:60-64) and seduction of the people (Lk 23:1-2). Since a strict legal prescription (*m. Sanh.* 4.1) had to be followed, the Sanhedrin was allowed to vote on a death sentence only after an interval of one night. So the definitive death sentence was pronounced on Thursday morning in the Chamber of the Hewn Stones.

That same morning Jesus was brought to the Roman prefect Pontius Pilate, who alone had power to execute their death sentence. Sensing that Jesus had done nothing to deserve death, he sent him to Herod Antipas, who as ruler of Galilee should be consulted on the case of his subject (Lk 23:8-12). Jesus was then sent back to Pilate, who called the accusing clan of high priests together again. They demanded his crucifixion. After that some petitioners arrived asking for the customary Passover amnesty and suggested the name of Barabbas

(Mk 15:6-15). Pilate jumped to the occasion and offered them a choice — Jesus in place of Barabbas. They may come back the next day and choose for themselves. The next day, Friday, was the eve of the Temple Passover. Most Jews were busy with preparations for the feast, so the enemies of Jesus gathered together some sort of rabble-rousing mob and came up to the Stone Pavement in the Praetorium (Jn 19:1-16), the ancient Hasmonean palace to be sought in the area of the so-called Herodian Mansion opposite the Western Wall of the Temple.[18] The mob demanded that Pilate release Barabbas and crucify Jesus. Finally Pilate gave in and Jesus was crucified, as Mark (15:25) has it, at the third hour (9 A.M.). Jesus died around 3 P.M.

The guesthouse with the upper room apparently continued to be hired by the first believers in Jesus.

In the "upper room" Jesus appeared to the disciples, Mary, and Jesus' brothers from Nazareth, who were gathered there for Pentecost (Lk 24:33; Acts 1:13). There must have been sympathizers among the Essenes on Mount Zion, for very soon it was said, "a large group of priests accepted the faith" (Acts 6:7). Since the *kohanim* (priests) came either from the Sadducees or the Essenes, many scholars think they must have been Essenes and belonged most likely to the Mount Zion establishment. The reason why the primitive Judeo-Christian community on Mount Zion adopted the community of goods (Acts 2:44-45; 4:32-35), not practiced anywhere else in Christian communities, is that they could not have lower standards than their neighbors, the Essenes. This thesis seems now confirmed by the thorough research of Brian J. Capper.[19] Both groups shared similar eschatological expectations, but while for the Essenes the community of goods was a sine qua non, the Jewish Christians practiced it rather on a voluntary basis.

One of the most astounding facts is the important role played by James the brother of Jesus. After the departure of Peter in 42 C.E. (Acts 12:19), he became the head of the first community, although he was not one of the Twelve, and John was still in Jerusalem. There are hints that his ideology was close to that of the Essenes. It was he who spoke the decisive voice during the Apostolic Council of Jerusalem (ca. 48). Accepting the mission to the heathen, he used a proph-

---

18. See B. Pixner, "Was the Trial of Jesus in the Hasmonean Palace? A New Solution to a Thorny Topographical Problem of Jerusalem," in *Jerusalem — City of Ages*, ed. A. L. Eckardt (New York and London: Professors for Peace in the Middle East, 1987), pp. 66-88.

19. Capper, "The Palestinian Cultural Context of Earliest Christian Community of Goods," in *The Book of Acts in Its Palestinian Setting*, ed. R. Bauckham (Grand Rapids: Eerdmans, 1995), pp. 323-56; Capper, "'With the Oldest Monks . . .': Light from Essene History on the Career of the Beloved Disciple?" *JTS* 49 (1998): 1-55. Also, see Capper's chapter in the present volume.

ecy of Amos about the "fallen hut of David" (9:11-12) in a manner reminiscent of Qumran exegesis (Acts 15:15-18; cf. 4QFlor 1.10-13).[20] In 62 James died as a martyr, lynched with the connivance of the high priest Ananus (*Ant* 20.197-203), also from the clan of Annas, who plotted against Jesus, his followers, and other pious Jews.

20. See R. Riesner, "James's Speech (Acts 15:13-21), Simeon's Hymn (Luke 2:29-32), and Luke's Sources," in *Jesus of Nazareth: Lord and Christ,* ed. J. B. Green and M. Turner (Grand Rapids: Eerdmans, 1994), pp. 263-78.

Excavating Caiaphas, Pilate, and Simon of Cyrene: Assessing the Literary and Archaeological Evidence

Craig A. Evans

Almost all historians and interpreters of the New Testament agree that the arrest, examination, and execution of Jesus of Nazareth constitute the most important series of events in the Gospel narratives. Who killed Jesus, why he was killed, and the juridical factors involved have been hotly debated for centuries. The two most prominent figures in this drama are Caiaphas the Jewish high priest and Pontius Pilate the Roman governor. As fortune would have it, we are in possession of significant literary and archaeological materials. It is the purpose of this paper to review these materials and to offer a somewhat revised assessment of the administrative functions and dispositions of Caiaphas and Pilate. As an addendum, the literary and archaeological evidence that pertains or may pertain to Simon of Cyrene, the man who carried Jesus' cross, will also be briefly considered.

Caiaphas in Literature and Archaeology

Caiaphas appears in the Gospels and the book of Acts.[1] In the earliest account of Passion Week, the Markan Evangelist states that the "ruling priests (οἱ ἀρχιερεῖς) and scribes were seeking how to arrest (Jesus) by stealth, and kill him" (Mk 14:1). The Matthean Evangelist expands this notation, adding Caiaphas: "Then the ruling priests and the elders of the people gathered in the palace of the high priest (τοῦ ἀρχιερέως), who was called Caiaphas (Καϊάφα)" (Mt 26:3). Likewise, while Mark says simply that Jesus was led to the high priest (Mk 14:53), the Matthean parallel identifies this high priest as "Caiaphas"

---

1. For a very helpful and current interpretation of Caiaphas in history and in the New Testament and Josephus, see B. Chilton, "Caiaphas," in *ABD* 1:803-6.

(Καϊάφα; Mt 26:57). The Lukan Evangelist links Caiaphas with Annas (cf. Lk 3:2: "in the high-priesthood of Annas and Caiaphas"; Acts 4:6: "with Annas the high priest and Caiaphas and John and Alexander, and all who were of the high-priestly family"), perhaps because Caiaphas was the son-in-law of Annas (according to Jn 18:13). The close association of the two high priests is seen in the Fourth Gospel (Jn 18:13-28), in which Caiaphas appears and is remembered for his "prophecy" that it is better for one man to die than for the nation as a whole to perish (Jn 11:49-51; 18:13; Caiaphas was high priest "that year," that is, the year Jesus was executed).

The Gospels tell us very little about Caiaphas the high priest. Mark says Jesus was led to the high priest (and we should assume, along with Matthew, that Caiaphas is meant). But it is the other ruling priests who are said to seek testimony against Jesus, at least initially (Mk 14:55). Caiaphas becomes involved in verses 60-64, when he asks Jesus to reply to the accusations and then asks him directly if he is the Messiah, the Son of God (v. 61). When Jesus says he is, and that as "Son of Man" he will be seated at the right hand of God and will come with the clouds of heaven (v. 62), implying that he will be seated next to God on the chariot throne (alluding to Ps 110:1 and Dan 7:9-14), thereby further implying that he will at that time judge the high priest and his associates, Caiaphas "tore his garments" and accused Jesus of blasphemy (vv. 63-64). The other ruling priests condemned Jesus as deserving death (v. 64). The following morning the ruling priests convene and decide to hand Jesus over to the Roman authorities (15:1). What role, if any, Caiaphas played in this deliberation is not said.

In the Matthean Gospel Caiaphas plays only a slightly more active role. He accommodates the ruling priests, who plot against Jesus, by allowing them to gather in the courtyard (αὐλὴν) of his home (Mt 26:3). And, as already noted, Caiaphas is mentioned by name when the arrested Jesus is brought to the ruling priests (Mt 26:57). In Luke, as in Mark, the name of Caiaphas is not mentioned during Jesus' hearing before the ruling priests and elders. He is mentioned by name when the apostles are brought before the council and are ordered to cease their proclamation (Acts 4:1-6). In the Fourth Gospel Caiaphas utters his ex cathedra pronouncement (Jn 11:49-50), which is recalled at the time of Jesus' arrest (Jn 18:14). Later, colorful portraits of Caiaphas in Christian apocryphal literature, some of which is passed on uncritically by ecclesiastical authorities (such as Justin Martyr and Eusebius), have no historical value.

All in all, the role played by Caiaphas is essentially what one would expect of the high priest, as we may surmise from the evidence from Josephus and other sources. The ruling priests have taken offense at Jesus' teaching and conduct in the Temple precincts, have contrived to effect a quiet arrest, and have presented him before members of the council, with Caiaphas the high priest presiding.

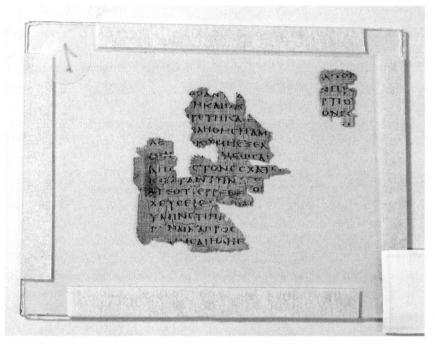

Figure 52. Second-century Greek papyrus of Mt 3:9, 15; 5:20-22, 25-28 [P⁶⁷]; **Biblioteca de la Abadía de Montserrat.** By permission of the librarian, Dr. Armand Puig i Tàrrech

What personal interest in or antipathy toward Jesus that Caiaphas may have had is a matter of pure speculation. Even the action of tearing his robe has more to do with Jesus' remarkable assertion than with Caiaphas's views of Jesus and his movement. Tearing his clothes was the appropriate response of the judge who hears what may be regarded as blasphemy (cf. *m. Sanh.* 6.5).

Another important first-century witness to the life and career of Caiaphas is Josephus. The Jewish historian tells us that Tiberius appointed Valerius Gratus as governor over Judea. The latter then "deposed Ananus from his sacred office, and proclaimed Ishmael, the son of Phabi, high priest. Not long afterwards he removed him also and appointed in his stead Eleazar, the son of the high priest Ananus. A year later he deposed him also and entrusted the office of high priest to Simon, the son of Camith. The last-mentioned held this position for not more than a year and was succeeded by Joseph, who was called Caiaphas ('Ιώσηπος ὁ Καϊάφας). After these acts Gratus retired to Rome" (*Ant* 18.2.2 §34-35). Later in his narrative Josephus explains that the Syrian legate Vitellius, having sent Pilate to Rome to explain his conduct toward the Samaritans, returned the high priestly vestments to Jewish custody. He goes on to relate that after

Vitellius "had bestowed these benefits upon the nation, he removed from his office the high priest Joseph surnamed Caiaphas (τὸν ἀρχιερέα Ἰώσηπον τὸν Καϊάφαν ἐπικαλούμενον), and appointed in his stead Jonathan, son of Ananus the high priest" (*Ant* 18.4.3 §95). Josephus makes no comments regarding the person or conduct of Caiaphas. What inferences, if any, may be made will be considered when the administration of Pontius Pilate is taken into account.

The high priest Caiaphas apparently is not mentioned in rabbinic literature, though the family name may appear. In a discussion concerning the ashes of the red heifer, the Mishnah asks, "Who prepared them (since the time of Ezra)? Simeon the Just and Yoḥanan the high priest prepared two each, and Elyoʿēnai the son of ha-Qayaf and Hanamel the Egyptian and Ishmael the son of Piabi prepared one each" (*m. Par.* 3.5). This Elyoʿēnai the son of ha-Qayaf (הקיף) may have been a son of Joseph Caiaphas.[2] Some manuscripts, however, read ha-Qoph or ha-Quph (הקוף), thus making the identification uncertain. According to the Tosephta, Rabbi Joshua said: "I hereby give testimony concerning the family of the house of ʿAlubaʾi of Bet Šebaʾim and concerning the family of the house of Qayapha (קיפא) of Bet Meqošeš, that they are children of co-wives, and from them high priests have been chosen, and they offered up sacrifices on the Temple altar" (*t. Yebam.* 1.10). The identification of this "house of Qayapha" with the Caiaphas family is probable. However, we learn nothing from this tradition beyond the simple fact that this family was a high priestly family that offered sacrifices on the Temple altar. A slightly different version of the Tosephta tradition appears in Babli: "I testify to you concerning two great families — the house of Zeboʿim of Ben ʿAkmai and the house of Ben Quphai [קופאי] of Ben Meqošeš, that they were sons of rivals and yet some of them were high priests who ministered upon the altar" (*b. Yebam.* 15b). This tradition adds nothing to what we already know, but the spelling variation in the name Quphai attests to the possibilities of variation, which in turn may have a bearing on the question of the spelling and identification of the name found in the famous ossuary. Finally, the Caiaphas family name may also be mentioned in Yerushalmi, where in *Maʿaśerot* 52a we hear of one "Menahem, son of Maxima, the brother of Jonathan Caiapha [יונתן קיפא]." Apart from the name itself, there is nothing here that suggests that this Jonathan was related to the high priestly family of Caiaphas.[3]

2. As suggested by M. Stern, "Herod's Policies and Jewish Society at the End of the Second Temple Period," *Tarbiz* 35 (1966): 235-53.

3. Reich ("Ossuary Inscriptions from the Caiaphas Tomb," *Jerusalem Perspective* 4 [1991]: 13-21, here pp. 17-18) has argued that "Caiaphas" is a nickname and that Josephus's reference to Caiaphas should be translated "Joseph nicknamed 'Caiaphas.'" The name may have functioned as a nickname, as it seems to in the example from Yerushalmi. The name on the ossuary, how-

The recent discovery of an ossuary, on which the name of Caiaphas may have been inscribed, has generated interest and disagreement. In November 1990 workers in Jerusalem's Peace Forest, about one mile south of the Old City, accidentally uncovered an ancient burial cave in which one dozen ossuaries were found. Six had lain undisturbed for two millennia; the other six had been ransacked by grave robbers. Two of the untouched ossuaries bear the name קפא. On one of the boxes two inscriptions read (on one end) יהוסף בר קיפא ("Yehoseph bar Qaipha") and (on one side) יהוסף בר קפא ("Yehoseph bar Qapha"). This ossuary contained the bones of a sixty-year-old man (and those of two infants, a toddler, a young boy, and a woman),[4] and could be the ossuary of Caiaphas the high priest, to whom Josephus refers as Joseph Caiaphas (cf. *Ant* 18.2.2 §35 ['Ιώσηπος ὁ Καϊάφας] and 18.4.3 §95 [τὸν ἀρχιερέα 'Ιώσηπον τὸν Καϊάφαν ἐπικαλούμενον]). The sloppy inscription on the side of the ossuary, perhaps made with one of the two iron nails found in the tomb, may be the writing of the relative who placed his bones in the box (to keep a record of whose bones were in which box).

The ornate and well-preserved "Caiaphas" ossuary is housed in the Israel National Museum in Jerusalem. The skeletal remains have been interred on the Mount of Olives. In the nearby "Akeldama" field and ravine, the tomb of Annas (Lk 3:2; Jn 18:13, 24; Acts 4:6; cf. *Ant* 20.9.1 §197-198), the high-priestly father-in-law of Caiaphas, may also have been identified.[5] According to Josephus, five of the sons of Annas served turns as high priest (*Ant* 20.9.1 §197-198). It is probable therefore that the influence of Annas extended well beyond his tenure in office.

Several archaeologists have identified the Yehoseph bar Qaipha of the ossuary with Joseph called Caiaphas of the narratives of Josephus and the New Testament Gospels. These include Zvi Greenhut and Ronny Reich,[6] among oth-

---

ever, seems to read as patronymic: "son of Qayapha." Could this work as a nickname, that is, as "son of (a man nicknamed) Qayapha"? On p. 19 Reich allows that Qayapha may have been a family name.

4. For analysis of the skeletal remains, see J. Zias, "Human Skeletal Remains from the 'Caiaphas' Tomb," *'Atiqot* 21 (1992): 78-80.

5. L. Ritmeyer and K. Ritmeyer, "Akeldama: Potter's Field or High Priest's Tomb?" *BAR* 20, no. 6 (1994): 22-35, 76. On the possible identification of the family house, see A. Rupprecht, "The House of Annas-Caiaphas," *ABW* 1 (1991): 4-17. On the possible identification of an ossuary in which the remains of a relative of the high priest Annas were interred, see D. Flusser, "Der Hohepriester Hannas und sein Geschlecht," in Flusser, *Entdeckungen im Neuen Testament. Band 2: Jesus — Qumran — Urchristentum,* ed. M. Majer (Neukirchen-Vluyn: Neukirchener Verlag, 1999), pp. 185-92.

6. Z. Greenhut, "Burial Cave of the Caiaphas Family," *BAR* 18, no. 5 (1992): 28-36, 76; R. Reich, "Caiaphas Name Inscribed on Bone Boxes," *BAR* 18, no. 5 (1992): 38-44, 76; Reich, "Os-

ers.[7] Spelling agreement with the rabbinic traditions noted above and especially the agreement with Josephus, who alone in the literature tells us that Caiaphas's full name was Joseph Caiaphas, has convinced these scholars that the identification is probable. Indeed, Dominic Crossan and Jonathan Reed have said with confidence: "There should be no doubt that the chamber was the resting place of the family of the high priest Caiaphas named in the gospels for his role in the crucifixion, and it's very likely that the elderly man's bones were those of Caiaphas himself."[8] In fact, there is substantial doubt.

Voices of dissent have been heard, however. William Horbury and Emile Puech have expressed doubts about the Caiaphas identification, arguing that the Qayapha' reading is difficult and improbable.[9] Rather, they think the name is probably Qôpha', Qûpha', or even Qēpha'. The consonants inscribed on the ossuary favor a two-syllable name (e.g., Qôpha'), not a three-syllable name (e.g., Qayapha'), which would be required to make the identification with the Greek Caiaphas found in Josephus and the New Testament. Perhaps, but Greek forms of Jewish names often expand, and so add another syllable. The name Qatros or Qadros may offer a pertinent example, for this high priestly figure, whose name appears as Qadrôs (קדרוס) in t. Menah. 13.19, 21 and as Qatrôs (קתרס) on a stone weight in the ruins of the "Burnt House" in the Old City, may very well be the Cantheras (Κανθήρας) mentioned in Josephus (cf. Ant 20.1.3 §16).[10] If so, we have a relevant example of how a shorter Semitic form of a name transliterates into a longer form in Greek. Part of the difficulty is the relative rarity of the Qayapha' name, which results in inadequate data for comparative analysis, as well as the poor quality of the ossuary inscriptions them-

---

suary Inscriptions from the 'Caiaphas' Tomb," 'Atiqot 21 (1992): 72-77; Reich, "Ossuary Inscriptions from the Caiaphas Tomb," pp. 13-21. This ossuary is one of the most impressive ever discovered, the beauty of which lends a measure of support to the Caiaphas identification.

7. W. R. Domeris and S. M. Long, "The Recently Excavated Tomb of Joseph Bar Caipha and the Biblical Caiaphas," JTSA 89 (1994): 50-58; D. Flusser, Jesus, rev. ed. (Jerusalem: Magnes Press, 1997), pp. 195-206.

8. J. D. Crossan and J. L. Reed, Excavating Jesus: Beneath the Stones, Behind the Texts (San Francisco: HarperSanFrancisco, 2001), p. 242.

9. W. Horbury, "The 'Caiaphas' Ossuaries and Joseph Caiaphas," PEQ 126 (1994): 32-48; E. Puech, "A-t-on redécouvert le tombeau du grand-prêtre Caïphe?" MdB 80 (1993): 42-47; Puech, La croyance des Esséniens en la vie future, EBib 21 (Paris: Gabalda, 1993), 1:193-95. Horbury points out problems in the Qayapha reading, while Puech remarks that the tomb itself is not really an impressive crypt, as one would expect of a high priest's tomb. Moreover, the tomb is not very close to Akeldama, the site of the more impressive tombs. Finally, the "Caiaphas" ossuary lacks the ornate inscriptions found sometimes on other ossuaries of the wealthy (e.g., the ossuary of Nicanor).

10. Reich, "Ossuary Inscriptions from the Caiaphas Tomb," pp. 18-19.

selves, making certain identification of the yod (so Reich et al.), as opposed to the waw (so Horbury and Puech), very difficult.[11] The Caiaphas reading and identification of this ossuary name has not been conclusively ruled out, but we must recognize how tenuous it is.

One final point may be mentioned briefly. Another box in this crypt contains the bones of a woman, bearing the name מרים ברת שמעון ("Miriam, daughter of Simeon"). In it a coin minted during the reign of Herod Agrippa I (42/43 C.E.) was found in the mouth of the skull, probably reflecting the pagan custom of payment to the Greek god Charon for safe passage across the River Styx.[12] Although we should not read too much significance into this curious feature, it may testify to the extent of penetration of pagan culture into Jewish life, even within priestly circles of the highest rank.[13]

11. I review the morphological and phonetic issues in C. A. Evans, *Jesus and the Ossuaries: What Jewish Burial Practices Reveal about the Beginning of Christianity* (Waco, Tex.: Baylor University Press, 2003), pp. 104-8.

12. See Greenhut, "Burial Cave," p. 35; Greenhut, "The 'Caiaphas' Tomb in North Talpiyot, Jerusalem," ʿAtiqot 21 (1992): 63-71, esp. p. 70; Reich, "Caiaphas Name," p. 43; R. Hachlili and A. Killebrew, "Was the Coin-on-Eye Custom a Jewish Burial Practice in the Second Temple Period?" *BA* 46 (1983): 147-53, here pp. 148-49. Knowledge among Jewish priestly aristocrats of Greek afterlife mythology is attested by Josephus (*War* 2.8.11 §155-156), by at least one epitaph (*IG* no. 1648; *NewDocs* 4:221-29, no. 114; W. Horbury and D. Noy, *Jewish Inscriptions of Graeco-Roman Egypt* [Cambridge: Cambridge University Press, 1992], pp. 234-35, no. 141: "O pitiless Charon") and by later rabbinic tradition (*b. Moʿed Qatan* 28b, in a comical lament for the departed: "tumbling aboard the ferry and having to borrow his fare"). Depictions of boats on Jewish ossuaries or crypt walls may also allude to the belief of the deceased ferried across the water to the land of the dead, as in B. Mazar, *Beth Sheʿarim: Report on the Excavations during 1936-1940*, vol. 1, *Catacombs 1-4* (New Brunswick, N.J.: Rutgers University Press, 1973), pl. XX (= Beth Sheʿarim, Hall P, catacomb no. 1); see also E. R. Goodenough, *Jewish Symbols in the Greco-Roman Period*, vol. 1, *The Archaeological Evidence from Palestine*, Bollingen Series 37 (New York: Pantheon Books, 1953), pp. 97-98 (cf. *Jewish Symbols in the Greco-Roman Period*, vol. 3, *Illustrations*, Bollingen Series 37 [New York: Pantheon Books, 1953], nos. 67 and 77), for examples in Palestine; and Goodenough, *Jewish Symbols in the Greco-Roman Period*, vol. 2, *The Archaeological Evidence from the Diaspora*, Bollingen Series 37 (New York: Pantheon Books, 1953), p. 43 (cf. *Jewish Symbols*, vol. 3, no. 836), for an example in Rome. S. Lieberman ("Some Aspects of After Life in Early Rabbinic Literature," in *Harry Austryn Wolfson: Jubilee Volume on the Occasion of His Seventy-Fifth Birthday*, ed. S. Lieberman, et al. [Jerusalem: American Academy for Jewish Research, 1965], 2:495-532, here pp. 512-13) thinks the "numerous boats on the Jewish graves in Palestine most probably represent the ferry to the other world, i.e., either the divine bark of the ancient Orientals, or Charon's ferry of the Greeks." Lieberman is probably correct.

13. Numerous coins have been found in ossuaries (cf. Greenhut, "The 'Caiaphas' Tomb," p. 70). During conference discussion, Joe Zias remarked that many if not most of these coins had been placed in the mouths of the deceased and that after decomposition and reburial in the ossuaries, became loose. L. Y. Rahmani ("A Note on Charon's *Obol*," ʿAtiqot 22 [1993]: 149-50, here p. 150) opines, rightly in my judgment, that this practice "may well have been seen, by stan-

Pilate in Literature and Archaeology

As in the case of the high priest Caiaphas, so also for Governor Pontius Pilate our best literary sources are the Gospels and Josephus. According to all four Gospels, Jesus is brought before the Roman governor, where evidently he is accused of claiming to be the "king of the Jews" (Mk 15:2). At least, that is how Pilate understands the accusation (cf. Mt 27:11; Lk 23:3; Jn 18:33). Had Jesus indeed accepted the recognition as the Lord's Messiah, soon to be seated at the right hand of God, and as "Son of Man" who would come with the clouds of heaven, then his presentation to Pilate as a royal messianic claimant does seem plausible. Luke adds the accusation that Jesus had taught the people to refuse payment of tribute to Caesar, in view of his own kingship (Lk 23:2). It is unlikely that Jesus taught such things in so transparent and explicit a manner. But the accusation nevertheless may reasonably summarize the implications of Jesus' program and claims. Beyond the trial narrative itself, which results in Jesus' condemnation to the cross, and the later granting of permission for burial (Mk 15:42-44; cf. Mt 27:58; Lk 23:52; Jn 19:38), the Gospels tell us almost nothing of Pilate — the man or his career. The only exception is the grim reference to the Galileans slain by Pilate (Lk 13:1), an event that will be taken up below. Outside of the Gospels Pilate is mentioned four times in the New Testament (three times in Acts [3:13; 4:27; 13:28] and in 1 Tim 6:13). In all of these occurrences Pilate is referred to in connection with the death of Jesus.

What has generated most of the debate is the Gospels' portrait of Pilate as wavering, weak, and even seemingly concerned to seek justice in Jesus' behalf.

---

dards of Jewish law, as an act of idolatry." Nevertheless, we must be cautious in our assumptions about how widespread this practice was among the Jewish people. This caution is recommended by Rahmani and Hachlili and Killebrew in the studies mentioned above. Besides Annas, Caiaphas, and Qatros, there is significant archaeological data pertaining to other Jewish high priests in our period. On an ossuary we have "Yehohanah, daughter of Yehohanan, son of Theophilus the high priest"; cf. L. Y. Rahmani, *A Catalogue of Jewish Ossuaries in the Collections of the State of Israel* (Jerusalem: Israel Antiquities Authority, 1994), p. 259, no. 871 and pl. 132. Theophilus succeeded his brother Jonathan, who served briefly after the removal of Caiaphas (cf. Josephus, *Ant* 18.5.3 §123). On an ostracon found at Masada we have: "A[nani]as the high priest, 'Aqavia his son" (Mas no. 461); cf. Y. Yadin, J. Naveh, and Y. Meshorer, *Masada I: The Yigael Yadin Excavations, 1963-1965, Final Reports; The Aramaic and Hebrew Ostraca and Jar Inscriptions/the Coins of Masada* (Jerusalem: Israel Exploration Society, 1989), p. 37 and pl. 30. The name on the ossuary may refer to Ananias, son of Nedebaeus, who served as high priest from 47 to 59 C.E. (*Ant* 20.5.2 §103). We may also have an ossuary inscription in reference to Simon, son of the high priest Boethos (as in *Ant* 15.9.3 §320-322); cf. Rahmani, *Catalogue*, pp. 85-86, no. 41 and p. 6. And finally, Joezer, son of Boethos, may be attested on an ossuary (cf. *CIJ* no. 1354; Josephus, *Ant* 17.6.4 §164; 18.1.1 §3).

We are told that Pilate found no guilt in Jesus (Lk 23:4, 14-16, 22), that he recognized that he had been handed over out of envy (Mk 15:10; Mt 27:18), that he washed his hands of the matter and told the Jews that he is innocent of the man's blood (Mt 27:24), and that the Jews themselves took full responsibility for his death (Mt 27:25). Many critics find this portrait incredible and assign it to early Christian apologetics in which Pilate is exculpated and, in contrast, the Jewish participants are blamed. It is pointed out, for example, that Pilate was vicious, was insensitive to Jewish religious sensibilities, thought nothing of killing Jews who were troublesome, and even indulged in anti-Semitic policies, including the minting of offensive coins, perhaps encouraged, even urged, by his political ally Sejanus.

In my judgment, the truth of the matter probably lies somewhere between the Gospels' portraits of a passive, almost benevolent Pilate and the portrait of Pilate as insensitive and villainous, as we have it in the writings of Philo and Josephus. Much of my thinking has been shaped by recent work by Daniel Schwartz and Helen Bond[14] and takes into account recent archaeological findings.

Let us begin with a brief review of the negative assessments of Pilate that we find in Philo and Josephus. Philo of Alexandria describes the governor of Judea as a "man of an inflexible, stubborn, and cruel disposition," adding that "briberies, insults, robberies, outrages, wanton injuries, executions without trial, and endless and supremely grievous cruelty" marked his administration (*Legatio ad Gaium* 38 §301-302). Philo's remarks here are primarily in reference to the incident of the golden shields that Pilate had placed in Herod's palace in Jerusalem, an incident that is probably related in some way to an episode reported by Josephus, in which Pilate is said to have attempted to relocate Roman standards to Jerusalem (cf. *War* 2.9.2-3 §169-174; *Ant* 18.3.1 §55-59).[15] Schwartz rightly recognizes that Philo's negative depiction of Pilate "is part of his exaltation of Tiberius," in which the late emperor becomes a role model for the vain and reckless Gaius Caligula, whose ambition for divine honors could have incited a Jewish rebellion.[16] Likewise, Josephus's largely negative portrayal evaporates under close scrutiny. Pilate had only two serious disagreements with the Jewish people. The first involved the standards, in which he backed down. The second involved dipping into the Temple treasury reserved for national sacri-

---

14. D. R. Schwartz, "Pontius Pilate," in *ABD* 5:395-401; H. K. Bond, *Pontius Pilate in History and Interpretation*, SNTSMS 100 (Cambridge: Cambridge University Press, 1998).

15. For arguments that these events were probably one and the same, see Schwartz, "Pontius Pilate," p. 399; Schwartz, "Josephus and Philo on Pontius Pilate," *Jerusalem Cathedra* 3 (1983): 26-45.

16. Schwartz, "Pontius Pilate," p. 399.

fices, to finish paying for the aqueduct being constructed in Jerusalem (*War* 2.9.4 §175; *Ant* 18.3.2 §60-62).[17] This time Pilate did not yield, with the result that hundreds of Jews were killed or injured. As Richard Horsley and others have pointed out,[18] Pilate could not have removed funds from the Temple treasury without the approval of Caiaphas and (probably) other ruling priests, such as the captain of the treasury. Indeed, it is probable that this is the same incident to which reference is made in Lk 13:1: "There were some present at that very time who told him of the Galileans whose blood Pilate had mingled with their sacrifices." If this is the same incident,[19] then those who opposed Pilate's use of sacred funds were not the residents of Jerusalem, but pilgrims from Galilee, perhaps during a festival. In other words, what Caiaphas and colleagues approved, and the residents of Jerusalem accepted (even if not with enthusiasm), devout Galileans in town for the offering of sacrifices could not tolerate. Parts of this aqueduct in and near Jerusalem are still visible to this day.

In both incidents related by Josephus, the ruling priests are conspicuous by their silence. This is especially startling in the case of taking money from the *qorbōnas,* for Pilate could not have done this, nor would he have dared do this, without permission and assistance from the ruling priests themselves. Evidently, Caiaphas the high priest and Pilate the governor worked well together. It is not surprising that when Pilate was removed from office in early 37 C.E., after his brutal assault on the Samaritans, Caiaphas was removed from office shortly afterward (*Ant* 18.4.2 §88-89; 18.4.3 §95).[20] Finally, the Samaritan incident itself probably offers further important evidence of Pilate's cooperation with his Jewish colleagues, for his surprisingly harsh action taken against the Samaritans was probably encouraged by the ruling priests, who not only despised their northern neighbors (especially for placing bones in the Temple during the ad-

17. The account from which the money was taken was the "sacred treasure known as *qorbōnas* (κορβωνᾶς)" (*War* 2.9.4 §175). Josephus is here referring to the dedicated offering known as "qorban" (קרבן, *qorban;* cf. Mk 7:11: "'qorban' [κορβᾶν], that is, 'gift'"; cf. Mt 27:6: "It is not lawful to put them [i.e., Judas's pieces of silver] into the *qorbanas* [κορβανᾶν]"), that is, a gift given to God. To take such consecrated items and put them to a secular use would have given offense.

18. R. A. Horsley, "High Priests and the Politics of Roman Palestine," *JSJ* 17 (1986): 23-55.

19. Schwartz, "Pontius Pilate," p. 398; so also E. M. Smallwood, *The Jews under Roman Rule: From Pompey to Diocletian; A Study in Political Relations,* SJLA 20 (Leiden: Brill, 1981 [orig. 1976]), p. 163. Bond (*Pontius Pilate,* pp. 194-96) disputes the identification.

20. For further discussion of these and other incidents, see R. E. Brown, *The Death of the Messiah: From Gethsemane to the Grave; A Commentary on the Passion Narratives in the Four Gospels* (New York: Doubleday, 1994), 1:698-705; J. S. McLaren, *Power and Politics in Palestine: The Jews and the Governing of Their Land, 100 BC–AD 70,* JSNTSS 63 (Sheffield: JSOT Press, 1991), pp. 81-87; Bond, *Pontius Pilate,* pp. 24-93.

ministration of the Roman governor Coponius, who had succeeded the deposed Archelaus; cf. *Ant* 18.2.2 §29-30), but would have had little sympathy for the refounding of the Samaritan temple at Mount Gerizim.

Let us now consider numismatic and archaeological evidence. It has been claimed from time to time that Pilate minted coins, perhaps at the urging of Sejanus, that would be offensive to the Jewish people, perhaps as part of a larger anti-Jewish program.[21] Of the coins minted during his administration, most date from 29 to 32 C.E., and most fall into three basic configurations (with combinations thereof). Following Bond's recent study, they may be laid out accordingly:

Obverse	Reverse
1. symbol: three ears of barley	*simpulum* (cultic wine vessel)
legend: IOYΛIΛ KΛICΛPOC	TIBEPIOY KΛICΛPOC
	date: 29/30 C.E.
2. symbol: *lituus* (augurs wand)	wreath with berries
legend: TIBEPIOY KΛICΛPOC	date: 30/31 C.E.
3. symbol: *lituus* (augurs wand)	wreath with berries
legend: TIBEPIOY KΛICΛPOC	date: 31/32 C.E.

In her review of Jewish coinage from the Hasmoneans down to the time of Herod I and the Roman governors of Judea, Bond finds nothing provocative about the coins Pilate struck.[22] Although the *simpulum* and the *lituus* may have been offensive to the religiously devout, given these symbols' pagan cultic associations, they are hardly more offensive than many other images pressed on issues of coinages in Palestine in the previous century or later. What is significant is that Pilate did not strike any coins with the image of the Roman emperor or with offensive legends claiming divine status. This is hard to explain, if Pilate had in fact attempted to offend his Jewish subjects. Moreover, Pilate's coins remained in circulation for several years, with no new minting until halfway

---

21. For example, E. Bammel, "Syrian Coinage and Pilate," *JJS* 2 (1950): 108-10; P. L. Maier, "Sejanus, Pilate and the Date of the Crucifixion," *Church History* 37 (1968): 3-13; H. W. Hoehner, "Pontius Pilate," in *Dictionary of Jesus and the Gospels,* ed. J. B. Green, S. McKnight, and I. H. Marshall (Downers Grove, Ill.: InterVarsity, 1992), pp. 615-17 (p. 616: "Sejanus, whose anti-Semitic policies he had followed").

22. H. K. Bond, "The Coins of Pontius Pilate: Part of an Attempt to Provoke the People or to Integrate Them into the Empire?" *JSJ* 27 (1996): 241-62. For older, different assessments of these coins, see A. Kindler, "More Dates on the Coins of the Procurators," *IEJ* 6 (1956): 54-57; B. Oestreicher, "A New Interpretation of Dates on the Coins of the Procurators," *IEJ* 9 (1959): 193-95.

through the brief reign of Agrippa I (41-44 C.E.). This too is very difficult to explain, if Pilate's coins had been widely regarded by Jews as offensive. Why wait ten or more years to replace them?

Brian McGing finds the Gospels' portrait of a cautious, opportunistic Pilate wholly credible.[23] This explains his lengthy tenure, the lack of conflict with the Jewish leaders, the fact that he did not appoint a single high priest, and finally his removal from office, in all probability for acting uncritically and incautiously according to the wishes of Caiaphas in the Samaritan affair. It seems clear that the Roman governors of Judea and Samaria were guided by the counsel of the ruling priests, who would have explained the significance of the actions of men like Theudas and the anonymous Jew from Egypt. This would explain why the governors reacted the way they did. In all probability Caiaphas urged Pilate to quash Samaritan hopes to rebuild the temple at Mount Gerizim, not because such a program would have fomented sedition (with which Rome would have been very concerned), but because the Jewish high priest was not about to allow a rival temple to be rebuilt and a rival priesthood to be reestablished. Thus, Caiaphas's professional jealousies may have clouded his better political judgment.

Perhaps the most dramatic archaeological datum concerning Pilate is the stone found at Caesarea Maritima bearing his name and title. In the New Testament the full name "Pontius Pilate" occurs three times (Lk 3:1; Acts 4:27; 1 Tim 6:13) and in most manuscripts is spelled Πόντιος Π(ε)ιλᾶτος (cf. *Ant* 18.2.2 §35). Pilate normally resided in Caesarea Maritima (on the Mediterranean), but at Passover and other festivals took up residence in Jerusalem, either in the Antonia (which is doubtful), which overlooked the Temple precincts, or in Herod's palace (cf. *War* 2.14.8 §301, which says Gesius Florus, the last governor before the outbreak of war, resided in Herod's palace). The Roman historian Cornelius Tacitus (ca. 56–ca. 118 C.E.) states that "Christus . . . had suffered the death penalty during the reign of Tiberius, by sentence of the procurator Pontius Pilate [*per procuratorem Pontium Pilatum*]" (*Ann* 15.44). Calling Pilate a "procurator" is anachronistic, as some scholars have surmised,[24] for prior to the brief reign of Agrippa I (41-44), the Roman governors of Judea were prefects. This conjecture was confirmed by the inscription found at Caesarea Maritima in 1961. Antonio Frova's reconstruction is as follows:[25]

23. B. C. McGing, "Pontius Pilate and the Sources," *CBQ* 53 (1991): 416-38.

24. For example, A. H. M. Jones, "Procurators and Prefects in the Early Principate," in Jones, *Studies in Roman Government and Law* (Oxford: Blackwell, 1960), pp. 115-25.

25. A. Frova, "L'iscrizione di Ponzio Pilato a Cesarea," *Rendiconti dell'Istituto Lombardo* 95 (1961): 419-34, esp. pp. 424-25. This restoration is frequently cited, though its reconstruction is much debated. For discussion and bibliography see L. Boffo, *Iscrizioni greche e latine per lo studio della Bibbia* (Brescia: Paideia Editrice, 1994), pp. 217-33.

[CAESARIEN]STIBERIÉVM   [Caesarean]s' Tiberieum
[PON]TIVSPILATVS   [Pon]tius Pilate,
[PRAEF]ECTVSIVDA[EA]E   [Pref]ect of Juda[ea]
[D]É[DIT   ]   [d]e[dicates   ]

According to this reconstruction, Pontius Pilate has dedicated a "Tiberieum" to the people of Caesarea (i.e., *Caesarien[ibu]s*).

The immediate value of the inscription is that it finally settles the question of Pilate's rank and title. According to the third line, Pilate held the rank of prefect *(praefectus)*. In the Gospels, Pilate is called a ἡγεμών (cf. Mt 27:2; Lk 3:1), which is a general term that means leader or governor, and can serve as the Greek equivalent for either prefect or procurator. Although there are variations and inconsistencies in the terminology, *praefectus* is usually rendered ἔπαρχος, "procurator" ἐπίτροπος, and "governor" ἡγεμών. Mark does not mention Pilate's rank (though the plural ἡγεμόντες appears in the eschatological discourse, in conjunction with kings; cf. 13:9). The prefect is more of a military office (i.e., a military governor), while the procurator has broader civil authority and was concerned to protect the emperor's financial interests.

Pilate's rank, however, is about the only important element in this inscription that commands agreement. The first line of the inscription has been the object of a great deal of debate and speculation. Although Frova's restoration is widely cited, especially in popular literature, it has in fact been challenged by many. A whole host of alternative reconstructions has been offered. E. Weber recommends *[Kal(endis) Iulii]s Tiberiéum [M(arcus) ? Po]ntius Pilatus [praef]ectus Iuda[ea]e [dedicavit]* — "The Tiberieum of July First Marcus (?) Pontius Pilate prefect of Judea has dedicated."[26] A. Degrassi suggests *[Dis Augusti]s Tiberiéum [Pon]tius Pilatus [praef]ectus Iuda[ae]e [fecit, d]e[dicavit]* — "The Tiberieum of the Divine Augusti [i.e., Caesar Augustus and Livia his wife, the mother of Tiberius]. . . ."[27] S. Bartina offers a simpler solution: *[opu]s Tiberiéum* — "The Tiberieum building."[28] C. Gatti proposes an ethnic restoration: *[Iudaei]s Tiberiéum* — "The Tiberieum of the Jews."[29] V. Burr proposes a cultic restoration: *[nemu]s Tiberiéum* — "The Tiberieum of the [sacred]

---

26. E. Weber, "Zur Inschrift des Pontius Pilatus," *BJ* 171 (1971): 194-200.

27. A. Degrassi, "Sull'iscrizione di Ponzio Pilato," *Rendiconti dell' Accademia Nazionale dei Lincei*, ser. 8: *Classe di Scienze morali, storiche e filologiche* 19 (1964): 59-65.

28. S. Bartina, "Poncio Pilato en una inscripción monumentaria Palestinense," *CB* 19 (1962): 170-75.

29. C. Gatti, "A proposito di una rilettura dell'epigrafe di Ponzio Pilato," *Aevum* 55 (1981): 13-21.

grove."[30] G. Labbé proposes a municipal reading: *[munu]s Tiberiéum* — "The Municipal Tiberieum."[31] Other reconstructions could be mentioned,[32] but one in particular deserves special attention.

Recently Géza Alföldy has concluded that the inscription concerns a Tiberieum that Pontius Pilate restored for the seamen of Caesarea Maritima.[33] His restoration is as follows.

[NAUTI]STIBERIÉVM	[Seamen']s Tiberieum
[PON]TIVSPILATVS	[Pon]tius Pilate,
[PRAEF]ECTVSIVDA[EA]E	[Pref]ect of Jude[a]
[REF]É[CIT]	[restor]e[s . . .

Alföldy plausibly suggests that the inscription commemorates a rebuilding of the harbor of Caesarea Maritima (perhaps specifically a lighthouse), an achievement in which Pontius Pilate would have taken some pride. The Caesarea Maritima inscription may hint at what occupied most of Pilate's attention during his tenure in office. Recent archaeological work in Caesarea Maritima, including underwater work in the harbor itself, may lend support to this conjecture.[34]

Finally, there is one more significant issue that needs to be treated. It concerns the length of Pilate's tenure in office. Based on Josephus's comment that Valerius Gratus served eleven years (*Ant* 18.2.2 §35), scholars usually assume that Pilate became governor in 25 or 26 C.E. Schwartz, however, has offered impressive arguments that Gratus's tenure was much shorter, that in all probabil-

---

30. V. Burr, "Epigraphischer Beitrag zur neueren Pontius-Pilatus-Forschung," in *Vergangenheit, Gegenwart, Zukunft*, ed. W. Burr (Würzburg: Echter, 1972), pp. 37-41.

31. G. Labbé, "Ponce Pilate et la munificence de Tibère: l'inscription de Césarée," *REA* 93 (1991): 277-97.

32. For additional discussion, see especially G. Alföldy, "Pontius Pilatus und das Tiberieum von Caesarea Maritima," *SCI* 18 (1999): 85-108; I. Di Stefano Manzella, "Pontius Pilatus nell'iscrizione di Cesarea di Palestina," in *Le iscrizioni dei cristiani in Vaticano: Materiali e contributi scientifici per una mostra epigrafica*, ed. I. Di Stefano Manzella, Inscriptiones sanctae sedis 2 (Vatican City: Edizioni Quasar, 1997), pp. 209-15 and pl. 3.1.2; and Labbé ("Ponce Pilate," in *Palestine in the Time of Jesus: Social Structures and Social Conflicts*, ed. K. C. Hanson and D. E. Oakman [Minneapolis: Fortress, 1998], p. 78) thinks the Tiberieum was the theater, in which the stone was eventually unearthed.

33. Alföldy, "Pontius Pilatus," pp. 106-7.

34. See A. Raban and E. Linder, "Caesarea, the Herodian Harbour," *IJNAUE* 7 (1978): 238-43; R. L. Hohlfelder, "Caesarea beneath the Sea," *BAR* 8, no. 3 (1982): 42-47, 56; Hohlfelder et al., "Sebastos, Herod's Harbor at Caesarea Maritima," *BA* 46 (1983): 133-43; L. Vann, "Herod's Harbor Construction Recovered Underwater," *BAR* 9, no. 3 (1983): 10-14. The harbor is described in Josephus, *War* 1.21.5-7 §408-414; *Ant* 15.9.6 §331-341.

ity he retired to Rome not long after he appointed Caiaphas high priest in 18 C.E. Schwartz conjectures that Pilate took office in 19.[35] This would mean, then, that Pilate and Caiaphas served in their respective offices for a lengthy and almost identical period of time, some eighteen years for Caiaphas (from 18 to early 37) and seventeen for Pilate (from 19 to early 37).

What conclusions may we tentatively draw from our observations? I think we may conclude at least four things:

1. Relatively speaking, Caiaphas and Pilate enjoyed lengthy and peaceful terms in office. Compared to their predecessors and successors, their tenures were remarkably long. The importance of this observation should not be quickly passed over.

2. It is very probable that there was little friction between Caiaphas and Pilate. This is not to claim that their working relationship was cordial, or that they liked one another, only that they were able to work together peacefully. There is no hint in our sources, literary or archaeological, of any serious disagreement between the high priest and the governor. The few violent clashes that Pilate had, either with the Jewish people or with the Samaritan people, were probably undertaken after consultation with the ruling priests, and perhaps even with their support.

3. It is probable that Pilate occupied himself with major projects, such as the renovation of the harbor at Caesarea Maritima, and left Jewish matters in the hands of Caiaphas and his priestly colleagues. One might say that Pilate was westward facing, toward the Mediterranean and Rome, not eastward facing, toward Jerusalem.

4. Finally, the Gospels' portrait of a cautious Pilate who tests the political winds before reaching a decision as to the fate of the popular preacher from Galilee is consistent with our sources when critically read.[36] Pilate, who had only recently arrived in Jerusalem for the Passover, would be understandably reluctant to offend the Jewish people during the festival. Contrary to popular conceptions of Pilate, the governor was not ordinarily brutal or anti-Semitic. His long tenure in office and the relatively few incidents that could be construed as negative (by tendentious writers like Philo and Josephus) speak in his favor. Pilate's caution and hesitation in his examination of Jesus became the grounds for later Christian apologetic, but in the end, the Roman governor agreed with Jesus' accusers that he held to messianic pretensions and should be executed.

35. Schwartz, "Pontius Pilate," pp. 396-97.
36. On this point, see Brown, *Death of the Messiah*, pp. 694-95; Bond, *Pontius Pilate*, pp. 119, 205.

Our sources suggest that the portraits in Jewish and Christian writings indulge in either overly positive or overly negative assessments of the protagonists and antagonists in their respective narratives. In all probability Pilate was not as venal as Philo and Josephus would have us believe, nor was he as principled as Christian writers would have us believe. The same is probably true for Caiaphas, who was probably not as harsh and callous as the Evangelists depict.

Simon of Cyrene

As a concluding addendum, the ossuaries found in the Kidron Valley in 1941, one of which may bear the name of Simon of Cyrene, may be briefly discussed.[37] There is a brief reference to this man in the Synoptic Gospels. According to Mk 15:21, "they compelled a passer-by, Simon of Cyrene, who was coming in from the country, the father of Alexander and Rufus, to carry his cross" (cf. Mt 27:32; Lk 23:26). Inscriptions on ossuaries 9 and 5 raise the possibility that the ossuaries of children of this man Simon may have been found. They have been transcribed as follows:[38]

ossuary no. 9 front

| ΑΛΕΞΑΝΔΡΟC | Alexander |
| CΙΜωΝ | (son of) Simon |

ossuary no. 9 back

CΙΜωΝ ΑΛΕ	Simon Ale
ΑΛΕΞΑΝΔΡΟC	Alexander
CΙΜωΝΟC	(son) of Simon

ossuary no. 9 lid

| ΑΛΕΞΑΝΔΡΟΥ | of Alexander |
| אלכסנדרוס קרנית | Alexander QRNYT |

ossuary no. 5

| CΑΡΑ CΙΜωΝΟC | Sara (daughter) of Simon, |
| ΠΤΥΛΕΜΑΙΚΗ | of Ptolemais |

37. Although discovered in 1941 by E. L. Sukenik, who published a very brief announcement in *BASOR* 88 (1942): 38, the inscriptions and a detailed description were not published for another twenty years. See N. Avigad, "A Depository of Inscribed Ossuaries in the Kidron Valley," *IEJ* 12 (1962): 1-12 and pls. I-IV. See also "Tomb South of the Village of Silwan," in N. Avigad, "Tombs," in *NEAEHL* 2:750-53, here p. 753.

38. Avigad, "Inscribed Ossuaries," pp. 4-11.

In ossuary 9 we read of an Alexander the son of Simon (front and back). The inscriptions are carelessly executed. On the front the given name Alexander and the surname Simon are both in the nominative. This error is corrected on the back, with Simon in the genitive (σίμωνος). But the inscription is marred in its first line by starting with Simon, the name of the father, and the first three letters of Alexander's name. The inscriber catches his error and restarts in lines 2 and 3. This time he gets it right. On the lid the inscriber presents us with Alexander's name in Greek (line 1) and in Hebrew (line 2). The genitive "of Alexander" means that the ossuary and bones within it belong to Alexander. The Hebrew line provides us with either the man's nickname or a place-name. קרנית is thought by some to mean "Cyrenean" (or Cyreanite). If this is true (and it is disputed), then we have a very interesting constellation that suggests that we may actually have the ossuary of the person mentioned in Mark's Gospel.

Ossuary 5 refers to a Sara daughter of Simon, of Ptolemais. It is *Sara* who is from Ptolemais, not *Simon*. Ptolemais is on the Mediterranean coast, equidistant from Tyre to the north and Caesarea Maritima to the south. J. T. Milik thinks קרנית is an engraver's error and that קרניח ("[the] Cyrenean") was intended.[39] Avigad doubts this explanation, but he too thinks קרנית is related to Cyrene.[40] The name Sara (sara), who is probably Alexander's sister, is common to Cyrenaica.[41] Finally, on one ostracon from Masada השרני appears, possibly in reference to a village in Judea. But it may also mean "the Cyrenean" or "Cyrene" (cf. Mas no. 424).[42] On an ossuary lid from Bethphage, Milik reads בן קרנו.[43] But given the similarity and frequent confusion of waw and yod, the inscription may read בן קרני, "son of (the) Cyreanite."

Mark reads clumsily, "Simon of Cyrene, who was coming in from the country, the father of Alexander and Rufus," which may mean that Simon, recently arrived from Cyrene, was on hand for the Passover and happened to be among the onlookers when the crucifixion party chanced by. This Simon is said to be the father of Alexander and Rufus. If it can be shown that קרנית does indeed

39. In B. Bagatti and J. T. Milik, *Gli Scavi del 'Dominus Flevit'* (Jerusalem: Francescani, 1958), p. 81.

40. Avigad, "Inscribed Ossuaries," p. 11. The Hebrew New Testament renders "Cyrene" as קוריני (e.g., Mt 27:32; Acts 2:10; 11:20; 13:1).

41. Avigad, "Inscribed Ossuaries," p. 9; cf. *SEG* ix, s.v. Σάρρα, index, where a Σάρα Σίμωνος is recorded; see D. M. Robinson, "Inscriptions from the Cyrenaica," *AJA* 17 (1913): 166-67, no. 24; W. Horbury and D. Noy, *Jewish Inscriptions of Graeco-Roman Egypt* (Cambridge: Cambridge University Press, 1992), p. 330.

42. Yadin, Naveh, and Meshorer, *Masada I*, p. 26 and pl. 24.

43. J. T. Milik, "Le couvercle de Bathpagé," in *Hommages à André Dupont-Sommer* (Paris: Adrien-Maisonneuve, 1971), pp. 75-96, here p. 78.

mean "Cyrenean," then this Simon may be the man mentioned in the Gospels. Martin Hengel and Pieter van der Horst entertain the possibility.[44] To be sure, the names Alexander and Simon are common,[45] but the ossuary under consideration attests the only known instance of an "Alexander, son of Simon." That and the possibility that father and son were from Cyrene are very suggestive.

There are other supporting factors. The Christian church quickly spread to Cyrene, and converts from there visited Jerusalem (cf. Acts 11:20; 13:1). It is possible that Simon of Cyrene played a role in spreading the new faith in his native country.[46] Moreover, in his epistle to the church at Rome, Paul refers to one Rufus (Rom 16:13). This datum, in combination with the ancient and probably reliable tradition that Mark's Gospel was published in Rome, lends a small measure of additional support to this identification. In other words, the Markan Evangelist mentioned that Simon of Cyrene was the father of Alexander and Rufus because these men were known to the Christians of Rome (and, as it turns out, one of them was known to Paul also).

To date, the identification of Alexander's ossuary remains inconclusive, but very suggestive. If it can be shown to belong to the Alexander mentioned by the Markan Evangelist, then it may shed important light on the spread of Christianity in its earliest stages. From an apologetic perspective, it may also lend important support to the probability that the passion narrative (as well as Easter?) rests upon eyewitness testimony.

This last remark, however, should not be taken to imply that the most important role played by biblical archaeology is an apologetical one. On the contrary, the importance of archaeology lies primarily in the clarification and contextualization that it provides for the biblical literature itself and the assistance it offers interpreters of this literature. The archaeological materials reviewed in this chapter have provided just this kind of exegetical contextuality.[47]

44. M. Hengel, The "Hellenization" of Judaea in the First Century after Christ (London: SCM; Philadelphia: Trinity, 1989), p. 67 n. 39; P. W. van der Horst, Ancient Jewish Epitaphs: An Introductory Survey of a Millennium of Jewish Funerary Epigraphy (300 BCE–700 CE) (Kampen: Kok Pharos, 1991), pp. 140-41. Van der Horst remarks that "there is at least a good chance that we have here the ossuary of the son of the man who carried Jesus' cross."

45. As emphasized by D. Luhrmann, Das Markusevangelium, HNT 3 (Tübingen: Mohr-Siebeck, 1987), p. 259.

46. On the Jewish presence in Cyrene, see Acts 6:9 (which mentions a "synagogue of the . . . Cyrenians"); Josephus, Apion 2.44; Ant 14.7.2 §114-118; 16.6.1 §160. We may rightly wonder whether Simon's assistance in carrying Jesus' cross put him into contact with Jesus' following, which in turn led to his adoption of the new messianic faith.

47. I wish to take the opportunity here to record my thanks to Jim Charlesworth for organizing a splendid conference in Jerusalem. The conference was of great benefit for all participants and attendees.

"Stone House," *Birah,* and Antonia during the Time of Jesus

Daniel R. Schwartz

Nehemiah seems to use the Hebrew term *birah* — which may mean "citadel" or "fortress" — about a building on the Temple Mount or thereabouts (Neh 2:8; cf. 7:2). Josephus, writing in Greek, reports the existence of a Hasmonean fortress termed *baris* in the same general area. Given the similarity of *birah* with *baris,* it is commonly assumed that the two terms refer to the same fortress at the same site. But Josephus also reports, repeatedly and explicitly, that Herod renovated the *baris* and renamed it "Antonia" (*War* 1.75, 118, 401; *Ant* 13.307; 15.409; 18.92). Now, if *birah* equals *baris* and *baris* denotes the Antonia, the result is what Joshua Schwartz has termed "the *birah* = *baris* = Antonia" equation. Indeed, such an equation is widely assumed.[1] Moreover, we might actually prefer to speak of "the *birah-baris-*Antonia-*birah* equation." Why? Because it is often assumed that rabbinic references to the *birah* in connection with the Temple Mount refer to the building noted by Nehemiah.

J. Schwartz has assembled two types of evidence that undermine this extended equation. First, he cites archaeological evidence that tends to locate Nehemiah's *birah* on the Temple Mount itself and not to its northwest where the Antonia was. We now add to this argument that D. Bahat has adduced archaeological evidence for the Hasmonean *baris* being somewhat south of the Antonia.[2]

---

1. J. Schwartz, "The Temple in Jerusalem: Birah and Baris in Archaeology and Literature," in *The Centrality of Jerusalem: Historical Perspectives,* ed. M. Poorthuis and Ch. Safrai (Kampen: Kok Pharos, 1996), pp. 29-49. For a recent, detailed discussion of the Antonia, see A. Lichtenberger, *Die Baupolitik Herodes des Großen,* ADPV 26 (Wiesbaden: Harrassowitz, 1999), pp. 35-39.

2. See D. Bahat, "The Western Wall Tunnels," in *Ancient Jerusalem Revealed,* ed. H. Geva (Jerusalem: Israel Exploration Society, 1994), p. 185; Bahat, "Jerusalem Down Under: Tunneling along Herod's Temple Mount Wall," *BAR* 21, no. 6 (1995): see esp. p. 45 (with map on p. 33); and J. Ådna, *Jerusalemer Tempel und Tempelmarkt im 1. Jahrhundert n. Chr.* (Wiesbaden: Harras-

Figure 53. The Herodian Temple, southern extension, with the triple Huldah gates.
Courtesy of J. H. Charlesworth

Second, J. Schwartz studied the rabbinic use of the term *birah* and argued that it too, usually, referred to the Temple Mount itself, or to some part of it.

These are all involved issues, which we do not intend to open. We would like to address only one point. Schwartz was skeptical about the propriety of locating at or near the Antonia any parts of the Temple cult, such as those the rabbis located at or near the *birah*. His doubts were based on the apparently reasonable notion that a Herodian or Roman fortress is not a proper place to store the priestly garments, since these require purity and sanctity. For this reason, Schwartz specifically expressed skepticism regarding an oral suggestion of mine, several years ago, based on a passage in Josephus's *Antiquities,* that the high-priestly vestments were stored in a chamber in or at the Antonia.[3] However, Schwartz gave no details of my argument (which was perfectly understandable, since it had not yet been published), and a misprint in his reference to the *Antiquities* (he refers to *Ant* 17 instead of *Ant* 18) makes it impossible for readers to explore the issue themselves. In what follows, I will present my sug-

sowitz Verlag, 1999), pp. 22-25 ("Die Lage der hasmonäischen Baris"). Also, see my review of Ådna in *JQR* 91 (2001): 509-10.

3. See Schwartz, "The Temple in Jerusalem," p. 44 n. 38. For a response to Schwartz's argument, see below, n. 12.

gestion, emphasizing again that it has to do with only one datum among many in the substantial and complex dossier on *birah/baris/*Antonia/*birah.*

According to Josephus, Pontius Pilate's stormy term as governor of Judea included two incidents in which he was perceived to have violated the sanctity of Jerusalem and the Temple (*Ant* 18.55-59; 60-62).[4] Accordingly, it is not surprising that when Lucius Vitellius, the Roman governor of Syria, finally suspended Pilate and sent him off to defend himself in Rome, he added a conciliatory gesture bespeaking a Roman hands-off policy toward the Temple. What did Vitellius do? He relinquished Roman control of the high-priestly garments, transferring them to the custody of the priests themselves. The background for this move, which constituted a measure of separation between religion and state, is explained as follows (*Ant* 18.91-95, trans. L. H. Feldman [LCL]):

(91) At that time the vestments were stored in Antonia — there is a stronghold of that name — for the following reason. One of the priests, Hyrcanus, the first of many by that name, had constructed a large house *(baris)* near the temple and lived there most of the time. As custodian of the vestments, for to him alone was conceded the right to put them on, he kept them laid away there, whenever he put on his ordinary clothes in order to go down to the city. (92) His sons and their children also followed the same practice. When Herod became king, he made lavish repairs to this building *(baris)*, which was conveniently situated, and, being a friend of Antony, he called it Antonia. He retained the vestments there just as he had found them, believing that for this reason the people would never rise in insurrection against him. (93) Herod's successor as king, his son Archelaus, acted similarly. After him, when the Romans took over the government, they retained control of the high priest's vestments and kept them in a stone building (ἐν οἴκῳ λίθοις οἰκοδομηθέντι), where they were under the seal both of the priests and of the custodians of the treasury and where the warden of the guard lighted the lamp day by day. (94) Seven days before each festival the vestments were delivered to the priests by the warden. After they had been purified, the high priest wore them; then after the first day of the festival he put them again in the building (εἰς τὸν οἶκον) where they were laid away before. This was the procedure at the three festivals each year and on the fast day. (95) Vitellius was guided by our law in dealing with the vestments, and instructed the warden not to meddle with the question where they were to be stored or when they should be used.

---

4. See also Lk 13:1 and Philo, *Legatio ad Gaium* 299-305. For the argument that the latter is another version of the first of the two incidents reported by Josephus, see my "Josephus and Philo on Pontius Pilate," in *The Jerusalem Cathedra*, ed. L. I. Levine (Jerusalem: Yad Izhak Ben-Zvi Institute; Detroit: Wayne State University Press, 1983), 3:26-45.

This passage deals with a period of perhaps a century and a half. In the present context, however, we shall focus only on the period of Jesus (§§93-94) and a point of Jerusalem's archaeology that, as we shall see, Josephus's diction seems to illuminate in a somewhat roundabout way.

Our points of departure are two stylistic anomalies in the text as translated by Feldman — which, however, quite accurately reflects Josephus's Greek (which we added parenthetically above). First, after we have been told in 91-92 that the vestments were stored in the Antonia, which was a fortress, it is surprising to read in 93 that they were stored in "a stone building" (lit. "in a building made of stones"). If the Antonia is meant, why does Josephus not say "in the Antonia"? And why the indefinite article?[5] But if another building is meant in 93, how is the reader to resolve the contradiction between the statements in that passage and the information in 91-92? Upon consideration, perhaps the reader will settle the matter by assuming that the stone building was some sort of secondary structure associated with and considered part of the Antonia. Nevertheless, such a reader might justifiably be puzzled as to why Josephus left such confusion in his text.

The second rough passage is as the first one: in 94 Josephus refers to the return of the vestments to "the building where they were laid away before." Again, the attentive reader is puzzled. Why did not Josephus just say "the building" or "the Antonia"?

Although I know of no explicit discussion of this problem, a review of translations over the centuries clearly shows that it bothered just about everyone. There can be no doubt for translators that the normal translation of *oikos* is "house" or "building." Indeed, some translators, as Feldman, translated its occurrences in 93-94 that way, thus perplexing their readers (as we observed).[6] But if Whiston gave "stone chamber . . . chamber" and Clementz went for "steinernen Behälter . . . Behälter,"[7] it is clear that they were seeking a way to avoid the problem. This they accomplished, as did some others, by having Josephus refer, in both passages, not to the Antonia itself but rather to something within it (a room or container). Others went one better and eliminated both difficulties: they reduced the first *oikos* to something smaller (room, cabinet, container) and substituted something general (such as "place") for the second one. Thus, a 1510 Latin translation has "tabernaculo . . . loco" and — perhaps on its basis — half a century later a German one gave "Kammer . . . Ort,"

5. In English, corresponding to the lack of any article in the Greek.

6. So too the Latin translation in the great 1726 Hudson-Havercamp edition (1:880 ["domo ex lapide constructa . . . domum"]).

7. *The Works of Flavius Josephus,* trans. W. Whiston (London, 1872), p. 490; *Des Flavius Josephus Jüdische Altertümer,* trans. H. Clementz (Berlin and Vienna, 1923), 2:521.

just as later translators were to give "Gehäuse . . . Ort," "cabinet . . . place," and "construction . . . lieu."[8] These all create a totally smooth text — at the price of requiring us to accept a rare (or worse) meaning for *oikos*.[9] Any Greek text that uses so elementary a word as *oikos* and yet engenders such difficulties and variety of translations, invites further examination.

Now when the normal translation (such as Feldman's) of a Greek text engenders a stylistic roughness, it is admittedly *possible* that — as was assumed by those responsible for the translations cited above — the author in fact intended a rare meaning. However, as a rule, rare meanings occur only rarely. So when there is some reason to suspect, given the author or the contents or both, that the Greek text might reflect usage in another language, it is worthwhile to consider another frequent possibility, viz., that the text we are reading reflects an idiom or proper noun in some other language. For if an idiom was rendered too literally, or a proper noun translated instead of transliterated, difficulties could easily ensue in the target language.[10] Given that Josephus was a Jerusalemite priest and is referring here to matters pertaining to the Jerusalem priesthood, we might wonder if recourse to Hebrew (or Aramaic) might help us out with the stylistic anomalies in his Greek text.

8. In order: *Iosephus de Antiquitatibus ac de Bello Iudaico* (Venice, 1510), p. cxlix (a); Flavius Josephus, *Des hochberuempten Historibeschreibers alle Bücher,* trans. D. Caspar Hedion (Strassburg, 1556), p. cccxxvi (b); *Des vortrefflichen Jüdischen Geschicht-Schreibers Flavius Josephus Sämtliche Wercke,* trans. J. B. Ott (Zürich, 1736), p. 445; *The Whole Genuine and Complete Works of Flavius Josephus,* trans. G. H. Maynard (New York, 1794), p. 290; T. Reinach, ed., *Oeuvres complètes de Flavius Josèphe,* trans. G. Mathieu and L. Herrmann (Paris, 1929), 4:150. Note also the middle way taken by A. Schalit in his 1963 Hebrew translation: *ḥeder . . . bayyit* (room . . . building).

9. True, it *can* mean something as partial as "room," "chamber"; see H. G. Liddell and R. Scott, comp., *A Greek-English Lexicon,* ed. H. S. Jones et al., 9th ed. (Oxford, 1940), p. 1205, s.v. (§I.2). But such an unusual translation seems to be only a last resort, to be weighed against other options, such as the one to be suggested below.

10. For an example of the latter type, which will especially interest us here, note that the Hebrew name for the lowlands that separate Israel's highlands from the coastal plain is *ha-shephela,* and it is usual simply to transliterate it; see, for example, *Encyclopaedia Judaica* 14 (1972), cols. 1380-81. But the word means "the low [region]." Accordingly, when 1 Maccabees, which is a Greek translation of a Hebrew work, refers at 6:40 to τὰ ταπεινά, translators and other scholars have differed, and continue to differ, on whether to translate with uppercase "the Shephelah" or lowercase "the low [region]," in which case referring to the low part of some place, not necessarily the Shephelah. Or, for another case, *ha-aretz* is a standard Hebrew term for the land of Israel, but the word itself means only "the land." In some passages it even denotes "the world." Accordingly, when a Greek text that may reflect a Semitic background uses ἡ γῆ, which is the usual translation of the Hebrew common noun, we may wonder whether it should be translated "the Land [of Israel]" or just "the land" (or "the world"). See my "The End of the GH (Acts 1:8): Beginning or End of the Christian Vision?" *JBL* 105 (1986): 669-76.

In pursuing this avenue of thought, it is important to note that Josephus gives, in our passage, a detail that was probably meaningless for many of his readers: the *oikos* in which the vestments were stored was *made of stone*. This is an item that only Jewish readers were likely to appreciate.[11] According to Jewish law, stone cannot contract impurity, so a stone house would be an ideal place to store the high-priestly garments.[12] The same is also true of other details in this report, such as the reference to Archelaus as king (§93), which was inaccurate but reflects a habit of ancient Jewish sources to make lesser figures into "kings."[13] So too the references to "the fast day" in 94 and "our law" in 95; it all sounds very much as if Josephus is thinking of Jews or insiders.[14]

That being the case, before we agree to settle for either a rough text or an unusual translation, we should ask whether "house built of stones" may have meant something special in Hebrew or Aramaic, as an idiom or proper noun. Here we are in luck, for it turns out that the Mishnah, in describing one of the most sacred rites performed by the high priest (Num 19), mentions a place *called* "Stone House": "Seven days prior to the burning of the Red Heifer the high priest should be separated from his house to a chamber on the northeastern face of the *Birah* — it was called *Bet Even* [lit. 'Stone House']. And water of purification is to be sprinkled upon him during all seven days" (*m. Parah* 3.1). That is, when the high priest had to be, for seven days, in a place that allowed for maximum purity, he was taken to the chamber *called* "Stone House," which is said to have been "on the northeastern face of the *Birah*." It is difficult to imagine that it is a coincidence that Josephus speaks of a "house built of stone" in connection with the purity of the high-priestly vestments and what happens

---

11. The matter is somewhat like the passage attributed to Hecataeus cited in Josephus's *Apion* 1.198, which underlines that the altar in Jerusalem was made of unhewn stones — a point only Jewish writers and readers, familiar with Ex 20:25, could appreciate. See B. Bar Kochva, *Pseudo-Hecataeus "On the Jews": Legitimizing the Jewish Diaspora* (Berkeley: University of California Press, 1996), pp. 149-50.

12. See, in general, E. P. Sanders, *Jewish Law from Jesus to the Mishnah* (London: SCM; Philadelphia: Trinity, 1990), p. 357 n. 64; R. Deines, *Jüdische Steingefässe und pharisäische Frömmigkeit* (Tübingen: J. C. B. Mohr [Siebeck], 1993), esp. chap. 4. Josephus's emphasis here on the special measures taken to protect the sanctity of the vestments would seem to overcome J. Schwartz's a priori objection about the Antonia being an unlikely place to seek especial purity (see above, at n. 3).

13. Note, similarly, Mt 2:22 (βασιλεύει); *Ant* 14.157, 165, etc.; H. Hoehner, *Herod Antipas* (Cambridge: Cambridge University Press, 1972), pp. 149-50.

14. For the argument (based on chronological and other considerations) that *Ant* 18.90-95 is based on a source composed by a Jerusalemite priest, see my *Studies in the Jewish Background of Christianity* (Tübingen: J. C. B. Mohr [Siebeck], 1992), pp. 202-17. In the present context, it does not matter which Jerusalemite priest — Josephus or another — authored the passage.

to them seven days before each festival; and since treatment of Josephus's *oikos* as a common noun leads to a puzzling text, it is all the more attractive to accept the invitation to view "house built of stone" as his attempt to represent the Hebrew proper noun — *Bet Even.*

Our conclusion, then, is that Josephus is here doing his best to render into Greek the Hebrew *name* of a chamber that served as an especially pure place serving the needs of the Temple cult. This is important, first of all, because it allows us to use Josephus as an outside control to confirm that a particular datum in the Mishnah is at least as old as the first century c.e.[15] Moreover, since rabbinic usage of the term *birah* has been the subject of some debate,[16] our discussion of *Ant* 18.93-94 is useful insofar as it lets us pin down at least one text where that term seems clearly to refer to the Antonia.

Beyond that, however, our explanation of Josephus's rough style in *Ant* 18.93-94 also leads us to contribute an item to an ongoing debate about the archaeology of Jerusalem in the time of Jesus. For although it used to be assumed, on the basis of some rather explicit Josephan statements (which we listed at the outset of our paper), that the Hasmonean *baris* became the Antonia,[17] it has more recently become fashionable to distinguish between their sites, with the *baris* just north of the original Temple quadrate and the Antonia yet farther to the north. Now in general I tend to think scholars looking — even digging — back into the matter should be very wary of positing that they know the Temple Mount and its immediate environs better than did a first-century Jerusalemite priest and historian, even if he were the sole witness to the matter. Now we may add to this general prejudice that our juxtaposition of *Ant* 18.90-95 and *m. Parah* 3.1 shows, as we have seen, that the proper noun *Bet Even* was indeed in use in the first century. That, in turn, entitles us to assume that this Mishnah's usage of *birah* too reflects first-century usage. So whatever we think of the

15. It might be objected that use of Josephus to confirm the Mishnah is circular and so illegitimate, in this case, since we established his meaning only by using the Mishnah. However, comparison with the following hypothetical case should dispel that objection. Suppose a scholar of the year 4000 uncovers a document of the year 2006 that refers to "JC's book on JC and archaeology." The use of "JC" will probably puzzle him. However, if he then discovers, in a text of 2300, a reference to the present volume naming its editor and title but not its date, he will legitimately infer that he probably has *two* pieces of evidence attesting to the existence of the same volume: one clarifies its editor and title, the other supplies its terminus ad quem.

16. See Schwartz, "The Temple in Jerusalem"; P. Mandel, "'Birah' as an Architectural Term in Rabbinic Literature" (in Hebrew), *Tarbiz* 61 (1991/92): 195-217. The debate began already in the Talmud; see Schwartz, p. 35, referring to *p. Pesaḥim* 7.8 (35a, top) and parallels.

17. Note that of Bahat's two publications cited in n. 2, in the 1994 one he posited some lack of clarity in Josephus's testimony, whereas in the 1995 one he more reasonably suggested that Josephus mistakenly identified the *baris* and the Antonia due to their proximity.

baris = Antonia part of the extended equation, the Antonia = *birah* part turns out to be very old, documented by two local witnesses who precede us, essentially, by two thousand years. That is impressive evidence of how first-century locals viewed the matter. If it is an error, it is a very old one — one that takes us back almost to the days of Jesus.

Miracles, *Maleficium,* and *Maiestas* in the Trial of Jesus

John W. Welch

Few legal subjects are more complex than the so-called trial of Jesus. Too little is known about the substantive laws and normative procedures, whether Jewish or Roman, in Jerusalem during the second quarter of the first century C.E.,[1] and too little can be determined about why various people acted as they did for anyone to speak with certainty about the wide array of legal technicalities presented by this case. Without presuming to resolve all these perplexities, I hope to shed new light on these proceedings by seeing the accounts in all four Gospels through one overlooked part of their common sociolegal context. While many religious, social, and legal factors undoubtedly propelled the case forward, deep-seated fears were behind them all. One underlying and commonly shared fear — the fear associated with magic or the supernatural — may have played a much more instrumental role in this case than is usually thought. Laws throughout the ancient world regulated the use of "magic," a concept that was highly variegated and whose manifestations were not often legally differentiated. The term "magic" typically covers a broad range of numinous activities, including sorcery, divination, astrology, wonder-working, exorcism, and all other such activities that cross over into the realm of the supernatural.[2]

---

1. Little is known about the specific legal rules of the Sanhedrin in Jesus' day. Talmudic laws may or may not have applied at that time. [Professor Welch was permitted to quote from the KJV; he also gives some of his own translations. — JHC.]

2. Magicians and diviners are known by many titles in antiquity. In ancient Palestine and Syria such nomenclature includes the terms "man of God," "spellbinder," "seer," "priest," "dream interpreter," "healer," "enchanter," "soothsayer," "lot drawer," "evildoer," "astrologer,"

This paper was first read at the annual meeting of the Classical Association of the Middle West and South, April 2001, and was updated for presentation to the Biblical Law Section of the Society of Biblical Literature, November 2005.

Modern people have difficulty understanding the pervasive roles and driving fears associated with unseen spirits, demons, powers, names, curses, and wonders in the world of the New Testament. But awareness of this factor brings into focus an overlooked dynamic in the trial of Jesus. In sum, the Jewish chief priests were deeply concerned about Jesus' wonder-working and therefore considered him worthy of death under biblical law, which made it a capital offense to engage in various forms of improper magic and, especially, to use miraculous signs or wonders to deceive people or to lead them into apostasy (Deut 13:1-5). For tactical reasons, the chief priests took Jesus to Pilate in the hope that he might find Jesus similarly guilty under Roman law of sedition *(crimen maiestatis)* through illicit magical wonder-working *(maleficium)*. Impelled largely by a fear of Jesus' apparent supernatural powers, they hurried the matter through to the prompt crucifixion. Although rarely noted in legal analyses of the trial, these Jewish and Roman laws best explain the conduct of virtually everyone arrayed around Jesus in his final hours on earth. Indeed, each of the four New Testament accounts of the death of Jesus makes coherent sense when read in this light.

A Background of Uncertainty and Confusion

Too often, traditional approaches have attempted to reconstruct the trial of Jesus as if it were a logical, rational affair, viewing it as a modern legal proceeding conducted by enlightened, scientific, postmodern minds. The accounts, however, suggest otherwise. These hearings and proceedings were neither orderly nor systematic; they were neither precisely focused nor well structured. For this reason most past legal explanations have failed, making it impossible to give clear, one-word answers to such questions as "Precisely what cause of action was brought against Jesus?" (as if ancient courts followed anything like modern pleading practice), or "Specifically who was responsible for the death of Jesus?" (as if lines of legal jurisdiction were clearly established). Many charges and many people were involved.[3] A more holistic

---

"sheep tender," "ensnarer," "wicked one," and "magician." Ann Jeffers, *Magic and Divination in Ancient Palestine and Syria* (Leiden: Brill, 1996). On the distinctions between magic and miracles, see Edwin Yamauchi, "Magic or Miracle? Diseases, Demons and Exorcisms," in *Gospel Perspectives: The Miracles of Jesus,* ed. David Wenham and Craig Blomberg (Sheffield: JSOT Press, 1986), pp. 89-183.

3. Some of the main studies in recent decades, arranged alphabetically, that tend to recognize the joint and dual complicity of the Jews and the Romans in the death of Jesus include E. Bammel, ed., *The Trial of Jesus* (Naperville, Ill.: Allenson, 1970); E. Bammel and C. F. D. Moule, eds., *Jesus and the Politics of His Day* (Cambridge: Cambridge University Press, 1984); H.-W.

approach to this situation is needed, which would be consistent with ancient, premodern sensitivities.

By way of illustration, consider the question of intent. One scans the New Testament for indications of what specifically motivated Judas, Annas, Caiaphas, Herod Antipas, Pilate, or the ever present chief priests, and finds precious few. One may guess, of course, what their precise purposes may have been, and various people have favored any number of political, commercial, social, personal, religious, or legalistic motives. Some commentators place culpability squarely on the Jews,[4] while others implicate the Romans.[5] While some

---

Bartsch, "Wer verurteilte Jesus zum Tode?" *NovT* 7 (1964): 210-16; H. Boers, *Who Was Jesus?* (San Francisco: Harper and Row, 1989); R. E. Brown, *The Gospel according to John, XIII–XXI* (Garden City, N.Y.: Doubleday, 1970); Brown, *The Death of the Messiah,* 2 vols. (New York: Doubleday, 1994); D. R. Catchpole, *The Trial of Jesus: A Study in the Gospels and Jewish Historiography from 1770 to the Present Day* (Leiden: Brill, 1971); E. Dabrowski, "The Trial of Christ in Recent Research," *SE* 4 (1968): 21-27; K. Haacker, "Wer war Schuld am Tode Jesu?" *TBei* 25, no. 1 (1994): 23-36; P. Hofrichter, "Das dreifache Verfahren über Jesus als Gottessohn, König und Mensch: Zur Redaktionsgeschichte der Prozesstradition," *Kairos* 30-31 (1988-89): 69-81; J. Jeremias, "Zur Geschichtlichkeit des Verhörs Jesu vor dem hohen Rat," *ZNW* 43 (1951): 145-50; K. Kertelge, ed., *Der Prozess gegen Jesus: Historische Rückfrage und theologische Deutung* (Berlin: Herder, 1988); G. D. Kilpatrick, *The Trial of Jesus* (London: Oxford University Press, 1953); M. Limbeck, ed., *Redaktion und Theologie des Passionsberichtes nach den Synoptikern* (Darmstadt: Wissenschaftliche Buchgesellschaft, 1981); G. Lohfink, *Der letzte Tag Jesu: Die Ereignisse der Passion* (Freiburg im Breisgau: Herder, 1981), trans. S. Attanasio, *The Last Day of Jesus* (Notre Dame: Ave Maria, 1984); P. J. Maier, "Who Killed Jesus?" *Christianity Today* 34, no. 6 (1990): 16-19; F. Millar, "Reflections on the Trials of Jesus," in *A Tribute to Geza Vermes: Essays on Jewish and Christian Literature and History,* ed. P. R. Davies and R. T. White (Sheffield: JSOT, 1990), pp. 355-81; J. Pawlikowski, "The Trial and Death of Jesus: Reflections in Light of a New Understanding of Judaism," *Chicago Studies* (Anniverary Volume) 25, no. 1 (1986): 79-94; G. S. Sloyan, *Jesus on Trial* (Philadelphia: Fortress, 1973); G. S. Sloyan, "Recent Literature on the Trial Narratives of the Four Gospels," in *Critical History and Biblical Faith,* ed. T. Ryan (Lanham, Md.: University Press of America, 1979), pp. 136-76; M. Sordi, *The Christians and the Roman Empire* (Norman: University of Oklahoma Press, 1986); J. A. Stalker, *The Trial and Death of Jesus Christ* (Grand Rapids: Zondervan, 1983); A. Strobel, *Die Stunde der Wahrheit,* WUNT 21 (Tübingen: Mohr, 1980); E. M. Yamauchi, "Historical Notes on the Trial and Crucifixion of Jesus," *Christianity Today* 15 (1971): 634-39.

4. Among the studies that tend to place primary responsibility on the Jews are J. Blinzler, *The Trial of Jesus* (Westminster, Md.: Newman, 1959), trans. from the 4th German ed. (Regensburg, 1969); F. F. Bruce, "The Trial of Jesus in the Fourth Gospel," in *Gospel Perspectives,* ed. R. France (Sheffield: JSOT Press, 1980), 1:7-20; D. R. Catchpole, "The Answer of Jesus to Caiaphas (Matt. 26:64)," *NTS* 17 (1970): 213-26; K. P. Donfried, "Paul and Judaism: 1 Thessalonians 2:13-16 as a Test Case," *Int* 38 (1984): 242-53; P. J. Maier, "Who Was Responsible for the Trial and Death of Jesus?" *Christianity Today* 18 (1974): 806-9; B. C. McGing, "Pontius Pilate and the Sources," *CBQ* 53 (1991): 416-38; P. W. Walaskay, "The Trial and Death of Jesus in the Gospel of Luke," *JBL* 94 (1975): 81-93; D. Wead, "We Have a Law," *NovT* 11 (1969): 185-89.

5. H. Cohn, *The Trial and Death of Jesus* (New York: Ktav, 1977), p. 114. Other studies that

focus on religious factors, others conclude that the trial "was political through-out in its intent and purpose."[6] Most experts would agree that a relatively small group of Jewish leaders in Jerusalem rejected Jesus and his disciples,[7] but previous scholarship has not made it sufficiently clear *why* their rejection of him was so intense that they felt compelled to stop at nothing short of his death.

---

have focused on the ultimate Roman responsibility for the death of Jesus include H. Bamberger, "New Light on the High Priest," *JES* 18 (1981): 653-55; S. G. F. Brandon, *The Trial of Jesus of Nazareth* (New York: Stein and Day, 1968); T. A. Burkill, "The Competence of the Sanhedrin," *VC* 10 (1956): 81-96; Burkill, "The Trial of Jesus," *VC* 12 (1958): 1-18; Burkill, "The Condemnation of Jesus: A Critique of Sherwin-White's Thesis," *NovT* 12 (1970): 321-42. W. A. Campbell, *Did the Jews Kill Jesus?* (New York: Peter Eckler, 1964); J. T. Carroll and J. B. Green, *The Death of Jesus in Early Christianity* (Peabody, Mass.: Hendrickson, 1995), p. 202; H. Cohn, "Reflections on the Trial and Death of Jesus," *Israel Law Review* 2 (1967): 332-79; Cohn, "Reflections on the Trial of Jesus," *Judaism* 20 (Winter 1971): 10-23; Cohn, *Reflections on the Trial and Death of Jesus,* 2nd ed. (New York: Harper and Row, 1971); Cohn, *The Trial and Death of Jesus* (New York: Ktav, 1977); M. Enslin, "The Trial of Jesus," *JQR* 60 (1969): 353-55; P. Fredriksen, *Jesus of Nazareth* (New York: Vintage, 2000), pp. 234, 256; G. Mamlok, "The Two Trials of Jesus," *Midstream* 35 (1989): 29-32; H. Mantel, *Studies in the History of the Sanhedrin* (Cambridge: Harvard University Press, 1961); R. L. Overstreet, "Roman Law and the Trial of Christ," *BSac* 135 (1978): 323-32; P. Richardson and D. Granskow, eds., *Anti-Judaism in Early Christianity* (Waterloo, Ont.: Wilfrid Laurier University Press, 1986); E. Rivkin, *What Crucified Jesus? The Political Execution of a Charismatic* (Nashville: Abingdon, 1984); A. N. Sherwin-White, *The Trial of Christ: Historicity and Chronology in the Gospels* (London: SPCK, 1965); J. G. Sobosan, "The Trial of Jesus," *JES* 10 (1973): 70-93; W. Stegemann, "Gab es eine jüdische Beteiligung an der Kreuzigung Jesu?" *Kirche und Israel* (Neukirchen-Vluyn) 13, no. 1 (1998): 3-24; P. Winter, "The Trial of Jesus and the Competence of the Sanhedrin," *NTS* 10 (1963): 494-99; Winter, *On the Trial of Jesus,* rev. and ed. T. Burkill and G. Vermes, 2nd ed. (Berlin and New York: Walter de Gruyter, 1974); Winter, "The Trial of Jesus as a Rebel against Rome," *JQR* 16 (1968): 31-37; S. Zeitlin, "The Crucifixion of Jesus Reexamined," *JQR* 31 (1941): 327-69; Zeitlin, "The Crucifixion: A Libelous Accusation against the Jews," *JQR* 54 (1964): 8-22; Zeitlin, "The Trial of Jesus," *JQR* 53 (1962): 77-88; Zeitlin, *Who Crucified Jesus?* (New York: Bloch, 1964).

6. Rivkin, *What Crucified Jesus?* based on his articles from the 1950s and 1970s; see pp. 27, 87, and 124.

7. Placing culpability on only a small group of Jewish leaders are R. J. Cassidy and P. J. Scharper, eds., *Political Issues in Luke-Acts* (Maryknoll, N.Y.: Orbis, 1983); J. B. Chance, "The Jewish People and the Death of Jesus in Luke-Acts: Some Implications of an Inconsistent Narrative Role," *SBL Seminar Papers,* 1991, pp. 50-81; F. D. Gilliard, "The Problem of the Antisemitic Comma between 1 Thessalonians 2:14 and 15," *NTS* 35 (1989): 481-502; H. Kosmala, "His Blood on Us and Our Children," in H. Kosmala, ed., *ASTI* 7 (1970), pp. 94-126; F. J. Matera, "Responsibility for the Death of Jesus according to the Acts of the Apostles," *JSNT* 39 (1990): 77-93; Matera, "The Trial of Jesus: Problems and Proposals," *Int* 45 (1991): 5-16; J. R. Michaels, "John 18:21 and the 'Trial' of Jesus," *NTS* 36, no. 3 (1990): 474-79; A. Schalit, "Kritische Randbemerkungen zu Paul Winters 'On the Trial of Jesus,'" in H. Kosmala, ed., *ASTI* 2 (1963), pp. 86-102; D. Schmidt, "1 Thess 2:13-16: Linguistic Evidence for an Interpolation," *JBL* 102 (1983): 269-79; R. Schippers, "The Pre-Synoptic Tradition in I Thessalonians ii 13-16," *NovT* 8 (1966): 223-34.

Pilate's motivations are equally obscure. Should he be seen as a weak, servile, incompetent, middle-management functionary who was easily intimidated, manipulated by his wife, and motivated by trepidation, having recently lost his power base in Rome; or should it be recognized that Pilate held in his hands great legal and military powers, unhesitantly asserting himself on several occasions to maintain public order? Above all, he probably was deeply frustrated; having tried in several ways to get the chief priests to drop their complaint against Jesus, Pilate saw that nothing was working and instead "a riot *(thorubos)* was beginning" (Mt 27:24). Still, what motivated Pilate to give the crowd "a firm bond" *(to hikanon)* remains unsatisfactorily obscure: Did he act out of impatience, indifference, hope that the crowd would just go away and leave Jesus alone, worry about Rome, fear for his own safety or station, or all or some of the above?

It is likewise difficult to determine the legal charges leveled against Jesus by his captors.[8] Several legal charges were raised, but none of them stuck. Significantly, none of the stated causes of action is consistently invoked throughout the record. This fluidity reminds us that Jesus' captors came out against him as "against a robber" (*epi lēstēn;* Mt 26:55; Mk 14:48; Lk 22:52). Robbers were out-

---

8. For focus on the specific charges brought against Jesus, especially blasphemy, desecration of the Temple, or political offenses against the Romans, see O. Betz, "Probleme des Prozesses Jesu," in *ANRW* 2.25, 1 (1982), pp. 565-647; D. L. Bock, *Blasphemy and Exaltation in Judaism and the Final Examination of Jesus* (Tübingen: Mohr Siebeck, 1998; reprint, Grand Rapids: Baker, 2000); F. Connolly-Weinert, "Assessing Omissions as Redaction: Luke's Handling of the Charge against Jesus as Detractor of the Temple," in *To Touch the Text,* ed. M. Horgan and P. Kobelski (New York: Crossroad, 1989), pp. 358-68; G. Dautzenberg, "Der Prozess Jesu und seine Hintergründe," *BK* 48, no. 3 (1993): 147-53; C. A. Evans, "In What Sense 'Blasphemy'? Jesus before Caiaphas in Mark 14:61-64," in *SBL Seminar Papers,* 1991, pp. 215-34; D. Hill, "Jesus before the Sanhedrin — on What Charge?" *IBS* 7 (1985): 174-86; T. Horvath, "Why Was Jesus Brought to Pilate?" *NovT* 11 (1969): 174-84; E. E. Jensen, "The First Century Controversy over Jesus as a Revolutionary Figure," *JBL* 60 (1941): 261-72; D. Juel, *Messiah and Temple: The Trial of Jesus in the Gospel of Mark* (Missoula, Mont.: Scholars, 1977); J. S. Kennard, Jr., "The Jewish Provincial Assembly," *ZNW* 35 (1969): 25-51; P. Lamarche, "Le Blasphème de Jesus devant le Sanhedrin," *RSR* 50 (1962): 74-85; S. Légasse, *The Trial of Jesus* (London: SCM, 1997), p. 65; O. Linton, "The Trial of Jesus and the Interpretation of Psalm CX," *NTS* 7 (1960-61): 258-62; J. R. Michaels, "John 18.31 and the Trial of Jesus," *NTS* 36 (1990): 474-79; M. A. Powell, "The Plot to Kill Jesus from Three Different Perspectives: Point of View in Matthew," in *SBL Seminar Papers,* 1990, pp. 603-13; D. Rensberger, "The Politics of John: The Trial of Jesus in the Fourth Gospel," *JBL* 103 (1984): 395-411; J. Schlosser, "La parole de Jesus sur la fin du temple," *NTS* 36 (1990): 398-414; G. N. Stanton, "Aspects of Early Christian-Jewish Polemic and Apologetic," *NTS* 31 (1985): 377-92. Peter Stuhlmacher, *Jesus von Nazareth, Christus des Glaubens* (Stuttgart: Calwer, 1988), translated by S. Schatzmann as *Jesus of Nazareth, Christ of Faith* (Peabody, Mass.: Hendrickson, 1993). W. O. Walker, Jr., "Jesus and the Tax Collectors," *JBL* 97 (1978): 221-38; F. Watson, "Why Was Jesus Crucified?" *Theology* 88 (1985): 105-12; F. M. Young, "Temple Cult and Law in Early Christianity," *NTS* 19 (1972): 325-38.

laws who were typically given virtually no legal rights by the legal establishment, let alone the full formalities of indictment on specific charges, arraignment, due process, or other such legal particularities.[9] The confusing assemblage of allegations apparently included blasphemy (Mt 26:65; Mk 14:64), "perverting the nation, and forbidding to give tribute to Caesar, [and] saying that he himself is Christ a king" (Lk 23:2), or usurping the title of "king of the Jews" (Mt 27:37; Mk 15:26; Lk 23:38; Jn 19:19). Most modern writers assume that the trial of Jesus was driven by political charges, but in fact, it is unclear that Jesus ever called himself "*the* king of the Jews." In what appears to be something of a derisive afterthought at the end of the proceeding, the Jews called him "king of the Jews" (Mk 15:12), but nowhere does Jesus say, "I am the King of the Jews." Instead, he insists that his kingdom is not of this world (Jn 18:36). Consistent with such silence or denials, Pilate refused to add the words "*He said I am King of the Jews*" to the inscription above the cross (Jn 19:21).

So, which cause of action provides the main reason for Jesus' crucifixion? The matter is complex and confusing, and not only for us today but also for the writers of the Gospels. In the Jewish proceeding, oddly, the leading official did not state a clear case but asked, "What [or why] do these bear witness against you?" (Mt 26:62; Mk 14:60). Later, even Pilate seemed unclear and had to ask, "What accusation bring ye against this man?" (Jn 18:29), to which he never received a straightforward answer. In the end, we simply learn that Jesus was accused of "many things" (Mt 27:13; Mk 15:3-4). Yet none of the traditional charges or purported motivations of the people standing against Jesus (whether religious or political) explains his case satisfactorily.

At best, all legal commentators agree that the situation is very complicated. And therein may lie the key to a solution. Seeking a specific, rational answer to the puzzle is wrongheaded precisely because the situation cannot be reduced to a few easy, modern labels. But this should not come as a surprise. Trials and legal procedures in the ancient world were not always orderly matters. For example, in a heated trial in Rome in 31 C.E., very close to the time of the trial of Jesus, Sejanus was accused of conspiracy against Tiberius. His case was tried in an exceptional way due to the highly charged emotional, urgent nature of the case. Sejanus's trial was accompanied by a popular demonstration of frantic violence, boisterous jeers, and savage rejoicing; he was condemned to death, and his body was abused for three days before it was thrown into the Tiber.[10] As

9. J. W. Welch, "Legal and Social Perspectives on Robbers in First-Century Judea," in *Masada and the World of the New Testament*, ed. J. Hall and J. Welch (Provo, Utah: BYU Studies, 1997), p. 145.

10. As reported in Seneca, *Tranq* 11.11.

Robert Rogers observed, "The judicial procedure, if it may be so dignified, was, to be sure, most exceptional, but so also was the emergency."[11]

Moreover, the simultaneous handling of multiple legal charges, as was common, must have heightened the confusion. Many of the trials during the reign of Tiberius featured multiple causes of action, the defendants concurrently facing various combinations of charges of *maiestas,* murder, adultery, hostile disloyalty *(perduellio),* sacrilege, bribery, counterfeiting, or falsification *(falsum).*[12] Under Jewish law, nothing prohibited a multiplicity of actions in a single proceeding, and nothing prohibited new charges from being added as the case went forward. The case of Jeremiah, for example, began with a charge that he had "prophesied against this city," but the accusation shifted during the proceeding to the somewhat different allegation, "he has spoken to us in the name of the Lord our God" (Jer 26:11, 16). The greater the public outcry, the fewer concerns about legal formalities. Indeed, a high degree of fluidity characterized the interrogations and accusations initiated against Jesus, who was charged on several counts.

Adding to this confusion was uncertainty about what to make of Jesus. Even before his arrest and trial, the general populace was bewildered. Jesus asked his own disciples, "Who do men say that I the Son of man am?" They reported a variety of popular opinions, including the idea that Jesus was John the Baptist or Elijah brought back from the dead (Mt 16:13-14; Mk 8:27-28). Uncertainty and puzzlement was a common reaction to Jesus. At the conclusion of his Temple speech on the Feast of Tabernacles, "there was a division among the people because of him" (Jn 7:43). "Some said, 'He is a good man,' others said, 'No, he is leading the people astray *(plana).*' Yet for fear of the Jews no one spoke openly of him" (Jn 7:12-13).

A Driving Factor of Fear

When people feel confused, they often become afraid. When they are afraid, they may act irrationally. Although New Testament commentators rarely mention the fear factor, fear provides the driving undercurrent that best explains the irregularities and vagaries in all four accounts of the trial of Jesus. More powerful than a mental motive or a purposeful intent, and broader

11. R. S. Rogers, *Criminal Trials and Criminal Legislation under Tiberius* (Middletown, Conn.: American Philological Association, 1935), p. 116.

12. For a list of criminal cases and their charges during the reign of Tiberius, see Rogers, *Criminal Trials,* pp. 206-11.

than a motivating stimulus or circumstance, the one consistent factor that runs through the entire story as told in all four Gospels is an underlying emotion of fear, especially of the supernatural. Of course, this fear did not always manifest itself in the same way among the various parties, but sooner or later *everyone* seems to be afraid of one thing or another. The array is considerable, and the fact that many kinds of fear are involved only adds to the unsettling confusion.

The followers of Jesus were afraid of the Jewish leaders. Joseph of Arimathea kept his loyalty to Jesus secret "for fear of the Jews" (Jn 19:38). The disciples fled from the scene of the arrest (Mk 14:50), and their fear only intensified after Jesus' death (Jn 20:19).

The chief priests were also afraid. They worried that if Jesus became too popular, the Romans would come and take away "the place [the Temple; cf. Acts 21:28] and the people" (*ton topon kai to ethnos;* Jn 11:48); and they also "feared the people" (Mt 21:46; Mk 11:32; Lk 20:19-20; 22:2). But even more than these concerns, the chief priests feared Jesus. Mark states that after Jesus spoke powerfully against the Temple, reportedly threatening to destroy the place by some extraordinary means (Mk 14:58), they "sought how they might destroy him: for they feared him" (Mk 11:18).

The scheme to destroy him, however, seems to have gone quickly awry. After being arrested, Jesus was passed abruptly from one hand to another with no one wanting to take the responsibility either for his death or his release. The original plot to do away with Jesus seems to have quickly begun to unravel, becoming far more complicated than probably any of the participants had expected. And they were not the only ones who were frightened. According to John, when Pilate heard the Jews say "He has made himself the son of God," his reaction was fear. Indeed, John states that Pilate "was really afraid" (*mallon ephobēthē;* Jn 19:8). True to life, Pilate's response is paralleled by the trepidation of the Roman judge Tigellinus, who thirty years later interrogated the miracle-working sage Apollonius and released him in admitted fear of his "demonic," superhuman powers, not wanting to offend a god.[13]

---

13. Philostratus, *The Life of Apollonius of Tyana* 4.43-44; related to the trial of Jesus in D. Zeller, "Jesus und die Philosophen vor dem Richter (zu Joh 19,8-11)," *BZ* 37 (1993): 88. The appearance of Apollonius before Tigellinus in the 60s parallels the trial of Jesus in many significant respects: Apollonius was viewed with suspicion and kept under surveillance for prophesying a near disaster for Nero; he was charged with impiety; the written testimony of the key witness for the prosecution turned up futilely blank; Tigellinus realized that he was dealing with a demon, so he interrogated Apollonius alone in a secret chamber; he asked, "Who are you?" and the accused claimed that his knowledge came from God; the judge asked how Apollonius exorcised apparitions of fantasia; the judge felt personally accused and in danger;

Similarly, the scene of gruesome death became a theater of fear, especially fearing the prospect of having offended some divine beings. One of the thieves on the cross rebuked the other: "Do you not fear God, since you are under the same judgment?" (*oude phobē;* Lk 23:40). And the centurion and those with him, when they felt the earth quake, "feared exceedingly" (*ephobēthēsan sphodra;* Mt 27:54). All the people left the crucifixion pounding their breasts (Lk 23:48) out of fear and worry about what they had done. These blows were not simply doleful signs of lamentation but forceful expressions of anxiety (cf. Mt 27:30; Lk 18:13; Acts 18:17; 23:10).

The abrupt ending of Mark, which concludes with the words "for they feared" *(ephobounto gar)* in Sinaiticus and Vaticanus, has puzzled many commentators. But if a strong underlying thread of fear runs throughout the Gospel narratives, then punctuating such an account with the words "for trembling and astonishment had come upon them; and they said nothing to any one, for they were afraid" (Mk 16:8) becomes understandable. For the faithful followers, this fear was not necessarily a symptom of gloom, but a concluding sign of awesome obeisance in the face of a powerful presence. Phobias are everywhere in this story — in far more places than people usually think.

Indeed, a fear that has been mostly overlooked as a factor in the trials of Jesus is the fear associated with magic and the supernatural. The widespread reputation of Jesus as a miracle worker or exorcist would have been especially unsettling to the chief priests who operated the Jerusalem Temple complex, who sought a legal pretext on which to reprimand or accuse him. Reports of his miracles — even if they were only unsubstantiated rumors — would have laid him open to obvious charges, both under Jewish and Roman laws, that he was a sorcerer, necromancer, or magician (Latin, *maleficus;* Greek, *kakopoios*). Such conduct would have raised already-heightened Jewish concerns in and around the holy places of Jerusalem, especially when such signs or wonders of Jesus were coupled with teachings that threatened to lead people into apostasy; and such behavior could also have easily intensified or given rise to Roman allegations of treason committed against the dignity or security of the emperor Tiberius.

---

he asked Apollonius to prophesy, but the accused declined on this occasion and explained that his previous prophecies were not based on a gift to him but rather on wisdom revealed from God; Apollonius felt no fear and denied any ill will toward the emperor; when asked to post a body bond, he cleverly replied, "Who can post bond for a body which no one can bind?" As Pilate found no fault in Jesus, so Apollonius was released by the Roman judge, who did not want to get involved in a conflict with a god, admitting that Apollonius was too powerful to be ruled by him. Apollonius, reputedly, then went out and raised a girl from the dead in the very hour of her marriage.

Figure 54. A woman in a chariot pulled by two winged serpents.
Courtesy of J. H. Charlesworth

Was Jesus' Conduct Religious or Magical?

From the facts leading up to the trial of Jesus it is evident that his conduct presented a difficult borderline legal case. For one thing, it is very difficult to distinguish licit from illicit uses of the supernatural. In the ancient world, no strict legal line divided the two.[14] Dividing the supernatural into legal categories of

14. Everett Ferguson, *Backgrounds of Early Christianity* (Grand Rapids: Eerdmans, 1987), pp. 212-31, comments that "what was regarded as religious by one person might be regarded as magic or superstition by another." Numerous other authors discuss the relationship between magic and religion and the problems that arise in distinguishing between them. Such discussions include Keith Bradly, "Law, Magic, and Culture in the *Apologia* of Apuleius," *Phoenix* 51, no. 2 (1997): 203-23; Matthew W. Dickie, *Magic and Magicians in the Greco-Roman World* (London: Routledge, 2001); Eric Eve, *The Jewish Context of Jesus' Miracles* (London: Sheffield Academic Press, 2002); C. R. Phillips III, "*Nullum Crimen sine Lege:* Socioreligious Sanctions on Magic," in *Magika Hiera,* ed. Christopher A. Faraone and Dirk Obbink (Oxford: Oxford University Press, 1991), pp. 260-76; Naomi Janowitz, *Magic in the Roman World* (London: Routledge, 2001); Jeffers, *Magic and Divination in Ancient Palestine and Syria;* Georg Luck, *Arcana Mund: Magic and the Occult in the Greek and Roman Worlds* (Baltimore: Johns Hopkins University Press, 1985); James B. Rives, "Magic in Roman Law: The Reconstruction of a Crime," *Classical Antiquity* 22, no. 2 (2003): 313-39; G. H. Twelftree, *Jesus the Exorcist* (Tübingen: Mohr; Peabody,

acceptable and unacceptable magic was sometimes impossible; many practices of these two domains overlapped. Nevertheless, maintaining the social and legal boundaries between them remained important, for magical activities were common enough. From priests performing sacrifices at temples to wanderers offering love potions, the supernatural was virtually omnipresent in ancient life. Perhaps most difficult of all, Jesus' actions appeared to be beneficial to humanity and divinely motivated, but they went well beyond ordinary social and legal boundaries.

Religion and magic are often distinguished by the ways they interact with the divine.[15] For example, religion represents the practices of a certain ethnic or political group and is institutionalized. Its priests are publicly legitimized and recognized, and they receive authority from a sanctioned organization, which is generally dedicated to a specific deity. Magic, on the other hand, is outside of strict sociopolitical boundaries. Teachers of magic have to be sought out in secret, and their authority lies in their ability or knowledge. Jesus' conduct clearly fell in the latter of these two.

For instance, religion tends to ask, appeal to, and maybe coerce the divine; sacrifices, oblations, prayers, and worship all contribute to the practitioner's appeal for a deity's actions; religion makes petitions to God. Magic typically tries to command, control, or manipulate the supernatural by esoteric knowledge, imprecations, or special communication with deity. People made special note of the fact that Jesus commanded the unclean spirits (Mk 1:27) and the winds and the waters (Lk 8:25), making him appear "more like a god . . . than like a mere charismatic healer or prophet."[16]

In many ways Jesus must have appeared to some to be acting outside of the boundaries of Jewish religion and inside the realm of magic, providing his opponents a convenient and serious prima facie complaint against him. Several events in his life would have raised serious legal concerns about whether he was operating within the context of religion or magic.[17] Jesus was openly heralded

---

Mass.: Hendrickson, 1993); David E. Aune, "Magic in Early Christianity," in *Aufstieg und Niedergang der Römischen Welt,* ed. Hildegard Temporini and Wolfgang Haase (Berlin: Walter de Gruyter, 1980), 2:1510-16.

15. Rives, "Magic in Roman Law," p. 326, states that it is the magician's "distinctive ability to communicate with the gods that gives the *magus* his unusual powers."

16. Todd Klutz, *The Exorcism Stories in Luke-Acts: A Sociostylistic Reading* (Cambridge: Cambridge University Press, 2004), p. 150. In Kahl's terminology, Jesus crossed over from being merely a "petitioner of numinous power" or a "mediator of numinous power" to being a "bearer of numinous power." Werner Kahl, *New Testament Miracle Stories in Their Religious-Historical Setting: A Religionsgeschichtliche Comparison from a Structural Perspective* (Göttingen: Vandenhoeck & Ruprecht, 1994).

17. Twelftree, *Jesus the Exorcist,* p. 207, has argued that because the Gospels do not specifi-

as a miracle worker and exorcist.[18] As Eric Eve's analysis of the Jewish context of Jesus' miracles concludes, "There is a consensus among virtually all the scholars reviewed here that Jesus did indeed perform healings and exorcisms that his contemporaries thought remarkable, and that this can be regarded as virtually certain. There is also a growing consensus that this miraculous activity formed an integral part of Jesus' ministry, and should not be brushed aside to leave room for a Jesus who was almost entirely a teacher."[19] If this assessment rings true of the ministry of Jesus, it is a fortiori even more the case with respect to his trial and death. Such activities could not have escaped legal cognizance.

Throughout the Gospel of Mark Jesus performed healings and miracles by touching and speaking (Mk 3:3; 4:39; 5:41; 6:48-51; 7:33; 8:22; 9:27). These techniques were also used by magicians who performed miracles.[20] In several healings Jesus' use of spit could have carried magical overtones (Mk 7:33; 8:22; Jn

---

cally name Jesus as a magician and refute him, he could not have been seen as one by his contemporaries, and the apocryphal evidence is only a latter interpolation. While it is impossible to know how Jesus' audience perceived him, so many sources have components that could have been seen as magical that it is dangerous to ignore the possibility. Why the New Testament writers chose not to address the issue is likewise impossible to know, but several explanations are reasonable. Jesus appearing as a magician may not have been a significant problem only for those who accused him. The Gospel writers may have been willing to admit the types of things Jesus did, but did not want to argue about Jesus' authority, just as Jesus himself did not. Perhaps the Gospel writers, writing years later, chose not to emphasize that particular way that Jesus was misunderstood. It had become less relevant than other views of Jesus. Another concern that is justifiably raised is how much of the events recorded in the Gospels were known to Jesus' accusers. The sources are simply not clear enough to determine any charge with certainty. It is possible that Jesus' accusers knew very little of the specifics that his later followers would write (such as the star at his birth or his time in Egypt). However, they must have known enough of his popularity and power that did not fall within established norms to feel threatened. This makes the charge of magic at least possible and perhaps highly probable.

18. P. Samain, "L'accusation de magie contre le Christ dans les Évangiles," ETL 15 (1938): 449-90, discusses especially Mt 27:63; Mk 3:22-30; Jn 7:20; 8:48; 10:20; and the temptation; M. Smith, Jesus the Magician (New York: Harper and Row, 1978); Twelftree, Jesus the Exorcist; R. Shirock, "Whose Exorcists Are They?" JSNT 46 (1992): 41-51. For an assessment of the fact that the miracles of Jesus do "exemplify some of the traits of magic," see E. P. Sanders, Jesus and Judaism (Philadelphia: Fortress, 1985), pp. 165-69.

19. Eric Eve, The Jewish Context of Jesus' Miracles (Sheffield: Sheffield Academic Press, 2002), pp. 16-17. Aune, "Magic in Early Christianity," p. 1538, also finds that Jesus made "use of magical techniques which must have been regarded as magical because they were effected within the socially deviant context of a millennial movement and because he was able to harness supernatural power in such a way that he and his followers believed that success was virtually guaranteed." See also Graham N. Stanton, Jesus and Gospel (Cambridge: Cambridge University Press, 2004), pp. 144-47.

20. Twelftree, Jesus the Exorcist, p. 158.

9:6).[21] Jesus also was reputed to have supernatural control of the elements, multiplying loaves and fishes, calming a storm, walking on water, and cursing a fig tree. The cursing of the fig tree especially would have appeared magical, as Jesus performed the act himself, not appealing to a supernatural power to act. Additionally, Jesus appeared to have a relationship with evil spirits or demons. Those possessed with demons or evil spirits often recognized Jesus and obeyed him (e.g., Mt 8:29; Mk 3:11-12; 9:25; Lk 11:14).

These incidents regularly caused an uproar in the region where they were performed. It is not surprising that many people reacted to this wonder-working with fear (Mk 1:27; 5:15).[22] After Jesus healed a man's withered hand, some people immediately began to talk about "how they might destroy him" (Mt 12:14; Mk 3:6; Lk 6:11). In a world that feared demons "as we fear microbes"[23] or anthrax, it is not surprising that the most common and consistent reaction of people to all the miracles of Jesus was fear (see, for example, Mt 9:8; Lk 5:26; 7:16; 8:37; Jn 6:19), for either he worked these wonders by the power of God or he was possessed by Beelzebub (Mt 12:22; Mk 3:22). Such actions leave no middle ground. To the extent that Jesus' healings and control over physical elements were open and impressive, these signs and wonders must have caused profound concern to anyone who did not believe that Jesus was benevolent. In one case in Galilee, scribes from Jerusalem became involved in a legal effort to determine whether he performed these miracles by the power of Satan or of God (Mk 3:22-23). Hollenbach concludes that the scribes and Pharisees "accus[ed] him both of practicing sorcery (witchcraft) and being possessed himself by Satan,"[24] although that alone was not enough to precipitate legal prosecution at that time.

Members of the Jewish aristocracy who opposed Jesus feared not only his popularity, but the source of his powers.[25] If Jesus' power came from magic,

21. Twelftree, *Jesus the Exorcist*, p. 141. Jesus' connection with prostitutes, who were often associated with magic, might also have linked Jesus in some minds with magic; see Dickie, *Magic and Magicians*, p. 99.

22. Paul W. Hollenbach, "Jesus, Demoniacs, and Public Authorities: A Socio-Historical Study," *Journal of the American Academy of Religion* 49, no. 4 (1981): 572.

23. J. D. M. Derrett, "'Archontes, Archai': A Wider Background to the Passion Narratives," *Filologia Neotestamentaria* 2 (1989): 177. See also S. B. Noegel, "Moses and Magic: Notes on the Book of Exodus," *JANES* 24 (1996): 58-59, pointing out that "fundamentally associated with Egyptian magic are notions of *nrw*, 'terror,' *qβ*, 'dread,' and *sfy.t*, 'fear.'"

24. Hollenbach, "Jesus," p. 572. Hollenbach is concerned only with social constructions, tensions, deviance, and hostility. Although he does not consider any legal provisions, he finds ample grounds to conclude that "Jesus' first exorcism led inevitably to his crucifixion" (p. 583).

25. Phillips, *"Nullum Crimen sine Lege,"* p. 269, concludes that "In the Roman Empire there was no question of the existence of persons with the ability to influence natural phenomena in

then he was a sorcerer worthy of death. If his authority came from God, then he was a prophet. Likewise, from a Roman point of view, certain healings would be entirely acceptable if performed by a Temple priest, but healings or other actions might make the performer a magician and as such an "enemy of the Roman order."[26] The question of the source of Jesus' power became so important that Jesus was asked explicitly, "By what authority do you do these things?" (Mk 11:28). Jesus never answered the question. His silence must have only heightened their concerns.

One week before his trial, according to John's account, Jesus raised Lazarus from the dead.[27] Jesus had raised others from the dead in Galilee, but the raising of Lazarus, just over the eastern hill from Jerusalem, brought his miracle working uncomfortably close to the temple city. For the Gospel of John, this was the culminating event that precipitated the action that had long been brewing.[28] Immediately thereafter, "the chief priests and the Pharisees gathered as a council [*synedrion*], and said, What do we do? for this man does many miracles [*sēmeia*]" (Jn 11:47). The mention of miracles here is an important disclosure. Jesus' miracle working stood at the root of the ultimate concern of his legal opponents. If these miracles were mere illusions, then Jesus was an illegal trickster,

---

ways that did not coincide with traditional religious usages. The question lay, rather, in the presumed source of the power and its utilization. There was no problem if one were aligned with what those with coercive power considered the 'right' source of power and if one used that power for the 'right' ends."

26. Ramsay MacMullen, *Enemies of the Roman Order: Treason, Unrest, and Alienation in the Empire* (Cambridge: Harvard University Press, 1966), p. 125: "There was thus no period in the history of the empire in which the magician was not considered an enemy of society, subject at the least to exile, more often to death in its least pleasant forms." See also Aune, "Magic in Early Christianity," p. 1518: "Magical practices and practitioners were generally illegal throughout the history of the Roman empire, though that which the Roman authorities regarded as constitutive of 'magic' varied considerably from one period to another." Aune cites M. Mauss and Jonathan Z. Smith for the proposition that "the essence of magic" was "in its illegality" (p. 1514).

27. One need not agree that "there was, at the time of Pilate's procuratorship, no story of this miracle." Alan Watson, *Jesus and the Jews: The Pharisaic Tradition in John* (Athens: University of Georgia Press, 1995), p. 49. It is possible that Pilate knew nothing about this recent development, even if many in the Jewish community did. Division among the Jews over the issue may have led them not to raise the issue with Pilate. Mentioning this incident may have only precipitated what they feared most, namely, that Pilate would remove them from control over the city and the Temple. On the historicity of the Lazarus incident, see Murray J. Harris, "'The Dead Are Restored to Life': Miracles of Revivification in the Gospels," in *Gospel Perspectives: The Miracles of Jesus*, pp. 310-15.

28. F. J. Matera, "Jesus before Annas: John 18,13-14.19-24," *ETL* 66 (1990): 54. Note also that the Secret Gospel of Mark inserts an episode between Mk 10:34 and 35, in which Jesus raised a young man from the dead, only a few verses before reporting the triumphal entry into Jerusalem.

wizard, or deceiver. Immediately after the report of what Jesus had done in Bethany, an illegal order went out for his arrest (Jn 11:57). To make legal matters even worse for Jesus and his friends, the chief priests also sought to arrest Lazarus (Jn 12:10), presumably on the legal ground that he had colluded with Jesus in perpetrating this deception.

The Gospel of John is not alone in reporting miracles as Jesus approached Jerusalem. As he drew near to Jerusalem, Jesus healed two blind men, Matthew says, by touching their eyes, and they heralded him as "Lord" or "Son of David" (Mt 20:31-34; Mk 10:46-52; Lk 18:35-43). In the Gospels of Matthew and Mark, as Jesus came to Jerusalem from Bethany, he cursed a fig tree and it mysteriously withered (Mt 21:19; Mk 11:20). Significantly, the magical-appearing curse of this tree is conjoined directly with the cleansing of the Temple (Mt 21:12-13; Mk 11:11-15).

Coupling these manifestations of numinous power with what his opponents would consider an incantation against the Temple — "I will destroy this temple that is made with hands, and within three days I will build another made without hands" (Mk 14:58) — yields a potent formula for fear and the need to take action against these out-of-boundary signs and wonders. These events were clearly disturbing to certain Jews. Such a slander against the Temple could rather easily have been taken as a magical curse. In fact, it would be considered blasphemous precisely because it called upon powers alien to the Temple. Not only did these words sound sinister, but they also further separated Jesus from the Temple and also institutional Jewish religion, placing him outside the sphere of organized and sanctioned religion and into the only other alternative, the realm of magic, and indeed not only outside licit religion, but threatening to it.

To people who took such forces seriously, trying to arrest Jesus would have been terrifying. The chief priests could not have undertaken this venture lightly. Being fearful, they would have steeled themselves against the unexpected and felt the need to move quickly. Jesus was reputed to have supernatural powers. He presented himself as a new Moses, and many of the miracles he reputedly performed exceeded those of Moses. The chief priests were well aware of the stories about what Moses had done to Pharaoh and his army. Moreover, when the men of Nazareth had attempted to kill or banish Jesus, he had passed mysteriously "through the midst of them" and slipped away (Lk 4:30); the chief priests may have been involved personally in the similar attempt in Jerusalem to stone him, when "Jesus hid himself, and went out of the Temple, going through the midst of them, and so passed by" undetected (Jn 8:59). With Jesus known as something of an escape artist, the leaders in Jerusalem would have sensed that they had their hands full in trying to take him at the height of his power.

Even during his arrest, Jesus continued to invoke miraculous powers. Matthew reports that Jesus told Peter to put away his sword, assuring him that he could call forth more than twelve legions of angels (Mt 26:53); and Luke recounts that when one of the disciples cut off the right ear of the high priest's servant, Jesus "touched his ear, and healed him" (Lk 22:51). Anyone in the group of arresters hearing or seeing such things would have been stunned; stumbling, they "went backward and fell to the ground" (Jn 18:6).

Supernatural factors play a dominant role in the New Testament account clear to the end. Herod Antipas hoped to see Jesus perform a miracle (Lk 23:8). People standing by the cross seriously wondered if Jesus could save himself; they saw him as a trafficker in evil spirits and thus waited to see if God would want him (Mt 27:43). They waited to see if the miracle-working prophet Elijah would rescue him from the cross (Mk 15:36). While that did not happen, the rocks were said to split apart, graves opened, and spirits appeared out of the ground (Mt 27:51-53). Behind everything here lurks a strong undercurrent of seeing Jesus as a powerful, and therefore worrisome, wonder-worker.

Indeed, ultimately the chief priests worried that Jesus, whom they specifically called a "trickster" or "deceiver" *(ho planos),* would somehow appear to rise after three days as he had prophesied he would (Mt 27:63). Early on the Pharisees had chided the Jewish officers for being "also deceived" or "tricked" *(peplanēsthe,* Jn 7:47; also 7:12). Now these people together worried that this, his last "trick" *(planē)* of appearing to rise from the dead, would be worse than his first trick (Mt 27:64). When they asked Pilate to place a guard at the tomb to prevent any such sleight of hand perpetrated with assistance from his followers, Pilate told them to use their own Temple guard, and they were concerned enough actually to do so (Mt 27:65-66).

What they feared most was some kind of ultimate, evil trick. The term *planos* especially means one who deceives by seduction through evil powers or misguided miracles. This term is applied to Satan himself (Rev 12:9), and to "the false prophet who performs miracles" (Rev 19:20). The evil Beliar is called a "deceiver" *(planos)* in the *Testaments of the Twelve Patriarchs* (*T Benj* 6.1); and in the *Sibylline Oracles,* Beliar is said to deceive many men, including the faithful elect, through nature miracles, including raising mountains, churning up the sea, raising the dead, and performing many signs (*Sib Or* 3.63-70). The word *planos* is also associated with the seduction by unclean spirits or polluted demons that led to the destruction of Noah's grandchildren in *Jub* 10.1-2.[29] Being a *planos* would obviously raise serious concerns at the time of Jesus.

29. See *TDNT* 6:238.

Magic as Criminal Conduct under Jewish Law

Although it is evident that certain forms of white magic or wizardry were not problematic at this time in Jewish culture, difficulties could easily arise. Magicians such as Simon Magus (Acts 8:9) seem to have walked the hills of Samaria freely without prosecution, but if magic went too far or was coupled with improper conduct, such action could be severely punished, even by death. Theudas, described by Josephus as a Jewish wonder-worker,[30] lawfully gathered a large following in Judea, but when he turned his alleged miracle powers against Rome in 45 or 46 C.E., he was attacked and beheaded by a squadron of Roman horsemen, and many of his followers were killed or taken prisoner.

This is not the place to review the extensive literature regarding Jewish attitudes toward magic in the Second Temple period. Much has been written about miracles, magic, charismatic holy men, sign prophets, exorcists, healers, sorcerers, and diviners in Josephus, Philo, Jewish wisdom literature, the Pseudepigrapha, and the Qumran library.[31] Suffice it to say that scarcely any attention has been given in these books to the legal dimensions of magic at the time of Jesus.[32]

The exception is in recent Qumran studies, where it has become evident that "magic is integral to the worldview of Qumran"; there magic was "a learned magic" that was extensive but "markedly restrained."[33] Armin Lange exhaustively surveys the Essene positions and practices concerning magic, exorcisms, incantations, and divinations.[34] As he shows, although "the wide range of different forms of magic and divination known by the Essenes is not re-

30. Josephus, *Ant* 20.5.1. This is apparently the same person referred to in Acts 5:36. See Eve, *Jewish Context,* pp. 296-99.

31. See particularly Aune, "Magic in Early Christianity," pp. 1523-57; Eve, *The Jewish Context of Jesus' Miracles;* Klutz, *The Exorcism Stories in Luke-Acts;* Barry Blackburn, *Theios Aner and the Markan Miracle Traditions* (Tübingen: Mohr, 1991); Susan R. Garrett, *The Demise of the Devil* (Minneapolis: Fortress, 1989); Wenham and Blomberg, eds., *Gospel Perspectives: The Miracles of Jesus;* John M. Hull, *Hellenistic Magic and the Synoptic Tradition* (Naperville, Ill.: Alec R. Allenson, 1974).

32. Even Garrett, while stating that "Jesus and his followers were themselves highly vulnerable to charges of practicing magic" (*Demise of the Devil,* p. 2), does not extend the point to the trial of Jesus.

33. Philip S. Alexander, "'Wrestling against Wickedness in High Places': Magic in the Worldview of the Qumran Community," in *The Scrolls and the Scriptures: Qumran Fifty Years After,* ed. Stanley E. Porter and Craig A. Evans (Sheffield: Sheffield Academic Press, 1997), pp. 335-36. See also Eve, *Jewish Context,* pp. 174-216.

34. Armin Lange, "The Essene Position on Magic and Divination," in *Legal Texts and Legal Issues: Proceedings of the Second Meeting of the International Organization for Qumran Studies, Cambridge, 1995,* ed. Moshe Bernstein, Florentino García Martínez, and John Kempen (Leiden: Brill, 1997), pp. 377-437.

flected in their legal texts," and "while magic and divination were widespread in late Second Temple times and were an integral part of Jewish belief and thought,"[35] some forms of magic were clearly rejected by the Essenes.[36] For example, Deut 18:9-22 was included in the Temple Scroll. Eric Eve similarly concludes, "The Beelzebul controversy indicates that the same kind of ambiguity surrounded Jesus' exorcisms."[37]

Biblical and Jewish laws, however, clearly prohibited various kinds of sorcery, soothsaying, or necromancy. The challenge was to distinguish acceptable forms of exorcism or miracle working from the unacceptable. For this reason, the Talmud required some "knowledge of sorcery" in order to be appointed a member of the Sanhedrin, so that such cases could be properly distinguished and prosecuted: "None are to be appointed members of the Sanhedrin, but men of stature, wisdom, good appearance, mature age, with a knowledge of sorcery."[38] The last qualification was required "so as to be able to detect those who seduce and pervert by means of witchcraft"[39] or to tell the difference between its proper and improper uses. According to Talmudic law, magic could be studied, but only so that it could be understood, not practiced.[40]

More than that, magic was forbidden in every layer of biblical law. Ex 22:18 states that "a woman who practices sorcery, shall not sustain her soul," i.e., shall not be allowed to live.[41] This provision, however, was not understood as applying only to women. The Septuagint, Mishnah, *Targum Neofiti,* and *Targum Pseudo-Jonathan* all understand this interdiction to apply to men as well, to "anyone who practices sorcery."[42]

Moreover, Num 23:23 assures that "there is no enchantment against Jacob, neither is there any divination against Israel," and Deut 18:10-11 concurs: "Let no one be found among you who makes his son or daughter pass through fire, no augur or soothsayer or diviner or sorcerer, no one who casts spells or traffics with ghosts and spirits, and no necromancer." All these are abominations to be flogged and driven out.

Lev 20:27 likewise provides that "a man also or woman that has a familiar spirit, or that is a wizard, shall surely be put to death." Having a familiar spirit

---

35. Lange, "Essene Position," pp. 408, 433.

36. Lange, "Essene Position," pp. 397-408.

37. Eve, *Jewish Context,* p. 216; see also Lange, "Essene Position," p. 435.

38. *b. Sanh.* 17a. Discussed in Janowitz, *Magic,* pp. 24-25.

39. *b. Sanh.* 17a, note 3 (Soncino, *Talmud,* p. 87).

40. *b. Sanh.* 68a.

41. J. A. Wagenaar, "'A Woman Who Practices Sorcery, Shall Not Sustain Her Soul,'" *ZABR* 6 (2000): 189.

42. Wagenaar, "A Woman," p. 186; *b. Sanh.* 67a.

refers especially to "calling out of the earth" or conversing with the spirits of the dead.[43] Being a wizard has to do with giving signs or wonders that "evoke recognition or knowledge."[44] Perhaps more than coincidentally, the expression "being worthy of death" *(thanatō thanatousthōsan, enochoi eisi)* in Lev 20:27 (LXX) contains the same words that appear in Mt 26:66 and Mk 14:64 to condemn Jesus as "worthy of death" *(enochos thanatou estin).*

Most pertinent to this discussion of the trial of Jesus is the law in Deut 13:1-5. Even if a prophet were able to give "a sign or a wonder," Deut 13:1-3 made it illegal to follow such a person to "go after other gods," and the punishment for the one who leads people into apostasy in this way was death (Deut 13:5). August Strobel and Otto Betz argue that this text is crucial to the accusation brought against Jesus by the Sanhedrin, that he misleads the people; but they unnecessarily focus their attention on Jesus' words instead of also considering his deeds; and Graham Stanton makes a strong case that Jesus' opponents marginalized him with the double accusation that he was both a magician and a false prophet, but he does not draw legal consequences from these two "closely related" allegations.[45] It well appears that "Jesus is best understood not as a magician but as a prophet,"[46] but

---

43. *TDOT* 1:131, and also p. 134. See also J. Milgrom, *Leviticus 17–22* (New York: Doubleday, 2000), p. 1768.

44. *TDOT* 5:46; Milgrom, *Leviticus 17–22,* p. 1765.

45. Strobel, *Die Stunde der Wahrheit,* pp. 81-86, focuses on the words of Jesus *(spricht, Sprache, demagogische Tricks, Demagoge),* which make Jesus a "misleader" *(Verführer)* and ultimately expose him to the accusation of blasphemy, pp. 92-94. But more than words are involved here. Strobel is followed by Stuhlmacher, *Jesus von Nazareth, Christus des Glaubens,* pp. 42-43 n. 6. Betz, "Probleme des Prozesses Jesu," pp. 575-80, 593-97, mentions *Zauberer* and *Wunder,* but the focus remains on false teaching and misleading. Stanton, *Jesus and Gospel,* pp. 129, 135, 137, sees magic and false prophecy as "closely related," but stops short of correctly seeing them as two constitutive elements of a single crime. Stanton makes no mention of magic or false prophecy in connection with the trial of Jesus in his *The Gospels and Jesus,* 2nd ed. (Oxford: Oxford University Press, 2002), pp. 281-88. Barry Blackburn, in *Theios Aner and the Markan Miracle Traditions,* p. 258, mentions Deut 13, but only in pointing out that without invoking the miraculous, Jesus remains simply another teacher whose opinions can be accepted or rejected through ordinary debate: "Such sign-working [prohibited by Deut 13] is deceiving and seducing precisely because of the widespread presumption that miracle-working demonstrates one's right to speak and act for God." Bernard Jackson draws extensive parallels between the trial of Jesus and the trial of Jeremiah, keying on Deut 18:18-22 and charges in both cases of false prophecy; while Jackson mentions the miracles of Moses and Jesus in passing, he looks primarily at the offending words of Jesus and Jeremiah; see *Cardozo Studies in Law and Literature* 4 (Fall 1992): 123-66; yet the lack of purported miracles by Jeremiah may be the needed factor that most distinguishes the successful case of Jeremiah from the opposite outcome in the trial of Jesus. On the connection between false prophecy and the utilization of magic in the Jewish context generally, see Garrett, *Demise of the Devil,* pp. 13-17.

46. Eve, *Jewish Context,* p. 17.

that misses the legal point. Seeing Jesus as a prophet is not inconsistent with seeing him in violation of Deut 13. In fact, this provision of the law presupposes this. Thus, on the Jewish side, the law in Deut 13 is even more applicable to Jesus and to his being called a "trickster" or "deceiver" *(planos)* than has been previously emphasized.

Any signs or wonders performed by Jesus, especially his raising people from the dead coupled with his soothsayer-like spell against the Temple, would readily have presented to some people a prima facie case of serious misconduct that could have warranted the death penalty under Jewish law. By itself, the alleged use of magic was problematic enough. The Mishnah, which may well reflect legal conditions around the time of the trial of Jesus, said "A sorcerer, if he actually performs magic, is liable [to death], but not if he merely creates illusions."[47] When used for leading people to worship other beings (including oneself) as God, the case became all the more unlawful (Deut 13:1-5). Trypho the Jew asserted that Jesus had been executed as a sorcerer *and* seducer of the people,[48] and the Talmud preserves the remark that "on the eve of the Passover Yeshu [the Nazarene] was hanged . . . because he has practiced sorcery *and* enticed Israel to apostasy."[49]

Early Christian sources likewise echo the view that Jesus' Jewish accusers considered his supernatural powers to be offensive. Lactantius did not deny this allegation, but explained it away: "We might have supposed him to be a magician *(magum)*, as you now suppose him to be, and the Jews then supposed him, if all the prophets did not with one accord proclaim that Christ would do those very things."[50] In the apocryphal letter of Pilate to Claudius, the chief priests were said to have accused Jesus of being a sorcerer and acting contrary to their law,[51] while

---

47. *m. Sanh.* 7.11. See further, Brigitte (Rivka) Kern-Ulmer, "The Depiction of Magic in Rabbinic Texts: The Rabbinic and Greek Concept of Magic," *JSJ* 27, no. 3 (1996): 289-303. As she points out, "The centuries that followed the return from the Babylonian Exile in the sixth century B.C.E. witnessed the growth and intensification of interest in magic in the Jewish sphere. From the second century B.C.E. until the redaction of the Talmudic documents the Jewish perspective of magic was in a state of constant flux"; eventually "the rabbis in their legal and interpretative literature generally tended to obliterate the vestiges of magic" (p. 289). Distinguishing between beneficial magic and mere illusions, however, proved very difficult. The "rabbinic discussions of magic are very subtle and elaborate." Janowitz, *Magic*, p. 20.

48. Justin Martyr, *Dialogue with Trypho* 69.

49. *b. Sanh.* 43a. R. E. Brown, "The Babylonian Talmud on the Execution of Jesus," *NTS* 43 (1997): 158-59. See also Josephus, *Ant* 18.3.63, and the Slavonic additions between *War* 2.174 and 175, which, although disputed, emphasize Jesus' status as a wonder-worker and attribute his legal difficulties to concerns about his miraculous powers.

50. Lactantius, *Divine Institutes* 5.3; PL 6:560-61. Regarding related comments from Justin, Celsus, and other early Christians, see Stanton, *Jesus and Gospel*, pp. 135-39.

51. M. R. James, *The Apocryphal New Testament* (Oxford: Clarendon, 1969), p. 146. See also

an Ethiopic fragment attributes to the Jews the line "Behold the sorcerer," as they present to Pilate a corpse that was supposedly the body of Jesus.[52] To these traditions may be added the additions to the Slavonic Josephus that emphasize the mighty miracles performed by Jesus the wonder-worker. Of unknown origin, these insertions show that Jesus was regarded in some circles as a man who worked copious wonders "through an invisible power . . . by word alone." Pilate "had that wonder-worker brought up," but pronounced him "a benefactor, not a malefactor, [nor] a rebel, [nor] covetous of kingship."[53] Moreover, in mainstream fourth-century Christian art Jesus was often depicted, on sarcophagi, on glass bowls, and in catacombs, as a magician holding a wand in raising Lazarus or in performing other miracles.[54]

None of this requires one to conclude, with Morton Smith, that Jesus truly was a magician or that he actually was convicted of being a sorcerer, but these legal items show that he easily could have been mistaken for or characterized as a magus and suspected of being a sorcerer. It is enough to see that under Jewish law the mere presence of this factor in his case would have considerably aggravated and unified the many charges lodged against Jesus, especially when coupled with the specific concern of Deut 13 about leading people into apostasy, and this element would have spilled over easily into potential offenses under Roman law as well.

Maleficium and *Maiestas* under Roman Law

Easily, the element of magic would have been relevant to accusations against Jesus under Roman law as well. Sorcery or magic was also a serious offense under Roman law at the time of Jesus, especially when it threatened in any way the security

---

Acts of Pilate 1.1: "They say unto him: He is a sorcerer, and by Beelzebub the prince of the devils he casteth out devils," in James, p. 96.

52. James, *The Apocryphal New Testament,* p. 151.

53. Josephus, *War* IV-VII, trans. H. St. J. Thackeray, LCL (Cambridge: Harvard University Press, 1928), pp. 648-50.

54. Robin Margaret Jensen, *Understanding Early Christian Art* (London: Routledge, 2000), figures 22, 30, 48, and pp. 120-24; Thomas F. Mathews, *The Clash of the Gods: A Reinterpretation of Early Christian Art,* rev. ed. (Princeton: Princeton University Press, 1993), figures 34-37, 51, 65, 68, and pp. 54-91; Antonio Ferrua, *The Unknown Catacomb: A Unique Discovery of Early Christian Art* (New Lanark, Scotland: Goedes and Grosset, 1991), pp. 55, 150; Leonard Victor Rutgers, *Subterranean Rome: In Search of the Roots of Christianity in the Catacombs of the Eternal City* (Leuven: Peeters, 2000), p. 115. Likewise, the *Infancy Gospel of Thomas* had no compunctions against recounting numerous magical feats performed by the childhood Jesus; for example, 2.1-2; 3.3; 4.1; 5.1; 7.2; 8.2; 9.3; 10.2; 11.2; 12.2; 13.2. I thank Josh Probert for this art history.

of the emperor. From the time of the Twelve Tables, magical incantations were prohibited: *Qui malum carmen incantassit,* "He who shall have sung an enchanted evil spell."[55] This long-standing Roman law proscribed the enchantment of grain standing in a field or the enticement of fertility from one field to another.[56] In the Roman state cult, "only a king possessed the necessary magic power, . . . [due to] the rightful king's closeness to the gods, . . . [whose status] was revealed by the gods through a sign (especially through the flight of birds)."[57] Hence, a magician who claimed to be a king might not only imperil the emperor but also treasonously impersonate the divine powers of the ruling monarch.

In Roman legal terminology, *maleficus* is "common parlance for 'magician'"[58] and "commonly denotes a sorcerer."[59] Its cognate *maleficium* is "not a technical juristic term" as such, but it is sometimes synonymous with *magia,* which covered a variety of types of sorcery, magical formulae, nocturnal sacrifices, or supernatural effects, and was a capital offense when "performed with an evil intention to harm or defraud another."[60]

State action could be taken against such people. According to Valerius Maximus, who wrote during the reign of Tiberius (14-37 C.E.), an edict was issued in 139 B.C.E. expelling deceitful Eastern astrologers from Rome and Italy who were fomenting trouble by their "fallacious interpretation of the stars."[61]

At the time of Jesus, certain forms of spell casting or divination had recently become punishable by death. In 11 C.E. Augustus Caesar himself issued a new edict forbidding mantics from prophesying about a person's death, which apparently had become a serious political and social problem in the Roman world.[62] The main thrust of this decree was to expand the law of *maiestas,*[63]

55. Table VIII, 1b. Pliny quotes these words while discussing "the alleged power in incantations" (Loeb edition, p. 475). W. Kunkel, *An Introduction to Roman Legal and Constitutional History,* 2nd ed. (Oxford: Clarendon, 1973), p. 29.

56. Kunkel, *An Introduction,* p. 29.

57. Kunkel, *An Introduction,* pp. 13-14.

58. Smith, *Jesus the Magician,* p. 41, allowing that "whether or not used before Pilate, the charge may have been brought against Jesus during his lifetime; its role in the gospels proves that it was important in the hostility between the high priests and the early Jerusalem church." Smith does not mention the Jewish laws against magic, and he considers the stories in the Synoptic Gospels about a nighttime Jewish proceeding to be "fictitious" (p. 39).

59. A. Berger, *Encyclopedic Dictionary of Roman Law* (Philadelphia: American Philosophical Society, 1953), p. 573.

60. Berger, *Encyclopedic Dictionary,* pp. 572-73.

61. F. H. Cramer, *Astrology in Roman Law and Politics* (1954; reprint, Chicago: Ares, 1996), p. 235.

62. Cramer, *Astrology,* p. 250.

63. R. S. Rogers, "Treason in the Early Empire," *JRS* 49 (1959): 90-94. It would appear that anyone, whether a Roman citizen or not, could commit treason.

which had long punished people who harmed the state by actions, to now include treasonous divination especially against the imperial family. Mantic activity had become popular during the time of Augustus, whose reign had begun with the propitious appearance of a comet, ushering in "an era of almost universal acceptance of astrology by the Roman upper class."[64] The new law curtailed "the hitherto unlimited freedom of astrological practice" through a "durable empire-wide imperial legislation [that would] circumscribe astrological and other divinatory activities everywhere."[65] Demons know no political or geographical boundaries.

The edict of Augustus was bolstered by a *senatus consultum* in 16 C.E. The need for further action only five years after the initial decree indicates that the problem remained unchecked. Tacitus, Suetonius, Ulpian, and Cassius Dio all confirm that foreign astrologers and sorcerers *(magi)* and their confederates were executed at this time, while Roman citizens who persisted in these practices were banished and expelled from Italy.[66] Tiberius, however, "pardoned those who petitioned him and promised that they would give up their craft."[67]

Erratic enforcement of such occult activity was perhaps inevitable. For example, during the Principate, although "no one [was] permitted to have books on the art of magic in his possession," and any such books were to be "burned in public," and offenders of humble rank were to be executed,[68] this law against the possession of such paraphernalia was not enforced in Ephesus until the seven sons of Sceva were fully exposed. Those practitioners were not executed (apparently they were of high rank; Acts 19:14), but they brought forward their enormously valuable collection of magical books (likely under threat of law), which were then publicly burned (Acts 19:19). Significantly, Luke reports without any embarrassment that Jesus was known to these demons (Acts 19:15).

Over the years the problem persisted. The practice of magic was condemned in 198/99 by the prefect of Egypt, Q. Aemilius Saturninus, whose edict imposed the death penalty on anyone involved in divination; he banned the use of "written documents ostensibly emanating in the presence of the divine," "the procession of images or similar trickery," or claims "to have knowledge of the supernatural or . . . of future events." Local administrators who failed to enforce this law were also "laid under the same chastisement" of death.[69]

During the reign of Tiberius, criminal trials were plentiful in Rome. Robert

---

64. Cramer, *Astrology,* pp. 78-79; Berger, *Encyclopedic Dictionary,* p. 418.
65. Cramer, *Astrology,* p. 249.
66. Cramer, *Astrology,* p. 238.
67. Suetonius, *Lives of the Caesars* 3.36.
68. Cramer, *Astrology,* p. 277.
69. S. R. Llewlyn, *NewDocs* 1 (1976), doc. 12.

Samuel Rogers lists over two hundred known defendants, many of them charged concurrently with multiple offenses. The most common charge, and one that could be coupled with an accusation of *maleficium,* was *maiestas;* it was involved in approximately one hundred known trials during the reign of Tiberius alone, although these accusations resulted in relatively few convictions.[70]

The law of *maiestas* condemned all types of treasonous conversation or libelous speech or action (p. 79), including the writing of libelous poetic verses (p. 83), the selling of a statue of the emperor (p. 88), or "spreading slanderous stories in the army with a seditious intent" (p. 99), if such conduct was directed against "the deified Augustus, Livia while she lived, and Tiberius, but not Tiberius' heir" (p. 130). *Maiestas* comprehended the old charge of *perduellio* (hostile treason) as well as the less serious charge of *libellus famosus* (malicious accusation, defamation, or lampoon) (p. 134), and it encompassed numerous charges, "many of them trivial if not actually absurd" (p. 190). For example, Faianius and Rubrius were indicted for *maiestas* for slighting Augustus's divinity by selling a statue of the deified emperor and breaking an oath sworn in the name of Augustus, but these indictments were quashed. Likewise, Cotta Messalinus, a friend of Ovid, called a banquet a funeral feast, alluding to the fact that Livia's deification had been refused, and found himself in legal trouble (p. 133). Dio reports that an ex-consul was executed for *maiestas,* having "carried a coin bearing a Tiberius type into a latrine" (p. 171). Other cases of *maiestas* involved the murder of a slave in front of a statue of Augustus, changing one's clothes beside a statue of Augustus, allowing oneself to be elected to an office on the same day that Augustus had been so elected, or "criticism of any word or action of the emperor" (pp. 171-72).

The potential penalty for such an offense was death,[71] and later Roman law would specify that the punishment for enchanters or spellbinders was crucifixion.[72] Mourning the death of anyone convicted of *perduellio* was forbidden,[73] and the name of the convict was blotted out of records and public memory under a decree of disgrace *(damnatio memoriae)* (p. 116). In a parallel fashion, the disciples of Jesus were prohibited by Jewish authorities from speaking in his name or of his memory following his death (Acts 4:17-18).

---

70. Rogers, *Criminal Trials,* identifies 106 named defendants accused of various forms of *maiestas,* which is "more than one half of the recorded indictments" of all kinds (p. 195). The parenthetical page references in the following text are to Rogers. See further Erich Koestermann, "Die Majestätsprozesse unter Tiberius," *Historia* 4 (1955): 72-106.

71. Cramer, *Astrology,* p. 249.

72. Smith, *Jesus the Magician,* p. 75, citing *Sententiae Receptae Paulo Tributae* 23.15-18.

73. Rogers, *Criminal Trials,* p. 140. The parenthetical page references in the following text are to Rogers.

During the reign of Tiberius, at least three cases of *maiestas* grew directly out of the use of astrology or magic. In the complicated case of Aemilia Lepida (20 C.E.), "the charge of *maiestas* was based on the alleged consultation of the astrologers regarding the imperial family. . . . But the indictment for *maiestas* was refused at Tiberius' specific injunction. What Lepida had asked and what answer she had received from the astrologers we are not told" (p. 52).[74]

Claudia Pulchra (26 C.E.) was entangled in a web of charges including adultery, "a plot to assassinate Tiberius by poison, and dealing in charms and incantations against the emperor." At this trial Agrippina interceded for Claudia, saying that Tiberius's worship of Augustus "was inconsistent with his persecution of Augustus' granddaughter," claiming that she herself was "the true image of Augustus, blood of his divine blood." Claudia was convicted and had likely been engaged in a conspiracy against Tiberius in the interests of Agrippina (pp. 92-93).

Mamercus-Aemilius Scaurus obtained the office of *consul suffectus* in 21 C.E. He was indicted in 34 for involvement five years earlier with magic rites of astrologers, which Rogers infers "inevitably suggests treasonable conspiracy" (pp. 139 and 152).

The closing years in the reign of Tiberius were troubled by many criminal cases right around the time Jesus was brought before Pontius Pilate in Jerusalem. Indeed, the year 32 C.E. saw "the largest number of criminal cases known in any one year of Tiberius' reign, a total of twenty-five," one-third of which grew out of the conspiracy of Sejanus against Tiberius the year before (pp. 112-14 and 128).

In addition, another law that may well have been used in these trials during the reign of Tiberius was the *Lex Cornelia de sicariis et veneficis,* a law that imposed capital punishment (burning alive) against magicians who murdered by poisoning.[75] According to the *Chronicle of the Year A.D. 354,* Tiberius executed forty-five sorcerers and eighty-five sorceresses, probably during the events of the years 16-17, only about fifteen years removed from Jesus' trial. Tacitus relates the story of Numantina, a woman prosecuted for having made her husband insane by incantations and spells.[76] Dickie believes that it was most likely the *Lex Cornelia* under which she was charged. A contemporary of Apuleius, Hadrian of Tyre, stated that this law was often broadened to take effect against sorcerers in general rather than used just for crimes resulting from *veneficia.*[77] It has also

74. She was a great-granddaughter of Augustus.

75. Dickie, *Magic and Magicians,* p. 147.

76. Tacitus, *Ann* 4.22.

77. See Rives, "Magic in Roman Law," p. 321, for an explanation of how *veneficium* is extended to include *maleficium.*

been observed that the actions of the populace or their leaders sometimes encouraged the Roman authorities to move against magicians, as was the case with Jesus and the Jewish leaders.[78] The fact that the *Lex Cornelia* covered *sicarii* as well as *venefici* may have been another reason why the Jews thought they could interest Pilate in taking action against Jesus as a malefactor, and the possibility of judicial liability for mismanaging such a case may also help to explain Pilate's hesitancy to condemn Jesus.[79]

While not implying that Jesus was crucified for somehow predicting the death of Tiberius Caesar or invoking incantations against the emperor, this legal background may explain why the Jewish chief priests (wrongly) thought they could get Pilate to take action against Jesus. If Jesus, who had been born under an unusual star and who was visited as an infant by magi from the East, spoke evil predictions against the Temple and the lives of the Jews, and prophesied about the manner of his own death, perhaps he would next turn to treason in the form of criticizing the emperor or laying spells on him. If that were to happen, letting Jesus go would certainly make Pilate no personal friend of Caesar.[80] In their final petition, the chief priests argued before the Praefectus that anyone who made himself a king "speaks against [*antilegei*] Caesar" (Jn 19:12). This looks like the making of an allegation of *maiestas*.[81] When coupled with a charge of *maleficium*, even a tenuous concern about treason begins to look more like something that the Praefectus might take an interest in. Indeed, Luke records that the chief priests sent out spies to record words that Jesus spoke "so they might deliver him unto the power and authority of the governor" (Lk 20:20). In seeking such evidence, they must have been looking for words whose effect went well beyond blasphemy under Jewish law, for they

78. Dickie, *Magic and Magicians,* p. 156. Rives, "Magic in Roman Law," p. 318, argues that although the contents of this law are known to apply only to the area less than a mile outside of Rome, the missing portions of the law (sections 2-4) likely contained information about cases that took place more than a mile from Rome.

79. See Krzysztof Amielanczyk, "In Iudicio Convenire (Circumvenire): Judicial Crimes according to the Lex Cornelia de Sicariis et Veneficis (81 B.C.)," *Pomerium* 2 (1996): 59-70, who shows that the clause in the *Lex Cornelia* imposed capital punishment on judges who conspired to execute an innocent defendant. Technically, this clause applied only to senators, but by the time of Tiberius's reign its scope may have expanded to provincial governors as well. I thank Julie Frederick for researching these points about the *Lex Cornelia*.

80. G. Lohfink, *The Last Day of Jesus* (Notre Dame: Ave Maria, 1984), p. 50, suggests that Pilate himself was at risk of being accused of *maiestas populi Romani*.

81. S. Légasse, *The Trial of Jesus* (London: SCM, 1997), p. 65, identifies *maiestas* as the reason for the death of Jesus, concluding: "Jesus was executed for having laid claim to royal power over his own people. Such a claim . . . fell under the accusation of *crimen maiestatis populi romani*." Légasse thinks, however, only in terms of political sedition or treason.

could not expect a Roman magistrate to take much interest in a purely Jewish dispute, as Gallio's dismissal of Sosthenes illustrates (Acts 18:14-17). And while the chief priests eventually had to be satisfied with weak hints of disloyalty *(laesa maiestas)* and not full-blown *perduellio,* they certainly would have latched onto any possibility that Jesus had insulted or threatened the persona of Tiberius himself, especially if any form of supernatural conduct could be implicated. Being far from Rome, the most likely way for a person in Jerusalem to hurt the emperor directly would have been through some form of magic or incantation.

The Charge of Magic in the Trial of Jesus

Laws against magic are mentioned occasionally by commentators writing about the trial of Jesus, but this underlying cause of action is not usually taken very seriously.[82] The main reason for this disregard is that no formal accusation of magic or *maleficium* ever seems to be made. But in light of the foregoing discussion, a closer look at Jn 18:30 is required.

The Greek manuscripts are not identical, but their differences are probably of no legal consequence. In Jn 18:28-29 the chief priests take Jesus to the Praetorium and Pilate asks, "What sort of accusation do you bring against this man?" They answer, "Unless this man was a *kakopoios* or *kakon poiōn,* we would not have submitted him to you" (Jn 18:30). On the one hand, the noun form *kakopoios* (the Latin equivalents of which are *maleficus* or *malefactor*) appears in codices Alexandrinus, Petropolitanus Purpureus, Codex 087 (Sinai/St. Petersburg), Ephraemi Rescriptus (third corrector), Basilensis, Seidelianus, Campianus and Bezae Cantabrigiensis (supplied), in several important families of other manuscripts, as well as in the Old Latin, Vulgate, and several patristic writers from the fourth century onward. On the other hand, three different participial forms, "making evil," "having made evil," or "evil-making," appear in other manuscripts; if this verb group can be taken together, it has slightly stronger cumulative support than does the noun, being found in Sinaiticus (perfect participle in the original hand, present participle in the corrector's hand), in Vaticanus and in the original hand of Ephraemi Rescriptus (present participles). The noun form, however, is present in "the overwhelming bulk of extant manuscripts" and would be the more natural Greek grammatical construction.[83]

---

82. For example, D. Hanks, *Christ as Criminal* (Lewiston, N.Y.: Edwin Mellen, 1997), p. 12.

83. I thank J. Bruce Prior, Kairos Research, 2004-04-05, for his assessment of the variant readings in the manuscripts. The construction "unless + he/it was" is most often followed by a

The use of the noun indicates that the chief priests accused Jesus of being a *kakopoios* or criminal wonder-worker. Perhaps they hoped Pilate would take cognizance of the case on that ground, knowing how voguish and volatile such charges had become back in Rome. But the participial phrase could also carry the same technical-legal weight, so long as the making of *kakos* or *malus* implied the use of some form of evil magic, which is conceivable. Recognizing that a term such as *maleficus, kakopoios,* or *kakon poiōn* should be understood in a general sense "save where it is qualified to take on a specific meaning,"[84] the argument that Jn 18:30 demands a technical-legal reading of this term is supported by the following:

1. The legal setting. Ordinary words carry technical-legal import when used in a judicial context. English words such as "action," "motion," "bench," or "arise" all have regular meanings in ordinary speech, but they assume a legal meaning when we know they are being spoken in court, as is the case here.

2. The legal request. When Pilate asked, "What sort of accusation do you bring against this man?" he was not saying, "What's going on here?" His words call for a specific legal response. He would expect the petitioners to formulate their answer in terms of cognizable causes of action under Roman law.

3. The logic of the exchange. In the Synoptic Gospels (of which John was presumably aware), Pilate had previously asked, "What *kakon* has he done?" (Mt 27:23; Mk 15:14; Lk 23:22). In their discourse with Pilate, if the chief priests were simply to respond, "Oh, he was doing *kakon*," their response would be circular, evasive, and probably insulting. Their answer must have been understood as more specific than simply a repetition of the question back to the magistrate.

4. The strong meaning of the word. Many astrological treatises, magical papyri, and other documents use the word *kakopoios* to describe bad mystical agents. While there are other words that are more distinctly used for magic, most have ambiguous connotations; they are sometimes negative words, sometimes not. *Kakopoios* is one word that not only carries the meaning of magic, but has an inescapably negative connotation. For example, the Scholiast on Aeschylus, *Seven against Thebes,* lines 720-25, sees Fury as a *kakopoios* "who ut-

___

noun or adjective, e.g., "unless he was a philanthropist and good man," "unless God was the absolutely free one," "unless it was indivisible," "unless it was the eternal truth," "unless he was the grandson of Kiron," or "unless there was something earthlike in the cosmos"; but it is possible for "unless + he/it was" to be followed by a participle, e.g., "unless he was the doer," "unless it were for hearing."

84. Twelftree, *Jesus the Exorcist,* p. 204. In a similar way, in order for the literally comparable Hebrew term *poʿᵃlê ʾawen* ("evildoers" or "workers of iniquity") to be connected with sorcery, "it has to be in a context which people already associated with supernatural forces." Jeffers, *Magic and Divination,* p. 104.

ters truth in the power of evils, for she spoke those words by night and they were fulfilled." In an emotionally charged setting, such as the hearing before Pilate, typical speakers or writers do not use strong words in a weak sense.

5. Early Christian reputation. The early Christians themselves were seen as being involved in magic. Suetonius states that "Christians" in the first century were accused of being involved in *superstitionis novae ac maleficae,*[85] a label that no one seems to doubt may imply charges of magic.[86] Christians were not simply being labeled "bad neighbors," but as "evildoers" or "workers of magic." Ironically, this charge makes them imitators of Jesus.

6. Contemporaneous legal prosecution of other miracle workers. Apollonius — who coincidentally was raised in Tarsus about the same time as Saul — was another miracle worker in the first century C.E. He was "tried for his life by Domitian," who accused him, among other things, "of divination by magic for Nerva's benefit"; his emphasis "on supernatural revelations inevitably led to his being accused of magical practices" on other occasions as well.[87] In the second century, Apuleius also found himself entangled in a lawsuit on charges of magic.

7. Exorcism of demoniacs. Jesus and his disciples were indisputably depicted as exorcists, the implications of which have been quite thoroughly explored in other contexts.[88] One may concur with Graham Twelftree that the historical Jesus was indeed an exorcist and yet not a magician,[89] but even exorcism used for improper purposes in an open and notorious fashion would have produced legal trouble. Carl Kraeling argued persuasively that people generally said Jesus "has a demon," meaning he "has a demon under his control," a concept commonly applied in the ambient culture to people having access to "the spirits of persons [such as John the Baptist] who had died a violent death" and helping them "to revenge themselves upon those who had done them violence, and to compensate themselves for the frustration the abrupt termination of their bodily existence had entailed."[90]

85. Suetonius, *De vita Caesarum* 6.16 (Nero).

86. R. Wilken, *The Christians as the Romans Saw Them* (New Haven: Yale University Press, 1984), p. 98. Perhaps to counteract such allegations, *Didache* 2.2, 3.4, and 5.1 specifically prohibited Christians from any involvement whatsoever with magic, enchanted potions, divination, sorcery, incantations, astrology, rites of purification.

87. Cramer, *Astrology,* pp. 222-23.

88. Smith, *Jesus the Magician,* pp. 30-36; Aune, "Magic in Early Christianity," pp. 1523-44; Shirock, "Whose Exorcists Are They?" pp. 41-51; C. K. Barrett, *The Holy Spirit and the Gospel Tradition* (London: SPCK, 1947), chap. 4, "Conflict with Evil Spirits — Temptation and Exorcism," and chap. 5, "Jesus as Miracle-Worker — the Words ΔΥΝΑΜΙΣ and ΕΞΟΥΣΙΑ."

89. Twelftree, *Jesus the Exorcist,* pp. 190-207.

90. C. H. Kraeling, "Was Jesus Accused of Necromancy?" *JBL* 59 (1940): 153-57.

8. Use in 1 Peter. The word *kakopoios* appears in two passages in 1 Peter. Although it is possible this term conveys only a general sense of "social deviancy," it can also "refer to an individual guilty of legally defined crimes."[91] Peter wrote that people generally were talking about Christians as "evildoers" *(kakopoiōn),* but he is confident that judges and others will see their good works, glorify God, and pronounce them not "evildoers" but "doers of good" *(agathopoiōn,* 1 Pet 2:12, 14; cf. Mt 5:16). In this context the label of "evildoers" was intended by outsiders to be deeply insulting, not weakly pejorative; turning the tables on these accusers at the day of judgment would thus be most dramatic. Even more definitively, in 1 Pet 4:13-16 "Christians" were exhorted to share the suffering of Christ, but not as a murderer, a thief, a *kakopoios,* or a fourth kind of offender (the nature of which is more general and indeterminable). Clustered grammatically together with the first two very serious offenses in this list,[92] the word *kakopoios* points to a particular crime of unacceptable magnitude, not merely a general indicator of moral misconduct. Edward Selwyn noted that Tertullian translated this word "here by *maleficus,* 'magician,'" as do others as well.[93]

9. Early Christian attestations. Some early Christians, such as Lactantius in the late third or early fourth century, openly acknowledged that the Jews had accused Jesus of being a magician or sorcerer.[94] Christians did not answer by arguing that this word in Jn 18:30 should be understood in some weak sense. They answered by arguing that the miracles of Jesus were acceptable because the prophets had predicted them.

His birth under an auspicious star would suggest a suspicious relation to astrology. In an age when astrology had become increasingly prominent and problematic in Roman culture, this concern may have carried more legal weight than a modern reader would realize.[95] The Gospel of Matthew makes a

---

91. J. H. Elliott, *1 Peter* (New York: Doubleday, 2000), p. 468.

92. "The repetition of *hōs* between *ē* and *allotriepiskopos* indicates that our author has passed from his catalogue of legal crimes to the social nuisance of interfering in other men's business and professing to put them to rights." E. G. Selwyn, *The First Epistle of St. Peter* (London: Macmillan, 1958), p. 225.

93. Tertullian, *Scorp* 12, and Tacitus, *Ann* 2.69, are cited by Selwyn, *First Epistle,* p. 225. Elliott, *1 Peter,* pp. 784-85, adds Cyprian, *Quir* 3.37, to the same effect, but nevertheless concludes that "it is likely that *kakopoios* here refers in general to 'one who does what is wrong,' acting contrary to prevailing custom and norms of conduct." Elliott, however, leans too heavily on 1 Pet 2:14 and 3:17, where the verbal form is not the same as 4:15, and he gives too little weight to the noun list of crimes in the immediate context of 4:15. If Jesus had been *falsely* accused of sorcery, the admonition to share his suffering but *not* as a sorcerer becomes all the more apropos.

94. See n. 50 above.

95. Bruce J. Malina, "Jesus as Astral Prophet," *Biblical Theology Bulletin* 27, no. 3 (1997): 83-98.

point of mentioning Jesus' connection to Egypt, which Celsus interpreted to mean that Jesus had received magical training there.[96]

Ultimately, however, Pilate found no such cause of action against Jesus and so held: "I find in him no fault," literally "no legal cause of action against him" (*oudemian . . . aitian,* Jn 18:38). Pilate claimed that the kind of kingdom Jesus asserted for himself was not treasonous per se; Jesus had not committed *maiestas,* and no evidence of *maleficium* was forthcoming. Jesus claimed that his kingdom had nothing to do with Caesar's world, and Pilate was satisfied that the man from Nazareth had not broken any Roman law, even by doing what some might have considered magical treason. Nevertheless, Pilate was apparently still fearful enough about the situation that he was willing to permit or take action.

Concluding Assessment: An Overriding Explanation That Makes Sense

While the Evangelists certainly wanted to avoid giving any false impression that Jesus somehow was a magician, and while most modern readers prefer to analyze the death of Jesus in terms of political or secular categories, perception of the supernatural evidently had more to do with the death of Jesus than most commentators have noticed. Recognizing this element unlocks many unresolved problems in the trial of Jesus. Speaking of the many complaints voiced against Jesus by his opponents, Morton Smith has argued that if Jesus' control of demons is taken out of the picture of his dialogues with his opponents, all that remains "is a collection of unrelated complaints, most of them not very serious; introduce it, and these complaints can be seen as component elements of a comprehensible structure."[97] This general insight applies even more potently to the legal analysis of the trial of Jesus.[98]

First, the legal factor of magic and wonder explains the overall behavior of the disparate parties. Of the many charges voiced against Jesus, none of the explicitly stated allegations or motivations accounts for the sufficient willingness on all determining sides (both Jewish and Roman) to execute Jesus or see him executed. Concerns about the use of supernatural powers, however, gave both Jews and Romans a strong interest in this case, thus explaining their common concerns and cooperation in this proceeding.

96. Robert L. Wilken, *The Christians as the Romans Saw Them* (New Haven: Yale University Press, 1984), p. 100, discusses how Celsus did not deny Jesus' ability to work miracles but instead attributed that ability to some training in Egypt.
97. Smith, *Jesus the Magician,* p. 31.
98. Smith, *Jesus the Magician,* pp. 36-43.

Second, the pervasive mood of fear and concerns over magic or witchcraft, and its closely related crimes of blasphemy and idolatry, explains otherwise strangely abrupt conduct. Concerns about blasphemy, false prophecy, or other such offenses would not have demanded the immediate attention of Jesus' arresters. Yet the parties acted precipitously. Fearing supernatural developments explains this urgent nighttime action. On the night Jesus was arrested, many people presumably stayed up all night, involved in this case. They may have assumed that he would invoke his powers that night, nighttime being when witchcraft is typically performed. Ironically, this night was also the time when Jesus' followers believed he fought the forces of evil and emerged victorious. Jesus quickly turned the tables on his approaching captors, pointing out that *they* were at work at night: "this is your hour, and the power of darkness" (Lk 22:53). In contrast, he affirmed that he had worked not only day after day (see Mt 26:55), but "right before" people's very eyes (*pros humas;* Mk 14:49), openly where all Jews come together (Jn 18:20). To Pilate, Jesus averred that his power came "from above," not from the realms below (Jn 19:11). In light of the sorcery factor, Jesus' statements can be understood as preemptive responses to any accusations that he was an evil-worker. These fears were real. As the Oedipus cycle and other popular literary tropes attest, people in the Hellenistic world believed that mantics could bring down kings and kingdoms in ways that even mighty military forces could not.

Third, the role of fearful power also explains the otherwise perplexing problem of how the Gospel accounts glide so smoothly from "a temple-focused offence in stage one [of the trial to] a kingship-focused offence at stage two."[99] The concern that existed in premodern societies over occult powers bridges the sacred and secular worlds. Witchcraft has often been seen "as the epitome of both religious and political rebellion," equated concurrently with "heresy and sedition."[100] Only a modern preconception strongly separates the spheres of church and state. Within a Jewish context, when Jesus appeared at Jerusalem during the Feast of Tabernacles, he went to the Temple of Herod and spoke publicly of himself in messianic terms (Jn 7:14-39);[101] because it was the role of the king to read the Law and speak from the Temple during the Feast of Tabernacles, Jesus was seen as usurping a royal prerogative under Jewish Law, and a

99. D. R. Catchpole, review of *The Trial of Jesus*, by S. Légasse, *NovT* 40, no. 3 (1998): 308.

100. T. O. Beidelman, review of *Witchcraft and Its Transformations, c. 1650–c. 1750*, by I. Bostridge, *Anthropos* 93 (1998): 587.

101. He stated: "If any man thirst, let him come unto me, and drink," for "out of [my] belly shall flow rivers of living water" (Jn 7:37-38). Such claims evoke allusions to the Lord God as the fountain of living waters (see Jer 2:13; 17:13), as well as the prophecy that living waters shall flow from Jerusalem in the day of the Lord (see Zech 14:8).

debate immediately ensued over the royal seed of King David (Jn 7:42). Religion and politics, Temple and kingship, play interrelated roles here. Likewise in the Roman sphere, politics and religion blend. The emperor, as *pontifex maximus,* was the head of the Roman cult as well as the chief of state. In either environment, any claim of authority from heaven (Mt 21:25-27; Jn 18:36), coupled with ostensible manifestations of supernatural powers, simultaneously raises questions about religious deviance and political malfeasance. These concerns expressed themselves not only in the forms of general rejection, name-calling, and accusations of social deviance,[102] but also as complaints and indictments with legal consequences.

Fourth, the secretive nature of miracle working also contributes to an understanding of the evidentiary and procedural problems involved in trying to identify and punish people who are improperly engaged in magical conduct. Recognizing this opacity and the difficulties it will always present to prosecutors helps to explain the multiplicity of accusations raised against Jesus. Multiple allegations increase the chances of success and thus, understandably, were raised in other trials of that very day, especially when charges of *maiestas,* disloyalty, *maleficium,* or occult practices were involved. The factor of *maleficium* could compound any minor offense. Lesser allegations, such as "we found him disturbing our people, telling them not to pay tribute to Caesar, and calling himself a king,"[103] assume much more serious proportions when coupled with a charge of magic or sorcery in violation of the Law of Moses and the Mishnah or the edict of Augustus and a *senatus consultum.*

Fifth, this factor also offers a solution to the legal puzzle of the punishment by crucifixion. The normal form of execution for blasphemy under Jewish law was stoning, and several times previously people took up stones to stone Jesus for blasphemy (e.g., Jn 8:59). Why, then, did Jesus' execution take the form of crucifixion? Contrary to widespread opinion, crucifixion was not exclusively Roman.[104] With the discovery of the *Temple Scroll,* scholars now acknowledge

102. B. J. Malina and J. H. Neyrey, *Calling Jesus Names: The Social Value of Labels in Matthew* (Sonoma, Calif.: Polebridge, 1988), see "witchcraft accusations" as having only "two possible effects," namely, expulsion or fission (see p. 29). They do not explore the legal effects of such allegations, even in their otherwise fine discussion of the roles of negative labeling and status degradation in the trial of Jesus, pp. 71-91. More is at stake in the capital trial of Jesus than names alone.

103. Sherwin-White, *Roman Society and Roman Law in the New Testament* (Oxford: Clarendon, 1963), p. 25.

104. Scrutinizing the legal and religious implications of crucifixion, which may have been a Jewish form of execution at the time of Jesus and not merely a Roman procedure, see J. M. Baumgarten, "Does *TLH* in the Temple Scroll Refer to Crucifixion?" *JBL* 91 (1972): 472-81; O. Betz, "The Temple Scroll and the Trial of Jesus," *SwJT* 30 (1988): 5-8; J. M. Ford, "'Crucify

that hanging on a tree (or crucifixion) could serve in Jesus' day not only as a form of exposing the body of a person who had been stoned to death, but also as a mode of execution under the prevailing Jewish law. Killing by suffocation was one of the four manners of execution permitted under Jewish law,[105] and the cause of death in a crucifixion or hanging was usually asphyxia or suffocation.[106] Especially pertinent to the case at hand is one notorious Jewish case a century before the time of Jesus, in which eighty witches were hung (or crucified) in Ashkelon without proper trials, because the court saw the case as a matter of emergency. The writers of the Talmud later looked back on this event and condemned it as an irregular, illegal decision by an ignorant or wicked court,[107] but this legal incident shows that such things could and did happen around the time of Jesus, even if it were virtually impossible under normal circumstances to convict a person of any such charge. Thus, on an emergency charge involving fear of demons, Jewish law was capable of putting someone to death by crucifixion. A case of normal blasphemy called for death by stoning; presumably a case compounded by additional offenses would call for a more painful mode of execution, which would have also been acceptable to the Romans, of course. Paulus later summarized Roman law as having held that "those who know about the magic art shall be punished with the highest penalty; they shall be thrown to the beasts or be crucified."[108]

Finally, the fear factor unifies the four Gospel accounts. While each reports its own idiosyncratic and conflicting technical details, the Gospels all share a broad but definite common view that these proceedings were full of fear, especially of the supernatural. Transcending the differences between the poles of Mark and John, the aura of supernatural powers ties the trial of Jesus together, not only literarily but also historically and theologically. Jesus is seen, not alternatively as prophet or wonder-worker, but as both: as a prophet who gave signs and wonders. Unless readers are willing totally to discount all the miracles, healings, exorcisms, signs or wonders (real or perceived) reported in the Gos-

Him, Crucify Him' and the Temple Scroll," *ET* 87 (June 1976): 275-78; S. Rosenblatt, "The Crucifixion of Jesus from the Standpoint of Pharasitic Law," *JBL* 75 (1956): 315-21; M. Wilcox, "'Upon the Tree' — Deut 21:22-23 in the New Testament," *JBL* 96 (1977): 85-99; Y. Yadin, "Pesher Nahum (4QpNahum) Reconsidered," *IEJ* 21 (1971): 1-12.

105. See generally, G. Horowitz, *The Spirit of Jewish Law* (New York: Bloch, 1953), p. 646. "By every unspecified death in the Torah strangulation is meant," but stoning came to be inferred, by analogy, as the preferred punishment for witchcraft. *b. Sanh.* 52b-54a. In later Jewish law, suffocation was not used for sorcery.

106. W. R. Litchfield, "The Search for the Physical Cause of Jesus Christ's Death," *BYU Studies* 37, no. 4 (1997-98): 98.

107. *b. Sanh.* 45b-46a.

108. Cramer, *Astrology*, p. 276.

pels and explicitly reemphasized in Acts 2:22-23 as the prelude to the anomalous *(anomōn)* death of Jesus, it is hard to imagine that these works of Jesus did not play an important role, directly or indirectly, in his trial and execution.

In the end, a few people who became afraid primarily because of his open association with the supernatural put Jesus to death. Some observers would come to view these wonders as signs that Jesus was divine. But for those who became afraid and thought Jesus was demonic and was acting in contravention of the laws against sorcery and the deceptive use of wonder-working, the only legal option was to reject and eliminate him. Of course, hate, envy, politics, prejudices, and economics all played their parts, but these factors do not come close to telling or explaining the whole story.

Ramat Hanadiv and Ein Gedi:
Property versus Poverty in Judea before 70

Yizhar Hirschfeld

In his book on the ruling class in Judea, Martin Goodman points to the enormous socioeconomic gap that characterized Judea in the first century C.E.[1] The Hasmonean aristocracy, comprised of families with a long line of distinguished ancestry, was physically removed by Herod and his loyal subjects and replaced by a new aristocracy based on wealth, power, and proximity to the ruling family. In this respect Herod implemented the accepted method used in the Hellenistic world of creating an aristocratic, feudal-like class, whose status, wealth, and property were beholden to the king. In return for their personal loyalty to the monarch, the members of this new class received large estates of very fertile tracts of land that belonged to the kingdom. Thus, for example, Herod's sister Salome received extensive tracts of land on the coastal plain, in the area of Yavneh (Jamnia), and in the Jordan Valley.[2] Ptolemy, Herod's personal friend and a high minister in the king's court, also received a large estate on the hill of Samaria, where the village of Arus was located.[3] Ptolemy's estate is estimated to have stretched over at least 1,000 hectares.[4]

Until Herod ascended the throne, most of the Jewish population in Judea

1. M. Goodman, *The Ruling Class of Judaea* (Cambridge: Cambridge University Press, 1987), pp. 59-66.

2. Josephus, *Ant* 18.31 (ed. L. H. Feldman, LCL [Cambridge: Harvard University Press, 1965], p. 27). Salome, Herod's sister, bequeathed her lands in the Yavneh (Jamnia) region and in the Jordan Valley (Phasaelis and Archelais) to Livia, wife of the emperor Augustus. See D. W. Roller, *The Building Program of Herod the Great* (Berkeley: University of California Press, 1998), pp. 120-21.

3. Josephus, *War* 2.69 (ed. H. St. J. Thackeray, LCL [Cambridge: Harvard University Press, 1927], p. 349). On Ptolemy, Herod's friend, see Roller, *Building Program*, pp. 63-64.

4. S. Dar, "The Estate of Ptolemy, Senior Minister of Herod" (in Hebrew), in *Jews and Judaism in the Second Temple, Mishna, and Talmud Periods*, ed. I. Gafni, A. Oppenheimer, and M. Stern (Jerusalem: Yad Izhak Ben-Zvi, 1993), pp. 33-50.

was comprised of independent farmers who cultivated their own private lands. Josephus distinctly characterizes the Jewish people as a nation of farmers: "Well, ours is not a maritime country; neither commerce nor the intercourse which it promotes with the outside world has any attraction for us. Our cities are built inland, remote from the sea; and we devote ourselves to the cultivation of the productive country with which we are blessed."[5]

The Hasmonean kings, who were originally farmers from the village of Modein, did not impinge upon the right of their people to own private property. The private land estates of the Hasmoneans existed only in areas they had conquered, such as the Jezreel Valley.[6] During Herod's rule, the situation took a complete turn. By using unconventional means, the Herodian aristocracy became the controlling force over private lands. The larger population consequently hated the estate owners in the first century C.E., and thus they could not carry out the traditional role of the local aristocracy in the Roman period, i.e., to mediate between the throngs of simple folk and the Roman authorities. Goodman also points to the inability of the Herodian aristocracy to control the people of Judea as one of the main reasons for the outbreak of the revolt of 70 C.E., which led to the destruction of the Temple.

The Excavations at Ramat Hanadiv

The excavations I conducted at Ramat Hanadiv, the results of which have recently been published,[7] uncovered manorial complexes that, I believe, belonged to one or two of the above-mentioned landowners. Ramat Hanadiv stretches over a large area (ca. 450 hectares) at the southern end of Mount Carmel, some 7 to 8 kilometers northeast of Caesarea. Two sites were exposed: Horvat Aqav at the western end of Ramat Hanadiv, and Horvat Eleq at the northeastern end of Ramat Hanadiv. At both sites, with 1.5 kilometers between them, we found large complexes dating from the last decade of the first century B.C.E. and continuing until the Great Revolt against Rome in 70 C.E. The cessation of the settlement in 70 indicates that the inhabitants of these sites took part in the events connected

---

5. Josephus, *Apion* 1.60 (ed. H. St. J. Thackeray, LCL [Cambridge: Harvard University Press, 1926], p. 187). On the agricultural settlement in Judea in the Second Temple period, see Y. Hirschfeld, "Jewish Rural Settlement in Judaea in the Early Roman Period," in *The Early Roman Empire in the East*, ed. S. E. Alcock, Oxbow Monograph 35 (Oxford: Oxbow Books, 1997), pp. 72-88.

6. S. Applebaum, "The Agrarian Question and the Revolt of Bar Kokhba" (in Hebrew), *ErIsr* 8 (1967): 287.

7. Y. Hirschfeld, *Ramat Hanadiv Excavations* (Jerusalem: Israel Exploration Society, 2000).

Figure 55. Map; location of Ramat Hanadiv.

Courtesy of Y. Hirschfeld

to the Great Revolt, thus implying they were Jewish. This is corroborated by the discovery of water installations at both sites that probably served as Jewish ritual baths *(mikvaot).*

Of the two sites, Horvat Eleq is the superior one. The perennial spring of Ein Tzur runs through the site. Near the spring, remains were found of an aqueduct, a swimming pool (with a capacity of over 300 cubic meters), and a heated bathhouse built according to Roman technology par excellence. The great similarity between the bathhouse at Ein Tzur and the Herodian bathhouses found at Masada, Jericho, Herodium, and Cypros indicates that the builder of this structure at Ramat Hanadiv was directly influenced by the king and was probably one of his close associates.

Above the spring, at the top of the hill, a fortified, orthogonal structure of especially large dimensions (4,800 square meters) was exposed. The structure boasted a solid wall (ca. 2 m. thick) with four corner towers and four intermediate ones. In the center of the structure a large, solid, main tower was uncovered that, by the thickness of its walls (1.3 m.), probably stood over 20 meters high. The construction of towers in Herod's day was unprecedented. Ehud Netzer's studies of the Herodium have demonstrated that the towers at the top of the mountain were built to a height of 40 meters.[8] The tower was a symbol of power and rule, and thus it is understandable why the estate owner of Horvat Eleq chose it as the principal feature of his complex. The tower also served as a place for storing the estate treasures (and indeed, in the basement of the tower we found dozens of clay jars *in situ*) and as the temporary dwelling of the land-owner when he visited the site (many estate owners were absentee landlords whose permanent dwellings were in the city).[9] Next to the tower, a large residential quarter and storage wings were discovered adjacent to the walls.

The agricultural nature of the complex at Horvat Eleq is exhibited by two additional structures that were uncovered at the site: a round tower that functioned as a dovecote *(columbarium)* and an olive press.[10] The main purpose of the *columbarium* was to supply pigeon manure as fertilizer for cultivating the land, and the olive press is indicative of olive growing and the production of olive oil. The estate, of which Horvat Eleq was its center, most probably stretched over the fertile soil of Hanadiv Valley, east of Ramat Hanadiv. On the fringes of this valley were springs that supplied drinking water to Caesarea via an aqueduct.[11] Thus, the complex at Horvat Eleq was located at a strategic point commanding the water sources of Herodian Caesarea. All these factors indicate that the estate owner was a figure from the king's closest circle, one of his sons — perhaps Archelaus or Antipas, whose mother, one of Herod's wives, was a Samaritan[12] — or one of his close associates, such as the above-mentioned Ptolemy, whose estate was located on the hill of Samaria.

The second site, Horvat Aqav, was a smaller complex (ca. 2,500 square meters) at the western end of Ramat Hanadiv. There the same elements were discovered: an orthogonal complex surrounded by a wall (1.3 m. thick) containing remains of a residential wing, agricultural installations (a cistern, two wine presses, an olive press), and a tower with thick walls (1.2 m.) incorporated into

8. E. Netzer, *Greater Herodium,* Qedem 13 (Jerusalem: Hebrew University of Jerusalem, 1981), pp. 96-98.

9. This phenomenon was treated extensively by Z. Safrai, "Ancient Field Structures — the Village in Eretz Israel during the Roman Period" (in Hebrew), *Cathedra* 89 (1998): 8-9. However, based on the archaeological remains, it is hard to say whether the owner was an absentee landlord or a landowner who lived in his manor permanently.

10. B. Zissu, "The Dovecote at Horvat 'Eleq,'" in *Ramat Hanadiv Excavations,* pp. 617-27.

11. Y. Porath, "The Tunnel of Caesarea Maritima's High Level Aqueduct at the Kurkar Ridge (Jisr ez-Zarqa)" (in Hebrew), *'Atiqot* 30 (1996): 23-43.

12. E. Schürer, *The History of the Jewish People in the Age of Jesus Christ (175 B.C.–A.D. 135),* I (Edinburgh: T. & T. Clark, 1973), p. 321. See also B.-Z. Rosenfeld and A. Borenstein, "The Jewish Settlements of Ramat Hanadiv in the Second Temple Period and Their Identification," in *Ramat Hanadiv Excavations,* pp. 656-58.

Figure 56.
Proposed
reconstruction
of Horvet Eleq in
first century C.E.

Drawing by B. Balogh

the southwestern corner of the complex. This combination of wall and tower characterizes a significant number of estate manors discovered in Second Temple–period Judea. In an earlier article I presented parallels to this site, including the central structure at Qumran, also comprising a wall and fortified tower incorporated into its southwestern corner.[13]

Roland de Vaux's excavations at Qumran in the early 1950s uncovered various wings, including many installations for the processing of agricultural produce outside the central complex. On the basis of this comparison, I reached the conclusion that it was not the Essene community, or any other religious sect for that matter, that settled at Qumran, but rather a wealthy landowner, his slaves, and servants who cultivated the oasis of Ein Feshkha located nearby (in the Dead Sea region the balsam plant was cultivated, and the perfume that was produced from it was considered the best). On the assumption that large, well-planned, and well-built dwelling complexes indeed reflect the wealth and status of the landowner, we would then have no difficulty in assuming that sites such as Qumran — the Ramat Hanadiv sites as well as about a dozen others throughout Herodian Judea — were inhabited by wealthy landlords, frequently mentioned in the writings of Josephus, the New Testament, and other sources.[14] As we shall see below, the simple folk, including the Essenes and recluses who withdrew from society, lived in simple, and much more modest, structures.

13. Y. Hirschfeld, "Early Roman Manor Houses in Judea and the Site of Khirbet Qumran," *JNES* 57 (1998): 161-89.
14. M. Feinberg Vamosh, *Daily Life at the Time of Jesus* (Herzalia: Palphot, 2000), p. 66.

The Ein Gedi Excavations

The social oppression and land theft that characterized Judea during Herod's reign and afterward, in the first century c.e., left many of the country's inhabitants in a state of poverty and bankruptcy. As a result, we are witness to two phenomena that characterized first century c.e. Judea. First, the significant rise in the number of bandits and thieves made the roads unsafe.[15] Many of these road thieves were probably originally farmers who became impoverished and subsequently turned to violence. The second phenomenon that characterized pre-70 Judea was retreating to the desert for religious reasons. According to Josephus, many people, both individuals and groups, withdrew from society for the Judean Desert and the Jordan River region, searching for personal redemption and the fulfillment of messianic expectations.[16] Among these were John the Baptist and his many followers, as described in the New Testament (Mt 3:1-13). Josephus himself lived in the Judean Desert with a recluse called Bannus,[17] an ascetic who fed on wild plants, dressed in tree bark, and frequently immersed himself in cold water — indeed, features very reminiscent of the description of John the Baptist.

Members of the Essene sect were among those who sought seclusion in the Judean Desert because of religious motives. Pliny the Elder informs us that a large group of Essenes lived a life of solitude and asceticism above Ein Gedi. Pliny describes the Essenes as people who shunned property and money, and led a life of celibacy and modesty in the bosom of nature. "On the west side of the Dead Sea . . . is the solitary tribe of the Essenes, which is remarkable beyond all the other tribes in the whole world, as it has no women and has renounced all sexual desire, has no money, and has only palm-trees for company."[18]

In the archaeological expedition at Ein Gedi, under my direction, we systematically excavated in 1998-99 what has been called "the Essene site."[19] First discovered by Yohanan Aharoni in a survey conducted in 1956 at the Ein Gedi oasis, the site lies on a natural rock terrace about 200 meters above the Dead Sea. At this site we were able to identify, even prior to the excavation, remains of

15. B. Isaac, "Bandits in Judaea and Arabia," *HSCP* 88 (1984): 176-84.

16. Josephus, *Ant* 20.97-98, 167-68, 188.

17. Josephus, *Vita* 2: "he (Bannus) dwelt in the wilderness, wearing only such clothing as trees provided, feeding on such things as grew of themselves, and using frequent ablutions of cold water, by day and night, for purity's sake."

18. Pliny, *Natural History* 5.15, 73 (ed. Rackham, LCL [Cambridge: Harvard University Press, 1942], p. 277).

19. For a preliminary report of the excavation results and conclusions, see Y. Hirschfeld, "A Community of Hermits above Ein Gedi" (in Hebrew), *Cathedra* 96 (2000): 7-40.

Figure 57. Ein Gedi,
waterfall.

Courtesy of Y. Hirschfeld

about thirty small cells, as well as a pool and the source of a dry spring. During the excavation another pool was exposed near the first one, and the dry spring became reactivated, issuing water as in antiquity. On the basis of pottery and glass fragments found in the cells, the site was dated to the first and second centuries C.E., or more precisely, from the mid–first century C.E. until the Second Revolt, which began in 130. Later on, in the Byzantine period (fourth to sixth century), two to three cells were resettled; however, this stage of occupation is relatively unimportant in comparison to the first one.

During the site's main stage of occupation, i.e., the first to second centuries C.E., there were about twenty-five small dwelling cells and three larger cells, perhaps intended for communal purposes. The two pools found near the spring and the lime furnace (used for producing plaster for the pools) indicate the agricultural occupation of the site's inhabitants. And indeed, agricultural terraces were found next to the pools, over an area of 0.4-0.5 hectares.

Did farmers or laborers live at this site as a temporary camp, or was this the place where the Essenes lived, as described by Pliny? Of course, we have no unequivocal proof that this was an Essene settlement, but Pliny's historical source and the archaeological finds, when combined, correspond with the overall picture of the settlement along the Dead Sea in the Second Temple period. Surveys

Figure 58. Ein Gedi, the Early Roman structures ("huts") that Hirschfeld thinks belonged to Essenes.

Courtesy of Y. Hirschfeld

Figure 59. Aerial view of the "Essene Gate" above Ein Gedi, looking south.

Courtesy of Z. Radovan

conducted along the western shore of the Dead Sea have brought to light about fifteen sites resembling the one above Ein Gedi.[20] At these sites, dating from the Roman period (as per the ceramic finds), clusters of an average of five to six cells were discovered on the fringes of the desert oases, along the Dead Sea, from north to south: Ein Feshkha, Ein Turabeh, Ein Gedi, and Ein Boqeq. We may conjecture that the recluses who, according to the sources, left for the desert in search of religious and spiritual redemption settled these groups of cells. Indeed, it would be difficult to prove this, since these people did not have any definitive cultic structures, as was the case later on, for instance, when the monks reached the Judean Desert in the Byzantine period.[21] Nevertheless, the multiplicity of sites and the clusters of cells of the type we excavated above Ein Gedi correspond with the sources attesting to the relatively large numerical presence of recluses in the region at the end of the Second Temple period.

Summary

The recent archaeological finds — including those from the excavations at Ramat Hanadiv and Ein Gedi — confirm the picture painted by Martin Goodman. On the one hand, the large and magnificent estate manors such as those uncovered at Ramat Hanadiv, Qumran, and elsewhere are an archaeological expression of the power and status of the ruling class in Judea. These were the wealthy landlords who, since Herod's time and onward (also after the kingdom's annexation of Judea), controlled the quality lands in the country. On the other hand, the poor clusters of cells discovered above Ein Gedi and along the western shoreline of the Dead Sea are an archaeological expression, indeed meager, of what those who retreated to the desert left behind — either owing to economic distress or to expectations of messianic redemption. Undoubtedly, the material remains left by recluses in the desert are modest, but their religious and spiritual legacy is great and has left its mark until today.

---

20. The sites along the Dead Sea were surveyed by Bar-Adon in the late 1960s and early 1970s. See his "The Judaean Desert and Plain of Jericho" (in Hebrew), in *Judaea, Samaria, and the Golan — Archaeological Survey, 1967-1968,* ed. M. Kochavi (Jerusalem: Archaeological Survey of Israel, 1972), pp. 92-152.

21. On the monastic-type chapel in the Judean Desert, see Y. Hirschfeld, *The Judean Desert Monasteries in the Byzantine Period* (New Haven and London: Yale University Press, 1992), pp. 114-17.

Between Jerusalem and the Galilee: Samaria in the Time of Jesus

Jürgen Zangenberg

Samaria in the New Testament

Why have a chapter on Samaria in a book entitled *Jesus and Archaeology*? The NT passages mentioning the region in general, localities in the region, or people from it are few (Mt 10:5-6; Lk 9:51-56; 10:25-37; 17:11-19; Jn 3:22-30; 4:4-43; 8:48; 11:54; Acts 1:8; 8:4-25; 9:31; 15:3) and provide little specific historical information on where and how Jesus might have had contact with this region in the heart of ancient Palestine.[1] Mark does not mention Samaria; Matthew refers to it only once, and that in a negative way by having Jesus instruct the Twelve *not* to go to the Gentiles nor enter a city of the Samaritans *(polis Samaritōn)*.[2] The passage is so unspecific that it is not even possible to say if Matthew had Samaritans (i.e., adherents of the biblically inspired cult on Mount Gerizim) or Samarians (inhabitants of the region of Samaria in general) in mind.[3] The par-

---

1. See the overview by A. Lindemann, "Samaria und die Samaritaner im Neuen Testament," *WuD* 22 (1993): 51-76, and the recent, very instructive article by J. P. Meier, "The Historical Jesus and the Historical Samaritans: What Can Be Said?" *Biblica* 81 (2000): 202-32, with ample references.

2. See Meier, "Historical Jesus," pp. 218-21; J. Zangenberg, *Frühes Christentum in Samarien: Topographische und traditionsgeschichtliche Studien zu den Samarientexten im Johannesevangelium,* TANZ 27 (Tübingen: Francke, 1998), pp. 181-91; A. J. Levine, *The Social and Ethnic Dimensions of Matthaean Salvation History: "Go Nowhere among the Gentiles . . ." (Mt 10:5b)* (Lewiston, N.Y.: Mellen, 1988); Y. Anno, "The Mission to Israel in Matthew: The Intention of Matthew 10:5b-6 Considered in the Light of the Religio-Political Background" (Th.D. diss., Lutheran School of Theology at Chicago, 1984).

3. This distinction was introduced by R. Egger, *Josephus Flavius und die Samaritaner. Eine*

I owe many thanks for valuable comments to Gabriele Fassbeck, Kurt Erlemann, and Wolfgang Zwickel.

allelism of *hodos ethnōn* and *polis Samaritōn* suggests that Matthew saw no difference between Samaritans and Gentiles (cf. Acts 14:16; Jer 10:2 LXX with similar figurative use of *hodos*, a position that is well established in contemporary Jewish literature).[4] For Matthew, Samaritans are not part of Israel, but belong to the Gentiles. Furthermore, Mark and Matthew have Jesus travel via Jericho to Jerusalem, thus indicating that he did not cross Samaria but rather seems to have taken the route around it through the Jordan Valley (Mk 10:1, par Mt 19:1; and further Mk 10:46, par Mt 20:29).

Luke's Gospel seems more promising,[5] but only at first sight. In Lk 9:51-56 Jesus, being on his way from the Galilee to Jerusalem, tried to travel through Samaria like so many other Jews, but was turned away by the inhabitants of a *kōmē Samaritōn*. The reason Luke gives for the inhospitable behavior of the villagers — that Jesus was traveling to Jerusalem — makes it very likely that they were Samaritans (we know of some unfriendly actions by Samaritans against Jewish pilgrims traveling from the Galilee to Jerusalem);[6] the rest, however, re-

---

terminologische Untersuchung zur Identitätsklärung der Samaritaner, NTOA 4 (Fribourg: Universitätsverlag; Göttingen: Vandenhoeck & Ruprecht, 1986), and has in many cases proven a valuable tool in describing the cultural diversity of the region of Samaria. Egger rightly stressed that Samaria by no means was inhabited only by Samaritans, but was home for many different groups. One has to keep in mind (which Egger certainly does), however, that most ancient authors, including Josephus and the New Testament writers, do not differentiate terminologically between specific groups in Samaria, and one has to find circumstantial evidence clearly to identify a person's religious or cultural affiliation. In this article I use the term "Samaritan" only when there is firm evidence that the person(s) under consideration adhered to the biblically inspired cult of Yahweh and worshiped on Mount Gerizim (cf. Meier's "religious definition" in "Historical Jesus," p. 205). In all other cases I use "Samarian" and qualify it with adjectives, wherever possible. Cf. also S. Freyne, "Behind the Names: Galileans, Samaritans, *Ioudaioi*," in S. Freyne, *Galilee and Gospel: Collected Essays*, WUNT 125 (Tübingen: Mohr Siebeck, 2000), pp. 114-31; J. Zangenberg, "Überlegungen zur Möglichkeit einer 'Topographie religiöser Gruppen' in Samarien zur neutestamentlichen Zeit," *Biblisches Forum* 1999 (2000): 69-97; R. J. Coggins, "Issues in Samaritanism," in *Judaism in Late Antiquity Part III: Where We Stand; Issues and Debates in Ancient Judaism*, ed. J. Neusner and A. J. Avery-Peck, HdO I/40,3 (Brill: Leiden, 1999), 1:63-77 (esp. pp. 67-68).

4. Consult *b. Sanh.* 63b (referring to 2 Kgs 17 and the "foreign" origin of the Samaritans); *y. Abod. Zar.* 44d.41–45.53-57 and *Gen. Rab.* 81.3 (referring to Gen 35:4-18 and the pagan idols the Samaritans allegedly hide under Mount Gerizim); *t. Abod. Zar.* 2.4-8; *t. Ohal.* 18.6; *m. Sheb.* 8.9f., but also *t. Ter.* 4.12. All texts are collected, translated into German, and introduced in J. Zangenberg, *SAMAREIA: Antike Quellen zur Geschichte und Kultur der Samaritaner in deutscher Übersetzung*, TANZ 15 (Tübingen: Francke, 1994).

5. Consult recently Meier, "Historical Jesus," pp. 222-27; M. Böhm, *Samarien und die Samaritai bei Lukas: Eine Studie zum religionshistorischen und traditionsgeschichtlichen Hintergrund der lukanischen Samarientexte und zu deren topographischer Verhaftung*, WUNT II/111 (Tübingen: Mohr Siebeck, 1999).

6. Josephus, *War* 2.232-247; *Ant* 20.118-136; Tacitus, *Ann* 12.54.

mains vague. Jesus and the disciples move on to another village, but Luke does not say anything about its character. Was it Samaritan or Jewish, was it in Samaria or elsewhere?

Lk 10:25-37 certainly provides no information either on possible contacts Jesus might or might not have had with Samaria. The pericope tells more about Luke's pedagogical skills and the prejudices of his congregation against Samaritans (and Luke's sympathy with them as a marginalized group; see below) than it helps us identify any historically or archaeologically relevant material.[7]

Only Lk 17:11-19 is more specific, but it is not actually a story about Samaria. In the complicated opening verse, 17:11 *(dia meson Samareias kai Galilaias)*,[8] Luke seems to indicate that Jesus met the ten lepers not in Samaria proper, but outside of it in the border region between Galilee and Samaria. If Luke or his sources actually were so well versed in geographical matters as some assume, this passage can only mean that the encounter took place in the city territory of Scythopolis or around Gaba, i.e., in the Jezreel Valley, which separated Samaria from the Galilee (cf. Josephus, *War* 3.37).[9] But the *kōmē* Luke mentions in 17:12 is just as unspecific as the one mentioned in 9:56. So, in the end, John Nolland might be correct in pointing out: "Luke has no interest in the geographical features of the journey. The location between Samaria and Galilee merely accounts for the mixed Jewish and Samaritan makeup of the group of the lepers."[10] The fact that the only leper who returns, praises God, and gives thanks to Jesus is a Samaritan, might — just like the "good Samaritan" in Lk 10:25-37 — be more indicative of Luke's narrative pedagogy toward his audience than of his historical or geographical reliability.[11] Moreover, the fact that all these passages belong to Luke's special traditions has made many exegetes rightly doubt if they are of any value for our question at all.[12] Lacking a

---

7. Consult M. Gourgues, "The Priest, the Levite, and the Samaritan Revisited: A Critical Note on Luke 10:31-35," *JBL* 117 (1998): 709-13, with ample references about the strategy of the narrative. Gourgues summarizes Luke's point: "Paradox of paradoxes, it is the Samaritan who, by means of reversal of roles, becomes the very model of neighborly love" (p. 713).

8. On the text-critical problems of this verse, cf., e.g., Böhm, *Samarien*, pp. 260-61; J. Nolland, *Luke 9:21–18:34*, WBC 35B (Dallas: Word, 1993), pp. 844-46.

9. On possible geographical implications, if Luke really *was* interested in giving an accurate location (cf. Nolland's skepticism below, n. 10), see, e.g., Böhm, *Samarien*, pp. 271-74.

10. Nolland, *Luke 9:21–18:34*, p. 846.

11. On the christological significance of the passage, see D. Hamm, "What the Samaritan Leper Sees: The Narrative Christology of Luke 17:11-19," *CBQ* 56 (1994): 273-87.

12. Too overconfident is Böhm, *Samarien*, esp. pp. 277: "Alle drei Perikopen [scil. Luke 9:51-56; 10:25-37; 17,11-19] zeigen palästinisches Lokalkolorit und viel Vertrautheit mit den jeweiligen realgeschichtlichen Verhältnissen vor Ort."

consistent geographical trait, the special traditions referring to Samaria or Samari(t)ans clearly cannot be pieced together to reconstruct even a most tentative form of itinerary. It is therefore not surprising to see Luke take up Mark's narrative thread again at the end of his *Reisebericht* and have Jesus enter Jerusalem via Jericho (Lk 18:31, 35; 19:1). Given the character of our sources, there seems only one conclusion for a historian: No matter how diverse the episodes the Synoptics transmit, in the end they all agree that Jesus seemed uninterested in Samaria.

Jn 4:4-43, however, draws a very different picture.[13] This is the only text that clearly reports an intensive encounter between Jesus and the region of Samaria, but its value ultimately depends on how much we trust John as a historian of the "life of Jesus" in general. Even if we assume that John's sources *are* somewhat reliable in this respect, the picture they convey brings us in open contrast with the negative result from the Synoptics. Since there are no convincing criteria at hand to decide which option is historically more likely, we cannot but leave the question open.[14] Meier also concludes his detailed study by stating the "disappointingly meager" result that, apart from possible but unlikely passing encounters between Jesus and Samari(t)ans, "by either explicit statement or telling silence, all the Gospels agree that there was no programmatic mission to the Samaritans during Jesus' lifetime."[15] So, in this regard, there would seem to be no need of a chapter about Samaria in a book on Jesus and archaeology.

We have to move to a different level to justify this study in the present book. None of the NT texts mentioning Samaria brings us into firm contact with the "historical Jesus," but they provide us with interesting glimpses into how early Christian communities interacted with the cultural diversity of late Hellenistic and early Roman Samaria. Apart from Jn 3:22-30, 8:48, 11:54, and

---

13. On Jn 4:4-43, see Meier, "Historical Jesus," pp. 227-31; Zangenberg, *Frühes Christentum,* pp. 97-196; R. G. Maccini, *Her Testimony Is True: Women as Witnesses in John* (Sheffield: Sheffield Academic, 1996); B. Hall, "Some Thoughts about Samaritanism and the Johannine Community," in *New Samaritan Studies of the Société des Études Samaritaines Volumes III and IV,* ed. A. D. Crown and L. A. Davey, Festschrift G. D. Sixdenier (Sydney: Mandelbaum Trust, 1995), pp. 207-15; J. E. Botha, *Jesus and the Samaritan Woman: A Speech Act Reading of John 4:1-42* (Leiden: Brill, 1991); H. Boers, *Neither on This Mountain Nor in Jerusalem: A Study of John 4* (Atlanta: Scholars, 1988); T. Okure, *The Johannine Approach to Mission: A Contextual Study of John 4:1-42* (Tübingen: Mohr, 1988); J. D. Purvis, "The Fourth Gospel and the Samaritans," *NovT* 17 (1975): 161-98; H. Odeberg, *The Fourth Gospel Interpreted in Its Relations to Contemporaneous Religious Currents in Palestine and the Hellenistic-Oriental World* (Uppsala: Almquist & Wiksells Boktryckeri, 1929).

14. Zangenberg, *Frühes Christentum,* pp. 195-96.

15. Meier, "Historical Jesus," pp. 231-32.

Acts 1:8,[16] only two texts provide a sufficient degree of *Lokalkolorit*[17] to allow a more detailed historical investigation: Jn 4:4-43 and Acts 8:4-25. These two texts,[18] however, clearly draw from a different milieu. While John 4:4-43 plays out in central Samaria close to Mount Gerizim, is full of allusions to Samaritans, refers to central elements of their theology, and is deeply shaped by the Judeo-Samaritan controversy over competing claims to the biblical traditions, Acts 8:4-25 breathes different air. Here Samaritanism does not feature at all, but instead we witness a world of miracles and two "dynamic" performers, Simon Magus and the apostle Philip, competing about whose power is greater. The local setting of the story is Sebaste, which (as we will see below) is a truly pagan city.[19] Both traditions reflect different ways of contact that Christian communities established with various groups in Samaria. The Hellenists to which Philip belonged were interested in reaching out to cities and their diverse, sometimes pagan inhabitants (cf. Acts 8:26-40; 15:3), whereas Peter and John preached in the *kōmai tōn Samaritōn*,[20] while John very likely counters strong reservations

---

16. On Jn 3:22-30 and baptismal groups in Aenon near Salim in Samaria, see Zangenberg, *Frühes Christentum,* pp. 58-81; on the charge in Jn 8:48, see pp. 197-204; Jn 11:54 mentioning Ephraim is discussed on pp. 214-19 and in J. Schwartz and J. Spanier, "On Mattathias and the Desert of Samaria," *RB* 98 (1991): 252-71.

17. I adopt this term from G. Theissen's pioneering studies on the cultural and historical context of Synoptic traditions: G. Theissen, *Lokalkolorit und Zeitgeschichte in den Evangelien: Ein Beitrag zur Geschichte der synoptischen Tradition,* 2nd ed. (Fribourg: Universitätsverlag; Göttingen: Vandenhoeck & Ruprecht, 1992), see esp. the introduction, pp. 1-24 ("Lokalkolorit und Zeitgeschichte in der Erforschung der synoptischen Tradition").

18. On Acts 8:4-25, see J. Zangenberg, "Simon Magus," in *Religionsgeschichte des Neuen Testaments,* ed. A. v. Dobbeler, K. Erlemann, and R. Heiligenthal, Festschrift Klaus Berger (Tübingen: Francke, 2000), pp. 519-40, and G. Theissen, "Simon Magus — die Entwicklung seines Bildes vom Charismatiker zum gnostischen Erlöser: Ein Beitrag zur Frühgeschichte der Gnosis," in the same work (pp. 407-32) (presenting Simon as a Samaritan who competed with Christianity in addressing both Gentiles and Samaritans); F. Heintz, *Simon, le "Magicien": Actes 8,5-25 et l'accusation de magie contre les prophètes thaumaturges dans l'antiquité,* CahRB 39 (Paris: Gabalda, 1997); W. A. Meeks, "Simon Magus in Recent Research," *RSR* 3 (1997): 137-42.

19. On the localization of the conflict in Sebaste, see Zangenberg, "Simon Magus," pp. 520-25. Böhm, *Samarien,* pp. 279-308, firmly rejects Sebaste and pleads for a very general reading in the sense of "(irgend) eine Stadt Samariens" (any city of Samaria) (pp. 288-89). But even *if* the "indeterminierte Textvariante" in Acts 8:5 is to be preferred on text-critical grounds (which I doubt, following M. Hengel, "Der Historiker Lukas und die Geographie Palästinas in der Apostelgeschichte," *ZDPV* 99 [1983]: 147-83, 177; cf. also Theissen, "Simon Magus," p. 416 n. 22), there is absolutely no alternative site that would fit into the category of a *polis* in pre-70 Samaria but Sebaste. Contrary to Böhm, I think the diction in Josephus, *War* 1.403, *is* in fact significant for the interpretation of Acts 8:5 that refers to *the* city in Samaria. There is not enough evidence to show that Luke had towns like Qedumim, Umm Rihan, or Sychar in mind (cf. Böhm, pp. 307-8).

20. On Philip, see A. v. Dobbeler, *Der Evangelist Philippus in der Geschichte des Ur-*

in his community against accepting former Samaritans as full members. Both authors and the communities behind them clearly do not relate to "Samaria" in general, but selectively target specific groups and regions within it. In their different theological approaches to Samaria (for John, Samaria is the home of the Samaritans, who compete with his Judeo-Christian community about the patriarchal traditions, for Luke it is the place of undifferentiated *allogeneis*), both authors reflect different strands in contemporaneous Jewish literature; in their different *Lokalkolorit* they mirror the fact that Samaria is not a monolithic entity, and that conflicts and contacts are always tied to localities. This emerging, complex picture of a "region of many cultures" (to borrow a catchy phrase from Israel Finkelstein) provides the background of how Christian communities interacted with the region, regardless if Jesus traveled through it or not.

Geographical Factors

The province of Samaria lies between Galilee and Judea. Its character differs in no way from that of Judea. Both regions consist of hills and plains, claim a light and fertile soil for agriculture, are well wooded, and abound in fruits, both wild and cultivated; both owe their productiveness to the entire absence of dry deserts and to a rainfall for the most part abundant. All the running water has a singularly sweet taste; and owing to the abundance of excellent grass, the cattle yield more milk than in other districts. But the surest testimony to the virtues and thriving condition of the two regions is that both have a dense population.

Josephus's description of Samaria in *War* 3.49-50 provides an interesting range of information. Shaped by gentle hills and wide plains, rich in natural resources and above all in water and fertile soil, densely populated, enjoying a mild and fructuous climate (see Aristeas 107-20 on the regions surrounding Jerusalem, including Samaria), Samaria is depicted as the almost ideal environment for human habitation, the development of culture, and the creation of wealth. Certainly, some of this almost hymnic description is due to literary convention, but as we will see shortly, Josephus does not grossly exaggerate.[21]

---

christentums: Eine prosopographische Skizze, TANZ 30 (Tübingen: Francke, 2000); F. S. Spencer, *The Portrait of Philip in Acts: A Study of Roles and Relations,* JSNTSS 67 (Sheffield: JSOT Press, 1992). Acts 15:3 shows the same combination of Phoenicia (apparently the coastal plain) and Samaria that is implied in chap. 8 (different is Theissen, "Simon Magus," p. 416 n. 21, who [unjustifiedly] takes Acts 15:3 as indication that Luke distinguishes between converted pagans and the "Gemeinden in Samarien" in Acts 8).

21. Z. Safrai, "The Description of the Land of Israel in Josephus' Works," in *Josephus, the*

Figure 60. Alabaster pitcher. It is perhaps Herodian, found west of Jerusalem. Courtesy of J. H. Charlesworth

Geographically, Samaria forms the northern sector of the central Palestinian hill country that reaches from the Negev in the south into the Galilee and farther into Lebanon, separated by the Litani River (Eleutheros) from the mountains of southern Syria up north.[22] Josephus mentions only the northern and southern boundaries of Samaria, of which only the former is a clear topographical feature. A steep drop and the fertile plain of the Jezreel Valley mark the northern end of the Samaritan hill country. This wide plain separating Samaria from the hills of Lower Galilee has for most of the time played an independent role in history, dominated by the cities of Megiddo on its western and Bet Shean (Scythopolis) on its wider, eastern side. At least in the period that in-

---

Bible, and History, ed. L. H. Feldman and G. Hata (Detroit: Wayne State University Press, 1989), pp. 295-324.

22. On the historical geography of Samaria, see Zangenberg, *Frühes Christentum,* pp. 12-14; Y. Magen, "Samaria (Region): Hellenistic and Roman Period," in *NEAEHL* 4 (1993), pp. 1316-18. Also see the recent survey reports like I. Finkelstein and Z. Lederman, eds., *Highlands of Many Cultures: The Southern Samaria Survey; The Sites* (Tel Aviv: Institute of Archaeology, 1997), pp. 73-130; P. Richardson, *Herod: King of the Jews and Friend of the Romans* (Minneapolis: Fortress, 1996), pp. 137-39; S. Dar, *Landscape and Pattern: An Archaeological Survey of Samaria, 800 B.C.E.–636 C.E.,* BAR International Series 308 (Oxford: BAR, 1986). Still valuable is A. Alt, "Zur Geschichte der Grenze zwischen Judäa und Samaria," in Dar, *Kleine Schriften* (Munich: Beck, 1954), 2:346-62.

terests us, the Jezreel Valley was not considered part of Samaria but was known as the "region of Scythopolis" (cf. Lk 17:11; *War* 3.37) and since 63 B.C.E. belonged to the Decapolis.

The southern limit of Samaria is more a product of history and politics than of geography. In fact, while the Samarian hills slightly drop in elevation the farther south one gets, there is no topographical feature that clearly marks the transition from Samaria to the Judean sector of the Palestinian hill country. The line between Samaria and Judea was drawn when the formerly south-Samarian districts Ephraim, Lydda, and Ramathaim were, among other privileges, transferred by the Seleucid king Demetrios II Nicator (145-139/38 and 129-125 B.C.E.) to Judea around 145 (*Ant* 13.5.127; 1 Macc 11:34) to ensure Jonathan's support in Demetrios's struggle against his rival Alexander Balas (150-145).[23] From that time on, these territories belonged to Judea. However, such artificial lines certainly did not pose ethnic barriers, and the Judeo-Samarian border territory very likely housed a strongly mixed population during the first centuries B.C.E. and C.E.

It is striking that Josephus's excursus does not refer to the eastern and western borders of Samaria, perhaps because they were so conspicuous. True, in the east the Jordan Valley posed a distinct but not insurmountable border, but the western boundary of Samaria is less prominent. Despite their marked appearance, the western foothills (which are lower than the hills in the center of Samaria and formed by wide valleys cutting into them from the west) did not separate the hill country population from the often culturally and ethnically different inhabitants of the northern coastal plain. On the contrary, western and central Samaria functioned as the agricultural hinterland of many of the coastal cities. Much of the produce consumed in or shipped away from harbors in Caesarea or Ioppe came from the Samarian hills, especially wine and olive oil. Grain, the main crop of the coastal plain, found customers inland. Caesarea

23. Regarding the identity of these three towns, Ephraim/Aphairema is et-Tayibe (see Zangenberg, *Frühes Christentum*, pp. 214-19, on Jn 11:45); Lydda is modern Lod; Ramathaim/Arimathea can be identified with Rentis, 14 kilometers north of Lydda, the possible home of Joseph of Arimathea. Consult R. E. Brown, *The Death of the Messiah: From Gethsemane to the Grave; A Commentary on the Passion Narratives in the Four Gospels* (New York: Doubleday, 1994), pp. 1213-19; S. Porter, "Joseph of Arimathea," in *ABD* 3 (1992), pp. 971-72; E. V. Dobschütz, "Joseph von Arimathia," *ZKG* 23 (1902): 1-18. Demetrios's decision marks a large transfer of territory. According to 1 Macc 11:57, Antiochos VI Dionysos Epiphanes (145-143/32 B.C.E.) granted Jonathan possession of four (!) districts, but there is no mention of the name of the fourth. J. A. Goldstein, *1 Maccabees: A New Translation with Introduction and Commentary*, AB 41 (Garden City, N.Y.: Doubleday, 1976), pp. 434-40, suggests that this may have been Acrabattene, but Josephus's description of the territory of Samaria quoted above indicates that Acrabattene was at least later still part of Samaria.

Maritima might actually have been founded to "drain" the rich agricultural revenues to be gained from Samaria. Such economic osmosis made sure that, as in the south of Samaria for different reasons, we find a highly mixed population on the western foothills.

Internally, Samaria is characterized by numerous winding valleys separating the hill country in small units — most notably east and west of the central watershed ridge. While the semiarid eastern slopes of the Samarian hill country were less populated (*War* 4.452-454), its northern and southern sectors were more densely inhabited from very early times. Apart from agriculture and settlement, the natural east-west valleys were perfect for traffic and trade.[24] Despite its hilly, sometimes almost mountainous character, Samaria was never isolated from the wider region.

Several transregional roadways ran through Samaria. Of particular importance was the north-south route that followed the watershed line on the ridge of the Samarian hill country and connected up with the population centers to the south (Beersheba and Jerusalem) and the north (Galilee, southern Syria). Unlike its western and eastern parallels in the coastal plain and the Jordan Valley, the watershed route runs almost solely through regions inhabited by Jews or Samaritans. This road, which offers a direct but not always untroubled passage, enters the northern Samarian hill country at Ginaea/Jenin (grid ref.: 178 207), the "gateway to Samaria." Close to Ginaea it met an important east-west route coming from Pella and the Decapolis, touching Scythopolis and continuing via Legio/Kfar Otnay (grid ref.: 167 220) to the coast.

At Sichem the north-south road crossed another important east-west route that, branching off from the Jordan Valley highway at Coreae/Tel es-Simadi (grid ref.: 196 171), ran west through Wadi el-Farah and Wadi Bedan to Shechem. From there it continued west through Wadi Nablus via Sebaste in the region of Caesarea Maritima. Above all, the western sector of this route was of prime importance for central Samaria. It connected the entire region to the coastal plain and its harbor cities and tied the entire fertile western and central hill country to the cities on the coast as their agrarian hinterland. After its construction between 22 and 10 B.C.E.,[25] Caesarea quickly became the commercial

---

24. On roads in Samaria, see Zangenberg, *Frühes Christentum*, pp. 14-22; D. A. Dorsey, *The Roads and Highways of Ancient Palestine* (Baltimore: Johns Hopkins University Press, 1991); Dorsey, "Shechem and the Road Network of Central Samaria," *BASOR* 268 (1987): 57-70; Dar, *Landscape and Pattern*, pp. 126-46; M. Avi-Yonah, "Historical Geography of Palestine," in CRINT I/1 (1974), pp. 78-116 (110-13). While the main routes certainly were used since early times (cf. Dorsey), there must have been a notable increase in local tracks and paths to connect the growing number of settlements in the Roman and especially Byzantine period.

25. With these dates I follow P. Richardson, "Archaeological Evidence for Religion and Ur-

outlet for Samaria similar to what Ptolemais was for the Lower Galilee and Tyre was for the Upper Galilee.[26] It is not surprising that Caesarea housed a strong Samaritan population in late antiquity.[27]

A third east-west highway branched off from the north-south road at Gofna/Jifna (grid ref.: 170 152) and cut through the former southern districts Ephraim, Lydda, and Ramathaim; at Antipatris it connected up with the coastal highway. Also from Gofna, an eastern road went to Jericho, and farther east to Esbus/Hesban (grid ref.: 226 134).

Apart from these transregional routes, each village could be accessed by tracks and country roads. In this respect Samaria did not differ much from all other regions in the Hellenistic and Roman East. Like anywhere else, local routes carried most of the everyday traffic: farmers bringing produce to market, herdsmen driving cattle to pasture, merchants traveling from town to town. Part of this track network was water reservoirs and fountains especially at junctions, inns, and (not only in pagan areas; cf. Jn 4:4-6) local shrines. Given the short distances between the Mediterranean and the Jordan River, travelers could easily cross Samaria west to east in two days and north to south in three days. George Adam Smith makes the point by stating, "the openness of Samaria is her most prominent feature."[28]

Samaria: A Region in Constant Transition

Given its strategic location in the heart of Palestine, no historian would wonder that Samaria, like so many other regions in the Levant, underwent dramatic ethnic changes during the Hellenistic, Roman, and Byzantine periods. Apart from "normal" regional migration, new groups of people were settled in the region by

banism in Caesarea Maritima," in *Religious Rivalries and the Struggle for Success in Caesarea Maritima*, ed. T. L. Donaldson (Waterloo, Ont.: Laurier University Press, 2000), pp. 11-34; see esp. p. 13.

26. Z. Safrai, *The Economy of Roman Palestine* (London and New York: Routledge, 1994), p. 113; K. Holu et al., *King Herod's Dream: Caesarea on the Sea* (New York and London: Norton, 1988), pp. 72-75.

27. R. Pummer, "Samaritanism in Caesarea Maritima," in *Religious Rivalries and the Struggle for Success in Caesarea Maritima*, pp. 181-202; Pummer, "Religions in Contact and Conflict: The Samaritans of Caesarea among 'Pagans,' Jews and Christians," in *Samaritan Researches Volume V: Proceedings of the Congress of the SES (Milan July 8-12 1996) and of the Special Section of the ICANAS Congress (Budapest July 7-11 1997)*, ed. V. Morabito, A. D. Crown, and L. Davey, Studies in Judaica 10 (Sydney: Mandelbaum Trust, 2000), pp. 3, 29-53, with ample references.

28. G. A. Smith, *The Historical Geography of the Holy Land* (1966; reprint of the 13th edition, Jerusalem: Ariel, n.d.), p. 219.

political powers to control this strategically important region by altering its ethnic composition toward a more favorable ratio of indigenous groups and new colonists. Perhaps the most infamous was the settlement of Mesopotamians after the conquest of the Samarian hill country by the Assyrian kings Shalmaneser V and Sargon II between 723/22 and 720 B.C.E. (2 Kgs 17:24-41).[29] Later, Alexander the Great secured the inland region of Palestine by placing a garrison of Macedonians in the city of Samaria (Curtius Rufus 4.8.9).[30] At the same time, we hear of a colony of Sidonian merchants in Shechem (*Ant* 11.340-346). At what point these Sidonians arrived is unclear, but it might not be coincidental that the MB-II[31] defenses on Tell Balatah were repaired and the site resettled in the late fourth century B.C.E. (see below on Shechem). Around the same time, the Samaritans established their sanctuary on Mount Gerizim (see below on Gerizim) through the merger of dissident priests from Jerusalem with elements of the indigenous Yahwistic population;[32] and other Semitic and non-Semitic groups with mostly pagan affiliation were living in the city of Samaria (see below on Samaria/Sebaste). While it is not clear if the Sidonians were the only inhabitants of Shechem, they reappear in the days of Antiochus IV Epiphanes petitioning the Seleucid king to dedicate the unnamed sanctuary on Mount Gerizim to Zeus Hellenios (*Ant* 12.257-264; 2 Macc 6:2f.).[33] They clearly are pagans, although they have adopted strange habits like keeping the Sabbath.

29. E. Stern, *Archaeology of the Land of the Bible*, vol. 2, *The Assyrian, Babylonian, and Persian Periods, 732-332 B.C.E.*, ABRL (New York: Doubleday, 2001), pp. 49-51; K. L. Younger, Jr., "The Fall of Samaria in Light of Recent Research," *CBQ* 61 (1999): 461-82; N. Na'aman, "Population Changes in Palestine Following the Assyrian Deportations," *TA* 20 (1993): 104-24; B. Becking, *The Fall of Samaria: An Historical and Archaeological Study*, SHANE 2 (Leiden: Brill, 1992); J. H. Hays and J. K. Kuan, "The Final Years of Samaria (730-720 B.C.)," *Biblica* 72 (1991): 153-81. On surveys and excavations in Bronze and Iron Age Samaria see now: H. Hizmi and A. De-Groot, eds., *Burial Caves and Sites in Judaea and Samaria: From the Bronze to the Iron Ages*, Judaea and Samaria Publications 2 (Jerusalem: Israel Exploration Society, 2004).

30. H.-P. Kuhnen, *Palästina in griechisch-römischer Zeit*, HA Vorderasien II/2 (Munich: Beck, 1990), p. 43; F.-M. Abel, "Alexandre le Grand en Syrie et en Palestine," *RB* 43 (1934): 528-45; 44 (1935): 42-61.

31. MB = Middle Bronze.

32. I follow F. Dexinger, "Der Ursprung der Samaritaner im Spiegel der frühen Quellen," in *Die Samaritaner*, ed. F. Dexinger and R. Pummer, WdF 604 (Darmstadt: Wissenschaftliche Buchgesellschaft, 1992), pp. 67-140; see also Coggins, "Issues in Samaritanism"; A. D. Crown, "Another Look at Samaritan Origins," in *New Samaritan Studies of the Société des Études Samaritaines Volumes III and IV*, pp. 133-55; J. D. Purvis, "The Samaritan Problem: A Case Study in Jewish Sectarianism in the Roman Era," in *Tradition in Transformation: Turning Points in Biblical Faith*, ed. B. Halpern et al. (Winona Lake, Ind.: Eisenbrauns, 1981), pp. 320-50; R. J. Coggins, *Samaritans and Jews: The Origins of Samaritanism Reconsidered* (London: SCM, 1975).

33. C. Breytenbach, "Zeus und Jupiter auf dem Zion und dem Berg Garizim: Die

This hodgepodge of ethnic groups was profoundly changed during the Hasmonean conquest of the region. The radical destruction of its urban centers in the city of Samaria, Shechem, and on Mount Gerizim by Hyrcanus I and his sons between 128 and 107 B.C.E. (*Ant* 13.254-257; 13.257-281; 13.395-397; *War* 1.62-65; cf. *Megillat Ta'anit* 18 and 22) and the subsequent colonization of key sub-regions with Jewish settlers resulted in a completely new picture. Large parts of Samaria were converted into crown land, the old elites were depositioned. Apart from the influx of new settlers, we can also assume a significant degree of internal migration resulting in a reorganization of land use assigned to each group, completing a process that had already begun in the south of Samaria with the transfer of the districts of Lydda, Efraim, and Ramathaim under Maccabean administration (see above). The harsh actions taken by Hyrcanus and his sons were intended to once and for all break any possible resistance against the sustained integration of the region into the Jewish state. It is significant that the new settlers did not occupy the destroyed cities, but mainly chose to live in new towns or farmsteads. According to Shimon Applebaum, "numerous field towers scattered around the villages and fortified centers" are the main evidence for a systematic Hasmonean occupation.[34] The fringes and fertile valleys of Samaria seem to have been most attractive to the occupants; a rabbinic passage (*m. Men.* 10.2) might imply that Jewish farmers in the central Samarian plain at Sychar supplied grain for use in the Temple in Jerusalem.[35] Only the city of Samaria was an exception and slowly recovered, probably because of its pagan profile; Shechem and the city on Mount Gerizim remained abandoned. Even though the Samaritans were not forced into conversion, the conquest boosted the internal consolidation of central elements in Samaritan religiosity and fostered an alienation between Samaritans and Jews.[36]

Hellenisierung und Romanisierung der Kultstätten des Höchsten," *JSJ* 28 (1997): 369-80; Zangenberg, *SAMAREIA,* pp. 67-68; U. Rappaport, "The Samaritans in the Hellenistic Period," in *New Samaritan Studies of the Société des Études Samaritaines Volumes III and IV,* pp. 281-88; M. Mor, "Samaritan History I: The Persian, Hellenistic and Hasmonean Period," in *The Samaritans,* ed. A. D. Crown (Tübingen: Mohr Siebeck, 1989), pp. 1-18.

34. S. Applebaum, "Hasmonean Internal Colonization: Problems and Motives," in *Man and Land in Eretz Israel,* ed. A. Kasher, A. Oppenheimer, and U. Rappaport (Jerusalem: Yad Izhak Ben Zvi, 1986), pp. 75-79 and IXf (X). Cf. Dar, *Landscape and Pattern,* pp. 213-29, and the critique by I. Shatzman, *The Armies of the Hasmoneans and Herod: From Hellenistic to Roman Frameworks,* TSAJ 25 (Tübingen: Mohr, 1991), pp. 67-69.

35. Samaritan farmers would obviously not have done so; on the Askar plain and its history, cf. Zangenberg, *Frühes Christentum,* pp. 96-106.

36. L. L. Grabbe, "Betwixt and Between: The Samaritans in the Hasmonean Period," in *Society of Biblical Literature 1993 Seminar Papers,* ed. E. H. Lovering, Jr. (Atlanta: Scholars, 1993), pp. 334-47; Mor, "Samaritan History I," pp. 16-18. At that time it is likely that the specifically sec-

Of course, large numbers of Samaritans and pagan Samarians remained in the region during the early Roman period,[37] but the population was now supplemented by a significant number of Jews. This overall picture proved to be irreversible. The reorganization of Syria-Palestine by Gabinius between 57 and 55 B.C.E. only led to a "restitution" of Samaria's status as a Hellenized city; the rest of the region seems to have been left unaltered (*Ant* 14.88; *War* 1.166). Herod, appointed *stratēgos* of Coele Syria and Samaria by Sextus Caesar in 47/46 B.C.E., developed a special relationship to the city and made it his supply base during the war with Hyrcanus II (*Ant* 14.408; *War* 1.299f.; Appianus, *Civil War* 5.75). He repaid its strong loyalty by lavishly refounding the city between 27 and 12 B.C.E. as Sebaste. A massive building program, including an official temple dedicated to Roma and Augustus with cult personnel and a city constitution in Greek style, secured Sebaste's enduring pagan character. The 6,000 colonists, mostly loyal veterans, that Herod settled in the city and its environs do not seem to have changed its pagan identity; even if there were Jews or Samaritans among the colonists, their presence was not ultimately felt. No comparable urban center existed in Samaria at that time, and Sebaste is the only place where we can risk an informed guess about its ethnic and cultural profile. This is even more significant because the lack of sufficiently explicit or early literary sources and the common material culture prevent us from identifying any other site as either clearly Samaritan or Jewish.[38]

After the death of Herod, Samaria was, together with Idumea and Judea, ruled by his son Archelaus (*War* 2.96f.) until he was deposed and exiled to Vienna in Gaul by Augustus, thanks to a rare cooperation between Jewish and Samaritan leaders who complained about Archelaus's mismanagement (*Ant* 17.342-344). But the rule of the Roman procurators that succeeded Archelaus in 6 C.E. was no better. Tensions between various groups in Palestine and Roman authorities grew in Samaria as well, and the alienation between Jews and Samaritans increased. Already during the governorship of Coponius (6–8/9 C.E.), Samarians defiled the

---

tarian alterations in the Decalogue were introduced into the nonsectarian Samaritan recension of the Pentateuch to secure the continued religious role of Mount Gerizim and compensate for the loss of political and religious freedom; cf. Zangenberg, *SAMAREIA*, pp. 180-86.

37. On the Samaritans in the early Roman period, see A. Kasher, "Josephus on Jewish-Samaritan Relations under Roman Rule," in *New Samaritan Studies of the Société des Études Samaritaines Volumes III and IV*, pp. 217-36.

38. On the problem of distinguishing Samaritan from Jewish material remains at such an early stage, see Zangenberg, "Überlegungen zur Möglichkeit einer 'Topographie religiöser Gruppen' in Samarien zur neutestamentlichen Zeit"; L. DiSegni, "The Samaritans in Roman-Byzantine Palestine: Some Misapprehensions," in *Religious and Ethnic Communities in Later Roman Palestine*, ed. H. Lapin, Studies and Texts in Jewish History and Culture 5 (Bethesda: University of Maryland Press, 1998), pp. 51-66; R. Pummer, "Samaritan Material Remains and Archaeology," in *The Samaritans*, ed. Crown, pp. 135-77.

sanctity of the Jerusalem Temple by scattering human bones on its premises (cf. *Ant* 18.29-30).[39] Pilate (26-36 C.E.), too, had to deal with religiously motivated unrest when many Samaritans followed a man who pretended to show them the holy vessels that Moses had hidden on Mount Gerizim. When the mass seized arms and gathered at Tirathana, Pilate routed them with his cavalry (*Ant* 18.85-89).[40] The inhabitants of Caesarea and Sebaste celebrated the death of King Agrippa I with sarcastic mock processions (*Ant* 19.356-361). Under Cumanus (48-52 C.E.) the situation further deteriorated when Jewish pilgrims en route to Jerusalem were killed in Samaria (*Ant* 20.118-136; *War* 2.232-247; cf. Tacitus, *Ann* 12.54) and only massive military force was able to contain rapid escalation.

All three groups (pagans, Jews, and Samaritans) were affected by the atrocities of the Jewish Revolt (66–73/74). The sack of Sebaste by the insurgents at the beginning of the revolt destroyed an already very fragile *modus vivendi* between Jews and pagans in the city (*War* 2.458-460). The following reconquest of the region by the Romans brought destruction on the Samaritans who, apparently in expectation of some divine intervention, assembled their forces on Mount Gerizim (*War* 3.307-315). Only the pagan population was able to really recover, and in fact dominated the region until the Byzantine period. After Samaria was first occupied by the Roman army (*War* 5.50), a massive influx of veterans and foreigners centered around the newly founded city of Neapolis (*War* 4.449; Pliny, *Natural History* 5.69; see the following discussion). Here we witness the same pattern as in Assyrian and Hasmonean times: the colonization of occupied territory with loyal newcomers to dispossess and control the old, seemingly unreliable inhabitants.

Economic competition and marginalization of Jews and Samaritans by the growing pagan population characterized the second and third centuries. The systematic Romanization and urbanization since the mid–second century had

---

39. On the textual and historical problems of this passage, see J. S. McLaren, *Power and Politics in Palestine: The Jews and the Governing of Their Land, 100 B.C.–70 C.E.*, JSNTSS 63 (Sheffield: Academic Press, 1992), p. 80; Egger, *Samaritaner,* pp. 237-46. It is not clear if the perpetrators actually were Samaritans.

40. I. Kalimi and J. D. Purvis, "The Hiding of the Temple Vessels in Jewish and Samaritan Literature," *CBQ* 56 (1994): 679-85; F. Dexinger, "Josephus Ant 18,85-87 und der samaritanische Taheb," in *Proceedings of the First International Congress of the Société des Études Samaritaines, Tel Aviv, April 11-13 1988,* ed. A. Tal (Tel Aviv: Chaim Rosenberg School for Jewish Studies, Tel-Aviv University, 1991), pp. 49-59 (with the comments in Zangenberg, *Frühes Christentum,* pp. 156-57 n. 612); A. Zeron, "Einige Bemerkungen zu M. F. Collins 'The Hidden Vessels in Samaritan Traditions,'" *JSJ* 4 (1973): 165-68; M. F. Collins, "The Hidden Vessels in Samaritan Traditions," *JSJ* 3 (1972): 97-116. This text not only confirms the continuing veneration of Mount Gerizim long after the destruction of the sanctuary, but also indicates (just like *Ant* 17.342-344) that the Samaritans had some kind of internal civic authority, most likely the heads of influential families.

opened better economic perspectives for all inhabitants of the region, but all progress occurred under a clear dominance of pagan culture. It is quite possible that Samaritans and Jews gradually fell back even to a numerical minority during the Roman era. Both groups, however, consolidated their own social and religious basis (codification of the Mishnah and Samaritan reforms)[41] and continued the process of mutual alienation. If the Samaritans rebelled against Hadrian at all, they certainly did not join the explicitly Jerusalemite agenda of Bar-Kokhba and his followers (132–135/36 C.E.).[42]

In the fourth century the situation seems to have changed again with lasting results.[43] The Samaritan community grew considerably and spread out into the neighboring regions (esp. Mount Carmel, Sharon plain) and cities (notably, Caesarea, Scythopolis, and Apollonia) and farther into the Mediterranean.[44] The reasons for the Samaritan expansion, despite a precarious legal position after Constantine, are not entirely evident, nor can we simply assume that all this happened at the cost of the Jews.[45]

The apparent increase in settlements in the Hellenistic to the Byzantine period,[46] therefore, is no continuous development, much less a result of peaceful

41. See the third-century date for the life of the Samaritan reformer Baba Rabba as put forward by P. Stenhouse, "Fourth Century Date for Baba Rabba Re-examined," in *New Samaritan Studies of the Société des Études Samaritaines Volumes III and IV*, pp. 317-26.

42. On this issue see M. Mor, "The Samaritans and the Bar-Kokhba Revolt," in *The Samaritans*, ed. Crown, pp. 19-31, though I remain skeptical if one can really speak of an even limited "Samaritan rebellion." The evidence Mor uses often seems too circumstantial.

43. On the Samaritans in the Byzantine era see, e.g., N. Schur, *History of the Samaritans*, BEATAJ 18 (Frankfurt: Lang, 1989), pp. 51-54; A. D. Crown, "Samaritan History 4: The Byzantine and Moslem Period," in *The Samaritans*, ed. Crown, pp. 55-81; Crown, "The Samaritans in the Byzantine Orbit," *BJRL* 69 (1986): 96-138; Crown, "Samaritan Religion in the Fourth Century," *NTT* 41 (1986): 59-95.

44. On the Samaritan diaspora, see V. Morabito, "The Samaritans in Sicily and the Inscription in a Probable Synagogue in Syracuse," in *New Samaritan Studies of the Société des Études Samaritaines Volumes III and IV*, pp. 237-58; P. W. van der Horst, "The Samaritan Diaspora in Antiquity," in van der Horst, *Essays on the Jewish World of Early Christianity*, NTOA 14 (Fribourg: Universitätsverlag; Göttingen: Vandenhoeck & Ruprecht, 1990), pp. 136-47; A. D. Crown, "The Samaritan Diaspora," in *The Samaritans*, ed. Crown, pp. 195-217; Crown, "The Samaritan Diaspora to the End of the Byzantine Era," *AJBA* 2/3 (1974/75): 107-23.

45. See the caveats by DiSegni, "Samaritans," pp. 56-57; and DiSegni, "Mutual Relations between Samaritans, Jews and Christians in Byzantine Palestine, as Revealed through the Epigraphic Finds," in *New Samaritan Studies of the Société des Études Samaritaines Volumes III and IV*, pp. 185-94. On the legal position of Samaritans in the Byzantine era, see Zangenberg, *SAMAREIA*, pp. 291-96; A. M. Rabello, *Giustiniano, Ebrei e Samaritani alla luce delle fonti storio-letterarie, ecclesiastiche e giuridiche*, 2 vols. (Milan: A. Giuffrè, 1987-88).

46. See the chart in S. Lev-Yadun, "Flora and Climate in Southern Samaria: Past and Present," in *Highlands of Many Cultures*, pp. 85-102.

growth, but the product of sometimes turbulent events, even though we presently do not have the archaeological means at hand to exactly retrace development by assigning the known settlements to specific groups. The situation only improves in the Byzantine period when the number of archaeological indicators increases due to the development of specifically Samaritan elements of art and decoration.[47] Because of the fragmentary nature of our literary sources and the virtual absence of any archaeological indicators of ethnicity especially for the early periods, we can be sure that these events were not the only changes that took place. Even if it were difficult to assess the impact of each of the events described above individually, the general picture remains irrefutable: as a result of Samaria's strategic position in the heart of the Palestinian corridor between Syria and Egypt, its fertility and accessibility, the ethnic composition and cultural and religious profile of Samaria's population were in constant transition.

Rural Life in Samaria

Villages and Towns

There is no reason to assume that village life in Samaria was in any way different, less lively, less complex, and less widespread from what we know about other regions in the Hellenistic and Roman East.[48] Josephus emphasizes that Samaria was dotted with villages (*War* 3.48-50); Luke mentions them also (Lk 9:52; Acts 8:25). Despite the importance of villages for the economy and social history of the region, not a single village site from the Hellenistic or Roman period has ever been systematically excavated in Samaria, its stratigraphy and settlement history established, and the results properly published. Surveys have recorded a notable increase in population in Samaria from the end of the Hellenistic period through the Roman period, reaching its peak in the Byzantine era.[49] To a large

47. R. Pummer, "How to Tell a Samaritan Synagogue from a Jewish One," *BAR* 24, no. 3 (1998): 24-35; DiSegni, "Samaritans," pp. 53-57.

48. See W. Ball, *Rome in the East: The Transformation of an Empire* (London and New York: Routledge, 2000), pp. 207-45; G. Tate, "The Syrian Countryside during the Roman Era," and Y. Hirschfeld, "Jewish Rural Settlement in Judaea in the Early Roman Period," both in *The Early Roman Empire in the East*, ed. S. E. Alcock, Oxbow Monographs 95 (Oxford: Oxbow, 1997), pp. 55-71 and 72-88, respectively; Hirschfeld, "Farms and Villages in Byzantine Palestine," *DOP* 51 (1997): 33-71; Safrai, *Economy of Roman Palestine*, pp. 64ff.; D. A. Fiensy, *The Social History of Palestine in the Herodian Period: The Land Is Mine*, SBEC 20 (Lewiston, N.Y.: Mellen, 1991), pp. 119-53.

49. Consult the survey results in southern Samaria in Finkelstein and Lederman, *High-

extent this process must have gone along with the expansion of existing, or the foundation of new, villages, because it was the villagers who provided the produce to sustain a growing population.[50] No village was like the other. There were significant differences in size and material culture. Villages with several hundred, even up to 2,000, inhabitants were not rare. The inner structure was also very diverse. Some sites show no social differentiation, others display signs of clear social and economic stratification.[51]

In general, most of the rural life in Samaria was more or less "anonymous," although quite a few villages are mentioned by name in the literature.[52] While many elements of everyday rural life in Jesus' time can be reconstructed from later sources such as the Talmudim or inferred from sites outside Samaria, it is almost impossible to assign a certain Samarian village exclusively to a specific religious group before the Byzantine period. While one could speculate that due to a strong family-based social fabric villages in general were culturally and religiously homogenous, this would not rule out the possibility that the majority in or even totality of the neighboring village belonged to a different group.[53] But there are enough indications to suggest that adherents of different religious milieus sometimes lived together even in one and the same village, and that the model of a homogenous village culture needs qualification.[54]

---

lands of Many Cultures; E. F. Campbell, Jr., *Shechem II — Portrait of a Hill Country Vale: The Shechem Regional Survey,* ASOR Archaeological Reports 2 (Atlanta: Scholars, 1991).

50. Safrai, *Economy of Roman Palestine,* pp. 64-82. Dar, *Landscape and Pattern,* provides the most comprehensive study of rural culture in western Samaria (but see the critique in the review by C. Edens in *AJA* 92 [1988]: 445-46).

51. Dar, *Landscape and Pattern,* pp. 42-47.

52. Apart from Mamortha, the predecessor of Flavia Neapolis (Josephus, *War* 4.449; Pliny, *Natural History* 5.69), other villages are mentioned: Anuathu Borcaius (Josephus, *War* 3.51), Arous (Josephus, *War* 1.69; *Ant* 17.289), Beeroth (1 Macc 9:4), Beer Zaith (1 Macc 7:9; 9:4; Josephus, *Ant* 12.397, 422), Beth El (1 Macc 9:50; Josephus, *War* 4.551; *Ant* 13.15); Dothan (Jdt 3:9; 4:6; 7:1, 18; 8:3), Gerasa in Samaria (Josephus, *War* 4.487, 503), Ginaea (Josephus, *War* 2.232; 3.48), Isana (Josephus, *Ant* 14.458; *War* 1.334), Salem in eastern Samaria (Jdt 4:4), and Tirat Ana (Josephus, *Ant* 18.86) are already mentioned in the first century C.E. or earlier. Justin Martyr, *Apologia* 26, adds Capparatteia and Gittha. Many more village sites can be found in Eusebius's *Onomastikon* (Adasa near Gofna, Amir, Ataroth, Berea, Beth Zaith, Eduma, Gaba near Gofna, Galgulis, Merous, Rama, Rimmoni, Salem, Salaba, Silo, Thebes). More could be added from rabbinic and Samaritan sources; many others are only known under their modern names (such as Umm Rihan, Qasr el-Lejah, Qasr el-Haramiyye, Khirbet el-Buraq). All data and orthographic variants are taken from *TIR.* I am currently working on a detailed analysis of the relevant material for M. Küchler and W. Zwickel, eds., *Orte und Landschaften der Bibel. Vol. III: Der Norden* (forthcoming).

53. Possible exceptions are Belemoth/Bethulia (Jdt 7:3; 8:3) and Salaba in the territory of Sebaste (Eusebius, *Onomastikon* 158.22), which might be taken as Jewish villages.

54. Zvi Uri Ma'oz's researches in the Golan, e.g., "Golan"; *NEAEHL* 2 (1993), pp. 534-46.

Only in the Byzantine period (which is beyond the scope of this paper) are sources available that enable us tentatively to connect single sites or certain subregions in Samaria with ethno-religious groups. Amoraic sources speak of the "district of the Samaritans" (with different terminology: *y. Hag.* 3.4, 79c; *b. Hag.* 25a; *Lam. Rab.* 3.7 [ed. Buber, p. 124]); the famous seventh-century "Halakhic Inscription" from the Rehov synagogue lists the names of eighteen or nineteen "permitted villages in the district of Sebaste."[55] It seems that the inscription informs observant Jews on their way to Jerusalem, or from Beth-Shean to the west, traveling through the district of Sebaste, where they "may purchase local agricultural produce without fear of transgressing the laws of tithes and the sabbatical year."[56] (The Targumists, *t. Dem.* 1.11; 5.24, mention "Samaritan villages along the road.") The reason for the permission is not given; Demsky points out that "the named villages may have been populated by either Samaritans, gentiles or both. Whatever the case, at the end of the Byzantine period their home-grown produce was exempt from tithes and sabbatical restrictions."[57] While many of the villages and hamlets listed in the inscription are older (two of them even appear to have been mentioned in the Samaria ostraca), it is clear that the overall situation implied does not predate the fifth century C.E.[58]

Given the sometimes fundamental changes in the population structure of Samaria (see above), we should be very cautious not to read any Byzantine data back into the Roman or even the pre-70 C.E. period without further evidence.

The assumption that pagans always lived in (Hellenized) cities while Jews or Samaritans lived exclusively in rural areas[59] is clearly wrong. One can expect village life to be as much a phenomenon of pagan culture as of Jewish or Samaritan culture, although the sources to positively prove that "on the ground" are admittedly scarce. The lack of systematically analyzed and published data about pagans in general is worse when it comes to a nonurban environment, which usually does not leave many literary traces either.[60] We know that cities like Sebaste were surrounded by a rural area that legally was considered part of

---

55. A. Demsky, "The Permitted Villages of Sebaste in the Rehov Mosaic," *IEJ* 29 (1979): 182-93.

56. Demsky, "Villages," p. 185.

57. Demsky, "Villages," p. 186.

58. Demsky, "Villages," p. 184.

59. Contrary to Theissen, "Simon Magus," p. 417.

60. See J. Geiger, "Aspects of Paganism in Late Antiquity," in *Sharing the Sacred: Religious Contacts and Conflicts in the Holy Land, First to Fifteenth Centuries C.E.*, ed. A. Kofski and G. G. Stroumsa (Jerusalem: Yad Izhak Ben Zvi, 1998), pp. 3-17; J. Zangenberg, "Realizing Diversity: Reflections on Teaching Pagan Religion(s) in Late Hellenistic and Early Roman Palestine," in *Between Text and Artifact: Integrating Archaeology in Biblical Studies Teaching*, ed. M. C. Moreland, Archaeology and Biblical Studies 8 (Atlanta: SBL, 2003), 179-92.

it *(chōra)*, and Josephus implies that some of the colonists Herod settled in Sebaste actually ended up in the *chōra* of the city (*Ant* 15.296). The detailed discussion of points of contact between Jews and Samaritans during everyday practices relating to agriculture and village life in the Talmud suggests that both groups must have lived very closely together (or very closely alongside each other) and does not exclude the possibility of "mixed villages."[61]

The site of Qedumim 10 kilometers west of Nablus (grid ref.: 1650 1793) offers rare insight into the material culture of a Samarian village.[62] Like so many other villages in the region, Qedumim was engaged in the production of oil and wine.[63] Although the majority of the finds date to the late Roman and Byzantine periods (and can be left aside here), some traces of earlier habitation were discovered. The most significant discovery was six ritual baths dating from the first to the eighth century c.e., attesting for the first time that some elements of "Jewish" material culture actually were also used by Samaritans.[64] Apparently, the development of parts of Jewish and Samaritan halakah ran parallel for a sufficient period of time to produce common elements of material culture.

Although it is not easy to distinguish between "villages" and "towns,"[65] some sites clearly belong in the latter group: Acrabba,[66] Aphairema/Efraim,[67] Arimathia/Ramathaim,[68] Gophna,[69] Thamna,[70] and Narbatta in western

---

61. Consult the texts collected in Zangenberg, *SAMAREIA*, pp. 117-29 (*m. Dem.* 3.4; *t. Dem.* 3.3; 4.24-27; 6.3f.; 7.11; *t. Abod. Zar.* 2.4; 2.8; 3.1; 3.5; 3.11; *t. Shab.* 6.20; *y. Abod. Zar.* 44d.64-65; *b. Abod. Zar.* 15b; *b. Git.* 45a).

62. On Qedumim, see Zangenberg, *Frühes Christentum*, p. 24 n. 65, and various reports by the excavator: Y. Magen, "Qedumim," in *NEAEHL* 4 (1993), pp. 1225-27; Magen, "Qedumim: A Samaritan Site of the Roman-Byzantine Period" and "The Ritual Baths (Miqva'ot) at Qedumim and the Observance of Ritual Purity among the Samaritans," both in *Early Christianity in Context: Monuments and Documents*, ed. F. Manns and E. Alliata, Festschrift E. Testa, SBF.CMa 38 (Jerusalem: Franciscan Printing Press, 1993), pp. 167-80, 181-93; Magen, *The Archaeological Discoveries at Qedumim: Qedem Museum* (Qedumim: Eretz Israel Academy, 1992).

63. On oil and wine production in Samaria, see Dar, *Landscape and Pattern*, pp. 147-90.

64. Magen, "The Ritual Baths (Miqva'ot) at Qedumim and the Observance of Ritual Purity among the Samaritans"; cf. DiSegni, "Samaritans," pp. 54-57.

65. Safrai, *Economy of Roman Palestine*, pp. 39-61; Dar, *Landscape and Pattern*, pp. 36-76.

66. Headquarters of a toparchy; cf. Jdt 7:18; *Jub* 29.14; 1 Macc 5:3; Pliny, *Natural History* 5.70; Josephus, *War* 3.48, 55; 4.504, 511, 551; *Ant* 12.328.

67. Headquarters of toparchy; cf. 1 Macc 11:34; Jn 11:54; Josephus, *Ant* 13.127; *War* 4.551; Zangenberg, *Frühes Christentum*, pp. 214-19.

68. Headquarters of toparchy; cf. 1 Macc 11:34; Mt 27:57; Josephus, *Ant* 13.127.

69. Headquarters of toparchy; cf. Pliny, *Natural History* 5.70; Josephus, *War* 1.45, 222; 2.568; 3.55; 4.551; 5.50; 6.115, 118; *Ant* 14.275.

70. Headquarters of toparchy; cf. Pliny, *Natural History* 5.70; Josephus, *War* 2.567; 3.55; 4.444; *Ant* 14.275.

Samaria[71] were not only bigger than normal villages, they also fulfilled some kind of local administrative function.

Apart from villages and towns, which formed the traditional fabric of rural life in Samaria, a third type of settlement must be mentioned. The Hasmonean dynasty as well as the Herodians granted lots of their land to influential members of the upper classes as signs of gratitude and to secure their further loyalty. When a dynasty ended, the next rulers would reacquire the lots and redistribute them to persons they considered important, so that the owners of such domains changed over time but the legal status and economic structure of them did not.[72] These domains were not only a onetime gift, the revenues collected from them were meant to supplement the regular income of these persons. All income from the villages on the domain as well as from lands of the domain itself belonged to the estate owner, keeping many villagers in a status of landless tenant farmers.[73] As many of these domains were located in exceptionally fertile territory, they became an important factor in the regional economy. These domains were among the few elements of the previous political system that the Romans continued after 70 C.E.[74]

Samaria, which had become crown land after the Hasmonean conquest, was a region of particular prominence in this respect. In his attempt to locate royal and imperial estates, Shimon Applebaum listed a good dozen sites in the vicinity of Caesarea, the Sharon plain, and western Samaria that date to the Hellenistic through Byzantine periods.[75] Of special importance are Haris (grid ref.: 163 169), ancient Arous, the site of a large estate owned by Ptolemy of Rhodes, Herod's minister,[76] and the settlement at Qarawat Beni Hassan, just 3 kilometers from Arous (grid ref.: 159 170).[77] Ptolemy's estate was protected by a

---

71. 1 Macc 5:23; Josephus, *War* 2.291, 509; *m. Neg.* 7.4. Cf. A. Zertal, "Hammam, Khirbet el-," in *NEAEHL* 2 (1993), pp. 563-65.

72. Fiensy, *Social History,* pp. 35-38.

73. Fiensy, *Social History,* pp. 80-85.

74. On estates in general, see, e.g., Safrai, *Economy of Roman Palestine,* pp. 82-99 and 358-65; Fiensy, *Social History,* passim; the rural farmhouse in Samaria is discussed by Dar, *Landscape and Pattern,* pp. 77-87.

75. S. Applebaum, "Royal and Imperial Estates in the Sharon and Samaria," in Applebaum, *Judaea in Hellenistic and Roman Times: Historical and Archaeological Essays,* SJLA 40 (Leiden: Brill, 1989), pp. 97-110.

76. On Arous, see Josephus, *Ant* 17.289; *War* 2.69; Dar, "The Estate of Ptolemy, Senior Minister of Herod" (in Hebrew), in *Jews and Judaism in the Second Temple, Mishna, and Talmud Period,* ed. I. Gafni, A. Oppenheimer, and M. Stern, Festschrift S. Safrai (Jerusalem: Yad Izhak Ben-Zvi, 1993), pp. 38-50; Fiensy, *Social History,* p. 42; F.-M. Abel, "Sappho et Arous," *JPOS* 7 (1927): 89-94.

77. Qarawat Beni Hassan might be Qarawa mentioned in late Samaritan sources as site of a

strong fort surveyed by Dar. Apart from extensive Roman and Byzantine settlement remains, Qarawat Beni Hassan features an "impressive fortress, of Herodian construction," and to the east of the present village a "rockcut hypogaeum, Deir el Darab, possessing an impressive architectural facade, whose style is characteristic of the last days of the Second Temple." A fortified enclosure north of the modern village contained "a number of long storebuildings,"[78] and many field towers dot the surroundings.

Applebaum's and Dar's research made evident that royal estates did not only consist of a single, large, and often well-fortified farmstead, but usually also enclosed "normal" villages, farms, and other agricultural buildings located on the domain's territory. It is hard to decide whether the inhabitants of these villages were settled when the estate was first built or rather belonged to the traditional social and economic texture of the region that had already existed for a much longer time. Perhaps these two scenarios are not alternatives, and we can assume an interesting overlay of segments of traditional village life and new forms of an almost "colonialistic" way of life.

On a smaller scale, domains such as Arous and Qarawat Beni Hassan offer good ways to picture what the "refounding" of Sebaste might have meant for the surroundings of the city. The surroundings were measured and split up in lots, which were assigned to individual newcoming settler families that had to till the land and make sure the region stayed calm. Fiensy estimates that the land given to the veterans exceeded 10 percent of the entire region of Samaria.[79] It would be interesting to know if and how the population already present on the land before the founding of the city was integrated, or if Herod simply evicted them.

Due to their significance in NT or early Christian literature, three sites deserve closer attention: Shechem, Sychar, and Gitta.

Long Lost Glory: Shechem (Tell Balatah) in NT Times

Shechem was correctly located on Tell Balatah by Hermann Thiersch and first excavated in 1913-14, 1926-28, 1931, and 1933-34 by Ernst Sellin and others.[80] Ini-

---

synagogue built by Baba Rabba (*TIR* 206). On the site, see Fiensy, *Social History*, pp. 38-42; Applebaum, "Estates," pp. 108-9; Dar, *Landscape and Pattern*, pp. 230-45.

78. Applebaum, "Estates," p. 108.

79. Fiensy, *Social History*, p. 43.

80. On Shechem, see Zangenberg, *Frühes Christentum*, pp. 27-30; E. F. Campbell, "Shechem," in *NEAEHL* 4 (1994), pp. 1345-54; L. E. Toombs, "Shechem (Place)," in *ABD* 5 (1992), pp. 1174-86; G. E. Wright, *Shechem: Biography of a Biblical City* (New York: McGraw-Hill, 1965), and the reports in the Tell Balatah/Shechem excavation reports series.

Figure 61. Magdala in Lower Galilee. Note the tower (*migdal* in Hebrew).
Courtesy of J. H. Charlesworth

tially, four strata were observed, but the pioneering years' lack of knowledge about stratigraphic methods and local pottery chronology led to incorrect dating and required constant revision. Important among the small finds were a hoard of 850 bronze and 7 iron arrowheads from the upper "Greek" level; bronze weaponry, including a sickle sword; and two cuneiform tablets, one dealing with judicial proceedings, the other a letter written by a teacher to his pupil's father asking for his fee to be paid. Sellin worked on the final report, until his manuscript and many artifacts were destroyed during an air raid on Berlin in 1943. Most of our current information on Shechem is based on the results of the Joint Drew-McCormick Archaeological Expedition that dug the tel and surveyed the region in several campaigns between 1956 and 1973, under the directorship of G. E. Wright.

Shechem was one of the most important Canaanite cities in the central hill country, on the main road between Mount Gerizim and Mount Ebal leading from Jerusalem to the north. The surrounding region is extremely fertile, and plenty of springs have favored intensive settlement (cf. *Ant* 2.18). The city appears in Egyptian Execration Texts of the nineteenth century B.C.E., and its king Lab'ayu features in the El Amarna letters of the late fourteenth century

B.C.E. It is possible that a reference in the Egyptian Anastasi papyrus of the end of the thirteenth century B.C.E. is also to this city. Biblical Shechem is identified with Tell Balatah, 2 kilometers east of modern Nablus. This location is supported by Eusebius (*Onomasticon* 164.11: Sikima), the Pilgrim of Bordeaux, the Madaba map, and other Byzantine sources. The city occupies a prominent place in the patriarchal tradition. On arrival in Canaan, after leaving Haran, Abraham built an altar to the Lord at Shechem (Gen 12:6-7). When Jacob came from Paddan-Aram, he pitched his tent outside the city and bought property there (Gen 33:18-19). Because Shemer "the Hivite" had raped Dinah, all male inhabitants of Shechem were killed and the city was plundered by the sons of Jacob (Gen 34). After the conquest of Canaan by the Israelites, the border of the territories of Ephraim and Manasseh met at Shechem (Josh 17:7), which was one of the cities of the Levites (Josh 21:21). Before his death Joshua gathered the Hebrews there; and they brought from Egypt the bones of Joseph, son of Jacob, for burial on the land his father had bought (Josh 24). After Gideon's death the Shechemites enthroned his son Abimelech, and gave him "threescore and ten pieces of silver out of the house of Baal-Berith" (Judg 9:1-16); but when they rebelled against him, he "sowed the city with salt" (Judg 9:45-47). In this connection we hear of the "tower of Shechem." It seems that the city retained its special status in the time of the kingdom of Israel, because Rehoboam went there to be enthroned by "all Israel" (1 Kgs 12:1); and when the tribes of Israel revolted against him, Jeroboam, son of Nabat, rebuilt Shechem as his first capital (1 Kgs 12:25).

After the destruction of the Israelite settlement in 722 B.C.E., only limited occupation can be attributed to the Assyrian period (stratum VI), and even less material to the Babylonian and Persian periods (combined stratum V). Fragments of Greek pottery attest to Shechem's connection to the Mediterranean trade network during the sixth through fourth centuries B.C.E. Despite some administrative function as district capital,[81] the great days Shechem enjoyed during the MB IIB and MB IIC periods were clearly over. The beginning of the Hellenistic period (strata IV-I) marks new activity. In the late fourth century B.C.E. Shechem was rebuilt, the tops of the MB IIC fortifications were excavated and rebuilt, and building terraces were created to provide space for houses and workshops. Under Ptolemaic influence the quality of the town houses in Shechem improved and its role as trade and craft center also continued under Seleucid dominion. It is possible to assign at least part of this activity to a colony of Sidonians mentioned by Josephus (*Ant* 11.342-346; 12.257-264: "Sidonians of Shechem"), who seem to have used the site for

---

81. Stern, *Archaeology*, pp. 422-23.

inland trade.[82] Despite much confusion about how to interpret Josephus, these Sidonians have to be distinguished from their Samaritan neighbors on Mount Gerizim (see below), although the pagan Sidonians have adapted certain customs from their biblically inspired neighbors (*Ant* 11.343f.; 12.259). From Josephus we learn that their main sanctuary was located on Mount Gerizim (Tell er-Ras), overlooking Tell Balatah (*Ant* 12.261). All activity on Tell Balatah ends abruptly when John Hyrcanus I conquers the region in 128 or slightly after 111/110 B.C.E. at the latest (*Ant* 13.254-257). From that time on, Tell Balatah virtually remained unsettled; its former inhabitants apparently were absorbed by other settlements in the region without leaving any trace.

Thus, when Jesus is said to have met the Samaritan woman at Jacob's well, Tell Balatah was a bare hill with only a few sherds indicating temporary use in the early Roman period (certainly not even a village). Despite much confusion in the ancient and modern literature, Shechem must be distinguished from Sychar, today's al-Askar (see below). In 73 C.E. the newly founded Roman colony Flavia Neapolis took over Shechem's role as an urban center between Gerizim and Ebal; it is only 1 kilometer west and is clearly without any continuity to its famous neighbor.

Competition at the Patriarch's Well: Sychar (al-Askar)

Located at the eastern opening of the valley between Mount Ebal and Mount Gerizim, just opposite Shechem (Tell Balatah) at a very important crossroads in the northern hill country, Sychar is a good example of a large number of townlets and villages that dotted the fertile plain east of the mountain ridge in antiquity.[83]

Most of what we know about Sychar is from texts. A site with that name probably already existed in Hasmonean times, as can be inferred from a passage in *Jub* 34.4 (second century B.C.E.; the Latin text going back to Hebrew *mahane Sakir:* fields of Sakir = Sychar). The Mishnah mentions the "plain of the spring of Socher" (*m. Men.* 10.2) as one of the places from which the grain was harvested to prepare the shewbread for the Temple. This passage is especially important, because it presupposes that at least a number of Sychar's inhabitants

---

82. On other Sidonian merchant colonies, see B. Isaac, "A Seleucid Inscription from Jamnia-on-the-Sea: Antiochus Eupator and the Sidonians," *IEJ* 41 (1991): 132-44.

83. On Sychar, see Zangenberg, *Frühes Christentum*, pp. 96-106; Campbell, *Shechem II*, pp. 21-23; Z. Yeivin, "'Askar," *RB* 81 (1974): 94-95; H.-M. Schenke, "Jakobsbrunnen — Josephsgrab — Sychar: Topographische Untersuchungen und Erwägungen in der Perspektive von John 4,5.6," *ZDPV* 84 (1968): 159-84.

before 70 c.e. were Jewish, since Samaritans (whose holy mountain was just 1.5 km. to the south) obviously would not have sent any gifts to Jerusalem. It is very likely that Jewish settlers came to this fertile area in the wake of John Hyrcanus's campaigns at the very end of the second century b.c.e. The settlers might not only have been attracted by the fertility of the area. John refers to Sychar to locate the plot of land "that Jacob had given to his son Joseph" for burial, where pious tradition also venerated a well named after Jacob (Jn 4:5; cf. Gen 33:18-19; Josh 24:32). There was enough reason, therefore, for both Samaritans and Jews to be present at a site so charged with religious significance and to underscore their position over against competing claims on the heritage of the patriarchs and the right way to worship the God of Israel. John's story of Jesus' encounter with the Samaritan woman at this very place indicates early contacts between unknown Christian missionaries (Jn 4:37) and Samaritans. Some of these Samaritans were converted and came into contact with the Johannine community.

No excavations have taken place at al-Askar so far, but surveys were carried out that produced evidence for habitation from the late second/early first century b.c.e. until the Byzantine period.[84] Earlier material (Iron I and II) found in the area belongs probably not to a settlement but to the extended necropolis of Shechem that occupied a long stretch along the lower flanks of Mount Ebal. A middle-Roman mausoleum found on the eastern slope of Mount Ebal might have belonged to Sychar, but could as well have been part of the large cemetery outside the city of Flavia Neapolis, which lies just 2 kilometers to the west. Especially notable is a particular second/third century c.e. type of sarcophagus sometimes called "Samaritan," which in fact might better be explained as a local tradition not exclusively associated with Samaritans.[85] Many of the names engraved on these sarcophagi, however, are "biblical" and could have been used by both Samaritans and Jews — and possibly even by indigenous pagans.

In an influential article published in 1968, Hans-Martin Schenke claimed

84. Campbell, *Shechem II*, pp. 21-23; Schenke, "Jakobsbrunnen," pp. 162-66.

85. On these sarcophagi, see Y. Magen, "The 'Samaritan' Sarcophagi," in *Early Christianity in Context*, pp. 149-66; R. Barkay, "Samaritan Sarcophagi of the Roman Period from the Land on [*sic*] Israel," in *Proceedings of the First International Congress of the Société des Études Samaritaines, Tel Aviv, April 11-13 1988*, pp. 83-98; E. Damati, "The Sarcophagi of the Samaritan Mausoleum at 'Askar (En Sychar)" (in Hebrew), *Israel People and Land* (Haaretz Museum Yearbook) 2-3 (1986): 87-106. Similar sarcophagi have been found at various places; see R. Barkay, "A Roman-Period Samaritan Burial from Talluze," *BAIAS* 7 (1987/88): 8-20 (see the distribution map on p. 17!). As Magen has conclusively shown, however, these sarcophagi cannot be used to identify the religious affiliation of the inhabitants of 'Askar (my notes in Zangenberg, *SAMAREIA*, pp. 319-21, need to be corrected).

that Sychar was the place to which the Samaritan population fled after the destruction of nearby Shechem in 107 B.C.E., and that the town subsequently functioned as the central settlement for this community. Others, like Hengel, followed him.[86] The evidence for this intriguing interpretation, however, is too weak. First, Schenke's scenario presupposes that we are able to see the historical sequence of events from the destruction of Shechem to the establishment or at least a significant expansion of Sychar reflected in the archaeological record. This is only partly the case. While the date for the destruction of Shechem seems firmly established, the survey material collected in and around al-Askar cannot bear the burden of proof for Schenke's theory. Its chronological range is too unspecific, its occupational context entirely unclear and not indicative of the size and character of the settlement. Apart from these chronological problems, there is the question of cultural profile. We have no evidence that the inhabitants of Shechem were Samaritans, nor that Shechem was any kind of Samaritan center at all; on the contrary, the only texts explicitly mentioning an ethnic/cultural group present in Shechem before 107 B.C.E. refer to Sidonians who were clearly not Samaritans. The city on the main summit of Mount Gerizim (which Schenke could not have been aware of) most likely served as civic and cultic center for the Samaritans, and not Shechem. Of course, the presence of Sidonian colonists does not exclude the theoretical possibility of Samaritan inhabitants, too. But — following Schenke's model for a moment — these Sidonians might also have fled to Sychar, which certainly would have affected the development of Sychar as a Samaritan center. It seems that, while its pivotal religious role was retained, no other single town succeeded Mount Gerizim as the civic center of the Samaritans after the disaster of 107.[87]

Presently, almost nothing is known about the actual size of the town in the first century C.E., nor about its cultural character. Sychar seems to have been one of the many small towns in the fertile central Samarian plain. Its location on a road junction, the vicinity to both Mount Gerizim and traditional biblical holy sites such as Jacob's well and Joseph's field, but not its specifically Samaritan character, made Sychar the ideal place for the encounter between Jesus the Jew and the unnamed Samaritan woman in Jn 4.

86. Hengel, "Das Johannesevangelium als Quelle für die Geschichte des antiken Judentums," in Hengel, *Judaica, Hellenistica et Christiana: Kleine Schriften II*, WUNT 109 (Tübingen: Mohr Siebeck, 1999), pp. 293-334; Hengel, "Historiker Lukas," pp. 180-82.

87. See below on Mount Gerizim, and Zangenberg, "Simon Magus," pp. 522-23. *If* there really was a single successor to Luza/Mount Gerizim as civic center (which I doubt), only Tirat Ana (perhaps to be identified with Kh. et-Tira, grid ref.: 174 174, about 5 km. south of the Gerizim) seems an appropriate candidate considering its role in an uprising mentioned in Josephus, *Ant* 18.86, 88, but even here the evidence is not sufficient.

The Hometown of the Magus: Gitta (Jatt)

Recent salvage excavations in Jatt, ancient Gitta, have provided interesting glimpses into the cultural world of a small townlet at the fringes of the Samarian hill country and Sharon plain (grid ref.: 1540 2005).[88] The origins of Gitta date back to Early Bronze (EB) I, further occupation was identified in EB II and III, MB II, and Late Bronze (LB). In the Iron Age the site shrunk to a sizable village that continued through the Persian and Hellenistic periods. Sometime after the annexation of the region by Alexander Jannaeus, the settlement shifted down the tell, whose slopes were further used for quarrying burial caves since the first century C.E. Since the foundation of Caesarea Maritima, Gitta belonged to its *chōra*.[89] Two very large burial caves on the northeastern slope of the hill were excavated and published by Porath, Yannai, and Kasher. Cave 5, which "consisted of an open courtyard, a passageway and three narrow burial halls arranged in a T-shaped formation,"[90] is of particular interest. Not only are the size and the form of the cave significant (it resembles Cave 1 of Maresha from the early second century B.C.E.), it is the sheer number of inscriptions that makes Cave 5 so important. All *kokhim* of the burial hall opposite the entrance were inscribed with names (ten inscriptions: one over each of the *kokhim*, one over all three side chambers, and two additional ones in side chamber 24 facing the main hall and entrance), the same with five of eleven *kokhim* in the southern burial hall; only the northern hall did not produce any inscriptions. Nineteen names are mentioned altogether, representing at least forty-two individuals. Apart from the number of inscriptions (its density is not matched by any of the Jerusalem tombs),[91] it is significant that all of them were written in Greek. The names belong to several categories. Traditional Hebrew names are transliterated (different versions of the name Miriam are represented four times, Rebecca three times, and Sara twice) and feature next to Greek names (Zoilos four times, Berenice five times, Mnaseas twice, and Dioskoros once) and Roman names (Paulus three times, Marcus and Agrippa twice, Tiberius once). Interesting is the high percentage of names that allude to Herod and his dynasty

---

88. Y. Porath, E. Yannai, and A. Kasher, "Archaeological Remains at Jatt," *'Atiqot* 37 (1999): 1-78 and 167*-171*; other reports on these graves in *ESI* 7/8 (1988/87): 83-87; *ESI* 9 (1989/90): 43. MB II, LB, and Iron II pottery from deposits are mentioned in *Hadashot arkhe'ologiyot/Excavations and Surveys in Israel* 110 (1999): 35*-36*; *ESI* 7/8 (1988/89): 83-84; *ESI* 4 (1985): 120.

89. Porath, Yannai, and Kasher, "Archaeological Remains at Jatt," p. 168*. *Pseudo Clement II* 22.2 localizes Gitta "six miles away from the Capital," which, of course, must be Caesarea Maritima, the provincial capital of Palestine in the second century C.E.

90. Porath, Yannai, and Kasher, "Archaeological Remains at Jatt," p. 168*.

91. Which could be the result of environmental influence (climate, etc.).

(Herodias is mentioned twice, Agrippa, Antipater, Berenice might also be mentioned), but most of these names are well attested in Jewish families in general.[92] Kasher and Porath tentatively date the bulk of the inscriptions to the late Hellenistic and early Roman periods and suggest the burial cave belonged to a wealthy Jewish family "somehow related to the Herodian dynasty."[93]

Cave 4, which housed fifteen *kokhim* surrounding a single rectangular chamber, contained three names (Rivqah, Ya'aqob, Yeshua') written in Hebrew square letters. Since, contrary to Kasher and Porath, Samaritans *did* use Hebrew square script,[94] it is not entirely clear if Cave 4 really was used by Jews.[95] As already pointed out above, it is notoriously difficult to identify Samaritan material remains before the fourth century and distinguish them from Jewish objects. So far, I do not see any convincing evidence why Cave 4 could only have been used by Jews.

Certainly, two burial caves are no basis for far-reaching conclusions about the cultural profile of Gitta. However, the names in Cave 5 clearly do indicate that the multiculturalism of first-century Caesarea Maritima also infected at least some parts of the population of the surrounding towns and villages.

Apart from its location, Gitta is of particular interest since it features as the place of origin of Simon Magus in several ancient sources (Justin, *1 Apology* 26.2; Pseudo-Clementine, *Homilies* 2.22.2). According to Acts 8:5, 9 (which does not mention Simon's place of origin), Simon performed miracles and proclaimed himself as "something great" in the "city of Samaria," which can best be identified as Sebaste (see above). So, at some time in his life Simon appears to have migrated from the *chōra* of Caesarea to Sebaste. It is interesting to see that Simon's move in a certain way reflects just that close interrelationship between the coastal plain and the central highlands that we discussed above. Given the location of Gitta on the fringes of the coastal plain and Samarian hill country, it is no wonder that a pagan miracle worker comes from that village and seeks followers in Sebaste, which was also deeply influenced by paganism. Simon's ori-

92. Porath and Kasher assume that this attests "the affinity, sympathy and loyalty of certain Jewish circles to the Herodian dynasty" ("Archaeological Remains at Jatt," p. 170*).

93. Porath, Yannai, and Kasher, "Archaeological Remains at Jatt," p. 168*.

94. See contemporaneous inscriptions in square script from Mount Gerizim in Y. Magen, L. Tsfania, and H. Misgav, "The Hebrew and Aramaic Inscriptions from Mt. Gerizim," *Qad* 33, no. 120 (2000): 125-32; J. Naveh and Y. Magen, "Aramaic and Hebrew Inscriptions of the Second Century B.C.E. from Mount Gerizim," *'Atiqot* 32 (1997): 9*-17*.

95. Kasher tries to support his observation by pointing out that "the Hebrew name Yeshua' [. . .] is unfamiliar in the Samaritan onomasticon with this spelling" ("Archaeological Remains at Jatt," p. 170*). We do not have much contemporaneous onomastic material that is undoubtedly Samaritan to compare with, and orthography varies considerably in burial inscriptions anyway.

gin in Gitta, therefore, is no indication that his movement was rooted in the rural world of Samaria and no proof that he was a Samaritan.[96] On the contrary, western Samaria seems to have been a breeding ground for all sorts of "heretics." Apart from Simon Magus, the Samaritan first-century heretic Dositheos is reported to have come from Socho (esh-Shuweike, north of Tulkarm, grid ref.: 153 194). According to Justin (*1 Apology* 26.4), Simon's alleged pupil Menandros came from Capareteia, which is to be identified with Kfar Hatta in western Samaria (grid ref.: 146 169).[97]

Cities in Samaria

There are only three sites in Samaria that justify the label "city," but only one of them (Sebaste) was extant during Jesus' lifetime. The Hellenistic temple city on Mount Gerizim was long destroyed, and Neapolis had not yet been built when Jesus is said to have met the woman at the well. All three sites deserve a closer look, as they illustrate the cultural diversity and historical volatility of the region better than anything else.

The Samaritan Sanctuary and City on Mount Gerizim

The conversation between Jesus and the Samaritan woman in Jn 4 centers around some of the most hotly debated issues between Samaritans and Jews. The Fourth Evangelist not only shows a genuine interest in these questions, he also seems sufficiently informed about the arguments on both sides. One of these issues has dominated the controversy from its beginning: the question of the legitimate place of worship. In Jn 4:20 the Samaritan woman points out: "Our fathers have worshipped on this mountain, but you say Jerusalem is the place where one must worship."[98]

96. Contrary to Theissen, "Simon Magus," p. 417.

97. On Dositheos and "the prophet like Moses," see, e.g., Zangenberg, *Frühes Christentum,* pp. 157-64, with references; J. E. Fossum, "Sects and Movements," in *The Samaritans,* ed. Crown, pp. 293-389; S. Isser, *The Dositheans: A Samaritan Sect in Late Antiquity,* SJLA 17 (Leiden: Brill, 1976).

98. On Mount Gerizim in general, see Zangenberg, *Frühes Christentum,* pp. 35-47 and 140-48. The religious role of the mountain for Samaritans is discussed, e.g., in R. T. Anderson, "Gerizim (Mount)," in *A Companion to Samaritan Studies,* ed. A. D. Crown (Tübingen: Mohr Siebeck, 1993), pp. 99-103; R. Pummer, *The Samaritans,* IoRJ 5 (Leiden: Brill, 1987), pp. 8-10; Anderson, "Mount Gerizim: Navel of the World," *BA* 43 (1980): 217-21; F. Dexinger, "Das

Mount Gerizim indeed features prominently in the Old Testament. According to Gen 12:6, Abraham entered the Promised Land through Shechem "at the oak Moreh." Gerizim and Ebal were the mountains on whose slopes the tribes of Israel assembled under Joshua, fulfilling Moses' command by hearing the curses and the blessings connected with the observance of the Law (Gerizim being the mount of blessing; Ebal the mount of cursing; Deut 11:29; 27:11-13; Josh 8:33-34). Mount Gerizim remains *the* religious center of the Samaritans (who dismiss Jerusalem as the "place of blessing"). Their cult on Mount Gerizim is legitimized by redactional insertions and changes to their version of the Pentateuch, most prominently to the Decalogue (the commandment to erect an altar on Gerizim).

Mount Gerizim consists of three peaks: the main summit (881 m. above sea level), Tell er-Ras to the north (a steep, conical peak rising to 831 m.), and the wide flat western hill (807 m.), and commands, together with Mount Ebal to the north, the entrance to a narrow valley containing the remains of Roman Flavia Neapolis and Tell el-Balata (ancient Shechem). As this pass gave the only access from east to west into the mountains of Ephraim and was situated on the main road from north to south, it was of strategic importance from earliest times. The earliest archaeological remains on Gerizim are those of a temple excavated in 1931 on the lower slope of the main summit (Khirbet et-Tananir) belonging to the MB IIC. Further excavations in the late 1920s revealed remains of an octagonal Byzantine church on the main summit. R. J. Bull and his team excavated a sequence of two temples on Tell er-Ras between 1964 and 1968. Many questions, especially on the character of the Samaritan sanctuary, whose existence was well established in written sources, remained open. It was only when renewed excavations under Yizhaq Magen took place (since 1982) that new evidence was produced that completely changed our understanding of the history of the mountain in the Persian, Hellenistic, Roman, and Byzantine periods, showing a complicated sequence of Samaritan, pagan, and Christian structures located on different parts of the mountain.

Two of the three peaks are crucial to our understanding of the historical and religious importance of Mount Gerizim in the late Hellenistic and early Roman period. As it turned out after decades of archaeological and textual re-

---

Garizimgebot im Dekalog der Samaritaner," in *Studien zum Pentateuch,* ed. G. Braulik, Festschrift W. Kornfeld (Freiburg, Basel, and Vienna: Herder, 1977), pp. 111-33; H. G. Kippenberg, *Garizim und Synagoge: Traditionsgeschichtliche Untersuchungen zur samaritanischen Religion der aramäischen Periode,* RVV 30 (Berlin: de Gruyter, 1971) passim; J. Macdonald, *The Theology of the Samaritans* (Philadelphia: Westminster, 1964), pp. 327-33; still valuable is the pioneering study by J. A. Montgomery, *The Samaritans: The Earliest Jewish Sect, Their History, Theology, and Literature* (Philadelphia: J. C. Winston, 1907).

search, the main peak and Tell er-Ras underwent significantly different phases and kinds of habitation and construction, making Mount Gerizim one of the few localities in the ancient world that at various periods was used by different, often conflicting religious groups.

a. The earliest archaeological remains on the main summit reported so far[99] belong to the Iron Age. Three proto-Aeolic capitals dating to the seventh century B.C.E. have been found reused in Persian period contexts, but might well have belonged to a cult place from the Assyrian period. In addition to the usual decoration with triangles and volutes, these capitals also show the edge of a Phoenician palmette "and, in one capital, the facade of a temple guarded by seven uraei."[100] In the late Persian period (fourth century B.C.E.), the summit was fortified and the first cultic installations were erected. These remains are the first traces of a particular Samaritan cult that was established as a result of tensions with the Jerusalemite priesthood and with support from the authorities of Samaria (cf. *Ant* 11.302f., 306-332 and 321-325; 13.74, which dates these events to the end of the Persian period and the coming of Alexander the Great). A massive expansion and reconstruction of the cult place took place around 200 B.C.E., and the slopes were built up with elaborate houses forming a spectacular ensemble of an acropolis with a paved *temenos* and massive fortifications surrounded by a large, very prosperous town. It is clear that this ensemble is to be identified with the main settlement of the Samaritans in the Hellenistic age (possibly called Bet-El/Luza), housing merchants as well as the priestly aristocracy. Fragments of inscriptions mentioning a "high priest" and "priests" in paleo-Hebrew script suggest that the *temenos* served as the Samaritan cultic

99. On the archaeology of the main summit, see the analysis in Zangenberg, *Frühes Christentum*, pp. 43-47; the summary in Magen, "Gerizim (Mount)," in *NEAEHL* 2 (1993), pp. 484-92; the detailed reports in Magen, "Mount Gerizim and the Samaritans," in *Early Christianity in Context*, pp. 149-66; and the older Hebrew reports, Magen, "A Fortified Town of the Hellenistic Period on Mount Gerizim," *Qad* 19, no. 75-76 (1986): 91-102; Magen, "Excavations at Mt. Gerizim: A Temple City," *Qad* 23, no. 91-92 (1990): 70-96. All previous discussions, however, including my own on the beginning of the Samaritan cult place and the possible relationship of the Persian and early Hellenistic strata with the origins of the Samaritans, have to be revised on the basis of new data published in *Qad* 32, no. 120 (2000): Magen, "Mt. Gerizim — a Temple City," pp. 74-118; E. Stern and Y. Magen, "The First Phase of the Samaritan Temple on Mt. Gerizim — New Archaeological Evidence," pp. 119-24; Y. Magen, L. Tsfania, and H. Misgav, "The Hebrew and Aramaic Inscriptions from Mt. Gerizim," pp. 125-32; Magen, "Mt. Gerizim during the Roman and Byzantine Periods," pp. 133-43. After the completion of my article, the official full publication of the Mount Gerizim Excavations has bugun. See Y. Magen, H. Misgav, and L. Tsfania, *Mount Gerizim Excavations I: The Aramaic, Hebrew and Samaritan Inscriptions, Judaea and Samaria Publications* 4 (Jerusalem: Israel Exploration Society, 2004). For the latest reconstruction of the stratigraphy and building history of the main summit of Mount Gerizim see esp. pp. 1-13.

100. Stern, *Archaeology*, p. 52.

center where, in accordance with Pentateuchal regulations, they performed their sacrifices and rituals.

Both the city and the acropolis were completely destroyed by John Hyrcanus I in 111/110 B.C.E. at the latest (*Ant* 13.255). Traces of later occupation indicate a small Hasmonean military post, but in the early Roman period the main summit seems to have been deserted. Despite the eradication of all cultic structures by Hyrcanus, the Samaritans continued to focus on Mount Gerizim in their religious and political aspirations (cf. *Ant* 18.85-89, which mentions a Samaritan "messianic" uprising in the year 35/36 C.E., and cf. the Samaritans' last stand against attacking Roman cavalry in 67 C.E. in *War* 3.307-315, also with possible eschatological undertones), but for many centuries without an identifiable building (Jn 4:20 cannot therefore point to an existing Samaritan temple). Samaritan sources from late antiquity indicate that a synagogue was built under Baba Rabba, the great Samaritan teacher and reformer, but no clear archaeological traces of the building have survived. Greek inscriptions from the third through fifth centuries C.E. mentioning Samaritan pilgrims (e.g., a cook named Zosimos from Caesarea), point to the continuing importance of the main summit. These inscriptions must predate the Christian use of the summit, since they were used as pavement slabs in the large octagonal church, built in 486 C.E. by the emperor Zeno and dedicated to Mary Theotokos (Procopius, *Buildings* 5.7.1-17). The church, which seems to have been built right over the Samaritan altar, marks the violent Christian takeover of the summit. It was expanded by a fortress under Justinian (ca. 530) and supplemented by substantial barracks. It continued to be in use until the end of the Byzantine rule. In the sixteenth century a Muslim *weli* was built on top of the Byzantine ruins.[101]

b. The second focus of activity on Mount Gerizim is Tell er-Ras, its northern peak.[102] Tell er-Ras, separated from the main summit by a small plain and a deep, artificial ditch, has always been oriented toward the settlements in the valley below. Excavations by Robert Bull and the Drew-McCormick Expedition

---

101. The Byzantine church has been separately discussed in Magen, "The Church of Mary Theotokos on Mt. Gerizim," in *Ancient Churches Revealed,* ed. Y. Tsafrir (Jerusalem: IES, 1993), pp. 83-89; the more detailed report is Y. Magen, "The Church of Mary Theotokos on Mount Gerizim," in *Christian Archaeology in the Holy Land: New Discoveries,* ed. G. C. Bottini, L. DiSegni, and E. Alliata, Festschrift V. Corbo, SBF.CMa 36 (Jerusalem: SBF Press, 1990), pp. 333-42. On the inscriptions, see L. DiSegni, "The Church of Mary Theotokos on Mount Gerizim: The Inscriptions," in *Christian Archaeology in the Holy Land,* pp. 343-50.

102. On archaeological discoveries on Tell er-Ras, see Zangenberg, *Frühes Christentum,* pp. 37-39; R. J. Bull, "Tell er-Ras (Mount Gerizim)," in *EAEHL* 4 (1978), pp. 1015-22; Bull, "The Excavations of Tell er-Ras on Gerizim (1964 and 1966)," *BA* 31 (1968): 58-72; Bull, "A Preliminary Excavation of an Hadrianic Temple of Tell er-Ras on Mount Gerizim," *AJA* 71 (1967): 388-93.

between 1964 and 1968 have revealed a massive, two-phased substruction that, according to architectural and decorative remains, including inscriptions, can be associated with a huge temple of Zeus. The temple was connected with the city below by a wide flight of stairs and had several administrative buildings in its vicinity. This impressing ensemble is depicted on city coins minted in Neapolis from the reign of Antoninus Pius (138-161 C.E.) to Volusianus (251-253). Although the archaeological remains clearly suggest a date for the temple in the mid–second century C.E. (with a refurbishment phase around 200 C.E.), it is very likely it had a predecessor dating back at least to Hellenistic times, since 2 Macc 6:2 and *Ant* 12.258-261 mention that Antiochus IV Epiphanes (re)dedicated a temple on Mount Gerizim in 166 B.C.E. to Zeus Xenios/Hellenios. In addition, a Dead Sea Scroll, the *Copper Scroll* (3Q15 12.4f.), confirms that stairs connecting Tell er-Ras with the valley must have been in existence in the late first century C.E. at the latest.[103] It would not be surprising if this sanctuary was used (or even first built?) by a group of Sidonian colonists living in the Hellenistic settlement on Tell Balatah/Shechem (cf. *Ant* 11.340-342; 12.257-264). The settlement on Tell Balatah and the temple on Tell er-Ras were destroyed by John Hyrcanus shortly after 111/110 B.C.E. (*Ant* 13.254-257; *War* 1.62-63). There are no clear traces indicating a continuation of worship on Tell er-Ras, but the stairs featured in the *Copper Scroll* should make one cautious about ruling out a use in the period between Hyrcanus's destruction and the erection of the mid–second century C.E. temple. Above all, the Roman building activities might have obliterated all archaeological traces. The pagan sanctuary gradually went out of use during the late fourth and early fifth century C.E.[104]

Although some problems need further discussion, the overall picture seems fairly clear. The pagan temple must not be confused with the contemporaneous Samaritan sanctuary on the main summit. Both were tied to different traditions and practices and used by different groups of people. Much speculation on the "syncretistic character" of Samaritan worship in earlier publications ensued because the Roman Zeus temple was found first and was then interpreted as belonging to the Samaritans.[105] Many texts that actually deal with

103. J. K. Lefkovits, *The Copper Scroll 3Q15: A Reevaluation; A New Reading, Translation, and Commentary*, STDJ 25 (Leiden: Brill, 2000), pp. 409-12. The stairs are mentioned well into the fourth century; cf. Bordeaux Pilgrim 13; Eusebius, *De duodecim gemmis* 190 (CSEL 35).

104. R. L. Hohlfelder, "A Twilight of Paganism in the Holy Land: Numismatic Evidence from the Excavations at Tell er-Ras," in Hohlfelder, *City, Town, and Countryside in the Early Byzantine Era* (Boulder, Colo.: East European Monographs; New York: Columbia University Press, 1982), pp. 75-113.

105. Note different positions proposed by R. T. Anderson, "The Elusive Samaritan Temple," *BA* 54 (1991): 104-7; R. J. Bull, "An Archaeological Context for Understanding John 4:20," *BA* 38

activities at two different spots on Mount Gerizim were read as referring to one and the same religious group. While we cannot rule out "syncretistic tendencies" among some members of both groups, there is no reason to suppose that the Samaritans in general were openly or clandestinely worshiping Zeus as their God. The Jewish claim, based on 2 Kgs 17, that Samaritans are an offspring of idolatrous foreigners meets no support in archaeology. Mount Gerizim, therefore, is one of the few places frequented by competing, sometimes even conflicting, religious groups.

Samaria/Sebaste

Samaria was the capital of the ancient kingdom of Israel until 723/722 to 720 B.C.E.; the capital of the Assyrian, Babylonian, and Persian province of Samirina; and a major urban center in Hellenistic and Roman Palestine.[106] Built on a hill about 100 meters above the surrounding fertile agricultural area, the city occupies a strategic point that gives access in three directions: west to the coastal plain, east to Shechem and from there to the river Jordan or to Jerusalem, and north to Megiddo and the Jezreel Valley. Extensive excavations of the site were conducted in 1908-10 by Harvard University, under the direction of G. A. Reisner and S. Fisher, and in 1931-35 a joint expedition under the directorship of K. Kenyon with the participation of British institutions, the Hebrew University, and Harvard University continued the work. Small excavations were undertaken by the Jordanian Department of Antiquities in 1967.

The city of Samaria in the time of Jesus had little in common with its famous predecessor, the capital of the northern kingdom of Israel. After this city was destroyed and the upper-class population deported, a new chapter began with the resettlement of the steep hill that once housed kings, princes, and prophets. Under Persian rule (sixth-fourth century B.C.E.) Samaria remained a provincial capital for most of central Palestine. The influence of the governors (many of which had the name Sanballat) seems to have extended into the Jewish community of Egypt (cf. the papyri from Elephantine). Fragments of Greek painted pottery found in Persian strata reveal the economic potential of the inhabitants, their far-reaching trade connections (especially to the coast), and a growing influence of

(1975): 54-59, and the critique of the "heretical interpretation" of Samaritanism by E. F. Campbell, "Jewish Shrines of the Hellenistic and Persian Periods," in *Symposia Celebrating the Seventy-fifth Anniversary of the Founding of the American Schools of Oriental Research (1900-1975)*, ed. F. M. Cross (Cambridge: Harvard University Press, 1979), pp. 159-67, esp. 159-61.

106. On Samaria and Sebaste, see Zangenberg, *Frühes Christentum*, pp. 47-55, and N. Avigad, "Samaria," in *NEAEHL* 4 (1993), pp. 1300-1310.

Greek culture on the city.[107] A cache of papyri discovered by P. W. Lapp in the caves of Wadi Daliyeh in the Jordan Valley, east of Samaria, throws light on the life of the inhabitants during the fourth century B.C.E. These unique documents date from about 375 to 335 B.C.E. and record transactions concerning property and land, loans, contracts and the sale, transfer, and manumission of slaves.[108] The iconography of the seals from these papyri as well as that of fourth-century coins displays the cosmopolitan profile of the political elite of late Persian Samaria; their names show their strong affiliation with Yahwistic tradition.[109] After the Jews returned from the Babylonian exile and began to rebuild the Temple in Jerusalem, some northerners who seem to have retained some form of Yahwistic religion (Jer 41:4-5) offered help, but the Jerusalemites declined (Ezra 4; Neh 2). This group of non-Judahite Yahwists could have constituted one stratum of the group that later came to be called Samaritans ("proto-Samaritans").

In 332 B.C.E. Samaria was captured by Alexander the Great. After his governor was killed by the local elite (cf. Curtius Rufus 4.8.9), Alexander brought local leadership to an end and placed a garrison of Macedonian veterans in the city. This step certainly strengthened the Greek element in the city. In the Hellenistic period the city was a center of pagan culture (inscriptions mentioning, e.g., Isis and Serapis; remains of a temple of Kore); massive fortifications around the acropolis (huge round towers were added, one of which is about 21 m. in diameter and is still standing to a height of about 9 m.) and scores of stamped handles from amphorae containing imported products indicate its economic power. A new wall, enclosing an area of some 250 by 130 meters, was built around the acropolis in the second century B.C.E., about 6.5 meters thick at its base and strengthened with rectangular towers. The city was completely destroyed by John Hyrcanus's sons Aristobulus and Antigonus in 108/107 B.C.E., and the whole population sold off into slavery (*War* 1.64-65). After Pompey annexed Samaria to the Roman province of Syria (*War* 1.156) in 63 B.C.E., the city underwent

107. On Persian period finds from the city and its vicinity, see Stern, *Archaeology*, pp. 422-28; on Attic ware, consult R. Wenning, "Attische Keramik in Palästina: Ein Zwischenbericht," *Transeuphratène* 2 (1990): 157-67.

108. P. L. Lapp and N. L. Lapp, eds., *Discoveries in the Wadi ed-Daliyeh*, AASOR 41 (Cambridge: ASOR, 1974); D. M. Gropp, "Samaria (Papyri)," in *ABD* 5 (1992), pp. 931-32; Gropp, "The Samaria Papyri from the Wadi ed-Daliyeh: The Slave Sales" (Ph.D. diss., Harvard University, 1986).

109. M. J. W. Leith, "Seals and Coins in Persian Period Samaria," in *The Dead Sea Scrolls Fifty Years after Their Discovery: Proceedings of the Jerusalem Congress, July 20-25, 1997*, ed. L. H. Schiffman, E. Tov, and J. C. VanderKam (Jerusalem: Israel Exploration Society, 2000), pp. 691-707; *Wadi Daliyeh I: The Wadi Daliyeh Seal Impressions*, DJD 24 (Oxford: University Press, 1997); Y. Meshorer and S. Qedar, *The Coinage of Ancient Samaria in the Fourth Century B.C.E.* (Jerusalem: Numismatic Fine Arts International, 1991).

considerable reconstruction under Governor Gabinus in 57-55 B.C.E. (*War* 1.166). Sextus Iulis Caesar, the governor of Syria, gave the region of Samaria and also the city to Herod around 47/46 B.C.E. (*War* 1.213). In 43 B.C.E. Herod visited the city and "restored it" by settling an unspecified kind of "unrest" *(stasis)* (*Ant* 14.284). The region of Samaria considerably supported Herod during his campaigns against the last Hasmoneans, providing supplies and soldiers. During the siege of Jerusalem Herod married Mariamne in Samaria (*Ant* 14.467), further deepening the very special relations between him and the city. Marcus Antonius and Augustus subsequently reaffirmed Herod's rule over the region and the city (Appianus, *Civil War* 5.75; *Ant* 15.217). In 25 B.C.E. Herod paid back what he owed the city: he settled 6,000 veterans, renamed it Sebaste in honor of the emperor, and gave it a civic constitution in Greek style. Herod's ambitious building activities contained renewed defenses and a magnificent temple dedicated to Roma and Augustus (*Ant* 15.296-298), possibly also a large basilica below the Roman *forum*, the first phase of the stadium in the northeastern part of the lower city, and an aqueduct. Herod's activities, which clearly presuppose the pagan character of the city, certainly represent the apex of Hellenistic culture in Sebaste.[110]

The city continued to be a cornerstone of Hellenistic culture in Palestine. The Roman governors recruited soldiers from among the inhabitants of Sebaste (*Sebastenoi;* cf. *Ant* 19.356, 364-366), who were much hated by the Jews for their ruthless behavior. Due to its strong pro-Roman attitude during the First Revolt, Sebaste was destroyed by Jewish rebels (*War* 2.458-460), but was soon afterward rebuilt. Just like after the destruction by Hyrcanus, the events at the beginning of the First Revolt do not seem to have changed the overall cultural profile of the city. Septimius Severus gave it the status of *colonia* in 200 C.E., after the city had remained loyal to him in his struggle with Pescennius Niger. Severus built a large basilica in the civic quarter and a colonnaded market street 13 meters wide and running from the west to the east gate over nearly 900 meters and consisting of 600 columns. He also had the defenses and the Augustus temple repaired. On the northeastern slope of the acropolis a theater was excavated that belonged to the early third century C.E., and a mausoleum and several other tombs from the Roman period were found outside the city.

Many Christian sources mention a bishop in Sebaste and indicate a strong affection for John the Baptist, whose tomb was located in the city by popular Christian tradition.[111] Several churches were constructed there for this reason,

---

110. On Herod and Samaria and Sebaste, see A. Lichtenberger, *Die Baupolitik Herodes des Großen,* ADPV 26 (Wiesbaden: Harrassowitz, 1999), pp. 80-92; D. W. Roller, *The Building Program of Herod the Great* (Berkeley: University of California Press, 1998), pp. 209-12; Richardson, *Herod,* pp. 174-202.

111. On the alleged tomb of John the Baptist, see Zangenberg, *Frühes Christentum,* pp. 82-86.

the latest by the Crusaders in the twelfth century. Today, parts of the ancient city are covered by the Arab village of es-Sebastiyye.

A New City in Samaria: Flavia Neapolis (Nablus)

Strictly speaking, Flavia Neapolis does not belong to the period under consideration.[112] The city was founded by Emperor Vespasian in 72/73 C.E. to consolidate Roman control over central Palestine after his victory in the First Jewish War (cf. Emmaus, Jaffa, and Jerusalem [Aelia Capitolina]). The founding of the city marks the beginning of a period of deliberate Romanization in the region after the First Revolt that must also have affected the composition of the population in central Samaria. The Romans built the "new city" *(nea polis)* over an older village named Mabartha (i.e., "passage": *War* 4.449; Pliny, *Naturalis historia* 5.69), just 1 kilometer west of Shechem. Much of the surrounding rural region, including Mount Gerizim and the plain east of the valley, was transferred to the city-territory *(chōra).* Designed as a bridgehead of Roman civilization surrounded by occupied territory, Neapolis was built on a Roman grid plan (as far as the awkward geography would allow), settled with veterans mostly from the victorious legions and other foreign colonists (cf. the names of Justin Martyr's father Priscus and grandfather Baccheios, who were citizens of Neapolis; *1 Apology* 1.1), and enjoyed all of Roman city life. An inscription mentions wrestling games in Neapolis in the second century C.E., and coins show depictions of Zeus, the Ephesian Artemis, Serapis, and Asklepios, and notably many emblems of military units. Especially famous are large city coins minted in Neapolis that show the city in the valley with magnificent colonnaded streets connecting up through a stairway to a large temple on Mount Gerizim (Tell er-Ras). Excavations revealed parts of a large hippodrome (with an amphitheater integrated late; cf. Beth Shean), a wide colonnaded street, a theater seating up to 7,000 people, segments of a city wall and probably also large baths. Many of these buildings might have been erected only after the Second Jewish War (132-135/36), when Romanization was enforced on an even broader scale, but they remained in use well into the seventh century C.E. Elaborate mausolea were found at several places lining the main routes leaving Neapolis (cf. Sychar). The city flourished until the civil war between Septimius Severus and Pescennius Niger in 198/99 C.E., when it was temporarily stripped of

---

112. On Neapolis, see Zangenberg, *Frühes Christentum,* pp. 30-35; Y. Magen, "Shechem (Neapolis)," in *NEAEHL* 4 (1993), pp. 1354-59, with further references. See now the full publication of Magen's excavations: Y. Magen, *Flavia Neapolis: Shekhem in the Roman Period* (in Hebrew), Judaea and Samaria Publications 6 (Jerusalem: Israel Exploration Society, 2005).

legal privileges because it sided with the defeated Niger. Instead of Neapolis, Septimius promoted its rival, Sebaste, located only 20 kilometers to the northwest. However, the city soon recovered and remained one of the most powerful and affluent urban centers in Palestine well into late antiquity.

For a long time Neapolis was an entirely pagan city. Justin Martyr, who was born there around 120 C.E., came into contact with Platonism in his hometown, but not with Christians (*Dialogus* 2.6; about Justin's conversion in general cf. *Dialogus* 3.1–7.1). But there is already a bishop mentioned among the signatories at the council of Nicea in 325 C.E. In the fourth century we also have the first clear literary and epigraphic evidence for the presence of Samaritans in the city. There is no sign so far suggesting any Jewish presence in ancient Neapolis before the Byzantine period.[113]

Outlook: Samaria Slipping out of Sight

The origin of most of the NT traditions and subsequent early Christian literature falls in the period of continuing Judeo-Samaritan tensions (a long-term effect of the Hasmonean conquest) and the rising power of paganism and growing presence of foreign colonists after the fall of Jerusalem (70 C.E.). Jews and Samaritans responded to this situation in various ways, first and foremost by internal stabilization (the Mishnah or religious reform under Baba Rabba among the Samaritans) and, connected with it, by attempts to set out rules of contact with others. It is interesting to see that NT and early Christian authors played only a minor role in this enterprise. Given the strong Jewish roots (both Galilean and Jerusalemite) of the very foundations of early Christianity, it is no wonder that wherever there *were* contacts with Samaria and its inhabitants, these contacts necessarily were reflected over against this Jewish background. The Fourth Evangelist is a good example of that strategy. To convince reluctant members in his community of the legitimacy of integrating former Samaritans into his congregation, he resorts to typically "Christian" positions to overcome the traditional controversy of where to worship the biblical God ("neither on this mountain nor in Jerusalem, but in spirit and truth," 4:23-24). At the same time, however, John emphasizes that "salvation comes from the Jews" (4:22).[114]

Obviously, there were no theological concepts at hand that would open a

---

113. G. Alon, *The Jews in Their Land in the Talmudic Age (70-640 C.E.)* (Cambridge: University Press, 1989), p. 144.

114. Zangenberg, "'Open Your Eyes and Look at the Fields': Contacts between Christians and Samaria according to the Gospel of John," in *Samaritan Researches Volume V*, pp. 3, 84-94; Zangenberg, *Frühes Christentum*, pp. 192-96.

way of salvation especially referring to the Samaritans. For example, there are no indications that the old prophetic traditions about the eschatological return of the ten lost tribes were ever applied to the Samaritans in intertestamental literature (*Ant* 11.131-135; 4 Ezra 13:40-47, 48-50; *m. Sanh.* 10.3; *m. Yad.* 4.4; cf. also Commodianus, *Carmen apologeticum* 941-996 in CCL 128), and it is no wonder that this tradition was never invoked when NT authors deal with Samaritans.[115] A "third way" between Samaritans and Jews was obviously only viable by theologically distancing oneself from both groups. Whenever John deals with Samaritans, his underlying agenda also is to reassure his own position over against Judaism as his prime sociological and theological background *and* opponent.

For Luke, who shows a much more stereotyped approach to everything Samarian, Samaritans never are of any importance on their own. Instead of getting involved in a discussion of their theological tenets, as John did to a certain extent, Luke follows the undifferentiated categorization of 2 Kgs 17:24-41 and labels both Samaritans and Samarians as *allogeneis* of a special kind. For him, their behavior either functions to illustrate Jesus' peaceful intentions (Lk 9:51-56) or as a paradox example to promote his understanding of ethical behavior (Lk 10:25-37) or to exemplify a proper response to Jesus' purifying power (Lk 17:11-19).

Consequently, the more Christianity lost contact with Judaism in the second century due to growing numbers of converted non-Jews in its ranks, the more Christian authors also lost sight of Samaritans who — due to their emphasis of Torah and priesthood — probably were very much considered part of the Jewish world. Thus, Christian authors ironically continued and intensified the marginalization Samaritans always had been subject to in most of contemporaneous Jewish literature. John's model of a "third way" on the basis of introducing a new category of worship and belief might have opened up that direction. Having no identity of their own, pagan Samarians were soon absorbed into the general theological approach toward the Gentile world. Luke's narrative of the encounter between Simon and Philip could have helped pave the way. As in Jn 4, the Spirit functions as the category to overcome "the other" and to formulate the new basis of religious life and group affiliation.[116]

It is striking that Justin Martyr, who had been born in Neapolis (*1 Apology*

---

115. Not even in Jn 10:16 ("lost sheep"). On the lost tribes, see Zangenberg, *Frühes Christentum,* pp. 206-9; J. Charlesworth, "Lost Tribes," in *ABD* 4 (1992), p. 372. Contrary to Böhm, *Samarien,* p. 310 and passim, I cannot see that Luke attempts to retrace the fulfillment of Isa 49:6 in history when dealing with Samaritans.

116. O. Cullmann, "Von Jesus zum Stephanuskreis und zum Johannesevangelium," in *Jesus und Paulus,* ed. E. E. Ellis and E. Grässer, Festschrift W. G. Kümmel (Göttingen: Vandenhoeck & Ruprecht, 1975), pp. 44-56.

1.1) and proudly called himself a *Samareus* (*Dialogus* 120.6), does not appear to have any intimate knowledge of Samaritan theology.[117] Samaritans do not even feature in his *Dialogue with Trypho*. He, like Irenaeus and Tertullian, was more interested in Simon Magus from Sebaste who, not himself a Samaritan, soon advanced to the status of a "messianic" figure for some or an arch-heretic for others. By elevating Simon to such prominent roles in many branches of early Christian literature, Simon lost touch with the region of his origin, and it soon did not matter anymore where he came from.

It is doubtful if Christian missionary activity was at all successful among Samaritans, despite or perhaps because of some interesting structural similarities between Christian beliefs and (heretical?) Samaritans like Dositheos.[118] Given theological positions like the ones featuring in John and Luke, Samaritans must have perceived Christians as part of the heretical, southern Jewish world. They might have been even more opposed to Christians because Christians not only disagreed about the proper interpretation of Torah and halakah, they even relativized and replaced Moses and his institutions with new religious categories. I cannot but conclude that the attraction of Christianity for Samaritans must have been very limited, and I agree with Martin Hengel, who called the Samarian mission of the Hellenists a mere "episode." I would be very willing to extend Hengel's statement to include Samaritans as well and cover the entire early Christian era.[119]

---

117. See B. Hall, "The Samaritans in the Writings of Justin Martyr and Tertullian," in *Proceedings of the First International Congress of the Société des Études Samaritaines, Tel Aviv, April 11-13 1988*, pp. 115-22; R. S. MacLennan, *Early Christian Texts on Jews and Judaism*, BJS 194 (Atlanta: Scholars, 1990), pp. 49-88.

118. On Dositheos, see above and Zangenberg, *Frühes Christentum*, pp. 157-64.

119. Hengel, "Historiker Lukas," p. 177; Zangenberg, *Frühes Christentum*, pp. 231-33.

The Sanctuaries of the Baptism on the East Bank of the Jordan River

Michele Piccirillo, O.F.M.

The Gospel Narratives

The Gospel accounts of Christ's public mission open with the preaching of repentance by John the Baptist in the region of the Jordan River: "Then Jerusalem and all Judea and the whole Jordan district made their way to him, and as they were baptized by him in the river Jordan they confessed their sin" — the Evangelists write unanimously.[1] Among them also Jesus "came from Nazareth in Galilee and was baptized in the Jordan by John" (Mk 1:9-11).

John the Evangelist particularly mentions two locations along the river in which both Jesus and John preached and baptized: "Bethany, beyond the Jordan" (Jn 1:28) and Aenon near Salim, located west of the river in the Beisan territory.[2] While John was in Bethany, beyond the Jordan, a delegation from the leaders at Jerusalem was sent to him, to ask whether he was the Messiah, Elijah, or the promised Prophet. It was there that John presented Jesus as the Lamb of God to the crowd and to his disciples.

The presence of Jesus at Bethany beyond the Jordan is again recalled in a discussion between the disciples of John (who was baptizing at Aenon) and some Jews: "So they went to John and said, 'Rabbi, the man who was with you beyond the Jordan, the man to whom you bore witness, is baptizing now, and everyone is going to him'" (Jn 3:26). Furthermore, the Evangelist relates that to avoid the imminent danger of being arrested during his visit to Jerusalem, Jesus "went back again beyond the Jordan to the place where John had previously

---

1. See Mt 3:1-6; Mk 1:4-5; Lk 3:2-3; most of the notes to this chapter are added by J. H. Charlesworth, the editor.

2. Jn 3:22-23; Eusebius, *Onomasticon* 40.1.

433

been baptizing and stayed there, and many of them in that place believed in him" (Jn 10:40-42).

An Exegetical Contribution

Let me add here an exegetical study prepared by Professor Giuseppe Segalla regarding the Gospel narratives: "This happened at Bethany, beyond the Jordan, where John was baptizing" (Jn 1:28). This topographic clause, placed at the end of the first scene narrated in the Fourth Gospel, has not attracted much attention from exegetes. Nearly all the last great commentaries ignore it, interpret it symbolically, or hastily dismiss it. In my opinion, the most significant exegetical treatment remains that by R. Schnackenburg in his monumental commentary.[3]

Among the very scant specific bibliography of the last two decades, the only article worthy of note — both for its amplitude (thirty-four pages) and the seriousness with which it presents the *status quaestionis* of modern research since 1658 (J. Lightfoot) — is the one by Reiner Riesner, published in the 1987 *Tyndale Bulletin*.[4] I believe that this article led to him being asked to write the entry "Bethany beyond the Jordan" in the *Anchor Bible Dictionary*.[5] In his *Tyndale Bulletin* article, Riesner defends as "worthy of consideration" (pp. 43 and 58) the hypothesis that identifies Bethany with the region of Batanaea, basing his arguments on the Targum and Talmud (pp. 53-54). Having treated the text-critical problem, which strengthens the customary use of "Bethany" in the text (pp. 32-34), he puts forward eight separate hypotheses regarding locations supported by first-class documentation and incisive critique. He finally concludes: "In our review of the various proposals for a solution we have found that along with the view that identifies Bethany with the Wadi al Kharrar opposite Jericho, only this other attempt at a solution, namely that Bethany is to be identified with Batanaea, is worthy of consideration" (p. 43).

According to him, the two hypotheses that carry the most weight are those regarding Wadi al Kharrar and Batanaea. In his treatment of the subject, Riesner

---

3. R. Schnackenburg, *The Gospel according to St John,* trans. K. Smyth, 3 vols. (New York: Crossroad, 1987).

4. R. Riesner, "Bethany beyond the Jordan (John 1:28): Topography, Theology and History in the Fourth Gospel," *TynBul* 38 (1987): 29-63. Also see B. Pixner, *Wege des Messias und Stätten der Urkirche,* ed. R. Riesner, 3rd ed. (Giessen: Brunnen Verlag, 1996); see pp. 14, 77, 178, 209-10, 383; see esp. "Bethanien jenseits des Jordan" on pp. 166-79.

5. R. Riesner, "Bethany beyond the Jordan," in *ABD* 1:703-5. Also, see the bibliography he supplies on p. 705.

does not use exegesis nor archaeology, but rather historical topography. The Gospel texts are used to give a local perspective, such as the distance between one location and another as presupposed by the text. There is no critical consciousness of the chronology in the documents cited as proof of the thesis, as in the texts from the Targum and Talmud, for the magical change of "Bethany" to "Batanaea."

I get the impression that he supports the "Batanaea" thesis in deference to his friend Bargil Pixner, O.S.B., to whom he dedicates the article. Pixner, albeit with less critical clarity and more fantasy, proposed and defended the same thesis in a more recent article (1991) published as part of a series of his studies, duly edited by Riesner. As an exegete I will limit my exposition to the exegetical aspect of Jn 1:28, leaving others to treat the archaeological aspect, which moreover is decisive, this being a historic geographical site. I will thus examine the text from three perspectives: that of (1) textual and philological criticism; (2) morphological criticism as a parenthetical clause of location; and (3) its significance within the narrative logic of the Fourth Gospel.

The Text

Not only the majority of codices but also the most ancient papyri from the third (P[75]) and second (P[66]) centuries propose the reading "Bēthania(i)," while the other, "Bēthabara(i)," is treated as secondary. Despite his support for it, Origen himself admits that nearly *(schedon)* all the manuscripts in his possession read "Bēthania(i)." It is therefore useless going over the same ground. A short critical discussion can be found in B. M. Metzger,[6] while a more detailed treatise appears in the commentary by C. K. Barrett.[7] Apart from having the majority of codices in its favor, "Bethany" is also the *lectio difficilior*. One could not explain the reading "Bēthania(i)" if the original were "Bēthabara(i)"; whereas the inverse can be, and has been, explained by Origen himself — not as a text-critical issue but because of the difficulty of identifying the location.

As for the philological aspect, one must note that no definite article precedes "Bēthania(i)," but the article is always used with the name of a region like Galilee or Judea. Therefore the name refers to a locality (Bethany) and not to a region (Batanaea).

---

6. B. M. Metzger, "ἐν βηθανίᾳ ἐγένετο {C}," in *A Textual Commentary on the Greek New Testament*, 2nd ed. (New York: American Bible Society, 1994), p. 171.

7. C. K. Barrett, *The Gospel according to St John* (London: SPCK, 1965), p. 146.

The Literary Form: A "Parenthesis Indicating a Place"

G. Van Belle has studied the "parentheses" in John's Gospel in an excellent and massive monograph, even though, unfortunately, the meticulous effort of classification is not matched by a critical guiding stand.[8]

Parenthetical notes are frequent in the Fourth Gospel; they are a stylistic characteristic and usually contain explanations and specifications the author offers to his readers. Regarding their content (pp. 106-12), Van Belle identifies as many as seventeen different categories: the translation of Hebrew and Aramaic words (Jn 1:38, 41, 42), the explanation of Jewish custom (2:6; 4:9; 18:28; 19:40), etc.

Our text is classified under "indication of place" (p. 108). The twenty-two texts classified under this category are further subdivided. Jn 1:28 is classified as "an indication inserted at the end of the scene." The texts in Jn 6:10, 18, 23, 59; 8:20; 11:18, 30; 21:8 belong to the same form. The precise indication of the location is aimed at rendering the account historic, that is, set in a precise place as opposed to "out of place." These specifications, as is the case of the remaining "parenthetical" indications, have an objective value for the Evangelist. The precise localization of the scene, as well as the translation of a word or the explanation of a Jewish custom, was addressed to readers that by his time were physically and culturally remote from Palestine, the place of origin of the tradition.

The parenthesis identifying the location in Jn 1:28 is in strict relationship with Jn 10:40 that recalls it, but without repeating the name "Bethany." Another text related to Jn 1:28 is 3:23. Here the place where John was baptizing is called Aenon near Salim. From the context (3:26) it is evident that this is yet another location different from "Bethany beyond the Jordan," and is to be sought to the west (3:22). It seems therefore that John was baptizing in diverse places, as would an itinerant prophet. There are many hypotheses regarding this locality.

The most ancient tradition places "Bethany beyond the Jordan" at Wadi al Kharrar in the Perea region, ruled by Herod Antipas, who imprisoned and later killed John the Baptist. The small Jordan tributary, about 2 kilometers long, could well be considered the Jordan River. Ever since Origen the difficulty of locating "Bethany" here is archaeological, inasmuch as no remains have been found that witness to a first-century settlement. The name had already been lost in the third century (Origen). But the historical memory of John the Baptist and Elijah is found in the most ancient itinerary, that of the pilgrim from Bordeaux (333 C.E.). According to R. Schnackenburg, this memory could explain the question asked as to whether John was "Elijah" (Jn 1:21).

8. See G. Van Belle, *Les parenthèses dans l'Evangile de Jean* (Leuven: Leuven University Press, 1985). Page references to this work are placed in parentheses in the text.

Figure 62. Upper Galilee and beginning of the Jordan Rift Valley below Mount Hermon.   Courtesy of J. H. Charlesworth

If, as some maintain, "Bethany" had been an invention, one would not understand the reason for choosing a name that caused difficulty to the reader. If it does create difficulty, this means it is the result of a historical record, even if the name has been lost through history.

"Bethany beyond the Jordan" in the Narrative Setting of the Fourth Gospel

Apart from being an indication of place or time for the reader cut off from the original traditions, the parenthetical notations serve a symbolic narrative function in the Evangelist's narrative setting. The inclusive narrative in the first section of the Fourth Gospel (Jn 2:1–4:54) is renowned: it begins and ends in Cana (2:1-11; 4:46). Another more beautiful example is the narrative of the passion (Jn 18–19): the action moves from the Garden at Gethsemane (18:1) to the garden in which there was a new tomb in which Jesus was laid (19:41).

What then is the narrative-symbolic function of the indication "Bethany beyond the Jordan"? It is the primary location in which John the Baptist witnesses to Jesus (1:19ff.), in negative (1:19-27) and positive (1:29-34) forms. The indication of the locality acts as a hinge between the two testimonies. The narrated testimony then passes through chapter 3 (3:22-30), Jesus himself referring to it in chapter 5 (5:34-36), and concludes in 10:40, where Jesus physically returns "to the far side of the Jordan," to indicate narratively the end of the *synkrisis* (shared role in the economy of salvation) between Jesus and the Baptist. Jesus returns to the place where he started, to avoid being arrested (10:39). The conclusion in 10:41-42 synthesizes the witness of John the Baptist at the end of the ministry of Jesus, who had performed "signs." Those "who believed in him" cited two reasons as proof that Jesus, and not John, was the Messiah, Son of God. The first — a negative reason — was that John had performed no sign. The second was the assertion that "all John said about this man was true." Now, what did John say about Jesus? John proclaimed that Jesus was "the Lamb of God that takes away the sin of the world"; that he "would baptize in the Spirit" and "was the Son of God." But all this becomes clear only at the end of the Gospel.

What is more interesting is the relationship with Bethany, to which Jesus goes in the following chapter 11. One can suppose that Jesus goes from "Bethany beyond the Jordan" to Bethany in Judea, home to Lazarus, Martha, and Mary. Is this the reason why 10:40 does not mention the former? In his moving from "Bethany beyond the Jordan" to Bethany in Judea, Jesus carries out that which was said of his relationship with John the Baptist: (1) in fact, Jesus performs his greatest sign, the resurrection of Lazarus, a prelude to his own resurrection, the supreme sign (2:18-19); and (2) the second part of chapter 11 (11:45-53) relates that the *synedrion* (Jewish council) gathers to decree the condemnation of Jesus, interpreted by the Evangelist as a death "not for the nation (Israel) only, but to gather together in unity the scattered children of God" (11:52). Thus John's first revelation comes true, "Behold the Lamb of God that takes away the sin of the world" (1:29).

The two Bethanys are the places of both the initial and final revelations of Jesus, in relation to the witness given by the Baptist, whose witness dominates the first part of the Gospel. In the second part of the Fourth Gospel (Jn 13–21), the witness of "the Beloved Disciple" comes to the fore.[9]

---

9. See J. H. Charlesworth, *The Beloved Disciple* (Valley Forge, Pa.: Trinity, 1995).

Exegetical Conclusions

We could summarize the results of this analysis of Jn 1:28 in a few short theses.

1. Bethany is undoubtedly the name of the place, beyond the Jordan, where John was baptizing. If the first rule of exegesis is to respect the original text, "Bethany" is not to be changed to "Batanaea."

2. C. Kopp, cited in a note by R. Schnackenburg, maintains that the identification of "Bethany beyond the Jordan" with Wadi al Kharrar "is the most serious archaeological lacuna" (n. 43). It is certain that the Evangelist intended to indicate a locality known during his time, or at least remembered in the tradition of his Gospel. The Synoptic Gospels speak only of the baptism of Jesus "in the river Jordan." The Fourth Gospel is more precise and has more detailed traditions about John the Baptist in relation to Jesus. The name "Bethany beyond the Jordan" is not justified by any direct symbolic motivation; neither by that of Joshua who crossed the Jordan. This is because it would have sufficed to say "beyond the Jordan." Neither is the connection of Bethany with Elijah mentioned. The reason for which Bethany is remembered must therefore only be a result of a historical tradition.

3. The unusual location "Bethany beyond the Jordan" enables the Evangelist to create a narrative unity in the *synkrisis* between John and Jesus. In this narrative the place where Jesus was first revealed is also the location from which Jesus sets out on his final journey to Jerusalem, where he would die as the "Lamb of God" (Jn 1:36), and to which he returns, among his disciples, to bestow upon them the Spirit (20:21-23). Bethany in Judea is the passage to fulfillment (13:1; 19:30).

As often happens in the Fourth Gospel, the symbolic value is built upon the narrative, in space and time, even if the actual storytelling is reduced to the barest minimum to allow more room for its theological significance. The concise and essential language used by the Evangelist creates problems. "Bethany beyond the Jordan" creates problems both for the exegete and the geographer. For this very reason there remains room for further research.

The Pilgrims

We find the first mention of the localization of the place of the baptism on the river Jordan in Origen (toward the mid–third century), who places the baptism of

Jesus and his stay beyond the Jordan, at Bethabara.[10] Eusebius of Caesarea (in the *Onomasticon* under the entry regarding Bethabara ["beyond the Jordan where John baptized for penance"]) takes up Origen's text and adds that the place was known to "many believing brothers who, wishing to be reborn, are baptized there in the living current" — a wish that, in the words of the same Eusebius, was also that of Emperor Constantine which he confided to the bishops gathered at Nicomedia: "Finally time is ripe (to receive) the salvific seal (baptism) which I once thought I could receive in the waters of the Jordan, where, we are reminded, the Savior was baptized as an example for us" (*Vita Constantini* 4.62.1-2).

The third witness is that of the anonymous pilgrim of Bordeaux who identifies the site of the baptism at a place five miles from the Dead Sea: "(From the Dead Sea) to the Jordan, where the Lord was baptized by John — there are five miles," near the crossing point of the Roman road that united Jerusalem and Jericho with the Via Nova Traiana on the Transjordanian high plateau to the east, passing through Livias and Esbus, the road used by pilgrims to reach the Memorial of Moses on Mount Nebo.

The Byzantine Buildings

The first to mention a sacred building in relation to the Jordan River is Theodotius, who stated that Emperor Anastasius ordered the building of a basilica on the bank of the river (ca. 530).

The witness of the anonymous Pilgrim of Piacenza (570) and John Moschus (second half of the sixth century) distinguishes topographically between the baptism of Jesus commemorated on the riverbanks and the place near the spring of Aenon/Sapsafas two miles eastward, where Jesus and John stayed. The same distinction is made in the Madaba Mosaic Map (sixth century):[11] Bethabara on the river and Aenon Sapsafas, beyond the Jordan. The Pilgrim of Piacenza is the first to note that the site of the baptism was in front of the monastery of Saint John: "Not very far from the Jordan where the Lord was baptized there is the monastery of Saint John, very big; in it there are two hostels for the pilgrims" (*Itinerarium* 12.4).

The pilgrims agree in remembering a votive column that was crowned by a metallic cross, infixed in the water in the middle of the river. The most explicit

10. The texts are conveniently collected by D. Baldi in *Enchiridion locorum sanctorum, documenta S. Evangelii loca respicientia*, 2nd ed. (Jerusalem, 1955).

11. M. Piccirillo, ed., *The Madaba Map Centenary, 1897-1997* (Jerusalem: Studium Biblicum Franciscanum, 1999).

Figure 63. The Saint John Monastery on the west bank of the river Jordan (Qasr al-Yahud). Courtesy of M. Piccirillo

is Theodotius: "At the place where the Lord was baptized there is a marble column, and on top of it there has been set an iron cross." Moreover, the Georgian calendar of the church of Jerusalem (sixth to seventh century) recorded three liturgical meetings by the riverbank on the Feast of the Epiphany: on the fourth of January, on the eve of the feast of the baptism, the assembly meets on the other side of the Jordan; on the fifth of January, the vigil of Epiphany, it gathers on the banks of the river; and on the sixth of January a solemn assembly is held at the Jordan, to commemorate the baptism in the Church of Saint John the Baptist, built inside the monastery.

From the sixth century on the monastery of Saint John, known by the Greek monks as the Prodromos and by the Arabs as Dayr Mar Yuhanna or Qasr al-Yahud, remained the topographical point of reference for the localization of the Sanctuary of the Baptism on the corresponding banks of the river. The Georgian calendar and other pilgrims until the medieval period relate the existence of a second church on the eastern bank of the river in front of the monastery of Saint John. The political situation during the Crusades — when the river Jordan became a frontier line between the Latin Kingdom of Jerusalem and the Sultanate of Damascus — resulted in the abandoning of the sanctuaries across the river, due to the "fear of the Arabs." From Jerusalem the pilgrimage to the west bank of the river has continued till today.

441

Figure 64. The Tell Mar Liyas on the south bank of Wadi al-Kharrar near the spring east of the river Jordan.   Courtesy of M. Piccirillo

The Rediscovery of the Eastern Sanctuaries

Modern exploration of the eastern sanctuaries, started in 1899 by Fr. Federlin, had partially identified the remains of the church on the eastern banks of the river in the estuary of the Wadi Kharrar, in front of the Monastery of Saint John, and the remains of the laura of Sapsafas near the spring of Kharrar on the tell Mar Liyas, 2 kilometers to the east. The two sites had been visited until February 1947. Fr. Augostinovich was the last to describe the ruins. As a result of the 1967 war, the river Jordan became once again a fortified boundary. The peace process and the celebrations of the Christian millennium opened a new period of research.

The government of Jordan has in fact chosen the Jordan River with its sanctuaries as a symbol of the Jordanian participation in the jubilee celebrations: "Jordan, The Land, and River of the Baptism," as can be read in the logo chosen for the celebration. A decree promulgated by King Hussein, on September 10, 1997, set up a "Royal Commission for the development of the park of the Baptism of the Lord the Messiah (Peace be upon him) in the Jordan Valley." As a result of the royal decision, the Department of Antiquities of Jordan started the archaeological exploration of the wadi, which resulted in the discovery of a large ecclesiastical complex in the estuary of the Wadi Kharrar near the river Jordan, and of a chapel paved with mosaics on the northern slope of Tell Mar Liyas overlooking the spring of 'Ayn Kharrar.

The interest that led to the setting up of this royal commission for the development of the sanctuaries of Wadi Kharrar is primarily due to the enthusiasm of Prince Ghazi ben Mohammed. On August 11, 1995, he took Fr. Eugenio Alliata (from the Archaeological Mission on Mount Nebo) and me to visit the Wadi Kharrar, an area the military situation had rendered inaccessible.

On the tell near the spring, we saw only what had been seen and noted by Fr. Augustinovich in 1947. About 50 meters from the bank of the wadi, we were able to collect potsherds pertaining to the Byzantine period and others belonging to different first-century pottery types, together with some fragments of stone vases typical to the Jewish environment. These are well-known types and are in fact the first archaeological witness to establish an area of human habitation by the spring during the first century. They help us affirm that the later writings of the Byzantine period, witnessing to the existence of the village of Bethany beyond the Jordan, should be considered seriously. This notwithstanding, the historical weight of the witness of Origen, who probably precipitously gave heed to his informers, had concluded that the village did not exist on the eastern bank of the river. Origen also proposed emending the Gospel text by substituting Bethany with the toponym Bethabara. Thus there are two topographic realities that do not exclude each other — Bethabara at the river Jordan and Bethany at the spring of Wadi Kharrar, just as we read in the Madaba Mosaic Map. The publication of the new material found during the three-year excavations by the Jordanian mission will substantiate the conclusion we have proposed after our first visits to the site.

The Cemeteries of Qumran and Celibacy: Confusion Laid to Rest?

Joseph E. Zias

While nearly all serious scholarship on the Dead Sea Scrolls has focused on the texts themselves, there has been an ongoing and unresolved argument over the nature of the site since its excavation in the 1950s, with many conflicting theories. As with many other archaeological controversies in the Holy Land, Qumran and the Dead Sea Scrolls have engendered debate and dissension among scholars,[1] and have destroyed careers and brought lawsuits between individuals as well. For decades, much of this debate has centered around whether or not Qumran is the Essene settlement site referred to by Pliny the Elder and Dio Cocceianus,[2] and the relationship of the 850[3] documents found in

---

1. H. Shanks, "Blood on the Floor at New York," *BAR* 19, no. 2 (1993): 63-68.

2. While Philo and Josephus discuss the Essenes, they never refer in specific geographical detail to the community west of the Dead Sea as Pliny and Dio Cocceianus do. See M. Stern, *Greek and Latin Authors on Jews and Judaism* (Jerusalem: Israel Academy of Sciences and Humanities, 1974), 1:538-40; G. Vermes and M. D. Goodman, *The Essenes: According to the Classical Sources,* Oxford Centre Textbooks 1 (Sheffield: JSOT Press, 1989).

3. According to Emanuel Tov in a November 10, 1999, seminar on "The Greek Texts from the Judaean Desert," sponsored by the Orion Center, the estimated number of documents from Qumran is presently about 850.

Special thanks are due to Dr. Olav Rohrer-Ertl, who was kind enough to permit a brief study of the anthropological material in Munich, and Stephan Pfann from the Center for the Study of Early Christianity (Israel), who provided me with his English translations of de Vaux's field notes on which this analysis is based. I would also like to thank Magen Broshi for his helpful and insightful advice on the last stages of the writing and Joan Taylor, who graciously allowed me to read her most comprehensive and encyclopedic latest article prior to publication. Thanks are also due to the Orion Foundation and the Foundation for Biblical Archaeology for their partial funding and the critical eye of Emile Puech and Marcel Sigrist at the Ecole Biblique for allowing me the use of their library facilities. All errors in interpretation are mine alone.

444

eleven caves in and near the settlement. Parallel to this ongoing controversy has been a renewed interest and challenging debate over the role in the community of women and children, whose graves were found in the cemetery, and thus the inevitable question of alleged Essene celibacy. While the debate over the role of women in Qumran began in the 1950s,[4] within the last decade it has intensified and generated a spate of articles dealing with the cemetery[5] and celibacy,[6] in particular the role of women and children within the Essene community.[7] While these scholars have produced some excellent scholarly works on the topic, they have neglected, in my opinion, to fully understand that the solution to the Qumran cemetery in particular must involve several disciplines, particularly physical anthropology. Therefore, we have attempted to reassess these difficult issues by expanding the research domain, employing a combination of archaeological, anthropological, historical, and literary disciplines.

The Cemetery

While the majority of scholars have theorized for decades that Qumran was the Essene settlement described by Pliny and others, and that the scrolls found there belonged to the Essene community, there is a small but very vocal dissent put forth by N. Golb that disavows any connection between the settlement on the plain and the documents found mainly in the caves to its west and northwest.[8] One of the principal arguments against the orthodox Qumran/Essene hypothesis put forth by F. M. Cross and J. T. Milik and popularized by

---

4. N. H. Richardson, "Some Notes on IQSa," *JBL* 76 (1957): 108-22.

5. R. Hachlili, "Burial Practices at Qumran," *RevQ* 16 (1993): 247-65; O. Rohrer-Ertl, F. Rohrhirsch, and D. Hahn, "Uber die Grabenfelder von Khirbet Qumran, insbesondere die Funde der Campagne 1956," *RevQ* 19 (1999): 3-47.

6. H. Stegemann, *The Library of Qumran: On the Essenes, Qumran, John the Baptist, and Jesus,* English trans. of German original (Grand Rapids: Eerdmans; Leiden: Brill, 1998), pp. 193-98.

7. L. Elder, "The Woman Question and Female Ascetics among Essenes," *BA* 57 (1994): 220-34; Z. J. Kapera, "Some Remarks on the Qumran Cemetery," and E. Schuller, "Evidence for Women in the Community of the Dead Sea Scrolls," both in *Methods of Investigation of the Dead Sea Scrolls and the Khirbet Qumran Site: Present Realities and Future Prospects,* ed. M. O. Wise et al., Annals of the New York Academy of Sciences 722 (New York: New York Academy of Sciences, 1994), pp. 97-113 and 252-65; Puech, "The Necropolises of Khirbet Qumran and Ain el-Ghuweir and the Essene Belief in Afterlife," *BASOR* 312 (1998): 21-36; J. Taylor, "The Cemeteries of Khirbet Qumran and Women's Presence at the Site," *DSD* 6 (1999): 285-323.

8. N. Golb, "Khirbet Qumran and the Manuscripts of the Judean Wilderness: Observation on the Logic of Their Investigation," *JNES* 49 (1990): 103-14; Golb, *Who Wrote the Dead Sea Scrolls?* (New York: Scribner, 1995).

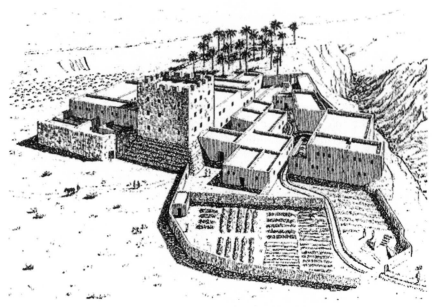

Figure 65. Proposed reconstruction of Qumran in first century C.E.
Courtesy of B. Balogh

G. Vermes,[9] is that researchers have known from the 1950s that the finding of women and children in several graves that lay east and southeast of the main cemetery presented certain diagnostic problems if the site was Essene and its inhabitants were exclusively a community of celibate adult males, as described by Josephus (*War* 2.120), Philo of Alexandria (*Hypothetica* 11.14), and Pliny the Elder (*Natural History* 5.17.4).

Five individual burials (Q32-36) containing women and children, excavated by R. de Vaux in the *extension sud* of the main cemetery, are all orientated along an east-west axis.[10] Furthermore, these burials are archaeologically dissimilar in several ways from the estimated 1,100 burials of males in the main cemetery with their strict north-south orientation,[11] of which 28 have been ex-

---

9. Schuller, "Evidence for Women," p. 253.

10. Along with these burials was T37, which was orientated along a north-south axis and conforms archaeologically to those burials from the main cemetery. The skeleton interred there was "uncertain (later male?)" in Elder's table ("The Woman Question," p. 227), indeterminate in Pfann's notes of de Vaux. In both Taylor and Rohrer-Ertl, however, this skeleton is suddenly sexed as female, which is difficult to understand, as it was not even present in the sample in Munich. Moreover, Rohrer-Ertl lists its height as 159 centimeters, which makes it highly doubtful that this person was female.

11. Tomb 4 was oriented east-west, with the head in the east. It was very similar in style to

---

446

cavated. South of these tombs is another sector labeled the *cimetière sud,* which contained about 30 burials of varying direction. Of these estimated 30 tombs, 4, containing one woman and three children, were excavated. Moreover, these burials along the margins of the main cemetery are relatively shallow, one (T35) being but 40 centimeters beneath the surface, whereas the burials in the main cemetery are 1.5–2.0 meters below the surface. The issue now facing us arises because all the adult male burials in the main cemetery are laid out in orderly rows along a north-south axis with their heads to the south and their feet to the north, while the women/children are east-west with their heads to the west. Common to many of the burials is a large stone marking one or both ends. Thus all individuals, regardless of age and gender, are buried beneath a pile of field stones with marking stones occasionally denoting the head and/or feet. Anthropologically, this is where the similarity ends. These anomalous east-west tombs, relatively few in number, are almost without exception on the margins of the main cemetery. De Vaux,[12] the French Dominican archaeologist in charge of the excavations, regarded these burials in the extensions as contemporaneous with the main cemetery at Qumran, an assertion based on the appearance of ceramic sherds in the fill. While we will later discuss this assertion — also recently advocated by E. Puech[13] — de Vaux's cemetery chronology has been accepted uncritically by the entire academic community, whether they be Dead Sea Scrolls scholars or archaeologists. While it is perfectly understandable why textual scholars may have misinterpreted the archaeological evidence, it is difficult to understand why two generations of field archaeologists have overlooked some of the most fundamental and basic tenets in the profession of burial archaeology.

For example, this apparent spatial separation by age and gender along the cemetery margins, unknown in Jewish burial practice, has led to numerous theo-

---

the tombs of the main cemetery, and as the head was in the east, it could be neither Christian nor Islamic. According to Emile Puech (personal communication), this could have been from the earlier period of the Essene settlement when the north-south burial axis had not been formalized, or it may have been from a later phase, as it was on the margin of the main cemetery. Elder ("The Woman Question," p. 226) has it north-south while it appears on de Vaux's map as east-west, and therefore it seems that there is some confusion here among scholars. As the tomb contained the remains of an adult male, it may be of little concern to our argument, other than possibly serving as the basis for the intrusive Bedouin cemetery. The Bedouin, perceiving a southwest burial, easily could have mistakenly regarded this interment as Islamic. The fact that the Bedouin burials are spatially adjacent to T4 gives a certain amount of credence to this argument.

12. R. de Vaux, *Archaeology and the Dead Sea Scrolls* (London: Oxford University Press, 1973).

13. Puech, "Necropolises," p. 25.

ries that attempt to explain the inclusion of the women and children in what was originally believed to have been an exclusive all-male community at Qumran. Several theories have been put forth to explain the anomaly. One theory proposed by Vermes is that these women and children were not members of the Essene community living at Qumran but were sectarians living elsewhere who were brought to the site for burial, thereby explaining their anomalous burial along the margins of the main cemetery.[14] Others, such as L. Elder, have posited that there are two differing phases at Qumran in which celibacy and noncelibacy alternate, whereas M. Broshi[15] claimed that these women and children were Essenes living elsewhere, who upon death were brought to the site for burial.[16]

The Anomalous Burials

Five tombs (T32-36) excavated in the southern extension by de Vaux,[17] believed to be Essene, were orientated along an east-west axis. Tombs 32 and 33 reportedly contained botanical evidence that the deceased were buried in coffins, which appears highly doubtful because if they were Islamic burials — a point I will discuss later — burying in coffins would have been strictly forbidden. Secondly, as they are chronologically and culturally intrusive, the wood — had it existed — would have been better preserved than the wooden coffins found in tombs 17-19 of the main cemetery. What was reportedly found and described as brown dust is either funerary clothing, which had in time disintegrated, or the remains of palm branches used as a funeral bier.

14. G. Vermes, *The Complete Dead Sea Scrolls in English* (New York: Allen Lane/Penguin Books, 1997), p. 45.

15. Elder, "The Woman Question," p. 229; M. Broshi, "The Archaeology of Qumran: A Reconsideration," in *The Dead Sea Scrolls: Forty Years of Research*, ed. D. Dimant and U. Rappaport, STDJ 10 (Jerusalem: Magnes Press and Yad Izhak Ben-Zvi; Leiden: Brill, 1992), p. 112.

16. As a result of extensive archaeological excavation to date, we have an ever increasing body of knowledge concerning Jewish burial practices, particularly extended family burial in Jerusalem during the Second Temple period. See A. Kloner, "The Necropolis of Jerusalem in the Second Temple Period" (Ph.D. diss., Hebrew University, 1980); L. Y. Rahmani, "Ancient Jerusalem's Funerary Customs and Tombs," *BA* 44 (1981): 171-77, 229-35; *BA* 45 (1982): 43-53, 109-19; B. Zissu, "The Necropolis of Jerusalem in the Second Temple Period: New Discoveries, 1980-1995" (M.A. thesis, Hebrew University, 1995). There is also a vast amount of material found in the Mishnah and other Jewish sources upon which scholars can draw, which, although written later, reflects normative burial traditions during the late Second Temple period. Consult D. Zlotnick, *The Tractate Mourning* (New Haven: Yale University Press, 1966).

17. De Vaux, *Archaeology*, p. 58.

These five burials and the four in the southern cemetery contained the skeletal remains of four children and five adult females. Three of these nine tombs contained grave goods, which is quite rare for normative Jewish burial practices.[18] Two burials (TS1 in the southern cemetery and T32 in the southern extension) presented a total of forty-nine beads fashioned from glass paste, agate, carnelian, amber,[19] and other hard stones that had apparently been worn around the ankles. A finger ring was also found in T32 while earrings were found in T33. Only on rare occasions has jewelry been found in Jewish tombs from the Second Temple period such as the tomb excavated by V. Sussman and J. Zias,[20] and when it is found it is usually such items as finger rings or rings in pierced ears that are difficult to remove without injuring the body of the deceased. Glass, stone, or metal beads are rarely if ever found in a Jewish tomb for reasons of halakah that expressly prohibit the "wanton destruction" of objects that are valuable and still usable.[21] Therefore, the finding of forty-nine beads, a finger ring, along with a pair of earrings in T32 — which the excavator described as a "different type" of tomb — along with the east-west orientation of both tombs immediately prompted our skepticism as to whether or not these anomalies were culturally part of the normative Essene burial tradition, whether it be at Qumran, Ain el-Ghuweir,[22] or any other Jewish cemetery of the

---

18. In family tombs, particularly in the Jerusalem area and Jericho (R. Hachlili and A. Killebrew, "Jewish Funerary Customs during the Second Temple Period in the Light of the Excavations at Jericho Necropolis," *PEQ* 115 [1983]: 115-25), grave goods will be found. These grave goods, however, usually fall into the category of items of daily life, which after use in the burial would either be broken (e.g., cooking pots) to prevent their reuse or oil lamps left in the tombs for halakic reasons. Ceramic spindle bottles and glass perfume bottles will also be found in tombs from this period. However, if one takes into account the number of items and types found in tombs, divided by the number of individuals interred there, one can see that the ratio is very low. Secondly, rings, beads, and earrings are items of a highly personal nature as opposed to objects of daily life and are seldom if ever found in Jewish tombs. If and when they do occur, as in Jericho, they are found in wooden coffins of women and children. According to Ann Killibrew (personal communication), one of the archaeologists involved in the Jericho excavations, no bead necklaces were found, and the number of beads that appeared in the wooden coffins totaled less than five. While beads were found in an Essene-type tomb at Hiam el-Sagha, the lack of information from the site and the beads that have been lost make assigning any ethnic affiliation on the basis of this one tomb a complicated prospect (Puech, "Necropolises," p. 33 n. 28).

19. The amber beads commonly used in Bedouin folk medicine are in such near perfect condition that one cannot escape the impression that they have not been in the ground for any length of time. Due to their softness, such beads usually become fragile, dull in texture, and pitted, whereas these beads still retain their luster.

20. V. Sussman and J. Zias, "A Burial Cave on Mount Scopus," *'Atiqot* 21 (1992): 89-103.

21. Evel Rabbati 9.23. Cf. Zlotnick, *The Tractate Mourning*, p. 72.

22. P. Bar-Adon, "Another Settlement of the Judean Desert Sect at 'En el-Ghuweir on the

period.[23] Surveying the M.A. thesis of B. Zissu,[24] which documents the excavation of tombs in Jerusalem during the years 1980-95 and includes a catalogue comprising 140 Second Temple tombs, one finds no mention of beads, particularly around the feet, among the few small finds mentioned.[25] Therefore, based on burial practices and traditions, our initial suspicion that these anomalous tombs excavated in the southeastern end of the Qumran cemetery may be neither halakically Jewish nor datable to the Second Temple period appears to be confirmed in light of the known archaeological evidence.[26]

Islamic Burial Practices

Like all cultures, Islamic burial practices are well defined with a certain set of rules that culturally define the individual in death as in life. In the desert regions of the ancient Near East such as the Judean and Negev deserts, Islamic, particularly Bedouin, burials are found atop all archaeological tells, nearly without exception. At sites such as Arad, Tell Sheva, Tell Malhatta, Tell el-Hesi, to name just a few, hundreds of Bedouin burials were excavated. Due to time constraints as

---

Shores of the Dead Sea," *BASOR* 227 (1977): 1-25 (originally appeared in Hebrew in *ErIsr* 10 [1971]: 72-89).

23. A survey of the literature of known Jewish tomb sites such as Meiron with 197 individuals from the first century to the fourth century C.E., produced no beads. E. Meyers et al., *Excavations at Ancient Meiron, Upper Galilee, Israel, 1971-72, 1974-75, 1977* (Cambridge, Mass.: American Schools of Oriental Research, 1981). No beads were found in the tomb atop Mount Scopus; see Sussman and Zias, "A Burial Cave on Mount Scopus." This tomb contained an additional eighty-eight individuals.

24. Zissu, "The Necropolis of Jerusalem in the Second Temple Period."

25. As many of the more than 900 Second Temple tombs discovered to date in Jerusalem have not been adequately published (Amos Kloner, personal communication), we asked the last four district archaeologists for Jerusalem (L. Y. Rahmani, A. Kloner, D. Bahat, G. Avni) if they had ever come across such a find, and their answers were in the negative. See Kloner, "The Necropolis of Jerusalem in the Second Temple Period," in which he reported 650 burial tombs, all of which failed to show any evidence of bead necklaces.

26. Frank Cross, one of the original scholars involved in Qumran research, acknowledged at the SBL meetings in Boston in 1999 that the skeletal material "emerging from the cemeteries in 1956 appeared to be unusually fresh to the excavators." As these graves were exclusively from the eastern extensions and the southern cemetery, it is precisely this material that is problematical and has the highest concentration of women and children in relation to the cemetery as a whole. This may in fact be one of the reasons why de Vaux and others over the years paid scant attention to the material from the extensions, whereas others have believed and argued that it was an attempt at marginalizing the role of women at the site. Panel discussion on meaning of the Dead Sea Scrolls, November 21, 1999, Hynes Center Ballroom B, 7:00–8:30 P.M.

well as pressure from certain religious circles in Israel, these burials, though frequently encountered in the field, are unfortunately seldom reported or published, aside from an occasional footnote. One notable exception to this underreporting is the site of Tell el-Hesi, which has been studied by J. K. Eakins.[27] In the series of volumes documenting the excavations at this site, volume 5 deals exclusively with the Bedouin cemeteries from fields V, VI, and IX, which comprise a total of 861 burials spanning the years 1400 to 1800 C.E. What is remarkable and perhaps defining in this report is the inclusion of grave goods in the Bedouin burial complex. Unlike Jewish and to a lesser extent Christian burials, in which the individual is (not) rarely buried with accompanying personal items, these individual burials of men, women, and children that contained grave goods, mainly necklaces, ear and finger rings, and bracelets, ranged from 13.3 percent in field V (19 graves out of 143) to 31 percent in fields VI and IX (96 out of 310). In field V, for example, out of 15 adult female graves, 10 (i.e., two-thirds) contained bead necklaces. Of the 96 adult females interred in fields VI and IX, 57, or nearly 60 percent, were buried with bead necklaces. Therefore, in Bedouin burials, burial with jewelry — particularly bead bracelets and necklaces — is normative for women despite the assertion by some Islamic scholars that such a custom was forbidden by Islamic law.[28] Other defining factors in Islamic burial custom are the practice from early times of burying the individual along an east-west axis with large field stones marking both head and feet, and the relative shallowness of depth in comparison to other ethnic groups. Lastly, in hostile desert environments where hyenas and other predators roam freely, an elongated pile of undressed field stones both marks the burial and prevents hyenas from scavenging the body of the deceased.[29] These five burial practices (east-west orientation, grave goods, shallowness of depth, field stone coverings, marking stones for the head and feet) define Bedouin burials with a high degree of certainty, whether they are atop archaeological tells, near Qumran, or in cemeteries adjacent to isolated Bedouin encampments in the region.[30]

27. J. K. Eakins, *Tell El-Hesi: The Muslim Cemetery in Fields V and VI/IX (Stratum II)*, ed. J. R. Spencer with K. G. O'Connell, ASORER, Joint Archaeological Expedition to Tell el-Hesi 5 (Winona Lake, Ind.: Eisenbrauns, 1993).

28. N. Brosh, ed., *Jewelry and Goldsmithing in the Islamic World: International Symposium, the Israel Museum, Jerusalem 1987*, Catalogue — the Israel Museum 320 (Jerusalem: Israel Museum, 1991), p. 3; Brosh, ed., *Islamic Jewelry*, Catalogue — the Israel Museum 281 (Jerusalem: Israel Museum, 1987).

29. Human skeletal remains are often found in zoological surveys of hyena dens in the Judean Desert, apparently coming from these shallow Bedouin tombs that have been violated by predators (L. Horowitz and J. Kerbis, "Hyenas at Home," *Land and Nature* 16 [1991]: 162-65).

30. While these five criteria are well known to the experienced field archaeologist and

When one views the Qumran cemetery in light of these five defining Islamic burial traditions, one simply sees that these east-west burials (T32-36) of men, women, and children, which lie on the southeast margin of the Qumran cemetery and were originally believed to imply spatial segregation by gender, are chronologically intrusive and thus are post-Byzantine, Islamic burials. Likewise, the same is true for the four anomalous tombs in the *cimetière sud*. Precise dating of these burials on the basis of the jewelry and beads contained therein is difficult, as there is scant published research on the topic of late Islamic jewelry. However, because the burials themselves are oriented along an east-west axis, and conform completely to Islamic burial patterns, one could infer that they date from the early periods of Islam up until the present. According to Islamic specialists, the beads from T1 and T32, totaling forty-nine, are relatively recent and common to the Mamluk (1250-1517 C.E.) and later Turkish periods.[31]

Osteo-archaeology and the Question of Women

Following excavation of the main cemetery, de Vaux excavated the tombs to the east (T32-37) — two in the northern extension and four from the southern extension — in 1955 and 1956. The human skeletal remains were transferred to two European laboratories and two Jerusalem institutions for further examination. The material transferred to France unfortunately has neither been published nor adequately studied by scholars. The remaining material that was excavated in 1953 and studied by Kurth and allegedly lost is housed in the Ecole Biblique in Jerusalem. The remaining material from T20

within the Islamic community, they apparently are lesser known to the community of scholars working within Qumran studies. It is perhaps ironic that the French archaeologist/diplomat C. Clermont-Ganneau opened one tomb on November 29, 1873, that he noted could not be Moslem, due to its north-south orientation (*Archaeological Researches in Palestine* [London: Palestine Exploration Fund, 1896], 2:15-16). Over 130 years later, Qumran scholars attempting to interpret the field excavations of de Vaux have overlooked this fundamental rule of burial archaeology.

31. Similar beads can be found in the collections of the Israel Museum, according to N. Brosh, the curator in charge of Islamic art, as well as in the Museum of the Bedouin in Kibbutz Lahav (special thanks to Orna Cohen, curator in charge of the Museum of the Bedouin). According to Palestinian collectors of ethnic jewelry, the beads are commonly referred to as *halabat* beads on the belief that they have curative powers for a wide variety of diseases. One of the Qumran beads is similar to a bead exhibited in the Museum of the Bedouin and is catalogued as having curative powers for one suffering from dental pain. As one of the women in the cemetery was suffering from severe dental abscesses in the upper maxilla that had eroded away much of the alveolar bone, it is not surprising that this bead was found in the burial.

to 37 and the southern cemetery has recently been published in an extensive study by O. Rohrer-Ertl.[32]

De Vaux's field notes indicate that aside from one problematic burial in T7, which Professor H. Vallois of the Laboratory of Anthropology in Paris labeled "Female?" the human remains from the main cemetery, some of which are now reportedly in Paris, were found to contain adult males only.[33] (The question mark Vallois appended after "Female" indicates that precise sex determination for that burial was difficult to assess with a high degree of exactitude.) Furthermore, he noted that the estimated stature of this individual was 160 centimeters, which statistically is decidedly out of the stature range of females of the period. For example, in the nearby site of Ein Gedi, the average stature of adult females during the Second Temple period was only 150.8 centimeters. Reviewing stature estimates reported in the anthropological literature compiled over the past twenty-five years for the region, one clearly sees that the possibility of a female during the late Second Temple period reaching 160 centimeters is practically nonexistent, as the mean stature for females from a random sample of five Jewish sites was 148.7 centimeters (see table 1). Therefore, although Professor Vallois was indecisive on the sex determination of this individual (Q-7), estimated stature alone, which is easier to determine, clearly reassigns this individual to the category of male.

Table 1: Estimated Stature of Jewish Females in the Second Temple Period

Site	Number	Minimum	Maximum	Mean
'En Gedi	10	146.7	154.5	150.8
Meiron	7	142.0	151.2	148.0
Mount Scopus	7	144.0	153.0	149.0
Gush Halav	7	142.9	156.7	147.0
Averages	Total: 31	143.9	153.8	148.7

Recently, two individual burials from the main cemetery (T22 and T24-II), originally regarded as male by Professor G. Kurth in the 1950s along with T37 in the extension, now appear as female in the latest study by Rohrer-Ertl.[34] These reassignments, however, again appear problematic in light of the estimated statures reported, 163, 159, and 159 centimeters, respectively, as well as on the ba-

32. Rohrer-Ertl, Rohrhirsch, and Hahn, "Über die Grabenfelder von Khirbet Qumran, insbesondere die Funde der Campagne 1956."

33. Puech, "Necropolises," p. 26.

34. Rohrer-Ertl, Rohrhirsch, and Hahn, "Über die Grabenfelder von Khirbet Qumran," p. 43, table 4.

sis of morphological characteristics that physical anthropologists employ to delineate males from females.[35] All four individuals for whom sex was indecisive (T7) or has been reassigned by Rohrer-Ertl (T22, T24-II, T37; see his catalogue at the end of the article, page numbers are not provided) statistically fall outside of the probable range of estimated statures for females of that period. Moreover, all four fall well within the range (159-168 centimeters) of stature that he and Kurth report for the males from the main cemetery. See the table I have prepared for this data. Therefore, as these estimated statures reported by Kurth and Rohrer-Ertl greatly exceed both individually and collectively the stature of Jewish females during the early Roman period, one must, in my opinion, statistically and methodologically now regard all four individuals as male. While some may argue that the stature difference of 11-14 centimeters between men and women is trivial by today's standards, one must note that of the four sites chosen at random, this difference exceeds that between males and females in antiquity in general. Thus, although variation is the rule in human biology, one can safely generalize regarding a feature such as stature in antiquity because the degree to which it varied in antiquity was less than that of today. One reason for this is that individual stature is a variable largely controlled by genetics,[36] and therefore, the endogamous nature of ancient societies tended to limit the range of biological variability within these groups as compared to today's world.

De Vaux, along with other scholars,[37] understandably also found it difficult to reconcile this indisputable evidence of women and children in the cemetery with Pliny's belief in celibacy. Furthermore, the fact that the women and children were on the margins of the site led to inevitable questions about the mar-

35. Morphological features that would be characteristic of male crania include large supraorbital ridges and low, sloping forehead (W. M. Bass, *Human Osteology: A Laboratory and Field Manual, Missouri Archaeological Society* [Columbia: Missouri Archaeological Society, 1985], p. 81). One diagnostic example would be illustration 9 of Rohrer-Ertl's recent article, which is labeled "Cranialansichten, Frauen," and contains two photos depicting the skulls recovered from T22 and T32. Contrary to the label, one can clearly see that T22, which was originally regarded as male by Kurth, possesses the above-mentioned masculine morphological features, especially when juxtaposed with T32, which is clearly female by all anthropological features. Furthermore, the fact that the stature of T22 is 163 centimeters makes it highly improbable that Q22 can be regarded as female.

36. D. Ortner and W. Putschar, *Identification of Pathological Conditions in Human Skeletal Remains,* Smithsonian Contributions to Anthropology 28 (Washington, D.C.: Smithsonian Institution Press, 1985), p. 33.

37. Elder, "The Woman Question and Female Ascetics among Essenes"; Schuller, "Evidence for Women in the Community of the Dead Sea Scrolls"; Taylor, "The Cemeteries of Khirbet Qumran and Women's Presence at the Site."

ginality of the women at Qumran. One way of reconciling this evidence was de Vaux's suggestion that women were not members of the community, or at any rate not in the same sense as the men buried in the same cemetery.[38] Later, Vermes was to propose serial celibacy for the community, with celibate and noncelibate groups coinhabiting the site.[39]

Chronological Incoherence

J. Taylor has published a detailed study on the cemetery material in which she correctly points out some issues associated with the sex determination of skeletons. Sex variation, she notes, quoting R. M. Weiss, will vary depending on the ethnic group, and "one must sex a new-found individual only in comparison to a well-analyzed population which requires multivariate methods and a very good knowledge of the particular characteristics of the population group under discussion."[40] While neither Kurth nor Vallois had that database available for comparison, today that is no longer the case, and to ignore the large databases available is to risk error. Suffice it to say, however, that experienced anthropologists can determine sex quite accurately when scientifically controlled blind studies on complete skeletons of known age and sex are available for comparison. This point is affirmed by D. Ortner, one of the most prominent forensic paleopathologists of today.[41] Therefore, with several reservations,[42] I believe that most of the preliminary sexing by experienced anthropologists such as Kurth and Vallois, while never adequately published, is essentially reliable though not 100 percent accurate, as the comparative data did not exist until the late 1960s. Fortunately, the material allocated to Germany, though very selective and incomplete, aside from tombs 32-37 and the southern cemetery, was restored in a proper manner by Rohrer-Ertl.

38. De Vaux, *Archaeology*, pp. 128-29.
39. Vermes, *Complete Dead Sea Scrolls*, p. 14.
40. R. M. Weiss, "On the Systematic Bias in Skeletal Sexing," *AJPA* 37 (1972): 239.
41. Ortner and Putschar, *Pathological Conditions*, p. 32.
42. After studying the material under the curacy of Rohrer-Ertl, I would reassign the very incomplete skeleton from tomb 34 that was assigned as "female?" as male. The femur has many of the physical characteristics that one would assign as male, in particular its length, which indicates that this individual had been 162 centimeters in height — highly unlikely for a woman of any age in antiquity. The width of the head of the femur is 43.5 centimeters, which is in the "gray area," the problematic range in which it is difficult to say whether this skeleton is definitely male or female. Had the dimensions of the femur been more gracile, I would have assigned it as indeterminate. As the estimated height of the individual is 162 centimeters, however, I would have to assign this as male.

Methodologically, it would appear that the material that was complete and in an exceptional state of preservation had been selected by de Vaux for further study and sent to Europe, whereas the material from the main cemetery that was fragmentary and thereby necessitating extensive laboratory reconstruction was reburied at the site. This assumption is based on the fact that in the Munich collection the only complete skeletons are those from the extensions, whereas the material from the main cemetery is incomplete and required much restoration by Rohrer-Ertl. This in and of itself is telling and arouses suspicion as to the chronology of the material. If one looks at the recent publication of Rohrer-Ertl[43] and the photographs of the crania (illus. 3-11), one clearly sees that the standardized anatomical measurements (table 2 of his report) taken of the crania of the males in the main cemetery are for the most part missing. This lacuna in the published data, all things being equal, means that due to the poor preservation of the material, the anthropologist was working with skeletal material that was incomplete and fragmentary and thus not amenable to measuring. As a consequence, important metrical data is not reported. Normally, this occurs with subadults or females, as the cortical bone is thinner and fragile, and therefore recovery is often incomplete and preservation is often poor at best. What is of particular interest in tombs from the cemetery extensions and the southern cemetery is that it is specifically those loci containing women and children, normally the least resistant to preservation, where one finds near total skeletal recovery and documentation. As time is an important factor in the preservation process, we have here this highly unusual situation in which the remains that have the least chance of being preserved are the best preserved. To the experienced anthropologist this means that the chronological coherence of the women and children, in comparison to the material from the main cemetery, is highly suspect. It was clear to me, upon seeing the material for the first time recently in Europe, that there was near total recovery of the unbroken skeleton remains from burials T32-33, 36, and from the tombs in the southern cemetery excavated in 1956. This material included the very fragile bones from the skeletons of the children, which is why Rohrer-Ertl was able to publish a nearly complete record of his anthromorphic data from these loci. When one has the opportunity to see the skeletal material firsthand, along with the burial data and grave goods, and to compare it to the poorly preserved and fragmented material from the main cemetery, it is difficult to avoid the obvious conclusion that these anomalous burials are simply Bedouin burials from recent periods (post 1450 c.e.) and thus chronologically intrusive.[44]

43. Rohrer-Ertl, Rohrhirsch, and Hahn, "Uber die Grabenfelder von Khirbet Qumran, insbesondere die Funde der Campagne 1956."
44. One need not see the material physically to come to this conclusion, as the published

Dental Evidence

Unlike bone, the highly mineralized nature of teeth makes them unique markers of human biological events. Bone is subject to remodeling, whereby cortical defects in the skeletons of young individuals or minor fractures disappear during growth, thus obliterating traces of one's biological past. Teeth, however, are incapable of altering their mineral structure, and therefore defects such as caries, abscesses, and attrition leave a permanent record of one's personal history.[45] This personal history is clearly seen in the skeletal remains from the ancient Near East due to the widely differing environments in the region that continue to leave their imprint on the dental record of the region's population. Desert environments subject the dentition to differing environmental stresses due to the highly abrasive nature of the foods consumed there, the way this food is prepared, and the difficulty in keeping windblown sand out of the daily diet. As a result, the dental attrition rate for individuals living in desert areas is greatly accelerated compared to those living in higher elevations, such as the Judean hills, Samaria, and Galilee, where the inhabitants do not face these environmental conditions to the same degree. Studies in Israel have shown that the attrition rate, expressed as the wear on the occlusal surfaces, differs greatly among populations, depending on the environment they inhabit.[46] When comparing peasants *(fellahin)* with desert Bedouin, significant differences already appear in young adults (twenty to twenty-four years old), and these rates nearly double in later years (thirty-five to forty-four years old). Thus the permanent molars for desert dwellers are worn down at an alarming rate when compared to nondesert dwellers. When viewing the dentition of the adults in the cemetery at Qumran, one clearly sees two differing lifestyles, that of the desert versus that of the uplands. Those individuals living in the desert for extended periods presented severe dental pathologies, including dental abscesses, antemortem tooth loss, and enamel wear in which the dentine was exposed. These pathologies typically associated with desert environments were present in the Bedouin skeletal material coming from the southeastern extensions. In comparison, the dentition of the males unearthed in the main cemetery was markedly different from the females in type and frequency of dental pathology. The surprisingly

photographs by Rohrer-Ertl, Rohrhirsch, and Hahn ("Über die Grabenfelder von Khirbet Qumran," pp. 37-45, illus. 3-11) clearly show the tremendous differences in preservation between the crania of the women and children and the males, the latter all having required extensive cranial reconstruction.

45. G. H. Sperber, "Paleodontopathology and Paleodontotherapy," *Journal of the Canadian Dental Association* 52 (1986): 835-38.

46. P. Smith, "Diet and Nutrition in the Natufians," *AJPA* 37 (1972): 233-38.

little wear on the posterior dentition was clear evidence of a differing diet and environmental history between the two groups. Therefore, it is clear from the dental evidence that the males interred in the main cemetery were not indigenous to the desert region but came to the site after their formative years, thus explaining the differential between the contrasting dental pathologies seen in the two populations. Had both groups shared a common past since birth, living under identical environmental conditions, these marked dental differences would not have been present.

The dental evidence (observed in the skeletal material) presented from the main cemetery, when compared to the females and children, supports the literary evidence of Philo and Pliny that males only came to Qumran from towns sometime after their twentieth year to join the desert brotherhood.[47] Their life span, however, was not long, as the average age at death, according to my calculations, was only thirty-four years.[48]

Discussion: Is Qumran Essene?

Much has been written about whether or not Qumran is the Essene site mentioned by the ancient sources.[49] Golb has been the most vociferous if not the

47. Vermes, *Complete Dead Sea Scrolls*, p. 42.

48. Stegemann (*The Library of Qumran*, p. 47) estimates thirty years as the average age of death, whereas I would estimate thirty-four years on the basis of the material I viewed in Munich. The difference between our estimates is probably due to his factoring in the females, as the mortality data for females in antiquity shows that their longevity was shorter than that of males. Josephus (*War* 2.151) writes that the Essenes are long-lived, most of them remaining alive over a hundred years. This he attributes to the simple and disciplined lives they led. As few actually lived past forty, many dying in their twenties, this is a gross exaggeration and raises the question of the truthfulness of Josephus's account of the Essenes. In fact, if longevity is a measure of the quality of life, then the mortality rate expressed by the cemetery data suggests that their health status was seriously compromised. One of the cardinal principles of paleopathology, the paradox of pathology, is that the lack of observed skeletal pathology may indicate a population that is unhealthy. If one enjoys good health and one's immune system is not compromised, then one survives these inevitable illnesses that all populations are subject to. The marks these chronic illnesses leave on the skeletal system show that their immune system was in fact robust and healthy enough to enable them to withstand these pressures. Thus, what was once believed to be a very unhealthy population in terms of observed pathology is today regarded as relatively healthier than one that evidences no gross pathology. In other words, they simply came down with an acute or chronic illness and were so immunologically compromised that they died immediately, leaving no skeletal signs of the illness.

49. Golb, "Khirbet Qumran and the Manuscripts of the Judean Wilderness"; Golb, *Who Wrote the Dead Sea Scrolls?*

most prominent scholar arguing against any possible connection between the Essenes and Qumran, with much of his argument being based on the cemetery finds. A portion of his argument rests on the eleven skeletons from the south cemetery, excavated by H. Steckoll and reported by N. Haas, which are clearly Bedouin burials.[50] Golb argues that the finding of women and children in the main cemetery "considerably reduced the chances [of connecting Khirbet Qumran with the Essenes], insofar as the claim had originally been built upon Pliny's description of a celibate community." Therefore, as "Pliny alone placed the celibate Essenes in a defined region of Judaea, the archaeologists insisted that Qumran was the place that he was alluding to."[51] Golb thought the 1,200 graves at Qumran were simply of "warriors who fought at Qumran" who had been massacred by the Roman army.[52] The absurdity of this was recently pointed out by Broshi in that the small site simply cannot sustain 1,200 individuals.[53] While Golb perhaps cannot be faulted for his naive belief that this is a military cemetery, what is beyond belief is his assertion that "approximately 10 percent of the skeletons . . . had broken bones" and therefore were soldiers.[54] Nearly all osteoarchaeological material that has lain in the ground for circa 2,000 years has broken bones due to taphonic changes. Furthermore, Qumran is located in the

---

50. N. Haas and H. Nathan, "Anthropological Survey of Human Skeletal Remains from Qumran," *RevQ* 6 (1968): 344-55. The ten graves excavated by Steckoll (Q38-47) are in my opinion scientifically totally unreliable and thus omitted from the report. The same conclusions regarding Steckoll can be drawn from Puech's ("Necropolises," p. 31) well-thought-out analysis of the problems surrounding the cemetery and the role of Steckoll in the excavating process. The latter was eventually ordered by the Israel Department of Antiquities to cease and desist digging these tombs in 1967, though not before he removed some objects from the site itself that were later sold on the open antiquities market. Since he published some of his illegal excavations, many scholars not working in the field of archaeology/anthropology have uncritically assumed that he was a trained archaeologist. For example, Elder ("The Woman Question," p. 224) cites Steckoll as a trained archaeologist, perpetuating the myth that his work is objective and scientific, whereas he was a journalist by profession and was more interested in the sensationalist side of the discipline than its historical and scientific aspects. Unfortunately, Taylor ("The Cemeteries of Khirbet Qumran and Women's Presence at the Site") likewise relies heavily on the observations of Steckoll. While it may strengthen the position of those in favor of engendered archaeology, it will ultimately severely weaken their arguments, some of which are creditable.

51. Golb, *Who Wrote?* p. 18.

52. Golb, *Who Wrote?* p. 34.

53. M. Broshi, "Was Qumran, Indeed, a Monastery?" in *Caves of Enlightenment: Proceedings of the American Schools of Oriental Research Dead Sea Scrolls Jubilee Symposium (1947-1997)*, ed. J. H. Charlesworth (North Richmond Hills, Tex.: Bibal Press, 1998), p. 30.

54. Golb, *Who Wrote?* p. 34. Y. Yadin (*The Temple Scroll* [Jerusalem: Israel Exploration Society, 1983], 1:324) also believed that the cemetery was a military cemetery, being the central cemetery for the region's fortresses dating from the time of John Hyrcanus.

Syrian-African Rift, an area susceptible to seismic activity where fragmented skeletal remains are the norm. De Vaux notes in his field notes time and time again that the skeletal material from the main cemetery was poorly preserved and fragmentary.[55] Moreover, had a massacre occurred in the region, one would expect to find a mass grave and not a well-planned cemetery. No mass grave was reported, nor was there any evidence of violence or trauma on the skeletal remains — something that would have been easily seen by the physical anthropologists — from the tombs in the main cemetery. Secondly, experience has shown that military cemeteries are somewhat unique and easily recognizable by the high level of traumatic injuries in the population, generally on the left side of the body, where soldiers usually attempt to ward off blows from a right-handed attacker. None of this was apparent in the Qumran cemetery. What is readily apparent is a uniform cemetery of adult males, laid out in well-arranged rows, suggesting that the cemetery had in fact been in use for an extended period of time. Furthermore, the cemetery presented criteria, although in some way different, that can unmistakably be associated with Jewish burial practices: individuals buried singularly or together, as in T16 and T24,[56] each of which contained two adult males; absence of personal grave goods; three burials in wooden coffins (T17 to T19); and three secondary burials (T11, 24, 37). Although interring two individuals in the same grave may appear unusual, in the light of Jewish burial practices, it is normative for one to be buried with "his brothers," and this simply implies a familial relationship among the deceased.[57]

55. J.-B. Humbert and A. Chambon, *Fouilles de Khirbet Qumran et de Ain Feshkha I,* NTOA Series Archaeologica 1 (Fribourg: Editions Universitaires; Gottingen: Vandenhoeck & Ruprecht, 1994), pp. 213-28.

56. While Kurth originally reported that tomb 24 contained two males, Rohrer-Ertl has since reexamined the remains and reassigned them as one male and one female. Having personally examined the material in question, I disagree with this reassignment, which was based on very fragmentary material. In fact, while studying the material, there appeared to be evidence of a third individual in the sample, unrelated to the other two. Therefore, I strongly suspect that mixing of the material occurred sometime after its transfer from Qumran to the laboratories, thus adding to the confusion. Taylor ("Cemeteries," p. 300 n. 52) alludes to these problems of material being mixed that Kurth was having while he was in Jericho prior to their shipment to Europe. Unfortunately, the material that was exceptionally well restored did not, with few exceptions, have any locus numbers or field numbers marked on the bones that could have prevented mixing. Working with human remains from an unfamiliar ethnic group is always problematical and can pose problems even for the experienced physical anthropologist. Furthermore, when the investigators (Kurth and Vallois) carried out their research nearly fifty years ago, they did not have access either to the comparative material or to the database — both of which are extremely important — available today. With these analytical constraints, some diagnostic errors are not inconceivable.

57. I disagree with Hachlili's assertion that burying the dead with their ancestors did not

The absence here of extended family tombs comprising several generations, as seen in other nearby Jewish sites such as Ein Gedi and Jericho, along with the absence of females and children, strengthens in my opinion the belief that we are dealing here in fact with a celibate community of males. Anthropologically, the only deviation from the Jewish burial norm seen here is the strict orientation of the graves along a north-south axis, which might reflect their opposition toward the priestly class in Jerusalem whom they disdained. According to Puech, Paradise and the New Jerusalem for the Essenes lay in the north,[58] and therefore these two factors alone would seem sufficient reason for the north-south orientation of the graves in the main cemetery.

Zissu has argued that some of the tombs found at a cemetery recently excavated near Jerusalem may belong to the Essene community. He bases this on the tomb typology, internment, the near total absence of grave goods, and the north-south axis of several tombs, as also found in the desert communities of Qumran and Ain el-Ghuweir.[59] As in Ain el-Ghuweir, men, women, and subadults are found in the Jerusalem cemetery,[60] confirming the belief that inferred spatial separation based on age and gender found in Qumran is untenable, whether it be the Judean Desert, Jerusalem, or elsewhere in the region. What is problematical and confusing with this cemetery is that several of the burials were later reused in the late Roman or Byzantine periods. One empty ossuary, grave goods dating from the second to the fourth-fifth century C.E., and the fact that many of the shaft graves are orientated both east-west and north-south further complicate matters. Thus, while some of the tombs are ethnically Jewish and probably Essene, without the final scientific report it is difficult to compare this cemetery with the cemeteries of Qumran and Ain el-Ghuweir.[61]

---

occur at Qumran ("Burial Practices at Qumran," p. 263). In two tombs we find two males, and in one of them the tomb appears to have been reopened for a subsequent burial at a lesser level, implying burying with one's family/relatives at a later date.

58. Puech, "Necropolises," p. 29 (quoting Milik).

59. B. Zissu, "'Qumran Type' Graves in Jerusalem: Archaeological Evidence of an Essene Community?" *DSD* 5 (1998): 158-71.

60. A total of forty-seven individuals were found (personal communication from Y. Nagar).

61. Hirschfeld's belief (Zissu, "'Qumran Type' Graves," p. 167 n. 21) that the Qumran cemetery actually belongs to the lower classes of the Jewish population of the Second Temple period, and that there is no reason to relate the cemetery to Qumran, is in my opinion unsustainable, as it would require males, females, and children to be represented, a datum totally different from what one observes at the Qumran cemetery. Furthermore, an all-male Jewish cemetery, in which women and children would be separated, is totally at variance with Jewish burial customs for the period.

The recent publication by K. D. Politis[62] in which he refers to the recent, systematic pillaging of 3,500 Nabatean tombs in Jordan, which are identical in style to those tombs in the main cemetery at Qumran, inevitably has raised some questions regarding the possible connection between Qumran and the cemetery east of the Dead Sea.[63] These 3,500 second-third century c.e. tombs contain grave goods of a type clearly indicating that they belong ethnically to another group in the region, the Nabateans. One need not be an archaeologist to realize that for looters to pillage 3,500 tombs without the prospect of enormous financial gain from the grave goods is unthinkable. At Qumran, however, because of the absence of grave goods, there was little looting following the cessation of the excavations.[64] It is clear that one cannot infer ethnicity during this period merely from the style of the tomb, as there are several other sites that in my opinion may not be Jewish, though they conform to the tomb style used in the main cemetery at Qumran. For example, C. M. Bennett writes that of the 507 tombs excavated in Jericho, 7 were from the Roman period, and these 7 can be divided into four types. The point I wish to make is that Qumran-style tombs, architecturally speaking, may not necessarily be Essene. Four of these tombs are similar to the tombs in the main cemetery of Qumran.[65] Because they contained grave goods, they, like the Nabatean tombs discussed by Politis, probably belong to another ethnic group inhabiting the region. Unfortunately, not enough information is contained in the Jericho report to infer either ethnicity or religious affiliation. Clearly, ethnicity in the archaeological record is a complex and multifactorial issue, and many different criteria are needed to infer ethnicity from burials, as tomb morphology alone tells us little. To categorize a cemetery as Essene, it must contain a minimum of four shared criteria: orientation, tomb architecture, demographic disparity, and few if any personal grave goods. Without these defining criteria, all appearing in the Qumran and Ain el-Ghuweir cemeteries, any attempt to assign definite Essene affiliation will remain unconvincing.

62. K. D. Politis, "Rescue Excavations in the Nabatean Cemetery at Khirbet Qazone 1996-1997," *ADAJ* 42 (1998): 614-16.

63. H. Shanks, "Who Lies Here?" *BAR* 25, no. 5 (1999): 49-53.

64. Experience has shown that much of the destruction to the region's archaeological heritage comes from the workers who have excavated the sites under the direction of foreign archaeological expeditions. Unfortunately, when the expeditions return home, the workers at times continue digging and looting the site for financial gain.

65. C. M. Bennett, "Tombs of the Roman Period," in *Excavations in Jericho*, vol. 2, *The Tombs Excavated in 1955-58*, by K. M. Kenyon (London: British School of Archaeology in Jerusalem, 1965), pp. 516-45. Puech has recently pointed out ("Necropolises," p. 33) that a proposed Essene occupation at Murabba'at, solely on the basis of a body buried in a shallow shaft, is not enough for a Jewish identification. It could be, he argues, a cemetery of some pre-Islamic nomadic people.

What is particularly noteworthy of the fifty-five individual remains cited here, which in my opinion are Essene (thirty-five from Qumran — this figure excludes T4, T32-36, which I have identified as Islamic burials — and twenty from Ain el-Ghuweir), is that there are few women, with the ratio of males to females being 8 to 1 (see table 2). Furthermore, in this Essene population from the two cemeteries, there is but one child. When viewing the demographic data in antiquity, subadult mortality (under eighteen years) usually averages around 50 percent, with some reported figures for this period as high as 68 percent.[66] Therefore, if on the average 50 percent or more of the Jewish population perished before the age of eighteen, which was normative in late Second Temple Jerusalem, the figure of less than 2 percent among the Essene community indicates that one is not viewing a community in which "be fruitful and multiply" was an ascribed norm.

Table 2: Demographics

Site	Total	Men	Women	Subadults
Ain el-Ghuweir	20	13	6	1
Qumran	35	34	1 (?)	0
Totals	55	47	7	1
as a %		87%	13%	
		47 of 54	7 of 54	

ratio of males over females is 8-1

Conclusions

Much of what has been written about Qumran during the past fifty years, particularly on the gender issue, has centered around the authors of antiquity, especially Pliny the Elder's (23-79 c.e.) remark on the "tribe of Essenes, that it has no women and has renounced all sexual desire" (*Natural History* 5.73). Further supporting the view that the Essenes did not bring wives into the community, Josephus wrote that they were regarded as sources of dissension (*Ant* 18.21), and Philo stated that "no Essene takes a wife, because a woman is a selfish creature, excessively jealous and an adept at beguiling the morals of her husband" (*Hypothetica* 11.14). These misogynistic passages, which reflect the commonplace negative attitude toward women in Hellenistic times, have been explained by scholars "as simply reflecting the desire of Greek writers to describe Jewish sectarian practices in terms understandable to the non-Jewish

---

66. J. Zias, "Human Skeletal Remains from the Caiaphas Tomb," *'Atiqot* 21 (1992): 78-80.

world."[67] If this is correct, perhaps one can and must redefine the Essene community in light of these negative remarks, as E. Schuller, Taylor, and Elder have attempted to do, as well as question the widely held view concerning the issue of male celibacy at Qumran in particular, which nearly all Qumran scholars have addressed.

Since the 1980s, L. H. Schiffman and others, including H. Stegemann, Schuller, Elder, and Golb, have mounted a literary as well as a theological attack that questions many of these views on the marginality of women at Qumran and attempts to accommodate the anthropological evidence.[68] Elder poses some interesting solutions to this difficulty, based on the literary and archaeological evidence found at the cemetery of Qumran, in that celibate males lived and were buried in Qumran whereas noncelibate males and females and their families lived at Ain Feshkha and Ain el-Ghuweir, even though no cemetery was found at the former site.[69] The absence of a cemetery may imply that upon death the sectaries living there were buried at Qumran. Unfortunately, her premises, like those of other scholars, are dependent on the belief that the anomalous Bedouin tombs of Qumran are chronologically contemporary with those in the main cemetery as well as an uncritical acceptance of the findings of Steckoll.[70]

Reviewing the archaeological evidence from the site of Ain el-Ghuweir, some 15 kilometers south of Qumran, which was excavated by P. Bar-Adon in the late 1960s, one finds nineteen graves contemporaneous with Qumran that, with one exception, are oriented in a manner identical to those found at the main

67. L. H. Schiffman, *Reclaiming the Dead Sea Scrolls* (Philadelphia and Jerusalem: Jewish Publication Society, 1994), p. 129.

68. L. H. Schiffman, *Sectarian Law in the Dead Sea Scrolls: Courts, Testimony, and the Penal Code*, BJS 33 (Chico, Calif.: Scholars, 1983), pp. 12-13, 214; H. Stegemann, "Some Aspects of Eschatology in Texts from the Qumran Community and in the Teachings of Jesus," in *Biblical Archaeology Today: Proceedings of the International Congress on Biblical Archaeology, Jerusalem, April 1984*, ed. J. Amitai (Jerusalem: Israel Exploration Society, 1985), p. 410; Schuller, "Evidence for Women in the Community of the Dead Sea Scrolls"; Elder, "The Woman Question and Female Ascetics among Essenes"; Golb, "Khirbet Qumran and the Manuscripts of the Judean Wilderness"; Golb, *Who Wrote the Dead Sea Scrolls?*

69. Elder, "The Woman Question," p. 229.

70. Puech critiques her article by pointing out that her hypothesis cannot be proven on the basis of either archaeology or the textual evidence ("Necropolises," p. 33 nn. 14, 17). Aside from de Vaux, Broshi, and Puech, few if any recognized Qumran scholars have come from the world of archaeology, which unfortunately has resulted in numerous errors and misunderstandings in attempting to interpret the site. In my opinion, it is precisely these three scholars who have come the closest to correctly interpreting the site and the cemetery, whereas textual scholars and others understandably have not been able to critically understand and evaluate the somewhat complicated archaeological and anthropological data at hand.

cemetery of Qumran. The one anomaly (T15), like those found on the southeast margins of Qumran, is interred along an east-west axis and, according to the excavator, may be intrusive.[71] What is interesting about these burials is that demographically, while they contain both sexes, only one subadult was reportedly discovered.[72] Secondly, a very short distance across the wadi is clearly a small Bedouin cemetery of unknown age, in which all the graves are defined by piles of stones along an east-west axis.[73] This is responsible in my opinion for the confusion among Qumran scholars, and is perhaps the crux of the entire gender issue. Collectively, in both the Jewish and Bedouin cemeteries of Qumran and Ain el-Ghuweir, the field stone–covered tombs on the surface are virtually identical visually down to the large marking stone on one or both ends. The Essene males in the main cemetery at Qumran had the head (south) and foot (north) ends of their tombs marked with a large stone, while the Bedouin did the same for men, women, and children in both sites, although they usually placed the larger stone near the head. On the surface, only the axis of orientation differs visually and culturally between Bedouin and Jew. Thus it is apparent from the archaeological evidence that the nomadic Bedouin, inhabiting the area for centuries, were well aware of the Qumran cemetery with its estimated 1,100-1,200 burials and simply utilized the available space on the margins according to the prevailing Islamic customs of the times. Referring specifically to Ain el-Ghuweir, Bar-Adon mentions that "Bedouin in the area are expert in differentiating, according to orientation of tomb, between ancient graves and Bedouin burial sites of recent origin."[74] This may explain why the Bedouin tombs of Qumran and Ain el-Ghuweir have not been pillaged, unlike the region's caves, as the chance of finding scrolls or grave goods of commercial market value is nil.

Unfortunately, the academic community has overlooked the obvious and regarded all the Qumran burials as being chronologically from the same period and cultural horizon.[75] Certain obvious criteria, however, including the rela-

71. Bar-Adon, "Another Settlement," p. 12.

72. The anthropological report was never published, which is unfortunate as twenty individuals were noted among the nineteen tombs excavated, again suggesting multiple burials as in Qumran, though they are not mentioned specifically in the publication. Elder ("The Woman Question," p. 225) misstates the gender ratio here as eight women and children and twelve males, whereas Bar-Adon clearly states that the correct figure is six women, one child, and thirteen males. Almost everyone misstates the number of tombs excavated. Instead of citing the correct figure of nineteen, Zissu ("'Qumran Type' Graves," p. 169) and Hachlili ("Burial Practices at Qumran," p. 253) both quote seventeen while Puech ("Necropolises," p. 27), Taylor ("Cemeteries," p. 310), and Elder ("The Woman Question," p. 225) all quote twenty.

73. Bar-Adon, "Another Settlement," p. 12.

74. Bar-Adon, "Another Settlement," p. 12.

75. Clermont-Ganneau, *Archaeological Researches in Palestine*, 2:15-16. In 1873 Clermont-

tively shallow depth of graves — one of which (T35) was 40 centimeters below the surface[76] — the presence of women's grave goods, the east/west axis, the head in the west facing Mecca to the south in T35 and T36, and the near complete recovery of fragile subadult skeletal material, should have immediately raised serious questions regarding the chronological coherence of this sample. The failure of scholars to recognize these defining, differing burial traditions has led to confusion in the scholarly world, in Qumran studies in particular, for nearly five decades.

Demographically, serious interpretive problems are encountered here if one argues in favor of the nuclear family unit in a reproductive or biological sense, however modified, as part of the Essene tradition. Whereas no published text from Qumran mandates sexual abstinence, there are six passages in which celibacy can clearly be inferred,[77] and thus the picture emerging from the two cemeteries[78] lends support to Pliny and Philo's belief that celibacy was the rule and that continuity was facilitated via adoption or proselytizing.[79] S. J. Pfann's recent reading of 4QSerekh ha-'Edah' (4Q249a), in which he presents textual evidence for celibacy for both married and unmarried members of the community, appears rather convincing, thus adding an additional passage to inferred celibacy.[80] The early date for the text (mid–second century B.C.E.) is significant here, as it implies that celibacy was an important ideological theme within the

---

Ganneau opened one grave and remarked that these north-south graves "are clearly distinguished from the modern Mussulman graves by their orientation, the longer axis in every case pointing *north and south,* and not east and west." These remarks suggest that the Bedouin cemetery probably was in existence, and he, like many other scholars of the nineteenth century, knew from their orientation that these burials were chronologically and culturally intrusive as they do not appear on his map of the site, which includes the extensions to the east of the main cemetery (2:15, cemetery of Kumran, illus. A, "General Plan of the Burying-Ground").

76. The majority of Bedouin graves in Tell el-Hesi average 30-140 centimeters in depth (Eakins, *Tell el-Hesi,* p. 8).

77. Elder, "The Woman Question," p. 225.

78. It is not without a note of irony that de Vaux's helper E. M. Laperrousaz always spoke of cemeteries in the plural. See E. M. Laperrousaz, *Qoumran, l'établissement essénien des bords de la mer Morte: histoire et archéologie du site* (Paris: A. & J. Picard, 1976), pp. 19-25. Unfortunately, Laperrousaz's habit seems to have been ignored by the scholarly community aside from a brief footnote here and there.

79. Totally celibate communities can survive quite well for hundreds of years and increase their numbers at a rate greater than natural biological conditions could produce. A case in point is the Shaker community in the United States, which began in 1774 with 9 members coming from England. Celibacy for men and women was strictly enforced, and by proselytizing and conversion they totaled 6,000 in nineteen communities by 1840. Cf. L. Foster, "Shakers," in *The Encyclopedia of Religion,* ed. M. Eliade (New York: Macmillan, 1987), 13:200-201.

80. S. Pfann et al., *Qumran Cave 4,* DJD 36 (Oxford: Clarendon, 2000).

community from its founding, thus providing further corroborative evidence that celibacy existed in Qumran from its inception.

Philo mentioned that the Essene community accepted members from the outside, but he expressly stated that they were "men of ripe years" (*Hypothetica* 11.3), and the absence of women in his account correlates with the cemetery evidence of Qumran. Josephus believed that some Essenes ascribed to total celibacy, which was definitely a norm for a large proportion of the community, but described another group of Essenes in which marriage was permitted. For those celibate members, adoption was permitted in order to instruct the adoptees in the rules of the community (*War* 2.120; *Ant* 18.20), but again no mention of sex is specified. The accounts of Pliny and Philo therefore conform completely to the demographic picture in the Qumran cemetery, whereas the second scenario of Josephus, the marrying Essenes, is problematical unless one accepts Pfann's reading of 4QSerekh ha-'Edah,' that they did marry but were obligated by Essene law to practice celibacy, which the cemetery evidence from all three cemeteries certainly suggests. The total number of burials which I regard as Essene is 103, taking into account that some of the burials from the Jerusalem cemetery may be later. In this population of 103 individuals there are no infants and but 3 children between the ages of five and ten. Normally, one could expect around 50 subadults in a population of 100 adults, whereas we have but 3. Demographically, therefore, the only viable alternative for the population to increase over time is that proselytizing and adoption take preference over procreation, thus permitting historical continuity. Furthermore, the total lack of infants as well as the absence or near total absence of women at Qumran strongly implies that, demographically, one is not observing a transitional phase in cultural norms, progressing from nuclear families to institutionalized celibacy, but rather a fully evolved and mature phase of development that had already coalesced prior to its existence in Qumran. That is to say, the picture emerging from the Qumran data implies that the ideological and theological beliefs for this community had developed elsewhere and had not evolved there within the community itself.[81] Had it been otherwise, the evidence from the Qumran cemetery would have presented a different demographic pattern; instead, what we perceive here appears to be exclusively a homogenous population of mature adult males (with the exception of the female from T9 on the margin of the main cemetery), thereby substantiating both 1QSa 1.8-9 ("At the

---

81. In Vermes' work on the history of the community (*Complete Dead Sea Scrolls*, p. 58), he clearly echoes this belief: "It goes without saying, however, that the initial phases of the community's existence must have preceded by some years or decades the actual establishment of the sect at Qumran."

age of 20 years [he shall be] enrolled") and 1QM 7.3-4 ("No boy or woman shall enter their camps, from the time they march out of Jerusalem to war until they return").[82] In a recent article, Puech estimated that the percentage of females in the population at Qumran was in the area of 2.0 to 2.5 percent,[83] challenging Elder's earlier figure of 30 percent,[84] whereas on the basis of this new analysis I would have to reduce this figure to 0 to 2 percent.[85] Women and children simply are not buried separately from men in Judaism, which is why the discovery of a female in the northern extension may be somewhat problematical as well as questionable. The findings from the cemetery at Ain el-Ghuweir and Jerusalem, where one finds men, women, and children interred without any spatial segregation based on age/gender, confirm this most basic and fundamental fact in Jewish burial practices. Therefore, one could reasonably ask, was the female in the northern cemetery (T9) at Qumran a member there or simply an outsider brought in for burial or even perhaps someone who died there during a visit? The fact that she is buried "outside" the main cemetery may have far-reaching implications for any attempted historical reconstruction. While some scholars may argue that the sample size is too small and nonrepresentative in relation to the main cemetery, one must realize that demographically in a "normal" Second Temple Jewish cemetery, approximately 50 percent or more of the skeletons in the sample will be subadults and not sexed and the remainder will be male or female. Therefore, the chances of being sexed as an adult male are one in four. With this in mind, the chances of thirty-five male skeletons in the main cemetery and extensions being all male, argues rather convincingly that the gender there is all male and that the sample size is more than adequate. In fact, given these probabilities, a sample size one-half to one-third this number would have been adequate.

Thus, while the biblical command "be fruitful and multiply" may have been a dominant theme in Judaism throughout the centuries, the literary, archaeological, and anthropological evidence presented here strongly suggests that it was not a universally held belief among all, particularly within the Essene community of Qumran, where instead a group of males chose to live "with only the palm trees for company" (Pliny, *Natural History* 5.7). The question before Qumran scholars now is, how and where were they "multiplying," or were they

82. Cf. Y. Yadin, *The Scroll of the War of the Sons of Light against the Sons of Darkness* (Oxford: Oxford University Press, 1962), pp. 71-72.

83. Puech, "Necropolises," p. 29.

84. Elder, "The Woman Question," p. 224.

85. I arrive at this figure by excluding the Bedouin tombs in the eastern and southern extensions as well as the material excavated by Steckoll in the 1960s for reasons stated above in n. 50.

multiplying at all? Insofar as Pliny said no one is born into the race (5.73), this total absence of infants is perhaps not so surprising and may be a defining characteristic in all Essene cemeteries. If our assumptions are correct, this could have far-reaching historical implications for the Jerusalem cemetery examined by Zissu, which spans four or five centuries and hints that it may in fact be a relic of the original Jerusalem Essene community because, despite the problematical time span, it shares several characteristics with the Qumran and Ain el-Ghuweir cemeteries.

The cemeteries of Ain el-Ghuweir and Qumran, in which only a single child was found,[86] call into account the veracity of Josephus's statement that there were two Essene groups, one celibate and one marrying. Marriage in and of itself does not necessarily mandate sexual intimacy, nor are the two mutually exclusive. Therefore, either Josephus is incorrect in his description of marrying Essenes, or if they did marry, celibacy may have been the rule as Pfann suggests, though Josephus specifically mentions that sex was for reasons of procreation only (*War* 2.161).[87] It is perhaps interesting that no other writer describes a second group of "marrying Essenes," which may call into account the accuracy of Josephus's description of the group as well as the contradictions inherent in the evidence. Modern historians who have studied the works of Josephus in fact have reported that he "can invent, exaggerate, over-emphasize, distort, suppress, simplify, or occasionally, tell the truth. Often we cannot determine where one practice ends and another begins."[88] The veracity and trustworthiness of his chronicle of Masada have been severely critiqued by S. Cohen, J. Magness, N. Ben-Yehuda, and lately Zias,[89] which may give one pause when one attempts

86. A thorough search of the archival material in the Israel Antiquities Authority failed to reveal the anthropological report upon which Bar-Adon's article was based. As one tomb was oriented east-west, however, my feeling is that this could very well have been the tomb of the child or from the Islamic period.

87. Stegemann, attempting to show that the celibacy issue was illusory, calculated the number of times an Essene could have sexual relations, according to halakah, at but twenty times over a ten-year period (*The Library of Qumran*, p. 197).

88. S. J. D. Cohen, *Josephus in Galilee and Rome: His Vita and Development as a Historian*, Columbia Studies in the Classical Tradition 8 (Leiden: Brill, 1979), p. 181.

89. S. J. D. Cohen, "Masada: Literary Traditions, Archaeological Remains and the Credentials of Josephus," *JJS* 33 (1982): 385-405; J. Magness, "Masada: Arms and the Man," *BAR* 18, no. 4 (1992): 58-67; N. Ben-Yehuda, *The Masada Myth* (Madison: University of Wisconsin Press, 1995); J. Zias, "Human Skeletal Remains from the Southern Cave (2001) at Masada and the Question of Ethnicity," in *Proceedings of the 50th Anniversary of the Dead Sea Scrolls*, ed. L. H. Schiffman, E. Tov, and J. VanderKam (Jerusalem: Israel Exploration Society, in press); Zias, "Whose Bones?" *BAR* 24, no. 6 (1998): 40-45, 64-66; see also the replies to critics of Zias, "Whose Bones?" in *BAR* 25, no. 2 (1999): 101-6.

to use Josephus as an accurate primary source on this issue, despite his assertion that he underwent a partial Essene education.[90] Cohen notes that Josephus, in the tradition of Greek authors, was expected to embellish the narrative and create something new, and that some of his changes were often the result of resolving theological difficulties posed by the text.[91] In the context of Second Temple Judaism and the narrative of the Essenes, the Jews had very serious theological problems over celibacy that may have been of less concern to Pliny and Philo, though the latter was a Jew. Marriage is the ideal in Judaism (Gen 1:28; 2:18, 24), and rabbinic writings even viewed celibacy as an unnatural state of affairs (e.g., *b. Yev.* 63a: "he who has no wife is not a proper man"; *b. Ned.* 64b: "a single man is called a dead man"). Therefore, to minimize problems over this difficult halakic issue for the Jews, the inclusion of the "marrying Essenes" may simply have been a literary device to cover up the difficult theological problems inherent in the narrative for a Jewish audience.

In light of the cemetery evidence, the hypothesis put forth by Cross, Milik, Vermes, and summarized by Schuller[92] now appears correct, as opposed to that of J. Baumgarten, Schiffman, and Stegemann,[93] who viewed marriage as a norm within the Essene community, particularly outside of the settlement at Qumran. While the beliefs of the latter three scholars may have some validity for Essenes living outside of the Dead Sea region, they appear untenable regarding Qumran and Ain el-Ghuweir and perhaps Jerusalem as well. As to whether or not the Essenes were celibate, single, or married, archaeological, anthropological, and mortuary evidence alone will, in and of themselves, tell us little. In my opinion, however, by combining all the evidence along with the demographic data emerging from the cemeteries of Qumran, the evidence speaks for itself.

Lastly, the ultimate interpretation of the cemetery at Qumran lies with the

90. Broshi ("The Creditability of Josephus," *JJS* 33 [1982]: 379-84) is somewhat less critical of the historical value of using Josephus for understanding the period in which Josephus lived and wrote. Others, however, have pointed out that his claim to have spent three years with the Essenes as part of his early education is clearly a fabrication, and if he was indeed with them, it was at most for six months (M. Black, *The Essene Problem* [London: Heffer and Sons, 1961], p. 34). Furthermore, Josephus's assertion that the initiation period to the community was three years is at variance with 1QS 6.21, which clearly states that the period was but two years. Broshi attempts to explain this contradiction by stating that the extra year was an additional year of study prior to the probationary period (M. Broshi, "A Day in the Life of Hananiah Nothos: A Story," in *A Day at Qumran: The Dead Sea Sect and Its Scrolls*, ed. A. Roitman [Jerusalem: Israel Museum, 1997], p. 68).

91. Cohen, *Josephus*, p. 233.

92. Schuller, "Evidence for Women," p. 253.

93. Schiffman, *Reclaiming*, p. 129; Stegemann, *The Library of Qumran*, pp. 193-98.

physical anthropologists, whereas its final historical interpretation lies with the Qumran scholars of today. I certainly believe it will eventually be solved, and hope that something can be learned from these fundamental but difficult lessons of the recent past that have led all of us astray for nearly five decades. Meanwhile, there is nothing in the cemeteries that should lead anyone "along the road to Damascus" to believe that Qumran, lying between Jericho and Ein Gedi, was anything but a monastic community of adult males, preferring the company of palm trees to women.[94]

94. Despite allegations that de Vaux and the Dominicans of the Ecole Biblique were interpreting the Essene community in light of Christian concepts of monasticism, it was actually the Americans who first associated the community at Qumran with monasticism. Recently, Broshi addressed this issue of monasticism in which he ended his article, independently and prior to my study, with the following sentence, which in my opinion sums up the issue: "If they were Essenes, then something seems to be quite clear: Qumran was a monastery" ("Was Qumran?" pp. 19-37).

Essene Community Houses
and Jesus' Early Community

Brian J. Capper

Discovering the Extent of the New Covenant Network of Poorhouses in the Judean Heartland around the Time of the Arrest of Jesus

Jesus' parable of the laborers in the vineyard (Mt 20:1-16) shows that there was a numerically significant, virtually floating population of underemployed in Galilee at the time of his public ministry, and that Jesus endorsed generosity toward this "underclass" and related care for them to the expression of God's will and kingdom. The purpose of this paper is to show, through the combination of evidence for the density of settlements in the Judean hills from Avi Ofer's archaeological survey of the region with close reading of ancient literary sources related to Essenism, that there existed a network of poor-care houses in southern Palestine at the time of Jesus' arrest. This well-organized network of poorhouses, run by the Essenes, extended to most if not all the villages and towns of the Judean heartland, and was of sufficient economic strength largely to relieve the problem and consequences of destitution in the region. The supporters and staff of these poorhouses had entered a relationship of mutual social and economic support that they called the "New Covenant." This social organization, a kind of "friendly society," offered social security to, and was deeply rooted in, the poorest classes of the region. It drew large numbers of members from the laborers and artisans who worked in the agricultural economy of rural Judea. The movement also had patrons from among the wealthy elite. Some of its Jerusalem patrons wanted to see Jesus installed as the Messiah and leader of the covenanted organization of the Poor.

The present author has elsewhere argued that the early community of Jesus' followers in Jerusalem embraced organized structures of poor-care similar to those employed by the Essenes (cf. Acts 2:42-47; 4:32–5:11; 6:1-6).[1] This pa-

---

1. See B. J. Capper, "Community of Goods in the Early Jerusalem Church," in *ANRW*

per supplies the wider socioeconomic context for understanding the appearance of these structures within the post-Easter community of Jesus' followers in Jerusalem. I will attempt to show that the activities of one of the village poorhouses of Judea, at Bethany near Jerusalem, are reflected in an event of the Gospel passion narratives, the anointing of Jesus as Messiah by his supporter from the Jerusalem elite, Mary (Mk 14:3-9; Jn 12:1-8). The etymology of "Bethany" will be shown to derive from *beth 'anya,* "house of the poor," or more precisely, "poorhouse," confirming the village's important role in providing alms and assistance to the poor of the Jerusalem area and to pilgrims. This poorhouse sought to acknowledge Jesus as the hoped-for Messiah, and many of its clientele accompanied Jesus on his triumphal entry into Jerusalem as Messiah of the Poor (Jn 12:12-19). The attempt by Jesus' supporters in and around Jerusalem to install Jesus as the leader of the New Covenant network of the Judean heartland contributed to the Sadducean authorities' actions against him. Thus this chapter aims to serve the goals of this volume by showing how new insights into the aims of Jesus and into events in his life can be won through the combination of archaeological evidence with close reading of literary sources.

The Distribution of the Essene Covenant in Rural Judea

Our first step to understanding the social character and role of the Essenes of Judea is to explore the distribution of the celibate male Essene population. Josephus is quite clear that there were over four thousand celibate male Essenes. He writes: "[T]hey hold their possessions in common . . . the men *(andres)* who practice this way of life number over four thousand. They do not bring wives into the community."[2] He says these celibate male Essenes live "in no one town *(polis),* but settle in large numbers in every one."[3]

This statement of Josephus has led some modern interpreters to assume that the Essenes at the time of Jesus were distributed throughout the towns of all Palestine,[4] but this is probably an incorrect deduction. Philo explicitly links

---

2.26.2, pp. 1730-74; Capper, "The Palestinian Cultural Context of Earliest Christian Community of Goods," in *The Book of Acts in Its Palestinian Setting,* ed. R. Bauckham, Book of Acts in Its First Century Setting, vol. 4 (Grand Rapids: Eerdmans, 1995), pp. 323-56.

2. *Ant* 18.1.5 §20-21; cf. Philo, *OmnProbLib* §75, where the number of four thousand is also given for the celibate male Essenes.

3. *War* 2.8.4 §124.

4. See E. Schürer, *The History of the Jewish People in the Age of Jesus Christ,* rev. G. Vermes, F. Millar, and M. Black (Edinburgh: T. & T. Clark, 1979), 2:563.

these male celibate Essenes to Judea. He writes that they live "in many towns of Judea, and in many villages in large and numerous societies."[5]

It seems likely that Philo's account, which is the earlier, gives a more accurate impression of the distribution of Essene celibates, occupying many of the villages and towns of the Judean heartland. Josephus's account, written after the massive upheaval of the revolt against Rome (66-70 C.E.), which led to huge movements of population, probably accommodates the description (possibly drawn from a common source) to the later situation.

Since Philo's description suggests the presence of celibate male Essenes in most if not all the villages and towns of the Judean heartland, it is useful to inquire about the number of villages and towns in this region during the early Roman period. If we exclude the essentially unpopulated wilderness of Judea and the only sparsely populated Beersheba-Arad Valley (the biblical Negeb), the number of villages and towns in the remaining, densely populated parts of Judea can be estimated, with some confidence, to around 200. A useful starting point for reflection on this question is the number of villages Josephus says were in Galilee, which covered a similar area to the Judean heartland. He says there were 204 villages in Galilee in his day.[6] E. W. G. Masterman, who lived in Palestine for many years,[7] estimated the area of Galilee as enclosed by the borders that Josephus describes at 900 square miles (2,300 square kilometers).[8] Roughly, we can think of every piece of terrain of about 11 square kilometers, or about 2 miles by 2 miles, containing a village or town (2,300/204 = ca. 11.3).

Interestingly, a similar density figure can be deduced from analysis of Avi Ofer's archaeological survey of the hills of Judah.[9] Ofer found 90 village or town settlements from the early Roman period in this area, which he put at some 1,000 square kilometers.[10] His figures imply a density of about one village to about every 11 square kilometers of terrain (1,000/90 = ca. 11.1). It thus appears that around the time of Jesus, villages in Judah and Galilee were distributed across the countryside in similar density. One could suggest that this is quite natural, as the key socioeconomic factors determining such distribution would have

5. Philo, *Hypothetica* 11.1.

6. Josephus, *Vita* §235.

7. See C. C. McCown, "The Density of Population in Ancient Palestine," *JBL* 66 (1947): 425-36; see p. 426.

8. E. W. G. Masterman, *Studies in Galilee* (Chicago: University of Chicago Press, 1909), pp. 131-34.

9. Avi Ofer, "The Highland of Judah during the Biblical Period" (in Hebrew with English summary) (Ph.D. diss., Tel Aviv University, 1993).

10. See Avi Ofer, "Judah," in *OEANE* 3:253-57, see p. 256. The estimate for the area of the Judean heartland is taken from this article; see p. 253.

been largely the same in both regions. On the one hand, the rural population gathered for society and safety in settlements; but on the other hand, few wanted to live far from the farmland on which most work was done. A journey of more than a mile to work in local fields seems to have been considered excessive. Even though the density of the rural population seems to have varied somewhat between the two regions (Josephus emphasizes that the agricultural fertility of Galilee led to a denser population),[11] this variation appears insufficient to have led to a noticeably denser coverage of settlements in Galilee than in Judea.

We can obtain a reasonably reliable estimate for the number of villages and towns in the semifertile regions of the Judean heartland by extrapolating from Ofer's result for the Judean hills. The Judean heartland consisted of the Shephelah, the Benjamin and Judah hills, and the Jerusalem "saddle." By Ofer's reckoning, these covered some 2,250 square kilometers. Ofer's figures suggest that in the early Roman period there were perhaps a little over 200 villages in the region (2,250/11.1 = ca. 203). This is about the same number of villages and towns Josephus reports for Galilee, which covered an almost identical area. The extrapolation is given in the following tabular form. A breakdown is given of the area of the basic constituent parts of Judea, with an estimate for each region based on the density of settlements given in Ofer's survey of the Judah hills. The final estimate is rounded to 200, a figure I would suggest is accurate within a 10 percent margin of error. This rounded figure for the Judean heartland gives an average density of settlements largely identical to that suggested above for ancient Galilee (ca. 1/11.3 square kilometers).

Table 1: Estimating the Number of Villages in the Heartland of Judea

Region	Area (sq. km.)	No. of sites of settlement over 1,000 sq. m.	One village or town per x sq. km.
Highlands of Judah	ca. 1,000	90 (survey, Avi Ofer)	ca. 1/11.1 sq. km.
Benjamin hills and Jerusalem "saddle"	ca. 500	ca. 45 (estimate assuming same density)	ca. 1/11.1 sq. km.
Shephelah	ca. 750	ca. 67 (estimate assuming same density)	ca. 1/11.1 sq. km.
Totals	ca. 2,250	ca. 200 (rounded estimate)	ca. 1/11.3 sq. km.

11. *War* 3.3.2 §42-43; 3.10.8 §518.

A figure of around 200 villages and towns in the Jewish heartland coheres with the data from other sources. Dio Cassius states that the Romans destroyed 985 villages and 50 fortresses in Palestine in the Bar-Kokhba war.[12] The Jewish guerrilla forces, holed up in caves, proved a difficult enemy. They used underground tunnels from which to attack Roman patrols, and were able to obtain a constant supply of food from the peasantry. The Romans, whose forces were almost disastrously sapped in their initial campaign, were forced to denude the countryside, driving off the Jewish peasant population, to achieve lasting victory. Dio Cassius's figure is therefore likely to include most of the significant sites of settlement in Palestine. A figure of around 200 villages and towns for Judea corresponds well with his information that there were something over a thousand in all the area that revolted, which included parts of Transjordan. The Jewish heartland of Judah, the Benjamin hills, the Jerusalem "saddle," and the Shephelah is similar in size to both Galilee and Samaria. The coastal plain occupies a similar area again. The wilderness and Negeb regions, while covering a large area, had a much lower density of settlements. In all, literary sources record 675 place-names for the whole of Palestine;[13] it would appear that the names of something like two-thirds of all villages and towns appear in literary sources.

The next step toward understanding the distribution of celibate male Essenes across rural Judea in the early Roman period is to consider the minimum size for a functioning group or association in any particular village or town. There are several indications in the sources that it would have been very unlikely for celibate male Essenes to live together in groups of less than ten. The first source to consider is the *Rule of the Community*. This document regulated the lives of celibate male Essenes and was found in multiple copies. In it we find this stipulation: "In every place where there are ten men of the Council of the Community, there should not be lacking amongst them a priest. And every one shall sit before him and in this way they shall be asked for their counsel in every matter" (1QS 6.3-4). This passage strongly implies that it would have been unacceptable for communities of celibate Essene males located in any of the villages and towns of Judea to have numbered less than ten.

The second source is the account of the Essenes given in Josephus's *Jewish War*. When Josephus emphasizes the orderliness of Essene communal behavior, he uses a group of ten as his example of a small gathering: "If ten sit together, one will not speak if nine desire silence."[14]

12. Dio Cassius, *Roman History* 49.12-14.

13. Gottfried Reeg, *Die Ortsnamen Israels nach der rabbinischen Literatur* (Wiesbaden: Reichert, 1989), p. vii.

14. *War* 2.8.9 §146.

Both sources deal with the *minyan* of ten adult males that constitutes the quorum for liturgical purposes in rabbinic Judaism.[15] The ideal of the *minyan* of ten was clearly based on the smallest subdivision of the people of God employed by Moses in the wilderness wanderings.[16] Thus, Scripture enjoined that the smallest possible subdivision of the ideal people of God was the group of ten men. The Essenes certainly saw themselves as the reconstituted, ideal people of God, so we must assume that the smallest acceptable size for a locally based group of celibate males was ten. A third source, the *Rule of the Congregation* (1QSa = 1Q28a), also divides the people into groups of ten: "These are the men appointed to the council of the community . . . all the wise of the congregation, the understanding and knowledgeable, who are blameless in their behavior and men of valor, together with the chiefs of the tribes, all judges, magistrates, captains of thousands, hundreds, fifties, tens, and the Levites" (1Q28a 1.27–2.1).

According to the *Rule of the Congregation,* a man aged thirty was eligible to lead a group of ten (1Q28a 1.13-15).

As the period of Roman occupation progressed, a military factor seems to have begun dominating thinking about Essene organization, if it had not done so before. Moses' subdivision of the people into thousands, hundreds, fifties, and tens had been, in fact, at once both military and judicial. From the time of the writing of a further source to consider on this theme, the *War Scroll* (1QM),[17] many Essenes must have seen their organized movement as a holy army preparing for the eschatological conflict against the Romans for which this document plans. The squad of ten is the smallest military subdivision of the *War Scroll,* in which appear careful prescriptions concerning the commanders of tens and their subordinates.[18] For those Essenes who looked forward to such military endeavors, the smallest acceptable size for a community of celibate Essene males, whose celibacy marked the readiness of their squad for holy war, was undoubtedly ten.

There may have been sectors of the Essene group that were not warlike in intent. Philo, with probable exaggeration, claims that all Essenes were pacifists, for none took any interest in the manufacture of weapons or armor, or any in-

---

15. See "Minyan," in *The Oxford Dictionary of the Jewish Religion,* ed. R. J. Zwi Werblowsky and G. Wigoder (New York: Oxford University Press, 1997), p. 468.

16. Ex 18:21, 25; Deut 1:15.

17. The *War Scroll* is probably to be dated to the late first century B.C.E. or the early first century C.E. See P. R. Davies, "War of the Sons of Light against the Sons of Darkness," in *Encyclopedia of the Dead Sea Scrolls,* ed. L. H. Schiffman and J. C. VanderKam (New York: Oxford University Press, 2000), pp. 965-68; see esp. pp. 966-67.

18. 1QM 4.3-6. See 2 Kgs 25:25 (a military squad of ten).

struments of war.[19] The basic smallest subdivision of ten was always appropriate, however, as the ideal organization for the people of God, not only to those Essenes who sought to assume a war footing, but also for those who shunned the possibility of revolt against Rome.

R. de Vaux, the excavator of Qumran, estimated that 200 people at most could have lived in huts and caves associated with the desert site.[20] Thus a substantial majority of the over 4,000 celibate male Essenes probably lived in the villages and towns of the semifertile heartland of Judea. The figures and information given about Essene distribution by Philo and the implication of a *minyan* of 10 in the sources cited cohere well with our estimate of around 200 villages in the Judean heartland. Philo's description can be satisfied if there were Essene community houses accommodating, say, between 10 and 20 celibate males in many of the towns and villages of the densely populated regions of Judea. *Three* thousand celibate males would have been enough to provide a group of 15 celibate Essene males to staff a community house in all the villages and towns in the Judean heartland — yet Josephus and Philo claim there were over 4,000 celibate male Essenes. In fact, only half the Essene celibate males numbered by Josephus and Philo would have been sufficient to staff viable community houses in most if not all villages and towns. Two thousand celibate males would have been sufficient to provide a staff of 15 for community houses in over 130 villages, or communities of a dozen male celibates in around five-sixths of the area's villages and towns. It is thus unimportant that our figure of around 200 villages and towns in Judea has only the accuracy of an extrapolation from a limited survey. The figure of over 4,000 given by Josephus and Philo is more than sufficient to satisfy Philo's description of a region saturated with communities of celibate male Essenes.

I would suggest that there were probably about 3,000 celibate male Essenes resident in the villages and towns of rural Judea. Celibate male Essenes resident elsewhere included the occupants of major communities of perhaps 100 or 200 in Jerusalem and at Qumran,[21] and the staff of other, smaller Essene settlements in the lower Jordan Valley, at other points on the Dead Sea, including perhaps Engedi, in some of the sparsely distributed settlements of the Beersheba-Arad Valley, and perhaps in far-flung areas of Jewish settlement.[22]

19. *OmnProbLib* §78.

20. R. de Vaux, *Archaeology and the Dead Sea Scrolls* (London: Oxford University Press, 1973), pp. 24-27.

21. On the question of Essene settlements at different periods at Qumran and in Jerusalem, see B. J. Capper, "'With the Oldest Monks . . .': Light from Essene History on the Career of the Beloved Disciple?" *JTS* 49 (1998): 1-55; see esp. pp. 19-29, 47, and 54-55.

22. B. Pixner has suggested that there was an area of Essene settlement in Batanaea, re-

Most of the celibate male Essenes in the region will have found employment outside their community houses in the local rural economy, as emphasized by Philo.[23] They brought home their wages each evening and shared them with each other and those they supported through their common purse (we will look more closely at this evening meal gathering later).[24] Since celibate male Essenes found employment in the local rural economy, and would have to travel to and from work each day, we should expect a fairly even distribution of small communities throughout the region. Moreover, large concentrations of celibate male Essenes in particular areas would have distorted the rural economy, causing resentment. Excessive local numbers of celibate male Essenes, not personally responsible for families, would have forced down the wages paid to local workers. A widespread, thin distribution is also likely because the Essenes, as Jews, probably saw a comprehensive "occupation" of the villages and towns of rural Judea, their own tribal land of Judah, in symbolic terms, demonstrating their own claim to be the reorganized Jewish nation.

These widely distributed communities of celibate male Essenes must have had an immense influence on the religious and social life of the peasantry, artisans, and laborers of rural Judea. Their disciplined and devoted lifestyle was easily visible to all the rural populace, for whom it must have been a topic of constant interest and examination. All Judea must have had a good understanding of Essene ideas and community practices. Indeed, especially in view of the high level of commitment and social cohesiveness involved in belonging to the Essene "New Covenant" as articulated in the principal Essene rule documents,[25] our statistical deductions suggest that the Essenes were the dominant religious and social force in rural Judea.

---

lated to Herod's settlement of Jews in this region. See *Wege des Messias und Stätten der Urkirche*, 2nd ed. (Giessen: Brunnen Verlag, 1994), pp. 159-69, where his other publications relevant to this theme are cited. There were probably no Essene celibates in Samaria, and few if any in the coastal plain or Galilee. Hence H. Stegemann, *The Library of Qumran* (German 1993; Grand Rapids: Eerdmans, 1998), p. 153, concludes: "The union of the Essenes was certainly, from its foundation onward, the most numerous religious group in the Judean heartland of Israel."

23. Philo emphasizes the rural occupations of the male Essene celibates in his description in *Apology for the Jews (= Hypothetica)* 11.8. All the occupations he mentions are typical of the day laborer in the agricultural economy of Palestine. See A. Ben-David, *Talmüdische Ökonomie* (Hildesheim: Georg Olms, 1974), pp. 65-69.

24. Philo emphasizes the daily receipt and pooling each evening of wages by the celibate male Essenes in his description in *Hypothetica* 11.10. On this passage see also Capper, "Palestinian Cultural Context," pp. 331-32.

25. The term "New Covenant" appears at *Damascus Document* (CD) 6.19; See *Rule of the Community* (1QS) 1.16–2.18.

The Social Level of the Celibate Male Essenes of Rural Judea

To understand the social role and impact of Essenism in the rural environment, it is important to assess the social level of the majority of those celibate male Essenes and their supporters who lived in the villages and towns of rural Judea. I would take the view that the physically isolated Qumran Community is not a good guide for understanding the social character of Essenism in rural Judea. While clearly a part of the broader Essene movement, the Qumran Community seems to have been somewhat sui generis. The intensity of scholarly activity at the desert site suggests that it may have housed what was in effect the Essene "university," a center of learning, where the most able members of the Essene group received a higher training in the context of a virtually enclosed religious community.

It is plausible that some of the aristocratic youth of Jerusalem were sent to the Qumran Community for a course of discipline and study. Josephus himself, who came from a wealthy priestly family and who clearly received a high-quality Greco-Roman education, claims to have pursued Essene training,[26] which he says lasted three years.[27] He did not go on to join a community of celibate Essene males. His claimed involvement with the Essene training may typify ways in which the Qumran Community served the interests of at least some elite families of Jerusalem, only sixteen miles away.

Philo describes celibate male Essenes, who worked in the rural Judean economy, as people who brought home their wages at the end of the working day and shared them to enable the purchase and consumption of a common meal.[28] Josephus, however, describes more tightly communal arrangements, including communal bathing before a shared midday meal.[29] He may be describing the Qumran Community, which was able to pursue, on its own estate, a more communal daily regime than was possible for Essenes who worked outside their communities in rural Judea, on whose lifestyle Philo's account is based. Josephus may even have been personally acquainted with the daily regime of the Qumran Community. It certainly seems possible that those living the highly regularized, scholarly life of the Qumran Community may have had greater connections with the social elite than the celibate male Essenes who lived in the villages and towns of rural Judea, and who worked daily on local farms and estates.

Philo's accounts of the Essenes give strong indications that the majority of

26. *Vita* 2 §10-11.
27. *War* 2.8.7 §137-142. We know from 1QS column 6 that the procedure probably lasted between two and three years. See J. C. VanderKam, *The Dead Sea Scrolls Today* (Grand Rapids: Eerdmans, 1994), pp. 137-39.
28. Philo, *Hypothetica* §8-11. See below for quotation of this passage and further analysis of it.
29. *War* 2.8.5 §129-131.

Figure 66. An assortment of inkwells from MB II to the Roman period.
Courtesy of J. H. Charlesworth

celibate male Essenes belonged to the ordinary mass of laborers and artisans employed in the rural Judean economy. Five powerful indicators point in this direction.

1. Daily Receipt of Wages

In his tract *That Every Good Man Is Free,* Philo explains that the unique Essene form of association involved a common roof, a common life together, and a common table *(homōrophion, homodiaiton, homotrapezon).* This high degree of social integration was realized by the daily collection and sharing each evening of the *misthos,* the "pay" or "wages"[30] that each working member had received during the day: "[F]or whatever they receive as wages *(epi misthō)* for their day's work is not kept to themselves, but is deposited before them all, in their midst, to be put to common employment."[31]

The Greek term *misthos* is cognate with two words used to denote the day laborer, *misthios* and *misthōtos.*[32] Day laborers constituted the lowest employed

30. W. Bauer, W. F. Arndt, and F. W. Gingrich, *A Lexicon of the New Testament and Other Early Christian Literature* (Chicago: University of Chicago Press, 1979), p. 523.

31. *OmnProbLib* §85.

32. Lev 19:13 (LXX) legislates that the *misthos* of the *misthōtos* may not be retained until the following morning.

group. It is apparent that the celibate male Essenes described by Philo worked on a daily basis outside their communities in the local economy of rural Judea as laborers and artisans and were paid every day. This is a strong pointer to their social position within the numerous classes of artisans and day laborers. It is well known that day laborers were among the economically weakest in ancient Palestine. Since they did not possess land, they were at the mercy of fluctuations in wage rates and demand for labor. Jewish law had long sought to protect this vulnerable class.[33]

2. Engagement in Agricultural Occupations and Crafts

In his *Apology for the Jews* (alternatively known as *Hypothetica*), Philo reports on the kinds of work the celibate male Essenes undertook each day, such as working the soil, shepherding, beekeeping, and crafts (11.4-9). All these activities are typical of the day laborer in the agricultural economy of Palestine, and confirm the social location of the rural celibate male Essenes within the class of day laborers and artisans.[34]

3. Dependence on the Daily Wage for Survival

Laborers were characteristically dependent on their daily wage for survival. Hence the Mosaic Law demanded that they be paid their wages at nightfall, when the working day came to an end. It was prohibited to hold over the wages of the laborer until the following day, since this meant laborers might not eat at all after a hard day's work — an unjust imposition on this vulnerable class (Lev 19:13; Deut 24:15). Philo's description of the evening meals of celibate male Essene laborers and artisans reveals this characteristic of dependence on the daily wage for survival: "Each member of the group, when he has received the day's wages *(ton misthon labontes)* for these different occupations, gives it to the person who has been elected as treasurer. As soon as he receives this money, the treasurer immediately buys what is necessary and provides food in abundance as well as whatever else human life requires. Thus having each day a common life and a common table they are content with the same conditions, lovers of frugality who shun expensive luxury as a disease of both body and soul."[35]

33. Lev 19:13; Deut 24:14-15; see Jas 5:4. In Deut 24:14 the day laborer *(śakîr)* is "poor" *('ebyon)* and "needy" *('anî)*.

34. See A. Ben-David, *Talmüdische Ökonomie* (Hildesheim: Georg Olms, 1974), pp. 65-69.

35. *Hypothetica* 11.10-11 (cited in Eusebius, *Preparation of the Gospel* 8.6-7), translation largely based on F. H. Colson, *Philo*, vol. 9 (LCL, 1941), see esp. p. 441. G. Vermes and M. D.

Philo is clear that the groups of celibate Essene males in the towns and villages of rural Judea pooled their daily wages to purchase food each evening. This shows that they lived a hand-to-mouth existence common to so many laborers and artisans of ancient Palestine. Indeed, Philo's description even suggests that this daily pooling was a survival strategy, by which the success of some in finding work could offset the plight of others who had not been as successful.[36] The frugal consumption that characterized the celibate Essene lifestyle, and indeed the celibate male Essenes' communal lifestyle, thus appears to have arisen out of real economic necessity.

4. Work from Sunrise to Sunset

Philo points in the *Apology* to the fact that Essenes labor with athletic virtue from before sunrise to near sunset: "Performing their accustomed tasks from before sunrise, they do not leave them till the sun has almost set, devoting themselves to them with no less joy than those who train for gymnastic combat."[37]

We may compare Philo's comment with Jesus' parable of the laborers in the vineyard (Mt 20:1-16). Those able to find work early in the day labored throughout the daylight hours, including the scorching midday heat. The Talmud informs us that workers in Palestine were conventionally taken on as dawn brightened the sky before sunrise, indicative of the full working day demanded of them.[38] Thus the celibate male Essenes of rural Judea described by Philo worked the full day typical of the day laborer.

Goodman, *The Essenes according to the Classical Sources* (Sheffield: Sheffield University Press, 1989), p. 29. It is important to note that at the beginning of this passage *hekastos* refers to "each man" or "each member" rather than "each branch" of the Essene organization. The text does not support this occasionally found assumption of common production. The present author would suggest that large-scale common production among the Essenes was only found on the estate at Qumran, whose residents had a more socially integrated day than in the village and town communities of Essenes, where celibate male Essenes worked outside their communities in the local agricultural economy.

36. It is important not to be misled by Philo's enthusiasm for Essene frugality, which expresses his own ascetic enthusiasm. The meager diet of the Essenes reflects the problems of the subsistence existence common to the peasant and artisan class, as does Jesus' prayer for "daily bread" (Mt 6:11 and Lk 11:3).

37. Philo, *Hypothetica* 11.6.

38. *b. B. Mes.* 83b offers the restraint that work should not start till the sun rises; *b. Yoma* 28b records that when the eastern sky was bright as far as Hebron, all were already on the way to work.

Josephus describes a break from the fifth hour for a ritual bath and common meal in the routine of the Essenes he describes. This divergence suggests that his own contact had been with Essenes who could avoid the heat of the day in their routine. The variation tends to confirm the suggestion made above that Josephus based his description of the celibate male Essenes on the more intensively communal daily routine of the Qumran Essenes. At Qumran, work was performed on the community's own estate, allowing it to set its own daily schedule more completely. There, work in the extreme midday heat by the Dead Sea was deliberately, perhaps necessarily, avoided.

5. Willing Acceptance of Any Kind of Work (Multiple Occupations Each Day)

Philo remarks that the Essenes "have to suffer no privation of what is indispensable to essential needs, and they never defer until the morrow whatever serves to procure for them blameless revenue."[39] This seemingly innocent description of Essene willingness to pursue a life of constant labor gives us an important insight into the socioeconomic level of the Essenes of rural Judea. It is important not to be misled by Philo's rhetorical vaunting of the hardworking Essene lifestyle as an expression of "athletic" virtue alone.[40] It would be naive to assume that men of a high social level voluntarily applied themselves to unceasing harsh labor throughout the sunlight hours. This is a mark of poverty, a characteristic of those who, with the ordinary working mass of the population, needed to work throughout the day to feed and clothe themselves and those for whom they assumed responsibility. It is also frequently characteristic of those in greatest economic insecurity in every culture and age to seek two or more different employments in a single day to garner a sufficient wage. The celibate male Essenes described by Philo habitually worked for the whole day, even in several employments, to secure the economic life of their communities.

The Work of the Essene "Houses of the Community" in Rural Judea

Josephus adds a concluding note to the account of the Essenes in his *Jewish War* to the effect that, alongside the order of celibate male Essenes, there also existed marrying Essenes, who composed a second order of the group. Unsurprisingly,

---

39. Philo, *Hypothetica* 11.9.
40. See Philo, *Hypothetica* 11.6-7.

the more striking and unusual celibate Essene life drew the attention of the ancient authors. Neither Philo nor Pliny the Elder even mentions the marrying Essenes.[41] Josephus's short reference to the order figures almost as an afterthought.[42] However, it is again important not to be misled by the rhetorical interests of the ancient authors. It is undoubtedly correct to assume that far more Palestinian Jews were attracted to, and able to abide by, the code of the marrying Essene order than joined the more difficult and rigorous life of the celibate male Essene order. It is likely that those incorporated into the marrying Essene order were several times more in number, at least, than the over four thousand celibate male Essenes. As we noted above, it is clear from Philo that a community of celibate male Essenes was found in many of the towns and villages of Judea. There were probably also groups of families in most, if not all, of the villages and towns of Judea. These family groups were incorporated into the Essene "New Covenant" (*Damascus Document* 6.19) and linked to local groups of celibate male Essenes.

The way of life of the second order of Essenes is given in the *Damascus Document.* Central to the life of the community was the institution of the *beth-cheber*, or "community house," where the community cared for those who received no or inadequate support within local kinship structures. For these destitute persons, the Essene "community houses" constituted substitute families or "fictive kinship groups."[43] The *Damascus Document* stipulates the tasks and means of support of these Essene community centers:

> And this is the rule of the Many, to provide for all their needs: the wages (13) of at least two days each month they shall place into the hands of the Overseer and of the judges. (14) From it they shall give to the orphans and with it they shall strengthen the hand of the needy and the poor, and the elder (15) who is dying, and to the wandering and to the prisoner of a foreign people, and to the girl who (16) has no redeemer, and to the youth who has no teacher, and for all the works of the community, and (17) the house of the community *(beth-cheber)* shall not be deprived of its means. (CD 14.12-17)

Since the monthly support given by family groups for the maintenance of the *beth-cheber* is defined in terms of daily wages rather than a proportion of

41. Pliny, *Natural History* 5.15 §73.

42. *War* 2.8.13 §160-161.

43. S. S. Bartchy has explored the anthropological concept of the "fictive kinship group" in relation to the sharing of property and lives in the early Jerusalem church; see his "Community of Goods in Acts," in *The Future of Early Christianity: Essays in Honor of Helmut Koester*, ed. B. A. Pearson (Minneapolis: Fortress, 1991), pp. 309-18.

crops, it is apparent that the members of the New Covenant who maintained these community houses were largely, if not entirely, drawn from the ordinary mass of laborers and artisans. These groups, who were dependent on a daily wage, did not own enough land from which to support themselves (if they owned any land at all). Hence this prescription defines their contributions in terms of the daily wage *(sakar* = Gk. *misthos)*. These ordinary working people were always in a potentially precarious economic position. They had created their cooperative "friends society" as a survival strategy to avoid descent through economic misfortune into destitution, begging, and worse. It is important to emphasize that the defined rate of two days' pay per month for the support of the economically weakest was a minimum contribution, as the phrase "at least" in line 13 makes clear. In line 17 we read that local communities were to ensure that the community house *(beth-cheber)* always had sufficient means to support those to whom it offered succor, implicitly at whatever cost to members necessary. It is thus quite possible that in hard times community officers eagerly canvassed those in work to give above the minimum to ensure that none of the indigent taken in at the Essene community center suffered from hunger or starvation. That such cooperative economic communities already existed in the towns and villages of Judea is of enormous importance for understanding the practices of the early Jerusalem Christians described in the opening chapters of Acts. The post-Easter followers of Jesus in Jerusalem, who also understood themselves to be a New Covenant community, employed similar economic mechanisms that enabled daily sharing with each other and economic support for the indigent (Acts 2:42-47; 4:32–5:11; 6:1-6).[44]

The *Damascus Document* defines the various classes that were to receive support in the Essene poorhouses of rural Judea. It is important to note that some of the classes of legitimate recipients of aid are clearly drawn from outside the immediate New Covenant community. The first (and therefore probably the most important) group mentioned is orphans, who are to be taken in and cared for (line 14). This interestingly corresponds very closely with Josephus's information about the celibate male Essenes, who "adopt the children of others while yet pliable and easily disciplined, and regard them as their own kin and shape them in accordance with their own principles."[45]

The problem of too many mouths to feed is common to all agrarian societies.[46] The ordinary mass of artisans and day laborers in first-century Judea,

---

44. On these passages see Capper, "Palestinian Cultural Context," pp. 323-56.

45. *War* 2.8.2 §120.

46. See G. E. Lenski, *Power and Privilege: A Theory of Social Stratification* (New York: McGraw-Hill, 1966), pp. 189-296; see esp. pp. 280-84.

along with those remaining peasants who held smaller plots of land, produced more than a few children who could not easily be provided for from the limited resources available in local kinship structures. Many of these children were adopted by the Essenes.[47]

The "girl who has no redeemer" and the "youth who has no teacher" of CD 16.16 are teenagers taken in by the community houses because the possibilities for their support within the local kinship structures of rural Judea had been exhausted. These also represent examples of what Josephus describes as the adoption practice of the Essenes. The danger for a poor girl whose family was unable to support her was that she might be sold into slavery or prostitution. Prostitution was essentially a consequence of poverty. As early as the fifth century B.C.E., Nehemiah had witnessed the problem of daughters who could not be fed on Judean farmsteads falling into the clutches of unscrupulous masters (cf. Neh 5:5).[48] The Essene practice of taking in teenage girls who could not be supported by their families, which had developed in the later postexilic period, helped avoid the phenomenon of prostitution in Judea. The Essenes thus sought to keep the stain of prostitution from the tribal territory of Judah and Benjamin, the lands most closely associated with the holy city of Jerusalem and the Jewish Temple. Essene activity in dispelling this extremely common consequence of poverty in the ancient world bears fascinating and direct comparison with Jesus' concern for the poor and his social interaction with prostitutes in Galilee (cf. especially Lk 7:34-50). Jesus must have viewed with approval the structures of organized support in rural Judea, begun by the Essenes, which, by taking unsupported girls into protective communal centers, prevented the fall of many into prostitution. Again, the prescriptions of column 14 of the *Damascus Document* show us the necessary backdrop for understanding the appearance of organized structures of communal sharing and support for the poor that appear among the early Jerusalem believers in Jesus in Acts 2–6.

Teenage boys taken in by the Essenes (CD 14.16) would be given a training that would eventually enable them to become contributory members, and per-

---

47. The problem was exacerbated by Jewish refusal to resort to infanticide, a common remedy in the Greco-Roman world; see J. R. Sallares, "Infanticide," in *Oxford Classical Dictionary*, ed. S. Hornblower and A. Spawforth, 3rd ed. (Oxford: Oxford University Press, 1996), p. 757; P. Brulé, "Infanticide et abandon d'enfant: pratiques greques et comparaisons anthropologiques," *Dialogues d'histoire ancienne* 18 (1992): 53-90; J. Boswell, *The Kindness of Strangers: The Abandonment of Children in Western Europe from Late Antiquity to the Renaissance* (New York: Pantheon Books, 1988), pp. 41-45.

48. See H. G. M. Williamson, *Ezra and Nehemiah*, WBC (Waco, Tex.: Word, 1985), ad loc. Compare also Herodotus's picture of poor Lydian women earning money for their dowries by prostitution; *Hist* 1.93.

haps found viable families of their own. This Essene work had an important consequence for the stability of Judean society. It helped prevent boys and youths without family support from drifting into bandit groups,[49] one of the few options open to such youngsters (along with mercenary service, travel to the coast for maritime work, and voluntary attachment where possible to a great house as a servant or slave). The period of at least temporary celibacy imposed on youths during training, or the alternative choice of lifelong celibacy within a celibate male Essene group, must have acted as a helpful population-limiting factor in rural Judea.

It is unlikely that many of the children taken in by the Essene community houses of rural Judea, if any at all, came from the higher social classes of retainers and families with larger landholdings. Jewish pride in having many children to continue the family name shines through the Hebrew Scriptures. A Jewish family with resources to support its children would not readily give them away. Nor did these unwanted children necessarily come from families that had already joined the Essene New Covenant. However, that the Essene poorhouses offered poorer families a way out of their principal economic difficulty will undoubtedly have led to great esteem for Essenism on the rural scene and will have contributed to an increasing adherence of local artisan and laboring families to the Essene covenant. Those who gave up children for adoption would probably want to make what contribution they could to the further upkeep of their own children, to gain standing with the care centers where their children were taken in and to observe and take pride in their offspring's training and progress. Though most were probably drawn from families outside the Essene covenant, at least initially, Essene adoptees were only taken in on the understanding that they would adhere to Essene principles. This must have been the principal route by which the celibate Essene order expanded its membership, and these good works of Essenism must have meant that the rural populace held the Essenes in high esteem. Over the several generations of the Essene movement's existence, large numbers of rural artisan and laboring families must have been drawn into the Essene New Covenant. This new form of voluntary, covenanted social organization provided a vehicle for the true expression of the ancient Israelite ideal of care for the poor, enshrined in the Mosaic Law, and offered social security in a period that saw great extremes of wealth and poverty.

49. On the banditry common to agrarian societies, including ancient Palestine, see E. Hobsbawm, *Bandits*, rev. ed. (Harmondsworth: Penguin Books, 1985); R. A. Horsley, with J. S. Hanson, *Bandits, Prophets, and Messiahs* (Minneapolis: Winston, 1985), pp. 48-87; R. A. Horsley, *Jesus and the Spiral of Violence* (San Francisco: Harper and Row, 1987), pp. 37-39; J. D. Crossan, *The Historical Jesus* (San Francisco: HarperSanFrancisco, 1991), pp. 168-206.

From this analysis of how the different sources of the *Damascus Document* and Josephus's account of Essene adoption in the context of his description of celibate male Essenes in his *Jewish War* mutually illuminate each other, I would suggest that the "community houses" in the villages and towns of Judea, which received monthly contributions from local families for the support of the poor, were actually staffed by celibate Essenes. The alternative — to assume that there were two types of Essene institutions that took in adoptees, one run by the marrying order and the other by the celibate order — is to multiply hypotheses unnecessarily. We should rather expect that unsupported girls and youths taken into the Essene poorhouses actually became, through their training, temporary or permanent members of celibate male and female orders based in these houses. We should assume that women of these orders worked at certain domestic tasks necessary in these houses, which might include spinning, weaving, and clothing manufacture. Male celibates, who usually worked outside the community houses, probably took boys with them as they plied their trades in the local rural economy, in order to train them (hence CD 14.16 speaks of the "youth who has no teacher," who could receive a training in this way). After work during the sunlight hours, male celibates returning to the community houses may have had a hand in teaching and leading prayers in the evening, during and after the communal evening meal.[50]

The *Damascus Document* goes on to prescribe support for the "elder who is dying" (14.14-15); here we find a close correspondence with Philo's description of the activities of the celibate male Essenes. Philo lays considerable emphasis on Essene care for the elderly:

> The old too, even if childless are treated as parents of a not merely numerous but very filial family and regularly end their days in an exceedingly happy and comfortable old age, honored with privileges and with the esteem of so many children who care for them. (*Apology for the Jews* 11.13)

> To the elderly is given the respect and care which natural children give to their parents, and they receive from numerous hands and minds full and generous maintenance for their latter years. (*OmnProbLib* §87)

The penal code of the *Damascus Document* defines penalties for speaking rebelliously against groups called the "mothers" and "fathers" of the community: "[If he has murmured] against the Fathers, he shall leave and not return again. But if he has murmured against the Mothers, he shall do penance for ten days" (4Q270 7.i.13-14).

---

50. See the activities of the early believers in Jerusalem described in Acts 2:42, 46; 6:1-6; 12:12.

I would suggest that these otherwise undefined groups of "mothers" and "fathers" are elderly men and women being cared for in the communal Essene centers, and that the centers carefully divided the sleeping accommodation and some recreational accommodation between men and women. It would have been easy and very much in line with common ancient practice to locate accommodation for males and females in different parts of a building or complex, perhaps separated by an open courtyard.[51] The elderly men were probably cared for by Essene male celibates and especially by the youths in their tutelage. These elderly men may also have had a particular role in the education of youths taken in by the community; hardened resistance could result in the expulsion of an adoptee. The elderly women constituted a widow order very much like the widow orders of early "Christianity,"[52] and were probably cared for by the young girls who were taken in and other unattached women who formed part of the staff of the community centers. The elderly women did not have the same authority in the community houses as the elderly men, as the more lenient punishment of those who spoke against them reveals. However, some (if not all) probably had particular roles in the tutelage of young girls taken in by the center.

The *Damascus Document* also prescribes care for the "poor and needy" (CD 14.14). These categories are echoed in Josephus's account of the Essenes. Josephus explicitly states that even the celibate male Essene, who was clearly under quite rigorous discipline, was able to use the resources of the community to help those in need: "Two things only are left to individual discretion, the rendering of assistance and compassion. Members may on their own decision help the deserving, when in need, and supply food to the destitute."

It is clear from this passage in Josephus's *Jewish War*[53] that the celibate male Essenes were prepared to treat with considerable kindness any destitute person they encountered in the villages and towns of rural Judea, their immediate social context. Josephus is here describing the latitude allowed to individual celibate male Essenes, who lived under considerable control from their superiors. Since such were allowed to give alms and assistance to the needy, we can be quite sure that communities of celibate male Essenes would have taken a significant role in helping the destitute of rural Judea. If the individual celibate male Essene could be allowed such leeway with his wages from the day before, pool-

---

51. See S. Walker, "Women and Housing in Classical Greece: The Archaeological Evidence," in *Images of Women in Antiquity*, ed. A. Cameron and A. Kuhrt (London: Croom Helm, 1983), pp. 81-91; C. Nepos, *Lives of Famous Men* (Lawrence, Kans.: Coronado Press, 1971), pp. 6-7.

52. On the widow orders of early Christianity, see B. Bowman Thurston, *The Widows: A Women's Ministry in the Early Church* (Minneapolis: Fortress, 1989).

53. *War* 2.8.6 §134; on the rigors of Essene discipline see esp. 2.8.6 §132-133, 135, 137-144, 150.

ing them with community resources in the evening after his day's work was done,[54] how much more would his community officers have been prepared to support and assist destitute and genuinely needy individuals who sought support from the community house.

The *Damascus Document* also prescribes care for the "wandering" (CD 14.15).[55] The "wandering" cannot be members of the local community. We know that celibate male Essene groups offered hospitality to those of their order who sought lodging with them when traveling.[56] However, it would be quite wrong to assume that all the wanderers for whom assistance is endorsed in this passage had to be members of the order. As we saw immediately above, compassionate assistance could be offered to those outside the community in genuine need. Support for the "wandering" in CD 14.15 points to the common problem of the poor in antiquity who wandered in search of work. The wandering poor figure greatly in the writings of Isocrates in the fourth century B.C.E., and were the principal factor in his development of a program for the invasion of Persian domains by Greeks and Macedonians.[57] Such invaders from the west, who later included the Romans, succeeded in transferring many of their own problems of land shortage and a multiplying, destitute underclass onto their subject peoples. Wandering workers figure in Jesus' parable of the laborers in the vineyard (Mt 20:1-16). Here, desperate Jewish workers have sought employment by walking from village to village, and are rescued by the generous treatment of the good vineyard owner who offers employment late in the day. From such an imagined or real occurrence, Jesus drew a lesson about how the kingdom of God was to be manifested (20:1). Here we find an interesting correspondence between the teaching of Jesus and the charitable activities endorsed by the *Damascus Document*. In southern Palestine (Judea), an organized network of Essene community houses helped secure the lot of the wandering poor. We should expect that Jesus took an interest in such well-organized forms of charitable support when he traveled in the south, and must ask if the artisan Jesus himself, and many of his fellow artisans from Galilee, availed themselves of

---

54. See Philo, *Hypothetica* 11.10-11 (see the discussion of this passage above). The daily collection of the celibate male Essene's wages is also implied in legislation of the *Rule of the Community*, where the novice's "property *and earnings* shall be caused to approach into the hand of the man who has the oversight *of the earnings* of the Many" (1QS 6.19-20) and community members are exhorted to abandon "wealth *and earnings*" (9.22).

55. The Hebrew term, which must be reconstructed, seems to be *yanua'*, "the man who is homeless" or "the wanderer."

56. See Josephus, *War* 2.8.4 §124-126.

57. See A. Fuks, "Isokrates and the Social-Economic Situation in Greece," in *Social Conflict in Ancient Greece* (Jerusalem: Magnes Press, 1984), pp. 52-79.

such assistance. We shall see below that Jesus appears to have received support from an Essene "poorhouse" near Jerusalem (known in the Gospels as "Bethany") when traveling as a wandering teacher, healer, and pilgrim.

The Social Impact of the Essene "Houses of the Community" in Rural Judea

It has already become clear from the above studies that the Essenes of rural Judea had a considerable impact on the welfare of the poorest classes of the region. We are able, by a statistical method, to gain a good impression of just how great the social impact of Essene poor-care is likely to have been.

M. Broshi has estimated the maximum possible population of western Palestine at 1,000,000, noting however that this figure was probably only reached in the Byzantine period. He bases his estimate on the total food resources that the region could produce.[58] He notes that for the early Roman period the ceramic intensity index is somewhat less than in the Byzantine period, perhaps suggesting a population of between 500,000 and 750,000 in the earlier period. The reliability of Broshi's method as a means to establishing the population of the coastal areas, where grain could be cheaply imported by sea from Egypt, is questionable. The high cost of overland transportation, however, means that the inland populations of antiquity had to be supported largely on locally grown food.[59] Thus Broshi's method can be trusted as a means for estimating the population of inland regions. The heartland area of Judea, some 2,250 square kilometers, constitutes about a quarter of the easily habitable areas of western Palestine (the areas of Samaria, Galilee, and the coastal plain are each of a similar order). If we assume, for the sake of argument, a population of some 650,000 supported on locally grown food at about the time of Jesus, one-quarter of this, or about 165,000, will have lived in Jerusalem and Judea. Jerusalem in this era probably had a population of around 60,000 to 80,000,[60] most of which will have been fed from food grown within Judea; this will have placed a limiting factor on the population remaining in the Judean countryside. The population of the villages and towns of the Jewish heartland of the Benjamin

58. M. Broshi, "The Population of Roman Palestine in the Roman-Byzantine Period," *BASOR* 236 (1979): 235-37.

59. See "Trade, Roman," in *Oxford Classical Dictionary*, pp. 1537-38; P. Garnsey, C. R. Whitaker, and K. Hopkins, *Trade in the Ancient Economy* (Cambridge: Cambridge University Press, 1983).

60. See W. Reinhardt, "The Population Size of Jerusalem and the Numerical Growth of the Jerusalem Church," in *The Book of Acts in Its Palestinian Setting*, pp. 237-65.

hills, Judean hills, and the Shephelah is unlikely to have risen above 100,000 in the early Roman period. As we have seen, this region contained some 200 villages and towns. Thus the average population of a settlement in the region, with its associated nearby farmhouses, will have been about 500, or less, including children.

As we have seen, most if not all of the villages and towns contained a community house, run by a group of perhaps twelve to fifteen celibate male Essenes. These central houses were supported by local family groups making their regular contributions of at least two days' pay per month, or about a tenth of their income.[61] There may also have been an important third stream of income supporting the poorhouse. Alongside the income of the celibate males who worked outside the center and the monthly contributions of associated families, there may have been occasional contributions from wealthy individuals who thought highly of the work of the poorhouse.

One must also ask if pious women from wealthy families did not make contributions of both money and practical assistance to the poor-care houses. On this it is worth comparing the wealthy women who supported Jesus as a traveling healer and teacher (Lk 8:1-3) and the expensive gift of perfumed oil that Mary of Bethany lavished on Jesus (Mk 14:3-9). Finally, a further source of income may have arisen from crafts pursued in the community center. These may have included pottery and basketwork, a source of income in later Christian monasticism. Basketwork could have been undertaken even by elderly members. The unattached girls and women resident in the center probably worked in spinning, weaving, and clothing manufacture.[62] An income surpassing the needs of the community center may have been raised from a surplus of such products.

We possess some information about the laborer's wage, and the cost of living, in the period. The wage paid to vineyard workers in a parable of Jesus is one denarius per day (Mt 20:1-16). The daily wage paid to the angel in the book of Tobit (5:15) is the same (one drachma). According to the Babylonian Talmud, Hillel, who was reckoned as very poor, survived on one *victoriatus* (half a denarius) per day (*b. Yoma* 35b). Heichelheim, who tabulated the evidence available for prices, calculated that the living cost of a single adult was a little less than one denarius per day.[63] We know according to the evidence of the

---

61. Stegemann, *The Library of Qumran*, p. 188, suggests that this monthly contribution was actually understood to be a tithe, once Sabbaths and rest days are removed from the 364 days of the solar year.

62. See the clothing made by Tabitha in Acts 9:36-43.

63. F. M. Heichelheim, "Roman Syria," in *An Economic Survey of Ancient Rome*, vol. 4, *Africa, Syria, Greece, Asia Minor*, ed. T. Frank (Baltimore: Johns Hopkins University Press, 1938), pp. 121-257, see p. 180.

Mishnah that a denarius would buy twelve loaves weighing around 550 grams each at the baker's shop.[64] A. Ben-David discovered, from personal experience, that an agricultural worker in Palestine might find work for only two hundred days in the year because of weather conditions.[65] Cato the Elder noted that while a slave working on an estate ate four to five pounds of bread per day and cost 312 sesterces (78 denarii) to maintain annually, a free worker and his family cost 1,000 sesterces (250 denarii) per year.[66] Thus it is clear that a Judean laborer earning a typical wage was probably able to keep only a small family in bare essentials. If his family grew, they might easily suffer want.

A valuable impression of the socioeconomic impact of the poor-care work of the Essene "house of the community" in a typical Judean village can be gained in the following way. Of the group of between twelve and fifteen male celibate Essenes living in the village, some will have been aged, and at any time there may also have been sickly brothers who could not contribute to the income of the house.[67] One brother may have been permanently employed in the center as the overseer.[68] A fair estimate would be that through the year the wages of working celibate males brought home and added to the finances of a typical community house amounted to the wages of about ten men. These wages will have included a substantial surplus over the needs of these celibates themselves. This surplus could be spread thinly, when necessary, to support those in need at the center. We should note the emphatic thread of extreme frugality that runs through the classical accounts of the Essenes. Josephus writes that they "do not change their garments or shoes until they are torn to shreds or worn threadbare with age," and of "the limitation of their allotted portions of food and drink to the demands of nature."[69] We can certainly assume that beneficiaries of charity at the Essene poor-care centers were given only a subsistence diet and simple shoes and garments. We may perhaps assume that a married working man on a laborer's wage could support at subsistence level a family of five, including himself. Hence the surplus income of ten celibates at a typical Essene poor-care center could probably be spread thinly enough to feed and clothe another thirty to forty souls, some of whom would be other male celibates who were sick, old, or working as the house officer. The remaining

64. See G. Hamel, *Poverty and Charity in Roman Palestine* (Berkeley: University of California Press, 1989), p. 40.

65. A. Ben-David, *Talmüdische Ökonomie* (Hildesheim: Georg Olms, 1974), pp. 65-69, 292.

66. Cato the Elder, *On Agriculture* 56.

67. Philo emphasizes care for the sick, *Hypothetica* 11.13; *OmnProbLib* §87. The *Damascus Document* likewise refers to care for the sick; cf. CD 14.15 (cited above).

68. See *Hypothetica* 11.10-11.

69. *War* 2.8.4 §126-127, 133; See Philo, *Hypothetica* 11.11.

surplus generated by the working male celibates could, when necessary, support through the community house up to thirty destitute children, women, and adults from the local area.

As we noted above, the influence of the Essenes on the religious and social life of the rural populace, grounded in their poor-care work and exemplary lives, lived out before the eyes of all, must have been very substantial. It would hardly be surprising if, over time, between a fifth and a third of the families of the village, at least, became incorporated in the Essene covenant. That is, it is quite plausible that up to 150 souls in a typical village could have been contributing members to the local Essene poorhouse. We may assume, in view of the high infant mortality typical of antiquity, that the average size of a nuclear family was perhaps five or six. Thus some twenty-five nuclear families, in a typical village of about five hundred inhabitants, may have been contributing members of the local Essene covenant. As their contributions were about a tenth of their annual income, their contributions could have supported, in difficult times, the equivalent of two or three whole families, or a further fifteen souls or more, at the poorhouse.

As we have noted, it would not be surprising if the poorhouse received occasional donations from wealthy patrons, especially in hard times, and that further extra income was derived from craft activities undertaken at the community house. It is thus quite likely that fifty souls or more, or about 10 percent of an average Judean village of about five hundred people, could easily be supported at the village's Essene poorhouse in hard times. In good times, especially in view of its culture of frugality, the house might easily accumulate a surplus.

In his classic study of agrarian society, G. Lenski seeks to calculate the typical size of the "expendable" or destitute class as a proportion of the population. He concludes that "[p]robably the best estimate we can make of the situation in agrarian society is that in normal times from 5 to 10 percent of the population found itself in this depressed class, with the figure rising as high as 15 percent on some occasions and falling almost to zero on others."[70]

It is thus probable that the poorhouses run by the Essenes had grown to such a scale by the early first century that they were able to support the destitute class of Judea. Their "New Covenant" was in fact preeminently a cooperative economic group that alleviated the key socioeconomic problems of agrarian society. It represented an effectively reformed Judaism, which by voluntary association largely eradicated the problems of poverty that had repeatedly appeared in Jewish history. Part of the economic secret of this innovative and effective form of voluntary association was the high value placed on temporary

---

70. Lenski, *Power and Privilege*, p. 283.

or permanent celibacy. Voluntary celibacy, as we have noted, functioned as a population-limiting mechanism. The combination of four thousand–plus celibate male Essenes and the two days' pay per month contribution from associated families created a socioeconomic equilibrium in rural Judea. The high number of males removed from child producing but enlisted in the support of the destitute and, especially, in the rearing of the children who could not be fed in laboring and artisan families, achieved a population balance without resort to the infanticide that was common in the Greco-Roman world. The Essene system eradicated the destitution that might force young girls into prostitution or cause youths to take to banditry. Thus the Essene work kept the territory of the Temple holy, and made atonement for the land through works of righteousness.

The Essene "House of the Poor" (Bethany) near Jerusalem

As we have seen, the Essenes most likely established poorhouses in most if not all of the towns and villages of Judea. How did they apply their poor-care system in the Jerusalem area? Did they found any special poor-care facilities within or near the city? As we have seen, the poorhouses of rural Judea cared for the elderly and sick as well as the poor. Since the Holy City raised special issues of ritual purity, it is likely the Essenes would have founded their Jerusalem poorhouse(s) outside the city. A passage from the *Temple Scroll* (11Q19) allows us to approach the question of the precise location of the Jerusalem poorhouse with confidence: "You shall make three places, to the East of the city, separate from each other, to which shall come the lepers and those afflicted with a discharge and the men who have an emission" (11Q20.13).

The passage immediately preceding this prescription defines a radius of 3,000 cubits around the city within which nothing unclean shall be seen (11Q20.12-13). Thus we should expect that an Essene care-center would be located farther than 3,000 cubits (about 1,500 yards) from the city. Three villages to the east of Jerusalem correspond well with the prescription of the *Temple Scroll:* Bethany, Bethphage, and En-shemesh. B. Pixner emphasized that information from the Gospels suggests that Bethany was where the Essenes cared for lepers. It is striking that Jesus is found, at Mk 14:3-10, dining in the house of Simon the leper at Bethany.[71] The correspondence with the prescription of the *Temple Scroll* shows that the story of this particular Essene care-center in the Jerusalem area, Bethany, is continued in the Gospels. It may also be significant

---

71. Pixner, *Wege des Messias und Stätten der Urkirche*, pp. 208-11.

that Lazarus, a very close friend of Jesus about whom we learn from John's Gospel, was cared for at Bethany while ill with an unknown disease that proved terminal (Jn 11:1–12:11). The Fourth Gospel notes that Bethany is fifteen stadia (about two miles) from the Holy City (11:18). The village was invisible from the city and Temple since it lay on the farther slope of the Mount of Olives. Its location was thus well suited to fulfilling Essene purity requirements.

The name Bethany itself confirms the village's function as a poorhouse of Jerusalem. Jerome's *Onomasticon* defines the meaning of Bethany as *domus adflictionis*, "house of affliction."[72] Jerome's Latin interpretation shows that he understood the name to be derived from the Hebrew *beth 'ani* or the identical phrase in Aramaic, *beth 'anya*. Both could mean either "house of the poor" or "house of affliction/poverty." The Christian Palestinian and Syriac versions of the New Testament both give the Aramaic version of this name and confirm Jerome's understanding. Unfortunately, modern commentators, beginning with Nestle, have rejected Jerome's explanation as a fanciful invention, preferring most often a derivation from the personal name Anaiah (Neh 8:4 and 10:22).[73] However, the Greek transliteration found in the New Testament, *bethania*, precludes this possibility, since no second alpha (a-vowel) appears after the iota (i/y), implying that none appeared after the yod (i/y) in the Semitic name. Rather, the Greek form *bethania* suggests that a consonantal yod (y) follows directly after the nun (n), as in the Aramaic form *beth 'anya*. Another, yet more speculative suggestion is that the name derives from *beth hini*, "house of figs."[74] This suggestion has arisen since the name of the nearby village Bethphage derives from *beth phage*, "house of unripe figs." However, the Greek *bethania* clearly demands a second component with an a-vowel in the first syllable. This precludes a derivation from *hini*, "figs." It is also unlikely that one of these two neighboring villages, which experienced exactly the same climate, would have been named for a difference in its fig crop. The Christian Palestinian and Syriac versions were undoubtedly correct to render Bethany as *beth 'anya*, "House of the Poor." The explanation of the expert Semitic philologist

72. See F. Wutz, *Onomastica Sacra: Untersuchungen zum Liber Interpretationis Nominum Hebraicorum des hl. Hieronymus*, Texte und Untersuchungen zur Geschichte der altchristlichen Literatur, vol. 41, pt. I (Leipzig: Hinrichs, 1914), p. 557.

73. E. Nestle, *Philologica Sacra* (Berlin, 1896), p. 20; see G. Dalman, *Sacred Sites and Ways: Studies in the Topography of the Gospels* (London: SPCK, 1935), p. 250. A contraction from the name Ananiah, which appears as a village of Bethel in Neh 11:32, is also sometimes mooted.

74. *Beth hini*, an unknown location, appears in the Babylonian Talmud, *b. Ḥullin* 53a. G. Dalman expressed different opinions of the correct etymology of Bethany. He rejected this possibility and preferred derivation from *beth 'anya* in his *Grammatik des Jüdisch-palästinischen Aramäisch*, 2nd ed. (Leipzig: Hinrichs, 1905), p. 419.

Jerome, who spent the last thirty-four years of his life as abbot of the monastery at Bethlehem, only about six miles to the southeast, was correct. The modern semantic equivalent of *beth 'anya*, "Bethany/bethany," is "Poorhouse/poorhouse."

Bethany was the last station on the route of pilgrims traveling from Galilee to Jerusalem. The Talmud notes that Bethany and Bethphage were celebrated for their reputation of hospitality toward pilgrims.[75] Galilean pilgrims avoided potential conflict with Samaritans by traveling south on the eastern side of the Jordan. Bethany was the last station on their route to Jerusalem after crossing the river and taking the road through Jericho up into the highlands. The Essene choice of Bethany as a place for care of the poor and sick is completely intelligible. A respectful distance from the city and Temple, and on the pilgrim route, Bethany was a most suitable location for a charitable institution. Jewish pilgrims who had made the longest overland journey (from Galilee) could be intercepted and cared for. The location was also suitable for a center that cared for the sick, who were best ministered to out of view of the Temple, and at a distance great enough to preclude any possible ritual affront to the Temple and Holy City. Josephus records that the individual celibate Essene was allowed to offer assistance and alms to the destitute without reference to his superiors (*War* 2.8.6 §134, cited earlier). It is thus not surprising that a communally organized Essene care-center had been established at Bethany on the Mount of Olives to care for pilgrims at the end of a long and potentially arduous journey from Galilee. The house naturally combined this work with care for the sick and destitute who drifted toward the city of Jerusalem. Thus Bethany received its name because it was an Essene poorhouse par excellence, the poorhouse that alleviated poverty closest to the Holy City.

We would expect the Essene poorhouse known as Bethany to have received important support from pious patrons belonging to the wealthy Jerusalem elite. We now examine the actions of one of these patrons as recorded in the Gospel passion narratives.

Mary of Jerusalem Announced Jesus as Messiah to the Poor by Anointing Him at the "House of the Poor" (Bethany) Near Jerusalem

According to the passion narratives of all the Gospels, Jesus made Bethany his place to stay, traveling into the city each day to teach in the Temple and returning at night across the Kidron Valley (cf. Mk 11:1, 11, 12-14, 20-21; 14:1-9). A Gali-

---

75. *b. Pesahim* 53.

lean artisan who had often made the long pilgrimage to Jerusalem for the feast, Jesus had probably always used the guest facilities at Bethany. He had a lifelong association with those who administered hospitality in the village. Several features of Jesus' association with Bethany suggest that he received considerable recognition from the Essene alms-administrators there. He was able to billet his whole traveling party in premises in the village, and continued to receive hospitality at Bethany even after his provocative action against the money changers of the Temple (Mk 11:15-19). During the week of his passion he was even honored at Bethany with a celebratory feast (Jn 12:2). The purpose of this feast was the open declaration of Jesus as Messiah, through a ritual of anointing.

B. Pixner pointed out that an ancient ritual bath still visible at Bethany in the garden of the Sisters of St. Vincent de Paul may be related to Jewish purification practices going back to pre-Christian times. Jewish pilgrims who went up to Jerusalem may have sought to purify themselves before entering the city (cf. Jn 11:55). Pilgrims may have used the ancient ritual bath at Bethany for this purpose. The dust of the last stretch of road would still cling to the feet of those who had purified themselves before entering the city. This may cast light on Jesus' washing of his disciples' feet (Jn 13:1-20). When Peter objected to Jesus' action, Jesus replied that "He who has bathed does not need to wash, except for his feet" (13:10). This may suggest that Jesus took the view, according to local custom with which he was familiar but which was unknown to his disciples, that after they had ritually bathed at Bethany their feet still needed to be washed when they entered the city of Jerusalem.[76]

We have already suggested that Jesus' interest in the poor and the outcast, which typifies his Galilean activities, would probably have led to an interest in the type of covenanted social organization through which Essenism addressed the problem and consequences of poverty in Judea. We must also ask how the Essene poorhouse with which Jesus had associations at Bethany responded to Jesus' inspiring and effective ministry of teaching and healing, which had already created a huge following among the ordinary mass of the population in Galilee.[77] The Gospels record an event that probably answers this question for

---

76. Pixner, *Wege des Messias und Stätten der Urkirche*, pp. 212-18. In a story of Jesus preserved in Oxyrhynchus Papyrus 840, a chief priest confronts Jesus in the Temple with the question: "Who gave you leave to tread this place of purification and see these holy vessels when you have not bathed and your disciples have not washed their feet?" The formulation of this question may imply that priestly circles regarded a foot washing as the necessary completion of a ritual bath, if movement from the bath into holy space might involve the contamination of the feet with dust. For the passage see F. F. Bruce, *Jesus and Christian Origins outside the New Testament* (London: Hodder and Stoughton, 1984), pp. 159-60.

77. See Mk 1:32-34, 45; 2:12; 3:7-12, 20; 4:1; 5:21, 24, 31; 6:30-34, 53-56; 8:1, 34.

us. At the feast made in his honor at Bethany, Jesus was anointed with costly perfumed oil by his disciple Mary (Mk 14:3-9; Jn 12:1-8). When objections were raised against Mary's action on the grounds of expense, Jesus defended it. His concluding remark in Mark's account gives us the key to understanding the significance of Mary's action: "Truly, I say to you, wherever the Gospel is preached in the whole world, what she has done will be told in memory of her" (14:9).

In the cult of the emperor, the term *euangelion*, "gospel," had attained high significance. *Euangelion* indicated joyful tidings such as were associated with the birthday, attainment to majority and accession to power of the Roman emperor. A calendar inscription of around 9 B.C.E. from Priene in Asia recorded, concerning the emperor Octavian (Augustus): "the birthday of the god was for the world the beginning of joyful tidings *(euangelion)* which have been proclaimed on his account."[78] Jesus has been anointed by Mary at Bethany as *meshiach,* the anointed one, the Messiah, the ruler of Israel and of the world. Only this explanation of Mary's anointing of Jesus can account for the universal significance Jesus ascribed to her action, and the universal fame he stated that Mary herself had gained through her deed. The proclamation of the gospel is that Jesus is the Messiah (Christ), the hoped-for universal Lord and redeemer of the oppressed. Mary had made the first public declaration of this good news for the world.

It was because Mary saw the proclamation of Jesus as Messiah and universal lord as the high significance of her action, that she had employed such a large quantity of expensive perfumed oil. At least one embarrassed onlooker commented that it could have been sold for three hundred *denarii,* a good annual income for a laborer (Mk 14:5). The high value of her perfumed oil shows that Mary was a wealthy woman, a member of the Jerusalem elite[79] who was a patron of Bethany, the poorhouse nearest to Jerusalem. Her action suggests that at least some members of the Jerusalem elite were eager for Jesus to be declared openly as the Messiah.[80] The danger inherent in Mary's action was obvious. Her anointing of Jesus as Messiah would inevitably provoke the Sadducean authorities, whom Jesus had openly challenged by overturning the money changers' tables in the Temple (Mk 11:15-18; Jn 2:13-22). A severe reaction from the Temple

---

78. See G. Friedrich, *TDNT* 2:724-25 *(euangelion* section A2b).

79. The important possible evidence for the elite status of the group of siblings who appear at Bethany, Mary, Martha, and Lazarus, has been recently assessed by F. W. Baltz, *Lazarus and the Fourth Gospel Community* (Lewiston, N.Y.: Mellen Biblical Press, 1995).

80. Others may have included Martha and Lazarus (see note above); Nicodemus and Joseph of Arimathea, who took care to bury Jesus' body with great honor (Jn 19:38-42); and the Beloved Disciple of the Fourth Gospel. See the study of Baltz cited in the note above and that of the present author cited first in the next note.

authorities was all the more certain since Mary seems to have sought to engage the staff, supporters, and guests of Bethany, the poorhouse nearest to Jerusalem, possibly the most important of all the Judean poorhouses, in open support of Jesus' messianic claim. Mary had sought to make Jesus the Messiah of the poor, as the leader of the highly organized New Covenant network of Judea.

Jesus was himself well aware of the inevitable consequences of Mary's action. We know this from his response when objection was made to the expense of the oil with which she anointed him Messiah (Mk 14:5; Jn 12:4-6). The words with which he chose to refer to his inevitable death, however, first addressed the immediate problem of the objection made against Mary's generosity. Rich women such as Mary, who associated themselves with Bethany, were expected to perform good works on behalf of the poor, such as ensuring that any destitute persons who died in the Jerusalem area were given proper burials. They were expected either to perform these works themselves or to provide for their undertaking, in a "beautiful" way, showing care and honor to the poor. Jesus declared that Mary has indeed performed a work of the kind expected of her, a beautiful work of the kind expected to flow from the gifts that she brought to the house from her great wealth: "She has done a beautiful thing to me . . . she has anointed my body beforehand for burial" (Mk 14:6-8). The deeper meaning of Jesus' words, however, is clear: "By anointing me thus, Mary has signed my death warrant. I will now be killed by those jealous of my popularity. I will now be gotten rid of by those who have failed to come to the true realization of my identity that Mary has announced to all in her action. They will see me merely as a declared political rival who must be put to shame before the people and killed." Commentators who attend only to the immediate rhetorical function of Jesus' remark, his exoneration of Mary, have assumed that anointing for burial was the real significance and intent of her action. This reading of the incident wrenches the act of anointing from its larger context, the faith of those supporters of Jesus who had come to regard him as the hoped-for King of Israel, the Messiah, and had worked to see him anointed as such.

The role of Bethany as the poorhouse closest to Jerusalem is confirmed by the hubbub of objection caused by Mary's use of such an expensive gift. Some witnesses to Jesus' anointing (Mk 14:4), including Judas (Jn 12:4-6), felt intense embarrassment that such wealth had been poured away (Mk 14:3). How could witnesses to the scene not feel embarrassment when Mary had chosen as the location for her action a poorhouse where the destitute of the Jerusalem area (always numerous) gathered at a respectful distance from the city to receive alms? Jesus referred to the poor who constantly gathered at Bethany for alms, in his response: "For you always have the poor with you, and whenever you will, you can do good to them" (Mk 14:7; cf. Jn 12:8). The crowds who acclaimed Jesus on his triumphal entry into Jerusalem as Messiah and King (Jn 12:12-19; note v. 2) were undoubtedly drawn from the destitute who received support from this Essene poorhouse at Bethany and saw Jesus as their champion.

Jesus went from Bethany to celebrate his last meal with his disciples at the "Upper Room" on Zion, the southwest hill of Jerusalem, where his associations with Essenism continued.[81] I hope this chapter has set out some wider context for reading B. Pixner's brilliant contribution to this volume, his exposition of the archaeological evidence for connections between the Essenes of Mount Zion and the earliest community of Jesus' followers in Jerusalem.

81. See Capper, "With the Oldest Monks," pp. 1-55. Further comments on the New Covenant that already existed in Judea at the arrest of Jesus are made in Capper, "Two Types of Discipleship in Early Christianity," JTS 52 (2001): 105-23.

Judas and Jesus:
A Message on a Drinking Vessel
of the Second Temple Period

William Klassen

One of the most intriguing challenges of research is to interpret the artifacts of ancient life and culture. Archaeologists, philologists, and historians need both training and special gifts to unravel these ancient mysteries that have grown incrementally due to the sheer mass of the material that has come to light.

The purpose of this investigation is to look at a delicate, translucent-glass drinking vessel inscribed with four words. It appears to come from Sidon in what is now southern Lebanon. Experts agree that it probably dates from the first part of the first century C.E. Some fifteen such vessels now lie in museums in Italy; Berlin; Birmingham, England; and Toledo, Ohio. The fact that three of the four words inscribed on the vessel appear in Mt 26:50, as part of the dialogue between Judas and Jesus, lends considerable interest to our research. If a connection can be shown to exist between these words — or even if there is a likelihood of such a connection — it behooves us to do our best to interpret it. Yet as far as I know, no New Testament scholar has broached the subject. We can then consider this as part of a much larger and particularly energetic search for the "historical Jesus."[1]

It is surely important to find out, as much as is possible, about the encounter between Judas and Jesus at that fateful moment of their lives when they met in the Garden of Gethsemane. It is just possible that a careful study of Matthew's text, the text on a glass beaker, and drinking customs of Jesus and his disciples may yield a better understanding of the relationship between Judas and

---

It is my pleasure to dedicate this chapter in gratitude to my colleagues at the École Biblique in Jerusalem. Since I first worked in their library in the fall of 1973, they have been gracious partners in biblical research and teaching. *Merci!*

1. For a sensitive and comprehensive survey and appraisal of that quest, see J. H. Charlesworth, "The Historical Jesus and Exegetical Theology," *PSB* 22 (2001): 45-63.

Figure 67. Ceramic Canaanite
bichrome ware with animal
(perhaps a ram) and with wavy
lines that seem to depict serpents
or water. This jar was found in
1999 northwest of Jericho in a cave.

Courtesy of The Cousins Foundation

Jesus. It is to John Meier's credit that he recognizes the need to study Jesus' relationship to others if we are ever to understand him. Unfortunately, while he devotes eight pages (213-21) of *A Marginal Jew* to John and twenty-four pages
(221-45) to Peter, he has only a few pages for Judas (208-11) and seems to over-
look the proportionately keener interest the four Gospels display in Judas and
his relationship to Jesus.[2] While Meier does admit that "betray" is not the most
accurate term to use for Judas's action, for the sake of "convenience and convention" he continues to use the term.[3]

Classical writers bear abundant witness to the glass-blowing industry in
the area of Sidon and Tyre during the Hellenistic period.[4] Numerous goblets
and bulbous cups or beakers found by modern archaeologists or tracked down

2. As noted in my book *Judas,* the Gospels, starting with Mark and continuing to John,
show increasing degrees of interest in Judas, a phenomenon that continues to this day.

3. J. P. Meier, *A Marginal Jew* (New York: Doubleday, 2001), 3:178. Meier argues for the existence of the Twelve during Jesus' ministry but unfortunately pays no heed to the way Jesus is depicted as relating to Judas in contrast, say, to Peter or others.

4. One classical text is Pliny's *Natural History* 36.190, cited in E. M. Stern, *Roman Mold-Blown
Glass: The First through Sixth Centuries* (Toledo: Toledo Museum of Art, 1995), pp. 65-73. Pliny's
description of how the glass industry began has been treated with skepticism by historians.

by glass collectors confirm early literary reports and encourage investigation. The relation of artifacts used for drinking, as well as drinking customs, to the literary sources of early Christianity and Second Temple Judaism in Galilee is an intriguing subject to explore.

A distinct class of glass drinking vessels inscribed with writing is of particular interest to historians and biblical scholars. Such writing ranges from primitive scrawling of the name of the artist who designed and created the vessel (perhaps the owner writing a brief message to the user with, say, an admonition to "seize the victory") to elaborate scenes of victory or comments on bucolic beauty.[5] In addition to hunting and sports scenes, after the Second Temple period there are some biblical scenes, such as Adam and Eve in the primal garden with the message, "Rejoice in God. Drink and may you live."

Perhaps most important for our study is the frequency of slogans such as "Life to you and yours, drink and live," "Life to you and yours," "Life to the Strong," "Marcianus . . . drink and live," "Wine gives life," "Rejoice with Yours. Drink and live."[6]

Glass drinking vessels have been discovered at many sites. Two beakers found at Masada were dated before 70 C.E.[7] Tel Anafa, occupied almost contin-

---

5. On wine vessels see G. Hagenow, *Aus dem Weingarten der Antike, Der Wein in Dichtung, Brauchtum und Alltag*, Kulturtum der alten Welt, vol. 12 (Mainz: Philipp von Zabern Verlag, 1982). The section "Sprechende Becher," pp. 135-48, documents a very common practice of writing something on a drinking vessel, a note of cheer or encouragement or name of the person who made the vessel, e.g., "Rejoice and Drink," etc. Considerable research and publishing has taken place on this topic. In addition to E. M. Stern's excellent book, I have found most helpful D. B. Harden, "Romano-Syrian Glasses with Mould-Blown Inscriptions," *JRS* 25 (1935): 163-86; Harden, "The Glass of the Greeks and Romans," *JRS* 25 (1935): 140-49; R. Harris, "Glass Chalices of the First Century," *BJRL* 11 (1927): 1-10.

6. M. Taylor and D. Hill, *Roman Engraved Glass Reproductions* (1998), pp. 1-10, published catalogue.

7. D. P. Barag, "The Contribution of Masada to the History of Early Roman Glass," in *Roman Glass: Two Centuries of Art and Invention*, ed. M. S. Newby and K. S. Painter, Society of Antiquities Occasional Papers 13 (London, 1991), pp. 137-140, here p. 139. G. D. Weinberg, "Mold-Blown Beakers with Mythological Scenes," *Journal of Glass Studies* 14 (1972): 26-47, here pp. 46-47, describes unpublished fragments of two beakers from Masada, assigned to the period before 75 C.E. on the basis of coins. It would appear that they have some similarities (color, shape, size), but, of course, significant differences are the absence of writing and the prominence of the nude human form on the Masada goblets. Clearly they were not brought there by the Zealots! I agree with Weinberg's statement that one would have "to be very rash" to "arrive at unassailable conclusions" on the basis of these finds, agreeable as it might seem (p. 47). O. Dussart, *La Verre en Jordanie et en Syrie du Sud*, Bibliothèque Archéologique et Historique, vol. 152 (Beirut, 1998), provides a broad representative treatment beyond our immediate area of interest but presents nothing like the Sidon beaker's inscription.

Figure 68. Ceramic beer
mugs from the Iron Age,
found in or near Jerusalem.

Courtesy of J. H. Charlesworth

uously from the early Bronze Age to about 75 C.E., revealed some artifacts, probably imported.[8] Jalame (also known as Jolame), located some 20 kilometers south of Nazareth, was a center for glassmaking at a later period and could well have been a center earlier, although there is no convincing proof of that.[9]

This paper examines a drinking beaker with a mold-blown inscription almost certainly dating from the first half of the first century. Copies of the beaker exist in numerous locations, with a dozen almost identical artifacts,[10] all with the words "Rejoice! That's why you are here."[11]

8. S. C. Herbert, "Anafa, Tel," in *ABD* (1992), 1:219-21.

9. G. Weinberg, ed., *Excavations at Jolame, Site of Glass Factory in Late Roman Palestine (351-383 C.E.)* (Columbia: University of Missouri Press, 1988).

10. Stern says they are "found throughout the Mediterranean. Two appear to be from Lebanon, four in South Russia, one each from Asia Minor and Cyprus, three from Greece, two or three from Italy and one from Tunisia. Fragments belonging to this type were found in Vindonossa, Switzerland and at Colchester, England. This distribution is characteristic of first century products associated with Sidon" (*Roman Mold-Blown Glass*, p. 97).

11. εὐφραίνου ἐφ' ὅ πάρει. Harden, "Romano-Syrian Glasses," pp. 173-75 n. 2. A chart of their locations is provided by G. Sangiorgi, *Collezione di vetri antichi* (Milan and Rome, 1914), table 19.

These words, in Greek uncial letters in continuous script embedded in molded glass (apart from the first word, which in Mt 26:50 is "Friend"),[12] reproduce exactly the greeting Matthew puts into the mouth of Jesus after he meets Judas at the time of the arrest. In Matthew's text Judas greets Jesus bilingually and respectfully with the words "Hail, Rabbi."[13] As Matthew, following Mark, describes it, Judas "kissed him warmly."[14]

Jesus replies: "Friend, this is why you are here."[15] E. V. Rieu translates it as an imperative, as do many others: "My friend, do what you have come for."[16]

The similarity between the two salutations, one recorded by Matthew and the other on the beaker, was apparently noted by Adolf Deissmann eighty years ago.[17] Since the days of Deissmann virtually all have rejected his opinion that the relative pronoun begins a question.[18] In the 1923 edition of *Licht vom Osten*, Deissmann wrote: "A Greek saying which is to be found on Syrian goblets from the time of the Roman Empire teaches us that the greeting, *eph' ho parei* [ἐφ' ὅ πάρει] was a fixed phrase in popular speech."[19] Deissmann described "it as an

12. ἑταῖρε.

13. χαῖρε ῥαββί.

14. So R. Brown, *The Death of the Messiah* (New York: Doubleday, 1993), pp. 1584, 1591, translates the Greek aorist verb *kataphileō*. Most commentators recognize that both Mark and Matthew intensify this kiss, Judas says he will *"phileō"* Jesus but in fact "keeps on kissing" = *kataphileō*. But commentators (preferring an ingressive aorist to a durative aorist) cannot bring themselves to allow this to be a genuine kiss. They tend to use that detail to denigrate Judas and to highlight his "treachery" or "callousness." It seems not to occur to them that for such a kiss to take place, it really takes two people! There is no indication that Jesus rebuffs Judas or turns him aside. To be sure, in Luke's version Jesus asks: "Would you hand over the Son of Man with a kiss?" (Lk 22:47-48). Surely that kiss no one would invent! See below at notes 39 and 41.

15. ἑταῖρε, ἐφ' ὅ πάρει.

16. E. V. Rieu, *The Four Gospels* (Penguin Classics, 1953).

17. A. Deissmann, *Licht vom Osten*, 4th ed. (Tübingen, 1923), p. 104: "jetzt im Besitze vom Theodor Wiegand" (not in the 1908 edition, "now in the possession of T. Wiegand"). Deissmann urged scholars to pursue the significance of this striking coincidence. It did not strike me as important to pursue when I first encountered it some years ago (see *Judas, Betrayer or Friend of Jesus?* [Minneapolis: Fortress, 1996]). I wondered then what an invitation to drink might possibly have to do with Matthew's account of Jesus and Judas's encounter on that fateful night. I am grateful for Professor James Charlesworth's encouragement to follow Deissmann's prodding.

18. The best summary of the options is Stählin, "φιλέω," in *TDNT*, vol. 9, trans. G. W. Bromiley (1974), pp. 140-41. James Moffat's translation is similar to the TEV's: "Be quick about it friend."

19. By the time the English edition of his book, *Light from the East* (1927), had appeared, the beaker on which Deissmann had based his observation had changed hands. Dr. Theodor Wiegand had purchased it in the Crimea from a dealer by the name of Seleko (Harden, "Romano-Syrian Glasses," p. 175). He assigned the inscription to the first century of the common

accurate inscription" and concludes that it is a question: "What are you here for? Rejoice!"[20] Since Deissmann, few have defended the interrogative form of the relative pronoun, and the majority of commentators and translators make it a straight affirmation, some even an imperative; specifically what Jesus said to Judas was: "Friend, do what you have come for," or "Friend, this is what you are here for."

The brevity of the expression, its apparent elliptical nature, but not least the preconceived opinions on what might have been going on between Judas and Jesus, and even some feelings about what Jesus *should* have said to Judas all make it more difficult to arrive at conclusions avoiding theological or dogmatic clutter.

Nevertheless, the effort is worthwhile. On several important fronts we are moving toward consensus. First, we can rejoice in our good fortune for having such an interesting artifact available in so many places in the world.[21] Stern notes that no cups have been recorded from datable contexts, "but a few examples of closely related types have been found in contexts dated to the first half of the 1st century . . . this Series was probably created before the middle of the 1st century."[22]

Deissmann's urging that this lowly bit of evidence be diligently studied has been virtually ignored by all commentators. However, it was heeded by Friedrich Blass and A. Debrunner, the ninth edition of whose *Grammar* was translated by Robert W. Funk. They describe it as a "reminiscence of a toast like the one attested on a goblet from Syria."[23]

Another grammarian, Nigel Turner, devotes a separate discussion to this passage, which he describes insightfully as "Linguistically one of the most difficult passages in the New Testament, and the suggestion that the words were inscribed on the drinking cup at the Lord's Supper is neither helpful nor probable."[24]

What, however, of the possibility that Matthew knew these words from a

---

era. It had by 1927 passed, thanks to Deissmann's generosity, into the hands of Rendel Harris. Wiegand may also have placed it in the Berlin Museum 11866 (Collection von Gaus No. 212).

20. See Harden, "Romano-Syrian Glasses," pp. 173-75 n. 15.

21. The Toledo Art Gallery has several (see Stern, *Roman Mold-Blown Glass*, pp. 97, 102), as do the British Museum, Birmingham Art Gallery, and Giorgio Sangiorgi collection in Rome.

22. Stern, *Roman Mold-Blown Glass*, p. 98.

23. F. Blass, A. Debrunner, and R. W. Funk, *A Greek Grammar of the NT* (Chicago: University of Chicago Press, 1961), §300. The qualifying adjectives "painful, ironic," since they carried the day, perhaps made it more difficult to allow the evidence to be evaluated without bias.

24. Nigel Turner, *Grammatical Insights into the New Testament* (Edinburgh: T. & T. Clark, 1965), pp. 68-71.

drinking cup in his environment or Jesus and Judas from theirs?[25] Can one imagine them as part of the oral tradition that came to Matthew?

Scholars continue to be baffled by the content of what Jesus was saying to Judas.[26] F. Rehkopf, W. Eltester, and G. Stählin worked hard to untie the knot,[27] but in the end could not do so with any degree of certainty or unanimity. In addition, monographs on Judas by W. Vogler, H.-J. Klauck, and W. Klassen do not take this evidence seriously at all.[28] Few commentators on Matthew show any awareness of this inscribed beaker, much less take it into consideration in trying to unravel this mystery.[29] To conclude then that "the meaning of this saying is not unequivocal and has always been debated"[30] is a slight understatement. Still, it is worth investigating in light of new evidence and a new openness to look at the figure of Judas in particular.

We are dealing here with a genuine piece of *realia:* real evidence. That it relates in some way to a piece of dialogue between Jesus and his most maligned disciple adds immeasurably to its value, for precious few (are there any others?) words between Jesus and any of his disciples have been preserved outside the Gospels.

At the same time, to make a connection with Jesus we must ask what the likelihood is that Jesus and his disciples were familiar with beakers bearing this drinking slogan. Surely the question, "What light does this cast on Matthew's perception of the Judas-Jesus encounter?" deserves consideration. We can leave to other, more romantic souls the pursuit of the Holy Grail. We will also not pursue the suggestion of Rendel Harris that Jesus and Judas drank from this beaker at the Last Supper.[31] Nevertheless, this type of beaker may well have

25. M. D. Goulder, *Midrash and Lectionary in Matthew* (London: SPCK, 1974), concludes from this response to Judas that Jesus had no resentment but accepted the coming tragedy (p. 445). The drastic ellipse (he supplies the verb "to do") makes the saying "extremely difficult."

26. Deissmann likely mentioned this first in his essay, "Friend, Wherefore Art Thou Come?" *ET* 33 (1922): 491-93.

27. F. Rehkopf, "Matt 26:50," *ZNW* 52 (1961): 109-15; W. Eltester, "'Freund, wozu du gekommen bist' (Matt XXVI.50)," in *Neotestamentica et Patristica (Festschrift für O. Cullmann)*, NovTSup 6 (Leiden, 1962), pp. 70-91; G. Stählin, "φιλέω," in *TDNT* 9 (1973), pp. 113-46; see esp. pp. 140-41 n. 241.

28. W. Vogler, *Judas Iskarioth* (Berlin: Evangelische Verlagsanstalt, 1985); H.-J. Klauck, *Judas — ein Jünger des Herrn* (Herder, 1987); Klassen, *Judas, Betrayer or Friend of Jesus?*

29. So W. D. Davies and D. Allison, *A Critical and Exegetical Commentary on the Gospel according to St. Matthew*, 3 vols., ICC (Edinburgh: T&T Clark, 1988-97), 3:508-10, who deal with the beaker evidence but lean toward an "ironic riposte to Judas's greeting" (p. 510) and are confident that "Judas conceals his evil intentions behind a greeting and a kiss" (p. 508). The drinking slogan can hardly be "ironic."

30. Stählin, "φιλέω," p. 140 n. 241.

31. Notes in the R. Harris file at Woodbrooke College Library, Birmingham, indicate that Dr. Wiegand gave the vessel to Harris and that it arrived "broken into a mass of fragments." It

been used in inns in Galilee, if not in Jerusalem, although to my knowledge no
wine glasses of this type and period with any inscriptions have so far been discovered *in situ* in either Galilee or Jerusalem.[32]

We can pursue the mood of the moment of the arrest and what light this
casts on the relation between Judas and Jesus. If we agree with the majority that
it is highly likely that Jesus and his disciples were familiar with such an inscription on a drinking cup, then we may follow Blass-Debrunner-Funk in taking
this greeting as a "reminiscence of a toast"[33] and try to place the cup into the
context of Jesus Research.[34]

With such a brief fragment, enigmatic as it is, the probabilities of authenticity
are increased — for editors do not usually invent problems. Indeed, this encounter
of Jesus with Judas as recorded in Matthew's Gospel is an addition to Mark's account. Certainly if Matthew was composed in the Tyre-Sidon area or around
Antioch, it is not fanciful to suggest that he would have known such a beaker.

We certainly may wish to affirm that the call to rejoice is a natural dimen-
sion of Judaism and then ask whether joining and rejoicing with wine may accord with Jewish values as reflected in Jewish sources.[35] Deissmann already
called attention to Ps 104[103]:15: "You make wine to gladden the human heart,
oil to make the face shine."[36]

---

was mended with great care by a Jewish craftsman, Mr. Byron of London. Harris "suggested that
a few hours previously Jesus and his disciples had been drinking from a similar cup and the
words were quoted as a prod to Judas." The note goes on, "Others did not agree with him"
(Woodbrooke Library file on "Chalice or Woodbrooke Cup"). Note Harris's article "Deissmann
on the Holy Grail," *ET* 35 (1923-24): 523-24. After Harris's death, the cup was again broken, this
time at a Woodbrooke College board meeting where its fate was being discussed. It was partially
restored with a few letters missing, and can be seen in the Birmingham Art Gallery.

32. Inquiries at the Israel Museum, at the Bible Lands Museum, and at the Ecole Biblique
have thus far always confirmed this.

33. Blass, Debrunner, and Funk, *A Greek Grammar,* §300. N.B. the absence of the qualifying
adjectives "painful, ironic."

34. Bernhard Dieckmann, *Judas als Sündenbock. Eine verhängnisvolle Geschichte von Angst
und Vergeltung* (Munich: Kösel, 1991), calls for a detailed survey of the biblical evidence; his work
is a theological treatment focusing on the relation of Judas to the death of Jesus and on the image
of the enemy. This research is a most valuable piece of work in addition to Klauck's and Vogler's.

35. That joy is a central element of both Jewish and early Christian life can be easily demonstrated. The invitation to joyful celebration is authentically Jewish. C. Arnold concludes that
"Good wine can bring joy" and cites Ps 103:15: "Wine rejoices the heart of man" (LXX), and Judg
9:13: "new wine which gladdens gods and humans"; see "Joy," in *ABD* (1992), 3:1022-23. In both
cases the language of the LXX is close to that of the beaker's inscription.

36. For the place of wine among the Jews, see Gustaf Dalman, *Arbeit und Sitte in Palästina:
Brot, Öl und Wein* (Hildesheim: Georg Olms Verlag, 1964), 4:386; see esp. p. 393 for the various
uses of wine. In the OT it is presupposed that the beaker of wine is taken as symbol of God's

Given the cloud that hangs over Judas and the fixed opinions of many scholars about the Judas-Jesus relationship, we can be sure that every word attributed to Jesus and Judas has become a battleground.

Five essential aspects need to be dealt with here:

- Judas's greeting of Jesus, "Hail, Teacher!"
- The kiss between Judas and Jesus
- The words Jesus speaks to Judas in response
- The meaning of drinking the cup
- A brief glimpse at some evidence from the early church

Judas's Greeting of Jesus, "Hail, Teacher!"

Commentators have noted that the greeting Judas extends to Jesus, "Hail, Teacher!" is what one would expect from a student. While the Gospel writers (Mark has only "Rabbi," Luke omits any greeting) translated it into Greek, it may originally have been in Hebrew or Aramaic — in which case Judas would have greeted his master with the wish that Jesus might have *shalom*. The greeting is a prayer in Hebrew, which means that Judas is praying that God may grant Jesus wholeness and lack of conflict.[37]

The Greek translation of this *shalom* greeting weakens it somewhat, but at least makes sense to both Mark's and Matthew's readers.

Much has been made of the fact that Judas addresses Jesus as "Rabbi." It is noted that the other disciples always address him as "Lord," and it is precisely in Matthew that the disciples are told not to allow themselves to be addressed as or to address each other as rabbi (Mt 23:8). At the same time, that text urges them to call Jesus rabbi, for he is their teacher and it is natural for a Jewish student to address his teacher as rabbi. There is no reason on the face of it, especially since Matthew here simply follows Mark, to conclude that Judas was deliberately disobeying the orders of his teacher. In this conclusion we concur with Raymond Brown. The thesis that the address "Rabbi" and the kiss "are unusual and therefore hypocritical signs of respect and friendship is dubious."[38]

---

help (Ps 116:13: "I will lift up the cup of salvation"). See also S. Krauss, *Talmudische Archäologie*, 3 vols. (Hildesheim: Georg Olms, 1966 [1st ed. 1911]).

37. Johannes Pedersen, *Israel: Its Life and Culture*, 2 vols. (London: Oxford University Press, 1926), p. 303: "The covenant is confirmed . . . still more by the intimate touch, through the kiss." "Those who meet . . . bless each other with good words and through them they give each other peace" (p. 303).

38. Brown, *Death of the Messiah*, pp. 1385-86.

The Kiss between Judas and Jesus

First let us proceed with a philological inquiry. A clear distinction between two words for kiss, *phileō* and *kataphileō*, is made in Xenophon's *Memorabilia*, in which Socrates and Critobulus are discussing the art of wooing. Socrates rejects "laying hands on the fair and forcing them to submit." For he has learned from Scylla that when you try to force people they flee. The Sirens, however, laid hands on no one but through enchanted singing would encourage all to yield to their charms. Socrates then teaches Critobulus a "good plan for making friends."

"Then won't you lay lip to lip, either?" asks Socrates. To which Critobulus answers: "not unless the owner is fair." Socrates then replies that the "ugly" like being kissed "supposing that they are called fair for the beauty of their souls." To this Critobulus replies: "A kiss *(phileō)* for the fair, and a thousand kisses *(kataphileō)* for the good!"[39]

There can be no doubt that kisses are sometimes planted on people's cheeks or lips for the wrong reason.[40] There is, however, no reason to think that

---

39. Xenophon, *Memorabilia* 2.6.33, ed. and trans. E. C. Marchant, LCL (London: Heinemann, 1923): Ὡς τοὺς μὲν καλοὺς φιλήσοντός μου, τοὺς δ᾽ ἀγαθοὺς καταφιλήσοντος. The translator inserts the word "thousand" to bring out the difference. Unfortunately this reference does not appear in Danker's new version of Bauer. The verb form does not appear in G. W. H. Lampe's *Patristic Greek Lexicon* (Oxford, 1961) but is well represented in Liddell and Scott's *Greek-English Lexicon*. According to Hatch and Redpath's *Concordance of the LXX,* it appears over twenty times in the LXX. The three occurrences in Josephus are inconclusive. Perhaps the most interesting usage is in his retelling of the Joab-Amasa kiss of betrayal where Amasa is killed by Joab under the ruse of a kiss (LXX, καταφιλέω, 2 Kgds 20:9). He follows the LXX usage (*Ant* 7.284). Since Joab had seized Amasa by the beard and forced the kiss, the case is not parallel to Jesus and Judas in any regard.

40. W. Klassen, "The Kiss as Sacred Act in the New Testament: An Example of Social Boundary Lines," *NTS* 39 (1993): 122-35. Also W. Klassen, "Kiss (NT)," in *ABD* (1992), 4:89-92. C. S. Keener, "Kissing," in *DNTB*, pp. 628-29, relates Judas's kiss to the practice of a student kissing his teacher on the head (attested in much later rabbinic sources), which he calls a "betrayal kiss." "That the outward act should have signified friendship, respect or devotion made the treachery all the more heinous (Prov 27:6)" (p. 629). Unfortunately he says nothing about Matthew's use of *kataphileō* here. A detailed analysis of the use of the term is needed, not only in Josephus, Philo, and classical writers, but also to determine whether the juxtapositon of the two terms dominates in a context where genuine love and the show of affection are contrasted. It surely appears that way in both Xenophon's usage and especially in Philo's generous use of this term for kiss in his meditation on who Masek (= From a kiss) is. He affirms that "we do not have love (φιλέω) in kissing (καταφιλέω)," for he goes on, "people even in hundreds of cases have to kiss their enemies." Conversely others, like Laban, are not held worthy even to kiss their children or daughters (following the text of the LXX Gen 31:28, he uses καταφιλέω). Philo concludes: "Hold then the virtues dear, we who have trained to hate dissimulation, embrace them

Judas kissed Jesus for any other purpose than that Jesus and the disciples normally kissed after they had been separated. It was, we can be sure, a sign that they confirmed their covenant of living together. Never in their common life together did they need it more.

What is especially important in this context is that we do not import into the text the mountains of ill will that have reigned for centuries in the church against Judas. Moreover, it is very important that we do not import into this encounter "sarcasm" or "irony,"[41] but rather allow words to convey their usual meaning. The kiss, for example, is normally a sign of affection or bonding; there is nothing abnormal about it in this context, nor does either Mark or Matthew treat it as anything but a genuine mark of affection. Because greeting with a kiss is standard practice among first-century Jews, it can serve double duty as identifying Jesus for the party from the high priest. Recall that only in Mark and Matthew is the kiss an important element.

For Luke it is a conative kiss. By the time of the Fourth Gospel, there is no kiss and Judas is not "possessed of a demon" but is himself "a devil" (6:70). In this Gospel he has been demonized almost from the start. Early in the ministry of Jesus, according to John, Judas typifies the defector par excellence (6:59-71). Although he may be included among the disciples whom Jesus loved to the end (13:1) and had his feet washed by Jesus,[42] a kiss is not recorded as evidence of that love. There is virtually no interaction between Jesus and Judas at all except that Jesus orders him to "Do quickly that which you do" (13:27), thus bringing John's treatment of this act of "handing over" during the last days "in harmony with" the Matthew text here.[43]

As James Charlesworth has demonstrated, while there was one writer who argued that Judas was "the Beloved Disciple," this position has not been taken seriously by other scholars.[44] It will be a while before Judas is treated as a

---

with your soul and love them truly and you will never desire to be the maker of that travesty of friendship, the kiss (καταφιλεῖν)" (*QuisRerDivHer* 8, pp. 40-44).

41. It can hardly be called "the worst type of hypocrisy," as S. T. Lachs does in *A Rabbinic Commentary on the New Testament* (Hoboken, N.J.: Ktav, 1987), p. 416. We must beware not to import later Talmudic discussions of the kiss into this period.

42. H. C. Orchard, *Courting Betrayal: Jesus as Victim in the Gospel of John* (Sheffield, 1998), argues that feet washing and betrayal(s) "are interlinked and should be interpreted together"; "both the reader and the protagonist know the act of perfidy is imminent, yet Jesus' behavior at this moment is utterly unexpected. He chooses to communicate with his disciples through an intensely intimate action, which renders him (Jesus) consciously and deliberately humiliated" (p. 160).

43. Brown, *Death of the Messiah*, p. 1386.

44. J. H. Charlesworth, *The Beloved Disciple: Whose Witness Validates the Gospel of John?* (Valley Forge, Pa.: Trinity, 1995).

"friend" of Jesus, much less as the Beloved Disciple. Progress will be made only if we take seriously David Daube's suggestion that behind Matthew's account of Judas's role stands the word $m^e sar$ ("deliver up" or "hand over"), with its wide and fluid notion.[45]

Moreover, we need to consider the vigilante system,[46] and especially the role and function of the high priest in first-century Jerusalem society.[47] Both Philo and Josephus speak of the important role the high priest played in keeping law and order, and the deep respect in which the people held him.[48] All sources agree that to "hand someone over" to a pagan ruler is a serious crime, punishable by death. There is not a hint of evidence that Judas had anything to do with non-Jewish authorities. This must be noted, for it drastically changes one's view of the nature of Judas's act in handing Jesus over to the high priest. This is especially true since Jesus surely expected the "handing over" to happen and saw it as the will of God. After Gethsemane he was ready to accept it.

With the new edition of Bauer's *Greek Lexicon*, Frederick Danker has made it possible for us to minimize the stress on "betrayal" and take the role of Judas seriously as an "informer" or as "the one who handed Jesus over." Behind that act, as the Gospels and Paul agree, stands God as the ultimate agent of "handing Jesus over to the High Priest."[49]

45. D. Daube, *Collaboration with Tyranny in Rabbinic Law* (London: Oxford University Press, 1965), pp. 10-11. Regrettably, Daube has Judas not handing over Jesus to the high priest but "dealing with non-Jewish authorities." I have paid more attention to this idea in "The Authenticity of Judas' Participation in the Arrest of Jesus," in *Authenticating the Activities of Jesus*, ed. B. Chilton and C. A. Evans (Leiden: Brill, 1999), pp. 389-410.

46. T. Seland, *Establishment Violence in Philo and Luke* (Leiden: Brill, 1995), discusses the "Punishing Agents" in Philo (pp. 125-31, 170-71). Philo is enamored by the example of the Levites who began with their nearest and dearest, acknowledging no love or kinship but God's love (*Vita Mosis* 2.170ff., 270ff.).

47. Excellently spelled out in the new edition of Emil Schürer, *The History of the Jewish People*, rev. G. Vermes, F. Millar, and M. Black (Edinburgh: T. & T. Clark, 1979), 2:234-313.

48. Josephus, *Apion* 2.185-188, waxes eloquent in praise of the Law in accordance with the will of God. All of life is under God and under the priests, not only general supervision, for it included "the trial of cases of litigation, and the punishment of condemned persons." In this "saintly government," this "sacred ceremony of administration of the law," the high priests play a key role. The gift of eloquence is theirs, but above all, discretion (2.186-187). See also *Ant* 11.111, 14.41: the Jewish people say, "It is the custom of their country [Jews] to obey the priests of the God who was venerated by them." What if Judas affirmed that and sought to make an encounter between Jesus and the high priest possible?

49. W. Reinbold, *Der älteste Bericht über den Tod Jesu: Literarische Analyse und historische Kritik der Passionsdarstellungen der Evangelien*, Beihefte zur ZNW no. 69 (Berlin: Walter de Gruyter, 1994), also concluded, "The word *paradidōmi* means not betray." Note also p. 235 n. 28: "Once more it should be specifically pointed out that *paradidonai* cannot be translated

Danker reminds us of Raymond Brown's observation that there is a tendency to translate the word *paradidōmi* as "betray," especially in connection with Judas.[50] In fact, the term "betrayer" is used only once in the New Testament to describe Judas's action (Lk 6:16), and the verb "betray" *(prodidōmi)* is never once applied to Judas. His role is rather that of the one, who along with God, hands the beloved Son over to the Temple authorities. Most often that role is assigned to God, but for some reason, as the decisive hour approached, a human agency became necessary. As the Gospel accounts illustrate (Mk 14:17-21// Mt 26:20-23; cf. Jn 13:21-30), each one of the Twelve asked whether he would be taking on that role. Every one of the Twelve asked, "It isn't I, is it?" Each, it seems, expected a negative answer. For Paul it was clear, God the Father handed the Son over as an act of love (Rom 8:32). It could even be said that Jesus "handed himself over" on our behalf (Gal 2:20). If Paul knew about Judas, it did not occur to him to mention his name. Without naming an agent he referred only to "the night when *he was handed over*" (1 Cor 11:23, emphasis added).

Jesus' Words to Judas

The banter between Jesus and Judas certainly can, and I believe should, be seen as a warm interchange between two comrades. This is certainly what the word "friend" conveys. We must first, however, deal with the evidence, which on the surface appears quite troubling.

Matthew is the only one who used the word in the New Testament and always in the vocative:[51] as in the king to the impudent guest without an appropriate garment at the wedding (22:12), or the landowner to grumbling workers about pay equity (20:13), or Jesus to Judas. As K. H. Rengstorf put it in an important study of the term: "Without putting too much into the word one may say that in all three (or four?) cases more is involved than merely a form. In each case a mutually binding relationship between the two, the one speaking and the one addressed, is being ignored and despised by the one spoken to."[52]

In all three cases, but especially in the case of Judas, he concludes, "guilt is incurred by the addressee who ignores the mutual agreement out of egotistic

---

betray." That Bauer (p. 1243) nevertheless speaks of the "betrayal" of Judas, "ist meines Erachtens nur wirkungsgeschichtlich erklärbar" (p. 235 n. 28).

50. F. W. Danker, ed., *A Greek-English Lexicon of the New Testament* (Chicago: University of Chicago Press, 2000), p. 762. See also p. 479: "the one who turned in Jesus," "Judas the informer" (p. 480).

51. Rengstorf, "ἑταῖρος," in *TWNT* (1935), 2:697-700.

52. Rengstorf, "ἑταῖρος," 698:34. The following two quotations also come from this article.

motives and considers only the other side as obligated." Rengstorf considers this so certain that Mt 26:50 "does not need any special comment." This is an astounding attribution of motive to Judas. Others wish to treat the whole incident as invented by Matthew (and Mark), but this is a strange fabrication and one would need to ask what purpose it serves.[53]

The Meaning of Drinking the Cup

To be sure, Jesus does not invite Judas to rejoice, as the full drinking slogan of Sidon does, but in using the words (in Greek), it is quite possible that he invited Judas to drink the cup, the cup of God's wrath, the cup of suffering, with him. Jesus had himself struggled and had overcome his own aversion to drinking the cup. Consistent with his striking invitation: "Are you able to drink the cup which I am about to drink?" (Mk 10:38//Mt 20:22; cf. Jn 18:11), he is now, having decided himself to drink it (Mk 14:36//Mt 26:39//Lk 22:42), inviting his disciple Judas to join in drinking the cup of suffering with him. Is it possible that he does so by citing a drinking slogan that may have been well known to Judas as well as to all the disciples? There is certainly other evidence that Jesus drank generously with his disciples ("wine-bibber," Mt 11:19//Lk 7:34). Such an invitation to drink the cup with Jesus is therefore quite in character. But it is also deeply emotional, and this surely could account for an elliptical allusion in an invitation to share his death with him.

But in this invitation, Jesus has shifted into another type of drinking. The cup was hardly one of imminent joy but one of pain and suffering and death. Only the later book of Hebrews (12:2) could refer to Jesus' suffering as something that he "endured for the joy that was set before him." It is difficult to fully fathom the enormous courage it took for Jesus to walk toward his death. Thus, we generally conclude: "Great exegetical difficulties are presented by this reply of Jesus."[54]

Perhaps we need to review again the rich imagery of the cup among the Hebrew people and allow for some new possibilities. Jesus had just gone through an agonizing night in which he pushed the cup away from himself three times (as he had many times earlier in his life), and now, feeling alienated from God, he reached out to Judas — the only disciple at that moment appar-

---

53. J. Klausner dismisses the details of the arrest narratives as "imaginary additions." See Klausner, *Jesus of Nazareth* (London, 1929), p. 336.

54. D. Haugg, *Judas Iskarioth in den neutestamentlichen Berichten* (Freiburg: Herder Verlag, 1930), p. 154.

ently capable of hearing the voice of God and following it — and offered him the cup as well!

For the Jews, the cup was a bonding symbol, a symbol of covenant.[55] By using this formula, "you are here for this," Jesus reassures Judas that the covenant is intact and, as they have shared the cup of wine on many previous occasions, they can do so again. Like all the other disciples, Judas declined the invitation, even though it had been spelled out often as a requirement for discipleship. The disciple is not above his Lord, and if the Shepherd is smitten the sheep will also be taken. In declining the invitation Jesus offered him, Judas made the most momentous decision of his life.

A number of scholars take this inscription on the drinking beaker seriously but hedge it with reservations. The reasons they give have to be taken seriously.

Raymond Brown, in his usual conscientious way, devoted considerable time to the role of Judas in the passion narrative and consistently translates the text by refusing to use the word "betrayal" to describe the act of Judas. Rather, Brown recognizes that it means to "hand over." He apologizes to the reader for being so literalistic, but what solid integrity is found in that decision. At the same time, Judas does not escape Brown's criticism.[56] When Brown comes to deal with this encounter in the garden, he concludes: "I find attractive the suggestion . . . (for which we have concrete evidence) . . . that this was a set phrase, usually in a context of convivial joy, but now used in the opposite situation. People could encourage others to a drink of companionship, 'Friend, rejoice. That's what you are here for.' To the irony that Judas comes with a kiss and says, 'Hail Rabbi,' Jesus responds with equal irony, 'Friend, that's what you are here for.'"[57]

Brown evidently assumes that Judas really did "betray" Jesus, but he gives no suggestion what it was that Judas betrayed, and therefore assumes irony although there is certainly nothing in the text that suggests irony.[58] On the face of

55. See the rich treatment of this theme by G. A. F. Knight, "The Cup of Wrath," *Int* 12 (1958): 412-17; A. W. Jones, "Eating and Drinking in the Old Testament," in *ABD* (1992), 2:250-54, good on symbolism of eating and drinking; L. Goppelt, "ποτήριον," in *TWNT* (1959), 6:148-60, with very ample documentation.

56. Jesus having recognized "the irrevocability of Judas' malice, hastened him on" (Brown, *Death of the Messiah*, p. 578). Judas "failed definitively" (p. 49), Judas is a "mysterious villainous figure" (p. 242), an "idle, otiose, iniquitous" person who acted against Jesus (p. 241). See my "Authenticity of Judas' Participation," pp. 405-6.

57. Brown, *Death of the Messiah*, p. 1388.

58. On the subject of irony see W. F. Stinespring, "Irony," in *IDB* (1962), 2:726-28. He uses the definition from Webster's dictionary: "a sort of humor, ridicule or light sarcasm which adopts a mode of speech the intended simplification of which is the opposite of the literal sense of the words." He lists Jesus' response to Judas as irony. Was Stinespring suggesting that Jesus

it, Jesus does not call Judas a traitor *(prodotēs);* he does not even call him a "Satan" as he did Peter (Mk 8:33//Mt 16:22-23) when Peter objected to Jesus' prediction that he would die.

Brown argues that he is simply reproducing Matthew's point of view and that the word "Friend" in Matthew — he is the only one to use it — always has the connotation of distance or censure. But surely it is wrong to take a word from one context and insert its meaning into another. In the other usages of the term in Matthew, it is quite natural to use it when the name of the person addressed would be unknown.[59]

Blaise Pascal the philosopher observed some 350 years ago: "when Jesus addresses Judas as 'Friend' he recognizes him not as an enemy but as someone who is carrying out the command of God, whom he loves. The word, 'friend,' is fully justified."[60] I suggest that we take it as Jesus' bold invitation that Judas drink with him. That is the most straightforward way of viewing this text, and it makes logical sense.

If indeed Jesus had spent most of the night deserted by his disciples, feeling alienated from God,[61] and praying that the cup might pass, then the friendliness with which he greets Judas comes as no surprise. It was normal for him to welcome Judas with a fervent kiss. He then invites him to drink the cup that was now ready.[62] Matthew makes that more difficult by leaving out Mark's strong affirmation, "the cup is prepared."

As Buchheit puts it: "In that moment when the traitor exchanges kisses with the Master, Judas carried out his duty. The task that had been assigned to him and which only he could do had been carried out."[63] Had Jesus wanted to rebuke Judas at this time, he could have chosen a different word from "friend."

Rather than speak of irony, I suggest we see in the way Jesus dealt with Ju-

---

really called him not a friend but an enemy? To accept that, one surely has to ask what in Matthew's view Jesus might be trying to tell Judas.

59. In Mt 20:13, while the master asks a question, it is surely not a rebuke but simply the way one might respond to someone whose name is unknown, as is the case also in 22:12. Here in the arrest narrative Jesus knows his name. Nevertheless, there is no reason to think that Jesus treats him "coolly" (J. P. Meier, *Matthew* [Glazier, 1980], pp. 327, 225, 249) or is "distant" from him based on this term, as some commentators conclude. If Jesus wanted to rebuke Judas, he surely would have other words in his vocabulary: "traitor," an "enemy" or a "hypocrite" or, as he did to Peter, a "Devil"!

60. G. Buchheit, *Judas Iskarioth* (Gütersloh: Rufer Verlag, 1954), p. 185.

61. See the fine study of this motif in R. Feldmeier, *Die Krisis des Gottessohnes. Die Gethsemaneerzählung als Schlüssel der Markuspassion,* WUNT 2/21 (Tübingen: J. C. B. Mohr, 1987).

62. If Klaus Müller is right, then Mark's unusual word, *apechei,* should be translated, [The cup of wrath] "has been poured": *ZNW* 77 (1986): 83-100.

63. Buchheit, *Judas,* p. 186.

das his capacity for the grotesque, the contradiction between the surface values and that which lies underneath. In that light what Jesus calls Judas remains: he is a "friend, comrade, associate." Moreover, the kiss stands as a provocative gesture only if one considers Judas' act as evil. Instead Jesus goes beneath the surface and addresses the question of the ultimate meaning of life (i.e., "This is what you are here for: to help your Master carry out God's will, the purpose for which we both have come to this hour").

The Judas Figure in the Later Church

In the later church Judas was not uniformly condemned.[64] There is certainly the clear possibility that Luke's account of Judas's death was meant to soften the blow of Matthew's account of his suicide. There is not only the *Gospel of Judas*, in which Judas is credited with having helped to bring salvation, there are also Jewish voices raised on his behalf.[65]

Then there is what we presume to be a Christian artist who in an ivory carving on a sarcophagus portrays Judas dying at the right hand of Christ as king of the Jews.[66] It is Judas over whose head — not over the cross — a bird (a dove?) feeds its young in the nest, a symbol of hope. Given its relatively late date, we must not read too much into this ivory carving. At the same time, we must allow it to bear witness, since it is often cited as the oldest extant portrait of Jesus on the cross[67] and the only one in which Judas is at the right hand of Jesus, who is described as "King of the Jews." Although it is on display in the British Museum, one does not see it often in books about Christian art. Indeed, the book published by the museum, *The Bible and the British Museum,* makes no reference to it. It is displayed without comment in Flusser's recent book on Jesus.[68] At the very least, the carving conveys Judas as dying with Jesus, hardly the negative view of Judas found so often in Christian biographies of Jesus.

64. On the Judas figure in the later church, see especially the excellent book by Kim Paffenroth, *Judas, the Lost Disciple* (Louisville: Westminster John Knox, 2001).

65. E. Bammel, "Judas in der jüdischen Überlieferung," in E. Bammel, *Judaica et Paulina: Kleine Schriften,* WUNT 91 (Tübingen: Mohr [Siebeck], 1997), 2:24-33. [The gospel of Judas has now been recovered in a Coptic manuscript, but the text is Gnostic. — JHC.]

66. The notes by the display in the British Museum describe it as the earliest known narrative representation of the crucifixion in Christian art.

67. Kurt Weizmann, *The Age of Spirituality: Late Antiquity and Early Christian Art* (Princeton: Princeton University Press, 1979), pp. 502-4.

68. D. Flusser and S. Notley, *Jesus* (Jerusalem: Magnes Press, 1997), p. 174. Curiously in the German Rowohlt edition (Hamburg, 1968) and as late as the recent 1986 edition, Judas has been cropped from the picture!

I suggest that this interpretation of the saying of Jesus, in the context of a drinking vessel from Tyre and Sidon, almost certainly found in abundance in Galilee, makes sense and unlocks a riddle that has been difficult to solve. We must, however, try to view the evidence without prejudice to Judas.

When we consider how little evidence we have about artifacts of daily life in Galilee in the first century, we can only describe this drinking glass as providing a remarkable insight into first-century drinking customs and vessels. The fact that so many glasses have survived twenty centuries is itself significant. More important is the almost unanimous agreement of archaeologists and historians that glass drinking-vessels were common enough among the middle-class Jews in Galilee that Jesus and his disciples could well have been familiar with this drinking slogan embossed in the glass itself. It could well have been used in taverns and homes throughout the region.

The cup, the embrace, the words exchanged — all are interwoven in the drama of the final moments in Gethsemane. In the famous painting by the Italian artist Giotto, the flowing yellow robe he puts on Judas denotes cowardice. Nevertheless, a careful review of the painting shows that Giotto has two real people meeting each other, not a spiritual Christ with a halo, nor Judas as a demon. Their eyes meet even as their lips come together. Judas is depicted as the one taking the initiative, with his flowing robe fully embracing Jesus as if Judas is enfolding Jesus to protect him from mob action. The bright colors of the two main characters, over against the sinister, threatening world with its obscene spears and armaments, reveal a genuine human relationship. In an hour of overwhelming anxiety, fear, and bewilderment, two male colleagues embrace and in that embrace bring strength to each other for the role God has called them to play. They did what they were there for.

ARCHAEOLOGY AND THEOLOGY

Archaeology and John's Gospel

Urban C. von Wahlde

The Context

The Gospel of John, known for its unique and profound theology, has often been accused of not being of substantial value for understanding the historical ministry of Jesus. Scholars who suggest this do not do so without reason, since substantial material in the Gospel is clearly "late" and indeed anachronistic to the ministry of Jesus. These features include the manner in which the words of Jesus are formulated and the small number of social groupings that do not fully reflect the variety of the actual ministry. There are also the many generalizing references to the religious authorities simply as "the Jews." There is the high Christology, the references to synagogue exclusion, the lack of concern for issues such as purity, fasting, and table fellowship that were so typical of the ministry of Jesus. All these features suggest that the Gospel of John reflects community issues at the end of the first century c.e. rather than an accurate portrayal of the ministry itself.

In addition to these anachronistic features, the pervasive interest in symbolism in the Gospel suggests that perhaps things should not be taken literally. Jesus, in his very words, is constantly speaking metaphorically: he is the bread from heaven, the true vine, the good shepherd, and the light of the world. Inevitably this orientation to the symbolic and cosmic encourages the tendency to suspect that the Gospel downplays attention to the specifics of history.

The Remarkable Number of Topographical
References Unique to John

If the above features suggest that the Gospel has little interest in the specifics of history, we find yet another feature that, to some, would suggest a significant element of history.[1] In the Gospel there are a remarkable number of topographical references that appear nowhere else in the New Testament. There are thirteen such references, and if we include features about which John gives us details not known from the other Gospels, the number swells to twenty. Understandably, this has given rise to a variety of interpretations. From the patristic period through the nineteenth century, the reaction might best be described as "naive historicism." Many critical questions had not yet been brought to consciousness and interpreters simply took all references to be historical and sought to confirm the locations, at times without a true critical sense. However, from the late nineteenth through the middle of the twentieth century, this "historicism" came to be replaced by a scholarly skepticism. This led some to believe that many of the topographical references in the Gospel were fictional, and in the light of the other features mentioned above, intended to convey symbolism rather than historical recollection.

The classic example of this approach was the article by N. Krieger. Krieger argued that all the places associated with John the Baptist in the Gospel are fictitious and intended to be symbolic.[2] Other scholars made similar arguments for other places, such as the pool of Bethesda with its five porches (said to symbolize the Torah), the pool of Siloam (which meant "Sent" and was said to have been chosen because Jesus "sent" the blind man to wash), and so on.[3] However, thanks in large part to the contributions of archaeology, the tendency to view the topographical references of the Gospel simply as fictitious or symbolic is now increasingly rejected by scholars.

Nevertheless, in spite of the general conviction that the Johannine topogra-

---

1. For a discussion of other aspects of the historicity of the Gospel, see the paper by P. Anderson elsewhere in this volume.

2. N. Krieger, "Fiktive Orte der Johannestaufe," *ZNW* 45 (1954): 121-23.

3. In fairness, it should be said that not all scholars have reacted to the various proposed symbolisms in the same way. Some have retained a skepticism; others have rejected all but the most obvious forms of symbolism. One other approach to the understanding of the topographical references in John should perhaps be mentioned, although it does not bear on the issue of historicity. K. Kundsin (*Topologische Überlieferungsstoffe im Johannes-Evangelium*, FRLANT, n.s., 22, ed. R. Bultmann and H. Gunkel [Göttingen, 1925]) argued that particular sites were mentioned in the Gospel because these were places with significant early communities. Thus the determining factor was not so much symbolism as etiology of communities. This view has not gained acceptance.

phy is neither fictitious nor purely symbolic, scholars have given little attention to this uniquely Johannine information. Although most commentaries discuss place-names briefly, and although Johannine topography is included in general studies of the Holy Land,[4] there have been almost no studies devoted exclusively to Johannine topography.[5]

By gathering together what is known of all the unique Johannine references as well as what is known of the singular details in John's other references, it is possible to put the Johannine data as a whole into better perspective. In this way not only can any vestige of claims of sheer fictitiousness or symbolism be rejected once and for all, but also the value of the Johannine information for understanding various aspects of the ministry of Jesus can be seen more clearly.

The Contribution of Archaeology

Building on, and adding to, the remarkable discoveries of the past, archaeologists continue to make more and more discoveries that are invaluable for understanding various aspects of the New Testament.[6] A great deal of this infor-

---

4. For example, G. Dalman, *Orte und Wege Jesu*, 3rd ed. (Gütersloh: C. Bertelsmann, 1924); C. Kopp, *The Holy Places of the Gospels*, trans. R. Walls (New York: Herder and Herder, 1963), unabridged German original, *Die heiligen Stätten der Evangelien* (Regensburg: Pustet, 1959); O. Keel, M. Küchler, and C. Ühlinger, *Orte und Landschaften der Bibel*, vols. 1, 2 (Zürich: Benziger; Göttingen: Vandenhoeck & Ruprecht, 1984); J. Taylor, *Christians and the Holy Places* (Oxford: Clarendon, 1993).

5. Beyond the articles of Krieger and Kundsin, there is the book of B. E. Schein, *Following the Way: The Setting of John's Gospel* (Minneapolis: Augsburg, 1980), and the article of B. Schwank, "Ortskenntnisse im Vierten Evangelium," *Erbe und Auftrag* 57 (1981): 427-42. With the exception of a series of appendices, Schein's book does not generally enter into a discussion of divergent theories regarding the location of particular sites nor the evidence for such identification. Schwank's article is not presented as his own proposal, but as a report of a group seminar in Jerusalem. An article by W. F. Albright ("Recent Discoveries in Palestine and the Gospel of St. John," in *The Background of the New Testament and Its Eschatology*, ed. W. D. Davies and D. Daube, Festschrift C. H. Dodd [Cambridge: Cambridge University Press, 1956], pp. 153-71) comments on the Lithostrotos (incorrectly), Aenon near Salim, and Sychar (which he identifies with Shechem) but focuses on the significance of the then-recently-discovered Nag Hammadi texts and the scrolls from Kirbet Qumran for the background of the Gospel of John.

6. Among the more recent, see J. H. Charlesworth, "Archaeology, Jesus, and Christian Faith," in *What Has Archaeology to Do with Faith?* ed. J. H. Charlesworth and W. P. Weaver (Philadelphia: Trinity, 1992), pp. 1-22; S. Freyne, "Archaeology and the Historical Jesus," in *Archaeology and Biblical Interpretation*, ed. J. R. Bartlett (London and New York: Routledge, 1997), pp.

mation is also proving to be pertinent to the understanding of the Gospel of John. Indeed, several sites unique to this Gospel are currently under active study, and our understanding of these sites is growing almost daily. Discussions with archaeologists indicate that discoveries already made, but not yet published, will provide even clearer insight into aspects of Johannine sites (as in the present collection).

As a result, the time seems ripe for a thorough review of Johannine topography with a particular focus on what archaeologists have to say, and to gather together in a kind of overview what has been, and what is being, achieved regarding the topographical information unique to the Gospel. Our primary focus is on the question of the historical reliability of this topographical information, but it is hoped that in the light of such review not only will our general understanding of the background of the Gospel increase but that we will be able to draw some more general conclusions about the curious interplay of the remarkably historical and the remarkably unhistorical elements of the Gospel.

A Survey of Unique and Distinctive Johannine References

I will begin with a listing of the most significant topographical references in the Gospel of John. This includes references both to the places Jesus himself visited and also to the various places mentioned in the Gospel in passing.[7]

Topographical References in the Gospel of John

1. **Bethany Beyond the Jordan** (1:28; 10:40)
2. **Bethsaida** (1:44)
   Galilee (1:43)
   Nazareth (1:45, 46)
3. **Cana in Galilee** (2:1, 11; 4:46-54; 21:2)

117-44; R. A. Horsley, *Archaeology, History, and Society in Galilee: The Social Context of Jesus and the Rabbis* (Valley Forge, Pa.: Trinity, 1996); E. M. Meyers, "Jesus and His Galilean Context," in *Archaeology and the Galilee: Texts and Contexts in the Graeco-Roman and Byzantine Periods,* ed. D. R. Edwards and C. T. McCulloch, SFSHJ 143 (Miami: University of South Florida, 1997), pp. 57-66; J. F. Strange, "Some Implications of Archaeology for New Testament Studies," in *What Has Archaeology to Do with Faith?* pp. 23-59.

7. References such as that Mary was from Magdala (19:25; 20:1, 18) or that Joseph was of Arimathea (19:38) are both found in the Synoptics and are too peripheral to be discussed here.

4. **Capernaum** (2:12; 4:46: 6:17, 24), **the harbor** (6:24-25), and **the synagogue** (6:59)
   Jerusalem for Passover (2:13; 5:1; 7:10; 12:12-18)
5. **Area of the Cleansing of the Temple** (2:13-16)
   The Judean Countryside (3:22)
6. **Aenon near Salim** (3:23)
7. **Sychar** (4:5)
8. **Jacob's Well** (4:4-6)
9. **Mount Gerizim** (4:20)
   Jerusalem for Feast (5:1)
10. **The Sheep Gate/Pool** (5:2)
11. **The Pool of Bethesda** (5:2)
    Sea of Tiberias (6:1; 21:1)
12. **Tiberias** (6:1, 23; 21:1)
    The Place of the Multiplication (6:1-15)
    A Crossing of the Sea of Galilee to Capernaum (see above)
    The Synagogue in Capernaum (see above)
    The Temple in Jerusalem for Tabernacles (7:14, 28, 37)
    Bethlehem (7:42)
    The Treasury in the Temple (8:20)
13. **The Pool of Siloam** (9:1-9)
    Solomon's Portico in the Temple (10:22-39)
14. **Bethany Near Jerusalem** (11:1-17; 12:1-11)
    The House of Lazarus (11:1-17)
    The Tomb of Lazarus (11:38-44)
15. **Ephraim** (11:54)
    Jerusalem (12:12-18)
    The House of the Last Supper (13:1–17:26)
16. **The Winter-Flowing Kidron** (18:1)
    The Mount of Olives (18:1)
    The House and Courtyard of Annas (18:13)
    The House of Caiaphas (18:24)
17. **The Praetorium** (18:28, 33; 19:9)
18. **The Lithostrotos** (19:13)
19. **Golgotha** (19:17-18, 20, 41)
20. **A Tomb in the Garden** (19:41-42)
    The Room Where the Disciples Were Gathered (20:19-29)

Of the places listed in the chart, some are well known and do not need to be discussed (regions such as Galilee and Judea; towns and cities such as Nazareth, Jerusalem, and Bethlehem). Others are, by their nature, not able to be defined since there would be little or no possibility of evidence that could corroborate the information (e.g., the exact house in Cana where the wedding took place, and the house of Lazarus in Bethany).[8]

When these texts are excluded, twenty references remain, references that are either unique to the Gospel of John or contain details unique to the Gospel. These references are identified in bold in the chart. It is these twenty sites that will be discussed in this chapter. Such discussion will involve not only reports on the fieldwork of archaeologists but also a critical review of the contemporary literary information (e.g., data in the New Testament and in Josephus). Although the primary emphasis here will be on a comparison of the archaeological finds with information provided in first-century accounts, later pilgrim reports can at times prove quite helpful in this quest and will also be included where appropriate.

1. Bethany Beyond the Jordan (1:28; 10:40)

The Johannine Context

The only knowledge we have of a place called "Bethany Beyond the Jordan" is from the Gospel of John. It is mentioned nowhere else in the New Testament or in ancient literature. It is identified as the place where John the Baptist sees Jesus and witnesses to him (1:28). Present with John are some of his disciples, two of whom are said to follow Jesus on the basis of John's witness. It is mentioned again later in the ministry (10:40), where it is said that Jesus returned there and many came to him and said that John performed no signs but everything John said about Jesus was true.

---

8. This is not to deny that popular piety has claimed to identify many of these locations. However, here we discuss only those sites for which archaeology can provide reasonable evidence. There would seem to be one extraordinary exception to this inability to identify specific houses: Peter's house in Capernaum. A considerable number of scholars would agree that the combination of literary and archaeological evidence together with (very early) traditions confirms the identification of this house in Capernaum. See the discussion below. Recently, J. Taylor (*Christians*, p. 200) has proposed identifying a cave in the area of Gethsemane, across the Kidron Valley, as the place where Jesus stayed overnight with his disciples and as the place of the arrest. While it is possible that Jesus would have slept in a cave when he was in Jerusalem for Passover, Taylor's proposal requires too much conjecture from both the Gospel texts and the archaeological evidence. See J. Taylor, "The Garden of Gethsemane: Not the Place of Jesus' Arrest," *BAR* 21 (July/August 1995): 26-35, 62. [On Bethany, see the chapter by Capper. — JHC.]

The Literary Evidence

The site of Bethany Beyond the Jordan continues to be disputed.[9] From the context in John, it can be situated in Transjordan at a river crossing. Since before the time of Origen, there has been no trace of the place archaeologically. Origen himself suggested that the name was incorrect and should have been Bethabara ("the place of crossing over").[10] This would identify it with the place where Joshua entered the Promised Land — about five miles north of the Dead Sea. The sixth-century Madaba map records a city of Bethabara at that site and identifies it as the place of John's baptizing. The map shows only one church, but there are pilgrim records of two churches since 530 C.E. Because the east side of the river was under Muslim control, the churches on that side were eventually abandoned.

In keeping with the tendency to see some place-names as symbolic creations, N. Krieger suggested that there was in fact no such place. The expression derived from *bet-aniyyah* ("house of response/witness/testimony") and was intended to communicate that this was where the disciples of John came to believe in Jesus.[11]

Today there are two main contenders for identification with the site.[12] The majority of scholars argue for a southern location, on the east side of the Jordan about five miles north of its entry into the Dead Sea, opposite Jericho, in the Wadi el-Kharrar. This is the site suggested by Origen but identified as Bethabara. However, B. Pixner and R. Riesner argue for a location in Batanea in the far northeast part of the country.[13] This is a region rather

9. The most thorough discussion of the various theories regarding the location of Bethany Beyond the Jordan can be found in R. Riesner, "Bethany Beyond the Jordan (John 1:28): Topography, Theology and History in the Fourth Gospel," *TynBul* 38 (1987): 29-63. Riesner in fact lists eight locations that have been suggested for the site. See also the most recent assessment by M. Piccirillo in this volume. I would agree (contra Piccirillo) that the evidence in the Gospel makes Batanea "worthy of consideration" as a possible site.

10. Origen, *Commentarium* 6.40; GCS 10:149.

11. Krieger, "Fiktive," p. 122.

12. In August 2004 S. Gibson published *The Cave of John the Baptist* (New York: Doubleday), in which he proposed that a cave near Jerusalem that functioned at one time as a water reservoir was used by John the Baptist as a site for baptizing. The identification is made on the basis of a carving on the wall said to be the figure of John the Baptist as well as other graffiti said to be Christian crosses. While the reservoir itself dates from the sixth century B.C.E., the graffiti and carving come from the Byzantine period (fourth–sixth century C.E.). The late date of the inscriptions as well as their ambiguity have led scholars to be skeptical of the identification. For a preliminary appraisal, with photos, see H. Shanks, "John the Baptist's Cave?" *BAR* 38 (November/December 2004): 18-19.

13. B. Pixner, *With Jesus through Galilee according to the Fifth Gospel*, English trans. (Collegeville, Minn.: Liturgical Press, 1996), pp. 20-21. Riesner, "Bethany Beyond the Jordan (John

than a town and the arguments are literary rather than archaeological, as we shall see below.

The Archaeological Evidence

From 1995 to 2002, archaeological excavations, under the direction of Moham-med Waheeb of the Jordanian Department of Antiquities, took place at Wadi el-Kharrar on the east side of the Jordan, across from the pilgrim site of Bethabara. M. Piccirillo, from the Studium Biblicum Franciscanum, was con-sulting archaeologist to the site and discusses this site elsewhere in the present volume. The wadi contains a tributary of the Jordan, and as Piccirillo describes in his paper, remains of an ecclesiastical complex from the Byzantine period have been found along its banks. Pottery (some of it fragments of stone jars dated to the first century) has been found there. This archaeological evidence confirms that the site was inhabited in the first century c.e. Coupling this with later pilgrim reports that identify this region as the location of Bethany Beyond the Jordan, Piccirillo argues that while this cannot "prove" that this is the Johannine site, it clearly makes this the most likely candidate. Mohammed Waheeb contends even more forcefully that this is the Johannine Bethany Be-yond the Jordan, a view now adopted by the Jordanian government, which has established the Baptism Archaeological Park on the site.[14]

The Literary Evidence

If there is a weakness to Piccirillo's otherwise impressive analysis, it is that he does not attempt to integrate the archaeological findings at the Wadi el-Kharrar with the data from the Gospel of John. Piccirillo confines his discus-sion to the archaeological data and pilgrim reports. The Johannine data pro-vide considerable details about this Bethany and need to be taken seriously.

Reconciling the literary with the archaeological evidence is not easy. As we have seen, the Gospel indicates that among those disciples who first followed

---

1:28)." See also R. Riesner, "Bethany Beyond the Jordan," in *ABD* 1:703-5, and M. Piccirillo's chapter in this volume.

14. The site is discussed in some detail (with photos and charts) in R. Khouri, "Where John Baptized," *BAR* 31 (January/February 2005): 35-43. The present archaeological remains date from considerably later than the first century c.e., although pottery remains indicate that the site was inhabited in the first century c.e. See also H. Shanks, "Site of Jesus' Baptism Found — Again," *BAR* 25 (May/June 1999): 14.

Jesus, Andrew, Peter, and Philip were from Bethsaida and Nathanael was from Cana of Galilee. These places are all in northern Galilee. The text of the Gospel would also suggest that while the unnamed disciple and Andrew were with John when he witnessed to Jesus, Peter was not because Andrew had to go get him. The same is true of Nathanael, whom Philip had to go get (we hear that Nathanael was under a fig tree before he came to Jesus). Thus it is difficult to imagine where Peter of Bethsaida and Nathanael of Cana were that Andrew and Philip could find them so easily if the scene of their encounter with Jesus took place in Judea.

The second piece of Johannine evidence comes from Jn 10:40, where "Bethany Beyond the Jordan" is seen as a place of retreat. This could perhaps suggest a location other than one in southern Judea, although a place in the Judean desert could not be ruled out. According to information at the beginning of the Lazarus account (11:6, cf. 17), it is three days' journey from Bethany Beyond the Jordan to the Bethany near Jerusalem. This also presents a difficulty for the proposed southern location. However, a northern location would fit the narrative sequence well. This information led Pixner, followed by Riesner, to suggest that Bethany Beyond the Jordan was located somewhere in the north.

Finally, as Pixner points out, it may be wrong to expect Bethany to be a city or village.[15] In 1:28 it is identified as a "place" or "region" *(topos)* rather than a village *(kōmē)* or city *(polis)*. This would suggest that any attempts to identify this Bethany with anything other than a general location may be mistaken and ultimately impossible unless additional literary evidence of the place is found, since there would be no archaeological evidence that could identify a region.

If these factors favor a northern location, there are also significant problems. From 1:19 one would get the impression that the site is fairly close to Jerusalem, since priests and Levites are sent to inquire about John. One must also explain the setting of 1:43, which seems to imply that when the disciples met Jesus, neither they nor Jesus was in Galilee but intended to go there. This would suggest a location in Judea, although a place across the Jordan in the north could also fit. However, on literary grounds, there are reasons to think that 1:43 was not a part of the original narrative. The information in 1:43 seems to be an addition by an editor, perhaps an editor who was familiar with the tradition of a southern site and erroneously presumed the Johannine scene to reflect that tradition also.[16] A third

---

15. In conversation with Pixner during the Millennium Conference. See also Riesner, "Bethany Beyond the Jordan," p. 55.

16. See, for example, R. Schnackenburg, *The Gospel according to St. John*, 3 vols. (New York:

problem for those who favor a northern location is the necessary textual modification from "Bethany" to "Batanea" — and the lack of significant manuscript evidence for such a change.[17]

John P. Meier has introduced Synoptic material into the discussion and suggested that the "desert" described as the place of John's baptism in Mk 1:4 and elaborated by Mt 3:1 as "the desert of Judah" would have referred to the area at the southern end of the Jordan Valley around Qumran. Thus baptizing by the Jordan would not be distinct from his activity in the desert because *the Jordan was the desert*.[18] This is also possible.

Meier also calls attention to Jn 3:22-26, which speaks of a period of baptizing activity in Judea by both Jesus and John.[19] However, this aspect of Meier's argument is less convincing. The Gospel of John presents more information than the Synoptics about the baptizing activity of John in general, and in it the meeting at Bethany Beyond the Jordan (1:28) is considerably earlier (at the beginning of the ministry) than the activity in the Judean countryside (3:22-26), which occurs after the first Passover. It is very possible that the accounts are intended to reflect activity in two distinct places.

In addition to the problems mentioned above, it is not clear just what "beyond" intends to convey. Does it mean simply that Bethany was on the eastern shore of the Jordan, or somewhere *beyond* the eastern shore? The Wadi el-Kharrar is not on the Jordan River proper but on a tributary of the Jordan. However, this is less a problem. Through the centuries the Jordan River has changed its course many times, and until the middle of this century it would swell to almost a mile wide during the rainy season. Consequently, in the first century C.E. the site may well have been immediately on the Jordan.

An additional problem concerns the pilgrim reports. Pilgrim accounts can be valuable in determining the location of biblical sites, but it is important to

---

Herder and Herder, 1966 [vol. 1]; New York: Crossroad, 1980-82 [vols. 2-3]), 1:313; R. Fortna, *The Fourth Gospel and Its Predecessor* (Philadelphia: Fortress, 1988), pp. 34-47; see esp. pp. 43, 46; U. C. von Wahlde, *The Earliest Version of John's Gospel* (Wilmington, Del.: Michael Glazier; Collegeville, Minn.: Liturgical Press, 1989), pp. 69-73.

17. So also G. Segalla in his comments to me in Jerusalem. He points out the extent of this problem. Yet it must be said that such a name change is not impossible. J. VanderKam (*Textual and Historical Studies in the Book of Jubilees*, HSM 14 [Missoula, Mont.: Scholars, 1977], p. 225) argues that the book of *Jubilees* preserves the first known reference to Sychar but reverses the vowels, making it Sakir.

18. J. P. Meier, *A Marginal Jew: Rethinking the Historical Jesus* (New York: Doubleday, 1991, 1994), 2:43-46. Meier also calls attention to R. W. Funk ("The Wilderness," *JBL* 78 [1959]: 205-14), who shows that in both Testaments the Jordan Valley was considered desert.

19. Meier, *A Marginal Jew,* 2:45. Meier also concludes that John's ministry was not confined to a single area but ranged the length of the country.

use them critically. There can be little doubt that Wadi el-Kharrar is the site visited by pilgrims during the Byzantine period. However, the earliest pilgrim report of Bethany Beyond the Jordan is that of the Bordeaux pilgrim in the first third of the fourth century. He takes the site to be in the south. However, the accuracy of his choice and the presumption that he witnesses to an unbroken tradition are put in doubt by the fact that early in the third century (almost one hundred years earlier) a person as learned as Origen had already visited the area himself and was able to find no evidence of a Bethany.

Conclusions

It would seem that whichever position one adopts, substantial problems remain. The central issue is the weight to be given to the Johannine information vis-à-vis pilgrim reports and the archaeological evidence. For this reason I will postpone my own final observations until the other topographical references have been studied and a judgment can be made on the accuracy of the Johannine information in general.

2. Bethsaida (1:44)

The Johannine Context

Although mention of Bethsaida is not unique to the Gospel of John and although the Gospel does not situate any of the actual activity of Jesus there, John gives us more detailed information about the town and its character than any of the other Gospels. It is mentioned (1:44) as the hometown of Andrew, Peter, and Philip. In 12:20-22 we are told that Greek-speaking persons wanting to see Jesus sought out Andrew and Philip (presumably because they could speak Greek).

The Literary Evidence

In addition to the Johannine references, Bethsaida is mentioned in the three Synoptic Gospels. The town is criticized for its lack of faith in Mt 11:21-24. Jesus healed a blind man there according to Mk 8:22-26. It is the site of the multiplication of the loaves according to Lk 9:10-17. The miraculous walking on the water also is said to have occurred near there (Lk 9:10).

533

According to Josephus, Bethsaida was a Hellenistic city.[20] Philip the Tetrarch (4-34 C.E.) raised it to the status of city *(polis)*, resettled it, refortified it,[21] and renamed it Julia. This was certainly in honor of Livia, the wife of Tiberius who was adopted into the Julian *gens* in 14 C.E.[22] Bethsaida became known as Julia and, later, as Livia.[23] Thus the Johannine portrayal of the disciples from this city as having Hellenistic names and as (presumably) speaking Greek is not only consistent within the Gospel but also fits well with what we know of Philip the Tetrarch's reshaping of the town's earlier character.

The Archaeological Evidence

In the last fifteen years, considerable evidence has been uncovered that indicates that the site of ancient Bethsaida is to be located at the modern et-Tell.[24] The archaeological remains at et-Tell were first identified by surface survey by means of ground-penetrating radar in 1987 by archaeologist Rami Arav. In 1991 the Bethsaida Excavations Project (BEP) was founded with headquarters at the University of Nebraska at Omaha, USA. Excavation of the site has been thoroughly documented in a number of scholarly articles and in three volumes of reports and essays on the excavations.[25] Subsequent work at the site has led the

20. *Ant* 18.2.1 §28.

21. This is the common translation of the text of Josephus. However, M. Smith has argued convincingly that this is not a correct translation and more accurately refers to the establishing of (or adding to) a military garrison stationed near the city. See M. D. Smith, "A Tale of Two Julias: Julia, Julias, and Josephus," in *Bethsaida: A City by the North Shore of the Sea of Galilee,* ed. R. Arav and R. A. Freund, 3 vols. (Kirksville, Mo.: Thomas Jefferson University Press, 1995, 1999), 2:333-46, here pp. 338-39.

22. Josephus says it was named Julia in honor of the emperor's daughter, but this is probably an error. Most scholars would accept the explanation above. The dating is disputed. If the resettlement was at the beginning of Tiberias's reign, it would have been in 14 C.E.; if toward the end, then 30 C.E. Around 30, Philip minted coins with the name Julia Augusta and the face of Tiberias's wife, Livia. This suggests that the later date is most likely the correct one.

23. So also M. Appold, briefly, in "The Mighty Works of Bethsaida: Witness of the New Testament and Related Traditions," in *Bethsaida,* 2:229-42; see esp. pp. 239-40.

24. The leaders of the Bethsaida Excavations Project credit an article by B. Pixner ("Searching for the New Testament Site of Bethsaida," *BA* 48 [1985]: 207-16) with being the first to make the case that biblical Bethsaida could be found at et-Tell. It was this that led to the first explorations of the site.

25. See, for example, R. Arav, "Et-Tell and el-Araj," *IEJ* 38 (1988): 187-88; 39 (1989): 99-100; Arav, "Bethsaida, 1991," *IEJ* 41 (1991): 184-86; Arav, "Bethsaida, 1992," *IEJ* 42 (1992): 252-54; R. Arav and J. J. Rousseau, "Bethsaida, ville perdue et retrouvée," *RB* (1993): 415-28; H.-W. Kuhn and R. Arav, "The Bethsaida Excavations: Historical and Archaeological Approaches," in *The*

State of Israel to officially recognize it as the location of the ancient city of Bethsaida. The site is now an archaeological park and part of the Jordan Park Recreation Area; it opened to the public in March 1998.

The location of the site is 1.2 miles north of the Sea of Galilee and a few hundred meters from the Jordan River.[26] It has been proposed by the excavators that in the first century C.E. the city was located on the shore of the Sea of Galilee but the shoreline has moved south over time, a process accelerated by a large deposit of sediment associated with flooding resulting from landslides in the upper Jordan River.[27]

The site was inhabited as early as 3100 B.C.E., and then continuously through the period of earliest Christianity. The city shows evidence of decline during the first century C.E., with some resurgence until struck by earthquake and flood. Afterward it lay abandoned for over a thousand years. Among the remains from the late Hellenistic-Roman period is a dwelling constructed around a central courtyard as was common in the first century. In it have been found lead weights for fishing nets, hooks, and anchors; it is now known as "the Fisherman's House." Another house has a cellar with four wine jars as well as tools associated with viticulture. Also discovered are the remains of what the excavators identify as a small temple from the Roman period.

In spite of this evidence, not all scholars agree that et-Tell is the true location of Bethsaida. El-Araj, another tel in the area, also has staunch proponents.[28] However, it is significant that members of BEP conducted a probe at el-

---

Future of Early Christianity: Essays in Honor of Helmut Koester, ed. B. A. Pearson (Minneapolis: Fortress, 1993), pp. 77-106; R. Arav, "New Testament Archaeology and the Case of Bethsaida," in *Das Ende der Tage und die Gegenwart des Heils,* ed. M. Becker and W. Fenske (Leiden: Brill, 1999), pp. 75-99. Earlier literature includes C. C. McCown, "The Problem of the Site of Bethsaida," *JPOS* 10 (1938): 32-58; Pixner, "Searching," pp. 207-16. The three volumes of reports and essays are those edited by Arav and Freund, *Bethsaida,* cited in full above. The site has also been the object of several articles and discussions in *BAR: BAR* 24, no. 4 (July/August 1998): 16; *BAR* 26, no. 1 (January/February 2000): 44-56; *BAR* 26, no. 3 (May/June 2000): 10-12; *BAR* 26, no. 5 (September/October 2000): 12, 14, 72, 74. See also F. Strickert, *Bethsaida: Home of the Apostles* (Collegeville, Minn.: Liturgical Press, 1998); J. Murphy-O'Connor, *The Holy Land: An Oxford Archaeological Guide from Earliest Times to 1700,* 4th ed. (Oxford: Oxford University Press, 1998), pp. 205-7. [Also see R. Arav's chapter in the present collection. — JHC.]

26. R. Arav, "Bethsaida," in *OEANE* 1:302-5; here p. 302.

27. Geological analysis reveals the presence of crustacean microorganisms in the clay at Bethsaida, indicating that it was once on the shore of the lake. More extensive study has confirmed that. See *BAR* 26, no. 1 (January/February 2000): 48, 56 n. 4. The most likely cause of the landslide was the catastrophic earthquake of 363 C.E.

28. The chief proponents of locating Bethsaida at el-Araj are M. Nun and D. Urman. See, for example, M. Nun, "Has Bethsaida Finally Been Found?" *Jerusalem Perspective* 54 (1998): 12-31. Nun argues for el-Araj, claiming that there are first-century remains there and that the fish-

Figure 69. Bethsaida; the large house of a fisherman. Courtesy of J. H. Charlesworth

Araj in 1987 that did not yield first-century materials, and then they surveyed the area with ground-penetrating radar during the summer of 1999 and concluded that only et-Tell was inhabited in the first century.

Some have also questioned whether the remains at et-Tell are consistent with what is known of Bethsaida from the Gospel of John and from information in Josephus. Josephus identifies the city by its later name, Julia, and places it on the eastern side of the Jordan.[29] This corresponds to the site at et-Tell. However, Jn 12:21 specifically identifies Bethsaida as being "in Galilee," and some have thought that John did so to distinguish it from another Bethsaida he knew of in Gaulanitis.[30] B. Pixner suggested that the course of the Jordan has changed due to earthquakes. Others have suggested that John was not being so

erman's house at et-Tell is too grand to be that of simple fishermen. He also claims that the fishing hooks found there are actually sewing needles. See *BAR* 26, no. 1 (January/February 2000): 52. See also D. Urman, "Public Structures and Jewish Communities in the Golan Heights," in *Ancient Synagogues: Historical Analysis and Archaeological Discovery*, 2nd ed., SPB 47.2 (Leiden: Brill, 1995), pp. 519-27.

29. Josephus, *War* 2.9.1 §168.

30. It is also proposed that John identifies Cana specifically as "of Galilee" to distinguish it from the other Cana near Tyre.

precise about his definition of Galilee as to exclude a site this close to the Jordan, the traditional eastern border. Certainly there is not even a suggestion of an alternative site on the Galilean side of the Jordan.

Notable also is the absence of a number of features at the site commonly indicative of Jewish presence, features such as a synagogue, ritual baths *(mikvaot)*, and stone vessels. Moreover, the archaeologists found a considerable number of pig bones, which suggests a sizable Gentile population.[31] Although from one point of view this may be disappointing, in the end this would tend to confirm Josephus's comment about the Hellenistic makeup of the city.

It is curious that the amount of pottery from the first half of the first century is less than the amount found in both earlier and later periods, suggesting that population wanes during the first century rather than waxes.[32] The lack of growth is also evident in the failure of the city to mint coins although it had been given the privilege of doing so. This is particularly puzzling because Bethsaida had been raised to the status of *polis* (city) by Philip in 30 C.E. Others have also questioned the identification of the city harbor with a location approximately twenty feet above the level of the lake. They argue that if the water level was up to this wall, all other harbors around the lake would be flooded.

In a recent response published in *BAR*, Arav has countered these concerns.[33] He points out that a number of towns were raised to the status of *polis* in the first century without the kind of expansion that one would normally associate with this honor. Arav also suggests that Philip's death soon after raising it to the status of city could also be a factor in Bethsaida's lack of growth. It could also have been due to the outbreak of the war with Rome; the population began to increase again at the end of the century, coming to a halt in the middle of the fourth century, presumably following the earthquake of 363 C.E.

Regarding "the misplaced harbor," Arav has explained that the discovery of a wall in 1993 was first hypothesized to be a harbor wall, but that theory has

---

31. According to Arav, "about 5% of the bones collected at the dig were of pigs" ("New Testament Archaeology," p. 84). Arav proposes that this is a substantial percentage and would suggest a mixed population. For further comment on the significance of such bones and a comparison with bone finds at Sepphoris, see M. Chancey and E. M. Meyers, "How Jewish Was Sepphoris in Jesus' Time?" *BAR* 26 (July/August 2000): 18-33, 61; see esp. pp. 23, 25. The fact that Philip was the first Jewish ruler to mint coins with human images suggests an attitude of tolerance to this either because of lax observance or because of mixed population.

32. See the lengthy letter of J. Zangenberg, "Reassessing the Bethsaida Identification," *BAR* 26, no. 3 (May/June 2000): 10-11.

33. R. Arav, "Show Me Your Bethsaida," *BAR* 26, no. 5 (September/October 2000): 12, 14, 72, 74.

been abandoned.[34] During a subsequent period of low water in the lake, the site was excavated and determined to be a water mill. It is the opinion of the BEP that in the first century C.E. the area to the west and southwest of Bethsaida was a lagoon, and so would not have had a true harbor.

Conclusions

In spite of the skepticism of some, the case for the identification of et-Tell with Bethsaida remains quite strong. Not only is the accumulated evidence for et-Tell impressive, the evidence for another location in the area is weak. It is correct that the archaeological evidence is not completely consistent with some of the details from Josephus, but the explanation of the discrepancies by Arav has been credible and may in fact help us understand more clearly details of Josephus's manner of describing such sites.

The Johannine information that suggests that Bethsaida was a Hellenistic city is confirmed by archaeology and agrees with Josephus's accounts except for John's designation of the site as being in Galilee. While there is no perfect solution to this latter problem, the suggestion that because of the site's proximity to the Jordan the author considered it to be in Galilee, is a reasonable one.

3. Cana in Galilee (2:1, 11; 4:46-54; 21:2)

The Johannine Context

Once again we hear about a town that is mentioned only in the Gospel of John within the New Testament. Yet, within John, Cana is mentioned four times (2:1, 11; 4:46; 21:2). Two miracles are said to take place there: the changing of water into wine and the healing of the official's son. It is also said that Nathanael, one of the named disciples of Jesus, was from Cana.

Archaeological Evidence

Although the town is known only from John, it is attested in Josephus and is said to be a place where Josephus, who had been a military officer at the beginning of the Jewish Revolt, established temporary headquarters while com-

---

34. In correspondence with the author.

manding Jewish forces in Galilee.[35] Consequently, although the existence of such a town in the first century c.e. is not in doubt, its precise location has been. Two primary locations have vied for identification as first-century Cana: Khirbet Qana and Kefr Kenna.[36]

Khirbet Qana is 9 miles north of Nazareth in the Bet Netofah Valley. This site has been under active investigation by the University of Puget Sound (Washington, USA) since the summer of 1998, with a plan to continue excavating for four years.[37] D. Edwards is the project director, aided by P. Richardson. Although the excavations are in a preliminary state, excavators report having found evidence of habitation from the fifth millennium b.c.e. to as late as the nineteenth century c.e.

The site itself is bounded by a series of large enclosure walls. One set of walls bounds an area of 2,500 square meters. The site, particularly in its upper strata, is compromised by modern quarrying everywhere. Nevertheless, there is considerable evidence of habitation during the early Roman period. Perhaps 20 percent of the total amount of pottery dates from the Roman period. Only the Byzantine stratum has more. A cave was found with Christian graffiti on plaster. This has been associated with pilgrim reports dating from as early as the sixth century.[38]

The second proposed site is *Kefr Kenna*, which is 3.5 miles northeast of Nazareth. A church was built on the site in 1881 by the Franciscans of the Holy Land. Archaeological excavations conducted in 1997 on the site uncovered the ruins of a fifth- or sixth-century church that contained within it a mosaic from the third century. On December 29, 1997, Franciscan Father Ignazio Mancini, who represents the Franciscans of the Holy Land in Rome, announced on Vatican Radio that a floor and stone basin were uncovered in the south area of the porticoed atrium of the church and could be dated to the first century c.e. According to this report, remains are from the first century c.e. at the earliest, and extend to the fourteenth century. Fr. Eugenio Alliata was in charge of the excavation.[39]

35. Josephus, *Life* 16 §86.

36. There is also a Cana in Lebanon that is proposed by the Lebanese Ministry of Tourism in a 1998 video as a place of pilgrimage. There is no substantial evidence that this is the authentic site. Moreover, the site is more than 100 kilometers from Capernaum and over 80 kilometers from Nazareth. See J. Herrojo, "Authenticité des Lieux Saints: Où était Cana de Galilée?" *La Terre Sainte* (French ed.) 65 (September/October 2000): 238-44, here pp. 238-39. J. H. Charlesworth (*The Millennium Guide for Pilgrims to the Holy Land* [North Richland Hills, Tex.: Bibal, 2000]) alludes to two other, even more unlikely possibilities.

37. In addition to the works cited in the footnotes, see also the chapter by P. Richardson in this volume.

38. J. D. Olive, "Field Director's Reports," in Excavations at Khirbet Cana: 1998-1999 Preliminary Reports, D. R. Edwards, http://nexfind.com/cana/thesite.html.

39. Fr. Alliata is quoted in *La Terra Santa* (Italian ed., February 1999, pp. 16-18) as saying

Stone jars are reported to have been found at Kefr Kenna as well as at Khirbet Qana.[40] Their presence indicates that the sites were inhabited by Jews in, or prior to, the first century, since such stoneware was not made after 70 C.E.

Literary Evidence

There have been numerous references to Cana in pilgrim (and other) reports. Recently these reports have been subjected to a thorough critical examination by Julián Herrojo of the Instituto Español Biblico y Arqueológico de Jerusalén.[41] This study by Herrojo has confirmed proposals made by other scholars that these pilgrim reports provide clear evidence not only of which site was considered the New Testament Cana in the earliest traditions but also the reasons for a shift in the identification of the site.

In his clear and careful study, Herrojo shows that the earliest reports (those of Josephus, Eusebius, Jerome) all locate Cana at Khirbet Qana.[42] Furthermore, in his evaluation of the reports up to the time of the Crusaders, Herrojo concludes that throughout this period there was no evidence of any doubt regarding the town's location. Herrojo analyzed each tradition and evaluated it in terms of its likely accuracy. In none of the descriptions could Cana's location be associated with Kefr Kenna either with "certainty"[43] or even with "high probability," and while at times the reports were unclear, no description was incom-

---

that there is a lack of archaeological evidence of early pilgrims to the site (e.g., graffiti), and that this is significant given the lack of continuity in the local tradition regarding the place. See Herrojo, "Authenticité," p. 242.

40. Although claims have been made at various times that "original" jars still remain at the site, this is not what is referred to here. Stone jars were used by Jews (and only by Jews) for purposes of ritual purity, thus presence of such broken remains indicates habitation by Jews. A factory for stone jars was found at Reina, not far from Kefr Kenna. See Y. Magen, "'Purity Broke Out in Israel' (Tractate *Shabbat*, 13b) — Stone Vessels in the Late Second Temple Period," *University of Haifa Catalogue No. 9* (Spring 1994), pp. 23-24; Magen, "Jerusalem as a Center of the Stone Vessel Industry during the Second Temple Period," in *Ancient Jerusalem Revealed*, ed. H. Geva (Jerusalem: Israel Exploration Society, 1994), pp. 244-56. As recently as December 23, 2004, Israeli archaeologist Y. Alexander reported finding shards of stone jars at Kefr Kenna and asserted that this is the correct site (Associated Press dispatch with a dateline of Cana, Israel, December 23, 2004, reported by MSNBC.com).

41. J. Herrojo, *Caná de Galilea y su localización: Un examen critico de las fuentes* (Paris: J. Gabalda, 1999). See also his "Authenticité des Lieux Saints," which summarizes many of the positions taken in his monograph, although from a different perspective.

42. Herrojo, *Caná*, pp. 23-35, 45.

43. The terms in quotation marks were established by Herrojo to evaluate the accuracy of individual pilgrim reports.

patible with Khirbet Qana. Consequently, Herrojo concluded that up to the time of the Crusaders there was only a single tradition of Cana's location, and this was consistently associated with Khirbet Qana.[44]

From a review of the considerable number of reports from the Crusader period itself, Herrojo concludes that Kefr Kenna and Khirbet Qana are recognized as distinct locations and are not confused. During this period ten pilgrim reports "certainly" identify Cana with Khirbet Qana and four others do so with "great probability." In addition, three are "ambiguous" and could refer to either place. None "certainly" identify Cana with Kefr Kenna; none are incompatible with Khirbet Qana. Finally, no report indicates doubt about the location of the town. In short, the results throughout the Crusader period are the same as for the earlier periods.[45]

The first indication of Kefr Kenna as a site of pilgrimage is in 1566, when a Greek Orthodox church was built there. Yet although the Greek Orthodox had begun a new tradition of the town's location, into the seventeenth century pilgrims (including Franciscans) continued to consider Khirbet Qana as the authentic site.[46] According to Herrojo, between 1630 and 1640 two events gave rise to uncertainty regarding the correct location of the town. First, "Khirbet" Qana ceased being populated and the town fell into ruins. Second, the tomb of Jonas, which had been located at Kefr Kenna and had helped distinguish it from the other town, was abandoned.[47] Both events led to a break in the tradition regarding the original site of biblical Cana. Because Khirbet Qana was no longer populated, there was less reason to visit it. Because the tomb of Jonas was neglected, the second factor that distinguished the two sites was also lost. As a result, it was easy to confuse the sites and indeed to consider Kefr Kenna as the biblical site. The first written indication of any uncertainty about the location of biblical Cana is expressed in the book of Francisco Quaresmio in 1626.[48] In it he expressed the conviction that Kefr Kenna was the correct site and that the Orthodox church was in fact the remains of a Byzantine church built by Saint Helena in the fourth century (and so indicating the true site).[49] Yet even then Fr. Quaresmio expressed this

---

44. Herrojo, *Caná*, pp. 36-45.

45. Herrojo, *Caná*, pp. 46-88. This refutes the arguments of those who have proposed that the Crusaders introduced the tradition of Khirbet Qana and that this interrupted the otherwise consistent tradition of associating Cana with Kefr Kenna.

46. Herrojo, "Authenticité," p. 240.

47. Herrojo, *Caná*, pp. 114-15.

48. F. Quaresmio, *Historica Theologica et Moralis Terrae Sanctae Elucidatio* (Antwerp, 1623 [1st ed.]; 1639 [2nd ed.]).

49. Herrojo, "Authenticité," pp. 241-42. Moreover, Quaresmio was the first to identify the

opinion with some hesitancy. But his opinion was readily adopted by subsequent investigators as one that was certain.

With this conviction, and within two years of the publication of Fr. Quaresmio's work, the Franciscan order began negotiations to buy property at Kefr Kenna, a difficult and complicated process that lasted almost two hundred years. In short, as described by Herrojo, the option to consider Kefr Kenna as the biblical city was an unfortunate and costly mistake. As indicated above, the scholarship of Herrojo is quite careful and confirms the views of earlier scholars who have proposed similar views.[50] As a result, it would seem that the identity of biblical Cana, which neither contemporary literary accounts nor archaeology was able to settle alone, can be established definitively by the critical reading of the pilgrim traditions.[51]

Conclusions

Archaeological work at both sites is ongoing. The excavations at Khirbet Qana are more extensive and so may be able to be evaluated more thoroughly.[52] In addition, the discovery and excavation of a pilgrim cave there, together with Christian graffiti, are consistent with the earliest pilgrim reports. Thus, although archaeology tips the scales in favor of Khirbet Qana, archaeology alone cannot be said to prove it. It is only the critical appropriation of the pilgrim reports that is able to settle the issue. J. Herrojo has shown clearly not only that the earliest Christian tradition is univocally in favor of Khirbet Qana as the proper location of the town, but also that the beginning of uncertainty (and of the tradition favoring Kefr Kenna) can be dated and explained.

---

tomb of Jonas as being not at Kefr Kenna but in another town (Meschad). See Herrojo, *Caná*, p. 119.

50. Herrojo is almost apologetic about the conclusions of his study out of respect for the Franciscans who now own the church at Kefr Kenna.

51. This view has been alternatively confirmed and rejected for over seventy years. See the discussion by Kopp, *Holy Places*, pp. 143-54. Kopp refers to his own study, *Das Kana des Evangeliums* (Cologne, 1940), which was later said by A. Alt to have settled the question. See A. Alt, *Kleine Schriften zur Geschichte des Volkes Israel* (Munich: C. H. Beck, 1959), p. 446. The judgment was premature.

52. See the chapter by P. Richardson elsewhere in this volume. See also the earlier article by J. Herrojo, "Nuevas Aportaciones para el Estudio de Kh. Qana," *LASBF* 48 (1998): 345-56, which describes the pilgrim cave, the well, tombs, and references to the possibility of remains of a Byzantine church at the site. Preliminary reports regarding the excavations each year are also posted to the official Web site of the excavation team: http://www.nextfind.com/cana/thesite.html.

4. Capernaum (2:12; 4:46; 6:17, 24, 59)

The Johannine Context

The mention of this town, like that of Bethsaida, is not unique to the Gospel of John and there is no doubt about its location, but archaeology has uncovered a number of features that are pertinent to, and need to be reconciled with, the Johannine data.[53] The first mention of Capernaum indicates that Jesus went there "for a few days" with his mother, his brothers, and his disciples after the wedding at Cana.[54] The second mention is of a meeting of Jesus with an official whose son was ill in Capernaum. Jesus grants the man's request and the son is healed.

The third, fourth, and fifth references all follow the multiplication of the loaves. In 6:17, it is said that the disciples set out in boats from the place of the multiplication to Capernaum. While at sea, they encounter Jesus walking on the sea; he gets into the boat with them; and they arrive suddenly at Capernaum. In 6:24 we read that the crowds that had witnessed the multiplication also come to Capernaum and are amazed to find Jesus there, knowing that he had not departed with the disciples. The final reference occurs in 6:59 and states belatedly that the preceding discourse (6:30-58) had taken place while Jesus was teaching in the synagogue in Capernaum.

Literary References

During the rule of Herod Antipas, Capernaum was a border town for those crossing over from the tetrarchy of Philip. There was a customhouse there (Mt 9:9) and perhaps a small Roman garrison (if the title of the official in Lk 7:2 indicates his purpose for being in the town).[55] J. Murphy-O'Connor speculates that the town was poor since a Gentile centurion built the synagogue for

---

53. It is known to archaeologists as Tell Hum. It is about 2 miles south of the mouth of the Jordan along the western shore of the Sea of Galilee and about 9 miles north of Tiberias.

54. The texts are given in the heading.

55. A considerable number of Roman coins have been found in the first-century stratum of the city, indicating a sizable Roman presence. It is unknown whether the *basilikos* of Jn 4:46 is to be identified as the Roman centurion of the Synoptics or whether the title was simply a general one that could also refer to the synagogue leader there. [A Roman bath has been found in eastern Capernaum, in the Greek Orthodox section. See von Wahlde's following discussion. — JHC.]

them (Lk 7:5).[56] Others suggest that it was relatively affluent given the size of the harbor.[57]

Archaeological Evidence

Capernaum, this small[58] town on the western shore of the Sea of Galilee, has been excavated extensively.[59] Four aspects are of potential interest for the Gospel of John: the harbor, the synagogue, the so-called Peter's House, and the remains of a Roman camp.

The Harbor   There are substantial remains of a quay on the lake's edge above the waterline. However, during a period of abnormally low lake levels from 1989 to 1991, remains of jetties and a breakwater were visible for the first time.[60] Some have suggested that the extensive remains indicate that this was among the more elaborate harbors on the Sea of Galilee.[61] As described by M. Nun, the harbor stretched for perhaps 600 meters along the lake and had ten jetties reaching out into the lake. Some were triangular; others reached straight out and then curved toward one another, creating a protected anchorage. There are, however, varying opinions about the age of the remains, some placing them in

---

56. Murphy-O'Connor, *The Holy Land*, p. 217.

57. See M. Nun, "Ports of Galilee," *BAR* 25, no. 4 (July/August 1999): 24.

58. J. Reed ("The Population of Capernaum," *Occasional Papers of the Institute for Antiquity and Christianity* 23 [1992]) estimates the population to have been about 1,700. Estimates vary, however. J. C. H. Laughlin ("Capernaum: From Jesus' Time and After," *BAR* 19, no. 5 [September/October 1993]: 54-61, 90, here p. 57) estimates that the population was about 1,000. [See Charlesworth's chapter for further discussion. — JHC.]

59. The first excavations at Capernaum took place in 1865. The synagogue was excavated in 1905. Beginning in 1969 and continuing through 1981, the Franciscans, under the direction of V. Corbo and S. Loffreda, cut a series of trenches beneath the third-century synagogue and found remains of an earlier one from the first century. For an overview by S. Loffreda, see "Capernaum," in *OEANE* 1:416-19. See also J. Finegan, *The Archaeology of the New Testament*, rev. ed. (Princeton: Princeton University Press, 1992), pp. 100-101; Laughlin, "Capernaum," pp. 54-61, 90. For a complete account of the excavations on the eastern property, see V. Tzaferis et al., *Excavations at Capernaum*, vol. 1, 1978-1982 (Winona Lake, Ind.: Eisenbrauns, 1989).

60. M. Nun ("Ports of Galilee," pp. 25-26) estimates that in modern times the normal water level of the lake is about three feet higher than in the first century. He estimates this from the fact that the site of "Peter's House" in Capernaum was flooded during high water and because the tops of modern quays tend to be about three feet higher than first-century ones.

61. The harbor is described by M. Nun, *The Sea of Galilee: Newly Discovered Harbors from New Testament Days* (Israel: Kibbutz Ein Gev, 1992). See also Nun, "Ports of Galilee," pp. 18-31, 64.

the first century C.E., others as late as the seventh century.[62] There is also evidence of fish pools near the harbor, indicating the presence of a substantial fish trade in the town.

In Jn 6:17, 24 it is said that both Jesus and the crowd that had witnessed the multiplication of the loaves crossed the lake and came independently to Capernaum. They would have landed at the town's harbor. If these remains are from the first century C.E., then undoubtedly this is where the boat carrying Jesus landed.

The Synagogue   There are impressive remains of a fourth-century synagogue not far from the shoreline of the Sea of Galilee in Capernaum.[63] These remains are well preserved and striking in their beauty. Consequently, it is unlikely that extensive excavation of this part of the site will be conducted in the future. However, in 1981 the Franciscans of the Holy Land excavated strategically placed trenches along the foundations of this synagogue. These trenches went down to virgin soil. Studies of the finds from these trenches confirmed the existence of another building, dating from the first century C.E., under the later synagogue. Because of the limited scope of the excavations, this previous building is detectable only as the black basalt foundation on which the later synagogue has been built. The basalt constitutes the foundation not only of the later synagogue but also of an earlier synagogue, as is evident from the fact that the later synagogue is not built squarely on the earlier foundation but has a slightly

---

62. M. Nun places them in the first century *(The Sea of Galilee)*. See also Nun, "Ports of Galilee," pp. 18-31, 64; see esp. pp. 25-27. Murphy-O'Connor *(The Holy Land,* p. 221) associates the harbor remains with the seventh-century city to the east of the first-century town. The remains of the harbor wall as it runs along the Greek Orthodox property to the east are clear in a photo in Laughlin, "Capernaum," p. 58. Laughlin dates the wall on the eastern property to the second or third century C.E.

63. Excavated by V. Corbo beginning in 1969. See his reports in V. Corbo, "Edifici antichi sotto la sinagoga di Cafarnao," in *Studia Hierosolymitana* (Jerusalem: Franciscan, 1979), 1:159-76; Corbo, "Resti della sinagoga del primo secolo a Cafarnao," *Studia Hierosolymitana* III (Jerusalem: Franciscan, 1982), pp. 313-57. See also S. Loffreda, *A Visit to Capernaum* (Jerusalem: Franciscan Printing Press, 1980) and *Recovering Capernaum* (Jerusalem: Edizioni Custodia Terra Santa, 1985), two treatments that are less technical but equally helpful. Also see the overviews presented by Finegan, *Archaeology,* pp. 99-104, and J. F. Strange and H. Shanks, "Synagogue Where Jesus Preached Found at Capernaum?" *BAR* 9 (November/December 1983): 24-31; Taylor, *Christians,* pp. 290-94. It is perhaps noteworthy that Taylor, who expresses general skepticism about the accuracy of many of the sites, recognizes that the later synagogue is built on the basalt foundation of what had also been a synagogue in the first century (pp. 292-93). However, controversy continues about the dating of the later synagogue. Many find it surprising that such a finely built synagogue would have been constructed, in the post-Constantinian period, in such a way as to overshadow the more modest Christian house church close by.

different orientation. This change in orientation is almost certainly due to a later, more precise calculation of the edifice's relation to the Temple in Jerusalem, which it was intended to face. Given the custom of building one synagogue immediately upon the site of previous ones, the earlier building is almost certainly the synagogue in which, according to the Gospel of John, Jesus taught (6:59) on the day after the multiplication of the loaves.

Saint Peter's House The existence of a house owned by Peter at Capernaum is known from the Gospel of Mark (1:29-31; cf. also Mt 8:14-17; Lk 4:38-41). About 130 yards south of the synagogue is a building venerated since Constantinian times as Peter's house. The site has been extensively excavated. This has revealed a complex history of construction, a complexity that is unusual for an ordinary house. Graffiti as well as other remains found at the site indicate that the original form of the house dates from the first century. Indeed, the archaeological features of the central room of the *insula* have suggested to experts that the room was in specifically Christian use as a house church already in the first century C.E. V. Corbo, who was in charge of excavations there, has also proposed that this is the actual house of Peter.[64] Almost all scholars now espouse this view.[65]

Remains of a Roman Camp In Jn 4:46-54 there is an account of the healing of an "official's" son who lay at the point of death in Capernaum. This account is very similar to the Synoptic accounts in which the child is identified as the son of a Roman centurion from Capernaum who, according to Luke, built the synagogue. However, in the Johannine account the father is described only as a "royal official," and so it is not certain that the Johannine tradition refers to the same incident, although it is certainly likely. Given the similarity of the Johannine account to that of the Synoptics, the possible existence of a Roman camp in the town is substantial.

---

64. V. Corbo, *The House of St. Peter at Capharnaum*, SBF.CMi 5 (Jerusalem: Studium Biblicum Franciscanum, 1969).

65. For example, J. H. Charlesworth, *Jesus within Judaism: New Light from Exciting Archaeological Discoveries*, ABRL (Garden City, N.Y.: Doubleday, 1988), pp. 109, 111; Murphy-O'Connor, *The Holy Land*, p. 218; J. Strange and H. Shanks, "Has the House Where Jesus Stayed in Capernaum Been Found?" *BAR* 8 (November/December 1982): 26-37. One of the few dissenting voices is that of J. Taylor (*Christians*, pp. 268-88), who argues that while the house was clearly a pilgrimage site from the fourth century on, the presence of beaten lime floors (which has been used to argue that the place was an early Christian house church) means only that the owner was of a higher economic class. She would also argue that graffiti in the house that have been claimed to be Aramaic (and therefore early) are in fact Greek.

V. Tzaferis has led excavations for a number of years on the Greek Ortho-dox property to the northeast of, and adjoining, the Franciscan property at Capernaum.[66] Close to the wall dividing the two properties, Tzaferis has found considerable remains of habitation, and most notably for our purposes the re-mains of a bath similar to the type used elsewhere by Roman soldiers. The re-mains date from the second or third century and are similar to a first-century Roman bathhouse at Ein Gedi. However, according to Tzaferis and J. C. H. Laughlin, who took part in the excavations, underneath this bathhouse was found evidence of a first-century building.[67] Because it would have been neces-sary to destroy what was above them, the first-century remains have not been extensively investigated. However, Tzaferis and Laughlin suggest that the struc-ture below was about the same size as the bath above and that these remains may well be those of a similar Roman bathhouse from the first century C.E. If such were so, then this might provide positive proof of a Roman garrison in Capernaum at the time of Jesus, and so would provide a specific location to which the centurion of the Synoptic Gospels was attached.[68]

Conclusions

As is evident from the above, there is no doubt about the existence or location of the town. More recent archaeology confirms what was already well attested by literary means. Yet at the same time, archaeology provides unique informa-tion. On the basis of excavations prior to 1981, we are able to determine the ex-act location of the synagogue in which Jesus taught. From the observations in 1989-90, we know something of the harbor at Capernaum.

It has always been puzzling that in John's Gospel, after the landing of Jesus at Capernaum (6:25), no reference is made to any movement of Jesus from the place where he landed to the synagogue where he teaches (the mention of the synagogue is given in 6:59, at the end of the homily). Of course, this awkward-

---

66. The site as well as the entrance to the property have been prepared for greater public access, a process that will undoubtedly make the site more accessible.

67. See Laughlin, "Capernaum." Laughlin has excavated at Capernaum with Tzaferis and acknowledged the contribution of Tzaferis to his article.

68. Matthew (8:5-13) and Luke (7:1-10) mention a Roman centurion at Capernaum whose ser-vant was ill and who had asked Jesus to heal him. In Matthew the centurion himself approaches Je-sus to ask for the cure. In Luke he sends elders of the Jews to ask for the cure. As they do so, they de-scribe the centurion as one who loves their nation and built a synagogue for them (7:5). There is a similar account in the Gospel of John in which a "royal official" *(basilikos)* approaches Jesus at Cana and explains that his son is at the point of death in Capernaum. Many scholars think these accounts are variants of one another. However, in John it is not clear that the man is a Gentile or a Roman.

ness may be due to editing that disrupted the sequence of the text, but now it could also be explained by the proximity of the synagogue to the harbor, as is evident archaeologically. Consequently, it is possible that this explains another minor, incidental, detail of the Gospel.

If Tzaferis is correct in his estimate of a first-century Roman bath underlying the ruins of the later edifice, this would give direct confirmation of a Roman presence in Capernaum in the first century and support the reference in Matthew and Luke to a Roman centurion in the town. It would lend weight to (but not prove) the suggestion of many that the "royal official" mentioned in Jn 4:46-54 was the centurion as proposed by Matthew and Luke.

Although the Gospel of John refers to Jesus as being "from Nazareth" (1:45), it gives no indication of a ministry by Jesus there, as do the Synoptics (Mt 13:54-58; Mk 3:20-35; 6:1-6; Lk 4:16-30). However, according to John, Jesus spends time in Capernaum *with his mother, his brothers,* and his disciples (2:12). This (unique) information would seem to imply that not only did Jesus regularly minister in Capernaum, but his family considered Capernaum in some sense a home. It is difficult to know how seriously to take this implication, but if we had only the Gospel of John, we would be inclined to think that although he was originally from Nazareth, he and his family had moved to Capernaum.

If this literary evidence suggests a change of home city for Jesus, archaeological evidence (as we have seen above) does the same for Peter. The Gospel of John describes Peter as being from Bethsaida (1:44). Yet there is strong early tradition bolstered by archaeological evidence that Peter lived in Capernaum. This would suggest that Peter had moved from Bethsaida to Capernaum. The combination of literary and archaeological evidence would thus reveal another detail from the lives of both Jesus and Peter.

5. Area of the Cleansing of the Temple (2:13-16)

The Johannine Context

If we follow the narrative order of the Gospel, the next relevant site is the place in the Temple in Jerusalem where Jesus found money changers and those selling animals for sacrifice (2:13-16). The Gospel account presents Jesus as making a whip of cords and driving out those selling sheep and cattle and pouring out the coins of the money changers and turning over their tables. He then told those selling doves to take them out of the Temple.

Here we are dealing with an incident that is reported in all of the Gospels. Moreover, the Johannine account does not give unique details about the location.

However, it does demonstrate correct understanding of the terminology uses for Temple precincts by distinguishing the outer court *(hieron)* (vv. 14-15), the place where the selling is said to take place, from the temple sanctuary itself *(naos)* (vv. 19-21). However, both the selling of animals and the changing of coinage are complex issues and need to be discussed separately. Yet with the aid of both archaeology and literary evidence, we are able to gain some clarity on the issues.

The Literary and Archaeological Evidence

Money changers were necessary to convert the common Roman currency into silver Tyrian coinage, the only coinage acceptable for the Temple offering. The actual place of conversion was in any of thirteen locations in the porticos surrounding the Court of the Women. The common view is that the money changers themselves were located in the Royal Portico on the south side of the Temple esplanade, where there were other shops. There is relatively little dispute about this conclusion.[69]

Roman coins were not allowed for such offerings. Coins minted in Jerusalem were either copper or bronze and would not qualify either. According to the Mishnah, the Temple offering was to be done in Tyrian coinage, which was silver.[70] The Tyrian mint was autonomous and not associated with the hated Roman Empire. Finally, the silver content of Tyrian coins was higher than that of Roman coins, and so the Tyrian coins were intrinsically more valuable.[71]

But what is the issue that makes the action of the money changers wrong in the eyes of Jesus? Was his reaction due to the very presence of the money changers in the Temple precincts, even in the customary place? Or had the money changers moved into an area that was not approved but was for some reason more convenient? If the first were the case, the issue would be one of a higher

69. See, for example, the discussion in D. Bahat's article "Jesus and the Herodian Temple Mount," elsewhere in this collection. See also E. P. Sanders, *Judaism: Practice and Belief, 63 BCE–66 CE* (London: SCM; Philadelphia: Trinity, 1992), p. 68. The presence of money changers in the Temple is mentioned in *Sheqalim* 1.3 (quoted in Bahat's article).

70. *m. Bekhoroth* 8.7.

71. [The Rabbis instructed that only the Tyrian silver coins could be used to pay tribute money to the Temple, and beginning in 66 C.E. Jewish shekels were introduced. Meshorer is convinced, rightly, that the term on them, "Holy Jerusalem," mirrors "Holy Tyre" on the earlier shekalim. See Meshorer, *Ancient Jewish Coinage* (New York: Amphora, 1982), 2:104-5. N.B. that according to the Tosephta, "silver," whenever it is mentioned in the Pentateuch, "is Tyrian silver." The tradition continues: "What is a Tyrian silver (coin)? It is a Jerusalemite" (*t. Kethubot* 13.20). See esp. D. Hendin, "Shekels of Tyre," in *Guide to Biblical Coins*, 3rd ed. (New York: Amphora, 1996), pp. 274-75. — JHC.]

standard of propriety on the part of Jesus. If the second were the case, it would be a matter of Jesus' reaction against what would be an (apparently tolerated) abuse of the normal procedure. However, there seems to be no way for us to determine which was in fact the case.

But there is another possibility. P. Richardson, now followed by J. Murphy-O'Connor, argues that Jesus was reacting against the money changers not because they were in the wrong place but because he considered the use of Tyrian coinage for the Temple offering wrong in itself.[72] As Richardson points out, the Tyrian shekel was not aniconic, and therefore was not a neutral or "holy" coin. On the obverse it contained an image, and in fact the image of a pagan god (Melkart-Herakles); on the reverse was a Tyrian eagle and the inscription "Tyre, the holy and inviolable." This would make the Tyrian half-shekel inherently offensive, at least to more devout Jews, and especially as a Temple offering. According to this argument, rather than change the law requiring silver coins, the authorities allowed the use of the Tyrian silver shekel, bowing to political and economic considerations. If this is a proper understanding of the situation, then it is not an issue of *where* the money changers were located but that they were there at all.[73] This would indicate that Jesus was demonstrating a higher level of rigor regarding what would be considered proper coinage for the offering.[74]

The issue of the reaction of Jesus to those selling animals is more complex. First, there is the matter of the specific animals mentioned in the Johannine text. Doves were among the most common animals used for sacrifice and were available for purchase so that worshipers would not be forced to transport them when coming a great distance. There are repeated references to the use and availability of such birds.[75] The use of sheep for sacrifice is also well at-

---

72. See P. Richardson, "Why Turn the Tables? Jesus' Protest in the Temple Precincts," in E. H. Lovering, Jr., ed., *SBLSP* 31 (1992), pp. 507-23; J. Murphy-O'Connor, "Jesus and the Money Changers (Mark 11:15-17; John 2:13-17)," *RB* 107 (2000): 43-55.

73. Richardson and Murphy-O'Connor also argue that the frequency of taxation may also have been an issue of some concern. Jewish males were required to offer a Temple tax each year. Yet the original text dealing with the tax (Ex 30:11-16) gives the impression that it was to be done only once. At Qumran it was made explicit that the tax was due only once in a life (4Q159 frag. l, col. 2). This would have been seen as another abuse within the Temple (Murphy-O'Connor, "Money Changers," pp. 48-49).

74. In his article referred to above, D. Bahat refers to Y. Meshorer (*A Treasury of Jewish Coins* [Jerusalem: Yad Yitshak Ben-Tsevi, 1997]) as saying that the so-called Tyrian coins were in fact minted in Jerusalem. It would seem then that these coins were not the same as those that were actually "Tyrian." [A "Tyrian shekel" minted in Jerusalem about 33 c.e. was unearthed in 2004 in Jerusalem's Old City. — JHC.]

75. See the texts in Jeremias, *Jerusalem in the Time of Jesus* (Philadelphia: Fortress, 1969), pp. 48-49.

tested, and it was very possible to purchase sheep; the numbers available, particularly at Passover, must have been quite large.[76] E. P. Sanders has suggested that the reference in the Johannine text to oxen available for sacrifice is an inaccuracy, on the grounds that such animals would be too expensive for all but the very rich and that, in addition, such animals were not required except in special cases.[77] However, the sacrifices prescribed for various feasts regularly include oxen (LXX: *boas*, the same term used in the Johannine account; see Num 28:11–29:39), and two young oxen (LXX: *boas*) were to be offered at the Feast of the Unleavened Bread (Num 28:17-19). Jeremias also cites rabbinic texts that indicate that such did happen: in one case R. Baba b. Buta "had three thousand head of small livestock brought to the Temple hill to be sold for whole burnt offerings and peace offerings."[78] Sanders himself admits that an ox or a calf could be sacrificed by an individual as a burnt offering or as part of a shared sacrifice, "but few could have afforded to do so." There is no indication that the oxen were to be used solely for individual sacrifices, and so Sanders's judgment about the Johannine account does not seem correct. All these animals would be available for purchase in the vicinity of the Temple so that those traveling would not be compelled to bring animals a great distance, something both inconvenient and possibly injurious to the animals.

We next discuss where the selling of animals for sacrifice took place. The problem is not providing animals for sacrifice (which was acceptable), but whether the commerce was being carried on in the proper place. Not only was there potentially a concern for the amount of commerce in the area of the Temple, but there were also the purity issues raised by the inevitable animal waste.

Scholars have made at least five suggestions regarding the location where these sacrificial animals were normally kept and sold. One common theory is that they were sold somewhere in the Court of the Gentiles.[79] A second proposal is that they were kept penned up outside the Temple Mount beyond the Sheep Gate, near the pool of Bethesda to the north of the Temple Mount.[80]

A third possibility is that the selling took place near the Hulda Gates in the southern wall of the Mount. This was the main entry to the Temple, and entrance was gained by a long corridor leading upward from the Hulda Gates into

---

76. See the discussion of numbers of sheep needed for Passover and speculation regarding the process of slaughter in Sanders, *Judaism*, pp. 136-38.

77. Sanders, *Judaism*, p. 88.

78. Jeremias, *Jerusalem*, p. 49.

79. This is the view expressed by D. Bahat in his article elsewhere in this collection. It is also the view of Jeremias (*Jerusalem*, p. 49).

80. This is the position adopted by Murphy-O'Connor, "Jesus and the Money Changers (Mark 11:15-17; John 2:13-17)."

the Court of the Gentiles. Under the southeastern part of the Temple terrace were the chambers now referred to as "Solomon's Stables." As a result of excavations in the area by B. Mazar, a passageway was found between the stables and the main entrance corridor leading up from the Triple Hulda gates.[81] This passageway extended along the southern wall of the Temple Mount and went as far as the Double Hulda gates. G. Cornfeld and J. Charlesworth propose that the animals for sacrifice could well have been kept in Solomon's Stables and brought forward as needed through this passageway.[82]

A fourth proposal has been made by E. P. Sanders, who has argued that if such animals were being sold, it would have to be on the streets below the Temple Mount.[83] Finally, J. Jeremias quotes references from the Talmud and *Midrash Rabbah* that indicate sacrificial animals were sold on the Mount of Olives.[84]

Of these, the first remains a possibility. The Mishnah (*m. Kelim* 1.890) speaks of zones of holiness within the Temple area. As is described by Bahat in his article elsewhere in this collection, it could well be that the Court of the Gentiles of the Herodian Temple consisted of the areas that extended beyond the bounds of the pre-Herodian Temple, and that was why the Court of the Gentiles was open to the ritually impure. This is confirmed in general by the notices posted in Greek and Latin on the balustrade that divided the Court of the Gentiles from those of the Israelite women and men.[85] Further, there are the general references to "shops" in the area of Solomon's Portico. But there is no direct evidence for the selling of animals in this court.[86]

81. B. Mazar, *The Mountain of the Lord* (Garden City, N.Y.: Doubleday, 1975), p. 126. The overall archaeology of the area is quite complex, and for details the reader is referred to the book by Mazar and to that by Cornfeld below.

82. G. Cornfeld, *The Historical Jesus* (New York: Macmillan; London: Collier Macmillan, 1982); Charlesworth, *Jesus within Judaism*, pp. 117-19. [See Charlesworth's discussion of the Ḥanot in the present collection. — JHC.]

83. Sanders, *Judaism*, p. 87 (cf. p. 69).

84. Jeremias, *Jerusalem*, p. 48.

85. On the basis of the inscription that prevents Gentiles from entering the restricted parts of the Temple on the grounds of purity, Bahat argues that the Court of the Gentiles would have been acceptable as a place for selling animals and that this is where it took place. The inscription Bahat refers to is reproduced in Bahat, *Atlas* (Jerusalem: Carta, 1990 [rev. ed. 1996]), p. 44, and Mazar, *Mountain of the Lord*, p. 114. This inscription is also described by Josephus (*Ant* 15.11.5 §417). That there were shops in the Temple Court is attested in rabbinic literature. See the texts cited in Jeremias, *Jerusalem*, p. 20.

86. Sanders cites Philo as saying that there was no sacred grove or tree in the Temple area because excrement of men or animals could not be brought into the Temple. Sanders, *Judaism*, p. 87, citing Philo, *De specialibus legibus* 1.74-75. But it is unclear whether this referred to the entire Temple Mount or the more restricted areas of the Temple.

The problem with the third proposal is that there is no clear evidence that the area under the southeastern corner of the Temple was used for animals during the first century c.e. J. Murphy-O'Connor has also pointed out that there would have been no reasonable way to bring the sheep into the stables except up through the Hulda Gates themselves.[87] This makes the third proposal unlikely. The fourth proposal is also a possibility, but if the selling were done in the streets below the Mount, the problem of bringing the animals into the Temple would remain, as it would also with the fifth possibility (that they were sold on the Mount of Olives).

However, the second proposal (that the animals were sold outside the Sheep Gate) is also a possibility. First, not only is this area outside the Temple Mount, at the time of Jesus it was also outside the city. This is the only side of the Temple Mount where such animals could be kept without defiling the city or the Temple. Second, because of the elevation and slope of the hill in the Bethzetha region, access to this gate would be more convenient than access to any other gate around the Temple area. Third, and perhaps most significantly, this gate had been known for centuries as the "Sheep Gate," and the naming of city gates was always related somehow to their use.[88] Yet how the worshiper would procure an animal from this area is not clear; it would clearly be out of the way since there were no major public entrances in that area. It may be that the animals were brought in by this gate and into the Court of the Gentiles for sale.

If the selling took place at any of the venues except the first, how it could be seen as violating the sanctity of the Temple is difficult to understand. But even if the first possibility were true, the reasons for Jesus' actions would not necessarily be clear. It could be that Jesus thought the Court of the Gentiles was not a proper place for such selling. It could also be that *on this occasion* the animals were not being corralled properly (and therefore being allowed to be in violation of Temple purity). Finally, it could be that Jesus' action was intended to be symbolic, reflecting a higher standard of eschatological purity for the Temple. The text regularly cited in this latter regard is Zech 14:21, which speaks of there being no more traders in the house of the Lord "on that day." But even this text

87. I am grateful to J. Murphy-O'Connor for his observations regarding various aspects of this problem.

88. See, for example, the "Garden" Gate discussed below, which reflects awareness of the "garden" near Golgotha. Some (e.g., D. Bahat) have suggested that the Sheep Gate is the same as that referred to in the Mishnah as the Tadi Gate, which is described as "serving no purpose." Bahat concludes that this means the gate was not functional. However, Mazar (*Mountain of the Lord*, p. 151) thinks this means that it had no particular function with regard to Temple rituals but was a kind of service gate.

is ambiguous. Does it mean that traders will not be necessary because everything will be holy (cf. vv. 20b-21a), or that concern for purity will demand the removal of traders?

One final issue may also be relevant. It is reported in the Mishnah (*m. Kelim* 1.7) that Simeon, son of Gamaliel I, complained about the exorbitant price of a pair of doves sold for sacrifice, that within a single day the price could be reduced from two gold dinars to one-half a silver dinar.[89] This would be a reduction in price of 900 percent. This account would suggest that price gouging could also be an issue in the sale of sacrificial animals. Although not specifically mentioned, such a practice could have been another element of abuse being condemned by Jesus. Such an abuse would be kin to the increased pressure to sacrifice larger and larger animals even though one was not required to do so. It is therefore clear that there were abuses of various sorts taking place in the Temple at different times.

Conclusions

Where then did the money changing and selling of animals take place? Perhaps the "proper" place was different for each. But it does not seem possible to determine with any certainty where this was. The most likely candidate for the changing of money is the Royal Portico. This was a place of some commerce and most likely to be the customary place for money changers. It may also be that the trade in animals also took place in the Court of the Gentiles, and that it was against this, together with the abuse of the money changers, that Jesus reacted. There seems to be no way to reconcile all the accounts and the conflicting evidence.

In the first century C.E. there were complaints on many sides about abuses associated with the Temple. The Essenes, who moved to the wilderness as a protest against such abuses, were only one example of this. If we prescind from the details, it would seem clear that Jesus was another such example. In spite of the many details that remain unresolved, it is clear that Jesus' actions were intended to demonstrate his concern for the purity of the worship, and nothing in this account would indicate his opposition to Temple worship in itself. It is also clear that in spite of some unresolved details, nothing in the Johannine account is patently inaccurate or could be said to demonstrate lack of knowledge of the Temple and its regulations. The Johannine account reflects the proper terminology for the various Temple areas. Moreover, contra Sanders, it seems it is ac-

---

89. A gold dinar is said to have been worth twenty-five silver dinars.

curate in reporting that there could be larger animals such as oxen among those for sale. In addition, archaeology continues to be helpful to the enterprise by providing an ever increasing knowledge of the layout of the Temple area, which enables a more precise discussion of the other issues.

6. Aenon Near Salim (3:23)

The Johannine Context

With the mention of Aenon near Salim, we return to information that is unique to the Gospel of John. Aenon is mentioned nowhere else in the New Testament nor in ancient literature. The name is highly evocative, since "Aenon" is from the Aramaic plural of "spring" and "Salim" is related to the word for "peace." Consequently, it is not surprising that some would argue that the name is symbolic and the place fictitious, as did Krieger.[90]

Yet there are early attempts to identify the place historically. The earliest reference to the location is on the Madaba map, which shows Aenon just northeast of the Dead Sea across the river from Bethabara. This would put it close to the Bethany beyond the Jordan (Jn 1:28) and may have referred to the springs at Ayn Kharrar, described above. Two other possibilities suggested with some regularity are Salim about three miles east of Shechem and the much more northerly Tel Salim, seven miles south of Beth-Shan (Scythopolis). Both places do indeed contain "springs" as their names would indicate. The earliest post-Gospel reference to Aenon is in Eusebius, who identifies it with Tel Salim, as do Jerome and the pilgrim Egeria (ca. 384 c.e.).[91]

Archaeological Evidence

Both sites have indications of habitation, but archaeological excavations are really not helpful. The only pertinent information is more properly geological: the presence of springs in the area. There are several springs within 300 meters of Tel Salim, and a majority of modern scholars (among them C. Kopp, B. Manzano, B. Pixner, and R. Riesner)[92] opt for this as the location of the

90. Krieger, "Fiktive," pp. 122-23.

91. Eusebius, *Onomasticon* 40.

92. Kopp, *Holy Places*, pp. 129-32; B. Manzano, "Les sources d'Aenon, près de Salim, où Jean baptisait," *Terre Sainte* 5-6 (1987): 124-30; Pixner, *With Jesus*, pp. 27-28; Riesner, "Bethany Beyond the Jordan (John 1:28)," p. 31.

Johannine site. Among those who argue for the site near Mount Gerizim are W. F. Albright and J. Murphy-O'Connor.[93] Murphy-O'Connor points to the continued existence of a town by the name of Salim in the area as well as springs spread along a 1 kilometer line at the base of Mount Gerizim. However, these springs are 5 kilometers to the west of Salim, a distance that is arguably too great to qualify as being "near."[94] At any rate, this southern location remains a minority position.

Conclusions

Given the paucity of details in the Johannine account, it has been understandably difficult to determine the location. A location at Ayn Kharrar is excluded because of the absence of a referent for Salim. At this time we are forced to rely on the consistency between the earliest pilgrim reports and the presence of springs at the site near Beth-Shan. Although a majority of scholars favor the more northern site, the case cannot be said to be decided. In fact, it may never be able to be decided, given the nature of the reference. But in any event, there is clearly no justification for treating the name simply as a symbolic one.

Samaria:
7. Sychar (4:4-6);
8. Jacob's Well (4:6);
9. Mount Gerizim (4:20)

The Johannine Context

According to Jn 4, in response to increasing pressure from the Pharisees, Jesus departs from Judea and returns to Galilee via Samaria. On the way he stops to rest at Jacob's well near the town of Sychar near Mount Gerizim. These three references make up the Gospel's references to sites in Samaria, and they are closely linked with one another. All three are unique to the Gospel of John within the New Testament. Because of their interrelatedness, we will treat them together.

---

93. W. F. Albright, "Discoveries in Palestine and the Gospel of St. John," in *The Background of the New Testament and Its Eschatology,* p. 159; Murphy-O'Connor, *The Holy Land,* p. 373.

94. So also Manzano, "Sources," p. 127.

The Archaeological Evidence

The most obvious of the sites under consideration is Mount Gerizim. It is referred to only in the Gospel of John within the New Testament, and even there it is not mentioned by name but is referred to as simply "this mountain," the mountain on which the (Samaritan) fathers worshiped. Yet the meaning is clear. There is no question concerning the identification of the mountain today. Considerable archaeological activity has been undertaken on Mount Gerizim since 1990,[95] but none is of specific relevance to the Johannine account.

Jacob's well is identified as being near the field given by Jacob to his son Joseph. This is a reference to the events narrated in Gen 33:18-20, where it is said that Jacob bought land at Shechem, and in Gen 48:22, where it is said that Jacob gave it to Joseph as his "portion" *(shechem)*. Joseph was buried there (Josh 24:32). This identifies the area with Jacob and also with Shechem. There is also little doubt about the site of Jacob's well. There is a well there today, about 250 feet outside the ruins of the town of Shechem. It lies directly on what was the main north-south road in the first century. This made it particularly suitable for travelers. This is, of course, consistent with the fact that Jesus stopped at the well as he was journeying north from Jerusalem to Galilee.

In verse 6 of the Johannine text this well is identified as a *pēgē* (a running spring), whereas in verses 11, 12 it is called a *phrear* (a dug-out well). The well near Shechem is just such a combination of dug-out well and running spring.[96] Thus once again the Johannine text reflects details of the well's location (near Shechem), of the site's history (given to Joseph by Jacob), of its particular makeup (both spring and cistern), as well as of its appropriateness for travelers.

The third of the three related sites is the town of Sychar. In the area close to both Mount Gerizim and Jacob's well there are two possibilities: the site of ancient Shechem and the town of Aschar. Some commentators, among them R. E. Brown, have proposed that the site be identified with ancient Shechem. Brown would deal with the difference in names by text criticism, pointing out that the Greek for Sychar *(Sychar)* is close to the Greek for Shechem *(Sychem)*.[97] However, the actual name Shechem is attested only in a single Syriac translation.[98] A

95. The excavations have been under the direction of Y. Magen. See Y. Magen, "Mount Gerizim and the Samaritans," in *Early Christianity in Context: Monuments and Documents*, ed. F. Manns and E. Alliata, SBF.CMa 38 (Jerusalem: Franciscan, 1985), pp. 96-97, 103-6; see in the same volume, Magen, "The Ritual Baths *(miqva'oth)* at Qedumim and the Observance of Ritual Purity among the Samaritans," pp. 167-80, 181-92, and "Samaritan Synagogues," pp. 193-230.

96. Kopp, *Holy Places*, p. 156.

97. R. E. Brown, *Gospel according to John I–XII* (London: Geoffrey Chapman, 1971), p. 169 n. 5.

98. It is curious that the United Bible Societies committee for the fourth edition saw fit to

more serious problem is that during the time of Jesus, Shechem was in ruins and uninhabited, having been destroyed by John Hyrcanus in 107 B.C.E. Yet the description of the disciples going into the town (4:8) and the woman returning to the city (4:28) implies that the city in question was still in existence.

In 72 C.E. Vespasian built the city of Neapolis (Nablus) a short distance from the site of Shechem, but this town was also not in existence at the time of Jesus. Pilgrim reports know of Shechem, Neapolis, and a Sychar distinct from Shechem. Eusebius speaks of "Sychar in front of Neapolis."[99] The Pilgrim of Bordeaux mentions Neapolis, Shechem, Gerizim, and Sychar. As a result, other scholars have sought to identify Sychar with the town of Aschar.[100] Kopp points to a comment by Epiphanius that suggests that Sychar was "opposite" Gerizim. This description fits the site of modern Aschar. However, according to W. F. Albright, the present town of Aschar only dates from medieval times.[101] But that of itself does not preclude the possibility of an earlier city on the site, and indeed the name is known from antiquity. The author of the book of *Jubilees* (second century B.C.E.) refers to a king of Sakir who is said to wage war against Jacob and his sons at Shechem (*Jub* 34.1-9).[102] This text has been studied in some detail by J. C. VanderKam, who confirms that this is probably the first literary reference to the town of Sychar.[103] There are also statements in the Talmud that indicate the existence of a town named Sakir in the vicinity.[104]

Conclusions

Although archaeology has not identified the precise location of Sychar, contemporary literary evidence together with pilgrim reports and the other nearby

discuss the problem and considered this single variant sufficiently important that it raised the issue. See B. M. Metzger (on behalf of and in cooperation with the Editorial Committee of the United Bible Societies' Greek New Testament), *A Textual Commentary on the Greek New Testament*, Companion to the UBS 4th ed. (Stuttgart: Deutsche Bibelgesellschaft, 1994 [2nd ed.]), p. 177.

99. Eusebius, *Onomasticon* 150.

100. It is argued for in detail by Kopp, *Holy Places*, pp. 155-66. It is also the view of Schnackenburg, *Gospel*, 1:423. Schnackenburg argues that it would be difficult to imagine an ancient name like Shechem being corrupted into Sychar.

101. W. F. Albright, "Recent Discoveries in Palestine and the Gospel of St. John," in *The Background of the New Testament and Its Eschatology*, pp. 153-71.

102. Kopp, *Holy Places*, p. 165.

103. VanderKam, *Textual and Historical Studies*, pp. 223-27. See also J. VanderKam, ed. and trans., *The Book of Jubilees: A Critical Text*, CSCOSA 87-88 (Louvain: Peeters, 1989), p. 226.

104. For references see Kopp, *Holy Places*, p. 165.

features that have been positively identified (Jacob's well, Mount Gerizim, proximity to Shechem) enable us to be reasonably certain that first-century Sychar was located on the site of modern Aschar. If evidence of first-century habitation could be found in the area, the case would undoubtedly be strengthened.

10. The Sheep Gate/Pool (5:2)

The Johannine Context

In chapter 5 of John's Gospel, Jesus comes to Jerusalem for a feast and meets a man who had been crippled for thirty-eight years. The man is lying next to a pool where there is a multitude of blind, lame, and paralyzed. The man explains that whenever the water is stirred up someone always reaches the water before him, and so is cured rather than him. Jesus commands the man to take up his pallet and walk. The man does so, and by thus doing reveals that he has been healed by Jesus. This is the miracle that is narrated; but our primary concern here is with the pool referred to in the narrative. The pool is described as being "near the Sheep Gate, a pool called in Hebrew *Bethesda*, having five colonnades." Again, we find a remarkably detailed description of the place in the Johannine account. Yet this has not deterred scholars from suggesting that the name is symbolic rather than actual.

The Literary Evidence

Our first concern is with the statement translated "being near the Sheep Gate." Actually there is some dispute about whether the adjective "sheep" refers to the gate or the pool. The translation of the verse given above is a relatively new one based on the textual decisions of the most recent critical editions of the Gospel. The reasoning for this reading can be explained briefly as follows. There are two textual problems in the verse. First, there is some uncertainty whether the Greek reads *epi* (or *en*) *tē probatikē*. The Nestle-Aland text prefers *epi* (at) to the alternative *en* (in).[105] The second problem is more substantive. It is clear that *probatikē* (sheep) is an adjective in the dative case. However, *kolymbēthra* (pool) can be taken as either dative or nominative. If "pool" is taken as the dative, then

---

105. B. Aland, K. Aland, et al., eds., *Novum Testamentum Graece*, 27th ed. (Stuttgart: Deutsche Bibelgesellschaft, 1993), ad loc.

"sheep" would be associated with "pool," but then there is no subject for the verb that follows. If "pool" is taken as nominative, then it would be taken as the subject of the following verb and then there is no antecedent for the *probatikē*. In favor of the first alternative is the observation of Barrett that church writers up to the end of the thirteenth century take *kolymbēthra* as dative and so associate *probatikē* with pool.[106] In favor of the second is the fact that there are no references to a "Sheep Pool" in ancient literature. But in Neh 3:1, 32; 12:39 there are references to the existence of *hē pylē hē probatikē* (the Sheep Gate) in Jerusalem. This gate was in the north wall, a short distance from the northeast corner of the city wall. This was of some significance in itself, but when a pool was discovered (see below), the confluence of archaeological and literary evidence made it more likely that the reference was to a *pool* near the Sheep *Gate*. As a result, textual critics now prefer the second alternative.[107]

Conclusions

Here again we see that the Gospel of John, with its reference to the relatively little-known "Sheep Gate," is not symbolic (i.e., it is not a reference to chapter 10 where Jesus refers to himself as the gate for the sheep) but an accurate reminiscence. In conjunction with the discovery of the pool, it reflects remarkably detailed (and unique within the New Testament) knowledge of Jerusalem at the time of Jesus.

11. The Pool of Bethesda (5:2)

The Johannine Context

There is a second important element in Jn 5:2, and that is the description of the pool with five colonnades. As in the text dealing with the Sheep Gate, there are textual problems with the name of the pool. The spelling of Bethesda is disputed in the manuscripts, and there are at least six variations: (1) Bethzatha, (2) Belzetha, (3) Bethsaida, (4) Bezatha, (5) Betzatha, and (6) Bethesda.[108] The

---

106. C. K. Barrett, *The Gospel according to St. John,* 2nd ed. (Philadelphia: Westminster, 1978), p. 251.

107. This differs from the opinion of Brown (*Gospel,* pp. 206-7), who preferred "Sheep Pool."

108. *Bethsaida* is most strongly attested (P[75], B, T, Wsupp; P[66] has *Bedsaidan;* P[66c] has *Bedsaida*) but is probably incorrect through confusion with the town name. On textual grounds

textual critics of the Nestle-Aland 27th edition of the Greek text have opted for (1) Bethzatha. The committee calls this "the least unsatisfactory" reading and suggests that (3) is an imitation of the town in Galilee and (5) is least attested and a likely adaptation to provide an etymology "House of Mercy."[109] Furthermore, the committee judged (4) Bezatha and (2) Belzetha to be simply variants of Bethzatha.

However, commentators have tended to prefer the reading Bethesda even though it is among the most poorly attested of the readings. In his monograph dealing with the archaeology of the site, J. Jeremias argues that if (3) Bethsaida is excluded because of possible confusion with the Galilean town of the same name, all the other forms can be explained as variations of (6) Bethesda. Schnackenburg argues that the form of the name attested in the *Copper Scroll* from Qumran (see below) is the Aramaic dual form of the Hebrew Bethesda and, since the Johannine text explicitly states that the form is *Hebraïsti*, Bethesda is the form to be preferred.[110] As a result, he and most commentators since have made their decision not on a strict textual basis but on these wider considerations.[111]

At one time, both the mention of the porticos and the Hebrew name were thought to be John's symbolic creation.[112] Bethesda (meaning "house of mercy") was taken to symbolize the mercy shown by Jesus to the crippled man. The mention of five porticos was thought to symbolize the five books of Moses and the inefficacy of the healing properties of the pool as compared with the healing power of Jesus.

Literary Evidence

Prior to the discovery of the Qumran scrolls, there was no direct literary evidence of a pool of Bethesda. The closest evidence was a notice in Josephus, who identified Bezetha as a region in the northeast section of the city;[113] Eusebius

---

the next most strongly attested form is *Bethesda*, but this is commonly rejected as an attempt at symbolism (i.e., "place of mercy").

109. This judgment is expressed in *A Textual Commentary on the Greek New Testament*, ed. Metzger, ad loc.

110. Schnackenburg, *Gospel*, 1:94.

111. J. Jeremias, *The Rediscovery of Bethesda, John 5:2*, New Testament Archaeology Monographs 1 (Louisville: Southern Baptist Theological Seminary, 1966), pp. 11-12. See, for example, Brown, *Gospel*, p. 207. Bultmann (*The Gospel of John*, Eng. trans., ed. G. R. Beasley-Murray, R. W. N. Hoare, and J. K. Riches [Philadelphia: Westminster, 1971], pp. 240-41) is an exception.

112. For example, J. Marsh, *The Gospel of Saint John*, Penguin New Testament Commentaries (Harmondsworth: Penguin Books, 1968), pp. 245-46.

113. Josephus, *War* 2.15.5 §328.

Figure 70. Bethzatha Pools;
Herodian period, Jerusalem.
Courtesy of J. H. Charlesworth

refers to it as Bezatha.[114] However, the text of the *Copper Scroll* from Qumran describes a treasure hidden "in *Bet 'Eshdatayin,* in the pool at the entrance to its smaller basin" (3Q15 11.12). Although the text is mutilated and the Hebrew difficult to reconstruct, the above text represents a reasonable reconstruction and is the one given by J. T. Milik.[115] J. Jeremias also proposes that the reference is a variant of Bethesda,[116] and others have agreed.[117]

The Archaeological Evidence

Archaeological excavations at the site began in the late 1800s and have continued in stages since that date. Excavations were renewed between 1957 and 1962

114. Eusebius, *Onomasticon* 58.21-26.

115. *Bet 'Eshdatayin* is a dual form in Aramaic ("place of twin outpourings") and reflects the fact that the pool had two basins. This is proposed first by J. T. Milik, "Le rouleau de cuivre provenant de la Grotte 3Q (3Q15)," in *Les Petites Grottes de Qumrân,* ed. M. Baillet, J. T. Milik, and R. de Vaux, DJD 3 (Oxford: Clarendon, 1962), p. 214. See also his earlier "Le rouleau de cuivre de Qumrân (3Q15). Traduction et commentaire topographique," *RB* 66 (1959): 321-57.

116. Jeremias, *Rediscovery,* pp. 34-36.

117. See, for example, J. H. Charlesworth, "The Dead Sea Scrolls and the Gospel according to John," in *Exploring the Gospel of John,* ed. R. A. Culpepper and C. C. Black (Louisville: Westminster John Knox, 1996), p. 67.

under the direction of J.-M. Rousée and R. de Vaux. The excavators discovered the remains of a pool with five sides as well as remains of covered colonnades, precisely in the area of the Sheep Gate and in the section of the city identified by Josephus as Bezetha.[118] The remains from the first century indicated the existence of a pool with two basins, lying one to the north and one to the south, in trapezoidal form, surrounded on four sides by porticos, with an additional portico dividing the pool from west to east.[119] At present, only part of the southern pool is actually exposed. Additional excavations revealed several smaller pools to the east of the large basins as well as a vertical shaft leading to the small channel between the two larger reservoirs and also leading to a lower chamber that empties into a canal leading away from the site.[120]

Unfortunately, although the pools have been studied repeatedly, relatively little of the work has actually been published.[121] The two main works are those by Duprez and by Pierre/Rousée.[122] However, the site is currently undergoing a comprehensive study under the direction of Shimon Gibson, who intends to publish a definitive description of the area, incorporating the discoveries of earlier archaeologists.[123] His work to date has led him to conclusions that are considerably different in a number of respects from those of his predecessors. We will point to some of his conclusions as they bear on the understanding of the pool from a Johannine perspective.

---

118. J.-M. Rousée and R. de Vaux, "Chroniques Archéologiques," *RB* 64 (1957): 226-28; J.-M. Rousée, "Chroniques Archéologiques," *RB* 69 (1962): 107-9; R. Mackowski, *Jerusalem, City of Jesus: An Exploration of the Traditions, Writings, and Remains of the Holy City from the Time of Christ* (Grand Rapids: Eerdmans, 1980), pp. 79-83; Finegan, *Archaeology*, pp. 230-32. A full account is also given in Jeremias, *The Rediscovery of Bethesda, John 5:2.*

119. Our interest here is only in the pools at the time of Jesus. The pools had a complex history. They were not built at the same time, and before the construction of the second pool, the first was used as a reservoir that fed water into a channel leading to the Temple. Herod built the Pool of Israel closer to the Temple, and this took over the function of the earlier pools. The pools at Bethesda were then shut off and became true pools. This was evidently the state of affairs at the time of Jesus.

120. Because the site contains remains of various periods and cannot be completely excavated due to private dwellings in the area, the archaeological site itself, although quite impressive, is difficult to visualize without detailed explanation.

121. One of the most readable accounts is that of Jeremias, referred to above.

122. A. Duprez, *Jesus et les dieux guérisseurs,* CahRB 12 (Paris: Gabalda, 1970); M.-J. Pierre and J.-M. Rousée, "Sainte-Marie de la Probatique, état et orientation des recherches," *Proche-Orient Chrétien* 31 (1981): 23-42. See also the brief J.-M. Rousée, "Chronique archéologique. Jérusalem (Piscine probatique)," *RB* 69 (1962): 107-8.

123. Dr. Gibson has graciously shared a brief draft of his paper with me, and it is on the basis of this that the following observations are made. He intends to publish his findings in the near future in an article in *Proche-Orient Chrétien.*

First, the current opinion is that of Duprez and Pierre/Rousée, that the healing by Jesus did not take place at the large pools but at the smaller eastern ones. This is based on their understanding that the steps along the western side of the southern pool are intended to break the force of water rushing into the pool from its entrance on the west. Thus because the steps were not for the purpose of entering the pool, they argue that the only pools readily accessible are those to the east. The fact that these "eastern" pools were the site of healing sanctuaries later (after 135 C.E.) also suggested that they were the site of healing in the first century.

However, Gibson proposes that, at the time of Jesus, healing took place only in the southern pool. Along its western edge, this pool has steps descending to the bottom, interrupted by a series of landings. Gibson is of the (new) opinion that these steps may have extended along the full western edge of this pool so that persons entering the water could descend on one side and emerge on the other. Both the size of the steps themselves and the presence of intermittent landings suggest that they were designed to allow considerable numbers of people to descend into the water. The northern pool, however, does not have such steps and served only as a reservoir. Water could be let into the southern pool via a small opening at the bottom of the transverse wall. It is clear that the pool also had a reputation as a place where healings took place whenever the water in the southern pool was churned up. It may well have been the churning caused by the entry of water into the pool that was thought to bring about the healing properties.[124] According to Gibson, the smaller basins to the east of the great pools[125] are not healing baths but simply remains of a large private dwelling, including a *mikveh*, which have no relation to the larger pools.

The original purpose of the larger pools continues to be debated. An early explanation was that they were intended for cleaning of animals being prepared for sacrifice in the Temple directly to the south.[126] This is entirely unlikely, but some think that the bright red streaking along the walls (from chemicals in the

124. The current view is that the northern pool is earlier and at one time served as a simple reservoir, with a channel at the bottom leading to a canal extending south to the Temple. When the second reservoir was built, the channel then led into the southern reservoir and the canal was covered over. Gibson would argue that both basins were built at the same time and that the canal was always covered.

125. Although referred to less often than the larger pools, there are three much smaller pools to the east of the main ones. These were created between 150 B.C.E. and 70 C.E. Duprez and Pierre/Rousée propose that they were also (pagan) healing sites built on earlier Jewish healing shrines.

126. This is the report of Eusebius, *Onomasticon*. The Greek text is given in Jeremias, *Rediscovery*, pp. 16-17. This was also reported by the Pilgrim of Bordeaux and others (see Jeremias, p. 17).

rock) gave rise to speculation that this was caused by the blood of the sacrificial animals. The present explanation given at the site is that arrived at by Duprez and by Pierre/Rousée, namely, that the two large pools were reservoirs that collected water for use in the Temple service and that the healings took place at the smaller pools to the east.[127] This is almost surely wrong. The steps in the southern pool are those typical of *mikvaot* and would never be found in a simple reservoir. Gibson himself suggests that the southern pool was used for "bathing" but observes that the arrangement of the steps is like that of *mikvaot*.

Mikvaot were constructed in a variety of ways.[128] In the most elaborate form, two pools were constructed side by side with a channel connecting the two. One pool was used as the *mikveh* proper and the other was termed an *otzer*. According to rabbinic opinion, the water in the *mikveh* proper could only be "living water," that is, water that came from a spring or rainwater that had flowed naturally into the pool. However, in a land where water was often scarce, the *mikveh* proper could be filled by hand and only the *otzer* would be filled with living water. Then the drawn water in the *mikveh* proper could be rendered clean by opening the channel connecting the two pools and allowing the (living) water from the *otzer* to come into contact with it. If the *mikveh* proper became unclean later, it could also be rendered clean by contact with water from the *otzer* by means of the channel.

At Bethesda, the juxtaposition of two pools in an area where the more northerly would easily collect large quantities of rainwater, the presence of steps in the southern pool with landings capable of accommodating numbers of people entering and leaving the water and the fact that such steps appear in only one pool, together with the presence of a conduit connecting the pools are features typical of a public *mikveh*.[129]

127. There is no mention of these other pools in the Gospel texts. It is the failure to recognize that the southern pool was a *mikveh* that distorted the conclusions of these scholars.

128. *Mikvaot* varied considerably in size. Sometimes they were a single pool; at other times they had an accompanying *otzer*. The *otzer* could be connected to the other pool by a channel built into the base of the pool, or the transfer of water could be made by connecting pipes. At times the steps were divided by a partition. An entire tractate of the Mishnah (entitled, appropriately, *Miqva'ot*) was devoted to the discussion of regulations of these pools. H. Danby, *The Mishnah* (New York: Oxford University Press, 1933), pp. 732-44.

129. The existence of a small channel between the two pools is similar to the *otzer* that connected the two pools of a *mikveh*. This channel is accessed by a shaft that leads down from the surface. But the understanding of the pools is complicated by the fact that under the above-mentioned channel is another that is said to lead under the southern pool and to exit into the Kidron Valley. See Jeremias, *Rediscovery*, pp. 37-38. Jeremias (p. 33) also considered it a Roman bath with separate pools for women and men and suggests a parallel at Siloam. The notion of parallel basins for women and men is unlikely, given the presence of steps only in the lower ba-

Conclusions

Whatever we may continue to learn about the original purpose of the pools, the discovery of this pool in close proximity to what was known from documents as the Sheep Gate was one of the most significant factors leading to a reappraisal of the topological data of the Gospel.[130] The discovery of the pools proved beyond a doubt that the description of this pool was not the creation of the Evangelist but reflected accurate and detailed knowledge of Jerusalem, knowledge that is sufficiently detailed to now be an aid to archaeologists in understanding the site. The Johannine account speaks of (1) its location near the Sheep Gate; (2) the name of the pool as Bethesda; (3) the fact that it has five porticos; (4) the fact of intermittent turbulence in the water. All these details are corroborated through literary and archaeological evidence of the site.

12. Tiberias (6:1, 23; 21:1)

The Johannine Context

In Jn 6:1 the Sea of Galilee is mentioned and is then identified also as the Sea of Tiberias. In 6:23 there is a passing reference to the fact that the boats that picked up witnesses to the miracle of the loaves on the previous day were from Tibe-

---

sin as well as the channel from the northern to the southern pool. The most thorough discussion of *mikvaot* is that of R. Reich, "*Mikva'ot* (Jewish Immersion Baths) in Eretz-Israel in the Second Temple Period and the Mishnah and Talmud Periods" (in Hebrew) (Ph.D. diss., Hebrew University, 1990). Also by Reich, "The Hot Bath-House Balneum, the Miqweh and the Jewish Community in the Second Temple Period," *JJS* 39 (Spring 1988): 102-7. B. G. Wright, "Jewish Ritual Baths — Interpreting the Digs and the Texts: Some Issues in the Social History of Second Temple Judaism," in *Archaeology of Israel*, ed. N. A. Silberman and D. Small, JSOTSS 237 (Sheffield: Sheffield, 1997), pp. 190-214. For a more popular discussion of the nature of *mikvaot* and how they can be distinguished from baths, see the exchange between H. Eshel and E. M. Myers regarding the identification of pools at Sepphoris: H. Eshel, "They're Not Ritual Baths," *BAR* 26 (July/August 2000): 42-45; and E. M. Meyers, "Yes, They Are," *BAR* 26 (July/August 2000): 46-49; H. Eshel, "We Need More Data," *BAR* 26 (July/August 2000): 49, and R. Reich, "They *Are* Ritual Baths," *BAR* 28 (March/April 2002): 50-55, esp. pp. 53-54.

130. The present author is currently at work on a detailed reappraisal of the site independently of that being conducted by Gibson. This will elaborate on the view sketched here and will differ significantly from the view presented by Duprez and by Pierre/Rousée. Advances in the study of *mikvaot* as well as a fuller contextualization of the pool in relation to other waterworks in the area will, I believe, advance the understanding of the pools and confirm the remarkable accuracy of the Johannine account.

rias. In 21:1, again the Sea of Galilee is referred to as the Sea of Tiberias. Yet John is the only New Testament document to refer to the sea by this name.

The Literary Evidence

Our extra–New Testament information about Tiberias comes from Josephus. It was a Hellenistic city on the western shore of the Sea of Galilee, founded by Herod Agrippa in about 20 C.E.[131] and named for the Roman monarch. The city had been founded on a cemetery, something abhorrent to Jews since it rendered those who lived there unclean. According to Josephus, it was first settled by persons of generally low standing and low character.[132] Yet it became a large city, with a palace, a stadium, and a house of prayer.[133] Josephus described the site as having hot springs and as being one of the most beautiful spots in Galilee. It was the primary rival of Sepphoris as capital of Galilee, and in fact the capital was moved from Sepphoris to Tiberias by Herod Antipas in approximately 24 C.E. and remained there for thirty years.

The Archaeological Evidence

Excavations at Tiberias have been conducted periodically since 1954 and were renewed in 1989 by Y. Hirschfeld. J. Reed estimates the population at approximately 24,000, which makes it the largest city in Galilee, surpassing Sepphoris by 6,000.[134] Because the city continues to be inhabited today and is a bustling, crowded city, archaeological study of the city is difficult. Nevertheless, some remains dating from the first century have been uncovered, including the original city gate and the main street of the town.

131. The date given is that of Hirschfeld (*OEANE* 5:203), but it is debated. Hirschfeld was the archaeologist in charge of the most recent excavations there. S. Freyne (*Galilee from Alexander the Great to Hadrian, 323 BCE to 135 CE* [Notre Dame: University of Notre Dame Press, 1980], p. 129) gives 13 C.E. as the date. At any rate, the town was not very old at the time of Jesus' ministry. There is no evidence that Jesus conducted his ministry there — or in Sepphoris, a fact that would suggest that perhaps he avoided the larger Hellenistic cities. [Numismatic studies reveal that Tiberias was founded between 17 and 22 C.E. See Charlesworth's chapter. — JHC.]

132. Josephus, *Ant* 18.3 §38. See also *Life* 85; *War* 2.614.

133. This would be true at least in the time of Josephus (*Life* 92, 277). These are not the remains that were identified by Hirschfeld in 1989-90.

134. Reed, "The Population of Capernaum." E. M. Meyers refers also to Reed's Ph.D dissertation: "Places in Early Christianity: Galilee, Archaeology, Urbanization, and Q" (Claremont, 1993).

During his observations along the waterfront at the time of the 1989-91 drought, Mendel Nun discovered five hundred feet of harbor quay and suggested that the complete harbor was much longer.[135] It has been pointed out that coins minted there regularly display anchors, vessels, and other symbols associated with the sea, such as Poseidon, the patron of sailors and fishermen. This may also indicate a close link between the city and the lake and fishing, although the dating of the coins raises questions.[136]

Conclusions

Both archaeology and literary evidence clearly attest the existence of the city as well as a harbor in the first century c.e. The Gospel of John, alone among New Testament works, reflects awareness of its existence. Given the size of the city, it would be appropriate that boats from this city be able to pick up those who had witnessed the multiplication and transport them to Capernaum. This is of course a minor detail, not significant for the theology of the chapter, but one that demonstrates once again the accuracy of topographical information in the Gospel.

13. The Pool of Siloam (9:1-9)

The Johannine Context

In Jn 9:1-9 Jesus encounters a man blind from birth and, after anointing his eyes with spit, sends the man to the pool of Siloam to wash. The man washes and gains the ability to see.

The Literary Evidence

The pool is referred to only in John within the New Testament[137] but is attested in the Hebrew Scriptures and in other contemporary literature.[138] It was at the

---

135. See Nun, *The Sea of Galilee*, p. 15; Nun, "Ports of Galilee," pp. 18-31, 64.

136. See Nun, "Ports of Galilee," p. 64. However, this evidence is ambiguous at best since, according to Meyers ("Galilean Context," p. 61), coins were not minted there until after 100 c.e.

137. Lk 13:4 makes reference to the "tower of Siloam" collapsing. What this refers to is not known, although it may refer to the same site. At any rate, the mention of a *pool* at Siloam is confined to the reference in the Gospel of John.

138. 2 Kgs 20:20; Isa 8:5; Neh 3:15; Josephus, *War* 6.7.2 §363. See the following note.

outlet of Hezekiah's Tunnel, the channel that led water from the Gihon Spring to the pool. At the time of Jesus, the pool was within the city walls and was a major source of water for the city.

The Archaeological Evidence

The site commonly thought to be the pool of Siloam was discovered by archaeologist Blis Vediki near the end of the nineteenth century. The form of the pool has been changed, perhaps as a result of the destruction of Jerusalem in 70 C.E. by the Romans.[139] In its present form, the pool dates from the Byzantine period (ca. 450) when a church was constructed at the site. Although the original size and shape of the pool are unknown, the pool itself still functions and is visible on the southern edge of the Ophel Ridge. It continues to serve as the southern outlet of Hezekiah's Tunnel. Neh 3:15 describes the pool as being near the king's garden and the "stairs that go down from the city of David." Vestiges of steps constructed during the Hasmonean period, which led from Mount Zion down to the pool, are also still visible in the vicinity of St. Peter in Gallicantu.

In June 2004 Israeli archaeologist Eli Shukrun reported that another pool had been discovered near the site of the "traditional" pool of Siloam during exploration of the area prior to the construction of a new sewage system in the area.[140] The site is being investigated by Ronny Reich and John Seligman as well as by Shukrun and lies close by and south of the other pool. It was reported in December 2004 that the archaeologists had revealed the full 50-meter length of the pool.[141] The pool is stone lined and has steps leading into it on all sides. On the south side, the retaining wall for the pool was part of the southern wall of the city. On the north side, the steps have been fully revealed and consist of a series of nine steps with every third step being broader than the others and serving as a kind of landing. The archaeologists have also discovered an "elaborately paved assembly area" adjacent to the pool. In addition, a water channel that brought water to the pool from the Gihon Spring has been revealed. Finally, steps leading from the site up the hill toward the Temple have been uncovered. At present, archaeologists are negotiating with the Greek Orthodox church that owns the property to further excavate the site.

---

139. Josephus speaks of the city of Jerusalem being burned "as far as Siloam" (*War* 6.7.2 §363).

140. *Jerusalem Post,* June 10, 2004, p. 5; *Jerusalem Post,* June 25, 2004, p. 12.

141. *Jerusalem Post,* December 24, 2004, p. 6.

Conclusions

Although incomplete, the most recent findings may well constitute a major breakthrough in the understanding of the pool and its extent. Among the issues to be dealt with is the relationship between the "traditional" pool and the "new" pool. Are they distinct pools? Are they related to one another? Does the water for the "new" pool come from Hezekiah's Tunnel? These questions remain to be answered.

Clearly the section of the "traditional" pool as revealed today does not indicate the original size of the pool. Excavations in the area have discovered the remains of the Hadrianic building constructed on the site. The extent of that building was considerably greater and may well indicate something closer to the original extent of the pool. It is not impossible that in the time of Jesus the "traditional" pool was the first of two related pools, not unlike the relation of the two sections of the pool of Bethesda. In both cases the "southern" pool is marked as a *mikveh,* and at the pool of Bethesda the "northern" pool served as the *otzer.* Certainly the northern ("traditional") pool at Siloam would qualify as an *otzer* also, since it was filled with the "living water" of the Gihon Spring. In any event, the accuracy of the Johannine information is clearly established, and further discoveries will only serve to amplify our knowledge.

14. Bethany Near Jerusalem (11:1-17; 12:1-11)

The town of Bethany near Jerusalem appears in the Gospel in connection with the raising of Lazarus who lived there. After the death of Lazarus, it is said that people came from Jerusalem to mourn with his sisters. It is then explained that Bethany was about fifteen stadia (about 1.75 miles) from Jerusalem.[142] Again in 12:1, when Jesus returns there for dinner with the family, it is said that people come from Jerusalem both to see Jesus and to see Lazarus who had been raised from the dead.

The town is identified consistently in all pilgrim reports with what is now el-Azariyeh, a town whose distance from Jerusalem agrees with the figures given in John.

Although this town is mentioned in all the Gospels (see Mk 11:1, 11, 12; Mt 21:17; 26:6; Lk 19:29) and it is recognized to be close to Jerusalem, only John includes the further detail of its precise distance from Jerusalem.

---

142. A *stadion* is about 218 yards, or one-fifth of a kilometer.

15. Ephraim (11:54)

The Johannine Context

After the raising of Lazarus from the dead, some of the people from Judea report Jesus' actions to the Pharisees and chief priests. They in turn convene a Sanhedrin and determine to put Jesus to death. Because of this, Jesus retreats "to the region near the desert, to the city called Ephraim." The mention of this city *(polis)* is unique to John within the New Testament.

The Archaeological and Literary Evidence

Although unique to John within the New Testament, Ephraim is mentioned several times in the Hebrew Scriptures as well as in the Mishnah and Talmud.[143] Josephus mentions it in connection with the movements of Vespasian in the Judean hill country.[144] After subduing the small towns of Bethel and Ephraim, he is said to progress to Jerusalem. That he could have attacked Bethel and Ephraim and then headed on toward Jerusalem would suggest that they were not far apart and that direct travel was possible. On the Madaba map (fourth century C.E.) Ephraim is located near Bethel. Commentators generally identify it with the modern village of Et-Taiyibeh, about twelve miles north of Jerusalem.[145] Its ancient name is also given as Ophras (Josh 18:23) and Ephron (Josh 15:9). There is little reason to think that this identification is not correct.[146]

Conclusions

Although no archaeological evidence has been found that would positively identify the city, the unique Johannine information is confirmed by the literary evidence.

143. 2 Sam 13:23; 2 Chr 13:19; 1 Macc 11:34. For other references see Str-B 2:546. For a full discussion see Schnackenburg, *Gospel*, 2:351.

144. Josephus, *War* 4.9.9 §551.

145. E.g., Brown, *Gospel*, p. 441; Schnackenburg, *Gospel*, 2:35. It is not mentioned in Finegan, *The Archaeology of the New Testament*, nor in Murphy-O'Connor, *The Holy Land*.

146. W. F. Albright ("The Ephraim of the Old and New Testaments," *JPOS* 3 [1923]: 36-40) proposed Ain Samieh as the site, but this has not been generally accepted.

16. The Winter-Flowing Kidron (18:1)

The Kidron Valley is another of the topographical references mentioned only in the Gospel of John (18:1). It runs along the east side of the Ophel Ridge and separates the Old City from the Mount of Olives. Parts of the valley are also known as the Valley of Jehoshaphat. Although the valley is well known and not in need of further identification or confirmation, its mention deserves to be included in the survey precisely because it is unique to John. It is an accurate geographical reference, and the fact that it is described as "winter-flowing" is further confirmation that the author's knowledge of the area is accurate in all details.

The Johannine Passion Story:
17. The Praetorium (18:28, 33; 19:9);
18. The Lithostrotos (19:13)

The Johannine Context

In the Johannine passion account, after Jesus' appearance before Caiaphas, he is taken to the Praetorium, the official residence of the Roman prefect[147] in Jerusalem, for trial. After discussion with the Jewish authorities and Jesus, Pilate assumes his official position upon the official judgment *seat* (the *bēma*), which had been put in place on the Lithostrotos, and pronounces judgment on Jesus. Here both the Praetorium and the Lithostrotos call for identification.

The Praetorium: Archaeological and Literary Evidence

Although the Roman prefect normally resided in Caesarea, he would take up temporary residence in Jerusalem at various times during the year, particularly during the major feasts when there was the possibility of disturbance in the city.

What is called the Praetorium in the Gospels was the Herodian palace *(basileia, aulē)* in the northwest corner of the city.[148] The palace was situated against the western wall of the city and extended southward along a major part

---

147. Although the term "procurator" appears in the New Testament (but not in the Gospel of John), this term was not used until after 41 C.E.

148. See the discussion in Brown, *The Death of the Messiah: A Commentary on the Passion Narratives in the Four Gospels* (New York: Doubleday, 1994), 1:706-10. See also B. Pixner, "Noch einmal das Prätorium. Versuch einer neuen Lösung," *ZDPV* 95 (1979): 56-86; R. Riesner, "Das Prätorium des Pilatus," *BK* 41 (1986): 34-37.

of that wall. Parts of the palace are still evident there today.[149] The city wall had been built during the time of the Hasmoneans, but Herod had modified it and added three large towers. Josephus describes the wall as "built on a lofty hill, and above the hill rose, as it were, a crest thirty cubits higher still; on this the towers stood and thus gained immensely in elevation."[150] Adjoining these towers was the palace proper. The towers are described as having been built of polished stone so smooth that they looked to be one single piece.[151]

Although the archaeological evidence is sufficient to identify and locate the Herodian palace, it is literary evidence that determines that this rather than the Fortress Antonia was the place where the prefect lodged. While it was once thought that Pilate resided in the Fortress Antonia, it is now clear that the Antonia, which was closer to the Temple, would have been used by the troops for close supervision of the Temple area whereas Pilate would have taken up residence in the more sumptuous quarters of the palace. This is confirmed by the fact that Josephus uses the term *aulē* (palace) only for the Herodian palace and regularly referred to the Antonia as a *pyrgos* (tower) or a *phrourion* (fortress).

The Lithostrotos

The Johannine Context   The Lithostrotos, mentioned in 19:13, indicates a specific location sufficiently well known to have its own designation in two languages. It refers to a place outside the Praetorium where the judicial bench of the Roman prefect was situated.

It is important to note that the Hebrew term *Gabbatha*, given as the equivalent of Lithostrotos, is not a *translation* but simply the Hebrew designation for the site. The difference is significant. The Hebrew term means "height" or "raised" place and so speaks of a different feature of the place than the Greek term, which means "stone pavement." Thus the Johannine account tells us two things: that the place was in a raised area *and* that it had a stone pavement where the judicial bench *(bēma)* was set.[152]

---

149. An overview of the excavations there is available in H. Geva, "Excavations at the Citadel of Jerusalem, 1976-1980," in *Ancient Jerusalem Revealed* (Jerusalem: Israel Exploration Society, 2000), pp. 156-67, and R. Sivan and G. Solar, "Excavations in the Jerusalem Citadel, 1980-88," pp. 168-76 in the same volume.

150. Josephus, *War* 5.4.4 §173.

151. Josephus, *War* 5.4.4 §176-181.

152. Although John is not the only New Testament writer to refer to the *bēma*, the fact that he mentions it by name is itself another indication of his knowledge of the practice.

The Literary Evidence   We will first look at the literary evidence. The description of the various elements of the Johannine scene is confirmed in a striking way by a scene in Josephus describing events some thirty years after the time of Jesus. The account begins with the arrival in 66 C.E. of the Roman prefect Florus in Jerusalem. The account continues: "Florus then took up residence at the palace, and on the following day having had the *bēma* put in place in front of the building, took his seat. The chief priests, the nobles, and the most eminent citizens then coming forward stood before the *bēma*. Florus ordered them to hand over those who had insulted him, declaring that they themselves would feel his vengeance if they failed to produce the guilty ones. The leaders declared that the people had peaceful intentions and sought pardon for the disrespectful ones."[153]

Florus was angered by this and ordered his soldiers to pillage the upper market of the city and to kill or arrest anyone they met. Josephus describes the brutal scene and then concludes: "[A]rresting many of the peaceable citizens, they [the troops] brought them before Florus, who had them scourged and then crucified."

It is unlikely that the location of the prefect's residence would have changed in the few years after the time of Jesus, and it is also unlikely that the location of such a formal proceeding as a judgment from the *bēma* would have changed. Consequently the scene in Josephus almost certainly represents what was undoubtedly a fairly common occurrence when the Roman prefect was in residence in Jerusalem. The scene described in John then constitutes simply an earlier occurrence of this same procedure — a scene preserved in remarkable detail in Josephus. The only detail lacking in Josephus is a mention of the Lithostrotos as the place were the *bēma* was located.

Archaeological Evidence   Is it possible to determine the precise location of the Lithostrotos? It is first of all clear that it must be in or near the Herodian palace. By recognizing this, we have already restricted its location to a small area of the city either within or adjoining the Herodian palace. But perhaps more can be said.

In a tour of the western wall of the city in August 2000, Shimon Gibson, who participated in excavations along the wall under the direction of M. Broshi during the 1970s, speculated that the Lithostrotos is to be located at a place near what was, in the first century C.E., the southern end of Herod's palace. Gibson points to the remains of a gateway approach into the city visible at this place. Gibson also points to the area adjacent to the remains of this entrance as being

---

153. Josephus, *War* 2.14.8 §301-302. This and the following translation are my own.

paved with stone and as providing a place where the Roman prefect (in residence at Herod's palace during Passover) would be able to hold court without bringing the persons into the palace proper.[154] This view has much to recommend it. It is clear that the section of the city that housed the Herodian palace was indeed not only the highest place in the city but was founded on bedrock rather than on fill.

It may be possible to take this theory one step further. It may well be that we are wrong looking for an area literally "paved with stone." It is of course true that normally "lithostrotos" can mean either "stone pavement" or "mosaic."[155] Yet simple stone paving or mosaic would not be so unusual in the city that such a place would merit having its own name. It is clear from the account in the Gospel that the term refers to a specific place, sufficiently well known to have a name in both Greek and Hebrew. Consequently, it may well be that the term was not intended to refer specifically to a *paved* area but rather to a place where the surface area consisted of bedrock. This would be true "stone pavement" and would be sufficiently distinctive to merit its own name. As firsthand inspection demonstrates, the area proposed by Gibson is both bedrock stone and a raised area — and has stone pavers in parts of the area — and so fulfills the definitions indicated by both the Greek and the Hebrew terms. Therefore it may well be that this is the true Lithostrotos.

Conclusions

The location of the Praetorium is now definitely identified. As for the Lithostrotos, while final determination must necessarily await Gibson's publication of a full report on the area, his view represents a new and viable theory and the best one since the collapse of the theory associated with the "stone pavement" of the Antonia Fortress.[156]

154. The existence of a gateway is reported in M. Broshi and S. Gibson, "Excavations along the Western and Southern Walls of the Old City of Jerusalem," in *Ancient Jerusalem Revealed*, pp. 147-55; see esp. p. 153. See also the illustration on p. 148.

155. In Josephus, *War* 6.1.8 §85, a soldier is said to slip and fall on the pavement because of his hobnailed boots. In *War* 6.3.2 §189, a soldier is described as falling, hitting his head on the pavement and being killed. In both cases, that a hard, slippery surface is involved is significant, but beyond that, the precise nature of the pavement is not certain.

156. In 1870 a stone pavement was found near the Antonia Fortress. On the pavement are the lines of a "king game" played by Roman soldiers. Such a game has parallels in the mockery of Jesus as king. Thus the form and the carvings in the rock suggested that this was the Lithostrotos mentioned in Jn 19:13. The find is described in detail by L.-H. Vincent, "L'Antonia et le Prétoire," *RB* 42 (1933): 83-113; Vincent, "Lithostrotos évangelique," *RB* 59 (1952): 513-30;

Jesus' Death and Burial:
19. Golgotha (19:17-18, 20, 41);
20. A Tomb in the Garden (19:41-42)

The Johannine Context

Jn 19:17-41 recounts the crucifixion, death, and burial of Jesus, and in so doing describes the location of both the crucifixion and the burial. The two places are treated together here because the sites are close to one another and best described in relation to one another.

The Johannine account of the crucifixion is quite specific and detailed. We learn that it occurred at "the place of the skull" (*Golgotha* in Hebrew, 19:17). The site is also said to be "near the city" (19:20).[157] We also learn later that there was a garden in the place (19:41) as well as at least one new (unused) tomb nearby (19:41).

After the death of Jesus, Joseph of Arimathea asked Pilate and was granted permission to take the body of Jesus for burial. It is said that he was joined by Nicodemus, and together they wrapped the body and anointed it with spices. They laid the body in a new tomb located in the same garden area where Jesus had been crucified.

While evaluating the information in the Johannine account, we should recognize that the account differs from the Synoptic accounts in several respects and provides considerably more detail. All the Gospels indicate that the tomb was hewn from rock. Matthew, Luke, and John report that the tomb was "new." But there is no mention in John that the tomb belonged to Joseph; only Matthew reports that.[158] Unique to John is the information that the tomb was in a

---

Vincent, "L'Antonia, palais primitif d'Herode," *RB* 61 (1954): 87-107. For many years it was thought that this was the actual "stone pavement" spoken of in the Gospel of John. However, later archaeological work by P. Benoit ("L'Antonia d'Hérode le Grand et le Forum Oriental d'Aelia Capitolina," *HTR* 64 [1971]: 135-67; Benoit, "Praetorium, Lithostroton, et Gabbatha," *RB* 59 [1952]: 531-50; Benoit, "Le Prétoire de Pilate à l'époque byzantine," *RB* 91 [1984]: 161-77) proved that this pavement actually dates from the second century and was part of a *forum* near the entrance to the later Roman city of Aelia Capitolina, which was built on the site of the earlier Antonia Fortress. This then is clearly not the stone pavement referred to in the Gospel of John.

157. There is no explicit reference in John, as there is in the Synoptics, to its being outside the walls, but that would seem to be the clear implication of the statement that it is "near" the city.

158. Some have argued that the Johannine information is inaccurate since it is unlikely that a rich person would have a tomb so near an execution site. This is not a problem for the Johannine account but is due to a conflation of the Matthean with the Johannine account. The

garden and that the garden and tomb were near the place of the crucifixion. In short, the Johannine account becomes potentially much more difficult to reconcile with the archaeological data since it provides considerably more detail than the Synoptics. Yet as we shall see, the archaeological data corroborate the Johannine account in considerable detail.

The Archaeological and Literary Evidence

Today the sites of both Golgotha and Jesus' tomb are commonly thought to be contained within the Church of the Holy Sepulchre. The first church on the site was built by Helena, the mother of Constantine, in the fourth century. The tradition that this was the site of the crucifixion is said to have dated from before that time. The site has been explored again and again by archaeologists. The most extensive excavations to date at the site of the present Church of the Holy Sepulchre began in 1960 and extended for twenty-two years under the direction of V. Corbo of the Studium Biblicum Franciscanum. The final report on the work was published by Corbo in 1980-81.[159] At present, the most accessible and readable account of the area and its archaeology is the book by Gibson and Taylor.[160]

The questions regarding the identification of the site of both the crucifixion and the burial are many, and debate continues about the correctness of the traditional identification. At the same time, it seems fair to say that many of the issues have been settled with reasonable certitude.

Around the place identified as Golgotha, the excavations reveal that as early as the eighth century B.C.E. the place had been a quarry. There is still evi-

---

location of the tomb is a problem for the Matthean account since it alone attributes ownership of the tomb to Joseph. In addition, while all the Gospels agree that a man named Joseph of Arimathea asked Pilate for the body, only John mentions Nicodemus.

159. The definitive report is that of V. Corbo, *Il Santo Sepulcro di Gerusalemme*, 3 vols. (Jerusalem: Franciscan, 1981-82). A preliminary report was published earlier by C. Coüasnon, *The Church of the Holy Sepulchre in Jerusalem* (London: Oxford University Press, 1974). For a helpful (and critical) review of the site and of Corbo's work, see D. Bahat, "Does the Holy Sepulchre Church Mark the Burial of Jesus?" *BAR* 12 (1986): 26-45. See also Brown, *Death of the Messiah*, 2:936-40, 1268-70; Charlesworth, "Archaeology," p. 9; J. Wilkinson, "The Church of the Holy Sepulchre," *Archaeology* 31 (1978): 6-13. The so-called Gordon's tomb, although more attractive and appealing, does not fit the New Testament data. See L.-H. Vincent, "Garden Tomb: histoire d'un mythe," *RB* 34 (1925): 401-31; Charlesworth, *Jesus within Judaism*, pp. 123-24; G. Barkay, "The Garden Tomb — Was Jesus Buried There?" *BAR* 12 (1986): 40-57.

160. S. Gibson and J. Taylor, *Beneath the Church of the Holy Sepulchre* (London: Palestinian Exploration Fund, 1994).

Figure 71. Church of the
Holy Sepulchre,
entrance from
the south.

Courtesy of J. H. Charlesworth

dence of chisel marks and of partly hewn blocks of the meleke limestone attached to the bedrock. This is consistent with the identification of the tomb as
hewn from rock, and also with the custom of constructing tombs in areas that
had previously been quarried. The identification of the place as like a skull also
reflects knowledge that the area where the crucifixion took place was a protrud-
ing, bare, and rocky area, probably a hillock not quarried because of the poor
quality of the stone there.[161]

There is also evidence that by the first century the surrounding quarry pit
had been filled in and overlaid with reddish brown soil. Corbo proposed that

161. It has been suggested that the presence of a quarry so near the walls provided not only
the obvious source of stone for building but also improved defense of this part of the wall by
lowering the level of the ground. See B. E. Schein, "The Second Wall of Jerusalem," *BA* 44 (1981):
21-26; see esp. p. 25 and the diagram on p. 24.

this took place about the first century and that the resulting arable land formed the garden mentioned in the Gospel of John.[162] This is possible, but there is some dispute about the age and nature of the fill and whether the vegetative remains were a result of planting or simple wild growth.[163] However, archaeology is aided here by literary evidence.

The quarry and the fill are located in the area adjacent to the city gate known from Josephus as the Garden (Gennath) Gate. And so the custom of naming Jerusalem's city gates on the basis of some feature relative to their location provides a strong indication that there was a garden in the area.[164]

Next is whether this location was inside or outside the walls of the city at the time of Jesus. Again we are helped by literary evidence. Josephus describes fully the various series of walls as they continued to expand as the city expanded.[165] According to Josephus, in the early years of the first century C.E. the northern city wall ran west along a line north of the site of Golgotha but then dropped south to a point just east of and below Golgotha itself before turning west. It was only later (between 41 and 44 C.E.) that Herod Agrippa extended the northern wall considerably, bringing the site of Golgotha within the walls of the city. Thus the Johannine account reflects accurate knowledge of the wall's location at the time of Jesus.[166]

The various archaeological shafts in the area have also aided indirectly in locating the wall by showing something of the extent of the quarry. U. Lux dis-

162. The garden is mentioned in 19:41 but also in 20:15, where Mary thinks Jesus is "the gardener."

163. Some would date the soil fill to the eighth century B.C.E. and claim that the quarry was not in use up to the first century B.C.E., as Corbo would claim. See M. Broshi and G. Barkay, "Excavations in the Chapel of St. Vartan in the Holy Sepulchre," *IEJ* 35 (1985): 108ff. Schein argues that the quarry also served to effectively increase the height of the city wall, thus making it less vulnerable to battering rams.

164. Brown, *Death of the Messiah*, 2:1269. Josephus speaks of the second wall of the city beginning near the gate called Gennath ("garden") (*War* 5.4.2 §146). In 1888, excavations under the Alexander Hospice (the Russian Mission in Exile) uncovered remains of a gate that was for some time thought to be the Garden Gate. Later study, however, has suggested that it actually comes from the fourth century. N. Avigad, excavating on the western hill of the city, discovered not only the remains of a wall but also a gap in the wall, which then continued after the interruption. This shows signs of being the Garden Gate. For his discussion, see N. Avigad, *Discovering Jerusalem* (New York: T. Nelson, 1980), p. 69, and the plan of the area on p. 50.

165. Josephus, *War* 5.4.2 §142-155.

166. The precise location of the second wall continues to be debated today. One of the most respected treatments is that of M. Avi-Yonah ("The Third and Second Walls of Jerusalem," *IEJ* 18, no. 2 [1968]: 98-125). G. J. Wightman has recently revived what is sometimes referred to as the minimalist view of the extent of the second wall in his long discussion of the matter (*The Walls of Jerusalem* [Sydney: Meditarch, 1993]).

covered evidence of a quarry beneath the present Lutheran Church of the Redeemer, and K. M. Kenyon also found evidence of the quarry in the area of the Martin Luther School.[167] That the quarry extends under the Church of the Holy Sepulchre was confirmed in 1981-82 by V. Corbo.[168] The overall area is approximately 150 by 200 meters.[169] This identifies the area that was the site of the limestone knob left by the quarriers, as well as the place of Joseph's grave, as being part of the quarry and outside the wall. Further, it shows that the quarry extended considerably south of the site of the crucifixion.[170]

One scholar opposed to the traditional view of the site of the crucifixion is J. Taylor, who has proposed that while the site of the tomb (see below) may be accurate, the actual site of the crucifixion was some 200 meters south of the traditional location, under what is now David Street.[171] Taylor proposes (correctly) that the city gates always led to major roads and that it is unlikely that such roads would have gone through the quarry. Rather they would have led west along the first wall and north along the second wall. She suggests that the place of crucifixion would have been near the juncture of these two roads at the Garden Gate, since it was the Roman custom to locate crucifixions along main roads in order to serve as a deterrent for others. Moreover, the references to the passersby who saw Jesus on the cross confirm a location along a public road. From various digs, it is clear that the quarry where the crucifixion took place extends considerably to the south (well under the present Church of the Redeemer).[172] As a result, Taylor argues, the traditional site of crucifixion could hardly be close to a road extending west along the north side of the first wall. While this is true, there is nothing, contra Taylor, that rules out the possibility that the traditional site of crucifixion could have been close to a road extending north along the second wall. Taylor also argues that pilgrim accounts of Melito of Sardis and Eusebius confirm this view. Yet these reports are ambiguous, and the places they refer to cannot be located with certainty. As a result, Taylor's conclusions based on their witness inevitably remain speculative.

---

167. U. Lux, "Vorläufiger Bericht über die Ausgrabung unter der Erlöserkirche," *ZDPV,* 1972, pp. 186-99; K. M. Kenyon, *Digging Up Jerusalem* (New York: Praeger, 1974), pp. 226-35.

168. Corbo, *Il Santo Sepolcro di Gerusalemme.*

169. So Gibson and Taylor, *Beneath,* p. 51. There is a helpful diagram indicating the contours of the quarry on pp. 52-53.

170. Gideon Avni, director of the archaeological team conducting the current archaeological survey of the church, has reported finding what appears to be evidence of the second wall under the foundation of one outer wall of the Church of the Holy Sepulchre, although no definitive search has been conducted. Avni reported this find during a tour of the Church of the Holy Sepulchre for members of the Millennium Conference, August 9, 2000.

171. Taylor's most recent view of the topic can be found in her article "Golgotha: A Reconsideration of the Evidence for the Sites of Jesus' Crucifixion and Burial," *NTS* 44 (1998): 180-203.

172. See Schein, "The Second Wall," pp. 21-26.

The Tomb of Jesus

The accuracy of the final element of the Johannine account (that Jesus was buried in a tomb nearby) is settled relatively easily. That there were tombs in the area is corroborated by Josephus, who makes reference to tombs of important people there.[173] Archaeologists have found ample evidence of tombs cut into the rock of the quarry, and these are reliably dated by stratigraphy to the first century C.E.[174] Among these tombs is one of an archosolium type, which corresponds to the description in the Gospel accounts.[175] The only question then is whether this tomb can be reasonably said to be that of Jesus.

That only one of the tombs has a niche of the archosolium type may suggest that this was the tomb of Jesus. The second factor is that, during his reign, Hadrian had leveled the area around the tomb and the place of crucifixion and built a temple to Venus on the spot. Moreover, after the construction of the third wall, the site was enclosed within the city. The fact that the area, which now lay well inside the city walls and bore no resemblance to the original, was remembered as the site of Jesus' burial up to the time of Constantine is perhaps the strongest argument for its authenticity. Finally, there is no other site with anything like the scholarly support that this site has had throughout the ages.[176]

---

173. Josephus (*War* 5.6.2 §229 and 5.6.3 §530) mentions the graves of John Hyrcanus and Alexander Jannaeus as being in the area. See Brown, *Death of the Messiah*, 2:936-40, 1269.

174. Given the amount of later construction in the area, it is almost certain that a number of other tombs existed in the area but were destroyed.

175. Rock-cut tombs contained either of two types of burial niches, the *kokh* or the archosolium. The *kokh* niche was a long narrow alcove cut back into the rock. The body was then wrapped and slid back into the alcove. The archosolium type was a shallow, transverse, bench-shaped resting place cut into the rock with an arch extending over it. In this type of niche, the entire wrapped body was visible. The Johannine account is the most explicit in indicating that the niche within the tomb was of the archosolium type. According to the Johannine account, it was possible to see that the tomb was empty by simply bending down, something not easily done if the niche is of the *kokh* type. Moreover, the fact that the headpiece could be seen separated from the other wrappings also indicates an archosolium niche.

176. In modern times, another tomb north of the city, the so-called Gordon's tomb, was proposed as the site of the crucifixion and burial. However, archaeologists have dated the original tomb to the First Temple period (Iron Age II — eighth to ninth century B.C.E.) based on the general form of construction. It was not used again for burial until the Byzantine era (fifth-sixth century C.E.). For a thorough history of the archaeological interest in the cave as well as the results of a thorough survey of the tomb, see Barkay, "The Garden Tomb," pp. 40-53, 56-57. See also the scholarly literature referred to in the article.

Figure 72. A tomb west of the walls of Jerusalem, often called Herod's family tomb. It is reminiscent of what the Evangelists describe concerning Jesus' tomb.
Courtesy of J. H. Charlesworth

Conclusions

The significance of this for our appreciation of the historical accuracy of John's reports is considerable. Not only does John provide several details present in the Synoptics (the name of the place, its location outside the city walls), but he goes on to provide more detail than the other Gospels. As has been so frequently the case, the Johannine account has introduced, casually and almost accidentally, details not essential to the narrative. If the presence of such details at first makes verification more difficult, the fact that they are corroborated by archaeological and other means demonstrates not only that the Johannine account contains remarkably accurate knowledge but also that the Gospel is in fact able to serve as a source of unique knowledge about the crucifixion and burial of Jesus.

General Concluding Observations

In this study we have examined a total of twenty topographical references in the Gospel of John, seeking to determine their accuracy. Of these, thirteen were unique to this Gospel. Having completed the review, we can now draw some general conclusions regarding the Johannine information.

The first conclusion has to do with the possibility of symbolic meaning for the sites. As we saw at the beginning, in the light of the numerous elements of the Gospel that are symbolic, anachronistic, or otherwise unconcerned with historical accuracy, the concern regarding the historicity of the topographical references is justified. But the survey reveals no credible evidence to suggest that any of the twenty sites is simply fictitious or symbolic. While some secondary symbolic meaning is possible in some instances, the intrinsic historicity and accuracy of the references should be beyond doubt.

The second conclusion has to do with how certain the identification of the various sites can be said to be. Of the twenty sites, sixteen have been identified with certainty. The Johannine information has proven to be accurate for Bethsaida, Cana, Capernaum, Jacob's well, Mount Gerizim, the location of Sychar, the Sheep Gate, the pool(s) of Bethesda, Tiberias, the pool of Siloam, Bethany near Jerusalem, Ephraim, the Kidron Valley, the Praetorium, Golgotha, and the tomb of Jesus.

Of the remaining four, two can be narrowed to within a relatively restricted locale: the place in the Temple precincts for the keeping of animals and the Lithostrotos.

There are then only two sites about which there continues to be substantial disagreement: Aenon near Salim and Bethany beyond the Jordan. Although plausible theories have been proposed regarding Aenon near Salim, the identification of the site cannot be said to be certain. There are no archaeological remains that can help in the identification, nor is there any reference to the site elsewhere in ancient literature that could be of help, and reports of later pilgrims are inconclusive.

As for Bethany Beyond the Jordan, the problem is that arguments made for identifying this Bethany with the site in the Wadi el-Kharrar do not take into account the Johannine information. Yet one of the results of the present paper has been to confirm the remarkable accuracy of the topographical information elsewhere in the Gospel of John. Given the consistent accuracy of the other Johannine references, the failure to take this information into account in identifying the location of Bethany is a drawback. In my opinion, the fact that not all the Johannine information agrees with the proposed southern location detracts significantly from the confidence that can be given to this identification. I am also inclined to put less weight on the pilgrim reports regarding Bethany, given an avowed ignorance of the site even in the time of Origen.

There are, of course, problems with the northern location also. There is no record of a Bethany in the north, and the proposed change in name from Bethany to Batanea is difficult to justify, although perhaps not impossible. My own view is that while there is considerable evidence for a northern location, it is impossible to be certain of either site.

The third conclusion we can make regarding the Johannine information concerns the amount of detail provided in the Johannine texts. We have noted throughout that such added detail could well make identification and corroboration more difficult. Yet in fact it has done just the reverse and demonstrates the full extent of the accuracy and the detail of the Evangelist's knowledge. It is precisely those places described in the greatest detail that can be identified with the greatest certitude. This is evident particularly for the pools of Bethesda, the place of crucifixion, and the location of Jesus' tomb. In attempting to identify Sychar, it was the added details regarding the nature and the location of Jacob's well, Mount Gerizim, and the detailed knowledge of the historical associations that "forced" the conclusion that the town referred to as Sychar is located at present-day Aschar.

But the regularity of minor details is also striking. Cana is described as "of Galilee"; Aenon is described as "near Salim"; Jacob's well is described as both spring and well. The two Bethanys are distinguished, the one described as "beyond the Jordan," the other as near Jerusalem and "about fifteen stadia" from the city. The Lithostrotos is identified by the Hebrew name for the location as well as the Greek, as is also the place of crucifixion.

In only two cases do details provided by the Johannine author remain ambiguous: the description of Bethsaida as being "of Galilee" and the description of Sychar as a *polis*. Yet even in these cases the surrounding detail is so consistent that we are left with the impression that it is our knowledge that is at fault, not the Johannine data.

The fourth conclusion is perhaps more of an observation. Although biblical archaeology has been a well-established field for over a century, the regularity with which new discoveries are being made is remarkable — and exciting! Impressive new gains have been made at Wadi el-Kharrar quite recently, and the archaeological park opened only in 2003. Bethsaida has been conclusively identified only recently under the direction of Rami Arav, and the site has been opened to the public only since March 1998. The work of Julian Herrojo on the pilgrim tradition regarding Khirbet Qana only appeared in 1999, and archaeological analysis of the site continues today under Douglas Edwards and Peter Richardson. What may be the original pool of Siloam was discovered as recently as June 2004. The pools of Bethesda are undergoing a major new study under Shimon Gibson, and it is already clear that there is more to be learned about them. A new proposal for the location of the Lithostrotos has been made recently, also by Gibson, and holds promise of providing greater knowledge of the site. The work of Gideon Avni at the Church of the Holy Sepulchre may provide further confirmation of the location of the second wall of the city, and so further corroborate the location of Golgotha. Because of advances in archaeology, our understanding of these sites is increasing at a remarkable rate, and there is no reason to think it will stop.

Further Ramifications for the Study of the Gospel

At the beginning of this essay we saw that much of the material of the Gospel of John is noticeably "late" and "developed" and/or "anachronistic." How do we relate the material that we have found to be so specific and so accurate to this other material that is so obviously "late" and "general" and "anachronistic"?

In one of the more influential books of the past quarter-century, J. Louis Martyn spoke of the Gospel as a two-tiered document that attempted both to speak of the historical ministry of Jesus and also to address the concerns of the later community.[177] Martyn argued that the Evangelist himself spoke on two levels. Martyn developed this thesis by a number of arguments, one of which was that the author took terms that were typical of the ministry and combined them with terms that were typical of the community at the end of the first century.

But little by little scholars are getting a clearer picture of what is historical, accurate, and specific in the Gospel and what is genuinely late, anachronistic, and symbolic. As a result of such studies, we are coming to see that the Gospel is indeed a mixture of early and late, but as our knowledge gains in precision, we will thereby be able to understand more clearly and more precisely exactly what is early and what is late. Martyn proposed that a single author constructed the Gospel on a dual level. The present study shows that at least for the topographical material of the Gospel, such a theory is not correct. The topographical references are not themselves constructed on two levels and do not exhibit any "late" features. They are entirely historical.[178] Rather the Gospel represents a mixture

177. J. L. Martyn, *History and Theology in the Fourth Gospel*, 2nd ed. (Nashville: Abingdon, 1979).

178. The same is true of other elements of the Gospel of John. For example, Martyn proposed that the combination "chief priests and Pharisees" was the unique creation of the Evangelist to reflect both the time of the ministry and the time of the Evangelist. However, that combination is not the creative work of the Evangelist but a historically accurate possibility. Yet the

of traditions some of which are quite accurate, detailed, and historical, and others that are late, developed, and anachronistic to the ministry. While the Gospel reflects two distinct historical periods, this is not the work of a single author. While for many this suggestion is not new, the precision and the confirmation of this earlier information would not be possible without the knowledge that archaeology is bringing to the discussion. The contribution of archaeology to the study of the Johannine traditions has been invaluable, and we can only look forward with hope for what it will continue to provide.

---

use of such historical terms for authorities does contrast with the use of other, less specific terms such as "the Jews" (in the contexts where they refer to religious authorities). See U. C. von Wahlde, "The Relationships between Pharisees and Chief Priests: Some Observations on the Texts in Matthew, John, and Josephus," NTS 42 (1996): 506-22.

Aspects of Historicity in the Gospel of John: Implications for Investigations of Jesus and Archaeology

Paul N. Anderson

Of the many tensions characterizing the Gospel of John, one of its perplexities most needing to be addressed critically is the set of issues related to aspects of historicity.[1] On one hand, John is the most spiritual, theological, and symbolic of the canonical Gospels, leading scholars in recent decades to take seriously the literary features of the work. On the other hand, there is more archaeological, topographical, and apparently historical material in John than in any other Gospel, or even in all three combined.[2] It is no surprise, therefore, that many of the essays presented at the millennial conference on Jesus and archaeology held in Jerusalem (August 2000) dealt with issues and details alluded to *directly* in the Gospel of John. And yet, because the prevalent opinion among New Testament scholars ascribes little if any historical weight to the Fourth Gospel, this trend presents a formidable obstacle to the scientific investigation of Jesus and archaeology. Consider, for instance, the opinion of Edgar J. Goodspeed regarding the purportedly ahistorical nature of the Fourth Evangelist: "It must be remembered that topography and chronology were among the least of the author's concerns. His head was among the stars. He was seeking to determine the place of Jesus in the spiritual universe and his relations to the eternal realities.

---

1. Tensions between the humanity and divinity of Jesus, the Son's egalitarian or subordinate relation to the Father, embellished and existentialized presentation of Jesus' signs, heightened or diminished sacramentology, present or future eschatology, and literary unity or disunity in John have been addressed especially in P. N. Anderson, *The Christology of the Fourth Gospel: Its Unity and Disunity in the Light of John 6*, WUNT 78 (Tübingen: J. C. B. Mohr [Paul Siebeck], 1996; Valley Forge, Pa.: Trinity, 1997); also included in *The Dialogical Autonomy of the Fourth Gospel — the Purpose, Development, and Meaning of John* (Eugene, Ore.: Cascade Books, 2006).

2. Professor von Wahlde's essay in the present collection examines over fifty archaeological and topographical passages in John, so the treatment of specific passages should be considered in his essay.

These were the matters that interested and absorbed him, not itineraries and time tables, so that practical mundane considerations that might apply to Mark, Matthew, or Luke have little significance for his work."[3] Clearly, John is greatly interested in Christology, but does that mean its narrator had *no* interest in the empirical details he includes in his narrative? If John's patent ahistoricity is a worthy thesis, this would be important to establish. This would mean that John's archaeological and topographical references would be disconnected: severed from the events narrated, thus requiring an alternative explanation. However, if this modernistic thesis itself emerges as less than resilient when subjected to critical scrutiny, the historical-critical scholar must explore alternative means of accounting for the distinctive character of the Johannine witness. This is especially important, given the fact of John's archaeological and topographical features, many of which appear also to be accurate.

Along these lines, several *serious errors* are made by otherwise critical scholars. (a) First, John's differences with the Synoptics are wrongly understood as three against one, with John being the lone Gospel out. If John and Mark may be considered the *Bi-Optic* Gospels,[4] John's differences with the Synoptics are better considered one against one, with at least some of them consisting of an individuated perspective providing an alternative — perhaps intentionally so — to Mark. (b) Second, it is a gross error to assume that because John is *theological* in its tone it is *ahistorical* in its character and origin. By analogy, the crucifixion of Jesus was of paramount theological significance to early Christians, but this fact alone does not *prove* its ahistoricity. Spiritualized reflection more often follows upon significant events rather than concocting them, and critical judgment must be used in discerning whether a theological comment in John betrays a spiritualized reflection upon an event or whether it reflects a projection of a theological notion on to the narrative. Facile conjecture alone does not meet the test of critical scrutiny. (c) A third error is to fail to notice the many ways John's traditional accounts appear more authentic than, and even historically superior to, those in the Synoptics. This is not to deny the many ways that the Synoptic presentations of Jesus are preferable to the Johannine; the point is that the multiplicity of issues between the Gospels must be consid-

3. See Edgar J. Goodspeed, *An Introduction to the New Testament* (Chicago: University of Chicago Press, 1937), p. 310.

4. See P. N. Anderson, "John and Mark — the Bi-Optic Gospels," in *Jesus in Johannine Tradition*, ed. R. Fortna and T. Thatcher (Philadelphia: Westminster John Knox, 2001), pp. 175-88. For the overall theory of John's relation to the other traditions, see P. N. Anderson, "Interfluential, Formative, and Dialectical — a Theory of John's Relation to the Synoptics," in *Für und wider die Priorität des Johannesevangeliums*, ed. P. Hofrichter, TTS 9 (Hildesheim, Zürich, and New York: Georg Olms Verlag, 2002), pp. 19-58.

ered — in their complexity — rather than moving simplistically in one direction or another.

Critical scholars are notably aware of fallacies related to affirming too much historical certainty based on an inferred apostolic origin of a Gospel tradition, but the obverse, assuming that one or more historical incongruities demonstrate the pervasive falsity of that tradition's historicity, is equally flawed.[5] This essay will endeavor to stay clear of such errors in the interest of analyzing critically the ways the Johannine witness might indeed be serviceable historically, and likewise where it is not. The goal of this essay is thus to evaluate critically the aforementioned opinions of modernistic scholars, seeking to cast new light on particular aspects of historicity in the Gospel of John, believing that such a prospect will inform the larger discussions regarding Jesus and archaeology. Before doing so, however, recent significant contributions on the subjects of archaeology, John, and Jesus deserve consideration.

Recent Breakthroughs on John, Jesus, and Archaeology

As a first consideration, the father of biblical archaeological studies, William Foxwell Albright, bolstered the historicity of the Johannine tradition impressively in his 1956 essay published in the Dodd Festschrift.[6] (a) He challenged the

---

5. Note the overreaching approach of R. L. Sturch, "The Alleged Eyewitness Material in the Fourth Gospel," *Studia Biblica* 2 (1978): 313-27, who seeks to overturn the works of Westcott and Dodd in their connecting of apparent eyewitness details in John with the eyewitness claims of the redactor. While some details "resist elimination" (an admission of his positivistic bias), he claims that alternative explanations *prove* that arguing that the "Evangelist was an eyewitness of nearly all that he reported . . . cannot in fact be achieved" (p. 324). He comes close, however, to committing the all-or-none fallacy in the *other* direction. Questioning the certainty of A does not demonstrate non-A. This is the fallacy of arguing an inference from ignorance. A second error follows. While Sturch rightly points out that many of the Johannine details cannot be confirmed, he also commits errors in his inference of Johannine "mistakes." He wrongly assumes that the forty-six years of building the Temple is an error, when it corresponds well with Herod's reconstruction program having begun in 19 B.C.E.; his determination that the weight of the spices must be an "inaccurate detail" (simply because he imagines it so) also fails to convince. While Westcott may have overstated his own case, Sturch's essay nonetheless falls short of overturning the Johannine eyewitness claims either on the basis of hard evidence or sound reasoning. Given an "if B then A" syllogism, the discounting of B does not demonstrate non-A. This is the fallacy of denying the antecedent. Not only is the conjectural questioning of B weak in these cases, but the structure of the argument is also logically flawed. Genuinely critical scholars will challenge claims in all directions, not just traditional ones.

6. See W. F. Albright, "Recent Discoveries in Palestine and the Gospel of St. John," in *The Background of the New Testament and Its Eschatology: In Honour of Charles Harold Dodd,*

purported *religionsgeschichtlich* origin of John's material as having been contemporary Hellenistic and Gnostic religious mythology, showing that the background was on firmer footing as a Palestinian work of Jewish origin. (b) Albright then presented many examples of John's familiarity with Palestine *before* the First Revolt (66-70 C.E.), challenging later datings of John. These early Palestinian and Jewish references in John appear to have been connected with Diaspora Christian settings in the Hellenistic world, probably by means of orally conveyed tradition.[7] (c) Archaeological finds in Jerusalem include a Roman stone pavement in the Antonia Tower (measuring 2,500 square meters, thus matching the Johannine *Lithostroton*) and the elevated ridge on which it stood (explaining the odd reference to the site in Aramaic, *gabbeta*, meaning ridge of the house).[8] (d) The topographic references to the places near Shechem where John was baptizing (Jn 3:22-30) include "Aenon near Salim," corresponding with the headwaters of Wadi Far'ah (near modern Ainun — similar to the Aramaic word for "little fountain," which itself is near the town of Salim) (pp. 158-60). These places in Samaria also would intersect with the fact that some Samaritans were later found to be followers of John the Baptist. (e) Likewise, the recent discovery of Jacob's well in Sychar (in the modern Arabic, *'Askar*) confirms the Johannine rendering (pp. 159-60). (f) The discoveries at Qumran have contributed an extensive understanding of Jewish dualism and models of redemption, making the Gnostic and Hellenistic cult inferences less and less plausible (pp. 160-70).[9] In summation, "both the narratives and *logia* of John's Gospel certainly or presumably date back to oral tradition in Palestine, before A.D. 70; they were probably transmitted orally in the Diaspora for at least a decade — possibly two decades — before being put into writing" (p. 170). Albright's archaeological contribution forced biblical scholars to consider again significant aspects of Johannine historicity, having been sidestepped by the previous century or more of critical scholarship.

A second major contribution to the study of John, Jesus, and archaeology is

---

ed. W. D. Davies and D. Daube (Cambridge: Cambridge University Press, 1956), pp. 153-71. The page numbers in the remainder of this paragraph refer to this essay.

7. Descriptions of Jesus as a *rabbi* and *didaskalos* are confirmed by pre-70 ossuaries, as are the common Jewish names: for Mary *(Maryam)*, Martha *(Marta)*, and Lazarus *(La'zar)* (Albright, "Recent Discoveries," pp. 157-58).

8. See also the extensive archaeological treatment of the Gabbatha site by J. F. Wilson, "Archaeology and the Origins of the Fourth Gospel: Gabbatha," in *Johannine Studies: Essays in Honor of Frank Pack,* ed. J. E. Priest, W. R. Clark, and R. L. Tyler (Malibu, Calif.: Pepperdine University Press, 1989), pp. 221-30, strengthening Albright's case further.

9. See also J. H. Charlesworth's important 1992 collection of essays connecting John with Qumran and thus the Essene movement: *Jesus and the Dead Sea Scrolls* (New York: Doubleday, 1992).

the 1988 monograph of James Charlesworth,[10] in which he outlines the top seven archaeological breakthroughs in the last half of the twentieth century. While Charlesworth does not call attention to this fact, amazingly *all seven of them* bear some connection with the Gospel of John! In addition to Johannine connections with the burned house in Jerusalem (confirming Jesus' double entendre prediction in Jn 2:19 that the Temple would be destroyed) in which stone jars for ritual purification were found (Jn 2:6) (pp. 106-8), the seven top archaeological breakthroughs are as follows: (a) The *seventh*-most-important archaeological discovery for Jesus studies is the discovery of Jewish synagogues in Palestine (pp. 108-15), and Charlesworth points out the locations of fifty-four of them (p. 110). Obviously, if Jesus preached in synagogues in Nazareth, Capernaum, and elsewhere, the widespread discovery of these ruins bolsters the plausibility of such presentations, especially in Mark and John (see Mk 1:21-29; 6:1-6; Jn 6:59). In addition, the discovery of what may have been the house of Simon Peter in Capernaum (adjacent to the synagogue) strengthens the account of the healing of Simon Peter's mother-in-law in Mk 1:29-34, which follows directly after the synagogue ministry of Jesus. It might explain also why the beginning of Jesus' ministry is connected with Nazareth (Jn 1:46) and Capernaum (Jn 2:12; 4:46).

(b) Charlesworth's *sixth*-most-important archaeological discovery for Jesus studies pertains to the walls and distinctive gates of Jerusalem (pp. 115-17). The distinguishing of various walls from those existent during the time of Jesus locates the traditional site of the crucifixion outside the city (although inside the Herodian third wall) as mentioned in Jn 19:20 and Heb 13:12. In addition, the only specific Jerusalem gate mentioned in the Gospels is the Sheep Gate,[11] described in Jn 5:2 as being near the pool of Bethzatha. The location of the Essene Gate as mentioned by Josephus is also in the region where Jesus' family and followers may have lived after his ministry, suggesting connections between the Essenes and the Palestinian Jesus Movement.

(c) The *fifth*-most-important discovery relates to the Temple Mount during the time of Jesus (pp. 117-19). The discovery of "double and triple Hulda gates" near which there were a massive stairway and passageways leading from the stables into the Temple area makes the driving out of oxen and sheep from the Temple area by Jesus in Jn 2:15 an entirely realistic scene — not just a con-

10. Charlesworth, *Jesus within Judaism: New Light from Exciting Archaeological Discoveries* (New York: Doubleday, 1988); see especially Charlesworth's fifth chapter, "The Jesus of History and the Archaeology of Palestine" (pp. 103-30). Page numbers referring to this work are placed in the following text.

11. Although see the reference to "the beautiful gate" of Acts 3:10, and note the Johannine (Solomon's Colonnade) detail included in Acts 3:11 and 5:12.

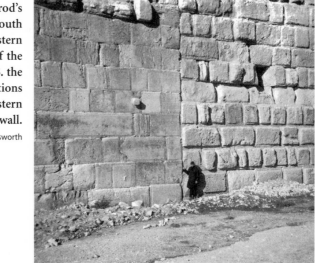

Figure 73. The seam that separates Herod's extension to the south and the earlier Eastern Retaining Wall of the Temple. N.B. the different constructions in the eastern retaining wall.

Courtesy J. H. Charlesworth

coction. Despite Charlesworth's preference for the archaeological detail in John, he nonetheless sides with the Synoptic view that the Temple disturbance led to the arrest and death of Jesus over and against the Johannine ordering of events. The huge stones found at the foundation of the Herodian Temple, and the way Josephus described the construction project, show Herod to have been the greatest builder in Palestine's history.[12] This being the case, the laudatory comments of Jesus' disciples about the magnificent stones and buildings in Mk 13:1 are confirmed by the archaeological evidence.

(d) The *fourth*-most-important archaeological discovery for Jesus Research is the discovery of two pools, just outside the Sheep Gate (cf. Jn 5:2) in Jerusalem, which appear to have been by five porticos — porches sheltering the four-sided circumference of the pools, with a fifth roof sheltering the area between the pools (pp. 119-20). Interestingly enough, until archaeologists began excavating this site, it was assumed that a five-portico pool must have been a Johannine fabrication — perhaps a theologized reference to the five books of Moses. With the discovery, however, of a central roof-structure supported by

12. An indirect reference to Herod's reconstruction project may be found in Jn 2:20, where the Jerusalem leaders exclaim that the project had been going on for forty-six years. As the reconstruction began in 19 B.C.E., according to Josephus (during the eighteenth year of Herod's reign; *Ant* 15.11.1), this would have marked that saying as taking place around 27 C.E., plausibly contributing to the chronological reliability of the Johannine rendering of an early Temple cleansing. If Jesus was born in 4 B.C.E., this would have been his thirtieth year.

columns, and one on each of the four outer sides of the pool complex, the Johannine rendering is entirely accurate from an archaeological and historical standpoint. It was *not* a "fabricated" detail. Even the name of the pool, Bethzatha (not to be confused with Bethsaida, the home of Andrew and Peter as some manuscripts have), is corroborated by the reference in the *Copper Scroll* of Qumran (Cave 3, col. 11) to a pool in Jerusalem called Beth Eshdathayin (meaning "the place of the twin pools" [Charlesworth, p. 120]). In these and other ways, the scene described in Jn 5:1-15 is impressively corroborated by recent archaeological discoveries, taking the above arguments of Albright further.

(e) In *third* place is the discovery of material near Pilate's Praetorium in Jerusalem, which appears to match very closely the presentation of the events, especially as rendered in Jn 18–19 (pp. 120-22). The Praetorium would have been the official residence of the governor, and because it was on an elevated ridge (*Gabbatha*, "high place," in Aramaic; Jn 19:13), the Temple area could have been monitored effectively. From there Pilate would also have exercised his judgment (the judgment seat of Jn 19:13), and the discovery of the large stone pavement matches the Johannine description of the Lithostrotos, also in Jn 19:13. This area, discovered in the excavations of Herod the Great's palace, is also mentioned by Josephus as "the Upper City" (p. 121), and once again the explicit references to topographical details in John are corroborated by the latest archaeological discoveries.

(f) The *second*-most-important discovery relates to the bones of a crucified man named "Jehohanan" (pp. 122-23). Actually, it is an ankle bone with a spike driven through it that is the most telling about the cruel Roman practice of crucifixion. Apparently, the victim would have had to raise himself up to breathe until death by suffocation transpired, thus making the dying process an extremely painful and prolonged one. This explains the surprise of Pilate in Mk 15:44 that Jesus had already died, and it explains why the soldiers would have broken the legs of their victims in order to hasten their death, as described in Jn 19:31-34. This also accounts, then, for the Johannine presentation of the soldier stabbing Jesus' side with a spear. He was already dead, so his legs need not have been broken, thus "fulfilling" the Scriptures of Ps 34:20 and Zech 12:10. The fact that Jehohanan was also given a proper burial erodes the inference that victims of crucifixion were characteristically dumped into a pit rather than buried in a tomb as is reported of Jesus in the Gospels — especially characteristic of the presentation of Jesus' crucifixion in *John*.

(g) Finally, the most important archaeological discovery for Jesus studies, according to Charlesworth, pertains to the growing evidence as to the site of the crucifixion (pp. 123-25). While Gordon's Calvary indeed looks like "the Place of the Skull" (*"Golgotha,"* as described in Mk 15:22; Mt 27:33; and Jn 19:17) and is outside the gate of the city (Heb 13:12), Charlesworth argues that the discovery that Herod's third wall was constructed *after* the death of Jesus plausibly confirms the traditional site of the crucifixion, found within the Church of the Holy Sepulchre (pp. 123-24). The exposed rock on that site rose 13 meters above the rest, and if this were the rock on which Jesus was crucified, the Petrine reference to the stone rejected by the builders would have had a double meaning (Mk 12:10; 1 Pet 2:7; Acts 4:11). That the area was a quarry is echoed by Jn 19:41, as it mentions a new tomb in which no one had been buried. If Jesus were to have been buried near the site of the crucifixion as John's narrative suggests, both the traditional site and the Garden Tomb site would corroborate those connections. In all seven of these archaeological breakthroughs, John features prominently — and in some cases *uniquely* — among the earliest Christian witnesses! While Charlesworth does not comment explicitly on the implications of these top seven archaeological discoveries as having Johannine connections, the fact of those connections is highly significant for the present study.

A third major contribution to the study of John, Jesus, and archaeology are the extensive historical investigations into the historicity of the Johannine narrative that have been undertaken. While all of them cannot be mentioned here, the point should be made that these studies have not so much been disproved or countered by critical analyses posing superior alternatives; they have simply been stepped over or disregarded by Johannine and Jesus scholars (primarily the *latter*).[13] Several of the most significant analyses of Johannine historicity over the last century include the following. (a) *First*, the work of Bishop Lightfoot (1904) amassed extensive evidence as to the internal and external "authenticity and genuineness" of the Johannine tradition.[14] (b) *Second*, the discovery of the P^{52} Papyrus in the Rylands Library, analyzed by Colin H. Roberts,[15] argues for a finalization of the Fourth Gospel by around 100 C.E. (rather than the middle or late second century C.E.), as it was already in circulation in Egypt by the first two or three decades of the second century. (c) *Third*, E. R. Goodenough, in his highly significant 1945 essay,[16] posits sev-

---

13. This excellent observation was made by Mark Allan Powell, chair of the Historical Jesus Section of the SBL meetings, who responded helpfully to the paper by Paula Fredriksen in the 2002 Toronto "John, Jesus and History Consultation" meetings. Those papers will be published in a future collection.

14. Building upon the works of Westcott and others, this work by Lightfoot (*Biblical Essays* [London: Macmillan, 1904], pp. 1-198, in addition to his commentary) established critical foundations for defending the traditional view — a venture continued by many others.

15. C. H. Roberts, *An Unpublished Fragment of the Fourth Gospel in the John Rylands Library* (Manchester: Manchester University Press, 1935).

16. E. R. Goodenough, "John: A Primitive Gospel," *JBL* 64 (1945): 145-82.

eral bases for reconsidering the originality of John, including John's independence from the Synoptics, omissions of virgin birth narratives and the institution of the Eucharist, and the distinctively unified character of the Johannine presentation of Jesus. (d) *Fourth,* in addition to other treatments of John's historicity, the 1960 book by A. J. B. Higgins poses one of the most measured treatments of aspects of John's historicity, including treatments of the healing of the official's son (4:46-54), the feeding/sea-crossing/discussion/confession narratives (6:1-71) in John and Mark, and Synoptic-like sayings of Jesus in John.[17] (e) *Fifth,* the massive *magnum opus* of C. H. Dodd on historical tradition in the Fourth Gospel established significant bases for the originative historicity of the Johannine tradition, outlining the independent developments of the passion narrative, the ministry of Jesus, the witness of John the Baptist, and the sayings of Jesus in John.[18] (f) *Sixth,* Franz Müssner's treatment of the historical Jesus in John[19] and the epistemological character of the Johannine Gospel as "anamnesis" — a memory of the ministry of the historical Jesus rendered in Johannine paraphrase — address plausibly most of the objections regarding the fact that Jesus' teachings in John are presented in the language and modes of the Fourth Evangelist. (g) *Seventh,* sustained energy has been invested in recovering the "priority" of the Johannine tradition, and John A. T. Robinson's postmortem monograph argues extensively for John's traditional priority rather than posteriority.[20] The above studies are but a sample of the most significant contributions to the critical analysis of John's historicity, and they deserve consideration for the critical scholar interested in a fair appraisal of the issues.

Impressively, the above findings demonstrate that John and Jesus specialists would do well to benefit from the latest archaeological and historical findings, and they demonstrate time and again how wrongheaded antihistorical treatments of Gospel narratives have tended to be. "The theological interests of the Evangelist" is one of the most pervasive phrases of *uncritical speculation and conjecture* employed by so-called scientific scholars seeking to account for a de-

17. Higgins, *The Historicity of the Fourth Gospel* (London: Lutterworth, 1960). Many other books and articles could be cited here, but Higgins's work is featured because of its particularly measured approach to the subject.

18. C. H. Dodd, *Historical Tradition in the Fourth Gospel* (London: Cambridge University Press, 1963).

19. F. Müssner, *The Historical Jesus in the Gospel of John,* trans. W. J. O'Harah (New York: Herder and Herder, 1966). See also a broader discussion of the issues in P. N. Anderson, "On Jesus: Quests for Historicity, and the History of Recent Quests," *QRT* 94 (2000): 5-39; and P. N. Anderson, "A Response to Professors Borg, Powell and Kinkel," *QRT* 98 (2002): 43-54.

20. J. A. T. Robinson, *The Priority of John,* ed. J. F. Coakley (London: SCM, 1985).

tail in one or more of the Gospels, and continuing discoveries demonstrate how flawed many such conjectures have been. In demonstrating the connectedness of Johannine, Jesus, and archaeological studies, Charlesworth rightly concludes his chapter by saying, "The Jesus of history is now less incomprehensible thanks to the archaeology of Palestine."[21] What I would like to add is that *the same applies to the Gospel of John.*

Indeed, it is puzzling that while John contains more archaeological, topographical, and chronological data than all three of the Synoptic Gospels combined, many scholars still fail to allow the possibility of *any* historicity within the Johannine tradition. If one regards the Fourth Gospel as patently ahistorical, the extensive presence of "archaeological" material presents a considerable problem. Where did this material come from, and why was it included? Was it simply added for rhetorical or "realism" effect, or does it lend insights into the character and origin of the Johannine tradition? Then again, much of John's tradition *is* spiritualized and theological in tone — especially the elevated teachings of Jesus — and this is why a critical appraisal of aspects of John's historicity is required.

Aspects of Historicity in John

Just as it cannot be said that because John is theological it cannot be historical, it is also wrong to assert that identifying John's historicity displaces its theological interests. Some points may be made for historical reasons in John, and some may be made for theological reasons. Likewise, the origin of other material may be historical, but the origin of some material may be theological; each investigation must be carried out specifically, with particular reference to the issue at hand. This being the case, without discounting the apologetic interests of the Evangelist to lead the reader to faith (Jn 20:31),[22] there are still aspects of historicity in John that are worthy of consideration in and of themselves. This is not to say they were entirely accurate, or even that their inclusion was motivated by historicizing interests; it simply is to argue that the phenomenology of these matters deserves to be investigated in determining aspects of historicity in John. This being the case, several Johannine features require critical consideration.

21. Charlesworth, *Jesus within Judaism*, p. 127.
22. See P. N. Anderson, *Navigating the Living Waters of the Gospel of John — on Wading with Children and Swimming with Elephants* (Wallingford, Pa.: Pendle Hill Press, 2000); also included in *The Dialogical Autonomy of the Fourth Gospel,* for a rhetorical analysis of how the reader is led toward a response of faith in John.

1. Rhetorical Claims to Firsthand Knowledge

The first fact to be considered is that the Johannine editor claims John's narrative is at least somewhat based on firsthand knowledge and testimony. In that sense John's editor makes a distinctive epistemological claim not found in the other Gospels. Whoever he may have been, the one who witnesses the death of Jesus and who was entrusted with the care of the mother of Jesus is mentioned as the Beloved Disciple (Jn 19:16-42), whose "testimony is true." Apparently after his death, the editor connects this person with three features: (a) he was the one engaged with Peter and Jesus in a dispute over honor and faithfulness, (b) he was the Beloved Disciple who leaned against the breast of Jesus (apparently between Peter and Jesus) in 13:23-25, and (c) he was the authorial source of the Johannine tradition (at least some of it) and was connected inferentially with the witnessing of the crucifixion by the communal assertion: "We know his testimony is true" (19:34-35; 21:18-25). While these claims do not necessarily imply that all of John is built on eyewitness material, it is also a fact that the identification of one or more fictive or spiritualized elements does not exclude the entirety of the Johannine narrative from the canons of plausible historicity.

Indeed, it might not be possible to know for certain who this figure was, and the Beloved Disciple clearly serves a typological function, representing ideal discipleship within the Johannine narrative. This being the case, however, it cannot be said that typological hero references cannot have been connected to a real person, who may have been identified before or after his death as the source of the Johannine witness. The extensive treatment of the Beloved Disciple by Charlesworth argues convincingly that whoever this person was, he is purported to have been the authoritative source of the Johannine witness — the one whose witness validates the Gospel of John.[23] While debates will continue as to who he might have been, several other claims also *cannot* be made.

First, it cannot be claimed that because this disciple presents an alternative view of "the Twelve" and Peter's authoritative place among them, he cannot have been one of the Twelve. Indeed, critiques of the use of the apostolic coin of authority may have risen from *within* the apostolic band rather than from without — especially if it were felt that such a coin were being co-opted by institutional aspirants within the church, perhaps even departing from the more informal and itinerant ministry of Jesus.[24] There probably never was a "single" perspective on Jesus' provocative ministry — even within his closest band of

---

23. J. H. Charlesworth, *The Beloved Disciple: Whose Witness Validates the Gospel of John?* (Valley Forge, Pa.: Trinity, 1995).

24. See Anderson, *Christology,* pp. 195-251.

disciples — just as there was never a single, straightforward memory of Socrates' symposium, forcing a disjunctive choice between Plato and Xenophon. In all four canonical Gospels the disciples are presented as miscomprehending Jesus' actions and teachings and discussing among themselves what he possibly could have meant. A moderate level of dissonance among the apostles and between their respective traditions is thus a sign of realism and authenticity rather than fictive adulteration.

Second, it cannot be said that the character of the Johannine tradition is epistemologically counter to an individuated reflection on the ministry of Jesus. John's dialectical presentation of Jesus' deeds and words betrays the epistemological character of first-order induction rather than second-order deduction.[25] In that sense, John's dialogical presentation of christological tensions — in contrast, say, to the more monological character of the Johannine Epistles — suggests proximity to Jesus rather than distance from him.

Third, even though much of modern New Testament scholarship has come to accept the opinion that the first to connect the apostle John with Johannine authorship was Irenaeus, in his opposition to Marcion around 180 C.E., this claim is *not* true. A first-century clue to Johannine authorship can be found in Acts 4:19-20, which has hitherto gone totally unnoticed by all sectors of the debate.[26] In this passage Peter and John speak (the only time John is presented as speaking in Acts), and two characteristically crafted sayings are listed. The first is clearly Petrine: we must obey *God* rather than humans (see Acts 5:29 and 11:17 for similar God-versus-humanity rhetoric attributed to Peter). The second, however, bears an unmistakably Johannine ring to it: we cannot help but speak about what *we have seen and heard* (see the testimony of the Johannine Elder in 1 Jn 1:3 and that of Jesus in Jn 3:32 for this being a characteristically Johannine

25. See the cognitive-critical analyses applying the works of James Loder and James Fowler to the scientific investigation of the origin and development of Gospel traditions in P. N. Anderson, "Cognitive Origins of John's Christological Unity and Disunity," *HBT* 17 (1995): 1-24; also in J. H. Ellens and W. Rollins, eds., *Psychology and the Bible: A New Way to Read the Scriptures* (Westport, Conn.: Praegers/Greenwood Publishers, 2004), 3:127-48. See also Anderson, *Christology*, pp. 137-66.

26. See Anderson, *Christology*, app. VIII: "The Papias Tradition, John's Authorship and Luke/Acts," pp. 274-77. The point here is not to argue that all of John is a factor of eyewitness memory; even if some of it was claimed to have been such, this does not mean all of it was. The point is to assess critically the claim that *none* of John's material is firsthand information. Even John the Baptist (or whoever is speaking in Jn 3:31-36) bases his testimony about Jesus on the basis that Jesus is reporting *what he had seen and heard* from the Father (Jn 3:32). These connections are further bolstered by the likelihood that the Johannine tradition (probably in its oral form) has come to serve as one of Luke's sources in his departures from Mark (see Anderson, "Interfluential, Formative, and Dialectical," pp. 43-48).

motif). Now this is not to say that Luke was *right,* or that the identity of the Beloved Disciple is thereby confirmed necessarily as John, the companion of Peter (although note the proximity of John and/or the Beloved Disciple to Peter in all four Gospels). As critical scholars know, the traditional view has serious problems to it, and Papias also mentions another John, the Elder, who apparently stood as a bridge between the apostles and Polycarp. It *is* to say, however, that the first connecting of the apostle John with the Johannine tradition *was not Irenaeus, around 180 c.e.* It was Luke, *a full century before Irenaeus,* and whether he was right or misguided, this first-century clue to Johannine authorship, which has been totally overlooked on all sides of the debate, approximates a fact.

Fourth, while not all of John's material can be connected directly to first-hand information, there are also many references to *empirically derived information* in John. This *is* a literary *fact.* For whatever reason, references to *all five senses* are used in John. That which is *seen* by someone (in the ocular sense) is reported 98 times[27] (*blepō,* 1:29; 13:22; 20:1, 5; 21:9, 20; *eideō,* 1:39, 46, 47, 48, 50; 4:48; 5:6; 6:14, 22, 24, 26, 30; 9:1; 11:31, 32, 33, 34; 12:9, 21; 18:26; 19:6, 26, 33; 20:8, 20, 25, 27; 21:12, 21; *emblepō,* 1:36, 42; *theaomai,* 1:14, 32, 38; 6:5; 11:45; *theōreō,* 2:23; 6:2, 19; 7:3; 9:8; 14:17, 19; 16:10, 16, 17, 19; 17:24; 20:6, 12, 14; *ide,* 1:29, 36, 47; 3:26; 5:14; 7:26; 11:3, 36; 12:19; 16:29; 18:21; 19:4, 14, 26, 27; *idou,* 19:5; *optomai,* 1:50, 51; 16:16, 17, 19, 22; 19:37; *horaō,* 1:18, 34; 3:11, 32; 4:45; 6:36, 46; 8:57; 9:37; 14:7, 9; 15:24; 19:35; 20:18, 25, 29); that which is *heard* (in the auditory sense) is reported 30 times (*akouō,* 1:37, 40; 3:29, 32; 4:1, 42, 47; 5:24; 6:45, 60; 7:32, 40, 51; 9:32, 35, 40; 11:4, 6, 20, 29; 12:12, 18, 29; 14:24, 28; 18:21; 19:8, 13; 21:7); that which is *smelled* is reported twice (*ozō,* 11:39; *eplērōthē ek tēs osmēs,* 12:3); that which is *tasted* is reported once (*geuomai,* 2:9); and that which is *touched* is reported 4 times (*haptomai,* 20:17; *ballō,* 20:25 [2x's], 27). Even references to temperature are mentioned *(psychos)* in 18:18, as the factor of coldness explains why Peter and others were warming themselves around a charcoal fire (18:18, 25). Again, some of these reports of empirical perception may have been added for historicizing effect, and they certainly represent a central feature of Johannine authorization (1 Jn 1:1-3), but claiming that *all of them were* fabrications-and-nothing-more has no compelling substantiation; it must be regarded a scholarly fiction. The literary fact that John possesses more appeals to empirically derived information than any of the other Gospels — canonical or otherwise — seems to sup-

---

27. Many other times seeing and hearing verbs are used in John, not in the empirical sense, but in the ideational or perceptual sense. And a few other times, hearing and seeing are used in the eschatological or obedience sense. The above references, however, appear to be used in the empirical sense.

port the claim of the Johannine editor. Whoever these persons may have been, the late first-century Johannine editor connects readers with the Evangelist's reflections on the ministry of Jesus and its implications for later generations. In several ways, therefore, the Johannine claims to firsthand information are thus not without substantiation.

2. Connections between the Jesus of Palestine and the Audiences of Asia Minor

Like the Gospel of Mark, John connects the Aramaic language of Jesus and the Jewish customs of Palestine with Gentile audiences in other places. This is an aspect of historicity that Matthew and Luke do not represent in the same way. Luke fails to pick up on the Jewish material in Mark, probably because of his selectivity — it was not material important to his purposes in telling the story of Jesus as a good and just man to his Hellenistic audience. Matthew, on the other hand, probably felt that his Jewish audiences did not need to be informed of Jewish customs or diction, and this may be why he omitted these sorts of Markan details. John, however, retains even more of this material than Mark does, and this suggests the preservation of the Palestinian ministry of Jesus for later Gentile audiences — probably reflecting an interest in maintaining vivid features of the Johannine oral tradition. For instance, John preserves such Aramaic words as *rabbi/rabbouni* (Jn 1:38; 20:16), *Messias* (1:41; 4:25), *Bethzetha* (5:2), *Siloam* (9:7), *Gabbatha* (19:13, actually having a different name in Greek — *Lithostrotos* — rather than a translation), and *Golgotha* (19:17) and "translates" most of them into Greek for Hellenistic audiences.

Further, John "explains" Jewish customs for Gentile audiences, informing them of particular ritual and purification practices, thereby explaining why things had to happen the ways they did. The sorts of jars used for Jewish purification rites are described (2:6); the Passover of the Jews is contextualized (2:13, 23); Jews having "no dealings with Samaritans" heightens the tension in the story of Jesus' encounter with the woman at the well (4:9); another feast of the Jews is mentioned (5:1); the Sabbath is mentioned as the day on which Jesus (perhaps provocatively) performed a healing (5:9, 10, 16, 18; 7:22, 23; see also 9:14, 16); a second Jewish Passover is mentioned (6:4); the Jewish Feast of the Tabernacles is noted (7:2); a third Jewish Passover is mentioned (11:55) with a reference to requirements for Jewish purification; events before the final Passover are mentioned with special importance (six days before, 12:1; before, 13:1); the Temple "where all the Jews gather" is described (18:20); it is explained that the Jews did not want to be made unclean for the paschal meal by entering the

Roman Praetorium (18:28); the Roman appeasement practice of releasing a Jewish prisoner at Passover time is mentioned (18:39); Jewish authorities are rendered as not wanting bodies to be hanging on crosses on the Sabbath lest it (and they) be defiled (19:31); the embalming practices of the Jews are explained (19:40); and the Jewish day of Preparation and the ceremonial purity of the tomb are described (19:42).

These prolific references to Jewish religious customs function to build connections between the Palestinian ministry of Jesus and later Gentile audiences. In that sense, interests in connecting religious aspects of John's originative history with the developing history of the Johannine situation can be clearly inferred. John's material shows evidence of originating in Palestinian memory and being rendered later for a Hellenistic audience. Thus, the impressive points made by Albright and Charlesworth are here confirmed and expanded.

3. Archaeological and Topographical Content

As mentioned above, an impressive fact within the scientific study of Jesus and the Gospels is that John includes some of the most explicit archaeological and topographical references to be found anywhere among the Gospels. Particular places locating events in the ministry of Jesus are not only mentioned, but they are described with information that seems more empirically oriented than theologically motivated. Consider, for instance, John's descriptions of the places where John was baptizing: *Bethabara* (or *Betharaba;* "Bethany" was a later corruption) beyond the Jordan (Jn 1:28);[28] *Aenon* near *Salim* (a place John was baptizing "because there was much water there") is mentioned (3:23); and it is implied that a particular place of baptism was different from the one "beyond the Jordan" where John had pointed out Jesus earlier (3:26). The disjunctive emphasis here between these diverse places implies particular topographical knowledge — it was *there,* not *the other place.* Upon receiving a harsh welcome in Judea, Jesus returned to the place where John had been baptizing — across the Jordan — and in contrast to the Synoptics, it appears that Jesus and John had been ministering contemporaneously with each other for at least a

---

28. It is more likely to infer that "Bethany" was added later than to infer that *Bethabara* or *Betharaba* replaced the more commonplace name. The speculation that because Bethany was not across the Jordan the Evangelist has thus made an inexcusable geographical mistake, is itself based on a flawed assumption. Leading archaeological investigations in Jordan are currently excavating a site east of the Jordan River (not far from Jericho), which have found both the remains of a village and a former tributary to the Jordan that had once formed pools of water — confirming the Johannine account.

period of time (10:41; 3:24). It appears also that Jesus' trans-Jordan ministry was successful, and even Mark reports Jesus ministering in that region (Mk 10:1) on his way to Jerusalem.[29] John's connecting the ministry of Jesus to the ministry of John the Baptizer not only is more plausible in terms of its multidimensionality; it also introduces archaeological information apparently rooted in empirical knowledge.

Likewise, John calls special attention to places where Jesus ministered. In the north, the region of Galilee (Jn 1:43-44; 4:3; 6:1; 7:1, 9) and the Sea of Tiberias (6:1, 23; 21:1) are mentioned with special emphasis, and Cana of Galilee (2:1-11; 4:43-54) is described as the place where Jesus' first two signs were performed.[30] Capernaum is also described as the hub of Jesus' ministry; it is the home of the Roman official whose son was healed, the place to which Jesus often went with his disciples, and the home of the synagogue in which Jesus preached (2:12; 4:46; 6:17, 24, 59).[31] From there Jesus travels to and from Judea several times (4:3, 47, 54; 7:1, 3; 11:7), and in doing so "must pass through" Samaria (4:4, 5, 7, 9) — a topographically correct detail.[32] Bethany gets the attention of Jesus as the home of Mary, Martha, and Lazarus — all people whom Jesus loved — and it was their home in which the anointing of Jesus is reported to have taken place (11:1, 18; 12:1-8). An interesting mention is also made of a Judean village near Ephraim to which Jesus withdrew upon an unfriendly reception by the religious leaders after the raising of Lazarus (11:54), and this detail seems unlikely to have been motivated by rhetorical or verisimilitudinal interests. It adds nothing to the story, either symbolically or rhetorically; it simply is mentioned but not developed.

Perhaps the most vivid archaeological details in John are connected with

---

29. On the trans-Jordan ministry of Jesus, John's and Mark's accounts corroborate each other, although John's account presents the visit with a greater sense of realism. Upon an uneven reception at the Feast of Dedication (Jn 10:22), Jesus returns to the original site of John's baptism, continues to minister there, and many believe in him, acknowledging his ministry's supersession of the Baptist's.

30. See Anderson, "John and Mark," pp. 180-85, for an argument regarding John's augmentation of Mark.

31. Incidentally, a large home with a Roman bath has been discovered in Capernaum, adjacent to the impressive synagogue site. While the synagogue is second century C.E., the present ruins were probably constructed on the earlier synagogue that had been destroyed by the Romans in the middle-late first century C.E.

32. John distinctively portrays Jesus' ministry in Samaria, and this could not have been a feature derived from the Synoptics. Mark makes no mention of Samaria or Samaritans, Matthew's Jesus instructs his disciples *not* to visit any village in Samaria (Mt 10:5), and Luke describes an unfelicitous visit by James and John where the Jerusalem-bound Jesus and his band were unwelcome (Lk 9:52-56). [See Zangenberg's chapter in the present volume. — JHC.]

Jesus' five visits to Jerusalem. They are described in graphic terms and refer to specific features rather than general ones. Jesus traveled "up to" Jerusalem's Temple courts for the Passover (2:13); he went "up to Jerusalem" for an unnamed Jewish feast to a pool named "Bethzatha," and particular knowledge of the site is mentioned. The Johannine tradition locates this pool near the Sheep Gate in Jerusalem, and the detail that it is surrounded by five covered colonnades (5:1-2) has been verified by recent archaeological findings. Jerusalem's details are portrayed in vivid and graphic ways during the early part of Jesus' ministry, and in this respect John differs radically from the Synoptic presentation.

While the Jewish feast of Jn 5 is left unnamed, the Feast of Tabernacles is explicitly described in Jn 7–8. Jesus apparently waited until the middle of the feast to go up to the Temple courts to teach (7:14), and part of the discussion gravitated toward his having healed the paralytic on the Sabbath earlier (7:23). On the last day of the feast he continued speaking publicly and did so in the treasury area of the Temple (8:20). Upon fierce engagements with the Judean religious leaders over his authority, Jesus' claims to authentication were experienced as blasphemy, and they picked up stones to kill him (the standard penalty for blasphemy; see Lev 24:14-16), whereupon Jesus left the Temple area, escaping danger (Jn 8:59). Within the same region, the story of the blind man picks up, and after Jesus placed mud over his eyes (having made the mud with spittle), he is told to wash in the pool of Siloam, a site confirmed by archaeological investigation (9:7). At the Feast of Dedication in Jerusalem, Jesus is described as walking in the Temple area in Solomon's Colonnade (10:22-23), another site confirmed by archaeological discovery. Likewise, the middle part of Jesus' ministry in John is remarkably different from its Synoptic counterparts in that events in, and descriptions of, Jerusalem are vivid and extensive.

After the Last Supper, Jesus and his disciples crossed the brook of Kidron and entered the garden there (18:1), and this topographical presentation is entirely accurate. The way one would have gone to the Garden of Gethsemane or the Mount of Olives involved crossing that wadi. John also includes amazingly vivid information associated with the trial of Jesus — content found nowhere else in the Gospel narratives. Because he was known to the high priest (18:15), the "other" disciple (but not Peter) was allowed to enter the courtyard of the high priest, and describing who was inside and outside the gate sets the stage for Peter's first denial (18:16-18). In the trial before the high priest, Jesus said he spoke openly in the synagogue and the Temple, "where all the Judeans gathered" (18:20), and Jesus was led from Annas to Caiaphas to the Praetorium, where Pilate met with the Jewish leaders outside — apparently honoring their religious convictions against defilement (18:28-29). Having gone inside and outside several times, Pilate came out and sat on a juridical seat, in Hebrew called *Gabbatha* (a term not actually translated into Greek; rather, the appellative name of the site in Aramaic, meaning "hill/ridge of the house" or perhaps "the palace mound"), on a site referred to in Greek as *Lithostrōton* (19:13), the stone pavement. Jesus then carried his cross to the Place of the Skull, which in Hebrew was called *Golgotha* (19:17), and the location of the crucifixion is mentioned as being near (and therefore outside) the city — a detail unique to John among the Gospels (19:20; although see Heb 13:12 for a more explicit reference). Knowledge of the surrounding area is suggested by the reference to the place Jesus was crucified having been near a garden and a new tomb in which no one had been buried (Jn 19:41). When Mary Magdalene arrived at the tomb, she saw that the stone had been removed from the tomb, and she later announced the resurrection of Jesus to the disciples (20:1, 18).

In these many references the Johannine narrator draws on knowledge of Galilean and Judean topography in ways that could not possibly have been concocted without some degree of familiarity. It is also true that familiarity could have originated from other sources or reports, but as the evidence for such hypotheses is lacking, a more plausible inference is that the Johannine tradition did have a considerable degree of origination in at least some sort of firsthand Palestinian experience. Once again, the judgment of Albright and others is confirmed regarding John and archaeological material.

4. Aspects of Spatiality and Topographical Incidentals

In addition to direct archaeological and topographical references, John has many spatial references and allusions to incidental physical realities within the ministry of Jesus. For instance, explicit distances are reported estimating how far one thing or event was from another. Bethany is described (accurately) as being fifteen stadia (about two miles) from Jerusalem (11:18), and particular distances to the shore are mentioned twice. When the disciples set off rowing across the lake to Capernaum, in contrast to the Markan general reference (the middle of the lake), the distance they had rowed was reported as twenty-five or thirty stadia (Jn 6:17-19) when Jesus appeared to them. Given that the lake is about seven miles across, this reference to three or four miles is not too far from the target. After the disciples had returned to their familiar fishing work, the boat was reported as about two hundred *pēchōn* (about one hundred yards) from the shore when they beheld postresurrection Jesus on the shore (21:8-9). These specific spatial references are unique to John among the Gospels.

In less direct ways, spatial uses of *anabainō* ("ascend" or "go up") and *katabainō* ("descend" or "go down") appear as topographical incidentals in

John. Jesus and the disciples "went up to" Jerusalem (2:13; 5:1; 7:8, 10; 11:55; 12:20), Jesus "ascended to" the Temple (7:14), and Peter "came up" out of the water into the boat (21:11). Conversely, Jesus and his disciples "descended to" Capernaum (2:12; 4:47, 49), the paralytic spoke of "descending into" the water (5:7), and the disciples "climbed down into" the boat (6:16). For the one who has traveled in Israel, elevation plays a major role in the experience of travel. As the way to Jerusalem would literally have involved climbing uphill, and traveling to Capernaum would always have involved going downhill, these incidental references to elevation betray the same sort of familiarity as measured references to spatiality. In that sense, spatial and topographic references appear to be used with knowing intentionality in John.

Other incidental topographical references make themselves manifest in John, suggesting familiarity with particular places featured in the narrative. For instance, the reference to there being plenty of water in Aenon near Salim functions to explain why John was baptizing there rather than the Jordan (3:23). The report of Jesus' visit to Jacob's well (the one Jacob had given to Joseph, his son) in Sychar of Samaria includes the incidental note that the well was deep, making it difficult to procure water, and the contact with the Samaritan woman is explained by Jesus' having had to go through Samaria on the most direct route between Jerusalem and Galilee (4:5). Within that discussion, knowledge of Samaritan worship conventions is demonstrated, and a universalizing point is made as a reconciling of northern and southern Semitic cousins. Neither the mountain of Samaria (Gerizim) nor Jerusalem is the credited place of worship (4:19-24); rather, worship must be in Spirit and in Truth. The Roman name is given for the Sea of Galilee, that is, "of Tiberias" (6:1; 21:1), and after the feeding of the multitude, Jesus fled again to the mountain alone (6:15). He was later found on the other side of the lake (6:25) by the crowd, which had crisscrossed the lake in boats, coming from the town of Tiberias, looking for Jesus. A reference is then made about the Bread of Life discourse having been delivered at the synagogue of Capernaum (6:59), and even some of Jesus' followers departed and followed him no longer (6:66). Lazarus's tomb is described as a cave with a stone lying in front of it (11:38), and after the ambivalent reception of the raising of Lazarus Jesus withdrew to the wilderness area near the village of Ephraim and remained there with his disciples (11:54). The location of the anointing was the home of Lazarus and his sisters (12:1-8), and the crowd that had come for the (Passover) feast met Jesus on his way to Jerusalem (12:12).

In these and other ways, incidental asides further suggest familiarity with the places and sites in which the events during the ministry of Jesus are purported to have taken place. One might indeed have known of Palestinian geography from afar and might have thrown in names of places in realistic-sounding ways, but the incidental references to the terrain of Jerusalem and the Temple area, the water in Aenon near Salim, the depth of Jacob's well, needing to pass through Samaria on the way to and from Jerusalem, and having to go "down to" Capernaum all give the sense of firsthand familiarity with the topography being described. As a subtle aspect of historiography, these incidentals and spatial references to places and their descriptions may be more telling than information that is more broadly known. The very fact of their indirect character makes it more difficult to imagine their having been concocted for ulterior reasons.

5. Aspects of Personal Familiarity

Another kind of familiarity implies knowledge of personal relationships, even connecting people with the places from which they hailed. Philip, Andrew, and Peter were from the town of *Bethsaida* (1:44; 12:20-21), and the present-day Bethsaida archaeological site on the north side of the Sea of Galilee shows evidence of fishing implements in it. Mentioned only in John is Nathanael, an authentic *Israelite* in whom there is nothing false, whom Jesus saw (and "knew") under a fig tree (1:45-48). In 21:2 it is mentioned that Nathanael hailed from *Cana* of Galilee. No explicit connection is made, though, between the encounter with Nathanael at the end of Jn 1 and the wedding of Cana at the beginning of Jn 2. In contrast to the authenticity of the Israelite Nathanael, the only southern disciple — Judas son of Simon — was mentioned as being from *Kerioth* in Judea (6:71; 12:4; 13:2). Pains are also taken by the editor to clarify that another Judas was *not* Iscariot, so as not to be confused later with the traitor (14:22). During the debate with the *Ioudaioi,* Jerusalem leaders declare their firm conviction that Christ would not come from the northern region of *Galilee,* but from Bethlehem, the city of David (7:41-52). *Bethany* is mentioned as the home of Mary, Martha, and Lazarus (11:1, 18; 12:1), and the one sought by the soldiers was none other than "Jesus of *Nazareth*" (18:7). During the crucifixion and after the resurrection, Mary of *Magdala* features prominently (19:25-26; 20:1; 18), and the man named Joseph, who provided a tomb for Jesus and who requested the body of the Lord, is identified by his place of origin: *Arimathea* (19:38). Thus, many people are identified by their geographic place of origin in John.

A second kind of personal familiarity in John relates to particular knowledge of people and their situations. This feature is especially vivid regarding Jesus' followers within his immediate band. *Andrew* (1:40, 44; 6:8; 12:22) is described distinctively in John as the one brother of Peter. *Nathanael* is mentioned only in John and is declared by Jesus to be an Israelite in whom there is no deceit (1:45-49; 21:2). *Philip* is featured more prominently in John than in all the other Gospels combined (1:43-46, 48; 6:5, 7; 12:21, 22; 14:8, 9). *Thomas* (11:16; 14:5; 20:24, 26-29; 21:2) is given the nickname *Didymos* (the Greek word for "twin," parallel to the Hebrew word for twin underlying the name "Thomas"; 11:16; 20:24; 21:2). While they are not mentioned by name, *"those of Zebedee"* are mentioned only in the last scene (21:2). The Aramaic word for rock — *Cephas* — is added to the Greek word for rock — *Petros* — with reference to *Simon's* appellative (1:42), and Peter (1:40, 44; 6:8, 68; 13:6, 9, 24, 36, 37; 18:10, 11, 15-18, 25-27; 20:2-4, 6; 21:2, 3, 7, 11, 15, 17, 20, 21) is identified as the son of a man named *Jonas* (1:42; 21:15-17). *Judas* is portrayed in characteristically negative light in John (6:71; 12:4; 13:2, 26, 29; 18:2, 3, 5), and his role as a keeper of the money (the holder of the money bag, into which he occasionally dipped) is contributed to the narrative as a reason for the disciples misunderstanding why he left the supper when he did. Also, upon the mention of *another disciple named Judas,* the main point to be made is that he was *not* Judas Iscariot, the one who betrayed the Lord (6:71; 12:4; 13:2, 26; 14:22). Two unnamed disciples are mentioned in John (1:35, 37; 21:2), and a singular unnamed disciple is also noted (18:15, 16; 20:3, 4, 8). The anonymous *Beloved Disciple* features prominently and climactically in the Johannine narrative (13:23; 19:26, 27; 20:2; 21:24). It is he who leaned against the breast of Jesus at the Last Supper, who alone among the Twelve was present at the crucifixion and to whom Jesus entrusted the care of his mother, who arrived at the empty tomb with Peter (allowing him to enter first), who pointed out the resurrected Lord to Peter on the lakeshore, and it is he who is credited with being the authorial source of the Johannine tradition.

The followers of Jesus are thus described with a great deal of personal familiarity. Their interests and foibles are drawn into the narrative as explanations regarding why some things turned out the way they did.

Beyond the immediate band of Jesus' disciples, other persons are also described with special familiarity in John. One of the interesting facts about these aspects of connectedness is that some of them cluster around leading persons and family groups. Most distinctively, the family circle of the high priest features prominently in John. *Annas* (18:13, 24) is singled out as *the father-in-law of Caiaphas,* the high priest that year (11:49; 18:13, 14, 24, 28), and the trial interviews and courtyard scenes are portrayed as happening in their homes. Uniquely in John, the servant of the high priest is mentioned by name, *Malchus,* and not only is it specified that this was the one whose ear was cut off (by *Peter* — another detail unique to John; 18:10), but the courtyard scene identifies the third fireside questioner of Peter as *a relative of the man whose ear Peter had severed* (18:26). These familiarities with otherwise unmotivated connec-

607

tions contribute to the plausibility that the *"other disciple"* may indeed have been known to the high priest, as asserted in 18:15-16. Even that comment serves to explain an odd detail: one disciple was admitted to the courtyard, but Peter had to wait by the gate until the other disciple was able to convince a servant girl (Peter's first questioner) to let him inside. This sequence of events does little to further the plot, and it seems unlikely to have been contributed as a factor of literary interests.

Regarding Jesus' family, *Jesus' brothers* are described as *not* believing in him (an odd detail to have concocted; 7:3, 5, 10), *Joseph* is referred to as the acknowledged father of Jesus (1:45; 6:42), and while *the mother of Jesus* is described as playing roles in two narratives, she is not mentioned by name (2:3; 19:25).[33] The *family of Lazarus* is also given special prominence in John, and both the final miracle and the anointing of Jesus in their house feature these bonds of connectedness. *Lazarus* is described as a close friend whom Jesus loved (11:1, 2, 5, 11, 14, 43; 12:1, 2, 9, 10, 17), and it is also emphasized that Jesus loved his sisters *Mary* (11:1, 2, 19, 20, 28, 31, 32, 45; 12:3) and *Martha* (11:1, 19, 20, 21, 24, 30, 39; 12:2). *John the Baptist and his circle* also play major roles in the pointing out of Jesus in John (1:6-8, 15, 19-35; 3:22-30), and *the followers of Jesus* are likewise described as gathering in familial ways before and after the crucifixion. Special prominence, for instance, is given *Mary Magdalene,* as she is not only the first to encounter the risen Lord (19:25; 20:1, 18), but also shares her witness with the others as *the apostle to the apostles.*

Beyond these familial circles, other figures are featured with special familiarity in John. While *Nicodemus* comes to Jesus by night (3:1, 4, 9; 7:50; 19:39), he is presented as assisting in the preparation of Jesus for his burial, and he also lends aid to *Joseph of Arimathea* (19:38), the one who generously donated the unused tomb and the one who requested the body of Jesus from Pilate. *Barabbas* is described as a thief (18:40), and of course, *Pilate* is described dramatically as "the impotent potentate" at the trial scene (18:29, 31, 33, 35, 37, 38; 19:1, 4, 6, 8, 10, 12, 13, 15, 19, 21, 22, 31, 38). In addition, several unnamed actors also are featured in the Johannine narrative, and these include *the steward and the servants* at the wedding miracle (2:7-10), *the Roman official and his son who was sick* in Capernaum (4:46-53), *an unnamed boy* who contributed his lunch (6:9), and *the Greeks who come to Jerusalem* to see Jesus (12:20-22). More promi-

---

33. Anonymity here, though, should not be construed to imply nonidentity. If the anonymity of the Beloved Disciple is taken as an indicator that this figure could not have been a known apostle, such as John or Thomas, by extension, the anonymity of "the mother of Jesus" must be taken as a statement *against* her identity as Mary. Neither of these is a sound move; rather, anonymity here, as for the Beloved Disciple, probably implies familiarity and respect rather than a disavowal of identity.

nently, *the woman of Samaria* becomes an effective evangelist to her people (4:7, 9, 11, 15, 17, 19, 21, 25, 27, 28, 39, 42), and *Samaritans, Jerusalemites, Judeans, Galileans, Hellenists,* and *Romans* play significant roles in the unfolding of the Johannine narrative — in addition to the nameless *crowd*.

While some of these features can indeed be explained as narrative devices employed to make the material seem more realistic, and some positive and negative presentation (for instance, the unbelieving crowd, Judas Iscariot, and the Beloved Disciple) is crafted for rhetorical reasons, one cannot claim on the basis of evidence that *all* (or even most) of these aspects of familiarity are devoid of historical or personal knowledge. In fact, the opposite seems implied by the character of these connections. They emerge in the story in ways that are sometimes unmotivated by the context, and aspects of relationality and personal familiarity get introduced to the narrative in ways that seem to "explain" unusual turns of events. Sometimes, however, their introduction adds very little to the story, and the only explanation is that the writer or narrator simply included a detail that for whatever reason appears to have borne more significance for the writer or narrator than the reader or hearer. For these reasons, Johannine aspects of personal familiarity fit better within the canons of traditional narration than fictive imagination. They may even reflect a degree of Johannine historicity, idiosyncratic as they may be.

6. Chronological References in John

While time is developed "kairotically" in John, it is also used chronologically in ways that imply intentionality. While the coming of the "hour" of Jesus is used about his glorification (2:4; 4:21, 23; 5:25, 28; 7:30; 8:20; 12:23, 27; 13:1; 16:21, 25, 32; 17:1), and while the climactic "hour" will have come for the disciples in the near future (11:9; 16:2, 4), *hōra* is also used in explicitly chronological ways in John. Jesus called his first disciples at the "tenth hour," suggesting the end of the day when finding somewhere to spend the night would have been a concern (1:39). Jesus met the woman at the well at the "sixth hour," obviously a noontime event during the heat of the day (4:6). Jesus healed the Roman official's son from afar at the "seventh hour," a specific time that was remembered as the coincidence of Jesus' word and the boy's recovery (4:52-53, although seven is also used symbolically at times). The crucifixion is also mentioned as taking place at the "sixth hour," locating the event in the middle of the day (19:14),[34] and upon the

---

34. Obviously, these numerological references could have denoted symbolic references: tenth could have implied the Ten Commandments, and six could have implied one short of a

entrustment of the mother of Jesus to the Beloved Disciple, things changed for them "from that time on" (19:27). Also, the early part of the day is mentioned three times in John (18:28; 20:1; 21:4), and the evening or darkness is mentioned four times (3:2; 6:16; 13:30; 20:19). In these ways the hour or the time of day is used both figuratively and chronologically in John, apparently with intentionality in both ways.

In the same way, "day" is used about a season of time in John (8:56; 9:4; 11:9, 53; 12:7; 19:31), and while it is at times used eschatologically (the "last" day; 6:39, 40, 44, 54; 11:24; 12:48), it also is used with apparent chronological intentionality. In general terms, the passing of several days is mentioned (2:12), and an emphasis is made on the *same* day wherein several events occurred (5:9; 20:19). More frequently, however, the explicit numeration of days is also used, and the association appears to be a chronological one. The wedding in Cana was on the third day (suggesting a brisk walk indeed if Jesus and his disciples were implied to be traveling from the south to Cana of Galilee; 2:1); the "temple" of Jesus' body would be raised up in three days (2:19-20); Jesus remained in Samaria two days after the encounter with the Samaritan woman (4:40, 43); and because he waited for two days before traveling to Bethany (11:6), Lazarus had been dead for four days by the time he arrived (11:17). The anointing of Jesus was reported to have taken place six days before the Passover (12:1), and Jesus is reported to have appeared to his disciples eight days after his earlier appearances (20:26).[35] Indeed, studies of numerology suggest symbolic meanings of numbers — a clear matter in the three days of 2:19-20 — but symbolic use does not imply a different timetable for the duration of Jesus' being in the tomb, nor does it prove that other time references were fictive. In these ways days are used generally and eschatologically in John, but they most commonly appear to be used with reference to chronological knowledge.

As a measure of time, the year is not explicitly used symbolically in John, although some scholars will attempt to make connections between numbers and symbolic associations. This being the case, particular years are mentioned (11:49, 51; 18:13), and the duration of time is several times measured in years.

---

perfect seven or half of the complete number twelve. It is a fact, however, that when there is nothing in the text to suggest an embellished symbolization of the numbers, such inferences must remain in the category of fanciful exegesis.

35. Again, as with hours, the numbers of days get developed symbolically in John, especially tied to days of creation in Gen 1–2 and other references to days in Hebrew Scripture. There is little if any value to such moves, however, given that commenting on the significance of the days is left undeveloped in the Johannine narrative. The inference must be made as a factor of the interpreter's ingenuity, rather than an apparent rhetorical device employed by the Evangelist.

The amount of time it has taken to rebuild the Temple is mentioned in passing as forty-six years (2:20, a dating that would locate the beginning of Jesus' ministry around 27 C.E.); the paralytic had been ill for thirty-eight years (a possible but unlikely reference to the thirty-eight years Israel had wandered in the wilderness; 5:5); and the age of Jesus is described as not yet fifty (not necessarily a claim that he *was* fifty; 8:57). Besides the many references to particular feasts in Jerusalem, the time of year is mentioned, or at least alluded to, in John. The mentioning of much grass at the feeding locates the event during the springtime (6:10), and the Feast of Dedication includes a mention of the wintertime setting in which it would have taken place (10:22). Indeed, references to time are used symbolically in John, but it would be an inexcusable mistake to assume that *none* of John's references to time intended to further some aspect of chronological knowledge. This is not to claim they were accurate, although many seem as though they could have been. The point is to assert that most claims of either their ahistoricity or their error are either fanciful or do not square with the character of the material. They are possibilities, but they fall short of critical demonstration.

7. The Fact of Empirical Detail in John

While some of the Johannine details are used rhetorically to further a point being made by the narrator, most of John's details do not appear to function in that way. They simply appear to reflect empirically derived details. In that sense they bear the closest resemblance to some of the material in Mark, perhaps reflecting the sort of material connected to oral traditions in contrast to the redacted uses of written Mark by Matthew and Luke. This is a highly important fact. It is often assumed that John's illustrative detail was added by a second-hand narrator as a means of "historicizing" the drama — the sort of thing that is assumed to have been common practice among ancient historians.[36]

---

36. While Philostratus's *Life of Apollonius* is often cited as the prime example, it cannot be assumed that there is no historical or firsthand information present in this narrative, or in all others regarding the heroic figure of Apollonius of Tyana. Indeed, much of the memory of Apollonius appears legendary and even embellished, but this likelihood does not in itself establish an alternative explanation for all reports about him. Likewise, to require all graphic detail in ancient historical narrative to have been a factor of "historicized dramatizing" supposedly would prove that Josephus's illustrative account of his own life must have been added fictively. Once again, the logic here is flawed. An even greater problem with attributing John's illustrative detail to "historicizing" additions — similar to contemporary conventions — is that the two closest examples, Matthew and Luke in their uses of Mark, demonstrate the exact

In addition to the many sensorily associated details mentioned above are these: Jesus is reported to have seen Nathanael under the fig tree (1:48); six ritual purification jars made out of stone are described as holding two or three *metrētas* of water each (2:6); Jesus is described as driving the animals out of the Temple area with a whip he had made out of cords (2:15); even 200 denarii would be insufficient to buy enough food to feed the multitude (6:7); the place where the 5,000 men were reclining for the feeding is described as having "much grass" (6:10); the food distributed and eaten is described as "barley loaves" (6:9-13) and *opsarion* (a prepared sort of fish rather than raw fish; 6:9, 11; 21:9, 10, 13) numbering five and two respectively; stones are picked up to kill Jesus (the prescribed punishment for blasphemy in the Torah; 8:59); Jesus made mud out of spittle and applied it to the blind man's eyes (9:6-15); worry over the opening of the tomb is associated with a bad odor (11:39); Lazarus emerged from the tomb with his hands and feet wrapped in strips of linen and with his face covered by a cloth (11:44); when the nard was prepared for the anointing of Jesus, its fragrance filled the house (12:3), and the high value of the perfume, described as worth 300 denarii, even raised an objection from Judas (12:5); Jesus was welcomed on his way into Jerusalem by a crowd waving palm branches (12:13); before washing his disciples' feet Jesus put on the clothes of a servant (13:4f.); not only was it night when Judas departed (13:30), but the soldiers and guards are described as bringing lanterns and torches to the garden for the arrest of Jesus (18:3); it was the *right* ear of the servant "Malchus" that was severed by Peter (18:10); the chilly temperature in the high priest's courtyard accounted for servants and disciples alike gathering to warm themselves around a charcoal fire (18:18); the sound of the cock's crowing was heard immediately after Peter's third denial (18:27); a crown of thorns was placed on Jesus' head by the soldiers, and they threw a purple robe around him (19:2, 5); the inscription ordered by Pilate was written in Hebrew, Latin, and Greek (19:20); Jesus was crucified between two men by four soldiers (19:18, 23); Jesus' clothing was divided into fourths and taken by the soldiers (19:23), but the seamless tunic of Jesus, woven from top to bottom in a single piece, was not divided, but the soldiers cast lots for it (19:23-24); a hyssop stick was used to lift a sponge dipped in a jar of sour vinegar to Jesus, which he drank (19:29-30); from the side of Jesus flowed water and blood (19:34-35); the spices are described as being a mixture of myrrh and aloes of about 100 *litras* in weight (19:39); Mary Magdalene came to the tomb

---

opposite! Matthew and Luke add units of tradition, but overall they omit names of persons and places and other illustrative details (see Anderson, *Christology*, pp. 185-92). This material is most prevalent in Mark and John, suggesting oral tradition in contrast to such secondary redactions as Matthew and Luke.

on the first day of the week early, while it was still dark, and found the stone had been removed from the tomb (20:1); an unnamed disciple and Peter arrived at the tomb and looked into it, seeing both the strips of linen cloth lying in one area and the headcloth folded up and located separately (20:5-7); it was in fear and behind closed doors that the disciples had gathered before the Lord appeared to them (20:19, 26); Thomas looked at the flesh wounds of Jesus (20:25-27); the disciples were instructed by Jesus to cast their nets on the right side of the boat (21:6); before jumping into the water, naked Peter threw on his coat (21:7); bread and fish were being cooked on a charcoal fire by Jesus on the shore (21:9); and the disciples' nets were not broken despite the number of large fish being as high as 153 (21:11).

As the above analysis suggests, John's narrative exhibits aspects of historicity in a variety of ways, not just one or two. Indeed, this may be one of the reasons for disagreements among scholars as to the historicity of the Johannine witness. Because one part of John's narrative fails to measure up to a particular mode of historicity, it is too easily assumed that none of it is historical. This is known as the all-or-none fallacy, which is equally problematic in whatever direction it is leveled. Another fallacy involves assuming that all aspects of historicity within a narrative need to be a particular form of historicity for them to be considered authentic. As the critical scholar distinguishes one aspect of John's historicity from another, each can be interpreted accordingly and thus more adequately. In that sense, asking *how* a narrative might be true is pivotal for being able to ascertain *whether* it might be true. The failure of scholars to make such distinctions is a leading reason for confusion and disagreement among them. Again, that some of the above examples might appear questionable from a blunt historicity standpoint does not mean that none of the above details is true, or that an alternative presentation of Jesus deserves to displace the Johannine automatically.[37] Discerning the particular aspects of John's historicity allows one's judgments to be more nuanced and measured — and one's claims to be more modest — and thus less likely to be false. Of course, the central importance of this issue is the degree to which our understanding of Jesus is enhanced by a clearer understanding of John and archaeology. Implications, then, follow accordingly.

---

37. Observe, for instance, the way M. Casey Maurice (*Is John's Gospel True?* [London: Routledge, 1996]) seizes upon aspects of John's differences with the Synoptics, claiming they are "inaccurate," thus leading to his central charge that John's renderings of Jesus (and especially John's christological claims) are "profoundly untrue." This case is hardly less apologetic than Craig Blomberg's defense of John's "historical reliability" (*The Historical Reliability of John's Gospel: Issues and Commentary* [Downers Grove, Ill.: InterVarsity, 2002]). The point here is that overstated claims for and against particular aspects of John's historicity do not necessarily apply to the others; each must be assessed on its own terms and weighed accordingly.

Implications for Archaeology and Jesus Research

The above analysis demonstrates that the bases for excluding the Gospel of John from the canons of historicity — and therefore from Jesus studies — are not as compelling as the prevalent opinion among modern biblical scholars has assumed. Conversely, neither is the above analysis intended to argue that everything in John is the result of eyewitness contact with Jesus; much of it shows evidence of later reflection, and it probably was the last of the canonical Gospels to be finalized (likely around 100 C.E.). It is also plausible that much of John's material came from secondhand or thirdhand accounts, rather than firsthand ones, despite the apparent presence of ample firsthand material.[38] What the above study does demonstrate, however, is that the Gospel of John is far closer to the historical Jesus than most scholars have claimed or thought for almost a century. Reasons for challenging John's historicity are often good ones, given John's theological interests, spiritualized character, and variance from the Synoptics, but a verdict of radical and pervasive ahistoricity is overreaching and wrong. While John's christological and spiritual interests are clear, it cannot be claimed now that the Evangelist's "head was in the stars" with topography and chronology being "the least of the author's concerns." Much of John's tradition appears authentic and even superior to the presentations of Jesus in the Synoptics, and this has extensive implications for Jesus studies.

Because John deserves to be considered within the mix of historical traditions, this must have an impact on historical Jesus studies. A more nuanced and balanced approach than assuming three "historical" Gospels versus a maverick "spiritual" Gospel might view the insight of Clement differently. Seeing John's as a "spiritual Gospel" might imply spirituality of insight rather than aloofness, just as the "bodily" aspect of the Synoptic witness might imply for Clement the outward structure of Jesus' ministry rather than facticity proper.[39] Indeed, both the Synoptics and John were *spiritual and corporal* in their interests, so their modernistic relegation in one direction to the exclusion of another is unsupported by the evidence and probably miscomprehends Clement's point to begin with. A more

38. Sturch, in "The Alleged Eyewitness Material in the Fourth Gospel," does outline several kinds of material that may have come from conjecture or secondhand knowledge, although suggesting a possibility is far short of demonstrating a likelihood — let alone a certainty.

39. In Hans Küng's impressive treatment of the implications of Jesus studies for Christian faith (*On Being a Christian* [New York: Pocket Books, 1966]), he reminds us that truth is beyond mere "facticity" (pp. 415-16). A modernistic reading of Clement's dictum might equate *sōmatika* with "facts" and therefore "truth," but this is likely a flawed reading of Clement. He might have been equating "truth" with the spiritual character of John, alluding to John's veracity rather than its distance from reality.

nuanced approach to the Synoptic and Johannine presentations of Jesus might thus involve a fresh consideration of the Markan and Johannine perspectives, appreciating the particular historical and spiritual points they make. As bi-optic presentations of Jesus' ministry, both perspectives deserve renewed critical consideration in performing state-of-the-art investigations of the historical ministry of Jesus. The fallacy is to primatize one perspective to the exclusion of the other.

This being the case, several implications for archaeology and Jesus studies follow. First, archaeological and topographical content in John should be taken seriously by scientific archaeologists. A priori claims to a Gospel's historicity or ahistoricity should be left on the shelf in deference to the first-order investigations that archaeological studies provide. When this is done, the evidence will speak for itself. Thus, the full benefit of archaeological information in John and the Synoptics may be valued and employed fully on its own merits instead of being marginalized due to preconceived grids of exclusion, which themselves are less than established.

Second, it also could well be that the archaeological material presented in John will be of great value if more nuanced means of approaching John's relation to the Synoptic traditions are employed.[40] In that sense, John's "independence" should be understood as *autonomy and nondependence* rather than isolation, and "influence" should be understood as possibly going both ways, thus involving *interfluence and engagement* rather than literary borrowing only. This will allow more measured judgments between the traditions, allowing scholars to appreciate ways that preferences for particular Synoptic and Johannine presentations of Jesus might be critically ascertained.

Third, aspects of the Synoptic renderings of Jesus' ministry more likely to be historically reliable include the following: (a) Jesus' teachings about the kingdom of God in parables probably do represent a clearer portrait of the teaching ministry of Jesus than the more christological "I Am" sayings of John. The latter reflect the Evangelist's preaching and teaching about Jesus in his own paraphrastic forms. (b) Jesus' use of short, pithy sayings illustrating the wisdom and way of the kingdom in the Synoptics is also probably more characteristic of his actual teaching ministry than the more interpretive Johannine discourses, although John still contains at least eighty of these pithy sayings. (c) Jesus' healing and exorcising ministries and his sending out his disciples to do the same, as presented in the Synoptics, seem authentic. (d) Jesus' confronting of religious authorities and cleansing the Temple as prophetic challenging of purity laws restricting access to God in the Synoptics indeed seem authentic and worth building on. (e) Jesus'

---

40. See Anderson, "John and Mark — the Bi-Optic Gospels" and "Interfluential, Formative, and Dialectical."

dining with "sinners" and healings on the Sabbath were intended as provocations intended to call attention to the renewal of Israel's covenant with God. (f) Jesus' extolling the love of God and love for others as fulfillments of the Law is indeed worth building on in understanding the intentional mission of Jesus. (g) Jesus' death and appearances as narrated in postresurrection consciousness, as represented in the Synoptics, have a fair amount of reliability to them. In at least these ways, the presentations of Jesus in the Synoptics are worthy material for constructing an understanding of the historical Jesus and his mission.

Fourth, aspects of the Johannine rendering of Jesus' ministry more likely to be historically reliable include the following: (a) Jesus' relationship with John the Baptizer in declaring the prolific availability of purification contributes significant insights for understanding the ministries of John and of Jesus. (b) Jesus' early cleansing of the Temple as an inaugural prophetic sign designed to get the attention of religious authorities and others regarding his message, explaining opposition to Jesus throughout his ministry, is worthy of critical consideration. (c) Jesus' ministry over more than one year, allowing the movement to build momentum, seems more plausible than the single-year ministry apparent in the Synoptics. (d) Jesus' public ministry beginning in settings other than the home of Simon Peter's mother-in-law and vicinities suggests a more public inauguration of his ministry as a complement to Mk 1. (e) Jesus' going to and from Jerusalem, as most observant Jews would have done in the first century C.E., and his performing signs in the south as well as the north, seem more plausible than the Synoptic presentations of a single visit to Jerusalem and an exclusively Galilean ministry. (f) Jesus' last supper being a common meal rather than a Passover meal seems more likely, as the seder references in the Synoptics are readily explicable as representing emerging Christian practice rather than historicity proper. (g) Jesus' teaching about the life of the Spirit and unmediated access to God's leading and love matches the view of the charismatic and itinerant teacher of the Synoptics, despite being couched in a Johannine paraphrase. In these ways at least, John's material contributes significantly to our understandings of the historical Jesus and his ministry.

Finally, considering different aspects of John's historicity (and likewise of John's literary, spiritual, and theological interests) prevents one from making sweeping generalizations regarding the epistemological character of Gospel material. Indeed, John has a great deal of rhetorical material and apologetic interest,[41] but this does not mean that such features can account for the episte-

41. Consider the dialogical modes of revelation and rhetoric (Anderson, *Christology*, pp. 104-7, 194-240, 259-63) and the rhetorical thrust of the Fourth Gospel (Anderson, *Navigating the Living Waters of the Gospel of John*).

Figure 74. Caesarea Maritima, Roman aqueduct built by Herod the Great. The Mediterranean Sea is on the left.

Courtesy J. H. Charlesworth

mological origin of all of its material. Aspects of historicity include: at least some sensorily derived firsthand content, evidence of complementarity to Mark, attempts to connect Hellenistic audiences with earlier Palestinian and Jewish aspects of Jesus' ministry, reflections of the evolving history of the Johannine situation,[42] archaeological and topographical content, spatial and topographical incidentals, aspects of personal and relational familiarity, chronological and sequential references, and the fact of empirical data in John. In at least these ways, aspects of historicity in John have extensive implications for performing state-of-the-art investigations of Jesus, and they likewise cast invaluable light on the character, origin, and development of the Johannine tradition itself.

While interpreting John's christological and theological interests remains a historic source of controversy, neither historicity nor ahistoricity should be confused with theology proper. Conviction for or against John's christological claims should not drive the acceptance of John's apparently historical material; neither should one's appraisal of the latter determine the former. Like theology, historicity must be explored on its own terms and assessed accordingly — whether this Evangelist had his head "in the stars" or not. Indeed, "practical and mundane considerations" *can also be genuine interests* of those interested in "the spiritual universe" and "eternal realities." The scandal of the Fourth Gospel is that it purports to address *both* poles, while negotiating the tension in between. It is the error of monological interpreters to insist on one pole at the expense of the other — a liability of traditionalistic and critical interpretations of

42. Consider the four crises inferred in a dialogical reading of Jn 6 (Anderson, *The Christology of the Fourth Gospel*); see also Anderson, Outline III in "Matters Johannine — Outlining the Johannine Riddles," in *The Dialogical Autonomy of the Fourth Gospel:* "A Historical Outline of Johannine Christianity — a Longitudinal Consideration of the Johannine Dialectical Situation."

John's historicity alike. While much of John is theological, to claim that all of its content — or even most of it — must be ascribed to canons of ahistoricity and concoction is more than the authentically critical scholar will want to claim. Given the multifarious aspects of John's historicity, this study will indeed have extensive implications for critical investigations of Jesus and archaeology.

Bultmann, Archaeology, and the Historical Jesus

John Painter

My assignment is to discuss *Rudolf Bultmann, archaeology, and the historical Jesus*. Here, in Jerusalem, I imagine the first question to be answered is, "Why Bultmann?" A partial answer would be that Bultmann stands as the outstanding New Testament scholar of the twentieth century. Today, his questions, conclusions, and methods continue to cast a long shadow over all that we do. Nevertheless, Bultmann, archaeology, and the historical Jesus must sound an improbable set of associations.

I think it unlikely that Bultmann was ever involved in an archaeological dig related to his field of research, or that he ever visited Israel and Jerusalem. One line of evidence suggests he might not have been interested in such matters. But if that is the case, it is clearly not because he saw no value in archaeological evidence and the light it can shed on the historical Jesus and the history of early Christianity. From another point of view, fundamental historical data is crucial for his understanding of Jesus.

We need to remember that Bultmann died on July 30, 1976, less than a month before his ninety-second birthday. He was one whose active years of scholarship were prior to the establishment of the present State of Israel. In those years travel to Palestine was not common and nothing like as easy as now. Bultmann lived in that period of German (Nazi) anti-Semitism that also made travel to Israel difficult for a German in the years immediately following the foundation of Israel. Nevertheless, travel to Israel and archaeological research by Germans were possible in these years.

The Historical Jesus

Recall again Bultmann's stunning claim: "I do indeed think that we can know almost nothing concerning the life and personality of Jesus, since the early Christian sources show no interest in either, are moreover fragmentary and often legendary; and other sources about Jesus do not exist."[1] This quotation has been taken as a rejection of historically established knowledge of Jesus. A closer examination shows that what Bultmann excludes is knowledge of the "life and personality of Jesus." In particular, Bultmann was rejecting the basis of a psychological study of the personality of Jesus. Because the sources ignore this aspect of Jesus' life, the modern scholar can make no progress here.

Secondly, John Macquarrie voiced a concern found throughout English-language critiques of Bultmann. The criticism is that Bultmann's existentialist interpretation of history brackets out "historical factuality."[2] In his reply to Macquarrie, Bultmann wrote:

> Further, Macquarrie objects to my understanding of history. He thinks that my existentialist interpretation of history ignores the factual character of historical events and thus also of the actual history of Jesus. Here I must reply that I do not regard the factual character of history and of Jesus as in any way irrelevant for faith and for theology. I say, rather, Christian faith declares the paradox that an historical event (precisely, Jesus and his history) is at the same time an eschatological occurrence. If the historical fact were stricken out, then the paradox would be abandoned. There is no existentialist interpretation of history at all which ignores the factual occurrence. I can also say that the existentialist interpretation of history attempts to answer the questions that the factual history in which we are entangled poses for us.[3]

Though this specific response was published in 1966, the same criticism of Bultmann remains common in the scholarly literature even today. It could be argued that the criticism remained valid in spite of what Bultmann said and thought. That seems unlikely but not impossible. In evaluating the possibility we need to assess Bultmann's own work. Prior to writing his book *Jesus* (1926) he published his *Die Geschichte der synoptischen Tradition* (1921). In this work he traces the tradition, now found in the Synoptic Gospels, back to its earliest

---

1. R. Bultmann, *Jesus and the Word*, trans. L. P. Smith and E. H. Lantero (London: Scribner, 1958), p. 14.

2. J. Macquarrie, in C. W. Kegley, ed., *Theology of Rudolf Bultmann* (New York: Harper and Row, 1966), pp. 129, 135; see esp. p. 141.

3. R. Bultmann, "Reply," in *Theology of Rudolf Bultmann*, pp. 274-75.

stage represented by the oldest Palestinian community. Even here there is the question of how accurately the earliest community preserved the Jesus tradition. Unlike some scholars, Bultmann was not willing to accept that the earliest tradition accurately preserved the Jesus tradition. Consequently critical criteria are established to identify probable authentic historical tradition preserved by the earliest community. Bultmann treated negatively some of the criteria other scholars found persuasive. Thus if the tradition did not fit a Palestinian context, Bultmann treated it as inauthentic; but fitting a Palestinian context did not demonstrate authenticity because not only Jesus but also the earliest community was Palestinian. Consequently Bultmann found the task of authenticating probable Jesus tradition more complex than did many other scholars.

The development of such criteria is often credited to later scholars who drew on Bultmann's work. One reason for this is that the discussion of such criteria is scattered through his book at points where discussion is relevant rather than gathered together in one place. Another reason is the widespread view that Bultmann rejected the project for which the criteria are designed and the commonly accepted assertion that he was not interested in the historical Jesus. How serious scholars could hold this distorted view when it is refuted so easily is, from one point of view, difficult to understand. For some reason Bultmann provoked strong, emotional reactions from some scholars. Such reactions are not inclined to seek understanding before entering into criticism and refutation. Karl Barth, in his essay "Rudolf Bultmann: An Attempt to Understand Him," noted how frequently Bultmann has had cause to complain about being misunderstood.[4] Why Bultmann provokes such misunderstanding has no simple answer.

An aspect of the answer is to be found in the response of many English-speaking scholars to existentialism. This reaction is thus not exclusively aimed at Bultmann. I remember a research paper delivered by an eminent British professor of philosophy on Sartre in the 1980s. The argument was that Sartre's language, when analyzed, was self-contradictory and his work could not be treated as serious philosophy. At no point in the paper was the question raised concerning the way Sartre used language. It was as if Wittgenstein had not drawn attention to the different ways in which language is used. And it is extraordinary to think that philosophers needed to be reminded of something so obvious.

A common misunderstanding of Bultmann's existential understanding is that it is individualistic and ignores reality outside the individual's consciousness. This blatantly ignores what is fundamental for him, that human life is al-

---

4. Karl Barth, "Rudolf Bultmann: An Attempt to Understand Him," in *Kerygma and Myth: A Theological Debate,* ed. H. W. Bartsch (London: SPCK, 1962), p. 84.

ways in the world and with others.[5] As we have seen, even an interpreter of Bultmann such as John Macquarrie falls into this error, charging Bultmann with bracketing out "historical factuality." Bultmann clearly repudiates the charge and clarifies the relationship of his interpretation to historical factuality. Consequently we should not be surprised to find Bultmann's concern to establish the historical evidence concerning Jesus.

Reference to the "historical Jesus" has more limited value than is often recognized. It is not meaningful to use the term to refer to the person and reality of Jesus as he actually was. This is a more ambitious goal than we are able to achieve. Rather, reference to the historical Jesus concerns what can be known of Jesus, with some degree of probability, on the basis of a critical use of the evidence, the understanding of Jesus established by the critical use of sources. From the historian's (Bultmann's) point of view, such criteria produce only the probability of authenticity. Given that Jesus left no writing from his own hand, and the description of his actions and record of his words come from the hands of others whose relationship to Jesus is unclear, a probable conclusion is significant. Thus Bultmann says, "By the tradition Jesus is named as the bearer of the message; according to the overwhelming probability he really was." Indeed, Bultmann says this is "the overwhelming probability." While this is a comment concerning Jesus as the source of the tradition, that is recognized through a detailed treatment of the various elements each of which is evaluated in terms of probable authenticity. Those elements considered authentic are judged in terms of varying degrees of probability. Thus his book *Jesus* could proceed without detailed critical discussion because this could be found in his *Die Geschichte der synoptischen Tradition.*

If we start at the most general point, Bultmann leaves no doubt that the evidence precludes discussing whether Jesus ever existed. The serious historical question concerns how accurately the oldest Palestinian community preserved the Jesus tradition. Bultmann states:

> Of course the doubt as to whether Jesus really existed is unfounded and not worth refutation. No sane person can doubt that Jesus stands as founder behind the historical movement whose first distinct stage is represented by the oldest Palestinian community. But how far that community preserved an objectively true picture of him and his message is another question. . . . It is precisely this complex of ideas in the oldest layer of the synoptic tradition that is the object of our consideration. It meets us as a fragment of tradition coming

5. See my *Theology as Hermeneutics: Rudolf Bultmann's Interpretation of the History of Jesus* (Sheffield: Almond Press, 1987), chap. 1, esp. pp. 19-27.

to us from the past, and in the examination of it we seek the encounter with history. By the tradition Jesus is named as the bearer of the message; according to the overwhelming probability he really was.[6]

Because of the critical work involved in the identification of Jesus with elements of the tradition found in the earliest layer, Bultmann says: "I see no objection to naming Jesus throughout as the speaker. Whoever prefers to put the name of 'Jesus' always in quotation marks and let it stand as an abbreviation for the historical phenomenon with which we are concerned is free to do so."[7]

Although Bultmann regards as overwhelmingly probable the identification of Jesus as the bearer of the message, he is willing to allow a more skeptical view, that Jesus was the source of a message that reaches us through a process of transmission. The point is that Bultmann recognized the difficulty of distinguishing Jesus from the process of transmission. While Bultmann believed it possible to do this in many cases with a high degree of probability, he sympathized with those who found the task problematic. Certainly he was more on their side than with those who thought they could read off the history of Jesus straightforwardly from the Gospels or from the earliest stratum of the tradition.

The Events of Jesus' Life

Nevertheless, it certainly can be argued that Bultmann pays little attention to the details of Jesus' life. That he had no confidence in the chronologies of the Gospels goes without saying. From his *Formgeschichte* perspective, the individual pericopae were the substance of the tradition. The frameworks were the works of the Evangelists. For the Synoptics, Mark provides the fundamental framework, which Matthew and Luke adapt. John has established an independent framework. But what of the events described in the individual pericopae?

> Hence, with a bit of caution we can say the following concerning Jesus' activity: Characteristic for him are exorcisms, the breach of the Sabbath commandment, the abandonment of ritual purifications, polemic against Jewish legalism, fellowship with outcasts such as publicans and harlots, sympathy for women and children; it can also be seen that Jesus was not an ascetic like John the Baptist, but gladly ate and drank a glass of wine. Perhaps we may

6. Bultmann, *Jesus and the Word*, pp. 17-18.
7. Bultmann, *Jesus and the Word*, p. 18.

Figure 75. Jerusalem
from the Mount
of Olives.

Courtesy of J. H. Charlesworth

add that he called disciples and assembled about himself a small company of
followers — men and women.[8]

This general picture of the activity of Jesus is dependent on isolating the earliest
layer of the tradition and subjecting it to critical scrutiny, excluding from it elements derived from the earliest Christian community. Bultmann, like many
scholars since the work of David Friedrich Strauss, restricted his construction
of the teaching of Jesus to the traditions found in the Synoptics. He specifically
notes that "the Gospel of John cannot be taken into account at all as a source
for the teaching of Jesus, and it is not referred to in this book."[9] His comment is
specific in reference to the teaching of Jesus. Even today most Johannine scholars agree with Bultmann that the teaching of Jesus in John has been radically
reformulated. This observation is supported by the way Jesus, the Evangelist,
and John the Baptist speak the same language in John and the language of the
later discourses of Jesus has much in common with 1 John. Even then we might
allow that fragments of authentic Jesus tradition can be recovered, as C. H.
Dodd argued. Building on Dodd's modest claims, some scholars today assert
that the failure to treat the Johannine tradition is unjustifiable. But the task of
recovery is much more difficult and less productive than in the Synoptics.

Having restricted his discussion to the teaching of Jesus, Bultmann does
not discuss historical elements contained in the Johannine narrative. It is certainly possible that, in some instances, John preserves a more authentic historical perspective than the one derived from Mark. Certainly, most scholars ac-

8. Bultmann, "The Primitive Christian Kerygma and the Historical Jesus," in *The Historical
Jesus and the Kerygmatic Christ*, ed. C. E. Braaten and R. A. Harrisville (New York: Abingdon,
1964), pp. 22-23.

9. Bultmann, *Jesus and the Word*, p. 17.

cept that Jesus' ministry spanned a period of something like three years, implied by John's account of three Passover festivals during it, rather than inside a single year, as implied by Mark. But is John's timetable a result of a concentration on the Jewish festivals rather than evidence of the time span of Jesus' ministry? Certainly the Passover is a significant festival for the early Christian understanding of Jesus' life and mission. Did Jesus eat his final meal with his disciples on the eve of Passover (John) or was it a Passover meal (Mark)? Finally, did Jesus cleanse the Temple at the beginning of his ministry (John), or was it the final offense that led to his arrest, trial, and execution (Mark)? In both of the latter cases arguments can be mounted to show that Mark's treatment suits Mark and John's treatment suits John. It is not possible to make a decision one way or the other with a high degree of probability. Only about the duration of Jesus' ministry do we find a preponderance of agreement with John, and even there it is difficult to show that it might not have been completed in the course of a year. Perhaps the authentic tradition can only be placed into a roughly chronological framework in which we can distinguish clearly the beginning and the end. Consequently, Bultmann treats what we might describe as the characteristic actions of Jesus rather than a sequential narrative of specific events.

Bultmann omits from his list of events, set out above, any reference to the crucifixion of Jesus and the belief in his bodily resurrection. That is not because he questions the historicity of either of these. Rather they are not treated as events *in* Jesus' ministry. Bultmann recognized the resurrection belief of the early Christians. This is evident in his criticism of Paul, who attempted to establish the bodily resurrection of Jesus by appealing to witnesses.[10] Concerning the crucifixion Bultmann wrote:

> Outsiders certainly could not recognize the essentially unpolitical character of both John and Jesus, especially as both aroused considerable popular excitement. Both movements were therefore suppressed quickly by the execution of their leaders. Jesus was crucified by the Roman procurator Pontius Pilate. What role the Jewish authorities, on whom the Christian put the chief blame, actually played is no longer clearly discernible. It is probable that they, as in other cases, worked hand in hand with the Romans in the interest of political tranquillity. At least there can be no doubt that Jesus like other agitators died on the cross as a Messianic prophet.[11]

10. 1 Cor 15:1-11; see his discussion of "Karl Barth, the Resurrection of the Dead" (1926), now in R. Bultmann, *Faith and Understanding*, ed. R. W. Funk, trans. L. P. Smith (Philadelphia: Fortress, 1987), pp. 83-84.

11. Bultmann, *Jesus and the Word*, p. 27.

However little we know of the life of Jesus, if we keep in mind that he was finally crucified as a Messianic agitator, we shall be able to light on the eschatological message to understand the fragmentary accounts of the end of his activity, overgrown as they are by legend. He seems to have entered Jerusalem with a crowd of enthusiastic adherents; all were full of joy and of confidence that now the Kingdom of God was beginning. It was a band like that which the Egyptian prophet attempted to lead to Jerusalem, which was halted and scattered by a division of troops sent by the Procurator Felix to meet it. Jesus entered Jerusalem, and with his followers took possession (as it seems) of the temple, in order to cleanse the holy precincts from all evil in preparation for the coming of the Kingdom.[12]

Here Bultmann obviously follows the Markan order of events leading up to the arrest, trial, and crucifixion of Jesus. It is interesting to note that already in 1926 he treats Jesus in terms consistent with other Jewish movements of the time. Jesus was crucified as a messianic prophet, a messianic agitator. It is notable that Bultmann does not think Jesus claimed to be the Messiah. Clearly he does think that others perceived Jesus as a messianic prophet, a messianic agitator. Given the tentative nature of any claim Jesus might make to be the Messiah in the Synoptic Gospels, it seems unlikely that Jesus made this claim of himself. Besides, there are Jewish texts that suggest that the Messiah remains hidden and does not make the claim himself. Rather, the Messiah is revealed. Any claim to be the Messiah seems to be evidence that the claim is not true.

Thus Bultmann portrays Jesus in terms intelligible to first-century Judaism. From this period on Bultmann portrayed Jesus as a Jewish messianic prophet, intelligible in the context of Jewish movements in the first century. Geza Vermes says (in his lecture in Sydney, July 2000) that the publication of his book with the title *Jesus the Jew* was controversial in 1973. It should be no surprise to learn how controversial this position was in Germany, a position Bultmann continued to defend from 1926.

Jesus as Teacher

All this in a book on the "teaching of Jesus"! More narrative follows where Bultmann tells of Jesus' celebration of a final Passover in the expectation of the imminence of the coming kingdom. What is more, Bultmann specifically asserts that these events provide the key to an understanding of the eschatological

12. Bultmann, *Jesus and the Word*, p. 29.

nature of the teaching of Jesus about the kingdom. From this perspective Bultmann does not seem so far from the reading of E. P. Sanders, though Bultmann describes "the cleansing of the Temple" where Sanders understands the event as a prophetic sign.

Nevertheless, although Bultmann had done the work to establish the nature of Jesus' activity and the actual actions that could be attributed to him, his book is not primarily about the actions of Jesus. That was not because Bultmann was unable to give an account of the events. Rather he considered that Jesus' purpose and ministry are best understood in his teaching.

> In the case of those who like Jesus have worked through the medium of *word,* what they purposed can be reproduced only as a group of sayings, of ideas — as *teaching.* . . . For his purpose can be comprehended only as teaching. . . . The subject of this book is, as I have said, not the life or the personality of Jesus, but only his teaching, his message. Little as we know of his life and personality, we know enough of his *message* to make for ourselves a consistent picture. Here, too, great caution is demanded by the nature of our sources.[13]

In reaction to Bultmann, Sanders set out to make the events of Jesus' life the basis for his studies of Jesus (*Jesus and Judaism* [1985] and *The Historical Figure of Jesus* [1993]). Given, as Bultmann argued, that Jesus was a teacher who operated by medium of the word, his actions will have been understood in the light of his teaching. Because uninterrupted actions can be understood in various ways, it seems likely that Sanders's understanding of the teaching of Jesus has guided the way he has understood the actions of Jesus, which he has overtly made the primary basis of his account. It also seems to be true that Bultmann's understanding of the actions of Jesus has had more impact on his account of the teaching of Jesus than he acknowledges. His account of Jesus' place within Judaism implies that this is the case.

Here it is important to set out Bultmann's distinction between what Jesus purposed, for which the task of reconstructing what he taught is crucial, and what Jesus achieved, for which a much wider scope of evidence is relevant. What Jesus actually achieved includes all the unintended consequences of his life as well as all that he purposed. Some of the consequences may well be consonant with what he purposed. Others may well be neutral to that purpose, or even contrary to it. From this perspective, the interpretation and proclamation of Jesus are part of what Jesus achieved, and this interpretation takes account of Jesus' death and the belief in his resurrection. It is hotly debated how far Jesus

---

13. Bultmann, *Jesus and the Word,* pp. 16-17.

purposed the circumstances of his own death or the belief in his resurrection that followed. These events are certainly part of the achievement of Jesus, whether he purposed them or not.[14]

Event and Interpretation, History and Kerygma

We have yet to draw out the significance of Bultmann's assertion that "There is no existentialist interpretation of history at all which ignores the factual occurrence. I can also say that the existentialist interpretation of history attempts to answer the questions that the factual history in which we are entangled poses for us."[15]

Jesus' life and mission, as known through historical research, pose questions for us about the meaning and purpose of our own lives that are also entangled in the events of factual history. The answers to these questions cannot be read off as necessary conclusions from the factual history itself. The New Testament bears witness to a believing response to the history of Jesus, and Bultmann seeks to elucidate this because he too came to believe as a consequence of his encounter and dialogue with the history of Jesus. But the reader of Bultmann's book on Jesus is free to follow or dissent from Bultmann's "point of view." "But because the book cannot in itself be for the reader *his* encounter with history, but only information about *my* encounter with history, it does of course as a whole appear to him as a *view*, and I must define for him the point of observation. Whether he afterwards remains a mere spectator is his affair."[16]

Here we are led to ask about Bultmann's understanding of the relationship of the historical Jesus to the kerygma and to Christian faith. The first disciples knew of Jesus' teaching and mission. Whatever they thought of him, they became his followers. What is more, when he was crucified they did not cease to be followers but came to believe in Jesus risen in a way that renewed their own lives. The paradoxical understanding of faith is clearly stated. The cross is both the saving event and the basis of faith out of which came belief in the risen one, in spite of the cross.

It is often said, most of the time in criticism, that according to my interpretation of the kerygma Jesus has risen in the kerygma. I accept this proposition. It is entirely correct, assuming that it is properly understood. It presupposes

14. On this see Bultmann's *History and Eschatology* (Edinburgh: Edinburgh University Press, 1957) and my discussion in *Theology as Hermeneutics*, chap. 1, esp. pp. 47-53.

15. Bultmann, "Reply," p. 275.

16. Bultmann, *Jesus and the Word*, p. 13.

that the kerygma itself is an eschatological event, and it expresses the fact that Jesus is really present in the kerygma. If that is the case, then all speculation concerning the modes of being of the risen Jesus, all the narratives of the empty tomb and all the Easter legends, whatever elements of historical fact they may contain, and as true as they may be in their symbolic form, are of no consequence. To believe in Christ present in the kerygma is the meaning of the Easter Faith.[17]

The relationship of the historical Jesus to the kerygma and Easter faith can be set out as follows. The historical Jesus gave rise to the Easter faith expressed in the kerygma. There is a material connection between the two, but they are not the same thing. Bultmann's portrayal of Jesus as a teacher or proclaimer of a message led him to formulate his position in a way that paradoxically affirms continuity between Jesus and the kerygma, "the proclaimer became the proclaimed."[18] While the teaching of Jesus is in continuity with the teaching of the great prophets, and elements of apocalyptic teaching are taken up into his eschatology, the belief that Jesus was the Messiah in spite of his crucifixion led to the recognition that his death was an essential part of God's saving action. It is this element that distinguishes the historical Jesus from the Christ of faith in Bultmann's thought. From this point of view it becomes clear why the historical Jesus is essential to Bultmann's theology but is not the same as his Christology.

The historical Jesus remains within the realm of Judaism. But Jesus set in motion a movement that Judaism could not contain. We can say that, for Bultmann, historical research shows Jesus to be in continuity with that movement but that belief in his saving death and resurrection took the movement beyond Jesus and the boundaries of Judaism. Historical research cannot establish the truth of that belief. Here Bultmann limits the value of historical research for theology because theology must work from the perspective of the believing response to the history of Jesus, his mission, death, and resurrection. Perhaps Bultmann paid too little attention to the role of historical research with its potential to falsify the basis of belief in Jesus, not by finding the bones of Jesus in the tomb but, for example, by showing that he was immoral and evil, a deceiver of his followers and so on.[19]

---

17. Bultmann, "Primitive Christian Kerygma," p. 42.

18. See Bultmann, "Primitive Christian Kerygma," pp. 38-39; Bultmann, *Faith and Understanding*, pp. 283-84.

19. On Bultmann's understanding of the relation of the historical Jesus to the Christ of faith, see my *Theology as Hermeneutics*, pp. 85-89, 92-93, 101-4, 168-77.

Jesus the Jew

At the Dead Sea Scrolls Exhibition in Sydney on July 17, 2000, Geza Vermes referred to his publisher's response to the suggested title of his 1973 book, *Jesus the Jew*. If that title was considered somewhat revolutionary in 1973, we need to remember that Rudolf Bultmann had portrayed the teaching of Jesus in thoroughly Jewish terms already in 1926 Germany in his book *Jesus* ("a Messianic prophet," "rabbi"). He went on to insist in his *Theology of the New Testament* that the proclamation of Jesus was not part of the theology of the New Testament but a presupposition of it.[20] This point of view is expressed clearly and concisely in his *Primitive Christianity in Its Contemporary Setting* (German ed. 1949):

> The proclamation of Jesus must be considered within the framework of Judaism. Jesus was not a "Christian," but a Jew, and his preaching is couched in the thought forms and imagery of Judaism, even when it is critical of traditional Jewish piety.[21]

> The preaching of Jesus is controlled by an imminent expectation of the Reign of God. In this he stands in a line with Jewish eschatology in general, though clearly not in its nationalistic form. He never speaks of a political Messiah who will destroy the enemies of Israel, of the establishment of a Jewish world empire, the gathering of the twelve tribes, of peace and prosperity in the land, or anything of that kind. Instead, we find in his preaching the cosmic hopes of apocalyptic writers. . . . All these elements are absorbed in the single all-embracing thought that God will then reign. . . . Jesus clearly believes that the present age is ebbing out. Mark's summary of his preaching ("The time is fulfilled, and the Reign of God has drawn nigh," Mark 1:15) is a fair representation of numerous sayings of Jesus which point to a new future and characterize the present as the time of decision.[22]

There is room to debate Bultmann's view of just where Jesus stood within Judaism. Again and again Bultmann asserted that the Judaism at the time was not uniform and that for the observant Jew the law was not a burden.[23] The critique of the law as a burden is made from the perspective of faith.[24] At the

---

20. Bultmann, *Theology of the New Testament*, trans. K. Grobel (New York: Scribner, 1951), 1:3, hereafter *TNT*.

21. Bultmann, *Primitive Christianity in Its Contemporary Setting* (New York: Meridian Books, 1956), p. 71.

22. Bultmann, *Primitive Christianity*, pp. 86-87.

23. Bultmann, "Reply," pp. 282-84.

24. Bultmann, *TNT* 1:191.

same time, he asserted that the critique of legalism was relevant in the face of a trend to broaden the application of the law often without questioning whether this led to the greater flourishing of human life.[25] Nevertheless, it is important to see that Paul looked back and saw his life as a law-observant Jew without any trace of having experienced an intolerable burden.[26] Jesus also refers to the heavy burdens placed on people's shoulders by the scribes and Pharisees (Mt 23:4) and contrasts his own "easy yoke" and "light burden" (Mt 11:28-30).

A good case can be made that Bultmann is on the right track in seeing Jesus in the tradition of the ancient prophets who proclaimed God's demand for righteousness and radical obedience that claimed the whole person. What separated Jesus from the prophets of old was that Jesus' message was delivered at a time when Judea was under Roman rule and his message was not addressed to the Roman rulers. Here Bultmann has underestimated the degree to which Jewish leaders participated in Roman exploitation of their own people. He also underestimates the degree to which Jesus' message was addressed to these leaders. Nevertheless, Bultmann rightly argued that there is evidence that suggests that Jesus used certain criteria to form the judgment that aspects of Mosaic Law were no longer applicable.

Jesus the Jew and Anti-Semitism

Bultmann's depiction of Jesus in Jewish terms continued throughout the Nazi period with its violent anti-Semitic policies. It is notable that his position involved not only the affirmation that Jesus was a Jew but also the negative denial that Jesus was a Christian. Bultmann's recognition of Jesus the Jew stands with his opposition to the implementation of the Aryan clause in German universities in the reorganization of the summer of 1933.

> The most decisive meeting of Bultmann and his pupils was no doubt the one held on the occasion of the visit from Emanuel Hirsch, pro-Nazi Dean of the Theological Faculty of Göttingen, to present to the Theological Faculty of Marburg the party-line objectives for Marburg and also to reorganize them, in the summer of 1933. After his address, there was the customary adjournment to the *Weinstube* to discuss the presentation — but Bultmann conspic-

25. Bultmann, "Reply," p. 282; R. Bultmann, *Essays Philosophical and Theological* (New York: Macmillan, 1955), p. 38.

26. Phil 3:4-8; Gal 1:13-14; see Bultmann, "Reply," p. 282, and Bultmann, *Essays Philosophical and Theological*, pp. 39-40.

uously withdrew to a side room, followed by his pupils, as a blunt act of rejection of the proposal.[27]

Bultmann and Hans Jonas

Bultmann's relationship to the Jewish philosopher Hans Jonas is well known. Jonas himself has frequently referred to and clarified the relationship. First, in the 1964 Festschrift marking Bultmann's eightieth birthday, Jonas wrote the following words of introduction to his "Philosophical Meditation" on Rom 7: "In 1930 I dedicated my first publication, *Augustin und das paulinische Freiheitsproblem,* to Professor Rudolf Bultmann 'in heartfelt gratitude.' The gratitude of the student was later joined by the friendship of maturity and the solace of loyalty. This bond has lasted through a life-time during which many another was broken and irretrievably lost in the dark abyss of our times."[28]

What he cryptically refers to here as "the dark abyss of our times" he elaborates more fully on two subsequent occasions when he also speaks of the bond that endured that dark abyss. The first of these is given in the substance of Jonas's lecture, given in Marburg in November 1976 at a memorial to Bultmann, who died on July 30. Jonas notes that his contribution was one of only two academic lectures given on the occasion and remarks of himself, that he is "not a theologian but a philosopher, not a Christian but a Jew." His paper opened with an explanation of his relationship to Bultmann:

> The appraisal of a thinker should perhaps separate the man from the work and confine itself to the substance of his thought. In the case of Rudolf Bultmann, I find this impossible for reasons both of compelling sentiment and of the objective conviction that this would leave out a too essential and precious part of the truth. Bultmann lived with what he thought, and his thought itself was such that this to-be-lived character stood forth as the true meaning of it. Foremost, however, is the fact that I have known him, that he was teacher to me and friend, a moving presence in my life that has shone through the years with a still and steady light.[29]

27. J. Robinson, introduction to *The Future of Our Religious Past: Essays in Honour of Rudolf Bultmann,* ed. J. M. Robinson, trans. C. E. Carlston and R. P. Scharlemann (New York: Harper and Row, 1971), p. 3.

28. Now in *The Future of Our Religious Past,* p. 333.

29. Now in *HTR* 75 (1982): 1.

Jonas tells how, in 1924, he followed Heidegger from Freiburg to Marburg, and there a fruitful exchange began between Bultmann and Heidegger and their students. There Jonas joined Bultmann's New Testament seminar. Through this contact Jonas became Bultmann's student and wrote his study on Gnosticism under Bultmann's supervision.[30] How Bultmann introduced Jonas to the New Testament and its intellectual environment is more fully elaborated by Jonas in "A Retrospective View."[31] What becomes clear from this is that Bultmann introduced his students to the latest archaeological discoveries as they became accessible. First there is reference to the newly discovered Mandean documents edited by M. Lidzbarski (1920; 1925). It was Bultmann who steered Jonas to the Mandean documents as relevant to the Fourth Gospel and to Gnosticism. His study also took in texts from Egyptology and Iranology, and when the Nag Hammadi library first came to light Jonas was one of the first scholars to study one of those Coptic documents, the *Gospel of Truth*.[32]

There were two Jewish students in Bultmann's New Testament seminar, Hannah Arendt and Hans Jonas. Here I raise the question of Bultmann's view of Jesus the Jew and his relationship to Jewish friends. Clearly an important friendship grew between Bultmann and Jonas. Jonas's account can be related impressively to fragments in Bultmann's "Autobiographical Reflections."[33] There Bultmann says, "I have never directly and actively participated in political affairs. I will simply survey my theological work through the Marburg years."[34] These of course were the years of what Bultmann calls "the Nazi terror."[35] Hidden here are events that we must learn of from others. There is first the event already referred to in the summer of 1933 when Bultmann led a protest against the Nazi policies introduced at Marburg by Emanuel Hirsch. Part of this reorganization was the introduction of the Aryan clause involving the exclusion of Jewish scholars. Jonas also tells of his horror when, as a result of Nazi policy, in the summer of 1933 the German Association of the Blind expelled its Jewish members. He went to Bultmann to report his decision to leave Germany and to say farewell. His report of the meeting with Bultmann is full of pathos, telling of the way Bultmann wordlessly entered into the agony of his decision.

This story also forms a background to the circumstances leading to the

30. Jonas, *Gnosis und spätantiker Geist* (Göttingen: Vandenhoeck & Ruprecht, 1934).

31. Jonas, "A Retrospective View," in *Proceedings from the International Colloquium on Gnosticism* (Leiden: Brill, 1977), pp. 1-15; see esp. pp. 4-10.

32. See his *The Gnostic Religion: The Message of the Alien God and the Beginnings of Christianity*, 3rd ed. (Boston: Beacon Press, 2001).

33. Bultmann, "Autobiographical Reflections," in *Theology of Rudolf Bultmann*, pp. xix-xxv.

34. Bultmann, "Autobiographical Reflections," p. xxii.

35. Bultmann, "Autobiographical Reflections," p. xxi.

publication of the first volume of Jonas's work on Gnosticism. Jonas tells how
Bultmann had taken his essay on free will in Augustine, written under
Heidegger, and published it in his prestigious research series in 1930. Then
came the time to publish Jonas's work on Gnosticism. But it was now 1933, the
year Hitler came to power, and Bultmann faced a reluctant publisher. Jonas tells
how Bultmann threatened to resign as editor if the publisher would not accept
his decision to publish Jonas's book. Thus Jonas says, "In 1934, 'Gnosis und
spätantiker Geist I' came out in German, with that remarkable Foreword by
Bultmann which was doubly so at the time."[36] Elsewhere he describes
Bultmann's preface in the following terms: "The famous preface with which he
finally sent that work on its way in 1934 (!) still stands as a shining testimony to
the courageous generosity of the man in a dark time."[37] Much more could be
said concerning the relationship of Hans Jonas to Bultmann. The best place to
read it is in Jonas's own words. His account of his visit to Bultmann at the end
of the war is also given in "Is Faith Still Possible?"

Bultmann and the Ethic of Jesus

Evidently Bultmann did not look on such intervention as political, though the
implications of the action were not lost on Jonas. In his "Autobiographical Reflections" Bultmann wrote, "I have never directly and actively participated in
political affairs."[38] His intervention at the level of his own activities was more
political than he seems to have allowed. Note his comments:

> The years at Marburg were troubled ones as a result of the political develop-
> ments after 1933, and the outbreak of the Second World War in 1939. . . . The
> work with the students, who were still motivated by the "Youth Movement" of
> the beginning of the century, was most gratifying. Then came the Hitler regime
> with its coercion and corrupting methods. Life in the university and in society
> at large was poisoned by mistrust and denunciations. Only within a small
> group of like-minded acquaintances could one enjoy the open and invigorat-
> ing exchange of the intellectual world. Many Jewish friends were forced to emi-
> grate. During the war, in the course of which my only surviving brother died in
> a concentration camp, came the worst pressure from the Nazi terror. When the
> Allies (in Marburg, the Americans) finally marched in, I, along with many

36. Jonas, "A Retrospective View," p. 10.
37. Jonas, "Is Faith Still Possible? Memories of Rudolf Bultmann and Reflections on the
Philosophical Aspect of His Work," *HTR* 75 (1982): 2.
38. Bultmann, "Autobiographical Reflections," p. xxii.

friends, greeted the end of Nazi rule as liberation. In the years of the Hitler regime my work was influenced by the struggle within the church. I belonged to the Confessing Church from the time of its founding in 1934 and, with my friend Hans von Soden, endeavored to see that free scholarly work retained its proper place within it in spite of reactionary tendencies.[39]

Günther Bornkamm says of the sources of Bultmann's theology, "They made him quite consistently take the way followed by the Confessional Church during the Third Reich."[40] This adds a little more to Bultmann's own brief factual acknowledgment. Bultmann's reference to many Jewish friends shows that his concerns went outside the internal troubles of the church and returns our attention to Hans Jonas, who tells of his return to Germany as a member of the British occupying forces in 1945. He had determined that it was the only way he would return. He describes meeting with only two people, one of whom was Bultmann. He came, having just learned the fate of his mother and their home, bearing a book from the publisher, and Bultmann inquired if it could be the second volume of his work on gnosis. It was in fact a copy of Bultmann's commentary on John. But the simple question, asked with continuing interest in his work, was enough to restore Jonas's faith in humanity.[41] He had resolved to abandon the work on Gnosticism, but Bultmann's question "became the bridge over the abyss; it connected the after with the before which grief and wrath and bitterness threatened to blot out, and perhaps more than anything else it helped, with its unique combination of fidelity and soberness, to make my life whole again."[42]

Bultmann did not think there was a distinctive Christian ethic. To know what is good or evil for the neighbor or society or the world has to be worked out using the faculty of reason. Certainly the Christian knows these demands, but Bultmann regards them as "general human demands." "Perhaps one may say that faith and love are manifest only in so far as there are Christians who, acting in faith and love and guided by their reason, take upon themselves responsibility for the world."[43] This again leads in the direction of an ethic that is not circumscribed by the boundaries of the church. This may be suggested by Bultmann's recognition that Jesus was a Jew, not a Christian. Certainly it is reason to oppose discrimination against the Jews in Nazi Germany. It is indirectly evidence that the historical Jesus was important theologically for Bultmann. It

---

39. Bultmann, "Autobiographical Reflections," p. xxi.

40. G. Bornkamm, "The Theology of Rudolf Bultmann," in *Theology of Rudolf Bultmann*, p. 4.

41. Jonas, "Is Faith Still Possible?" p. 3; see also Jonas, "A Retrospective View," p. 12.

42. Jonas, "Is Faith Still Possible?" pp. 3-4.

43. Bultmann, "Reply," p. 280.

gives weight to Bultmann's own claim, "I must reply that I do not regard the factual character of history and of Jesus as in any way irrelevant for faith and for theology."[44] There is other evidence that suggests that Bultmann opposed any form of racial discrimination. Some of this too can be gathered from the comments made by Hans Jonas.

Jesus and Paul, Jesus and the Kerygma

Another line supporting this view arises from Bultmann's essay "Jesus and Paul" (1936), at the end of which he concludes: "One cannot flee from Paul and return to Jesus. For what one encounters in Jesus is the same God who is encountered in Paul — the God who is creator and judge, who claims man completely for himself, and who freely gives his grace to him who becomes nothing before him. All that one can do is to go to Jesus *through* Paul."[45] While there are some differences between the two, we could say that the implicit claim of Jesus is made explicit in Paul. But again it becomes clear that the historical Jesus, knowledge of whom is recovered through historical evidence and work, is important for Bultmann's theology. Historical work cannot establish the truth of the kerygma or of Bultmann's theology. Involved in this is an existential decision, the decision of faith. But Bultmann's historical labors on *The History of the Synoptic Tradition, Jesus, The Theology of the New Testament,* and *Primitive Christianity in Its Contemporary Setting* provide evidence of a scholar for whom the historical Jesus is a matter of concern and for whom the historical evidence produced by archaeology had an important place.

Evidence and Historical Argument

The argument has outlined the role of evidence in establishing *an* understanding of the historical Jesus and the importance of this for Bultmann's theology. Bultmann also introduced Hans Jonas to the historical evidence made available by archaeology for his study of Gnosticism. Bultmann's own writings also show a scholar who was anxious to make use of all possible evidence. His work led the way in the use of the Mandean writings, the *Odes of Solomon,* and many other sources made available by archaeology.

---

44. Bultmann, "Reply," p. 274.

45. Bultmann, "Jesus and Paul" (1936), in Bultmann, *Existence and Faith* (New York: Meridian Books, 1960), pp. 183-201, here p. 201.

As early as 1925 Bultmann was looking to sectarian Judaism as the medium through which Gnosticism was mediated to Hellenistic and especially Johannine Christianity. He argued that the Gnostic movement found expression in baptizing sects around the Jordan: "If we could get a clear picture of the Essenes, we would perhaps make progress. In any case the Jewish and Jewish Christian baptismal sects, thorough investigation of which is urgently needed, show what possibilities there were."[46] Here we have clear evidence of Bultmann's enthusiastic use of newly discovered source material. It led him to draw conclusions about the nature of the sectarian Judaism that formed the context of the Gospel of John. In his commentary on the Gospel (1941) he frequently referred to early Oriental Gnosticism mediated by Judaism.[47] While the Mandean and Manichean evidence was too late to provide convincing evidence for the context of the Gospel of John, the use of these sources alongside other Jewish and Jewish Christian sources such as the *Odes of Solomon* led him to conclude: "At first, Gnosticism probably penetrated into the Christian congregations mostly through the medium of Hellenistic Judaism which was itself in the grip of syncretism."[48] The 1925 quotation shows that Bultmann allowed for Gnostic influence in Palestinian Judaism. Identifying the Essenes as a likely source of evidence now appears to be an extraordinarily accurate shot in the dark. Bultmann wrote: "While a pre-Christian gnostizing Judaism could hitherto only be deduced out of later sources, the existence of such is now testified by manuscripts recently discovered in Palestine."[49]

This is a rather general and imprecise reference to the texts from Qumran. Johannine scholars now generally recognize their relevance for the study of the Johannine writings.[50] The emphasis on knowledge and the dualistic language of light and darkness, truth and falsehood, life and death, God and the devil, used in similar phrases in John and some of the Qumran texts (see 1QS 3.13–4.26) has led to the reappraisal of John in Jewish terms. Strangely, the recognition of Jewish and Gnostic, which Bultmann advocated, tends to have given way to Jewish, not Gnostic. There may be more work to do on this issue before the case can be closed.

However this turns out, we conclude that there is nothing antithetical

46. Bultmann, "Die Bedeutung der neuerschlossenen mandäischen und manichäischen Quellen für das Verständnis des Johannesevangeliums," *ZNW* 24 (1925): 142-43.

47. See, for example, his *The Gospel of John,* trans. G. R. Beasley-Murray (Philadelphia: Westminster, 1971), pp. 28-31.

48. Bultmann, *TNT* 1:171.

49. Bultmann, *TNT* 2:13 n. *.

50. See my *The Quest for the Messiah: The History, Literature, and Theology of the Johannine Community* (Edinburgh: T. & T. Clark, 1991; Nashville: Abingdon, 1993), pp. 35-52.

about the association of Bultmann, archaeology, and the historical Jesus. In the quarter-century since Bultmann died a month short of turning ninety-two, the publication of the Qumran texts has taught us much and the material evidence of archaeological work has thrown much new light on our understanding of life in Galilee and Judea. I have no doubt that Bultmann would have embraced this with enthusiasm.

Jesus and Resurrection Faith in Light of Jewish Texts

Emile Puech

Beliefs in the fate of the individual were diverse and evolved in ancient Israel and Judaism before Christ. As is well known, according to Acts 23:8, "The Sadducees say there is no resurrection, nor angels, nor spirit, while the Pharisees accept them both."[1] This is supported by the Gospels (Mt 22:23; Mk 12:18; and Lk 20:27) as well as by Jewish literature (Mishnah, Talmud, *Abot Rabbi Nathan*, Josephus, Targumim), which present the Sadducees as denying any belief in resurrection, reward, and judgment in the world to come, and any kind of life after death, even the persistence of soul and body, because such beliefs have no scriptural basis in the Torah.

On these matters of afterlife, Pharisaic beliefs are quite the opposite. The Pharisees believed that God will fulfill the promises to the fathers, namely, the resurrection of the righteous and the judgment to come. According to Josephus, the Pharisees maintained that the soul is imperishable, and that only the souls of the good pass into another body, that is, to a new life. However, the souls of the wicked suffer eternal punishment (*Ant* 18.14).

Again according to Josephus, the Essenes subscribed to the doctrine of immortality of the soul (*War* 2.154): "although bodies are corruptible and their matter unstable, souls are immortal and live for ever." But according to Hippolytus of Rome, the Essenes did believe in the resurrection of the body

---

1. See recently B. Viviano and J. Taylor, "Sadducees, Angels, and Resurrection (Acts 23:8-9)," *JBL* 111 (1992): 496-98, even if I do not accept their explanations of the verse and on the intermediary state. On the different Jewish opinions and the New Testament passages, see E. Puech, *La croyance des Esséniens en la vie future: Immortalité, résurrection, vie éternelle? Histoire d'une croyance dans le Judaïsme ancien*, vol. 1, *La résurrection des morts et le contexte scripturaire*, vol. 2, *Les données qumraniennes et classiques*, Études Bibliques (nouvelle série n°s 21-22) (Paris: Gabalda, 1993), 1:201-85.

(*Refutatio* 9.27): "they acknowledge both that the flesh will rise again and that it will be immortal, in the same manner that the soul is already imperishable."

Resurrection in Jesus' Teaching

The teaching of Jesus took place in a historical context that well explains his position on the subject. In a controversy with Jesus on the law of levirate (Mt 22:23-33 and pars.), the Sadducees tried to convince him that the Pharisees' faith in the resurrection of the body was utopian. But Jesus answered on both issues advanced by them: (1) the power of God — for at the resurrection men and women do not marry, they will be like the angels in heaven; and (2) the proof from Scripture — using the rabbinic rule of the *gezera shewa*[2] ("I am the God of Abraham, the God of Isaac and the God of Jacob," that is, "the God not of the dead, but of the living"). Thus Jesus affirmed both points denied by the Sadducees, at their own level and manner: resurrection of the dead and proof from Scriptures. At the same time, Jesus refuted the concept of resurrection as a return to life on earth. The law of levirate and resurrection are not opposed. They belong to two different worlds — the present one and the one to come. On the other hand, Lk 20:35 speaks of "those who are judged worthy of a place in the other world and in the resurrection of the dead"; i.e., not all will be resurrected. The just alone can participate in the world to come and in the resurrection.

To arrive at Jesus' position on the afterlife seems hazardous, because his teaching is transmitted to us through the preaching in the Palestinian Jesus Movement that interpreted it. However, it does not seem that his thought has been changed, even if we do not have the *ipsissima verba Jesu*. According to his answer to the Sadducees, Jesus clearly belongs to the Pharisaic stream of thought. He accepts the belief in the resurrection at the end of time, and he stresses his "spiritualization" — the just will be like the angels.

As there were a variety of opinions among the Pharisees, so variety of perspectives characterizes Jesus' teachings. On one hand, the resurrection of the righteous is asserted in the parable of the invited guests (Lk 14:13-24), where Jesus links resurrection and rewards of the just in the afterlife, at the resurrection of the upright *(anastasis tōn dikaiōn)*, and also in the dialogue with Martha (Jn 11:25: "anyone who believes in me, even though he dies, he will live"); but note that here belief in Jesus could replace belonging to the Jewish congregation.

---

2. [This Hebrew expression means that the similarity of words between one passage and another indicates that the passages refer to the same idea or concept. — JHC.]

(Compare this statement with Josephus, *War* 2.163b and *Ant* 18.14.)[3] On the other hand, the universal resurrection is slated for the end of time, for the just and the wicked, the Jew and non-Jew according to the Greek version of Dan 12:2-3 (as found in Acts 24:15: "And I hold the same hope in God as they do that then will be a resurrection of the upright and the wicked alike") and supposed in Mt 25:32-46 (the parable of the last judgment); 12:41-42 (the sign of Jonah, the men of Nineveh, and the queen of the South); Lk 13:28-30 (the ones invited in the kingdom of God); John 5:29 (resurrection to life or to judgment). The same opinion is found in the School of Shammai.

About the Intermediary State after Death

To the belief in the resurrection at the end of time is attached the concept of an intermediary state. What about the time between death and the final judgment? What happens to the just and the wicked at and after their deaths? According to Pharisaic traditions, the dead are divided among three groups: (1) the just, whose names are inscribed in the book of life; (2) the wicked, who are inscribed for Gehenna, already after death; and (3) those not totally just nor totally wicked, who belong to an intermediary group — they need some time in Sheol-Hades for the purification of flesh. This was the opinion of the School of Shammai (*b. Rosh-hashana* 16b-17a; *t. Sanhedrin* 13.3), but the School of Hillel thought that God, who is gracious, will be merciful to those in the intermediate group.

Such ideas can be found in some passages in the Gospels. The parable of the rich man and Lazarus (Lk 16:19-31) first of all intends to teach the way of conversion, because the fate of the individual is fixed forever at his or her death. The message is: "Listen to the Law and to the Prophets and you will enjoy a blessed afterlife, not eternal chastisements in Gehenna!" The same idea is found in the dialogue with the good thief (Lk 23:39-43). Death by crucifixion would normally be suffered by someone guilty of a capital offense; it designates him as a wicked person, one whose fate after death should be Gehenna. In a mythical, spatial, and temporal use of language, Jesus' answer to the good thief, "Today, you will be with me in paradise," denotes that because of his confession of sin, and of Jesus as Messiah, his fate is no longer that of the wicked in Gehenna but is now of the just in paradise — with Jesus himself, the Just and Innocent par

---

3. *War* 2 §163b: "Every soul, they maintain, is imperishable, but the soul of the good alone passes into another body, while the souls of the wicked suffer punishment"; *Ant* 18 §14: "They believe that souls have power to survive death and that there are rewards and punishments under the earth for those who have led lives of virtue or vice: eternal imprisonment is the lot of evil souls, while the good souls receive an easy passage to a new life."

excellence — like the other just ones waiting for the resurrection and entry into the kingdom of God. His prayer has been granted because he converted before his death and the fixation of his eternal fate.

Such a presentation is not opposed to belief in the resurrection, as many have thought; on the contrary, it totally belongs to the schema of a historical eschatology, well known particularly in *1 En* 22. The intermediary state, supposedly necessary for some souls in need of purification of sins, is at the origin of purgatory in Christian theology. But the image of Abraham's bosom (*eis ton kolpon Abraam;* Lk 16:22) was another way to designate the abode of the souls of the just in *1 En* 22, like the paradise of the apocryphal books, or like the souls of the slain waiting underneath the altar (Rev 6:9-11), or underneath the throne of God (in Judaism), but not yet in the state of glory and bliss in the kingdom of God.

Resurrection of Jesus

That Jesus of Nazareth held this view of death and afterlife is apparent from Peter's address to a Jewish crowd at Jerusalem:

> This man, who was put into your power by the deliberate intention and foreknowledge of God, you took and had crucified and killed by men outside the Law. But God raised him to life, freeing him from the pangs of Hades, for it was impossible for him to be held in its power since, as David says of him . . . (citation from Ps 16:8-11). For David who is dead and buried and whose tomb is still with us, spoke with foreknowledge about the resurrection of the Christ: he is the one who was not abandoned to Hades, and whose body did not see corruption. God raised this man Jesus to life, and of that we are all witnesses. Now raised to the heights by God's right hand, he has received from the Father the Holy Spirit, who was promised, and what you see and hear is the outpouring of that Spirit. (Acts 2:23-33)

After his death on the cross when Jesus cried: "Father, into your hands I commit my spirit" (Lk 23:46), his soul went into paradise or Sheol-Hades (Lk 23:43; see also Mt 12:40; Rom 10:7; Eph 4:9-10; Heb 13:20), while his body was buried in a new rock-cut tomb, according to a Jewish practice for criminals. But on the third day, the day after the solemn Sabbath, he rose from the dead. The resurrection of the Messiah Jesus is unique in human history, in that it anticipates for him the day of judgment, at which he will preside. The descent into Hades in the realm of the dead — to be understood in the abode of the just —

and his resurrection mean the final defeat of death (Isa 25:8) and the salvation of all the dead in Christ *(en Christō)*. It is clear that the resurrection of Jesus is not a reanimation of the body or a return to the previous way of life, but rather the entry into the glory of God at the right hand of the Father, as the various appearances of Jesus show.

All the passages on this subject in the New Testament state that the death and resurrection of Jesus have fulfilled the Scriptures. But where do the Scriptures provide insights on beliefs about life after death and the resurrection?

Scriptural Texts on the Afterlife and Resurrection

As a Jewish religious group, the Essenes were very familiar with (in reading and copying) the normative books: the Torah, the Prophets, and other books *(kethûbîm)*, accepted or rejected later by the rabbis from the corpus that became the Hebrew Bible in the second century c.e. This means that the reference books upon which they were highly dependent included some influential apocryphal and pseudepigraphical works, which were unknown in their original language until the Qumran discoveries. And we now know that they included Daniel among the prophetic books (4Q174 1-2 ii 3) — as it is in the Septuagint — and not with the *kethûbîm*, as in the MT.

In the Bible, as in ancient Near Eastern literature, Sheol denotes the area under the earth where the dead reside, and from where God can rescue the individual, at first in a metaphorical sense but later on as expression of a belief in the power of God to raise from the dead (Ps 16:10).[4] Once Sheol ceases to be seen as a neutral place for the good and the wicked alike, it becomes a place of punishment, called Abaddon, Gehenna, and the Pit. Because of the perfection of creation by godly Wisdom (Prov 8:22-31), the wisdom literature is closely connected to human obedience to the divine Law and to maintenance of the justice of God. Consequently, moral conduct results in the teaching of the two ways: the way of life for the wise and righteous, and the way of death for the foolish and the wicked. Accordingly, two kinds of fates are awaiting them in this life or after death: rewards for the just and chastisements for the wicked, because if goodness is not rewarded and wickedness is not punished, God cannot be said to be just. Therefore, the prophets and wisdom literature mostly insist on individual responsibility for repayment after death in a form of life that will ensure that the just stand up at the last judgment while the wicked go into perdition (Pss 1; 16:10; 49:15; 69:28-29; 73:24; Prov 12:28; 14:32; 15:24).

---

4. On the Old Testament passages and apocryphal texts, see Puech, *La croyance*, 2:37-199.

The beliefs about the afterlife became more precise among the wise and pious people (the predecessors of the *Hasîdîm*), first in Isa 26:14-19, in which judgment and punishments of the wicked are opposed to the resurrection of the just in a context of collective eschatology, and God has destroyed death forever (Isa 25:8). This passage marks a clear evolution in belief, from national resurrection in the vision of the dry bones of Ezek 37:1-14, before this text became reinterpreted in a personal way by the author of *Pseudo-Ezekiel* (4Q385 2-3):[5] "I have seen many in Israel who loved thy Name and walked on the paths of righteousness. When will these things happen and how will they be rewarded for their piety?" At the end of days, the just will rise in a kind of restored life: the bones will reconnect, sinews will grow on them and they will be covered with skin; then the four winds of heaven will blow the spirit in them and they will live. This explanation of the resurrection of the dead was taken over by the School of Shammai, while the School of Hillel based its view on Job 10:10-12, to be understood like a new creation in the mother's womb.

Clearly, the belief in postmortem vindication of the righteous did not arise in Israel from the experience of righteous suffering or martyrs, as has been so frequently asserted in scholarly accounts. Beliefs about survival beyond death or eschatological vindication may have infiltrated the Jewish Palestinian world after the exile, mainly from Persia, before any crisis of religious suffering among Jews, as the texts quoted above seem to indicate.

In the eulogy of the ancestors, Ben Sira 48:11 knows a happy end for the just who would die during the days of the return of Elijah before the judgment (Mal 3:23-24[4:5-6]).[6] The prophet will have the power to give back life to the just who would die during this period of time: "Happy is the one who will see you and die, because you will give life and he will rise up!" (Hebrew text). But this return to life is before the eschaton.

Based on Isa 26 and 66:22-24, Dan 12:1-3 applies the concept of the resurrection of the just only to the time of great distress for the day of judgment and of the annihilation of the wicked. Many (the just and wise who are sleeping in the dust) will awaken to everlasting life and shine brightly as the stars of heaven forever, while the others, the wicked, will be destined for shame and everlasting disgrace. The same idea is seen again in the *Words of the Lights:* "All those who are inscribed in the book of life [*will rise and stand*] to serve you and give thanks to your holy name" (4Q504 1-2 vi 14-15).[7] The inscription in the book of life in Daniel and the *Words of the Lights* have also introduced a change from a

---

5. See Puech, *La croyance,* 2:605-16.

6. See Puech, *La croyance,* 2:73-78.

7. See Puech, *La croyance,* 2:564-68.

national eschatology to a more individual and personal one according to the ethic of the prophetic and wisdom literature based on the "Two Ways" theology, as it is also in *Pseudo-Ezekiel*.

Already, along the same lines, among the pre-Qumranic Apocrypha recovered, the resurrection of the just is probably present in a passage of *Visions of Amram* where "light, joy [and peace]" will be given to "the Sons of Light" at the last judgment, but "[darkness, death] and Abaddôn" to the sons of darkness (4Q548 1-2 ii 12-14).[8] More or less contemporary with this, the Book of Watchers of *1 Enoch* clearly affirms individual existence after death, a postmortem retribution for the righteous and the wicked. The immortality of the souls of the just and the impious waiting for the last judgment in separated compartments hardly precludes the resurrection of the righteous. Again in the Book of Visions there is a possible allusion to the resurrection (*1 En* 90.33), associated with the idea of a restoration of the people of God. The Book of Exhortations (91.10; 92.3; 102.4; 103.3-7; 104.1-5) may contain another possible allusion to resurrection as in Dan 12:3. The Lord shall come, judge and punish the wicked, and "the righteous shall arise from their sleep." The new life of the just whose names are inscribed before the glory of the Great, is presented as a transformation into eternal life and glorification. For this a glorified body bright like the stars must be implied and not a pure immortality of soul. The association of the blessed with the angels in glory is related to the day of great judgment and not to death (104.5). This same belief is found in the later Book of Parables. The author or authors of this Enoch book imagine the future to be essentially the resurrection of the just to eternal life on a new earth in company with the Elect of God, but the impious shall perish in eternal fire (*1 En* 51; 58; and 61). In *1 Enoch* the eternal life of the just is consistently described as a glorified life in light, radically different from the present earthly life, and generally associated with the resurrection at the time of the last judgment. There is no question of a reviving of spirits, as is generally considered, because the soul or the spirit does not die and that shining is expected at the day of the last judgment. The just will live forever in a glorious condition, and divine justice will be exercised in the future, retrospectively with respect to the dead.

Such are the revelations in *1 Enoch*, and alluded to in passing in Dan 12. The same doctrine is known in 2 Maccabees (mainly in chap. 7, about the martyrs for the Law) as an exhortation in the battle against impiety. The raising of the just as a new creation will take place "in the day of mercy" (2 Macc 7:23) — which corresponds to the last judgment and not to an individual eschatology. And there will be no resurrection to life for the impious king but torment for him and his de-

---

8. See Puech, *La croyance*, 2:537-40, and Puech, *Qumrân Grotte 4*, XXII, DJD 31 (Oxford: Clarendon, 2001), 4Q548.

Figure 76. Kidron valley,
Beni Hezir Tombs;
first century B.C.E.
Courtesy of J. H. Charlesworth

scendants. The same opinion is found in the *Psalms of Solomon* (3; 9; 13; and 15).[9] Resurrection functions as a recompense for the suffering of the just. They will be rewarded by eternal life at the day of mercy, while sinners will be punished.

In the book of Wisdom, the immortality of the soul of the just does not depend on a Platonic preexistence but is a gift of God as a reward for good deeds, just as Sheol is the punishment of the wicked. This will be "at the time of Visitation" (*en kairō episkopēs;* Wis 3:7, 13), where the just will shine out, judge nations, and rule over people after an eschatological battle (Wis 5:17-23). This supposes the same teaching as in Dan 12, even if a bodily resurrection is nowhere clearly mentioned (but see "the just will stand up boldly to face those who had oppressed him"; Wis 5:1, *stēsetai = qwm?*). Meanwhile, "the souls of the just are in the hand of God, at peace" (Wis 3:1, 3), reflecting the idea of the partition of Sheol-Hades already attested in *1 En* 22. As in the passages cited above, Wisdom knows a linear eschatology with two steps: death and visitation: "The just live forever" (Wis 5:15, *zōsin*) and "they *will* shine out" (3:7; *analampsousin*); this is not a purely-individual transcendent eschatology. Do we find something similar to this teaching in the Wisdom texts among the recently published Dead Sea Scrolls?

Qumranic Texts

Qumran Sapiential Instructions

The date of composition of the sapiential literature is debated but may predate the exile in Qumran and the composition of Dan 12. The best-preserved didactic

9. See Puech, *La croyance,* 1:125-27.

Figure 77. Qumran caves. From right to left: Cave 5, Cave 4.
Courtesy of J. H. Charlesworth

text is *Sapiential Work A*[d-a] (4QInstruction; 4Q415-418).[10] This text offers advice on how to relate to God and fellow human beings. It can be compared to Proverbs and Ben Sira, with ethical and professional admonitions and also cosmological and eschatological considerations. The wisdom contains divinely revealed mysteries *(rz nhyh)* for the elected ones, which enable them to discern between truth and iniquity (*Sapiential Work A*[b] [4Q416 2 iii 8-15]). It stresses the need to struggle in pursuing wisdom and the rewards afterward. An instruction, directed first to the foolish-minded and then to the truly chosen, offers a sharp contrast between their distinct fates, and an encouragement to the latter to persevere in the pursuit of wisdom and righteousness (*Sapiential Work A*[a] [4Q418 69 ii 4-15]):

> 4 . . . *(vacat)* And now, O you foolish-minded ones, what is good to him who has not been
> 5 fashioned? [And what] is tranquility to him who has not come into existence? And what is judgment to him who has not been established? And what lament shall the dead make over al[l] their [days?]
> 6 You were fashioned for S[he]ol and to the everlasting pit shall your return be, for it shall awaken to expo[se] your sin,[and the inhabitants of]

10. J. Strugnell, D. Harrington, and T. Elgvin, *Qumran Cave 4, XXIV: Sapiential Texts*, pt. 2, DJD 24 (Oxford: Clarendon, 1999). It may be placed between Proverbs and Sirach (p. 36).

7 its dark places shall cry out against your pleading, and all those who will en-
dure forever, those who investigate the truth, shall rouse themselves for your
judgment. And then

8 will all the foolish-minded be destroyed, and the children of iniquity shall
not be found anymore, [and al]l those who hold fast to wickedness shall
wither away.[And then,]

9 at the passing of judgment upon you, the foundations of the firmament will
cry out, and all [the ce]le[stial] ho[sts] will thunder forth [*and will live* al]l
those who love[*righteouness.*]

10 *(vacat)* And you who are the truly chosen ones, who pursue [understand-
ing] who seek [eagerly for *wisdom,* and] who keep vigil

11 over all knowledge, how can you say: "We are tired of understanding, and
we are vigilant in pursuing knowledge e[very time] or everyw[here]?"

12 But one is not weary in all the years of eternity! Does one not take delight
in truth forever, and does not knowledge [forever] serve oneself? But the
s[ons of]

13 heaven, whose lot is eternal life, will they truly say, "We are weary of doing
the works of truth, and [we] are exhausted

14 at all times"? Will [they] not walk in everlasting light [*all with an attire of*
g]lory and abundance of splendor? Yourselves [*you will stand*]

15 in the firmaments [of holiness, and in] the council of the divine ones all[
the days of eternity?(vacat). (our translation)[11]

The instruction first warns the foolish-minded that their fate is death and the
pit at the judgment, because to Sheol they must return. In its dark places they
will be accused by those who investigate the truth, and they will be annihilated.
Even the cosmos reacts, and the celestial hosts will help to separate those who
love wisdom and righteousness. In a corresponding paragraph, the instruction
tries to convince the faithful chosen ones to pursue righteousness and wisdom
despite their weariness, because there is no weariness in eternity, as the angels,
the sons of heaven, show forth as models for unwearied involvement in God's
truth and for eternal participation in God's glory.

The assumption seems to be that the righteous ones will participate, or be
witnesses, in the judgment of the foolish-minded ones for which they will rouse
themselves, when the cosmos will cry, and that the angels will separate the good
ones for the judgment. But contrary to the fate of the wicked, their fate is everlasting life in the eternal contemplation and happiness in the company of the
angels who dwell in the heavenly court. The instruction seems to know about

11. See Strugnell, Harrington, and Elgvin, *Qumran Cave 4,* XXIV, pp. 211-474; see esp. pp.
281-91, with my new readings and translation.

the resurrection of the just, when the pit shall awaken to expose the sin of the foolish-minded, and that its inhabitants shall cry out against their pleading, and that the just who investigate the truth and who will live forever, shall rouse themselves for their judgment. And all this will happen when the cosmos will cry out and the angels are acting for the last judgment.

A similar view is found in *Sapiential Work A^a* (4Q418 126 ii 3-10):

3 for] with a true e[ph]ah and a right weight God will measure all.[ ]
4 he has spread them out, in truth has he established them and according to their delight they study[ ]
5 everything will be hidden. And furthermore they will not come into being without his good pleasure, and *from* [his] wisdo[m]
6 judgment, to repay vengeance to the workers of iniquity and a ju[st] visitation[to]
7 and to imprison the wicked, but to raise up the head of the poor [ ]
8 in everlasting glory and peace eternal and the spirit of life to separate[ ]
9 all the children of Eve. And on the might of God and the abundance of his glory together with his bounty [ ]
10 and upon his faithfulness shall they meditate all the day. Continually shall they praise his name and . . . [ ]. (my translation)[12]

God will vindicate the righteous in a just visitation by imprisoning the wicked and raising up the head of the poor who will share the angelic life of everlasting praise of God. An accent is put on divine election, and although God is a just judge, there is a kind of determination by God that is not yet to be found in Proverbs. But as in the biblical wisdom, the fear of judgment and the afterlife dominate the present way of life. The teaching of this instruction on the world to come explicitly takes over the content of Proverbs. For example, Prov 12:28 (see also 14:32 and 15:24): "In the way of uprightness is life; but the ways of the vengeful lead to death."

That scenario is found later in early Jewish documents and in the New Testament, except that there is no resurrection for the wicked as in the previous passages of the "Old Testament" and in some teachings of Jesus. The idea of a kind of angelic existence for the just is also to be read in Jesus' answer to the Sadducees (Mt 22:30 and par.); and that the angels will assemble the just to separate them from the wicked is clearly developed in the parable of the last judgment in Mt 25, but is also present in the explanation of the parables of the darnel (Mt 13:36-43) and of the dragnet (Mt 13:47-50).

12. See Strugnell, Harrington, and Elgvin, *Qumran Cave 4*, XXIV, pp. 211-474; see esp. pp. 349-57, with my new readings and translation.

Damascus Document (CD)

The sapiential instruction that insists so much on understanding, knowledge, study of wisdom, and investigation of the truth prepares and anticipates the discourses preserved in the *Damascus Document*.[13] From the beginning, the author of this document asserts that God will judge those who spurn him. God has saved a remnant, chosen the Righteous Teacher to guide them on the truthful path. God had revealed his will to those turning aside from the path and abominating the precepts. These will be destroyed, because he has not chosen them from the beginning, he knew their deeds, and he hates them. But those who convert and remain steadfast in God's covenant and Law will acquire eternal life and all the glory of Adam, because God has pardoned their sin. This means that they will inherit all that Adam lost by his fall (CD 1–3; as in 1QS 4.23 and 1QH 4.27). "They will live a thousand generations" (CD 7.6). For Adam lost his immortality and died; and since the covenanters know death, the recovery of eternal life and the glory of Adam can be possible only through resurrection in a body of glory, and not be an eternal extension of the present life. This will arrive at the judgment, when God will visit the earth to punish the wicked by eternal destruction and give eternal life to the righteous, because the exact times, names, and deeds of the wicked and of the elect are known to God. But until the number of years is complete, the community is presently living in the time of the end — as in a closed fortress to better resist the assaults of Belial (CD 7–8; 19.5f.; 20.15f., 25-33).

Rule of the Community (1QS)

A theological and more explicit presentation of the fate of the just and the wicked is found in the famous "Instruction on the Two Spirits" (1QS 3.13–4.26), as the introduction says: "to teach all the Sons of Light about the origin of all the sons of man concerning all kinds of their spirits according to their signs for their deeds in their generations, and concerning the visitation of their afflictions and the times of their reward" (3.13-15, my translation).[14]

God is the creator of all and he established all and all depends on him. "He created man to rule the world and placed in him two spirits by which he has to walk until the moment of his visitation" (3.15-18). According to the paths of the spirit that man is following in the present life, rewards or chastisements will re-

---

13. See Puech, *La croyance*, 2:499-514.
14. See Puech, *La croyance*, 2:421-40.

sult at the visitation. As for the fate of the just: "And the visitation of all those who walk in it will be healing, 7abundant well-being in a long life, fruitful off-spring with all everlasting benedictions, eternal enjoyment with endless life, and a crown of glory 8with majestic clothing in eternal light" (4.6-8, my translation).

This list suggests not simply a prolongation of earthly life, but a transformation into a new and immortal, quasi-angelic life, involving altogether soul and body. By contrast, the fate of the wicked is as follows: "And the visitation of 12all those who walk in it will be an abundance of afflictions at the hands of all the angels of destruction, everlasting damnation by the scorching wrath of the God of revenges, eternal torment and permanent 13shame with the humiliation of destruction in the fire of the dark regions. And all their times for their generations (will be) in mourning of affliction and bitter deceit in the existent darkness until 14they are annihilated without remnant or survivor among them" (4.11-14, my translation).

At the visitation the fate of the wicked is torment and punishment before annihilation, because, for the requirements of justice, evil must be punished before it can be removed. But this does not require that the wicked resurrect for eternal shame, as it is assumed for the just, for instance in the phrases "crown of glory, majestic clothing in eternal light," "glory of Adam," and "the new creation" (4.7-8, 23, 25). God "will remove for ever the existence of injustice at the time of visitation," which is "the time of the judgment decided" (4.18-20). This time is "the appointed end and the new creation," and "thus] God will cast the lots of every living being according to his spirit at the ti[me of retribution of] the Visitation" (4.25, 26). All those explanations agree perfectly with the views on that topic already found in Dan 12, and the hope of a new world and a new heaven is based on Isa 65:17 and 66:22. Could the concept of resurrection be absent from 1QS since the *Rule* refers to Dan 12 and to Isaiah? The central theme of rewards and punishments at the time of judgment and new creation is the motivation for the members to become saints in association with the sons of heavens, the angels, although the group is presently living among sinful people. Entering into the community, the member is making the good choice for his life, but he does not yet know how far he can persevere. The final cleansing is not yet attained, and if anticipated, it is only in hope through an appropriate life.

War Scroll (1QM)

The same opposition between the two spirits "until the determined day of the great battle," when Belial will be imprisoned and the sons of darkness exterminated and the just be in an eternal light and joy, is found in the *War Scroll* (1QM 13).[15] In the Gospels, only the Father knows the final day, and not the angels or the Son (Mt 24:36). The defeat and punishment of all the wicked in the fire of Abaddon or Sheol at the Day is not without allusion to the victory of the righteous whom God will raise up (1QM 14). The names of the chosen are written in the heavenly books as in Dan 12 (1QM 12.2). This central view of the scroll is that of Daniel and other texts quoted above. There is no question of a continuing life on earth ignoring the postmortem fate of the just and the wicked.

The Thanksgiving Hymns (1QH)

Expressed in didactic hymns, the same theological point of view is found in the *Hymns* scroll where there is no pure realized eschatology. The present salvation of the pious is a promise for the future at the time of judgment, and an anticipation of communion with God. As the destruction of the wicked is still awaited, the same is true for the eternal life of the pious with God in the company of angels. Instructed in the divine mysteries, the author knows the present and the future, the struggle of the two spirits in the human heart and the final results, the everlasting punishment and the reward at the time of the end, of the universal conflagration and of the renewal of creation. To enter the community of those who have knowledge and to persevere in the trials are necessary to receive the promised inheritance and future rewards. The present community is not the final salvation, only the first step, for the *Hymns* knows a linear eschatology that ends with universal conflagration and total renewal, as well as the existence of an intermediary state in different spheres of heaven, earth, and Sheol — that means there are both an individual and a collective eschatology. In some hymns, judgment, rewards, and punishment depend on the results of the eschatological war with the fall of Belial and of all the enemies who will burn in Abaddôn (1QH 11.30-37; 14.32-39; 7.30ff.). By contrast, the rewards are the resurrection of the just and the transformation of the living as in Dan 12 and Isa 26:19 (1QH 14.37; 5.28-29; 19.15-16). The faithful know that they will receive the benefit of salvation by the grace of God after being purified of the great sin, which is an allusion to the original sin (1QH 11.21), and clothe themselves in the glory of Adam for the length of days (1QH 4.27), which means everlasting life. The curse that had fallen on mankind will be changed into blessing for the faithful, so that Paradise and life with God will be given back to them. This is compared to an exaltation to eternal height *(rwm ᵃwlm)*, an exal-

15. See Puech, *La croyance,* 2:443-98.

tation of the just above the angels in the eternal light of God himself (1QH 24.6-13), the creation being purified and renewed through the fire. All this agrees with the previous texts.[16]

> 30 Then the torrents of Belial will overflow their high banks
> by a fire devouring all their waterings
> to destroy every tree, green 31 or dry, from their canals,
> and it will roam with flames of fire
> until the annihilation of all that drink from them.
> It will consume the foundations of clay 32 and the seating of dry land;
> the bases of the mountains will become a burning
> and the roots of flint streams of lava
> and it will consume until the great 33 Abyss.
> Then the torrents of Belial will break into Abaddôn,
> the schemers of Abyss will howl in a roar of extractions of mud.
> The earth 34 will cry out at the calamity overtaking the world
> and all its schemers will scream
> and all that are upon it will go crazy
> 35 and will melt away by the great calamity.
> For God will thunder with the roar of his strength,
> and his holy residence will howl with the truth of 36 his glory,
> and the host of the heavens will add to their voice,
> and the eternal foundations will be melt and will shake,
> and the battle of heavenly 37 heroes will roam over the earth,
> and will not stop until the destruction, eternally determined
> and unparalleled. (1QH 11)

> Then the sword of God will pounce at the time of judgment,
> and all his faithful children will awaken
> to destroy [all the children of] 33 wickedness,
> and all the children of guilt will be no more.
> And the Hero will draw his bow
> and he will open the heavenly encirclements 34 into an endless open space
> and the everlasting gates to take out weapons of war,
> and they will be victorious from one end to the other.
> They will shoot 35 arrows and there will be no salvation for
> a guilty creature,
> they will trample to destruction without captive

16. See Puech, *La croyance*, 2:335-419, for the rearrangement of columns and text, our translation.

and without hope for the multitude of corpses
36 and for all the heroes of war there will be no shelter.
For to God Most High belongs the *ju[dgment]*
and . . . ,
37 and those who lie in the dust will hoist the flag,
and the worm of the dead will raise the banner to the rampart
and they will destroy the enemies cutting them down 38 in the battles
    of the insolent.
And the overwhelming whip, when it will pass,
will not enter into the fortress, but it will to[uch them with —]
39 and the stroke will destroy the works of Belial
[and it will be like the stone] for plaster or as the beam for fire. (1QH 14)

And their visitation will be in the abundance of 22 compassi]on
and everlasting favors for all their periods in peace,
or the ruin of their *de[eds of impiety,*
and You will reward them according to] 23 their judgments:
eternal glory and delight and unending joy for [good] deeds,
[but afflictions and pu]nishments for [ba]d 24 de[eds].
These are those [You] esta[blished before the wo]rld
to judge through them 25 all your works before creating them,
together with the host of your spirits and the congregation of [*your angels,*
with your holy vault and all 26 his hosts,
with the earth and all its productions,
in the seas and in the abysses,
[according] to all their designs for all the eternal ages 27 and the
    final visitation.
For You have established them before the world,
and you have [raised up] in them the work of man
so that 28 they may count your glory throughout all your dominion,
for you have shown them what they have never se[en,
destroying] what was old and creating 29 new things,
demolishing ancient things and erecting eternal beings,
for you have established them
and you will exist 30 for ever and ever. (1QH 5)

And for the sake of your glory, you have purified man from offence,
so that he may be holy 14 for you
from every abomination of impurity and guilt of unfaithfulness,
to become united with the children of your truth
and in the lot with 15 your holy ones,

to raise from the dust the worms of the dead to an
    everla[sting] community
and from a depraved spirit to your knowledge,
16 so that he can stand for service in your presence with the perpetual host
and with the spirits [*of eternity*]
and so that to be renewed with all that ex[ist 17 and] will exist,
and with those who know in a community of jubilation. (1QH 19)

25 Burning burns] the foundations of mountains
and fire [sears] the base of Sheol,
You have esta[blished them] by your judgments 26 [— ,
and] you [-] those who serve you loyally
so that their posterity will be before you all the days.
And [their] abo[de] you have established 27 [*in heaven,*
so that they refrain from] offence
and they cast away all their iniquities,
and they can inherit all the glory of Adam in the abundance of days.

(1QH 4)

You will settle the spirits of wickedness away from the e[arth
and all the — who are acting] 7 wrongly will be no more,
and you will place the abode of the wic[ked in the dark places
    of Abaddôn
and in the Sheôl] all 8 the spirits of impiety,
where they will be oppressed by sorrow [and — ,
and — , 9 and delight for everlasting generations.
And when the impiety will arise for the domi[nion upon the children
    of darkness,
—]10 their oppression will grow up to destruction.
Before all your creatures [you will judge them
according to the amount of] y[our compassion and] the abundance
    of 11 your favors.
In order to know everything in your glory
and to preci[se — and — of] the determined time,
you made known 12 your judgment of truth
and to the ear of flesh you revealed (it)
and [in your — you have taught] to the man the plan of 13 your heart
and you have explained the time of the instruction to the flesh.
[For the spirits of the ho]st from above, you will judge in the height,
14 and those who dwell on the earth, on the earth,
and also [the inhabitants of Sheô]l beneath you will judge,

and those who sit 15 in the darkness you will accuse,
when you will declare the just just
and when you will declare wic[ked the wicked — . (1QH 25)

And You, 13 man, above the g[ods, you will establish (him)
and you shut him like a bird] imprisoned until the time of your good will.
(1QH 24)

The insistence of all these Qumran texts — that without cleansing of the
spirit the body cannot be cleansed and that in the future God will purify the human body of all wickedness — suggests a strong unitary view of human nature,
which testifies clearly in favor of belief in the resurrection of the body as a condition of everlasting life. The anthropologies of these passages are consistently uniform, and not varying, as some scholars have claimed. But of course, they understood the resurrection only for the just people of God, while the living will be
transformed into glory at the time of judgment when the world will be renewed.
Putting aside the literary genre of the texts, it is difficult to find in them the possibility of human existence without a body for the eternal destiny of the righteous.
The clearest text on this topic is now *On Resurrection* (the *Messianic Apocalypse*).

On Resurrection (Messianic Apocalypse; 4Q521)

The manuscript asserts clearly the belief in resurrection.[17] Among the divine
benefits at the end, it says: "God will heal the deadly wounded and he will raise
the dead" (2 ii 12). Then, after the coming of the prophet and of the king Messiah, it describes the judgment: "The cursed one shall be for death [when] the
One who is giving life [will resurrec]t the dead of his people," in a form of short
credo (7, 5-6):

]see all t[hat has made 2the Lord, (the) ear]th and all that is in it,
(the) seas and all 3that they contain] and all (the) reservoirs of water
        and torrents.
4[Rejoice, al]l [of you,] who are doing good before the Lord,
5[the blessed but no]t like these, the accursed,
and [they] shall be for death,
[when] the Reviver 6[will resurrec]t the dead of his people.
7Then we shall give thanks and announce to you the justices of the Lord

17. See Puech, *La croyance,* 2:627-92, and Puech, *Qumrân Grotte 4,* XVIII: *Textes hébreux
(4Q521–4Q528, 4Q576–4Q579),* DJD 25 (Oxford: Clarendon, 1998), pp. 1-38.

wh[o has delivered] 8the mortals
and has opened [the tombs of . . . ,]
9and has o[pened the books . . . ,
10. . . ,]
11and the valley of death in[. . . ,]
12and the bridge of the Aby[ss . . . ,]
13the accursed have coagulated [. . . ,]
14and the heavens have welcome[d . . . ,
15and al]l the angels[. . .].

Quite clearly, this passage follows the concept in Dan 12. The resurrection is understood as a new creation: as the creator, the Lord can create anew when he is providing justice to the just of his people, by opening the tombs and raising the dead to life or glorifying the living. But there is more than what we have seen in the previous texts on the fate of the wicked and the just. Something is said about the place and condition of the accursed and the blessed. After crossing the bridge on the Abyss, the accursed will be rigid or coagulated, falling down into Abaddôn or Sheol, a freezing hell, while the blessed will be welcomed by the personified heavens to live in the company of the angels. This new and unique notion recalls the Bridge of the Sorter of Zoroastrianism on the one hand,[18] and on the other, the conviction found elsewhere in the Qumran texts that at the time of the visitation or judgment the just will stand before God in the company of angels and be similar to them, even above them. In other words, the state of the resurrected body is not a pure return to life on earth. Instead, it involves a spiritual transformation for the living as well as for the risen dead so that they can stand before God and serve him.

This eschatology recaptures the original state of Eden (the protology), that the just are waiting to enter the paradise lost: the restoration of the just in their bodies to the state of humanity before the original fall, on a renewed earth purified of wickedness by fire. Consequently, the state of the resurrected body or flesh, already present in *1 Enoch*, is that of the glory of Adam living in the company of God and of the angels. Thus it is easy to understand the passages of the New Testament speaking of a spiritual body *(sōma pneumatikon)* at the resurrection, and of the renewal of all *(palingenesia;* Mt 19:28; 2 Pet 3:13; Rev 21:1).

These Qumran texts show that after the messianic kingdom, the Essenes expect the day of visitation-judgment in the eschaton to usher in the

18. But Zoroastrianism has a fully developed doctrine of the resurrection of all mankind (see *Bundahishn* 34). Resurrection is associated with judgment of the just and the evil deeds of man that will be revealed when all mankind is resurrected and gathered for judgment. But the dates of these texts are difficult to establish.

glorification-resurrection-transformation of the just on a new earth, and the eternal destruction of the wicked in Sheol-Abaddon. There is no doubt about that, contrary to what scholars have stated for decades. Qumranic eschatology is much more unified and consistent than it could be expected at first.[19] And it agrees precisely with the statement of Hippolytus of Rome about the Essenes: "They acknowledge both that the flesh will rise again and that it will be immortal, in the same manner that the soul is already imperishable" (*Refutatio* 9.27). This view is proximate, if not identical, to the eschatology of the Pharisees, the separated branch of *Hasîdîm,* who based their view on the same biblical and apocryphal compositions.[20]

The eternal life of the just in the glory of Adam and in the company of God and angels does not agree with the concept of immortality or of an immediate assumption after death in an individual eschatology, but with the belief in resurrection-transformation at the end of time as rewards, whereas the wicked will be punished forever in a collective eschatology. Such a belief in the afterlife, based on the scriptures and the Jewish traditional texts, is what is also found in the teaching of Jesus.[21] The same view is found in the Qumran compositions so far published. But the death and resurrection of Jesus inaugurated the eschatological process (Acts 26:23; 1 Cor 15:20; Col 1:18). This is God's vindication of the persecution of Jesus (Rom 4:24; 8:11).

Selected Bibliography

Baumgarten, J. M. *Qumran Cave 4. XIII: The Damascus Document (4Q266-273).* On the basis of transcription by J. T. Milik. DJD 18. Oxford: Clarendon, 1966.
Cavallin, H. C. C. *Life after Death: Paul's Argument for the Resurrection of the Dead in 1 Cor 15.* Pt. 1, *An Inquiry into Jewish Background.* Coniectanea biblica, New Testament Series 7:1. Lund: Gleerup, 1974.

19. It is amazing to see how scholars contradict themselves along the pages trying to prove the contrary; for instance, see P. R. Davies, "Death, Resurrection, and Life after Death in the Qumran Scrolls," in *Judaism in Late Antiquity,* ed. A. J. Avery-Peck and J. Neusner, pt. 4, *Death, Life-after-death, Resurrection, and the World-to-Come in the Judaism of Antiquity* (Leiden: Brill, 2000), pp. 208-10.

20. The Qumran burial practices are in full agreement with the Essenes' belief in the afterlife. And if the south-north direction of the tombs were not exactly unique, it is the best one that agrees with their beliefs.

21. For many more Jewish texts, see Puech, *La croyance,* 1:99-199. See recently Viviano and Taylor, "Sadducees, Angels, and Resurrection," pp. 496-98, even if I do not accept their explanations of the verse and on the intermediary state. On the different Jewish opinions and the New Testament passages, see Puech, *La croyance,* 1:201-85.

Davies, P. R. "Death, Resurrection, and Life after Death in the Qumran Scrolls." In *Judaism in Late Antiquity,* edited by A. J. Avery-Peck and J. Neusner, pp. 189-211. Pt. 4, *Death, Life-after-Death, Resurrection, and the World-to-Come in the Judaism of Antiquity.* Leiden: Brill, 2000.

Puech, E. *La croyance des Esséniens en la vie future: Immortalité, résurrection, vie éternelle? Histoire d'une croyance dans le Judaïsme ancien.* Vol. 1, *La résurrection des morts et le contexte scripturaire.* Vol. 2, *Les données qumraniennes et classiques.* Études Bibliques (nouvelle série n°s 21-22). Paris: Gabalda, 1993. Includes a long bibliography.

———. *Qumrân Grotte 4.* XVIII: *Textes hébreux (4Q521–4Q528, 4Q576–4Q579).* DJD 25. Oxford: Clarendon, 1998.

———. "Immortality and Life after Death." In *The Dead Sea Scrolls — Fifty Years after Their Discovery: Major Issues and New Approaches; Jerusalem International Congress, 1997.* Jerusalem: Israel Exploration Society, 2001.

Strugnell, J., D. Harrington, and T. Elgvin. *Qumran Cave 4.* XXIV: *Sapiential Texts.* Pt. 2. DJD 24. Oxford: Clarendon, 1999.

Van der Ploeg, J. "The Belief in Immortality in the Writings of Qumran." *Bibliotheca Orientalis* 18 (1961): 118-24.

Archaeology and Early Christology

John Reumann

The Origins of Christology

Christology traditionally has to do with what believers confess about the work and person of Jesus Christ. It thus includes his teachings and his deeds, to help and heal, to call for repentance and to forgive sins; his expression of authority; death and resurrection; and the various titles people have employed to express his exaltation in their lives and that of the community of followers.[1] Vincent Taylor once listed no fewer than fifty-two of these titles in the New Testament alone.[2] Such exaltation arose early and pervasively. The full story of Christology would have to include efforts to assert the deity of Jesus while maintaining that he was a man of Jewish flesh from Nazareth. It would also have to include his place in the trinitarian Godhead, for which there is already triadic foreshadowing in the New Testament (2 Cor 13:13; Mt 28:19).

To illustrate: around 55 C.E., in his letter to the Philippians, Paul was citing a rhetorically splendid "hymn" (or, better, an encomium) about a figure in the form of God — indeed, of whom equality with God can be mentioned — who suffers humiliation and death but whom God exalts to lordship.[3] Traditionally

---

1. See A. Grillmeier, *Christ in Christian Tradition*, vol. 1, *From the Apostolic Age to Chalcedon (451)*, trans. J. Bowden, rev. 2nd ed. (Atlanta: John Knox, 1975); H. Schwarz, *Christology* (Grand Rapids: Eerdmans, 1998), which, while written from the standpoint of a systematic theologian, gives attention to the quests for the historical Jesus.

2. Taylor, *The Names of Jesus* (New York: St. Martin's Press, 1953).

3. Much of the enormous literature on Phil 2:6-11 is treated by R. P. Martin, *A Hymn of Christ: Philippians 2:5-11 in Recent Interpretation and in the Setting of Early Christian Worship* (Downers Grove, Ill.: InterVarsity, 1997), and in R. P. Martin and B. J. Dodd, eds., *Where Christology Began: Essays on Philippians 2* (Louisville: Westminster John Knox, 1998). Even if one should accept the notion that the "hymn" was originally written in Aramaic and stems from

660

Phil 2:6-11 is taken to present Christ as "with God" at the beginning, as fully human, and then given the title above all names, *Kyrios,* or Lord, thereby straining monotheism but retaining it by means of the final phrase, that all is "to the glory of God the Father." *Kyrios* here is often regarded as equivalent to the Hebrew Tetragrammaton, but this is not without problems when Septuagint manuscripts are considered like P. Fuad 266. Here in the Greek translation the four Hebrew letters are written in the text, and we have no idea whether in Greek a reader used *"kyrios"* at that point, "my Lord *(adonai),"* or something else.[4] More recently some scholars have explored Jewish speculation about Wisdom, Word, and the Spirit as a "second God,"[5] thus giving some background in Judaism for the Christology of Phil 2:9-11. More specifically, in Roman Philippi Jesus' title could be directed against the emperor, *Dominus Caesar.*[6]

Christology from Above and from Below

Christology has been developed not only "from above," as in the Philippians passage, with a figure who comes from God, but also "from below" *(von unten),* beginning with the man Jesus, who was baptized by John, went about doing good, etc., as in Mark's Gospel or Acts 10:36. Indeed, Albert Schweitzer maintained that attempts to recover "Jesus as he really was" could begin only when the Chalcedonian and trinitarian formulae were laid aside.[7] In our day, "historical Jesus" studies have more and more been concerned to find a Jesus like us. "Like us" may include a liberationist or pacifist Jesus, a feminist, gay, or celibate Jesus, and so on down the line of contemporary interests. One can list a dozen or more types of Jesus figures that writers have championed.[8] This does not necessarily mean a figure void of Christology, but most of the titles have been

Antioch — a view that appears increasingly unlikely — the passage in no way represents the beginning of Christology, for it includes a far earlier formula in v. 11, "Jesus Christ is Lord."

4. See G. Howard, "The Tetragram and the New Testament," *JBL* 96 (1977): 63-83; J. D. G. Dunn, *The Theology of Paul the Apostle* (Grand Rapids: Eerdmans, 1998), pp. 249-52.

5. See below, n. 66.

6. The passage will be discussed in my Philippians commentary, forthcoming in the Anchor Bible series.

7. Schweitzer, *The Quest of the Historical Jesus: A Critical Study of Its Progress from Reimarus to Wrede* (German 1906; English 1910; Baltimore: Johns Hopkins University Press, 1998), p. 3.

8. J. Reumann, "Jesus and Christology," in *The New Testament and Its Modern Interpreters,* ed. E. J. Epp and G. W. MacRae (Philadelphia: Fortress; Atlanta: Scholars, 1989), pp. 520-24. "Jesus the Jew and Jesus as seen by Jewish scholarship" is one of the categories. A particular aspect of it has been examined in my contribution to the Festschrift for Harry M. Orlinsky, *"Leben-Jesu-Forschung* in Eretz-Israel," *ErIsr* 16 (1982): 186*-92*.

placed in their development, if not their origins, in the period after Easter by recent scholarship. Christology in the career of the historical Jesus becomes indirect, something during Jesus' lifetime that foreshadows later development but was not yet overt. It is no accident, but instead reflects a trend, that my assignment in this area for the 100th anniversary volume of the Society of Biblical Literature in the 1980s was "Jesus *and* Christology," not a Christology of Jesus himself.[9] Such a trend was heralded by Morna Hooker's *Jesus and the Servant,* not a Jesus who (thought he) was the Servant of God.[10] Here is pointed up the question of whether such titles were post-Easter or were created by Jesus, or were pre-Christian and pre-Jesus and thus a part of Jewish "messianology."[11]

To illustrate: Phil 2:6-11 can be read as beginning not with a figure in heaven but with a human figure on earth, indeed one like the Servant, who is afflicted, indeed martyred, but then exalted, as in Wisdom of Solomon 2:10, 12-20.[12] The question that "Christology from below" poses is how much messianology is rooted in the lifetime of Jesus, even though it escalates after Easter. Another way of asking the question is not how much of a "messianic consciousness" the historical Jesus possessed (or that we can demonstrate), but how much of an "eschatological consciousness" did he express, that during his ministry the Day of the Lord and the kingship of God were at hand.

9. See n. 8 above, and contrast B. Witherington III, *The Christology of Jesus* (Philadelphia: Fortress, 1990).

10. M. Hooker, *Jesus and the Servant: The Influence of the Servant Concept of Deutero-Isaiah in the New Testament* (London: SPCK, 1959).

11. Thus some (cf. Hooker, *Jesus and the Servant*) argue that identification of Jesus with "the servant" is a post-Easter creation, as in 1 Pet 2:21-24 or in Mt 8:16-17 where Jesus' healings and exorcisms are identified with Isa 53:4 ("he took our infirmities and bore our diseases") by the Matthean community or the Evangelist. Others hold that Jesus was the one who first made the identification, during his ministry; cf. T. W. Manson, *The Servant-Messiah: A Study of the Public Ministry of Jesus* (Cambridge: Cambridge University Press, 1953). J. Jeremias, *"pais theou,"* in *TDNT* 5:667-717, sought to trace it back to connections in Jewish texts prior to Jesus. The Dead Sea Scrolls have led to further efforts to parallel and contrast the self-understandings of the Teacher of Righteousness and of Jesus; cf. J. H. Charlesworth, "The Righteous Teacher and the Historical Jesus," in *Earthing Christologies: From Jesus' Parables to Jesus the Parable,* ed. J. H. Charlesworth and W. P. Weaver (Valley Forge, Pa.: Trinity, 1995), pp. 46-61. Extreme views have been put forth by I. Knohl, *The Messiah before Jesus: The Suffering Servant in the Dead Sea Scrolls* (Berkeley: University of California Press, 2000), and M. O. Wise, *The First Messiah: Investigating the Savior before Christ* (San Francisco: HarperSanFrancisco, 1999). Such views had appeared (and generally been set aside) in earlier speculations on the scrolls by A. Dupont-Sommer and A. Nolan, *Jesus before Christianity* (London: Darton, Longman and Todd, 1977; Maryknoll, N.Y.: Orbis, 1978).

12. J. Murphy-O'Connor, "Christological Anthropology in Phil. II.6-11," *RB* 83 (1976): 25-50.

Early Christology

"*Early* Christology" can have several meanings, relative to different views about the topic generally. Here we exclude the later developments in the third-to-fifth centuries.[13] Some would tie it exclusively to the New Testament period, perhaps including the early decades of the second century, using terms like "apostolic age" and "subapostolic age." Others might limit it to Jewish Christianity, in a sequence that runs on into Hellenistic-Jewish, and then Gentile, Christianity. Still others might connect it with the Christology claimed during and from the lifetime of Jesus. While efforts are made in historical Jesus studies and the Gospels to distinguish sharply among the various titles like "Son of Man," "Messiah" (Christ), and "Son of God," it has been argued that titles soon came to be used loosely; one was interchanged with another, without regard to original meanings. All of them exalt Jesus.

It is not always realized how rapidly and completely a Hebrew term like *māšîaḥ* (messiah) dropped out of Christian usage, in favor of its Greek translation "Christ" (*Christos,* "anointed person"). Whatever one concludes from the history of anointed kings, priests, and occasionally prophets in Israel and about messianic figures and movements in Jesus' day, let alone development of the theme with regard to Jesus in Christianity,[14] the term in Greek, *ho messias,* occurs only twice in the entire New Testament. Surprisingly, both instances are in John, the Gospel often regarded as most christological and theological and even anti-Jewish, but which sometimes may preserve well-founded traditions. In 1:41 Andrew announces to his brother Peter, "We have found the Messiah," to which the explanation is added, "(which is translated Anointed)" or (NRSV note) "Christ." In 4:25 the Samaritan woman at the well in Sychar says to Jesus, "I know that Messiah is coming," which the Evangelist explains by the phrase "(who is called Christ)." The woman meant not an anointed king from the house of David but Taheb, "one who returns," a

13. This excludes developments precisely in a period when Christology was being most clearly and forcefully articulated in the councils of Nicea (325 c.e.), Ephesus (431), and Chalcedon (451) and a period from which we often have archaeological evidence. Is, e.g., the "beautiful new synagogue at Capernaum, dated now to about 370 c.e.," to be "interpreted as a restatement of the Jewish community's solidarity in the face of Christian encroachment at the House of St. Peter, just a few yards away"? So D. E. Groh, "The Religion of the Empire: Christianity from Constantine to the Arab Conquest," in *Christianity and Rabbinic Judaism: A Parallel History of Their Origins and Early Development,* ed. H. Shanks (Washington, D.C.: Biblical Archaeology Society, 1992), p. 302.

14. See, among many treatments, the chapters in J. H. Charlesworth and L. L. Johns, eds., *The Messiah: Developments in Earliest Judaism and Christianity; The First Princeton Symposium on Judaism and Christian Origins* (Minneapolis: Fortress, 1992).

Prophet-like-Moses figure.[15] The Evangelist explains her Samaritan beliefs for Christian readers with a Jewish designation, *Messias*. These are the only uses of the term in the Greek NT; elsewhere it is always *(ho) Christos*. NRSV, out of philo-Semitism or an attempt at historical verisimilitude, has inserted "(the) Messiah" at Jn 1:20, 25; 3:28; 4:29; Rom 9:5; and elsewhere. The matter is no different on use of *Messias* in related early Christian literature and in the church fathers.[16]

Archaeology's Contribution to Christology

How much can archaeology contribute to discussion about the rise of Christology? Very little, it would seem, when literature on each term is examined. In books on New Testament Christology there is seldom any reference to archaeology, and in treatments of (New Testament) archaeology, seldom is there a listing in the index to "Christology" or even "Christolatry" or the worship of Jesus Messiah.[17] To put it in negative terms, one often finds an ambiguity about archaeological evidence, just as there is frequently about the interpretation of literary texts. Discoveries of artifacts are differently interpreted and vigorously debated just as with the New Testament and Jewish documents. Presentations at this conference provide ample evidence of unresolved questions and competing answers about finds from a dig.

To illustrate: in 1945, when a new road was being cut from Jerusalem to Bethlehem, ossuaries with inscriptions were found at Talpioth. They were dated to 40-50 C.E., in part because a coin of Herod Agrippa from 42-47 was found in the tomb. Names included Simeon Barsaba, Mariam daughter of Barsaba, and Metai. With these names scholars sometimes compared those on ossuaries at the *Dominus Flevit* site on the Mount of Olives. One Greek inscription at Talpioth read *Iesous iou*, which, if pointed with a circumflex accent on the sec-

---

15. See R. Brown, *John*, AB 29 (Garden City, N.Y.: Doubleday, 1966), pp. 172, 176. Commentators and dictionaries like *TDNT* 9 (1974), pp. 566-68 (W. Grundmann), seldom make much of these two rare usages, amid the concatenation and sequence of titles in Jn 1:35-51 (in v. 38 "rabbi" is also explained as "teacher").

16. See BADG, p. 635, and *PGL*, where there is no entry for *Messias* or example of the noun in references under *Christos* (1531), even in connection with A, "of anointed persons in OT"; B, "of Jewish Messiah"; or C, "Jesus as the Christ."

17. So A. Deissmann, *Light from the Ancient East* (New York: George H. Doran Co., 1927), p. 382: "From the time of Paul there is not Christology but a Christolatry, recognizable as such by the historian of religion — a Christianity of Christ." In the index of M. F. Unger's *Archaeology of the New Testament* (Grand Rapids: Zondervan, 1962), the term "Christology" does not occur. The same situation obtains in most such treatments.

ond word, would mean "Woe" or "Alas for Jesus."[18] But with an acute accent, the same phrase could be rendered "Jesus, joy."[19] A second Talpioth inscription read *Iesous aloth,* perhaps referring to "aloes" for burial (Jn 19:39, *aloēs;* Hebrew *'ªhālôth*), but it was also read as a Hebrew form from the infinitive *'lh,* "Jesus has gone up" (ascended), or an appeal to the risen Jesus for the deceased, "Jesus, let (him who rests here) arise," or even "help!"[20] The inscriptions generated lively discussion for a time, even sensationalistic ones in some newspapers.[21] Little has been heard of these once-publicized finds since Fishwick in 1963 laid many of the existing theories to rest and proposed that we have here "the earliest evidence of Christian influences within Jewish syncretic magic," the name "Jesus" infiltrating what were "Jewish abbreviations of the Divine Name."[22] If correct, this reading would show how pervasive the deity of Jesus was, in some Jewish circles, at an early but uncertain date. Little has been heard since on the matter. NEAEHL (2:752) records simply that Sukenik's view of sorrow at the crucifixion of Jesus has not been accepted, and that any application of the *Dominus Flevit* inscriptions to Judeo-Christians is "doubtful." A final nail has been placed in the coffin of such speculations about these ossuary inscriptions

18. So E. L. Sukenik, "The Earliest Records of Christianity," *AJA* 51 (1947): 351-65. For this sense of *iou* one can cite Aristophanes, *Thesmophoriazusae* 245. Usually *iou* occurs twice in such instances, as in Sophocles, *Trachiniae* 1143; some took an oblique diagonal stroke to the upper right of the upsilon as a sign of repetition; others as an acute accent mark. The inscription is reproduced, among other places, in J. Finegan, *The Archaeology of the New Testament: The Life of Jesus and the Beginning of the Early Church* (Princeton: Princeton University Press, 1969), p. 241, hereafter Finegan, *Archaeology* (1969); less satisfactorily, without the diagonal stroke, in E. Dinkler, "Comments on the History of the Symbol of the Cross" (German 1951), reprinted in his collected essays, *Signum Crucis* (Tübingen: Mohr-Siebeck, 1967), translated in *The Bultmann School of Biblical Interpretation: New Directions? JTC,* vol. 1 (Tübingen: Mohr-Siebeck; New York: Harper and Row, 1965), p. 126.

19. As in Aristophanes, *Knights* 1096. Other guesses were *iou[da]* = of Judah (so Bagatti); or "(son of) Jehu." Cf. Dinkler, "Comments," p. 131, and Finegan, *Archaeology* (1969), p. 241.

20. Sukenik derived *aloth* on ossuary 8 from Hebrew *'lh* = lament; O. Moe from *'lh* = rise; references in D. Fishwick, "The Talpioth Ossuaries Again," *NTS* 10 (1963-64): 53 n. 7 and 51 n. 3. Some took it as a personal name. Cf. Dinkler, "Comments," pp. 127-31; Finegan, *Archaeology* (1969), pp. 242-43.

21. There is a good discussion for the general reader in Finegan, *Archaeology* (1969), pp. 240-43. Note the subtitle of his book — it does *not* use the word "Christology." Earlier, see A. Parrot, *Golgotha and the Church of the Holy Sepulchre,* Studies in Biblical Archaeology 6 (London: SCM, 1957), pp. 113-16; B. Gustafsson, "The Oldest Graffiti in the History of the Church?" *NTS* 3 (1956-57): 65-69. Much was made also of ossuaries found in the Kidron Valley in 1941, possibly containing burials of a Jewish family from Cyrenaica, more conjecturally the bones of Alexander and the Simon of Cyrene who carried Jesus' cross; see N. Avigad, "A Depository of Inscribed Ossuaries in the Kidron Valley," *IEJ* 12 (1962): 1-12.

22. Fishwick, "The Talpioth Ossuaries Again," pp. 61 and 58.

as references to Jesus and early Christians by the observation of J. Murphy-O'Connor that "[t]he XR (chi-rho) sign on one ossuary does not mean that the person was a Christian, it is attested as an abbreviation for 'sealed.'"[23]

Numerous other examples might be cited of archaeological finds that could have importance for the historical Jesus and/or Christology but have often turned out to be marked by uncertainties. Space limits the instances that can be discussed here.

a. At Caesarea Philippi (Paneas, Banyas), the environs of which provide the traditional site for Peter's confession in Mark and Matthew, a bronze relief on a stone has been said to represent Jesus healing the woman with a hemorrhage (Mt 9:20-22 pars.). Eusebius reports seeing it in the fourth century with his own eyes (*HE* 7.18). The woman was given the name "Bernice" (Latin "Veronica") and became part of the "Veronica legend" (about how she wiped the face of Jesus on his way to the cross and preserved this image on her cloth). The Banyas representation, said to have been before her house (for she was then a pagan), showed a woman on bended knee, beseeching a man in a double cloak. At his feet grew an herb that served as antidote for all sorts of diseases. Christians took the figure to represent Jesus. But quite likely it was originally a depiction of Asclepius or a Roman emperor.[24] There are references to Jesus as a powerful healer — indeed, of such a woman — but it is doubtful that the bronze statuary was erected by Christians to represent him. More likely it is a secondary identification of some other figure with their Savior.

b. Christ *the Good Shepherd* (Jn 10), certainly a christological theme relating him to God (Ezek 34), is often depicted as a figure with a lamb on his shoulders (Lk 15:4-7 par.). The pose found in statuary is similar to that of Hermes bearing a ram on his shoulders.[25]

23. J. Murphy-O'Connor, *The Holy Land: An Archeological Guide from Earliest Times to 1700* (Oxford: Oxford University Press, 1992), p. 131. Fishwick, "The Talpioth Ossuaries Again," pp. 51-52, notes that the "rectangular (+) and diagonal (x) crosses" at *Dominus Flevit* and Talpioth are precarious as references to Jesus' crucifixion, since the usual symbol for it was a tau (T).

24. See W. Safaris, "Jesus and Caesarea Philippi," at this conference. According to early Christian historians, what Eusebius saw was destroyed by Julian the Apostate later in the fourth century; this suggests that the monument was venerated by Christians of that period. The healing plant suggests Asclepius. Reference to a "a savior" or "god" in the accompanying inscription may have encouraged Christians to identify it with their Jesus. It thus tells us how much he was revered. See the discussion in E. von Dobschütz, *Christusbilder, Untersuchungen zur Christlichen Legende*, TU 18 (n.s., 3) (Leipzig: Hinrichs, 1899), and in SC 41 on the passage. B. Pixner, *Wege der Messias und Stätten der Urkirche: Jesus und das Judenchristen im Lichte neuer archäologischer Erkenntnisse*, ed. R. Riesner (Giessen: Brunnen, 1991 [2nd ed. 1994]), pp. 89-90, refers to the pagan environment and to the *petra Haemorrhoisae*.

25. E. Stauffer, *Die Theologie des Neuen Testaments* (Gütersloh: Bertelsmann, 1948), prints

Figure 78. Mount Hermon (right); Caesarea Philippi (left of center in valley).
Courtesy of J. H. Charlesworth

c. Inscriptions and art from *the catacombs* provide some evidence of Christology with regard to beliefs about the resurrection of believers and the after-

side by side as plates 63 and 64 (omitted in the English ed.) *Hermes Kriophorus* (copy of a fifth century B.C.E. Greek statue, honored in Christian times as one of Christ) and *Christus Pastor Bonus* (third century C.E. sarcophagus relief); cf. the Good Shepherd statue from El Mina, Gaza, fourth century, Israel Antiquities Authority 32.1802, and the Good Shepherd statue at Caesarea (fifth century?; see Finegan, *Archaeology* [1969], p. 76). G. Snyder, *Ante Pacem: Archaeological Evidence of Church Life before Constantine* (Macon, Ga.: Mercer University Press, 1985) — not Christology but "church life" — pp. 55-56; cf. pp. 22-24, 36-38. Snyder wishes to apply the figure to the *Christian community* as a "caring" one, and only after the peace of Constantine, to "the one who gave us that 'care.'" But note also his distinction: "the major difference between the Old Testament and New Testament in early Christian art lies in the presence of a deliverer (Jesus), rather than a delivered (Orante)" (p. 55); on the praying female figure, Orante, see pp. 19-20. But the inscription of Abercius (pp. 139-40; *RAC* 1:12-17; *JAC* 23 [1980]: 22-47), with its reference to this citizen (of Hierapolis) as a "disciple of the holy Shepherd," is pre-Constantinian. E. R. Goodenough, *Jewish Symbols in the Greco-Roman Period,* Bollingen Series 37 (Princeton: Princeton University Press, 1956), 5:40-41, argued for the "fish from the fountain," the "very great" and "pure" fish in the inscription as Jewish and kosher. Thus symbols, even when coupled with texts, in an inscription, often remain ambiguous. But it is likely that Christ as the Good Shepherd arose out of earlier (pagan) artistic representations and biblical texts in Christian use, prior to Constantine.

life, reflective of Jesus' resurrection. The materials may at times be related to liturgy, another area that can involve both texts and archaeological remains.[26]

d. The history of *the cross* as a theological symbol, not just a means of execution, has often been treated.[27] "[I]n the field of archaeology," Dinkler wrote in 1951, "it has been an absolute dogma that the symbol of the cross makes its first appearance in the age of Constantine."[28] But one piece of archaeological evidence reversed that view, at least for a time. The so-called "cross of Herculaneum," to which Sukenik had appealed in making his case for the Talpioth ossuary inscriptions as Christian (above, n. 18), was a cross-shaped recess on the wall in a room of a house excavated in 1938 at Herculaneum, as part of the 200th anniversary of excavations there (and hence dubbed the Casa del Bicentenario). Although the table or cupboard in front of it had dice in it, the room was called an early Christian sanctuary with a wall cross, to be dated before the eruption of Vesuvius in 79 C.E.[29] Subsequent examination, however, argued that it was a "wall cabinet" that was "anchored in the recess on the wall" by the nail imprints.[30] This resulting lack of evidence for *Christian* crosses led Dinkler to pursue a quest for *Jewish* cross-signs, including the tau marking in Ezek 9:4 as a protective sign from God for judgment. For Dinkler there were only "indirect connections" between Jewish and Christian cross symbols. Not the Jewish "signing with a taw" *(sēmeiōsis tou theou)*, but the Pauline "word of the cross" (1 Cor 1:18) was the start of "a new beginning" for the symbol.[31]

26. Finegan, *The Archaeology of the New Testament* (1969), surveys Jewish catacombs at both Beth She'arim (pp. 203-8) and Rome (pp. 208-12); sarcophagi and ossuaries (pp. 213-19). In his second volume, *The Archaeology of the New Testament: The Mediterranean World of the Early Christian Apostles* (Boulder Colo.: Westview Press, 1981), pp. 30-34, Finegan treats Christian *catacumbas* at Rome. Snyder, *Ante Pacem*, draws on Christian sarcophagi (pp. 35-43), cemetery structures including catacombs and martyria (pp. 82-115), and inscriptions from such sites. Cf. above, nn. 18-23 and 25.

27. Among the surveys are E. Dinkler, "Comments on the History of the Symbol of the Cross"; Finegan, *Archaeology* (1969), pp. 220-60; Snyder, *Ante Pacem*, pp. 26-29. M. Hengel has dealt with this widespread form of execution among Romans and non-Romans *(Ant* 13.380-383; *War* 1.97-98) in his *Crucifixion* (Philadelphia: Fortress, 1977) and treated separately the Christian meaning for Jesus' cross in *The Atonement: The Origins of the Doctrine in the New Testament* (Philadelphia: Fortress, 1981).

28. Dinkler, "Comments," p. 132.

29. A. Maiuri, *Herculaneum*, Guide-Books to Museums and Monuments in Italy 53 (Rome: La Libreria della Stato, 1945), pp. 47-49; Finegan, *Archaeology* (1969), pp. 249-50.

30. Dinkler, "Comments," pp. 133-34; Snyder, *Ante Pacem*, p. 27 ("three hundred years too soon"). Cf. also A. de Francisis, in *The Princeton Encyclopedia of Classical Sites* (Princeton: Princeton University Press, 1976), p. 387.

31. Dinkler, "Comments," pp. 134-45, with quotation from p. 145, a phrase from Origen,

A second piece of evidence to be considered is a drawing on the wall in the servants' quarters of the Imperial Palace on the Palatine in Rome. It depicts a man with his right hand raised toward a human figure who has a donkey's head, on a cross. The graffito reads in Greek, "ALE/ZAMENOC/CEBETE/ THEON." Even though the final two letters of the verb are slightly lower than the first four, it should presumably be read as an imperative, second-person plural, "Alexamenos, worship-ye god." But why plural? Others therefore take it as *sebet(ai)*, "Alexamenos is worshiping (his) god."[32] It would, in either case, be an early caricature of what Christians worship. Snyder allows that "there may very well be a place in early Christian art for the protective cross of the social matrix" (Ezek 9:3-8),[33] but "no place for the kerygmatic cross." That seems to assume that the cross represents only "victory, peace, and security," a so-called *Christus Victor,* Christ the King *(rex)* on a cross, but not "a crucified Christ." Yet texts as early as 1 Cor 1:23, 2:2 did speak of "Christ crucified" as the kerygma (cf. Phil 2:8), and ideas about the death of Jesus were being expressed in Jewish symbols like the "sin offering" (2 Cor 5:21) and Passover expiation (1 Cor 5:7; Rom 3:25), not to mention symbols from the Greco-Roman world like "reconciliation."[34] Did the significance of Christ's cross in Paul's day really recede until after Constantine? Was it a matter of reticence about too publicly employing a painful symbol?

e. *Miracles* are part of the identity of Jesus, in contrast to John the Baptist, who "performed no sign" (Jn 10:41); his great power is a part of Christology.[35]

Selecta in Ezechielem 9 (PG 13:800). Such Jewish cross marks were both rectangular (+ or T) and diagonal (X) (not "standing" and "reclining" as in the English translation, p. 136).

32. H. Leclercq, *DACL* 3 (1948), 3.2, pp. 3051-54, reads the third singular form; Snyder, *Ante Pacem*, pp. 27-28, the imperative, and argues that such use of the figure on the cross "hardly proves that the cross was an early Christian symbol." Finegan, *Archaeology* (1969), pp. 253-60, brings into the debate the Egyptian ankh-cross and the combination of tau and rho in some early manuscripts in abbreviations for references to crucifixion *(stauros* becomes *s + os).* On the latter item, cf. further W. Wischmeyer, "Christogram und Staurogram in den lateinischen Inschriften altkirchlicher Zeit," in *Theologia Crucis — Signum Crucis,* ed. C. Andresen and G. Klein, Festschrift E. Dinkler (Tübingen: Mohr-Siebeck, 1979), pp. 539-50.

33. *Barnabas* 9.8, which Snyder cites, is especially interesting: the figure 318 (from Gen 14:14 and 17:23), in Greek IH = 10 + 8, and T = 300, is taken to mean Jesus (first two letters of *Iēsous*) and his cross (T).

34. See the tradition history for *(apo)katallasō* terms in J. Reumann, "Reconciliation," *IDBSup*, pp. 728-29.

35. For rabbinical wonder-workers in Galilee, see G. Vermes, *Jesus the Jew: A Historian's Reading of the Gospels* (London: Collins, 1973). Vermes placed Jesus within charismatic Judaism in Galilee, as a Hasidic *zaddik,* helper, healer, teacher, and leader; this Jesus was venerated as "prophet, lord, and son of God," unsurpassed in "laying bare . . . the essence of religion" (pp. 223-25). E. Rivkin, *What Crucified Jesus? The Political Execution of a Charismatic* (Nashville:

The miracle stories in the New Testament, about mighty signs performed by Jesus in the Gospels or, under his power, by followers, as in Acts, have long been compared with stories about healings or exorcisms by rabbis or the votive tablets that recorded healings at pagan shrines like Epidaurus.[36] Form-critical analysis reflected such stories, as found in many sources, including those unearthed at healing shrines.[37] One place where we encounter a pagan shrine (with medicinal baths for clients of the god Serapis or Asclepius), Jewish tradition (about an angel troubling the waters; Jn 5:4), and a miracle story involving Jesus (Jn 5:1-13) was Bethzatha (or Bethesda) in Jerusalem.[38] The water-into-wine miracle at Cana of Galilee (Jn 2:1-11) has sometimes been seen to have a background in the Dionysus cult, for which in Galilee archaeology provides some support.[39]

f. *Numismatic evidence* has been employed by G. Theissen to argue that the

Abingdon, 1984), seems to follow this view in presenting Jesus as a "charismatic of charismatics," though miracles seem *not* to be involved in the qualities listed for such a figure by Rivkin. On the performance of miracles as a key to Jesus' self-understanding, i.e., as a charismatic with authority from God (messianic intermediary with no christological titles), see the overview in G. Theissen and A. Merz, *The Historical Jesus: A Comprehensive Guide* (Minneapolis: Fortress, 1998), pp. 212-23, 281-315.

36. So already P. Fiebig, *Jüdische Wundergeschichte des neutestamentlichen Zeitalters* (Tübingen: Mohr-Siebeck, 1911), and O. Weinreich, *Antike Heilungswunder,* Religionsgeschichtliche Versuche und Vorarbeiten 8,1 (Giessen, 1909). Further, L. P. Hogan, *Healing in the Second Temple Period,* NTOA 21 (Fribourg: Universitätsverlag; Göttingen: Vandenhoeck & Ruprecht, 1992); J. Meier, *A Marginal Jew: Rethinking the Historical Jesus* (New York: Doubleday, 1994), 2:535-37.

37. R. Bultmann, *The History of the Synoptic Tradition* (German 1921; New York: Harper and Row, 1963), pp. 220-44; Theissen and Merz, *The Historical Jesus,* pp. 281-85, 287, 289-90, 304-8 (charismatics), 314-15.

38. Up-to-date guidebooks like Murphy-O'Connor's *The Holy Land,* pp. 31-33, often pay more attention to the pagan healing sanctuary remains than do commentators, but cf. B. E. Schein, *Following the Way: The Setting of John's Gospel* (Minneapolis: Augsburg, 1980), ad loc. A reference in the Qumran *Copper Scroll* (3Q15 11.11-13) also enters into identifying the site. The folklore reference to an angel in 5:3-4 occurs in only some manuscripts. Some debate whether the Serapis (Asclepius) finds are post–New Testament. On the site generally, see J. Jeremias, *The Rediscovery of Bethesda, John 5:2,* NTAM 1 (Louisville: Southern Baptist Theological Seminary, 1966), summarized in Finegan, *Archaeology* (1969), pp. 142-47. J. F. Strange, "Beth-Zatha," in *ABD* 1:700-701, speaks of a "local healing cult" that later assumed "Roman dress" after 135 C.E.

39. R. Bultmann, *The Gospel of John* (Philadelphia: Westminster, 1971), pp. 118-19; H. Noetzel, *Christus und Dionysos: Bemerkungen zum religiongeschichtlichen Hintergrund von Johannes 2,1-11,* Arbeiten zur Theologie 1 (Stuttgart: Calwer, n.d.); Goodenough, *Symbols,* vol. 6 (1956), pp. 13-15, 43-84; note the Dionysus mosaic at "the Mansion" in Sepphoris (Murphy-O'Connor, *The Holy Land,* p. 413) and the temple (of Dionysus?) at Bet Shean (Murphy-O'Connor, p. 200).

phrase in Mt 11:7 (par. Lk 7:24) about "a reed shaken by the wind" is a reference by Jesus to Herod Antipas.[40] The phrase occurs in Jesus' tribute to John the Baptist (11:7-15), "Among those born of women no one has arisen greater than he" (11:11). But why the phrase about "a reed swaying in the wind," as the Revised English Bible renders it? It occurs in a series of questions. Jesus said to the crowds (NRSV):

7   What did you go out into the wilderness to look at?
    A reed shaken by the wind?
8   What then did you go out to see?
    Someone dressed in soft robes?
    Look, those who wear soft robes are in royal palaces.
9   What then did you go out to see?
    A prophet? Yes, I tell you, and more than a prophet.

The phrase in 7b has sometimes been taken to imply something extraordinary in the wilderness, a traditional place for God's revelation; or something of no lasting effect (the movement of the imprisoned Baptizer, 11:2, had subsided; John is then a figure wavering with every wind).[41] Or it has been read in light of Aesop's fable (which had penetrated even into rabbinic tradition, *b. Ta'an.* 20b; cf. *Der. Er. Zut.* 4; *'Abot R. Nat.* 41) about a sturdy oak tree uprooted by a storm and deposited among some reeds, frail and slender. The oak asked why they had weathered the storm but the tree was blown over. Their answer: "You fought against the storm, but we bow and bend to every breeze." The Baptist is the oak, the reeds represent the courtiers in the palace (v. 8).[42]

None of these answers can be regarded as completely satisfactory. Theissen therefore built a case for the reed as an emblem of Herod Antipas on the coins he had minted for the founding of his new capital, Tiberias, circa 19 C.E. The symbol was common on coins of cities on a river or lake (cf. the mosaic from the Byzantine Basilica of the Multiplication of the Loaves, with its water plants and Nilometer); it raised no problems for his subjects in either Galilee or Perea;

40. G. Theissen, *The Gospels in Context: Social and Political History in the Synoptic Tradition* (Minneapolis: Fortress, 1991), pp. 26-42. Theissen cites his numismatic evidence from Y. Meshorer, *Jewish Coins of the Second Temple Period* (Tel Aviv, 1967), and F. A. Madden, *History of Jewish Coinage, and of Money in the Old and New Testaments* (1864; reprint, New York: Ktav, 1967), p. 97 no. 1 and 2, p. 99 no. 1. Cf. *ABD* 1:1085-86 (J. W. Betlyon).

41. W. F. Albright and C. S. Mann, *Matthew*, AB 26 (Garden City, N.Y.: Doubleday, 1971), p. 136.

42. So D. Flusser, *Die rabbinischen Gleichnisse und der Gleichniserzähler Jesus*, pt. 1, *Das Wesen der Gleichnissse*, Judaica et Christiana 4 (Bern, Frankfurt, and Las Vegas: P. Lang, 1981), p. 52.

it accords with what Strabo (*Geogr* 16.2.16) and Pliny the Elder (*Natural History* 24.85) mention about the region (various aromatic reeds grow there). On the coin the reed replaces any head of an emperor or local ruler that might cause offense. Theissen suggests that "shaken reed" could have become a name for the king who swayed with and survived many a political wind, who wavered between wives, and even between Sepphoris and Tiberias as his place of residence. Compare "that (sly) fox" as another name that Jesus used for him (Lk 13:32). Herod Antipas later changed the image on his coinage to a sturdy palm tree (ca. 26-27 C.E.). Theissen thinks the vivid phrase goes back to Jesus himself and reflects local color of the day, as he contrasts the uncompromising prophet with the "shaking reed" of a kinglet from the Hellenistic Roman power elite. The archaeological impact of coins here does not provide us directly with any Christology about Jesus, but it does become part of a picture of Jesus speaking with authority about himself and John as messengers sent by God (Mt 11:10, cf. Mk 1:2, from Mal 3:1), Jesus greater than John because of the kingdom's imminence that he proclaims (11:11).

g. *Folklore* is sometimes invoked to explain a passage (see [e] above on Jn 5:2 and note 38). But on occasion such efforts to see reflected native (Jewish) customs may collide with other explanations. The detail in Jn 2:1 that there was a wedding in Cana of Galilee "on the third day" has sometimes been traced to the Jewish custom of holding weddings on a particular day of the week. The provision in *Ketub.* 1.1 was that a virgin marry on the fourth day of the week (Wednesday) and a widow on the fifth day, since in towns the court sat on the second and fifth days of the week; in case the groom discovered on Wednesday night that his bride was no virgin, he could bring suit in court the next day (Deut 22:14).[43] Some commentators see this fitting into a Johannine chronology where 1:39 ("four o'clock in the afternoon") preceded the Sabbath; "the action of 1:40-42 would have taken place on Saturday evening–Sunday; that of 1:43-50 on Sunday evening–Monday ['the next day']; Monday evening–Tuesday would have been the second day of the journey; and Jesus would have arrived at Cana on Tuesday evening or Wednesday morning."[44] That makes it "the third day" since Philip and Nathanael were called (in 1:43-51) on Sunday. But later Jewish provisions put weddings on the third day in the week to forestall Roman overlords in the period of the Hadrianic persecution from claiming the first night with the virgin bride.[45] If that custom held in Jesus' day, the wedding "on the third day" would have reflected an intent to thwart the occupying power

43. Str-B 2:398; *The Mishnah* (Danby), p. 245.
44. Brown, *John*, p. 98.
45. Str-B 2:398; *t. Ketub.* 1.1 (260), see 3[b].

and its soldiers. Jesus went along with the schedule. But others think "the third day" is just a round number, as in Lk 13:32;[46] still others, since Jesus' second miracle in Cana occurs "after two days" (Jn 4:43), think both allude to the resurrection of Jesus, "on the third day" after his death.[47] That would make the detail somewhat christological, hinting at the miracle of miracles to come on the third day. But no interpretation of the phrase has proven conclusive.

h. *House churches,* as places where Christians gathered, from the beginnings till the time of Constantine, provide an example where New Testament references, archaeological discoveries, and sociological analysis have brought to the fore a factor not without significance for Christology.[48] Paul's letters often refer to "the church in the house of *(kata oikon)* . . . ," and then follows a name like Philemon (and/or Archippus; Philem 2), Aquila and Prisca (1 Cor 16:19; Rom 16:5), and Nympha (Col 4:15); see also Lydia and the Philippian jailer and their households in Acts (16:15, 32). Archaeological finds as at Dura Europos provided evidence for private houses remodeled for use by religious groups. In Dura, cheek by jowl, were, along with a house church, a house synagogue, expanded from the dwelling of a well-to-do Jew, and a Mithraeum.[49] The *domus Petri* at Capernaum can illustrate how churches developed from a private home, though in that instance a "pilgrimage church" was also involved, not just a local cell of believers.[50] In Rome one can also speak of "tenement churches."[51] One should not think of these house churches in terms of lavish villas, as at Pompeii, but of much simpler homes, accommodating ten to thirty people in an extended household.[52] (The

---

46. R. Schnackenburg, *The Gospel according to St. John* (New York: Herder and Herder, 1968), pp. 1 and 326 (correcting his reference to 12:32). It implies "that the promise made by Jesus in 1:50 or 51 was fulfilled very soon"; 2:1 thus links to what preceded, through this general phrase.

47. Brown, *John,* p. 97; cf. R. Kysar, *John,* ACNT (Minneapolis: Augsburg, 1986), p. 44. But the Johannine resurrection narrative makes no reference to "the third day" (2:19-22 is ecclesial-christological). Kysar thinks the phrase may stem from the "Signs Source," with its numbering of miracles (2:11; 4:54).

48. See F. V. Filson, "The Significance of the Early House Churches," *JBL* 58 (1939): 105-12; H.-J. Klauck, *Hausgemeinde und Hauskirche im frühen Christentum,* SBS 103 (Stuttgart: Katholisches Bibelwerk, 1981); V. Branick, *The House Church in the Writings of Paul,* Zacchaeus Studies: New Testament (Wilmington, Del.: Glazier, 1989); L. M. White, *The Social Origins of Christian Architecture,* vol. 1, *Building God's House in the Roman World: Architectural Adaptation among Pagans, Jews, and Christians,* HTS 42 (Valley Forge, Pa.: Trinity, 1996); vol. 2, *Texts and Monuments for the Christian Domus Ecclesiae in Its Environment,* HTS 42 (Valley Forge, Pa.: Trinity, 1997).

49. C. H. Kraeling, *The Christian Building: Excavations at Dura-Europas* 8, part 2 (Locust Valley, N.Y.: J. J. Augustin, 1967); Snyder, *Ante Pacem,* pp. 68-71; H. O. Thompson, *ABD* 2:241-43.

50. Snyder, *Ante Pacem,* pp. 71-73; V. C. Corbo, *ABD* 1:867-68.

51. Snyder, *Ante Pacem,* pp. 75-82, on *Tituli* churches in Rome and their development in some cases from apartments in an *insula.*

52. Cf. R. Banks, *Paul's Idea of Community: The Early House Churches in Their Historical*

oikos was the basic unit in Aristotle's political, social, and economic theory.) There are all sorts of implications from house churches for organization and life among early Christians (often involving, of necessity, patrons and benefactors) and for liturgical settings in worship. Just as there were some fifteen Jewish synagogues in Rome, so likely there were seven or eight house churches there in Paul's day, especially in the Trastevere and Via Appia sections.[53]

How does all this relate to Christology? When one considers that in Rome some house assemblies were Jewish Christian and some were Gentile Christian (recall the expulsion of Jews and therefore also Jewish Christians for a time under Claudius in 49 C.E.; Acts 18:2), or contemplates how different in Philippi must have been the households of the woman from Lydia in Asia Minor, a pagan proselyte to Judaism, converted by Paul (Acts 16:13-15, 40), and of the jailer (Roman civil servant, perhaps army veteran, adherent likely of the Caesar cult), then one begins to grasp why Paul so frequently calls believers to unity. This is so with "the strong" and "the weak" in Rome (Rom 14:1–15:13) and in Philippi with calls to like-mindedness (Phil 2:2-5; 4:2). It is possible that different households treasured different Christologies.

i. Space does not permit exploring the parentage of Jesus — virginal conception or fathered by a legionnaire named Ben Panthera (cf. *parthenos* = virgin)? — or puzzling archaeological topics like the SATOR AREPO square.[54]

The discovery of documents at Qumran and discoveries about the same

---

Setting (Grand Rapids: Eerdmans, 1980), pp. 34-42; J. Murphy-O'Connor, *St. Paul's Corinth: Texts and Archaeology*, GNS 6 (Wilmington, Del.: Glazier, 1983), pp. 156-58; Klauck, *Hausgemeinde*, pp. 100-101.

53. P. Lampe, *Die stadtrömischen Christen in den ersten beiden Jahrhunderten*, WUNT 2/18 (Tübingen: Mohr-Siebeck, 1987), pp. 367-68, 10-52 (Rom 16), pp. 301-2; Lampe, "The Roman Christians of Romans 16," in *The Romans Debate*, ed. K. P. Donfried, rev. ed. (Peabody, Mass.: Hendrickson, 1991), pp. 216-30.

54. Cf. R. Brown, *The Birth of the Messiah: A Commentary on the Infancy Narrative in Matthew and Luke* (Garden City, N.Y.: Doubleday, 1977), though without discussion of names for Jesus in Talmudic tradition, like *Ben Panthera* ('Abod. Zar. 40d), and the sensation twists sometimes given to a legionnaire, stationed in Palestine but transferred to the Rhine in 9 C.E. The funeral urn of Tiberius Julius Abdes Pantera, an archer, was hailed in some accounts as of the man who had, as a soldier in the occupying army, fathered a son by the Jewish girl Mary; cf. M. Goguel, *Jesus and the Origins of Christianity*, trans. O. Wyon (New York: Harper Torchbooks, 1960), 1:73-74. W. Ziffer, "Two Epithets for Jesus of Nazareth in Talmud and Midrash," *JBL* 85 (1966): 356-57, wished to take it as "son of Pandora." The *sator* cryptogram, found at Dura Europos and elsewhere, meaning possibly "the sower, with his plow, holds, with purpose, the wheels," has been taken to reflect Jesus' parable of the sower (Mk 4:3-8); Ezek 9:6 (touch no one with the tau mark); Gnostic thought, or none of the above; cf. *DACL* 15.1, pp. 913-15; the *New Catholic Encyclopedia* 12 (1967), pp. 1098-99. [Also, see Chilton's chapter and the appendix to Charlesworth's chapter in the present work. — JHC.]

time at Nag Hammadi gave new impetus to efforts at explaining Jesus and early Christianity from, respectively, Jewish backgrounds and a Gnostic outlook. Both must be reckoned with. It is not impossible, as some have argued, that "Gnosis," however we define it, had Jewish elements in it. Qumran helps us see varieties in Judaism and, for Christology, the notion in the Dead Sea Scrolls community of two messiahs as well as a righteous teacher. Nag Hammadi materials have abetted understandings of the Q source and sayings tradition, especially through the *Gospel of Thomas*.

For all this, archaeology, while often showing how reverence for, confession of, and worship of Jesus grew, does not answer our questions about the origin and sequence of each title in Christology and how the titles relate to each other. The "fish" symbol is well known, as an acronym in Greek, *ICHTHUS*, for *Iēsous, Christos, Theou Huios, Sōtēr*. But is "Christ" here a title (originally "Messiah"), or has it become "Jesus' last name," so that the christological weight is borne by "Son of God" and "Savior"? Is "Son of God" here to be understood in an Old Testament–Jewish sense, or a Greco-Roman one? Or did it depend on who was tracing a fish symbol on the ground or interpreting the formula? "Savior," while possible in the Hebrew Scriptures to refer to God, more likely was derived from pagan use, employed by Christians in response to claims of Hellenistic deities and rulers and Roman emperors to be "saviors."

A Picture of Jesus' Christology

Putting data together concerning Jesus and Christology has produced many models over the centuries, and there is no end in sight. Traditionally, the view has been that Jesus spoke and presented himself with all the christological grandeur that the Fourth Gospel attests. But then how could the disciples have failed to understand who he was, as the Gospel of Mark depicts them, dull and without understanding? At the other end of the spectrum of possible interpretations — we exclude the "Christ myth school," that a person in Judaism named Jesus of Nazareth never lived — Jesus has often emerged as a noble teacher, but with no personal claim about himself. Such was the view in liberal Protestantism. It takes the form in Bultmann and Bornkamm of arguing that all christological titles are post-Easter.[55] Or in the Jesus Seminar, of a teacher or prophet or aphoristic sage devoid not only of Christology but also of much eschatology, certainly nothing apocalyptic in his makeup.

---

55. R. Bultmann, *Jesus and the Word* (German 1926; New York: Scribner, 1934); G. Bornkamm, *Jesus of Nazareth* (German 1956; New York: Harper, 1960).

Figure 79. Glass bottle found north of
Jerusalem; Herodian period.

Courtesy of J. H. Charlesworth

My own efforts at an account of Jesus that includes some Christology have included a picture of Jesus who used the term "Son of Man," though the early church did not, confessionally; who did not describe himself as "the" or even "a" Suffering Servant," but who exhibited what serving means, so that the depictions in Second Isaiah could be applied to him in the early church; who understood himself as "the Son" in a sense not found among contemporaries in Judaism (a reflection of his experience with God as "Abba"). This concept developed in the early church along lines familiar in the Greco-Roman world of Jesus as "Son of God." The term *mar* could have been used in Jesus' lifetime in polite address to him, in some instances meaning no more than "Sir," but developed after Easter into *Kyrios* as "Lord" (though equation, via the Septuagint, flat out with God is, as indicated above, dubious). The title "messiah" is one over which christological battles have been fought for centuries. On the two occasions when it was offered to Jesus — at Caesarea Philippi in Peter's "confession" (really, in Mark, a satanic misunderstanding) and in the trial scene of Mk 14:61-62 (par.) — I am uncertain whether Jesus rushed to accept it, deflecting it in favor of "Son of Man" and an expectation of suffering. This was because he rejected popular connotations of a zealotlike warrior figure who would fight the Romans and establish a political state. The term "messiah" had to be defined by what Jesus was, and soon became, in the Greek *Christos*, more a name than a title.[56] In the 1992 Oxford Bible Se-

56. J. Reumann, *Jesus in the Church's Gospels: Modern Scholarship and the Earliest Sources* (Philadelphia: Fortress, 1968), see esp. chap. 9.

ries,[57] my treatment of Jesus, of necessity quite brief, is along propositional lines. It suggests how his words and deeds spoke of and even for God, with himself as herald of the kingdom. After the resurrection he was elevated with further titles of exaltation. Such sketches must be made in light of the old and new quests for the historical Jesus, subsequent developments like the Jesus Seminar and what is somewhat presumptuously called "the third quest," for it includes all sorts of proposals that by no means fit together with one another. There are thus many ways to spell out what one thinks held true about Jesus during his lifetime and how and in what ways his lordship was expanded in the early church.

The Use of Archaeology in Christology

In these many accounts of Christology, on the part of Jesus and in the early church, archaeology usually plays a small role.[58] In Albert Schweitzer's famous account of the quest down through the beginning of the twentieth century, results of discoveries figure in only one chapter, 17, but there it deals with the Aramaic language, rabbinic parallels, and further afield, Buddhistic influence.[59] Even in his favorite area of apocalyptic eschatology, Schweitzer can be accused of not being on top of the latest in manuscript discoveries from the Middle East containing apocalypses. It is difficult to find many subsequent "lives of Jesus" that make much use of archaeology either. Perhaps W. Phillips, *An Explorer's Life of Jesus*, can be mentioned.[60] Charlesworth has put the matter well: "Historians can prove that the cross is historical, archaeologists may be able to show

57. J. Reumann, *Variety and Unity in New Testament Thought* (Oxford: Oxford University Press, 1991), pp. 39-45.

58. The volumes edited by J. H. Charlesworth and W. P. Weaver (Philadelphia and Valley Forge, Pa.: Trinity) in the series Faith and Scholarship Colloquies, *What Has Archaeology to Do with Faith?* (1992) and *Earthing Christologies* (1995, above n. 11), look promising and are on the right track for many readers. One can learn much about the historical Jesus and Christology as "unfinished business" (H. Anderson, in *Earthing Christologies*), but direct connections between Christology and archaeology are rare.

59. Schweitzer, *The Quest*, pp. 270-93. One of the few lives in Schweitzer's account that reflected the world of Palestine was Renan's *La Vie de Jésus* (1863), the author of which had traveled throughout the Middle East and lived in Lebanon while working on it (Renan also published Phoenician inscriptions); Schweitzer's reaction (pp. 180-92) to an account that admittedly was overly romantic, was devastatingly negative. See my comments in *Eretz-Israel* 16 (1982): 188-89*.

60. W. Phillips, *An Explorer's Life of Jesus* (New York: Two Continents and Morgan Press, 1975). Claiming influence from W. F. Albright, Phillips describes his work as "The biography of the Founder of Christianity that is true to fact as to faith."

us where he was crucified; but they cannot elicit a confession in the crucified Lord."[61] One is reminded of how Bultmann's program of demythologizing was sometimes summed up: we can demonstrate to a reasonable degree, in accord with the historical method, that Jesus died on such and such a date in Jerusalem by crucifixion, and that his disciples later said he was raised from the dead; we might even find some day a protocol copy of the records of the Roman trial. But we can never show by such means the meaning of the cross or any "fact of the resurrection." Those two things go together as matters of faith, and in fact the meaning of the cross is that Jesus lives, or, otherwise put, his vindication shows that his cross had the meaning claimed for it.

What, then, is the good of such historical studies? What is the value of archaeology? First and foremost, to help provide some of the setting for the arenas where Christology developed. Nowadays one can even speak of "a quest for the historical Galilee," an effort often connected with the hope that if we could come to a correct understanding of what the area was like where Jesus worked throughout his ministry, we would understand him better. From the phrase in Isa 8:23(9:1), "Galilee of the Gentiles," some in the period of National Socialism in Germany sought an Aryan Jesus. (Actually the Englishman H. S. Chamberlain had worked along such lines at the turn of the twentieth century.) More commonly, Galilee has been looked on as less orthodox than Judea and Jerusalem in its Judaism ("Galilee, Galilee, you hate the Torah," as Johann Ben Zakkai put it; *y. Shab.* 15d). Put more positively, "Judaism in a form directed towards the universally human or, if you like, a syncretistically weakened form."[62] More recently the approach has taken the form of seeing Jesus as a Cynic philosopher.[63]

Archaeology can, secondly, aid us in grasping how early and widespread was the growth of the Christian movement and with it the acclamation of Jesus by believers and expression of Christology. But it remains a *Hilfswissenschaft,* or auxiliary science, for it cannot tell us how titles and concepts arose or why and exactly how Christology functioned for faith. For that, textual accounts of human experiences are needed. Furthermore, archaeological evidence can run the danger of seeming, by its tangible nature, to prove too much for faith — that *Die Bibel hat doch Recht* (Werner Keller's famous title) runs the danger not sim-

61. Charlesworth, *Jesus within Judaism: New Light from Exciting Archaeological Discoveries,* ABRL (Garden City, N.Y.: Doubleday, 1988), p. 156, cited approvingly in *Earthing Christologies,* p. 14.

62. W. Bauer, "Jesus der Galiläer," in his *Aufsätze und Kleine Schriften* (Tübingen: Mohr-Siebeck, 1967), p. 104, cited in Theissen and Merz, *The Historical Jesus,* p. 163.

63. Among others, B. Mack in *The Lost Gospel* (San Francisco: HarperSanFrancisco, 1993), assuming Hellenistic influences.

ply of becoming *The Bible as History* (its English title) but "the Bible is always right," in every way.

The story is told — and ours is not the first generation where Vatican authorities and Roman Catholic scholars have been accused of suppressing or manipulating evidence in the interests of the church[64] — of how archaeologists found the tomb of Jesus, inscription, skeleton, and all. News was kept quiet until the Vatican was informed. Officialdom was at a loss on how to proceed with such a discovery until someone said, "We must call Union Theological Seminary in New York. There is a professor there who can tell us what to do." So they outlined the findings and their implications to Professor Paul Tillich. There was a long silence. Finally he said, "Oh, so he did live!"

That, of course, would be small gain for many, but one forgets how extreme some popular views sometimes are over the very existence of Jesus. Thus, a review in the Sunday *New York Times* for April 23, 2000, opined, "There is not a shred of historical evidence outside the Bible itself to support the existence of Jesus." This prompted a letter recalling the "shreds" in Josephus, Tacitus, and Lucian of Samosata.[65] One needs to know and keep informed about "the basics," old evidence that is often in our day little known, as well as new discoveries that may bear on Jesus, his world and person.

Self-Critique

Self-Critique: Three final remarks on much of what has been said in and after presentations at this conference, myself included.

a. To speak simply of "Jesus the Jew" is not completely helpful, any more than to speak of "Jesus, a Palestinian Arab activist," as some do in liberationalist, postcolonial analysis. One must try to specify *what kind of Jew* Jesus was. How did Jesus agree with, react to, and differ from the various Judaisms of his day? In discussing evidence about *mikvaot* and other means for ritual purity in his day, one must also bring in and reckon with passages like Mk 7:17-23

---

64. See O. Betz and R. Riesner, *Jesus, Qumran, and the Vatican: Clarifications* (New York: Crossroad, 1994). For examination of extravagant claims made about papyrus fragments of Matthew, cf. G. Stanton, *Gospel Truth? New Light on Jesus and the Gospels* (London: HarperCollins, 1995); the chapter on "archeological evidence" (pp. 111-21) deals, among other things, with R. A. Batey, *Jesus and the Forgotten City* (Grand Rapids: Baker, 1991), i.e., Sepphoris, but cannot be said to have turned up anything christological.

65. The original review was of Thomas Cahill's *Desire of the Everlasting Hills.* The references in the letter in the May 14 *Review,* p. 2, were to *Ant* 20.200 and 18.63-64; *Ann* 15.44.3; and *The Passing of Peregrinus.* Among other texts that might be mentioned are *b. Sanh.* 43a.

("thus he declared all things clean") and discuss Jesus' attitude toward ritual purity. At times it was not simply Jesus *in* his environment but Jesus *against* his environment, much as was the case sometimes with the Hebrew prophets. When Jesus makes such assertions as are reflected in Mk 7, are there not a charismatic authority and an indirect Christology being expressed?

b. It is to be appreciated that Christology in the early church developed by employing concepts from the Hebrew Scriptures and Judaism *and* also from the Greco-Roman, and even Gnostic, worlds. It is sometimes assumed that "biblical theology" includes only aspects that draw on what Christians call the Old Testament, as if what can be called "revelation involving non-Semitic concepts" is second-rate. Even within our analyses of Judaism there often seems a tendency to obscure a part of the variety within Judaism, namely, those speculations in connection with God about Wisdom, Word, and the Spirit. The book by Alan Segal, *Two Powers in Heaven,* opens up a world in light of which some christological understandings about Jesus may have developed, a world that pretty much disappeared in rabbinic Judaism.[66] There were factors in some types of Judaism that were immensely influential for Christology, factors about which both Christians and Jews may be surprised.

c. All this challenges the traditional model of Judaism and Christianity as a "mother-daughter" relationship. They are better seen as siblings, perhaps even sets of brothers and sisters in each family, at times in sibling rivalry. Both were emerging religions in the first century, after the ninth of Ab in 70 c.e. It is not simply that one is the source and the other derivative, but rather, this newer approach goes, they are two related religions that influenced each other, in a back-and-forth relationship. "The Parting of the Ways," as it has often been called, is not a single, final date on the calendar but a continuing feature for Jews and Christians. For while there have been partings of two ways, there have also been agreements on the way, from Jesus to the present. The possibility of discussing Christology together provides a good example of both some agreements and some basic differences.

---

66. A. F. Segal, *Two Powers in Heaven: Early Rabbinic Reports about Christianity and Gnosticism,* SJLA 25 (Leiden: Brill, 1977). Segal holds that Christology was "built through exegesis rather than through hypothetical preexistent titles" in first century c.e. debate, but speaks of "complementary" powers in heaven for Christians in contrast to "opposing" powers in heaven according to Gnosticism. Cf. also N. Deutsch, *The Gnostic Imagination: Gnosticism, Mandaeism, and Merkabah Mysticism,* Series in Jewish Studies 13 (Leiden: Brill, 1995); G. G. Strousma, *Savoir et salut,* Patrimoines (Paris: Cerf, 1992); Strousma, *Hidden Wisdom: Esoteric Traditions and the Roots of Christian Mysticism,* SHR 70 (Leiden: Brill, 1996), and Strousma and H. G. Kippenberg, eds., *Secrecy and Concealment: Studies in the History of Mediterranean and Near Eastern Religions,* SHR 65 (Leiden: Brill, 1995).

Annotated Bibliography on Christology
(other titles appear in the notes)

Charlesworth, J., et al., eds. *The Messiah: Developments in Earliest Judaism and Christianity.* First Princeton Symposium on Judaism and Christian Origins. Minneapolis: Fortress, 1992. Twenty-five papers from a conference in 1987, chiefly by Christians but including some Jewish scholars, trace various aspects of the transition from messianology to Christology.

Cullmann, O. *The Christology of the New Testament.* Translated by S. C. Guthrie and C. A. M. Hall. 2nd rev. ed. Philadelphia: Westminster, 1959, 1963. An influential treatment that groups titles around the earthly work of Jesus, his future and present work, and Christ's preexistence.

Dunn, J. D. G. *Christology in the Making: A New Testament Inquiry into the Origins of the Doctrine of the Incarnation.* Philadelphia: Westminster, 1980. One reaction to the debate, primarily in the British Isles, over "the myth of God incarnate."

————. "Christology (NT)." In *ABD* 1:979-91. There is no article in this dictionary entitled "Christology (OT)" or "Messianology," but see R. A. Horsley, "Messianic Movements in Judaism," 4:791-97.

Fuller, R. H. *The Foundations of New Testament Christology.* New York: Scribner, 1965. In contrast to his earlier *The Mission and Achievement of Jesus,* SBT 12 (London: SCM, 1954) and influenced by F. Hahn, Fuller traces the development of christological titles after Easter till their usage in written documents like the letters of Paul and the Gospels.

Fuller, R. H., and Pheme Perkins. *Who Is This Christ? Gospel Christology and Contemporary Faith.* Philadelphia: Fortress, 1982. Includes post–New Testament developments in the creeds and modern discussions.

Grillmeier, A. *Christ in Christian Tradition.* Vol. 1, *From the Apostolic Age to Chalcedon (451).* Translated by J. S. Bowden. London: Mowbray, 1965; Atlanta: John Knox, rev. 2nd ed., 1975. A noted Jesuit scholar traces Christology from New Testament beginnings, through "logos-sarx" and "logos-anthropos" Christology, to the decisions of the great church councils that move from kerygma and theology to dogma.

Hahn, F. *The Titles of Jesus in Christology: Their History in Early Christianity.* German edition of 1963 translated by H. Knight and G. Ogg. New York: World, 1969. While taking many titles as post-Easter, this major treatment shows some continuity with the historical Jesus, in the spirit of the new quest.

Jonge, M. de. *Christology in Context: The Earliest Christian Response to Jesus.* Philadelphia: Westminster, 1988. The context is "the dynamics of the first hundred years or so of church life" (p. 15), and follows de Jonge's *Jesus: Stranger from Heaven and Son of God,* SBLDS 11 (Missoula, Mont.: Scholars, 1977) and *Jesus: Inspiring and Disturbing Presence,* trans. J. E. Steely (Nashville: Abingdon, 1974).

Longenecker, R. N. *The Christology of Early Jewish Christianity.* SBT 2/17. London: SCM, 1970. While what one means by "Jewish Christianity" continues to be debated, this volume uses Qumran and Nag Hammadi materials to detail christological development among Jewish Christians.

Reumann, J. "Jesus and Christology." In *The New Testament and Its Modern Interpreters,* edited by E. J. Epp and G. W. MacRae. Philadelphia: Fortress; Atlanta: Scholars, 1989. Written for a 1980 deadline, revised in 1983, with a few bibliographical additions possible in 1985. The term "Third Quest" seems not to have been used in print till 1988, though N. T. Wright (in *ABD* 3:800-801) included under it some earlier titles (where the phrase seems not to occur).

Schillebeeckx, E. C. F. *Jesus: An Experiment in Christology.* Dutch edition of 1975 translated by H. Hoskins. New York: Seabury Press, 1979. Systematicians sometimes tire of waiting for biblical scholars to come to any conclusions, and, as in this case, do their own homework. The volume includes both historical Jesus and Christology. Schillebeeckx's second volume, *Christ: The Experience of Jesus as Lord,* trans. J. Bowden (New York: Crossroad, 1982; German ed. 1977), is ecclesiology as well as Christology.

Schwarz, H. *Christology.* Grand Rapids: Eerdmans, 1998. A systematic theologian who has taught in both the United States and Germany treats the quests for the historical Jesus and how the biblical testimony has been assessed through history, including relevance for today.

The Christian Apocrypha and Archaeology

J. K. Elliott

At first glance, archaeology and the early noncanonical literature, commonly referred to as the New Testament apocrypha, or (better) Christian apocrypha, may seem strange bedfellows. The one is a scientifically established uncovering and studying of antiquities, revealing lost civilizations, discovering battlegrounds, domestic artifacts, and dwellings and explaining them in the contexts of their original history or prehistory. Often archaeologists succeed in illuminating in a tangible way past events and even individuals. The Christian apocrypha are noncanonical writings, often written in imitation of the New Testament Gospels, letters, Apocalypse, and the Acts of the Apostles, and in most cases are imaginative writings intended to amplify the first-century events surrounding Jesus and his earliest followers. These works purport to be historical, but what they reveal are the beliefs, interests, and concerns of Christians after the first century C.E. The earliest apocryphal texts are from the second century, but other, often derivative, writings come from the centuries following.

It is expecting a great deal of archaeology to be able to verify the historical value of allegedly historical events and persons in essentially legendary tales. To call this genre of literature "apocryphal" implies, correctly, that its historicity is spurious, and its character secondary and unreliable. Obviously, we see value in these texts from the second century onward as ways of revealing the folk traditions of the average man or woman in the days of their composition, and their theology and Christian practices, but such are not normally the concerns of the archaeologist verifying the events related.

Our understanding of Shakespeare's *Hamlet* is not enhanced or affected by a visit to Elsinore Castle or a study of archaeologists' reports on it. These are a red herring. Similarly, it is fruitless to seek a historical person to match King Lear. As we shall argue below, a coincidence of a name in the apocrypha with a place or person known from outside (sometimes paralleled by archaeological

Figure 80. Ceramic inkwells, from the
second millennium B.C.E. to the
Hellenistic period, and an Early Roman
glass inkwell, and a Byzantine stylus. All
were found in or near Jerusalem.

Courtesy of J. H. Charlesworth

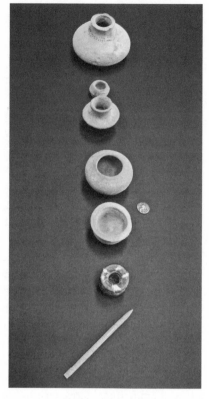

discoveries), means only that the name qua name was in the author's memory
or was common knowledge. Shakespeare probably knew only the name of
Elsinore Castle in Denmark and nothing else about it.

Many Christian apocryphal romances mention place-names like Rome, Corinth, Ephesus, Philippi, and Achaia, but all too often these are merely conventional
stock locations of early Christian settlements. The same is true of the names of
most dramatis personae. In these cases the books that were eventually called the
New Testament provide most of the names and inspiration for these later writers,
although names from the popular cultural background and collective memory
doubtless played their part too. Similarly, merely because one of the apocryphal
Acts sets a story in an arena or a temple does not imply that the author had a particular building in his mind's eye, and even if he did, that any results of archaeological work on such a site would verify or corroborate any details in the written account. Archaeology and contemporary literature may illustrate and parallel the
domestic scenes and daily life in the second-century apocryphal Acts, with their
settings in Roman households, and featuring their slaves, as well as prominent citi-

zens, amid the life of luxury enjoyed by many of the stories' characters, but all such an investigation may do is to confirm these books as typical products of their age, i.e., the second century, and as congenial stories for the leisured and moneyed classes that undoubtedly wrote, read, and enjoyed such literature.

Despite this, however, there are numerous parallels between the results of archaeology and these apocryphal texts. One particular area where archaeology and the Christian apocrypha regularly coincide is in the supposed or traditional burial places of the apostles.

For example, much effort has been expended, particularly in the 1950s as well as more recently, to identify an ancient tomb excavated beneath St. Peter's Basilica in the Vatican as the burial place of Simon Peter.[1] Those dependent on the canonical New Testament have no direct proof there that Peter ever traveled to Rome. The Acts of the Apostles effectively writes Peter out of its travelogue where he is said (laconically, and uncharacteristically vaguely) to have merely "gone off *elsewhere*" (Acts 12:17); the remaining missionary journeys in that book are Paul's journeys. A good case can be made that Peter visited not only Corinth (as implied in 1 Cor 9:5, as well as at 1:12 where a "Peter party" is flourishing) but that he also founded the church in Rome, to which Paul addressed a letter before his visit there, and where Paul later was met by Christians from that well-established and flourishing church. It is the apocryphal *Acts of Peter* and derivative texts that retail several episodes of Peter in Rome. And Peter is crucified in Rome (*ActsPet* 40).[2] The tradition linking Peter and Rome is strongly supported by early Christian tradition, although none prior to the mid–second century.[3] Conversely no other contradictory tradition links this prime apostle with any other resting place.

It is not only the martyrdom of Peter that gets a mention in the Christian apocrypha but also his imprisonment. The fourth-to-sixth-century apocryphon known as the *Martyrium Beati Petri* by Pseudo-Linus 5 tells of Peter in the Mamertinum, built over the Tullianum.[4] Gullible modern-day tourists are shown

1. A very full description of the situation linking Peter and Rome and including the archaeological evidence is Erich Dinkler, "Die Petrus-Rom-Frage," *TRu* 25 (1959-60): 189-230, 289-335; and 27 (1961): 33-60. The articles include in section 2, "Die Diskussion des archäologischen Befundes," sketches based on the archaeological evidence then published, and there are exhaustive bibliographical details here too. An earlier and influential study is O. Cullmann, *Petrus. Jünger — Apostel — Märtyrer* (Zürich: Zwingli Verlag, 1960), in the third section of which (pp. 78-128) the literary, liturgical, and archaeological evidence for Peter's death in Rome is examined in detail. See also A. A. di Marco, *The Tomb of St. Peter*, NovTSup 8 (Leiden: Brill, 1964).

2. References to apocryphal texts are in J. K. Elliott, *The Apocryphal New Testament* (Oxford: Clarendon, 1993), here p. 426.

3. See Cullmann, *Petrus*, p. 127.

4. R. A. Lipsius and M. Bonnet, *Acta apostolorum apocrypha* (Leipzig: Mendelssohn, 1891, 1898, 1903; reprint, Hildesheim: Olms, 1959), 1:1-22.

this prison as the place where Peter was held prior to his crucifixion. The cistern known as the Tullianum — so named from *tullius*, "a pool of water" — was restored as a jail by Tiberius (14-37 C.E.). The present-day church over the site, St. Giuseppe dei Falagnami, incorporates, as a consequence of this legend, a chapel named St. Pietro in Carcere and its altar displays a relief of Peter baptizing a jailor. According to Pseudo-Linus, Peter obtained the water with which to baptize the jailor miraculously by striking the rock walls of his cell. This pictorial image, with its parallel to Moses' striking the rock from which water gushed out, is found in many examples of early Christian art, such as in the Catacomb of Comodilla.

The derivative later apocrypha, the *Acta Petri et Pauli* and the *Passio sanctorum apostolorum Petri et Pauli,* locate the two apostles in Rome at the same time, and they share a parallel martyrdom in that city, Paul on the Via Ostiense and Peter on Vatican Hill. Early and common illustrations of the two men embracing, presumably in Rome, are doubtless intended to convey the unity of the church.

The apocryphal *Acts of Paul* (Martyrdom 5) records Paul's decapitation in Rome.[5] A site three miles south of Rome, the Trappist monastery known as Tre Fontane, commemorates the place in which Paul was beheaded. Here the written tradition seems the earlier and has been embellished to the extent that it is claimed Paul's severed head bounced three times on the ground and at each place a fountain gushed up — hence the name of the church. Probably this may be classed as an etiological cult legend, in which the name Tre Fontane is linked to the tradition of Paul's death in Rome. The actual burial place is believed to be beneath the nearby basilica of S. Paolo fuori le Mura.

Just as Peter's burial place has attracted archaeological investigation, so too has Thomas's. The apocryphal *Acts of Thomas,* another of the major apocryphal Acts dating probably from the second century, records Thomas evangelizing in India as well as his martyrdom and his first burial there. A strong and early Christian tradition has tended to accept that tradition, and it has been encouraged by the belief of the Malabar, Syrian Orthodox, Christians of Kerala that their church was founded in India by Thomas. As a result, there exists a church building at Mylapore near Madras on the site where it is said Thomas was buried prior to the translation of his body to Edessa in the fourth century. That church itself is from the sixth to the eighth century, and has a contemporary Pahlavi inscription on its tower. The story of the transience of Thomas's first burial place parallels the detail in *ActsThom* 170 that relates an episode after Thomas's burial when King Misdaus,[6] who had had Thomas executed, wished to take one of Thomas's bones from the grave to serve as a cure for his sick son, but found the

---

5. Elliott, *The Apocryphal New Testament*, p. 387.
6. Elliott, *The Apocryphal New Testament*, p. 510.

tomb empty because Thomas's disciples had removed the body and taken it to Mesopotamia (by which Edessa is to be understood) as the final destination.

At the beginning of the twentieth century several writers tried to argue for the general veracity of the tradition that Thomas evangelized India. The tales in this apocryphon are accepted by these scholars to be fanciful; nonetheless, Medlycott, then bishop of Tricomia, and Farquhar, another student of India, as well as Dahlmann were generally sympathetic to the historicity of at least the underlying tradition in the *Acts of Thomas*.[7] In so arguing, they were going against the general skepticism that greeted this apocryphon like other apocrypha, treating them all on the same level of fictitiousness. Their opinions had a certain vogue, albeit short-lived. One of the reasons they accepted the tradition associating Thomas with India was that coins had been discovered by archaeologists that identified a Parthian monarch Gudnaphar with King Gundaphorus of the early part of the *Acts of Thomas*. Gundaphorus reigned from 19 to 55 C.E. On some coins Gundaphorus is associated with a certain Guda, which may explain why in the *Acts of Thomas* the king has a brother named Gad. Other attempts to accept the verisimilitude of other details in the apocryphon, especially its local color, now look like special pleading. Few today outside Kerala would wish to treat the *Acts of Thomas* as anything other than a typical and imaginative Christian novel.

A more sober evaluation of the personal and geographical names in the *Acts of Thomas* is to be seen in an article by George Huxley,[8] who tries to establish the significance or reasoning behind the choice of the particular proper names in this apocryphon. He is concerned to trace the possibility that the author of the *Acts of Thomas,* thought to be a second-century Syrian from Edessa, was acquainted with these particular names.

Historical and geographical details in these Christian apocrypha are normally merely arbitrary, just as the names of the dramatis personae are purely fictitious. Even the eponymous heroes, Peter, Paul, and others, are merely conventional and are one-dimensional, cardboard characters. The apostles in these books are largely indistinguishable one from the other — one could not write differentiated character sketches, let alone biographies, from the details and stories found within them. Sometimes stories told in one apocryphon can be transferred

---

7. A. E. Medlycott, *India and the Apostle Thomas: An Inquiry with a Critical Analysis of the Acta Thomae* (London: Nutt, 1905); J. H. Farquhar, "The Apostle Thomas in North India," *BJRL* 10 (1926): 80-111; Farquhar, "The Apostle Thomas in South India," *BJRL* 11 (1927): 20-50; J. Dahlmann, *Die Thomas-Legende und die ältesten historischen Beziehungen des Christentums zum fernen Osten im Lichte der indischen Altertumskunde* (Freiburg im Breisgau: Herder, 1912). See also F. C. Burkitt, *Early Christianity outside the Roman Empire* (Cambridge: Cambridge University Press, 1899); see esp. pp. 63-89.

8. G. Huxley, "Geography in the Acts of Thomas," *GRBS* 24 (1983): 71-80.

to another apostle in a different apocryphal Acts. The famous *Quo Vadis?* episode is a case in point: it occurs in the *Acts of Peter,* where it seems to belong appropriately, and in the *Acts of Paul,* where it seems intrusive.[9] Often the particular hero's name and geographical references in the apocryphon itself are the product of a locality or church that wished to claim one of the twelve disciples or an early apostle for its own — especially if that person was believed to have brought Christianity to its region and founded a church there. In the *Acts of Thomas,* most of the names of the characters are Semitic, Iranian, or Greek — not Indian. In short, the Indian setting seems artificial, contrived, and purely fictitious.

It may, however, be more than a coincidence that Gundaphorus is a character in a fictitious apocryphon and was an actual king. The authors of these apocrypha did not live or write in a vacuum; the name of a real person, especially if it fitted the exotic location of the hero's exploits, could be dredged from memory or other sources and applied to a major character.

Just as church tradition links the martyrdoms of Peter and Paul with Rome, John is firmly linked with Ephesus, as references in Eusebius, Justin, Clement of Alexandria, and especially Irenaeus make clear. The death of this apostle is, as with Peter, Paul, and Thomas, significantly absent from the New Testament. The biblical authors seem not to have found stories of the apostles' deaths edifying. John's final working place in Ephesus is, however, recorded in the apocryphal *Acts of John,* where in chapter 62 he reaches Ephesus and later dies there.[10] The *Virtutes Iohannis* 8 attributed to Abdias and dating probably from the sixth to seventh century, has the Ephesian Christians building a church in John's name.[11] The Justinian Basilica in modern-day Seljuk, on the plain above Ephesus, stands on the supposed site of his burial. This basilica has replaced an earlier church, which marks the tomb traditionally associated with a Christian named John, and thus taken to be the disciple and author of the Johannine literature in the New Testament. F.-M. Braun in his full investigation into John devotes chapter 4 in part 3 of his *Jean le théologien*[12] ("Le tombeau de Jean à Éphèse") to examining the archaeological evidence uncovered at different levels of this site.[13]

Whether the apocryphal literature and the sources, oral and perhaps written, behind these second-century Acts encouraged the faithful to identify and

9. Elliott, *The Apocryphal New Testament,* pp. 384, 424.

10. Elliott, *The Apocryphal New Testament,* pp. 328-38.

11. Elliott, *The Apocryphal New Testament,* p. 345.

12. F.-M. Braun, *Jean le théologien et son évangile dans l'église ancienne,* EBib (Paris: Gabalda, 1959), 1:365-74.

13. Comparable studies into the traditional burial place of Philip in Hierapolis are conveniently recorded in the recently published F. Amsler, *Acta Philippi: Commentarius,* Corpus Christianorum, Series Apocryphorum 12 (Turnhout: Brepols, 1999).

give precision to the localities, especially the burial places, of the founding fathers of the church, or whether these written texts merely repeat known traditions explaining how sites already identified and venerated fit in with an eponymous hero's biography by using details from a local, popular, and oral tradition that may have sometimes encouraged the writer of an apocryphal romance, cannot be determined. Certainly, one must recognize that sometimes details from a local, popular, and oral tradition may have encouraged the writer of an apocryphal romance. In some cases it may well be that we are seeing parallel and largely independent traditions.

We now turn to other characters in these Acts that may reflect the memory of an actual, historical personage of the same name. Queen Tryphaena, who figures in the *Acts of Paul and Thecla*,[14] is the patroness and protector of Thecla. This is another name, like Gundaphorus, for which historians and archaeologists can attest a historical character that fits the name and period. A Queen Tryphaena of Pisidian Antioch existed. Coins of Pontus have been found that show on their reverse a queen of that name; on the obverse is her husband, or maybe son, the king who reigned from 37 to 63 C.E.[15]

The choice of the name Agrippa for the Roman official in *ActsPet* 26ff.[16] is unlikely to have been triggered by the name of the historical Jewish king Agrippa I, although Karasszan suggests that the contradictory role of the prefect in the *Acts of Peter* recalls the similarly held judgment made of King Agrippa.[17]

Acts of Paul 43 tells of Thecla's death in Seleucia. Not unusually, tradition has sought to identify her burial site in more than one place. The most convincing location (in that it fits the story line) is at a site in Memianlik, Seleucia, in present-day Turkey.[18]

---

14. Elliott, *The Apocryphal New Testament*, pp. 364-72; see esp. pp. 369ff.

15. Medlycott, *India*, pp. 231-32, ever willing to find historical evidence in these apocrypha, gives credence to this story, claiming that a consort of such a king would have been in a position to influence events as described in the *Acts of Paul* and to have been able to protect Thecla!

16. Elliott, *The Apocryphal New Testament*, pp. 418ff.

17. I. Karasszan, "Agrippa, King and Prefect," in *The Apocryphal Acts of Peter: Magic, Miracle, and Gnosticism*, ed. J. N. Bremmer, Studies in the Apocryphal Acts of the Apostles 3 (Leuven: Peeters, 1998), pp. 21-28.

18. See U. M. Fasola, "Il complesso catacombale di S. Tecla," *Rivista di archeologia cristiana* 40 (1966): 19-50, and Fasola, "Le basilica sotterranea e le regioni cimitiali vicine," *Rivista di archeologia cristiana* 46 (1970): 193-288. For attempts to plot the various Thecla materials of this very popular female saint (at least until 1969 when her cult was officially suppressed by the Vatican), and apostle and virgin, see G. Holzhey, *Die Thekla-Akten. Ihre Verbreitung und Beurteilung in der Kirche*, Veröffentlichungen aus dem kirchen-historischen Seminar 2:7 (Munich, 1905). See also G. Dagron, *Vie et miracles de sainte Thècle*, Subsidia Hagiographica 62 (Brussels: Société des Bollandistes, 1978).

Most of the examples in this investigation inevitably come from the apocryphal Acts, for these are the stories rich in characters and place-names, but at least a couple of parallels can be drawn from other types of Christian apocrypha. In the apocryphon known as the *Arabic Gospel of the Infancy* (the antecedents of which probably reach back to the second century), the holy family sets out on their journey into exile in Egypt. One of their resting places en route is Matarea, where a spring erupts miraculously. *(Arab) GosInf* 24[19] speaks of balsam originating in that place due to the sweat of Jesus having fallen there. Again, one suspects that a known place familiar for its balsam was chosen as the setting for yet another incident in the "1,001 Nights" tale that is this infancy gospel. I note that present-day travel operators in Egypt point to this legend when describing a spring at Matarea, now a suburb of Cairo. The permanence of an apocryphal tale is again thereby demonstrated.

The familiar story of Veronica with her handkerchief capturing an impression of Jesus' features is to be found in the medieval *Vindicta Salvatoris* and in the *Mors Pilati*. A *sudarium* preserved in St. Peter's, Vatican City, as a relic of Christ's passion came to be identified as Veronica's legendary handkerchief. Again, we see an artifact and a written legend being linked in popular tradition. The relic thus became important for pilgrims. Chaucer's Pardoner in *The Canterbury Tales*, for instance, had a reproduction of the vernicle.

On a comparable level we note that a belt known as the virgin's girdle is displayed as a relic in Prato Cathedral in a chapel dedicated to it, the Cappella del Sacro Cingolo. That chapel has a fresco showing Mary during her assumption handing her girdle to Thomas as a souvenir of her earthly presence. The written form of the story is in one of the several apocryphal stories about the dormition or *transitus* of Mary, the so-called "Narrative of Joseph of Arimathea."[20] Here Thomas, delayed by his priestly duties in India (!), is not present with the other disciples at Mary's death. Mary hands him the girdle while she is ascending to heaven. The disciples' rebuking of Thomas, here dubious about Mary's tomb, turns to blessing when he shows them the girdle.

A rare example of an artifact associated with the apocryphal epistles is the letter supposedly written by Christ in the *Doctrina Addai*, known to Eusebius in Greek and also found in a different form in Syriac. The basic story involves Jesus responding by letter to a request to come to Edessa and explaining that he will send his apostle in his stead. According to the *Pilgrimage of Etheria*, a letter of Christ (presumably this one, as no other tradition survives stating that Christ wrote anything else that was permanent) was preserved and copied and

19. Elliott, *The Apocryphal New Testament*, p. 103.
20. Elliott, *The Apocryphal New Testament*, pp. 714-16.

miraculous powers ascribed to it. Other evidence exists, stating that copies of this letter enjoyed wide circulation as an amulet affixed to doorjambs and walls. To my knowledge archaeology has not unearthed any such copies. Perhaps searching for such an item may be compared to the fruitless attempts to find the Holy Grail or pieces of the true cross.

But, generally, we would not be appreciating the literary conventions of these second-century stories if we were appealing to historical records or archaeological evidence to bolster the ostensibly historical milieu of the tales. This genre of literature should be appreciated — and enjoyed — as *theological* treatises or pious romances or indeed as edifying sermons, but only on their own terms.

On a different level we ought to note here that it is archaeology that has revealed actual (and sometimes hitherto unknown) apocrypha. We need think only of the Nag Hammadi find in the 1940s that brought to light a full Coptic version of the *Gospel of Thomas,* or the main fragment of the long-lost *Gospel of Peter,* unearthed in 1886-87, or the Oxyrhynchus fragments 1, 654, 655 containing sayings *(logia)* of Jesus in Greek paralleling parts of Coptic Thomas. Other similar recent archaeological digs have exposed hitherto unknown fragments of apocryphal texts, and these may be seen in modern printed editions of these Christian apocrypha.

Another tangible link between the Christian apocrypha and archaeology (unconnected, of course, with our earlier discussion about archaeology verifying the contexts of the New Testament apocrypha) is in discoveries not of texts but of illustrations that parallel Christian apocrypha. I am thinking here of such discoveries in catacombs in Rome such as the Catacomba Nuova under the Via Latina. Archaeological work also on the necropolis at El Bagawat has uncovered chapels that contain images paralleling stories in the Christian apocrypha, particularly the legends of Thecla.[21] The Cappadocian rock churches may also be mentioned, as they too contain similar images.

The link between the rhetorical (i.e., the written Christian apocrypha) and the iconic representation of the same scenes is debated. Which influenced the other? Are both sometimes independent but parallel and different representations of the same traditions? These are important questions for early Christian art, but this is not the place to rehearse that debate.[22]

21. See A. Fakhry, *The Necropolis of El-Bagawat in Kharga Oasis* (Cairo: Service des antiquités de l'Égypte, 1951), and A. Grabar, *Christian Iconography: A Study of Its Origins* (Princeton: Princeton University Press, 1968).

22. For a book on this theme, see D. R. Cartlidge and J. K. Elliott, *Art and the Christian Apocrypha* (London: Routledge, 2001).

The Historical Jesus and Biblical Archaeology:
Reflections on New Methodologies and Perspectives

James H. Charlesworth

The end of the eighteenth century, when the old search for the historical Jesus began, is appreciably unlike the beginning of the twenty-first century in many ways. Especially is this paradigmatic difference evident with regard to what can be known about life in ancient Palestine between the time of Herod the Great, who was declared king of the Jews by the Roman Senate in 40 B.C.E., and the destruction of the land and Jerusalem by the Roman armies, under the future emperor, in 70 C.E. During those 110 years ancient Palestine was profoundly reshaped by the increasing incursion of Roman subjugation, the massive building programs of Herod the Great, and the increasing power of influential high priests (especially Caiaphas and Annas). It was also during those years that Jesus from Nazareth lived and died, and the Palestinian Jesus Movement, which evolved into Christianity, emerged as one of the many Jewish groups and sects.

During the First Jewish Revolt of 66–72/73 many villages and cities were destroyed by the Romans. This destruction is palpably evident today in many places, especially in Jotapata (Yodefat), Gamla, Jericho, Qumran, Masada, and especially within the Old City of Jerusalem. In many of these sites, sealed beneath a stratum, often a layer of ash, archaeologists have recovered remains of humans who lived then, along with their possessions, including inkwells, pots, plates, tables, earrings, as well as evidence of destruction, especially thick layers of ash in which are embedded arrowheads and spears. In one real sense, the fate of those who lived then has been often a treasure trove for archaeologists and historians. In the midsixties we could not sit in houses destroyed in the conflagration of 70 C.E., but now we can. Only forty years ago we could not see the *mikvaot* south of the Temple Mount and the destroyed shops and broken streets with their sewers; now we can. These archaeological discoveries have disclosed a magnificent city with impressive monuments.

Thanks to the recovery of the Dead Sea Scrolls, we can now read and study traditions that might not have been known to Peter and Andrew but may have shaped the judgments of Caiaphas and Annas. We can observe and hold in our hands lamps and oil fillers that color Jesus' parable of the ten wise and foolish young women. We can hold in our hands coins, like the widow's mite and a silver coin with the face of an emperor; each of these brings to life Jesus' references and message.

Inter alia, thanks to archaeological discoveries and research we can begin to approximate provisional answers and insights such as the following:

- Nazareth was a small village when Jesus was a youth. A vineyard, winepress, walls, and towers have been discovered less than a mile from the heart of ancient Nazareth (and the well from which Mary, his mother, obtained water); perhaps Joseph (and conceivably Jesus) helped build these or similar constructions as a "builder."
- The claim that Cana has finally been located is to be taken seriously, and the evidence of Jewish life there during the time of Jesus helps us understand this village, which was between Nazareth and Capernaum.
- Bethsaida seems now to have been identified, and the evidence of fishermen living there in basalt houses helps us understand the setting for some of Jesus' actions and the hometown of some of his disciples.
- The massive and numerous excavations at Sepphoris reveal life there during the time of Jesus. The vast evidence of Jewish life helps us comprehend the traditions not only in rabbinics but also in the Gospels.
- Synagogues during the time of Jesus have clearly been located in ancient Palestine, and it is certain that while many "synagogues" were only meeting places or a reserved room in a private house, a synagogue did at times refer to a building (N.B. the inscription that refers to repairing part of a synagogue [discussed in "Jesus Research and Archaeology: A New Perspective"]).
- Evidence of life in Samaria during the time of Jesus is beginning to be impressive, although much of Sebaste is still not excavated. The evidence of Herod's building there, as at Caesarea Maritima, is monumental.
- Jerusalem was a metropolis during the time of Jesus. Not only did pilgrims come up to Jerusalem from all parts of the civilized world, but merchants frequented and defined the city. It is clear that Herod not only enhanced and extended the Temple Mount area, to increase his reputation among the Jews, but he also built a hippodrome and refurbished the Antonia Fortress, as well as expanded the Hasmonean palaces, to increase his prestige among the Romans and to make his own life more sumptuous.

Figure 81. Sunset, looking west from the Arbel, in Lower Galilee.
Courtesy of J. H. Charlesworth

- Clearly, the discovery of the magnitude of the Temple and its surroundings, as well as the massive size of the stones in the western retaining wall, help us appreciate Jesus' disciples' amazement at the grandeur of such stones.
- Archaeological evidence of Pilate, Caiaphas, and Simon of Cyrene, as well as the recovering of the bones of a man who had been crucified, helps historians re-create and imagine Jesus' so-called trial and his execution outside the western walls of Jerusalem.

It would be foolish to continue to foster the illusion that the Gospels are merely fictional stories like the legends of Hercules and Asclepius. The theologies in the New Testament are grounded on interpretations of real historical events, especially the crucifixion of Jesus, at a particular time and place.

While archaeologists may pursue pure research without any interest in possible historical or theological payoff, biblical scholars ultimately no longer have the presumed luxury of avoiding data from the times and places in which the biblical records took shape and were edited. For a New Testament scholar to disavow the importance of archaeology for New Testament studies, including Jesus Research, is a form of myopia. It leaves the Gospels as mere stories or relics of ancient rhetoric. Archaeological work, perhaps unintentionally, helps the biblical scholar to rethink and re-create the past. For the specialists in Jesus Research the rewards are unexpectedly surprising and rewarding, as the previous chapters prove. The ancient world known to Jesus and his fellow Jews is beginning to appear before our eyes, and we are obtaining phenomenal glimpses of what life was like back then when the Temple was the center of worship and sacrifice, over there in that land called "holy."

Glossary

Jacob Cherian

adyton	innermost sanctuary of an ancient temple open only to priests
agora	a gathering place; marketplace
amphitheater	an oval or circular building with rising tiers of seats ranged about a central space; used for contests and spectacles
amphora	a two-handled (ceramic) vessel used to transport wine, oil, or grain
aniconic	nonfigurative representation
apotropaic	designed to avert evil
apse	semicircular or polygonal end of a basilica or eastern end of a church
architrave	stone or timber horizontal beam above an entrance; the lowest division of an entablature resting immediately on the capital of the column
archosolium	arched recess for burial
ashlar	rectangular hewn or squared stone (elegantly prepared)
atrium	central room of a Roman house; forecourt of a church
balk/baulk	a vertical earthen face of the wall left around a trench caused by excavated squares (usually 0.5-1 m. wide); it reveals the stratigraphical progress of the dig
Bar-Kokhba	leader of the Second Jewish Revolt against Rome (132-136 C.E.)
basilica	elongated, rectangular public Roman building (or a church), with double (or more) internal colonnades on either side of a central nave, often with one or two apses
bastion	a projecting part of a fortification

bay	a principal compartment of the walls, roof, or other part of the building
bema	raised platform in a synagogue or church from which the Torah is read or the liturgy performed
beth midrash	Jewish house of study
Bit Hilani	a very distinctive palace architecture
boss	untrimmed projecting part of a stone
bouleutērion (-a)	council chamber in a Greek city
broadhouse	a rectangular house or room in which the entrance is located in one of the long walls
bulla	seal impression stamped on clay or other material
buttresses	a projecting structure for supporting a wall or building
caduceus	a symbol showing a staff with two entwined snakes at the top
caldarium	hot room in a Roman bathhouse
capital	uppermost member of a column or pilaster crowning the shaft and taking the weight of the entablature
carinated	having or shaped like a keel
casemate wall	double fortification wall with partitioned compartments
cathedra	bishop's official seat
Cave of Letters	the northern cave in the Naḥal Hever in the Judean desert in which fifteen Bar-Kokhba letters were found
cenacle	upper room; a retreat house
cenotaph	empty tomb or monument built to commemorate the death of a person
chalice	drinking or offering cup; eucharistic cup
clivi	streets climbing the slopes
colonia	status (of varying gradations and different privileges) granted to a town outside Roman territory
columbarium	a structure lined with rows of small recesses; thought to have been used for storing ashes of cremated bones, or for breeding doves
dating, carbon 14	a method to date an artifact by measuring the degree of disintegration of the carbon 14 content
dating, thermo-luminescence	dating of an artifact (such as pottery) by the amount of thermoluminescence it produces; used to estimate the time elapsed since an object was last heated
doorjamb	an upright piece forming the side of a door opening
dovecote	see *columbarium*

drum	cylindrical part of a column shaft, having a drumlike shape
dunam	a measure of land, equal to about a quarter of an acre
Eastern *terra sigillata*	red pottery common throughout the eastern Mediterranean region from the second century B.C.E. to the second century C.E.
epigraphy	study of forms of letters and of inscriptions
faience	a glazed ceramic material; used mainly to produce small vessels, decorations, and jewelry
fill	occupational debris, soil, stones, etc., moved to an area to fill, level, or raise a floor or other structure
fresco	painting on freshly spread moist lime plaster with water-based pigments
frieze	middle member of an entablature, often sculptured or richly ornamented
glacis	an earthen (or stone/brick) rampart sloping down from the exterior face of a city wall (usually for defensive purposes)
graffito (-i)	writing or drawing scratched on a public surface (rock, wall)
gridiron	something consisting of or covered with a network
griffin	a mythical animal, partly eagle and partly lion
hastae	diagonal strokes
header	a brick or stone laid in a wall with its end toward the face of the wall
Hippodamian plan	a town plan in which the streets intersect at right angles
hippodrome	an oval stadium for horse and chariot races
ḥuṣṣoth	(Hebrew) the space outside a building, sometimes "streets"
hypocaust	hollow areas in which heat could circulate beneath the floor of a Roman bath, usually supported by columns of bricks
hypogeum	the subterranean part of an ancient building; an ancient underground burial chamber
iconography	imagery or symbolism in pictorial material relating to or illustrating a subject
in situ	term used to denote artifacts found "in place," in the position in which they were excavated
insula (-ae)	city block of dwellings, usually quadrangular
intrusive	relates to an artifact originating from a later archaeological context than the one it was found in
Ionic order/capital	one of the three Greek orders of architecture, characterized by its volute simple capitals

joist	timber or metal beam used to support a ceiling or floor
kataphatic	refers to speaking about God by attributing to God positive predicates
khirbeh/khirbet	(Arabic) ruin
kokh (-im)	(Hebrew) Roman-period burial place cut from rock
lapidary script	engraved on stone (or metal), used for monumental inscriptions
laura	a monastery of an Eastern church; a group of hermit cells
Levant	countries of the eastern Mediterranean: Lebanon, Syria, Israel, and Jordan
lintel	a horizontal architectural member spanning and usually carrying the load above an opening
loculus (-i)	shelflike burial space within a tomb
locus (-i)	a specific three-dimensional feature or closed unit of excavation during archaeological work
Madaba map	a sixth-century map of the Holy Land represented on a mosaic pavement in a Byzantine church at Madaba
mamzer	a person with a mixed, uncertain, or illegal genealogy
menorah	a candelabrum with seven candles, used in Jewish worship
mikveh (mikvaot)	Jewish ritual bath used for ritual purification
Mishnah	collection of mostly halakhic Jewish traditions compiled after 200 C.E. and made the foundational part of the Talmud
naos	shrine; the main room of a Greek temple
nave	central part of a basilica or church
necropolis	a large and important cemetery
Neutron activation analysis	used to identify the provenance of stone or clay vessels; determination of an object's chemical profile, using spectroscopy
niche	a recess in a wall, to hold an object or for decoration
Nilometer	a staircase or graduated pillar that showed the heights to which the Nile rises
numismatic	related to the study or collection of coins
obelisk	an upright four-sided pillar that gradually tapers as it rises into a pyramid
odeion (-a)	a small-roofed theater, mainly for musical or poetical performances
ophidian	relating to or resembling snakes

opus reticulatum	Roman masonry facing, consisting of pyramidal blocks laid out diagonally, their bases facing outward
orthogonal plan	town plan of parallel streets intersecting at right angles
ossuary	a depository for bones of the dead
ostracon (-a)	inscribed sherd
otzer	(Hebrew) "treasure," used to designate the small pool of "living water" that purifies a *mikveh*
paleography	study of ancient handwriting
palmette	a decorative motif suggestive of a palm tree
pediment	a triangular space that forms the gable of a low-pitched roof, along with the horizontal and raking cornices
peristyle	an open space or court surrounded by columns
pilaster	an upright pier that projects slightly from a wall
polis (-eis)	Greek city-state
portico	a colonnade or covered ambulatory in a building
rampart	a broad embankment raised as a fortification
realia	artifacts discovered in excavation, such as pottery, arrowheads, bronze or iron utensils, and coins
redoubt	an isolated work forming an enclosure, often used to defend or reinforce a prominent point
relief	projecting detail, ornament, or figures
saddle	a device mounted as a support, often shaped to fit the object held
Sanhedrin	court of justice and supreme Jewish council (first century B.C.E.–sixth century C.E.)
sarcophagus (-i)	coffin (Greek: "flesh eater")
scriptorium	a room for the copying and writing of documents
Septuagint	Greek translation of the Hebrew Bible (third-second century B.C.E.)
shekel	an ancient Jewish weight and a silver coin
sherd/shard	broken piece(s) of pottery
sill	a horizontal piece that forms the (or one of the) lowest member(s) of a framework or supporting structure
slag	by-product of metal smelting, pottery or glassmaking or lime burning
spolia	stones used for buildings that were dismantled from older ones
stadium	large, usually unroofed building, with tiers of seats for

	spectators; a measure of length in ancient Greece, equal to about 185 meters
stela (-ae)	an upright slab or pillar, often with carvings and inscriptions
stratigraphy	study of occupational layers as they are uncovered during an excavation
stratum	a combination of all *loci* belonging to one historical and cultural period of habitation at a site
stretcher	a stone or brick laid with its length parallel to the face of the wall
stucco	a fine plaster used in decoration and ornamentation
stylobate	a continuous base supporting a row of columns
sudarium	a napkin or cloth for wiping the face; a portrait of Christ on a cloth
Targum	Aramaic translations or paraphrases of the Hebrew Bible
tel (Hebrew), tell (Arabic)	ancient mound, composed of remains of successive settlements
temenos	enclosed sacred precinct (of a temple)
terminus ante quem	latest datable period to which an event or artifact can belong
terminus post quem	earliest datable period to which an event or artifact can belong
Tiberium	a monument in honor of Tiberius (see Evans's chapter)
Tosephta	supplement to the Mishnah
tournette	slow potter's wheel
triclinium	a dining room; derived from the couch(es) extending around three sides of a table
typology	the study of features, development, and chronology of artifacts
vici	streets along the contours
votive offerings	offered in fulfillment of a vow or in devotion or gratitude
voussoir	one of the wedge-shaped pieces forming an arch or vault
wadi	(Arabic) usually dry streambed, except during the rainy season
wasters	discarded or broken pieces of glass
weli	(Arabic) monument dedicated to a Muslim holy man
xystos	an open colonnade, or walk planted with trees

Selected Bibliography

Jonathan E. Soyars

[The following selected bibliography is provided in the hope that the interested reader might find it a helpful guide to important and influential publications relevant to the current discussion. It is not intended to be comprehensive, nor does it provide an exhaustive compilation of all material cited in the present volume. Rather it provides a number of major publications, mostly in English, that should inform a serious discussion of Jesus, archaeology, and related fields. — JES.]

Applebaum, S. *Judaea in Hellenistic and Roman Times: Historical and Archaeological Essays.* SJLA 40. Leiden: Brill, 1989.

Arav, R., and R. Freund, eds. *Bethsaida: A City by the North Shore of the Sea of Galilee.* 3 vols. Kirksville, Mo.: Thomas Jefferson University Press, 1995; Truman State University Press, 1998, 2004.

Arnal, W. E., and M. Desjardins, eds. *Whose Historical Jesus?* Waterloo, Ont.: Wilfrid Laurier University Press, 1997.

Aviam, M., and P. Richardson. "Josephus's Galilee in *Life* and *War* in Archaeological Perspective." In *Josephus, Translation and Commentary,* edited by S. N. Mason, vol. 8, app. A, pp. 177-217. Leiden: Brill, 2000.

Avi-Yonah, M., ed. *Encyclopedia of Archaeological Excavations in the Holy Land.* English ed. 4 vols. Englewood Cliffs, N.J.: Prentice-Hall, 1975.

Bartlett, J. R., ed. *Archaeology and Biblical Interpretation.* London and New York: Routledge, 1997.

Barton, John, ed. *The Biblical World.* 2 vols. London and New York: Routledge, 2002.

Batey, R. A. *Jesus and the Forgotten City: New Light on the Urban World of Jesus.* Grand Rapids: Baker, 1991.

———. "Sepphoris and the Jesus Movement." *NTS* 47 (2001): 402-9.

Betz, H. D. *The Greek Magical Papyri in Translation, Including the Demotic Spells.* Chicago: University of Chicago Press, 1986.

Binder, D. D. *Into the Temple Courts: The Place of the Synagogues in the Second Temple Period.* SBLDS 162. Atlanta: Society of Biblical Literature, 1999.

Bruce, F. F. *Jesus and Christian Origins Outside the New Testament*. London: Hodder and Stoughton, 1984.

Chancey, M. A. *The Myth of a Gentile Galilee*. SNTSMS 118. Cambridge and New York: Cambridge University Press, 2002.

Charlesworth, J. H. *Jesus and the Dead Sea Scrolls*. ABRL. New York: Doubleday, 1992.

――――. "The Jesus of History and the Topography of the Holy Land." In *The Handbook of the Study of the Historical Jesus*, edited by T. Holmén and S. E. Porter. Leiden: Brill, 2005.

――――. "Jesus Research and Near Eastern Archaeology: Reflections on Recent Developments." In *Neotestamentica et Philonica: Studies in Honor of Peder Borgen*, edited by D. E. Aune, T. Seland, and J. H. Ulrichsen, pp. 37-70. Leiden: Brill, 2003.

――――. *Jesus within Judaism: New Light from Exciting Archaeological Discoveries*. ABRL. New York: Doubleday, 1988.

――――. *The Millennium Guide for Pilgrims to the Holy Land*. North Richland Hills, Tex.: BIBAL Press, 2000.

――――, ed. *Caves of Enlightenment: Proceedings of the American Schools of Oriental Research Dead Sea Scrolls Jubilee Symposium (1947-1997)*. North Richland Hills, Tex.: BIBAL Press, 1998.

Charlesworth, J. H., and L. L. Johns, eds. *Hillel and Jesus: Comparative Studies of Two Major Religious Leaders*. Minneapolis: Fortress, 1997.

Chiat, M. J. *Handbook of Synagogue Architecture*. BJS 29. Chico, Calif.: Scholars, 1982.

Chilton, B., and C. Evans, eds. *Studying the Historical Jesus: Evaluations of the State of Current Research*. Leiden: Brill, 1994.

Cohen, S. J. D. *The Beginnings of Jewishness: Boundaries, Varieties, Uncertainties*. Berkeley: University of California Press, 1999.

Crossan, J. D., and J. L. Reed. *Excavating Jesus: Beneath the Stones, behind the Texts*. San Francisco: HarperSanFrancisco, 2001.

Cryer, F. H., and T. L. Thompson, eds. *Qumran between the Old and New Testaments*. Sheffield: Sheffield Academic Press, 1998.

Dar, S. *Landscape and Pattern: An Archaeological Survey of Samaria, 800 B.C.E.–636 C.E.* BAR International Series 308. Oxford: BAR, 1986.

De Vaux, R. *Archaeology and the Dead Sea Scrolls*. London: Oxford University Press, 1973.

Dever, W. G., and J. E. Wright, eds. *The Echoes of Many Texts: Reflections on Jewish and Christian Traditions: Essays in Honor of Lou H. Silberman*. BJS 313. Atlanta: Scholars, 1997.

Edwards, D. R., and T. C. McCollough, eds. *Archaeology and the Galilee: Texts and Contexts in the Graeco-Roman and Byzantine Periods*. SFSHJ 143. Atlanta: Scholars, 1997.

Elliott, J. K. *The Apocryphal New Testament*. Oxford: Clarendon, 1993.

Evans, C. A., and S. E. Porter, eds. *Dictionary of New Testament Background*. Downers Grove, Ill.: InterVarsity, 2000.

Feldman, L. H., and G. Hata, eds. *Josephus, the Bible, and History*. Detroit: Wayne State University Press, 1989.

Fine, S., ed. *Jews, Christians, and Polytheists in the Ancient Synagogue*. London and New York: Routledge, 1999.

Fine, S., and E. M. Meyers. "Synagogues." In *OEANE* 5:118-23.

Finegan, J. *The Archeology of the New Testament: The Life of Jesus and the Beginning of the Early Church*. Rev. ed. Princeton: Princeton University Press, 1992.

Flusser, D. *Judaism and the Origins of Christianity*. Jerusalem: Magnes Press, 1988.

Freyne, S. "Archaeology and the Historical Jesus." In *Archaeology and Biblical Interpretation*, edited by J. R. Bartlett. London and New York: Routledge, 1997.

———. *Galilee: From Alexander the Great to Hadrian, 323 B.C.E. to 135 C.E.; A Study of the Second Temple Judaism*. Rev. ed. Edinburgh: T. & T. Clark, 1998.

———. *Galilee and Gospel*. WUNT 125. Tübingen: Mohr (Siebeck), 2000.

———. *Galilee, Jesus, and the Gospels: Literary Approaches and Historical Investigations*. Philadelphia: Fortress; Dublin: Gill and Macmillan, 1988.

Geva, H., ed. *Ancient Jerusalem Revealed*. Jerusalem: Israel Exploration Society, 2000.

Gibson, S., and J. Taylor. *Beneath the Church of the Holy Sepulchre*. London: Palestinian Exploration Fund, 1994.

Goodenough, E. R. *Jewish Symbols in the Greco-Roman Period*. 13 vols. New York: Pantheon Books, 1953-68.

Grabbe, L. L. "Synagogues in Pre-70 Palestine: A Reassessment." *JTS* 38 (1988): 401-10.

Green, J. B., S. McKnight, and I. H. Marshall, eds. *Dictionary of Jesus and the Gospels*. Downers Grove, Ill.: InterVarsity, 1992.

Guijarro, S. "The Family in First-Century Galilee." In *Constructing Early Christian Families*, edited by H. Moxnes, pp. 42-65. London and New York: Routledge, 1997.

Gutmann, J., ed. *Ancient Synagogues: The State of Research*. BJS 22. Chico, Calif.: Scholars, 1981.

———, ed. *The Synagogue: Studies in Origins, Archaeology, and Architecture*. Library of Biblical Studies. New York: Ktav Publishing House, 1975.

Haase, W., and H. Temporini, eds. *Aufstieg und Niedergang der römischen Welt*. Berlin and New York, 1979-.

Hachlili, R. *Ancient Jewish Art and Archaeology in the Land of Israel*. Leiden: Brill, 1988.

Hanson, K. C., and D. Oakman. *Palestine in the Time of Jesus: Social Structures and Social Conflicts*. Minneapolis: Fortress, 1998.

Hirschfeld, Y. *The Palestinian Dwelling in the Roman-Byzantine Period*. Jerusalem: Franciscan Printing Press/Israel Exploration Society, 1995.

Hoffmeier, J. K., and A. Millard, eds. *The Future of Biblical Archaeology: Reassessing Methodologies and Assumptions*. Grand Rapids and Cambridge: Eerdmans, 2004.

Horbury, W., W. D. Davies, and J. Sturdy, eds. *The Cambridge History of Judaism*. 3 vols. Cambridge and New York: Cambridge University Press, 1984-.

Horsley, R. A. *Archaeology, History, and Society in Galilee: The Social Context of Jesus and the Rabbis*. Valley Forge, Pa.: Trinity, 1996.

———. *Galilee: History, Politics, People*. Valley Forge, Pa.: Trinity, 1995.

———. *Jesus and the Spiral of Violence: Popular Jewish Resistance in Roman Palestine*. Minneapolis: Fortress, 1993.

Horsley, R. A., and J. S. Hanson. *Bandits, Prophets, and Messiahs: Popular Movements in the Time of Jesus*. Minneapolis: Winston, 1985.

Jeremias, J. *Jerusalem in the Time of Jesus: An Investigation into Economic and Social Conditions during the New Testament Period*. Translated by F. H. Cave and C. H. Cave. Philadelphia: Fortress, 1969.

Kee, H. C., and L. H. Cohick, eds. *Evolution of the Synagogue: Problems and Progress.* Harrisburg, Pa.: Trinity, 1999.

Kenyon, K. M. *Digging Up Jerusalem.* London: Ernest Benn, 1974.

Kloppenborg, J. S. *Excavating Q: The History and Setting of the Sayings Gospel.* Minneapolis: Fortress, 2000.

Kloppenborg, J., and S. G. Wilson, eds. *Voluntary Associations in the Ancient World.* London: Routledge, 1996.

Kloppenborg Verbin, J. S. "Dating Theodotus (CIJ II 1404)." *JJS* 51 (2000): 243-80.

Levine, L. I. *The Ancient Synagogue: The First Thousand Years.* New Haven: Yale University Press, 2000.

———. *The Galilee in Late Antiquity.* New York: Jewish Theological Seminary of America. Distributed by Harvard University Press, 1992.

———. *Roman Caesarea: An Archaeological-Topographical Study.* Qedem 2. Jerusalem: Hebrew University of Jerusalem, 1975.

Levine, L. I., ed. *The Synagogue in Late Antiquity.* Philadelphia: American Schools of Oriental Research, 1987.

Madden, F. A. *History of Jewish Coinage, and of Money in the Old and New Testaments.* 1864. Reprint, New York: Ktav, 1967.

Mare, W. H. *The Archaeology of the Jerusalem Area.* Grand Rapids: Baker, 1987.

Markoe, G. E. *Phoenicians.* Los Angeles: University of California Press, 2000.

McRay, J. *Archaeology and the New Testament.* Grand Rapids: Baker, 1991.

Mendels, D. "Jesus and the Politics of His Day." In *Images of Jesus Today,* edited by Charlesworth and W. P. Weaver. FSC 3. Valley Forge, Pa.: Trinity, 1994.

Meshorer, Y. *Ancient Jewish Coinage.* New York: Amphora Books, 1982.

———. *Jewish Coins of the Second Temple Period.* Tel Aviv: Am Hassefer, 1967.

Meyers, E. M., et al. *The Excavations at Ancient Meiron, Upper Galilee, Israel, 1971-72, 1974-75, 1977.* Cambridge, Mass.: American Schools of Oriental Research, 1981.

Meyers, E. M., and J. F. Strange. *Archaeology, the Rabbis, and Early Christianity.* Nashville: Abingdon, 1981.

Meyers, E. M., ed. *Galilee through the Centuries: Confluence of Cultures.* DJSS 1. Winona Lake, Ind.: Eisenbrauns, 1999.

———, ed. *The Oxford Encyclopedia of Archaeology in the Near East.* 5 vols. New York: Oxford University Press, 1997.

Millard, A. R. *Reading and Writing in the Time of Jesus.* New York: New York University Press, 2000.

Murphy-O'Connor, J. *The Holy Land: An Archeological Guide from Earliest Times to 1700.* 4th ed. Oxford: Oxford University Press, 1998.

Negev, A., and S. Gibson, eds. *Archaeological Encyclopedia of the Holy Land.* Rev. ed. New York and London: Continuum, 2001.

Oakman, D. "The Archaeology of First-Century Galilee and the Social Interpretation of the Historical Jesus." In *SBL Seminar Papers, 1994,* pp. 220-51. Atlanta: Scholars, 1994.

Pearson, B. A., ed. *The Future of Early Christianity: Essays in Honor of Helmut Koester.* Minneapolis: Fortress, 1991.

Perring, D. "Spatial Organization and Social Change in Roman Towns." In *City and Coun-*

try in the Ancient World, edited by J. Rich and A. Wallace-Hadrill, pp. 273-93. London: Routledge, 1991.

Pixner, Bargil. *With Jesus in Jerusalem: His First and Last Days in Judea.* Rosh Pina: Corazin, 1997.

———. *With Jesus through Galilee according to the Fifth Gospel.* Collegeville, Minn.: Liturgical Press, 1996.

Reed, J. L. *Archaeology and the Galilean Jesus: A Re-examination of the Evidence.* Harrisburg, Pa.: Trinity, 2000.

———. *Kingdom-Building in Galilee.* Claremont, Calif.: Institute for Antiquity and Christianity, 2002.

Rich, J., and A. Wallace-Hadrill, eds. *City and Country in the Ancient World.* London: Routledge, 1991.

Richardson, P., with C. Hixon and A. Spurling. "3-D Visualizations of a First-Century Galilean Town." In *Virtual Reality in Archaeology,* edited by J. Barceló, M. Forte, and D. H. Sanders, pp. 195-204. BAR International Series 843. Oxford, 2000.

Roller, D. W. *The Building Program of Herod the Great.* Berkeley: University of California Press, 1998.

Rousseau, J. J., and R. Arav. *Jesus and His World: An Archaeological and Cultural Dictionary.* Minneapolis: Fortress, 1995.

Safrai, Z. *The Economy of Roman Palestine.* London and New York: Routledge, 1994.

Sanders, E. P. *Judaism: Practice and Belief, 63 BCE–66 CE.* London: SCM; Philadelphia: Trinity, 1992.

Sawicki, M. *Crossing Galilee: Architectures of Contact in the Occupied Land of Jesus.* Harrisburg, Pa.: Trinity, 2000.

Segal, A. *Theaters in Roman Palestine and Provincia Arabia.* Mnemosyne 140. Leiden: Brill, 1995.

Shanks, H. *Jerusalem: An Archaeological Biography.* New York: Random House, 1995.

Shanks, H., and D. P. Cole, eds. *Archaeology in the World of Herod, Jesus, and Paul.* Washington, D.C.: Biblical Archaeology Society, 1990, 1992.

Sperber, D., ed. *The City in Roman Palestine.* New York: Oxford University Press, 1998.

Stanton, G. *Gospel Truth? New Light on Jesus and the Gospels.* London: HarperCollins, 1995.

Stern, E., ed. *New Encyclopedia of Archaeological Excavations in the Holy Land.* 4 vols. Jerusalem: Israel Exploration Society & Carta; New York: Simon and Schuster, 1993.

Taylor, J. E. *The Immerser: John the Baptist within Second Temple Judaism.* Studying the Historical Jesus 2. Grand Rapids: Eerdmans, 1997.

Theissen, G. *The Gospels in Context: Social and Political History in the Synoptic Tradition.* Minneapolis: Fortress, 1991.

Thiede, C. P. *The Cosmopolitan World of Jesus: New Findings from Archaeology.* London: SPCK, 2004.

Urman, D., and P. V. M. Flesher, eds. *Ancient Synagogues: Historical Analyses and Archaeological Discovery.* SPB 47. Leiden: Brill, 1995.

Wilson, S. G., and M. Desjardins, eds. *Text and Artifact in the Religions of Mediterranean Antiquity: Essays in Honour of Peter Richardson.* SCJ 9. Waterloo, Ont.: Wilfrid Laurier University Press, 2000.

Index of Scripture and Other Ancient Texts

CLASSICAL SOURCES

Aeschylus
Seven Against Thebes
ll. 720-25 376

Appianus
Civil War
5.75 405, 428

Aristotle
Nicomachean Ethics 229

Cato the Elder
On Agriculture
56 494n.66

Curtus Rufus
Alexander
4.8.9 403, 427

Geographical Index